Empire of Things

Empire of Things

HOW WE BECAME A WORLD OF
CONSUMERS, FROM THE FIFTEENTH
CENTURY TO THE TWENTY-FIRST

Frank Trentmann

HARPER
An Imprint of HarperCollins*Publishers*

HarperCollins books may be purchased for educational, business, or sales promotional use. For information, please e-mail the Special Markets Department at SPsales@harpercollins.com.

Originally published in the United Kingdom in 2016 by Allen Lane.

FIRST U.S. EDITION

Library of Congress Cataloging-in-Publication Data has been applied for.

ISBN: 978-0-06-245632-8

16 17 18 19 20 OFF/RRD 10 9 8 7 6 5 4 3 2 1

For Oscar & Julia

Contents

List of Illustrations

List of Figures

Introduction

We live surrounded by things. A typical German owns 10,000 objects.
In Los Angeles, a middle-class garage often no longer houses a car but
several hundred boxes of stuff. The United Kingdom in 2013 was home
to 6 billion items of clothing, roughly a hundred per adult; a quarter of
these never leave the wardrobe. Of course, people always had things,
and used them not only to survive but for ritual, display and fun. But
the possessions in a pre-modern village or an indigenous tribe pale
when placed next to the growing mountain of things in advanced
societies like ours. This change in accumulation involved a historic
shift in humans' relations with things. In contrast to the pre-modern
village, where most goods were passed on and arrived as gifts or
with the wedding trousseau, things in modern societies are mainly
bought in the marketplace. And they pass through our lives more
quickly.[1]

In the last few hundred years, the acquisition, flow and use of
things – in short, consumption – has become a defining feature of our
lives. It would be a mistake to think people at any time have had a single identity, but there have been periods when certain roles have been
dominant, defining a society and its culture. In Europe, the High Middle Ages saw the rise of a 'chivalrous society' of knights and serfs.[2] The
Reformation pitched one faith against another. In the nineteenth century, a commercial society gave way to an industrial class society of
capitalists and wage workers. Work remains important today, but it
defines us far less than in the heyday of the factory and the trade union.
Instead of warriors or workers, we are more than ever before consumers.
In the rich world – and in the developing world increasingly, too –
identities, politics, the economy and the environment are crucially shaped
by what and how we consume. Taste, appearance and lifestyle define
who we are (or want to be) and how others see us. Politicians treat public
services like a supermarket of goods, hoping it will provide citizens

with greater choice. Many citizens, in turn, seek to advance social and political causes by using the power of their purse in boycotts and buy-cotts. Advanced economies live or die by their ability to stimulate and maintain high levels of spending, with the help of advertising, branding and consumer credit. Perhaps the most existential impact is that of our materially intensive lifestyle on the planet. Our lifestyles are fired by fossil fuels. In the twentieth century, carbon emissions per person quadrupled. Today, transport and bigger, more comfortable homes, filled with more appliances, account for just under half of global CO^2 emissions. Eating more meat has seriously disturbed the nitrogen cycle. Consumers are even more deeply implicated if the emissions released in the process of making and delivering their things are taken into account. And, at the end of their lives, many broken TVs and computers from Europe end up in countries like Ghana and Nigeria, causing illness and pollution as they are picked apart for precious materials.[3]

How much and what to consume is one of the most urgent but also thorniest questions of our day. This book is a historical contribution to that debate. It tells the story of how we came to live with so much more, and how this has changed the course of history.

Like other key concepts in history, consumption has not had a fixed meaning over time. The term originally derived from the Latin word *consumere*, which first arrived in French in the twelfth century and from there found its way into English and other European languages. At that time, it meant the using up and physical exhaustion of matter. Food, candles and firewood were consumed. So was the body when attacked by an illness – hence the English use of 'consumption' for the 'wasting disease' (tuberculosis). To confuse matters, there was the similar-sounding *consummare*, which meant to complete something, as in Christ's last words: 'It is finished' (*consummatum est*). In actual usage, 'waste' and 'finish' were often rolled into one.[4]

Between the seventeenth and twentieth centuries, the term underwent a miraculous metamorphosis. Consumption progressively ceased to mean waste or destruction and instead became something positive and creative. From the late seventeenth century, economic commentators began to argue that the purchase of goods and services not only satisfied individual wants but, in the process, enriched a nation by enlarging the market for producers and investors. Personal vanities, like a snuffbox or extravagant clothes, could yield public benefits, at least in material terms. Such linkages unsettled earlier moral certainties. A major milestone was Adam Smith's *The Wealth of Nations* in 1776, in which he argued that 'consumption is the sole end and purpose of all production.'[5] Notwithstanding this dictum, Smith and his immediate successors were some way from making consumption the centre of economics, let alone from imagining that there could be sustained growth. This had to wait until the 1860s–'70s, when W. S. Jevons, Carl Menger and Léon Walras argued that it was consuming, not labour, that created value.

The apotheosis of the consumer may have started in economic thought, but it was completed by politics. In the years around 1900, 'the consumer' arrived on the political stage as the twin of the citizen, using the power of the purse to promote social reform, first in the United States and Britain but soon in France and elsewhere in Europe, too. It was only after this, in the interwar years when mass-produced, standardized goods took off, that companies and advertisers made the customer the 'king' of the marketplace. In the next few decades, users of health, education and sports services started to be addressed as 'consumers', until, by the 1960s, observers sighted a whole new type of society: a 'consumer society'. By the late twentieth century, it was no longer just goods and services but emotions and experiences that were being consumed. Nevertheless, the older association with 'using up' was never completely lost. Wilhelm Roscher, the founding father of historical economics in nineteenth-century Germany, once remarked that a coat was not consumed until its fibres were coming apart. Tellingly, the Japanese term – specially created in the 1880s – remains *shōhi*, which combines 'to spend' (*hi*) with 'to extinguish' (*shō*). In an age when we are once again becoming aware of the finite resources of the planet, this broader, material conception of consumption has a lot to say for itself.

The changing meaning of the term reflects the advance of capitalism since the fifteenth century, which spread markets, purchase and choice more widely across society. Yet it would be too narrow to focus our attention exclusively on shopping and changes in spending power. Consumption is about more than purchasing. Even as shopping has been in the ascendant in the modern world, people have continued to access things and services via other channels, including gifts, company-sponsored gyms and holidays and, especially in the last fifty years, through health, housing, education and welfare provided by the state. Shopping will receive its fair share of attention in this book. But we must also appreciate how goods are used, for this is how they give shape and meaning to social life and identity.

This book, then, aims to follow the life cycle of consumption as fully as possible from demand and acquisition through to use, collection and, ultimately, disposal. This means it will give attention to the desire for goods that lay behind demand, including the fashion for Indian cottons in eighteenth-century Europe, that for European dress in nineteenth-century Africa, or the emergence of new European tastes for exotic goods such as coffee, tea and chocolate. Preferences for these goods were neither pre-existing nor stable but had to be created. And they changed over time, as colonialism and capitalism rebranded such products for Western mass markets. Cultures, too, varied in the kind of goods they prized. Some (like Ming China) valued antiquity, while others (like the Dutch Republic and early modern England) increasingly pursued novelty. Acquisition is the next link in the chain of consumption. Here, in addition to purchase and purchasing power, we will need to examine the contribution of credit and saving. But we should also not forget ways that do not involve shopping through which goods reach people, such as when households pass on goods to family, friends and charity, or the remarkable recent transformation of cooking and gardening from work into hobbies that take up considerable amounts of time and money. The final link in our chain is when goods reach the end of their social life: broken, outdated or simply no longer wanted by their owner. It is about waste but also storage and reuse.

Just as important as time and money are the spaces of consumption. Here the department store has dominated the scene as the icon of modernity. Equally fascinating, though, is the vibrant mix of shops and retailing surrounding it, from street sellers and the co-operative shop to the neighbourhood store. And so, more generally, are the spaces where leisure time was (and is) spent. These range from commercial enterprises, like the early cinemas and dance halls, to public swimming pools and company-sponsored fashion shows. And we need to follow the link between public and private life; in particular, the crucial entry into the home of running water, gas and electricity which set in motion new habits and expectations and attracted new appliances. We also want to know not only how much money was spent on a radio, a washing machine or an air-conditioner, and who bought them, but how they changed the character and rhythm of daily life. Comfort, cleanliness and convenience – to use an eighteenth-century phrase – were dynamic drivers of consumption.

Today, consumption is at the centre of a heated public debate between two rival camps pointing their moral artillery at each other.

On one side stand progressive and social democratic critics who attack the juggernaut of shopping, advertising, branding and easy credit for turning active, virtuous citizens into passive, bored consumers. In this view, people have been made to desire and buy things they do not want and which they have neither the money for, nor the time to enjoy. 'Artificial wants' have replaced 'authentic needs'. People are overwhelmed by too many choices and increasingly short-sighted. Like a hamster on its wheel, they are trapped in a spend/work/consume cycle, leaving them unhappy and lonely, mentally unstable and deeply in debt. Years of such mindless consumption and the search for instant gratification have dulled their hearts and minds to the plight of others. Private, self-centred hedonism has killed the public spirit. 'Consumerism', to give it its unfriendly label, is a new kind of totalitarianism: 'the gulag replaced by Gucci', in the words of one commentator.[6]

On the opposite side are the champions of consumption, first and foremost classical liberals who cherish freedom of choice as the bedrock of democracy and prosperity. Citizens, in this view, should have the right to follow their preferences and make their own choices without some authority telling them what is good or bad. Making choices in the marketplace is like voting in elections. To interfere with the former would undermine the latter. To be *Free to Choose*, as Milton and Rose Friedman put it in 1979 in their popular American book and the ensuing TV series, was not only the best but the only way to promote 'both prosperity and human freedom'.[7] How this vision conquered the United States has been elegantly told by Lizabeth Cohen in *A Consumers' Republic*.[8] Similar views are heard today across the globe, often grouped under the umbrella of neo-liberalism. They have had support, too, from some social democrats who accept that people have the right to comfort, fun and little luxuries. Greater choice of more goods and services, some hoped, would weaken old hierarchies of class and taste and nurture a more pluralistic society. In 2004, Britain's New Labour prime minister Tony Blair declared: 'I believe people do want choice, in public services as in other services.' Giving parents and patients greater choice as 'citizens and consumers', he insisted, would improve schools and hospitals.[9]

Such a political and moral defence of choice has not occurred in a cultural vacuum. It benefited from wider changes in society that created a more tolerant and favourable atmosphere for goods and pleasure in the 1970s and '80s. Perhaps, the French writer Michel de Certeau noted, people were not all passive dupes but creative, even rebellious, defending their autonomy with their own distinctive lifestyle. Youth subcultures, others observed, used fashion, mopeds and popular music to challenge conformity. Shopping, writers in gender studies added, was not all frivolous but could be empowering, giving women, who did most of it, new identities and public presence. Postmodernism swept across a simple divide between 'authentic' and 'artificial' desires and scrambled the hierarchy of 'good' and 'bad' taste. If reality did not contain a singular point of view but was constructed by different discourses and interpretations, who was to say whether a person's love of Elvis was any less genuine or worthy than someone else's for Wagner? Anthropologists carried out fieldwork in affluent societies and reported that shopping and consuming were profoundly meaningful social experiences, not acts of mindless accumulation. People found and expressed themselves through their possessions.[10]

This book does not set out to adjudicate a moral debate, let alone decide whether consumption is 'good' or 'bad'. Consuming is too diverse and its history too rich to fit either extreme model: complacent mass consumption or individual freedom. The book's main aim is a different one: it wants to step back and give readers a chance to look at the subject from a historical perspective, to explain how consumption evolved the way it did over the last five centuries. This means it is, above all, interested in questions of process. To be precise, it concerns the interplay between two processes: one is how institutions and ideas shaped consumption over time; the other is how consumption, in turn, transformed power, social relations and value systems.

In order to observe the changing interplay between these forces effectively, we cannot restrict our view to either individual preferences or general abstractions. Recent psychologists have shown how misleading it is to view preferences as rational in the way mainstream economists tend to do. What people choose depends on how the choice is framed; people are more likely to buy meat that is labelled positively, as 75 per cent lean, than negatively, as containing 25 per cent fat, to give a very simple example.[11] This is a fundamental insight, but there is no reason to apply it only to the present, as recent psychological experiments have done. History is a vast laboratory within which this kind of framing took place. Trade, empires, cities and ideologies all framed the context in which people lived their lives, tickling some desires and repressing others, shaping habits and spreading ideas about taste, comfort and what constituted the good life. Money and time matter, as we shall see. Economists have asked how and when households and their members trade leisure for income, deciding to sell their labour on the market to enable them to buy goods in return. This is important but too narrow a conception of demand, for it does not tell us what compelled households to want more goods in the first place, nor what they then did with them. We therefore need to look at the forces that impinged on households as well as the choices they made. Material desires are not a modern invention. But they can be cultivated and amplified or neglected and silenced. The last five hundred years were a period of sustained amplification. This book offers a history of demand broadly understood.

One major framing force has been morality, and it remains so today. People and rulers have carried with them notions of good and bad behaviour, proper and improper spending, fair and unfair prices, excessive and moderate ways of living. But these also change over time, as ideologies rise and fall and material realities change. The positions in today's moral debate briefly sketched above are echoes of a much longer historical battle. Once viewed like this, their main value is as part of the historical puzzle rather than as analyses that are either right or wrong; as chapters in the history of ideas more interesting for revealing the force and legacy of traditions of thought than for telling us what consumption is actually like. Instead of rushing to join today's moral debate, then, we should realize that these positions are steeped in history. To say that consumption is totalitarian, for example, can obviously be challenged by pointing to the very real differences between power in one of Stalin's labour camps and that exerted by luxury brands, however seductive. More interesting is to explore how such thinking travels in the furrows ploughed by earlier thinkers. The critique of consumerism as a new fascism goes back to the 1960s, to Pier Paolo Pasolini, the Italian film director and writer, and the Marxist émigré Herbert Marcuse. Marcuse warned of the coming of a *One-dimensional Man*, a book that became a best-selling consumer article in its own right.

While Marcuse's pessimistic diagnosis of social control and repression may have gone out of fashion, a good deal of today's public debate continues to take its lead from the critique of consumerism that flourished during the post-war boom. No single book has cast as long a shadow as John K. Galbraith's *The Affluent Society*, first published in 1958. An economist by profession – he had been in charge of keeping prices stable in the United States during the Second World War – Galbraith was a liberal intellectual with a social mission. He portrayed a new and dangerous kind of society emerging from the war. With peace restored, mass consumption was called upon to absorb the expanded manufacturing capacity created during the war. To make this happen, Galbraith wrote, production could no longer just satisfy wants: it had to create them, with the help of advertising and salesmen. A vicious cycle was set in motion that propelled people to live beyond their means (with the help of consumer credit), entrenched business more deeply at the centre of power, and, perhaps most worryingly, favoured individual materialism over civic-mindedness, creating, in his famous phrase, an atmosphere of 'private opulence and public squalor'.[12]

More generally, as we shall see, the idea that citizens are dehumanized, enslaved and corrupted by the lure of things reaches back to Karl Marx via Jean-Jacques Rousseau all the way to Plato in ancient Greece. In the later Middle Ages and early modern period, spending on fashionable clothes, lavish weddings and fine furniture was met with widespread disapproval and even prohibition. It was denounced for setting off a spiral of emulative spending – what is often called 'keeping up with the Joneses' – and for undermining values and social hierarchies. It was also attacked for draining money from public coffers. Perhaps most troubling, avarice and the lust for things were said to distract Christians from the true life of the spirit. In his *City of God*, begun in 413, St Augustine, one of the fathers of the Church, had traced the lack of restraint all the way back to original sin and Adam's eviction from paradise: the 'error and misplaced love which is born with every son of Adam'.[13] The lust for things and the lust for flesh sprang from the same source.

The view that being and having are opposites thus has a very long history. But so has an alternative trajectory that sees people as only becoming human through the use of things. From the seventeenth century onwards, there were a growing number of voices which gave consumption new legitimacy. The longing for more, in this view, was driving human ingenuity and civilization.

Readers, like this author, will have their own moral point of view. What is 'extravagant' or 'frivolous' to one may be an 'essential' need for another. For an understanding of history, however, it is not very enlightening to view the past only through one's own moral filter. Rather, we need to take the changing attitudes of historical actors seriously – the positive and ambivalent as well as the critical – especially if we want to understand how 'needs' and 'wants' came to expand as much as they did. Pointing the finger at the manipulative power of advertisers and brands has tended to shut the door too quickly on this richer story of the human engagement with goods.

The aim, though, of this book is not only to appreciate consumption as the outcome of historical forces. Consumption, in turn, also changed states, societies and daily life. To see this clearly, we need to break with a tradition that has treated material culture as a separate sphere of everyday life. In 1912, Theodore Roosevelt, the progressive ex-president of the United States, told American historians that the 'great historian' of the future would not only portray great events but 'will in as full measure as possible present to us the every-day life of the men and women of the age'.[14] Just over fifty years later, the French historian Fernand Braudel opened his trilogy on civilization and capitalism in the early modern world with an entire volume on *The Structures of Everyday Life*. Such a distinct treatment provided a feast of insights, not least about the power of eating and drinking habits and the routines of daily life that persisted alongside a market economy. But it came at a price. Treating daily life, the market and politics as separate spheres made it all but impossible to follow the interplay between them. This made the approach particularly cumbersome for modern history, broadly the period from the eighteenth to the twentieth century, when these spheres became ever more entangled. For Braudel, whose creative vision had emerged while working on the sixteenth century, 'material civilization' was a 'shadowy zone'.[15] In the modern world, by contrast, it advanced to the centre of politics, with the standard of living, housing and eating, leisure time, shopping and waste establishing themselves as core elements of public concern and policy.

The growth of consumption – in terms of its sheer bulk, change and material throughput – means that we are dealing with a new dynamism that has left few aspects of public life untouched. This book follows this momentum and assesses its consequences for social life and politics. To do so, it presents an alternative account to that of the 'affluent society', which has continued to inform the popular imagination and treats consumption as a phenomenon – or disease – of the decades following the Second World War: the era of the boom, the *Wirtschaftswunder* or *les trente glorieuses*. This is the period commonly associated with the rise of hedonism, the power of marketing and advertising men, the coming of the credit card, self-service supermarkets and, above all, the American way of life. It is to these years that commentators trace the root cause of today's fixation with consuming more and more. Consumption, in this view, stands for private choice, rampant individualism and market exchange. Chronologically, it is largely a post-'45 story, with the United States the model for others to follow.

This book breaks with this approach in four fundamental ways. It, firstly, widens the time frame. The 1950s and '60s saw unprecedented gains in disposable income in the West, but this does not mean that people's lives before this period had been barren. Rather than a new beginning, the post-war boom is better viewed as a late chapter in a longer story of the global expansion of goods. When precisely this expansion began has been the subject of heated debate. Thirty years ago, the historian Neil McKendrick confidently dated the 'birth of consumer society' to eighteenth-century Britain.[16] He set off a race to discover its origins in ever more distant periods, some finding its first signs in the new taste for beer and beef in late-medieval England. The great wave of historical research that followed has been a mixed blessing. On the one hand, it amply documented that new clothes, domestic comforts and tastes for exotic tea, coffee and porcelain were already arriving before the Industrial Revolution. Contrary to conventional wisdom, mass consumption preceded factory-style mass production; indeed, Western demand for Indian cotton and Chinese porcelain was one factor that would stimulate innovation in European industry. While not starting from zero, the fifteenth to seventeenth centuries saw a blossoming of material life in Renaissance Italy and late Ming China, and then in the Dutch Republic and England. This book begins with the different dynamics and qualities of consumption in these societies.

On the other hand, the attempt to pin down a particular moment for the birth of consumer society had unfortunate side-effects. In particular, it distracted historians from the larger task of charting the evolution of consumption across time and space. 'Birth' was an unfortunate metaphor, because, unlike a baby, consumption was not set on a natural, almost universal path of growth and development. In the course of modern history, it was moulded by states and empires and responded to changes in culture and society, with resultant shifts in lifestyles, tastes and habits, prompting new identities and relationships.

The book's second shift in perspective is geographical. In the Cold War era of affluence, the United States appeared to be the *Ur*-consumer society, exporting its way of life to the rest of the world. The flow was largely in one direction: part of 'America's advance through twentieth-century Europe', as a recent historian has put it.[17] What the thesis of the 'birth' of consumer society did was to make eighteenth-century England the nursery of an Anglo-Saxon model of choice and markets.

Today, in the early twenty-first century, this Anglocentric story stands in radical need of reassessment. With the rapid growth of China, and material advances in India, Brazil and other so-called emerging nations, it is hard to treat consumption as a uniquely Anglo-American export. Though a billion and a half people continue to live at the edge of starvation, it is clear that the bulk of the world's population is living with more. They have not, however, simply followed in American footsteps. Of course, the British empire and its twentieth-century successor, the United States, were active in spreading their material civilization across the globe. But other societies were not empty vessels: they had their own cultures of consumption. African kingdoms that succumbed to European colonizers in the nineteenth century brought pre-existing tastes and habits to the imperial encounter. In the twentieth century, Japan and West Germany joined the club of affluent societies with a ticket stamped 'savings', not cheap credit. Instead of suspecting everywhere a creeping monoculture, we need to appreciate the continuing hybridity and diversity amidst shared trends in rising comfort and ownership of consumer goods.

Nor are all consumers liberal capitalists. Fascist and communist societies consumed, too. Hitler's Germany and Mussolini's Italy were materialistic as well as militarist regimes. They promised their chosen people not only greater living space but a higher standard of living within it. That they left behind destruction and genocide instead does not make their material ambition any less important. In the case of socialist countries, there was less choice and more shortage than in capitalist ones. Consumption always remained subordinated to production, even after Brezhnev and Honecker made concessions to the demand for greater variety, fashion and comfort. Still, it would be wrong to write these societies out of a history of consumption simply because they were not capitalist and their cars and televisions took longer to be delivered and were more prone to break down. Doing so would only make sense if free choice and market exchange were the only criteria of judgement. No society before 1900, not even Britain, the cradle of industrial capitalism, was able to match either the volume or the throughput of goods in socialist Europe.

Widening the story in time and space in this way has a third implication for the approach taken in this book, and this concerns its cast of characters. The conventional picture of shopping and choice is crowded with advertisers, brands and malls. This book does not deny their contribution, but consumption has been framed not only by market forces.

It has been shaped by states and empires, through war and taxes and the often violent transplantations of people and goods from one part of the world to another. Ideas of the 'good life', and the goods and services needed to make it a reality, have come not just from marketing gurus on Madison Avenue but from social reformers and city planners, moralists and churches, and, at crucial moments, from consumers themselves, who have rallied together, using the combined force of their purchasing power to improve their own lives and, sometimes, those of others.

Politics, broadly defined from the top and from below, is therefore a running theme in these pages. This is partly to give attention to how, in addition to reflecting disposable income and time, people's lifestyles have been the subject of political conflict and intervention. (Some of these were macro-changes, such as tightening or freeing credit and the availability of mortgages, while others were micro-interventions in the very fabric of daily life, down to the size and layout of homes and the wires and switches provided for appliances.) Partly, it is to find out how consumers' own ambitions have changed over time. What has living with more done to politics?

But I am also interested in those bits of consumption which are directly sponsored by states and public policy. Here, I think, the narrative of affluence, with its twin forces of choice and markets, has a blind spot that is particularly troubling, from the point of sustainability as much as history. The consumer boom of the 1950s and '60s was not entirely a market phenomenon. These were the same years that saw the unprecedented expansion of social services which funded or subsidized a growing share of housing, education and health-related expenses, in addition to channelling some income directly to the poor, the elderly and the unemployed. These boom years were the very decades when developed societies were becoming more equal than ever before. This historic era of greater income equality has been reversed since the 1970s – with Turkey a rare exception – but even after recent austerity cuts, the amount of public social spending on benefits, housing and pensions remains huge. In the rich countries that make up the OECD, government social spending peaked at 21.9 per cent of GDP in 2009 and has fallen only slightly since the 'Great Recession', to 21.6 per cent of GDP in 2014. Britain, Germany and a few other countries have reduced their social spending-to-GDP ratios by 2 per cent since 2009, but that still leaves public social spending at levels unparalleled in any previous century of human existence; in fact, Japan, Finland, Denmark and Spain increased their social spending by 4 per cent in this period.[18]

Without the coupled rise of welfare services and social equality, 'mass consumption' would have been less massive. To exclude the contribution of social services and transfers in accounts of consumption simply because they are not bought in a market is a mistake. I have, therefore, included a chapter that looks beyond the marketplace at the role states and companies have played in raising material standards and expectations. Rising levels of consumption cannot just be put at the feet of neo-liberals and blamed on the rich setting off a cascade of excess, shopping binges and debt that trickles down to the rest of society.[19] States, including social democratic ones, have played a significant role, too. The fate of Greece and other countries since the recession shows what happens to private consumption when the public belt is tightened. States – and the people benefiting from services and transfer payments – may not be the biggest beneficiaries of a high-consumption system, but they are nonetheless implicated in it. Any discussion that seriously tries to come to grips with the material intensity of our lives needs to address this.

Finally, the book takes a larger view of what is consumed and why. Studies of consumption draw on powerful views of human behaviour and what lies behind the appetite for more. Mainstream economists imagine an individual consumer who has rational preferences and seeks to maximize pleasure and minimize pain; these preferences might change with age, but the model presumes that the individual knows about this ahead of time. Whether people are always this rational is a matter of debate,[20] but for our purpose perhaps the greatest shortcoming is that this approach tells us very little about change over time. An alternative view is more psychological and takes in social motivation, seeing the root cause of consumption in the human desire to feel superior. Here, consumption is relational rather than an individual preference (rational or not), part of a social positioning system that tells people where they stand. Particular kinds of clothes and other goods simultaneously signal that an individual belongs to one group and keep others at a distance. This is a very old view, going back to the ancients, but perhaps its most influential version today is the notion of 'conspicuous consumption', a term made famous just over a century ago by Thorstein Veblen in his critique of the American rich and their flashy display of luxury.[21] Since people want to be loved and admired, such luxury enjoyed by the few causes envy and emulation by the many, triggering a race in which no one wants to be left behind.

This view of human behaviour remains the single most dominant strand in popular debates about affluence, shopping binges and debt. It is also, as I have said, a partial view of humanity and the dynamics of consumption. Showing off and status seeking does occur, but this does not mean it is the only or the main force quickening the material metabolism. Here a fixation with shopping can be especially distracting. A lot of what we consume happens outside shopping malls and follows a different logic. People consume many goods and services simply as they go about their daily lives, to express duty and affection to each other, and to accomplish tasks of many different kinds. The family meal is a classic example. It involves the purchase of food, its preparation (using energy and stoves or microwaves), dishes served in a particular sequence, gender roles and rituals of eating and sociability. Some goods, of course, can play multiple roles – a new kitchen might be bought to impress or to satisfy the hobby chef as well as to bring the family together. A car can be a symbolic status good, but also a hobby that demands time and expertise, as well as a practical means to commute or drive the children to their music lessons. A lot of goods and resources are used for domestic comfort, such as heating and cooling. And, frequently, they are a means to some other end – for example, the pursuit of leisure activities, hobbies and entertainment. Skiing, playing tennis and fishing require a lot of kit. But skis and fishing rods are rarely purchased for display on a wall, although playing one sport may carry more prestige than another. A radio can be a status item, but its main use is for listening to, often while eating or doing the washing-up. The world of consumption is full of these more inconspicuous items and practices, which do not follow the logic of individual choice and behaviour so dominant in economics and psychology. We are mainly dealing here with social habits and routines, not expressions of individual motivation or desire.[22] The arrival of gas and water, the washing machine and the radio, and the growing pull of leisure activities were all important catalysts for rising levels of consumption.

A better understanding of habits and routines matters for two connected reasons. One is social. The attention given to conspicuous display, while often inspired by a progressive concern with improving the condition of the poor, has inevitably led writers to focus on the very rich and on luxury goods. Emulation and imitation is assumed to explain the demand among the majority of the population. This can sometimes look pretty patronizing. Since it is taken as given that most people ape those richer than themselves, it is not necessary to find out much more about their own habits and motivations. If only they stopped hankering after bigger cars and extravagant accessories and focused on their 'real needs'! Yet it is far from clear whether most people always 'look up' like this. In many situations they look side-ways, taking their cues from their peers rather than those wealthier than themselves.[23] A good deal of change has been widespread and taken place in daily life with the diffusion of materially more intensive forms of comfort and convenience such as lighting, heating, air-conditioning and home entertainment. Giving greater attention to such inconspicu-ous aspects allows us to see more of the texture of society.

A second reason is to aim at a more measured evaluation of consum-ing and its consequences. 'Conspicuous' consumption is easily treated as 'wasteful', as squandering resources that could be put to much better use for society at large; this was what made Veblen such a passionate critic. It might be easier to feel outrage at a £2,000 handbag or a 400-foot luxury yacht complete with swimming pool and hand-cut crystal stair-cases than at an ordinary bathtub, central heating or a pair of trainers. The former suggest excess and extravagance whereas the latter may seem modest and useful. But, from an environmental perspective, the moral equation of private excess with public waste is too convenient. Carbon-dioxide missions from hot showers and baths, heating and cooling the home to ever higher standards of comfort, rushing from place to place, are far greater than those from luxury yachts and acces-sories – although diamonds throw up a lot of mining waste and pollution. The problem, then, is not that critics of conspicuous con-sumption go too far but that they do not go far enough. The environmental challenge is out of proportion to their diagnosis. To put it differently, 'waste' does not just stem from morally suspect forms of consuming. A lot of it comes from practices that are considered 'nor-mal'. It is precisely the usefulness of such habitual forms of consumption and their 'normality' that makes changing them so difficult. This does not mean we should not try, merely that the point of intervention needs to be social practices – what people do that uses up things and resources – not individual morality or motivation.[24]

This book tells the story of the global advance of goods. It does so in two parts which complement each other. The first is historical and takes readers from the blossoming of the culture of goods in the fif-teenth century to the end of the Cold War in the 1980s and the resurgence of Asian consumers since. While it is broadly chronological, it is also thematic, following how the essential building blocks took shape in different regions. It traces the impact of empire on material desires, comfort and identities; looks at how modern cities shaped leisure and infrastructures, and vice versa; examines the transformation of the home; considers how modern ideologies (fascism, communism and anti-colonialism as well as liberalism) seized on the promise of a higher standard of living; and explores how Asian consumers came to join their cousins in the West. Part Two moves in the opposite direction. It takes central topics of concern today and places them in a historical context. These chapters ask about excess and credit; whether we have become a 'harried' society addicted to quick and superficial stimuli; how consumption has transformed generational identities (for the elderly as well as for teenagers and young children); how it has changed religion and our ethics, sense of fairness and connection to distant others – all the way to how we get rid of stuff: have we become a 'throwaway society'?

The last thirty years have seen a veritable boom in consumption studies, with thousands of specialist books and articles, divided by region and period, by particular products and practices, right up to studies of individual department stores and consumer movements.[25] Comparisons are few and far between and, where they exist, tend to focus on Western Europe.[26] For all the insightful detail, this has left behind a bewildering fragmentation of knowledge, with so many trees obscuring a view of the forest. This book attempts to put together these scattered pieces and fill in holes to create a synthetic picture. Instead of focusing only on points of origin or on contemporary affluence, it seeks to understand how we got from the fifteenth century to the present.

Inevitably, a book of this scope cannot cover everything. My intention has been to follow major themes across time and space, not to try to be encyclopaedic. This has required difficult decisions about what to include and what to exclude. In general, I have started by identifying core questions and problems, rather than proceeding from a settled belief in certain causes or consequences. Uncertainty is a useful friend of the historian. Many chapters, indeed many sections, could have grown into books of their own. But this would have defeated the overall purpose of creating a synthetic picture in a single volume. The kinds of examples and case studies I have drawn on in each chapter are not random but are carefully chosen to illustrate larger developments and to signal divergence as well as parallels. Behind them lurk many others which could have been drawn upon for similar effect.

The book is not a global history in the strict sense of covering the entire world, nor does it offer portraits of individual countries. I have tried, rather, to take topics out of their usual habitats and follow them across other parts of the world. In addition to the United States and Britain, which have dominated past accounts, I roam across Europe and Asia, with shorter excursions to Latin America along the way. I would have liked to say more about contemporary Brazil, but here, as in other omissions, I hope that readers with an interest in a particular country will find at least some compensation in the thematic consideration I offer on topics of shared concern, such as the lifestyles of the new middle classes, where I chose to concentrate my energies on China and India. My main focus is on what is called the developed world, but this does not mean it is exclusively on the rich North. I consider the effect of imperialism on colonial Africa and India as well as the impact of migration and remittances on changing lifestyles in not so rich parts of the world. People in the South are not just producers and objects of moral concern for affluent consumers in the North. They are consumers, too, including of fair-trade products.

Moving across time and place like this raises the daunting challenge of moving from the micro to the macro (and back) but has also been one of the pleasures of writing the book. Historians tend to focus on one or the other, but there is much to be found out from following the flow between them.

Since this book is about how we came to live with more things, it also tries to give some attention to the material properties of those things. This may strike the general reader as an obvious point. But it has not always been that obvious to academics, and particularly not to historians. In the 1980s and '90s, when studies of consumption took off, historians took their inspiration from anthropologists. Their main questions were about the cultural meanings of goods and about identities and representation. This book could not have been written without the rich research emerging from this tradition. But, as has become clear once more in recent years, things are not only bearers of meanings or symbols in a universe of communication. They also have material forms and functions. They can be hard or soft, flexible or stubborn, loud or quiet, manual or fully automatic, and much else. They are not just looked at but are handled and require care. Above all, we do things with them. There are good reasons for the adjective in 'material culture'. Only by appreciating that goods matter, so to speak, can we hope to see how and why our lives have become so dependent on them.

As a whole, the book will give readers a chance to look at

consumption in a fresh light. As we will see, morality is woven deep into the fabric of our material lives. This is unlikely to change. The book does not expect to settle the moral debate but tries instead to give readers a more complete toolkit with which to engage with it, and with the urgent task of finding more sustainable lifestyles, too. If we want to be able to protect the future, we need to have a more rounded understanding of the processes by which we reached the present.

PART ONE

I

Three Cultures of Consumption

How fashions and comforts had advanced since his youth, a sixty-year-old chronicler marvelled in 1808. Napkins were no longer just for 'very refined dinner guests' but found on tables everywhere. Rich men paraded about town with their watches dangling from elaborate hooks. Once the habit of the few, tobacco was now smoked by everyone and stored in precious boxes. Some novelties were so recent they could be dated, like the craze for wind screens on houses that had started ten years earlier. Others could be measured by the inch. The sleeves of women's jackets used to be one foot wide. Now, it was fashionable to have them six inches wider. The height of fashion was the 'hundred-pleats skirt', 'a new style', made of crêpe, which ensured it would fall 'very softly'. But change was not confined to the upper levels of society. Even ordinary people were wearing 'new and curious clothing'. One example was the easily removable collar that put new life into an outdated coat. Another was a short-sleeved linen jacket perfect for the summer season and, we are told, especially popular with fat people. 'Frivolous servants' dressed up in black double-threaded silk trousers. There was, perhaps, no better sign of the wave of new fashions than the keeping of animals as trendy pets.[1]

Our chronicler was not writing from Paris or London but from Yangzhou, a prosperous Chinese city on the lower Yangzi river, a little over 200km inland from Shanghai. In his writings, published in 1808, the poet Lin Sumen recorded a fast-changing world of goods, something that in the next two centuries came to be seen as a hallmark of Western modernity. Of course, what was fashionable on the streets of Yangzhou was not exactly the same as in a Paris salon or a London pleasure garden. Lin, for example, describes a 'butterfly shoe', graced by a large satin butterfly on heel and toe, with an inner lining of English wool or Ningbo silk. Popular pets were chickens from Canton and rats from 'the West'. Still, substitute the manifold designs of English shoe-buckles for differently shaped butterflies; silver snuffboxes for tobacco holders made of jade; exotic parrots and goldfish for 'Western' rats; add the legion of European commentators complaining of servants imitating the dress of their masters; and the differences between the two scenes rapidly fade.

Histories of consumption have mainly mirrored those of the rise of the West. Just as it was the cradle of modernity, we used to be told, the West was also the birthplace of consumer society. For all their differences, the influential historians Fernand Braudel and Neil McKendrick saw fashion as the heart of Western capitalism, the force behind its dynamism, desire and innovation. Eighteenth-century France and Britain, they were convinced, had fashion and, with it, modernity; China did not. McKendrick dated *The Birth of a Consumer Society* confidently to the third quarter of the eighteenth century, and located it in Britain.[2]

But was consumer society 'born' in eighteenth-century Britain? Researchers have collected indisputable evidence of the rising volume of goods in eighteenth-century Britain and its American colonies. Yet historians working on earlier European periods were not entirely happy to see their subjects treated as static or defective, little more than a 'traditional' backdrop to the main drama of the birth of modernity in Hanoverian Britain. A race got under way, as one after another claimed a 'consumer revolution' for their own period. Stuart historians have spotted it in seventeenth-century England, Renaissance scholars traced its roots to fifteenth-century Florence and Venice, while medieval historians detected its embryonic stirrings in a new taste for beef and ale and playing cards. Scholars of China added that the Ming dynasty (1368–1644), too, had a cult of things and deserved to be recognized as 'early modern'.[3]

The birth metaphor alerts us to the importance historians attach to origins, and to the tunnel vision this can produce. The focus on national origin has tended to distract historians from comparison across cultures and to reduce the past to an antecedent of the present, a stage on the road to today's throwaway society. This has made it sometimes difficult to appreciate what was distinctive about the use and meaning of goods in earlier times. The next two chapters attempt to provide a more rounded, evolutionary view that allows us to see parallels as well as the ultimate divergence in the global diffusion of goods between 1500 and 1800. There was no single modern consumer culture. Renaissance Italy, China in the late Ming dynasty (1520s–1644), and the

Netherlands and Britain in the seventeenth and eighteenth centuries all saw a notable increase in possessions. All had shops and lexicons of taste. Each was dynamic, but in different ways. Which direction the flow of goods took was, in part, shaped by states and markets, income and prices, urbanization and social structure. Ultimately, however, as I hope to show, it was the values that these societies attached to things that set them apart from each other and made some hungrier consumers than others.

THE WORLD OF GOODS

One of the achievements of the three centuries between 1500 and 1800 was to join together distant continents in a world of goods. Trans-regional trade already flourished in earlier periods. The Silk Road had connected Asia with the Mediterranean since 200 BCE. By 800 CE, the Indian Ocean was a dynamic, integrated trading zone. This early phase used to be associated by historians with pepper and spices, fine silks and other luxury goods. It is now clear that sugar, dates, cloth and other bulk goods such as timber were a significant part of cargo even then. By the twelfth century, dyed and block-printed cottons from India were traded in Cairo and East Africa.[4] Venice, Florence and Genoa acted as gateways between Europe and the Orient, pulling in oriental silks and Turkish carpets in exchange for European metals and furs. What was new after 1500 was not only that the Americas were opened up but that all these trading zones became connected in a truly global manner. A good deal of getting and spending continued to be in regional markets, but these now received an injection of global goods. Tea, porcelain and even sugar flowed from China to Europe and the Americas as well as Japan.[5] American tobacco, turkey, maize (corn) and the sweet potato went to China; cotton textiles from Gujarat and the Coromandel coast found new customers in Europe and her Atlantic colonies, in addition to established markets in Japan and East Asia.

Trade and consumption, of course, are not the same thing. One is about the exchange of goods. The other is about people's acquisition and use of them. Still, the former is a major facilitator of the latter, and so an important backdrop to our story. In the three centuries between 1500 and 1800, global trade was expanding at an unprecedented rate, growing by 1 per cent a year on average.[6] It added up: in 1800, twenty-three times as many goods were floating on the world's oceans as there had been three centuries earlier. These growth rates are particularly impressive when we bear in mind that this was in a period before the Industrial Revolution, in a world which did not know of large, sustained economic growth. By one estimate, the GDP of both Europe and China grew no more than 0.4 per cent a year in these three centuries, and even this reflects mainly population growth. If adjusted per person, their annual rate of growth of GDP drops to 0.1 per cent and 0 per cent respectively.[7] In such an environment of low or zero growth, the rise in trade made a big difference. It brought more goods in greater variety, and even some goods that had never been seen before, such as printed cottons from India and cocoa from the New World. And by widening the channels of commerce, trade encouraged specialization and the division of labour. Instead of mainly consuming the fruits of their own labour – like most peasants growing their own food had for most of the Middle Ages – more and more people sold and bought goods on the market. The growth of trade did not trigger a complete transformation. Even in advanced European societies, many housewives continued to sew and knit at least some of their family clothes and hand them down well into the twentieth century. Elsewhere, some peasants continued to live from hand to mouth. But the rise of commerce did lead to a shift in the balance and orientation of consumption as well as its volume. Choosing and buying things in the market became more significant, home production and gift giving less so. In this sense, commerce and consumption went hand in hand.

In the sixteenth and seventeenth centuries, the main trade current was from East to West. Unlike Spain and England, the Ming was not a global empire. Ocean trade was banned for most of the dynasty; a formal 'sea ban' was introduced in 1371 in an attempt to root out pirates and smuggling, and not abolished until 1567. The ambitious seven voyages to India and the Persian Gulf by the eunuch Zheng He between 1405 and 1433 commissioned by the Yongle emperor were exceptional, and subsequent rulers reverted from an active policy of mercantile expansion. In reality, however, traders continued to find a way through informal and illegal channels. Foreign merchants were officially not allowed to enter the Middle Kingdom except as members of a diplomatic mission. In addition to offering tribute goods to the Chinese court, many such embassies effectively operated as trade delegations. Smuggling took place on a much larger scale. The pirate trader Wang Zhi had several hundred vessels and a 100,000-strong crew under his command in the mid-sixteenth century.[8] Many Chinese merchants simply got around the 'sea ban' by basing themselves on the islands off the south-eastern coast of China; one main route for textiles was via Ryukyu (today, Okinawa). The first European merchants to set up a trading post were the Portuguese, at Macao, also on the south coast, in 1557. A few years later, in 1573, Spanish galleons began to anchor at Manila in the Philippines. In 1609, Antonia de Morga, the president of the Crown of Castile's tribunal (*audiencia*) in the East Indies listed the emporium of Chinese goods that the junks unloaded there for sale to the Spanish. Some of these were in the luxury range: ivory, velvets embroidered with gold, pearls and rubies, pepper and spices. Yet there was also:

> white cotton cloth of different kinds and qualities, for all uses . . . many bed ornaments, hangings, coverlets, and tapestries of embroidered velvet; . . . tablecloths, cushions, and carpets . . . copper kettles . . . little boxes and writing-cases; beds, tables, chairs, and gilded benches, painted in many figures and patterns; . . . numberless other gewgaws and ornaments of little value and worth, which are esteemed among the Spaniards; besides a quantity of fine crockery of all kinds; . . . beads of all kinds . . . and rarities – which, did I refer to them all, I would never finish, nor have sufficient paper for it.[9]

The international marketplace was becoming more crowded with things. But until the middle of the eighteenth century, transactions were lopsided. Europeans paid China not in goods but largely in silver, mined and shipped from the New World. Silver was a crucial lubricant in the growth of markets, because it oiled the wheels of commerce and monetized society, making it easier to buy and sell goods. It was also one thing that China was desperately short of. Its own silver mines were limited, while the demands of the imperial bureaucracy, for which it was the lifeblood, were limitless. Chinese merchants were hungry for the silver that foreign traders brought with them in exchange for Chinese porcelain and textiles. Until the 1520s, the bulk came from silver mines in central Europe and Japan. In the next century, this would be outshone by the bullion from New Spain. Spanish officials had their fingers so deep in corruption that it is impossible to know how much silver was actually shipped in addition to that which they chose to record. But it is clear that the galleons were creaking under the weight as they sailed from Acapulco in the New World to Seville in the old, and on to Amsterdam and London, where the Dutch and English East India Companies put it on their ships sailing to Asia to pay for spices, porcelain, silk and cotton. In the early seventeenth century, at least 60,000kg of Spanish silver reached China every year. In 1602, one official in Acapulco told the Spanish Crown that 345,000kg had been sent to Manila.[10] Still, even then China was not hermetically sealed. In the classic novel *The Dream of the Red Chamber* (*Hong Lou Meng*) (1791), European clocks and textiles make an appearance, as do Western wine and even a Western spotted dog.[11]

This was not a simple success story. Trade wars, piracy and treacherous oceans disrupted the traffic of goods. Vasco da Gama's fleet first reached Calicut on India's south-western Malabar Coast in 1498. Two centuries later, the biggest of the European chartered companies in the East Indies, the Dutch Vereenigde Oost-Indische Compagnie (VOC), still had only two hundred ships. As late as 1700, all European ships combined brought back from Asia 230,000 tons of goods a year, an amount that would fit into two big container ships today. In the early eighteenth century, the VOC dispatched no more than thirty to forty ships a year to Asia. But ships were getting bigger and returning with bigger cargoes; in an average year in the 1680s, VOC ships returned with 9,800 tons from Asia; by the 1700s, it was more than double that (22,000 tons).[12] More boats and goods were crossing the Baltic and Mediterranean, and the continuing importance of these markets must not be forgotten; the Dutch controlled the herring trade in the seventeenth century; the fish was caught mostly in the North Sea and then exported, together with salt, to the Baltic and the German states. Direct comparisons between the European and Asian trade are fraught with difficulties. The voyages, the cargo, its quality and value were all radically different. It is 13,500 nautical miles to sail from Amsterdam to the Dutch East Indies, but only 641 to reach Copenhagen. The profits on a ton of pepper or porcelain vastly exceeded that on a ton of herring. However small comparatively in weight and volume – the VOC's share of all Dutch commerce never exceeded a quarter – it was the precious value of the goods that made the Asian trade so significant. By one estimate, their combined annual value had reached 20 million guilders by the mid-eighteenth century, greater than that of everything the Dutch brought back from the Baltic.[13]

From the late seventeenth century, commerce started shifting towards to the Atlantic world, and this pull was nowhere stronger than for the English economy. In the 1630s, the bulk of goods England sold abroad had been woollens, to the rest of Europe. By 1700, these were being outpaced by the exotic crops from the new world: sugar, tobacco and, to a lesser extent, coffee.[14] But the Atlantic world provided more than cheap new commodities harvested by slaves. It also, and in contrast to China and imperial Spain, contributed a fast-growing customer base. Richard Ligon sailed from England to Barbados in the summer of 1647 on the 350-ton *Achilles*. At the end of his three-year stay, he noted the goods the sugar economy was attracting. A hundred ships a year landed at the island. In addition to 'servants and slaves', they brought 'cloth of all kinds, both Linnen and Wollen; Stuffs; Hatts, Hose, Shoes, Gloves, Swords, Knives, Locks, Keys, &c. Victuals of all kinds, that will endure the Sea, in so long a voyage. Olives, Capers, Anchovies, salted Flesh and Fish, pickled Macquerells and Herrings, Wine of all sorts and the boon Beer *d'Angleterre'*.[15] These were humble beginnings. When Ligon crossed the Atlantic, there were barely more than 100,000 English settlers in the West Indies and North American colonies. By the time American patriots declared their independence in 1776, the figure was approaching 3 million. In trade, the real take-off came in the decades after 1700. In that year, England exported goods worth £205,000 to the West Indies. Seventy years later, the value of exported goods was £1.2 million. Exports to North America grew even faster in this period, from £256,000 to £2.5 million, especially metalware and woollen goods. In the course of the eighteenth century, the American colonies, the West Indies and West Africa grew into an important extension of Britain's home market, taking, by its end, one third of British manufactured exports; in 1700, it had been a tenth.[16]

This new era of global exchange had a profound effect on daily life. A single plant could have transformative effects. In seventeenth-century China, the arrival of the nutritious and high-yielding sweet potato from America allowed millions of peasants to switch from growing rice to cultivating silk, which, in turn, could be traded for other goods. (Sweet potatoes were eaten baked or boiled, dried and preserved, made into flour for noodles and even brewed into wine.)[17] American corn, similarly, freed up land and hands, enabling Chinese peasants to pick tea leaves and cultivate sugar for the market instead of having to grow their own rice to survive. There were losers as well as winners. When the Dutch introduced price controls for cash crops, Indonesia and Malaysia plunged from prosperity to poverty, as peasants reverted from selling sugar, pepper and cloves on the market and buying cloth and other goods in exchange to a hand-to-mouth existence of subsistence farming. In the Atlantic world, Europeans' appetite for sugar spawned an organized form of capitalism based on slavery and the

cultivation of a single crop. This was the most extreme form of commodification. People's thirst for goods in one continent was quenched
by enslaving millions of humans as goods for sale in another. What
difference empire made to consumer culture, and vice versa, is a subject
that will receive sustained attention in a later chapter. Before that, we
need to discover where the demand for things was coming from in the
first place.

MAGNIFICENCE AND MAJOLICA

The expansion of interregional and then global trade intersected with
the commercialization of everyday life. Signs of the latter can be
observed in Renaissance Italy in the fifteenth century and in late Ming
China, as well as in seventeenth-century Britain and the Netherlands.
At a time when the vast majority of people in Europe and the rest of the
world led a rural existence, struggling for survival, these precocious
societies were hotspots of consumption. In each of them, people
acquired more things than they had had before. The spread of markets
and the division of labour that came with it enabled growing numbers
to buy items they had not made themselves. In economic terms, these
developments could be summed up as a growth in demand, and, as we
shall see, high wages and the ability to buy more goods were important, especially in the Low Countries and England. But we must attend
to quality as well as quantity if we want to understand the role goods
played in these societies, that is, we must follow their meaning, value
and function. Demand was shaped by culture and social structure, and
these differed in these societies. While all benefited from greater trade
and spending, Renaissance Italy, Ming China and early modern Britain
and the Low Countries ultimately developed different cultures of consumption. It is to these differences that we now turn.

Between the eleventh and the fourteenth centuries, Europe enjoyed a
commercial revolution in which Florence, Venice and Genoa emerged
as the prosperous link between the Byzantine and Muslim world and
the courts and fairs scattered across a predominantly agrarian Europe.
Initially, traders from these North Italian cities brought back from the
Levant silk, spices and other luxury goods which they exchanged for
grain, furs and metals from Europe. The next two centuries saw a
reversal of fortunes. The European economy expanded while that of

the Levant declined. Tuscany developed a flourishing wool industry, favoured by its marshy maremme south of Pisa which attracted sheep from the Apennines. By the thirteenth and fourteenth centuries, Lucca, Florence and Venice had learnt the art of making silk fabrics, paper and glass themselves. Alongside banking and commerce, it was these artisanal trades that made these cities prosper and expand, turning Northern Italy into the most urbanized region in Europe. Florence began building its wall in the late thirteenth century: two centuries later, it enclosed an area fifteen times as big. The city fed its citizens with grain from Puglia and Sicily. By 1575, Venice's population was close to 200,000, twice its size before the Black Death hit in 1348. The fortune of these cities was tied to their luxury trades, and these, in turn, were tied to Europe's uneven recovery from the bubonic plague. At first, the demographic catastrophe reduced the pressure on land and raised the wages of workers lucky enough to survive. By 1500, growth had come to a halt, as the population had recovered and each acre had to feed more mouths. Prices were rising, especially for food. This hurt ordinary workers, but it benefited nobles in Scandinavia and central Europe, as well as the aristocratic landowners in Italy and, by extension, the Florentine and Venetian artisans who were making the luxury goods for their palaces and tables.[18]

Possessions were becoming more numerous and refined. Increasingly sophisticated tableware was symptomatic of this trend. Households accumulated more spoons, forks and drinking glasses. In 1475, the Florentine banker Filippo Strozzi ordered four hundred glass beakers from Murano. In the same year, the silk merchant Jacopo di Giannozzo Pandolfini bought a set of twelve silver forks and spoons. When Domenico Cappello, son of the Venetian admiral Niccolò, died in 1532 – a time when Europeans elsewhere had never held a fork, let alone owned one – he left behind 38 table knives with silver handles, 12 decorated and gilded spoons and forks, and 42 plainer forks.[19] Instead of individual plates, the elite table was increasingly graced with a complete service. By the late sixteenth century, that of the Marquis of Squarciafico in Genoa, contained 180 pieces of pewter and 104 dishes of different sizes. The neighbouring Brignole family could claim over 115 plates of silver. Some new objects made their appearance, such as the eggcup or silver and gold *spazadente* and *stuzicatoio da orecchi*, which allowed more elegant cleaning of teeth and ears. Pewter was sometimes ordered from London and stood on fine linen cloth from Flanders. Most of the silver spoons and bowls, the glass and pottery, however, were the product of local craftsmen, such as those enamelling gilded glass goblets in Venice or glazing the colourful majolica pottery in Montelupo in Tuscany and Casteldurante in the Marche (see Plate 1); in the sixteenth century, local textiles also gained the upper hand over imported ones. What made these objects precious was their increasingly sophisticated design and decoration rather than their material or novelty.[20]

Silver and tableware were signs of an emerging culture of domestic sociability and politeness. Rooms were increasingly separated by function, creating distinct spaces for sleeping and eating and for libraries and picture galleries. In their homes, merchants and aristocrats introduced a special room for more intimate entertaining: the *salotto*. By the late sixteenth century, the home and its possessions displayed a family's character as well as its riches. A guidebook of the period for the new bride advised her to 'guide' her guests 'around the house and in particular [to] show them some of your possessions, either new or beautiful, but in such a way that it will be received as a sign of your politeness and domesticity, and not arrogance: something that you will do as if showing them your heart'.[21]

Politeness looked outward but also inward, for it put a new premium on private comfort and self-fashioning. In his classic *The Civilization of the Renaissance in Italy* (1860), Jacob Burckhardt, the Swiss pioneer of cultural history, was among the first to note the growing attention to personal beauty and self-fashioning in *cinquecento* Italy: 'No sort of ornament was more in use than false hair, often made of white or yellow silk.' Alongside hair extensions – some made of real hair (*capelli morti*) – false teeth and perfumes, Burckhardt observed the wider interest in cleanliness, manners and comfort, unique at the time. In Bandello's novellas, he noted, 'we read . . . of soft, elastic beds, of costly carpets and bedroom furniture, of which we hear nothing in other countries.' Linen was abundant and beautiful. Everywhere, 'art enobles luxury', from the toilet-table with 'numberless graceful trifles' to carpets with intricate designs. Foreign visitors were impressed when they received their own clean napkin at meals.[22] In more recent years, historians have filled in Burckhardt's depiction of domestic comfort. In the course of the sixteenth century, armchairs appeared alongside traditional stools. There was an influx of Turkish carpets, books, prints and musical instruments. Children played with spinning tops and wooden horses, while adults would entertain themselves with backgammon or the riskier (and illegal) new betting game *biribissi*. And precious objects came to be viewed not only in their own, separate terms but as part of a tasteful ensemble that had to be built up over time with knowledge as well as money. For connoisseurs like the Florentine humanist Niccolò Niccoli with his rich book collection, and Isabella d'Este, the Marchioness of Mantua, who assembled coins, vases and statues, acquisition became a life project.[23]

Previous accounts have often traced the 'civilizing process' to the influence of the court,[24] but it was in fact far more widespread than a court could reach. Artisans in Genoa, for example, left behind six, sometimes twelve silver spoons. Most had a bed, a table, sheets and linen.[25] When a fairly modest innkeeper died in Siena in 1533, his own bedchamber contained a bed with a pair of curtains and coverlet, and a chest with several decorative bedspreads. In addition to seventeen shirts, his wardrobe included a silk headdress, satin gloves, a velvet hood and a pair of sleeves made of embroidered silk damask.[26] In Venice, fifty years later, death – and the inventory that was drawn up to record his household possessions for inheritance purposes – gives us a snapshot of the living conditions of an artisan in Venice, the wood-carver Andrea Faentino, who had done some work for the great architects of that city. Unlike a growing number of his contemporaries, Faentino worked and lived in the same space, in a rented house. He was working on two sculptures of apostles and angels when he died. Like his contemporaries, he stored most of his possessions in a *cassa*, or chest, but his four were made not of cheap, ordinary wood but of more precious walnut. They contained clothing, blankets, textiles and shoes. He also owned twelve gilded knives with ivory handles and eight silver forks. In the kitchen there were four walnut stools and a table described as 'old' in the inventory. He had two pans, two salt shakers, forty pieces of pewter and fifty-eight white majolica plates – the recent fashion had been for whiteware over coloured plates. His bed, by contrast, was modest and lacked the soft refinement found in merchant homes. On the wall, however, hung not only a simple painting of the Madonna but also one of a woman with a lute, and another of 'il Turco', revealing the widespread influence of oriental images at the time. Faentino also had an impressive number of books on religion, architecture – including a book by Leon Battista Alberti – and history (one about the Albanian national hero George Skanderbeg, who led Pope Pius II's crusade and contained the Ottoman Muslim expansion until his death in 1468). And he owned a lute.[27]

Faentino's material world was one of modest comfort, quite inferior to that of merchants and aristocrats. In 1620s Florence, for example, Piero d'Agnolo Guicciardini, who had made his riches in the local wool and silk industry, had 151 pictures on display in just one room of his town house.[28] A century earlier, the poor noblewoman-turned-courtesan Elisabetta Condulmer had six gilded chests filled with linen, abundant silver spoons, down-filled mattresses, and, alongside the *Adoration of the Magi*, paintings of the nude Andromeda and of naked men.[29] In Venice in the 1570s, even a better-off illuminator of manuscripts owned twenty-five paintings (one of Nero), a mirror and a map of the world as well as rugs from Cairo and Persia.[30] Still, however limited or old, Faentino's possessions were clearly part of a shared material culture which included tableware, books and music-making – a lute or harpsichord could be found in most Venetian households at the time – as well as an appreciation of pictures as objects of art to be owned and displayed rather than used purely for religious or devotional purposes.

It can be tempting to think of pre-modern societies as extremes of inequality, where a few rich lords feasted off the many ragged poor, and this was true for much of Europe, still then predominantly rural. Urban Northern Italy was different. Florence in 1500 was no more unequal than the United States in 2000. The city consisted not of two cultures, with a sharp divide between the elite and the homogeneous plebs. Rather, most Florentines found themselves somewhere on a spectrum that ranged from the marginalized poor to more comfortable artisans and shopkeepers. Books were not only bought by the patrician elite but by bakers, carpenters and metalmakers. In small doses, some artisans were even sharing a taste for a few exotic goods, such as oriental rugs. Imported Hispano-Moresque ceramics found ready buyers among shoemakers, blacksmiths and textile workers; one wool weaver owned a set of 7 jars, 13 bowls and 34 plates.[31] A similar picture can be found in the bustling commercial centres of Northern Europe such as Antwerp, which saw a rapid diffusion of pictures and majolica in the seventeenth century.[32]

Still, to see in the Renaissance the 'seeds of our own . . . bravura consumerism' would be to go one step too far.[33] While possessions and ideals of comfort had begun to fill the home, they remained part of a civic culture that continued to be oriented towards public display and posterity, not private pleasure or the lure of novelty. Its animating spirit was magnificence, its goal perpetuity. The spending on personal possessions was trivial compared to the outlay on monumental town palaces and public banquets. These were the main drivers of Renaissance consumption. The Palazzo Strozzi, for example, begun in 1489, cost the Florentine family half as much as Henry VII's royal palace at Richmond.[34] Aristocrats tried to outshine each other with the most richly decorated chapel, but the goal was to demonstrate one's magnificence and *virtù*, not simply to show off one's wealth. The point of reference was Aristotle, who had praised the appropriate display of private wealth as a sign of civic virtue and pride in a community governed and defended by like-minded brave, propertied citizens. The patrician elite in Renaissance Italy were pioneers in shifting the symbolic currency of power from people to things. Unlike landed aristocrats elsewhere in Europe, the Strozzis and fellow nobles asserted their status through splendid objects and buildings, not by keeping a large camp of retainers. Suitably presented, paintings and vases could reflect the cultured character of a citizen at home. Yet private pleasure and *comodità* (comfort) for their own sake remained suspect. They had to mirror a devotion to the public good. The admired life was that of the active citizen who increased the splendour and strength of his city by erecting monumental buildings, commanding an army and sponsoring communal feasts and public works. Large-scale consumption was safe – and could be enjoyed – when it occurred in the pursuit of such public ends. In that sense, a richly decorated chapel like that of the Salviati family in San Marco, Florence, was very different from – say – a modern Ferrari. Luxury stood in the service of posterity, to engrave the family name in the annals of the city for generations to come. The civic humanism of the Renaissance favoured solid things. Money was spent to last.

The conservative character of Renaissance consumption can be seen in the type, function and circulation of goods. Though Italian cities imported oriental silks and by 1500 had started to produce their own for the European market – the first chapter in what would become a Western success story of copying and replacing Eastern wares – silk was exceptional. Overall, material culture was one of notable continuity. There was more of everything, and a few new items arrived on the scene, such as the upholstered chair, but a household in 1600 still mostly had the same kind of things as two hundred years earlier. It was a culture of refinement rather than novelty. The design on goblets became more elaborate, the wood carving on furniture more ornate, the wall hangings more splendid, but the materials and type of goods hardly changed.

As well as being useful, and sometimes decorative, goods functioned as assets. In a cash-poor economy, and especially in times of inflation, clothes, linen and silverware were important ways to store value. For rich and poor, the pawnshop served as a local bank. If an individual needed some cash, they pledged their clothes or household goods, then, a few months later, redeemed them. Because goods were storehouses of wealth, they needed to be durable. A cloak, a ring or a detachable velvet sleeve was of little use if it was so fashionable that in a year's time it would have lost its value as a pledge. The vast majority of people dressed like their grandparents.[35] When Renaissance people accumulated goods, then, it was not because they had discovered fashion and went through things more quickly but because they were building up their assets. In 1633 in Venice, one oar-maker left his widow 43 shirts, 25 sheets, 63 tablecloths and napkins and 105 pewter plates.[36] Most textiles and silver spoons in inventories like this one were probably never or rarely used but stored away as material life insurance. Linens, of course, were worn out through regular use and had to be replaced, but silks and other high-quality goods were carefully maintained and reused for as long as possible. When in 1580 the Milanese Livia Tollentina was widowed, she recycled her married wardrobe to upholster her coach and make ecclesiastical hangings.[37]

Gifts, pawns, personal loans and securities connected high and low in a circle of mutual dependence. The Castellani, an elite Florentine family, are a good example. In 1460, Francesco di Matteo Castellani deposited his wife Lena's embroidered dress with a money-lender to raise cash to pay back a loan. Yet Lena was set to attend an aristocratic wedding, so he simultaneously borrowed a large pearl set in gold, a diamond set 'in the Parisian style with white and red flowers and green foliage', and, for good measure, a ruby set in gold. In reverse, he loaned a family heirloom and cloth hangings bearing his coat of arms to a noble friend who had brokered his sister's marriage. To a local schoolmaster, he sent freshly purchased manuscripts of Suetonius and Justinian, and, on feast days, lent some of his clothes and swords to local blacksmiths. Possessions were always on the move.[38]

Possessions thus circulated within a social orbit of reciprocity and trust, rather than expressing an act of individual choice. Their free flow was further restricted by moral boundaries. In Renaissance thought, to be virtuous and independent, a citizen had to be self-sufficient. Leon Battista Alberti and other writers idealized the citizen who consumed the fruits of his own estate without needing to resort to shops and strangers. The lesson of the ancients was that Rome was strongest when it was simplest. Too many possessions produced over-sensitive weaklings incapable of defending their republic. In reality, aristocratic men certainly did shop in markets, but such excursions were more about civic bonding than shopping for leisure, as the historian of Renaissance shopping Evelyn Welch has shown. Drawing on Cicero, Renaissance morals approached trade with a double standard that justified a social order with patrician merchants at the top and plebeian shopkeepers at the bottom. On a large scale, commerce was virtuous and added to the glory of the community. Merchants brought back their wealth to their landed estates. On the small scale of a shop, by contrast, trading was 'vulgar', the Venetian writer Tomaso Garzoni stressed in the late sixteenth century. Patrician merchants might have made their wealth in trade, but they retained a foothold in the country, on their estate, which provided them and the community with food. Shopkeepers just sold. Could they be trusted? That shops were a vital link in the chain of distribution, connecting merchants and customers, and, indeed, creating demand, would have been anathema to contemporaries. Shopkeepers continued to labour under a stigma of low status. In Milan in 1593, the Senate banned them from entering the nobility.[39]

The suspicion of shopping was part of a larger fight against luxury and all the evils that came in its train. The argument reached back to Plato, who had reasoned that the material world was a mere shadow of reality. While his ideas had never been entirely lost in the Middle Ages, they gained new prominence in the Renaissance through the Platonic Academy at Florence, where Marsilio Ficino translated his complete works into Latin. In his *Republic*, Plato followed the decline of a virtuous, frugal city as it was corrupted by the lust for luxurious living. When citizens kept to the basic needs set by nature, the city was in 'sound health'. Once people started to follow the desire of their flesh, however, they set in motion an insatiable drive for more that ended in war and corruption. First, they wanted to 'lie on couches and dine from tables, and have relishes and desserts', but, rather than being satisfied with that, this only whetted their appetite for 'painting and embroidery . . . and gold and ivory'.[40] The quest for luxury was insatiable and forced the city to expand and go further and further afield in search of resources, leading to war and conquest. Aggression abroad was worsened by decay at home, as luxury emasculated formerly virile citizens. The loss of self-control turned vigorous citizens into weak brutes, incapable of defending themselves. Inevitably, the corruption of the flesh led to the corruption of a republic. This link between a frugal lifestyle and republican greatness on the one hand, and private excess and public corruption on the other, was a central theme for Cicero, who would become the Renaissance's favourite Latin author.

Christianity gave these classical ideas a fresh thrust and urgency. Just as Plato had argued that bodily pleasures interfered with the soul and the pursuit of true knowledge, so the Church warned that the desire for earthly possessions distracted Christians from the life of the spirit. In the Sermon on the Mount, Jesus had said: 'Lay not up for yourselves treasures upon earth, where moth and rust doth corrupt, and where thieves break through and steal; but lay up for yourselves treasures in heaven, where neither moth nor rust doth corrupt, and where thieves do not break through nor steal: for where your treasure is, there will your heart be also.'[41] By tracing the lack of self-control all the way back to original sin and Adam's eviction from paradise, Christian teaching also sexualized luxury. The desire for goods, money and carnal lust all sprang from the same source.

That luxury easily led to lechery was common knowledge in the Renaissance and contributed to the moral disquiet about shopping and excess. A mercer in late-sixteenth-century Venice, for example, was accused of living 'luxuriously' because he was suspected of having extramarital affairs.[42] Only in the hands of the Church, where it was used appropriately to proclaim the glory of God through splendid buildings and paintings, was luxury safe. On the eve of a daughter's wedding, a Venetian patrician might proudly show off trousseaus full of clothes richly embroidered in silk or gold, but conspicuous consumption was tempered by no less powerful displays of frugality, such as choosing to be buried in the coarse brown habit of a Capuchin monk. The path to heaven started with simple living. According to a popular Venetian proverb, he who 'disregards the world and its things within it, is given wings to go to the summit of heavens'.[43]

Suspicion of luxury was the kindling with which the Dominican friar and fanatical preacher Girolamo Savanarola started the 'bonfire of vanities' in the middle of Florence's Piazza della Signoria in 1497. On the bottom step of the pyrotechnic pyramid lay precious foreign tapestries; higher up were images, board games, musical instruments and books by Boccaccio.[44] It is important to remember that many Florentines not only owned paintings, lutes and domestic furnishings but many also happily piled them up 20 metres high and danced around the flames as they burnt.

Opulence and excess did not only trouble fanatics like Savanarola. In the fifteenth and sixteenth centuries, the Venice senate passed more than a dozen laws and regulations against such a 'sumptuous' lifestyle. Lavish weddings and expensive fur-lined coats made visible inequalities in wealth and status that threatened the republic's ideal of equality and restraint. They also triggered a competitive spending spree which pushed some citizens into debt. For a republic frequently at war, this was a serious concern, for money that had been spent on ermine or gilded furniture could not be collected as a special war tax. A first law in 1299, by the then Great Council, tried to curb spending on weddings, and applied to everyone except the doge and his family. Another in 1334 complained about the 'inordinate and especially superfluous expenses by both men and women' and justified restrictions because cupidity, 'the root of all evil', was all too easily creeping up on its citizens. In the fifteenth century, the senate's principal concern shifted to dress. The wide sleeves of mantles (socha) were prohibited in 1400. Deprived of that distinction, wealthy Venetians started to line theirs with precious furs. The senate responded with a new law in 1403 that outlawed the use of ermine and marten. A string of restrictions followed, from the allowed size of the trousseau to the use of gold and silver in gowns and coats. In 1512, the senate stipulated that no more than six forks and six spoons were to be given as wedding gifts and banned a whole range of luxurious home furnishings, including gilded chests and mirrors and highly decorated bed linens. Two years later, a special magistracy was set up, with three noblemen empowered to check, regulate and punish extravagant behaviour. Some offenders, they reported, threw bread and oranges at them. 'The fickleness of unbridled appetites of men as well as women,' the senate concluded, 'continues to grow so much that few care about spending.' Still, it would not give in without a fight. In 1562, the senate launched its most comprehensive attack, outlawing tapestries that were 1.5 metres high, prohibiting gilded fireplace furnishings, and stipulating in fine detail what was permissible at banquets, all the way to specifying that desserts were to consist only of small pieces of 'ordinary pastry' and fruit in season.[45]

While precocious, then, consumption in Renaissance Italy also remained precarious, kept in check by a series of material and moral constraints. Excess and opulence retained a stigma of sin and corruption. Splendid possessions could not simply satisfy individual desire but needed civic legitimation. Tableware and furnishings were becoming more numerous and sophisticated, but, overall, they were part of a culture of refinement rather than of novelty and its twin, disposal. Quality, storing wealth and reuse retained the upper hand, for

patricians as well as artisans. While the number of stools and chests
was on the rise in the homes of craftsmen, the choice of words used by
many inventories is telling: they are described, simply, as *vecchio* or
vechissimo (old or very old).[46] We are not dealing with a consumer culture of high throughput; it was geared towards luxury rather than the
mass market. The tone of consumption thus reflected and reinforced
the extraordinary accomplishment of the highly skilled artists and artisans in these urban luxury industries. At the same time, this left these
societies highly vulnerable, heavily dependent on the fortunes of small
luxury markets and sensitive to shifts in international trade and politics beyond their control. The Portuguese discovery of a new sea route
to the East in 1497 sidestepped Venice. Competing traders from Northern Europe arrived in the Levant in the wake the Holy League's defeat
of the Ottoman fleet at the Battle of Lepanto in 1571, off western
Greece. The rise of Atlantic trade in the next two centuries pulled the
centre of commercial life north to Amsterdam and London, further
marginalizing Venice and Florence. Plagues in 1575–7 and 1630 deci-
mated their populations, and the Thirty Years War (1618–48) cut them
off from the German fairs and cities, one of their remaining markets.
The Mediterranean chapter of magnificent luxury consumption had
come to a close.

The clash between commerce and custom, between desire and restraint,
was a European-wide phenomenon in the late Middle Ages and early
modern period. Venice and Florence may have been at the forefront,
but markets extended their reach in this period, from respectable cities
like Nuremberg to small towns in the Black Forest. And as they did
they brought with them more goods and tastes that posed a challenge
to the social order. In addition to financing trade and buying and selling in bulk, merchants were themselves ambassadors of new fashions.
Hans Fugger, for example, the head of the powerful creditor-merchant
family firm in sixteenth-century Augsburg, southern Germany, was a
discerning lover of shoes made in the Spanish fashion. He ordered his
from Spanish shoemakers in Antwerp with detailed instructions, down
to their small, ornamental perforations.[47] Such new fashions and
imported goods were vehicles of distinction and emulation that could
unsettle existing hierarchies and codes of behaviour. What if a
style-conscious apprentice were to copy Fugger's shoes? And what of
the local shoemakers who might lose their livelihood to foreign competitors? Things did not have to come from very far to be threatening.

In 1453, for example, Nuremberg passed a sumptuary law outlawing long peaks on shoes, a fashion blamed on nearby Swabia.[48]

Between 1300 and 1600, a great wave of sumptuary laws swept across Europe. In parts of central Europe, such legislation retained its force into the nineteenth century. At first, regulations banned extravagant meals and gifts at weddings and funerals. In the fifteenth century, the focus shifted to clothes.[49] In German-speaking central Europe, over 1,350 ordinances were passed regulating clothing alone between 1244 and 1816.[50] These laws reveal a world in flux and give us an opportunity to explore a little further how early modern societies responded to the challenge posed by the advance of goods. The laws' fixation on clothing is simple to explain. These were the most visible markers of one's place in the social order, denoting status, rank, age and gender. Unlike in Venice, where many restrictions had an egalitarian motif and hit all patricians and citizens alike (except the doge), most European sumptuary laws were instruments of inequality, seeking to preserve a finely graded hierarchy. Thus, Nuremberg fairly typically reserved silk, furs and pearls for aristocrats, princes of the church and respected professions; only knights and doctors of law were also allowed to wear gold threads.

Societies reacted in three ways to transgressions. One extreme was a sweeping ban. In Strasbourg, an ordinance of 1660 fined anyone who dared to imitate 'new' clothes from foreign nations, 'regardless of whether it looks good or bad'. The other was to give in. Under Henry VIII, in 1532–3, the English Parliament had passed an act 'for Reformacyon of Excesse in Apparayle' which, among other things, limited the wearing of purple silk and cloth of gold tissue to the royal family (dukes and marquesses were allowed to wear it in their doublets). It forbade anyone not in receipt of at least £100 a year to 'weare any satene damaske silke chamlett [a mixed fabric of silk and wool] or taffata in his gowne cote with sleeves or other uttermost apparell [sic]' nor any foreign fur.[51] In London in 1574, a member of the Merchant Taylors' Company was sent to prison for wearing a 'pair of hose lined with taffety, and a shirt edged wieth silver contrary to the ordinances', and a few years later, the Lord Mayor ordered that apprentices were allowed to wear only hand-me-downs from their masters.[52] But, overall, English justices of the peace showed little enthusiasm for enforcing the restrictions. Elizabeth I issued several clothing proclamations, but by the end of her reign such bills routinely died in the House of Commons. The Tudors' sumptuary legislation lapsed in 1604. The Netherlands had not even bothered to introduce any. Significantly, these two were the most advanced societies not only commercially but, as we shall see, also in learning to live with change and trusting people to monitor and fashion themselves. Still, in the seventeenth century, they were the exceptions, not the norm.

Most societies steered a third, middle path, making some allowance for new tastes by creating ever more finely detailed codes of dress. In a new regulation in 1693, the patricians of Nuremberg tolerated the fashionable short jacket that replaced the customary long coat, but when it came to caps and accessories imposed an elaborate set of gradations. Ladies of old noble families were allowed to wear a silken velvet cap with a sable or marten border that, during public festivities, could be adorned with buckles of gold and pearls, though not diamonds. Wives and daughters of 'respectable merchants' could also wear a velvet cap, but the cost was not to exceed twenty-four gulden and they were prohibited from attaching gold buckles or gold lace. Matrons and maidens of regular trading families and other members of the third rank were allowed a cap of velvet with dyed marten, to cost no more than ten gulden, without any gold whatsoever. Shopkeepers – the fourth rank – were limited to tripp-velvet with rims of simple fur (not marten) and neither silver nor gold. Similar rules reached into other spheres of life. Their visibility made coaches, for example, potent carriers of status. Only the first class was permitted to ride in a dream of silk. Coaches for the second class had to be upholstered in cloth, but red and blue were prohibited. Third-class people had to pay fifty thalers for the privilege of renting a coach and then had to make do with plain grey cloth, horses without shiny harnesses and coachmen without livery.[53]

Enforcement varied. While many communities relied on their citizens to restrain themselves, others were more punitive. In eighteenth-century Basel, thousands of women were fined for dress abuses. Few went as far as Mustafa III, the sultan of the Ottoman empire, who in 1758 went out in disguise into the Aya Kapisi quarter in Istanbul to check whether non-Muslims were respecting his clothing laws. When he stumbled across a Christian and a Jew wearing yellow leather boots reserved for Muslims, he had them promptly hanged.[54] In general, enforcement depended on local allies in guilds, churches and community courts with an interest in disciplining offenders and defending the social order. On their own, states and central governments were able to do very little. That was one major difference between England on the one hand and central Europe, France and Scandinavia, on the other, where local authorities actively fined and admonished transgressors in their midst.

Such laws expressed a view of the world as one of fixed horizons. A society had limited resources and needed order and self-restraint to survive. For early moderns, to consume literally meant to use something up or to exhaust it. This latter sense – for example, burning wood or wearing a coat until it is entirely worn through – was still alive as late as 1900.[55]

In societies with limited technological innovation and no sustained growth, the flight of money and resources was a natural cause of concern. A burgher's wife in Nuremberg who wanted a silk dress from Lombardy threatened to put local artisans out of business. Money was scarce and once spent on luxuries escaped the reach of the tax officer. That spent on foreign luxuries left the local economy altogether. This was the background for many sumptuary laws which tried to stop wealth from going to waste through luxurious living. Moreover, if one group in the community started to consume more, it diminished what was left over for everyone else. How people dressed, what they ate and how they spent their money was therefore treated as a communal matter, not an exercise of private choice. Consumption had to be subordinated to production. Dress marked one's guild and profession. Social stability required people to know their place and consume within their limits. New fashions, especially when coming from outside, were an assault on this conservative order. Those who lusted after new styles, the Strasbourg law of 1660 explained, were losing 'the commendable steadfastness for which our old German forefathers had a singular reputation in other things as well as in clothing'.[56] Fears of extravagance were directed at conspicuous patricians as much as at uppity plebeians. The limits placed on wedding feasts, jewels and expensive caps and gold buckles all targeted status competition at the top. If wedding costs were allowed to spiral out of control, the children of burghers would marry later or never, sending a community on the road to extinction.

These were the fears. What about the reality? How much difference did these restrictions make? Clearly, they were unable to arrest the march of time and completely freeze societies in a static mould. Artisans would innovate with new styles and materials to stay ahead of the rule book. In many parts of Europe, living conditions picked up again after the ravages of the Thirty Years War. In the early seventeenth century, for example, men and women in Bondorf and Gebersheim, two villages in Württemberg, Germany, owned 3 and 12 articles of clothing respectively. A century later, the number had shot up to 16 and 27 pieces. By 1800, it had doubled again.[57] Not far from there, in the town of Laichingen in 1796, the wardrobe of the merchant Georg Christoph Nestel included 17 short fashionable vests cut with a high waist, in colourful patterns as well as in black and white, and including ones made of cotton and silk. Eighty years earlier, the merchants and members of the local town council had accorded themselves the privilege of wearing cotton as well as gold and silver. But the lower orders continued to have to wear local dress made of a mix of linen and cotton. By the mid-eighteenth century, half the clothes of married women were inventoried as 'old' or 'semi-old'. The authorities forced artisans and the poor to appear in black dress in church and at town gatherings. Consequently, the town was a sea of plain, black dress. Light cottons and bright colours – the twin marks of the fashion revolution, to which we shall return – started to make their slow appearance only in the 1790s, a full century after they had reached the Netherlands and England.[58]

That some people transgressed the regulations and authorities felt required to update them repeatedly, does not mean they had no effect. After all, transgressors oriented themselves by the clothing order and, by aspiring to the silk ribbon or gold buckles of the rank above, indirectly acknowledged it as a point of reference. By ranking goods and fashions, such laws could reinforce a social pyramid of taste. This was why, in France, the royal court played 'the motor role in sartorial distinctions', in the words of the historian Daniel Roche.[59] All eyes were fixed on king and queen.

And defiance could be costly and painful. The Justices of the Peace might have looked the other way in Elizabethan England, but in central Europe the authorities were far less forgiving. In Germany's Black Forest in 1708, the pastor of Ebhausen delivered a sermon against 'over-dressed women' and had the church court impose an 11-kreuzer fine on one of them for wearing a neckerchief too large for her station. This was one month's pay for the average maidservant. Five years later, in the nearby small town of Wildberg, one in ten inhabitants were fined for clothing offences in the course of the year. The average fine was a week's wages. Almost all those punished were women. Public shaming was widespread and risked long family feuds, if not complete ostracization. In communities like these ones in Württemberg, sumptuary legislation was powerful because it was part of a wider regime of social control by guilds and churches which used simultaneous checks on work and spending to keep women subordinate and labour cheap. Single and young women and widows were not allowed to earn their living independently by weaving or selling other products in the marketplace. Instead they had to live in and work as servants for artificially low, fixed wages. Masters ensured, too, that their apprentices were kept in place and their guilds did not have to face competition; the guilds excluded migrants and Jews as well as women. It was a double screw. Husbands tightened one end to limit what their womenfolk could earn and then turned the other to restrict what they could spend it on. The local courts gave a husband the power to take his wife's earnings, and if he wanted to, to forbid her to make purchases altogether. Husbands thus monopolized both production and consumption, and this explains why in some towns their wardrobes continued to be fuller than those of their wives.[60]

This was a rural area, but it was not cut off from the world or locked into some timeless agrarian self-sufficiency. These small towns and villages were tied into markets, weaving and spinning for export. They lent and borrowed money. The women there clearly had desires for novelties, like the unfortunate miller's maidservant who spent a day in jail in 1736 because she had been spotted buying ribbons at a fair. What distinguished such communities was not an absence of desire but a social and institutional straitjacket which kept desire and spending in check. It was difficult for consumption to flourish in such an environment.

PHOENIX HAIRPINS AND
REFINED ANTIQUES

In the second half of the nineteenth century, after the Opium Wars, a picture of China as static and closed began to take root in the Western mind. This was, we now know, the distorted result of seeing the recent success of the Industrial Revolution in Europe as proof of a unique Western talent for modernity, and of China's backwardness. In 1582, when the Italian Jesuit Matteo Ricci set foot in China, a more positive view prevailed. Ricci was impressed by the dynamism in Nanjing – 'they say there are two hundred thousand weavers here' – and by how, elsewhere, the Chinese 'now weave a cloth made entirely of silk', 'in imitation of European products'. The long, loose sleeves worn by Chinese men and women reminded him of the Venetian style. He, too, noted the 'exceedingly large number of books in circulation . . . and the ridiculously low prices at which they are sold'. Ricci was struck less by difference than by the 'similarity of customs': 'Their use of tables, chairs, and beds is wholly unknown to any of the peoples of the states that border on China ... there are numerous points of advantageous contact between ourselves and the Chinese people.'[61]

Ricci had an interest in emphasizing parallels, but his observations – like those of the Portuguese Jesuit Álvaro Semedo, who admired the 'traffic and commodities' in China in the 1620s–'30s – do record how commercialization was sweeping across Ming China, releasing a torrent of goods, fashions and desires; and with it anxieties about social disorder and moral decay.[62] One channel was via smuggling and the tribute trade. Another was legal coastal shipping. In 1548, one official counted over a thousand boats in a period of thirty-nine days along the Zhejiang–Fujian coast in the south-east of the empire.[63] Such coastal trade connected with a much larger regional trade across this vast land empire. Its major artery was the 1,794km-long Grand Canal, the oldest man-made waterway in the world. Reopened in the 1510s, it ran from Hangzhou on the eastern coast to Yangzhou and the Yangzi, and all the way to Beijing in the north. The primary purpose of this grand piece of infrastructure was military, allowing army barges to carry grain to Beijing, the Ming's new capital from 1421. But while government boats had priority, the Grand Canal inevitably facilitated the movement of food and goods in general. Grain from Guangzi in the south-east was ferried north to the cities along the Yangzi. From farmers in the central interior, rice travelled down the Yangzi to reach consumers in Jiangnan, the area around Shanghai. From the north, raw cotton was shipped to Sung-Chiang prefecture, south of Shanghai, where it was turned into cotton cloth and then sold on to the rest of China. Cups and bowls from Jingdezhen, the porcelain capital in the north-east, a few hundred miles inland from Canton, were traded by merchants from Huizhou in the south (see Plate 3). In reverse, tea and sugar from the south travelled north. Soybean cakes were transported down the coast from Manchuria. Books printed in Sichuan ended up in the hands of readers in Nanjing and the Yangzi delta.

The Jesuit Semedo felt the Chinese were 'naturally inclined to be merchants' and found the 'traffic' they made 'incredible', not only between provinces but within cities: 'for almost whatsoever is found in the shops, is sold in the streets in a lesser quantity.'[64] In the sixteenth century, this web of commerce was growing rapidly, and as it did, producers became connected to more distant consumers, enabling farmers and artisans to specialize and earn their living by selling in the market and buying a

Ming China, 1600:
internal and external trade routes

0 _____ 500 miles
0 _____ 500 km

N

MANCHURIA

Great Wall

Beijing ■

Cotton

SHANDONG

Cotton
cloth

Grand
Canal

PACIFIC
OCEAN

Xi'an

Cotton cloth

Nanjing • • Yangzhou
• Shanghai

Hangzhou

SICHUAN

Chengdu

Jingdezhen •

ZHEJIANG

Silk, cotton,
porcelain,
lacquer
and sugar
to Japan

Yangzi River

Cotton
cloth

Rice

FUJIAN

Books

Silver
from Japan
and
Spanish America

Grain

Tea
and sugar

Porcelain

GUANGXI

Huizhou

Guangzhou •
Macao •

VIETNAM

BURMA

Silver from
Europe and
Spanish
America

Silk, cotton and
porcelain
to Europe

PHILIPPINES
(Spanish)

to Europe

• Manila

growing portion of their food and clothing. In Shandong, in northern China, for example, it became so profitable to cultivate cotton that many farms stopped growing their own grain. Increasingly, barter was being complemented by getting and spending.

The sprouts of consumption were nowhere stronger than in the Yangzi delta, the commercial heart of China, and home to around 30 million peasants who made and sold cotton cloth in exchange for rice, raw materials and household goods. Although late Ming China was far less urban than Northern Italy, the Netherlands or England, there was an overall increase in market towns and, by 1700, in the most advanced regions, such as Jiangnan, perhaps as many as one in six people lived in towns. Unfortunately, we lack for China the detailed inventories that would allow us to paint a picture of the material world of the late Ming with the same sharpness as for early modern Europe; it is not possible to itemize tableware, furniture and other possessions. We are much more dependent on surviving reports from social observers who wrote local gazettes, novelists and authors on taste and household management. Inevitably, what we see has been filtered through their own values, which are often nostalgic for an idealized, simpler past and condescending about the new desires of lower-ranking groups. But, if read carefully, they let us at least reconstruct the main characteristics of the material environment in which they lived. The memorialist Zhu Guozhen, for example, offers a short description of a household in Jiangnan around 1600. Here the head of the household wove cotton into cloth, which he then exchanged for silver with which he bought the rice for his family. 'A family's rent, food, clothing, utensils, and what it spends for social occasions, for raising children, or for burying the dead all come from cotton.'[65] The account is silent on how much is spent on social occasions, what he buys for the children, their clothes and lifestyle, but it leaves no doubt about how specialization was fuelling greater consumption.

Cities sported new fashions and more advertising. The historian Gu Qiyuan (1565–1628) noted how in Nanjing in his youth, women's fashion had changed once in ten years, but in his ripe old age it changed every two or three years. Hairstyles were reaching unprecedented heights, with so-called 'peony heads' held up with the help of false hair.[66] In addition to porcelain from Jingdezhen, urban markets sold embroideries from Hangzhou and cloisonné wine cups made by Muslim craftsmen in Beijing. Commercial culture was thriving, with a growing number of shops, more literate consumers, and shopkeepers and artisans battling for their attention with increasingly adventurous advertising and early attempts at trademarks and branding. Print culture and books reached a mass market in the seventeenth century, made possible by simpler fonts, woodblock cutting and a greater division of labour. There were textbooks and plays, erotic handbooks and novellas, some selling for as little as 0.1 taels, an affordable sum for middle-ranking officials, scholars, merchants and their wives. In Jiangnan, perhaps as much as half the population were literate.[67] This more textual culture considerably widened the possibilities of advertising. Shops sported trademarks on hanging banners. Butchers in Suzhou, for example, announced that they were the 'Authentic Lu Gaojian' or, even better, the 'Real Authentic Lu Gaojian', hoping to cash in on the reputation of the famous original Lu. In Beijing, some signs were 10 metres tall; others were illuminated by lanterns at night. Women wore hairpins with the characters 'Zhu Songlin', the trademark of the high-quality bamboo craftsman Song Lin. On Nanjing's bustling Sanshan Street, bamboo-furniture shops traced their craft back to Pu Zhongqian. From Japan came folding fans, lacquered tables and gold-painted screens and cosmetic boxes. The main customers for luxury goods were the gentry and literati-scholars; some penned poems and biographies in praise of artisans, which boosted their name recognition further.[68] Yet, in rich, developed regions like Guangdong (Canton) in South China, peasants, too, were increasingly consumers as well as producers, buying sugar, shell jewellery, betel nuts and rain cloaks.

Style was trumping substance everywhere, according to local Chinese gazettes. 'A family without as much as an old broom,' one gazetteer wrote in 1591, 'go about in carriages . . . and dress themselves up in the hats and clothing of the rich and eminent.' In villages, rustic frugality was giving way to a bewildering obsession with fashion. The scholar Chen Yao noted in the 1570s how 'young dandies in the villages say that even silk gauze isn't good enough and lust for Suzhou embroideries . . . Long skirts and wide collars, broad belts and narrow pleats – they change without warning.' It was all about *shiyang*; literally, 'the look of the moment'.[69] A new genre of almanacs appeared, offering 'the Complete and Categorized Essentials for the Householder' (undated but in circulation by 1600), a kind of guidebook on household management that also gave tips on interior decoration. Such books mainly targeted the gentry and urban merchants. That one surviving copy has also been found in the grave of a small rural landowner, however, suggests that porcelain and other goods found their way into the hands of at least some aspiring farmers in the countryside, too. Advice on decorative objects would have been of little value without objects to begin with.[70]

Growing abundance was most visible among merchants. The Confucian novel of manners, *Jin Ping Mei* (*The Plum in the Golden Vase*), completed in 1618, paints a vivid picture of it. The book is about the social climber Ximen Qing, who is about to take a third wife, Meng Yulou, the widow of a textile merchant. The matchmaker introduces her by listing her possessions: 'She owns two Nanking beds, with retractable steps; four or five trunks full of clothing for all four seasons, figure gowns and so forth . . . ; pearl headbands and earrings, gold jewelry set with precious stones and gold and silver bracelets and bangles . . . And she has two or three hundred bales of fine cotton drill as well.' When Ximen finally meets her, she wears 'a kingfisher blue surcoat of figured silk, emblazoned with a mandarin square . . . On her head: Pearls and trinkets rose in piles; a phoenix hairpin was half askew.' A manservant brings tea 'flavored with candied kumquats in carved lacquer cups inlaid with silver and provided with silver teaspoons in the shape of apricot leaves.'[71]

A merchant's wife wearing a phoenix hairpin may not sound much but it signalled how things were challenging the social order in the late Ming. Phoenixes and dragons were the Chinese equivalent of pearls and marten. They were meant to be reserved for empresses and princely consorts. In 1593, the scholar-official Zhang Han complained that they were now worn by wives of the Fourth and Fifth Rank. Since the first Ming emperor, Hongwu (1368–98), customs had become more 'lavish' and 'people all set their resolve on venerating riches and excess'. 'Nowadays men dress in brocaded and embroidered silks, and women ornament themselves with gold and pearls, in a case of boundless extravagance which flouts the regulations of the state.'[72]

Excess knew no limits, and there are some striking parallels between extravagance in late Ming and early Qing China and that recorded in Europe. Just as the Venetian senate worried about excessive spending on ceremonies, a Beijing magistrate in the 1590s noted how the cost of funerals was reaching astronomical proportions.[73] The great salt merchants of Yangzhou were notorious for their intense competition for status, trying to outspend each other on horses, weddings and funerals. 'There was one,' one writer recalled in 1795, 'who erected wooden nude female statues in front of his inner halls, all mechanically controlled, so as to tease and surprise his guests.' Another 'wished to spend ten thousand taels in a single day. One of his guests suggested that he buy gold foils. From the tower on top the Golden Hill he threw down the gold foils which, carried by the wind, soon scattered amidst trees and grass and could not be gathered again.'[74] Giacomo da Sant'Andrea, a spendthrift from Padua, had already perfected this art in 1300, throwing silver and golden objects into the river Brenta.[75]

The salt merchants' original source of wealth was their exclusive right to sell salt at monopoly prices, which they had acquired in exchange for delivering grain and fodder to the empire's armies in border regions. In the 1490s, the exchange of grain for salt was relaxed, and traders now branched out into silk and tea as well as money-lending. In Yangzhou in the eighteenth century, the new Qing emperors elevated the salt merchants to official positions, exempting them from the rigorous civil-service examination. Merchant houses announced their new status with palatial halls and exotic gardens, with pavilions and bridges. Some merchants added verandas. Red sandalwood came from Arabia, jade from Burma and marble from Sichuan. In 1795, the Yangzhou writer Li Dou noted nine types of coloured glaze roof decorations. Four gardens, he wrote, were built in a Western style. Many merchants decorated their homes with clocks and mirrors from Guangdong and Europe.[76]

As in Italy, then, so in China: the rising tide of goods reached merchants and peasants as well as the landed elite. The royal court was far less important for the diffusion of new goods and manners than has been assumed. The main source was in market towns and in an increasingly commercialized countryside. The opulence of merchant houses challenges the standard view, handed down by nineteenth-century Western visitors, that the Chinese were a frugal people. All this does not, however, mean that fashion, novelty and conspicuous consumption were embraced with open arms. Quite the contrary, they were condemned for upsetting established social hierarchies and morals. Like Renaissance Europeans, the Ming ranked land above trade. The state, an ancient proverb said, was like a tree: its roots were agriculture; traders and artisans were mere branches. Prosperous merchants were challenging this natural order. A chronicler in Jianning (Fujian province), in 1543, was horrified that some people actually chose to become merchants.[77]

The Ming gentry and the scholar-official elite viewed novelty with suspicion. Affluent merchants and plebeian consumers were disorderly elements in society. A barrier was erected against uppity consumers and their unwanted things: taste. Wen Zhenheng was a powerful landholder whose challenge to the Ming court landed him in prison. In 1645, he starved himself to death when the Manchu conquered Suzhou. In his prime, however, he had also been a new type of style counsellor, the author of the *Treatise on Superfluous Things* (1615–20). The title was deliberately ironic, for his real subject was the things 'essential' to a cultured life. 'Bed curtains for the winter months should be of pongee silk or of thick cotton with purple patterns. Curtains of paper or of plain-weave, spun-silk cloth are both vulgar.' For the art historian Craig Clunas the *Treatise* signalled how China was developing its own 'proto-consumer culture'. In one sense this is right. Style, too, could now be learned from a manual. In Wen's world, status was no longer just the result of birth but of refined consumption, that is, the aesthetic skill of discriminating between the elegant (*wu*) and the vulgar (*su*). Taste created cultural capital. What mattered was not the number of possessions: rather, the aesthete showed his sensibility by creating a 'harmonious' (*yun*) relationship between an object and its surroundings. A vase had to be the right size for a room. It ought to be of bronze in winter and spring, porcelain in summer. And it certainly should never hold more than two varieties of flowers, 'since too many gives the appearance of a wine shop'.[78]

Although the *Treatise* celebrates the pleasure gained from things, it was in other ways the antithesis of the consumer culture that would transform the modern world. Novelties held few attractions. Things produced for the market were suspect. True value resided in antiquity, and could be appreciated only by the connoisseur. As one of Wen's associates wrote in the preface to the *Treatise*, sons of the nouveau riche and 'one or two dullards and persons of mean status' were trying to pose as 'aficionados', but they inevitably failed, 'besmirching anything which comes into their hands with their wanton fumbling and grabbing, to an utter pitch of vileness'.[79] The quest for antiques set off its own kind of demand, including grave robbing. It sparked a wave of imitations. 'How many authentic antiques can there be?', one poet asked, warning readers to watch out for forgeries in late-seventeenth-century Suzhou; one technique was to apply vinegar to brass to create the illusion of an ancient patina.[80] Still, this kind of demand was ultimately about digging up old bronzes of the Shang period (*c.*1600–*c.*1046 BCE) and collecting antique pieces of calligraphy from the Jin dynasty (265–420) – that is, goods that already existed – rather than attracting various new kinds of possessions. One exception was newly commissioned pieces of fine art and calligraphy, but even here the brushwork often followed the style of ancient masters. Instead of releasing a current of new articles, antiques and original pieces of art were stocks to be cherished for life; indeed, even in the afterlife. Many merchants as well as members of the imperial elite chose to be buried with antique jades and bronzes, old paintings and books. In 1495, the merchant Wang Zhen was interred with twenty-four paintings and two scrolls of calligraphy – two of the paintings were signed Yuan dynasty (1279–1368) but have been exposed as fakes; several others were by fourteenth- and fifteenth-century court painters and scholar-officials.[81]

If goods were circulating more quickly, then they did so in a conservative cultural environment. Like Renaissance Italy, late Ming China failed to generate a sense that consumption might make a positive contribution to state, society and economy. Confucian literature was full of warnings about how extravagance led to corruption. *The Plum in the Golden Vase* offered several volumes' worth. Ximen Qing's decadent lifestyle is a morality tale of how his lust for things and sex fed off each other until they overpowered him. Fine clothes and ornaments constantly arouse Ximen. In one scene, he observes a maidservant, Chun-mei, 'wearing a blouse of aloeswood-colored moiré [a wavy silk] with variegated crepe edging, which opened down the middle, over a drawnwork skirt of white glazed damask. Shoes of scarlet iridescent silk, with white soles, satin high heels, and gold-spangled toes were visible beneath her skirt.' In addition to a tiara of jade, 'enchased [sic] with gold', her 'hair was further adorned with plum-blossom shaped ornaments with kingfisher feather inlays . . . which had the effect of further enhancing:

> The fragrant redness of her ruby lips, and
> The glossy whiteness of her powdered face.
> Before he knew it, Hsi-men Ch'ing's [Ximen Qing's]
> Lecherous desires were suddenly aroused.

Soon he is fondling her breasts, 'sucking at the teats like a young calf'. The desire for things and the desire for flesh propel each other forward on the road to self-destruction. Ximen lays out fifty taels of silver and buys four sets of silk clothes for a singing girl he kept in a brothel, 'explaining that he planned to deflower' her. 'Amid dancers' skirts and singers' clappers, he is forever seeking novelty.'[82] The novel played relentlessly on the double meaning of the 'silver stream'. Letting it flow too freely drained the body of its physical and financial strength. At thirty-three, Ximen dies from an overdose of aphrodisiac. By implication, too much consumption would be equally fatal to the health of the nation.

The elite did not put on a hairshirt, although literati circles and scholarly women did favour simple attire, and courtesans in late Ming China were known for their plain robes.[83] What the gentry, scholar-officials and literati did was to promote an alternative canon of values and behaviour. Rather than competing directly with the conspicuous consumption of some rich merchants, they sidestepped it, elevating an aesthetic disposition and the disinterested appreciation of art for art's sake above material wealth and the accumulation and waste of possessions that came with it. Cultural capital trumped economic capital, to use the language of later sociologists.[84] High status was demonstrated through connoisseurship, the collection of antiques, the writing of poems, playing the *guqin* (zither), studying the classics or spending idle time with an exclusive group of friends. Drinking games with poetry competitions are the principal form of leisure in the novel *Dream of the Red Chamber* (1791). In the sixteenth century, the elite formally forbade villagers such pleasures, including the collection of rocks and antiques. Pleasure required mental rather than material resources. It could not simply be purchased like any other commodity. A lot of it was contemplative, spiritual and aesthetic, such as admiring mountain scenes and gardens in nature or paintings. Sociability could involve heavy drinking, but even this was valued as an act of transcendence that left the physical world behind.[85] It resembled the classical Aristotelian ideal of leisure as contemplation – reserved for the elite who did not need to work – more than our busy contemporary pursuit of material satisfaction and productive leisure.

This learned, contemplative culture of consumption continued to set the social tone in late Ming and Qing China. Commerce had unleashed a diffusion of goods and created new classes of consumers, but it had not yet created its own lifestyle or value system. The conflicted identity and soul-searching of the salt merchants of Yangzhou here is revealing. True, some were nouveau riche flouting their wealth. But many others took their cue from the official scholar elite and its ideal of the cultured life, learning to play the zither, sending their poems and calligraphy to scholars for approval, and preparing their children for the official examinations, hoping to secure a place among the elite for future generations. As we have seen, already in the late fifteenth century a merchant such as Wang Zhen would try to enhance his status by surrounding himself with paintings by the educated elite. By the eighteenth century, the Hung merchant family entertained famous scholars, astronomers, poets and calligraphers. Ma Yueguan and his brother Ma

Yuelu became poets in their own right and used their wealth to build up a rare book collection and host a literary salon; they also generously supported historians and poets through sickness and financial difficulties.[86] Culture, not material wealth, was the ticket into the elite, and this was a successful strategy for many merchant families, if not in the second, then in the third generation, when sons became degree-holders and officials. All this is not to say that China was stagnant or closed. As we have seen, Japanese lacquer, European glass and Western pet rats found their way into the empire. But how much bigger would the trade in foreign goods have been if the Ming had had its own Western Ocean companies along the lines of the European East India companies. European goods remained on the margins of Ming and Qing culture. They were mere curiosities with no assigned place in a value system which looked for meaning in the past.[87] The cult of antiquity pulled in the opposite direction from the pursuit of novelty that would distinguish an acquisitive consumer culture. In that sense, China was commercially advanced but culturally backward looking.

MORE STUFF

It was in the north-west of Europe, in the Netherlands and Britain, that a more dynamic, innovative culture of consumption came to take hold in the seventeenth and eighteenth centuries. The growth in shops, markets and personal belongings was well under way in Renaissance Europe and Ming China, but their further expansion in the Netherlands and Britain was only in part a continuation of this earlier trend. For the two countries separated by the North Sea changed after 1600 in ways that, together, created a new kind of consumer culture. The exponential rise in stuff went hand in hand with a rise in novelty, variety and availability, and this was connected to a more general openness to the world of goods and its contribution to the individual self, to social order and economic development. What distinguished the basket of goods in the eighteenth century was the combination of novelty, variety and the speed of change. Tobacco, tea and porcelain were new things that spawned new forms of consuming, socializing and self-representation. Equally important was the jump in variety. The manufacturer Matthew Boulton, who sold tea kettles, buckles, buttons and toothpick cases, had 1,500 designs on his books.

There was, perhaps, no better indicator of the change than the shift in the meaning of the word 'consumption' itself. After centuries in which the body politic had been modelled on the human body, the consumption of goods began to be distinguished from its epistemological cousin, consumption as a wasting disease. Personal excess, of course, continued to attract moral critics, but it was no longer a dangerous social disease. Instead, a chorus of new voices defended man's appetite for more as the impetus of human advancement. Here was a fundamental transformation, overturning centuries of received wisdom: less is more gave way to more and more. Once regarded as a drain, to be checked and kept under control, consumption was now defended as a source of wealth. In 1776 Adam Smith pronounced it the 'sole end of all production'.[88]

The first signs of this change were apparent in the Dutch Republic, which declared its independence from Spain in 1581. The Netherlands pioneered a new type of society and economy that provided a favourable environment for greater consumption. Its distinctive twin features were an integrated market and a mobile, open society. Land was not in the hands of the aristocracy, as in most of Italy and the rest of Europe, but belonged to smallholders. Secure in their tenure, thanks to long leases, they made the most of the rising demand and price for food from a growing urban population by switching from basic wheat and rye to higher value butter and cheese, meat and garden vegetables. Peasants turned into market-savvy farmers. Grain was profitably imported from eastern Germany and the Baltic. In the towns and cities, money and labour flowed into increasingly specialized and successful industries. Haarlem became the centre for fine linen, Delft for ceramics. Leiden, in 1584, produced 27,000 pieces of cloth: eighty years later, it churned out six times that number, and with a growing share of pure woollens (*lakens*).[89] If Ming China saw signs of specialization, the Dutch raised the division of labour to a new art form. Their villages were characterized by a proliferation of skills and trades, of shoemakers, wagon-makers and horticulturalists as well as farmers and small traders. In contrast to the wool trade in Flanders, guilds were absent in the new Dutch export trades, which had little interest in having obstacles placed in their path. Even where guilds existed, as in the north of the Netherlands, they were subordinate to urban governments and lacked the independent power to restrict trade and labour they possessed elsewhere on the continent.[90] Instead, in the Netherlands, the textile trade acted as a magnet for workers from Flanders and Liège. The United Provinces were one commercial zone, without the many regional barriers and taxes that required goods to be unloaded and assessed every few miles in the German-speaking lands. More than anywhere else in the world, labour, capital and land were allowed to find their most productive outlet.

It was this virtuous mix of flexibility and fluidity that enabled the Dutch to attract and expand trade, and to absorb the pressures that a growing population and seventeenth-century wars were putting on living conditions elsewhere on the continent; the Dutch population doubled between 1500 and 1650, reaching 1.9 million. All this was not enough to trigger an industrial revolution. But, and crucially for our interests, it did manage to convert a growing population to high wages and a growing demand for goods; in turn, rising real wages prompted the search for labour-saving devices such as windmills and the horse-powered butter churn. Thus, a typical dairy farmer at the end of the sixteenth century was able to buy one third more rye for every pound of butter he sold than at its start. He could afford to buy more things.[91]

The domestic interior and everyday life were transformed. Farmhouses were filling up with things. By the late seventeenth century, it was common for a farmer to own a clock, carpets and curtains, paintings and books, and some porcelain dishes standing on eight-sided tables, items rarely seen a century earlier. At the time of his death in 1692, the rich farmer Cornelis Pieterse de Lange owned sixty-nine silver buttons, in addition to a number of silver spoons and knives. Few of his neighbours in Alphen were able to match that, but the rise in comfort and possessions was palpable everywhere. By 1700, mirrors had become ubiquitous. Proliferation, though, was uneven. Some things, such as the number of tablecloths, saw little change; the number of bedsheets might even have slightly declined. Others, however, were multiplying apace. In the village of Lisse, the widow Anna Nannige Beverwijk had sixty-one table napkins, for example. Linen, in particular, was a deposit of wealth, and many farmers poured their new earnings into it. On modest dairy farms, men and women had eighteen linen shirts each in their wardrobes by the 1670s, three times the number a century earlier. Fashionably decorated linen was replacing cheaper wool.[92]

The new scale and taste for abundance was nowhere more apparent than in the great townhouses of Dutch cities. The Bartolotti house, on Amsterdam's Herengracht, was an opulent burgher's palace. In 1665, its great hall had a long oak table with twelve red velvet-upholstered

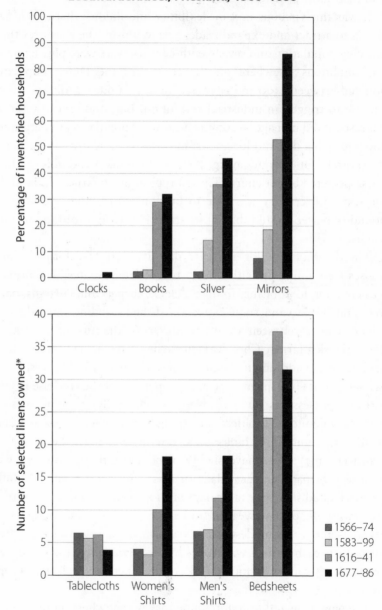

Possessions among rural households in Leeuwarderadeel, Friesland, 1566–1686

Percentage of inventoried households

100
90
80
70
60
50
40
30
20
10
0

Clocks   Books   Silver   Mirrors

40
35
30
25
20
15
10
5
0

Number of selected linens owned*

Tablecloths   Women's   Men's   Bedsheets
               Shirts   Shirts

■ 1566–74
☐ 1583–99
■ 1616–41
■ 1677–86

* By farm households with ten or more milk cows.

Source: Jan de Vries, *The Dutch Rural Economy in the Golden Age, 1500–1700* (1974), pp. 219, 221.

chairs, an ebony-framed mirror and paintings of the Nativity, family members and the Princes of Orange on the wall. Even the maid had seven paintings in her room. Typically, such townhouses integrated several worlds of consumption, bringing together fine silverware made in Amsterdam and Utrecht with cabinets from east India, tiles from Delft and carpets from the Orient. In 1608, the Dutch East India Company put in an order for over 100,000 pieces of Chinese porcelain.[93] Some of this would be re-exported, but a good deal would find its way on to Dutch tables and walls. As Simon Schama has brilliantly shown, there was nothing especially plain or thrifty about the Dutch, not even among more modest merchants and shopkeepers.[94] In 1717, a tailor's household on the Prinsengracht contained five paintings, Delft earthenware, pewter tankards, seven lace curtains, two dozen chairs, several books, six sets of bed linen, forty-one napkins and a birdcage. There was a general appetite for more possessions and finer, decorated articles that went right across the population, as illustrated by the lotteries organized by many towns to raise money for charities. In Veere, in the south-western Netherlands, the lottery in 1662 offered wine goblets and standing salts, silver jars and silver sword handles. And these were just the minor prizes. Those lucky to win the top prize took home a silver table service of dishes, plates, tankards, candlesticks and forks worth 4,000 florins.

After the Reformation, Calvinists continued to repeat ancient warnings about wealth as a mother of extravagance. But, importantly, local magistrates refused to listen. To the contrary, towns staged lavish banquets, allegorical masques and fireworks to celebrate their greatness and wealth. It is worth noting how, by contrast, in China, the late Ming emperors repeatedly forbade their subjects to 'make their pleasure' and set off fireworks in New Year celebrations.[95]

In the Dutch Republic, an acceptance of pleasure simultaneously gained hold with a taste for new things. Commercial success and an openness to the world of goods went hand in hand, not least because growth relieved some of the age-old pressure against 'sumptuous' lifestyle and luxury manifest elsewhere. Consumption no longer automatically threatened national ruin and to eat up finite resources. Rising earnings meant the Dutch were able to consume more and still invest, belying the simpler morality tale made famous by Max Weber in *The Protestant Ethic* (1904/05), where Calvinist thrift appeared as the cradle of modern capitalism. For the Dutch, the temptations of luxury could be managed as long as burghers did not forget they were also citizens. It was possible to steer a path between excess and austerity. This acceptance extended to smaller pleasures in everyday life, not only to drinking beer (as long as it was downed in licensed public houses) but also to new habits developing with exotic foods, drugs such as smoking tobacco, and sweetening food and drink with sugar. As early as 1620, tobacco was being smoked for pleasure. Puffed in moderation, in a clay pipe made in Haarlem or Groningen, it was acceptable. Some militant Calvinists smelled self-indulgence and stupefying lethargy, but there was little taste for prohibiting the crop in Amsterdam, where it was dried and cut. In fact, the major growers who started to cultivate a domestic variety included a deacon of the Reformed Church.[96] Here were portents of an emerging mass culture which diffused previously exclusive exotica and integrated them into daily life. The world of consumption was beginning to be navigated with a new moral compass.

Across the North Sea, in England, the volume and variety of goods also grew exponentially in this period. They would reach unprecedented dimensions in the eighteenth century, but the first effects of greater spending can be traced back all the way to the late Middle Ages. In England, real wages in 1500 were three times higher than they had been in 1300, thanks to the Black Death (1348–9), which had wiped out over one third of the labouring population. Higher wages and cheaper food created demand for more varied, higher quality goods. Instead of making do with the bread and cheese of their ancestors, English workers by the late fourteenth century were enjoying meat and ale. Peasants started to wear shoes made of cattle hide rather than the cheaper sheepskin. In the fifteenth and sixteenth centuries, most of the higher quality goods that marked this rising standard of living were foreign imports, such as silks and velvets from Italy or stoneware from the Rhineland (see Plate 4). Tellingly, beer was introduced from the Netherlands – its hops made it last longer than native ale, which went off in a week, and thus assisted the spread of alehouses.[97] In the sixteenth century, the domestic market became the backbone for products made in England. Imitations joined imports, often with the help of skilled immigrant labour. London emerged as a production centre for glass and silk. The biggest trade was that in the new draperies, the lighter, finished kinds of wool which artisans from the Low Countries introduced to England.

The shift towards lighter fabrics, new mixes of silk and wool, and changes in fashion unsettled the social hierarchy of dress and threatened confusion. Elizabethans started to complain about servants sporting coats made of the finest cloth and hose dyed with Flanders dye. In his *Description of England* (1577–87), William Harrison yearned nostalgically for a time when an Englishman had been known abroad by his own cloth and, at home, contented himself with wearing simple woollen clothes. But, he acknowledged, those days were gone for good:

> Such is our mutability that to-day there is none to the Spanish guise, to-morrow the French toys are most fine and delectable . . . by-and-by the Turkish manner is generally best liked of, otherwise . . . the short French breeches make such a comely vesture that, except it were a dog in a doublet, you shall not see any so disguised as are my countrymen of England.

It had come to a point 'that women are become men, and men transformed into monsters'. So enthralled by fashion and constant change were his countrymen that Harrison prayed to 'God that in this behalf our sin be not like unto that of Sodom and Gomorrah'.[98]

Under the Stuarts in the early seventeenth century, the elite picked up where their Italian Renaissance counterparts had left off, amassing art, books and antiquities and mingling in shopping halls such as the New Exchange in London, opened by James I in 1609.[99] Less magnificent but more consequential were mundane changes that reached across society to produce elements of mass consumption. New, cheap products made their appearance. The knitting frame made it possible to mass produce stockings, in a growing variety of types and patterns. Gregory King in 1688 estimated that 10 million pairs of stockings were bought a year, or two pairs per person.[100] There were clay pipes, pins and white soap, brass and steel thimbles. These were made in small workshops and show how wrong it is to assume that mass consumption needed factory-style mass production. In the home, the move from wood to coal led to the introduction of saucepans and kettles that could be placed directly on a stove or grate instead of having to be hung over the fire. Pottery, too, was becoming more versatile and widespread. When Daniel Defoe stepped into a 'large hollow Cave' in Derbyshire inhabited by a poor lead miner and his family in 1727, he was surprised to find 'shelves with earthen ware, and some pewter and brass'.[101]

Not everything was new. In Stuart England, the upper gentry continued to eat a lot of beef and go hawking, as in medieval times. For them, shopping trips to London coexisted with home production and gift-giving through an extensive patronage network of yeomen, tutors and wet nurses looking for work and support. In that sense, consumption was part of a labour exchange as much as a purchase in a marketplace. Still, even where products were not intrinsically new, they often came in a growing number of varieties. In the first half of the seventeenth century, for example, Lady Alice Le Strange of Hunstanton, in Norfolk, bought sixty-two different kinds of fabric, including fine linen cloth from the Netherlands, Spanish cloth, linen damask, plush (an expensive silk velvet), satin, camlet (a soft angora wool), plain woollen broadcloth and 'best scarlet', a singularly expensive type of wool. The Le Stranges first bought a piece of Indian cotton in 1623 – a calico border for one of Alice's gowns. Their beds were dressed in black velvet and gold, crimson damask and scarlet as well as in the new draperies made in England, such as the so-called jollyboys, and decorated with Indian nicanee cotton. This household belonged to the upper five hundred of the kingdom – Sir Hamon was a knight – and spent in excess of £2,000 a year. But, however privileged, the Le Stranges were not living in a world apart. There was no sharp antithesis between old luxury and modern novelty, which is sometimes thought to have separated the aristocracy from merchants and shopkeepers – at least not in England. Gentry families like the Le Stranges also ate off pewter plates and were drawn to some of the same new tastes and products that circulated in commercial society at large, such as the lighter, new draperies and Indian cotton.[102]

New goods began to spread even more rapidly after 1700. Inventories give a snapshot of the gathering momentum. In 1675, no household in London owned china or utensils for tea and coffee. By 1725, 35 per cent owned the former, and 60 per cent the latter. In the earlier year, one in every ten households had a clock, pictures and some earthenware. By the latter, every second home did.[103] In Tudor times, curtains, cottons and looking glasses could generally be found only in the homes of local elites. On his death in 1554, Thomas Harrison, a Southampton girdler (belt-maker) and bailiff, owned 'painted curtains' for the window in his chamber. His parlour included a bed with yellow curtains of saye, a fine-textured cloth resembling serge.[104] By the 1720s, such furnishings were a common sight, facilitated by a new room plan. Beds left the parlour, which now assumed its modern purpose as a room reserved for socializing and entertaining.

The new material culture did not reach all parts of England with the same speed. In some ways, progress was so uneven that it created two nations. In London, Bath and Liverpool people sipped tea behind drawn curtains in 1700, but such novelties were virtually unseen in

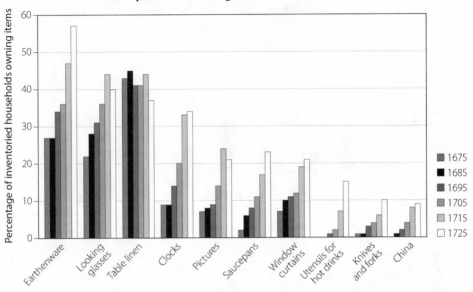

Source: Lorna Weatherill, *Consumer Behaviour and Material Culture in Britain 1660–1760*, 2nd edn 1996, table 2.1.

Cornwall as late as 1750. Still, new goods reached well beyond cities. They appeared in Kentish villages close to London as well as in industrializing Yorkshire and colonial Virginia. The transition from stool to chair and from chest to drawers and wardrobes was a provincial and colonial as well as a metropolitan story. Comfort, however, rarely arrived in one block. For most, it involved trade-offs. In England, the same worker who enjoyed tea, put up curtains and retired to a feather bed often suffered from malnutrition and damp. In the United States in the 1790s, travellers noted how their Virginia hostesses sat on handsome furniture, elegantly dressed, but served drink in broken glasses while the wind whistled through cracked windows.[105] The eighteenth century prioritized highly visible and immediate forms of consumption – dress, furnishings and tea sets – over hidden pipes, baths and utilities.

Inventories, inevitably, give a distorted picture of the ownership of goods across society as a whole, since they are heavily clustered around the gentry, traders and professions. One needs to own goods to make an inventory in the first place. Fortunately, some parishes had an interest in recording the possessions of the poor as part of a bargain that allowed an indebted person who was entering a workhouse to keep his

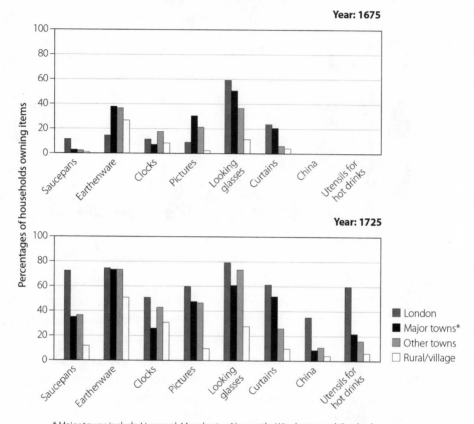

Selected possessions in town and country, England, 1675–1725

Year: 1675

Percentages of households owning items

Saucepans · Earthenware · Clocks · Pictures · Looking glasses · Curtains · China · Utensils for hot drinks

Year: 1725

London
Major towns*
Other towns
Rural/village

Saucepans · Earthenware · Clocks · Pictures · Looking glasses · Curtains · China · Utensils for hot drinks

* Major towns include Liverpool, Manchester, Newcastle, Winchester and Cambridge
Source: Lorna Weatherill, *Consumer Behaviour and Material Culture in Britain 1660–1760*, 2nd edn 1996, table 4.4.

belongings until the end of his life in exchange for leaving them to the parish thereafter. It comes as no surprise that in eighteenth-century Essex fewer paupers had clocks (20 per cent) and looking glasses (27 per cent) than did artisans and traders (71 per cent and 62 per cent). What is remarkable, however, is that half the paupers owned tea-related items, feather bedding and candlesticks, well in line with the rate among tradesmen. While some paupers owned nothing, poverty no longer barred the door to the world of things for all.

The more fortunate labourer John Tadgell occupied a dwelling room with two additional chambers with his wife and two children in 1810. Each of the two chambers had a four-poster bed with feather bedding.

In the dwelling room he kept tea cups, glasses and crockery, sixty-seven pieces in all, plus a set of sixteen Delft plates. Together with a mahogany tea chest and a long oak table with plenty of chairs, here were all the basic requirements of a new culture of politeness and sociability.[106] Tadgell's possessions may have eclipsed those of the average labourer, but they do suggest how goods and comforts began to enter the homes of ordinary Britons as well as those of the middle and upper classes. Those who did not own such goods directly often had access to them as servants or lodgers. By the late eighteenth century, tea kettles, curtains, feather beds and looking glasses were all customary in London lodging houses.[107] Visitors from other parts of Europe were routinely impressed by the well-dressed appearance of the London poor – not 'even a beggar, without both a shirt, and shoes and stockings', the German writer Karl Philipp Moritz noted in 1782. This was in stark contrast with the shoeless poor in Berlin and Paris, or, for that matter, in Dublin and Glasgow.[108]

New clothes and a culture of self-fashioning had a ripple effect across the imperial economy, all the way to those who had been reduced to chattels themselves. Unlike the mother country, the American colonies kept sumptuary laws alive. The 1735 South Carolina Negro Act forbade negroes to wear their masters' cast-off clothes and restricted them to white Welsh plains and other cheap fabrics. Such legislation proved increasingly difficult to enforce, partly because masters used dress to buy loyalty, partly because slaves were asserting themselves as consumers, spending the little hard-earned money they made from raising chickens or growing cotton on the side on silk ribbons and looking glasses. In 1777, Charles Wakefield of Maryland offered eighty silver dollars for the return of his house-slaves Dick and Lucy. The advertisement identified their wardrobe on the run. Dick had taken with him not only a 'pair of Russia drab overalls' but also 'a green cloth coat, with a crimson velvet cape, a red plush [coat], with blue cuffs and cape, a deep blue camblet jacket, with gold lace at the sleeves, down the breast and round the collar . . . [and] a pair of pumps and buckles'. In addition to several petticoats, Lucy had with her two cotton gowns, 'one purple and white, the other red and white', a 'jacket, and black silk bonnet, a variety of handkerchiefs and ruffles . . . a pair of high heel shoes, a pair of kid gloves and a pair of silk mitts, [and] a blue sarsenet [soft silk] handkerchief, trim'd with gauze, with white ribbon sew'd to it'.[109] Such apparel was very different from that worn by slaves fifty years earlier.

The fashionable novelty par excellence was cotton, and by following its rise to prominence over the next few pages we can appreciate more fully the attributes of an emerging new consumer culture: its aesthetic appeal and variety; its cheapness and practicality; the consequences for more frequent changes and combination with accessories; and marketing and the creation of a fashion system that integrated consumers and producers living on different continents (see Plate 6).

Spain's colonial ventures in the New World and European trade with China had already introduced a transoceanic commerce of silk and wool in the sixteenth century. Spain took silver from the Americas and sent them cloth from Castile. The Manila galleons which sailed annually from the Philippines to Acapulco after 1579 brought both raw silk and dyed, embroidered pieces to the New World; the Spanish also planted mulberry trees in Mexico to grow silkworms on the spot. In Peru, indigenous weavers, alongside skilled migrants from the old world, turned wool and silk into tapestries with Chinese floral motifs and red-blue ponchos with a green phoenix. New hybrids made their appearance, blending traditional garments like the Andean *lliclla*, or shawl and the *anacu*, a wrapped dress, with Chinese silk and Castilian damask. In Quito, in 1596, the wardrobe of Maria de Amores – an affluent lady of Inca and Ecuadorian descent twice married to Spanish husbands – included one Chinese *lliclla*, another made of green Castilian damask with golden edging, and an *anacu* of green Castilian satin with a golden edging; she also owned a 'large Chinese porcelain'.[110]

Cotton, however, was the first truly global mass consumer good. Indian dyed cottons had been sent to East Africa in the eleventh century, and been carried deep into Asia. By the second half of the seventeenth century they were sold across Europe and the Ottoman empire, but it was in England that they first reached the middling sort and then the masses. In 1664, the English East India Company (EIC) shipped a quarter of a million pieces of cloth to England. Twenty years later, it shipped over a million. Designs that flopped in London found ready buyers in the empire, circulating all the way to trading stations near the Arctic Circle in Canada. Chintzes – that is, cottons hand-printed in India – put a splash of colour into people's wardrobes. In England at that time, some linens were block printed in imitation of Italian silk damask, but these could not rival the more sophisticated Indian designs. Cotton took colour much better than linen and could be washed without losing its shine, unlike textiles dyed in Europe. Printed cottons offered fashionable dress and vivid designs at an affordable price; the European alternative of wool patterned on the loom was far more expensive. Colourful chintzes, 'the ware of Gentlewomen in Holland', the EIC noted in 1683, were worn by the middling sort in England – the wives and daughters of merchants, traders, lawyers, manufacturers, clergymen, officers and farmers who occupied the middle strata of society between the landed aristocracy and the working masses.[111]

Indian cottons threatened local wool, linen and silk industries, which led to a virtually European-wide ban on calico (France: 1689; Spain: 1713; Britain: 1700 and 1721; Russia: 1744); only the Netherlands stood apart. In Spitalfields, London, in 1719–20, women had their calico dresses torn off their backs by rioting silk weavers. But prohibition failed to kill the 'calico craze' – quite the opposite. Manufacturers circumvented the ban by mixing cotton and linen. East India Company ships would arrive in the port of London and be boarded by textile workers who turned the calico cloth into shirts and handkerchiefs and then sold the finished articles illegally on land. Officers and sailors tried to bring calico into the country, concealed among their private possessions; British diplomats and foreign ambassadors, too, were not infrequently found smuggling silk into England. And cotton was part of the wider smuggling network, alongside spirits, tea, tobacco and other taxed goods. In 1783, the Parliamentary Committee on Illicit Practices noted how, on entry, calicoes and linens were often hidden among other goods, mixed with those already stamped by the excise, or stamped with a counterfeit mark; in France, similarly, Asian textiles were unloaded and sold in Lorient before they had been inventoried. Smuggling gangs liked cotton because the prohibition made it particularly profitable on the black market. In the port of London alone, 4,099 pieces of calico and muslin were seized in 1780, giving a sense of the large volume of contraband goods that went undetected. In 1783, the House of Commons estimated several hundred coastal vessels were involved, from 30 to 300 tons, carrying crews armed 'with clubs and heavy whips, generally inflamed with liquor, and assembled in such numbers as to reduce the revenue officers to be quiet spectators of the proceeding'. Scouts and riders set up signals for the boats, then loaded the cargo on to wagons and headed to London and provincial towns with fake permits.[112]

The ban on cotton might appear reactionary but it also illustrates how far the spirit of the sumptuary laws had been left behind. The authorities no longer cared whether ordinary housewives sported the colours or fabrics of aristocratic ladies. The issue was where the product was made, not who bought it. The ban was a textbook example of how an infant industry could be nurtured behind a shelter. Its main objective was to help the domestic linen and silk industries, but in due course it built up a powerful British cotton industry. British producers used the protection from foreign competition to develop new fabrics, to copy and to innovate, until by the late eighteenth century they surpassed their Indian rivals in the Gujarat and along the Coromandel Coast.[113] The ban was initially on cottons printed and painted in India (1701) and was then extended, in 1722, to those printed in Britain. But it did not cover fabrics mixed with cotton. By the 1730s, most linen in Manchester was mixed with cotton into fustian. Colourfast printing with copperplates – first developed by Francis Nixon in Ireland in 1752 – and the rotary printing machine in 1783 finally gave British cotton masters the edge over Indian cottons printed by hand. In 1774, Britain rescinded its ban on printed cotton. Twenty-five years later, it consumed some 29 million yards of home-produced cotton cloth.

We speak of cotton in the singular, but for contemporaries the appeal lay in its variety as much as its novelty. Cotton was traded in two hundred types and offered unprecedented versatility. And this confronted shoppers with an entirely new burden of choice. How was a customer to distinguish between all the various fabrics, their uses, quality and price? The arrival of consumer guides is indicative of the transformation under way. *The Merchant's Ware-House Laid Open* (London, 1696; just before the import ban was imposed) offered an A–Z survey of Indian cottons and European textiles aimed at 'all sorts of Persons', starting with Alcomore-holland, a Dutch flax, and ending with Vehemounty, a French fabric. The greater the variety, the more easily people were cheated. Ascertaining quality by appearance was difficult. Some cloth looked lovely in a shop, 'yet wear like Paper', while others 'look well to the Eye, but . . . falls into pieces' in the first wash. Readers were told how to avoid deception by 'the most crafty Dealer'. Long cloth, that is, cotton up to 40 yards in length, used for shirts and shifts, sold for 15 pence a yard. It came in two kinds: one from India, which was then dyed in England; and the other, which arrived ready-dyed. It was best to avoid the former and pick the latter because 'they never lose the colour in washing as the English-dye cloth.' How would a customer spot the difference in a shop? Answer: 'you may know the English-dye from the Indian by the colours, for the Indian dye is much evener dyed than the English, for the English hath brown and dark spots in it.' 'Mulmuls', a kind of muslin or plain-woven fabric, was even worse in the view of the author: 'very thin ... generally fray'd, and it not only wears extraordinary ill, but when washed two or three times, wears very yellow'. It was commonly sold at a precious price by hawkers, 'but in the wear is a perfect Cheat'. Among the many colourful chintzes, it was important to distinguish between the very fine ones, painted with birds and beasts, which 'retain their colours till they are worn to pieces', and the chintz serunge, somewhat 'coarser, yet ... of very pretty Flowers' that kept their colours equally well and were perfectly good for gowns and petticoats as well as quilts.[114]

By the late eighteenth century, the clothing revolution was in full swing. Silk remained France's most valuable textile export and Britain sent growing volumes of it to North America and Jamaica as well as to Denmark and Norway. Virginian ladies liked a bit of rococo, too. In England, silk lost some of its exclusiveness, as tradesmen began to sport silk waistcoats and breeches. At the other end of the market, linen remained cheap and hung on as underwear for a little while longer. But for outerwear, cotton was increasingly becoming the norm and people were prepared to pay slightly more than for the cheaper but also duller linen, although the poor would switch to cotton only in the next century. In France, by the time of the Revolution in 1789, artisans, shopkeepers and servants all wore more cotton than wool or linen; it was only in the wardrobe of aristocrats and the professions that it was beaten into second place by silk. By this time, cotton had also outpaced silk in New York and Philadelphia. Unlike in the case of watches, where rising consumption was the child of new technology and lower prices, cotton was a textbook example of how fashion was the decisive driver of demand. And once artisans and servants, too, were wearing cotton, their superiors began to look for more elegant and expensive cotton stockings.[115]

As an article of consumption, clothing is uniquely sensitive. There is no other thing which has such a tactile and visual presence in our lives. We touch it, see it, feel it. The clothes we wear contribute to our sense of our bodies. The line between 'us' and 'the thing' is therefore a fuzzy one. One recent philosopher has even generously accorded clothes a kind of 'half-life', since they move with our bodies: 'We live our clothes as though they were alive. Your trousers do the walking.'[116]

But clearly, the liveliness of clothes depends on material and cut. The shift in fabrics in the eighteenth century had huge consequences for people's experience of themselves. Cotton was a material manifestation of the new culture of comfort. It was softer on the skin and lighter than linen and wool, reinforcing the fashion for a looser fit already under way in the seventeenth century. The way it took dyes democratized colour and fashion. In 1700, European capitals were largely a sea of black and white with shades of brown and grey. A century later, there was a rainbow of colour, with reds and blues, yellows and greens, a common sight among labourers' clothes as well as those of aristocrats and their servants. Before cotton, fashionable clothes had been a monopoly of the few, not only because of sumptuary legislation but because they were expensive and costly to maintain, silk notoriously so. When the painter Lorenzo Lotto bought himself a new wardrobe in Venice in the 1540s, it cost him a small fortune; the woollen cloak and tunic alone took three months of his wages.[117] Printed cotton cost more than plain worsted (wool) but was cheaper than silk or patterned wool. In the 1770s, a ready-made cotton gown could already be had for 8 shillings new, and 3 shillings second-hand (there were 20 shillings in the pound), at a time when an artisan earned between £20 and £40 a year. A market in ready-made garments sprang up. Bright, fashionable clothes with patterns or flowers provided workers and the poor with a new sense of identity. Victims of theft recorded their favourite dress in fine detail. One poor British woman described 'a small running sprigged Purple and White Cotton Gown, washed only once, tied down with red Tape at the Bosom, round plain Cuffs, and the Bottom bound round with broad Tape'.[118]

The relative cheapness and growing variety of dress had paradoxical effects. Lighter fabrics meant adding layers to keep warm – Europe is not India. And this opened up fresh opportunities for fashionable combinations and accessories such as ribbons, hats and handkerchiefs wrapped around the neck. Patterned neckerchiefs moved within the reach of poor workers and peasants. The wheel of acquisition and replacement accelerated. While the price of a coat or gown was declining, the actual proportion of income spent on clothing went up, as people's wardrobes became more varied and changed more frequently. In 1700, French servants spent 10 per cent of their earnings on clothes. By 1780, it had risen to a third. Ironically, it was probably the urban poor who changed their clothes most frequently, for theirs wore out most quickly, without the benefits of soap, laundry and repair.[119]

Branding and labelling can be traced back as far as ancient Egypt and Mesopotamia, where courts and bureaucracies used them to add value by distinguishing quality and origin.[120] In the eighteenth century, traders and makers raised branding, product differentiation and sales promotions to new heights. In 1754, Robert Turlington first sold his 'Balsam of Life' – a remedy for kidney stones, colic and 'every malady' – in pear-shaped bottles with the name and royal patent moulded into the glass. The kings of marketing were the pottery-maker Josiah Wedgwood and his partner Thomas Bentley. Neil McKendrick gives a sense of their innovative salesmanship. They used:

> inertia-selling campaigns, product differentiation, market segmentation, detailed market research, embryonic self-service schemes, money-back-if-not-satisfied policies, free carriage, give-away sales promotions, auctions, lotteries, catalogues . . . advanced credit, three-tier discount schemes, including major discounts for first orders, and almost every form of advertisement, trade cards, shop signs, letterheads, bill heads, newspaper and magazine advertisements, fashion plates and fashion magazines, solicited puffs, organized propaganda campaigns, even false attacks organized to produce the opportunity to publicize the counter-attack.[121]

As we have seen, it would be wrong to write off earlier societies as static, and this was true of fashionable goods as well as of consumption more generally. Already in the fourteenth century, the court of Burgundy had acted as a European fashion centre. The Dukes of Burgundy were renowned for their lavish dress. Philip the Bold (1342–1404) had a scarlet doublet, with pearls embroidered in the shape of forty lambs and swans which carried gold bells around their necks and in their beaks. Burgundian ladies introduced tall, peaked hats. Travelling to foreign courts made the Dukes of Burgundy fashionable trendsetters among the European aristocracy. It was then that hemlines were getting shorter while men replaced long, loose tunics with tailored doublets and jackets that fell just below the waist. In the course of the fifteenth century, fashion switched from wide funnel-shaped sleeves to the 'bag-pipe' style which ended in a tight cuff.[122] Ming China had fashion, as we have seen earlier in sixteenth-century complaints about the frequent change in the lengths and widths of skirts and pleats. European merchants trading in the East knew that many Asians were discerning customers. In 1617, the director-general of the Dutch East India Company noted how locals were 'very particular about the quality' of their tapis or wrap-around skirts and were ready to pay good money for a good design. Peasants might do with coarse cotton, but richer customers wanted theirs colourful, patterned on the loom, with borders, and often incorporating gold thread. Order books reflected the detailed attention given to local tastes. In 1623, for example, VOC directors in Batavia, the capital of the Dutch East Indies, asked producers in Coromandel to make tapis with 'bright red borders and small flower work in lively colour'.[123]

What was new in late-seventeenth and eighteenth-century Europe was that fashion was institutionalized into an industry, with its own spaces, calendar and media. This was a global as much as a local achievement. Paris set the pace, but it needed Indian weavers to follow. The Dutch and English East India companies played a critical role in connecting the trendsetter with the producer and the consumer. In the 1670s, the English East India Company took samples of clothes fashionable in Paris and sent them via Syria to India to be copied there by local weavers. In the next decade, the loop was closed, with new designs and samples from India having their appeal first tested in Parisian salons before going out to European markets. 'Note this for a constant and General Rule,' the EIC directors explained in 1681: 'in all flowered Silks you change the fashion and flower every year, as much as you can – for English ladies, and they say the french [sic], and other Europeans – will give twice as much for a new thing not seen in Europe . . . than they will give for a better Silke of the same fashion worne the former yeare.'[124]

Those without immediate access to a salon or royal court could take advice from the new fashion magazines. The French *Mercure* started to give fashion tips in 1672. Ladies' almanacs multiplied in the next century and included engravings of the newest designs and recommendations on where to shop. In its January 1777 issue, the *Magazine à la Mode, or Fashionable Miscellany* listed the gentleman's dress for the drawing room as worn on the queen's birthday earlier that month: 'The waistcoat lined with fur . . . The make of the coat is the same as has been for some years, except that the waist is shorter – the skirts of course longer . . . The cuff is small, and close, with three buttons on the upper side.' For a lady, the 'most fashionable morning dress . . . is a deshabilié, which consists of a short jacket and petticoat: the coat is generally puckered round the bottom about a quarter of a yard deep, with gawze [a translucent, loosely woven fabric], or the same silk. But fur is more in vogue this month than any other trimming'. The cap was French. To be in style, it needed to have a 'full lappet across the head, but none descending behind . . . an alteration which has taken place this month'. Fashion-conscious ladies were directed to Mr Kluht of London's

Covent Garden for the dress, and to Mrs Taylor of Rathbone Place for the cap.[125] Readers had two black-and-white engravings to consult. It was around this time that colourful fashion plates and fashion dolls made their entry (see Plate 8). Initially made of wood, the fashion doll had by the 1790s evolved into an article fit for mass consumption: a flat-pack cardboard-cut-out figure, 8 inches high and sold at 3 shillings. From here it was a short step to a children's toy with a set of six dresses and other exchangeable accessories. Fashion had crossed the generational divide.[126]

Thus, a new regime of consumption came into being in the north-west of Europe in the seventeenth and eighteenth centuries, characterized by volume, variety and innovation. The circular flow of the Renaissance did not disappear but was channelled into a dynamic system that injected constant novelty. Second-hand clothes, pawnshops, auctions and the giving of gifts brought cotton gowns and teapots to everyone. Novelty, not antiquity, fired the pistons, unlike in late Ming China. British historians have quibbled about the precise date of this shift. The bigger question, however, is 'why?', not 'when?' Why did this switch happen in Britain and the Netherlands and not in China or Italy?

There are three leading answers competing with each other: the standard of living (Britons had higher real wages); emulation (they copied their superiors); and the 'industrious revolution' (individuals worked harder in order to buy more things). Let us consider them in turn.

Appreciation of China's commercial vitality in the early modern period has led to a vexed controversy over whether the Dutch and English really were so much better off. In the most advanced area of China, the Lower Yangzi, people in 1800 enjoyed a standard of living comparable to that in England and the Netherlands, according to the China historian Kenneth Pomeranz. The 'great divergence', he has argued, happened in the nineteenth century and resulted not from Europe's genius for modernity but rather, in Britain's case, from geographic luck and imperial force that provided the first industrial nation with abundant coal, slaves and cheap food.[127]

Recent calculations confirm that British wages did decline between 1740 and 1800, but they also highlight that this was a comparatively small dip from a unique high-wage plateau that Britain had enjoyed for four centuries following the Black Death. High wages preceded imperial expansion and were in large part the result of a small population and cheap energy, which encouraged innovation and productivity, with big inventions, such as Thomas Newcomen's steam engine (1710), but also smaller ones of tinkering and adaptations, such as James Watt's development of the separate condenser in the 1760s, which made Newcomen's engine even more efficient. Already by the seventeenth century a divergence was under way that cut across Europe as well as separating East from West. Workers in Delhi and Beijing lived near a subsistence level comparable to those in Florence and Vienna. Those in London and Amsterdam were in a different league again, enjoying a more varied and high-quality diet of meat, alcohol and wheat (instead of plain oats). During the Industrial Revolution, English workers were getting poorer relative to their superiors, but this left them still better off than their fellow labourers in Asia or Southern Europe.[128]

One riposte to these calculations is that wages may not offer a good yardstick for comparison between these societies. Europe had a large and growing army of wage earners, while in China proletarians were a poor minority, marginalized and unmarried, whereas the families of the tenant farmers who dominated the Yangzi Delta were better off. In

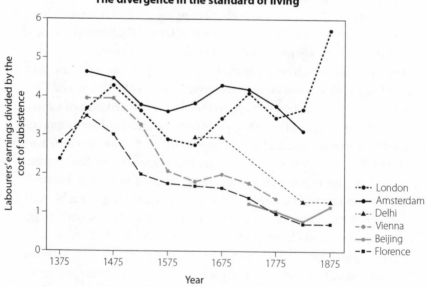

The divergence in the standard of living

(y-axis: Labourers' earnings divided by the cost of subsistence)
(x-axis: Year)

Legend:
- London
- Amsterdam
- Delhi
- Vienna
- Beijing
- Florence

Labourers' earnings divided by the cost of subsistence:
1 = just enough to survive
4 = earning four times what was needed to survive

Source: Robert Allen, *The British Industrial Revolution in Global Perspective* (2009), p. 40.

India, similarly, weavers received meals, housing and other benefits in addition to their wages, which makes direct comparison treacherous.[129] Data compiled by Bozhong Li suggests that life in 1820s Songjiang, near Shanghai, was respectable. Peasants enjoyed 2,780kcal a day, a figure China would not reach again until 2000 and slightly above the figure recommended by health experts today. They drank twice as much tea as Britons, ate half as much sugar and, on top, smoked a little tobacco and opium, 'the lusty friend'.[130] On the other hand, Britain's lead looks even larger when we take into account the much greater variety of affordable goods available to its population, which went well beyond the bread, cheese, linen and candles that feature in the standard basket of goods underlying statistical comparisons of the standard of living in this period. Chinese tenant farmers who produced cotton on the side managed to reach a level above subsistence. Yet this kind of labour might have made it harder to climb further up the ladder of development, because doing a bit of this and a bit of that limited the scope for specialization and innovation. In a world with industrializing nations this would prove a big handicap.

The standard of living debate has concentrated on workers, but equally important for our concerns is the group above them. Britain was distinguished by its large 'middling sort', the many merchants, members of the professions, officers and industrialists. Four in ten families had an income of £40 or more a year in the 1750s, twice as much as was considered necessary for survival. This group had a lot to spend on comfort and conveniences. In the course of the Industrial Revolution, Britain would become a more unequal society. Still, by comparison with China and India, as well as with Southern Europe, its middle class was enormous.[131] And it was increasingly self-confident, its members making the most of a dynamically growing world of goods to carve out their own place in society. Instead of emulating the old elite, this large group used new goods and tastes to establish new distinctions and create their own, more private culture of comfort.

In the original thesis of the British birth of consumer society, emulation was the parent of demand: its midwife was 'the mill girl who wanted to dress like a duchess', in McKendrick's words.[132] Contemporaries were constantly sneering at uppity consumers. This is hardly surprising. The clothing revolution ran roughshod over an inherited system of sartorial distinctions that had mapped dress on to rank. Instead of reflecting a person's origin, clothes suddenly seemed to make the person. Servants who dressed above their station were a cause of particular concern. 'It is a hard matter,' Daniel Defoe lamented in 1725, 'to know the mistress from the maid by their dress; nay, very often the maid shall be much the finer of the two.' This set off a spiral of aspirational spending: 'the maid striving to outdo the mistress, the tradesman's wife to outdo the gentleman's wife, the gentleman's wife emulating the lady, and the ladies one another'.[133]

Contemporary ridicule, however, is not the same as convincing historical argument. For one, similar complaints can be found in many societies then and before, including Ming China, as we have seen. Secondly, imitation was rarely the chief motivation for adopting new clothing styles. Servants often had little choice but to wear the dress given to them by their masters. British artisans and workers did not dress smartly in order to pass as a duke or duchess but to fit in with their own peers, to show their coming of age and independence, or in hope of a better job.[134] More generally, the spread of novelties belies notions of a simple trickle-down process. Elite women, for example, began wearing chintzes on the outside of their gowns only in the 1690s, after the calico craze had taken off. Rather than aping the aristocracy, the middling sort was often the trendsetter.

The 'industrious revolution', similarly, is a historical interpretation that takes its cue from contemporary observers. In the early eighteenth century, Daniel Defoe described textile districts where 'you see the wheel going almost at every door'. Everyone was busy: husbands, wives and children. Together, their wages made for 'a tolerable plenty'. By 1770, the enlightenment thinker James Steuart concluded that if, before, people had worked because they had been forced to, 'men are forced to labour now because they are slaves to their own wants.' The economic historian Jan De Vries has argued that this was precisely what happened in the early modern Netherlands and Britain. Drawing on the Nobel-prize-winning work of economist Gary Becker, De Vries pictures the household as an economic unit that makes rational decisions about how best to allocate its time. Instead of just producing what they needed themselves, households began to sell their labour so they could buy more stuff. The taste for tea, sugar and the many other new consumer goods made whole families join the ranks of wage earners. And it made them work longer and harder. The Industrial Revolution was preceded by a revolution in demand.[135]

At first glance, this thesis looks attractive. Instead of treating it as a reaction to supply, demand becomes the tail that was wagging the dog. It is a neat explanation of how consumption was able to expand in

Britain while wages were falling in the second half of the eighteenth century. Overall, however, the thesis runs into a barrage of frustrating problems. For one, it starts in the middle of the story and mixes cause and effect. People ended up buying more consumer goods, but that may not have been the initial motivation that drove them to work harder. The opposite was probably the case. Puritans started to preach 'industriousness' in the early seventeenth century as times were getting harder.[136] People started to work longer and sell more of their labour to stay alive, not to indulge themselves. Living conditions improved in the century after the English Civil War (1642–51), and when they did, labourers tended to spend their money on better furniture rather than tea and sugar or other novelty items. In other words, their preferences stayed pretty much the same. Industriousness, too, was a prescriptive ideal – not an innocent reality – that told people how they ought to live, which liberalism and imperialism would export to the rest of world. For most workers the shift from leisure to wage labour was probably by necessity, not choice. They were pushed by rising food prices rather than pulled by material desire. Working hours lengthened further in the second half of the eighteenth century – by a third [137] – but, again, this was in response to soaring inflation and an increasingly tough labour market in these decades.

In his survey of *The State of the Poor* in the 1790s, Frederic Eden gave the annual budget of a typical miner and his family in Cumberland. He earned £26 a year. His wife and seven children made an additional £18.[138] Of their expenses, which amounted to £44, a good £3 10 shillings went on tea and sugar. Did they 'occasionally, wash ore' to afford the tea and sugar, or to help with the rent (£3) and the costs of the many pregnancies and lyings-in of his wife, which added up to £20 over the years? Arguably, it was not an appetite for novelties or a desire to impress others that led his family to buy tea, sugar and candles but because these were enabling them to spin late into the night, stay warm and keep awake.

The link between wanting more and working harder was contingent. In Britain, the initial demand for consumer goods came from the middling sort without making them more industrious: their wives stayed at home. In seventeenth-century Friesland, Dutch farmers did specialize, selling more of their produce in exchange for novelties rather than making things themselves. By contrast, Catalonia in the following century was industrializing, yet here side jobs remained high and new consumer goods were conspicuous by their absence. In prosperous

Kent, meanwhile, households bought tableware and curtains but also did more of their own baking and brewing.[139] Developing societies, then, did not travel on a single highway from new tastes to growth and specialization. Desire and 'wants' were not just there, automatically compelling people to enter the market for labour and goods, as presumed in the 'industrious' model. Desire itself varied, as did the scope for its expansion, which was shaped by norms and institutions. While purchasing power favoured Europe's north-west, it was only one variable, and, on its own, it is insufficient to explain the step-change in consumption in the seventeenth and eighteenth centuries.

What set Europe apart from Asia was an expansionist state system which responded to competitive pressure by favouring innovation and creating future markets. Britain's simultaneous creation of an Atlantic market and imitation of superior Indian textiles, behind the shelter of an import ban, was the most pronounced example of this. Indian textile weavers at first lacked any incentive to innovate – after all, they were better – and then, by the late eighteenth century, when they were feeling the harsh wind of British competition, lacked a strong state to respond.

Yet the differences within Europe were at least as decisive. What set Britain and the Netherlands apart from the rest of Europe was a favourable climate of ideas and institutions that encouraged men and, especially, women to join the ranks of wage earners and consumers. As we have seen, places like Württemberg were held back not because the women there did not have material desires or the wish to be industrious and earn some money, but because they were punished if they acted on them. In 1742, for example, a knitter's wife who had been working independently was ordered by the local village court to stop and return to her husband. Shopkeepers made sure their towns barred pedlars, and husbands beat their wives for leaving the house in search of work, with the full support of the authorities. Guilds restricted labour mobility. Together, husbands, fathers, churches and guilds exercised a social discipline unknown in England.[140] Compare this to London in 1455, where the women who threw silk said they were 'more than a thousand', including 'many gentlewomen' who lived 'honorably' and supported their households.[141]

Blessed with an early central state, England was spared the multitude of local authorities and regional powers which interfered with the flow of goods on the continent. The English state directed its force outward. The contrast with the Spanish empire is instructive. The first to import exotic chocolate and tobacco, Spain might have been expected to make the most of its head start in the race for consumption. In reality, it quickly fell behind. Its main strategy was to extract resources from its colonies, not to develop them into an additional market for its goods. At home, on the Iberian Peninsula, it suffered from a fragmentation of regional authorities, currencies and taxes as well as long distances and poor transport. Castile and Navarra had their own import and export duties and could issue their own coins. Many towns had their own fiscal powers. A heavily indebted city such as Seville used consumption taxes to stay afloat.[142] Such obstacles inevitably constrained the choices and opportunities of the Spanish to make the most of new products and tastes. By the middle of the eighteenth century, for example, only one in four middle-income families owned a dish to serve hot chocolate. There were some signs of improvement, especially in the growing number and diversity of textiles. In the city of Palencia, in Spain's north-west, the average household managed to expand their clothing from forty-two to seventy-one items in the eighty years after 1750. Still, new consumer goods arrived in a trickle, not a wave. Outside Madrid, in provincial towns such as Santander, napkins and tablecloths – crucial indicators of growing refinement – became more widespread only in the early nineteenth century. Tellingly, even in many urban areas of Spain, cotton was displacing linen only in the 1830s.[143]

In Britain, the state and a more integrated market provided a more favourable environment for the diffusion of goods. This was an important factor for the advanced growth of consumption in this part of the world. But having a favourable terrain is not the same as making the most of it. It still leaves unexplained the underlying dynamic that made people turn more and more to a world of goods. As we have seen in the case of cotton, the British state gave a helping hand to British industry by protecting it against Indian calicoes. But the demand for these goods was already there – the state did not create it, it merely diverted it. To understand how goods became a more integral part of people's lives in modern societies, we now need to attend to cultural factors that gave goods new meaning and significance.

2

The Enlightenment of Consumption

The initial reaction was disgust. The Italian Girolamo Benzoni first observed the cultivation and preparation of cocoa in Nicaragua in the 1550s. Natives added water, a bit of pepper, sometimes honey, and beat the mixture into a froth. The result was a 'beverage more suited for pigs than for humans'.[1] Travelling in Turkey sixty years later, the English poet George Sandys noted how men there did not go to taverns but to 'Coffa-houses', where they chatted and sipped a drink made of a berry 'as hot as they can suffer it: blacke as soote, and tasting not much unlike it'.[2] Within a century, aristocratic and commercial elites alike were hooked. A quintet of exotic drug foods conquered Europe: tea from China; coffee and cane sugar from Arabia, and tobacco and cocoa from the New World. In Habsburg Spain and Austria, nobles held chocolate parties (*las Chocolatadas*). Across Europe, respectable burghers and learned gentlemen began to meet in coffee houses. By the mid-eighteenth century, servants and artisans, too, were enjoying a cup of tea or coffee. By 1900, the conquest was complete. Even chocolate had been transformed into a mass product, eaten by soldiers and workers as well as sipped by fine ladies. Once precious luxuries, exotic drugs had become everyday items.

BITTERSWEET

The introduction and popularization of new tastes is a critical feature of modern consumer culture. By following the dramatic change in fortune of these exotic beverages we can gain a clearer insight into how such new tastes emerged and the historical actors and processes responsible for them. The careers of tea, coffee and chocolate were marked by displacement and devaluation. They involved an unprecedented global transplantation of plants, peoples and tastes. In their colonies, European empires created a new tropical production zone. Under the Aztecs, cacao was grown mainly in Soconusco, along the Pacific coast of Mexico. The Dutch took it to Venezuela, Catholic missionaries to the Philippines. At the time of Sandys' travels, coffee was grown only in Yemen and shipped from the port of Mocca. Then the Dutch started growing their own in Surinam (1718), the French in Martinique (1723), the British in Jamaica (1728). In the 1840s, the British set up colonial tea plantations in Assam and Ceylon. Sugar cane – indigenous to South-east Asia and first introduced to the Mediterranean by Arabs – was moved by Europeans from Madeira and the Canaries to the West Indies. Contemporaries were aware of the significance of these migrations. Whether coffee and sugar were decisive for Europe's fortune, he did not know, the French writer Bernadin de Saint-Pierre confessed in 1773. He was sure, though, that these two companions brought a great tragedy to the other two continents affected: America was depopulated because Europeans wanted land for cultivation; Africa was depopulated because they needed labour to cultivate America.[3]

Each of these drug foods has had its own literature, beginning with Sidney Mintz's pioneering study of sugar, *Sweetness and Power* (1985), which sparked a new genre of commodity biographies.[4] The attractions of that genre are easy to see. Following the life of a food reveals the interdependence between regimes of production and consumption separated by oceans and national histories. The warm comfort of a cup of sweetened tea served in Britain is connected with the brutality of slave plantations in the Caribbean. A second insight is that goods, like people, have a 'social life'.[5] Their character and value changes along the food chain and across time. For Aztec rulers, cocoa was tribute, money and religious ritual. A chest of tea can be sold or given as a gift.

The problem with commodity biographies is not that they explain too little but that they often explain too much, asking a single plant to bear the weight of world history. Exotic drug foods have thus produced a host of grand narratives. One recounts a civilizing process in which the new manners of the tea party and the coffee table trickled down from European courts to aspiring middle classes and then the rest.[6] Another points to the coffee house as the birthplace of a new public sphere.[7] Some have gone so far as to see in coffee's edge over chocolate the triumph of sober, modern and Protestant Northern Europe over the self-indulgent, baroque Catholic South.[8] In another view, British tea and sugar forged an imperial chain between colonial slavery and metropolitan factory labour.[9] The problem with these individual stories is that what appears unique and essential about one beverage in one place appears more contingent when placed alongside other stimulants in other settings. Factories in Protestant Europe, for example, served workers beer and gin as well as sober coffee. The great tea-drinking nations include Russia and China, with empires and labour regimes that were radically different from Britain's. We therefore need to look at these drug foods alongside each other. Ultimately, exotic beverages were winners because they were extraordinarily flexible, able to serve a variety of social groups, cultural meanings and economic regimes. This included colonies and small nations as well as imperial metropoles.

From a global point of view, the European adoption of drug foods was less an ingenious act of discovery than a belated catching up.[10] Drinks with the stimulant caffeine or theobromine (of which traces are also found in cocoa) had long been integral to other civilizations. Powdered green tea was widespread in Ming China, while the Manchu in inner Asia drank black tea with milk. Coffee had been drunk in the Middle East since the fifteenth century, when the Sufis devised a technique to roast the bean, spreading the new hot drink to Cairo and Mecca. In East Africa there was khat, further west, the kola nut, chewed by the well-off in the morning 'to drive away the bitterness of sobriety', as the Haussa said.[11]

The impact of empire on taste and ritual was as profound in the New World as in the Old. In the Spanish empire, Jesuits moved cacao plantations from their original Mexican base to Caracas (Venezuela) and the Guayas Basin (Ecuador) in the late sixteenth century. Chocolate drinking swept across Central America. Many of the cocoa beans harvested in Venezuela were consumed on the spot. Colonial elites sipped it in Lima. In Guatemala and Nicaragua, chocolate was drunk by everyone. In the Philippines, too, it was the beverage of choice – prepared with unrefined sugar and sometimes with pili nuts and roasted rice mixed in – until coffee-drinking Americans took over in 1898.

The second beverage of the consumer revolution in Latin America, and often forgotten, was maté, a Paraguayan caffeine-containing tea made from the dried leaves of the evergreen holly *Ilex paraguariensis*. Initially it grew wild, but Jesuit missions turned it into a plantation crop. It was sold across the subcontinent, from Chile and Peru to Montevideo. Indeed, maté was as much an exotic novelty in Buenos Aires as coffee was in London and Paris. Maté was an even more social drink than tea or coffee. Drinkers passed the gourd around and shared the *bombilla*, or straw. The culture of accessories associated with European tea parties was in truth a shared international phenomenon. Silver straws and gourds mounted in silver made it all the way up to the high-lands of Ecuador. As in the European tea-party and *Kaffeekränzchen*, maté rituals marked out women as arch-consumers, simultaneously guardians of domestic sociability and potential spendthrifts. There 'is no house, rich or poor', one observer wrote in the 1780s, 'where there is not always maté on the table, and it is nothing short of amazing to see the luxury spent by women on maté utensils'.[12]

What lay behind the conversion of Europeans to exotic beverages? That they contained alkaloids, with their habit-forming potential, worked in their favour but was hardly sufficient. First, taste barriers had to be overcome. Nor should we exaggerate the beverages' addictive power. Many drank a diluted, watery brew. By 1780, for example, observers noted that mountain farmers in Saxony had taken up coffee, but 'it was so thin that it barely had the colour of the beans.'[13] In Voralberg, Austria, textile workers regularly drank coffee at that time.[14] But in many cases, the habit preceded the drug. In 1900, most people in continental Europe still sipped 'substitute' coffee, made from chicory or acorn, which contained no caffeine whatsoever; real coffee only displaced milk in rural Austria in the decades after that. That Europeans had the power to navigate the seas, conquer colonies and enslave Africans mattered, but, on the other hand, the Atlantic plantation system would have crashed had it not been for Europeans' growing taste for sugar and coffee in the first place. The fundamental question, then, is how and why taste and habits changed. It is also one of the most difficult ones to answer.

Unlike changes in individual taste, such as a child's sudden liking for bitter or acidic foods, the transformation of entire national taste buds proceeded slowly. Along the way, the criteria of taste changed, as well as the groups that acted as taste-makers. In the first phase, from the sixteenth to the early eighteenth century, appropriation and dissemination were an exclusive affair. In 1724, all of England made do with 660 tons of coffee. If shared equally, each inhabitant would have been able to enjoy one weak cup of coffee every three weeks – and this was an unusually good year. Tea consumption was only slightly higher.[15] Cocoa was traded regularly from the 1590s, but even a century later Venezuela still only shipped 65 tons to Spain each year. Coffee and chocolate, then, were luxuries, both because few people could afford them and because they were marked out as rare goods that called for a particular disposition, knowledge and art of consumption.

The original ambassadors of taste were missionaries, merchants and

The imperial flow of goods and slaves in 1770

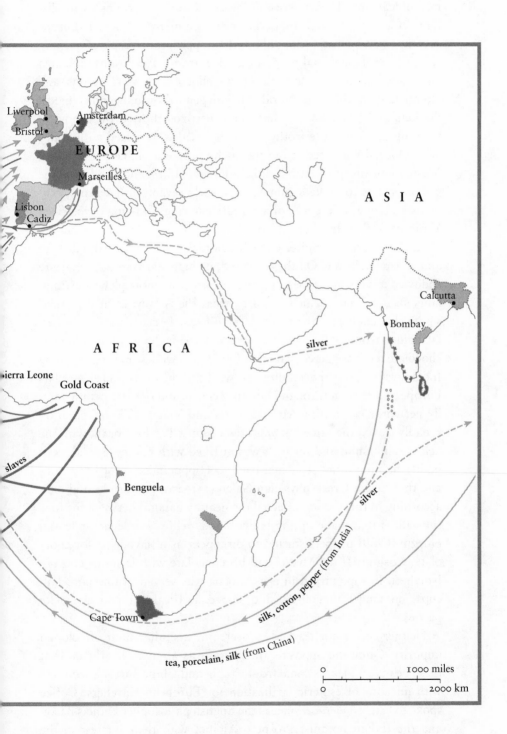

Liverpool
Bristol
Amsterdam
EUROPE
Marseilles
Lisbon
Cadiz

ASIA

AFRICA

Calcutta
Bombay

silver

Sierra Leone
Gold Coast

slaves

Benguela

silver

silk, cotton, pepper (from India)

Cape Town

silk, cotton, pepper (from India)

tea, porcelain, silk (from China)

0   1000 miles
0   2000 km

men of learning. Their interest in the exotic and their contact with distant cultures ensured that the new stimulants reached Europe accompanied by instructions about their appropriate preparation, consumption and medicinal properties, taken from observations in Arabia and New Spain. The first European chocoholics were Jesuits and Dominicans in the New World. They depended on indigenous maids, markets and know-how. Indians and mestizos showed them how to whip up and enjoy the frothy drink the local way, spiced with honey and coloured with seeds from the anchiote tree to make it a rich red; Mesoamericans preferred it hot, adding chillies and maize to the ground beans to make a soup. By the early seventeenth century, religious houses were the hub of a global drug ring, shipping cocoa from Veracruz to their brothers in Rome.[16]

At the heart of empire, cocoa's colonial provenance earned it an ambivalent welcome. On the one hand, its high status in Aztec culture endowed it with elite appeal, setting it apart from more plebeian stimulants such as maté, which failed to cross the Atlantic. On the other, sipping hot chocolate like a colonial signified a descent down the imperial ladder from civilizer to barbarian. Back in Spain, the colonists' chocolate habit triggered fears that Europeans were being corrupted by Indian ways. It was the nobility that sanitized the drink and ensured its European diffusion through Habsburg courts and the aristocratic family networks connecting Madrid, Paris and Vienna. The preparation broadly stayed the same but was now disguised as European, with the help of cinnamon and sugar. It was justified with reference to ideas of bodily humours that stretched back to Hippocrates (c.460–370 BCE) and the ancient Greek physician Galen (131–201 CE); drinks and diet, according to this theory, affected the healthy balance between the four substances that made up the body: blood, yellow bile, black bile and phlegm. Chilli peppers started to disappear as a flavouring for chocolate. Cosimo III de' Medici had his chocolate with jasmine; elites in Northern Europe mixed in eggs. Cocoa was served in fine porcelain cups, no longer in gourds, and sipped at breakfast and chocolate parties.

Neither coffee nor tea had to overcome a similar taint of colonial impurity. Quite the opposite: the exotic was an asset for them. That these beans and leaves came from Arabia and China surrounded them with an aura of esoteric civilization for European travellers. Coffee spoke to learned *virtuosi* such as the English philosopher Francis Bacon and the Italian botanist Prospero Alpino, with their interest in the natural world in all its variety. Europeans found in the Turkish coffee house a model of fellowship and conversation, and borrowed freely from Arabic medical knowledge. One of the earliest and most influential accounts of coffee drinking was by the French doctor and antiquarian Jacob Spon. In 1671, he described how the Turks took 'a pound and a half of the Kernels of this Grain', and after 'peeling off the skin roast it before the fire . . .[and then] boyl it in twenty pintes of water', before serving it in 'little dishes of porcelain'. Spon repudiated those who criticized coffee, like tea, for effeminizing body and mind. In its defence he cited not only 'an eminent Arabian Physician' but also Galen, who continued to influence European medical thinking. Hot coffee, Spon explained, maintained the balance of the four bodily 'humours', or fluids, by preventing the 'boyling of the blood, and the decaying of the strength'. He also noted how Arabs used it against indigestion, catarrhs and as a popular remedy against the 'stoppage of Women's courses'.[17] Back home, Spon and fellow physicians prescribed coffee to women suffering from painful periods.

Coffee's initial advance across Europe, however, was far from smooth. Imports and prices fluctuated greatly. Coffee made more profitable ballast than stones, but its original route from Yemen to Britain was treacherous. East India Company ships were easy prey for Red Sea pirates. In the years 1691 and 1693, no coffee reached British shores at all. Nor had Galen suggested that hot drinks were always beneficial. At the School of Paris, some physicians warned that hot things shortened life. In England, a Dr Willis sent patients with a 'cold heavy Constitution' to the coffee house to clear up headaches and lethargies. Patients with a hot temperament, by contrast, were advised to stay clear of the black drink because 'it may dispose the Body to inquietudes and leanness'. Too much coffee risked leaving such men 'paralytick, and does so slacken their strings, as they become unfit for the sports, and exercises of the Bed, and their Wives recreations'.[18] Indeed, the seventeenth-century German geographer Adam Olearius, who had been sent to Persia and Muscovy by Frederick III in 1633–5, observed that Persians drank coffee as a form of birth control. Chocolate, by contrast, was known as an aphrodisiac. Whether Britain's spectacular population growth would have slowed if it had become a nation of coffee instead of tea drinkers, we must leave to the reader's imagination.[19]

By the late seventeenth century, these drugs still enjoyed flexible uses and associations. Samuel Pepys, after a hard night's drinking, sipped chocolate to settle his stomach and cure his hangover. Many coffee houses served the whole range of hot beverages. It was coffee, however, that took the lead as a 'wakeful and civil drink'.[20] In expanding commercial societies, its sobering qualities set it apart from both aristocratic excess and the plebeian frenzy associated with sailors and prostitutes smoking marijuana. Coffee was recommended for clerks whose morning ale and wine, 'by the Dizziness they cause in the Braine, make many unfit for business'.[21] Coffee meant reason, control and moderation.

The early coffee houses attracted two groups of customers in particular: businessmen and scholars. The first coffee house in the West, The Angel, opened in Oxford in 1650. Venice and Amsterdam followed suit, in 1663, as did Bremen (1673), Boston (1690) and Prague (1705). By then, London had several hundreds of them. Immigrants and mercantile minorities played a decisive role in their diffusion. Oxford's was founded by a Jewish immigrant, the one in rue de Bussy, Paris, by an Armenian; it catered to the Knights of Malta. Unlike chocolate, coffee flaunted its exotic side. At Don Saltero's in London – real name: James Salter – visitors were able to sip their coffee while marvelling at crocodiles, turtles and other natural curiosities staring down at them from the ceiling. Countless establishments called themselves The Turk's Head.

Later commentators sometimes drew a sharp contrast between a sober, coffee-drinking commercial culture and that of a hedonistic court. This must not be overdone. In European principalities like Dresden, courts acted as magnets for exotic goods, attracting Italian and Levantine merchants who brought with them coffee, accessories and know-how. The coffee house was newsroom, business counter and university rolled into one. Here, one picked up one of the early newspapers, clinched a commercial deal and learnt of the latest scientific discovery. In the 1960s, the philosopher Jürgen Habermas celebrated the coffee house as a prototypical bourgeois public sphere governed by reason. At the time, however, few lived up to this lofty ideal. Most served brandy as well as coffee. Some served Turkish sherbets, others offered *bagnios*, Turkish baths complete with masseurs and barbers, and an opportunity to meet one's mistress. Reasoned conversation was interrupted by gossip, the occasional fight and illicit sexual encounters (see Plate 11). The public character of the coffee house had its limits. In Dresden, the authorities imposed a stiff tax on coffee to drive out plebeian establishments. In Prussia, Frederick the Great banned coffee altogether in 1769 to keep money in the country and protect domestic chicory against the colonial beverage. Such responses to coffee drinking were not just an assault on civil society by absolutist states. They also came from within civil society itself. In England, early coffee-house regulars worried that too much openness would corrupt the young and undermine order and respect for intellectual authority.[22] Drinking coffee required the right cultural disposition. Luxury, not democracy, was the animating spirit. In a discourse on coffee in 1764, one Italian writer concluded that all authorities were agreed that 'the virtue of sociability, humanity, and sweetness, the perfection of arts, the splendour of nations, and the cultivation of intelligence' always grew with luxury.[23] These were still virtues of the few, not the many.

The popular breakthrough came in the private, not the public sphere. By the mid-eighteenth century, there were growing signs of coffee and tea's invasion of the home. New daily routines and domestic sociability sprang up. In bourgeois families, husband and wife began the day with a joint morning coffee and returned home to drink tea or coffee with the family in the afternoon. For gentlewomen, the tea party was a ritual of female sociability but also an occasion to do business with traders and tenants' wives.[24] The beverages' conquest of the home was important, not least because it triggered a secondary wave of pots, tables and accessories. A court official in Wolfenbüttel, Germany, was recorded in 1745 as owning a coffeepot, milk jug, teapot, sugar caddy and eleven teaspoons – all in silver; a brass tea urn, with spirit stove; a pewter chocolate pot; and eleven blue-and-white porcelain cups, a sugar bowl in the same style, six small coloured cups, three chocolate mugs and six brown coffee cups.[25]

In 1715, the traveller Jean de La Roque, famous for his voyage to Arabia, noted in his treatise on the progress of coffee in Europe that in addition to 'men of quality', an 'infinite Number of Persons' had become 'accustom'd to Coffee . . . who are not in a Condition to appear handsomely at the publick Coffee-Houses'.[26] Diffusion was fastest in the heart of the commercial empires, Britain and the Netherlands. Inventories are especially numerous for these two countries, and they provide snapshots of how quickly the habit spread. Just north of Amsterdam, for example, lay the small town of Weesp, home to linen weavers, gin distillers and small farmers. In 1700, inventories recorded no tea or coffee wares at all. By the end of the 1730s, virtually every household had some cups and a pot. In Aalst, in Flanders, two thirds of the poorest quintile drank tea at the end of the eighteenth century, one third also coffee. The main difference was that the rich had porcelain pots, the poor only copper ones. In Antwerp, even people living in single rooms brewed their own tea or coffee. In London lodging houses, teapots for lodgers were a must by the end of the century.[27]

Coffee and tea were sold by booksellers and mercers as well as grocers and chemists. And exotic goods were offered in a growing variety, for every taste and budget. In 1683, an ironmonger in Cheshire, England, sold four grades of tobacco; two generations later, Alexander Chorley in Manchester offered ten different types of sugar. Dealers advertised tea 'for the benefit of the poor' at 'reduced prices in small quantities not less than 2 ounces'.[28] How strong a hold these new tastes had on habits is suggested by the case of Samuel Bauer, a Dresden wine merchant. At his home he had built up a modest tea and coffee service, including pewter cans and six coffee cups, in red and white, from the local Meissen manufactory. When the burgher fell on hard times, he took his caffeine habit with him to the poorhouse. He ordered coffee in the morning and afternoon, spending as much on the black brew as on all his other food and beer combined, until his death in 1787.[29]

Bauer's modest Meissen set was tangible proof of the expanding market for tableware that was simultaneously fashionable, affordable and durable. Yet Meissen and contemporaries like Wedgwood were resourceful beneficiaries of the demand for semi-luxuries rather than its instigators. A century earlier, no prophet could have foreseen the dominance of European-made chinaware. No European cup or bowl could rival porcelain from China (see Plate 4). The Dutch had produced tin-glazed Delftware since the sixteenth century, but it easily cracked. Earthenware did not agree with hot beverages. Europe was behind in techniques of production, glazing and painting: a continent of brass and rough pewter, not fine china. Ehrenfried von Tschirnhaus discovered how to produce hard-paste porcelain in Saxony in 1704, but the process was kept secret and was initially so expensive that only Augustus the Strong and his court could afford his wares. Meanwhile, the Chinese of Jingdezhen fired many hundred kilns that supplied 4,000 local factories. It was a truly global centre of production, not only providing Europe with several hundred tons of chinaware a year by the 1740s, but shipping even larger volumes to Japan and across South-east Asia. Novelty, fashion, adaptation and innovation – the fuel of consumer societies – were the product of East–West exchange.

Chinese porcelain was a hybrid thing. On the inside, a bowl carried liquids; on the outside, stories and dreams. In Asia, pottery painting evolved in tandem with woodblock printing and calligraphy.[30] One popular motif of late Ming porcelain was the 'Red Cliff', a scene of a wine-drinking boating party inspired by a story from the eleventh century. Such bowls circulated in Asia but also found their way to seventeenth-century Paris and Istanbul. Some European writers like the poet Alexander Pope and the essayist Joseph Addison worried that women were selling their soul for a porcelain cup: porcelain dishes transported their beholders into a virtual pleasure-dome. Yet, overall, European respect for Chinese civilization was still strong enough to surround chinaware with an air of refinement and virtue. In addition to their technical expertise and capacity, Chinese producers were adaptive. They responded to the evolving craze for chinoiserie, giving Europeans the Orient they wanted; these were often second-best articles as far as the Chinese were concerned. In Canton, European merchants began to arrive with their own patterns, but in the early eighteenth century their execution was still entirely in the hands of local decorating shops. Patterns and fashions changed quickly. What was the latest craze one year was 'old' China the next. Markets segmented. European dealers offloaded unwanted stock on the American colonies.

The demand for Chinese semi-luxuries set in motion a feverish wheel of imitation and innovation. At first, Europeans were little more than copycats. In the middle of the century, the tide turned. In Bow, east London, a factory started to produce bone china, making it Britain's 'New Canton'. In the 1760s, Wedgwood found a way to cover earthenware with a shining glaze that was both attractive and strong enough to withstand sudden changes of temperature, crucial for hot beverages. Creamware was born, a cheap yet smooth substitute for porcelain, ideally suited for the growing middle-class market. Porcelain manufactories mushroomed across Europe, benefiting from princely subsidies but also from a European network of painters and designers, who took their inspiration from the *New Book of Chinese Design* (1754) and similar pattern books. Transfer printing enabled manufacturers to move illuminations from engraved copperplates to paper and then on to ceramics. Innovation extended to marketing. Wedgwood opened showrooms and distributed catalogues of his patterns across Europe from Nice to Moscow. Qinghua under-glaze of blue and white now faced competition from home-grown 'Egyptian black'. Fashion was a fickle master. Porcelain was a Chinese monopoly in 1700. By 1800, tableware was firmly in European hands. In 1791, the East India Company had stopped bulk imports from China altogether.[31]

The diffusion of beverages and tea ware was in part a trickle-down process. Servants were introduced to the new hot drinks by their masters and, in turn, asked for a few grams of tea or coffee in addition to their pay. In 1757 the philanthropist Jonas Hanway, a friend of foundlings, the sick and the poor and the first Englishman to carry an umbrella, complained that servants and labourers had become 'enslaved by [the] foolish customs' of the rich and would rather give up a loaf of bread than a cup of sweetened tea. As far as Hanway was concerned, the 'national frenzy' was a 'criminal excess'. It was bad for 'national welfare' (China had to be paid in silver), bad for character and enterprise (sipping tea wasted precious time) and bad for health (tea was 'unnatural' for people in a cold northern climate, 'unwholesome' and close to 'poison'). Worst, it added to the 'beggary and distress' of the poorest, for 'the more wants the poor have, the more discontented they will be if they are not gratified.'[32] In Paris a few years later, the historian Legrand d'Aussy wrote, 'there is absolutely no shop girl, cook, or chambermaid who does not have coffee with milk for breakfast.'[33] In alleys and markets, he added, female vendors served the lower orders with *café au lait* made from used coffee grounds and sour milk.

Emulation, however, was only part of the story. For people in cities with little money and less time, tea and coffee offered a cheap substitute for a hot meal. The addition of sugar shifted their appeal further from exotic medicine to nutritious pleasure. Initially, most coffee was probably drunk without or with very little sugar. By 1715, La Roque noted that there were those who drank coffee no longer for the sake of health but to 'please their pallats', loading it 'excessively with Sugar' until it turned into a syrup.[34] By the end of the century, tea and coffee were recognized as 'vehicles of nourishment' for sugar; still, even then champions of coffee advised moderation, because 'it is apt to become acid, if made sweet: and this is the one reason why many people forbear drinking Coffee.'[35]

The engine of expansion was empire. It was in the eighteenth century that European empires began the large-scale exploitation of their tropical colonies and intensified their trade in tea from China. In the 1720s, the various East Indies companies still brought only 770 tons of tea a year back to Europe. By the 1760s, it was ten times that, accompanied by millions of pieces of chinaware; by the 1820s, it had doubled again. At a time when the price of wheat and other domestic foods was rising, tea became cheaper and cheaper. In Amsterdam, the wholesale price of coffee plummeted from 10 gulden per kilo at the beginning of the eighteenth century to 1 gulden at its end. In the same period, Britain increased its sugar consumption almost ten times, to 20 pounds per person a year. This was the peak of the Atlantic slave trade that was so crucial for coffee and sugar plantations. On the eve of the abolition of the slave trade, in 1807, the West Indies supplied a quarter of Britain's total imports. Never again would the colonial world play such a large role in the imperial centre. Malachy Postlethwayt, who worked as a publicist for the Walpole government and the Royal Africa Company, acutely perceived the architecture of the British empire: it was, he wrote in the 1750s, 'a magnificent superstructure of American commerce and naval power on an African foundation'.[36]

By the late eighteenth century, the human cost of slave sugar started to cause public outrage, as we shall see in the next chapter. Meanwhile, in economic terms, the costs and benefits of empire continued to be the subject of debate. In a strict sense, mercantilism was bad for consumers, certainly when compared to its successor, the liberal empire of free trade and cheap food. Sugar, tea and especially coffee bore heavy taxes, which encouraged smuggling, especially from France via the Isle of Wight. Similarly, sound economics tell us that free labour is more productive than slave labour. The whip does not encourage efficiency or ingenuity. But history is bloodier and messier than economics. The new order of consumption was built on the backs of slaves. China showed that it was possible to grow sugar on small farms, but there were not many European labourers eagerly waiting to embark for Jamaica or Haiti, nor many plantation owners willing to pay the high wages that would have been necessary to attract them. If Britain had opened her colonies to the rest of the world, it would have prompted a French takeover, not a free market. Clearly, this mercantilist empire enriched traders and plantation owners at the expense of slaves and ordinary people back home. British consumers paid through the nose for the British navy and the Atlantic colonies. Yet the reality was that, without the navy and slaves, they would have had even fewer tropical goods.[37]

Consumption is not a simple function of either economics or culture. Fluctuating prices and changing tastes can reinforce each other. Britons' growing preference for tea over coffee is a case in point. In the 1710s – the golden age of the coffee house – coffee still had the edge. A century later, the tables had turned. A Briton now consumed almost 2 pounds of tea per year, but only two thirds of a pound of coffee. As 1 pound of tea makes as much beverage as 3 pounds of coffee, Britons thus drank around eight cups of tea for each cup of coffee. Price helped.[38] Duties on coffee were raised in 1724 but lowered on tea in 1745. Some historians have suggested that tea was favoured by the convenience of preparation – just add hot water, no roasting required – and built-in economy; tea leaves can be reused, as the poor and adulterators knew. Evidence from other countries urges caution. Americans switched to coffee after Independence and apparently did not mind the extra fuss and utensils. Coffee beans, too, were reused. La Roque advised that the 'same Coffee, which has been once us'd, retains still Vertue enough to serve a second and even a third Time', a recommendation echoed in German advice books.[39] More decisive was that ordinary Britons liked the affordable Bohea tea grown in northern Fujian while mercantilism drove up the price of good coffee. British taste reflected the political economy of the British empire: a sweet alliance between the sugar lobby of the West Indies and the East India Company, which imported tea from China. Empire left its mark on quality as well as price. West Indian planters used prime land to grow the crop that was most profitable: sugar. Coffee was treated as second class. The quality told. Even the champions of Jamaican coffee conceded the 'smell, the rankness in the taste, and disgusting return', which made it 'unpleasant' for anyone accustomed to beans from Mocca or the French islands.[40] For British coffee it was a vicious circle: high taxes meant low consumption, which, in turn, depressed investment, quality and taste. The failure of British coffee offers a history lesson that is easily forgotten: some new tastes were acquired thanks to mercantilist empire; others were spoiled by it.

The Chinese state might not have blocked trade, but it did not promote it either. Wealth created in the Yangzi Delta was siphoned off and transferred to the poorer north, a kind of cross-subsidy for the sake of political stability. The British state was no charity bazaar, but it squeezed its people's wallets to build up trade and colonies as well as to subsidize the elite. And trade spurred demand, as contemporaries appreciated. 'It is not because an English washerwoman cannot sit down to breakfast without tea and sugar, that the world has been circumnavigated,' the champion of colonization Edward Gibbon Wakefield noted, 'but it is because the world has been circumnavigated that an English washerwoman requires tea and sugar for breakfast.'[41] The Atlantic empire gave the new textile industries, too, a much bigger outlet than they would have had otherwise.[42] The promotion of trade intersected with a domestic culture receptive to experimentation, as was the case in the new cotton and pottery manufactories. All this favoured growth and development.[43] And it enlarged the basket of goods for Britons at home and in the colonies. Trade was significant because it cheapened consumer goods at a time when food prices were rising. It was those with disposable income, the middling sort and the rich, who were the main beneficiaries.

URBAN LIVING

All societies had capitals and major cities. China had Beijing and Yangzhou; France had Paris, with half a million inhabitants by 1700. What set the Netherlands and Britain apart was the density of their urban landscape. Towns and cities grew by leaps and bounds. In England and Wales in 1500, fewer than one in thirty people lived in a town with a population of more than 10,000; by 1800, it was one in five. In the Netherlands, this proportion increased from 16 per cent to 29 per cent. Meanwhile, a mere 5 per cent lived in towns in the lower Yangzi in 1800, the most developed region in China at the time; in Latin America and India, it was around 6 per cent.[44] France and Germany were overwhelmingly rural societies, while Italian cities suffered from stagnation or decline. Why should this matter? After all, commerce expanded in the Yangzi in the absence of towns, as revisionist historians have recently shown. For consumption, however, urban life was decisive – for four main reasons.

First, thanks to their size and social complexion, towns and cities provided a favourable space for product differentiation and specialized services. The sheer variety of tea sets, wallpapers and ready-made gowns is unthinkable without them, as is the arrival by the mid-eighteenth century of dedicated glass and china shops alongside the general mercer of old. Cities thus accelerated and fed the specialization made possible by trade. Secondly, towns provided a stage where desires were tickled and new tastes diffused. Urban tradesmen acquired porcelain, curtains and saucepans faster than their counterparts in the country.[45] In other words, urban living did more to increase demand than rising income or falling prices did. The countryside was not entirely cut off, but there were only so many novelties that a pedlar could carry on his back. What urban shops began to offer in the eighteenth century was a whole ambience of consumption, with goods behind plate glass and mirrors, display cabinets and comfortable chairs for customers. Shopping became part of urban leisure. Provincial shops played a crucial role in the cultural as much as the commercial

integration of Britain. In Chester in the 1730s, for example, the upholsterer Abner Scholes assembled two showrooms of an ideal home, with
chairs and tables, modern fabrics and framed prints of Lilliputians,
made fashionable by the suceess of *Gulliver's Travels*.[46] Urban living,
thirdly, cut into self-provisioning. True, the French bourgeoisie continued to draw on wine from their vineyards and urban workers kept
chickens into the twentieth century but, in general, 'autoconsomma-
tion' was much harder for city folk than for their country cousins.
Cooking requires an oven, time, skill and coal. Urban workers lacked
most of these. Clothing, too, was increasingly purchased ready-made.

Booming cities, finally, created a particular arena of communication. Growth and mobility constantly brought new faces together.
Reputation and identity were more fluid. Dress was a way to signal who
one was, or wanted to be. A new culture of appearance took hold. 'Fine
Feathers make fine Birds,' the Dutch-born physician and philosopher
Bernard Mandeville noted in *The Fable of the Bees* in 1714, 'and People
where they are not known, are generally honour'd according to their
Cloaths and other Accoutrements they have about them; from their
richness of them we judge of their Wealth, and by their ordering of
them we guess at their Understanding. It is this,' Mandeville concluded,
that made a person 'wear Clothes above his Rank, especially in large
and Populous Cities, where obscure Men may hourly meet with fifty
Strangers to one Acquaintance, and consequently have the Pleasure of
being esteem'd by a vast Majority, not as what they are, but what they
appear to be.'[47] The anonymity of towns made it easier to seek approval
and be treated above one's station. 'This Golden Dream', as Mandeville
called it, unleashed a game of imitation and disguise that made demand
self-perpetuating.

It is not necessary to be quite so cynical, but the general point about
the importance of consumer goods for identity formation stands. Dress,
accessories and comportment provided a social positioning system. A
trader, new to town, was less likely to attract business if he dressed like
a country bumpkin, a customer less likely to receive credit. Perhaps as
significant as building trust and impressing others was fashioning oneself. One of the first things young workers bought with their wages was
a decent set of clothes: it announced a new, mature identity. Simultaneously, the commotion of cities more generally put a premium on privacy,
as people drew their curtains and looked for comfort inside the home
and in its possessions. The stage was set for 'self-fashioning' three centuries before literary critics coined the term.[48]

THINGS ON THE MIND

Karl Marx believed that Western capitalism divorced humans from the world of things. The rise of the West, in this influential view, entailed a unique ability to look at an object as an abstraction, a lifeless thing that could be exchanged for money, in contrast to tribal cultures which fetishized goods for their magical powers. The more goods the West accumulated, the less they cared about them. Many have blamed the enlightenment for the West's 'self'-importance. For Theodor Adorno and Max Horkheimer, the founders of the neo-Marxist Frankfurt School of social research, it left behind an 'instrumental rationality'. For some anthropologists, the sharp line between people and things set the West apart from the more organic material cultures of Africa or China. In Ming China, man was part of the world of things (*wu*). In Europe, according to this view, however, they were torn asunder by René Descartes, who, in the 1640s, argued that the mind was an entity separate from the body and the material world. A century and a half later, Immanuel Kant is said to have completed 'humankind's victory over . . . things'.[49]

This fixation on humans as independent subjects is, we are told, the source of our own current mess. Modernity gave Western man the delusion that he controlled matter. Our dependence on things was forgotten. Objects became subordinate and disposable. The throwaway society was the inevitable result. In recent years, the French social scientist and tireless champion of things Bruno Latour has been at the forefront of a campaign to give things back the respect they deserve and reclaim them as actors in our lives. What is required, Latour insists, is nothing less than a break with the intellectual foundations of modernity. From Hobbes and Rousseau to Rawls and Habermas in the late twentieth century, political thought has been the 'victim of a strong object-avoidance tendency', dreaming up assemblies emptied of stuff, where people meet as if 'naked', equipped only with reason.[50]

It would be foolish to deny parts of the critique – the enlightenment did sponsor the idea of critical reason and undermined folk ideas which, for example, had invested trees and other objects with the power of speech and action. The real question is whether dematerialization captures the overall thrust of modernity and whether it led to a distinctly carefree attitude to things in the West. After all, that the Chinese saw persons and things as one has not stopped them from consuming a

lot in recent decades. Nor did Western modernity have a single tradition. Arguments for the authentic self were paralleled and sometimes
drowned out by a new fascination with things as handmaidens of
knowledge and identity; even Descartes did not believe in a strict dual-
ism between mind and matter or subjects and objects. Instead of falling
into a sudden material amnesia, artists and scientists were, in fact,
thinking about things, including in political economy, philosophy, literature and law. Seventeenth- and eighteenth-century minds were, for
want of a better word, becoming stuffed.

The embrace of things had its roots in natural philosophy. Renaissance culture had made people more attentive to objects. Collections of
books and exotic herbs reflected the expertise and taste of the collector.
This provided the foundation from which Dutch and English scientists
and travellers in the seventeenth century would develop a fresh approach
to knowledge. Instead of proceeding from general principles, they
began with the detailed description of objects. Understanding could
not be achieved by mental exertion alone but required going out into
the world, to smell, touch and catalogue the many things that filled it.
In the decades after 1598, fleets of Dutch ships returned from the East
and West Indies with collections of shells, nutmeg, armadillos and the
bones of an elk. Expeditions to the Spice Islands added a Hottentot
spear. Cabinets of exotic plants and artefacts like those in Enkhuizen
and Leiden appeared in travel guides and attracted artisans and merchants as well as students and royalty. Commercial expansion and
'tasteful objectivity' fed each other.[51] Both reached out into the world
in search of new things.

The empirical, material approach to knowledge made trade a virtuous partner of science and sociability. Goods and goodness advanced
hand in hand. Trade did not just line the pockets of the merchant. It
opened up the world for the general good. Like science, trade taught
people to appreciate objects and to work together, as Caspar Barlaeus,
the Renaissance polymath, argued in his lectures at Amsterdam's Ath-
enaeum in the 1630s. This was a much more dynamic and open view
than that of civic humanism, where magnificence had been the privilege of the few. Trade validated objects in the home in a new way. The
Chinese dishes and Turkish carpets that Dutch burghers displayed in
their homes were symbolic of this 'positive relationship to the world', in
the words of the Ming historian Timothy Brook, and stood in contrast
to the late Ming, where the foreignness of objects carried little value.[52]

The established position had been that the desire for things was simultaneously a costly drain on the nation and corrupted the individual. This was well expressed by the English merchant Thomas Mun. The Dutch were beating us, Mun wrote in 1664, because they were industrious, while the English were suffering from a:

> general leprosie of our Piping [smoking], Potting [drinking], Feasting, Fashions, and mis-spending of our time in Idleness and Pleasure (contrary to the Law of God, and the use of other Nations) [that] hath made us effeminate in our bodies, weak in our knowledge, poor in our Treasure, declined in our Valour, unfortunate in our Enterprises, and contemned by our Enemies. I write the more of these excesses, because they do so greatly wast[e] our wealth.[53]

Yet even as Mun was writing, this orthodoxy was coming under fire from the new champions of things. Desire was a divine gift, the scientist Robert Boyle wrote in 1655. While 'other creatures were content with . . . easily attainable necessaries', God had furnished man with 'a multiplicity of desires'. 'Superfluities and dainties' were not bad. 'Greedy appetites' inspired an 'inquisitive industry to range, anatomize, and ransack nature'. Instead of distracting people from the world of the spirit, the lust for goods gave them a 'more exquisite admiration of the omniscient Author'.[54] God wanted people to be consumers, not ascetics.

The classical suspicion of luxury lost ground as the culture of improvement gathered steam. For the Royal Society, founded in 1660, Venetian glass and other foreign luxury goods advanced new technologies and useful knowledge. Patents proliferated. In his *History of the Royal Society* (1667), the Bishop of Rochester presented luxury and novelty as vehicles of progress. At the beginning, he wrote, society had been divided into the powerful and the rest. The powerful increased their pleasure and conveniences through luxury; the rest did so through work. The result was opulence and cities. So far, so good. Where the bishop broke with earlier writers was in daring to imagine that progress could continue, thanks to the 'discovery of new matter, to imploy men's hands' and the transplantation of the same matter from the colonies, such as silk. 'We have no ground to despair.' The microscope, optical glass and other new instruments showed that 'we have a far greater number of different things reveal'd to us, than were contain'd in the visible Universe before.' Trade and novelties injected constant fresh energy into Britain: the more the better.[55]

Novelties were also news, and the latest goods were promoted by the

burgeoning market for printed news. In addition to selling tea and coffee, the apothecary John Houghton, a fellow of the Royal Society, ran
a weekly, single-folio commercial newsletter between 1692 and 1703.
Sold at two pence, the *Collection for Improvement of Agriculture and
Trade* mixed information on the price of coal and company stock with
adverts for chocolate and spectacles.

These texts were about more than this or that novelty item. They
expressed a fundamentally new view of human nature. The critique of
luxury had drawn on the principles of the ancients. Aristotle presumed
that man had limited needs. The best way to satisfy them was to lead a
simple life, according to Socrates. The moderns raised their sights. An
early exponent of a more expansive vision of desire was Nicholas Barbon, a pioneer of insurance and banking in London in the 1680s
Mankind, according to Barbon, was born with two general wants: the
'Wants of the Body, and the Wants of the Mind'. And the latter were
'infinite'. Desire was the 'Appetite of the Soul', and as natural to it 'as
Hunger to the Body'. 'Man naturally aspires' and 'his wants increase
with his wishes, which is for everything that is rare, can gratify his
senses, adorn his body, and promote the ease, pleasure and pomp of
life.' England's resources were, similarly, 'infinite and can never be consumed'. Consumption was not fixed by physiological limits. Barbon
knew what he was talking about – a wheeler-dealer, he was a fashionable dresser and a speculative builder who profited from Londoners'
wish for greater comfort in the aftermath of the Great Fire. Fashion
was not wasteful. Rather it was the 'desire of novelties and things
scarce, that causeth trade'. The more the nation traded, the more people
earned, the more they consumed, the fatter the king's coffers.[56]

In *The Fable of the Bees* (1705/14), Bernard Mandeville sharpened
the blade of this argument and delivered the *coup de grâce* to the old
moral order. Private vices, in his famous phrase, made for public
benefits:

> Envy it self, and Vanity
> Were Ministers of Industry;
> Their darling Folly, Fickleness
> In Diet, Furniture, and Dress,
> That strange ridic'lous Vice, was made
> The very Wheel, that turn'd the Trade.

Vice had raised 'Pleasures, Comforts, Ease/ To such a Height, the very
Poor/ Liv'd better than the Rich before'.[57] The argument cut through the

moral unity of civic humanism, which imagined a symmetry between individual virtue and the public good. It divorced social benefits from individual character. Bad intentions did not matter, if the results were good. A glutton made a good citizen. Strong nations were built by vice, not virtue.

In sixteenth-century China, the writer Lu Ji had already questioned the notion that extravagance impoverished society. The luxurious living of the few encouraged commerce. It is unhelpful, however, to see here a Chinese Mandeville *avant la lettre*.[58] Unlike the Dutch doctor, Lu Ji did not imagine a 'wheel' of perpetual growth. The amount of wealth created by heaven and earth was fixed. One person's loss was another's gain. What made Mandeville so revolutionary was that he portrayed a society where individuals' lust for things fed everyone's gain, making the whole nation wealthier and stronger.

The fresh appreciation of consumption mirrored a more positive view of wages. In the past, the poverty of the many was taken as given. There was only so much to go around. If weavers' wages went up, so would the price of cloth, resulting in fewer sales, fewer jobs and more poverty. It was the massive increase in trade and the confidence in useful knowledge in the decades after the Restoration (1660) that opened contemporaries' eyes to what had been a fact for two centuries: Britain was a high-wage economy. John Cary argued in 1695 that improved skills and labour-saving technologies made it possible to be competitive and pay high wages. Instead of being condemned to a struggle for survival, the bulk of the population could enter the ranks of consumers. Higher spending was feasible. In fact, it was desirable, Daniel Defoe argued in *A Plan of the English Commerce* in 1728. For the entire nation depended on the many labourers and shopkeepers and 'the largeness of their Gettings': 'by their Wages they are able to live plentifully, and it is by their expensive, generous, free way of living, that the Home Consumption is rais'd to such a Bulk, as well of our own, as of foreign Production.' 'We are a luxurious, expensive People.' Life was 'full of Excesses', Defoe wrote, 'even criminally so in some Things'. Still, cutting wages to cut consumption was a bad idea. Pay them less and they would spend less. The whole kingdom would suffer.[59]

Not everyone was convinced. When a mild earthquake hit New England in 1727, the Puritan Cotton Mather, a Harvard graduate, preached it was a sign of God's displeasure at the vanities of his flock. The luxury wars were a pan-European phenomenon. What distinguished the debate in Britain was less the absence of critics than its more fluid, mercantile tone. Expanding commerce and arguments for consumption were supporting each other. Getting rid of the crypto-absolutist James II in 1688 helped, by reducing fears of courtly excess. Instead of a sharp divide between luxury and necessity, contemporaries discovered a spectrum of 'modest' or 'innocent luxury' in between. What once was luxury could mutate into necessity, as in the case of sugar. Why try to stop the lower orders from joining in? By 1776, as we have seen, Adam Smith could present consumption as 'the sole end of production' as if it was the most uncontroversial fact of life.

On the continent, by contrast, the luxury debate was rekindled by the crisis of the nobility and the rise of despotism. Once a sign of magnificence and virtue, critics complained, luxury was corroding the Spanish nobility, as nobles tried to outspend each other on showy dress and gardens. Strong, productive landowners turned into soft, effeminate puppets. Their power ended up in the hands of an absolute monarch. In France, similarly, Denis Diderot denounced luxury as a source of corruption, centred on the court. And the Church! Voltaire added. Elaborate banquets and liveried servants diverted wealth from more productive employment which had justified luxury in the past. Luxury no longer helped the poor, Baron d'Holbach concluded, it created them.[60]

Critics of luxury were not automatically traditionalists and anti-trade, just as its defenders were not all modernizers, let alone democrats. The English Nicholas Barbon was a Tory. In France, the Marquis de Mirabeau attacked his fellow noblemen for being decadent 'bloodsuckers' but looked for salvation to free trade and agrarian development, not a return to Spartan frugality.[61] The excesses of the nobility, like those of bankers today, attracted attention because they seemed to explain a deeper crisis – French losses in the Seven Years War (1756–63) did wonders for the sale of the Marquis' *L'Amis des hommes*. Consumption remained first and foremost a political, not an economic question. When it was sweet and when sour depended on the system of government. Luxury was vital in a monarchy where the rich supported the poor, Montesquieu argued, but evil in a republic of equals.[62]

In the course of the Enlightenment, the luxury debate crystallized two opposed yet equally radical views of human nature and social order. One celebrated the authentic self. In this view, the self existed prior to and separate from the material world. For Jean-Jacques Rousseau, the desire for things turned free men into slaves. Fashionable clothes and excessive comforts alienated people from their true self. Rousseau himself donned a simple Armenian coat, much to the ridicule of high society. His great achievement was to extend this idea of a pure self into a political argument for social equality. A republic needed free, active citizens, and this required equality. Luxury destroyed it and reduced people to things. Despotism and slavery were twins.

An alternative view was advanced by David Hume, Rousseau's friend and host in London in 1766 until their heavily publicized falling-out when the exiled Rousseau, known for his belligerence, accused his host of secretly plotting against him. Taken to extremes, Hume wrote in his *Essays*, luxury was pernicious, but the general 'increase and consumption of all the commodities, which serve to the ornament and pleasures of life, are advantages to society'. The difference between the two men was beautifully captured by Allan Ramsay in his famous portraits of 1766, with Rousseau appearing in his plain Armenian coat while the Scottish philosopher sported bright scarlet, gold brocade and fine lace. Luxury, Hume argued, made a nation stronger and happier. Where 'there is no demand for such superfluities, men sink into indolence, lose all enjoyment of life, and are useless to the public'. 'Slothful members' made poor citizens and poor soldiers. Rather than leading to despotism, the desire for more was the bulwark of liberty. For it enlarged the 'middling rank' which neither submitted to slavery (like poor peasants), nor had the hope of tyrannizing others (like barons).[63]

Hume's project was nothing less than 'a science of man', and his positive view of luxury was part of a larger appreciation of the role of objects in the making of the self and civil society. Mandeville had left the door wide open to accusations of vice and immorality. Hume closed it, connecting ethics and emotions to the economic defence of material desire. The desire for things made people better as well as richer. By nourishing commerce and industry, it brought them together in clubs, conversation and entertainment, all of which made them 'feel an encrease of humanity'. 'Thus,' Hume concluded, 'industry, knowledge, and humanity, are linked together by an indissoluble chain, and are found, from experience as well as reason, to be peculiar to the more polished, and . . . more luxurious ages.'[64]

That curiosity about objects encouraged civilized sociability had already been the argument of Dutch natural philosophers. In *A Treatise of Human Nature* (1739), Hume extended this to the self. Hume had studied at La Flèche, Descartes' college, but the *Treatise* presented a full-scale alternative to Cartesianism. The mind was not its own entity, separate from the body and nature. Rather the self was a fiction, a kind of work in progress, the composite result of impressions and ideas. It is not clear whether Hume had read Spinoza, who argued that thought originated in sense and sensibility and was thus rooted in matter. He was certainly familiar with his disciples, Pierre Bayle and Mandeville, and frequented the Rainbow Coffee House, on Fleet Street in London, which was popular with Spinozists. Hume showed how bodily pleasure and pain shaped our identity and passions. An encounter with a new object was one way in which intelligence and feeling were inspired and strengthened. When the 'soul' applied itself to understand a novelty, Hume wrote, it moved with difficulty at first. This difficulty excited 'the spirit' and was 'the source of wonder'. Over time the stimulus wore off.[65] This was just as well, added Hume's friend Lord Kames in his reflections on novelty a few years later. If it did not, we would suffer from overload and 'have no room left either for action or reflexion'.[66] To trigger the sense of wonder, new objects needed to keep coming. Novelty's psychological effect fascinated the Scottish Enlightenment and put fashion and obsolescence in a new light. Far from being artificial or alienating, new things helped make us who we were. Stop their flow and the self would lose some of the impressions that kept it alive.

Today, consumption is so often associated with selfishness that it is worth emphasizing how the eighteenth century appreciated that individuals' desire for things had social benefits. Wealth, social order and an interest in doing good sustained each other. How did possessions achieve this? The utility of an object pleased its owner, Hume pointed out, by permanently reminding him of the pleasure that object would give in serving its purpose. What had not been noticed, Adam Smith added in *The Theory of Moral Sentiment* (1759), was that the means for attaining pleasure were often valued higher than that pleasure itself. People stuffed their pockets with 'little conveniences' and contrived 'new pockets' to carry more. They walked about 'loaded with a multitude of baubles' of so little direct use that it 'is certainly not worth the fatigue of bearing the burden'. And yet, people accumulated more and more. People were in love with 'numberless artificial and elegant contrivances', Smith wrote, because they imagined them to be '*means* of happiness'. On its own, a tweezer case looked frivolous and contemptible. Yet, 'in our imagination', it was part of a harmonious system that made the pleasures of wealth 'grand and beautiful and noble'.[67] The deception energized mankind and prompted men to cultivate the soil, build cities and improve science and communication.

Self-interest was tamed and civilized by an interest in the approval of others. The faculty of sympathy – the ability to put oneself in another's shoes – made for social order: a poor man who could imagine himself one day as master of a mansion was unlikely to want to get rid of the rich. In the past, it was felt that consumption had to be regulated because reckless spending would otherwise wreck society. This was nonsense, said Smith. Extravagance was driven by 'the passion for present enjoyment'. It was 'sometimes violent' but 'momentary and occasional' compared to the stronger desire to better our condition which we carried from the cradle to the grave. This prompted us to save to accumulate wealth. On balance, the frugal many always outnumbered the profligate few. The increase in England's wealth was proof of this. Consumption could safely be left in the hands of individuals. It was 'the highest impertinence and presumption', Smith concluded, for 'kings and ministers to pretend to watch over the economy of private people, and to restrain their expense, either by sumptuary laws, or by prohibiting the importation of foreign luxuries. They are themselves always, and without any exception, the greatest spendthrifts in the society.'[68]

In the *Wealth of Nations* (1776), Adam Smith looked back on the decline of feudalism and rise of commerce in Europe. It was the great barons' appetite for diamond buckles and 'trinkets and baubles' that made them gradually barter away their authority, he argued. They literally consumed their power. To fund their growing appetite for goods they first reduced the number of their retainers. The barons' 'expensive vanity' then gave the remaining tenants a chance to extract longer leases and win greater independence in return for a promise of higher rents. Merchants and artisans were happy to supply the goods. Thus, a 'revolution of the greatest importance to the public happiness' was unleashed, the unintended consequence of the 'folly' of one, and the 'industry' of the other. The wealth of commercial society was set free. And with it greater peace. The 'pride of man makes him love to domineer', Smith observed in the same section.[69] Much better if that desire found an outlet in snuffboxes and hats, however silly, than in owning other people. Material possessions constrained personal aggression and social strife. People would be too busy acquiring things to kill each other.

William Blackstone, the father of common law, devoted the largest book of the *Commentaries on the Laws of England* (1765–9) to 'the Rights of Things'. He drew distinctions between everything from movable things and land to domestic and wild animals. The right of inheritance ensured that possessions had a virtuous effect on society. It 'sets the passions on the side of duty, and prompts a man to deserve well of the public, when he is sure that the reward of his services will not die with himself', but be transmitted to those for whom he has 'the dearest and most tender affections'; the initial origins of the right, Blackstone suggested, were probably simply that a person had his family around him on his death bed.[70]

Blackstone was reacting to a trend. Possessions were becoming increasingly central to personal identity and family memory. Plates and cutlery started to carry stamped initials. Sometimes identity was literally carved into furniture, as in the cupboards and drawers in eighteenth-century America which their female owners emblazoned with their names. Heirlooms constructed family memory and kept the self alive for future generations. In 1756, an English lady set down that 'the old china cup with the gilt cover and saucer, that has a setting in gold belonging to it, Mary must have, and give it to her daughter', as was family tradition. 'These trifles I give to renew in her mind whenever she sees them, the constant tenderness of her truly affectionate mother.'[71] Objects forged a similar bond for the growing number of mercantile and imperial families separated by the Atlantic and Indian Oceans in this period. The early modern ascendance of the conjugal family oriented towards its children no doubt stimulated such practices of material remembrance, and also explains why women played such a significant role as its custodians. Personalizing objects was a way simultaneously to serve the family ideal and to carve out a private space in its midst.

But the material culture of the self was never easy. By blurring the line between person and object, it made it difficult to say where one ended and the other began. Possessions helped create the self, but what if consumption depleted it? In Scotland, Hume and Smith's paean to commerce and innocent luxuries faced some critics, for example, the judge and philosopher Lord Monboddo, who worried that modern comforts would sap the strength of Highland warriors and lead to population decline.[72] The rising circulation of goods also raised fears that their worship might possess the soul. Daniel Defoe reflected this ambivalence. On the one hand, he reported on the virtuous circle between consumer goods, industriousness and a higher standard of living. On the other, in *Moll Flanders* (1722), he told the story of a young woman whose lust for silk handkerchiefs and golden beads led her to thievery, prostitution and imprisonment: the more she desired things, the more she herself was reduced to a thing for sale.

The transmigration of souls from person to thing became a running theme in eighteenth-century literature. The 'souls of fashionable folk are to be found in their garments', the great satirist Jonathan Swift wrote. A genre of 'it narratives' took off, in which watches, coins and lapdogs gave accounts of their lives. For the ancient philosopher Pythagoras, belief in the transmigration of souls had led to greater sympathy for other creatures. Eighteenth-century stories narrated by objects, by contrast, often painted a grim picture of human vice and folly. Owners were selfish and careless, slaves to their consuming passion – pretty much the opposite of the philosophical ideal of sympathy and sociability. In the *Adventures of a Black Coat* (1760), the garment narrated the fall of Susan Sirloin, the daughter of a humble tradesman, whose desire for more drove her to prostitution. If anyone in this tale had moral sentiment it was the coat, who concluded that the power of reason was wasted on humans: they ignored the road to true happiness in their hectic craving for instant satisfaction. That the real authors behind these 'it narratives' were themselves adapting to an increasingly competitive literary market might in part explain their cynical tone. Other commentators worried that women were becoming wound up like clockwork, fixated on fashion and tea parties. A good century before Carlo Collodi put speech and cunning into *Pinocchio* (1883), contemporaries were already fascinated by the grey zone between human subjects and animated puppets. The two mingled in puppet theatres, where it was left to the audience to figure out what were the life-sized puppets and who was the aptly named wooden-legged actor Samuel Foote.[73]

A CULTURE OF IMPROVEMENT

Since the earliest moments of exchange, human communities have had to confront the challenges that new things, tastes and desires brought with them. The spectacular rise of consumption in the late seventeenth and eighteenth centuries reflected the reach of colonial power, technological advances and the growth of an urban, wage-earning population, but none of these would have mattered had society not also chosen to live in a fast-changing world of goods. Goods did not just arrive. They had to be invited in. In the past, societies were stand-offish. The Dutch in the seventeenth, and even more so the British in the eighteenth century, were more accommodating. Ideas about innocent luxury and a fluid self offered supporting arguments. But, in the final analysis, consumption is a lived experience, and it was here that a decisive compact emerged between values and practices that justified the arrival of 'more'. For all the fears it continued to generate, consumption was welcomed as an integral part of personal and social improvement. It was made safe.

Few habits brought out the dangers of luxury more clearly than overeating. Gluttony was one of the seven deadly sins, austerity its remedy. Eighteenth-century doctors changed the diagnosis and the cure. 'Hypochondria', as contemporaries labelled melancholy and depression, was a disease of luxurious living, the result of gorging on food, drinking too much wine and a sedentary lifestyle. The patient was left constipated, melancholic and listless. It was one of the nervous disorders that the physician George Cheyne called the 'English malady'. Unlike the older theory of bodily humours, which identified black bile as the cause of melancholia, this diagnosis rested on the novel idea that bodily organs were connected through nerves. The stomach signalled to the brain. Pumping it full of tea, brandy, chocolate and tobacco curdled the mind. Hypochondria was a particular worry for the elite, whose superior capacity for sympathy and sensibility was traced to their delicate nerves. Luxurious living threatened their fitness to lead. It was difficult to govern a country, let alone an empire, from a sick bed, convulsed by dyspepsia, spasms and depression. The collapse of the Roman empire was an oft-cited case in point.

The orthodox solution had been fasting, purging and bleeding. Eighteenth-century Britons increasingly felt they could manage without resorting to such drastic measures. Hypochondria medicalized and at the same time normalized excess. In medical as in social knowledge, there was growing faith that greater consumption did not have to lead to ruin. Today remembered for his *Fable of the Bees*, Bernard Mandeville was also a doctor of medicine, trained at Leyden, who, in 1711, presented a *Treatise of the Hypochondriack* in the form of a dialogue. Your disease has been misdiagnosed, the foreign doctor Philopirio explains to the patient Misomedon, once of 'gay, even Temper' but now 'peevish, fickle, censorious, and mistrustful'. The 'hypo', as the condition was dubbed, was located in the nervous coat of the stomach. The cure was to abstain temporarily from excessive suppers to give the stomach time to regain strength and to go riding for physical and mental invigoration. Then, 'you will eat your Suppers with as much Pleasure as ever.' In support, Philopirio cites the case of a pregnant Dutch woman who 'being prodigiously in love with Pickled Herrings, fed on them daily in great quantities, and before her longing was satisfied, which in all probability must have lasted some Weeks, had eaten Fourteen Hundred, without receiving the least Injury by them' – 'A very good Observation for a Dutchman', Misomedon dutifully responds.[74] The occasional binge was safe. Where Mandeville opted for self-regulation, other physicians turned to drugs. A lively market in manuals and medication sprang up.[75] Some doctors prescribed more tea, coffee and brandy, not less. Luxury thus fed itself.

Originally, as we have seen, 'consumption' contained a double meaning that referred to 'wasting diseases' as well as the using up of goods. Shakespeare played on this when he had Falstaff complain 'I can get no remedy against this consumption of the purse: borrowing only lingers and lingers it out, but the disease is incurable' (*Henry IV*, Part II). All use was cyclical and had its passage of waste. Consuming and being consumed (in the physiological sense) were inseparable, and nowhere more visibly than in the ingestion and digestion of food and drink. While the debate over overeating did not completely cut the connection, it certainly loosened it. Instead of scaling back when dyspepsia mounted, consumption marched on by opening up a new market in treating the consequences of high living.

The culture of politeness gave consumption an additional lift. Coffee houses and the taste for exotic beverages were just one part of an expanding universe of social spaces – from clubs and restaurants to promenades and pleasure gardens – that were simultaneously dedicated to leisurely entertainment and genteel self-fashioning. Fashionable clothes, tea sets, the latest novel and appropriate wallpaper and furnishings were vital to the polite lifestyle through which the expanding middling sort defined itself and asserted its place in a fluid, post-aristocratic society. Politeness put the enlightenment ideals of sympathy and sensibility into material practice. Refined emotions were demonstrated by making oneself agreeable to others and gaining their esteem. In this social game, consumer goods were essential because they revealed polite people's sensitivity to style and aesthetics – which set them aside from the uncouth labouring masses – and at the same time facilitated sociability and conversation.

How to dress, what food to eat and how: all this could be learnt, just like how to carry on a conversation. There was an explosion of self-help manuals on polite behaviour. 'In your Cloaths,' *The New Help* advised in 1684:

accommodate yourself to the fashion of your Equals ... with respect to
times and places and if you do exceed them in any thing, let it be in Plain-
ness and Gravity ... Put not your meat to your mouth with your knife in
your hand, as the Country clowns do ... Wipe not your hands ... on
your bread, nor on the tablecloath, but on a corner of your napkin ...
carry not your Handkerchief in your hand, Mouth ... or under your
Arm, but in some secret place ... Every action ... ought to be done with
some sign of respect to those that are present.[76]

For discourse to be polite, bodily gestures and the correct use of objects,
from clothing to toothpicks and napkins, were as important as the
words spoken. Politeness made consumption socially productive. Such
manuals took their inspiration from Renaissance courtesy literature,
but they were now addressed to 'persons of all ranks and conditions'
and sold at one shilling, within reach of clerks.[77]

In Japan during the Tokugawa period (1600–1867), the standard of
living also rose for merchants and commoners, but wealth was spent on
better walls, wooden floors, drainage and clean water. The interior
remained sparse, with core possessions kept in a trunk, and a solitary
vase on display. Additional possessions were put in storehouses, out of
sight.[78] This culture of simple comfort, in part inspired by Zen Buddhism, made eminent sense in a country with few natural resources.
Arguably, it gave Japan a higher well-being than Europe.

In Britain and the Netherlands, by contrast, the domestic interior
was the centre stage for sociability and self-fashioning; the built environment was secondary. Furniture, wallpaper, chinaware and other
possessions showed that one was in harmony with refined taste. They
needed to change with the times. In the year 1713, 197,000 yards of
wallpaper were sold in England. Seventy years later, it was over
2 million.[79] By that time, it was common to repaper the home every few
years. There was a powerful symmetry, then, between the rise in consumption, the culture of politeness and the philosophical notion of the
self as a fiction. Just like the self, the polite person was always adapting,
making himself affable and facilitating sociability with the help of fashions and accessories.

Taste – or the 'polishing principle', in the words of Frances Reynolds,
sister of the artist Joshua – made consumption respectable. But what
exactly was it? 'Taste is at present the darling idol of the polite world,'
one critic noted in 1756. 'The fine ladies and gentlemen dress with
Taste ... fiddlers, players, singers, dancers and mechanics themselves

are all the sons and daughters of Taste. Yet in this amazing superabundancy of Taste, few can say what it really signifies.'[80] In fact, plenty of people felt they knew exactly what it was for. However frustrating to the philosopher, it is this extraordinary surge of competing definitions of taste that is so compelling to the historian. Frances Reynolds defined virtue, honour and ornament as the three pillars of taste, but this was of little practical use to a lady standing in a showroom having to decide between teacups with various classical and Chinese motifs.

Historians used to argue that the matter was simple: the monarchy and nobility set the tone, the middle classes followed – some sociologists still believe this story. Reality was more interesting. What was tasteful in the exclusive circle of the *beau monde* was not the same as in the homes of the average merchant or lawyer. Few could afford to spend a whole year redecorating their house, as the countesses of Strafford did in St James's Square in 1712; the japanned cabinets had to have frames specially made to match those owned by the Duke of Marlborough. For the middling sort, it was as big a mistake to be showy, as it tended to look cheap. Taste had to be in line with one's station. It meant modest elegance, not gaudy ostentation. Cabinet-makers and china merchants served as style counsellors. And if 'any gentleman is so vain and ambitious as to order the furnishing of his house in a style superior to his fortune and rank,' one manual advised, 'it will be prudent in an upholsterer, by some gentle hints, to direct his choice to a more moderate plan.'[81] A range of taste registers developed, catering for different ranks, wallets and social horizons.

To critics, the preoccupation with apparel and decorum was a dangerous trend that put ornamentation ahead of self and substance. Fashion, it was said, sapped the strength of the nation by reducing strong Britons to effeminate fops or, worse, Frenchmen. It is easy to see here a precursor of more recent fears that 'consumerism' hollows out individuals and public life. This is too simple. The pressure to please others did indeed put a strain on individuals. Yet politeness and the material trimmings that came with it also created a space for social interaction that was free from violence and conflict. In Britain – a society which was undergoing rapid economic change and had torn itself apart in a civil war, sectarian conflict and a glorious yet bloody revolution – such a social space was welcome. Without it, the spread of clubs, associations and conversation societies in the eighteenth century would be unthinkable. Consumption and civil society advanced hand in hand.

Everyone had to be polite, but women especially so. They were presumed to have a heightened sensitivity that made them better at refining morality, and society more generally. The cult of sociability cast women as civilizing consumers and reinforced an increasingly stylized but widespread view of the division of labour between the sexes: women consumed, men produced. In China, the diffusion of opium from Qing officials and eunuchs downwards created a distinctly male collectors' culture of snuff bottles and phials with rich depictions of celestial birds and caves filled with peach blossom.[82] That European men also shopped and bought coats, coaches and cigars was all but forgotten. One result was that the evils of consumption came to be portrayed through the corruption and fall of the 'weaker sex', from Moll Flanders to Madame Bovary. Fashion and tea parties pulled mothers away from their domestic duties, eighteenth-century observers complained. The disintegrating household was a microcosm of the entire economic order coming undone. Instead of spinning and knitting at home, women were wasting money on tea.

On the whole, however, the Enlightenment put the figure of the female as consumer in a more glowing light. Not only did it set out the economic gains from moderate luxury, it presented the growing admiration of women and their social talents as a sign of human progress and refinement. Barbarians treated women as workhorses or slaves. It was private property and commerce that softened men's warlike disposition and made them appreciate women's delicacy and gift for multiplying the comforts of life. 'Women become, neither the slaves, nor the idols of the other sex, but the friends and companions,' Adam Smith's protégé John Millar wrote in the *Origin of the Distinction of Ranks* in 1771. Unlike ancient Greece, modern 'refined and polished' societies like Britain and France valued women's social as well as domestic skills. 'They are encouraged to quit that retirement which was formerly esteemed so suitable to their character . . . to appear in mixed company, and in public meetings of pleasure. They lay aside the spindle and the distaff, and engage in other employments more agreeable to the fashion.' In turn, their 'polite accomplishments' would refine men. The love of pleasure could be carried to excess, Millar warned, pointing to 'the voluptuousness of the Eastern nations' where polygamy ruled. In commercial society, women and pleasure were safer. Comfort and conversation were schools of civilization. In his own family, the 'commerce of the sexes' proved more frustrating – four of his six daughters never married.[83]

BACKLASH?

The American and French revolutions demonstrated the political force generated by the expanding culture of consumption. Never before had what one wore and what one drank been so important in a rebellion. In New England, throwing tea into Boston harbour and shedding imported clothes in favour of a home-spun coat moulded a nation of patriots. In France, freedom of religion and speech were joined by the freedom of dress (8 Brumaire, 29 October 1793). These were not consumer revolutions in the literal sense. People rallied as 'citizens', 'the people' and 'daughters of patriots', not as 'consumers'. Rights and liberty mattered more than the price of tea. The influence was indirect. Goods connected rebels in shared experiences and offered a symbolic platform for oppositional politics.[84]

According to the Tory view in London in the 1760s, the American settlers were meant to produce, not consume. Luxury might be innocent at home but in the colonies it was a drain and should be taxed accordingly. Even fifty years earlier, Westminster would have had its way. But the colonists had been on a spending spree, filling their homes with teacups and cutlery and their bellies with tea, all imported from the mother country. They were in no mood to have their new standard of living taxed away. It was a momentous miscalculation. Rumours spread of a conspiracy: the British deliberately exaggerated Americans' wealth so they could overtax and impoverish them. The colonists faced a choice between frugality and industry: 'keep the British manufactures we purchase longer in use or . . . supply their place by manufactures of our own.'[85] The boycotts of tea and the pledges not to buy or sell imported goods became demonstrations of patriotic virtue. This was not a renunciation of goods in general, only of British ones. The American Revolution defeated both Tory imperialists and American frugalists. Instead of going down, imported luxuries skyrocketed in the young Republic. The founding fathers hoped to steel manly virtue against corrupting luxury, but as John Adams, the United States' second president, was amongst the first to note, in reality, material distinctions became more, not less important in a democracy.[86]

Similarly, in France, attempts to harness private dress to public politics were short-lived. The long trousers of the sans-culottes – the militant lower-middle classes and artisans – briefly became the uniform of revolutionaries in 1792, but their symbolic power was almost

instantly undercut by the ease with which aristocrats and other suspected enemies could slip into them. After 9 Thermidor, 27 July 1794,
revolutionary politics left private taste alone. Clothes, music and theatre ceased to serve official ideology. Fine dress returned, albeit in
classical style.[87] For an event that introduced its own calendar and terror, the French Revolution was remarkably insignificant when it came
to consumer culture. Except for the compulsory tricoloured cockade, it
left behind no distinctive dress, furniture or lifestyle. In France, as in
America, consumption had a far greater impact on the revolution than
the other way around.

Revolution and war dampened faith in the power of desire and
novelty to improve and enrich society. The fear of luxury made new
converts, right and left. Instead of making people more industrious,
more goods and comforts made them bloody revolutionaries, conservatives argued. They needed a firm hand, not greater freedom to spend.
In turn, counter-revolutionary measures proved to radicals that tyranny really was the twin of luxury. John Thelwall had first-hand
experience. A champion of natural rights, universal suffrage and peace
with France, and, according to the authorities, the most dangerous
man in Britain, 'Citizen' Thelwall was charged with high treason and
thrown in the Tower in May 1794. What better place to compose a
sonnet on 'The Source of Slavery'. 'Ah! why, forgetful of her ancient
fame/ Does Britain in lethargic fetters lie?' It was because once free-born
Englishmen:

> slight the once-lov'd name
> of rustic Liberty, and deify
> Luxurious Pride. To her the pliant soul
> We bend degenerate! her vain pomps adore,
> And chace the simple virtues from the shore
> They wont to guard. Hence to the base controul
> Of Tyranny we bow, nor once complain;
> But hug with servile fear the gilded chain.[88]

Thelwall was acquitted after a few months and later turned his radical
energy to the science of elocution, but the idea of the tyranny of things
continued with early socialists, cooperators and Romantics who experimented with model societies of self-sufficient, simple living.

Karl Marx took the critique of consumption to a new level by turning the republican argument that luxury bred slavery into a full-blown
analysis of industrial capitalism. The argument came in two giant

leaps. The French Revolution, Marx wrote in 1844, did not bring free-dom but split the human soul in two: a citizen in public life and a bourgeois in the comforts of his private home.[89] With another failed revolution (1848) under his belt, Marx then traced alienation further, to the soul of objects and human labour. *Das Kapital* (1867) made the commodity the 'elementary unit' of the entire economic system. Robin-son Crusoe, Marx explained, made all his furniture and clothes with his own bare hands. They were personal products. Under capitalism, by contrast, they were social products, made by one and bought by another: commodities. Exchange stripped objects of their essence. Prices made them interchangeable: '20 yards of linen = 1 coat or = 10 lbs of tea or . . . = ½ ton of iron or = etc.'[90] To the capitalist, it did not matter whether a particular coat brought back memories of winters past or whether tea was sipped with family. They were all the same, as long as they could be exchanged for profit. Buying and selling estranged things from the people who made them. The result was a modern fet-ishism, where people worshipped goods for their price tag. Exchange value hid the human love, sweat and tears that went into making the world of goods. In a famous passage in *Das Kapital*, a table, the minute it appears for sale, acquires transcendental qualities, 'standing itself on its head' in relation to other commodities, 'stranger than if it were vol-untarily beginning to dance'.[91]

Once he had converted them into abstract commodities, Marx lost interest in the life of objects. His 'materialism' was preoccupied solely with production. By making the exploitation of labour the source of surplus value, he effectively wrote consumption out of the story. What people did with the goods after they bought them was irrelevant. This way of thinking had two fatal effects. One was the delusion that getting rid of profit would bring human freedom. The other was an instinctive suspicion that the desire for goods had to be unnatural, the result of manipulation, which blinded socialist leaders and intellectuals to the simple fact that people not only lost but found themselves in their possessions.

In real life, the Marx family had to be more attentive to things. Exiled in London in the 1850s and '60s, their life was a constant strug-gle to make ends meet and placate shopkeepers and debt collectors. Next to the monthly income of £5 from Friedrich Engels, it was the pawnbroker who kept the Marx family from being thrown into the street. Without him, there would have been no *Das Kapital*, no Russian Revolution, no Stalin or Mao. 'I do not think that more has ever been written about "money" when money was so short,' Karl admitted to Friedrich.[92]

The little house in Kentish Town had few permanent possessions. Jackets, shoes and silverware went to the pawnbroker when Marx was short of journalistic work and when butchers, landlords and schools demanded their due; once, desperation drove his wife to try to sell his books, unsuccessfully. He would hide upstairs, writing to Engels, leaving her to deal with 'the hungry wolves' down below. '9 Graftonterrace [sic], 15 Juli 1858. Lieber Engels! I urge you not to be frightened by the content of this letter.' The 'daily struggle with the mere necessaries' had 'completely disabled' him. His wife was a nervous wreck. It was 'disgusting'. His wife had not spent a farthing on new clothes, which was particularly hurtful given her aristocratic upbringing. What his children wore was 'subproletarian'. Marx included a list of his expenses. In May he had to pay £7 for water and gas, and £3 to the pawnbroker for interest. He now rented a jacket and trousers, at 18s. Shoes and hats for the children cost £1 10s. And yet, he still owed £9 in rent, £6 for schooling, £7 to the butcher and £30 to the pawnshop. The situation had reached a critical point. This time it was impossible to avoid tough decisions – a dire warning that usually extracted more money from Engels. Even if he took the children out of school, sacked the servants and 'lived off potatoes', he would still need to sell all the furniture to clear his debts. But here lay the crunch. Possessions were not just abstract commodities. They meant respectability and self-esteem. In 1852, when all his jackets were in pawn, he could not go out – 'everything is shit, and I fear that this dirt will eventually end in scandal.' Marx was painfully aware of his family's shame and his children's worry that they might be visited by their friends while their shoes and toys were pawned. He himself, Marx said, slightly exaggerating, had no problems with moving to 'a truly proletarian flat' in Whitechapel, but it would be the death of his wife, Jenny, a born 'von' Westphalen who liked to lay out her Argyll silverware and damask napkins in the parlour, when they were not at the pawnshop.

Life was not always cheerless. Jenny had a piano – bought on hire purchase. The generous Engels sent bottles of Bordeaux and port. Children and family were delighted when the 'basket of spirits' arrived. The Marx household lived the different modes of consumption that coexisted in Victorian times. It combined stock and flow, circulation and novelty, restraint and excess. Clothes were assets and needed to be conserved. Come winter, and the coats were reclaimed from the pawnshop – not so different from Renaissance times. In July 1864, his wife returned from an auction with household goods, including a carving knife and fork for Friedrich: 'I had told her that those were missing in your household.' New things, however, also tickled the imagination. When the closest communist ally in exile, 'Lupus' Wilhelm Wolff, died in 1864 and left Marx £600, Marx immediately dreamt of fitting out the entire family in the finest Manchester silk. When possible, the family holidayed at the seaside in Ramsgate. Paying off the greengrocer and worrying about the bare necesseties did not preclude bingeing, now and then. One evening he took the socialists Wilhelm Liebknecht and Edgar Bauer on a pub crawl from Oxford Street to the Hampstead Road until they were so drunk that, by two o'clock, they turned to smashing gas lanterns with paving stones.[93]

The irony was that Marx was about fifty years behind the times with his diagnosis of accelerating immiseration. Around 1800, the engine had indeed stuttered. In the first industrial nation, wages were stagnant at best, and their share of GNP falling. In the long run, however, industrial development was achieved by investment and technology – by making work more productive, not by paying workers starvation wages. Notwithstanding pain and suffering, from the 1830s British labourers were earning more and spending more;[94] the pattern would be repeated in Germany, Italy and other 'second industrializers' just two generations later. Rising expectations made it more appealing to reform capitalism than to crush it.

The decades after the French Revolution, then, are best understood as a reaction, not a reversal. Infatuation with 'affluence' after 1945 made it tempting to paint a dark picture of the early nineteenth century. For 'the ordinary individual', the 'normal expectation was to live on the edge of starvation', the economist John Kenneth Galbraith assured us. 'Progress would enhance the wealth of those who, generally speaking, were already rich but not of the masses. Nothing could be done about it.'[95] Not even the Revd Thomas Malthus, the poster-boy of the 'dismal science' was that gloomy. In the first edition of his *Essay on Population* in 1798, Malthus did indeed have no hope for improvement: higher wages and more children would end in a subsistence crisis and famine. In subsequent editions, however, there were rays of hope. Instead of breeding, people with good money in their pocket might decide to postpone marriage and opt for more comforts and fewer children. The thought of depriving themselves or their children of a respectable life would simply be too painful. The taste for comforts and conveniences would thus teach the lower classes prudential habits. Malthus believed this was precisely what had set more prosperous England apart from impoverished Ireland: 'It is the diffusion of luxury therefore among the mass of the people, and not an excess of it in a few, that seems to be most advantageous, both with regard to national wealth and national happiness.' There would always be rich and poor, but in Malthus's mind there was at least a chance now that the proportion of the poor would diminish by joining the middle class. More consumption was one step in the right direction.[96]

In the short run, the Napoleonic Wars gave way to the restoration of the monarchy but, in the longer term, Europe would be convulsed by two new forces: nationalism and liberalism. While their main object was to free nations and create liberty, they also added to the growing support for consumption. Compared to Marx's leap into abstraction, most contemporaries kept consumption down to earth. Wilhelm Roscher was the father of *Nationalökonomie* in Germany, the science of national or historical economics then in the ascendant. 'The person,' Roscher explained in 1854, 'who pays twenty dollars for a coat has consumed that amount of capital only when the coat has been worn out.' Roscher drew, among others, on Mirabeau, who had hoped to turn ostentatious aristocrats into agrarian modernizers. Consumption was everything that was 'lost in utility'. A landlord who pocketed the rent without making any repairs was consuming because he was using up his fixed capital. This way of looking at it gave consumption a role in national development. National character determined consumption but, equally, consumption shaped the nation. For Roscher, British and Dutch comfort and cleanliness were examples of the increasingly benign character of consumption, towards the 'real, healthy and tasteful enjoyment of life' and away from 'inconvenient display'. Roscher followed on the heels of writers like Moritz von Prittwitz, a lieutenant general in the Prussian infantry, who were making their peace with pleasure and who had emphatically announced: 'enjoying more means living more means being more human!'[97] For the nation, what mattered was that consumption was productive, not wasteful. Interestingly, national economists were convinced that civilization cut down waste. 'The more civilized a people are,' Roscher wrote, 'the less do they completely destroy values by use; and the more do they use their old linen etc. as rags.'[98]

When producers and consumers clashed, the state was to side with the latter, Roscher advised. Nationalism made social balance the ultimate goal. Few serious liberal thinkers went as far as the popular French economist Frédéric Bastiat, who wanted consumers to rule everything. Still, liberalism changed the tone of political debate and introduced a more emphatic defence of the consumer. Again, one example must suffice to indicate the drift of things, and what better place to look than in an anonymous pamphlet written by 'a consumer' attacking the protection of silk producers in England in 1833. The consumer was not a sectional group: 'each of the labourers is a *consumer*'; that the author felt the need for italics shows just how unusual the term still was at the time. There was 'no other standard of the public utility of any productions than that of their being suited to the wants and demands of consumers'. Anyone who thought that public life should be guided by other considerations was mistaken. Experience proved beyond doubt that 'men or nations are rich by the possessions of useful commodities [and] that the object of trade or barter is the acquisition of things which we desire.'[99]

The Dutch and English middle classes had been the first to let little luxuries into their lives and make their peace with the world of goods. Elsewhere on the continent, a culture of frugality, restraint and self-denial retained its strength among bourgeois families, but even here the wind of change is palpable by the late nineteenth century. In few places was the ideal of a simple life and self-discipline more pronounced than in Switzerland; Geneva had been Rousseau's home town. The essential instruments of a rational conduct of life were saving, keeping accounts and planning for the future. This would allow oneself to rise above brute economic forces and reach a higher cultural sensibility. Traditionally, the thought of self-indulgence filled the Swiss bourgeoisie with horror. In the second half of the nineteenth century, fewer and fewer lived up to this ideal. There were still those, like the prosperous state archivist of Zurich, Gerold Meyer von Knonau whose household and appearance were modest and sober; typically for bourgeois families, his son received pocket money from the age of ten and had to keep detailed accounts to develop discipline and thrift. But there was also Josefine von Weiler, a rich widow from Bern who remarried into even more money in 1855 and who rented holiday homes in Nice and Paris, spending heavily on new dresses, carriage and horses during her travels. In the late nineteenth century, the puritan interior of bourgeois homes was giving way to plush and decor. Previously blank walls and floors were covered with wallpaper and carpets. Chandeliers multiplied, and dinners became more lavish. In the 1860s, the young Ameli

Moser justified her spending on a new wardrobe by telling her bourgeois parents that excessive modesty was just as conspicuous and bad
as excessive luxury.[100]

For those raised on Puritan virtues, these new comforts made for a
sometimes difficult psychological balancing act. At the breakfast table,
bourgeois families showed their restraint by having either butter or
jam, never both. Yet, in the evening, the soirées were lavish, champagne flowed and a growing variety of fish and fowl was served. For the
Bern surgeon Emil Theodor Kocher, who would later receive the Nobel
Prize in medicine for his work on the thyroid gland, domestic comfort
and conveniences were a dangerous 'idol', and he urged his wife to
throw their material 'ballast' overboard so they could reach the higher
spheres of existence. But this was a fantasy. Greater consumption and
convenience were now a part of their lifestyle. While some, like the
senior Bernese official Emmanuel von Fischer, worried about consumption being a drain on wealth – worst were the many 'useless daily
expenses' – others now stood up in defence of a richer lifestyle. In 1890,
the liberal theologian Konrad Kambli revisited luxury from a
reformed-Christian perspective.[101] Luxury, he argued, was not a sin.
Rather, it was a civilizing force. That was, after all, why societies which
did not enjoy luxuries were barbarians. True, he wrote, not all luxury
was good. But, as long as it was measured and appropriate to the rank
of a person, it assisted his own cultivation and that of society overall.
Kambli was not an original thinker. But, from the more general perspective of a change in mentality, what mattered was that, in the end,
he had reached a similar conclusion to David Hume's great defence of
'innocent luxury' a century and a half earlier.

The seventeenth and eighteenth centuries put in motion the pendulum
of consumption. Possessions, comforts, tastes and desires were all
growing and becoming more elaborate, setting off a backlash of worries about excess and corruption. More goods provoked greater fear of
goods. What was new and radical was that there were now values and
practices that favoured greater consumption and kept the momentum
going. It was only the beginning.

3

Imperium of Things

Perhaps the greatest single omission from mainstream theories of consumption is geopolitics. Economists tend to focus on individuals seeking to maximize pleasure and minimize pain. Sociologists, meanwhile, see consumption as a sign of emulation and distinction between groups. Other writers look at mentalities, such as the romantic imagination, with its dream-like disposition for future pleasure, or at practices, such as cooking or home improvement. Global power is conspicuous by its absence from all these approaches. Conversely, the classic theorists of imperialism had little to say about the desire, appropriation and use of things. For J. A. Hobson, Heinrich Friedjung and Joseph Schumpeter, all writing in the immediate aftermath of the European scramble for Africa in the late nineteenth century, imperialism was driven by finance capitalism, aggressive nationalism, or an 'atavistic' aristocracy that was clinging on to feudal power and glory. Consumers featured, if at all, as victims of a jingoist conspiracy that enriched the few at the expense of the many.

This lack of interest is curious, since, as we have already seen in the case of cocoa, coffee, tea and sugar, empires long played a critical role in channelling new goods, tastes and lifestyles. One reason for the silence is, simply, that the social-democratic Hobson, like the Marxists Rudolf Hilferding and Vladimir Lenin who followed him, was interested in what was new about the 'new imperialism' rather than in empire more generally. If we take a longer view and compare the world in 1492, when Columbus first set sail, with that in 1900, by which time one fifth of the world dominated the rest, what is striking is how the phenomenal expansion of goods happened alongside the equally massive expansion of European power. In the next two chapters, we will follow the new material culture as it carved its way through the city and the home. But we need to start by placing it in its larger geopolitical context to appreciate the uneven dynamics of global consumption.

Empire changed the terms of consumption. The flow of goods, in turn, shaped the workings of imperial power. What this interplay looked like depended on the politico-economic arena in which it took place, and this underwent a major overhaul in the modern period. In the seventeenth and eighteenth centuries, the context was set by mercantilism, a mix of trade barriers, monopolies and shipping restrictions with which states tried to seize trade and power at the expense of their rivals. In this view, one country's gain was another's loss. Empires were locked in a tug of war, each determined to protect its own colonies, ships, goods and silver. In Britain, after the Glorious Revolution of 1688, some Whigs began to develop a more liberal view and see overseas markets as a source of growth and power,[1] but omnipresent threats from French and Spanish rivals ensured that, in reality, trade remained a branch of warfare, not a vehicle for peace and plenty. While early modern empires thus paved new pathways for exotic foods and drugs, they simultaneously put a brake on the traffic of goods by erecting trade barriers to keep out foreign articles, forbidding their own goods to be shipped in foreign vessels and sponsoring national industries. Such mercantilist policies were expensive and it was ordinary people who paid for the wars, navies and the higher prices that came with them.

After Waterloo (1815), everything changed. The military defeat of France on the one hand, and China's internal convulsions on the other, handed Britain a hegemonic position. In the Indian Ocean, rivalry between the powers had been bad for shipping. In the decade after Waterloo, with Britain in control, the number of ships crossing to India and China doubled; the end of the East India Company's monopoly on trade in India in 1813 opened the door for other British and European vessels.[2] And more voyages and bigger tonnage meant cheaper cotton, pepper, tea and other goods for consumers. Naval power and industrial superiority gave Britain the confidence to switch from mercantilism to free trade. Instead of planting 'Keep Out' signs around its colonies, Britain threw the door wide open. Instead of a zero-sum game, trade was now believed to benefit all. The free-trade empire set itself the mission of creating one integrated world market. Liberal imperialism and globalization became almost indistinguishable. The 1850s–'70s saw the emergence of the first European free-trade zone, as Belgium, France and other nations joined a more open trading network.

For consumers, the switch to liberal empire had profound consequences. Free-trade Britain created the world's first consumer-friendly empire. Most immediately, it meant cheaper goods and lower taxes for Britons. Instead of squeezing its people, the British state switched to a path of growth, with low taxes on a rising volume of goods. Consuming more was now public policy. But for the rest of the world, liberal imperialism had effects that were at least as great. The 'open door' to the British market indirectly benefited consumers from Vienna to Buenos Aires. But the legacy was more profound than cheaper prices. It affected the very conception of civilization, humanity and property.

British hegemony spread a new dominion of things that unsettled alternative material cultures. After a century of dominating the slave trade, Britain abolished it in 1807 and then led the international battle against the trade in human chattel. Liberal empire insisted that people were not things – with dramatic effects for African kingdoms built on man-ownership.

Goods are not neutral. In the age of empire, they were intensely associated with superior European technology, science and gunboats. The rising tide of goods brought mixed fortunes to all sides. For indigenous societies, European shirts, sofas and umbrellas upset existing hierarchies. For imperial masters, goods were signs of power, too, but ones to mark the distance between ruler and ruled. Consumption amongst colonial subjects had to be controlled. By the 1880s, when the scramble for Africa got under way, the internal contradictions of liberal empire were in plain view. Global levels of trade and consumption were rising fast, but so was the pace of conquest and annexation.

Here was the paradox of this phase of globalization. Economically, the world was more open in the 1870s and 1880s than a century or two earlier, but in terms of political and cultural power it was becoming more rigid and closed. The hardening of racial thinking in these years interacted with Europeans' ambivalence towards the expanding world of goods they had done so much to bring about. On the one hand, there was a liberal opening, as Europeans discovered the consumer at home and thought in positive ways about the contribution of that person to the creation of value, wealth and social order. On the other, there was a closure of the European mind, as Africans and other colonial subjects were relegated to a subordinate position, coolies working for Western mass markets or 'backward' peasants, rather than consumers in their own right. This racial asymmetry was the opposite of the democratic widening from aristocratic to bourgeois and then to mass consumption within Europe. While one was not the direct cause of the other, the two were part of the same story. Europeans' subjugation of colonial populations ran in parallel to the European apotheosis of the consumer and the 'standard of living' at home. While we therefore start in Africa and India, we ultimately return to Europe to appreciate the transformation of consumption in the age of empire.

DISPOSSESSION AND REPOSSESSION

It is now commonplace to write about the nineteenth century in terms of the 'great divergence' between East and West. In industrial growth and global power, Europe raced ahead of China. The causes of this disparity remain the subject of debate.[3] Imperial trade and expansion, Atlantic slavery and easily accessible domestic coal gave Britain a unique edge. What ultimately proved decisive, however, were the gains accrued from three centuries of high wages. High wages encouraged British entrepreneurs to innovate and develop labour-saving machinery and to exploit a sophisticated European network of technology. And it was serendipitous timing: after the Napoleonic Wars (1803–15), Europe enjoyed a favourable spell of peace and stability, just as China was struck by a series of natural disasters, ineffective emperors and debilitating rebellions.[4] Hunger for Indian cottons and Chinese porcelain played their part in stimulating growth and innovation, as did the Atlantic colonies, which provided additional outlets for some of Britain's most rapidly developing sectors, such as textiles. In the final analysis, however, it was engineering, iron and steel, and steamboats – producer-goods industries – that really powered Britain's sustained growth, not cotton shirts or creamware.[5]

Alongside the East/West divide, there was another development that caused a seismic shift in both the quality and scope of consumption: the end of slavery. Free labour and free trade (after 1846) were the two legs of Britain's liberal empire.[6] When Britain abolished the slave trade in 1807, it set in motion a process of world-historical significance. Emancipation in 1833, the American Civil War and the abolition of slavery in Cuba and Brazil in 1886 and 1888 were followed by the end of domestic slavery in Africa in the years around 1900; Russia abolished serfdom in 1861. In truth, slavery in many places was not replaced by genuinely free labour but by indentured and coerced labour. In French West Africa, slavery actually increased in the century after Britain abolished the evil trade. Germany never did away with slavery in its colonies, and Hitler and Stalin would devise their own forms of forced labour. But however imperfect and partial, the imperial attack on slavery redefined the order of things: people were no longer possessions that could be traded like other goods.

The slave plantations of the Americas and the Caribbean have, understandably, shaped our understanding of the trade in humans: over 11 million Africans were forced across the Atlantic passage. Yet slavery also flourished within many African societies. In 1800, to own slaves was a sign of power and prestige in many kingdoms. Economically, slavery was a rational response to the continent's principal constraint: labour, not land. Capturing and commanding slaves was a way to harness that scarce resource. Most slaves were clients, not chattels; they were soldiers, servants and peasants, rarely plantation labour. Consumption, even luxury, was not altogether absent in slave-holding societies – royal wives and concubines were richly decorated in fine cloth and jewels. In general, though, domestic slavery depressed both the absolute volume of demand and the relative significance of goods for conferring status and power. A good deal of pre-colonial consumption in Africa consisted of tributes or gifts, distributed by elites to their clients. This was in sharp contrast to Western Europe, where serfdom had died out by the sixteenth century, although it would resurface in Central and Eastern Europe. Slavery *within* Britain was formally outlawed in 1772, although, in reality, some owners chose to ignore it by apprenticing their slaves. At that time, around 15,000 people of African descent were living in the British Isles – some free, some unfree – a tiny number in a country with half a million comfortable middle-class families or when compared to the half-million slaves in the West Indian colonies. We now know that, in addition to merchants and planters, many widows, clergymen and other small investors living in Britain profited from slaves in the colonies.[7] Yet they did not surround themselves with a large retinue of servants at home. The number of footmen was limited and declining. Instead, the profit from the bloody trade was sunk into mahogany chairs, porcelain, elegant dresses and jewels.[8] Status came to reside in the ownership of objects, not people. By 1914, the liberal European model ruled. After first spreading slavery across the world, the British empire extirpated it.

Abolition had profound implications for value, desire and identity. Once owning people was no longer an option, wealth and power were channelled into things (or saved for future consumption). Britons entered the crusade against slavery with a baggage of Enlightenment ideas about the dominion of things and its virtues. The hunger for comforts and possessions, it was believed, would lead people from trading in humans to trading in goods. Thus the abolitionists set out to save the 'dark continent'.

To know what difference empire made to African consumption, it is essential to have a pre-colonial baseline. In the late nineteenth century, when imperialism was in full swing, missionaries and critics of empire typically portrayed African colonies as a dumping ground for European gin and shoddy guns. The more industrial and modern Europeans became, the more such commentators represented Africa as 'traditional', untouched by inequality and materialism until brutalized by the slave trade. The African was 'half devil and half child', in Rudyard Kipling's phrase. The notion of sub-Saharan Africans as untouched by commerce was, however, Western fantasy and imperial rhetoric. Africa was not frozen in some pre-commercial ice age. Trade and a passion for things had been expanding for several centuries before imperial conquest. Coastal regions in West and East Africa recorded rising imports of textiles, beads and iron. From a European perspective, these quantities might have looked tiny. West Africa took a mere 4 per cent of English exports in 1800. When viewed from the Gold Coast, the valleys of the Senegambia and Zanzibar, however, the volume of European and Indian goods was impressive. By the sixteenth century, the Portuguese were shipping half a million *manilas* (bracelets) to the Gold Coast a year. In Southern Central Nigeria, people started wearing Holland Linen in 1600. In the course of the eighteenth century, the value of imports in West Africa rose tenfold. Rouen and Liverpool shipped hats, glasses, smoking pipes and, especially, textiles. The value of the cargo often exceeded that of the ship and crew.

Africans were becoming increasingly discriminating consumers with their own regional tastes and fashion cycles. Accra demanded linen, Offra block-printed chintzes, preferably in red. In the Senegambia – the sub-Sahara region closest to Europe – Indian *niconees* (striped calico) and *tapseals* (a mix of silk and cotton) were popular. European traders had to adapt to local fashions. In eighteenth-century Senegambia, people demanded not just any kind of knife but a 'Flemish' type, first introduced by Dutch and Portuguese merchants. British traders managed to get a foothold in the market only once they arrived with similar models. Among the most lucrative and widespread articles were beads, shipped in billions, and used for decoration, religious offerings and as currency and a symbol of wealth. Beads were immensely varied in style and quality. Glass beads were round or tubular, transparent or speckled. Some were imitation pearls and crystal from Venice and Bohemia.[9] The slave trade was part of this expanding world of goods, enriching local rulers and their followers. The King of Dahomey, for example, made £250,000 from the sale of slaves in 1750.

It is impossible to do justice here to the rich literature about different regions, but three general points can be made. First, consumption was on a long, upward curve before the scramble for Africa got under way in the 1880s. The abolition of the slave trade in 1807 accelerated this process, as West African communities started to trade ever greater amounts of palm oil, gum and other export crops. But it did not originate it. A taste revolution was already creating distinct regional styles. In other words, Africans did not need imperial masters to teach them how to become consumers. Communities had their own vocabulary of material desire. For Mombasans, desire (*moyo*) and possessions were considered integral to selfhood and status. European travellers in East Africa noted how 'natives like to display all their finery by putting it up in their rooms, so that people may see their plates, coffee cups, trinkets, baskets and many other things.'[10] The second point is about sequence. Not only was the volume of goods rising, but the direction of imports shifted well before Europeans imposed formal rule over Africa: goods no longer simply flowed from India to Europe and Africa. Britain started to wrest control from India in textiles, the biggest prize in African markets, in the early nineteenth century. In 1850, Britain sent 17 million yards of fabric to West Africa; twenty-five years earlier, it had been a mere million. Finally, the share of consumer goods was itself rising. In Senegambia in the early eighteenth century, for example, iron was still a major import, to be turned into hoes and tools by local smithies. A century later, iron was marginal, outpaced by textiles. The 'guns and gin for slaves' picture is largely a myth; alcohol was never a dominant import and guns arrived in large numbers only after the end of the slave trade.

Outside coastal towns, European contact with Africans in the early nineteenth century was largely limited to missionaries. Missions were divided about the best strategy for conversion. For many early missionaries, going native was an opportunity to lead a life of voluntary poverty as servants of Christ. Western comforts were an obstacle to salvation. Poor pay and poor transport left them isolated, adding to the pull of indigenous life. Among the Bethelsdorp mission in the Cape Colony, Mr I. G. Hooper learnt to live in a straw hut, sleep on a board and be 'as pleased with a fare chiefly of dry bread as with the best provisions when in my native land'.[11] Such missionaries dropped their shirts and neckties, forsook tea and coffee, and often took a Khoekhoe wife. Champions of indigenization never disappeared altogether, but abolition shifted the focus to westernizing Africans. The battle against slavery and sin would not be won until Africans embraced 'legitimate trade' as a profitable alternative. Africans had to learn from Europeans, not the other way around. Mission stations became islands of Western lifestyle, with houses that had windows, tables, beds and candles. On baptism, a convert received a white shirt and a blanket. The path to salvation was paved with goods.

Spiritual rebirth would inspire new habits, comforts and desires. 'The same Gospel which had taught them they were spiritually miserable, blind, and naked,' Robert Moffat, a veteran of the London Missionary Society (LMS) in Africa wrote in 1842, 'discovered to them also that they needed reform externally, and thus prepared their minds to adopt those modes of comfort, cleanliness and convenience which they had been accustomed to view only as the peculiarities of a strange people.' Body smearing was 'very disgusting'. Animal hides needed to be swapped for shirts and gowns. Saving souls and winning customers now went hand in hand. New clothes, Moffat wrote, would 'sweep away the filth and customs of former generations, and . . . open up numberless channels for British commerce, which, but for the Gospel, might have remained for ever closed'.[12] Commerce and conversion propelled each other forward in missionary propaganda. 'God has clearly chosen England to be the great Missionary nation,' the Church Missionary Society explained in one of its many tracts, since why else would He have put her at the centre of world trade?: 'just see how every thing around us comes from Heathen or foreign countries. Our coats are dyed with indigo bought from Bengal; . . . we have our tea from China; our coffee from Arabia . . . even our railway cars have palm-oil from Guinea for oiling the wheels'. British factories would have to shut their doors were it not for the Heathens' demand for British goods. 'Thus we are bound, by close ties of common interest, to multitudes of nations who are ignorant of God and of His Christ.' It was sinful to think that, with this interdependence, God had not given Britons a particular duty to carry salvation to the heathen.[13]

Consumption, too, would work away on the African mind. John Philip of the LMS spelt it out for the governor of the Cape: 'Tribes in a savage state are generally without houses, gardens and fixed property: by locating them on a particular place, getting them to build houses . . .

cultivate corn land, accumulate property, and by increasing their artificial wants, you increase their dependence on the colony, and multiply the bonds of union.'[14] A man with an address and possessions did not steal cattle. Abolitionists and champions of African expeditions like Thomas Fowell Buxton saw a natural affinity between the slave trade and African laziness on the one hand, and peaceful trade and industriousness on the other. The ultimate remedy for the slave trade lay in Africa, not in Europe. Western things would initiate a virtuous circle of greater wants, work, property and peace.

Optimism about raising Africans to Western levels of comfort and commerce reached its peak in the 1830s. It is well illustrated by a letter from Mr Ferguson, the head of the medical department in Sierra Leone, the British colony founded for freed slaves, and was publicized at length by Buxton, the leading campaigner against the international slave trade. The 'grade' of liberated Africans was directly visible in their houses and interiors, Ferguson wrote. The highest grade lived in comfortable two-storey stone houses built from their earnings. Here they enjoyed 'mahogany chairs, tables, sofas and four-post bedsteads, pier glasses, floor cloths and other articles indicative of domestic comfort and accumulating wealth'. Liberated Africans had a 'great love of money', Ferguson wrote. But this was not a vice. Unlike the 'sordid' miser, they devoted their income to 'the increase of their domestic comforts and the improvement of their outward appearance of respectability'. It is difficult to imagine higher praise from a British observer. There 'is not a more quiet, inoffensive, and good-humoured population on the face of the earth'.[15] In other words, these were model consumers close to the kind imagined by Adam Smith. They put their energy into peaceful industry and possessions, not into dominating their fellow men.

The Revd Samuel Crowther, who had been a slave boy in Yoruba country in 1821 before taking the voyage to Freetown and freedom, returned to the Niger in 1854 and noted the 'striking change in the habits of the people' since his earlier expedition in 1841. Soon after reaching the village of Angiama, a few miles inland, he was greeted by Brass people in canoes, there to buy palm-oil. In 1841, 'very few' of the people he encountered 'were to be found with any decent articles of clothing'. Now, 'among a group of about forty people on shore, fifteen who I could distinctly see had English shirts on.' For Crowther, who was on his way to become the first black bishop of the Church Missionary Society, it was 'an evident mark of the advantage of legal trade over that in men'.[16]

Evangelicalism, the animating spirit behind the crusade against the slave trade, placed a heavy burden on individuals to atone for their sins and bring their world closer to God's design. British consumers, as well as Africans, had to reform their ways. After all, they were the ones enjoying slave-grown sugar. The colonial food chain tied European consumers to the fate of African slaves. 'The consumer of the West India produce may be considered as the Master-Spring that gives motion and effect to the whole Machine of Cruelties,' one abolitionist pamphlet put it in 1792.[17] Consumers had a moral duty to abstain from slave-grown sugar. It was bloodstained, polluting, even cannibalistic. In 'every pound of sugar used . . . we may be considered as consuming two ounces of human flesh'.[18] The boycott of slave-grown sugar grew into a transatlantic mass movement. Women were at the forefront, capitalizing on their control of the purse, ideas of domestic virtue and their much-cited ability to sympathize. Ethical consumerism was born (see Plate 15).

It has been tempting to see this episode as a radiant light in the dark history of colonialism, pointing forward to human rights and more responsible shoppers. In fact, abolition in 1833 prompted a moral retreat. At first, the anti-slave movement continued with national petitions. At its London conference in 1854, it called on its members to abstain from buying slave-grown cotton, rice and tobacco, but after that, it is the silence of European consumers that is resounding. Imperial consumers did not rally to boycott the growing mountains of cheap sugar, coffee and cocoa produced by indentured labourers or slaves in other countries. By 1900, Europeans reserved their ethical buying power to target sweatshop conditions and help local matchstick girls. When the media turned its spotlight on Cadbury's use of slaves in São Tomé and Príncipe, the Portuguese islands in the Gulf of Guinea, in 1904–9, British consumers went on sipping their cocoa regardless.[19] Campaigners and industrialists agreed that it was for firms, not private consumers, to tackle labour abuses. Quaker calls for a consumer boycott came to nothing. As a political weapon, the boycott was now turned inside out. Instead of an instrument of the affluent few in the imperial metropole eager to lift up colonial producers, consumer boycotts on the eve of the First World War were used by the weak against their imperial overlords, by Poles in Eastern Prussia against German shopkeepers, and Indians opposing Britain's partition of Bengal. The Chinese diaspora used boycotts across Asia to protest against the United States' detention and deportation of Chinese immigrants.

Imperialism left consumer society with a split identity. While establishing themselves as colonial masters, Europeans also seized control as master consumers, relegating the rest to the role of coolies or peasants. The European discovery of the consumer in economics and the emergence of the Western concept of the 'standard of living' were one part of this story, to which we shall need to return. Here, we must follow the colonial story a little further, to see how the African consumer was squeezed out of the imperial imagination.

The gradual fading away of the figure of the African as discriminating consumer resulted from several converging developments. Missionaries were impatient: the millennium was nigh. In evangelical dreams, commercial societies would spring up overnight. But the Niger and other inland regions proved more treacherous than explorers had reckoned. Above all, the free-labour colonies in West Africa turned out to be troubled experiments. This, together with the Indian rebellion of 1857, spread doubts about whether non-white subjects could be refashioned in their masters' image. A harder, scientific racism began to colour the imperial mindset.

This more aggressive stance was partly a reaction to the difficulties European traders and missionaries encountered on the ground. Commerce and consumption did in fact continue their forward march in the second half of the nineteenth century. In West Africa, many indigenous traders followed the evangelical script. They turned from slaves to palm oil, and built houses and filled them with furniture, pictures and wall clocks. A Mr Lawson, a mixed-race merchant in Togo, smoked cigars, served imported tongue, and prided himself on his European dress and furniture.[20] The frontier of consumption was being pushed further and further inland. John Tobin, one of the big British importers of palm oil, told a parliamentary committee in 1865 that 'white men' used to 'fancy that anything was good enough for black men', but now the people in the Niger Delta 'are as well able to distinguish between genuine articles and fictions as any person in this country'.[21] In East Africa, caravans spread the cash-commodity nexus to the foothills of Kilimanjaro. Peasants insisted on being paid in cash. Each tribe, one explorer noted, 'must have its own particular cotton, and its own chosen tint, colour, size among beads . . . Worse still, the fashions are just as changeable' as in England.[22]

For Europeans, native middlemen posed a threat to their control of trade and access to crops in the hinterland. At the same time, the dual advance of traders and new objects of desire corroded local power structures. By the 1880s, after decades of doubt and caution, European governments were finally ready to seize control. The details of the scramble for Africa lie beyond the scope of this book. Superior arms, technology and logistics gave Europeans an overwhelming advantage. Ultimately, however, the defeat of African societies was a sign not of their backwardness but of their dynamism. What made them simultaneously vulnerable and attractive to European empires was that they were trading and consuming more, not less. Things spurred conquest.

Patronage and clientage remained important, but the corrosive effect of the world of things on African kingdoms was visible everywhere. Prior to the 1880s, direct European control was limited to a few coastal forts, but the indirect effects of empire spilled over into the hinterland. In the palm-oil belt of the Niger, the ex-slave Ja Ja established himself as a powerful rival both to British merchants and old slave-trading elites. Ja Ja controlled the palm trade in Opobo and set up a blockade in 1871 to stop European encroachments. To pay for defence and administration, Sierra Leone and other colonies had to levy more and more taxes on trade and markets. To escape these duties, local traders abandoned Freetown and moved upstream. With them, they took shirts, boots, mirrors and other articles, bartered in exchange for palm and cola nuts. Goods and commodity production propelled each other forward, deeper and deeper inland, triggering a crisis for *anciens régimes*. In Sierra Leone, chiefs started to complain that Creoles were moving into Susu and Limba territories and buying up crops before they were harvested. Creole merchants opened inland depots and struck deals directly with farmers, bypassing the old elites who had controlled trade in the days of slavery. The material culture of this moving commercial frontier was plain to see. The houses of Creole traders were filled with Western furniture. Some chiefs tried to contain the incursion within Creole quarters, with limited success. In the Mende territory, one chief's belongings included a mirror, a dressing table and a four-poster bed. A wave of Western goods was sweeping across West Africa. In Freetown, a Dress Reform Society tried to resist it, in vain. Women rejected the suggested loose robes. Instead, Muslim men started to wear trousers under their gowns, while their wives copied the tight-laced dresses of the Christian elite.[23]

The impact of consumer goods was doubly explosive because they also functioned as credit. Traders left textiles and other goods with native merchants for six to twelve months, waiting for the next palm-oil harvest to pay for it. This 'trust system' had worked well in the past. But the arrival of new merchants and the drop in the price of oil during the great depression in the 1870s–'80s put the system under strain. Some traders ran up 'double debt' with newcomers, pushing established players to seize goods in retaliation. If West Africa suffered from a problem, it was not too little but too much competition. Trade expanded by force. British trading vessels increasingly brought gunboats in their wake. Trading posts became flashpoints of conflict. At Onitsha in central Nigeria in 1879, for example, natives attacked the trading post and pillaged British goods. HMS *Pioneer* was sent up the Niger in reprisal. It confiscated £50,000 worth of British goods. After three days of bombardment, the crew descended on the inner town and burnt it to the ground. The lower town was levelled. British traders and missionaries expressed their thanks to the local Consul.[24]

The shift from trade in humans to trade in goods was disastrous for many rulers. For states built on slavery, commerce was a Trojan horse. In the Ashanti kingdom (Ghana), slaves and taxes were the sinews of power. The more slaves, the higher an individual's rank. The Ashanti practised mercantilism on a grand scale. The government controlled trade and levied hefty tributes on merchants; the tribute tax took around half a person's income and interest was at a stiff 33 per cent. Tribute was paid in gold, cloth and slaves. But the growth of the rubber and cocoa trade challenged this order.[25] A new class of middlemen emerged, the *asikafo*, who wanted to trade free from government interference. Here was, more or less, an African version of Adam Smith's virtuous transition from feudal to commercial society, from a dominion over people to a dominion of things – with one important qualification. It was not an internal struggle: looming on the sidelines was the British empire. For 'new men' like John and Albert Owusu Ansa, Western goods were part and parcel of their identity. They sought British protection against the interference by the Ashanti state.

Commerce and things ate away at the foundations of tribal authority. Ashanti became a British protectorate in 1896. The next few years saw the great Edwardian boom, when the trade in palm oil and cocoa expanded in leaps and bounds. And, as it did, Ashantis shifted from harvesting the kola nut and small-scale gold mining to the more profitable cultivation of cocoa. By 1910 Ghana had become the world's biggest exporter of cocoa. Overall, this probably paid off, raising the standard of living for the Ashanti population. But, as the cash-commodity nexus tightened, it also triggered new conflicts over land and power. Slaves and land were fast losing their value as guarantors of status and power. Chiefs were 'destooled', or toppled, more and more quickly. Shrewd chiefs undertook a portfolio review and began to build up possessions as a kind of private pension plan for life after destoolment. In 1910, the Ashanti Council of Chiefs finally agreed that two thirds of all property accrued by a chief during his rule would revert to the individual on his removal or abdication. Property now resided primarily in the person, not the office. It was another triumph for the dominion of things.

European steamships, guns and goods were manifestations of a new material order. Local leaders picked up on this quickly. On the southern slopes of Kilimanjaro, Mandari, the ruler of the municipality of Moshi, described power as a geopolitical hierarchy of things. At the top, immediately below God, were the English. They controlled most 'good things': valuable manufactures, guns and medicine; Mandari named his son Meli after the British 'mail boat'. A rung below was the Hindoo merchant: Indian textiles had kept their edge in East Africa. Only then, and in spite of their presence on the coast, came the Germans: they simply did not have the goods. To Mandari and local elites, where things came from mattered more and more. They were impatient with traders who tried to unload their second best or came with goods from nearby Zanzibar. Only authentic articles from Europe would do.[26]

The end of domestic slavery intensified this process because it created a more crowded marketplace for goods. Slavery had constrained choice. Male slaves were forbidden from wearing a *kofia* to cover their head, women from wearing a veil. Being a slave trumped being a Muslim. Clothes were visible markers of who was free and who was not. In East Africa, free Arabs wore colourful block-printed Kanga cloths, whereas African slaves had to make do with off-white 'merikani' sheets from America. Already before the end of slavery, slave women breached such sartorial rules and used local indigo to give their merikanis a splash of colour. Freedom unleashed a scramble for new wardrobes. The first thing a slave did was to buy a shirt or an embroidered *kofia*. The Zanzibar archipelago was a thriving fashion scene (see Plate 13). A Swahili saying went in 1900: 'Proceed cautiously in Pemba. If you come wearing a loincloth, you leave wearing a turban. If you come wearing a turban, you leave wearing a loincloth.'[27]

Colonial rule gave this spiral an additional twist. Colonial administrations controlled jobs, money and status. Spending on Western goods simultaneously indicated one's proximity to colonial rulers and one's distance from native groups at the bottom of society. In French Cameroon after the First World War, the Duala elite spent a small fortune on European clothes. They drank imported wine, finished their meals with Western-style desserts and drove automobiles and motorbikes. It was men, with their greater public presence, who were in the vanguard of conspicuous consumption. A Duala man easily spent 1,000 francs a year on his European wardrobe, three times as much as his wife.[28]

It is still sometimes said that Europeans entered the scramble for Africa because they wanted to capture new customers to offset the great depression. The opposite is closer to the truth. Europeans had little interest in African consumers. Colonial subjects were meant to be coolies for mines and plantation labour, not shoppers. Imperialists happily suspended the laws of the market when it suited them. Africans were pushed into the labour force by land theft and the Maxim gun, not pulled by the prospect of a living wage. The conceit of the 'lazy African' was a justification for paying low wages or no wages. This was, arguably, short-sighted. A high-wage economy makes for better customers. European nations might have reaped big benefits had they been more liberal and invested in their subjects.

African middlemen were a thorn in the side of imperial administrators and businessmen. Richard Butler, the consul at Fernando Pó (an island in the Gulf of Guinea now named Bioko), wanted to tax native shopkeepers out of existence. A vice-president of the Anthropological Society in London, he saw Africans as farmers, not traders. In its French colonies, the Third Republic sought to model its colonial subjects on the French peasantry. Britain's United African Company, run by George Goldie, tried to monopolize trade up and down the Niger with the help of gunboats and local treaties. Frederick Lugard, the High Commissioner for the Protectorate of Northern Nigeria, introduced caravan tolls in Nigeria in 1904 to squeeze out local traders and turn weavers of durable, local cloth into cotton growers for Lancashire.[29]

African consumers were abandoned by their missionary friends, too. As early as the 1840s, Wesleyans were complaining that trade made Africans shifty and materialistic. By the end of the century, all missionary groups saw commerce and consumption as sinful, not the training ground for a Christian life. The desire for goods and money was now blamed for the small number of converts. Missionaries had talked about inculcating new material wants and habits but were rarely interested in putting their money where their mouth was. The Moravian Mission started to pay wages only in 1904. Children worked for eight hours and were lucky to receive a few pennies; after all, they were paid in kind in 'civilization' and *Kultur*, missionaries pointed out. At mission stations, shops were reserved for Europeans. Missionaries despaired of their flock. Natives had become more industrious but they were now obsessed with things, a pietist missionary in Togo noted in 1894. They treated his photo album like a mail-order catalogue, comparing dress styles again and again and asking him to order them the finest collars and ties for Christmas. They wanted good clothes and food – too much so. In the early days of Christianity in the Roman Empire, he balefully pointed out, new believers had dressed simply; they did not show off like Africans.[30] In East Africa, the local bishop despaired of the way in which coastal towns lured away souls and destroyed 'clean living': Zanzibar was 'Piccadilly, Sodom, and a public bar.'[31] That missionary leaders were at all surprised by this exodus is telling. At missions, a superior teacher was paid a fraction of what a clerk earned in town, barely enough to feed the family and buy a couple of shirts (see Plate 14).

Missionaries broadly split into three camps. All demoted the African consumer. Friedrich Fabri of the Rheinisch Mission and J. K. Vietor of the Norddeutsche Missionsgesellschaft were examples of the new chauvinist generation emerging in the 1880s. Africans had to be disciplined into becoming productive, tax-paying subjects of the German empire. They still paid lip service to Africans' potential as customers. The problem with Africans in this view was that they were either living in a state of subsistence or were middlemen who spent their money on mahogany-panelled wardrobes and other luxuries which bypassed the fatherland. Africans needed to be made to buy simple German goods. Their main role, however, was as an agrarian proletariat that would produce raw materials for German industry.[32]

Other missionaries scoffed at the idea of Christianity serving imperialist policies. Imagine, one critic said, St Paul telling the Corinthians they needed to buy 'their carpets at Aquila'.[33] Far better to turn Africans into self-sufficient peasants. Africans, in this view, had to be protected from material temptations and imperialist plantations alike. This paternalistic approach placed Africans on an even lower stage of development, effectively asking them to leave the world of goods altogether. Africans were not ready for markets, wages and higher wants. The scars of slavery ran too deep. They first needed to cleanse themselves by learning the 'dignity of honest toil'. The guiding watchword was St Benedict's rule: *ora et labora*, prayer and work. The path to a true Christian life involved hoeing, and more hoeing, not getting and spending. Once they had reached a truly Christian state, they might earn some wages and become customers, perhaps, but this was in the very distant future. Their zeal for turning Africans into ascetic peasants reflected missionaries' disillusionment with the effects of industrialization on workers in Europe. Africa was a second chance to put modernity right and save Christianity from the unholy spiral of satanic mills, cheap entertainment and family breakdown.[34]

A final group went yet further and took refuge in the 'spirit of tribal society'. God's design was already visible in Africans' tribal and familial order. For the Lutheran Bruno Gutmann, who lived with the Chagga in East Africa, this 'original' tribal state had to be protected at all cost against the incursion of material civilization. Kinship and the shared struggle for survival created a bond between men. 'As soon as money comes in . . . which will buy things of purely material value, immediately we see the destruction of the vital interdependence of men, which is alone the source of their spiritual and moral nature – in a word, of their existence as human beings.'[35] Imperialism, then, gave the seesaw of consumption another push: as the volume of goods went up, European imperialists and missionaries came down on consumption as inauthentic and alienating.

The craze for fashion and goods has continued to be a frequent target of attack. Africans, in the words of the Nigerian-born journalist Chika Onyeani, writing in 2000, have perpetuated their colonial bondage, degenerating into a parasitic 'consumer race' instead of investing in human capital and development like other 'productive races'.[36] Consumer goods have been tainted by their entanglement with slavery and conquest, and some Western historians continue to characterize them as a 'contagious' disease that destroyed native cultures.[37] Such readings do injustice to the longer history of exchange, the active role played by indigenous groups, and the liberating elements of consumption. Material desires were not a sudden import of empire but reached back to pre-colonial times. The contrast between 'traditional' tribal Africa, where *homo economicus* had not yet set foot, and a 'modern' Western world of goods, inequality and individualism was a convenient figment of the imperial imagination. We cannot simply stamp consumption as inauthentic or frivolous. For former slaves and migrants, things were a great emancipator. A shirt, a hat, a watch and a mirror were tickets to social inclusion and self-respect.

Europeans at the time had only contempt for such sartorial display. A colonial official complained about the extravagant appearance of Swahili 'clad in fezes with coloured shirts and bow ties, blue serge suits, wearing shoes and socks . . . a monocle, and smoking cigarettes in long, gold-tipped cigarette-holders. Such caricatures are not pleasing sights to see, and even worse perhaps are the gentlemen who have taken to soft hats and heavy boots.'[38]

We can see the schizophrenic nature of empire in this early wave of globalization. The growing unease with African consumers was a shared experience of imperialism, felt in liberal Britain as well as in nationalist Germany and republican France. Free trade after the mid-nineteenth century accelerated the global circulation of goods, yet when these goods reached colonial subjects they rang imperial alarm bells. Free trade did away with trade barriers, but empire erected new racial hurdles in their place. In Britain, free trade stood for cheap goods for all. Everyone was a consumer, and every consumer was a citizen. In the colonies, however, these inclusive, democratic credentials were seriously compromised. Britain stood for free trade, but it was also an empire, and as such found it difficult to embrace the African consumer, because consumption challenged the very distance between races that empire was founded on. When Africans put on bowler hats or corseted dresses they came uncomfortably close to their imperial masters. A researcher in 1930s Northern Rhodesia observed that 'many Europeans . . . are less courteous in their relations with well-dressed Africans than they are in their relations with those in rags, for they resent and fear the implied claim to a civilized status.'[39]

A comparison with the United States is instructive. American racism was most passionate at home. Americans did not carry the same burden of territorial empire into the world of goods. They worried far less about other races mimicking them. Africans, Indians and Chinese, all were potential customers for Singer sewing machines and other American products.[40] It was the United States, not the British empire, which took on the older mission of things, promising to raise other races up the ladder of material civilization. This would give it a critical edge in the mid-twentieth century.

Empire, then, qualifies the traditional story of consumer society as a democratic advance from elite to bourgeois to mass consumption. As class barriers were softening, racial divides were hardening. In Europe, elites had gradually given up attempts to regulate status through sumptuary laws in the seventeenth and eighteenth centuries. Imperialism can be understood as a regression, re-exporting an informal sumptuary policy to the colonial world. Indeed, in the Second World War, colonial administrators in East Africa tried to formalize it by limiting Africans once again to merikani cloth.

JEWELS AND BY-LAWS

Wajid Ali Shah, the last king of Oudh (Awadh), was in exile in Calcutta when the Indian Mutiny erupted in 1857. Here, at the southern outskirts of the city, he reconstructed the noble court and lifestyle of his lost Lucknow. Matija Burji, the Eastern Dome, was a collector's dream. The entire animal kingdom was assembled, from lions, leopards and bears to giraffes from Africa and a two-humped camel from Baghdad. In his pigeonries, Wajid Ali Shah had over 20,000 birds. He paid 24,000 rupees for a pair of 'silk-winged pigeons', it was said, and another 11,000 for a pair of white peacocks. A cage on a hillside offered the entertaining sight of thousands of snakes in pursuit of helpless frogs. If Wajid was not a scholar like some earlier nawabs, he was certainly a collector on a grand scale, gathering the finest animals, Urdu poetry and at least three hundred wives.

Noble leisure had its plebeian counterparts. Birds of prey were reserved for the nobility, but quail fighting was popular with poor and rich alike. A bird fight was treated as fine art. Contenders were carefully hardened for battle. First the bird was starved. Then it was given a purgative rich in sugar to cleanse its insides. At night, the trainer would wind up the quail with shouts of 'ku', so 'he loses his surplus fat.' Finally, as battle loomed, the beak was sharpened with a penknife. Some owners administered drugs so an injured bird would keep fighting 'like one possessed', the historian Abdul Halim Sharar reminisced in 1920.[41]

Here were the last vestiges of an oriental culture of consumption that had flourished under the Mughal empire. British rule brought armies and tax collectors, but it also spread new norms, habits and behaviours. It changed the terms of consumption. Quail fighting became a base act of cruelty, no longer a fine leisure pursuit. A poetic recital of a young nawab's sexual exploits was now shamefully obscene, admiring thousands of song birds idle waste. In the early days of British rule, in the second half of the eighteenth century, Robert Clive (Clive of India), the nabob par excellence, accumulated filigree boxes, betel-nutcrackers and other Mughal elite artefacts, while governors such as Warren Hastings learnt Urdu and Persian. Many Europeans collected Indian birdcages and antiques, sat under embroidered tents and slept with Indian mistresses.[42] But as the British empire dug its teeth deeper into the subcontinent, the rift between the two cultures grew wider. As the

Mughal empire crumbled, its material culture lost its appeal for Europeans. 'Year after year has witnessed the introduction of fresh European refinements,' a contributor to the *Calcutta Review* wrote in 1844: 'our dwellings have grown internally less and less Oriental . . . Our rooms are no longer bare and unencumbered; they are chock-full of European furniture; the walls are hung with paintings; the floors covered with warm carpets. The 'eye is pleased; the spirit is raised; there is a greater feeling of home'. The 'unquestionable accession of mosquitoes' was a prize worth paying for having curtained rooms and enjoying European comforts in the tropics.[43] The 1857 rebellion accelerated the withdrawal into a cocoon of white-only country clubs.

The historian Christopher Bayly has offered a powerful interpretation of the switch from Mughal to British rule. Consumption regimes echoed a shift from archaic to modern globalization, and from artisanal skill to modern mass production. 'Whereas modern complexity demands the uniformity of Levi's and trainers,' Bayly concludes, 'the archaic simplicity of everyday life demanded that great men prized difference in goods . . . In one sense archaic lords . . . were collectors, rather than consumers.'[44] This is too harsh a verdict on modernity, echoing older notions of how consumer culture leads to disenchantment and loss of authenticity. In reality, collecting and consuming have reinforced each other in the last two hundred years; in museums but also in private households, with their stamps, antiques, rare beer cans, or exotic nutcrackers from distant places.[45] 'Cosmic kingship' has been democratized: everyone can be a collector and play the role formerly reserved for rulers, protecting exotic objects or discontinued toys from extinction. Fashionable youths, meanwhile, personalize their jeans and trainers. Standardization is always undercut by diversification, or 'customization', as it is called in the world of fashion.

Bayly nonetheless put his finger on two critical qualities of earlier consumption regimes. The first is their hybridity. Until around 1800, rulers demonstrated their divine authority by amassing exotic spices and animals, fine furs and fine books from distant lands; Wajid Ali Shah's ancestor Asaf ud-Daula had a stockpile of English watches, pistols, mirrors and furniture in his palace in Lucknow. 'Fusion' is not a recent invention. The second point is about the tributary flow of consumption. Nawabs and other rulers were more than private connoisseurs. They controlled the flow of goods and services for the rest. Shawls, jewels, brass and silver: their acquisition was mainly a result of tribute and gift, not individual choice. Instead of market transactions between buyer and seller they were exchanges between ruler and client conducted at public feasts and ceremonies. The British empire cut through these networks of rule and mobilized consumption for its own ends. It was a two-pronged offensive. One was on the production side – cheap factory textiles from Lancashire flooded the Indian market. The other, equally important, went to the heart of the luxury regime – the central state took control of taxes and bazaar duties and slashed elites' tributes and pensions.

Indian courts practised conspicuous consumption on a grand scale. At durbars (courts or ceremonial gatherings), courtiers brought *nadhr* gifts for their superiors and valuable *pishkash* presents for the emperor. In return, the emperor awarded gifts, *khil'ats* (robes of honour), *jagirs* (land titles) and allowances.[46] Armies were another transmission belt for goods and loyalty. In Nagpur, in central India, the Maratha court was by far the biggest consumer in the region, buying up three quarters of all fine muslins, shawls and *kinkhabs* (silk brocades with gold and silver thread) for itself, its retainers and soldiers. The Maratha maintained 150,000 men. In the eighteenth century, the East India Company participated in this network of gifts and patronage, but the tributary system came to an end with the company's loss of its trade monopoly in India in 1813.

Formal British rule brought down the architecture of this court-based luxury and the local producers supporting it. When princely armies disbanded and court retainers lost their allowances, regions contracted like deflating balloons. Artisans lost their elite customers for fine cloth, leather and sweetmeats. Many towns witnessed an exodus.[47] The precise impact of British power differed from city to city. For example, in the Gujarati city of Surat, just north of Mumbai, the main textile industries shrank, but artisans who made the famous gold thread *jari* managed to hang on.[48] Notables, meanwhile, tried to keep up their former lifestyles as best they could, even as their pensions were being cut back by the British. While undermining old elites, the British empire simultaneously promoted new ones, such as the Parsis. Still, with all these nuances and qualifications, it is clear that, overall, the British empire was bad for luxury consumption in India.

This was fully intentional. India was 'backward', one English observer argued in 1837, because 'princes and nobles were engrossing all the wealth of the country,' while its people were 'groaning' under the burden. There was no harm done at all if cheap British textiles killed local manufacturers. Much better for them to move into more efficient employment on abundant land. 'As to the Indian people generally, they are clear gainers; or they would surely not take the British goods, unless they were either cheaper or better than their own.'[49] This was the voice of the free-trade empire: trade would bring specialization, greater efficiency and welfare. British rule was benign because it shifted resources from idle princes to the Indian people. The sad truth was that the British empire managed to do the first without accomplishing the second. Simply put, Indian society under colonial rule moved from the shape of an hourglass into that of a pyramid. At the top, the rich elite was slimmed. At the bottom, the poor were not getting poorer, but there were many more of them. The middle class and affluent workers remained few.

Why India under British rule became locked into a cycle of pauperization has been one of the longest-standing debates in history and economics. Some of it had to do with geography and timing rather than imperial rule. Globalization was under way in the nineteenth century, and it made sense for India to buy British textiles, which were getting cheaper, and to grow and export those raw materials which were commanding rising global prices, especially opium, raw cotton, indigo, sugar and wheat. Britain did not need imperial control to sell its cotton shirts: India's switch from the workshop of the world to its farmyard would probably have happened with or without empire. Cheap yarn from Lancashire, moreover, benefited Indian consumers and handloom weavers. India's main problem was that its industries were labour intensive. Without new technologies, artisans worked harder, not more efficiently. Big industries remained few and far between. British investment was too small to jumpstart the economy. All this had a paradoxical effect on Indian patterns of consumption. On the one hand, Indians reaped the benefits of a mass market of cheaper and more varied goods. On the other, their real wages were restrained, at best growing modestly in the late nineteenth and early twentieth centuries.[50]

Where British rule left its mark was on the style of consumption. Some historians have stressed the 'ornamentalist' nature of the Raj after the Mutiny, marked by an inflation of titles and orders, the crowning of Victoria as Empress of India in 1877 and the great Delhi Durbar of 1911, the huge assembly to celebrate George V's coronation. Native princes covered in gold and diamonds were joined by 100,000 people to watch the arrival of the new king, who was spectacularly dressed in a robe of imperial purple, white satin breeches and silk stockings, and adorned with the collar of the Order of the Garter, rubies, emeralds and the Star of India.[51] Such imperial spectacle was part of a strategy to shore up old Indian princes and present the British Raj as a legitimate successor to the Mughals, but they never reinstated the older tribute system. Gifts and goods no longer oiled the wheels of power.[52] A centralized state bureaucracy took their place. Instead of a public demonstration of fealty and status, gifts were reduced to bribes collected in secret.

This fundamental switch deserves emphasis, because ever since the economist Joseph Schumpeter wrote his *Sociology of Imperialism* in 1918, it has been fashionable to treat imperialism as an 'atavism', a living museum in which an outdated feudal elite could recreate traditional hierarchies and the 'life habits of the dim past'.[53] In fact, the opposite happened. The Raj spawned a new material culture. Private was separated from public life, leisure from work, administrative rules from native networks. For the British in India, leisure was about polo, not patronage. Moderation and individual restraint took the place of excess and public display. Consumption was to be productive, not spectacular. Spending (and saving) had to be for a purpose.

British imperialism advanced through by-laws and new ideals of private comfort. Together, they reshaped two critical sites of consumption: the city and the home. In 1850, the Government of India Act allowed Indian cities to form municipal bodies and follow the path of urban improvement pioneered in Manchester and Birmingham. Incorporation left few aspects of urban life untouched, from the style of housing and the look of local shops, via what alcohol could be sold where, when and by whom, all the way to where to dump one's rubbish. For local elites, municipal bodies were new instruments of influence and co-optation. At first, members were nominated by the British, but from 1883 an equal number of deputies were elected by propertied voters. British rule imported British ideas of urban living. The local *manzil*, or courtyard house, with its small openings to keep out heat and dust, was a particular thorn in the side of Victorian reformers preoccupied with fresh air and windows, and ignorant of local knowledge about climate control. In Lucknow, new houses were denied planning permission unless they followed an English-style bungalow, with rooms for different functions and an outside garden instead of the customary internal courtyard. The shopping experience, too, was streamlined. Shopkeepers had to get rid of exterior decoration in favour of neat and simple fronts. For local residents, these interventions had contradictory effects. The free-trade empire was committed to opening markets and extirpating aristocratic excess. At the same time, the British levied new taxes on food, tobacco and salt; the local elite made sure that the house tax hit them least hard. Food and drink were regulated for the sake of public health. This meant the end for distillers of local booze, pushing many people to seek refuge in opium and hashish. The local elite turned to whiskey, gin and sherry.[54]

The pull of British culture was never complete. Religious gift-giving, for example, continued, in spite of utilitarian appeals to thrift. Local elites performed a balancing act, seeking to maximize their influence with the new rulers without losing their standing in their own communities. English education and standards of middle-class discipline and probity were gaining ground. The luxurious lifestyle of the Mughal gentry and the splendour of Hindu religious festivals, once celebrated, were condemned by Nagar Brahmins and Parsis alike as sheer waste. When scribal communities such as the Kayastha started to work for British administrators they dropped the customs of their former Muslim rulers, such as lavish weddings. For the aspiring middle class, consumption was harnessed to professional advancement.[55] Not all these predispositions were new or imposed from the outside. Here and there, British rule was able to draw on pre-colonial attitudes, such as the more austere strand of Hinduism which radiated out from the Ramanandis – Nepalese followers of Rama and courtiers of Muslim nawabs – to other service elites and Muslims.[56]

If not always an innovator, the British empire was a fertile soil for ideals that favoured less ostentatious and more 'rational' consumption. The social capital to be gained from education, in particular, reordered the priorities of spending and the role of women. Advice literature told Hindu women that their true religious place was in the home, not with priests in public festivals. Their energies needed to be channelled into household management in the service of their husband's career.

In other colonies, as in India, empire introduced an ideal of domesticity that ran roughshod over local customs. In Dutch Sumatra, for example, Karo women worked the fields and had some control over money. Missionaries wanted them to be housewives. Ironically, it was the growing fashion for fitted clothes, first adopted by their husbands, that broke the mould. The desire for Western clothes made many send their daughters to missionary schools that offered sewing clubs.[57]

For the Western world of goods, the imperial dance meant two steps forward and one step back. Indians were caught in a crossfire of messages: to consume more, to consume less, and to consume differently. British feminists were shocked by Bengali women in their transparent saris with heavy jewellery and no undergarments. Indians had to be put into shoes and stockings. Too close an emulation of Western styles, on the other hand, made imperial rulers and Indian nationalists alike uncomfortable. British attempts to impose a uniform order on the subcontinent and fix Indian customs were doomed from the start. Britons were prohibited from wearing Indian dress at official functions in 1830. Affluent Indians began to put on European suits, shoes and stockings, though often with turbans and never with a Western hat. In 1854, the Governor-General allowed Bengalis to appear in boots and shoes at official and semi-official occasions. By the time a new resolution had been passed, Indians pressed for further changes. After gaining the right to wear shoes, Bengalis in the 1870s appealed to be exempted from the rule requiring them to wear a turban in the office. Turbans, they pointed out, were not a regional custom. They preferred a light cap. The Lieutenant-Governor, Ashley Eden, was livid and refused. Dress was meant to exhibit the difference between East and West. A cap was a dangerous hybrid that signalled 'a prevailing laxity' among native officials who no longer knew their place.[58]

The Indian middle class, too, was torn about the appropriate style of consumption. While many professional Indian men inclined towards a Western lifestyle, they urged their wives to be traditional. Nationalist periodicals frowned upon Indian women who opted for Western make-overs.[59] Their husbands meanwhile were satirised by Indian writers as *baboos*, a 'modified Anglo-Indian', as if 'civilization could be brought about by wearing tight pantaloons, tight shirts and black coats of alpaca or broadcloth.' The *baboo* exchanged modesty and practical sense for 'must-have' leather shoes from Cuthbertson and Harper, shoemakers to the British in India (see Plate 39). He owned a piano rather than a native instrument, ate mutton chops, drank brandy and smoked cigars, all in violation of Hindu law.[60] Nationalism turned the marketplace into a moral minefield.

These moral restraints intensified as caste and gender roles were loosening. In the early twentieth century, Indian women started to do more of the shopping, to eat out and go to the movies. While the poor continued to spend heavily on religious festivals and weddings,[61] they were not entirely bypassed by the current of goods either. 'Half hose or full stockings' were worn by 'the wealthiest Baboo to the commonest fruit seller', an Indian critic noted in 1881.[62] Poor labourers in Calcutta, previously naked except for a loincloth, began wearing shoes and stockings, increasingly made in Japan. In rural society, caste-based restrictions were softening. The poor started to sport artificial-silk saris and wear cloth previously reserved for Brahmins.[63] Consumer culture would probably have changed the fabric of Indian society even if there had been no empire. What British rule did was to create a material nursery for a new colonial elite. Nationalists inherited a middle-class ideal of disciplined consumption. From the more cyclical mode of the Mughal tributary festival, which was about recycling loyalties and maintaining status, consumption shifted to a more dynamic, if less flamboyant, style committed to maximizing future earnings and status. In East as in West, conspicuous consumption now bore the stigma of decadent waste.

The imperial advance of European things was nowhere clearer than in the home, both for its ambition and its limits. The decades after the Mutiny brought a rising wave of European families. By 1914, close to 200,000 Europeans were living in India. Setting up home in the colony was a demonstration of imperial strength and identity. Armchairs and paintings of the English countryside, the ritual of changing for dinner, corsets and stiff collars: these were material reminders of where one came from and why one was there. Advice books drummed home the unbridgeable divide between the two cultures:

> One of the characteristics of an Englishman is to make his surroundings, wherever he may be stationed, as like as possible to those of his own country. The representative Indian changes but little in his ways, and he, too, likes to be amongst his own country people: consequence, as a general rule in India, the European quarters and the Indian or native city are separate.[64]

The Indian bungalow was as different from the English home as 'a temple from a church', one commentator wrote in 1904.[65] Bungalows often lacked wallpaper and curtains. Rooms intercommunicated with each other, instead of creating discrete spaces for separate members of the family. Servants were thus more visible, as were children. Rooms were often characterized by their temperature ('hot', 'cold', 'wet'), not their social function.

Britons in India worked hard to anglicize the domestic interior. The lists of goods arriving in Calcutta on British ships give a flavour of the British taste and the lifestyle that arrived with it. On 15 July 1784, the *Calcutta Gazette* advertised the investment of Captain Johnson of the *Berrington*. It consisted of an 'elegant assortment of goods, which are of the latest fashions', including pianofortes, 'Salisbury kitchens', fine Irish linen, claret, porter and ale, cheese and pickled salmon, and a set of the House of Lords and Commons debates. Other sales in the same year included 'superb full dress suits', 'silk and cotton hose' and Hogarth's complete works.[66] John Paterson, the Calcutta agent of the P&O Steamship Company, in 1869 owned a 'Victoria couch; an Albert couch; a Victoria easy chair; an Albert easy chair; a mahogany easy chair; . . . a set of six Genoa chairs . . . a mahogany square piano forte; seven volumes [of] music books and a lot of loose music books' and a 'mahogany marble top centre table'. The local objects in his possession were limited to two 'inlaid marble dishes of Indian workmanship' and models of Indian servants.[67]

Ruling a tropical colony, however, made smooth transplantation impossible. For many imperial families, home in India was a mobile affair, closer to a camper van than a country cottage, as they moved between hill stations and administrative centres. Rents were high. Families brought their eiderdowns, chintzes and dinner sets from Britain, but plenty of rugs, furniture and accessories were picked up in India in shops, auctions or second-hand marts. British women could not 'resist the temptation of collecting brasses, rugs, embroideries and treasures of all kinds', returning from the hill stations to their winter quarters laden with trophies.[68] Some memsahibs slept on a *charpoy*, a rope bedstead. The respectable tea planter George Williamson of Assam had armchairs and sideboards but neither pictures nor textile furnishings. Families used Indian matting and *purdahs* for door screens. Even in 1900, British men in the Raj still outnumbered British women by three to one. They often shared lodgings and made do with minimal furnishings. Many homes resembled curiosity shops. 'The chair on which we sit,' one resident noted in 1872, 'was bought from a distinguished civilian . . . That table was picked when the inspector of railways gave up housekeeping . . . That davenport [sofa] was purchased when the late judge left the country on his retiring pension.'[69] Whatever the ideal, for imperial families, Westernization was a partial affair.

In homes of the local elite, European goods and furnishings started to cross the threshold more frequently after the mid-nineteenth century but often stopped at the reception room. Gooroo Churn Singh, a Calcutta merchant, owned several two-storey brick houses, furnished with an Albert couch, a carpet from Brussels and a cut-glass twelve-light chandelier with frosted and engraved shades.[70] Past the reception room, however, Hindu merchants kept an exclusive zone for their extended family. This dual lifestyle was a continuation of the flexible cultural adaptation that stretched back to the eighteenth century: the Khatris of Benares had maintained palaces and worn Mughal jewellery and Persian dress in public but for their home opted for simple dhotis and a mud-walled house in town.

The rising river of Western goods reached furthest into colonial societies where racial and cultural barriers were lowest, as in Ceylon (Sri Lanka), where the Dutch left behind a high degree of intermarriage and where an Indian merchant diaspora flourished. The local elite wore trousers underneath Indian jackets and dressed their children in sailor uniforms. Their houses were filled with upholstered furniture, pictures and chandeliers. On Mr Peiris's Belvedere estate, 'one of the finest and best appointed country seats of the Western Province', interior arrangements were 'on the latest English lines'. Indeed, for the mosaics of pictures that lined the walls and floors, all materials were specially imported from England (see Plate 16). Mr Peiris had also been caught by the English passion for cycling at the time: he was captain of the Moratuwa Cyclists' union. Not very far away lived the cinnamon and coconut plantation owner Mr N. E. de Croos; the family originated from India. He served on the local board of his town, Negombo, was a 'pillar of the Catholic Club' and president of the cricket club. 'He used to play tennis and football, and has lately become a keen horseman.' 'Barbeton', his town house, was 'one of the finest residences in the Western Province'. Its drawing room included chandeliers, paintings and photos, carpets as well as matting, armchairs and a piano. For his official photograph, Mr de Croos appeared in morning suit, complete with top hat.[71]

THE DISCOVERY OF THE CONSUMER

In Europe, the era of high imperialism (1870s–'90s) took consumption to new heights. In part, this was the result of the fast-advancing global integration of markets, made possible by steamships, imperial expansion and trade liberalization. The price of wheat, sugar, beef, cooking oil and much else plummeted. Cooling technology and canning brought Argentinian steak and Canadian salmon to dining tables in Bordeaux and Bristol. The cost of clothing fell, too. At the same time, European and American labour became more productive, thanks to factory production and new technologies, boosting exports and raising wages. In 1899, a British worker had twice as much spending power as fifty years earlier. Americans enjoyed even higher real wages.[72] In the old world and the new, Europeans and their descendants had never had it so good.

The quickening pace of consumption had equally important cultural and political dimensions. New spending power and the growing influx of goods drew attention to the way in which consumption was reordering norms, relations and identities. How people spent their money came to matter as much as how much they earned. The power of the purse handed shoppers a personal weapon for social justice. Thinkers and activists discovered 'the consumer' and started to flesh out this person, recognizing their contribution to wealth and welfare. Slowly but surely, Europe and America were developing a sense of themselves as consumer societies.

The new prominence of consumption was part of a mental shift in industrial societies. In the wake of the French Revolution of 1789, earlier optimism had given way to an emphasis on natural limits. Things might improve a little, thanks to prudent policy and habits but, ultimately, most political economists agreed the economy would hit a ceiling. The deeper one had to dig for coal and the less fertile land one put under the plough, the higher the cost and the lower the yield. That was the law of diminishing returns. From the mid-nineteenth century, America and Britain realized that they had broken through that ceiling. Other industrial nations followed. They were now in uncharted territory, politically and morally as much as economically. Growth unsettled assumptions about the social order, the nature of wealth, its origin, use and distribution. Was destitution ordained or was it man-made, the result of bad policies and institutions? If the latter, what share of riches should go the poor? Excessive display and debt continued to set off alarm bells. Contemporaries did not ignore the role of land and production as sources of wealth. But the balance was shifting. By the late nineteenth century, economists, radicals and social movements were picking up the story where the Enlightenment had left off. Everyone was beginning to talk about the consumer.

The career of the concept of the 'standard of living' is a good indication of the hopes and anxieties that came with growing spending power. Household budgets had first been studied in seventeenth-century France and England. From the mid-nineteenth century, they developed into the central tool of an increasingly global enterprise of social investigation. By 1930, several thousand inquiries had been conducted everywhere from Boston to Bombay, Shanghai to Rome and St Petersburg, showing in pounds and pennies exactly how much money households with different incomes spent on food, lodging, clothes and 'sundries', or small assorted items. Any social reformer worth the name carried a budget study in their pocket.

One driving force was Ernst Engel, director of the Statistical Bureau in Saxony and then, after 1860, in Prussia. The next two generations of social policy experts passed through his research seminar – the first in the world. Engel injected a bracing statistical precision into government and scholarship. His goal was to build up statistics into an independent science with a social mission. Engel had sat at the feet of Frédéric Le Play at the École des Mines in Paris in the 1840s. For Le Play, who compiled thirty-six volumes on the budgets of European workers, material improvement dangerously undermined patriarchy and religion. Engel, by contrast, was a liberal at heart and a constant thorn in Bismarck's side. For twenty years, the Iron Chancellor tried to sack him for briefings that exposed how official policy was often based on fantasy and inference rather than hard fact, before finally managing to give him the boot in 1882. For men like Engel, statistics not only clarified 'the social question', they held part of the answer. Budget studies could defuse social conflict by documenting how people were progressively better off. As a family's income improved, the proportion spent on food declined. This became known as Engel's law, the first economic law derived from inductive analysis. Freed-up money went towards better education, healthcare and recreation. In good time, Engel believed, the working class would pull itself up from vice, misery and revolutionary temptations to a middle-class plane of comfort, order and self-improvement. Engel was no naïve utopian. Towards the end of his life (1896), he compared his own studies with data from the United States and Belgium. As important as the rise in incomes itself, he noted, was that it was smooth and gradual. If it was too sudden, it might produce a moral regression, as happened with the Belgian workers who spent rising wages on drink in the 1850s. Still, Engel was convinced that people wanted to improve themselves and, given the chance, would do so. He looked forward to the day when 80 per cent of a budget would be devoted to needs, leaving 20 per cent free spending money. At the time, this was generous. In 1857, in his seminal study, a middle-class household in Saxony still spent 85 per cent on food, clothing, housing and fuel, a poor worker as much as 95 per cent.[73]

Budget studies gave consumption a new visibility. Well-being, they showed, was a result of the art of spending, not just earning. Politically, this made the standard of living a double-edged sword. What good were higher wages if they went towards alcohol and tobacco? critics asked. Greater purchasing power might unhinge the entire economy. A budget analysis of forty-three families convinced the Massachusetts Commission on the Cost of Living in 1910 to blame a rise in prices on the increasing 'waste of income' that resulted from a 'national habit of extravagance'. On the other hand, household budgets also gave reformers and trade unions new ammunition in the battle for a 'living wage'. *Round about a Pound a Week* (1913) in Britain and similar investigations elsewhere demolished the idea that poverty was caused by drink. In the United States, organized labour started to fight for an 'American' standard of living. They could not be expected to live like an Irish peasant or Russian serf, they insisted.[74] By 1919, investigations were no longer just concerned with the share of expenditure on food, lodging and recreation but with establishing a basic consumption norm, down to the precise number of shirts, shoes and stockings purchased. A 'fair standard of living', according to the Bureau of Municipal Research in Philadelphia, required every year two new dress shirts, six washable collars and one suit (50 per cent wool) for him, and one skirt, nine cotton stockings, one corset and one and a half hats for her. This kind of wardrobe would have cost $78 a year for a man and $66 for a woman, at a time when workers in the garment industry earned between $350 and $600 a year; an experienced female printer would earn $16 a week.[75]

Many studies at the time, in fact, jarred with Engel's law. In 1911 Hawaii, for example, Portuguese and Chinese labourers increased the share they spent on food as their earnings improved. The same was true for European peasants. One criticism that has plagued the theory since its inception is that the standard of living is not a universal, objective yardstick. Judgements about what makes for a high quality of life vary from culture to culture. One investigation in Shanghai found that even the poorest spent up to a third of their income on festivities, leisure, drugs and other 'sundry items', a much higher share than amongst workers in European cities with higher earnings. Which of the two were better off? Importantly, it was the universalist standard which attracted the greatest amount of followers, and only in the last two decades have subjective and culture-specific approaches to well-being made a comeback. What made the standard-of-living concept so attractive around 1900 was precisely that it offered reformers a yardstick of how far a society had advanced towards the material well-being associated with a modern way of life.

A report on Bombay mill workers in 1923 was typical. Of these

The annual requirements of a fair standard of clothing, Philadelphia, 1919

Hats 1

Collars 6
Ties 3
Dress shirts 2
Working shirts 4
Gloves 1
Overcoats 2
Suits 1

Summer underwear 3
Winter underwear 1

Extra trousers 1

Socks 12

Shoes 2
Shoe repairs 2

Hats 1.5

Coats 0.5
Suits 0.5

Shirtwaists 0.5

Petticoats 2
Corsets 1

Gloves 1

Summer underwear 3
Winter underwear 2

Skirts 1

Stockings 9

Shoes 2
Shoe repairs 1

Gentlemen's suits, from Simpson's
Catalogue for Fall and Winter, 1918-19.

Spring fashions for women, from a catalogue
published by Sears, Roebuck & Co., 1920.

Source: William C. Beyer, Rebekah P. Davis and Myra Thwing, *Workingmen's Standard of Living in Philadelphia: a report by the Bureau of municipal research of Philadelphia* (1919), p. 67.

families, 97 per cent lived in a single room. Half of them were in debt to money-lenders. Yet they spent 19 per cent of their earnings on liquor, tobacco, betel nuts and haircuts. Weddings, funeral rites and customary expenses pushed them deeper into debt; a marriage cost Rs 214, or half a year's wages. Such behaviour was plain wrong, the investigator concluded. People needed to be weaned off old customs and irrational spending habits. They were caught in a vicious circle of idleness and stimulants, lacking the necessary desire to accumulate things. To become better workers, they first had to acquire a modern ethic of consumption: 'Spending wisely may be regarded as the crux of the whole labour problem'. 'When once the workers have unsatisfied desires for something different from idleness they are on the road to efficiency where each step taken makes the next easier.'[76]

That idea that material desire prompted people to be more industrious had been commonplace in the eighteenth century, as we have seen. It was only now, though, in the late nineteenth century, that an economic theory of consumption began to emerge. Adam Smith's famous remark that 'consumption is the sole end and purpose of all production' was about all he had to say on the topic. For his successors, David Ricardo and John Stuart Mill, economics was about land and production. In the 1840s, the extreme liberal Frédéric Bastiat in France raised the flag for the consumer in his crusade for 'free exchange'; Bastiat's dying words in 1850 supposedly were 'we must learn to look at everything from the point of view of the consumer.' Still, even that did not amount to much of a theory, since free markets would take care of everything. Mill – the pre-eminent public moralist of the Victorian era and a champion of social justice and representative government as much as economic logic – made sure to nip such laissez-faire dogmas in the bud. Consumption, he repeated in 1844, was not a separate branch of economic analysis.[77] The matter was closed. Or so it seemed until the 1870s.

'The theory of economics must begin with a correct theory of consumption,' W. S. Jevons announced in his *Theory of Political Economy* in 1871.[78] The Ricardo–Mill school had it fundamentally wrong. Jevons had devoted his entire life to throwing off 'the incubus of bad logic and bad philosophy which Mill's Works have laid upon us'.[79] That as a young lecturer he was forced to teach Mill, while his own early writings were ignored – his first book on logic sold four copies in twice as many months – did not help. Still, ethics and economics went together for Jevons, as they had for Mill. The goal of maximizing pleasure was balanced by a Unitarian commitment to doing good. Measuring demand, protecting consumers and improving the working conditions of young mothers were all part of the same job.

For Ricardo and Mill, the value of goods was determined by their cost: a coat was worth the cloth and sweat that went into making it. Jevons turned the matter inside out. Value was created by the consumer, not the producer. What a coat was worth depended on how much an individual desired it. And that desire was variable. One loaf of bread was essential, a second might be desirable, but a third was superfluous. Goods had a 'final utility': each additional portion had less utility than the one before because the final one was less intensely desired. On the continent, Carl Menger and Léon Walras were independently coming to similar conclusions. 'Marginal utility', as it became known, introduced a radically new way of looking at economic life. It moved the individual consumer to the centre. Jevons bolted together Bentham and calculus; he had passed through University College School, set up by Bentham's disciples. Pleasure and pain were the 'springs of human action'. Their ratio, however, changed in the course of consumption, as in the case of the first loaf and the third. And this could be measured. Economics was becoming a mathematical science.[80]

In the twentieth century, this approach would be christened the 'neo-classical revolution'. Given the ultimate triumph of mathematical formulae in economics, it is tempting to see the 1870s–'80s as the birthplace of the ideals of consumer sovereignty, choice and markets which would reach their apex with neoliberalism a century later. This would be misleading and teleological. At that time, the wind was blowing in the opposite direction: away from leaving everything to markets and towards a belief that consumers deserved public aid and protection.

Jevons and his contemporaries did not look to choice and the utility-maximizing consumer as a panacea. 'If the pattern of a dress is pleasing to the intending wearer,' Jevons acknowledged, 'that settles the matter; no government inspector can make it unpleasing.' But a lot of life was not like this. It was full of risk, ignorance and natural monopolies, such as gas and water. 'He who selects the greenest pickles may be unaware of the copper which gives the attractive tinge.'[81] These sentences are from the last book he would write: *The State in Relation to Labour* (1882). In August that year, Jevons took his wife and children for a holiday on the English coast, near Hastings. He went for a swim in the cold sea and drowned, at the age of forty-six; it was probably suicide.

The English sea took with it his planned *Principles of Economics*. The economist Lionel Robbins later noted that Jevons 'formed no school. He created no system.'[82] This was left to Alfred Marshall, who not only established economics as a proper discipline at Cambridge in the 1890s but softened the harsh image of the 'dismal science' by adding a sense of duty and caring for others to the existing catalogue of selfish motives. Marshall used Jevons's core idea: the consumer was the 'ultimate regulator of all demand'. He then gave it an evolutionary twist. Jevons's theory had focused on wants. This was too static. While 'wants are the rulers of life among lower animals,' it was 'the changing forms of efforts and activities' that revealed 'the keynotes of the history of mankind'. Marshall's argument was as brilliant as it was simple. Human wants and desires, he wrote, were 'generally limited and capable of being satisfied. The uncivilized man indeed has not many more than the brute animal.'[83] Progress increased both their variety and the effort devoted to satisfying them. Material satisfaction was guided, or ennobled, to use a Victorian term, by a natural urge for self-improvement. Leisure was 'used less and less as an opportunity for mere stagnation', such as idleness and drink, and more and more for sport and travel. Consuming was like climbing a ladder of ever higher tastes and faculties, with each activity releasing new energy to move up to the next rung. It was an optimistic view in keeping with ideas about social evolution that characterized the period. The 'neo-classical' discovery of the consumer, however, was accompanied by a socio-cultural critique of unrestrained mass consumption. 'The world would go much better,' Marshall wrote, 'if everyone would buy fewer and simpler things, and would take trouble in selecting them for their real beauty; . . . preferring to buy a few things made well by highly paid labour rather than many made badly by low paid labour'.[84]

Consumption was attracting growing attention from economists of all stripes, but there remained a vehement disagreement about exactly what it was. Some wanted to limit it to physical goods; others included services, taste and experience; some even clung to Jean-Baptiste Say's concept of 'reproductive' or 'technical' consumption, which included the coal and materials used up in a factory. Historical economists turned to consumption as an indicator of national power. German writers were especially sceptical about individual choice. On the eve of the First World War, Karl Oldenberg worried that affluence had brought in its train the civilizational diseases of drink and tobacco. New desires eroded customs. Peasants wanted soft white bread instead of solid German rye. In cities, the 'cult of meat' caused arterial sclerosis, rheumatism and nervous dyspepsia. And yet, he stressed, consumption played a vital role in raising nations to a higher level of civilization. Pure, self-centred satisfaction of desire existed only at the rawest stage of civilization. After that, nation and family harnessed their energy for collective strength. Unlike for the liberal Marshall, the movement was not all 'upwards' and peaceful, though. It was a struggle between rising and declining nations. Resources were limited. Two kinds of nations would survive, Oldenberg speculated: those whose growing needs generated high energy, and frugal ones with barely any needs at all. Nations with middling needs would go to the wall.[85]

The first general account of a society of abundance came from the place with the highest standard of living: the United States. In 1889, Simon Patten announced 'a new order of consumption'.[86] Patten was the chair of the Wharton School of Business and, as was true for so many leading American scholars of his generation, was inspired by the German historical school of economics; he himself had studied at the University of Halle. The economy, in this view, was the product of historical evolution and enmeshed in social and political life, rather than a timeless system of universal laws. The big change that occupied Patten was that, for the first time, modern societies were producing more than enough to secure a basic existence. The task now was to organize wealth in ways that maximized welfare for all. People had a right to leisure. Libraries and parks would cultivate a love of beauty and nature. Tariffs and taxes on tobacco would discourage 'bad' wants. The battle against 'vice', however, would be won not by restraint but by greater welfare and greater pleasure: 'society is not safe until to-day's pleasures are stronger than its temptations.'[87]

Material desire had found a new evangelist. To get a sense of what this sounded like, let us listen in on a speech Patten gave at a Philadelphia church in 1913: 'I tell my students to spend all that they have and borrow more and spend that . . . It is no evidence of loose morality when a stenographer, earning eight or ten dollars a week, appears dressed in clothing that takes nearly all of her earnings to buy.' Quite the contrary, he said, it was 'a sign of her growing moral development'. It signalled her ambition to her employer. A 'well-dressed working girl . . . is the backbone of many a happy home that is prospering under the influence that she is exerting over the household'. This was not exactly what the congregation of the Spring Garden Unitarian Church was used to. There were cries from the floor: 'absolutely untrue'. How could Patten be so naïve? one member asked. 'The generation you're talking to now is too deep in crime and ignorance . . . to heed you.'[88] Whether they liked it or not, that day in 1913 the audience had been witness to a historic shift: abundance had begun to create its own morality.

The intellectual discovery of the consumer was the crest of a rising wave of social activism that swept across industrial societies around 1900. Received wisdom is to see citizenship as a series of steps, from civil liberties in the early modern period, to the political right to vote in the nineteenth century, to the social rights established by the welfare state in the middle of the twentieth century.[89] This story misses a critical stage: that of the citizen-consumer. The 1890s and 1900s were not just the golden era of the department store and shopping for pleasure. They were also the time when social movements began to mobilize consumers to reform society. Rather than seeing this period as a flight into selfish materialism, then, we should recognize that individual spending and civic activism propelled each other forward. For every new department store, there was a group of ethical shoppers outside who attacked the exploitation of its shopgirls. Organizations ranged from the millions of workers in the co-operative movement to the 6,000 middle-class Britons in the Christian Social Union who boycotted sweatshop tailors in Oxford. In France in 1902, reform-minded bourgeois Catholics formed the Ligue Sociale d'Acheteurs. Similar buyers' leagues mushroomed elsewhere.

Ethical consumerism was a metropolitan affair, in the sense both that it involved mainly middle-class women in European and American cities and that their causes were local. The moral energies devoted to the plight of slaves during earlier consumer boycotts were now redirected to exploited wage-workers at home. There was more than a bit of irony in this, since caring consumers burst on to the scene in Paris, London and Berlin at the very time when imperialism and globalization moved into top gear, and since it was the cheap palm oil, cotton, coffee and rubber from colonies and overseas plantations which underpinned mass markets in the first place.

If it was the consumer who directed the economy, not the producer, liberals, socialists and feminists asked: How was it that the consumer was treated as serf rather than king? Consumers needed to arise, assert their rightful place at the centre of society and put the power of their purse to civic use. What this meant in practice depended on national traditions and political cultures. We can nonetheless identify three broad goals. One was individual: be a conscientious shopper. The second was collective: consumers organize. The final one was political and directed at the state: give consumers rights and protection.

'The nineteenth century has been the century of producers,' Charles Gide, the leader of the French co-operative movement, told students in 1898. 'Let us hope that the twentieth century will be that of consumers. May their kingdom come!'[90] Gide's vision of a new social order mixed republican ideas, Christian values and a French associationist vision of socialism by small groups. All social life evolved around consumption. Did not eating at the same table automatically bring people together? Consumption had a better claim to create solidarity than production, especially given the modern division of labour. Everyone was a consumer. Yet, at present, he wrote, manufacturers and department stores were in charge and planted 'false needs'. Consumers needed to throw off the yoke of 'commercial feudalism', join co-operatives and buy responsibly. Once they controlled the wholesale trade, they would take over production and land as well. Consumers had it in their power to achieve social harmony and raise the condition of workers.[91]

Co-operative societies were run by men, but it was ultimately the 'women with the baskets' who did the shopping, and who were in the vanguard of ethical consumerism. Well-off women discovered their toiling sisters. In 1891, a Consumers' League was set up in New York to fight sweatshops. By 1914, it had grown into a national federation with 15,000 activists, headed by Florence Kelley.[92] The first 'white labels' were attached to underwear from certified manufacturers (see Plate 38). Now a respectable woman could know that her clothes were not stained by the blood of factory girls. Boycotts of sweated goods followed. There were links with the earlier campaigns against slave-grown goods which had been directed by Kelley's aunt, Sarah Pugh, a Quaker abolitionist.

Buyers' leagues sprang up in Paris, Antwerp, Rome, Berlin and Bern. International exhibitions publicized the harsh realities of home manufacturing and child labour. 'The consumer,' a German woman explained, 'is the clock which regulates the relationship between employer and employee.' If the clock was driven by 'selfishness, self-interest, thoughtlessness, greed and avarice, thousands of our fellow beings have to live in misery and depression'.[93] Love of fashion and control of the household budget gave women a special duty not to take advantage of shopkeepers and artisans. Buyers' leagues provided the ethical shopper with a checklist: start your Christmas shopping early, stop buying after 8 p.m. and pay small traders immediately, in cash. The leagues campaigned for Sunday closing; those in America and Switzerland also pressed for the minimum wage and the right to collective bargaining.[94]

Some of this was little more than a charitable hobby for the local elite. The president of the German league, founded in 1907, was the wife of Theobald von Bethmann-Hollweg, the Prussian minister of the interior and future German chancellor. Who could disagree with women exercising their duty as caring mothers and housewives? 'To live is to buy. Buying is power. Power is duty,' was the motto of the first international conference of buyers' leagues in 1908.[95] But ethical consumerism was also about rights. For the growing number of educated, reform-minded and ambitious women, it was a way to demonstrate their public spirit. Suffragettes on both sides of the Atlantic saw a symmetry between choice and the vote. If a housewife on a tight budget could choose wisely in the marketplace, day in, day out, and feed her family, how could she not be competent enough to make a cross on a ballot paper every few years? Consumption taught women to be 'chancellors of the exchequer'. In Britain, fourteen women formed a separate Women's Co-operative Guild in 1883. Twenty years later, the guild had 20,000 members and targeted poorer working-class areas. Co-operatives were mini-democracies. Here, members learnt the skills of citizenship: deliberation, voting and representation. In the past, radicals had praised the 'art of association' for creating virtuous and self-reliant male bread-winners who did not make any claims on the state. The WCG turned it into a justification for women's political and social rights, including state aid for maternity care and a minimum wage.[96]

The feminist and socialist case for a consumer revolt was put most forcefully by Teresa Billington-Greig, a British suffragette who had horsewhipped a steward for ejecting her from a Liberal Party meeting and seen the inside of Holloway Prison. It was idle, she said, to complain about capitalist profiteers. 'We are all more or less profiteers.' Consumers' love of cheap goods implicated them in low wages and social injustice: 'We are a shoddy people.' Women were especially prone to poor taste and conservative inaction because they were imprisoned in their homes. Capitalism had made man the producer who controlled public life. At the time of writing, in 1912, the rise in the standard of living of the previous three decades had levelled off. Organized labour had failed, she concluded, and it had especially failed women. As one of the few women organizers in the young Independent Labour Party, Billington-Greig knew what she was talking about. Female emancipation and the consumer-led reform of capitalism were one and the same battle. Organized as consumers, women would free themselves from both degradation and the cult of cheapness. Co-operatives were no longer enough. Consumers needed to pursue direct political action, enter into partnership with trade unions and establish a consumers' council to lead the fight for better-quality goods and improved working conditions.[97]

The discovery of the consumer acted as a catalyst for the idea of social citizenship. Political rights required the right to leisure, Simon Patten had stressed. A parallel economic argument made sure that this was no empty phrase. If modern nations had moved from scarcity to abundance, this meant they were producing a 'surplus'. Where did this surplus come from, and where did it go? The progressive answer was given by J. A. Hobson, the most prolific of a new generation of British radicals. As early as 1889, he had challenged the orthodox wisdom that production always created its own demand (J.-B. Say's famous law) together with his friend, the businessman and mountaineer A. F. Mummery. The rich, the two argued, were unable to consume all their income. The result of such 'underconsumption' was over-investment, gluts and depression. Six years later, Mummery was dead, lost in the Himalayas. Shunned by the establishment, Hobson pressed on alone. In 1899, he went to South Africa as the *Manchester Guardian*'s special correspondent to cover the Boer War. He returned with a book, *Imperialism* (1902), that revolutionized the terms of political debate – quite literally, since Lenin borrowed from it freely before adding a revolutionary edge.

Hobson's great idea was that aggression abroad was connected to 'under-consumption' at home. Poverty persisted, he argued, not because of natural, Malthusian pressures but because wealth was unfairly divided. Productivity was rising steadily. The profits, however, went to a small clique of investors. Finance was 'the governor of the imperial engine', constantly seeking new outlets for investment, by force if necessary, as in the South African war. All the time, the remedy was waiting at home. 'If the consuming public in this country raised its standard of consumption to keep pace with every rise of productive powers, there could be no excess of goods or capital clamorous to use Imperialism in order to find markets.'[98] A vast market lay at home, untapped, with Britons hungry for better food, better homes and better cities.

Enlightenment thinkers had looked to the merchant as an agent of peace. Hobson looked also to the consumer. Like Marshall, Hobson believed that people would not just consume more, but better. Gambling, racecourses and the 'flash music-hall' were the cultural byproducts of imperialism and inequality. The lower classes aped the manners of financiers and aristocrats; Hobson admired the American economist Thorstein Veblen, who who had attacked the luxurious lifestyles of the American rich as a form of social waste, and would meet him in Washington, DC, in 1925. Together, Hobson hoped, social welfare and free trade would purify the air. Ordinary Britons would 'begin to demand better commodities, more delicate, highly finished and harmonious'. Enjoyment would increase 'without . . . exhausting the store' of nature. Greater appreciation of quality, in turn, would provoke interest in how goods were made and put an end to 'anti-social competition'. The 'more qualitative consumption becomes, and the more insistent each individual is upon the satisfaction of his peculiar tastes, the smaller will be the probability that two persons will collide in their desires, and struggle for the possession of the self-same commodity'. Here was a progressive counter-argument to the charge by Conservatives and Marxists that free trade created a downward spiral of cheapness, materialism and apathy. Instead, in a more equal society, consumers would show an 'increased regard for quality of life' and care more deeply for things, the people who made them and their community. Hobson joined two subjects that previously had been kept apart: 'the citizen-consumer'.[99]

Governments still paid little attention to consumer issues, with the partial exception of food safety and public health. Still, there was a perceptible change in the atmosphere around the turn of the century. The concept of a decent standard of living broadened the political arena, with millions engaged in battles over tariffs and the cost of food. This was a truly global moment, with protests from Vienna to Santiago,[100] and reflected the global integration of the food system. As steamships moved wheat and beef across the oceans, people became used to more and better cuts of meat and a cheaper cup of coffee. In the 1890s, this trend hit a buffer. Many producers and farmers experienced globalization as a threat to their existence. With the exception of Britain, all states raised their trade barriers, and with them prices. Trade policy thus gave the issue of the standard of living fresh political urgency.

The space assigned to the consumer in these battles differed depending on each country's traditions, as well as its socio-economic make-up. In Germany, the Social Democratic Party (SPD) launched a crusade against the *'hunger tariff'*. Here the language was that of class. It was workers whom tariffs robbed of their hard-earned bacon, not the consuming public. Stretching the German language to its limit, contemporaries warned against the *Nurkonsumentenstandpunkt*, the point of view of consumers alone.[101] In a corporate tradition, where producer and professional identities prevailed, the consumer seemed a sectional interest, at best a clerk, at worst an idle rentier. In France, social hierarchies and the large number of small workshops also favoured a split identity. Henriette Brunhes' Ligue Sociale d'Acheteurs treated artisans and shopgirls as workers, not fellow consumers.[102] In the United States, the simultaneous advance of wage labour and mass manufacturing made spending more of a shared concern. Virtually every American bought their clothes with their wages. Progressives turned to consumers as a unifying force in the battle against trusts and plutocracy. It was consumers who would 'displace our present duality of resplendent plutocracy and crude ineffective democracy with a single,

broad, intelligent, socialized, and victorious democracy', trumpeted
Walter Weyl, a student of Patten's and one of the founders of the *New
Republic*.[103]

The apotheosis of the consumer occurred in Britain. Britain, unlike
high-tariff America, had been a free-trade nation since 1846. Victorian
politics laid a supporting platform: the consumer as tax-payer, represented in town councils and parliament. The heated defence of free
trade after 1903 raised the citizen-consumer to new heights. Initially
focusing on 'the cheap loaf', the campaign added more and more goods
to its political shopping basket. On high streets, shop windows taught
lessons in the standard of living with displays of branded goods like
Colman's mustard and hats and jackets from Britain alongside more
costly samples from protectionist Germany. That this was a biased
comparison – Americans and Australians lived even better behind trade
barriers – did not make the message any less forceful. Britain's higher
standard was advertised as evidence of the superiority of its liberal institutions and its high regard for the consumer. Industrialists rallied to the
defence of 'that most important person', as did cooperators, trade
unionists, feminists and the Treasury. The consumer was the national
interest.[104]

VALUE ADDED

A concern for consumer welfare and a critique of imperialism went
hand in hand for radicals like J. A. Hobson. The debate about the costs
and benefits of empire has been conducted as an accounting exercise
ever since: how much capital did Britain send to its colonies and what
was the consequence of having an empire for investment and welfare at
home? The short answer by scholars who have calculated investments
in railway and securities is that it paid to invest in colonies more than
at home, but that it paid even more to invest in neutral overseas markets, especially the United States and Latin America.[105] Empire, in
other words, attracted investment that might have gone into British
schools, roads and power stations. But the scope and return from
investment within the empire was dwarfed by more attractive opportunities beyond it. This was the era of finance imperialism, and whether
empire was keeping capitalism going was the big question of the day.
There is no reason, however, why the debate should be limited to capital investments. Empire affected the flow of goods more broadly. As

cultural markers, 'visible' goods mattered more than the 'invisible' exports of pounds and securities. Just as there are terms of trade, we thus need to think about the terms of consumption, terms that change between groups, products and regions. We have already observed how empire altered status. It also redefined the value of place.

Ironically, Hobson launched his attack on empire during the heyday of free trade, when the empire had come to matter less to Britons' welfare than ever before. Trade liberalization – sometimes free, sometimes forced – and steamboats opened up the world for late-Victorian consumers. Victorians enjoyed beef from Argentina, sherry from Portugal and sugar from Brazil. The round of second industrial revolutions in France, Germany and the United States created new markets for finished goods which, again, lay outside the empire. Most colonies were growing, but their share in metropolitan markets was falling: in 1805, one quarter of British imports came from the West Indies; by 1855 it had dropped to 5 per cent. It was when the global economy went into free fall in the inter-war years that Britons rediscovered the value of their colonies, with empire shopping weeks, appeals to 'Buy British', Kenyan-coffee-roasting demonstrations and competitions for the biggest Empire Christmas pudding.[106] Overall, under free trade, it was tropical colonies that were dependent on the imperial centre, not the other way around. On the eve of the First World War, Jamaica bought 44 per cent of its imports from Britain, the Gold Coast 89 per cent.

Radicals characteristically worried about the effect of imperialism on social equality. Again, we need to take a long view. All empires affect status and income, but some do so more than others. The mercantilist empire had been one long gravy train for aristocrats, planters and monopoly traders. True, it created some positive spillovers for regional economies tied into imperial trade, such as the wool trade in the West Riding of Yorkshire or workers producing glassware and copper in Liverpool. Overall, however, the transaction was one-sided. Consumers paid for the navy; the elite reaped the profits. The eighteenth-century empire magnified social inequality in Britain, but even more sharply in the colonies. Jamaican planters accumulated vast riches. By 1800, the average white man in Jamaica was over fifty times as wealthy as a free white person in the United States. Consuming united the white master class. Colonial planters were famed for their lavish entertainment and hospitality, dances and tea parties, French brandy and pickled crabs.[107] Riches and poverty did not disappear with the end of slavery and tariffs, but after 1846 the cost of empire was more fairly shared than before, as the imperial state lifted a large tax burden off the shoulders of British consumers.

The increasingly open, global trading system after 1850 transformed the imperial architecture of consumption. The British taste for sweetened tea has served as a shorthand for the link between empire and consumption. As a vessel for sugar, the teacup tied consumers in London and the Scottish Highlands to slave plantations in Jamaica and Barbados. After the 1840s, the British shifted the cultivation of tea from China to their Indian empire. Tea was an essential part of British life, from domestic rituals to the tea shops that began to crop up in the 1880s, all the way to Widow Twankey, the pantomime dame in *Aladdin* – a play on 'twankay', a green tea past its prime. Tea, and other such exotic products, 'embedded colonial meanings as well as colonial trade in ordinary lives', in the words of one historian[108] Sugar, according to Sidney Mintz, reflected 'the growing strength and solidity of the empire and of the classes that dictated its policies'.[109] This is all true for the eighteenth century, but for the nineteenth century the opposite can be argued. The British empire became more powerful as the fruits of its tropical colonies became ever less important to its metropolitan consumers.

In the seventeenth and eighteenth centuries, empires had opened crucial pathways for exotic tastes, but at a price. The taxman encouraged the smuggler. When duties on tea were lowered in 1745, the legal sale of tea in Britain suddenly tripled.[110] In France, too, smuggling softened a little the impact a regime of taxes and restrictions had on consumption. To circumvent the 'French Farm', which had the monopoly on collecting the taxes on imported tobacco, traffickers brought Virginia tobacco into France via Dutch ports and Alsace, where they then blended it with home-grown weeds.[111] Still, such contraband trade only satisfied so much demand. Other empires also had liberal moments that boosted consumption, but these tended to be temporary and short-lived, for example when Spain lowered duties in Guayaquil, in Ecuador, and introduced a colonial customs zone in the 1770s. In the longer perspective, however, the break-up of the Spanish empire after the Napoleonic wars turned out to be a step backwards, as Venezuela and other newly independent states raised their own barriers and export taxes to finance themselves. The conclusion is clear: in the long run, mercantilism was not fit for mass consumption. That was the historic achievement of free trade from the 1840s.

The phenomenal spread of tropical goods in the second half of the nineteenth century was driven by two forces: trade liberalization and a massive increase in cash-crop production. Unlike sugar, cocoa resisted industrial-style cultivation. It thrived in shade and needed surrounding plants to protect it from wind and disease. Economies of scale were few. Slavery was not absent – the Portuguese used it on São Tomé and Príncipe, their cocoa islands off West Africa, while the Germans tried 'scientific' planting and coerced labour in Cameroon, without much success. In general, cocoa favoured smallholders or, at least, a mix of day-labourers working alongside slaves at harvest time. Cocoa was a direct beneficiary of the end of slavery, which swelled the number of smallholders in search of a plot of land. In the Amazon, in Brazil, mixed-race and Amerindian small farmers gained ground over large planters after the Cabanagem Rebellion of 1835–40. In Colombia, the abolition of slavery was followed in 1851 by land grants to freed slaves. Coffee, by contrast, thrived on slave plantations. Virgin forests, long-distance railway and slave labour (until emancipation in 1888) made Brazil the world's premier producer. In 1914, the world consumed fifty times as much coffee as a century earlier. Colonies now provided only a small fraction of this.[112]

Mercantile empires were never entirely sealed off from outside trade. A good portion of Britain's colonial sugar and coffee was re-exported down the Rhine and Danube to landlocked central Europeans. Still, Britain's free-trade empire provided the lubricant for the global (rather than colonial) flow of goods. What mattered now was cheapness, not origin. By the 1880s, a Briton's spoonful of sugar contained no more than a few colonial grains. The bulk came from Brazilian cane and East European beet sugar. From a global point of view, the British link between tea, empire and mass consumption was the exception, not the rule. The other big European tea consumer, after all, was Russia. By 1914, Europeans got virtually all their coffee from Brazil. The coffee harvests in German colonies were minute, and even the French West Indies only filled 3 per cent of cups in Parisian cafés.[113] Chocolate, similarly, came less and less from the colonies. It was a dramatic reversal of fortune.

To look for direct influences of colonial produce on metropolitan sensibility, therefore, is to miss the forest for the trees. The liberal empire of consumption was not a one-way street. It involved reverse flows in the colonial world as well as lateral exits and flyovers via which goods reached societies without colonies. The power of the free-trade empire was precisely to make all producers, including tropical colonies, look to global demand. Colonial products became more diffused and invisible. Sometimes they were completely detached from the imperial core. By the 1880s, the biggest consumers of sugar from British Jamaica sat in Chicago and Boston, not London and Liverpool. The Dutch had Java, but cocoa manufacturers like van Houten did not like the insipid taste of its beans. Most Javanese cocoa was consequently sold on to the United States. The German *Kolonialwarenladen* (colonial-goods shop) effectively made a business out of their neighbours' more successful empires. In a mercantilist world, colonies had been a necessary ticket to consumption. In a liberal world economy, mass consumption no longer cared about the colour of the flag. Take the world's premier league of coffee drinkers on the eve of the First World War. The Dutch still drank more coffee than anyone – now largely from Brazil – but hard on their heels were Norwegians, Danes, Swedes and the Swiss. Consumption was not centred on imperial metropoles. Cubans drank more coffee (from Costa Rica) than did the French and the Germans; the average Chilean twice as much as a Spaniard or Italian.[114] The 'South', it is all too often forgotten, were not only producers. They were consumers, too.

National policies and class cultures shaped who drank what where. After Independence, Britain shut out the United States from its West

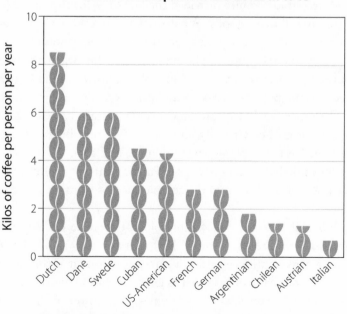

Coffee consumption in the world in 1913

Source: Ernst Neumann, *Der Kaffee: Seine geographische Verbreitung, Gesamtproduktion und Konsumtion* (1930), pp. 69, 151.

Indian colonies and prohibited American ships from carrying colonial goods. It was a blow to the United States' re-export trade. Thomas Jefferson's response was to switch to France and its Caribbean colonies. Trade in and consumption of coffee became a patriotic act. After the 1820s, the United States reached further south, to Brazil. By 1880, Americans consumed almost half a billion pounds of coffee a year.[115] Care must be taken, however, not to produce nationalist caricatures. Nations were not monocultures. American revolutionaries had boycotted British tea, but in the nineteenth century tea was almost as popular as coffee. The Japanese customarily drank tea, but migrants returning from Brazil also created a taste for coffee; the first Brazilian café opened in Tokyo in 1908. Britons were a nation of tea drinkers, but never exclusively so. By 1900, they drank as much chocolate as the Spanish, belying the idea of a fault line between a sober, rational Protestant North and a debauched Catholic South.

Commodity biographies can have a triumphant, Whiggish flavour, with one exotic food conquering all before it. History written by the winner tends to miss the remarkable resilience of many local and class-based tastes. Social emulation could be counteracted by an equally strong sense that each class should stick to its own food. Such norms acted as a buffer against national homogenization as well as global fusion. Averages hide large disparities between classes and regions. In France, for example, sugar consumption increased, but most of it ended up in bourgeois mouths. According to one estimate in 1873, a Parisian labourer made do with a total of 10 grams of sugar a day – two spoonfuls – a fraction of the British sweet tooth. In the rest of the country, workers, miners and farmers largely abstained from sugar altogether. If at all, sugar was used as a condiment (like pepper or salt), or for medication, administered to the sick. A 1906 survey by a Paris hospital found that the majority of labourers disliked sweet things: sugar spoiled one's appetite and weakened one's vigour. Sweets and pastries were something for leisured elites, not workers, who turned to red meat, cheese and wine for physical strength. It is, therefore, dubious to see a pre-existing taste for sugar as a European gateway for tropical foods. Coffee, too, had some difficulty winning over workers. In Paris, sans-culottes had already acquired a taste for coffee at the time of the French Revolution, and it appeared in working-class cafés. Outside Paris, though, the uptake was more modest. One canteen in Lyons served a good thousand meals a day in 1896 but merely thirty-seven cups of coffee.[116]

Tea and sugar were more widespread in the first industrial nation,

Britain, but to see cause and effect here is misleading. Industrialization did not need sucrose or caffeine. It proceeded just as well with beer and wine. Belgium, France and Germany all industrialized while their factory labourers still tasted very little sugar. In fact, the people with the biggest sweet tooth at the end of the nineteenth century lived down under, in agrarian Queensland – consuming around 60kg per person a year. Coffee's popular success as a sober and industrious drink was more a consequence of industrialization than its stimulant.

In continental Europe, the real take-off came in the 1870s–'80s, as Brazil cut deeper and deeper into its forests and prices fell. An inspector in Düsseldorf, Germany, noted how 'the working classes now routinely drink coffee three times a day'.[117] Industrial firms and social reformers opened canteens and coffee huts. It is easy, however, to exaggerate the intake of caffeine. In 1909, after twenty years of activity, the Union of People's Coffee-Halls served Hamburg workers 75,000 cups of coffee but 2 million cups of caffeine-free substitute coffee. At home, many families diluted coffee beans with the cheaper chicory.[118] Temperance groups championed coffee as the energizing antidote to alcohol. Whether it worked is another question. Port cities such as Hamburg were never sober. In fact, the Union of Coffee-Halls served alcoholic drinks as well. In France, male workers took their coffee with brandy, in the Netherlands and Germany with rum or schnapps. If the rise of industrial society meant more coffee, it also involved more liquor. Krupp, the big German steel-and-arms manufacturer, served its workers seventy times as much beer as coffee.[119]

By 1914, sugar, coffee and chocolate had conquered those parts they had previously found difficult to reach. National food cultures and eating and drinking habits were becoming more integrated. In contrast to the early luxury phase, led by Jesuits, merchants and scholars, the driving forces behind this later mass phase were business, state and nutritional science. Exotic beverages were pushed as essential foods for strong industrial nations, no longer the discerning choice of the refined few. Industrial firms rationalized the work schedule to boost workers' energy and concentration. Instead of a long pause in the middle of the day, firms introduced shorter meals and coffee breaks. Some handed out free coffee in place of drinking water. An additional push came from the state and science. German prisons and hospitals put coffee on their list of staple foods in the 1870s.[120] A new alliance emerged, made up of the army, nutritional experts and national beet-sugar interests. Sugar's calorific energy, they preached, made it vital for national strength. In 1876, the

French army included sugar and coffee in a soldier's daily ration. Around this time, the Dutch technology of extracting the butter from cocoa unlocked chocolate's potential as a mass consumer good. Cocoa powder and chocolate bars were born. Unlike tea or coffee, chocolate had nutritional value. It now shook off its association with leisured ladies and idle priests and was repackaged as a 'flesh-forming' and 'heat-giving' energy drink for North Pole explorers, athletes, workers and busy housewives. In Cadbury advertisements, Professor Cavill swore its cocoa was 'the most sustaining beverage he could take during his swim across the Straits of Dover'.[121] Rebranded as a 'motor for health', with testimonials from doctors and the medical journal the *Lancet*, cocoa entered infant food. Children's palates would never be the same.

By 1900, nationalism was at least as vital a prop for this mass consumer culture as imperialism. Many small states without colonies introduced ordinary folk to chocolate through their armies. In Switzerland, Suchard started sending 'military chocolate' to barracks in the 1870s and sold chocolate in the shape of bullets (*Schokoladen-patronen*). The first soldiers to try it spat it out, but it soon became a standard ration. Some recruits ate the dry powder pure.[122] Once the 'food of the gods' for the Aztecs, cocoa had evolved into a mass-produced national commodity: the food of the people.

Things travelled further and further, stretching commodity chains to unprecedented lengths by 1900. Already in the late seventeenth century, almost 150,000 metric tons of grain crossed the Baltic Sea each year, largely ending up in the bellies of Dutch burghers.[123] In the second half of the nineteenth century, liberal policies, faster steamships and cooling technologies lowered prices and stretched the food chain to new extremes. In the 1830s, a Londoner's wheat and flour came from 2,430 miles away. By the 1870s, it was almost double that. It was now that many foodstuffs became international travellers. A Londoner's butter, cheese and eggs used to come from a few hundred miles away. By the 1870s, they took a journey of over 1,300 miles.[124]

Together, liberal empire and mass consumption changed the visibility and value attached to the place of origin. Some goods suffered geographic displacement. Coffee in the late nineteenth century was like air travel in the late twentieth. Once everyone could go there, exotic places lost their charm. Distance became affordable and, consequently, devalued. To ordinary consumers in 1900, it mattered that coffee had a kick and was cheap, not where it came from, as it had for earlier connoisseurs. A few places preserved an interest in the Orient, for example smoking salons in Berlin with Moorish interiors but, in general, the more goods entered the mass market, the more the exotic was left behind. Blending beans and processing foods meant that value was added in Europe. Coffee might not have been home grown but the appearance, packaging and taste was European. In the early 1900s, most Britons drank a concoction made of beans from Mysore (for body), Kenya (for acidity) and Mokka (for aroma).

For drug foods in general, the age of mass consumption was strikingly conservative in character. *Fin-de-siècle* Europeans drank more coffee and tea than ever before, but they pretty much lost the curiosity about new, untried foreign substances that had driven their forebears to experiment with coffee, tobacco and cocoa in the earlier age of luxury and exploration. European tastebuds dulled. Once caffeinated drinks had taken hold, it was difficult for new stimulating rivals to dislodge them. No khat houses opened in Vienna or Paris in 1900, and no popular taste for chewing betel nut developed. There were some practical and aesthetic reasons for this – the khat leaf, which contains cathinone, loses its stimulant force during shipping, while chewing betel produces red saliva and wears down the teeth's calcium; chewing khat can also lead to constipation.[125] Still, black teeth and smoke had not stopped tobacco in earlier centuries. What was decisive was culture and ideological bias; after all, since the 1950s, khat could have been easily shipped by air fresh from East Africa, but, instead, most Western countries have banned it. Tea and coffee promoted a culture of politeness that discriminated against spitting, except in the baseball dugout. Chewing khat is very slow and relaxing, and quite the opposite of the purposeful atmosphere of an eighteenth-century coffee house. And tropical articles such as khat had the added weight of new-found European supremacy against them. Unlike Arabian coffee or Chinese tea in the seventeenth century, Europeans in 1900 associated khat with racially inferior people in East African colonies; some continue to do so today. Chewing khat appeared a barbarian habit, not a civilized practice to be emulated. In the West, khat became stigmatized as a dangerous drug.[126] Where exotic extracts made it, as kola did, their origin was disguised, blended into a soft drink and packaged as all-American. When it came to exotic drugs, therefore, the era of free trade was paradoxically less open and vibrant than mercantilism had been.

Value followed power. From around 1850, exotic goods came to bear the stamp of a new racism and nationalism. Empires and nations started to authenticate goods for their subjects, highlighting certain places of origin and erasing others. Victorians branded Chinese tea as 'slow poison' from untrustworthy 'heathen[s]', no match for the new Assam leaves from colonial plantations safely in British hands. Imperial origin became a sign of racial quality control. Experts doubted whether the colouring in green tea caused serious harm, but the adverts and testimonials were relentless, from stories of toenails found in Chinese tea to claims that it was 'mixture of tea-dust with dirt and sand, agglutinated into a mass with a gummy matter, most probably manufactured from rice-flour . . . lastly, dried and coloured . . . either with black lead, if for black tea, or with Prussian blue, gypsum, or turmeric, if intended for green'.[127] In 1884, a health exhibition, with over 4 million visitors, displayed the superiority of Indian plantations managed by 'skilled Englishmen'.[128] Two years later, the Colonial and Indian Exhibition featured a tea court which served 300,000 cups of Indian tea. A decade later, and Indian tea had overtaken its Chinese rival. Origin and the food chain mattered, where it served an imperial purpose.[129]

This was a movement in which local actors manipulated the centre as well as the other way around. The Indian tea syndicate, made up of the Assam Tea Company and similar firms, used the exhibitions to market their colonial goods directly to consumers, circumventing metropolitan merchants. Similarly, in France, it was the peasant vine growers and *négociants* (merchant-manufacturers) of the Marne who successfully led the campaign to have their sparkling wine recognized as the only authentic Champagne in the world.[130] Nationalism's belief in the unique personality of the soil was converted into the idea of *terroir*, which offered a flavour of the nation to consumers who should learn to appreciate the distinctiveness of their own grapes and cheeses. Champagne's *appellation d'origine* in 1908 signalled the coming of a new era of a local–national politics of origin, which brought us Chianti Classico, Lübecker Marzipan and Melton Mowbray Pork Pies. Local authentication was part of the explosion of brands in the pre-war years, which itself was a response to the growing mass market for manufactured foods with its many unknown new products and fears of adulteration; in Germany alone, 75,000 brands of food, drinks and tobacco were registered between 1894 and 1914.[131]

If the creation of value moved into the hands of advanced Western consumer societies, it also had a boomerang effect. Once wine and coffee were associated with superior European culture, overseas elites adopted them, too. The earlier spatial logic of luxury was now reversed. How far goods had travelled mattered less to consumers in Boston,

Paris and London but ever more to local elites in Santiago and Buenos Aires, who ordered direct from London or the Bon Marché department store in Paris. Chile and Argentina used to be thought of as marginal for British exports but, in fact, they grew into a fast-expanding market for British cottons. By 1880, inhabitants in the Southern Cone received ten times as much cotton as they had in 1815. But Latin American consumers were never passive sheep. 'Did you really suppose,' one Bahia merchant wrote to a British textile trader in 1814, 'because you shipped them, the Portuguese were obliged to buy them? The fact is that your goods could not be sold at any price . . . We could not compel people to buy goods they did not want.'[132] Locals wanted handkerchiefs in the newest styles and patterns, and British merchants were busy assembling fashionable samples.

Already in the 1820s, travellers noted how the craze for British goods was cutting its way into the Colombian interior. 'The ale which came from England was considered a great luxury' by local officials. In Popayán, in the Valle del Cauca, a merchant had a Broadwood piano brought all the way from England; on the last stretch from Buenaventura, porters had to carry it on their backs across the mountains. When John Potter Hamilton, Britain's First Commissioner to the new state of Colombia, reached the secluded valley, he was stunned to find his assigned bedroom and curtains 'completely in the French style', with eau de Cologne, Windsor soap and brushes on a side table.[133] A good deal of the English goods were smuggled into Colombia via Jamaica. In Chile, maté imports from nearby Argentina declined, as the elite turned to coffee and tea from far-away India. Local fermented *chichas* was uncouth. People of distinction served French-style wine in French-style houses behind French windows. From the 1850s, Chile cultivated its own Medoc.[134]

Empire made origin matter more than ever before at the periphery. For settlers in Canada and Australia and other parts of the Anglo-world, a can of Bristol tripe and a bottle of Worcester sauce contained a sense of 'home'.[135] This extended beyond white-settler elites. In British Honduras (now Belize), the imperial experience left behind tastebuds that favoured smoked tongue, brandy and lemon cordial over local foods. For slaves and their descendants, eating English food was a way of claiming respect and equality, not unlike the emancipated slaves who sported Western clothes in Zanzibar. Such longing for long-distance luxury goods reinforced a developmental model based on the export of minerals and raw materials – nitrate in the case of Chile, mahogany in that of British Honduras – in exchange for processed foods and manufactured goods. British Honduras even imported its tapioca from the metropole. This gave commodities a rather unpredictable spin in the game of imperial power and resistance. On the one hand, the taste for imported Scottish whiskey, Horlicks malted milk and Oxford sausages asserted the supremacy of the imperial palate. On the other, this transfer made colonial consumers more stubborn and less responsive to the designs of the imperial centre. British Honduras's trade deficit was a direct result of its hunger for British goods, and a heavy drain on Westminster. Once imperial tastes had formed, people were unlikely to respond to pleas to 'buy local', as the Colonial Office learnt the hard way in the inter-war years.[136]

In the era of the 'new imperialism' in the 1880s–'90s, imperial symbols and slogans gained ground in advertising. The craze for African explorer H. M. Stanley ('Dr Livingstone, I presume') was an advertiser's dream. Stanley appeared in ads for soap and Bovril, and sipped tea with the Emin Pasha in his tent at Kavalli, on the southern shore of Lake Albert. 'Stanley: "Well, Emin, old fellow, this Cup of the United Kingdom Tea Company's Tea makes us forget all our troubles." Emin: "So it does, my boy."' What else was the Emin to say? In a pioneering study, the literary scholar Thomas Richards argued that these imperial adverts showed the 'homogenizing power of the commodity'.[137] Ads for Bovril and Pear's soap used African settings and placed indigenous people all over the world in the same subservient position: as grateful recipients of civilizing goods. The nineteenth century, Anne McClintock has argued in an influential study of race and gender, saw a shift from scientific racism to 'commodity racism'. Exhibitions, advertisements and branded goods meant that 'as domestic space became racialized, colonial space became domesticated.'[138] The Pear's Soap advert of a white boy scrubbing a black boy to white purity and progress is a classic example.

Yet, looking through adverts and newspapers of the period, what is noteworthy is not that racial images appear but that they do so far less often than we might expect. The picture of a grinning 'sambo' serving up cocoa was exceptionally rare. On the contrary, the representation of goods was increasingly national. In 1881, Cadbury's adverts still showed the entire food chain of its cocoa, from African workers collecting the pods to the roasting process, the cooling cellar and the packing machines in its Bournville headquarters outside Birmingham.[139] By the 1900s, Africa and Africans had all but disappeared. Cadbury now advertised its cocoa as 'nature's best gift to mankind' but was silent about its origins. Cadbury's cocoa was 'the standard English article', 'the good Old English Cocoa', 'the typical cocoa of English manufacture'.[140] Where people appeared, they were white English scientists in testing rooms and white women workers in Bournville. It was they who guaranteed Cadbury's 'authentic' quality, what made it a 'perfect food', free of 'foreign substances'. The 'fresh air, wholesome exercise and bright surroundings', one advert explained, made for healthy workers, which in turn ensured the 'keenness on the part of every employee to assist in maintaining the rigid standard of purity that is required in everything bearing the name and mark of Cadbury Bournville'.[141] A British shopper would have been forgiven for thinking that Cadbury's cocoa grew in Bournville.

Cadbury was no peculiarity. The creation of milk chocolate added to the European makeover of exotic goods. Tobler turned chocolate into a 'Swiss' article, with a bear on an alpine rock, while Milka advertised happy milkmaids amidst alpine cows. Colonial and oriental associations never entirely disappeared: Karl Hofer's 1900 poster for Kaffee-Messmer showed a Moor drinking Turkish coffee, as did some coffee shops in Berlin and Vienna. In France, advertisements for the Café du Comptoir de Colonies showed a black couple in loincloth and parasol leaning on coffee bags from Martinique and Guadeloupe (French colonies) as well as from Java (Dutch East Indies) (see Plate 17). Arguably, such ongoing representations benefited from a particular situation in France, where the Third Republic fixed colonial preferences for coffee, cocoa and a whole host of spices. Colonial goods were more visible here, partly because they were treated as such by the taxman: coffee from the French colonies paid 78 francs per 100kg instead of the 156 francs levied on foreign beans. Minstrel shows and African street sellers of chocolate did their bit to keep racial associations in the public eye.[142] In the 1930s, Hava advertised its authentic 'café du Bresil', showing its passage from the plantation to Le Havre. Racial images were most prominent in advertisements for Banania, a drink made of chocolate and banana flour. Even here, though, the true origin and producers were eventually driven out of the picture. The original recipe hailed from Nicaragua and was sourced in the French Antilles. In the First World War, Banania adverts replaced Antilles women with Senegalese soldiers. In Germany, people were more likely to see images of the Rhine on their package of coffee than palm trees. Black people appeared in only 3 per cent of all German coffee adverts. One company floated a brand made of purely colonial beans to please the Kaiser, but this was the exception.

What sold was the familiar – regional pride and national belonging – not the exotic. Locals bought 'Rheinland Kaffee', or 'Arminius Kaffee', named after the German warlord who annihilated the Roman army in the Teutoburg Forest in CE 9. At the 1893 world fair in Chicago, the candy manufacturer Stollwerck moulded 30,000 pounds of chocolate into a temple of Germania standing 38 feet tall; the French had 'Jeanne d'Arc' chocolate bars.[143] In the United States, coffee was advertised as 'New Orleans', marking the national point of entry rather than the place of origin. The global expansion of 'Italian' coffee since the 1950s would be the culmination of this new spatial reordering made possible by the European command of goods, processing and marketing.[144]

By 1900, Europeans and their cousins across the seas held the global reins of consumer culture more firmly in their hands than ever before. Industry and income lifted European demand to unrivalled heights. The rise of the mass market, however, was much more than a separate Western story. It was complemented by imperialism, which constructed a new material hierarchy between Europe and the rest of the world, between consumers and coolies. It was in the more liberal atmosphere of the nineteenth century that Europeans truly took command of global consumption. Power extended from commodities to knowledge, branding and value. It was the West that embraced 'the consumer'. That colonial rulers developed an increasingly visceral dislike of natives apparently mimicking their lifestyle did not, of course, extinguish their subjects' appetite for goods. What it did do was to justify paying Africans low wages or no wages – or, to use economic language, to depress their purchasing power. The promotion of the consumer in the West and their demotion in Africa were two sides in the widening geopolitical divide of economic fortunes. Empire wrote out the colonial producer from the world of goods as it was displayed, marketed and enjoyed. It was this that was, perhaps, the clearest demonstration of the power of empire to change the terms of consumption.

4

Cities

Cities consume. They feed off the surrounding countryside and spit out new goods and tastes. One hundred years ago, the great historian of capitalism Werner Sombart characterized sixteenth- and seventeenth-century Paris, Madrid and London as consuming cities par excellence. These cities were so dominant, he wrote, because they were the home of the two biggest consumers at the time: the court and the Church.[1] Catering for luxury made these cities the engine of modern capitalism. In his view, the period after the French Revolution witnessed the decline of the consumption city, as kings were overthrown and cardinals fled. True, there would be seaside resorts and retirement communities, but the future belonged to producing cities and port towns like Manchester and Marseilles. Sombart's contemporary Max Weber, one of sociology's founding fathers, similarly defined the consumer city by its 'non-productive' clientele, such as rentiers who drew interest on dividends or retirees in the 'pensionopolis' of Wiesbaden on the Rhine, the 'Nice of the North'.[2]

This neat distinction between consuming and producing cities, alas, has one weakness. All inhabitants consumed, including workers, traders, housewives and maids. And, in nineteenth-century Europe and the Americas, they did so increasingly in cities. The nineteenth century saw a deepening divide between urbanizing and de-urbanizing regions. In 1800, around 12 per cent of Europeans lived in towns. By 1910, it was 41 per cent. In Latin America, numbers rose more gently, to 20 per cent. China, by contrast, moved in the opposite direction, dropping from 12 per cent in 1600 to 6 per cent by 1900. Africa was largely untouched by cities, but even here there were boom-towns such as Cairo, where the population jumped from 250,000 in 1859 to 700,000 in 1914.[3] The period from around 1850 to 1920 saw a great transformation. Cities were not only getting bigger, they were consuming more, and faster. The best-known point of entry into this story has been through the doors of the department store. But this is to start

mid-stream. For, in addition to shopping and spectacle, the city transformed the entire infrastructure of consumption and, with it, daily
routines, needs and entitlements. What constituted a 'civilized' way of
life changed for ever.

FLOW AND DISRUPTION

Right in the heart of the city a golden spot appeared, another here, a third
one there, then a fourth – it is impossible to say how quickly they spread,
let alone count them. One cannot imagine anything more beautiful, but
now comes the most beautiful part. The spots turn into lines, the lines
into figures; sparks join sparks . . . into endless avenues of light. Some,
which run across the valley, appear like the richest garlands of sparkling
flowers. Others, which crown the heights, resemble the outlines of fantastic buildings.

Paris had switched on its lights. *La ville lumière*, the city of light,
entranced travellers. Illumination made its temptations irresistible.
Paris was like 'Circe's magic castle with shining halls full of music and
sweet women . . . with brilliant streets, with arcades full of sparkling
jewels, shining eyes on one side of the shop windows and longing and
yearning on the other.'[4]

In 1800, Paris and London made do with a few thousand oil lamps.
Most areas were plunged in darkness outside of daylight hours. By
1867, when the above impressions appeared, Paris was lit by around
20,000 gas lamps. By 1907, it had 54,000; London had as many as
77,000 lights, most of them fitted with incandescent burners; each
burnt 140 litres of gas a night.[5] When the First World War broke out in
1914, Paris was seventy times brighter than during the 1848 revolution.
The famous lament by Edward Grey, the British Foreign Secretary, that
the lights were going out all over Europe, was as moving in August
1914 as it would have been meaningless three generations earlier.

Gas, water and transport transformed the emotional and physical
space of the city and, with it, the rhythm of urban life. Streets, neighbourhoods and their inhabitants were networked, connected through
pipes, gas lines, the omnibus and the tram. Electricity would add
another layer, but before the 1920s it was mainly just used to power
trams and trains. In the second half of the nineteenth century, any
modern city worth the name aspired to be networked. By the 1870s,

Buenos Aires, which had around 180,000 inhabitants, had 268km of gas pipes. In Edo (Tokyo), the first gas lights were lit in the Ginza district in 1874. In the most developed corners of Europe, such networks were built in even smaller towns, such as Yeovil in Somerset or Hamilton in Scotland, which in 1913 provided gas to almost 3,000 homes each. British firms were especially active in spreading the know-how and capital from the booming towns at home to cities abroad, an imperialism of gas and water that stretched from Rosario in Argentina to Sydney in Australia.[6]

These were works in progress rather than perfectly functioning systems. Urban planners and engineers were prone to compare their creations to hearts and arteries. Yet the city was not a body, organic and circular. Miles of pipes meant miles of roads broken up. Water leaked, gas exploded. Water and gas were natural monopolies with huge start-up costs. Networks sparked conflicts about who should run them and who should pay for what. And they impinged on established patterns of everyday life. With the flow of gas and water came battles over the very essence of consumption. Were baths and water closets 'basic needs' or 'luxuries'? For thousands of years, people had lived without gas and running water. Their adoption would not be as simple as flipping a switch.

Gas and water consumption was rising dramatically in the course of the nineteenth century. Initially, most of it was for industry. Gas had been first used in mills in the 1790s and business remained the main consumer into the 1870s, followed by cities themselves. Many providers overcharged their small private customers to keep their bigger, commercial ones happy. Liverpool was one of the first cities to woo households and small shops with discounts for 'perennial users' in the 1840s. It was only in the 1880s and '90s, however, that gas entered the home in earnest, helped by rising incomes, cheaper prices and the slot meter. The slot meter was ideal for working-class tenants who managed tight and fluctuating budgets and moved house frequently. By 1913, Leeds provided gas to 112,000 consumers, twice the number thirty years earlier; almost half were on the slot meter and 15 per cent had gas cookers. New gas stoves, which doubled the radiant heat of the older convection model, provided warmth and comfort. In Zurich by 1908, most gas was no longer for lighting but for cooking and heating. Three quarters of all tenements now had gas. Consumption had almost tripled in ten years to 1 billion cubic feet per year. London, on the eve of the First World War, consumed a staggering 50 billion. Latin American cities such as São Paulo were not far behind.[7]

It was in the same period that cities developed their modern thirst for water. In 1802, it was estimated that the average Parisian made do with five litres of water a day. By the end of the century, it was more than ten times that. Anyone who thinks heavy water use is a recent problem should look at the United States in this period. American cities quickly established themselves as *über*consumers. The bigger the city, the greater its thirst. Small New England towns supplied around 35 to 45 gallons per head per day in the 1860s. In Boston, Chicago and other large cities, it ranged from 60 to 100 gallons. Atlanta in 1884 pumped a phenomenal 225 gallons (855 litres) per person, ten times the amount in Madrid or Berlin.[8] Growing cities needed bigger reservoirs, aqueducts and ever more distant sources. Wells and water-carriers gave way to piped supply. The initial demand was not from private individuals but from business – factory owners and commercial users, who dominated town councils and pressed for more, better water for their industries. The discovery of waterborne disease also pointed to the need for clean, abundant water for everyone. Public fountains and free water for schools became a matter of civic pride.

In water as with gas it was in the last quarter of the century that private consumption took over. A broad phalanx of health reformers, philanthropists and commercial interests urged people to consume more. That cleanliness was next to godliness was nothing new in Europe and North America, but in the eighteenth century it had referred to neat appearance and clothing.[9] It was in the following century that the emphasis shifted to the body. Washing oneself, reformers argued, was vital for civic life as well as public health: as long as the better-off reached for smelling salts when they passed one of the 'great unwashed', social conflict was inevitable. Yet it was not only the poor who were unclean. Three decades after cholera was identified as a waterborne disease in 1854, London's Dr John Simon was emphatic in his sanitary handbook that many among the better-off classes, too, had yet to reach a 'high standard of sensibility to dirt'.[10]

Epidemiology, the germ theory of disease and sanitary reforms had social democratic implications. Infectious disease could jump classes. No one was safe unless everyone was cleaner. This concerned public authorities, water companies, builders and landlords, but also private conduct. Regular washing meant self-respect and respect for others. Elementary schools held cleanliness checks to inculcate new habits. In France, exercises drummed into pupils the connection between hygiene, decency and love. A mother did not want to kiss a daughter with a dirty face, one dictation read in the 1890s. Being nice and studious, another explained, was no compensation for being dirty: friends would turn away in disgust. 'Conjugate: I know my duty. I wash my hands.'[11] Dirt, then, bred social exclusion as well as disease. The washroom was to be the training ground of little citizens, soap and running water its civic curriculum.

By 1900, the tap and the gas light were as much symbols of urban modernity as the museum and the department store. The volumes of water pumped to city dwellers increased dramatically. Water closets and bathrooms added exponential pressures – with every flush, two to three gallons went down the pan. One London engineer found that, on average, taking a public or private bath used between 90 and 120 US gallons.[12] 'Constant supply' was first introduced in London in the 1870s–'90s. Instead of having intermittent service, pumped during certain hours, then stored in tanks and cisterns, cities set out to provide water at high pressure around the clock, on demand. Constant supply epitomized the universal ambition of networked consumption: flow was to be a twenty-four-hour reality for everyone. London in 1913 pumped over 200 million gallons to its 7 million inhabitants every day and night. By 1912, Leeds supplied its 480,000 inhabitants with 26 million gallons a day via 510 miles of pipes. The Alexandria Water Co. took 5 billion gallons from the Nile to 400,000 people.

Such triumphs of engineering, however, should not distract from limits and failures. In most cities, constant supply remained the exception. On the eve of the First World War, when all of London was on it, only every fifth Parisian was. Foreign students visiting Paris were advised to boil their water for at least fifteen minutes. In Hamburg, water was pumped unfiltered from the Elbe, spreading cholera in 1892. In Shanghai, a city of a million people, the waterworks company supplied only 30,000 premises – in the thousands of squatter huts, occupants dug their own shallow water holes. Hangzhou, the big city at the southern end of the Grand Canal, got its waterworks only in 1931; twenty years later, a mere 1 per cent there had piped water. Even in inter-war Europe, where running water had become a defining distinction between city people and country folk, many cities lacked a complementary sewage system; in Italy, two thirds of homes had no running water as late as the 1950s.[13]

To understand the changing patterns of urban consumption we cannot look at the network just from the centre outwards, as engineers and urban planners tended to do. We also need to view it from the other direction, that is, from the point of view of the women, men and children who opened the tap, went to the standpipe or ran a bath. Aggregate demand was made up of many diverse everyday practices. There was no typical networked city, just as there was no universal consumer.

Cities, districts – even neighbouring streets – had unequal access to water. Location, class and housing type mattered. In the Berlin neighbourhood of Louisenstadt in 1900, for example, workers fortunate enough to live at the back of an apartment block with more prestigious, already connected flats at the front were twice as likely to have running water as their comrades elsewhere in the city. Moreover, running water is one thing, having a private bathroom, toilet and hot water something else. Water closets spread quickly from the 1860s in some cities, such as Liverpool, London, Boston and New York. In others, toilets strained already overstretched systems and led the authorities to discourage, even prohibit them, as in Manchester. By the 1880s, most urban Americans still emptied their waste into cesspools. In Tampere, Finland's first industrial city, dry and ash toilets continued to predominate well into the twentieth century. The Municipal Council in Shanghai passed 'Foreign Building Rule 76' in 1905: 'no connection shall be made to any drain, public or private, whereby ordure will be discharged into the same.' It reserved the right to grant special permission for 'an approved watercloset system' upon condition that the content of any cesspool was removed by the council at whatever cost it saw fit. In British slums in the 1950s, homes had televisions and vacuum cleaners but neither indoor toilets nor hot water. Across Europe, a separate bathroom remained a luxury into the 1960s.[14]

In Asia, it was the treaty-ports – colonial mini-states where Europeans and Japanese enjoyed trading privileges and extraterritorial sovereignty – that introduced piped water. In Tianjin (Tientsin), near the Bohai Gulf, a British company started to provide the British settlement with tap water in 1899. Four years later, it was joined by the Tientsin Native City Waterworks Company. Few Chinese residents had the money or fittings necessary for running water in the home. Instead, this Chinese–Western joint venture built a network of street hydrants. People went to a 'water shop', where they bought a ticket, allowing them to fill their buckets at a hydrant; Beijing operated a similar system. Instead of dealing with thousands of individual customers, the Tientsin water company took its earnings from one or other of the five hundred franchised 'water shops', a kind of liquid McDonald's. Neither the British nor the Tientsin system, however, managed to make a clean break with established customs. British elites had water pipes going into their homes, but no pipes taking the sewage away. Water carriers, well organized in guilds, were understandably reluctant to collect the dirty water only. The hydrants, meanwhile, offered carriers new commercial opportunities. Buckets were filled halfway then topped up from the river and the mix sold on as company water to unsuspecting customers.[15] Networks, in other words, were porous, not closed, and self-regulating. There was a flow between imported, modern systems and established local ones. Most people washed and drank from both.

In Europe and North America, water carriers disappeared from city streets, but running water did not always flow smoothly. Many working-class families shared a tap in the yard. Water pressure could be uneven or lacking altogether. In Philadelphia in the 1880s, a respectable engineer had the water brought up in cans to his bathroom, to the amazement of a visiting English colleague.[16] And constant supply brought new vulnerabilities. Not only did tenants come to expect running water around the clock, but so did landlords. Cisterns were troublesome to look after and took up valuable space. Much better to rip them out, landlords concluded, in poorer neighbourhoods like the East End of London, with the full support of local authorities keen to eliminate potential reservoirs of dirt and disease. When a series of frosts and droughts in the 1890s brought the constant system to its knees and forced water companies to switch back to intermittent service during the summer, East Enders were left in a stinking mess, unable to catch the water when it was turned on, let alone flush their toilets (see Plate 26).[17]

The spread of gas and electricity networks was similarly uneven. Gas, like water, promised to civilize the home. Adverts for early gas stoves showed housewives leaping in joy from the dirty hell of coal to the paradise of clean fuel. Sometimes, men, too, were urged to throw off the shackles of the time-consuming routine of heating their bathwater with briquettes or charcoal. What running water did for water closets, baths and, later, showers, gas did for toasters, irons and other domestic helpers. The home turned into a 'consumption junction'.[18] Gas and electric labour-saving devices entered American homes in earnest only in the 1920s, and Europe and Asia after the Second World War. When Georges Brassens, the singer-songwriter, moved to the 14th arrondissement in Paris in 1944, the house in impasse Florimont had neither gas, electricity nor running water.[19] As late as 1949 in Shanghai, a mere 2 per cent had gas. The foundations, however, were already being put in place by gas networks fifty years earlier. For social reformers, gas brought happiness to the home and safety to the streets. The slot meter enabled the poor to enjoy better light, promoting domestic happiness. Temperance advocates held out the slot-gas stove as the greatest enemy of the publican. One penny cooked a healthy meal. Instead of running off to the pub for a bite to eat and a bit of warmth, and getting drunk in the process, husbands stayed at home. Economy, family life and public morals all gained – it was even a step towards female emancipation. Women lecturers stressed how gas freed housewives from staying at home to start and maintain a fire. Outside, it was hoped, gas lights would eliminate the hiding places of thieves and prostitutes.[20]

Yet light and darkness bounced off each other. Illumination was incomplete and had paradoxical effects. Gas lighting most effectively enhanced the spectacular atmosphere of spaces devoted to entertainment. Our visitor to Paris was not for nothing so taken with gas-lit shop windows and restaurants. Gas lights expanded the repertoire of magical illusion. In Buenos Aires, the Argentine Theatre on Reconquista Street switched on its lights in 1856. Libraries extended their hours, although the sulphuric acid produced by the combustion of frequently impure gas had the unfortunate side effect of destroying more than one fine book.[21] In the home, however, the much-lauded social benefits of lighting were counteracted by fears that gas, when burnt, overexcited the organs and led to blood clots. For decorators, almost as terrifying was the effect on wall hangings and soft furnishings; they championed electricity instead. In bourgeois apartments in Paris, gas in the 1880s was mainly used in corridors and antechambers – in the dining room and intimate spaces, candles were said to be much better for illuminating the faces of guests.[22]

The writer Jun'ichirō Tanizaki worried that street lighting would destroy the appreciation of shadows in Japanese aesthetics.[23] But in the streets, too, lighting remained patchy. Most cities, even large ones, remained a far cry from the Parisian ideal of the nocturnal city decked in garlands of light. Beirut introduced gas lights in 1889, but these were planted at street corners only. At night, whistles flew through the air, as police signalled to pedestrians at the next corner when it was safe to cross the road in the darkness.[24] In Edo, Kabuki theatres were lit by gas from the 1870s but hardly any streets in the plebeian Low City had lighting. Even London, with its tens of thousands of lights, was known to be 'the best and the worst lighted city in the world'. In 1911, photometers had difficulty picking up the dim light in poorer areas.[25] The axial lighting of thoroughfares was a frequent target of complaint. Lights suspended in the middle of the street left bus passengers jumping off into the shadows and put pedestrians at risk. In cities that burnt a lot of coal, fog sometimes overwhelmed gaslights for days. Mr Goodenough, a London engineer, noted in 1910 how 'he had gone down [from his flat], and stood at the foot of the column, and could not see the light, though the lamp was only 18 feet above the road-level.' And where there is light, there is shadow. In the City of London, the epicentre of the world economy, the lights on Cannon Street left triangular patches of darkness, creating dangerous 'refuges for objectionable persons'.[26] The more cities were lit, the more darkness inspired fear and fascination. For every additional watt, there was another Gothic story of metropolitan shadowlands.[27]

Gas and water confronted cities with unprecedented challenges. One was to decide who should provide them. Massive investments were required. Initially, these were shouldered by private firms that, in exchange, secured monopolies with price guarantees for several decades. These arrangements were a source of endless conflict about fair prices, quality and supply. Shareholders had little interest in connecting remote neighbourhoods or carrying water from hills and rivers far away. From the 1860s, more and more cities were taking on the job of providing consumers directly. By 1880, there were more public than private waterworks in British and American towns. Sweden was solidly municipalized by 1913, and in France most communes had also taken over, although Paris still received its water from the Compagnie Générale des Eaux. Spain was a singular exception to this trend, in part because its towns historically lacked strong civic authorities. In London, with its fragmented administration, public takeover of water was also delayed until 1902.[28]

This movement is known as 'municipal socialism', though the driving force behind it had little to do with socialist parties, which were still in their infancy. The main pressure came from urban growth and the limits of nature. Unlike food and clothing, water became more, not less, expensive in the late nineteenth century. Urban sprawl meant longer pipes to suburbs and more distant, expensive sources. Private companies had maximum prices set by legislators early on, and so had little incentive to invest. Cities were forced to take over. Many businessmen were happy to swallow the pill of public ownership as long as it ensured enough water for their factories. In gas, the opposite logic was at work. Unlike water, gas was highly profitable, thanks to technological innovations. Especially for new, expanding cities without a strong revenue base, it was an attractive cash cow. As one historian has suggested, we should really be talking of 'municipal capitalism'.[29] It was the profits from gas that allowed cities to emerge as major providers of public consumption, from parks and libraries to playgrounds and swimming pools.

What has been less appreciated is that the challenges for consumers were equally profound. Water and gas raised vexed questions about the very essence of consumption. Was water a 'gift of God' or a commodity? If the latter, what should be its price and how did you make people pay? At how many gallons did 'essential' use become 'luxury'? From around 1850, many cities were caught in a fifty-year war over these questions. It was in these battles that many citizens for the first time came together in 'consumers' leagues'. Some householders and shopkeepers felt robbed by their private monopoly providers and set up their own bodies. In Paris they formed the Union des Consommateurs de Gaz Parisien (1879). In Marseilles and several provincial cities, small traders and restaurateurs tried to force down prices in the 1890s by boycotting the gas companies, without much success. Across the Channel, angry residents formed the South London Gas Consumers' Mutual Association.[30] Households were charged for lights that often flickered and gas meters that exaggerated – hence the Victorian saying 'You lie like a gas meter.' Engineers tore their hair out over how to stop people misreading their meters – the middle dial moved counter-clockwise – from manipulating them with magnets, or, worse, dangerously enlarging tiny gas openings with the help of a local plumber. Gas and electricity could not be sold by the kilo. What exactly were people buying: voltage, or energy and candle power? When voltage dropped, the lights dimmed, but the meters kept turning. In Paris, in 1893, the Compagnie Parisienne de l'Air Comprimé was fined and lost its monopoly for routinely supplying low voltage.[31]

Battles over water took grievances to a new level. Water, like bread or sugar, could be sold by the kilo, exactly one litre, and this was what water carriers had done for aeons. As networks spread, however, water underwent a metamorphosis. Companies metered big customers by volume, but this made little sense for millions of small private households. Meters were too expensive and started to spread only from the 1880s. In their place, providers resorted to rough rules of thumb. In some countries, the charge was based on the number of individuals in a household. In the United States, the frontage of a house was used to estimate the number and comfort of the people within. In Britain, land-lords paid water rates based on their local property tax, and then added a lump sum to the rent of their tenants. A frugal bachelor in his large villa paid more than his neighbour who lived with a large family in a smaller house next door.

Just as sanitary reforms were resolving the early-Victorian crisis of public health, new conflicts began to flare up over the rights and inter-ests of consumers. The first battles were over water rates. Some openly called for a 'water parliament'. Others turned to law and consumer advocacy. In the early 1880s, a network of 'consumer defence leagues' sprang up across London with legal advice centres explaining to resi-dents how they had been overcharged by the private water companies and how to resist payment. A second front was opened by the battle of the bath. Legislation in the 1850s required water companies to provide water for 'domestic' use. The problem was that the standards of domes-tic life were in flux. The middle classes were installing baths and water closets. For water companies, these were not for 'essential' or 'domes-tic' use but 'extras', like gardens, to be charged in addition – 8s per item, to be precise, for a London house with an annual rental value between £100 and £200. The middle classes were furious. Sheffield's mayor said, 'if it was not a domestic use for a man to wash his skin and keep himself clean, he did not know what was.' His fellow townsmen formed a Bath Defence Association and boycotted extra charges. Some painted a red line around the inside of their baths to monitor the bath water actually used and demanded to be charged accordingly. Judges were not impressed and enforced existing rates.

Consumption and politics had come together in earlier boycotts of tea and slave-grown sugar and would do so again in campaigns against domestic sweatshops. What was remarkable about the water consumer movement was that it was initially led not by female shoppers but by propertied men. It was their stake in the community as tax-paying property owners that pushed these respectable Victorians into con-sumer activism. As far as they were concerned, they were fighting for their rights as citizens as much as for cheaper water for their homes. That they paid for water on the basis of local taxes (rather than gallons used) may explain why this wave of activism was so pronounced in Britain. The consumer was thus helped on to the political stage by a particular system of citizenship and government, based on the proper-tied male tax-payer. We should not romanticize these activists. Cities were divided. Many respectable townsmen took a myopic view: why should a city spend their hard-earned tax-payers' money on bigger waterworks or other improvements to benefit the masses who paid no taxes at all?[32] But nor should we ignore their role in introducing consumer rights into politics.

Droughts in the 1890s opened a final, third offensive in the water wars. By now, Londoners were used to constant supply, which made the return of taps running dry all the more irritating. Attacks on water companies now came from workers and women, progressive liberals and socialists, as well as the propertied classes.[33]

Consumer activists talked about rights, but what about their responsibilities? One reason why 'the consumer' moved to the centre of debate was that water companies laid scarcities and high prices at their door. It was the 'wasteful' consumer who was to blame, not the networks, their engineers or shareholders. Everywhere, contemporaries were prisoners of a simple, guiding assumption: progress involved higher levels of consumption; indeed, demanded it. 'When iron pipes and high-pressure engines were introduced,' Archibald Dobbs, the lawyer who spearheaded the consumer leagues in London, wrote in 1890, 'a much larger quantity of water was used. The requirements of householders are *naturally and properly always on the rise*: the standard of comfort constantly improves.'[34] In New York, a decade later, when the city was pondering what to do as it was fast exhausting the flow of the Croton River, a detailed report concluded: 'Water should be supplied in the most lavish abundance and instead of restricting its use, every inducement should be held out to encourage a greater, or more lavish use than is now prevalent.'[35] Asking citizens to be more economical was unimaginable. This left waste as the only target.

The literature is full of figures of consumption per person. These need to be treated with caution. Cities did not know what individuals consumed. They recorded how much was pumped. In between lay cracked pipes and leaking taps. A British inquiry produced the following exchange in 1892 between the Royal Commission and the eminent engineer Sir Frederick Bramwell, chairman of the East Surrey Water Company. 'The population of London having been . . . accustomed to consume large quantities of water,' the commission asked, 'do you not think that there would be very great difficulty in bringing down the consumption?' 'May I take objection to your word "consuming",' Bramwell interjected. 'One moment. I used the word "consuming" because I thought it was the most general word that we could take.' Bramwell disagreed: he preferred 'provided'.[36] What was consumed depended on one's perspective. Was it only the water that was purposely used for washing, cooking and drinking, or should it also include the many gallons lost through dripping taps? Might it even include all the water lost through leaking mains, a kind of invisible consumption?

Contemporaries were divided, and for good reason. In some areas, waste exceeded personal use. In Shoreditch, just north of the City of London, residents were supplied with 37 gallons a head a day in 1882. Waste inspectors and improved fittings brought this down by half. In the slightly posher Finsbury Park nearby, inspectors found that in June of that year people used 18 gallons during the day but 105 gallons whilst asleep – 'letting their hoses run all night in the gardens'.[37] If anything, constant supply and modern conveniences encouraged such practices. Laundry was left under constant running water to save on soap, the toilet flush nailed open to keep pan and pipes clean. In Newark, New Jersey, during the harsh winters of 1895–8, inhabitants kept the taps open to prevent pipes from freezing, stretching the city's supply to its limits. An educated guess is that around 1880, before metering spread, European cities lost between a quarter and a half of pumped water through leakage. This was mainly due to faulty plumbing and worn-out faucets, rather than wilful waste – 'tenants do not rob landlords,' the most comprehensive inquiry into metering concluded.[38]

The more cities were built upward into the skies, the less waste there was. After the greater number of baths and WCs, this was the other reason why American figures were so stunningly high. New American cities were less compact than old European ones, and more detached houses meant more fixtures and pipes. In 1890 Berlin, each service pipe supplied seventy households. In Detroit, it was a mere handful. Put differently, if 30 per cent of water was lost through leakage, this meant 5.4 gallons per Berliner a day but 75 gallons in Detroit. These factors force us to revise actual consumption figures downward, but they do nothing to change the three-tier hierarchy that had emerged by 1900, with German cities at the bottom (5–30 gallons per head per day), British cities in the middle (17–40, with Glasgow ahead, thanks to the Scottish preference for a three-gallon flush); and Americans on top (30–100+ gallons). In 1903 spot checks in Manhattan – not yet metered – suggested 30 gallons were truly used by the average person, while over 50 gallons leaked away or could not be accounted for at all; another 50 gallons went on commercial and public use. Even this figure obscures class differences within the city. After deducting leakage, engineers found that

Thirsty cities: water consumption, 1870–1904

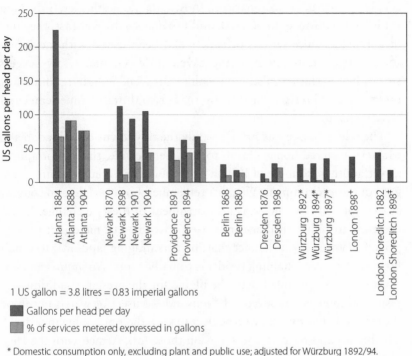

1 US gallon = 3.8 litres = 0.83 imperial gallons

■ Gallons per head per day

■ % of services metered expressed in gallons

* Domestic consumption only, excluding plant and public use; adjusted for Würzburg 1892/94.
† New River Company area (North London) with a mix of houses representative of London.
‡ After waste inspection and installation of fittings by the New River Company.

Source: J. H. Fuertes, *Waste of Water in New York* (1906); *Royal Commission on Water Supply* (1900),
Cd 25. Final Report; E. Grahn, ed., *Die Städtische Wasserversorgung im Deutschen Reiche* (1902); J. T. Fanning,
A Practical Treatise on Hydraulic and Water-supply Engineering, 15th edn (1902).

a typical resident in a Brooklyn tenement used on average 39 gallons a day. In a richer apartment house on the Upper West Side, it was five times that.[39]

There was a lively exchange of knowledge and technologies between cities. Liverpool's Deacon waste-water meter helped locate waste by strategically monitoring mains in select districts overnight and then comparing their flow during the day. It was tried out in Boston and briefly also in Yokohama and Frankfurt; in Boston, it reduced consumption by a third in 1883–4. Newark forced meters on several thousand wasteful culprits. Berlin went for comprehensive metering and was much admired by American authorities. We do not have exact figures for the impact of meters on personal consumption; Berlin metered owners of entire apartment houses, not individual tenants. We do know, however, the percentage of services metered. This allows a rough but instructive comparison. In Atlanta, domestic meters dramatically reduced waste. In Newark and Providence, by contrast, they had little impact. Once serious offenders had been served with a compulsory meter, additional metering saved little. Germany saw success stories like Berlin but also failures like Dresden. Würzburg and many other cities still resisted meters. By 1920, two thirds of American cities were metered.

The odd man out was Britain – only the tiny towns of Abingdon and Malvern metered homes. From today's perspective, this might appear as yet another example of British exceptionalism, a laissez-faire disregard of the environment. We must remember, however, that no country at the time saw the meter as an instrument of lifestyle change. It was designed to reduce leakage, not use. Advocates of metering, in fact, prided themselves on the fact that, by encouraging landlords to repair fittings, they were enabling residents to bathe more. An inquiry in New York in 1906 concluded that 'the blame for the present conditions . . . rests not upon the hundreds of thousands of users of water, but upon the relatively few owners who neglect to keep their plumbing in order'.[40] The British approach was to focus on those few. Armed with the Deacon meter, waste inspectors tracked down careless landlords and made them install fittings tested and stamped by the company; Manchester conducted 40,000 inspections in 1905 alone. In some districts, this cut 'consumption' by half.[41] No British city confronted waste on the scale of Detroit or Atlanta. London's thirst was manageable. But so was Berlin's. That, unlike Berlin, London and other British cities did not think it necessary to charge consumers for what they really used also reflected political values and realities. Taking on all landlords Prussian-style was not an attractive option in liberal Britain. As the engineer Bramwell told the Royal Commission, 'if out of 100 persons who are supplied 10 are wasting and 90 are not, you do not trouble the 90 . . . you simply trouble the 10 who deserve it.'[42]

What were the effects of taps and running water on people's habits? One claim, inspired by Michel Foucault, is that they made people turn inwards, physically and mentally. Toilets were enclosed private cubicles. Hygiene and running water inculcated the self-discipline needed by liberalism, teaching individuals to rule themselves. 'Liberal governmentality' came through the pipes.[43] In reality, spaces and practices were less secluded and private than one might think. As we have already seen, by tying households together into an interdependent network, constant supply also forged public connections. Technologies spread slowly and unevenly, depending on class-specific spaces and habits. In the 1890s, a bathroom with a shower was such a novelty even in affluent homes in London that hosts would show them off to dinner guests. In Berlin, there was one bathtub for every seventy-nine people. As late as 1954, only one in ten French homes had a bathroom.[44]

Water closets spread more quickly – by 1913, they were the norm in London as much as in Leipzig and Lille. Still, for most people, these were not entirely private spaces. An inspection of the 14th arrondissement in the south of Paris in 1904 found that only every fifth flat had its own toilet. The rest shared a WC on the stairs or on the ground floor; private taps were equally rare.[45] Personal hygiene and neighbourly contact and conflict remained intimately connected. In Hanover, every third family shared the loo with a dozen or more persons, often in a communal courtyard – a commentator after the war recalled the foul smell from the proximity of human and kitchen waste.[46] In working-class Barcelona in the 1930s, the toilet was often in the kitchen. In Britain, concerned parents made their teenage boys leave the toilet door open to keep sinful hands in view.

Personal hygiene routines continued to diverge. Even where homes had a fixed bath with hot water, bathing was still a long way from the daily shower. By their own count, the middle-class citizens of Sheffield only ran a bath sixty-two times a year – for the entire household. Schoolteachers preached cleanliness, but by the 1920s half the schools in France still did not have a washroom, and most teachers were waiting for running water to arrive at their own home. For many, cleanliness was a communal ritual, in school showers, the local river, or in municipal pools built to celebrate the joy of water as a shared, social democratic good. In Helsinki, men and women paddled around naked in the city's swimming bath, on alternating days. In Europe as in Asia, public baths were spaces of sociability and gossip as well as private cleanliness. Given the labour involved in preparing a hot bath for those without piped water – that is, the majority – bathing routines varied considerably. Some took a weekly bath on Saturdays, others washed at the sink every night. Some kids shared the tub, others did not, with Mother emptying the bath and boiling fresh water, for one bath after another. One woman, born in 1897, recalled growing up in a family of eight in Bradford. Her father was a railway engineer. They had a 'good sized bathroom' with a 'large zinc bath', but the water had to be boiled on a gas stove in the kitchen. She and her three older sisters had their bath once a week, on Saturday afternoon. Her two brothers went to the swimming baths instead: 'they got showers regularly you see. So we managed fairly well.'[47]

GOING SHOPPING

Beijing, the new capital of the Republic of China (1911–28), was a city bustling with shops and entertainments. In overthrowing the Qing dynasty, the 1911 revolution snuffed the life out of the markets that had catered for the court, its princes and eunuchs. A hotchpotch of shopping spaces emerged. Along the periphery, temple markets survived. At Wangfuijing in the south-east, where many foreigners lived, department stores opened their doors. But it was in the south-west where the biggest market of all emerged: Tianqiao, 'the Bridge of Heaven' (see Plate 23). The new Republican rulers were keen to clean up the Inner City. The transport network was expanded. Tianqiao was lucky. It became the end of the trolley-bus line. Roads were widened, marshes filled in. Within a generation, the once-swampy village resort had grown into a lively hub for anyone looking for a bargain and a bit of fun. Visitors to Tianqiao market could choose between three hundred shops. One quarter sold silks and fabrics, another second-hand clothes. Seven shops specialized in foreign manufactured goods, one in Western suits. There were 116 snack dealers competing for hungry customers, alongside 37 restaurants. There was barely any need the market did not cater for. It had photostudios, grocers, drug dens and a brothel. While shopping, visitors were able to watch acrobats, singers and magicians. In 1918, a state-of-the-art leisure complex was added, the South City Amusement Park, open from eleven to eleven, where, for 30 cents, students and the middle classes could go bowling and roller skating or enjoy the theatre and dance halls; a 'foreign meal' at one of the restaurants cost extra. Tianqiao was a happening place for poor and better-off alike. The hero in Lao She's famous novel *Rickshaw Boy* (1936) found it impossible to leave the city, such was Tianqiao's magnetic pull.[48]

Republican Beijing fits awkwardly into the conventional story of the 'modern city'. On the one hand, it exhibited certain trends that can be seen as emblematic of mass consumption. On the other, large department stores were accompanied, even outflanked, by an equally dynamic sector of small shops and stalls. Here prices were not fixed but negotiable, arrived at through haggling or cheating. Shops were known as 'tiger booths': the retailer was the tiger, the customer the prey. Tian-qiao's South City, similarly, had a touch of Coney Island, but in the main market it was troupes of actors and acrobats who dominated street and stage. Yet these were no longer 'traditional' either. *Laozi*, or lotus singers, had shed their provincial origins and become commercial entertainers, professionally organized, with stage names and news-paper rankings. Far from being the preserve of primitive customs, Tianqiao was a vibrant source of novelties, including female perform-ers and fake wrestling. Street entertainment and a large-scale leisure park developed side by side.

In West as well as East, the century after the 1820s witnessed a revo-lution in shopping. People had shopped since ancient times,[49] but this period saw a shift in gear. Shopping became a popular leisure activity – an end in itself as well as a means to acquire goods – and people talked of 'shoppers'. Shops proliferated, boosted by urban growth and a rise in real wages, which was especially pronounced in Europe and the Americas from the 1860s. This story has often been told via the rise of department stores epitomized by the Bon Marché, founded in Paris in 1852. Paris, in the phrase of the cultural critic Walter Benjamin, was the capital of the nineteenth century, the epitome of bourgeois modern-ity at its peak. For Werner Sombart, department stores were the children of modern capitalism.[50] As late as the 1960s, this point of view had a certain intuitive logic to it, as department stores continued to expand their market share. Since then the tables have turned: the giants have been in crisis, squeezed by discounters and a renaissance of street mar-kets. Beijing, therefore, is a good point of entry into the world of shopping because it broadens our view from the outset to take in the many different types of retail spaces and practices that expanded along-side each other. In Europe and America, as in Beijing, modernity came in all shapes and sizes. Innovation, in short, must not be confused with size and concentration. This does not mean we can ignore the depart-ment store – far from it. Rather, we must place it next to the pedlar, the market hall and the co-operative shop, which were all equally creative responses to the growing demands of urban populations.

Historical opinion about the department store has diverged sharply. A generation ago, historians presented it as the apex of the shift from court to mass consumption. The Bon Marché and its ilk wrought a social and psychological revolution, inflaming new desires and elimi-nating human interaction. 'The numbed hypnosis induced by these places,' one historian wrote, 'is a form of sociability as typical of modern mass consumption as the sociability of the salon was typical of prerevolutionary upper-class consumption.'[51] The department store, in this view, catapulted people previously accustomed to having nothing into a world of desire. This is too strong. As we have seen, the early modern period was not a pre-consumerist dark age.

More recent writers have been gradualists. The department store, they stress, did not ring in a new era. Virtually all its innovations can be traced back in time. To see and be seen was already a feature of the shopping galleries in seventeenth-century Antwerp, Paris and London. How these galleries aroused first a desire for goods and then sexual desire was already made fun of by Pierre Corneille in his 1632 comedy *La Galerie du palais*. Around this time, the bazaars in Istanbul counted more than 10,000 shops and stalls.[52] In the eighteenth century customers already browsed and compared goods and prices, while shopkeepers used mirrors, skylights and displays to create a seductive atmosphere. By 1800, many grocers displayed their tea and other articles with fixed prices on counters and shelves and used trade cards for advertising. In Newcastle, the draper Bainbridge showed fixed prices on its fabrics as early as the 1830s, to take the anxiety out of shopping. It was drapers, too, who switched to a business model of high turnover and low mark-up, opening 'emporia', *magasins de nouveautés* and 'monster shops' with large showrooms where several hundred sales assistants offered quality goods at wholesale prices for ready cash. Smoother and more transparent plate glass began to turn high streets into fantasias in the 1840s. Rather than a radical break, from this perspective the department store appears the culmination of a long-drawn-out evolution in retailing.[53]

Nonetheless, contemporaries in the late nineteenth century did experience the department store as a sign of a new society. Its forgotten antecedents did not make their sensation any less intense. What the department store did was to bring together various innovations under one enormous glass roof supported by a massive iron frame. The biggest stores imposed themselves on the urban landscape like civic buildings and royal palaces. A. T. Stewart in New York City was the 'Marble Palace' (1846). In 1906 the Bon Marché covered 53,000 square metres (see Plate 19). Glass plate created a virtually continuous shop-window from pavement to roof. Some buildings were architectural set pieces, like the art nouveau Innovation in Brussels, designed by Victor Horta in 1901 or Paris's Printemps by René Binèt (1907). Stores were often technological pioneers. Marshall Field's introduced electric lights in 1882. Muir and Mirrielees was the first building in Moscow with an elevator (1908). At Corvin's in Budapest, the elevator was such an attraction that the store decided to charge visitors to ride it.[54]

Department stores were self-conscious global institutions in ways not seen before, working in tandem with those other forces of globalization at the time: the world exhibition, the steamship, the postal service and migration. The 1851 Great Exhibition in London, the Exposition Universelle in Paris 1867 and later exhibitions displayed the products of the world in a way that blurred the lines between culture and commodity. Stores, in turn, were likened to museums. Here people could behold the world as a collection of goods, carefully displayed under glass. William Whiteley saw his West London store as the Great Exhibition's direct successor, bringing goods from across the world within the reach of every shopper.[55] In Berlin, Tietz put a 4.5-metre globe on top of its store on Leipziger Straße, lit from the inside at night. Department stores were a global family, held together by transnational flows of capital, knowledge and taste. The Bon Marché inspired namesakes in Brixton and Liverpool. In 1912, Harrods opened a branch on Buenos Aires' exclusive Calle Florida. As well as moving outwards from European cities, these flows operated sideways, drawing on home-grown enterprise. Gath and Chaves' store in Buenos Aires was the result of a partnership between the creole Lorenzo Chaves and Alfredo Gath, a British migrant. Ma Ying, who established the four-storey Sincere Company in Shanghai in 1917, had first been impressed by fixed prices and customer service in Anthony Hordern's shopping palace in Sydney.[56]

Global ambition was on show in the range of goods on offer. London's Whiteleys christened itself the 'Universal Provider'. Stores concentrated on clothing, furniture and fabrics, but the range of goods and services was impressive nonetheless. *Harrod's Catalogue* of 1895 offered everything from Cambric Knickers ('trimmed Deep-Muslin Frill, Button-hole Edge, handmade' or slightly cheaper machine-made kinds), kettles and cuckoo clocks, to Japanese-lacquer toilet cabinets, a lady fortune teller ('in Gypsy Costume', two hours for £2 2s), all the way to funerals, with coffins and gravestones in a range of materials, hearses, mourning carriages and a number of attendants and coachmen depending on one's budget.[57] Selfridges introduced a children's floor and a children's day. At the department store, it was possible to shop from cradle to grave.

The key to success was flow – flow of people and of goods. Cheap prices demanded large, rapid turnover, and this fundamentally changed the atmosphere inside the store as well as its relationship to the urban environment outside. In comparison to early modern shops, the department store was an extrovert. Instead of creating an exclusive, semi-private space for elite customers, it reached out into the city to grab the masses and pull them in. In the 1890s, large shop-windows became a stage for a new profession of window dressers to live out ever more ambitious fantasies. At Marshall Field's in Chicago, Arthur Fraser turned the entire shopfront into a seventeenth-century manor house. Provincial stores tried their hands at wire battleships and models of St Paul's made out of handkerchiefs. Selfridges lit its store from 8 p.m. until midnight to attract nocturnal window-shoppers. Shops added covered arcades that extended their displays into the street. It was hard to tell where commercial space ended and public space began.

Once inside, the pull continued. At Harrod's, a 'moving staircase' started rolling in 1898, transporting up to 4,000 customers per hour.[58] Conveyer belts transported merchandise. Messages flew through pneumatic tubes. Rapid turnover ruled. 'Sales' had existed for a century or more. The department store turned them into seasonal rituals. Muir and Mirrielees held sales on gloves in March, perfume in April and carpets in August. All stores had 'white weeks', mostly in January, as well as 'special price' or '95-pfennig' weeks. During sales, customers could quadruple, to 70,000 a day in the Bon Marché. Stores turned over stock six times a year. Sales-mania excited cartoonists, moral reformers and shoppers alike. 'Sale' was, as the *Prejudiced Guide to London Shops* put it in 1906:

> [the] magic word that stocks our wardrobes, deletes our purses, disorganizes our routine, fascinates us, repels us, delights us, disappoints us twice a year regularly in London . . . The ethics of sales are so disturbing, one time so morally and clearly good, the next minute so conspicuously disappointing and bad, that no woman, I believe, is quite settled in her mind regarding them.[59]

It was the birth of total shopping. Department stores held concerts, installed picture galleries and libraries, and provided tea and smoking rooms. Openings and promotional weeks turned shop floors into magical stage sets. No one captured the atmosphere more vividly than Émile Zola, who devoted a good twenty pages to the exhibition of white in his *Au Bonheur des dames* (*The Ladies' Paradise*), published in 1883 after meticulous research in the real Bon Marché. 'There was nothing but white, all the white goods from every department, an orgy of white, a white star whose radiance was blinding at first.' In the gallery of haberdashery and hosiery, 'white edifices were displayed made of pearl buttons, together with huge constructions of white socks, and a whole hall covered with white swansdown.' In the central gallery, bright light illuminated white silks and ribbons. 'The staircases were decked with white draperies . . . running the whole length of the banisters and encircling the halls right up to the second floor.' The 'ascending whiteness appeared to take wing, merging together and disappearing like a flight of swans. The whiteness then fell back again from the domes in a rain of eiderdown, a sheet of huge snowflakes.' In the main hall, over the silk counter:

> there was the miracle, the altar of this cult of white – a tent made of white curtains hanging down from the glass roof. Muslins, gauzes, and guipures [large-patterned decorative lace] flowed in light ripples, while richly embroidered tulles and lengths of oriental silk and silver lamé served as a background to this gigantic decoration, which was evocative both of the tabernacle and of the bedroom. It looked like a great white bed, its virginal whiteness waiting . . . for the white princess . . . who would one day come . . . in her white bridal veil. 'Oh! It's fantastic!' the ladies kept repeating. 'Amazing!'

In the perfume department, the salesmen had made a display of white china pots and white glass phials, with a silver fountain in the centre and a shepherdess standing in a harvest of flowers. But the crush of customers was greatest in the lace department, 'the crowning glory of the great display of white', where 'the most delicate and costly whites' were on display. 'The temptation was acute; mad desires were driving all the women crazy.'[60]

Zola's novel, the most successful of the emerging genre of the department-store novel, mixed social observation with moral anxiety. In Zola's store, a dream world of virginal innocence (the white bed, the shepherdess) collides with animalistic lust. He described women 'pale with desire' and with an 'irresistible desire to throw themselves' into silks and velvets, 'and be lost'. The department store replaced the satanic mill, a microcosm of social evil. Mouret, the fictional head of *The Ladies' Paradise*, is the successor to the pitiless factory-owner in earlier Victorian novels. 'When he [had] extracted his fortune and his pleasure from them [the women], he would throw them on the rubbish heap.' Zola describes the store as a ruthless 'machine' designed to seduce and conquer women. During sales, the 'current' of the store grew into an 'ocean' that took everyone and everything with it.[61]

The Ladies' Paradise is a brilliant catalogue of contemporary fears. One was that these 'cathedrals of commerce' were displacing the true Church, with the worship of goods leading away from the worship of Christ. Small retailers and conservatives worried that the big stores were destroying family shops and, with them, social balance and national strength; one shopkeeper in Zola's novel throws himself in front of an omnibus in despair. Department stores, critics charged, deprived millions of shopkeepers of their daily bread. Society would be split in two: a small group of businessmen and an army of consumers. Family, religion and morality, all would be destroyed. Into the 1890s, many shop assistants lived in and were not allowed to marry – love was bad for business, Zola noted. On the other hand, sex sells, and the press was full of claims that stores attracted prostitutes or hired good-looking male assistants to seduce the weaker sex. The Swedish novel by Sigfrid Siwertz *Det stora varuhuset* (1926) opens with a sex scene in the bedding department; Swedes were always one step ahead. Everywhere, the department store was in the crossfire. In Spain, shopping was blamed for the decadence of a once-great empire.[62] In Germany, Jewish-owned chains were seen as sapping the strength of a rising empire.

In reality, department stores took only a small slice of the retail trade. They created new work for specialist crafts, and they pulled more shoppers into city centres, as some small shopkeepers learnt to appreciate. Nonetheless, these fears drew strength from several important trends: the growing visibility of women in urban life; the impact of urbanization on religious devotion; and a more aggressive nationalism. Some prophesied that sexual and national crisis would be the result. In eighteenth-century London, 'macaronis' – foppish men with a love for Italian song and feathered hats – had been derided for weakening the nation;[63] it was such effeminate traits among the American colonials that British troops mocked in the original version of 'Yankee Doodle' during the Seven Years War, before the song would be given its patriotic makeover by the new republic.

But the shop was not necessarily a space of moral danger. In *Emma* (1816), Jane Austen has Harriet Smith take shelter from the rain in a draper's, where she meets the respectable Mr Martin, with no hint of threat or corruption. In real life, middle- as well as working-class women walked the streets unaccompanied.[64] By the end of the century, the atmosphere had changed. As female emancipation and professional employment gathered pace, unchaperoned middle-class women became a lightning rod for wider fears. The department store seemed to unleash the passionate beast in otherwise respectable ladies. Often it was women with a purse full of money who were caught shoplifting, like Zola's Madame de Boves, who was in the grip of a 'neurosis' caused by 'her unsatisfied desire for luxury when confronted by the enormous, violent temptation of the big stores'.[65] The lust for things erupted from deep within the female body. Many kleptomaniacs, according to criminologists, were menstruating women.

Lurking behind these sexual anxieties were fears about the loss of self-control and individuality. The department store simultaneously repelled and attracted, because it seemed to hold within it a new mass society. One contemporary likened it to an ocean liner where classes were temporarily thrown together.[66] Writing in 1900, the German sociologist Georg Simmel highlighted two complementary processes. One concerned the effect of money and metropolis on an individual's relation to objects. The harmony between things and humans was torn asunder. In the metropolis, according to Simmel, relations with objects had become false and superficial. Fashion, novelties and promotions accelerated and diversified to win attention. 'The broadening of consumption,' Simmel wrote, 'is dependent upon the growth of *objective* culture, since the more objective and impersonal an object is the better it is suited to more people.' Things lost their personal touch. Formerly individual works of art, they were now interchangeable mass products. The second process concerned the relation between individuals and social groups. Metropolitan life estranged people from their community and class. In earlier periods, it was said that 'city air makes you free,' but freedom now was a costly illusion. People might be free to move and shop. But, Simmel argued, they were really a 'grey' mass. Valued as customers, they were devalued as individuals. Shop assistants no longer distinguished between a decorated officer and a lowly soldier, between a simple student and Herr Professor Dr Simmel; they were all treated alike, as long as they had money to spend. In the modern city, the 'decolouring' of objects and individuals went hand in hand.[67]

This dehumanizing portrait of the modern shopper reached a new melancholic depth in the 1930s in the work of the German philosopher and essayist Walter Benjamin. Benjamin took his own life on 10 October 1940 at the French border with Spain, rather than face deportation to Nazi Germany. He left behind a legendary archive of fragmented scraps and thoughts on nineteenth-century Paris that has entranced critics ever since, the so-called 'Arcades Project'. Benjamin mixed Marx with Proust and added a dash of Freud. Reality was not what it seemed. A dream had fallen over Europe in the nineteenth century. This was why capitalism had not, and would not, die a natural death. To wake up his contemporaries, Benjamin set himself the role of historical therapist, interpreting the advance of 'dream-time' (*Zeit-traum*) in nineteenth-century Paris.[68]

Unlike Max Weber, Benjamin did not believe modernity had disenchanted the world. Quite the opposite: shops, novelties and advertisements were the new gods. The shopping arcades of the 1820s–'40s were collective 'dream houses',[69] passageways into the past; Benjamin likened them to 'caves containing the fossil remains of a vanished monster: the consumer of the pre-imperial era of capitalism, the last dinosaur of Europe'.[70] With their shops and promenades, these covered arcades provided the habitat of a new type: the *flâneur*. Strolling the city without aim or purpose, the *flâneur* was like a walking camera, creating an album of private impressions from the scenes of public life. The crowd was his home. Haussmann's rebuilding of Paris in the 1860s flushed him out. Grand boulevards encouraged crowds to move along in a regular flow. This left the department store as a rare, surviving haunt for meandering. But here, Benjamin stressed, freedom was further compromised by uniformity and surveillance. In the department store, 'for the first time in history . . . consumers begin to consider themselves as a mass.'[71] Whether he liked it or not, the *flâneur* was himself on display.

These pessimistic readings have cast a long shadow over the twentieth century. They need to be placed in their historical context. For all their brilliance, they tell us more about the theorist than about the reality of shopping in the late nineteenth century. Benjamin was writing with the Nazis at his back. For him, there was a straight line from the department store to Adolf Hitler. Totalitarian states picked up 'the mass' as their model: 'the *Volksgemeinschaft* [racial community] . . . aims to root out from single individuals everything that stands in the way of their wholesale fusion into a mass of consumers.'[72] But in 1900 there were no Nazis. For many contemporaries, shopping did not automatically lead to mass conformity and moral decay. Zola, after all, ended *The Ladies' Paradise* by marrying off Denise, the shop assistant, to Mouret, the owner – a master stroke of social reconciliation, which united community and commerce, morals and Mammon, the virtuous petit-bourgeoisie and the nouveau riche. In real life, many defended shopping for opening up public spaces to women. Shopping did not have to be frivolous, the Lady Guide Association preached when it began organizing tours in London in 1888. With rest stops at museums and public sights, shopping trips made women more rational consumers and taught civic duty and imperial pride. For Gordon Selfridge, who opened his store on Oxford Street in 1909, shopping combined recreation with emancipation; he supported women's suffrage.[73]

Defenders of the big stores were more vocal in liberal England than on the continent, but even there, where small retailers were more numerous and better organized, it is easy to exaggerate the opp sition. Special taxes on department stores were only temporarily levied in Germany, Hungary and a couple of American states, but they were tiny and ineffective, little more than 1 per cent of turnover. Some contemporaries looked to the department store for cultural uplift. Entering one of these temples of merchandise was 'an act of joy, pleasure, a celebration', one German observer mused in 1907. At last, even the 'simple people' had a chance to share in this 'abundance and all this beauty, without spending a penny', and gain 'a sense of beauty and inner happiness more generally'.[74] Modernist artists celebrated the hedonism of the new woman. In *Child of the Big City*, a 1914 Russian film by Yevgeni Bauer, the pretty, orphaned seamstress Mania is mesmerized by the department store and becomes a vamp, milking her admirers to fund a life of tango, bars and glamour. The corruption of innocent girls by the big city was a set piece of literature, but Bauer turned the moral convention on its head. Mania is the heroine, not the victim. In the end, it is Victor, one of her rich admirers, who is driven to suicide, unable to let go of his bourgeois fantasy of her as an object of desire and to recognize her for the real woman she is.[75]

The uniformity of 'mass society' has been exaggerated, in part because the department store has been idealized as typically bourgeois and metropolitan. In fact, stores differed in size, customer base and shopping practices. Most were a far cry from the palatial Bon Marché. In Imperial Germany, the stores Wertheim, Tietz and Karstadt started in Stralsund, Gera and Wismar, towns with fewer than 30,000 souls. Twenty-five of these provincial stores would have fit into the Bon Marché. In Britain, many stores were knocked together from neighbouring buildings. If the Bon Marché catered for the bourgeoisie, other stores were less exclusive. Working families with greater disposable income were a growing customer base and one reason for the take-off of urban stores in the late nineteenth century. When the Wertheim brothers opened their first branch in Berlin, it was a cheap bazaar (*Billigbazar*) in the working-class district of Kreuzberg, and even after moving into the more prestigious Leipziger Straße in 1897 it continued to depend on working-class customers and commuters. Dufayel catered for similar groups on the outskirts of Paris. Many stores struggled to live down their early associations with cheap, shoddy goods. Respectable ladies, it was said, would ask staff to wrap up articles in brown-paper bags to pretend that they were shopping for their servants. It is impossible to give a social breakdown of shoppers, but one department store in the Rhineland did keep a register of its delivery service, classifying its customers by profession. Together, artisans, pensioners and blue- and white-collar workers made up one third. Most people did not leave the stores laden with packages. The average sales price was less than a Mark – a worker earned 60 Marks a month on average.[76]

Men went shopping, too. Harrod's offered one hundred different kinds of briar pipes for the discerning gent. Department stores advertised ready-made suits for every season and included self-measurement forms in their catalogues. Lewis's in Liverpool had started as a menswear store. In the 1890s, men got their own New Look: an athletic outfit, complete with fitted jackets, padded shoulders and corsets to accentuate a narrow waistline. The first magazine dedicated to the fashion-conscious man was launched in 1898. It was called simply *Fashion*. Far from seeing the rise of grey uniformity, these years brought

Customers of a department store in Germany in 1900

Source: Julius Hirsch, *Das Warenhaus in Westdeutschland* (1909), p. 26.

a gradual liberation from the identical three-piece suit. Sportswear and leisure clothes took off. At the same time, the growth of office work made fashion a legitimate investment in career development. An up-to-date suit announced a man of ambition. 'Tailor your way to opportunity,' Royal Tailors urged American men.[77] Other bits of male fashion developed bottom-up, as tailors incorporated stylistic elements from dandies and the music-hall.[78]

Nor were women simply passive prey. At Selfridges, they made up half the private investors. The knowledgeable shopper could rely on a growing literature of guidebooks with advice on how to determine quality, secure a good price and avoid being taking advantage of. One early *Lady's Shopping Manual* warned, 'three fourths of the *male* assistants in the trade know nothing of the goods which it is their business to exhibit. Their object too frequently is to sell *by any means*.'[79] Department stores did most of their business in cash, but in smaller and specialist stores credit survived. Legally, a wife lacked economic independence, but the 'law of necessities' gave her the right to pledge her husband's credit for 'necessary' goods – and what was 'necessary' depended on social rank and convention. A fashionable hat might be a luxury for a washerwoman but a necessity for a merchant's wife. By pretending to be more than they were, some women ran up a long list of credit that they had no intention of repaying. For retailers, it was a nightmare, since courts ruled that traders could not recover 'unnecessary' debts incurred without a husband's consent.[80] In addition to glitz and magic, therefore, a good deal of shopping involved a cat-and-mouse game between retailer and customer, each side trying to escape being cheated by the other.

Music-hall song celebrated shopping as free entertainment for honeymooners:

> *Chorus*: Shopping's a pastime simply sublime,
> Nothing to spend but a real good time,
> Examining every pretty thing that the shopmen politely display.
> 'That looks neat! Awf'lly nice! Simply sweet!
> 'What's the price? Thank you, we'll call another day.'[81]

Actually, there were all sorts of obstacles to browsing, let alone being a *flâneur*. Many stores employed shopwalkers and doormen to stop so-called *palpeuses* and 'tabbies' – people who loved to touch but did not buy. When Gordon Selfridge checked out his London competitors, he was told to 'move on' when he answered that he had come just to look around. There were obstacles to buying, too. In German stores, each department, however small, had its own cashier. Customers had to wait in line and pay before proceeding to another section. Retailers, meanwhile, complained that German shoppers were helpless and lacked the independence of their French counterparts.[82]

Glass cabinets and displays created a new intimacy between consumers and goods. 'Perhaps more than any other medium,' one historian has written, 'glass democratized desire even as it democratized access to goods.'[83] This did not mean, however, that human relations vanished from the shop floor. Shop assistants were taught to be polite and neutral and to suppress any character trait that might cause offence: no loud make-up, silly laughs, or personal remarks. Still, provincial stores knew it was vital to build up a loyal customer base. In Buffalo, New York, a city with half a million inhabitants, Mr Gibson, the store manager, would stand in his morning coat at the entrance of Adam, Meldrum and Anderson and greet female customers by name. In the toy department, assistants made sure to know the names of their next generation of customers. Stores worked hard to counter the image of a dehumanizing monster and threw themselves into the life of the community, organizing war veterans' parades and teaching housewives how to roast a suckling pig.[84]

It is easily forgotten that department stores also did business in other parts of the world, for example Egypt, with its rich mix of religions, customs and languages. There, sales clerks carried notebooks to record preferences and build up personal relationships with customers. Veiled Muslim women had to be addressed differently to Jewish or Christian customers. In Cairo, Orosdi-Back employed Muslim salespeople as well as Greeks, Italians, French, Russians, English, Spanish and Sephardi Jews. The Egyptian feminist nationalist Huda Sha'arawi recalled her early trips to the shops around 1900. She loved going to the department stores in Alexandria. Her eunuch did not. Every planned trip threw the household into:

> heated debate for days. They looked upon me as if I were about to violate the religious law or commit some other crime . . . They insisted . . . I must be accompanied by Said Agha [the eunuch] and my maids . . . When I entered Chalon, the staff and clientele were visibly taken aback by this veiled apparition and her retinue. In the lead Said Agha stared into the surrounding faces, silently warning them to look the other way . . . The eunuch proceeded straight to the store manager and brusquely demanded

the place for the harem. We were led to the department for women's apparel, behind a pair of screens hastily erected to obscure me from view.[85]

Huda Sha'arawi was not to be a mass consumer, on display. But even though she was segregated behind screens, shopping gave her a sense of empowerment. 'Not only was there a wide range of goods to choose from but there was money to be saved through wise spending.' She persuaded her mother to join her and eventually was allowed to shop on her own.

What the telegraph did for communication, the department store and mail order did for shopping: they compressed time and space. Of course, the countryside had never been a commercial desert. Sombart recognized the revolutionary role of pedlars, long accused of seducing the farmer's wife with fashionable things she had not even known existed.[86] By the middle of the nineteenth century, most farmers in North America and Europe were part of a cash nexus, buying and selling in the market. Nor was this limited to the more developed Western regions of Europe. In Russia, serfs were breaking out of self-sufficiency and began buying and selling goods at weekly markets and nearby fairs in the 1820s, a generation before their emancipation in 1861. Items for sale included tobacco, linen cloth, wine, mustard and honey, as well as coffins. When the serf Avdot'ia Yefremov died in Voshchazhnikovo in 1836, she left behind a wardrobe that included five coloured dresses, three French headscarves in pink, blue and black, two nightshirts with cotton sleeves, a coat with sable trim and winter stockings. In addition to several rings and earrings, she also owned a pearl necklace. Then, there were the possessions she had brought with her in her dowry, including three tablecloths, one cotton blanket, a napkin, one feather bed, a pair of green curtains, several towels (one trimmed with lace and ribbon), and two samovars (one copper, the other iron). A neighbouring serf owned a silver coffee pot and a forty-piece silver tea set.[87]

In general, there were two conveyor belts for new tastes and products: the country fair and war. In the middle of the nineteenth century, the Illinois state fair had stalls selling fine watches, sporting goods, wigs and perfumes. Farmers returned from the Civil War with a taste for ready-made clothes and other novelties.[88] The department-store catalogue turned such currents into a torrent. By 1900, Eaton's in Toronto, for example, sent out 1.3 million copies of its 200-page catalogue, or one for every fifth Canadian.[89] The city came to the log house.

Karl Marx observed that the entire economic history of society was summed up in the changing relation between town and country.[90] He was mainly concerned with the division of labour, but the flow of consumer goods and tastes was just as important. The cultural boundaries between city and country were increasingly porous. Harrod's maintained a postal service that stretched from Argentina to Zanzibar. Moscow's Muir and Mirrielees delivered across the Russian empire from Poland to Vladivostok, as long as items were worth 50 roubles or more. In 1894, the Bon Marché distributed 1.5 million catalogues, half to the provinces, another 15 per cent abroad. It sent packages worth 40 million francs a year to provincial towns and villages.[91] Pieces of urban fashion and comfort could be had thousands of miles away from the metropole. When Anton Chekhov was recovering from tuberculosis in Yalta in the late 1890s, he continued to get his hats, detachable collars, curtains and stoves from Muir and Mirrielees.[92]

American writers, preoccupied with the melting pot, have emphasized the role of the department store in fusing a new national identity. Globally, however, such unifying forces were counterbalanced by social and ethnic distinctions. The department store cultivated a transnational style that gave national elites a chance to demonstrate their modernity and distance themselves from 'traditional', 'lower' social and ethnic groups. Paris and London were the centre of this fashion network. In São Paulo, the daughters of coffee barons bought their French dresses at the Mappin store, before retiring at five o'clock to its salon for English tea. Cairo's Au Petit Louvre – a marble palace with Louis XVI-style columns set up by the Chemla brothers from Tunis – sold the newest hats from Paris and boasted its own French milliner and corset maker. Street sellers and haggling were disdained as something for indigenous people and peasants.[93]

In reality, it was impossible to draw a sharp line between modern and traditional shopping. Aristide Boucicant, the founder of the Bon Marché, had started out as a pedlar's associate. Haussmann's bulldozing of old Paris – boulevards instead of barricades – set the stage for the big stores, but it was quite unique. Even in Cairo, which tried to follow his example most faithfully, small shops and street traders continued to find their niche in the new downtown area of Ismailia. The boulevards were dominated by grand stores selling Western clothes, but the tiny passageways connecting them were home to hundreds of tailors, trinket sellers and food shops selling nuts and spices in open sacks. On Fu'ad Street, unlicensed hawkers continued to peddle their wares. Most locals moved between these spaces unbothered by an academic divide between 'traditional' and 'modern'. They went to the department store for special occasions, bought their regular Western shoes from one of the cheap small cobblers, and tried some sweets from Damascus on the way. They were, in short, parallel shoppers.[94]

It is tempting to see in the global spread of the department store a sign of its advancing dominance, but that is an optical illusion. The world of shopping was expanding in all directions in the late nineteenth century. The big stores rang up sales, but so did a host of rivals, from pedlars to the co-operative shop. In Western Europe in 1914, department stores controlled less than 3 per cent of the retail trade; in the United States, it was slightly more.[95] The stores rarely reached 10 per cent of all clothes and furniture sold. Their competitors were not asleep. Small shops multiplied. By 1910, for example, there were 21,000 shops in Hamburg, one for every 44 inhabitants, double the density half a century earlier. Across Europe, family-run shops provided employment for millions, especially women. And their swelling ranks explain both their paranoia about new competitors and their drive to innovate in the hunt for customers. Small shops led the way in advertising, packaging and display, and put colonial and processed goods on the shelf.[96]

Urban growth, a mobile workforce and a rising standard of living created opportunities for pedlars as well. Far from being the dying remnants of the Middle Ages, itinerant traders adapted remarkably well to the flexible needs of the city. Since many hawkers could or would not sign their name, British census data is unreliable, but experts estimate their urban number probably doubled in the second half of the nineteenth century, to around 70,000, in line with population growth. In Prussia, their number was twice that high, in spite of various taxes and restrictions.[97] In Hamburg, around 3,000 costermongers sold everything from fruit and vegetables to pulp fiction. In town and country alike, pedlars increasingly carried mass-manufactured goods rather than home-made baskets and crockery. The abolition of guilds and greater freedom of trade earlier in the century also opened the door for discounters, the *Wanderlager*, a kind of mobile outlet centre that, in premises rented for a few weeks at a time, brought remainders, cheap clothes, delicatessen foods and carpets from bankruptcy sales to small-town consumers. In 1910, there were a thousand of these in Germany.[98]

The radical alternative to the department store was the co-operative shop (see Plate 21). Like the big stores, co-operatives sought to lower prices by eliminating the middleman, but they went one step further, turning the shop into a mutual enterprise, owned by the shoppers themselves. Profits were handed back as a dividend: the 'divi'. In England, some friendly societies began to sell food for mutual benefit in the 1760s; in Japan, co-operative finance was already practised by the Mujin societies in the thirteenth century. The real take-off came after 1844 when a group of flannel weavers and Owenite socialists opened a co-operative store in Rochdale, Lancashire. The 'Rochdale Pioneers' became stars of international radicalism, attracting admirers from as far away as Russia and Japan. It was Rochdale's moment on the world stage. When the failure of the 1848 revolutions left behind a suspicion of the 'wilder sort' of social reformers, as the leading cooperator George Jacob Holyoake would call them, the co-operatives seemed the acceptable face of social improvement.[99] Instead of violent overthrow, co-operatives sought to tame the merciless, capitalist beast from within by growing virtuous cells of voluntarism, mutualism and self-help. Signing up promised a better world as well as cheaper food.

The export success of this model depended on what domestic alternatives were available and, in particular, on the size and attitude of local socialist parties. In Denmark, for example, the Social Democrats believed that co-operatives would worsen, not improve, the condition of the people by pushing small shopkeepers into destitution. In late-nineteenth-century Britain, by contrast, in the absence of a strong Labour Party, it grew into the biggest social movement of the day. By 1910, some 3 million Britons belonged to 1,400 consumer co-operatives – or roughly every fourth household, and most working-class families. Co-ops were particularly strong in the mid-sized towns of the industrial north-west, previous retail deserts. On the eve of the First World War, they controlled 8 per cent of all retail sales in Britain, three times that of the department stores and just ahead of the chain stores. In Germany, they counted 1.6 million members; in France a million; and half a million in Italy, concentrated in the north; in Japan they took off in the inter-war years. Peasants joined in Scandinavian countries.

Basic foodstuffs made up the bulk of their wares; in the Belgian La Maison du Peuple half the sales were of bread. But the co-ops were extending their range, too. They developed their own brands and advertising. Stores began to sell jewellery and furniture, and to decorate their shop windows. 'Basic needs' were expanding. The co-ops sought to overcome cultural as much as material poverty. To create a more cultivated self and community-oriented lifestyle required nothing less than a revolution in taste and leisure. They offered a working-class version of total shopping with a good conscience. Like the department stores, local co-ops put on concerts, tea parties and cooking lessons. They opened libraries and reading rooms. Exhibitions displayed a world of goods in miniature, except that they were not the latest fashions from Paris but wholesome flour, boots and cutlery made by partners in the International Co-operative Alliance, founded in 1893.[100]

To see the rise of shopping as the decline of public space would, therefore, be too simple. Shopping created new public spaces, sociability and sensibilities as well as cutting into old ones. Cities were battle zones between rival visions of spatial order. More than anyone, it was street sellers who were in the firing line, and their fate shows us both how urban authorities tried to regulate the flow of goods and people, and how difficult that proved to be. For a start, the sanitary revolution spread to the street. Hawkers were considered carriers of disease and disorder, difficult to check, easily slipping away. Standing at street corners, moving and stopping their carts, shouting out their wares, they were an eyesore to every self-respecting mayor and health inspector. Across the world, cities turned to market halls to bring them under central control (see Plate 22). Such halls offered additional stalls for teeming urban populations. They made it easier to license retailers and control quality and prices. And they promised to regulate people and behaviour. Prohibition of street selling, sanitary reforms and the erection of a market hall often went hand in hand. Bolton's grand market hall, over an acre in size, required the clearance of almost two thousand slum dwellings. Roughs and undesirables would be kept out. Inside, spitting, swearing and shouting were forbidden. Market halls showed what a city was made of. Bradford's Kirkgate Market was an octagonal pavilion with a glass-and-iron roof and ornamental ironwork painted in gold and bronze. The opening of Derby's market hall in 1866 involved a grand procession of the town's worthies and a performance of the *Messiah* by a chorus 600-strong.[101] For their champions, these halls were veritable schools of progress. They taught the lower orders better manners and gave them cheaper and healthier food, thanks to bulk purchases, freezers, hygienic storage and health inspections.

Transforming shopping spaces and habits proved more complicated than reformers had reckoned, however. In Berlin, the market halls were booming with wholesalers of food and flowers, but small retailers deserted them. By 1911, observers began to notice their 'growing insignificance' for ordinary people.[102] Several halls closed down. It could be cheaper to buy from a street dealer, who did not carry the extra expense of renting a stall. Moreover, small stores offered credit while market halls dealt in cash only. Many halls lacked the splendour of Bradford's. Shanghai had fourteen municipal markets, for example. Elgin Road market was 'an old wooden erection' propped up by supports. Purdon Road market was a cement structure, but only half the space on the first floor was occupied. Wuchow market was 'difficult to keep clean' because of the many dealers of cooked food. Behind the town hall, in Maloo market, the Chinese section was doing well, but the foreign section was deserted. In Tsitsihar Road, market stalls were empty while hawkers thrived. If cities involve what Henri Lefebvre, a pioneer in the study of everyday life, has called the production of 'spatial consensus',[103] the authorities in Shanghai had few illusions that they were achieving it. 'The enormous number of foodhawkers in the Settlement is a constant source of anxiety, and even with the assistance of Sanitary Police it is found impossible . . . to control this class of trade.' They stored food in their bedrooms or used as 'a refrigerant . . . the commodity known as natural ice, but more accurately described as frozen sewage'.[104]

The simple fact was that street sellers offered cheap and flexible shopping. The minute a fixed store pulled down its shutters, a street seller arrived at the corner. And they were everywhere. Buying some food in a market hall often meant a long walk or the extra expense of a tram fare. Centralization had visible limits, often ignored in portrayals of the modern city in terms of boulevards and department stores. Push carts and street stalls remained common sights on New York's Lower East Side and in other cities with mobile, migrant communities. Weekly markets continued to flourish in Cologne, just as they survived in Quito and São Paulo.[105] Even in Britain, cities were pushed to reverse their earlier regulations because market halls proved incapable of catering to growing populations with more money to spend. Around the turn of the twentieth century, after two generations of abuse and fines, street sellers and open-air markets were allowed back.[106]

Nor were street sellers easily pushed around. The provincial Mexican city of Morelia provides a good example of the twisted history of spatial politics. Modernity here arrived in 1888, with electric lighting. A department store opened – the Port of Liverpool. Merchants and city officials joined forces to clean up public spaces and create an attractive shopping environment. Stores introduced glass display cases. But this sparkling new setting was rudely disrupted by street vendors, who added injury to insult by taking away custom, according to a 1913 commission. Instead of entering respectable stores, customers would linger outside, where street stalls sold everything from shoes to ice cream. Kiosks, too, sprang up. The vendors had to go. The order to relocate, however, had unexpected consequences. Instead of packing up and dispersing, one by one, vendors united and formed a union. In 1917, during the revolution, they returned.[107]

We have stressed the contribution of old and new to the consuming city. It was a story of diversification rather than homogenization. Let us now move from the spaces to the rhythms of shopping. Many writers have claimed that, in the modern city, movement became regulated, disciplined and anonymized. Numbed customers trotted along boulevards and moved through department stores in an orchestrated flow. Lefebvre likened modernity to 'dressage', where, like horses, people are trained in a sequence of automatic, repetitive movements. Liberty is an illusion: 'people can turn right or left, but their walk, the rhythm of their walking . . . do not change for all that.'[108] We might object that routines can be liberating as well as disempowering,[109] but here we ask whether modern urban life was in fact a heartless, monotonous cycle.

In fact, the modern city impressed many contemporaries with its multiple rhythms. The journalist George Sims took the pulse of the British metropolis in 1904 in a panoramic tour of *Living London*. He observed how shopping districts differed 'not only in their general appearance, but in their methods, their manner and their language as though they belonged to different cities'. The scene in Westbourne Grove, home of Whiteley's department store, where ladies chatted about 'prices, bargains, catalogues, and such things' was a far cry from that in the East End, where enterprising shopkeepers hawked furniture and crockery 'amidst clustered pillars of linoleum and carpet, like lay priests in ruined temples' and 'buyers are stopping to haggle with the sellers.' On Saturday evenings, tailors and toyshops on Whitechapel Road had their doors open and costermongers' barrows stood 'thickly by the kerb'. Here the 'baked potato merchant passes and repasses, sowing sparks from the big black can on his barrow. The public houses are full; the pavement is covered with men and women and children, well-dressed, shabby and disreputable, shopping, or leisurely promenading.' When the audiences poured out of the theatres, the current changed again.[110]

New spaces such as the market hall, too, remained home to a range of rhythms. On weekdays, there was the flow of customers in search of a good cut of meat, or a gramophone. No spitting, please. On Saturdays, however, many markets stayed open until midnight. For youths, they were a place to promenade and flirt. Others stopped to watch clog dancers or to be weighed. Haggling returned. Tea rooms offered a place for rest and refreshment. For those in a hurry, there was fast food from one of the pie shops or ice-cream vendors. Jugglers, acrobats and other street performers were allowed back in; Glasgow's Bazaar had a rifle range.[111] Except for the absence of second-hand shops, it was not so different from Tianqiao market.

ENTERTAINING SPACES

Space, as Lefebvre points out, is not just there, a physical assemblage of streets and buildings. It is social, the product of communication, practices and exchange.[112] It involves the senses, a perception of one's personal space in relation to the surrounding world. In the modern city, that sense of space underwent a transformation as remarkable as the physical changes brought about by water pipes and glass windows. Entertainment was crucial to that change. In addition to goods and people, cities were channelling emotion. To be sure, cities remained spaces of work, and they had offered bread and circuses since ancient times. All the same, the period roughly from the 1880s to the 1920s witnessed a dramatic proliferation of commercial spaces dedicated to fun – the music hall, the cinema the amusement park, the football stadium and the velodrome. Their holidays and spending money may look miserly to today's reader, but most working people of the period were enjoying more disposable income and holiday time than ever before. Some towns made pleasure their primary business. The English resort Blackpool entertained 4 million visitors in 1893. Many factory workers enjoyed their first 'day-tripping' holiday here; Sigmund Freud, too, stayed twice and loved paddling in the Irish Sea.

Ambivalence about the city ran deep in European culture. The Romantic William Wordsworth warned in 1800 that its many stimulations induced an 'almost savage stupor'. A century later, such diagnoses were reinforced by new experiences of time and space. Instead of ticking like a clock, time moved like a stream, ebbing and swelling. Modernist writers stretched minutes and compressed years, even reversed the flow of time.[113] There was a widespread feeling that society was accelerating and fragmenting under the strain. Individuals were being tossed about,

cut loose from stabilizing norms and hierarchies.[114] Speed and dynamism made the city the crucible of a new mental state, what Georg
Simmel in 1903 called the 'blasé attitude' in what remains the most
influential essay on the metropolis: 'The blasé attitude results . . . from
the rapidly changing and closely compressed contrasting stimulations
of the nerves.' In the big city, two forces were at work. One was the
'boundless pursuit of pleasure' which 'agitates the nerves to their
strongest reactivity for such a long time that they finally cease to react
at all'. The second was the bombardment of the mind with so many
sensations that, however small and harmless in themselves, their sheer
number exhausted the nerves. The result was an inability 'to react to
new sensations with the appropriate energy. This constitutes the blasé
attitude which, in fact, every metropolitan child shows when compared
with children of quieter and less changeable milieus.' It was characterized by numbness and a loss of depth. The city was all head, no heart.
City dwellers acquired the soulless intellect of a calculating machine,
responding to the metropolitan pressure for punctuality, precision and
coordination. Ultimately, metropolitan people were a lonely crowd of
pseudo-individuals. To the 'blasé person', Simmel concluded, all things
appeared in 'an evenly flat and gray tone'.[115]

Cinema, with its fast-moving images, came to epitomize metropolitan overstimulation, exhaustion and homogenization. 'Movies are the
mirror of today's society,' wrote Siegfried Kracauer in a 1927 newspaper article on cinema audiences for the *Frankfurter Zeitung*, where
he was film and theatre critic. 'Stupid and unreal film fantasies are the
day dreams of society.' They forged a 'mass taste', typical of the
metropolis. Everything about cinema was fake, from the escapist
romances of poor girls marrying rich men to the architecture itself; the
baroque pretence of Berlin's Gloria-Palast typified the 'refined pomp of
superficiality'. In small towns, cinemas were for the lower classes, while
the middle classes kept their distance. In Berlin, by contrast, the current of metropolitan life sucked everyone into mass society, including
the rich and educated. The result was a 'homogenous metropolitan
public . . . from the diva to the typist.' Kracauer had little doubt who
epitomized this metropolitan mass: his series bore the title 'The Little
Shopgirls Go to the Movies'.[116]

Interpretations like this have had considerable influence, and it is
easy to understand why. We know what followed: the totalitarian use
of film and entertainment, and the ubiquity of standardized Hollywood fare. The benefit of hindsight, however, can blind us to what

there was before. References to 'mass society' are essentially ahistorical. They suggest a universal, passive consumer across time, as if movie-going was always the same. When Kracauer deplored the 'cult of distraction', the cinema was already celebrating its thirty-second birthday. And its childhood was quite different from its middle age.

The first kinetoscope opened on Broadway in New York in 1894 in a converted shoe store. It showed pictures through a peep-hole. In the early years, moving pictures were part of an existing ensemble of entertainment, rather than a separate activity. They were shown in music halls and swimming baths, at fairs and in mission halls. Travelling cinemas passed through small towns and rural areas and were crucial in spreading a taste for the new medium. In the Netherlands, for example, they reached 1 million viewers. Utrecht's Tivoli Park had a tent especially reserved for travelling shows. A typical local Varieté cinema in 1904 showed moving pictures to around 70,000 viewers a week. Some travelling cinemas were palaces on wheels, with mirrors 13 metres tall, gilded decorations, an organ, hundreds of light bulbs and silk-covered seats in the front row. They comfortably seated seven hundred people. A typical format was that of Guido Seeber's *Wanderkino* in 1904. Starting with a musical concert, this travelling cinema then showed the audience a short film of the Gordon Bennett Cup – the first international motor race in 1903 – before taking them on a walk through London's zoological garden and to a bullfight in Madrid in front of the Spanish king. The show ended with *Sleeping Beauty* and a tour of the 'fascinating lumber trade to Canada' – all for 40 pfennigs.[117]

It was in 1906 that cinemas began to settle down. In the United States and Western Europe, most cities, large and small, now got a fixed movie house. London's first was the Balham Empire, with seating for one thousand. In the States, Lexington, Kentucky, had two cinemas for its 25,000 inhabitants. The growth in the following years was phenomenal. By 1914, Britain had 3,800 cinemas. London alone had almost five hundred, with seating for 400,000, more than five times that in music halls. Within a decade, cinema had become the dominant form of popular entertainment. In 1913, 250,000 Londoners went to the cinema, every day. In New York City, the weekly attendance was closer to a million; almost a third were children. Fun had never been cheaper. Almost everyone had a nickel for the nickelodeon. In Britain, children often got two pennies pocket money – one for the ticket, the other for sweets to go with it.[118]

Far from being a sudden shock to the raw nerves of innocent

viewers, early cinema worked in tandem with a range of established technologies of marvel. In its travelling days, it built on the customary culture of fairs. In music halls, short pictures were interspersed with song and humour. There is little evidence that the first generation of viewers found cinema unnerving. The magic lantern and the panorama had prepared audiences from all classes for the sensation of moving images and illusions of reality, in rural Ireland as well as the centre of Paris. Panoramas went back to the 1790s and immersed spectators in landscapes and battle scenes painted on vast canvases that often stretched to over 200 square metres. The next generation added the diorama, which moved the scenes themselves in front of an audience. By 1889, there were seventeen of these in Paris. The La Tourraine diorama offered a life-sized model of a steamer. Sitting inside it, workers and peasants who had never seen the Atlantic experienced a sea passage along the French coastline, with moving canvases of waves, beaches and hotels. Over a million visitors went. Another simulated voyage took Parisians from Venice to Constantinople, in under half an hour, including the smell of sea water and the motion of the sea. Even once they were permanent, cinemas did not necessarily operate as separate entertainment. The Hippodrome in Paris, 'the biggest cinema in the world', opened on 14 December 1907 and aimed at total spectacle. It was a circular hall with an open area in the centre for horses and, later, elephants. A full-size orchestra played. On opening night, the audience was treated to eighteen short films, choral singing and a boxing match.[119]

Audiences were everything but passive spectators in a trance. They cheered on heroes and booed villains. For producers, the volume of applause was an indication of a star's worth. Sometimes the audience was the main entertainment. Showings were frequently disrupted. One Londoner recalled his childhood visit around 1910 to a local cinema that sat thirty, with kids at the front. Every time the short film broke down again, 'a stout lady who always sat on a cushioned stool near the Exit . . . tugged at a little chain hanging from the gas-lamp near the door.' The room flooded with light: 'the management had learned not to leave a company of children in the dark with nothing to engage their attention.' At a 'more stately pleasure-dome', brown-uniformed attendants 'paraded the aisles from time to time squirting deodorant over our heads'.[120] Cinemas had narrators and musicians who built up scenes in their own, individual style. Many ran a continuous programme, from morning to midnight. People came and went as they pleased. A structured viewing format, where audiences arrived during the trailer and left after 'the end', only slowly emerged in the 1930s.

Until 1909, film length had an upper limit of 300 metres, or sixteen minutes. In the next few years, *Quo Vadis* and *Les Miserables* were the first to offer two continuous hours. The initial response, however, was one of scepticism, and gives us a sense of dominant viewing habits. The editor of the French *Ciné-Journal* observed in October 1911:

> the public enters and leaves in the middle of the show . . . Our spectators tend to be people who go the cinema for an hour to experience diverse emotions and have their curiosity satisfied quickly. They love short drama and pretty comedies. They appreciate the news of the week and films about distant lands, exotic tribes and natural history. How can we possibly open our programmes with a long film that is the entire programme?[121]

The succession of genres shown across a programme required audiences to switch between modes and speeds of viewing. This was not conducive to mass hypnosis.

For Simmel, the mind had two layers. Deeply felt and emotional relationships were located in the 'more unconscious layers of the psyche and grow most readily in the steady rhythm of uninterrupted habituations', associated with rural life. The intellect occupied the 'transparent, conscious, higher layers of the psyche'.[122] Metropolitan life, he believed, simultaneously drained the lower layers and exhausted the higher ones. What he failed to appreciate was that movies also cultivated new faculties. Local films, shot at the factory gate, gave workers a chance to watch themselves on screen. Audiences shouted in delight at recognizing themselves and friends. Nature and travel films created a sense of moving through time and space. 'I love the cinematograph,' one Frenchman confessed in 1907. 'It satisfies my curiosity . . . I tour the world and stop where it pleases me, in Tokyo and Singapore. I follow the craziest itineraries', from the Rocky Mountains to the waterfalls of the Zambezi.[123]

By 1914, most people in American and Western European cities went to the movies routinely, but this did not automatically make them a homogeneous public. Taste and habits reflected class, education, gender and ethnicity. For working-class wives the cinema was a liberator. Instead of spending Saturday alone at home, they, like their husbands, now went out to entertain themselves. Girls tended to go to the movies less often than boys, who enjoyed greater control over their time and money. Migrant communities had their own theatres. The Jewish cinema in New York's Lower East Side mixed Yiddish vaudeville with biblical films. For Italian migrants, Italian imports were as important as movies about the American way of life. Arguably, it was films such as *Dante's Inferno* (1911) that turned Sicilians into Italians in the first place. In Chicago, African-Americans went to the black movie theatre on the South Side. For affluent shoppers, there were cinemas alongside department stores with special afternoon showtimes. By 1910, cinema attracted audiences from all classes and in all kinds of cities.[124]

The most nuanced picture of audiences we have is for Germany, where in 1913 the student Emilie Altenloh observed movie-goers in Mannheim for her doctoral thesis on the 'sociology of cinema', the first academic study of its kind. Mannheim was a city with 200,000 inhabitants and a dozen cinemas. Cinemas were stratified. Workers paid 50 pfennigs but the local elite paid ten times that for a box seat and arrived in evening dress. In between these two groups sat officers, engineers and traders. It was academics who went to the movies least often – a point worth remembering, given the often patronizing accounts of early movies and movie-goers by Kracauer and other intellectuals. Tastes diverged considerably, including among the lower classes. Industrial workers, Altenloh found, liked humour and love stories best. The petit-bourgeoisie enjoyed historical drama and war. Artisans, on the other hand, preferred nature and educational films. For them, entertainment had to have a practical value. It is impossible to disentangle entirely the social bias from these findings. Altenloh was convinced that the proletariat was culturally impoverished, with a passion for Indians and robbers but immune to anything requiring deep appreciation. Still, her interviews do bring out the range of cultural practices missing from accounts of homogeneous mass consumption. 'I visit almost everything,' a fifteen-year-old machine fitter reported. 'Mondays I go to the cinema. Tuesdays I stay at home. On Wednesdays I go to the theatre. Fridays I have gymnastics' and 'Sundays I go for a walk in the woods with the girl from next door.'[125] He does not tell us what happened next, but he did list his preferred genres. He especially liked romantic love stories and films about Indians and aviators. But he also adored Wagner and Schiller. This skilled worker suggests that tastes might have been more complex a century ago than has been assumed. Cowboys and Fantomas, the arch-criminal genius of evil, did not push *Lohengrin* off the stage.

Warnings of cinematic overstimulation were part of more general anxieties about leisure. Attempts to regulate recreation and drive out plebeian entertainment from public space went back to the seventeenth century and before. Industrialization gave them fresh urgency. Industry required discipline, and less drink and leisure at the workplace. Once separated from work, leisure turned into a social problem that called for further discipline. What if people wasted their spare time on immoral and stupefying distractions instead of improving themselves? Victorians launched a crusade for 'rational recreation'.[126] Cities, churches and companies established libraries, working men's clubs, YMCAs and athletic teams. This unease expressed a deeper ambivalence about consumer choice: could individuals be trusted to choose their own recreation? The simultaneous shortening of the work day and rise in spending power set off a frightening growth in commercial temptations. In the 1850s, industrial workers in the United States worked almost seventy hours a week. By 1890, this had dropped to sixty hours; by 1918, it was fifty-four. The whole balance of national life seemed to be shifting. The 'land of labour', was turning into a 'nation of idlers', the president of Colgate University in upstate New York warned. America was heading the way of ancient Rome, amusing itself to death. Commercial leisure was so dangerous because it gave free rein to instinctive impulses, previously sublimated by hard labour. It was 'cheap, enervating and deteriorating' and resulted in 'moral and intellectual degeneration'.[127] Across the Atlantic, there was similar unease about the corrupting force of cinemas, gambling and dance halls. A militaristic climate heightened fears that the national body was softening.

The growing visibility of children and adolescents as consumers gave these anxieties a new generational complexion. Friedrich Nietzsche and youth leaders called on the young to shed the 'pseudo-wants' of city life. Significantly, it was at this time, in 1904, that the American psychologist Stanley Hall defined adolescence as a separate life-stage, a period of 'storm and stress' prone to perversion and vice.[128] Troublesome youths were nothing new in history, but it was now that they were diagnosed as a distinct problem: juvenile delinquents. Moral panic was fuelled by an awareness of the growing independence of youth, in terms of both money and mobility. Scavenging for tin cans, bottles, paper and discarded furniture and selling the loot to the local junkman gave city kids new freedom as consumers. Rising wages freed adolescent workers from parental control. A welfare officer in Germany commented on the mixed blessing of the eight-hour day introduced just after the First World War. Youths now had so much money and time on their hands that they rushed to any kind of entertainment to relieve their boredom.

They were 'tempted into a life-style change that severely damaged their still developing bodies'.[129]

The street and the dance hall were flashpoints in the war over leisure. American reformers like Jane Addams felt they were waging an uphill battle. The cinema and corner candy store were much more attractive than the school settlement house. In New York City 95 per cent of children played in the street. A 1909 survey of the Lower East Side – an area of barely one third of a square mile between East Houston, Grand and Suffolk Streets – counted 188 candy shops and stands, 73 soda shops, 9 dance halls and 8 movie houses. There were nine synagogues and churches, one police station and not a single playground. If the saloon was the 'poor man's club . . . the candy shop and ice cream parlor are the youngster's club.' Here they socialized and skylarked. Candy stores had slot machines and lotteries. Juvenile Protective Agencies warned that sweets and gambling tempted children to steal and pawn their school books. The street was a magnet for delinquency; it was not until the 1920s that cars took over and paper boys disappeared from city centres. Part of the blame fell on overcrowding. Home was no longer 'sweet home' but a mere 'sleeping box and eating den', in the words of the secretary of New York City's child welfare committee.[130] Adolescents looked for fun in the street.

Delinquency, however, was not the monopoly of the poor. Recreation was so contested precisely because adolescents from comfortable families also ended up in court. A survey in Cleveland traced delinquency to upwardly mobile families. 'Their recent prosperity has permitted their children a sudden accession of comfort and money and spare time.' Such youths had thrown off a 'patriarchal notion of family control'. 'The only standard they seem to have substituted is that of cutting a dashing figure with "the crowd". They . . . represent a nascent social energy permitted to run wild.' The most frequent offence was staying out at night. Street gangs formed. Girls were going out unsupervised. Girls from families with a decent income were found to spend between two and five hours a day at home on chores, but four and a half hours or more on each school day on street corners and in movies, seven hours on the weekends, 'often meeting boys'. Girls in seventh grade went skating with boys and had sex. Some ended up in institutions. It was a 'good' neighbourhood, the report stressed, that displayed 'one of the worst failures in developing wholesome uses of spare time'.[131]

The dance craze spawned fresh dangers. In the early years of the twentieth century, dancing grew into one of the most popular spare-time activities, second only to reading. Dance halls and academies mushroomed, and introduced girls between the ages of sixteen and twenty-one to slightly older boys. One dollar bought six group lessons. By 1919, Cleveland, for example, a city with 800,000 inhabitants, was home to 115 dance halls. The two at Luna Park and Euclid Beach Park, on the shore of Lake Erie, sold over 120,000 tickets a week. A well-managed academy had rules against 'tough dancing', which included 'hugging, twisting, "spieling" '.[132] At Euclid Beach Park, the dance floor was managed with 'rigid standards of propriety'. Only the schottische, waltz and two-step were allowed. Couples who thought they could put in an extra glide had to leave the floor. The problem was the many halls where booze and bodies moved freely. In Manhattan, half the dance halls sold liquor. Many dance academies rented out their halls for 'run off' affairs. 'Peculiarly undesirable' were those that invited 'the mixture of the hardened girl and the corrupted man with the unsophisticated who come into such contacts for the first time'. 'Pick-up acquaintances' were spreading. To keep 'this undesirable practice at a minimum', Cleveland's recreation experts pressed for more dance-hall inspectors and for 'alert and wise chaperones' to police not only the floor but 'even the sidewalks and streets near the building'.[133]

Attempts to clean up youth leisure took two main directions. One was a flight from the city. Boy scouts, *Wandervögel* and organized youth movements took to the woods and mountains to cleanse and recharge their bodies. If there was to be dancing, it would be folk dancing, or in a loin cloth around a tree. The other approach was to raise the quality of leisure within the city. Youth protection agencies waged a battle against dirt and trash. In Hamburg, teachers and pastors distributed white lists of respectable literature and organized boycotts of bookshops that corrupted the young with stories of crime and Buffalo Bill. On Sunday afternoons, youth centres screened approved films, read fairy tales and held Punch and Judy shows.[134] These never reached more than a small minority of the population.

More significant were the new leisure spaces sponsored by city authorities. European cities had started to open botanical gardens to the public in the middle of the nineteenth century, not without resistance from some middle-class burghers. American cities took this initiative to a new level. City people needed play not Puritanism, reformers argued. This was partly a defensive move, prompted by fears of militant workers. Urban, industrial life was stressful: far better to give workers some entertainment than for their frustration to breed revolution. Strikes taught early critics to accept the movie house as a safe outlet.

There was also, however, a genuine appreciation of the positive role of play in human development. The pursuit of pleasure was a 'normal impulse', the secretary of New York's recreation committee emphasized in 1912. Psychology 'teaches that joy is power; that right recreation is not merely wholesome but developmental'.[135] The problem was not leisure but cities' failure to channel it in healthy directions. Dance halls and candy stores were to be supervised and regulated, not shut down. Above all, cities needed to offer more leisure themselves. Parks were laid out. Swimming pools opened. By 1890, Worcester's Lake Park in Massachusetts attracted 20,000 visitors a day, roughly one in five of its population. In Cologne, the city built its first municipal sports ground in 1892; twenty years later, in the district of Poll, it added an athletic field, five football pitches, one hockey field and ten tennis courts. In England, Manchester bought Platt Field in 1908 and turned the former country park into a municipal leisure complex with 46 tennis courts, 13 football and 9 cricket pitches, a boating lake and a paddling pool. American cities built playgrounds with sports equipment. 'Shall we Provide a Playground? Or Enlarge the Jail?', leaflets asked. In 1910, Worcester offered the first of its summer playground programmes. The city paid for fifty staff and offered athletics, singing, games and sewing lessons at twenty locations. Close to 7,000 children took part every day.[136] Investment in public recreation continued to grow after the First World War. Between 1925 and 1935, leisure budgets doubled. By then, there were almost 10,000 playgrounds and 8,000 softball diamonds across the United States.[137] Commercial and public recreation, then, grew in tandem. Leisure in the city was a mixed economy.

The biggest beasts were the amusement parks within easy reach of the big cities. The famous Tivoli Garden opened in Copenhagen in 1843, with a merry-go-round, scenic railway and oriental buildings. The years around 1900 witnessed a dramatic expansion. Coney Island, in Brooklyn, encompassed Dreamland, Steeplechase and Luna Park. Luna Park alone occupied 36 acres with a 200-foot high Electric Tower, reflecting pools, waterslides, a 'trip to the moon' and a submarine ride inspired by Jules Verne. It was a fairyland with 1,200 towers, domes and minarets. Two hundred thousand lights glimmered in the night sky (see Plate 27). Resorts such as Luna Park blended nostalgia and technology, relaxation and thrill, carnival and curiosity. In one tour, a visitor could enjoy a daring rollercoaster ride, visit a freak show, flirt and take in an Inuit village.

What were the effects of this cocktail on urban crowds? One thesis is that commercial leisure blended diverse immigrant cultures into a more homogeneous crowd. True, in its early years, Coney Island attracted a wide range of visitors, although there was always an informal colour bar. Social and cultural mixing must not be overstated, however. By the 1920s, the elite had abandoned Coney Island, and affluent workers started to retreat to the more respectable Jersey shore. In other parts of the world, amusement parks developed their own distinct flavour, reflecting the particular social and cultural composition of their surroundings. Blackpool, the premier English resort, with a pleasure beach that catered for up to a quarter of a million visitors on a bank holiday, made much of its democratic quality. In the words of the *Blackpool Times* in 1904, the resort brought together, 'the merchant and the mechanic, the lady of fashion and the factory lass . . . the mightiest and the meanest'.[138] By comparison with Coney Island, Blackpool was always more uniform, a Protestant crowd from the same industrial hinterland, with a shared sense of respectable, orderly fun. Still, a class divide ran through the resort, and the town made sure to keep fairgrounds out of the middle-class North Shore. In colonial Singapore, the New World amusement park opened in 1923. Previously segregated public space was opened to all classes and races. From six o'clock to midnight there were boxing matches, gambling, movies, theatre and restaurants. The cabaret had the longest dance floor in Malaya. Its success, however, depended less on hybrid fusion than on the range of cultural genres it offered different ethnic audiences. Next door to a *bangsawan* Malayan opera, a Chinese troupe performed Chinese opera. Popular dances included the Malayan *ronggeng* but also European dances including flamenco. Theatre programmes alternated between Shakespeare, Dutch plays and Hindustani fairy tales.[139]

By 1914, cities in industrial nations were networks of gas, water and communication with a material lifestyle fundamentally different from that in the country. In summertime, residents in small towns and rural areas, used to fetching their water from wells in buckets, watched with trepidation the arrival of tourists from the city accustomed to baths and constant running water. At the same time, department stores, discount stores, advertising and mail-order catalogues spread urban tastes and fashions to the provinces. Consumer culture did not stop at the few remaining city walls. In that sense, the city was beginning to lose some of its uniqueness.[140] It was no longer necessary to live in Paris to look like a Parisian. As important as these general movements, however, was the diversity within and between cities. Metropolitan modernity was not cast from a single mould. Innovation and adaptation overlapped. Cities accommodated department stores and street sellers, cinemas and public playgrounds, hot running water in private bathrooms and stand-pipes in alleys and courtyards. Instead of a monotonous lifestyle and blasé mentality, cities were home to a diversity of practices, rhythms and spaces of consumption. It is unhelpful, then, to view this period as a solid shift from custom and community to commerce and individualism. Cities and their inhabitants were not passively swept away by a tsunami of goods and desires. At the same time as shops were mushrooming, cities were also forging new communities through consumption.

5

The Consumer Revolution Comes Home

Bruno Taut hated clutter. One of the leading modernist architects in Weimar Germany, Taut was responsible for iconic housing developments such as the Horseshoe Estate in Berlin (1925–33), a 350-metre-long semicircle of three-storey apartment blocks surrounded by several hundred terrace houses with gardens. The modernists' mission was to build new, better homes to create new, better people. The flats on the Horseshoe Estate had separate bathrooms and kitchens, revolutionary at the time. Modernists prized flat roofs, unadorned exteriors, functional steel and glass. But eliminating external frills was only half the answer. Reform also had to work from the inside out. Taut's *The New Home*, which he dedicated in 1924 to 'all women', was a declaration of war on stuff: 'Pictures of all kind, mirrors, throws and doilies, curtains over curtains, pillows on top of pillows, carpets, door-mats, clocks, photos and souvenirs on display, consoles crowded with trinkets . . .' Cultured elites bemoaning popular taste was nothing new, but for Taut the problem ran deeper. People had developed a superstitious fear of losing their precious little possessions. They were no longer kings in their castles: they had become serfs to things.[1]

This 'tyranny of the lifeless' was slowly eating away at family harmony and, most of all, at the housewife. Women – 'the true creators of the home' – had become slaves to dusting. The liberation of women required liberation from stuff. Taut's manifesto for simplicity was inspired by a mix of sources. In addition to the social-reform atmosphere of the Weimar years, he drew on Christine Frederick, the American prophet of domestic efficiency, whose time-and-motion studies had shown how much energy housewives could save in a more rationally designed kitchen. But his true passion was for Japan and the simple, clear lines of its interiors; after Hitler came to power in 1933, the Jewish Taut would flee to Takasaki. German homes needed to be more Japanese. Knick-knacks, tassels and fringes, little craft objects made by the children, all these had to go; together with excess chairs and 'shoddy department-store stuff'. Taut was not especially concerned whether things were art nouveau or Biedermeier. It was the cult of the 'ensemble', the seemingly endless combinations of objects that did not belong together that galled him. Built-in cupboards and functional furniture would take their place, restoring the housewife's health and sanity (see Plate 31). And people had to be educated out of the false sentimentalism inspired by all the stuff and into a more authentic appreciation of cultural objects. 'Mental hygiene', he wrote, was just as important as bodily cleanliness. Like the Japanese, Europeans should keep their pictures and objects locked away in a trunk, bringing them out only when they wanted to appreciate them. Unlike his fellow modernists, Taut was never a pure functionalist. He allowed for distinct colour combinations – on the Horseshoe Estate, front doors were painted yellow, red or green – but, otherwise, the walls should be bare.

Taut's programme for a domestic revolution carried a particular charge in Weimar Germany, where the project of building a democracy made architecture and design highly political.[2] Yet soul-searching about the home as a space of consumption was taking place across Europe, the United States and Japan. If fears (and hopes) about what consumption was doing to society had focused on the city and public space in the late nineteenth century, in the first half of the twentieth they increasingly revolved around private space. Inside the homes of the European elites and middling sort, the separation of private from public spaces had already begun in the seventeenth and eighteenth centuries, giving rise to a new ideal of separate male and female spheres. With greater privacy came a new culture of comfort, epitomized by upholstered chairs and, later, sofas. Around 1900, these longer trends took on a new significance. Industrialization had dramatically accelerated the exodus of paid work from the home. It left behind the domestic sphere as *the* quintessential space of consumption, a material haven managed by the housewife and waiting to be filled with possessions, new technologies and leisure activities.

We are entering the era of the living-room suite, the washing machine, the radio and home ownership. Mass-manufactured goods brought standardized comfort to the common man. Gas and electricity were filling the home with machines. The radio and gramophone opened it up to a new world of entertainment and sound. And the home itself became a prized possession.

This invasion of goods was about more than how much stuff people had. It transformed the heart and soul of everyday life, its rhythms and routines. Would these machines liberate people from drudgery and dependence and nourish a richer personality, thereby strengthening family and society? Or would they feed an addiction to ever higher levels of comfort and consumption, fostering a selfish materialism and withdrawal from the world? As with all revolutions, so with this one: there was no inevitable direction and no foregone conclusion. Home economists and manufacturers, politicians, designers and novelists, vied with each other for control of the home. In the end, however, the home was shaped by the people who lived in it, and by local norms and conventions

HOME, SWEET HOME

What was an affront to taste to some was big business to others. Across Europe and the United States, the last third of the nineteenth century saw a boom in home furnishing. Incomes were rising and, with them, spending on the home. In Boston and London as in Paris and Berlin, these were golden years for home decorators as the aspiring middle classes sought to bolster their social position and identity by tastefully arranging their domestic interior. Young couples setting up home were urged to view the living room as an 'important agent in the education of life', in the words of the popular American guide *The House Beautiful*, first published in 1881.[3] Decor expressed a family's culture, and was said to have long-lasting effects on its members. The spread of wallpaper captures the cult of home furnishings. By 1874, British wallpaper manufacturers produced 32 million pieces, six times as many as only a generation earlier.[4] In middle-class homes, porcelain pugs and brass peacocks jostled with Japanese radiator covers.

Better-off working families, too, were expanding and updating their furnishings, especially in the United States, where real wages were highest. For contemporary observers, carpets were the litmus test of home comfort. They were one of the benchmarks used in a pioneering survey of skilled workers in Massachusetts in 1874. One machinist's family earned just over a thousand dollars a year. Half of it went on food, yet all six rooms in their home had carpets. In half the houses visited, at least the parlour had a carpet.[5] Many homes had a sewing machine and an organ or a piano, the ultimate proof of respectability.

The lives of most industrial workers in Europe and Asia were a far cry from this level of comfort. In St Petersburg, some married workers had pillows and covers, but most single seasonal tenants slept on bare wooden planks in overcrowded flats, without any place for personal belongings.[6] Still, even outside the United States, there were signs of change. In Europe, miners bought pianos on instalment plans. The parlour became sacred, invested with the decorative 'superfluities' so hated by social reformers; workers bought things even when they could not afford to use them, like the brass fender which was kept in a locked parlour.[7] In late-developing Scandinavia, skilled workers, too, began to enjoy more home comforts. In Christiana (now Oslo), a textile worker's family still shared a kitchen with the neighbour but now had their own living room (12 by 15 feet), with 'two windows, with short lace curtains across the top . . . a bed made up as a single one; a wo[o]den sofa or settee that could be used for a bedstead; a table, cupboard, clock, pictures, flowers'.[8]

The sheer size of the new mass market in home furnishings raised a trinity of fears: it threatened to standardize life and culture, produce artificial desires and imprison women in a gilded cage. These fears tended to be voiced together. Typically, Taut complained that living rooms had begun to look like international hotel rooms, uniform and florid, preventing nations from cultivating their own style of living.[9] Cheaper chairs and sideboards were a threat to creative artists, but they were a boon for consumers. Attempts to counter this trend, such as the Arts and Crafts movement, often achieved the opposite: artist-designed wallpaper and carpets were also mass produced.

The late nineteenth century saw a vigorous interplay between the unique and the mass-produced, as individualization and standardization pushed each other to new heights. It reached its climax in the homes of the Parisian bourgeoisie. On the one hand, drawing rooms and corridors were filling up with copies and imitations, made possible by new materials and methods of large-scale reproduction. Rubber had a lot to answer for. Initially used for medical purposes, from the 1860s *caoutchouc* revolutionized the art market. Suddenly, it was possible to mass-manufacture hard-rubber figurines in their thousands and to produce decorative vases, frames and embossed photo albums on the cheap. Aluminium, linoleum and celluloid enhanced the scope of mass reproduction further. Vulcanization brought artificial flowers and miniature greenhouses. Electroplating made it possible to make zinc and brass look like bronze. In Ferdinand Barbedienne's legendary foundry in Paris, hundreds of workers were busy releasing from their casts armies of fake-bronze Davids shouldering their slingshots and Mozarts complete with violins in all sizes. The bourgeoisie had caught *statuomanie*, it was said. What rubber and bronze did to statues, lithography did to paintings. La Maison Legras in 1870 carried 2,000 different reproductions in its catalogue, from still lifes to landscapes. It was no longer necessary to visit the Louvre. For 20 francs, famous statues and paintings now came home.[10]

Fears of falling into shallow conformism spurred a feverish pursuit of individualized taste. By the late nineteenth century, the bourgeois home had become a sanctuary of the private self. In part, this was a retreat in a very real, physical sense, as the middle classes turned their apartments into safe havens from the revolutionary danger of the street. But, from the middle of the century, privatization was also increasingly visible in people's relationship to objects. Safety meant more than a lock on the front door. Cabinets, desks, wardrobes, boxes and many other personal belongings were fitted with locks by enterprising locksmiths. Personal items had to be secured against servants but also against family and peers. Carpets and curtains became more elaborate to create a cocoon of silence. The longing for safety was reinforced by a quest for individual comfort, control and order through things. The growing fixation with personal cleanliness in these years extended to possessions. With dusting, disinfectants and special 'Chinese powders', the bourgeoisie brought their material world up to their standard of personal hygiene. Genuine *confort*, a term the French adapted from the English in the 1840s, did not only concern the 'satisfaction of the body' or even the spirit, one manual stressed, but 'even more so that of the heart'.[11] *Drapes artistiques* over chairs, coverlets and a harlequin statuette on a side table showed one's individual taste and character. *Le Journal des demoiselles* and similar home magazines which took off in this period ran articles on 'Home, Sweet Home' and proffered advice on how to give the interior the right personal touch. In Britain, it has been argued, liberalism strongly encouraged people to develop their individual style in home decoration,[12] but a similar trend can be found in countries which did not enjoy the same liberal climate. The home emerged as a temple to the self across Europe.

By 1914, middle-class families could choose from thousands of differently designed chairs, sofas, beds and side tables. The London department store Liberty began to experiment with lifestyle marketing, offering Moorish-style furniture alongside Eastern pots to customers fearful of 'common' taste.[13] And the production of the new sparked a craze for the old. Early modern Paris had already seen a profitable trade in 'demi-luxe' furniture, sold via upholsterers from cash-strapped aristocrats to an aspiring bourgeoisie.[14] But, in general, the demand for the old was limited. A survey of the apartments of Parisian merchants, bankers and shopkeepers found that antiques were completely missing in the 1830s–'50s. By the 1890s, they were full of them. Paris and London experienced an antiques boom. Curiosity shops, antique dealers and furniture brokers multiplied by leaps and bounds.[15] There was a craze for copies of Louis XVI consoles and rococo chairs. For the lover of trinkets, there were monthly magazines such as *La Curiosité* (1886) and *Le Bibelot* (1907). Collecting antiques became a shared pastime among the bourgeoisie. The desire for the authentic ranged far and wide, from Asian vases and Turkish carpets to spinning wheels from Brittany, which wove a thread between the Parisian bourgeoisie and an idealized bygone rustic past. Far from destroying the old and 'authentic', the spread of mass comfort increased the value of such objects, leading to an almost archaeological interest in all things past, both common and elite. People hunted down old furniture, had it repaired or simply broken up and rebuilt with other pieces. For upholsterers, it was the best of times.

If this trend was international in scope, it had a particular thrust in the United States. It was no accident that the man most responsible for streamlining conveyor-belt mass production was also in the vanguard of collecting ordinary objects made by ordinary people: Henry Ford, the father of the Model T automobile. Ford started to gather mundane stuff in 1906. By 1929, his collection had grown into a museum of junk, a kind of Smithsonian of the common man, and is still open to the public today, in Dearborn, just outside Detroit. Edith Roosevelt, wife of President Theodore, was another 'junk snupper'. These years saw the 'transubstantiation of junk', in the words of a leading scholar of collecting.[16] The yard sale was born. In the sixteenth and seventeenth centuries, collecting prized objects from afar had been a way for kings to show the global reach of their power.[17] Around 1900, cosmic kingship was being democratized. Everyone could be a collector.

Here was one source of Taut's despair. Unlike for many later critics of 'consumerism', for Taut the problem was not that of a 'throwaway society'. It was that people were not throwing away enough. One person's attic became another one's living room.

The diffusion of goods around 1900 disrupted established codes of status. Accumulation and display were a way to reassert social hierarchies. In 1899, the heterodox Chicago economist Thorstein Veblen christened this phenomenon 'conspicuous consumption'. In his *Theory of the Leisure Class*, he focused primarily on the super-rich and their use of costly entertainments and fine arts to distinguish themselves from those below. For the elite, 'vicarious consumption' was a way to assert their high station in life at a time when goods were becoming available to the many.[18] The pivotal figure in this competitive game was the lady of the house. Through her leisure, her jewels and a tastefully assembled interior, she could demonstrate the high reputation of the middle-class family, and its distance from the grubby world of work.

As Veblen showed, much of this was a charade. The lady of the house was not necessarily idle. Domestic work was simply disguised to uphold the ideal of leisure. Real comfort and leisure, Veblen argued, were never the goal, and it was 'a more or less fortuitous circumstance' if they were achieved. All these exercises followed what he called 'the great economic law of wasted effort'. Instead of turning resources to productive use, 'conspicuous consumption' wasted them on accumulation, display and imitation. While Veblen directed his sharpest, most cynical observations at the new American elite, he stressed that this status-fuelled rivalry also continued 'at a lower point in the pecuniary scale than the requirement of vicarious leisure'. The cult of comfort and decency compelled all wives to 'consume some goods conspicuously for the reputability of the household and its head'.[19]

In an age of progress, none of this made for very happy reading. Veblen was no Darwin or Spencer. Social evolution was regressive. Consumption was merely the latest chain in man's enslavement of woman. The wife had evolved from the 'drudge and chattel of the man . . . [as] the producer of goods for him to consume', into 'the ceremonial consumer of goods which he produces' – an 'unfree servant'.[20] For feminist reformers such as Charlotte Perkins Gilman, Veblen provided authoritative support, notwithstanding his own notoriety as a womanizer who was constantly trying to seduce his students and his colleagues' wives; his own wife eventually divorced him. It was because 'playing house' was the one thing that women were allowed to do, Gilman wrote, that women indulged in decoration and stuff. The home was a material monster that 'grows by what it feeds upon' and kept women from contributing to the real world. The only limit to this 'senseless extravagance' appeared to be 'the paying capacity of the man'.[21]

Lust for distinction had been the stuff of satire and literature since ancient times. Veblen's originality was to make it the engine of an entire social system. The argument's simplicity is the key to its continuing appeal, but also its fundamental weakness. For Veblen, human nature was pretty much a constant. He saw goods as instruments of social reputation and power. People put up a picture or bought furniture more to impress others than for their own personal pleasure. The use of things was directed outwards rather than inwards. Those who, like Veblen and Taut, championed plain living ignored or belittled the feelings, meanings and memories that objects often carried. Taut mocked the 'emotional fetishism' of the housewife who could not let go of a little craft object made by her son – 'our darling Billy made this, do you remember, Hubby, when he was just . . .'[22]

While some consumption was (and remains) conspicuous, Veblen's contemporaries were also increasingly turning to possessions and hobbies for self-fulfilment. In part, this compensated for an increasingly regimented world of work. By 1900, hobbies were advertised as a cure against boredom and nervous exhaustion. Yet hobbies were more than a retreat. They were also a way of exploring and affirming the material dimensions of the self.

Home improvement was self-improvement. Few captured this creed better than George and Weedon Grossmith in *The Diary of a Nobody*, the greatest satire on the suburban home in the English language, first published in *Punch* in 1888. Mr Pooter and his wife Carrie had barely moved into their six-room, semi-detached 'villa' in one of the new suburbs in north London, just around the corner from where the Arsenal football stadium stands today, when Pooter was caught by the bug of home improvement. Nothing was quite as good in Pooter's life as he aspired for it to be – the house was in a decent neighbourhood, but the back garden ran down to the train tracks, saving him £2 in rent. He was intent on putting it right. Pooter's motto was 'Home, Sweet Home', and it was within its four walls that he found his pride. Carpets had to be nailed down, curtains put up. Pooter was unstoppable. After painting some flower-pots in the garden red, he went upstairs and painted the servant's washstand, towel-horse and chest of drawers. 'To my mind it was an extraordinary improvement'; that the servant disagreed was 'an example of the ignorance of the lower classes'. What drove him on was not the opinion of others but a feeling of accomplishment. One project fed the next. Pooter got more red enamel paint – 'red, to my mind, being the best colour' – and painted the coal scuttle and the backs of his Shakespeare plays. He even painted the bathtub red – 'delighted with the result. Sorry to say Carrie was not, in fact we had a few words about it.' In the end, Pooter was punished for his folly, when, two days later, he rose from the bath in a fright, with what looked like blood running down his hands.[23]

THINGS ARE US

Such satires are entertaining, but they also contain a serious point, forcing us to reconsider what still is an influential interpretation of the years around 1900. Veblen and Taut, in their different ways, looked on the advance of goods as alienating. In this, they stood in a tradition that stretched back to Marx and Rousseau, and which continued with many socialists and consumer advocates into the twentieth century. These thinkers did not have a single ideology. What they shared was an instinctive suspicion that consumption was estranging people from their true selves. Modernity, in this view, destroyed an organic unity between man, things and nature. People became divorced from the products of their own hands, science and reason from nature and emotion, and the male public from the female private sphere. The result was disenchantment, inequality and conflict.

In *The Protestant Ethic and the Spirit of Capitalism* (1904–5), Max Weber offered one influential version of this story. Modern people were alienated from the world. All they cared about was their own salvation and success. People, Weber wrote, were sucked into an 'objectified economic cosmos', fuelled by exchange and the desire for goods. In the process, they lost the authentic, full experience of life enjoyed by the peasant and the warrior. The peasant was able to die 'saturated with life', like Abraham, having completed the full cycle of their being. Modern civilization spat out so many cultural goods that one only ever tasted a slice of life. To counter this 'devaluation', people made the pursuit of culture a 'calling' (*Beruf*). But with more culture came more goods and greater comfort. It was a vicious cycle. At best, Weber concluded, modern man could hope to die 'weary of life'.[24]

Many historians who have written about the late nineteenth and early twentieth centuries have slotted their story into this grand scheme, as another chapter in the growing divide between self and things.[25] In his brilliant study of the changing image of abundance in modern America, T. J. Jackson Lears presents this period as a culminating stage in the 'dematerializing of desire'. Advertisers nurtured a restless self. There was always another new product around the corner promising greater self-fulfilment. New stuff was scarcely unpacked before it was left behind in the purchasers' never-ending journey to find themselves. Consumer culture, in this view, completed the Enlightenment project associated with Descartes: the creation of a self separate from the physical world, and master of it.[26]

Disenchantment, it is worth stressing, is an interpretation of modern history based on assumptions about human nature, rather than an account of how people actually engaged with the material world. If we are concerned with the latter, another story emerges. Rather than ongoing dematerialization, the 1890s–1920s witnessed a renaissance of the material self. The enlightenment story continued, albeit in a different key. The language of the passions, of sociability, refinement and sympathy gave way to a more hands-on, more private relationship with things. Mr Pooter, collecting, crafts and home furnishing, these were all elements of a renewed appreciation of the role of things in the development of the self. The self was not sealed off from the material world. It was touched and formed by things, while things in their turn carried the imprint of an individual's character and culture. Artefacts came to be seen as passageways into the self.[27] The world's first open-air museum, in 1891, was Skansen, on the island of Djurgården in Stockholm, where visitors could take a stroll through centuries of old houses, farmsteads and artefacts. In New England, 'living history' museums started to bring colonial households back to life. Anthropological exhibitions displayed living tableaux of indigenous tribes. In politics, contemporaries began to notice how flags, posters and badges created emotional ties that transcended the model of the sober, reasoning citizen.[28] Meanwhile, researchers of childhood were stressing the importance of toys for cognitive development. Societies were in the grip of a material turn – and this included literature, psychology and philosophy.

In 1890s America, this moment had a name: James. It came in two parts: Henry and William. The James brothers had their finger on the pulse of the passion for consuming. Henry, the younger by sixteen months, had dabbled as a playwright before shooting to success with *The Spoils of Poynton* in 1897, a sensitive exploration of the power of things. The novel captured the collecting craze of the period. Poynton was more than a house. It was a temple of objects carefully built up by the widow Mrs Gereth over the years. Her life and her identity have become inseparable from her collection. 'Yes, it is a story of cabinets and chairs and tables,' James wrote, but they were not 'magnificently passive'. They had a 'power in them', felt by a collector at first sight. Having, beholding and touching objects over the years reawakened those earlier 'passions' and 'faculties'.[29] Mrs Gereth's goal was not 'conspicuous consumption' – if only. Poynton was an object of private devotion that destroyed the most intimate relations around her. The problem was that her son was engaged to Mona, who appreciated the worth of Poynton enough to make its handover a condition of the marriage but who was blind to the soul of things. Mrs Gereth cared for her possessions as if they were her children. They had grown up with her, just as she herself grew with them. To hand them over to Mona was like sending off one's darlings into the charge of strangers. The novel follows Mrs Gereth's strategies to sabotage the marriage by building up the more aesthetically sensitive Fleda as a rival. The 'spoils' of Poynton spark a bitter and destructive war between the characters. In the end, Poynton goes up in flames.

Henry James laid bare the psyche of the consumer as collector. His portrayal of Mrs Gereth anticipates some of the psychological groundwork on repression and displacement by Sigmund Freud in the next generation. Goods as fetishes have an erotic quality. Things, not people, monopolize Mrs Gereth's love and desire. More than that, however, James described accumulation as an organic process of physical care. The widow had 'waited' for her treasures, 'worked for them, picked them over, made them worthy of each other and the house, watched them, loved them, lived with them'.[30] Through them she had created her personality. And by caring for them and setting them in relation to each other, she had breathed life and value into them.

Mrs Gereth is a pathological case, but what Henry James so brilliantly conveyed was a material outlook oriented towards possession but transcending the conventional portrayal of the consuming self as if it was separated from things. Desire here was more than the short-lived fix of buying yet another novelty. Collections gain in emotional investment the larger they grow and the longer they are cared for. It would be difficult to draw a clear line between Mrs Gereth's identity and her possessions. This way of looking at things could not have been more different from Rousseau's or Marx's. In the hands of a Mrs Gereth, a Mr Pooter or any ordinary person, things could be used to build social identities and relations, not just to obscure their connection to labour.

The Spoils of Poynton did not supplant *Das Kapital*, but it captured the broadening sensibilities at the time. Simply because people no longer made most of their own things, they did not automatically jump carelessly from one new item to the next. An opposite trend was also gaining ground. In their homes, people increasingly invested their selves in their possessions. This trend – the creation of value through consumption, not just production – is often associated with a switch from industrial society to consumer society that has taken place since the 1950s. It was already under way in the late nineteenth century.

When Henry James first thought of his story in 1893, his older brother, William, had just completed his two-volume *Principles of Psychology*. A professor at Harvard University, William James was an intellectual giant of the American scene, one of the founders of pragmatism. He tackled big subjects: truth, religion and the relationship between mind and matter. William had studied painting as well as medicine, and this, together with repeated bouts of depression, probably encouraged an interest in the emotional flow between people and things. To favour either thought or matter, he believed, was foolish and unnecessary. The two could not be separated; this point had been forcefully made by the German idealist Friedrich Schelling earlier in the century and was reiterated by James's contemporary C. S. Peirce. The self and the material world seeped into each other, with emotions and experiences running between them. A 'man's Self is the sum total of all that he CAN call his,' James observed. This did not mean 'only his body and his psychic powers' or his family, work and reputation, but also 'his clothes and his house . . . his lands and horses, and yacht and bank-account'. All these gave an individual 'the same emotions. If they wax and prosper, he feels triumphant; if they wane and die away, he feels cast down.'[31] People had a 'material self' as well as a social and spiritual self, and a pure ego.

The home was the nursery of that 'material self'. 'Its scenes are part of our life,' William James wrote, and it awakened 'the tenderest feelings of affection'. Any writer on domestic harmony could have written this. James went further. People, he wrote, had a 'blind impulse' to find a home and improve it. They had an 'equally instinctive impulse' to collect possessions, which became 'parts of our empirical selves'. This explained 'our depression at the loss of possessions'; it felt like 'a partial conversion of ourselves to nothingness'. This was precisely Mrs Gereth's fear.

With the material self came an emphasis on habit and doing. The world was a place of action, not pure sentiment. William James, who by all accounts was an exceptionally caring father and a generous teacher, scorned Rousseau, 'a nerveless sentimentalist and dreamer' who spent his life in a 'weltering sea of sensibility and emotion' while packing off his kids to a foundling hospital.[32] A lot of ordinary consumption was tied up in habits. There was 'no more miserable human being than the one in whom nothing is habitual but indecision' and to whom 'the lighting of every cigar, the drinking of every cup' was a matter of deliberation and choice. It was vital, therefore, James concluded, to make as many 'useful actions' automatic and habitual as early as possible. The more bits of daily life were handed over to 'the effortless custody of automaticisms', the more 'our higher powers of mind' were set free for higher tasks.[33] At the same time, people needed to keep alive their 'faculty of effort', for example by voluntarily abstaining from something – an 'insurance policy' for hard times. Here was a new view of ordinary consumption as something positive.

What the two Jameses were up to was a larger reclamation of the mundane in early-twentieth-century culture. Few philosophers would dare mention Martin Heidegger, the dark prince of twentieth-century philosophy, in the same breath as William James – indeed, Bertrand Russell felt it was best not to mention him at all.[34] There were fundamental differences between the philosophies and politics of the two men. James was a pragmatist, Heidegger an existentialist whose embrace of Nazism in the 1930s has cast a long shadow over his ideas. James practised radical empiricism; Heidegger believed that old Germanic words contained hidden wisdom: the very word 'thing', he noted, was originally connected to the *Ting*, or 'moot', a local assembly coming together to deal with a case.[35] William James, like his brother, was a transatlantic man, travelling a dozen times to Europe. His home in Cambridge, Massachusetts, was a comfortable villa with plenty of armchairs for his many visitors. The world looked very different from Heidegger's retreat in the Black Forest mountains, where his rustic cottage overlooked a working farm with its black-and-white cows grazing in a meadow.[36]

Still, there are interesting parallels when it comes to the growing appreciation of things. Like James, Heidegger tried to put the world back into the self. And, like James, this led Heidegger to emphasize the importance of ordinary things to the human spirit. In *Being and Time*, published in 1927, the handling of everyday objects acquired an almost spiritual force; Heidegger had started out as a theology student.

The authentic self required authentic living, or *Dasein*. The true person did not arrive ready-assembled but was created through 'being-in-the-world'. A person was grounded in a world of everyday objects. It was through handling things that the world announced itself to us. *Dasein* involved our caring for things, by eliminating the gap between them and us through appropriate use. Using a hammer created a deeper, more authentic relationship with the object than looking at it, what he christened, in typical linguistic overkill, *Zuhandenheit*, as opposed to *Vorhandensein*; or ready-to-handness versus simple prior existence.[37]

What William James and Heidegger illuminate is the wide spectrum of thought that registered a new respect for things in the early twentieth century: things are us. Of course, Heidegger's was a deeply masculine philosophy, one of the hammer rather than the needle; as a boy he had hammered barrels for his father, a cooper. Still, the sense he gives that things involved feeling and caring suggests that it is unhelpful to see the emotional history of objects as the domain of women alone, or to separate the symbolic from the functional qualities of consumption. Where Heidegger differed from James was over the kind of things that enriched the self, and those which debased it. The thinker from the Black Forest prized a simpler, more intense and unified life with things; the one from the Charles River a multilayered existence where some things supported routine tasks and freed up others to satisfy more emotional and creative faculties. These two positions would recur again and again as societies debated the good or evil of new technologies, from washing machines to computers.

In Heidegger's world, new technologies were dangerous intruders. Cookers, fridges and other domestic machines stifled our sense of smell and touch, robbing us of age-old sensations of being in nature, gathering food and making fire.[38] Behind this view of technological disenchantment lurked a deeper pessimism. For Heidegger, unlike for earlier Enlightenment thinkers such as Immanuel Kant, public opinion encouraged conformity, not critical reason. Most humans were like a herd following what 'people' liked and did. The tyranny of 'people' led to a culture of the average, blind to the distinct qualities of things.[39] Philosophically, Heidegger's quest for the primordial meaning of 'Being' presented itself as a deliberate break with all of Western philosophy since Plato. Politically, it led to the dangerous idea that authentic 'Being' might be nurtured in the pure racial community of the Nazis. Today, it is common to hear that we need greater respect for things in order to encourage a more sustainable lifestyle. Heidegger is a reminder that such respect is not automatically benign. Sympathy for things could mean a nasty indifference to human beings.

PROPERTY-OWNING DEMOCRACY

Home furnishings need a home. This is an obvious point, but one worth making. Residents of shack settlements in South Africa today, for example, have different attitudes to consumer goods than those who have moved to regular homes. In the latter, there is a drive to conformity, to show one is part of modern life. In the former, limited privacy and high visibility discourage people from bringing home new goods for fear of unleashing gossip and ostracism; some prefer to park them with relatives.[40] Not being able to put up a house has a palpable effect on what people buy. This was one reason why African mineworkers in Branch Hill in 1930s Northern Rhodesia (now Zambia) spent barely anything at all on furniture but almost 60 per cent of their hard-earned cash on clothes: they were a convenient movable asset and allowed people to wear their status literally on their backs.[41]

It is wrong, therefore, to think about the things people put in their homes as if they were free-floating objects. They derive part of their significance from their relation to the brick and mortar that surrounds them. This relationship underwent a fundamental change in the course of the twentieth century, as nations of tenants turned into home-owners. The home became the single largest consumer good in people's lives. This trend was uneven, influenced by tax regimes and financial systems that fall beyond the scope of this chapter. Nonetheless, by 1980, the majority of homes in Western Europe were no longer rented but owned – only the Netherlands, Sweden and Germany were just below the halfway mark.[42] What concerns us here is the shift in attitudes to the home as a consumer good.

The history of home-ownership is essentially a long experiment in 'behaviour change'. People do not have an innate desire to own their home. Like virtually everyone else in the nineteenth century, Mr Pooter was content to rent. In the twentieth century, ownership became the norm, not to own a home a stigma, first in the United States and Britain but then also more widely. Ownership also turned the home into a nest egg. This called for new habits of financial prudence and long-term commitment. And it encouraged a more intense and intimate love affair with the home and its possessions, making it feel more like 'ours'.

The roots of this ideal lie in the inter-war years. The man who first made home ownership a political mission was Herbert Hoover. Building more homes, raising standards of comfort and standardizing construction and fixtures were central planks in his programme to modernize America during his years as Commerce Secretary in the 1920s. Hoover's reputation would be tarnished by the Great Depression of 1929–32, but before his doomed presidency (1929–33) he was a much-admired new force: the progressive businessman. Hoover had a nose for gold – it was his discovery of it in Australia that launched his international career as a mining engineer in 1897. In character, Hoover could not have been further removed from the 'conspicuous consumers' derided by Veblen. A plain dresser, he was reserved, a man of action not appearances. Born into a Quaker family in Iowa in 1874 and orphaned at the age of nine, he had a serious outlook on life. Life was service: to oneself, to others, and to God. Many Quakers (and others) before him had held these values. What was extraordinary about Hoover was how he channelled them into a programme of material comfort and little luxuries for all: the American dream.

Hoover laid out his worldview in *American Individualism*, a slim book published in 1923, written in the shadow of the First World War. The war had given Hoover a large field in which to exercise his social conscience, first by organizing the Belgian relief effort, later at Versailles by advising President Wilson on the reconstruction of Europe. It also convinced him that the United States possessed a material civilization all of its own. The European war and the revolutions that followed were the result of backward hierarchical societies, of autocracy and class. In contrast to their vicious cycle of poverty, oppression and fanaticism, America had discovered a virtuous cycle of individual freedom, social mobility and democracy. 'Progressive individualism' was in part a way to increase efficiency. Give workers a chance to better themselves, and they will be more productive. Greater standardization of production, in turn, would cut costs and mean more goods for everyone, without having to raise wages.

Yet Hoover was a Quaker as much as a businessman. America 'cannot march toward better days unless it is inspired by things of the spirit'. There was a 'divine spark' in every heart. The key to unlocking it was to raise the standard of living. The ultimate goal of efficiency was happier homes. For Hoover, property and comfort were the 'real

fertilizers of the soil from which spring the finer flowers of life'. Governments were to concern themselves no longer just with basic food and
education. They needed to promote better homes, clothes and 'non-
essentials'. Tenants had to be raised to property-owners for their own
good and that of the nation. The 'right of property' stimulated individual
initiative, he explained, not only so 'he may gain personal comfort, security in life, protection of his family, but also because individual accumulation
and ownership is a basis of selection to leadership in administration of the
tools of industry and commerce.'[43] Individuals with a stake in their community were better parents, better neighbours and better citizens.

How novel was Hoover's American dream? Some historians have
echoed his view of a clash between a dynamic, individualist America
and a class-ridden, miserable Europe.[44] This is too harsh. In reality,
Europe was dynamic, too, as we have seen. Similarly, the idea of possessions and comfort as ways of nurturing character and celebrating
the richness of God's creation had cropped up at least since the seventeenth century. What was novel was the democratic quality of Hoover's
aspiration: everyone should be a home-owner and enjoy a rising standard of living.

Some writers have approached these years as yet another stage in the
battle between consumerism and citizenship fought by civic-minded
thinkers since Rousseau.[45] To Hoover there was no such conflict. He
christened his philosophy 'progressive individualism', but we might just
as well call it 'civic consumerism'. It grafted consumer desire and accumulation onto the civic ideal of the propertied, active citizen. Owning
a home gave people a stake in the community and at the same time
opened the door for more possessions, bathrooms and electrical appliances. In turn, having a more comfortable home would give people
the self-assurance to join civic clubs and engage in mutual advancement. The view of patriotic consumers here is much larger than in
later appeals to shop for the sake of the country. Property led to civic
engagement – as indeed it had, unbeknownst to Hoover, in the Victorian water wars.

These ideas expressed a growing conviction that home-owners were
more stable and cared more strongly about their community. This message had a middle-class flavour, but it was equally attractive to reformers
striving for greater social equality. In his pioneering study of *The Philadelphia Negro* (1899), the African-American W. E. Du Bois, for
example, concluded that slavery had destroyed 'proper home life'. This
was the reason African-Americans spent too much money on showy

clothes and too much time in church or at amusements. 'The mass of the Negro people must be taught sacredly to guard the home, to make it the centre of social life and moral guardianship.'[46] To Du Bois, those who joined building societies represented a sign of hope. 'Home ownership,' the home economist Hazel Kyrk wrote in 1929, 'is a widely accepted symbol of a family's thrift, industry and financial success.' It 'connotes order, good citizenship, prosperity, good housing'.[47]

In practice, building a property-owning democracy was not easy. Mortgages were few, down payments high. Banks introduced loans for real estate from the 1870s, but mainly to big customers. In Chicago, for example, where owner-occupied suburban developments took off after the great fire of 1871 saw rents skyrocket, Polish and other immigrant workers distrusted banks and instead borrowed from friends and family. From the 1880s, real estate developers started to offer them direct payment plans, typically with a 10 per cent down payment, and the rest in monthly payments, 'just like rent'. A two-bedroom house, with a parlour and kitchen, near Chicago's lumber docks, could be had for $1,000, although it was left to the new owner to finish the basement and attic themselves, and, in many cases, accept life without an indoor toilet and sewer system, which would not arrive until the 1920s; a factory worker typically earned $590 in 1890.[48]

The overall trend is impressive, nonetheless. In the United States almost a million new homes were constructed in 1925 alone. By 1930, virtually every other home was owner-occupied.[49] In most big cities, the number of renters was higher, but even here ownership was spreading fast. In New York and Philadelphia, 87 per cent and 61 per cent were renting in 1920. In 1930, this was down to 80 per cent and 42 per cent.

Government and business worked hand in hand to promote civic consumerism. One of the main companies was the Aladdin Company, which sold the 22 by 30 feet, two-storey 'Standard' house. A new home made a new person. 'The most uncouth,' a 1921 advert explained, 'would not dare stick his muddy brogans on the top of a finely polished mahogany table, or expectorate [spit] on a valuable rug. But in a hovel . . . would the same individual have any hesitancy about propping his feet on a barrel, and expectorating on saw dust?' A good home would 'subtly impart happiness and refinement.'[50] That home ownership should nurture family and community spirit was taken literally: Aladdin organized meetings for its extended 'family' of homebuyers, held photographic contests and announced children born into Aladdin houses.

Home ownership created new customers for home appliances. Moving house triggered new purchases to upgrade the interior. Things that had looked just fine suddenly appeared out of place in a new home. In the 1920s, this meant, above all, a 'modern' makeover of bathroom and kitchen. With the support of almost 2,000 local committees, the 'Better Homes in America' campaign promoted the ideal home across the country. In 1930, it sponsored over 6,000 home shows. Three million people stepped into the model Cape Cod-style cottage, which had running water, a built-in bath and a standardized kitchen with electric fridge and stove. These offered national belonging, a share in what Hoover had dubbed the 'American standard of living', as well as personal cleanliness and convenience. The Kohler Company set up an Anglo-Saxon model village in Riverside, Wisconsin. It had a simple message: modern bathrooms and kitchens turned immigrants into Americans. Walter Kohler, himself of Austrian stock, understood this well. At the same time, civic consumerism tempered innovation with tradition. Kohler's Cape Cod model family home advertised new fixtures in the bathroom, but the living room mixed colonial revival furnishings with hand-me-downs to show the continuity of family life across generations.[51] Making the family home the pivot of a national culture, then, gave consumption a new legitimacy, connecting past, present and future. Instead of being a threat to family and social stability, consumption now appeared its rock. This message would not be lost on future conservatives.

Not everyone agreed. A two-storey 22 by 30 feet home was not exactly a McMansion – by 2005, the median American home had ballooned to almost twice this size (2,300 square feet). Still, the spread of standardized homes raised fears about shallow conformity. No single source expressed this better than *Babbitt*, Sinclair Lewis's great American novel. Published in 1922, *Babbitt* sold a phenomenal 140,000 copies in its first four months.[52] H. L. Mencken, the leading critic of the time, praised it for showing the 'real America'.

Lewis had grown up in Minnesota, just across from Kohler's Wisconsin, and used the fictional mid-Western town of Zenith to unveil the darker side of home ownership. *Babbitt* is the story of a real estate agent who lives in the suburban development of Floral Heights, where only three houses are more than a few decades old. Part of it reads like an ideal home catalogue:

1. Wedding *cassone* (chest) from mid fifteenth-century Tuscany, with figures in Burgundian fashion.

2. This maiolica dish (tin-glazed earthenware) was part of a 178-piece dinner service made in 1559 for the wedding of Jacopo di Alamano and Isabella Salviati, of the Florentine banking family.

3. Porcelain bottle from Jingdezhen (c.1590–1620) depicting a scholar.

4. Simple stoneware bottle from the Rhineland (c.1600), with imperfect cobalt blue decoration.

5. Jasperware teapot by Wedgwood (c. 1790).

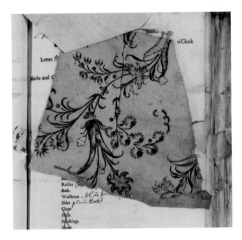

6. *top left* English jacket and petticoat (1770s) made from cotton painted and dyed in India.

7. *top right* Poor mother's flowered cotton token left with her daughter at London's Foundling Hospital in 1747.

8. *left* Fashion doll (66 cm tall), probably French, 1760s, dressed in a cotton gown, with linen underwear, and a collar of pink silk ribbon.

9. *top and middle* Drinking chocolate becomes a social custom in Europe: la xocolatada in Spain, 1710.

10. *left* Silver maté cup and *bombilla* (straw) from 19th century South America.

11. *above* Not always a place of sobriety and reason: a satirical print of a coffee-house mob, England, 1710.

12. *left* Old woman making tea; W. R. Bigg, *Cottage Interior*, 1793.

13. *top left* Young Swahili woman in fashionable *kanga* cotton, printed in Africa; Zanzibar, around 1900.

14. *top right* Mix of European and African clothes at the Kumase Mission in Asante (Ghana), 1903.

15. *middle left* English glass bowl promoting ethical consumption in the fight against slave-grown sugar, 1820s.

16. *bottom right* Living like the English: the coconut plantation owner Mr. William Augustine Peiris and family in Ceylon (Sri Lanka).

17. *left* Poster advertising coffee from French colonies and the Dutch East Indies, by Edward Ancourt, *c.* 1890.

18. *below* The 'Paula girl' (1926), promoting 'Finnish coffee' for the Paulig company, in traditional Sääksmäki costume, since 1920.

19. *top left* Aerial view of the Bon Marché in Paris, 1887.

20. *middle* The grand hall of the Bon Marché in the early 1920s.

21. *bottom* Co-operative shop in 1899 Newmarket, England.

In a corner by the front windows was a large cabinet gramophone. (Eight out of every nine Floral Heights houses had one.) Among the pictures, hung in the exact center of each gray panel, were a red and black imitation English hunting-print, an anemic imitation boudoir-print with a French caption of whose morality Babbitt had always been rather suspicious, and a 'hand-coloured' photograph of a Colonial room – rag rug, maiden spinning, cat demure before a white fireplace. (Nineteen out of every twenty houses in Floral Heights had either a hunting-print, a *Madame Fait la Toilette* print, a coloured photograph of a New England house, a photograph of a Rocky Mountain, or all four.)

The room, like Babbitt's life in general, was more comfortable than that of his boyhood. 'Though there was nothing in the room that was interesting, there was nothing that was offensive. It was as neat, and as negative, as a block of artificial ice.' The piano was unused. The books on the table were 'unspotted and laid in rigid parallels'. The grenadier dog-irons in front of the fireplace were 'like samples in a shop, desolate, unwanted, lifeless things of commerce'.[53]

The bedroom had two plain beds, with a table and 'standard electric bedside lamp' between them, and 'a standard bedside book with coloured illustrations' that had never been opened. 'The mattresses were firm but not hard, triumphant modern mattresses which had cost a great deal of money.' The hot-water radiator was of the exact standard size for the room. 'It was a masterpiece among bedrooms, right out of Cheerful Modern Houses for Medium Incomes. Only it had nothing to do with the Babbitts, nor with any one else.' The house was five years old, with all 'the latest conveniences'. It was a temple to electricity. There were plugs for lamps, the vacuum cleaner, the piano lamp, the electric fan and, in the dining-room, for the coffee maker and the toaster. 'In fact there was but one thing wrong with the Babbitt house: It was not a home.'[54]

It is unlikely that either Heidegger or Taut read it, but *Babbitt* expressed many of the concerns they had. A true home involved the art of dwelling, not just accumulation. Babbitt did not care about the things around him, because he did not use them. Things had lost their distinctiveness. Even books had been cut to standard. Once, when he was young, Babbitt had hopes of becoming a lawyer. Then he embarked on the restless pursuit of social expectations. The more expectations he fulfilled, the more possessions he stockpiled, the further he moved away from happiness and himself. In the end Babbitt finds he is nobody, an empty shell.

This was the main story, but Sinclair Lewis was too good a novelist –
the first American to win the Nobel Prize – not to capture some of the
positive feelings that attracted people to standardization. Seneca
Doane, Babbitt's college friend and a radical lawyer to boot, hated 'the
perpetual whine about "standardization"'. To him, standardization
was 'excellent, *per se*. When I buy an Ingersoll watch or a Ford, I get a
better tool for less money, and I know precisely what I'm getting, and
that leaves me more time and energy to be individual in.' William James
could not have put it better. And standardization created a shared culture and national identity. When Doane was in London and saw a
picture of an American suburb in a toothpaste ad, he was homesick.
'There's no other country in the world that has such pleasant houses.
And I don't care if they *are* standardized. It's a corking standard!'[55]

In the real America, the job of the many real estate Babbitts was
made easier by the housing shortage and by rent control. One reason
for the rise in home ownership was that rental property was taken off
the market and turned into a more profitable commodity for sale. A
study immediately after the Second World War asked one thousand
Americans why they had bought a home: 24 per cent saw it as an investment, 11 per cent were driven by a 'desire for independence'. Yet for
every fifth person who was motivated by the 'ideal of home-ownership',
there was one who felt forced to buy because they simply could not find
a home to rent. Many complained that rents had spiralled out of control and that, ultimately, ownership was cheaper.[56] People were pushed
into the property market as much as pulled.

The rise of home ownership was not a peculiarly American phenomenon. 'Small as it is, it's my happy home' was a line in the Japanese
version of 'My Blue Heaven', a popular jazz hit in the 1930s.[57] By then,
life-size show homes were on display on London's Oxford Street just
like any other consumer good. In fact, Britons enjoyed a more liberal
mortgage market than Americans, with low down-payments and
thirty-year mortgages. People could borrow up to 95 per cent of the
value of their home. The big difference between the Great Depression of 1929 and our recent one in 2008 was that, in the 1930s, silly
mortgages got Britain out of the slump instead of causing it. 'Cheap
money' made new homes affordable to clerks and workers. For a down
payment of £20, it was possible to buy a three-bedroom house complete with bathroom and kitchen worth £400. By 1938, one in five
working-class families owned their home.[58]

Although rent and mortgages were a major part of the household budget, we have little systematic knowledge about their impact on people's spending patterns, or vice versa. In English cities, for example, rents were galloping ahead of wages in the late nineteenth century – this must have put a brake on working-class consumption. The introduction of rent controls during the First World War offered some help but was soon rolled back. The proliferation of tenants' associations and rent strikes was testimony to a growing anger. Countries took different roads to better housing. In Belgium, strikes pushed the government in 1889 to give the national savings bank the power to invest in better homes for the poor; France followed with a similar law in 1894. British cities opted for slum clearances. The results were mixed. American observers at the time concluded that, in Britain, provisions for rehousing the displaced were completely inadequate. In Belgium and France, small towns put housing loans to better use than big cities; the building of boulevards in Paris and the beautification of Vienna put many of the new homes beyond the reach of the poorest inhabitants.[59]

In general, homes were becoming bigger, cleaner and more comfortable in the early twentieth century, but they were also getting more expensive. The first generation of public housing, too, charged high rents – when English workers moved into one of the new suburban council estates, their rents often shot up by a third or more. In 1928, a third of all tenants on Liverpool council estates were in arrears – and that is before the world depression hit. In the 1930s, workers spent around 20–25 per cent of their pay on rent and fuel – those who paid a mortgage, slightly more.[60] There were already some initiatives with more affordable housing in Austria in the 1920s, but mainly it was only with the expansion of welfare states after the Second World War that public housing, more rigorous rent controls and social transfers put down a supporting floor for poor consumers; how critical such public transfers were for affluent societies we shall see in a later chapter. Since the 1970s, the cost of housing as share of household consumption has once again been on the rise, at least in Western Europe.[61]

Better homes thus had many contradictory effects. Rising rents meant less spending money. A Liverpudlian woman recalls how in 1927 she moved with her husband and baby to one of the new suburban estates: it was an escape from living with her mother, aunt and cousin, squeezed into a two-bedroom terrace. It 'was so different. It made life so much easier being able to wash indoors and to have the electricity . . . [and] hot water'. At the same time, she recalled how 'we didn't have any

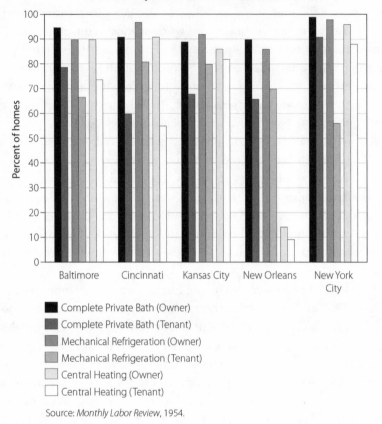

Standards of comfort in American owner- and tenant-occupied homes with kitchens, 1950–52

Source: *Monthly Labor Review*, 1954.

wardrobes, had to just hang the clothes on hangers on the picture rail. We had to . . . because you couldn't afford to buy things once you had moved in with having to find the big rent.'[62]

High rents encouraged other working-class families to take out a mortgage, but home ownership also had ambivalent effects. For some it was liberating to hold the keys to their own home. They devoted more money to home comforts. American surveys in 1950 show that owner-occupied homes were equipped with more private baths, fridges, air-conditioning and central heating than rental properties.[63] For other, less fortunate households, the financial strain proved greater than expected. In inter-war Britain, working-class families who moved out to the suburbs in some cases switched off heating and even lights to save for the next mortgage payment. Home ownership, then, could constrain as well as unleash consumption.

Owning one's home was gaining in popularity in other European countries, too. By 1960, every second Finn, Belgian and Italian owned their home; in Britain, the number had reached 42 per cent of the population. Today, owner-occupation is just as high across the European Union as in Britain (69 per cent); in fact, it is the United States (58 per cent) that lags behind Belgium, Italy and Spain (all around 80 per cent).[64] Belgian and German miners have for generations had a strong preference for ownership. Even where renting remained strong, the single family home had emerged as the dominant type by the middle of the century. In the Netherlands, 71 per cent of houses were single-family homes, although only 27 per cent contained owner-occupiers.

Across Europe, conservatives, home-builders and Christian reformers were singing variations on the same tune of civic consumerism: a man who owned his home had a stake in his country, making him an upright, loyal citizen, a buttress of family life and freedom against collectivism. In fact, not even Stalin's Soviet Union was altogether immune from the siren call. Late Stalinism dangled the ideal of domestic comfort and home ownership before its new elite, the over-achieving Stakhanovites. In a typical piece of middle-brow fiction from 1950 Russia, Dimitri returns home and muses about his new status in life: 'Homeowner! How the sense of this world has changed! Homeowners in Rudnogorsk were now the best shock-workers and engineers, working people. Dimitri was impatient to go with Marina to look at their new home, but it was late. His dreams carried him along with her into their own house, their new house where they would begin their life together.'[65]

MODERN LIVING

Home ownership was part of a larger dream of modern living. Modern homes promised to liberate their inhabitants from tradition, waste and exhaustion. This vision had enormous appeal for progressives, the middle classes and social reformers in Cairo and Tokyo as much as in Chicago and Berlin. It focused on the housewife as a scientific manager, but its ambition was to transform family life more generally. Modern living had three core ideals. One was the glorification of comfort and cleanliness. A second was the emphasis on individual privacy within the family: a home should have one room per person. Finally, there was a belief that, as in a factory, domestic spaces should be separated by function and equipped with machines to maximize efficiency. How much these ideals would be realized depended on material resources, such as purchasing power and housing stock, but equally on cultural traditions and practices. Inevitably, the diffusion of home technologies was uneven, but once we loosen the chronology slightly, interesting patterns of adaptation and resistance become apparent. Instead of a linear triumph of modernity, the outcome was a hybrid of old and new.

So much of our image of modern living is tied up with the washing machine and other consumer durables that it is important to stress that several core ideas were already gathering force before electricity arrived in the home. The separation of private from public spaces, and consumption from production, were already visible in the redesign of middle-class homes in seventeenth- and eighteenth-century Europe, as the more open hall gave way to the parlour, study and other private chambers. Private zones were not only for the rich. Social reformers blamed many problems of the poor on their lack of privacy. One of the first schemes for their physical separation was the three-room cottage designed in the 1770s by the architect John Wood. It had recesses to provide, if not fully separate bedrooms, at least a private sleeping space.[66] By 1919, the one room per person standard had been accepted for government employees in the United States. For the 'typical family' of two adults and three children, the US Bureau of Labor Statistics now estimated that a kitchen–dining room, a living room and two 'large, well ventilated and lighted bedrooms' were the 'irreducible minimum for decent, healthful living'.[67] Families had a right to comfort as well as decency, social reformers insisted.[68] Even in Stalin's Soviet Union, the grim realities of communal living were pierced through with initiatives to cultivate the sense of private space and self-discipline necessary in order to turn backward people into modern Soviet men and women. One of the first things the wives of the Soviet elite did in their effort to build a 'good society' (the *obshchestvennost* movement, born in 1936) was to replace the shared bunks in workers' barracks with free-standing individual beds.[69]

The expanding culture of comfort drew on two competing ideals, well illustrated in the main house patterns of mid-nineteenth-century America. One sought comfort in an aesthetic union between the inhabitant's body, the mind and the material environment. For architects such as Andrew Jackson Downing, the verandah was both a shelter from the elements and a place for the family to sit together. The other prized practicality. This was the approach of Catherine Beecher, a crusader for female education. For her, the mark of a comfortable home was a kitchen designed for efficiency, not a porch for lounging in.[70]

It was the United States that spearheaded the industrial revolution in the home. The take-off of new domestic technologies was rapid in the 1920s. By its end, 18 million of the country's 27 million homes were wired, 15 million had electric irons, 7 million a vacuum cleaner and 5 million a washing machine. In the top income group, 92 per cent had a bath, 63 per cent a radio and 83 per cent a car. Many skilled workers were now buying the things they were mass-producing. Every other Ford employee, for example, had an electric washing machine and a car.[71] Race and income continued to make for sharp divides. By the mid-1930s, for instance, every second African-American home had a bath but only 19 per cent had a radio and 17 per cent a car.[72]

By comparison, Europe, Japan and Canada were slow to adopt labour-saving devices. Electric irons and vacuum cleaners existed before the Second World War, but most families preferred to spend their disposable income on a radio or new furniture rather than a washing machine. In Western Europe, fridges and washing machines were almost exclusively found in middle-class homes until the late 1950s; in 1957, not even 5 per cent of the French and British population owned a fridge – in the USA it was 27 per cent.[73] What were the reasons for this lag? Part of the answer is money. No European worker was able to compete with the high wases paid by the likes of Ford, made possible by early mass production and superior productivity. An average washing machine cost $125 in 1924. By 1934, it could be had for $50 or less, easily affordable for the average American who brought home $300 a month. In France, by contrast, a standard Mors vacuum cleaner would have sucked up the entire monthly pay packet of a skilled worker.[74]

In addition to having money, and access to electricity and running water, people had to be convinced that it made sense to invest in these machines rather than spend on entertainment, traditional festivities, or looking good in a new dress. After all, as home economists at the time and historians since have shown, these labour-saving devices saved far less time than the producers and advertisers promised. The appeal of goods such as the automatic washing machine was far from self-evident. In the 1950s, the lower classes preferred to spend their hard-earned money on a TV set rather than a labour-saving appliance; by 1957, every second low-income household in Britain owned a TV set.[75] The modern home as we know it was reached via a crooked path littered with all sorts of obstacles, some economic and infrastructural, others cultural.

Modern consumption technologies depended in the first place on modern utilities. Societies, even individual households, often lived in several overlapping material eras at once. As we saw earlier, gas, electricity and running water did not arrive together but could be separated by as much as two or three generations. The United States was no exception. Urban America was quick to develop an appetite for new fuels. By the time of the Great Crash of 1929, three quarters of American homes were wired, and every second used gas for cooking.[76] Modernity in the form of plumbing, however, was slower to arrive. When the Lynds studied life in Muncie, Indiana, in 1925 for their famous social study of *Middletown*, they found one third of homes had no bathroom, a quarter did not even have running water or sewage, but that it was 'not uncommon' to observe the same families 'using an automobile, electric washer, electric iron, and vacuum cleaner'.[77] This was pretty much the national pattern. There was a shocking discrepancy between social reality and the ideal standard of comfort and cleanliness summed up in the 'one room per person' formula. In 1920s Texas, 20 per cent of white families and 43 per cent of African-Americans lived two or more to a room. In New York City, gas and electricity were nearly universal, but 290,000 rooms had no windows.

Nor did the eventual arrival of these utilities automatically modernize domestic life. In Paris and Birmingham, one third of homes still lacked a separate bathroom by the late 1950s. Diffusion of gas and electricity remained highly uneven, both between countries and between cities and villages in the same country. Societies that adopted gas early (like Britain) were not automatically slow to take up electrical appliances later. By 1938, for example, 1 million electric cookers stood in British homes, a quarter million more than in the German Reich, although here an impressive third of them stood in the kitchens of artisans and skilled workers.[78] It has been said that, with their expanding networks and grids, electricity providers created their own demand.[79] But this was far from smooth or simple. The electricity works tried hard to stimulate greater domestic consumption – a lot of capacity was under-utilized outside industrial peak hours – with the help of night-time storage radiators and special discounts for greater use. Outside the USA, however, the new clean power was slow to cross the threshold. Into the 1950s, most European homes used electricity for lighting and little else.

Together, price and habits were formidable obstacles. Electric plugs and switches were unfamiliar and could be mysterious novelties. In Germany in 1928, a guide explained that 'the only function of the switch is to switch electricity on and off. This observation may sound self-evident but it is not! Quite a few housewives think that the switch is a convenient point to hang up the broom or the shopping net or even a heavy coat.' Switches could get hot. He concluded with a list of ten prohibitions: 'avoid shaking lamps and appliances or throwing them about' (no. 8) and 'do not change a light bulb when the electricity is "on"; it could be damaged – and you too!' (no. 9).[80] After the Second World War, in the great rebuilding of European cities, it was often consumers who had to persuade developers and utilities to give them more electricity, not the other way around. A German survey in 1964 found that 41 per cent of all German flats had only a single socket in the kitchen; 4 per cent had none at all. And their circuits were often deficient. As one observer wondered aloud: 'Is it "comfort", if one has to switch off the radio in order to plug in the iron?'[81]

Across the globe, cities went through modernization in similar fits and starts. In 1920s Shanghai, for example, the municipal council actively promoted electric cookers and radiators with demonstrations at a showroom on Nanking Road and special hire arrangements; in terms of total demand for kilowatts it was on a par with European cities. Among the rich, the electric 'cooking apparatus' was found increasingly 'reliable despite the bad usage it is sometimes subjected to by the native servant'.[82] What was going on in most people's homes was another story. Most *li*, or alleyway houses, in the municipal settlement were turned upside down by landlords and tenants through a mindboggling range of partitions, lofts, enclosures and added floors, all designed to pack more people in and maximize rent. By 1935, houses that had initially been designed for a single family accommodated on average twenty-four persons, each with 30 square feet of living space. Not surprisingly in these cramped conditions, the kitchen was rented out as a living space. Instead of functional separation, modernity here meant the dissolution of the kitchen.[83]

Even where functionalist comfort was achievable, it often met with resistance and adaptation. As power companies and producers learnt quickly, the benefits of gas and electricity and the goods they powered were not obvious. They had to be marketed. The first electric kitchen was exhibited at the Chicago World Fair in 1893. In inter-war Europe, some cities had 'transparent restaurants' to show diners how an electric kitchen worked.[84] The masterwork of modern design was the Frankfurt Kitchen of 1926 by Grete Schütte-Lihotzky, the first professionally trained female architect in Austria. It was exactly 1.9 by 3.44 metres (70 square feet). In this mini-factory, everything was functional, from the electric range to the continuous work surface with height-adjusted cupboards. Storage chutes and pouring spouts saved the housewife from having to open doors and containers to get to sugar and flour; the containers were aluminium, except for the flour shovel, which was made of oak – the tannic acid kept away worms. An ironing board folded up flat against the wall. There was even a suspended, movable lamp.[85] As in modern kitchens advertised by the Everyday Life Reform League in Japan, this model had a single function: it was solely for cooking, not for eating or socializing. Not an inch was wasted. Everything had its standardized place and purpose, just as the average housewife was imagined to move along in a predictable rhythm established by scientific motion studies.

The problem was that housewives were not robots. They lived in enormously diverse conditions, with different ideas about what a kitchen should be. Enamelled sinks were better than steel, and ironing boards should be mobile, the Dutch housewives' organization told urban planners in The Hague.[86] Nor did builders, producers and ideal-home promoters agree on a shared design. The modern kitchen advertised in Shanghai in the 1920s looked very different from that in Frankfurt. It featured an electric range that stood alone in a sizable kitchen, with a sink and running water but without either continuous worktops or cupboards. Ideal-home shows in inter-war London advertised American labour-saving devices, but continuous kitchen surfaces were equally lacking here; the L-shaped kitchen first appeared in 1949. Even in California, adjoining counters spread only slowly. In Paris, organizers at the annual Salon des Arts Ménagers found that pure functionalism did not go down well with the bourgeoisie: modern kitchens were flanked by Louis XV parlours and dining rooms.[87]

The Frankfurt Kitchen was the culmination of modern functionalist design. To people's lives it was marginal. Barely 10,000 of its type were installed. For the vast majority of people (and housing associations) this cuisine Porsche was out of reach; it would have taken the average Frankfurt worker a year's income to buy one. As late as 1968, only every third German home had a standardized, built-in kitchen. The idea of the kitchen as a place of beauty and entertainment similarly encountered considerable resistance. At the German 'Informa' ideal-home show in 1963, Grete Meyer-Ehlers, the first female professor for home and design in Berlin, insisted that the kitchen, in the first place, was a 'workspace'. She found it hard to imagine how housewives would possibly prepare liver dumplings and potato pancakes in front of brushed-steel and plastic surfaces.[88]

For working-class people in the 1930s, a more normal domestic scene was that of the Mann family in Berlin, who shared an apartment with four other families. To get to their bedroom, the Manns and their two young daughters had to cross a communal corridor. The toilet was shared, as was the cleaning of the corridor, which caused endless friction. The Manns had their own kitchen, with water on tap and metered gas but no refrigeration: 'Everything that was bought was eaten instantly, so that nothing could spoil,' Hilla, one of the daughters, recalled. The kitchen was for much more than cooking. It was where the Manns mainly lived. It was the only heated room and included a bed, with a pillow embroidered by their mother, and a wall hanging with birds and flowers – 'that looked cozy'. Opposite the curtained windows was a table, built by their father, with a rinsing bowl underneath. Next to it stood a white cupboard, with glass doors on top, to show the good porcelain for guests, and wooden doors at the bottom to hide aluminium pots, day-to-day crockery and onion-patterned cutlery bought with loyalty stamps at the Kaiser's Kaffee chain. For light, there was only a petroleum lamp. The inventory shows how ordinary people relied on a mix of bought and home-made goods. In their living room, they had a mirrored wardrobe for their clothes, hand-woven chairs, a Rembrandt reproduction next to family photos and landscapes painted by their father, books, records and a self-assembled gramophone – the neighbour would knock at the walls and shout 'Encore!' when the music stopped.[89]

It was not just in Berlin that modern consumer goods were entering the home, only to come to some accommodation with local culture. In the early twentieth century the appeal of new goods was palpable across the globe. In Cairo, the bourgeois home was promoted as the microcosm of a new nation, leaving behind traditional culture and polygamy. Advice literature praised Western-style furnishings and warned against oriental carpets as carriers of disease. Over-stuffed and over-decorated foyers were out, comfortable chairs in. Modernity did not have to be austere, though. Louis XIV furniture and English tea services were prized. It was screens and other objects 'usually placed at the door of a harem' that were to be avoided at all costs. In reality, many middle-class families added an Ottoman touch to these Western ideals. Fashions followed the Paris look but were made of smooth and glossy 'oriental cloth' rather than British ripple wool. Daughters played on pianos ornately decorated with mother-of-pearl inlay and carved mahogany mouldings, and sometimes fitted with an additional pedal for mandolin sounds.[90]

Western goods spread much further across African societies than is commonly recognized. In sub-Saharan Africa, the Duala, a local ethnic elite who were traders and worked as clerks for the French colonists in inter-war Cameroon, spent substantial sums on houses, motorcars and bicycles.[91] Rooiyard in Johannesburg was a slum of 1,000 square yards, which has long since been demolished. In the early 1930s, it was the site of a material culture in rapid transition.[92] The longer people had lived there, the more Western objects they tended to have. These included beds and sideboards, tables and chairs, pianos and gramophones, chintz curtains and linoleum floors, all the way to framed pictures of movie stars looking down from wallpapered walls. The majority of families had either a gramophone, a bicycle, a sewing machine or a combination of these. Embroidery was a popular leisure activity among women. Younger girls wore lipstick. Men drank beer. How people sat, slept, ate and looked was changing. Pots and pans for the 'ready-prepared mealie meal' were taking the place of wooden mortar and pestle. Ellen Hellmann, an anthropologist who lived in Rooiyard and the first woman to receive a PhD from the University of Witwatersrand, was repeatedly assured by the local inhabitants that 'the Europeans' manner of cooking meat is a great improvement upon Native preparation of meat.' New goods and habits were financed through a daily struggle with money. Hardly anyone saved. Most families spent what they could scrape together from their miserly 20-odd shillings weekly pay on instalment plans for gramophones or furniture. One Southern Soto couple spent as much on the instalment for their sideboard as on rent. It is tempting to view this scene as another sad comment on the conquest of traditional culture by Western consumerism. Hellmann resisted this. What was emerging was a 'new composite culture', not the West transplanted. Half the families had children in the country and maintained contact with tribal life, sending clothes and furniture back home. Amongst the poor in Johannesburg, as amongst the rich in Cairo, pieces of consumer culture were fitted into local culture, creating a mix of new values and behaviours in the process.

The sanitary city created a favourable environment for new domestic technologies by diffusing a culture of hygiene and cleanliness. It is an illustration of how changes in private consumption were enabled by prior public reforms. In showrooms and demonstrations, producers advertised washing machines and electric stoves as clean technologies that allowed women to fulfil their role as guardians of private and public health. Durables spoke directly to a sense that the home and its contents were private and had to be shielded from outside pollution. This was evident in the growing aversion to sending out one's dirty clothes, or having a collective wash-day with neighbours and family. 'I can stand my own dirt but I can't stand the dirt of someone I never saw,' as one American housewife put it in 1934.[93] By the end of that decade, the washerwoman, a dominant and imposing sight only a generation before, had all but disappeared in the United States. In Europe, collective laundry facilities in working-class housing blocks faced a similar fate in the next generation: 'It is better to wash one's dirty clothes in one's own home!' a woman in Turin explained in 1956.[94] Hard-to-wash items and the sheer increase in people's wardrobes threw a lifeline to commercial laundries, but these were often avoided for personal clothes and underwear. Laundries were routinely blamed for destroying heirlooms, fading favourite blouses and much else. In return, commercial laundries made much of the dangers of the new machines to life and limb. Whether automatic or semi-automatic, early machines still required hands-on attention. Tubes needed to be changed and the spinning movement had to be kept in check. The laundry industry warned of women who had been scalped or electrocuted.[95] In Canada, wringer washing machines still outsold automatics in the late 1960s. Canadian women preferred durability and distrusted complicated machines with multiple cycles.[96]

In Japan, consumer magazines initially advised against washing machines: most people did not have enough clothes to fill a whole drum, and so the few items would merely be rubbing against water instead of getting clean. In cities, there were plenty of washerwomen who charged a pittance. In the countryside, salesmen of electrical appliances ran into all sorts of obstacles. Electricity needed to be shown to be safe. Then, custom dictated that men's and women's clothing and upper and lower garments be washed separately. Before there was any market for their washing machines, companies concluded, lifestyles had to change.[97]

The perhaps decisive factor, however, was a revaluation of housework itself. To buy labour-saving devices it was necessary in the first place to believe that labour was worth saving. The back-breaking routine of wash-day had been a feature of women's lives for a very long time. Why change it? In South Africa today, where homes have colour TVs and fridge freezers, many women insist on performing their duty as wives by washing by hand; the machine is denounced for tempting girls and daughters-in-law into laziness and disrespect.[98] New technologies required a willingness to transfer work done by hand to a machine. They asked people to see the home a bit more like William James did, and a bit less like Heidegger. And this meant appreciating that a housewife was worth more than her physical labour. Critics have said that consumer durables still left women enslaved – 'crypto servants', according to J. K. Galbraith.[99] This is, strictly speaking, true, but it misses a profound change in the nature of this subordination, as women turned from physical labour to household management.

The appeal of the modern home went hand in hand with the rise of the modern woman. We are so accustomed to thinking of the home as a site of female subordination that it is easy to forget that previous generations looked for empowerment and liberation within the home as well as outside it. The new wave of women's magazines of this period advertised the modern home as much as cosmetics and cinema stars. They were all part of the same dream of a freer, more consumerist modernity.

The campaign to brighten the housewife's lot began before the washing machine. In 1907, the washing powder Persil was born. In the next few decades, the German parent company Henkel created an international empire that promoted its magical 'self-acting' powers (see Plate 32). Instead of endless scrubbing, the laundry was left in a soaking lye of cold water overnight, then put to boil the next day, gently rinsed (first in warm then in cold water), and *voilà*, the previously dreaded white wash was done. Better powders and soaps saved the housewife precious time and money by protecting the fabric against aggressive scrubbing – Sunlight, the product of its main rival, Lever, promised the same. Unfortunately, this sequence ran entirely counter to established routines. Salesmen endlessly complained of the misapplication and 'prejudice' they encountered. New customers had to be 'enlightened', for example, Frau Meier of Cologne who complained that Persil had turned her clothes grey. Others continued to scrub in spite of the new powders and then blamed the holes in their handkerchiefs on Persil.[100] The celebration of washing as joy, then, was more than advertising whitewash. It had a practical purpose: for a new household product such as Persil to be effective, women had to learn to use their hands less and accept cleanliness as a result of technology instead of exertion.

In the inter-war years, Persil's empire grew threefold; over 100,000 tons were produced in 1938.[101] The company ran an evangelical campaign of missionary proportions. Henkel set out to persuade all housewives that they had a right to joy and that they could have it, too, as long as they followed the Persil way of washing. It sent flappers on stage in front of wash buckets. At home shows, Henkel had its own pavilion fronted by a gigantic, bubbling foam fountain, which attracted over 3 million visitors at the 1926 Gesolei exhibition for health, welfare and sport. It ran flying wash-advice bureaus and gave practical demonstrations in shops, pubs and schools, in small towns going door to door, and in apartment blocks. In 1928, alongside the pudding and baking-powder giant Dr Oetker, Persil started its own schools, where housewives received twelve hours of free instruction in the art of modern washing and cooking, including a chance to handle appliances. For young children, there were doll's clothes to wash. Henkel even had UFA, the leading movie studio in Germany, produce a film on the art of soaking. Its films reached an estimated 19 million housewives. One central feature of the campaign was the link between laundry and hygiene: charts illustrated that washing powder reduced infant mortality. To fight germs, the modern housewife needed modern products. 'Wäsche, Waschen, Wohlergehen' – laundry, washing, well-being – advertising vans blasted through their loudspeakers. The campaign was universal in its ambition: all housewives, rich and poor, rural and urban, young and old, needed to be carried into the modern age. Some salesmen recognized that in a country like Greece, where households lacked the necessary clothing for a whole Persil-white wash, it might be wiser to focus on the cold laundry of more delicate wool and silk clothes. In general, however, progress was open to all cultures, from Algeria and West Africa to rugged Sardinia, where, it was said, local women were unable to contain their joy about its magic power: 'Our laundry is now whiter than the snow of Gennargentu!'[102]

It would be a revolution without class struggle, turning hard work into joy. The housewife no longer returned from wash-day exhausted and irritable, but relaxed and happy, able to devote herself to husband and children: this was how advertisers imagined the modern home across the developed world. In reality, chores did not vanish. Still, the boundaries between production and consumption were blurred. There was glamour in the laundry, good housekeeping guides cheered. Women were entitled to leisure in the home. This was why many women home economists, although sceptical about the time-saving promises, supported the industrial revolution in the home. Together with greater comfort and better planning, 'economical equipment' would help align the home to 'the needs and wishes of *every* member of the family' and lead to more 'agreeable mutual relations and mutual help'. It would provide 'an outlet for the spirit of service that is the basis of a happy home'.[103]

Everywhere, liberation from traditional norms came with a new responsibility of care: to provide a modern home. It was too easy to blame technological obstacles for past difficulties, home exhibitions told the housewife. She should also blame herself 'as customer and consumer' for not making the most of new machines and training.[104] The housewife was elevated to a super-minister of health, nutrition and culture.

In Japan, this 'promotion' was reflected in the shift in meaning of *shufu*. Originally *shufu* had referred to the proprietress of a business. By the early twentieth century it meant 'housewife'. In Japan, as elsewhere, the new science of hygiene and nutrition gave housekeeping public and scientific authority. Being a housewife became a profession. A clean home and nutritious home-cooked food saved men from dirt, disease and drink, keeping family and nation healthy.[105]

The Japanese redefinition of women's roles was a joint project of housewives, civic organizations and the state. The four most popular women's magazines together had more than 1 million readers, professional women and housewives alike. One wife wrote to the magazine *Fujin koron* in 1920 that the time had come to overthrow the 'old-fashioned lifestyle' and eliminate the 'tremendous waste around us'. 'Among the many things we should learn from the American family's lifestyle, most important, I think, is that the housewife's duty is to make her home a happy and beautiful place to live.'[106] The home was rebranded as a space of scientific management and family-centred happiness (see Plate 37).

The push for modern living came from national policy and embourgeoisement as well as women's groups. Home science was already part of the school curriculum for girls at the end of the Meiji period (1868–1912), when Japan embraced modernization. The First World War turned it into a plank of national policy. In 1919, the Everyday Life Reform League (*Seikatsu kaizen dōmeikai*) was set up, a body initiated by the Home Ministry with support from women's schools, architects and middle-class reformers. National survival required thrift and health. Traditional living, with its elaborate ceremonies, gift-giving and dress codes needed to give way to a simpler life. 'Reform of the Home Begins with the Kitchen,' the League's posters and flyers told city dwellers. Instead of kneeling in a dark, dirty kitchen covered in soot and open to the environment, the modern housewife stood in a clean, enclosed space with electricity, running water and continuous worktops. From here, the modern spirit of rational and family-centred life spread. The poster 'Family Gathering rather than Tinkering with Antiques' showed how men in traditional dress, indulging in private hobbies, were transformed into doting fathers and husbands wearing Western suits. The League targeted domestic dwelling in all its dimensions. It championed chairs and sought to eliminate useless ornamentation. Gardens were to be practical, not decorative. The self-proclaimed motto was 'health and safety', but it also required thorough mental reformation. 'Everyday life is the expression of the nation's thought,' as the government official Tago Ichimin put it.[107]

Modern living involved a new division of labour. In a nineteenth-century Japanese household, cleaning, cooking and housekeeping had been shared among husbands, wives and male servants. By the 1920s, these had all become women's tasks. In Japan, as elsewhere, middle-class families relied on fewer servants. Most *shufus* still had one or two female servants, but the household itself was contracting into a self-contained nuclear unit. The housewife took on hitherto unknown authority within her four walls. If she was still dependent on her husband, she was no longer subordinate to her parents-in-law or bound by traditional festivals and ritual spending. The promotion of housewives' budget books in this period signalled the arrival of the Japanese housewife as a more independent consumer, in charge of family spending.

Women today may wonder where all their promised leisure time has gone. Home economists were already asking the same thing in the 1920s. In 1929, the home economist Amy Hewes asked a national sample of female students at Mount Holyoake College to report on the electrical appliances their families back home had acquired. In 1919, most families had had either none or were limited to one or two appliances, especially an electric iron. Ten years later, most had five or more, most commonly fridges, washing machines, waffle irons, toasters and coffee percolators. Families were then asked to record changes in their daily routines. More than a third reported that they were doing more washing and ironing. Sewing and baking, too, had increased. Only one fifth said that they had saved any time to engage in outside activities.

The actual time saved was clearly 'disappointing as compared to the promises of things possible made by the salesmen of electric appliances'. At the same time, Hewes wrote, '[i]t may often happen that a women's [sic] horizon is greatly widened by any outside activities.' By making this possible, even if only in modest degree, appliances were good for housewife and family alike.[108]

What we see here is the escalator of consumption at work. More possessions and domestic technologies induced new activities and raised standards and expectations, which opened the door for further technologies. Consuming was, as the economist Alfred Marshall had recognized, like climbing an infinite ladder, except that in this case activities did not lead to nobler activities but added new rungs of stuff. Cleanliness and pride in the home were not fixed states but infinitely expandable.[109] Companies understood this. There was always 'whiter than white', to use the Persil slogan. Much has been made of 'inbuilt obsolescence' as the engine of consumerism. Equally important was the inbuilt intensification of norms and practices introduced by new durables. A vacuum cleaner and washing machine did save two to nine hours per week, studies found at the time. But this gain was virtually wiped out by more frequent hoovering and laundry and higher standards of cleanliness. Sheets and clothes were changed and washed more often. Within a generation of its adoption, the washing machine transformed how it felt to be clean or dirty; a mere 5 per cent of German men changed their underwear daily in 1966; by 1986, it was 45 per cent.[110] In some cultures, women began to iron underwear. The sewing machine did not just make the same clothes with less effort. It encouraged more clothes and greater personalization, with diverse patterns and more ruffles, tucks and borders to be added. Housewives had long expressed their pride and care for the family in the state of their home. More goods and appliances multiplied the demands on their attention. Instead of throwing their energies into whitening the doorstep by scrubbing it with a soft lime stone, working-class housewives competed with each other about who kept the shiniest kitchen, the cleanest bathroom and the neatest parlour. Here was the cruel contradiction: new equipment promised to turn housework into leisure, but women had been brought up in a culture where idleness was considered unwomanly. Time saved went into another round of hoovering.

In a later chapter we will need to look more closely at the changing nature of leisure time. Here we are concerned particularly with the effect of new appliances on female housework. The historian Ruth

Schwartz Cowan, whose influential work picked up where earlier home economists had left off, has argued that the domestic revolution meant 'more work for Mother'. Studies from the 1920s showed that weekly housework took around forty-eight hours in urban and sixty-one hours in rural America. A 1965 survey clocked up fifty-four hours, with twenty-eight hours for housework and twenty-seven hours for child-care. New chores 'cancelled' any time gained.[111] This is strictly correct, but such an aggregate view only goes so far. We need to ask about the quality of time as well as the quantity. Housework is not all the same. Most women said they liked cooking better than childcare. Ironically, and especially since the Second World War, American women have spent more time with their children and less time at the stove. What happened, then, was a redistribution of time at home, as well as a rise in the time spent at paid work outside it. In addition, tasks were coordinated differently. Listening to the radio while doing the laundry at home and keeping an eye on the kids at the same time is different from doing a single task or doing them sequentially, even if the hours spent are the same. The domestic revolution was probably as important in creating more intense clusters of parallel practices as it was for the overall use of time.

Aggregates also hide class and regional contrasts. Research for Hoover's conference on the home in 1932 showed that housekeeping differed hugely across America. In cities, homemakers spent half as much on laundering as did their rural sisters, yet twice as much on 'care of family'. A woman in rural America was effectively on her own. By contrast, the urban housewife had twenty-seven hours of additional help. And labour-saving devices had different consequences for working-class and middle-class women. One reason why the hours of housekeeping appeared to stay constant was that the original data, like that on college families, was biased towards the middle class. Naturally, the time they spent on home-keeping did not decline: they lost their servants. For working-class mothers, the opposite was true: the washing machine saved them time, sweat and tears – as one 1950s housewife put it plainly, 'You could take away my bed, but just don't leave me without that automatic washing machine.'[112] This class divergence had already been noticed by the Lynds in their research for Middletown in 1925. If labour-saving devices did not erase the 'double burden', time-use data since then suggests it at least reduced it for women in employment.[113]

In general, the influence of appliances was probably smaller than often thought. The most extensive recent review of time-use data in twentieth-century America finds little evidence that the arrival of appliances prompted women to join the workforce. Female housework in the 1930s–'60s did shoot up, but this had less to do with hoovers and washing machines and more with the fact that single women were increasingly living in their own apartments rather than in boarding houses or with their families.[114] There is no simple cause–effect relationship between what is done at home and what is bought in the marketplace. Yes, ready-made food and microwaves have led people to cook less. In other aspects of domestic life, however, the two types of provision have supplemented each other: people spend more money on children's services, games and entertainment, but they also spend more time with their children.

In some contexts, household appliances brought empowerment in indirect ways. When fairly poor families in 1970s–'80s Egypt and other developing countries were buying consumer durables, they were partly doing so to demonstrate their status within their neighbourhood. But they also boosted a housewife's control over family finances. Putting spare cash into an instalment plan for a TV or a washing machine meant it could not be handed out to a needy neighbour or a cousin asking for help with wedding expenses or medical bills. Consumer durables locked in money, shielding their owners from the claims of customary reciprocity. When an opportunity for social improvement arose, such as a move to a better flat or the education of a child, they could be resold, releasing built-up capital.[115] White goods were a savings account with a dividend of greater control for the housewife. This kind of consumerism, which is never talked about in conventional critiques and media commentary, encouraged both greater autonomy and care for one's intimate family. Modern things could be a ticket out of the extended family and community into which one was born.[116]

Men continued to spend less time on housework than women, but they had their domestic revolution, too. It just didn't happen in the kitchen. It took place in the hobby basement, the garage and the garden. Mrs Clean was joined by Mr Fixit. Men and women came to the modern home from opposite directions. For women, industry came into the home, upgrading their domestic role to that of scientific manager. For men, on the other hand, the home and garden were refuges from the world of industrial labour. Several developments came together. The shift from artisan to factory worker or office clerk raised anxieties about masculinity. What did modern man actually accomplish, now that he was no longer *homo faber*? Do-it-yourself was a way to rebuild male pride. Hobbies and crafts, not the devil, would make work for idle hands. It also offered a moral defence of private recreation at a time when rising leisure time included the 'involuntary' leisure of high unemployment in the 1930s. Tools became consumer goods. By the middle of the century, Macy's department store was selling motor-driven jigsaws and other power tools; Black & Decker introduced its small hand-held drill in 1946.

As with the language of domestic appliances aimed at the modern housewife, the language of the male craft-consumer appealed to both rationality and fun. It was sold as an exercise in thrift and self-reliance. In truth, the average person would have saved money by buying a chair in a store rather than making it themselves. What mattered to many, however, was less the end result than the satisfaction of making things: 'I am sitting on a home-made chair . . . [and] the greatest reward coming out of this piece of work was the fun of making it with my own hands.'[117]

Gardening offered an increasingly popular way to consume the fruits of one's own labour. With the help of both companies and trade unions, industrial workers discovered allotments and window boxes. The First World War gave a natural boost to allotments, but their popularity carried over into peacetime. In inter-war France, the Société d'horticulture et des jardins ouvriers de la region du Nord grew from a sapling into a mighty oak, with 700,000 members. For 8 francs 50 centimes a year, a French miner would receive fifty packets of seeds, the bimonthly magazine, lessons about gardening and a chance to shine in competitions and win more seeds at the tombola. 'Auto-consumption', according to these associations, gave workers moral and material roots in a competitive, commercial world. What the home and DIY were to the middle classes, the vegetable garden would be to the worker: a stake in the country and a chance to leave 'his signature on the soil'. Care for plants heralded 'attentive work, order and family discipline,' garden magazines told their working-class readers.[118] In times of crisis, they were also a major strategy for survival, and nowhere more so than in Nazi and post-war Germany. In the mid-1930s, about 10 per cent of all fruit and vegetables in the German *Reich* was grown in allotments. In the late 1940s, many Germans would not have survived had it not been for access to one of the 1 million allotments.[119]

For most white-collar workers, a workshop at home remained out of reach. Recreational crafts were primarily a blue-collar and middle-class pastime. Still, the general phenomenon deserves recognition. American schools set up hobby clubs; big firms their own craft guilds. In Manhattan, the Museum of Modern Art even installed a woodworking shop for fathers and sons who did not have the privilege of their own hobby basement. In Europe, painting and wallpapering were increasingly done by husband and wife together.[120] The home was not gender equal but it was more of a joint project than before. Men spent roughly twice as much time on domestic chores and repairs in 1945 as in 1900.[121]

It is simplistic, then, to view consumer culture as passive and de-skilling. A good deal of the rise in consumption involved buying for the sake of making and personalizing the home. DIY, handicrafts and gardening attracted a sizable chunk of consumer spending, with their own magazines, stores and fairs. Consumerism encouraged new skills as often as it killed old ones. Men were drawn into a more active, home-centred culture. By the 1930s, most had a better grip on the hammer than their grandfathers. Perhaps Heidegger should have worried less. Machines were leaving their imprint on the home, but so was the hand. Ironically, *homo consumens* gave a helping hand to *homo faber*.

How, then, should we interpret the domestic revolution in the longer history of consumption? At one level, we can see electric irons and washing machines as completing a trend stretching back to the eighteenth century: things took the place of servants and retainers. Households downsized their human staff and upgraded their material helpers. At another level, however, it should also be viewed as a counter-revolution. The eighteenth and nineteenth centuries had seen a shift from making to buying things. By 1900, urban Americans bought their clothes instead of sewing them. Outside remote mountain areas such as the Appalachian highlands, baking bread, canning and pickling, making soap and home medicines, were all losing ground to cheaper, more convenient and heavily advertised commodities.[122] Commentators began to worry that the home was becoming an empty shell. What would be left of it when people's lives were all about getting and spending in the marketplace? The twentieth century showed such worries to be unfounded. It is wrong to presume that a rise in shopping automatically leads to a decline in homemaking. In the most commercial consumer culture, twentieth-century America, time spent on homemaking has remained constant at around fifty-two hours per week.[123] There are two main reasons for this. The first is the growing size of homes and the rise of 'solo living'. There is simply more floor space for the individual to take care of. The second is the influx of appliances. Washing machines, floor waxers, electric irons and fruit-juice extractors, drills and sewing machines, all of these either restored activities or invented entirely new ones. Consumption became more productive.

TUNING IN

The domestic consumer revolution was one of the ear as much as the hand. Western cultures in particular had long encouraged sight as the first sense, and the diffusion of consumption in earlier periods had worked primarily through visual stimuli via fashion, shop-window displays and the bright lights of the city. The gramophone and the radio added an aural sensibility. They literally opened people's ears. If the cult of cleanliness and domestic science looked inward, the radio reached out, carrying new dream worlds directly into people's living rooms.

The gramophone and the radio were not initially designed as instruments of domestic entertainment. The phonograph was first presented by Edison to the public in 1877. Early gramophones were used for a range of purposes, including dictation, court testimony, and to bring back the voice of loved ones from the dead. The Columbia Phonograph Company in 1890 advertised that it could give composers new ideas by allowing them to play music backwards. In France, Pathé introduced slot listening machines where people could listen to a song for 15 centimes. The Gramophone Co. and Victor had already opened recording studios in Singapore and Mexico in 1903–4, and it was at this time that Debussy was sufficiently impressed by the promise of immortality to record excerpts of *Pelléas at Mélisande* in the Paris studio. Mass-produced discs had started to displace wax cylinders just before the First World War. Still, as late as 1918, it was possible to record only three octaves.

The breakthrough came in the 1920s. In 1927, record sales reached 104 million in the United States. The opera singer Enrico Caruso alone brought in $2.5 million for the Victor recording company. Some artists feared that private music boxes would be the death of public music. In fact, the opposite happened. The gramophone and radio boosted live-music performances by giving people a taste for the Charleston, the black bottom and other novelty dances that could be practised at home. In Malaya, the record industry used stadium events to promote the hugely popular Miss Soelami, the 'undisputed Kronchong Champion of All-Java'.[124]

The radio's metamorphosis from boyhood gadget to family entertainment was more dramatic still. Between 1901, when Guglielmo
Marconi first sent signals across the Atlantic, and the First World War,
boys in their thousands experimented with building single receivers
and sending dot-and-dash signals. In 1920, the fifteen-year-old Harold
Robinson managed to send a signal from his home in New Jersey all the
way to Scotland. In the early 1920s, radios meant headphones attached
to a self-assembled crystal set. It was a hobby for 'hams' and schoolteachers. Boys saved up their pennies to buy parts from the local ten-cent
store. By 1922, there were some 600,000 radio hobbyists in the United
States.[125] An estimated 20,000 stations were operated by American kids
on lower wavelengths. Gothenburg and other European cities had radio
clubs with thousands of members. Schools were vital transmitters on
both sides of the Atlantic. In Prussia, almost half of them participated
in school radio, offering pupils a fairly balanced diet of music, literature, geography and languages; many of the sets belonged to teachers.[126]
In the States, 'colleges of the air' were run from universities and agricultural colleges. The radio was an unrivalled educator, the US
Commissioner of Education, John Tigert, emphasized in 1924. In addition to whetting an interest in the world, it taught 'lessons in thrift, in
handiwork, and in science that the best teachers in the land might well
contemplate with envy'.[127]

A hobby page from a 1932 magazine for radiophiles in Luxembourg
gives a sense of the skill and confidence required to set up a three-tube
receiver with loudspeaker. To be able to listen to Strasbourg and Rome
in the evenings, one needed an external antenna at least 25 metres long
and 10 metres high with a minimum of 120 volts. If the volume was
too low, the listener was encouraged to use a pencil and rubber to add
or remove graphite on the individual resistors of the low-frequency
amplifier. As anyone who has seen Laurel and Hardy's *Hog Wild* (1930)
will know, just putting up an antenna was fraught with disaster.
Battery-operated radios frequently leaked acid on to sideboard and
carpets. It was not until the late 1920s that fully electric models were
introduced – for example, the Radiola 17 in 1927 – and that external
cables, tubes and loudspeakers were absorbed into a finished mahogany body – as in the Telefunkensuper 653 in 1931 (see Plate 33).
Encased and polished, the radio now sat neatly alongside other furniture, with simple dials for an easy listening experience for the whole
family. The male gadget was fit to move from the attic to the sitting
room.[128]

It is difficult to exaggerate the scale of the radio explosion in these years. In 1925, Denmark and the Netherlands, for example, each had just under 25,000 receivers. By 1936, there were 660,000 and 940,000 respectively. This was almost one per household, the same as in the United States; in Argentina, one in ten people had a radio.[129] After an early stage of individual listening, the radio became sociable. The family was at the heart of this shared experience: hours of daily listening went up dramatically the more members a family had.[130] But the living room was not sealed off. Quite the opposite: by the late 1920s, Ozark and other makers were advertising portable devices: 'Camp, fish, hunt, tour with Radio. Make your vacation complete.'[131]

Above all, the radio amplified relations with neighbours. Sometimes this meant collective listening. Listeners were urged to take their radio to neighbours and to the office: 'There's no loneliness where there is Radiola.' Heinrich Weber recalled with pride how, when he was a young boy in Hildesheim, Germany, in the early 1930s, his father encouraged him to put his apparatus in the window so the whole neighbourhood could listen in. In South Carolina, early radio owners would entertain the whole town.[132]

Gramophone and radio transformed soundscapes and sensitivities to noise across the globe. At the flick of a switch, radio killed silence and loneliness. It could mean sleepless nights as much as shared joy. In 1934, Singapore's Legislative Council passed an amendment to the Minor Offences Ordinance which prohibited the playing of gramophones and wireless music after midnight except with the permission of the police.[133] Conflict cut two ways. Such was the sensitivity of transformers at the time that reception was easily disturbed by a neighbour switching on an electrical appliance. Studies at the time suggest that one third of the many thousand reported interferences came from private households. Some neighbours fought a war of noise with their new electrical weapons. Denmark was one of the first countries (in 1931) to pass a law protecting listeners from interference. In Germany, naturally, there were fines for troublemakers who deliberately used their electric iron or vacuum cleaner to interfere with their neighbour's listening habits.[134]

Radio transformed everyday life in ways that far exceeded anything earlier revolutionaries had tried to achieve with dress reform and other changes from above. People adjusted their daily schedules to follow their favourite programme. Some clergymen called for boycotts of Sunday-evening broadcasts, in vain.[135] Public stations such as the

British Broadcasting Corporation (BBC), founded in 1922, introduced 'Children's Hour' to nurture future citizens. Radio listening was easily coordinated with a range of other home tasks, injecting some fun into chores: 'Dishwashing does not seem like drudgery and goes much faster accompanied by sprightly jazz,' one woman wrote in 1925.[136] For people with lower education and income, in particular, the radio became the prime instrument of leisure. But even among American women with a college education, almost half listened to two hours of radio or more in the evenings. Early American audience surveys show that women had the radio on fairly constantly during the day – 'Oh, I tell you, it's company to me – someone with me all the time in the house.'[137] Men mainly listened over breakfast and in the evening. Children lay awake at night, mulling over what they had heard earlier. Some reported nightmares, but most parents endorsed their children's listening habits. The radio seemed both to educate and make home life more interesting. This was one of the main attractions for many: it diffused conflict, filled silence and got the family together: 'If we didn't have it, we wouldn't have a family.'[138]

The main critique of the radio came from across the Atlantic, via the émigré Jewish intellectual and music theorist Theodor Adorno. Adorno found refuge from the Nazis in New York at the Columbia radio research project, funded by the Rockefeller Foundation and run by another émigré, the Viennese Paul Lazarsfeld. Here Adorno consolidated his opinion about the 'social authoritarianism' of the radio.[139] It is a revealing episode for our story, not only because his ideas would become a central plank in the Marxist critique of the cultural industries which, through the Frankfurt School of Social Research, would inspire a new generation of critics after 1945. It also shows how a Marxist focus on production, combined with an inherited European elite sensibility, could lead a formidable thinker such as Adorno to misunderstand this new medium of consumer culture completely.

To Adorno, everything was serious, especially culture. He did not do fun. True listening meant an all-encompassing critical engagement with music as a *Gesamtkunstwerk*, a total work of art. Anything else was just passive entertainment. More was at stake than poor taste. Light, popular music was part of capitalism's strategy of imposing its commodified spirit on all spheres of life, snuffing out creativity and freedom. It was a short step from mass-produced pot-boilers like 'Yes, We Have No Bananas' to fascism.

Biography and theory were one in Adorno's case. He was born in 1903 to the half-French, half-Italian singer Maria Calvelli-Adorno, who had performed at the Imperial Court Opera in Vienna; his father was a Jewish wine merchant. At their Frankfurt home, life evolved around the piano. 'Teddie', an only child, played duets, learnt violin, attended the conservatory and composed several string quartets and works for piano. Shy and precocious, Adorno affected the guise of the intellectual artist – rather than wear a wristwatch, he carried his watch in his shirt pocket, on a chain. His first forays into music writing in the early 1920s mixed adolescent self-importance with a conviction that only true art, uncompromised by bourgeois sentiment, could save humanity from extinction. Even Stravinsky did not go far enough; Adorno panned his *Soldier's Tale* as 'a dismal Bohemian prank'.[140] Only twelve-tone music promised salvation. In 1925, he went to Vienna to study with Alban Berg. In brief, Adorno was the musical equivalent of Bruno Taut, in a Marxist vein: commercial fluff and bourgeois ornamentation had to go.

Radio, Adorno concluded, was the 'narcotic' loudspeaker of the bourgeois system. It made for 'retrogressive tendencies in listening, for the avalanche of fetishism which is overtaking music and burying it under the moraine of entertainment.' Such snobbery sufficiently irritated his boss, Lazarsfeld, for him to ask Adorno whether the true fetishism was not perhaps rather his indulgence in grand Latin phrases. Adorno was plainly disgusted by the idea of a farmer's wife listening to Beethoven while washing up. Radio destroyed symphony as a collective experience. It privatized listening, turning music into just another 'piece of furniture'. Classical music was 'trivialized' as it was broken up into recognizable theme songs and served like any other 'ready-made piecemeal product which can be enjoyed with a minimum of effort'. As the gap between serious and popular music widened, so people moved further away from true consciousness and freedom. What religion had been to Marx, commercial culture was to Adorno: the opiate of the masses. Popular or, as he called it, 'vulgar' music, including jazz, was how bourgeois society lulled people into servitude.[141]

Adorno did theory, not empirical research, and, with the benefit of hindsight, what is perhaps most interesting is how his analysis managed to evolve into its own kind of conformity, leading many in the next generation to rehearse pre-packaged condemnations of consumer culture. It is therefore worth emphasizing how out of touch he was. Radio listeners were intensely active, American researchers found in the 1930s. For men especially, the radio nurtured a love of music. 'I always liked music,' an Italian-born shoemaker reported, 'but being unable to hear much good music prevented my enjoyment of it. But then I began listening to the radio and now I am familiar with most of the great works. I never would enjoy it so much without the radio.' Some played piano less because 'I can see my own faults too clearly.'[142] But, in general, the radio and gramophone gave a boost to music making, spread new styles like jazz, and increased the number of orchestras. Records were sometimes used to challenge power and authority, as when rallying Indian nationalists to boycott British goods during the partition of Bengal in 1905. Instead of much-feared uniformity, the radio created openings for diverse genres and listening communities, including folk cultures on the brink of extinction. A Swedish machinist working in Norway was deeply moved when he tuned his radio in the evenings to 'Stockholm-Motala-Jönköping and heard a song of his childhood, sung in my childhood dialect'. Many stations broadcast local programmes in local dialect until the Swedish government took over in 1935.[143] In Japan, radio kept alive traditional instruments and forms of storytelling; in Malaya the music of *kroncong*; in the United States it transmitted the blues and popularized hillbilly music and hearth-and-home songs. By the 1930s, black families were able to listen to black DJs playing black music.[144] In a single week, over 30,000 hours of music programmes were presented to the American public.[145] The radio encouraged not conformity but a cornucopia of tastes.

How and what people consumed did not follow some prior logic of mass production. Adorno's shortcoming was to ignore what the radio did inside people's minds. Radio listening was a new, emotional experience. For men in particular, it opened up a world of feelings. Some early listeners switched off the light to heighten the sensation. Most people listened in the comfort of their home, but in all other respects the radio was everything but private. Commentators in the late 1920s who predicted that the radio's appeal would be limited to 'isolated persons like farmers, the sightless, and those who are nearly deaf' were soon proved wrong.[146] Radio stimulated the social imagination. Without an actual orchestra or group of actors, the listener had to imagine the scene and players. Fans of serial shows created a theatre in their minds. An early study of radio psychology compared the experience to people with vision having to learn to be like blind people and visualize the world through their ears. This 'practice in visualization is helping to restore in adults some of the keenness of imagery dulled since childhood'.[147]

Day-time serial listeners were not tuning in because of a 'vacuum' in their lives, Herta Herzog, a researcher and Lazarsfeld's wife, found; there was no evidence that active listeners stopped going to clubs and churches. Rather, the home was now the entrance to a virtual social world. Radio created a feeling of community with the thousands of others listening in to the same programme. For some, series such as *The Goldbergs* – a daily fifteen-minute soap about a poor Jewish family in the Bronx that ran in the 1930s and 1940s – were an escape from their real family. For others, they were a source of comfort, making them 'feel better to know that other people have troubles, too'. Characters became friends, even better than real ones – 'Friends are so unpredictable . . . But radio people are reliable.'[148] A large number felt they were learning about life from these programmes, from social etiquette and how to handle the kids to why a husband came home grumpy from work.[149]

The eighteenth century had assigned 'the spectator' a central role in the advance of politeness. Imagining themselves in someone else's position would foster sympathy. People were encouraged to be their own spectators and evaluate their effect on others. The radio was not about politeness. But, perhaps, we can see it as a twentieth-century version of the spectator, a cultural successor to the diary and the conversation club. In their radio imagination, people forged new social solidarities and acted out social roles. Listening to the wireless expanded the emotional horizon of the private person, who learnt to share the joy and pain of distant others.

The ancient Greek idea of the home was the *oikos*, a household that united production and consumption, family and servants. Long after it had vanished from the landscape, this ideal continued to exercise a hold on the modern imagination. The rise of industry and commerce and the competing demands of private and public worlds caused a crisis of identity. The home had to be more than just a place for consuming stuff. In the utopian novel *Looking Backward* (1887), Edward Bellamy offered a socialist answer. The hero falls asleep and wakes up in 2000 in the socialist city of Boston to behold the home transformed. Housework has disappeared. Cooking and laundry are done by communal experts. 'We choose houses no larger than we need, and furnish them so as to involve the minimum of trouble to keep them in order.'[150] In the 1950s, real researchers descended on one of the new suburbs outside Toronto and described a very different scene. The home had been entirely taken over by individualist consumerism: it was a dormitory with bloated leisure spaces and showrooms of stuff. The cult of personal possessions was splitting the family into 'an aggregate of persons with little reason or motivation to stay together'.[151]

In truth, the history of the home has been more mundane and more paradoxical than either of these two extremes. Production has not left the home. Rather, consumption and homemaking have reinforced each other. Practical usefulness justified the purchase and use of home equipment, including the radio. In the course of the twentieth century, people have spent more material and emotional resources on the home than ever before, just as one half of the population (women) was spending less time in it. Collections, pictures, souvenirs and other objects have become vital family bonds,[152] taking on the role once played by shared work.

Even the dystopian picture of acquisitive suburbia was belied by the fact that researchers in the 1950s found old furniture in new homes: inherited sofas, old dining-room tables and old sterling cutlery gave families a sense of stable identity.[153] In their kitchen, people preferred sociability to functionalism. Modern design faced formidable barriers of custom and habits. In Finland, working-class and rural residents converted the functional kitchen into the family space they were used to. When working-class families moved to new homes in Britain in the 1940s, one of the first things some did was to erect temporary partitions to create an eating area alongside the new, small kitchen. The partitions came down only when the rent-collector called. 'Modern' furniture was all but absent.[154] To design-conscious, middle-class observers, living-room suites and deep-pile carpets were all identical abominations of conformity and tastelessness. The people living there, by contrast, had an equally strong sense that they 'had their own taste' that set their home apart from their neighbours'.[155] What mattered was how things were arranged and the many little objects that said, 'This is who we are.' Rather than being primarily about emulation, things were signs of identity and respect.

In the battle between competing ideas of comfort, then, emotions had the edge over rational efficiency. Comfort was about feeling at home. It was 'good' consumption and justified spending and buying furniture on instalment plans. 'We're not lavish, but we like to be comfortable,' one British family explained in the 1980s. 'You feel comfortable in comfortable furniture. Other people buy cheap things to save money for . . . what we would regard as silly things. They're not concentrating on their home comforts and nice settee. It's not for people to come and see what we've got but to actually feel comfortable. They're not necessities but they are not luxuries either.'[156]

6

Age of Ideologies

She was just nineteen and lucky to be alive. Heidi Simon had been born the year Hitler came to power. Frankfurt am Main, her hometown, was among the cities worst hit by Allied bombing; the 1944 raids killed thousands and left half the population homeless. Now, in 1952, Heidi was one of the winners in an amateur photography competition to celebrate the American Marshall plan. Recovery had barely begun. The entries reflected the harsh realities of post-war Europe: 'Bread for all'; 'No more hunger'; 'New homes'. She scooped one of the top prizes: a Vespa moped plus prize money. The officials at the Ministry for the Marshall Plan may well have been surprised by her response. She was very happy about winning but, she wrote, to be honest and without trying to sound 'impertinent', she wondered whether she could not rather have a Lambretta than a Vespa. For the entire last year she had 'passionately' longed for a Lambretta. The Ministry refused and sent her the Vespa.[1]

This snapshot of young Heidi Simon, tucked away in the German federal archives, is a reminder of how the large forces of history intersect with the material lives and dreams of ordinary people. The Marshall Plan was a critical moment in the reconstruction of Europe and the advancing Cold War divide between East and West, but its recipients were far from passive. Heidi's outspoken desire for a particularly stylish consumer good in the midst of rubble also challenges the conventional idea that consumer society was the product of galloping growth in the age of affluence, the mid-1950s to 1973. It jars with the sometimes instinctive assumption that people turn to goods only for identity, communication or sheer fun *after* they have fulfilled their basic needs for food, shelter, security and health. It is no coincidence that this psychological model of the 'hierarchy of needs', initially proposed by the American Abraham Maslow in 1943, gained in popularity just as affluence began to spread. According to this theory, Heidi Simon should have asked to trade in the Vespa for bricks and mortar and perhaps some savings bonds, rather than hoping for an upgrade to the 123cc Lambretta with its sleek single-piece tubular frame.

In the era of the Cold War, consumer society became an American trademark. Consumerism, democracy and capitalism were promoted as one package. It could be embraced for exporting freedom or condemned for fostering soulless, selfish materialism, but there was no doubt amongst contemporaries that consumer society was as American as apple pie. It was at this point that general models were first assembled of what a consumer society really was, most notably by the economist J. K. Galbraith in his bestseller *The Affluent Society* (1958). The United States was presented as a new society, where people were driven to consume ever more to keep the engine of production running, at the expense of public welfare, the environment and their own happiness. This model has shaped the way we think and talk about consumption ever since. It continues to inform the worldview of many critics today, who trace the dangers of 'consumerism' to a post-1945 addiction to growth. The neo-liberal 1990s told a similar story, but celebrated the triumph of choice and markets. The end of our own era of affluence in 2009 and the decline of America are an opportune moment to take a broader view.

The golden years from the 1950s to the early 1970s – *das Wirtschaftswunder, il miracolo, les trente glorieuses* – brought annual growth rates of 5 per cent to Western Europe, unprecedented in history. Affluence, however, came in the wake of an equally extraordinary series of transformations that compressed into a single generation total war (1914–18), a world depression (1929–31), the rise of totalitarian regimes and another even more brutal world war (1939–45). To explore the connections between these eras does not mean to propose a simple continuity. Some of the drive for cream cakes and Coca-Cola in the 1950s can be understood as an immediate reaction, a liberation from rationing and austerity. But longer trends were at work as well. The 1950s and '60s bore marks of the '30s, in politics, culture and in the lives of ordinary people. Young parents who set up a home and bought their first TV and car in the 1950s had grown up as children of the Depression. Fascism cast a shadow long after the defeat of the Nazis; elites continued to fear that mass consumption might resurrect it. The inter-war years were a formative period for the growing power of consumption in public and private life.

Hard times nurtured dreams of a better life, in politics, cinemas and local committee rooms. The 1930s were the golden years of consumer activism. The consumer had found their voice in the Victorian period. Now, in countries reeling from war, inflation and world depression, everyone began courting the consumer – national governments, social reformers and advertisers. All mass ideologies promised their supporters a better life and developed strategies to harness consumption to their particular ends. This included the progressive New Deal as well as Nazism and Stalinism, colonial nationalists and popular imperialists. However limited the delivery on these promises, people acquired a taste for more. Even regimes marked by low growth, deprivation and colonial exploitation played their part in boosting consumption.

Modern societies had entered the twentieth century with an ideal of separate spheres. Culture was to be kept apart from commerce, private from public life, male from female spheres, reason from emotion. Social classes had distinct diets, clothes and amusements. As the flow of things and tastes accelerated, these divides became harder and harder to maintain. This made affluence a battleground in the 1950s – '60s. Societies that had been accustomed to coping with too little found themselves worrying about having too much. Yet, once the ideal of freedom was linked to personal lifestyle, no sphere was immune. To consume was endorsed as a liberating process of self-discovery, available to all. That this fundamental clash of values gave way to accommodation rather than class warfare or counter-revolution was one of the most remarkable outcomes of the twentieth century. In different ideological dialects, people had been promised a better life. Now they took their leaders at their word: was not everyone entitled to a TV, new clothes and satisfaction? A more intensive, material lifestyle was becoming a shared goal, East and West. Governments might roll in tanks, but none dared to roll back consumption. Instead of being controlled by elites, consumption gained control of culture and politics. By the 1980s, what to Adam Smith had been 'the sole end and purpose of all production',[2] looked almost like the sole end of being.

CLASH OF MATERIAL CIVILIZATIONS

For consumers across Europe, the First World War was a transformative experience. Before the war, consumer activism had been limited to liberal societies or middle-class groups such as the shoppers' leagues on both sides of the Atlantic. Total war made consumption a matter of national survival everywhere. All belligerents faced unprecedented problems in securing their food supply. Germany and its allies had to cope with a blockade, Britain with submarines sinking convoys of grain, and all with the internal dislocation wrought by recruiting, feeding and killing armies. Shortages sparked inflation and unrest. People who had previously seen themselves as workers or clerks discovered that they, too, were consumers. Whether they liked it or not, governments were driven to adopt what contemporaries called 'war socialism', running the economy, setting prices and commandeering resources. A tug of war developed between an increasingly organized consumer interest and governments making ever greater demands for frugality and self-sacrifice.

The heat of war forged a new consumer identity, and nowhere more so than in central Europe. In Germany, in December 1914, barely four months into the conflict, a national committee for consumer interests was set up. The Kriegsausschuss für Konsumenteninteressen represented a total of 7 million households, over one quarter of the population. Similar organizations sprang up in Allied Vienna, Budapest and Prague, as well as in neutral Switzerland and Luxembourg. The German committee included co-operatives and housewives' organizations, but now also those on fixed salaries, men working for the state railways and Christian trade unionists.[3] Inflation made the consumer outgrow the inherited clothes of the female shopper: Workers, too, were consumers, many argued. This left as the enemy the 'producer interest' – a small bastion of rich businessmen and cartels. Not all groups were happy with this shift away from status based on work and professional identity. Civil servants preferred to keep their distance, as did doctors and judges. Still, 'the consumer' could no longer be so easily dismissed as a sectional, selfish interest.

The German committee expressed the new confidence in the consumer as a source of national strength. By 1917, there were almost two hundred district bodies fighting against profiteers and for greater self-sufficiency. They offered everything from cooking demonstrations to advice on recycling and how to avoid being cheated. They distributed blacklists of profiteers and hoarders, set up complaints centres and introduced spot-check inspections to compare the price, quality and availability of goods in rival shops. Here were the hallmarks of the testing organizations that would spread everywhere in the next two generations, such as the Consumers' Union, *Which?*, *Stiftung Warentest* and *Que Choisir*. In their hands, greater awareness of price, quality and safety would increasingly focus on individual welfare. In the Great War, by contrast, individual and collective interests were two sides of the same coin. Robert Schloesser, a leading advocate of consumer representation, announced in 1917 that the war had forged a new collective mentality. In addition to looking for a good deal, consumers would concern themselves with raising the condition of the lower classes. And they would strengthen the nation, 'so that when an external enemy threatens Germany the next time, the nation will never again have to simultaneously fight an internal enemy, the exploitation of Germans by Germans.'[4]

The ink had barely dried before this optimistic vision was put to a devastating test. As it was failing to break through the Western Front in 1918, Imperial Germany lost the battle of the home front. Rather than unifying the nation, the regime's rationing system exacerbated tensions, producing a widening gulf between entitlements and a sense of unfairness that eventually swallowed up the old regime.[5] Poor consumers attacked soldiers' wives and mothers with many children for their 'unfair' special allowances.

In the short run, peace proved less favourable to the new consumer bodies than war. This was true for losers and winners alike. In Russia and central Europe, revolutionary councils were organized around workers and soldiers, not consumers. In Britain, the Consumers' Council died in 1920, divided and impotent. The government saw little reason to keep it alive; with the end of wartime controls, its *raison d'être* had gone. Soldiers returned to their industries and to the strike as their primary weapon for defending their livelihoods. In Weimar Germany, consumers still sent a few representatives in 1921 to the economic council, the Reichswirtschaftsrat, but they were quickly outwitted by corporate producers; tellingly, on the Coal Council, it was industrial users and coal dealers who spoke as the consumer interest, not housewives or tenants.[6]

Still, the war had important legacies. At one extreme, the new Soviet regime in Russia turned war socialism to its own use. The Bolsheviks applied the lessons of centralized control with harrowing consequences. The 1917 revolution started a brutal rollercoaster for shopkeepers and customers alike. After initial rationing and the suppression of private shops (1917–21), open buying and selling was encouraged (1922–8), before war was declared on shops once again (1929–35). Rationing was not abolished until 1935. By 1930, less than 6 per cent of the retail market was left in the hands of private traders. Shopping now meant a state shop, barter or the black market. By 1932, most workers in key industries ate their main meal in state cafeterias. All this had catastrophic consequences for people's standard of living, which by the following year was below that at the time of the October Revolution.[7]

Consumption marked one's place in the socialist order. That goods are markers of distinction was nothing new. Under the Bolsheviks, the state could manipulate distinction because it controlled the goods. The rationing hierarchy placed workers and engineers at the top, housewives and clerks in the middle, receiving only half as much food, and peasants at the bottom, receiving nothing. Entry to shops and cafeterias was screened. Peasants, for example, were not admitted to state stores, which offered cheaper prices than commercial stores. Even the bill in a cafeteria reflected one's rank in the workers' state: a construction worker paid 84 kopecks for lunch, an engineer two and half times that amount.[8] As is well known, Soviet Russia threw its energies into collectivizing land and nationalizing industry. For everyday life, the state was equally significant. The clothes people were able to buy (or not), the price they had to pay, whether they obtained things in a state store or from a speculator – people's lives as consumers were defined by their relation to the state.

Scarcity only bolstered state power. One of the first to appreciate this was Leon Trotsky. At the time he was exiled in 1928, it was routine for people to line up outside state stores and co-operatives to wait for goods to arrive, secure a share and then sell them on, a process known as 'queueism' (ocherednichestvo). To have blat, or good connections, was vital. In The Revolution Betrayed, written from his Mexican exile in 1936, Trotsky described scarcity as the breeding ground of state power. 'When there is [sic] enough goods in a store, the purchasers can come whenever they want to. When there is little [sic] goods, the purchasers are compelled to stand in line. When the lines are very long, it is necessary to appoint a policeman to keep order.' This was how Soviet bureaucracy grew. 'It "knows" who is to get something and who has to wait.'[9]

Even in countries that axed state controls, consumption remained on the political agenda. Consumer co-operatives had mushroomed during the war. Housewives' clubs, patriotic leagues and salvage councils trained millions of civilians in the art of thrift. Government propaganda and public opinion asked people to think of the public consequences of what they bought and used. To save the fatherland (or mother country), kings promised to eat fish rather than meat. Social movements instructed the young in how to salvage tins. Here was a reservoir for future appeals to consumption as a collective endeavour.

The war left behind a sense of a social bargain between state and consumers. Treating consumption as a civic project encouraged a greater sense of entitlement. Consumers expected to be protected against scarcity and profiteers. After inflation gave way to stability in the mid-1920s, governments proved unwilling to clamp down on cartels and price-fixing. Yet neither in Britain nor Weimar Germany were they entirely able to ignore demands for state supervision of fair prices. Some have seen this as a return to an older 'moral economy', where authorities confronted by food riots in the eighteenth century would temporarily step in to restore a 'just price'.[10] It was more than that. A fair price became part of social citizenship. Rent control in Weimar was one example. Wartime experiments emboldened social democrats and progressive liberals to look for permanent ways to stabilize prices and regulate food supplies.

Consumer politics was also expanding its repertoire. The Hamburg Konsumentenkammer, one of the local councils to survive until the Nazis, gives a sense of their broadening ambition. In addition to fighting the 'price terror' of guilds and cartels and supporting municipal market-halls, the council also defended the new self-service vending machines that offered cigarettes, chocolate and hot sausages outside legal opening hours. By 1929, there were 200,000 of these in German cities, but the Hamburg police had repeatedly rejected permit applications. The *Trumpf* sweet machines offered people the 'convenience' of being able to buy when they pleased. After years of being treated as an 'object', the consumer needed to grow into the 'subject' of economic life, the council insisted. The state should be responsive to the public in the services it provided, such as transport and electricity. Did the burghers of the free city of Hamburg not have the same right to travel on trains with comfortable, upholstered seats as those in big cities elsewhere?[11]

Having seen Fordism in America with their own eyes, some German trade unionists defended new desires as an engine of growth rather than a drain on productive resources.[12] That the satisfaction of some needs gave rise to new ones was a good thing. The big question in the inter-war years was how long this expansion of needs could go on. With the world depression (1929–31) it hit a major roadblock. The issues were in part economic – how much spending could the state afford? Did wealth not have to be produced before it could be consumed? But these were tied to a deeper, moral conflict. What if more goods produced not stronger citizens but reckless individuals without soul or spine? Such fears reached back to Rousseau and beyond, but the inter-war crisis of capitalism and the rise of totalitarianism gave them fresh urgency. To understand how these tensions were resolved, we need to look at the Depression alongside the dual expansion of commercial leisure and consumer politics.

The inter-war years were precarious times, but they were times with expanding horizons, in Europe as well as the United States. Europeans as a whole entered the Second World War better fed, over an inch taller and earning more than their parents; ironically, it was the Aryan master race that was not growing. These gains were, of course, unevenly distributed across class, regions and generations. In terms of income, the average European was more than 25 per cent better off, according to recent estimates.[13] This might look modest compared to the growth spurt of the 1950s and '60s, but contemporaries could only measure their lives against the past, not the future. For many, the gains were real enough; palpable in better housing, fancier clothes, cinemas, personal radios and cameras. The Depression was a step backwards in this slow movement forward. In 1929, for example, Americans purchased cars worth $9 billion. By 1933, this had sunk to $4 billion. Sales of furniture dropped to a third, that of radios and musical instruments to a fifth, of levels before the Wall Street Crash.[14]

Old industries were particularly hard hit. Entire communities were thrown out of work. In 1932, the sociologist Paul Lazarsfeld and his wife Marie Jahoda, a social psychologist, descended on Marienthal, a textile village south of Vienna, to find out how families were coping. The people of Marienthal had seen their share of ups and downs in the 1920s. In 1925, they had joined the national strike, then faced unemployment. A subsequent revival proved short-lived. By 1932, more than two thirds of the 478 families had lost their job. Mothers were no longer returning from day-trips to Vienna with toys and fashionable clothes but worrying about how to afford shoes; the researchers organized a clothes bank for the village. Depression really meant what it said. It sucked the life out of the town, turning a once-lively place into a 'tired community'.[15] The very rhythm of life was changing. Previously a blessing, leisure time was now a curse. Unemployed men were no longer in a hurry. Instead, they were 'drifting' through the day to kill time.

In their consumption habits, however, families responded to the loss of income in strikingly different ways. Some sold their radios and fine cutlery, cancelled the newspaper and moved back to self-provisioning, growing vegetables or raising rabbits. Others, by contrast, desperately clung to the pleasures of better times. Some used their plots to grow roses and tulips rather than potatoes: 'one cannot live by bread alone, one also needs something for one's heart,' as one villager put it.[16] A fifty-year-old woman, dependent on emergency aid, bought herself a curling iron on credit. Another welfare recipient purchased a coloured print of Venice. Many mothers skimped to buy their kids chocolates or doughnuts. Such responses looked like 'irrational housekeeping', but they were, in fact, quite understandable. People had become accustomed to a growing world of things. Children gave honest testimony to the resulting tension between harsh realities and rising expectations. Most downscaled their Christmas wish list for their poor parents but continued to dream of new clothes, picture books, toys and sports equipment. 'I did not get anything,' one eleven-year-old girl wrote, 'only glasses. I really wanted an atlas and a compass.' Jahoda and Lazarsfeld found many Christmas letters written in the subjunctive: 'If my parents were not unemployed, I would have liked . . .'[17]

Levels of wealth and deprivation differed across Europe and the United States, but rising expectations had taken hold. In downward cycles like war and depression, people no longer fell back to an earlier norm of scarcity. The episodes from Marienthal were mirrored in Maurice Halbwachs' contemporaneous study of workers in France, Germany and the United States. People cut back on necessities to preserve recent luxuries. The standard of living was not just a function of income or biological need. It was shaped by habits and expectations.[18] Amidst the sharp drop in spending during the Depression, therefore, we find a remarkable resilience of consuming habits. People did not stop buying but tried to find cheaper ways to maintain their lifestyle. In American cities, expensive cafés went bankrupt. Yet people continued to eat out, simply at more basic diners. They still bought new clothes, just cheaper ones. There was no change in the fashion cycle; women's dresses and hats went through as many transformations as before. Nor did the Depression reverse the trend to fill the home with electric helpers. Toaster sales were down, but American families bought four times as many electric refrigerators in 1932 as they had in 1929.[19] Nor did the Depression make people sell their cars; they simply hung on to their old model a little bit longer. In their study of Muncie, Indiana, the Lynds even reported a slight rise in the number of registered cars: the car had become a 'must'.[20] For petrol stations and recreation, the slump was good news, as people took to the roads and visited national parks. Even that most horrible fate – house repossession – was turned into entertainment with a perfectly timed new board game: Monopoly.

There were patches of light as well as darkness. For those in work, life was getting significantly better. As we have already seen, affluent workers were joining the ranks of homeowners and radio listeners. There were now growing islands of comfort and entertainment, especially among workers in new industries such as electrical engineering, people on fixed incomes who benefited from the drop in prices, and among the young. In 1930s Britain, young working-class men had considerable spending power; their income had more than doubled in a generation. Most handed half of their wages over to their parents, but this left another half for their own pleasure. Young women joined a new army of clerks, typists and shop assistants, earning less than their brothers but enjoying unprecedented independence nonetheless.[21] Here were the core customers for cinemas, dance halls, fashionable clothes, lipstick and brilliantine. The triumph of these new commercial dream worlds was not complete; older forms of leisure, including street entertainment and 'monkey parades' (dating promenades), were still around in the 1930s.[22] Their rise was breathtaking nonetheless. By 1930, more than half of all adolescent working-class boys went to the cinema at least once a week; girls only slightly less often. Consumerism was a life stage, separating members of the same class, indeed household. Young men would buy new shirts and suits, while their parents made do and mended. For most, it was the cry of the first child that meant the end of free spending.

While European societies as a whole, therefore, occupied rungs well below the high standard of living in the United States, some groups within them were climbing up the ladder fast, developing tastes and excitements similar to those of the better-off Americans. No space was more formative than the cinema. The effect on self-fashioning emerges powerfully from a study of 2,000 American students and pupils conducted between 1929 and 1932. One nineteen-year-old girl had studied Mary Pickford to learn the art of make-up. A high-school junior fell in love with Clara Bow's sleeveless jumper dress in *The Wild Party*: 'Nothing could be done about it. My mother had to buy me one just like it.' Movies were an etiquette book for increasingly self-conscious teenagers. 'Ways of address, conduct at the table, etc., have been incorporated into my conduct by seeing them in the movies,' a male sophomore reported. Young women imitated Greta Garbo, not always successfully: 'When I try to copy her walk, I am asked if my knees are weak. How insulting some people are!' Many a girl adopted Pola Negri's fierce look. Rudolph Valentino taught an entire generation how to be held and kissed. One nineteen-year-old recalled how at the age of eleven she had started putting perfume behind her ears, something she had learnt from Norma Talmadge, the glamorous star of the silent era.[23]

Movies are often condemned for lulling people into escapist fantasies, feeding day-dreams of 'lavish wardrobes, beautiful homes, servants, imported automobiles, yachts and countless handsome suitors', as one girl remembered. So it is worth stressing that they had liberating effects, too. 'Often I get ideas of how much freedom I should have' from movies, a black male high-school student noted, because there 'fellows and girls . . . can wear the best of clothes, make plenty of money, go nearly any place they choose . . . and enjoy all the luxuries of life.'[24] Movies encouraged girls in particular to challenge parental rules and press for greater freedom to go out or to receive company at home.

For Europeans, movies brought American style and a higher standard of living within touching distance. This did not mean a complete makeover. Most working-class girls did not aspire to look like vamps. Rather, celluloid dreams spoke to ideals of 'neat' appearance. Films 'show me that the best mode of dress is the simple one, as it is neat and at the same time gives a finished appearance', one female British bank clerk wrote. A private secretary recalled how in the early '20s, when she was seventeen, her then boyfriend had commented on a film star's 'lovely little feet' and how 'her shoes are always beautiful.' From that moment, 'I always bought the nicest shoes and stockings I could afford,' and shoes remained her 'pet luxury' into the years of war-time rationing.[25] Inevitably, these aspirations led to frustrations with the material reality of the present. One young British woman, a shorthand typist who went to the pictures four times a week, found that seeing 'marvellous places' like New York and California on the screen left her 'miserable and unhappy sitting in my stuffy little office all day with nobody to talk to but myself (which I don't) and to go home to a house that should have been knocked down five years ago'.[26] Such feelings were not all bad. Movies taught people to aspire to a better life. In societies marked by class, race and gender, greater expectations had public as well as private consequences. The screen encouraged a desire for travel and goods but also for greater equality of opportunities. People no longer resigned themselves to their fate so easily. Most viewers knew that the America on the screen was a glorified ideal, not the real thing, but this did nothing to diminish its appeal as a more classless society, nor the anxieties it provoked among elites.

That good times made people reckless had long been the complaint of social reformers. It was a leitmotif in studies of household budgets which sought to document how the standard of living might rise if only individuals drank less and gambled less. The 1920s heightened such fears, for three reasons. One was that people's demands on the state were rising just as states had to shoulder the huge costs left behind by war. The second was universal suffrage – what if the multitude lost their head? Finally, there was the example of the United States, which advertised a future built on mass consumption and individual pleasure. There was no simple divide between European 'traditionalists' and American 'modernizers'; France, Germany and Britain all had their modernizers.[27] Still, there was a widespread suspicion that American cars and movies lured Europeans towards moral and financial bankruptcy. Even consumer champions, like the Hamburg council, were worried about the rising numbers buying clothes, furniture and watches on credit. Whatever experts returning from New York and Chicago preached, American conditions were not applicable to the continent, they insisted. Purchasing power was too low and instalment plans merely diminished it further.[28]

All this helps to explain why one of the products doing really well during the slump was bestsellers warning Europeans of the evil of affluence. Georges Duhamel's *Scènes de la vie future* (1930) went through 187 editions. The American dream was really a nightmare, he wrote. Mass production and mass consumption had turned people into materialist slaves. Americans had traded in their freedom for a fridge and a car.[29]

America was the menace, not so much for what was really happening in Detroit or Hollywood, but because of European elites' deep-seated suspicion of mass society. Many of them had not believed women fit to vote, nor the many men without property and education. Now these same people were tempted by material desires they did not have the self-discipline or knowledge to control. Mass consumption challenged the intellectual elite's position as the guardian of civilization. This was especially pronounced in those parts of Europe, such as Spain, where they had assigned themselves a leading role in national regeneration, with the curious result that plenty appeared the greatest threat where it was furthest away. Few matched the thundering critique of the 'self-satisfied age' launched by the Spanish philosopher Ortega y Gasset in 1930 in *The Revolt of the Masses*; it would enjoy a second success in the 1950s. He supported the overthrow of the monarchy in 1931, but he was more against the king than for democracy. When civil war broke out he fled to Buenos Aires. Ortega y Gasset was a modernist, but when it came to culture, he was an elitist to the bone. 'The mass is the average man,' he wrote. 'Anybody who is not like everybody . . . runs the risk of being eliminated.' The cinema filled workers' minds with visions of 'fabulous potentiality', creating an 'inborn, root-impression that life is easy, plentiful, without any grave limitations'. *Superabundancia* was the enemy of civilization. Ortega y Gasset called 'the mass' 'the spoiled child of human history', obsessed with things, speed and instant gratification. Scarcity had been much better for human development, for character was formed by challenges and self-discipline. Abundance, by contrast, made individuals 'deformed', vicious and false.[30]

Across Europe, cultural elites manoeuvred themselves almost instinctively into the position once occupied by the Church, that of defenders of the spirit against the temptations of the flesh. Johan Huizinga, the great Dutch historian, to take an example from the liberal north-west, in 1935 attacked the 'permanent adolescence' of the age and 'the cult of self'. Morals were squeezed by materialism from two sides: by Marxism, with its appeal to class; and by Freudianism, with its obsession with sex. For Huizinga, these were symptoms of a deeper malaise. The Depression revealed how the world had lost its equilibrium. Spiritual and material values no longer balanced each other out. 'A highly refined economic system daily puts forth a mass of products and sets forces in motion which nobody wants and which bring advantage to none . . . which many scorn as unworthy, absurd and mischievous.' Artists and writers were no better. Everywhere, standards were declining, resulting in 'cultural disorder'. 'Serious activity' and 'play' had contaminated each other. Slogans and PR ruled. Decorum and respect were on the wane. Radio could not teach people to think, as the printed book once had. The one good thing Huizinga had to say for consumer culture was reserved for film, where the happy ending had at least preserved a 'solemn and popular moral order'.[31]

Eventually, consumption emerged stronger from this mid-life crisis. Consumers came to be seen not as the cause of the problem but as its cure. To some degree, this process can be summarized as the triumph of John Maynard Keynes, who justified public spending and condemned an older glorification of thrift. Keynes's *General Theory* of 1936 followed a string of more popular pieces that asked contemporaries to turn their morals upside down. In times of recession, he wrote in 1931, saving was evil: 'Whenever you save five shillings, you put a man out of work for a day.' He urged 'patriotic housewives' instead to 'go to the wonderful sales' and indulge themselves.[32] Governments, too, needed to spend, not cut. Yet Keynes himself was not an unqualified hedonist. Unlike his teacher Marshall, he did not believe that needs were insatiable. In 'The Economic Possibilities for our Grandchildren', published in 1930, he envisaged a future where absolute needs would be fulfilled and everyone devoted their energies to non-material purposes. 'We shall honour . . . the delightful people who are capable of taking direct enjoyment in things, the lilies of the field who toil not, neither do they spin.' In the short run, Keynes endorsed consumer spending. In the long run, however, he hoped for a return to 'some of the most sure and certain principles of religion and traditional virtue – that avarice is vice . . . and the love of money is detestable'.[33] In view of the rising level of consumption since, it is difficult not to conclude that Keynes had a better eye for the short than the long run.

Keynes was only one voice in a more general turn towards consumption. The consumer became an ever more frequent point of reference in the 1930s. French co-operatives started to address 'consumers of health', British teachers the 'consumer's view of adult education', others the 'consumer of art'. In South Africa, William Hutt, a classical liberal economist, coined the idea of 'consumer sovereignty'. Consumers, Hutt argued, did not necessarily know what was best for them, but in a market society their demand ensured that power was diffused, rather than controlled by state or producers, thus facilitating social harmony.[34] In Geneva, internationalists at the League of Nations looked to consumers to absorb excess production and restore world harmony. At the level of policy, the New Deal marked the capitalist apotheosis of this process, but we cannot understand it in isolation. All ideologies discovered consumption. The premise of cultural pessimists and old elites had been that goods bred a cult of the self. Mass ideologies had far fewer problems with mass society. The desire for things simply had to be turned into an instrument of collective strength. By the mid-1930s, gloomy predictions were drowned out by a chorus of 'joy', or *Freude*, which openly celebrated material pleasures.

In America, the transfer of power from the Republican Herbert Hoover to the Democrat Franklin Delano Roosevelt in 1933 changed the diagnosis of the crisis from over-production to under-consumption. New prescriptions brought new politics. The New Deal made the consumer an integral part of democratic state building. Freedom was 'no half-and-half affair', Roosevelt told the 1936 Democratic Convention. 'If the average citizen is guaranteed equal opportunity in the polling place, he must have equal opportunity in the market place.'[35] And for this a strong state was needed. Mr and Mrs Consumer went to Washington. The National Recovery Administration (NRA), set up in the summer of 1933, included a Consumer Advisory Board to protect the public against unfair pricing, poor quality and misleading labelling. Similarly, in the Agricultural Adjustment Administration and other branches of the New Deal state, there was an Office of the Consumer Counsel. The Federal Housing Administration and the Tennessee Valley Authority delivered cheaper housing and electricity.

In practice, diffuse consumer interests found it hard to match concentrated business interests when it came to setting codes and prices for fertilizers, underwear or any other of the five hundred articles regulated by the NRA. Advances in consumer protection were piecemeal and imperfect. Roosevelt himself pursued a double strategy, looking sometimes to consumers' political power, at other times to their purchasing power.[36] The 1930s showed that it was much harder for government to change institutions than to increase spending, which is where the thrust of policy came to lie. Still, the New Deal raised the political profile of the consumer to a new height. It renewed the alignment between state and consumers first noticeable in the First World War. More than that, it turned consumers into instruments of social policy.

If consumers went to Washington, Washington also encouraged them to build the New Deal back home. Over a million volunteers signed up housewives to put a Blue Eagle sticker on their front door and pledge to buy only at stores that paid the minimum wage. On the radio, *Consumer Time* taught the art of civic spending. The New Deal emboldened shoppers to take the fight against high prices into their own hands and boycott profiteers; in the spring of 1935, boycotts forced the closure of several thousand butcher's shops in New York City alone.[37] Rather than building a welfare state, the New Deal turned to consumers to redistribute income and strengthen the purchasing power of workers and farmers. As the post-war years would show, this was a shaky foundation for welfare policies.

The New Deal was the culmination of a more general appreciation of the consumer as citizen. The National Consumers' League had led campaigns for a minimum wage, the protection of women and to regulate child labour since the 1890s. In the course of the 1920s, it was joined by a new generation of muckrakers who exposed shoddy goods and fraudulent advertising. Consumers' Research was set up in 1927 as a private testing agency to empower people by giving them better information. The pinch of the Depression further enhanced the appeal of self-help. Why pay more for a brand name or extra packaging? CR's bimonthly bulletins and product checklist were shields against the onslaught of advertisers and salesmen. Stuart Chase and Fred Schlink, CR's founders, came from a communitarian tradition that viewed goods and desires with suspicion. Following in the footsteps of Veblen, Chase stressed the wastefulness of electric food mixers and many other gadgets.[38] At the same time, the recession upgraded the social function of spending. Mass unemployment was a serious shock to a value system based on work and self-denial. In the mid-1920s, President Coolidge had still preached that national strength and welfare rested on the simple virtues of industry and thrift.[39] From this view, consumption was something that had to be earned. Consumers came after workers. For the progressive Chase, by contrast, these values were outmoded. High productivity meant more leisure and less employment. America had changed from a society of scarcity into one of abundance. The moral union between working and spending had dissolved. In an 'economy of abundance', there was no longer a 'measurable relation . . . between work contributed and goods consumed'. The recession showed how society needed to ensure the 'unhampered flow of goods to consumers, involving the right to a minimum standard of living, regardless of work performed – if no work is available'.[40] People should spend more, not less; dividends and greater purchasing power should be extended to all. Consumers, in short, were productive citizens, too. Prosperity and stability rested on their shoulders.

Business and advertising endorsed the convergence of consumption and citizenship. To counter accusations of monopoly, American corporations presented themselves as mini-democracies. A 1921 advert for AT&T styled the giant telephone operator as 'Democracy . . . of the people, by the people, for the people.' General Electric likened the purchase of household conveniences to having the vote. Roosevelt's fireside radio chats were master classes in marketing, eyed with concern and envy by advertisers whose job it was to rehabilitate the corporate image in an anti-business atmosphere. Advertisers pitched democratic consumers against dictatorial politicians – 'under private capitalism, the Consumer, the Citizen is the boss' whereas in 'state capitalism, the politician is the boss', an ad by the J. Walter Thompson agency put it.[41]

The increasingly popular idiom of the consumer as king had a touch of hypocrisy; privately, advertisers saw shoppers as irrational, stupid or easily distracted; feminine stereotypes that, by the 1930s, were extended to men as well.[42] It did, however, capture an important political turn towards choice in American culture. In the inter-war years, choice stood for more than individualism and markets. It was also a way to foster citizenship. In addition to empowering people vis-à-vis state and business, progressives sought to develop their democratic character. Standardized goods threatened to replace individual taste and identity with conformity and anonymity. The Depression reinforced the sense that people were tossed about by an economic system too complex for them to understand. One remedy was to simplify the system – to return to the farm. This was, however, now the stuff of literary nostalgia, not practical politics. The other was to cultivate more intelligent citizens. This was the approach championed by the philosopher John Dewey and the home economics movement.

Dewey was America's most prominent public intellectual between the wars. His causes ranged from educational reform and women's rights to a defence of Trotsky against the charges of the Stalinist show trials. In 1931, on retiring from Columbia University, he founded the Third Party to give greater voice to consumers. Later, he opposed Roosevelt for being too inflationary and not doing enough for the poor; one of the many contradictions of the New Deal was that it relied on consumption taxes.[43] These skirmishes produced few results. Dewey's main legacy ran deeper. Building on William James, Dewey turned pragmatism into an instrument of democratic freedom. The core of this idea was simple: thought and personality emerged through experience. Life was about becoming, not about reaching a particular goal. This outlook prized experimentation, and with it choice. Through making decisions and reflecting on them, people learnt to think about the consequences of their actions and developed a democratic disposition. It was a philosophy of the common man, with radical implications. Its influence on progressive education was profound; it prized learning by doing. For consumers, it was no less empowering. Instead of regulation from above, it looked to change from below, confident that people had the ability to make intelligent choices. Desires should be nourished through critical reflection, not suppressed.[44]

Choice, then, was about more than calculating costs and benefits. This was almost a spiritual vision, a secular reworking of Christian ideas; Dewey himself had been raised a Congregationalist in Vermont. Actions were oriented outwards rather than inwards, connecting individuals to their communities and the universe at large. By the 1940s, his ideas had reached hundreds of thousands of young Americans in home economics classes in schools, colleges and local communities. Consumption, home economics taught, was about ethics as well as practical housekeeping. Key texts were inspired by Dewey. The consumer was more than a buyer, the leading home economist Hazel Kyrk stressed. Wise consumption raised 'questions of motives, of values, of ends', not just getting the best deal.[45] It was such social ethics that gave choice its broader influence in the 1930s. It could be a tool of citizens, not just of the utility-maximizing individual. This marked a fundamental shift in values. In the older republican tradition, goods and desires tempted people away from active citizenship. Now, choosing in the marketplace nurtured stronger citizens.

The sense that America was blessed with a mutually reinforcing union between freedom and plenty received an additional boost from totalitarian challenges abroad. Consumers, it seemed, saved America from *Führers* and commissars alike. Horace Kallen, a New York philosopher who had emigrated from Silesia, developed an entire worldview from the premise that '[w]e are consumers by nature and producers by necessity.' Fascism and communism were only the latest manifestations of a servile mentality arising from a division of labour that accorded primacy to the producer. It was the consumer, Kallen argued, who was a whole person, someone who overcame the 'false division of men' into competing roles.[46] True freedom lay with consumer cooperation. This association between freedom and consumption became increasingly central to America's self-image.[47] Yet this was not the only pairing. Totalitarian regimes discovered consumption, too.

In Germany, the Nazis consciously presented themselves as a break with bourgeois politicians who preached austerity. For Hitler, the standard of living was one front in the battle against Jews and communists. Simple living was for primitives. The Aryan master race was entitled to more. Every German should be able to climb the ladder, like the Americans. The problem was that Germany was not the United States: it was plagued by lower productivity, lower purchasing power and fewer resources. Hitler's answer was to break through these constraints by conquest. But, in the short run, rearmament sucked resources away from consumer industries like textiles and leather. The basic dilemma was that Nazi leaders, unlike the generals, were committed to defending private levels of consumption and not prepared to ask the German people to tighten their belts. They remembered with horror the collapse of the home front in 1918. Tourists were allowed to mingle, carefree, in the Black Forest. Cosmetics and toy production continued until the disastrous defeat at Stalingrad in 1943.[48]

Nazi policy was, consequently, shot through with contradictions. On the one hand, Nazis prophesied an era of abundance once the Aryan race had a chance to spread; the squandering of resources was hailed as a mark of racial superiority. On the other, the regime was struggling to pay for scarce resources and, in 1936, introduced a four-year plan to encourage the use of national materials – with very modest results. An unprecedented network of motorways was built, but the pursuit of self-sufficiency, with its restrictions on foreign fuel, put a brake on its use. The Nazis promised luxury for the masses and supported symbolic goods such as the *Volksempfänger* radio, which benefited from cartels and fixed prices. Newly-weds could get a special loan to fit out their first home, as long as the bride stopped working. At the same time, the regime's militarism was costly and repressed consumption. The Nazis could not simply maintain Germans' material comforts by making the enemy pay. The Aryanization of Jewish property and plunder in the occupied territories was brutal and rapacious, but it reduced only slightly the fiscal burden of war.[49]

Nazism was forced to stretch the temporal horizon of desire. 'Consumerism' is often characterized as being all about instant gratification. This ignores the fantasies which public regimes helped to feed, especially those that saw themselves in timescales of a thousand years. Consumption was increasingly driven by a joy of longing, something the sociologist Colin Campbell has traced to 'the Romantic imagination'.[50] In this future-oriented mode, pleasure comes from dreaming about stuff. The eventual moment of acquisition can be disappointing. Then the anticipation of something new starts the cycle again. The Nazis vigorously encouraged people to shift their material desires to the future. The more the regime failed to deliver the goods, the greater its promise of future wealth. During the war, savers were promised 15 per cent interest and more, and deposited over 80 billion Reichsmark. An amazing 340,000 well-off Germans paid into the Volkswagen saving scheme run by the Nazi trade union, the German

Labour Front (Deutsche Arbeitsfront), for a VW beetle, without any receiving a car; they did not even receive any interest.[51] Adverts continued to sing the praises of brands of cigarettes and detergents which were rapidly becoming unavailable.

The Nazis' promise of affluence was underwritten by the name of the organization motto *Kraft durch Freude (KdF)*, or 'Strength through Joy'. There is a certain symmetry with post-Depression America, albeit in a different ideological key. Private pleasure and national power would reinforce each other. Even the pursuit of autarchy was conducted within these parameters. The cheese substitute Velveta was to be savoured as a delicacy. With Nivea, young women were told, a little lotion could build a perfect tan. In 1937, the laundry and cosmetics giant Henkel launched its own 'two-front war against waste' in production and consumption. People needed to be more discerning, not consume less. Market researchers in the Gesellschaft für Konsumforschung saw their job as raising consumers to a higher cultural level.[52] Unlike the individual materialist in the United States, they argued, the German was a *Kulturmensch* with deep roots in the community. By 1938, the *KdF* catered for almost 9 million German tourists. Package tours were designed to pacify workers and to harden them for the collective struggle to come. They were also a relatively cheap way to show off the way in which race was erasing class. Cruise ships like the *Wilhelm Gustloff* introduced what recent budget airlines have since perfected: the classless cabin. Leisure provision was minimal; on board, travellers enjoyed sack races. Some lucky workers were able to enjoy a week in Norway, or Madeira, the most sought-after destination.

At one level, tourism strengthened the racial state. Photo diaries show how travellers appreciated the racial traits of 'our Nordic brothers' amidst the Norwegian fjords.[53] The problem was that – contrary to theories of 'mass society' – pleasure was intensely private. Once tickled, it tended to escape a uniform 'mass' taste. By endorsing hedonism, the Nazis inevitably created spaces for personal satisfaction and escape. *KdF* tours were notorious for heavy drinking and heavy petting. Once a ship had left the harbour, some passengers would simply drop the 'Hitler greeting'. Women used Mediterranean cruises for erotic adventures with local men, to the horror of security agents.[54]

The cult of the home only deepened these contradictions. In the 1937 exhibition Schaffendes Volk (A Nation at Work) a million visitors toured model houses and modern conveniences. Appropriately, the exhibition was opened by Hermann Göring, who had been placed in charge of the four-year plan the previous year and who embodied the taste for the good life; the organizers flew in his favourite chocolate Sachertorte from the Viennese patisserie Demel. Model homes reflected Nazi consumerism's combination of tradition and modernity. Rustic beams and embroidered curtains mixed with the latest technology. Henkel had its own pavilion and model house (complete with a cinema in the basement), which it used to demonstrate new easy-to-use paints. These were no longer just for professional decorators, visitors learnt. Everyone could now paint their own four walls. New products met the autarchy goal for pure, 100 per cent German materials: *rein deutsche Werkstoffe*. At the same time, they deepened a private culture of comfort and pleasure.[55]

It might appear self-evident that mass ideologies like fascism were a more receptive vessel for mass consumption than their bourgeois predecessors, but we must not exaggerate the natural affinities, nor imagine a clean break with older values. American movies were popular in 1930s Germany, while swing music developed into youthful resistance and was crushed. Nazi tourism did not eliminate an older middle- and upper-class travel culture. Regular tourists despised Nazi package groups, while the latter often complained about inferior food and accommodation on their holidays. In spite of its populist title, the 1936 Schaffendes Volk exhibition included houses built for a bourgeois lifestyle, with servants' rooms and separate kitchen and dining rooms.

The paradoxical relationship between mass ideology, mass consumption and bourgeois habits was nowhere more pronounced than in Stalinist Russia. In the 1920s, efforts to mould a new Soviet person focused on replacing petit-bourgeois with proletarian traits. Marxism stood for 'everything for the masses' according to Stalin; it was anarchism that looked to the individual (*lichnost*).[56] By the mid-1930s, the proletarian leather jacket had been replaced by crêpe de Chine. Two movies, a mere five years apart, register the shift. *Odna* (*Alone*) was made by the great Soviet directors Grigori Kozintsev and Leonid Trauberg in 1929–31. It was one of the first Russian movies to experiment with sound; the clicking of a typewriter and public announcements were added after filming. Dmitri Shostakovich wrote the score, lost during the Siege of Leningrad but reconstructed in 2003.[57] The film opens with Yelena Kuzmina, a newly qualified teacher, first in her Leningrad flat enjoying modern utilities, then going on a shopping trip with her fiancé to pick out furniture for their future home. Such petit-bourgeois desires are quickly crushed when she is given her first posting: a village in the Altai Mountains of Kazakhstan. Neither sha-men nor a corrupt village elder, however, manage to discourage her from her mission of bringing education to the 'backward' Asian brothers and sisters – Lenin, who had a strong belief that Asian 'hordes' needed to be civilized, would have been proud. About to report on illegal sheep-trading, she is left in the snow for dead. In the end, the villagers rescue her, and she is airlifted to safety. This was a typical Soviet *Bildungsroman*: individuals matured into comrades as they learnt to sacrifice personal comfort for the socialist good.

By the mid-1930s, movies such as *Odna* had disappeared from cin-emas, replaced by glamour, entertainment and melodrama. *Tsirk* (*Circus*) was a 1936 musical about an American circus artist – the star was the glamorous Lubov Orlova – and her black baby, who find love and acceptance among the welcoming Soviet people. *Tsirk* combined propaganda with vaudeville, parades, cheap jokes and sentimentalism; different ethnic groups of the Soviet people sing the baby a lullaby, each in their own language.

The shift from *Odna* to *Tsirk* was part of a second revolution. In the 1920s, Soviet energies concentrated on transforming political and eco-nomic institutions. Now, they turned to the individual. In the mid-1930s, Stalin tried to plant the roots of a new material civilization. As in New Deal America and Nazi Germany, it was the state, not the market, which pushed consumption forward. Material desires would advance communism. 'Life is getting better, life has become more joyous,' Stalin pronounced in 1935. This slogan was trumpeted from department stores, the fun fair at Gorky Park and in popular song. After years of deprivation, comrades were told to enjoy tennis, silk stockings and jazz by Antonin Ziegler's Czech band. Red Army officials learnt to dance the tango. Heroic workers, the Stakhanovites, received gramophones and a Boston suit (for him) and a crêpe de Chine dress (for her). A Soviet House of Fashions opened its doors in Moscow in 1936, and the USSR set out to overtake France in the production of perfume. Novelty was encouraged. Chocolate and sausage makers raced to expand their ranges; in 1937, Moscow's Red October factory produced over five hundred different kinds of chocolates and candies. From Moscow to Vladivostok, there were exhibitions of radios, cameras, fashionable shoes and even a Soviet washing machine. The campaign for a plainer domestic lifestyle was abandoned. Housewives were urged to join embroidery classes and personalize their living quarters. Personal prop-erty received official protection in Stalin's 1936 constitution.[58]

The campaign for *kulturnost* (a cultured lifestyle) touched all parts of everyday life, from personal hygiene and appearance to cream cakes and social dances. Red consumerism challenged the divide between needs and wants. Luxury was no longer decadent. It was the socialist future, to be enjoyed by all. This approach can be understood as a particular Soviet version of the 'politics of productivity' which all inter-war regimes wrestled with. Dangling watches and phonographs in front of workers would make them work harder. 'We want to lead a cultured life,' Party leader Miron Djukanov, a miner, told fellow Stakhanovites in 1935: '[W]e want bicycles, pianos, phonographs, records, radio sets, and many other articles of culture.'[59] Greater productivity, in turn, would allow socialism to overtake and crush capitalism. Stalinism aimed at an extreme version of the 'industrious revolution'. Hard work would catapult ordinary people into a new material era, as in the case of E. M. Fedorova, a garment worker in Leningrad's Red Banner Factory who was rewarded with a watch, a tablecloth, an electric samovar, an electric iron and a phonograph and records for exceeding her targets – in addition to the works of Lenin and Stalin.[60]

Stalin's consumerism had a paternalist touch: the 'father of the people' looked after all workers. At the same time, individuals were asked to take an active role in refashioning themselves. It was a socialist variation of 'the civilizing process' that the sociologist Norbert Elias traced back to early modern court culture.[61] Mirrors and soap would teach self-discipline. Polished shoes, clean shirts and a shaved face signalled an inner purity that could be monitored by others as well as by oneself. Caring for personal possessions would foster attentiveness at work. Cleanliness was now next to socialism, not godliness.

What is remarkable in retrospect is how much of the Soviet ideal of material culture continued to spin in a bourgeois orbit. Prized goods were a Boston suit and silk stockings, a gramophone and a watch, vases and chocolates. Civilizing the socialist self involved a shared ensemble of goods and habits, not difference. Everyone would climb up the same ladder of cultural progress, with Stakhanovites leading the way. Champagne would flow for all loyal workers. Recent research suggests that in the 1930s the gap between workers and the elite did narrow somewhat, although this was primarily because of better food and clothing rather than luxuries; all of Leningrad had to make do with a mere 25,000 bottles of champagne during the anniversary celebration of the October Revolution in 1940.[62] Class did not disappear, however. Rather, the drive for material uplift gave birth to a new communist elite; at the Kirov works in 1935, some workers demanded an end to the 'fattening-up' of managers.[63] The mid-1930s saw a widespread inflation of ranks, prizes, orders and medals. Many came with serious stipends or cash awards. Stalinism transmuted into a hybrid of bourgeois manners and Tsarist hierarchies.

This can be read as a betrayal of revolutionary principles. For many consumers, however, it was empowering. A cultured lifestyle required cultured shopping. Soviet people, too, had a right to be served courteously. Only discerning customers would be able to navigate the affluence that socialism would bring and force shopkeepers to raise their game. In theory, then, the absence of competition made consumers more, not less important. Soviet reformers returned from trips to American and European cities fascinated by customer service and convenience. In Berlin, people ate ice cream in paper cups and sausages off paper plates, easily disposable. Ingenious! At Macy's in New York, sales personnel were polite and attractive, advising customers on how to dress to their advantage; even teaching them how to play tennis or golf. The store offered home delivery and had an in-house barber and post office. Marvellous! The future lay with Western department stores, not the traditional Russian co-operative. Back home, they launched Soviet hamburgers, cornflakes and ice creams. The period saw a campaign to transform the shopping experience. Opening hours were lengthened and shops pressed to have better displays, plants, and chairs for tired customers. Salespeople were taught to wash their hands and keep shelves clean. Complaint books were introduced and promoted as a civic exercise in socialist criticism, although some shops hid them. In 1936, a series of customer conferences was launched, encouraging housewives to tell retailers and producers what they needed, what worked and what did not; some quite openly challenged sales staff about scarce goods and tactless treatment.[64] Consumers, like workers, were responsible for building socialism. The parallels to the New Deal are apparent. In Russia, as in America, an expanding state turned to the consumer to advance its social project.

These initiatives had limited success. Between 1932 and 1937, the sale of radios in the USSR did go up eightfold to 195,000 a year, gramophones to almost 700,000. There were 328 Gastronom shops operating in forty regions. Still, in a population of over 150 million, these were small numbers. A lot of fashion and electrical goods were symbolic, barely reaching beyond Leningrad's Nevsky Prospect or Moscow's Central Department Store, which occupied the old site of Muir and Mirrielees, where the Tsarist elite had once shopped. The typical Russian shop was a world apart from Macy's. In Odessa, for example, the problem was not that shop-window displays were dull but that they did not have a shop window in the first place. There was no glass; there were no shop signs, no packaging materials; some shops had no weights or measures.[65] Rural areas were not completely cut off from consumer culture. There were travelling cinemas, and half of all radios were sold in shops in the countryside, but most of them had no space for storing goods and many lacked soap. *Kulturnost* was easier said than done.

Stalinism was a type of internal imperialism. It tried to do with Soviet workers and peasants what European imperialists had attempted with the heathen in the colonies: impose external state control through the self-control of clean shirts and bodies. In the inter-war years, colonial nationalists were turning this 'civilizing' process back on their masters. Foreign goods were burnt in demonstrations as far apart as Egypt, China and India. Boycotts proliferated as substitutes for state power. Goods were a target that could be hit without guns and armies. Clothes, in particular, dominated the agenda. Clothes weave a thread between private and public, between the material self and global regimes of production. They are an extension of our body and signal who we are yet at the same time reflect fashion and group identity. In societies with high illiteracy and limited freedom, campaigns for national clothes were an attractive way to promote national identity. If clothes make the man, new clothes would make new citizens. Empires might control imports and exports, but what people chose to wear proved more elusive, although in India the British tried to outlaw items like Gandhi's cap. As simultaneous markers of difference and uniformity, however, goods also raised thorny questions for colonial nationalists. Was the goal to throw out imperialists and keep the goods? Or, were the goods themselves too contaminated by imperial power?

Mohandas Gandhi was a sartorial fundamentalist. As a young man, he had first set out for England in 1888 with a white flannel suit, carefully packed away during the crossing. When he disembarked on English soil in late September he found to his chagrin that he was surrounded by a sea of dark suits. In the next few decades, he would shed Western dress as he discarded layers of imperial civilization. In South Africa in 1913, he donned the mourning dress of indentured labourers to protest against the shooting of Indian workers. A few years later, back in India, he adapted the Kashmiri cap into a new national style. By 1921, he had settled on the dhoti, a waistcloth slightly longer than a loincloth that he would wear for the rest of his life.[66]

The dhoti had been sported by protesters in an earlier boycott of British goods over the division of Bengal in 1905; American revolutionaries had worn home-spun dresses in the 1760s. Gandhi tied such traditions to spiritual and political emancipation. Coarse clothes signalled a break with an unjust society, a refusal to consume akin to a hunger strike. They gave individuals a chance to purify themselves. As early as 1909, Gandhi had targeted material passions in his plea for self-government, *Hind Swaraj*, a slim book written on his return voyage from London to South Africa. In the past, people had been enslaved by force. 'Now they are enslaved by temptations of money and of luxuries that money can buy.'[67] Modern civilization had removed all checks on self-indulgence. Appetites had become insatiable. All this undermined community, taste and self-control. Political home rule and self-rule lay along the same path: a return to the 'proper use of our hands and feet'.[68] It was as if Rousseau had met Marx and Christ. India was poor because the British empire drained it of resources – here Gandhi followed earlier Indian 'drain theorists' – but also because the lust for things bred inequality and selfishness. For Gandhi, it was as sinful to covet imported cloth as to covet a neighbour's wife. Imperial exploitation was underpinned by self-exploitation and a disregard for others. Consumers were violent creatures.

Gandhi's answer was *khadi*. By spinning and weaving the coarse, unbleached *khadi* cloth with their own hands, Indians would liberate themselves. Like the Mughal emperors who had built imperial networks through gifts of elaborate textiles,[69] Gandhi aimed to use *khadi* to unite the nationalist elite with the poor. It was 'the soul of India'.[70] Swadeshi – the movement for indigenous goods – sought to rebuild society in the image of an ideal village. Swadeshi marriage songs renounced the suffering wrought by foreign clothes. Once spinning, weaving and finishing cotton were reunited, community spirit would revive. Instead of wanting more and more stuff, people would want only what everyone else had. Here was the starting point for future movements for simple living. Gandhi's genius was to turn an economics of autarchy into an ethics of global brotherhood. People who wore *khadi* showed their 'fellow-feeling with every human being on earth' by renouncing anything that did harm to others.[71] Gandhi appropriated the motto of free traders and turned it on its head: every 'revolution of the wheel spins peace, goodwill and love'.[72]

The wheel was slow to spin. Gandhi himself had at first confused the loom with the spinning wheel, and when he moved into the Satyagraha

ashram in the Bombay Presidency in 1917 to start *khadi*, the nearest
spinning wheel was in another state. But by 1920, the Indian National
Congress had endorsed swadeshi and non-cooperation. Four years later,
it adopted the 'spinning franchise': no *khadi*, no vote. Every member had
to contribute 2,000 yards spun by themselves and have a *charkha* (spinning wheel) in their house. *Khadi* became the anti-colonial uniform.

Few in the nationalist elite or society at large, however, were prepared to join Gandhi's fundamentalist revolt against things. Gandhi
himself urged a minimum of thirty minutes of spinning a day. In the
Congress Party, many middle-class leaders were happy to adopt *khadi*
as a symbolic token but had no problem with fashion as such; Sarojini
Naidu, the poet and president of the Indian National Congress in 1925,
liked her fine clothes, and Nehru asked for high-end, fine-spun cloth to
be brought to him in prison. Others doubted whether hand-weaving
was really the ticket out of poverty. In the population at large, *khadi*
clashed head on with caste and class cultures. In Madras, white, coarse
cloth was traditionally worn by widows living at the margin of society. Mothers complained that it was impossible to marry off their
daughters in such ugly clothes. By the mid-1920s, *khadi* was being
diluted, largely thanks to the marketing drive of Gandhi's nephew
Maganlal. Colourful patterns, regional styles and fancy fabrics were
launched (see Plate 40). There were exhibitions, posters and publicity.
By 1930, the Swadeshi League advertised clothes mass-produced at
Indian-owned mills.[73] It was no longer necessary to spin by hand in a
self-sufficient community. Purchasing a shirt or sari with a nice design
was fine, as long as it carried a certified label. Swadeshi could be bought.

Across the world, most nationalists came down on the side of
consumerist modernity, one with patriotic and increasingly ethnic
overtones but consumer friendly nonetheless. There were good historic
reasons for this. Nationalism and marketing had evolved alongside
each other, both using icons to construct shared communities, from the
cult of Washington to that of Bismarck and Garibaldi. Gandhi's
anti-consumerism was rather atypical in that it drew from a European
reaction against industrial society; he had absorbed Ruskin and Tol-
stoy. Elsewhere, nationalists wanted to gain control over consumer
industries. They understood what Marx had not: goods did not only
alienate, they could also unite. With the Treaty of Nanjing in 1842,
after the First Opium War, China lost the power to set its own trade
barriers. Consumer boycotts were an attractive substitute: people took
it into their own hands to keep out foreign goods. In 1905, Chinese

communities across Asia boycotted American goods in response to the United States' exclusion of Chinese workers. The transfer of German rights in Shandong to Japan during the First World War added to the sense of 'national humiliation'. In December 1919, around one thousand students paraded through the Chinese part of Shanghai, searched shops and 'burnt any goods which they considered to be of Japanese origin'.[74] 'Boycott Bad Goods' societies burnt bundles of Japanese cotton and other goods. In 1925, British goods were boycotted in protest at killings by British soldiers in Shanghai. In Egypt, the arrest of Wafdist nationalists in 1921 similarly sparked a wave of boycotts. In 1932, law students at Cairo University lit bonfires of fine European suits: 'The silk garment is from your enemy, take it off and trample it. Light the fire and burn his old clothes in it.'[75]

National products would rise from the ashes. National-product exhibitions like the one at Hangzhou's West Lake attracted some 18 million visitors. Women were assigned a new civic role. Just like soldiers on the battlefield, they were fighting for national survival in the marketplace.[76] In Egypt, shoppers were called on to be patriots and build 'Egypt's economic mosque'. Buying a national product meant that 'what you spend from your private budget returns to the budget of the nation (your big family)', as one advert put it in 1933.[77]

National products united consumers and producers. But what exactly made a sock or a dress 'national'? In China, the National Products movement made common cause with modern fashion and hygiene, urging 'compatriots' to use locally made Three Star toothpaste and add Three Star cologne to their bath. Fashion shows included Western-style suits and wedding dresses. In semi-colonial societies such as Egypt, national dress was a hybrid of Western and local modernity. If there was anything like a national dress, it was the *tarboosh*. The red felt cap was the centre piece of the Piastre Plan organized by students in the 1930s, which asked people to pledge a piastre – a hundredth of an Egyptian pound – to develop national textile industries. The *tarboosh* itself, however, was a modern creation and had been introduced by the military reforms of the 1820s, when Sultan Mahmud II banned turbans. A century later, middle-class men wore it with Oxford shoes and a two-piece suit. The drive for national industries promoted European-style socks, hosiery and silk stockings. Egyptian hosiery factories advertised themselves as successors to the pharaohs and showed young men posing in front of the Giza pyramids holding an Egyptian flag and a pair of socks. Artificial silk was rebranded as an Egyptian fibre. Territorial origin mattered more than national style. What was crucial was where a suit was made, not its particular cut.

Initially, European- or Jewish-owned stores such as the Cicurel department store lent their support to national products. By the 1940s, it was the shops themselves that had to be 'national'. Goods had to be sold by Muslim Egyptians, not just be produced by Egyptian hands from Egyptian materials. Egyptian ownership could even trump product origin. The *al-Bayt al-Misri* department store marketed itself as Egyptian even though its inventory included shoes and shirts made in Britain. During the Cairo Fire in January 1952, which erupted in protests against the killing of Egyptian policemen by British occupation troops and helped accelerate Nasser's military takeover in July of that year, rioters burnt the Jewish Cicurel and Orosdi-Back department stores as well as British shops, hotels and bars.[78]

In today's age of 'fair trade', it is tempting to see organized consumers as benign agents of internationalism who reach out to poor producers in distant lands. Historically, though, their contribution to nationalism was at least as important. Consumer boycotts had an ethnic as well as an ethical side. National products promoted a more exclusive nationhood, repelling not just imperial intruders but also compatriots without the right ethnic or religious credentials. Nor were they always anti-imperial. Empires played the same game, urging metropolitan consumers to buy colonial coffee and fruit to strengthen the imperial race. Again, such campaigns were especially popular where imperial groups were denied the more direct weapon of a tariff, as in Britain in the 1920s. Here, during Empire shopping weeks, Christmas-cake competitions and stalls for tasting Kenyan coffee, British housewives were urged to use their shopping basket to help their kith and kin in the empire. Why buy sultanas that had been trampled on by 'dirty' Turks, if it was possible to have 'clean', sweet ones grown, dried and packaged by Christian cousins in Australia?[79] Consumption was, indeed, a civic responsibility, but this could mean imperial or nationalist brotherhood as well as democratic citizenship.

MAKING FRIENDS

The Cold War was a second round in the ideological battle over affluence. The defeat of Nazism changed the rules of the game at two levels. One was geopolitical. The question of whether America or the Soviet

Union offered a superior material civilization was now fought over by two rival blocs. As one bloc tried to outproduce and out-consume the other, the material race accelerated. The second was domestic. Europeans had to come to terms with the Iron Curtain, but also with high growth. After the war, one cake became two cakes within fourteen years. Nothing like this had been seen before. Was such turbo-growth sustainable? Europeans worried. Indeed, was it desirable? The Nazi downfall brought back to power many conservatives and liberals who had looked at mass consumption with disdain. Was Nazism not the inevitable result of a devilish materialism? The miracle years were a period of conflict and anxiety.

The story was dramatic by any count. France gives a sense of just how rapidly consumer goods were spreading. In 1954, still only around 7–8 per cent of households had a fridge or a washing machine, 1 per cent a TV. By 1962, more than a third had a fridge and a washing machine, a quarter a TV. By 1975, it was 91 per cent, 72 per cent and 86 per cent, respectively. Eastern Europe was lagging behind, but only by a few years.[80] In developed societies, consumption grew by around 5 per cent per year in the period 1952–79; slightly faster in Japan (8 per cent); more slowly in the United Kingdom (3 per cent).[81] The figures for the USSR in the 1960s–'70s are comparable (c.6 per cent),[82] although it started from a lower point. And there was more leisure time in which to spend rising incomes. In West Germany in the 1960s, wages doubled and free time rose by an hour to three hours forty minutes a day, with free Saturdays and a rise in paid holidays from fourteen to twenty days.[83] On the other side of the Berlin Wall, in the socialist GDR, people had to work longer but nonetheless they, too, gained an extra hour of leisure a day between 1974 and 1985.[84] Travel, mobility and communication grew by leaps and bounds. The first charter flights for Spain and Corsica took off in the early 1950s. The same period saw the democratization of the car. In 1950, fewer than 5 per cent had an automobile in Western Europe. Thirty years later, most families did.[85]

If anything, such statistics underplay the dynamism of these years. Aspiration often predated acquisition. The 1957 Italian movie *Susanna tutta panna*, a cheesy comedy of errors about what happens when lust for women and lust for cream cakes collides, opens with the shapely daughter (Marisa Allasio) of the local pastry baker climbing out of a foamy bathtub, when few Italians had either foam or hot water. Later, she follows a family of petty thieves to their hovel, where they have a fridge, an electric range and a TV, cleverly hidden away from spying neighbours.[86] Even in the poorest pockets of Europe, such as Calabria, the young were busy watching movies like this one.[87] In Germany, only 5 per cent of the poor had a fridge at the time, but it was at the top of everyone's wish list.[88] In the Soviet Union, as elsewhere, magazines encouraged a craving for fashion and style: which shirt would go best with what suit?[89] Mascara ruled. There never seemed to be enough perfume or high heels.

The transformation of everyday life was especially dramatic in rural communities. In a typical French town such as Douelle, on the River Lot, fifty of the 163 houses already had a radio at the end of the Second World War but only two or three had a fridge, a cooker and central heating, and none a washing machine; only ten had an indoor toilet. By 1975, virtually everyone had all of these.[90] This, then, is the context of the changing language with which contemporaries came to discuss these developments. Consuming was no longer just one activity among others but defined an entire social system. It was a way of life: a 'consumer society', a 'mass consumption society', or a *Freizeitgesellschaft*, a leisure society.

In the 1950s, left and right were divided among themselves as well as between each other in their reaction. Among progressives, two texts marked the spectrum of responses: John Kenneth Galbraith's 1958 *The Affluent Society* and Tony Crosland's 1956 *The Future of Socialism*. Galbraith's book was one of a string of 1950s American bestsellers (David Riesman's *Lonely Crowd*; Vance Packard's *Hidden Persuaders*) which have shaped transatlantic debate about the destructive effects of consumerism to this day. Our addiction to goods, he argued, was at the heart of a new historic order – 'the affluent society' – geared towards growth and production. Sustained growth had lifted the ceiling on the economy but at the same time spread a new social disease. Production no longer satisfied real wants. Wants were now created and manipulated by advertising and a value system that equated the good life with personal possessions. This cycle relied on an 'inherently unstable process of consumer debt creation', he warned, pointing to Americans' growing use of instalment credit to buy new cars. Above all, it corroded public life. Affluence, in Galbraith's famous phrase, bred 'private opulence and public squalor'. It was this causal connection that was the core of his argument. In turning to private goods and leisure, people were turning away from their community. Private wealth led to the neglect of public welfare. With a prescient sense of environmental dangers, Galbraith described the average family driving their 'mauve and cerise, air-conditioned, power-steered, and power-braked automobile' through a city that is 'badly paved' and made 'hideous by litter', until they come to a picnic site where they enjoy 'exquisitely packaged food from a portable icebox by a polluted stream . . .' 'Is this,' he asked, really 'the American genius?'[91]

In *The Future of Socialism*, the British Labourite Crosland offered a more optimistic view. Writing just as Britain was coming out of austerity, Crosland argued that growth and goods would strengthen social democracy, not undermine it: '[H]igher personal consumption must form part of any statement of the socialist goal on fundamental egalitarian grounds.' As more people gained access to goods, class distinctions would soften. The very rich, he speculated, with a glance at the United States, would realize that the material rat race no longer made sense as a way to stay ahead of the crowd. In place of ostentation, they would turn to charity and education, a form of 'conspicuous under-consumption'. Even if abundance did not lower the average level of unhappiness in the population, Crosland argued, it brought public and private benefits. It was much better for grievances to be personalized than for them to sow social conflict. And rising material standards increased 'the individual's range of choice and area of cultural possibilities'. True socialists needed to be more 'anarchist and libertarian' and less 'the prig and the prude'. Crosland here targeted the anti-hedonist spirit in the Labour Party personified by Sidney and Beatrice Webb, the Fabian socialists whose devotion to research and parliamentary blue books meant they never took time for music or the theatre. A better society would not be built by 'abstinence and a good filing-system'. People deserved to have fun. Crosland jumped to the defence of the Teddy-Boys. These teenagers with their dandyish long jackets and tapered trousers were not all delinquents or barbarians. Rather, they showed the 'first awakening of a genuine, working-class interest in sartorial elegance' and of a 'genuine' youth culture: jazz. Greater abundance needed greater tolerance of individual choice, including a move away from censorship, unfair divorce and abortion laws, and the 'obsolete penalties for sexual abnormality'.[92]

The differing diagnoses were underscored by the different personalities of the two authors. Crosland had been raised in London and had returned, from his wartime experience as a paratrooper in Italy and France with a love of food and drink – if anything, a bit too much of the latter. He lived as he thought, enjoying jazz and nightclubs. Galbraith, by contrast, grew up on a farm in Southern Ontario. Behind his discomfort with urban life and its bars and other temptations lurked a nostalgia for a simpler life. In *The Affluent Society*, he lamented that schools were unable to compete with private glitz. The 'dubious heroes' of the movies, 'not Miss Jones, become the idols of the young';[93] he himself had gone to a one-room rural school; Vance Packard, the other great critic of consumerism, had also been raised on a farm, in Pennsylvania.

It is, perhaps, ironic that it was Galbraith's, a book that was self-consciously promoted as a challenge to conventional wisdom, that would itself become conventional wisdom. Crosland, meanwhile, found the time to write his book thanks to having lost his seat at the 1955 election. Many on the left insisted that affluence was tenuous and the poor more vulnerable than ever before. The path to the New Jerusalem could not be paved with fridges and TVs. Party activists were out of touch with a new generation of voters throughout the 1950s, one of the reasons for Labour's years in the wilderness.[94] Crosland's time would come only in the 1960s, with the liberation of sex and pleasure.

By contrast, Galbraith's diagnosis has informed critics of 'consumerism' pretty steadily to this day. His characteristic mix of clarity and confidence was so seductive that it is easy to forget that *The Affluent Society* was not a sober empirical study but a piece of advocacy to justify greater public spending. In the short term, his plea for a tax on consumption to fund social services was unsuccessful; as a member of John F. Kennedy's administration, Galbraith's influence was marginal. His effect on public debate, however, was enormous, and his ideas helped drive the increased spending on health and education in the mid-1960s under JFK's successor, Lyndon B. Johnson.[95] Yet as a historical source, however, Galbraith's work tells us more about the unease with affluence than about the phenomenon as such. Galbraith, tellingly, drew a line between 'simple modes of enjoyment' (he included here sport, food and houses as well as cars and sex) and more 'esoteric' ones such as music, fine art 'and to some extent travel'. The first group required 'little prior preparation of the subject for its highest enjoyment' and was thus the target of 'modern want creation'. The latter, by contrast, were more distinctly individual and had to be cultivated.[96] This was a classic middle-class trope of mass culture versus educated taste. Among the new generation of critics, there was little sense that individuals had the 'material self' that William James had identified half a century earlier, nor of the growing amount of preparation and sophistication contemporaries were devoting to food, the home and, indeed, sex.

Galbraith's worries about the end of thrift notwithstanding, Americans in the 1950s were, in fact, saving more, not less, than in the inter-war years – in 1957, the personal savings rate stood at 10 per cent,[97] an eye-wateringly high figure for anyone concerned about debt today. As a percentage of GDP, public spending was rising with affluence, not declining, as the model would lead one to expect.[98] Some of this can be reconciled with Galbraith's argument, but only so far. Government home loans and highway programmes supported a suburban consumer lifestyle and racial segregation.[99] Galbraith was right to attack the 'shortcomings' of municipal services, 'overcrowded' schools and 'filthy' streets. He was wrong, however, to presume this reflected a decline. Fifty years earlier, New York City waste had been dumped into the Hudson River. It was greater affluence and population growth that had led towns to introduce public parks, better schools and waste management in the first place. Arguably, *The Affluent Society* is itself the best evidence that private plenty led people to demand better public schools, hospitals and recreation.

Books such as *The Affluent Society*, which sold millions, were successful because they hit a raw nerve, in the United States and even more so in Europe. The Second World War had destabilized class, gender and racial hierarchies and made consumer culture a lightning rod for all sorts of anxieties. Americans were already worrying about the decline of happiness in 1948. Alongside colourful ads for supermarkets and Westinghouse fridge freezers, *Life* magazine sponsored a round-table at which Erich Fromm, the émigré psychologist, warned that people were using leisure to escape from reality; he himself admitted to reading detective stories. Other participants worried about 'moral anarchy' and a reported rise in drink, crime, divorce and mental illness. With their false romantic ideas, movies endangered 'the maintenance of a healthy democratic society'.[100]

Most Europeans had no problem with America; a 1953 French survey found that only 4 per cent saw the United States as a cultural threat.[101] For cultural elites, however, affluence was an American invasion, a glimpse of a dark future against which to measure the glorious national past. Few liked the look of it. The chorus was never shriller than in the 1950s. J. B. Priestley feared that Britain was turning into 'Southern California, with its . . . TV and film studios, automobile way of life (you can eat and drink, watch films, make love, without ever getting out of your car), its flavourless cosmopolitanism . . . and bogus religions'.[102] For the French, the Americans were *les grands enfants*, children fascinated by gadgets; all standard of living, no soul. The communist poet Louis Aragon labelled the United States a 'civilization of bathtubs and Frigidairs'.[103] Across Europe, the charge was the same. Consumer society bred shallow conformity and destroyed national traditions and communal spirit. In France, commentators feared that the American cult of busyness was destroying the national gift for *flânerie* and lounging about. In Germany, they bemoaned the retreat of deep thought and spiritual feeling before empty self-indulgence. *Reader's Digest* was taking the place of Voltaire, Goethe and Dante.

For Christian conservatives, materialism was as great a threat as Bolshevism in the immediate post-war years. It might nurture a new fascism. How could Europe be rebuilt as a Christian civilization if a new generation was sinking deeper and deeper into the morass of consumer culture? For several founders of the German Christian Democratic Union, the Nazis were proof that secularism bred materialism and destruction. Given the Nazis' open pandering to material desires, this was not an irrational reading of recent events. Radio programmes exhorted good Christians to practise self-denial.[104] Anxieties were not limited to Catholics and Communists. The Liberal Wilhelm Röpke, who had fled the Nazis to Switzerland in 1933, believed in free markets, yet was troubled when people bought goods on credit. The paternalism attacked by Crosland ran deep and wide. Welfarism was a wonderful ideal, but were the people ready for it? Many progressives were unsure. 'In order to satisfy the Welfare State must we provide television plus a dog & a garden, and if so, what is to happen to any new form of amusement that may be invented?' the British liberal Gilbert Murray wondered in 1955. Affluence was a dangerous spiral, tempting trade unionists to demand ever higher wages and wreck stability.[105]

The decline of organized Christianity added fuel to these fears. It is sometimes said about the miracle years that Europeans traded in God for goods. This is too strong. In Britain, religious attendance was already in freefall in the inter-war years. This was one reason why contemporaries were so nervous. Traditional institutions had been crumbling. It now just needed a little push to knock them over. In his social survey of York, Seebohm Rowntree, the philanthrophic industrialist and social researcher, found that the church-going population had dwindled from 35 per cent in 1901 to a mere 13 per cent in 1948. The decline of religion seemed correlated with the rise in shoplifting; one shop in London had 5,000 garments stolen a year. Rowntree summarized the advancing mindset as 'I see, I want, I take.' Decent folk were being misled by American films that advertised wealth and luxury as ends in themselves. Television ushered in a new dark age. As TV viewers dimmed the lights, 'not only intellectual pursuits such as reading, but also manual ones such as knitting and darning will become impossible'.[106]

The Cold War gave these domestic worries world-historical importance. Earlier superpowers like the British empire had, at times, attributed to goods a civilizing mission, but the United States was the first to tie its ambitions to the export of a way of life explicitly organized around consumer goods. The historian Victoria de Grazia has christened America a 'market empire'.[107] Salesmen took the place of missionaries, the fridge that of the bible. Trade fairs and American show homes were the new churches in a foreign politics of plenty. In September 1952, the Berlin trade fair included an American pavilion with an electric kitchen, a TV, a car in a carport and a hobby shop with DIY tools. Almost half a million Germans saw it and had a chance to browse through a Sears catalogue. Under Dwight D. Eisenhower, US president from the following year, such exhibits became centrepieces of US policy. A special fund was set aside for cultural programmes. Corporate donors jumped on board. By 1960, there had been ninety-seven official exhibits in twenty-nine countries, from Leipzig to Zagreb and from Bangkok to Damascus. About 60 million visitors had a chance to step into life-sized American show houses to understand why separate bathrooms were a 'basic dignity' and how washing machines brought freedom.

Earlier ambivalence towards consumer culture was settled by the Cold War. Left and right were pushed to take sides. Jean-Paul Sartre, for example, had returned from the United States in 1946 with a fairly nuanced view of American life. By 1953, the Korean War and the execution of Julius and Ethel Rosenberg for espionage had convinced him that America was like 'rabies'. French communists, with the support of wine growers, called for a ban on Coca-Cola – in vain. Marshall Plan exhibits faced an especially hostile reception from French labour. Elsewhere, defeat and ruin made labour movements more receptive.[108] Liberation from Nazism made it much harder for Germans to think of America as an evil empire. Here, consumer society seemed to promise security, democracy and free unions.

It was the Conservatives who were first to make peace with affluence.

Christian Democrats could not at the same time be in the Atlantic alliance and denounce American consumer culture. By the late 1950s, doubts about soulless materialism had been replaced by celebrations of consumer democracy – 'You've never had it so good,' in Harold Macmillan's 1959 British election slogan. Instead of worrying about Christ, the Conservatives discovered choice. This turned consumer politics upside down. Traditionally, the consumer champion had been the co-operatives, with strong links to Labour. The Conservatives had been the party of farmers and business. Now they reached out to housewives and workers, promising affluence for all. With the partial exception of Scandinavia and Japan, co-operatives were in decline by the 1960s, outflanked by a more competitive individualism manifest in popular testing organizations which compared and rated new products.

Consumer choice offered a way to rebuild family and nation. Rather than destroying Christian values and community, perhaps kitchens and TVs would strengthen family life? This was the hope of Ezio Vanoni, the Italian finance minister, and Ludwig Erhard, West Germany's economics minister. Erhard, the architect of the social market economy, was a chubby figure with a fondness for cigars and simple lentil-and-sausage soup. As early as 1950, he proposed an exhibition on the standard of living. The changing title captured the increasingly programmatic ambition. The initial name for the 1953 exhibition was 'We Can All Live Better.' It then changed to 'We All Want to Live Better,' before settling on 'Everyone Should Live Better.'[109] The official poster showed the benefits of productivity: a bulging wage packet. Visitors to the exhibition numbered 1.4 million. One pavilion was dedicated to the consumer's central place in society. For the first time, organizers proudly announced, consumers were not merely visitors but were themselves on display. All Germans yearned for a 'place in the sun'. This phrase was originally coined by Kaiser Wilhelm II. Whether intentionally or not, its reuse summed up the changing target of German ambitions: not overseas colonies, but a comfortable home.[110]

In this familial consumerism, women were assigned a central place. Consumer durables would free up time for the family to spend together. The Catholic Church hoped that families would be so immersed in home life they would be immune to communism. Even buying on credit found religious approval. Far from being a sign of reckless excess, leasing arrangements such as hire purchase were good for society, the Church of Scotland decided in 1957: regular payments taught people to plan ahead.[111]

The sovereign consumer and the caring, homebound housewife were supposed to be one and the same. This was a shared image in the United States and Western Europe. Men's function was to earn more for their families to spend. Acquisitiveness could spill over into family life. One American woman recounted the changes as she and her husband grew from a young couple in a small rented flat into a family with five children and an eight-room mansion on a lake. Her husband's income had almost doubled, to $25,000 a year. They had a boat, a horse, the children expensive musical instruments. Her husband constantly bought them new things: 'I feel he tries to own all of us in the family too much.'[112] Suburbanization reached new heights, and the ambition of American college girls was to get married and raise children, rather than pursue an independent career, as was the aim of the previous generation.

Historians have tended to view the post-war years as a new beginning. From a longer perspective, however, it might be better to see the 1950s as a conservative restoration, picking up and amplifying earlier trends. The cult of the home and family-centred leisure made affluence palatable, but it was hardly new. There were direct biographical connections between the 1930s and the 1950s. In Oakland, California, researchers followed children born in the early 1920s through the Depression and into their post-war adulthood.[113] Boys who earned money in the 1930s selling newspapers or peddling handicrafts tended to save regularly in the 1950s, much more so than boys without earnings or girls without allowances. Among men, there was a strong correlation between deprivation while young and a fixation with work later. Earning power was a way to give their children the material comfort and stability they had missed out on. Children of the Depression were suddenly big earners – one of the causes behind the post-war baby boom.[114]

In West Germany, Chancellor Erhard courted women as 'chancellors of the exchequer', echoing the slogan circulating in Britain and America before the First World War, when the power of the purse had been linked to the demand for women's right to vote. Families could receive tax credits for buying consumer durables, a subsidy with a Nazi past; Erhard had worked for a marketing firm during the Hitler years. What changed was the social project: the housewife was now recruited to build a democratic rather than a racial state. As citizen consumers, women had not just duties but rights, most notably the right to choose.

The consumer was the lynchpin of the conservative restoration more generally, too. In the 1950s, even public administration and schools were referred to as consumers.[115] In leisure magazines for their workers, German companies circulated articles from *Reader's Digest* that explained how all business hinged on happy customers.[116] It was the consumer, not the boss, who determined work and wages. Consumer satisfaction provided a shared goal for boss and workers: growth without social conflict.

The conservative restoration, however, was fraught with contradictions. On the one hand, it preached choice. On the other, it wanted individuals to stick to traditional roles. Not surprisingly, this created a zone of conflict with the group that, more than any other, turned to goods and fashion for their identity: youth. The 1950s saw a wave of youth riots. On New Year's Eve in 1956, several thousand youths fought running battles with police on the Kungsgatan in the centre of Stockholm. There were riots in Vienna (1957) and smashed concert halls during rock and roll performances in Milan (1957) and Hamburg (1958); in 1958, German youths clashed with police almost every other day. In Paris, the *blousons noirs* inspired fear and gangs fought each other in the 15th arrondissement. In Moscow, young men *flâneur*ed up and down the left side of Gorky Street – Broadway or simply 'Brod' to them – in extra-long jackets, tight trousers with wide flares and thick-soled shoes that could weigh up to 2.5kg. On both sides of the Iron Curtain, authorities, journalists and cultural elites voiced the same moral panic: youth was in crisis.[117]

These confrontations had particular local ingredients; West Germans, for example, worried about how to build a new army with young rebels. But it is helpful to see things in the round. How consumption redefined generations is a theme that will be explored in greater depth in a later chapter. Here we should note what the preoccupation with rebellious youth tells us about nervous elites as well as about teenagers. The actual number of youths in gangs and riots in the 1950s was tiny compared to those who dutifully went to Boy Scouts, saved for their trousseau or pottered about on an allotment. Fears of moral decay were circulating prior to mopeds and jeans. Already in 1952, a Dutch commission reported on youths running wild. It found a dangerous mix of excess and lack of purpose. Gerard and Piet, fourteen-year-old twins, for example, returned home from a family party with their parents at 4 a.m., 'drunk as a skunk'. Youth mirrored a world that had 'lost its form'.[118] They were whirling madly, dancing boogie-woogie. In Buiksloot, an Amsterdam suburb, seventeen-year-old workers spent most of their earnings on clothes, cinema and cigarettes. When they did not go dancing on the Nieuwendijk, they were 'hanging about' on street corners. Where would it all end? In fact, half of office girls never went dancing. But to the commission it seemed that parents and youth organizations were losing their grip – most boys and girls came home after 10 p.m., and membership of youth organizations was falling.[119] In many ways, youths in the 1950s were simply reclaiming the streets and some of the freedoms their grandparents had lost in the crackdown over juvenile delinquency at the beginning of the century. To the establishment, however, the behaviour of 'wild' youths raised doubts whether war-torn societies could ever rebuild themselves.

As the tide of goods rose in the 1950s and '60s, cultural authority looked ever more like a sandcastle at the surf's edge. Goods and images gave youths a chance to fashion their own identity, rituals and etiquette. The next decade saw the diffusion of subcultures. Rock'n'roll and denim, initially the preserve of proletarian and ethnic groups at the margins, spread to middle-class kids. Styles of consumption were so contested because they signalled two rival cultures. The bourgeois model had prized self-discipline and self-improvement. Pleasure required restraint, education and work first – 'in the sweat of thy face shalt thou eat bread' (Genesis 3:19). Youth culture, by contrast, was about emotional release and was intensely physical. It prized instant gratification. It was about sweat, speed and sex. It meant rock 'n' roll, the swinging hips of Elvis the Pelvis and the Italian *urlatori* – literally, 'the screamers' – with a young Adriano Celentano twisting as if he were a spring (*il molleggiato*). Its literary heroine was Françoise Sagan, who wrote *Bonjour Tristesse* at the tender age of eighteen and swapped her Catholic upbringing for whiskey and an Aston Martin, which she crashed in 1957 in a much-publicised accident. Critics deplored the 'animalistic' behaviour and ecstasy of the young. Rock'n'roll, teachers' magazines warned, was an expression of 'the philosophy of all that was ugly'.[120]

Governments' initial reflex was to shore up cultural authority. Stiffer juvenile protection laws were introduced to keep the under-eighteens from dance halls and dangerous movies. Many radio stations banned Elvis. But popular demand proved too strong. Spaces of consumption were expanding and ever easier to reach. In the Netherlands, a million people had a moped in 1960; it was in these years that stealing cars, motorbikes and scooters entered the list of 'delinquency'.[121] If songs were banned on public radio, there was always the jukebox in the ice-cream parlour. Kids were cleverer than censors – a survey in Paris and Amiens found that half the boys and girls watched censored films one way or another.[122]

And the young commanded growing purchasing power. In the United States, advertisers began targeting fashion-conscious college students as early as the 1920s. In Western Europe, the big leap came in the 1950s, when teenagers' discretionary spending doubled. In America in 1964, 22 million teenagers spent around $12 billion, while their parents spent another $13 billion on them. In West Germany, ten–fifteen-year-olds controlled DM180 million spending money. This meant a lot of records, suits and dresses. A twenty-year-old plumber's mate remembered his 1940s childhood in the East End of London: 'I think I had one new suit . . . but usually I wore second-hand clothing from Brick Lane.' In the course of the 1950s, 'things changed . . . Things just seemed to get much better. We started to buy new things.'[123] Adolescents like him had around £9 to spend a week, while a seven-inch single cost 6s 8d.

The expansion of the school system reinforced greater segregation between the generations. Peer groups flourished. By 1937, 80 per cent of all American teenagers attended high school. In France, half of eleven–seventeen-year-olds were in school by 1962.[124] It is no surprise that the term 'teenager' spread from the 1940s onwards. Cliques used fashions and accessories to mark who was 'in' and who was 'out'. Better-off cliques went bowling, poorer ones roller skating. Peer culture was competitive and acquisitive. A 1949 study of high-schoolers in the Midwest reported how for the typical boy 'the value of money is to use it to satisfy his search for pleasure; he has to have money to go places and to do things. The girl has to have dresses, hats, stockings, shoes, coats, purses . . . perfume, cosmetics, and the "right" hair-do.'[125] This was the constituency targeted by the new teen magazines, *Seventeen* (1944) in the States, followed in Europe by *Bravo* (1956), *Salut des copains* (1962), *Ciao amici* (1963) and *Jackie* (1964).

The international circulation of goods and styles, too, increased – in no small part thanks to the movement of armies in the Second World War and after. Western Europe saw hybrid styles of native and American genres; in youth gangs, 'Pierre' and 'Heinz' suddenly became 'Bob'. This phenomenon crossed the Iron Curtain. On the streets of Prague in the 1950s, the *pasek* teenagers pinned US cigarette labels to their Czech ties.[126] Tarzan films were hugely popular in the Soviet Union after the first one was released in 1951, and youths tried hard to copy Johnny Weissmuller's hair. Movies from Italy and Germany were equally popular. The Georgian capital, Tbilisi, came to a halt in 1947 when the German wartime movie *Girl of My Dreams* (*Die Frau meiner Träume*) was shown, starring the glamorous Marika Rökk, the Hungarian singer-dancer. In the Eastern Bloc there were also signs of a new age-specific culture of pleasure, separate from the demands of work and politics. In a Russian underground publication, a writer charged the older generation: 'You propose to spit on the operetta, study only [Friedrich Engels'] *Anti-Dühring*? and discuss politics? How boring are your ideals . . . How can a person live without jazz, funny songs, dance and laughter?'[127]

The moral panic about young consumers was so sharp because of related concerns about sexual promiscuity and a loosening of class and gender hierarchies. Sex was becoming an 'obsessional activity', of 'purely animal satisfaction', Seebohm Rowntree wrote in 1951.[128] Such fears drew on an earlier association between the temptations of the flesh and the lust for things, especially among the weaker sex. In 1917, in an earlier war on 'delinquency', one investigator in Cleveland, Ohio, met a girl keen on dating and dancing who claimed to be eighteen: 'What she wanted, she said, was a good time; she didn't care how she got it. If going to a hotel with a man was the price she had to pay, she was willing to go through with it.'[129] These girls wanted 'fun'. The 1950s cry over 'wild youth' extended these fears to men. And it expressed class fears.

Strictly speaking, the 1950s were the scene of a war between classes rather than between generations. Most youths did not have a problem with their parents but with the social conventions of other classes. In France in 1958, three quarters of young people felt very or reasonably happy and did not think their generation would be any different from that of their parents.[130] The rockers, *blousons noirs* and *Halbstarke* marked out as 'delinquents' were predominantly working class. Those arrested mainly came from the bottom of society and had little education. Leather jackets and wild screams threatened not only elders but also their bourgeois sons and daughters, whose superior status rested on manners instilled by the lyceum. In the words of one German teenager in 1960, she preferred parties where guests 'drink Cola or syrup', danced a bit of rumba and listened to music, 'but please without such screaming'.[131] 'Jailhouse Rock' drowned out 'The Well-tempered Clavier'. At early rock concerts, university and A-level students volunteered as security guards to keep mechanics and unskilled workers from dancing in the aisles.[132]

It would be too simple, however, to tell the rise of youth culture as a story of rebellion from below. There was also encouragement from above. By embracing consumer sovereignty, conservatives had opened Pandora's box. If voting in the marketplace was equivalent to democracy, how could the hundreds of thousands buying the latest Elvis record be wrong? The sales figures spoke for themselves, youth magazines and their readers pointed out. The authorities switched from outright prohibition to co-option. The need to break with the Nazi past had always limited the scope for prohibition; 'jazz' would be allowed in the West German army. If it was impossible to insulate civic life, perhaps a civic note could be injected into commercial culture? In Britain, children flocked to their local Odeon for Saturday-morning clubs, where, before the show, they had to sing the national anthem and pledge: 'I promise to tell the truth, to help others, and to obey my parents.'[133] *Ciné-clubs*, *Jugendfreizeitstätten* and youth clubs opened their doors, with help from governments and town councils. Designed as nurseries of citizenship, these turned into additional channels for commercial music, dance and entertainment. By the early 1960s, even churches had beat services.

Most academics have been critical of consumer society, and this has led them to follow earlier critics who, as it happens, were mostly also academics. We must not exaggerate their importance. What distinguished the 1960s and '70s from earlier periods was a growing acceptance of consumer culture. If 'choice' was one impetus for this shift, the other was self-expression. Critics of the 'affluent society' inherited the belief that mass consumption led to conformity. Rock'n'roll, it was said, bred bendy legs and empty heads, leaving the young susceptible to totalitarianism. This argument always rested on shaky ground. After all, with their subcultures, teenagers were challenging the conformist lifestyle of their elders, including that of the intellectual elite.

Goods enabled people to find themselves. We saw earlier how ideas of a 'material self' blossomed in the late nineteenth century. In the 1950s and '60s these ideas received fresh support from three sources: technology, advertising and a new generation of cultural leaders. Electric guitars (and later synthesizers) gave teenagers who had never taken a music lesson a chance to play and innovate – one reason for the rapid change and diversity in musical styles since. Business nurtured and harvested counter-culture from the outset. Advertisers and marketing helped elevate youthful nonconformity into the dominant idiom. Everyone and everything was turned into an act of creative self-expression, from the purchase of Booth's gin – a 'Protest against the Rising Tide of Conformity' – to Suzuki motorcycles, with their 'power to free you'. The generation of admen who arrived on Madison Avenue in the 1960s had read their Galbraith and Packard and consciously reinvented themselves as agents of nonconformity.

Men were urged to take off their grey suits and express their individuality through more fashionable and colourful clothes; by the late 1960s, menswear in America was growing almost as fast as women's fashion.[134] Opting for a VW showed that you were not a member of the herd but a critical, responsible driver who was not fooled by changing tail-fins and other gimmicks of planned obsolescence. Anti-advertising converted a bad conscience about 'consumerism' into a reason for buying more.

Self-expression also provided a bridge between the arts and commerce. Actors, like intellectuals, had had a deep suspicion of advertising. By 1959, serious artists like Vittorio Gassman and Anna Maria Ferrero were appearing in a promotional sketch for Baci chocolates on the Italian show *Carosello*, mocking precisely such high cultural pretensions.[135] Older critics such as Marcuse (born 1898), Adorno (1903) and Galbraith (1908), were overtaken by a new generation of public intellectuals who adopted a more balanced tone towards the world of goods. In 1964, Umberto Eco (born in 1932) came to the defence of mass culture. All of us might read Ezra Pound's poetry at one moment and pulp fiction the next. Sometimes, Eco wrote, mass culture diffused ready-made emotions and aided conformism, but at others it opened up social questions. It satisfied a genuine need for entertainment. And it was democratic, broadening access to culture and world affairs and diminishing the influence of class and caste. Eco noted that mass media had aided the anti-colonial struggle in Algeria.[136]

The guru of this more positive approach was the market researcher Ernest Dichter. Another refugee from Vienna – his psychoanalytic practice had been across the street from Freud's home – Dichter had moved to Paris in 1937, where he worked as a salesman (following in his father's footsteps), before settling in the United States in 1938. In one of his first jobs for advertisers he interviewed ordinary Americans about soap and hit on the basic premise of Motivational Research (MR): products had a 'personality' that spoke to deeper psychological needs. Objects were more than utilitarian. They had 'real expressive powers', even 'a soul'.

Dichter was a clever showman rather than an original thinker, adding a dash of Freudianism into a cocktail of pop psychology and marketing lingo. He gained notoriety as the target of Vance Packard's *The Hidden Persuaders* (1957). Equally interesting was Dichter's response to his critics. 'Growth of life,' he wrote in *The Strategy of Desire* in 1960, 'can be understood as an ever increasing variety of objects that we come into contact with and an ever increasing intimacy with these objects.' Wanting stuff was not frivolous. It was about self-fulfilment. This idea had affinities with the Enlightenment as well as with recent psychological theories of self-realization. Where Dichter went further was to see the profusion of possessions as a passage in human liberation. Market researchers were akin to therapists, teaching people 'to forget the guilt of original sin'. This psychological defence of the right to shop acquired added significance at the height of the Cold War. 'We are in the midst of a silent war,' Dichter wrote in 1960: 'on the outside with Russia, and on the inside with our old concepts of thinking.' Not only would the economy 'literally collapse overnight' if critics had it their way and consumption was scaled back to 'immediate and necessary needs'. It would weaken the American psyche. 'The real defenders of a positive outlook on life, the real salesmen of prosperity, and therefore of democracy, are the individuals who defend the right to buy a new car, a new home, a new radio.'[137]

Feminists pointed out how MR recycled gender inequality by glorifying housework.[138] Dichter, however, was no simple defender of the social order. Like Crosland, he believed that the spread of affluence would slow down competitive status-seeking. Instead of 'keeping up with the Joneses', individuals would spend more energy developing their 'inner Joneses', retire earlier, bake their own bread and design their own distinct outfits and home interiors. By developing a pleasurable relationship with things, we would make them 'our tools', 'freeing ourselves from their tyranny'. Dichter's *Handbook of Consumer Motivations* (1964) took readers from food and shelter to things of a 'higher order', including art, patriotism and plants. It mirrored his vision of personal progress from 'the human being as a *thing* person to the human being as a *think* person'.[139] There were affinities here with Christian Democrats in Europe who also embraced goods and appliances as a way of overcoming the brute materialism associated with communism. Dichter's plea for a new hedonism was not 'spend now, worry later'. Looking forward to leisure would encourage people to plan ahead and save, he believed – optimistically, as it turned out in the case of America.

In the wake of totalitarian manipulation of the masses, and in the midst of Cold War debates about mind control, the omnipresence of adverts and the use of psychological techniques made advertising and marketing intensely controversial subjects of public debate. The dream worlds spun by advertisers seemed to have lodged themselves in the human psyche for good. In his popular *One-dimensional Man* (1964), Marcuse concluded that the 'mere absence of all advertising and of all indoctrinating media of information and entertainment would plunge the individual into a traumatic void where he would have the chance to wonder and to think, to know himself . . . and his society'. It was, Marcuse added, 'an (unfortunately fantastic) example'.[140]

There are two classic accounts of the rise of marketing. The first treats the post-war era as a new dawn, where a homogeneous mass market gave way to differentiation and market segmentation. The second tells a story of how adverts and marketing techniques moved beyond the marketplace, taking over all spheres of life.[141] Marketing, in this view, started to colonize society and politics, recasting citizens as customers: the advertising wave of post-war affluence prepared the ground for the neo-liberal 1990s.

Both these accounts are too simple. Market segmentation and efforts to differentiate between customers were well under way in America in the inter-war years. The 'mass market' was never monolithic. The mail-order giant Sears was already classifying its customers on the eve of the First World War. After the war, department stores began to experiment with 'customer control'. This technique was driven by credit departments, which compiled ledgers of inactive customers and then targeted them directly to lure them back to the store. Managers knew that customers who used credit tended to spend more. Stores kept index cards with tabs to indicate whether customers had bought hats or shoes, at what cost and time of year, at which branch, and whether they were married or single. Instead of just checking accounts, credit managers moved into the business of promoting sales. In the 1930s, the punch card and data processing arrived, which enabled shops to segment customers by income. In Britain, market research was distinguishing people by the class of paper they were reading – *The Times* was 'A', *Good Housekeeping* 'D'. Personalized sales had entered the mass market.[142]

After the war and austerity, advertising expenditure grew fast; the 1950s and '60s, after all, were decades of phenomenal growth. But a longer perspective suggests it is misleading to see the post-war era of affluence as some sudden take-off into the stratosphere. In the United

United States advertising expenditure, 1920–2005

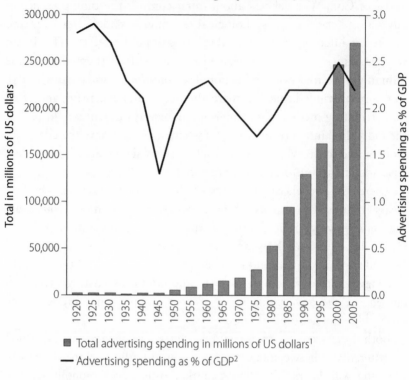

■ Total advertising spending in millions of US dollars[1]
— Advertising spending as % of GDP[2]

[1] Data from Robert Coen, structured advertising expenditure dataset, v. 1.15.
[2] Data from US Annual advertising spending since 1919.
Source: http://www.galbithink.org/cs-ad-dataset.xls.

States, advertising's share of GDP was above 2 per cent throughout the inter-war years, and peaked at 3 per cent in the early 1920s. Notwithstanding the glamour today associated with admen in the 1950s and '60s, at no point did these years manage to reach that high point. What changed was the type of advertising and the goods it promoted. In the years around 1900, most advertising was in newspapers or via mail order. The dominant product was patent medicine. By the 1970s, American firms spent almost as much on TV adverts as on newspapers. The leading products now were cars, toiletries, food, beer and alcohol.

Nor did commercial and pop-psychological techniques inexorably sweep all before them. In the early years, advertisers were widely criticized for lowering aesthetic taste and despoiling the landscape. In pre-1914 Germany, they were attacked for promoting 'Jewish' techniques or being American and vulgar. The great historian of capitalism

Sombart thought advertising was throwing money down the drain, as well as fraudulent and ruining good German taste. Local authorities objected that loud posters and night-time advertising were devastating town and countryside. To establish their credentials, advertisers needed allies in art and design. In Cologne, they collaborated with the Werkbund, the modernist association of artists and architects. Advertising, they told their critics, was about more than profit: it would be the cultural educator of the masses.[143] In America, the first courses in marketing appeared at universities in 1900. But, in reality, marketing never managed to put itself on a scientific footing. Most practitioners were practical men, not psychologists. There was a lot of trial and error. American agencies developed cutting-edge techniques, but when they reached Europe they had to be adapted to fit local markets and customs. A lot of knowledge was home grown. J. W. Thompson's London office accepted that they were working in a market where class mattered more than on Madison Avenue. Dichter himself opened an office in London in 1957, only to find that his techniques did not work there. In spite of their growing affluence, Britons, he despaired, were puritanical and did not use products to express themselves. Most firms never fully subscribed to 'motivational research' and remained openly sceptical of anything that smacked of subliminal manipulation.[144]

Rather than seeing marketing moving outward in one direction – from market to society – its success depended on a cross-fertilization with state and society. Market research became credible because it intersected with a more general advance of a whole variety of related forms of social research: mass observation, opinion polling, expenditure surveys, audience research and, also, direct attempts by the state to understand their citizens better in order to promote healthy or national products. The US Department of Commerce launched its own market research series in 1929. In Britain, there were marketing boards for milk and imperial goods which conducted research better to understand and shape buying behaviour. There was a revolving door between state departments and advertising agencies. It was a commercial–state–social-science research complex.[145]

What is remarkable in this general picture is how diverse the presence of advertising continues to be in similarly affluent societies. Intensity and visibility vary considerably. In the United States in 1980, advertising spend per person was more than double that in Japan or Germany and four times that in Italy. Interestingly, it was Switzerland and Finland that came closest to American levels.[146] Where ads appeared also

Advertising expenditure per capita in 1980, in US dollars

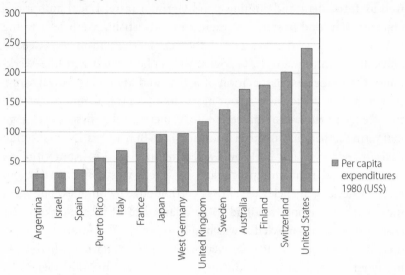

Source: *Sixteenth Survey of Advertising Expenditures Around the World*, 1982.

continued to diverge. In the US, Australia and Britain in the 1990s, a third of ad spend was for television. In Scandinavian countries, it was a mere 14 per cent. Most advertising continued to be in newspapers north of the Alps but, south on television. This may partly have to do with different shares of commercial stations and public providers, but it may equally reflect the fact that Northern Europeans do more reading for leisure and (still) have a more vibrant newspaper scene.[147]

To expand, goods need to be able to cross frontiers. With their emphasis on pleasure and experience, advertisers, market researchers and youth subcultures crossed an inner psychological frontier, as important as external territorial ones. Consumption now was acknowledged, indeed endorsed, as a way to reach deep into one's identity and libido. Some recent writers have suggested that, today, we live in a new 'experience society'. Things no longer matter primarily for what they do but for how they make us feel. Sports shoes and spectacles in all sorts of designs and colours are obvious examples. Affluence, according to this view, was a historic break with a system dominated by basic needs – before the post-war miracle, societies were preoccupied with utility; since, with feelings.[148]

This is dubious history. It underestimates the continuing importance of materiality; smart phones and skateboards need to work as well as feel good. It also ignores the longer history of emotional needs. For all his blindspots, Dichter (like the anthropologist Bronislaw Malinowski and the sociologist L. T. Hobhouse before him) was right to recognize that all societies, rich and poor, have emotional relationships with goods. Early economists had not altogether ignored the role of feelings. Hermann Gossen formulated his laws of pleasure in 1854 out of a realization that much human activity was not about filling the stomach but about avoiding boredom.[149] Alongside 'defensive' goods (bread, for example), which gave instant satiation, there were 'creative' ones (such as music or travel) to which people turned in anticipation of pleasure to come. These were 'experience' goods. Each pleasure, Gossen believed, had its own optimal frequency, maintained by greater or lesser repetition. What the 1950s and '60s did was to expand the range of frequencies. At one end, change accelerated, as in men's fashion. At the other end, however, new routine experiences sprang up. Week after week, for almost four years in the late 1950s, Italians tuned into the same evening game show: *Lascia o raddoppia?* The American *The Price is Right* ran from 1956 to '65, the German *Was Bin Ich?* soldiered on until 1989. Familiarity and novelty needed each other.

From this longer perspective, 1968 appears in the story of consumption as a climax rather than a sharp break, let alone a revolution. The material self had been growing. Now, pleasure became a right, and clothes, cars and pop music ways to exercise it. Some groups attacked consumption as a subliminal weapon of capitalist domination which, by planting artificial needs, reduced the masses to passive spectators. For the Situationist International, only spontaneous 'situations' and ironic actions, such as dressing up as Santa Claus and distributing teddy bears outside toy stores, could restore freedom and creativity. At the Sorbonne in Paris in May 1968, one poster declared that the 'consumer's society must perish of a violent death . . . Imagination is seizing power.'[150] For the vast majority of young people, however, consumer society was not a pressing issue.[151] Even English 'drop-outs', Dutch *provos* and German *Gammler* – small groups who had exchanged their apprenticeships for freedom – insisted on their right to enjoy drink, drugs and the latest record.[152] Some communes encouraged sympathizers to practise shop-lifting. It was a boycott of the cash register rather than of consumer goods.

The most violent attack took place in Frankfurt. On 2 April 1968, fire bombs with timers went off in two department stores, destroying

some toys and sports equipment. Even this, however, needs to be placed
in perspective. The incident was trivial compared to the Cairo Fire in
1952, when nationalists set fire to six department stores and seven hundred shops, dance halls and other properties. The context of the
German bombing was American imperialism and the war in Vietnam.
A year earlier, on 22 May 1967, 322 people had died in a fire in the
Brussels store Innovation. The cause was probably electrical, but the
fact that it broke out during an American fashion show, with protests
over Vietnam outside, raised suspicions of politically motivated arson.
In Berlin, the Kommune I, the first political commune, founded in
January 1967, distributed flyers that presented the disaster as a 'new
gag in the versatile history of American advertising', which had hit on
the idea of burning the customer himself. When, they wondered, might
someone discreetly light a cigarette in a changing room and set alight
the KaDeWe department store or Woolworth, so that Berlin could
share the burning feeling of Hanoi?[153]

The real bombs a year later failed to ignite a broader conflict over
consumer culture. Arguably, they helped extinguish it. The subsequent
trial escalated into a self-destructive stand-off between terrorists and
the state. The bombers, Andreas Baader and Gudrun Ensslin, saw
themselves as fighting a war against *Konsumterror*: 'Consumerism ter-
rorizes you, we terrorize the goods.' In their attitude to goods, as in
their use of force, they could not have been further from Gandhi. 'I also
like cars and all the things one can buy in department stores,' Ensslin
said. 'But when one has to buy them so that one does not gain consciousness, then the price is too high.'[154] Consumption was fine as long
as radicals did not have to pay for it. Ensslin appeared in court in a
shiny red leather jacket. Baader modelled himself on the French film
star Jean-Paul Belmondo and appreciated night-clubs and fine clothes;
during his stay at Hans Werner Henze's house in Rome, he liberally
helped himself to the composer's silk shirts. When he was finally
caught, in a speed trap, it was behind the wheel of a 300hp Iso Rivolta;
earlier cars included a white Mercedes 220SE and a Ford Fairlane, with
tail-fins. He was closer to Dichter's American consumer than to a Maoist peasant.

Ensslin was the daughter of a Swabian pastor and a typical example
of youth culture's challenge to hierarchies. Anti-authoritarian politics
worked with consumer culture rather than against it. Private pleasure
became a revolutionary principle; in the famous words of one German
communard, his orgasm mattered more to him than Vietnam.[155]

Soixante-huitards, or 68ers, had very little to say about the impact of their lifestyle on producers. For all the critique of 'consumer society', they accepted choice and self-fashioning, even reinforced it. Some radicals were fearful of 'selling out' and urged simplicity. Most, though, saw popular music and colourful clothes as vehicles of self-realization. For youth movements, this was a major change in direction. Around 1900, organized youth had turned to woods and mountains to escape commercial leisure and stimulants. Now they seized the latter pair as routes of liberation.

Consumer culture and radical culture lived together openly. In Berlin, the model Uschi Obermaier moved into Kommune 1, drank Coke and smoked Reyno; she had no interest in revolutionary texts, she confessed. Exotic fashion was part of anti-establishment politics. At criminal trials, 68ers, fresh from boarding school, appeared in green jackets and light blue trousers. That fashion and music could be turned to radical use shook at the foundations of the Marxist position that the culture industries were instruments of alienation and control. Activists might have Adorno and Marcuse on their shelves, but their lifestyle belied the thesis that 'technological society' had created a 'one-dimensional man', pacified through the 'repressive needs' created by entertainment, advertising and illusions of comfort.[156] To believe in self-actualization implied that individuals were able to evaluate the goods on offer and make their own choices. Radical magazines featured adverts from car and drink manufacturers. In counter-cultural literature, Donald Duck appeared next to Mao.[157]

The potential of such affinities was not lost on business. Barely a year after the 1968 revolts, counter-cultural shirts and dresses were hanging in department stores. The *soixante-huitards* may have scored anti-authoritarian successes in family life and education. As far as their material appetite was concerned, however, they continued where their parents had left off. Beards saved a few razor-blades. Communes turned orange crates into shelves. Some feminists burnt their bras, and early hippies gave away their watches. Yet, overall, the new generation was resource hungry. In New York, some young families joined together as communes but kept their personal cleaners and private showers: the air-conditioning was always on.[158] In Germany, in 1974, a researcher was surprised to find a greater number of TVs, stereos and washers and driers in communal 'alternative' flats than in conventional households; some flats had three cars.[159] Shared use, then, did not automatically entail simple living. Perversely, it could have the opposite effect, justifying the purchase of more appliances to avoid conflict over who controlled the TV or stereo.

By 1973, when the oil crisis hit, consumer culture was thus firmly entrenched. Critical voices did not disappear. Pier Paolo Pasolini, the Italian poet and filmmaker, lamented that television and cars had flattened customs and classes into the same materialist monoculture; the 'craving to consume' had led to a 'new fascism', degrading the Italian *popolo* far more than in Mussolini's day – rather downplaying the way in which leisure had been manipulated under Il Duce.[160] In France, Jean Baudrillard offered a new critique of consumer society as a total system of signs, in which people lived under a kind of magical spell, no longer choosing goods for their practical utility but for the images and messages they conveyed. As these were infinite, the system generated a continuous longing for more: 'affluence is . . . merely the accumulation of the *signs* of happiness.'[161] In 1972, the Club of Rome – a group of scientists, businessmen and professionals – published its first report, warning that in a world of finite resources there were limits to growth. In the Soviet Bloc, too, there were some sceptics. Alexander Solzhenitsyn, who had read the Club's report, in 1974 urged the leaders of the USSR to abandon a self-destructive path of greed and progress and return to small towns, gardens and silence.[162]

However noble, such views no longer held sway in either East or West. The centre of political gravity had shifted. In the previous decades, Conservatives had swapped their anti-modernism for family-oriented consumerism. Even Charles de Gaulle, for all his antipathy to America as a society without history, sponsored what one historian has called 'domestic Americanization'.[163] Social Democrats eventually accepted, however grudgingly, that workers wanted private comforts as well as work and welfare. Further left, European intellectuals rediscovered America, with its lifestyle communities, as the vanguard of revolution.[164] Instead of denouncing consumer culture as a method of oppression, writers like Michel de Certeau in 1974 presented shopping and eating as everyday practices where little people could regain some control of their lives through cunning, 'ruses' and 'making do'. In the next decade, the anthropologist Mary Douglas and the historian Simon Schama began to appreciate consumption as an integral part of the social system and of the creation of meaning, solidarity and identity, while scholars in gender studies rescued female shoppers from oblivion.[165]

A similar opening is perceptible among American civil rights activists. In the 1950s, Martin Luther King had warned that big cars were distracting African-Americans from God. By the 1960s, he preached a different theme: the evil was poverty in the midst of plenty. Poor whites needed to join hands with African-Americans. King came to recognize that his followers had material aspirations, and for civic as much as personal reasons: big cars won respect. Everyone craved distinction. The danger was when the 'drum major instinct' was not 'harnessed' but allowed to take over, prompting people to go on a spending spree to 'outdo the Joneses', to boast, lie and become snobs.[166]

For those at the margins, access to goods meant social inclusion and a sense of dignity. In the late 1960s, thousands of welfare recipients took to American streets to fight for their right to credit cards.[167] The closest anyone in power came to reviving an older moralism was President Jimmy Carter during the oil crisis. 'We've learned,' he told television viewers in 1979, 'that piling up material goods cannot fill the emptiness of lives which have no confidence or purpose.'[168] Even for Carter, however, the solution did not lie with a curb on consumption. His two main conclusions were that Americans needed to have faith and that, in future, increased demands for energy should be met by domestic sources, including 20 per cent from solar power by 2000. Americans got the former, not the latter; in 2014, solar power produced barely 0.5 per cent of electricity.[169]

Acceptance of affluence must not be confused with blind optimism or market euphoria. Rather, it involved a more balanced attitude to things. No one illustrated this new-found equilibrium better than Jean Saint-Geours in his book *Vive la société de consommation* (1971). Saint-Geours was establishment pure. With a socialist background, he had served as chargé de mission under Pierre Mendès France in 1954–5, before becoming inspector-general of finances, a top-ranking civil servant. At the time of writing, he was director general of the bank Crédit Lyonnais. As a founding member of the Club of Rome, he recognized the dangers of pollution, poverty and urban sprawl. Growth needed to be slowed down and managed. Still, he argued, it was foolish to think any progress could be made by forsaking consumption. The world of goods had brought collective as well as individual freedoms. People found genuine satisfaction in the use of things, something an older 'sacralization of labour' had denied them. Rather than leading to alienation, as the Marxists Lefebvre and Marcuse had it, consumer society lifted individuals out of ignorance and their dependence on Church and elites. Spending on books had tripled in the 1950s. Repression had given way to greater sexual freedom.

Saint-Geours' was a distinctly French way of making peace with affluence. Consumer society was not a social disease. It had not killed culture, he wrote. It had merely democratized it. The creative spirit was alive and well; Saint-Geours was one of the first to imagine a 'post-industrial society' where the pleasure and freedom to consume would revolve around new experiences. He could see what Galbraith, fifteen years earlier, could not. Affluent societies were spending more and more on health and education: in the early 1960s, public expenditure was 36 per cent of GDP in France (33 per cent in the UK; 35 per cent in West Germany); by the late 1970s it had reached 46 per cent in all three. This was no coincidence, according to Saint-Geours. *L'homme de consommation* was more than a private hedonist. Abundance allowed individuals to concern themselves with collective needs such as better healthcare and a cleaner environment. Private consumption and social progress were tied. To want pace-makers but not cars was impossible. Saint-Geours used his own life to illustrate how things were 'complicit' in who we were. He was on intimate terms with his car, even feeling a certain 'fraternity' with those who made it. Yes, the car polluted, but it was also liberating, giving access to the countryside and a whole world of sensations. Its curves gave him 'pure pleasure'. With the automobile, the dreams of man had produced a truly enchanted object. Beautifully designed cars reminded him of 'fish and fowl'.[170] Consumer goods were on par with nature.

SELLING OUT

For all the anxieties of priests and philosophers, Western societies managed to absorb the challenge of affluence. No regime collapsed under the weight of goods. It was in socialist Eastern Europe that material desires played a more destructive role. To switch to the Soviet Bloc after discussing affluence deserves some justification. Shortages, after all, were legendary, and choice limited or non-existent. It would be a mistake, however, to write a triumphant Whiggish history of consumer culture as if it were synonymous with the rise of market liberalism. Socialism was its own kind of consumer society, and people in it developed a hunger for things out of proportion to what was available in the shops. Today, it is tempting to think of materialism as a disease of capitalist societies with their spendthrift consumers, ubiquitous advertising and department stores filled to bursting. The socialist experiment suggests an inverse relation was also possible: finding it hard to get hold of goods could make them more, not less attractive. Lack of choice, moreover, did not mean people had no things. From the vantage point of any society before the twentieth century, these were enormously well-endowed societies. The 1960s–'70s were years of spectacular growth. In the USSR, consumer durables grew at a rate of 8 per cent a year. By 1976, virtually every family in Hungary, East Germany, Czechoslovakia and the Soviet Union had a TV, a radio and a fridge, although Bulgaria and Romania lagged behind. Leisure and tourism shot up as well. Deprivation, like affluence, is a relative experience. In the affluent West, poor consumers also suffered social exclusion. The problem for socialist societies was that aspirations were measured against the higher, rising watermark of the West.

In May 1960, in a speech to the Supreme Soviet, Khrushchev pledged that in the 'immediate future' the Soviet Union would reach the consumption level of the United States: after that 'we will enter the open sea in which no comparisons with capitalism will anchor us.'[171] Two years later, the Hungarian government promised its people 610,000 TVs, 600,000 washing machines and 128,000 fridges within the next three years. 'Frigidaire-socialism' was born.

What drove socialist consumer culture? One view is to see it as a Western import. True, Western jazz, jeans and rock exercised enormous pull – in the late 1960s, hippies went to the Latvian Academy of Sciences library to consult copies of Vogue. Socialist advertising, such as it was, took its lead from Western agencies. Yet the Eastern Bloc also had its own dynamics. As in the case of Americanization, stimuli travelled from the periphery as well as the centre. The USSR took its mass-production furniture from Czechoslovakia. Socialist brotherlands held joint fashion and music festivals.[172]

A second reading is more cynical and sees consumerism as a strategy of rule. Socialist leaders, in this view, bought domestic peace with goods. The lesson taken from the uprisings in East Germany in 1953 and Hungary in 1956 was that factories needed to produce things that people wanted. The Prague uprising in 1968 and conflict in Poland in 1970 were followed by promises of more goods and greater openness to youth culture. While there is some truth to this, it tells us little about how goods were changing daily life in these societies. Socialist consumption was a product of internal tensions as well as external stimuli.

American goods turned the Iron Curtain into a net curtain. Before

the Berlin Wall went up in 1961, it was easy for East Germans to visit
exhibitions or watch American movies in one of the border cinemas in
the Western zone, helped by a subsidized exchange rate. In June 1956,
Polish workers used the Poznań international trade fair, which in addition to the ubiquitous modern fitted kitchen had a packed American
fashion show, for anti-Soviet protests.[173]

The problem for socialist regimes was lack of vision as much as poor
economics. One after the other, they entered the material race on terms
set by the West, unable to develop an alternative, 'simpler' lifestyle less
dependent on things. Emulation was most intense in the eye of the
storm: the two Germanies. In 1953, the East German regime launched
its 'new course' with a greater emphasis on consumer goods.[174] As in
1930s Stalinist Russia, there were attempts to develop a more cheerful,
attractive sales culture.

When it came to gadgets, socialists were not to be beaten. The 1956
Purimix was an ingenious contraption. It did the vacuuming and, with
the right attachments, chopped vegetables and ground coffee. The East
German Fashion Institute, which opened its doors the following year,
looked to Paris, not Moscow. Heinz Bormann, the 'Red Dior', was
mimicking the newest Western designs.[175] In 1958, food rationing ended
in East Germany and Party chief Walter Ulbricht announced that in
three years the GDR would have 'overtaken' its capitalist neighbour in
consumer goods and per capita income.[176] By now, there was a socialist
mail-order catalogue and a push for self-service shops. Instalment plans
allowed socialist shoppers to buy on credit for up to 20 per cent of their
annual income; furniture and radios were the most popular items.

All these initiatives ran into the same difficulty. There was an institutional reason why socialist regimes neglected light consumer goods
in favour of heavy industry: big, centralized industry was the source of
political power. In addition, the barter regime of the Soviet bloc placed
a premium on food and raw materials at the expense of technological
innovation. The more developed members such as the GDR and Czechoslovakia were punished twice over. They had to trade their undervalued
industrial products for overvalued food and raw materials.[177] The law
of comparative advantage was turned on its head. Incapable of delivering on big white goods, the GDR in 1959 shifted its focus to the
'thousand little things needed in daily life' like screws, sewing needles
and spare parts. Delegations travelled to Sweden and West Berlin to
study dry cleaning and DIY.[178] If socialist consumers wanted things,
they would need to learn to repair them.

The material race, then, was already in full swing when vice-president Nixon sparred with Khrushchev in the famous kitchen debate at the international exhibition in Moscow on 24 July 1959. The fully equipped six-room ranch house cost $14,000. Any American worker could afford that, Nixon challenged Khrushchev. The Soviets had sent Sputnik into space two years earlier and the Soviet leader was not easily shaken: in the Soviet Union all new houses had this kind of equipment, he hit back. Variety was overrated: why have different models if one machine did just fine? The Soviet media, as if making Galbraith's point, showed images of American slums and garbage dumps. Almost 3 million visited the American pavilion in Sokolniki Park, three times the number who went to the Soviet exhibits (see Plate 43). The model kitchen prepared 16,000lbs of frozen foods for visitors amazed at the appearance of French fries or mash within minutes. Some Muscovites shook their heads at gadgets such as the toaster: why toast bread that had been cooked already? Consumer goods were an irresistible magnet. American models were mobbed by visitors who wanted to know how they lived, the price of their dresses, and whether false eyelashes needed to be removed at night. The American pavilion came fourth in the official competition; the Czechoslovakian one won. Presumably, the people who had carried away dirty Pepsi cups as souvenirs felt differently.[179]

Socialist leaders had been reared on Marx's vision of a future where the divisions between work and leisure, private and public, would be overcome. Under communism, people would no longer seek refuge in leisure and private comfort as an escape from work. With work no longer coercive, leisure would complete a rounded socialist man. As we have seen, in the 1930s fine clothes and consumer goods were used to reward productive workers. During the Cold War, leisure became a central battleground between socialism and 'capitalist imperialism'. Rock'n'roll, jeans and TV romances were weapons of 'ideological diversion' by which the class enemy tried to distract attention from building socialism.[180] They were a breeding ground of 'false needs'.

In truth, these pressures were home-grown as much as imported. Long before East Germany lifted its official ban on watching Western television, socialist regimes had been complicit in the creation of a more privatized lifestyle. In some ways, this paralleled the Nazis' predicament: it was difficult to control the living room, notwithstanding attempts to recruit children to denounce their parents. With the Thaw, from the mid-1950s, privatization accelerated. Self-service shops and supermarkets sprang up across the Eastern Bloc. Krushchev had championed a socialist norm of consumption, but variety and a private taste for little luxuries had little room in it. Consumer goods industries continued to be starved for the benefit of heavy industry. From 1964, under Leonid Brezhnev, Krushchev's successor, the Soviet Union changed direction. Factories had to establish direct links with shops to ensure that more of the goods they manufactured were actually wanted. Spies studied markets and conferences discussed how to improve distribution. Between 1966 and 1970, the output of consumer goods grew by half. Conveniently, the oil crisis raised the demand for Soviet crude and made it possible to import more goods at lower prices. The streets of Moscow became more consumer friendly, with more alteration and self-service shops. By 1972, two hundred shops in Moscow had their own cafés. *Pravda*, the party newspaper, printed a new truth with articles saying that 'the consumer is always right!' and calling for 'commodities – to the people'.[181]

From the outside, miles of brutalist housing blocks signalled drab uniformity. On the inside, a rush was under way to personalize one's flat. In 1960, a Polish magazine started a series called 'My Hobby is My Flat', with examples of how to blend new and old furniture, decor and belongings into a personal style.[182] Official designers preached functional modernity, but their despair at the resurgence of knick-knacks and 'bourgeois' furniture tells its own tale. The Soviet Union made ten times as many furniture sets in 1975 as it had ten years earlier. The home exercised an enormous pull in socialist societies and inspired a hot pursuit of novelty, fashion and updating. In the late 1960s and 1970s in Russia, the craze was for crystalware and tableware, often bought in the GDR. In East Germany, wall-to-wall carpets and all-round wallpapering were entering homes at record speeds. The regime's market researchers found that a third no longer bought sofas and living-room furniture to last for life but had replaced them in the last ten years.[183] When researchers asked teenagers in 1979 about their desires, 'to furnish a pretty flat' came out top for boys and girls alike, well ahead of 'going on holiday every year', 'dressing fashionably' or saving for a record player or car.[184]

The hybrid nature of socialist economies bred both desires and disappointments. Basic goods such as housing, education, electricity and food in schools and factories were provided by the state at heavily subsidized prices. Conversely, consumer goods came with a hefty price tag and long waiting lists. A large shadow economy emerged; in Poland, around a quarter of private income was spent in the black market in the early 1980s.[185]

Cheap public services are sometimes invoked as a positive counterweight to the many failures in private consumption. This misses the way in which defects in one aggravated problems in the other. One reason East Germans poured their money and souls into the interior was that this was the one aspect of housing they had control over. The housing stock itself was a disaster. In 1971 in East Germany, the average home was sixty years old. Two thirds were without bath or toilet; 29 per cent did not even have running water. According to an internal survey, 1.2 million flats or 20 per cent of the housing stock were in an 'entirely unacceptable' condition.[186] Sweden and West Germany were building new flats at more than twice the speed. The problem was not only the number of flats but their small size. The average flat (53 square metres) had one or two rooms. In the West, with its more spacious 79 square metres, it was three or four. Even after Honecker's house-building programme in the 1970s, in a place like Saßnitz, for example, a seaside town with 10,000 souls, 944 married couples were on a waiting list for their first flat, while 128 divorced couples were still forced to co-habit. Other areas of public consumption suffered from similar shortages, including the much-praised childcare system; in Zwickau, home of the Trabant car, which, with its two-stroke engine and hard plastic shell, came to symbolize life under socialism, more than half the children were waiting for a nursery place.[187] Socialism was hugely wasteful. Housing was so cheap that once a family had secured a large flat there was no reason to give it up once the children had moved out. At parties, hosts used to cool beer under (free) running water in the bathtub. Socialism was a recipe for private austerity and public squalor.

And cheap public goods encouraged private wants and social stratification. For socialist leaders, who bore the scars of austerity from their own upbringing, there was a simple moral logic why rent should be virtually free while a TV cost a monthly salary of 1,500 marks or more. The first was a 'basic need', the latter a 'luxury'. Luxury taxes and sumptuary legislation were nothing new, of course, but historically these had sought to shore up hierarchies, not to break them down. It was a counterproductive mix. The regime was effectively subsidizing a new class of consumers. Cheap housing left better-earning professionals and the intelligentsia with a vast unspent income. The result was a consumerist pressure cooker, as high-income groups competed for everything, from cars to fridges and showerheads. In the 1950s, collectivization, education reform (and bourgeois flight) had advanced social equality in East Germany. In the 1960s, social stratification returned in earnest in the sphere of consumption.

It is possible to follow this process fairly clearly, because the GDR was a dictatorship, and a very German one at that. It set up its own Institute of Market Research and kept immaculate records. In the 'workers and peasants' state', it was the intelligentsia, managers and clerks who owned washing machines, soaked in a hot bath and topped the waiting lists for cars. Most appliances were found in households with two earners. Single mothers were left behind. Pensioners were lucky to have a 'dry toilet'. Some of these divides narrowed as televisions and other new technologies diffused, only for new ones to open up. The introduction of the five-day working week in 1967 and freer travel within the Eastern Bloc sparked a tourism and camping boom. How you spent your weekend, whether you went on holiday at all, and whether you could relax on an air-mattress, became new status markers. White-collar workers were more likely to go on holiday than industrial workers. Camping equipment belonged disproportionately to the intelligentsia. The rich had hobbies; the poor did not.[188]

Additional divides cut across gender and generation. Human fulfilment through leisure was one of the core goals of socialism. Female labour participation rose dramatically in socialist regimes, but in a scarcity economy this only left women more pressured, as they were the ones who did the shopping. The real beneficiaries of a shorter working week were their husbands. East German time-use data shows that men's free time shot up from 37 to 48 hours a week between 1965 and 1971, while women gained only a single hour (26 to 27 hours). At a time when the temporal gulf between the sexes was narrowing in the West, it was wider than ever before in the East; women did 80 per cent of the shopping, cleaning and cooking in 1965, 79 per cent in 1970.[189] A good chunk of time was taken up by sewing, knitting and mending. Half of women's skirts and dresses were home-made because shops did not have the desired size, colour or pattern. Even among top earners, every third woman regularly sat at the sewing machine. Consumption involved a large share of self-provisioning, gifting, recycling and passing on, especially when it came to children's clothing. As late as 1980, in spite of various plans to improve quantity and variety, half the boys and girls were wearing hand-me-downs.[190] The regime tried to respond in the late 1960s by extending shop opening hours. Perversely, this only added to the frustration, as women spent their Saturdays roaming across neighbouring districts in the hunt for a dress, mostly in vain.[191]

Youth culture was a constant headache for socialist regimes. Ulbricht's public celebration of the virtuous reciprocal relationship between leisure and work was belied by an internal report on the leisure activities of 8,000 apprentices, students and teenagers: 'Freizeit 69'.[192] According to this, every second young East German in 1969 had a portable radio, one in three a moped, one in five a leather jacket. An active biker scene sprang up. For most teenagers, the goal in life was to earn money to buy goods, to be free and mobile. They liked listening to music, swimming or just hanging out, far more than spending time in the socialist youth group, the Freie Deutsche Jugend (FDJ). Working-class teenagers, in particular, disliked the FDJ. At first, regimes tried to ban beat music and crack down on drinking. Sex, drugs and rock'n'roll were an affront to socialist ideals. This only drove them underground. Many youth clubs kept going. Some held drinking championships. The Wall kept people in. To keep out radio waves, jeans and bootleg copies was more difficult. In 1971, the XI parliament of the FDJ openly conceded that 'bourgeois consumer culture' had taken root. With Honecker in power, after May 1971 the strategy shifted to greater tolerance for long hair and denim, including state-sponsored rock bands.[193] It is unclear what else the regime could have done, but it was an admission of defeat. The ideal of a uniform socialist culture had failed.

In one sense, consumer culture did the same in the East as in the West: it eroded the monopoly claim of one 'legitimate culture'. The crucial difference was that socialist regimes were built on an assumed symmetry between politics and culture, public and private. The proliferation of private lifestyles ran roughshod across this. Nor did greater tolerance win back hearts and minds. By the end of the 1970s, even the most 'socially engaged' young workers spent at best two hours a month with the FDJ, while they watched almost one hour a day of (mostly Western) television. Discos and gardening were vastly more attractive than FDJ clubs. What clothes one wore was a matter of private taste and social cliques, not Party directive. One in five teenagers wore badges with American stars and stripes or other Western logos on their clothes.[194] Hungary introduced youth shows where teenagers dressed like members of British rock bands. In the Soviet Union, sociologists found that the young no longer aspired to become communist leaders or join the intelligentsia: rather, they wanted to be manager of a shop and gain access to goods.[195] By the late 1970s, socialist culture had become a minority affair.

This *Kulturkampf* swept across the Eastern Bloc. In Hungary in the early 1960s, there was a lively debate about the social effects of consumerism. Fundamentalists warned that private possessions created political apathy. Far from it, revisionists argued. To succeed, socialism needed to raise the standard of living. Consuming was a socialist virtue. If possessions were anti-socialist, some said, then the most revolutionary people would be African bushmen, who had a loincloth and little else.[196] In Poland, commentators observed that people looked to private possessions for stability (*ideał małej stabilizacji*). When inhabitants of Łódź were asked in 1968 what they saw as the role of material goods in life, the majority answered that they were for convenience and fun. Hardly anyone worried about negative side-effects. However unrealistic, the many promises of more goods made by leaders such as Edward Gierek in 1970s Poland reinforced a materialist outlook. Young Polish workers looked for quick improvement in the standard of living. For university students, happiness meant material comfort.[197] Many dissidents maintained a distaste for 'consumerism', sometimes drawing on an older critique of technological domination stretching back to Heidegger, but, significantly, Václav Havel celebrated young people sitting around a record player listening to underground music for 'living the truth' and asserting the 'independent life of society' against totalitarian lies and encroachments.[198]

Greater openness to the West in the 1970s and '80s magnified the effects of stratification. It did not cause them. In East Germany, luxury shops first opened their doors in the 1960s. Exquisit sold fashionable dresses and fine lingerie, Delikat dry gin, olives and Western cigarettes, all at exclusive prices. There was a kind of luxury fever, and the freer flow of Western gifts and hard currency raised its temperature. So did the transmission of West German TV and packages from family across the Wall. We know from looking at Central America and China how remittances sent home by migrant workers can set off a spiral of rivalry and emulation that unsettled existing hierarchies.[199] Honecker's East Germany was an experiment of remittance-based consumerism on a national scale. Hard-currency-only Intershops had originally been introduced for foreigners. By the mid-1970s, the bulk of their revenue came from purchases made by the citizens of the GDR. A third of teenagers now got their clothes as presents from family in the West. East Germany was becoming two nations, those with access to Deutschmarks and those without. Instead of 'each according to his ability' – the official formula – the new reality was 'each according to the residence of his aunt', in the words of the dissident singer-songwriter Wolf Biermann.[200]

For the regime, it was a vicious circle. The economy simply could not satisfy more private tastes and build more public housing at the same time. Oranges did not grow in Leipzig. They had to be imported and paid for with exports. This, however, meant that an already weak consumer goods industry was further starved of investment. And the deficit was escalating. The regime was living beyond its means. Western credits provided temporary relief but, to service them, the regime needed to attract hard currency. One way to do this was to allow citizens to buy a Volkswagen Golf and other expensive goods as long as they found an aunt to send them the required Deutschmarks. The regime was on Western life support. To keep it going, it encouraged the people to want more.

It was a path to self-destruction. Daily tensions over consumption led to a growing estrangement between citizens and leaders. The regime maintained an extensive petitioning system which gave individuals a chance to complain directly to Party bosses. It had been designed to monitor opinion and to contain protest by individualizing grievances. Instead, it politicized everyday life. A good half a million petitions were posted every year in the 1980s. Petitioners vented their anger as frustrated consumers but in doing so began to question the fairness and legitimacy of the regime itself. Poor housing was a major grievance. Some traced the defects in public consumption to the parallel barter system for private goods and blamed the regime for doing nothing to stop it. How could it be, one Erfurt citizen complained to Party leaders, that people were able to advertise freely in the newspaper 'exchange heating system for a Wartburg car'. No surprise that builders were unable to finish their job. 'Something is not right here.'[201] Only one in five cars were sold on legally. Many perceived shoddy products, missing parts and absent customer service as disrespect. Waiting seven to ten years for a car, not surprisingly, created a deep bond between owners and products; the Trabant, little more than a moped with a Bakelite frame, became a member of the family, often with its own pet name. When their proud new 'fathers' picked up the car and it turned out to be in the wrong colour, or once it started to break down without a spare part in sight, understandably, it felt like a personal attack; it was particularly cruel for those who had their car stolen and were placed at the bottom of the waiting list once again.

Shortages and uneven distribution ate away at social solidarity.

Some openly challenged the regime's authority to decide what was 'luxury' and what 'basic need'. Richard Henning, for example, had put down his name and money for a Lada in 1975 but was still waiting for his car ten years later. It was not a luxury, he emphasized. They needed it because his wife had to get home from her night shift. Why a citizen of the GDR had to wait so long for a car was 'unfathomable' to him.[202] Sightings of Western models added to the sense that the regime was privileging some groups over others. Jealousy, corruption and intrigue spread. Anonymous writers accused their factory director of maintaining three cars: one for his wife, one for sunny days and one for rain.[203] It offended regional pride as well as justice to see VWs and Mazdas on the streets of East Berlin. Were Berliners better than the inhabitants of historic Leipzig? 'I am now fifty-eight years old,' a man from Bautzen complained in 1986, 'and have worked forty years for our state; forty years I have helped make the state what it is today. Is that not long enough to be entitled to a new car?' He reminded ministers that the GDR had a constitutional commitment to equality.[204] Consumption raised a litany of questions about fairness. Why did the new neighbours get a telephone when a decorated member of the 'Brigade of the Working Class' was still waiting after years? How was a hard-working father to explain to his children that other families had things they did not? What kind of socialist justice was that?

The regime stepped up the production of cars and fridges in the 1970s and early '80s, but at the expense of quality. Complaints poured in about unavailable exhausts, heating coils and bicycle tubes. 'Consumer durables' became a misnomer. The Kombinat Haushaltsgeräte (the publicly owned enterprise for domestic appliances) was deluged by angry petitioners whose new washing machines lasted less than a year. Goods also broke down in the West, but here complaints were dispersed across firms and institutions. Accountability was diffused. In East Germany, by contrast, the petitioning system channelled frustrations and directed them at the heart of the regime. Local officials reported how difficult it was to maintain socialist morale amidst everyday frustrations. 'Believe me, comrades,' one old Party activist in Dresden wrote in 1981 to Günter Mittag, the prickly minister in charge of the economy, 'I can explain the most complicated questions of international affairs to our workers, but their experiences with the thousand little things strain everyone's consciousness and leave doubts.' He gave the example of a mother of three who took a day off, hoping to combine buying new clothes for her teenage son – 'nothing special, simply a durable pair of trousers, socks, and shoes' – with the search for some coffee-filter bags, and a package of frozen spinach to make a quick dinner. 'The result was nil!! and that in a big city with plenty of shopping opportunities . . . As hard as it may sound, her day was stolen.' Why, he asked, should shopping be so hard? 'What kind of demand-oriented production was this?'[205] The regime had entered a crisis of legitimacy. Its end was a question of when, not whether.

By the time the Wall came down in 1989, socialist consumer culture was suffering from visible schizophrenia. On the one hand, queuing and waiting for things had reinforced an older culture of austerity which prized longevity, repair and conservation. The first fridge and TV were treasured and cared for, repaired rather than discarded. Like the birth of a child, their acquisition was imprinted deep in people's biographies.[206] On the other hand, the emotional investment in goods undercut workers' identity as producers. High-quality Western goods made them painfully aware of the low value of their own, socialist products. Hans-Peter Johansen, for example, worked in a factory that made typewriters and printers. For the physicist and reserve officer it was unbearably sad how East German products had fallen behind the West in every respect, from design to functionality. In his 1986 petition, he devoted an entire page to the various faults of the Granat record player, which had been in circulation for a decade. Counter to its name (the red gemstone garnet), it was a dark 'monotonous plastic box', so poorly designed that pressing the 'characteristically heavy buttons' made the needle jump across the grooves because of the lack of cushioning – 'in complete disregard of the basic laws of physics'. 'I dare contend, no radio amateur would have made such elementary mistakes.' Everywhere, socialist workers were the prisoners of outdated or defunct technologies. It was hardly a surprise, he wrote, that comrades arrived late to work with little motivation.[207]

It was one of the great ironies of modern history. Marxism, which had set out to overcome alienation and make people and their work one again, ended up destroying workers' pride in the products of their own hands. Instead of *homo faber*, socialism bred its own species of *homo consumens*. For goods like the Trabant the revolution of 1989 spelled a cruel fate. In their thousands, owners simply abandoned them on street corners as trash.[208]

7

Inside Affluence

The capitalist West prided itself on its superiority to the socialist East, but the historically unprecedented spread of affluence in the 1950s and '60s was not universally celebrated. Far from it: material riches triggered soul-searching about what affluence was doing to moral values and the social fabric. Half a century later, with the benefit of hindsight, we can re-examine the inner workings of these newly affluent societies. Three views have predominated. The first is that affluence from the 1950s onwards has changed the priorities of consumption from the material to the symbolic, typified by a shift in spending from food to communication. A second sees the diffusion of TVs, cars and holidays to the masses as putting an end to class society. Inequality persists, but, according to this argument, class tastes have been replaced by shared dreams and aspirations. Finally, there is the Americanization thesis. Consumer culture has tended towards convergence, spreading an American idiom at the expense of diverse national traditions. How much of this is true?

AFFLUENT BUDGETS

Expenditure is not everything, but our understanding of consumption would be incomplete without knowing how people spent their money. One defining feature of the post-war decades is the sharp decline of food as a proportion of Europeans' household budget. In the mid-1950s, Norwegians, like the French, still spent around 45 per cent of their earnings on food and drink. By 1973, it was a mere quarter; by 2007 just over 10 per cent.[1] There were regional and social gaps and lags – in Sicily, over 4 million people depended on food parcels and soup kitchens in 1959. Today's poor still struggle to afford an adequate diet, and food banks are spreading in Britain, Spain and other countries hit by austerity. The overall direction, however, was the same everywhere. By the early 1990s, Greek families spent little more than 15 per cent on food. In the lives of Europeans this was a revolutionary change, even more dramatic than the fall in food prices in the late nineteenth century. In 1958, industrial workers had to sweat four hours for a pound of coffee; by 1993, a mere eighteen minutes. People started to eat fewer potatoes and more meat, and drink soft drinks rather than milk. Scandinavians today sip ten times as much wine and soft drinks as fifty years ago.[2] Societies worry less about food security than about over-eating.

Where did the freed-up money go? One view, aided by the post-modern focus on consumption as a universe of signs, sees a paradigm shift: culture and symbolic experiences have taken the place of physical needs. This is misleading, as a brief look at France and Norway shows. Spending on recreation and culture has indeed doubled in the last half-century – more books are published than ever before. But so has spending on housing. In the half-century since the 1950s, the share of private expenditure devoted to housing, routine maintenance, gas and electricity has doubled in Norway (from 15 per cent to 30 per cent) and tripled in France (from 7.5 per cent to 23 per cent). If housing, transport and food are put together, they ate up the same amount of the household budget in 2007 as they did in 1958: 60 per cent.[3] It is an indication of how much the affluent society is about 'ordinary' rather than conspicuous consumption.[4] Spending more money on the home reflects a rising standard of comfort, warmer rooms and hot showers; central heating reached most French homes only in the 1970s and '80s. There is, then, a curious mismatch between real trends in spending and the ink most theorists have devoted to the consumer as a shopper buying yet another branded handbag. One reason, probably, is that many commentators continue to take their inspiration from Veblen's *Theory of the Leisure Class* (1899), written at a time when people spent more on clothing than on housing.

CLASS AND STATUS

The second debate concerns the effects of these shifts on class. In pure numerical terms, a simple trend presents itself: what the French call *moyennisation*. Household budgets show that the top and bottom of society have lost their distinct consumption profiles. In the 1960s and

'70s, workers began to spend disproportionately more on leisure and culture, while the *cadres supérieurs* cut back.[5] As far as food and drink are concerned, the gulf between the elite and the rest has diminished, as professionals and workers embraced new recipes, products and going out. The cultural divide now opened up further down the social scale, excluding the poor from the more dynamic lifestyles of the many.[6]

The trickier question is whether watching TV or going to a show means the same to a boss as to an employee. It would be nice to give a simple answer, but, in addition to countries having distinctive social structures, we have the complication that scholars have approached this question through national class preoccupations. Early American researchers took it as given that consumer culture was creating one burgeoning middle class. This was, after all, what the American dream was about; Ernest Dichter and his fellow émigré and psychologist George Katona studied almost exclusively middle-class households, as did their feminist critics. British observers, by contrast, were preoccupied with the working class and its presumed destiny of building social democracy. Were TVs and material aspirations destroying solidarity? In France, meanwhile, the focus was more on high culture, and how the elite was converting opera, paintings and table manners into social capital.

In early American accounts the middle class and suburbia blurred into one. Already in the 1930s, writers noted how suburbs were fuelling a more competitive material lifestyle of 'keeping up with the Joneses'. Asked what they would do if they had another $1,000, the members of a Parent–Teacher Association in Westchester put travel first, then 'desire for material goods and services', such as a better car or 'pretty clothes'.[7] Only after that came savings and better schools for the kids, at a time when the country was still in depression. Suburbanization also boosted home-based leisure – one of the reasons for the conservative restoration in the middle decades of the twentieth century. Once he had returned from his office job in the city, the commuter tended to stay home. Suburban families did puzzles and played board games together. Physical isolation and dependence on the car meant that they went together to the movies. Researchers in Westchester noted how the family was 'the most stable nucleus of recreational activities in the suburb'.[8]

For affluent suburbanites in mid-twentieth-century America, civic life and fun were increasingly one and the same. 'We are concentrating more and more on giving ourselves a good time,' one Westchester

woman noted in 1923. 'The newer members ... are more interested in
bridge, teas ... and Beauty Culture courses than in helping the community.' Suburban women's clubs were conveyors of new products,
tastes and recipes to be tried at home, such as 'Sunday Night Supper
Treats'.[9] From here it was a short step to the Tupperware parties of the
1950s, which turned the lounge into a sales floor. By 1954, over
20,000 belonged to the 'Tupperware Family'. Tupperware containers
were emblematic of the family-oriented consumption regime. They
were utilitarian, saving money and left-overs. They taught children to
have their lunch in 'an orderly and pleasing manner'. At the same time,
the parties offered housewives a way out of isolation and self-abnegation.
The vice-president Brownie Wise urged women affiliates to 'use it all':
instead of putting away their precious lingerie, women should wear it
and indulge themselves.[10]

Home leisure was helped by air-conditioning. When the writer
Henry Miller warned of *The Air-conditioned Nightmare* in 1945, the
controlled environment was largely limited to cinemas, department
stores and offices. It was in the 1950s that AC window units entered
middle-class homes; in 1957, the Federal Housing Administration
began treating AC as part of the mortgage cost rather than as an extra.
Families with air-conditioning, advertisers said, spent more time with
their kids at home.[11] AC was absent from European homes, but there
was a similar inward turn. The war reinforced the home's appeal as a
place of security. 'The home of tomorrow,' a popular guide for the
home owner stressed in 1954, 'is a bulwark against a hostile world, and
makes the family impregnable from the outside.'[12]

Suburbs, researchers concluded, nurtured a new kind of American,
characterized by sociability, aspirations and upward mobility. In fact, this
confused cause and effect. Material aspirations and a hyper-active social
life were the results of middle-class affluence, not of suburban living.
Working families did not share them. A study in the mid-1950s followed
Ford workers to their new suburban homes just north of San Jose.[13] There
was no increase in partying or going out. Many did not know what a
cocktail was. Most did not belong to any club or association. Consumer
culture did not automatically snuff out associational life – most workers
were not joiners to begin with. Nor did new-found domestic comfort drag
them on to a social treadmill. Workers hoped to stay in their jobs, not
move up in the world to outshine their neighbours.

By the late 1950s, American workers earned around $4,000 a year.
In the previous two decades, their income had seen a spectacular

ten-fold increase. And yet working families retained a material outlook of their own. Affluence did not create a classless monoculture. A study at the time compared the approach to money and goods amongst middle-class women and working-class housewives in Chicago, Louisville and Trenton.[14] For the middle class, material craving was sustained by a sense of a brighter future: 'As long as I want things and am not completely satisfied with what I've got I'll continue to be happy,' said one middle-class woman. 'I'm always wanting something more or different or new.' Working families, by contrast, suffered from 'depression phobia'. Two decades of rising incomes notwithstanding, wives were convinced that their husbands would never earn more in the future. These were not the optimistic, self-confident consumers painted by studies of the middle class. Fancy cooking pots, toys for the kids and other impulse purchases triggered feelings of guilt. Most had instalment plans but saw them 'as an almost immoral self-indulgence'. Affluence did not extinguish a working-class concern with how to make ends meet. Goods were measured by their usefulness – a large sofa that could be turned into a bed – not their beauty. Recreation was a frivolous waste of money better spent on 'important' things. Department stores in the centre of town were viewed with suspicion, alien to their own way of shopping, which was based on the familiar and the local. One bought in neighbourhood shops or through friends and family contacts.

The persistence of such class cultures in prosperous America is a reminder that we should be careful when talking of national styles of consumption. Katona and colleagues contrasted an American forward-looking mentality with a conservative German one: 'The average American consumer happily spends tomorrow's income while the German only likes to spend yesterday's savings.'[15] The problem is that there is no such person as the average national consumer. Treating the middle class as a norm tends to obscure differences across class and regions; Northern Italians, for example, continue to spend a larger proportion of their earnings on leisure and sport than those in the south. Unlike their middle-class neighbours, American workers were not that much more optimistic than Europeans. The contrast between American credit-addicts and continental European savers must not be overdone. Europeans, especially young industrial workers, also took out instalment plans. In the 1960s and '70s, the private savings rate in the United States was only marginally lower than in Western Europe.[16]

The 'embourgeoisement' thesis attracted the greatest attention in the motherland of the working class: Britain. The economic sociologist Ferdynand Zweig returned to England from a study tour to the United States in 1952 struck by how workers there had responded to his question about who the middle class were: we are, they told him. In the course of the next decade, Zweig found that British workers were moving along the same road.[17] Affluence, he argued, was eating away at working-class culture. A community of work and neighbourhood was breaking down into acquisitive individuals. Workers carried a mental checklist of what to buy next rather than thinking about the class struggle. In their aspirations and lifestyle, they no longer took their lead from their fathers and mates but from their social betters. The resulting clash of values was captured nicely by Alan Bennett in his play *Enjoy* (1980), set in one of Leeds' last back-to-back houses, itself awaiting demolition. 'I do not want love,' Linda, a call-girl, exclaimed to her parents, 'I want consumer goods!'[18] The 'new acquisitive society', Zweig warned, was self-destructive, no longer checked by old values of restraint and self-sacrifice. An inflationary spiral would pull down the welfare state.

Zweig's thesis – echoed by the market researcher Mark Abrams at the time – was soon subjected to sociological critiques and found wanting. In the mid-1960s, the sociologist John Goldthorpe and colleagues studied 250 affluent workers in Luton, an engineering and car manufacturing town.[19] That workers took home more money did not mean they were joining the bourgeoisie. Blue-collar workers, the sociologists wrote, swapped a community of work and neighbourhood for a world of private comforts. Hardly any manual labourer shared friends or leisure pursuits with the middle classes. At the same time, union membership and support for the Labour Party remained high. While blue-collar workers were shedding their traditional collectivism for a new individualism, white-collar workers were moving from their inherited individualism towards a pragmatic support for collective bargaining. What they shared was an orientation towards money and possessions. Otherwise, they kept their distance. The effects of affluence, then, were limited. If material aspirations were converging, social hierarchies remained intact.

Looking back on these debates half a century later, it is difficult not to be struck by the way in which the discussion of consumption was framed by an overarching concern about the future of the Labour Party. Private consumerism, it was feared, was destroying traditional close-knit communities built on solidarity and fairness and without selfish pleasures – Zweig compared it to a 'cocoon'.[20] Historically, this was a curious concern, for Labour parties had expanded at the very same time as commercial leisure, in the late nineteenth and early twentieth centuries. In reality, working-class communities had always been fractured by gender, ethnic, confessional and regional identities. Working-class conservatism, similarly, existed before affluence, while social networks and understandings of class continued to co-exist with new private comforts. Money was not everything. Luton workers understood social inequality as an inherited combination of power and pounds: 'ordinary people like us' versus 'Mayfair Johnnies'.[21] The references to material aspirations in the 1950s and '60s need to be viewed in the unique context of their time – high growth and the lowest peace-time unemployment of the century. When hard times returned, working families switched back to a concern with getting by. A researcher who revisited Luton in the gloomy mid-1980s – when unemployment stood at 14 per cent – found plenty of social networks. Affluent workers watched TV, but they also met with kin, neighbours and fellow workers. Nor did affluence eradicate gender segregation. Men participated more in domestic life, but they still had their outside world of drink and football.[22]

The British debate involved a new recognition that 'affluent workers' derived their identity and self-worth from the things they owned and used rather than from the things they made. But how exactly was what people liked related to social inequality? It was in France in the 1960s that Pierre Bourdieu assembled the most ambitious account of the nexus between class and culture, eventually published in 1979 as *La Distinction*, 'the single most important monograph of post-war sociology published anywhere in the world'.[23] Such has been its success that 'distinction' has entered everyday vocabulary to describe how we use things to send signals about who we are. For Bourdieu, it was much more. It was the centre of the social universe, the sun around which classes orbited. The gravitational force was taste. Taste distinguished in a double sense. It separated one group from another. And 'it distinguishes in an essential way, since taste is the basis of all that one has – people and things – and all that one is for others, whereby one classifies oneself and is classified by others.' The reference to 'people and things' is crucial, for Bourdieu insisted that each class had its own distinct taste regime: 'Taste is what brings together things and people that go together.' People's preferences and lifestyles, what they liked and how they consumed things, had a unity to them, embodied in an appropriate 'habitus', and socialized through a hierarchical educational system.[24]

Through interviews, surveys, theory and elaborate diagrams, Bourdieu drew a cultural map of French society. At the top was the well-educated elite, which defended its monopoly over 'legitimate culture' and claimed a 'superior' distinction ('art for art's sake'). Typical was 'S', a forty-five-year-old lawyer born into the Parisian grande bourgeoisie. S lived in a 300 square metre flat in the 16th arrondissement and had a country house in Burgundy. His guiding principle in life was refined pleasure. He despised people who bought 'not what pleases them but what has value'. He liked Matisse as well as Botticelli. Cooking was 'a state of mind' for him – 'To appreciate it, you have to be "relaxed": Sturgeons' eggs, some Russian cooking, is quite delicious.' He was a connoisseur of Bordeaux wines and kept ten bottles from 1923. Drinking fine wine was a 'liturgy', to be celebrated 'only with certain people, who are capable of enjoying it in the same way'.

It was this elite that interested Bourdieu most. It used taste to justify and maintain social hierarchies. The classes below had their own life-styles, which were oriented towards this 'legitimate culture' and affirmed its superiority. Thus, the petit-bourgeoisie put on Ravel's *Bolero* to demonstrate its 'cultural goodwill'. In its homes it introduced 'nooks' and 'corners' to show it was 'living beyond its means'. The manual working class, meanwhile, submitted to a 'taste for necessity'. Things were, first and foremost, about their function, not pleasure or aesthetic effect. Food was about calories, not cuisine. Clothes should be practical; Bourdieu found that working-class wives paid far less attention to fashion or beauty than their bourgeois superiors. Spending hard-earned money on a Bach recording was considered 'pretentious' and as 'foolish' as spending 2 million (old) francs on a fine watch.[25] 'Culture' was for the elite.

Distinction was a giant step forward. Marxist accounts of 'mass culture' pictured consumers as passive dupes of a culture industry. This made it difficult to explain change. Bourdieu, by contrast, saw them as actively involved in reproducing a class system. And he went beyond the fashionable attention to signs and discourse at the time, concerning himself with *how* as well as what people consumed. His critique of the elite's hold on 'legitimate culture' had a French republican agenda: political democracy required cultural democracy.[26]

The big question is whether this snapshot of France in the 1960s can be blown up to fit a wider frame. Were classes separate islands with their own uniform taste and habitus? Even for France in the 1960s this is doubtful. Bourdieu was mostly interested in the high culture that separated the elite from the working class, ignoring practices that cut across groups, such as watching television. Neither gender nor immigrant communities featured, somewhat ironically, since Bourdieu had made his initial mark with a seminal study of gender in Algeria. It is also debatable whether people had coherent, class-specific tastes. Let us recall the machine fitter in 1913 Bochum who liked Wagner as well as Cowboy-and-Indian movies.[27] The sociologist Bernard Lahire, who has painstakingly gone through French data on cultural practices since the 1970s, has found that 'dissonance' is more widespread than any coherent class taste. Individuals mix and match genres, creating their own distinct taste portfolio. In the same family, some love TV game shows, while others despise them. Distinction is more a personal accomplishment than a class attribute – there is a 'war' between 'high' and 'low', 'noble' and 'vulgar', 'sophisticated' and 'trash', but, according to Lahire, these battles are fought inside each individual, not between classes.[28]

Instead of unifying classes, the spread of mass media, TV and music equipment has, arguably, facilitated greater pluralism. This is partly the result of access to multiple genres via radio, TV and, most recently, the internet, and partly because of more domestic enjoyment. Participation in 'high' or 'low' culture used to be visible: a public act. With TV, all classes can watch a mix of programmes without fear of losing status. This does not mean class has gone away, however. Rather, its operating mode has shifted, from taste to degrees of participation. The most rigorous study of cultural consumption, conducted in Britain between 2003 and 2005, found similar preferences for music genres, sport and TV across groups; visual arts were an exception.[29] Only for a small executive elite did high culture still serve as capital. Taste has been democratized. The main divide was now between those who were participating in art and music and those who were not. Workers especially were unlikely to go to concerts, the theatre or museums, or practise sport, and more likely to spend their time at home or socializing with friends.

Affluence, then, has brought to a close the clash of class cultures, although for reasons other than those anticipated by pluralist reformers like Crosland. Workers are no longer in awe of high culture. At the same time, they no longer have a culture of their own. Everyone now is a football fan. The Labour Party abandoned a distinct culture of producers. Meanwhile, the middle and upper classes switched from snobbish elitism to cultural poaching. The new strategy of distinction is no longer to erect barriers to protect one's class from hoi polloi but to become an 'omnivore' and mix as many styles as possible – to listen to working-class bands and world music as well as string quartets; to watch TV soaps as well as Shakespeare on stage. Paradoxically, then, letting go of the claim to own culture has helped the middle class to consolidate its sense of superiority.[30]

How did consumption affect social identities in communities where class was not the dominant marker? African cities are an interesting case because here migrant workers' tribal identities were confronted with entertainment, new tastes and products. Accra in 1950s Ghana, for example, had eight large cinemas that showed American films, musicals and thrillers, as well as safari movies. There were twenty African dance bands and numerous social clubs. Consumption could reinforce ethnic divisions; the Indo-Ghana Club, for example, was for Indians only. Yet it also challenged hierarchies, both imperial and local. In French Equatorial Brazzaville, on the Congo River, football turned into a challenge to the colonial masters when successful native teams refused to take off their boots and play barefoot. At the same time, European hats, shirts and dresses rode roughshod over tribal dress codes, offering the young and poor a way to free themselves from a sartorial regime controlled by their elders. Young couples danced the rumba and waltz.[31]

There has been a tendency to see consumption as an all-powerful solvent of community, so it is worth stressing how at times it has functioned as a cement. The Xhosa who migrated to the city of East London in South Africa in the 1950s reproduced the rural division of 'Red' and 'School' factions. The more traditional Red (amaqaba), who smeared their bodies with red ochre, looked upon consumer culture with suspicion. Credit and spending money on leisure were frowned upon; 'calves in the postal savings account did not die,' went one of their sayings. Reds lived in communal quarters, cooked together and, after work, joined in tribal iseti drinking groups and shared memories of the homeland. The School Xhosa, by contrast, arrived Christian and literate and embraced consumer culture with open arms. Most joined sports clubs. Dance halls thrived. Some jived and played rugby, others preferred ballroom dancing, bars and the cinema. Going to the cinema, Reds said, had made School Xhosa thieves. When possible, School Xhosa moved into their own private quarters, bought consumer goods and decorated their homes with Western-style furniture and ornaments. A consumer lifestyle was a way to preserve their distance from the Reds and at the same time impose their own gradations on what had been a virtually classless rural society. In the end, it was not consumer culture that weakened tribal culture but urban planning and forced removal, which scattered Red Xhosa across new satellite towns.[32]

AMERICANIZATION?

The Americanization thesis can be thought of as a geographic extension of the idea that consumer culture flattens distinctions. The standardizing force attributed to America is not surprising. The age of affluence coincided with America's triumph as the new great power after 1945. Supermarkets, American marketing and Hollywood dream couples – all these were easily viewed by sceptical Europeans as vanguards of an imperialist monoculture. The decline of America as a superpower affords an opportune moment to look back and ask to what degree lifestyles really have converged. To do this we need to consider practices as well as products: that is, what people did as well as what they bought.

The supermarket epitomized what the US historian Victoria de Grazia has called America's 'irresistible empire'. It promised choice, convenience and cheapness. With its neon-lit aisles, freezers and pre-packaged foods in cheerful, air-conditioned surroundings, the supermarket was an icon of a futuristic modernity. Its origins, however, lay in the dark days of the Depression in the 1930s. Bigger shop floors and self-service increased volume while cutting overheads. Discounts attracted price-conscious shoppers. By 1939, one quarter of every dollar spent on food in the United States was spent in a supermarket. Twenty years later, it was 64 cents. By then, self-service had blossomed into a form of self-fulfilment. Pastel interiors, soothing background music and colourful packaging were introduced to make shoppers try something new and treat the trip to the supermarket as a journey of self-discovery.[33]

In Europe, Americans picked Italy and Belgium as the first bridgeheads. With the help of a low-interest government loan, Nelson Rockefeller's corporation (IBEC) opened its first Supermarkets Italiani store in Milan in 1959. It was no commercial D-day, however. American retail technologies were not easily transplanted – the imported shopping carts, one director noted, had been designed for Americans loading up Cadillacs, while most Italians could not yet afford a Fiat 500.[34] Frozen food made little sense without a fridge. Across Europe, there was a mix of obstacles, from restrictive planning laws, small buildings and limited opening hours to the political clout of shopkeepers and co-operatives. Advance was slow and uneven. By 1971, when Britain had over 3,500 supermarkets, there were only six hundred in all of Italy, and those were mainly in the north. A decade later, Italians still bought only 3 per cent of their food in supermarkets; in France, it was 14 per cent. Expansion was much more rapid in Britain, Germany and the Netherlands, where, by the early 1990s, around 60 per cent of the grocery market was controlled by big supermarket chains.

The real wave of concentration came in the 1980s and '90s and was the result of domestic forces rather than American invasion. For example, until 1966, Denmark prohibited chains from opening more than one outlet in any municipality unless they also had a manufacturing side (like the co-ops). Opening hours were extended to 8 p.m. only in 1994. When discount superstores took off, the Danish co-operatives made the most of it. In France, the 1973 Royer Law put shopkeepers on local zoning committees to slow the progress of supermarkets. Consequently, French chains looked abroad and opened stores in Spain and Latin America; half of Carrefour's earnings come from foreign operations.[35]

Nor did commercial exchange flow in only one direction, from America outward. Innovations travelled back and forth, and circulated. Along with urban megastores, the giant Swiss co-op Migros pioneered small self-service stores and travelling vans, which would be copied in Turkey and Brazil. It was Migros which first added electronic check-out to self-service, catching the interest of American retailers. On the ground, American models had to be modified to fit local space and habits. The result were local–American hybrids. Swiss supermarkets, for example, put quality ahead of choice. Instead of stocking 4,000 articles, as American stores did, they carried a selected assortment of brands. Standardization was kept in check by attention to local tastes and products. Book corners provided an aura of cultural respectability.[36] South of the Alps, Italian supermarkets found that it was easier to exploit existing habits than import foreign ones. Daily lotteries, gift promotions and the display of fresh, unpackaged food targeted Italians used to shopping daily rather than weekly. Unlike American stores, Swiss and Italian supermarkets had to set up their own supply chains from scratch, and ended up producing many of their products or importing them directly.[37]

Phobias of Americanization were inspired by older fears of what rationalization did to work, community and freedom. Small stores and artisan's workshops stood for a vibrant community; large self-service stores for soulless anonymity. In the 1962 Italian novel *La vita agra* (*Bitter Life*), the supermarket appears as a dehumanizing evil born of the boom. Disguised as ordinary shoppers, employees mingle among hypnotized women, encouraging them to fill their trolleys. Everyone buys the same thing. No one speaks a word. The meat counter resembles an assembly plant, where women mechanically seal slices of meat and cold cuts in cellophane. At the check-out, cashier girls sit like automatons, 'identical blue caps with the name of the shop on their heads, looking at the figures with dilated pupils, never blinking ... their complexion fading, their necks ever more wrinkled like so many little tortoises'.[38]

The experience of ordinary shoppers was rather different. After some instruction about how to use wire baskets and shopping carts, most people took to the supermarket, even finding it liberating. The warm, friendly glow of the small shop had often been more ideal than real. Encounters in the local shop involved class, dependence and, sometimes, humiliation. Working-class housewives left the butcher with a thicker cut of meat than they had asked for or could afford rather than lose face in front of the neighbours. Gossip was rife: why did the single young woman from next door suddenly buy twice her usual? In addition to convenience and longer hours, the supermarket had a democratic air, especially attractive to working women, singles and minority ethnic groups. Men, too, found supermarkets easier to navigate, and novelty products gave them a feeling of competence; in the 1960s, a third of the clientele was male. Supermarkets presented themselves as pillars of democracy: 'Choice is the same for everyone,' to use the slogan of the Italian Esselunga. It was the better-off who initially turned up their noses. After all, superior status was demonstrated through the personal attention they were given. In Britain, the wife of a judge swore violently at Alan Sainsbury at the opening of one of his first self-service stores when she found out that she was expected to be her own shop assistant. Self-service disrupted the age-old balance of power between customer and retailer.

It would be wrong, however, to conclude that the supermarket sparked a revolutionary switch from intimate human encounters to anonymous mountains of merchandise. Even where self-service spread fastest, as in Britain, most people kept up parallel shopping, buying some items in supermarkets, others in small shops. After years of decline, France still had some 600,000 small shops in the 1980s, not counting bakeries. The number of corner kiosks has gone up in Finland, not down. Other than for food, small retailing remains big business in most European countries. Not all chain shops, moreover, were necessarily soulless. Early supermarkets realized that they needed to overcome a sense of cold anonymity and, in response, introduced personal greeters and over-the-counter service. Oral histories of dozens of British shoppers about their first experiences with self-service suggest that customers often remained on familiar terms with shop assistants, at least in smaller supermarkets and smaller communities. One woman recalled: 'You still know the people, so there's still a bit of chatter . . . because you know them, the same as you did in the counter-service ones.'[39] In big urban supermarkets, that was more difficult. Still, this does not automatically make these stores places of lonely individuals. To this day, shoppers sometimes take their chatting and community with them into the store. In supermarkets in China today, in-store announcements are drowned out by the conversational noise of couples shopping together. In Taipei, Seoul and Hong Kong, teenagers have turned McDonald's into youth centres, even holding reading clubs there.[40]

What is remarkable is not that the United States has spread its wares but how uneven its influence has been. The dominance of Hollywood is matched by the resilience of local music cultures in many parts of the world – not unimportant, given that listening to music is the most popular form of cultural consumption. Scale matters. It costs far less to produce a record than a movie. Anglophone music came to rule in the Netherlands and Germany, but national styles, artists and record sales remain significant in France, Greece, Norway and Italy. Across Europe, American jazz and, later, rock'n'roll sparked innovation and diversification. In the 1950s, the Italian singer Domenico Modugno ('*Volare*') blended influences from Southern Puglia and Sicily with crooning and swing (see Plate 45). In 1959 France, Georges Brassens ('*La Mauvaise Réputation*') was more popular with the young than Paul Anka, the Canadian crooner who dominated the American charts with 'Diana' and other hits at the time.

Post-war reconstruction also involved cultural reconstruction. Regional music and folklore gained their own dedicated TV and radio programmes. Hamburg got its Haifischbar; Naples its Neapolitan song parade. Superimposed were national music festivals such as the Festival

di Sanremo, launched in 1951 and inspiring joy and bemusement ever
since. These were vital vehicles for new national cultures, especially in
societies sharply divided by region. The Eurovision Song Contest built
on this model. Sanremo illustrates the kind of exchanges lost in an
exclusive focus on Americanization. The festival did have American
guest stars, for example Louis Armstrong in 1968, but in the same year
the winning entry was a joint Italian–Brazilian hit, 'Canzone per te' by
Sergio Endrigo and Roberto Carlos, which turned the standard romantic formula on its head: 'the loneliness that you have given me, I cultivate
like a flower.' [41] The military coup in Brazil in 1964 led to an exodus of
Brazilian artists. Gilberto Gil moved to London, Chico Buarque to
Rome. Lucio Dalla's '4/3/1943' owed its Portuguese touch to the latter,
who later turned it into a Brazilian hit ('Minha História') which was
also successful in Japan. These years saw the birth of the cantautore, a
new breed of singer-songwriter (Tenco, Giorgio Gaber, Fabrizio de
André, Gino Paoli) who owed as much to the French chansonniers
Georges Brassens and Charles Aznavour as to Bob Dylan and Nat King
Cole.

Latin American influences have extended as far as the Arctic Circle,
where, inspired by travelling musicians, Finns developed their own
type of tango, performed in a minor key, blending Argentinian rhythm
with a folkloristic nostalgia for nature and the homestead (see Plate
46). With its own stars, festivals and competitions for Tango King and
Queen, it has become as central to Finnish culture as the sauna. In the
1960s, the rivalry between pop and tango was cast as a battle for the
Finnish soul, and for the survival of a rustic lifestyle in what was
becoming an increasingly urban society – the proportion of Finns living in urban areas almost doubled, from 32 per cent to 60 per cent
between 1950 and 1980. In the vanguard of pop music were the English
Beatles and the Rolling Stones; American influences were more marginal, and it was not until April 1966 that an American singer had a
Top 5 hit – Nancy Sinatra with 'These Boots are Made for Walkin''.
Defenders of Finnish tango worried about the moral decay and gender
confusion created by long-haired musicians and their fans. Tango lyrics
reinforced an image of the city as a cold and lonely place. Pop musicians, in turn, ridiculed tango as backward, loved by peasants cut off
from modernity. 'I say, brave is the band,' one musician wrote in 1967,
'that dares to travel north of Jyväskylä [in central Finland] without
tango covering 90 per cent of their repertoire . . . in Ostrobothnia a
band was threatened with a knife because it didn't play enough tango.' [42]

Things have relaxed a little since, and tango has also found admirers in Helsinki and Turku in the urban south. More generally, the fusion of hybrid styles has continued in recent genres, for example post-punk Suomi-reggae, with the inimitable hit: 'Hän haluaa huussin' ('He Wants a Dry Toilet').[43]

The resilience and vitality of national and regional music styles has in some cases been nurtured by cultural protection. France is a pronounced example. In 1986, it passed a law (Loi Léotard), which has since required 40 per cent of all radio time to be devoted to French songs and regional languages. French musicians singing in English or another foreign language did not benefit. Public TV stations had to spend at least 2.5 per cent of their turnover on producing French films. On television, 40 per cent of all films had to be French. Up to the present, France has refused to bow to American pressure and let free-trade agreements extend to its national treasures of music and film.[44]

It might be contended that even if people in the developed world cherished different music, food, and so on, affluence has nonetheless spawned an identical lifestyle in the way we consume. This is a tricky question, because research on Americanization and globalization has looked mainly at goods, not what people did with them. Still, some insights can be gleaned from time-use data that countries started keeping in the 1960s. One research team has recoded national data to allow a comparison of eating and reading patterns in the United States, France, Britain, the Netherlands and Norway. Between 1970 and 2000, eating out went up everywhere, but at significantly different rates. By the end of this period, Britons and Americans spent an average of twenty-five and thirty minutes a day eating out. Norwegians, by contrast, rarely went to restaurants or diners (fourteen minutes a day). The French were eating out more – and continue to do so – but they were also spending a good hour and a half each day eating at home, whereas the American figure for eating at home had plummeted to under forty minutes. Affluence, then, has not led to a convergence of daily habits and rhythms. French, Swiss and Italians sit down to a meal together and take their time. Americans snack, often alone, while doing other things.[45]

These are, of course, averages, and we must ask next how practices are distributed across the population. Are people devoting their leisure time to TV, sport, reading, and so forth in an increasingly similar pattern? On the eve of affluence, habits were highly uneven. In 1946, for example, two thirds of Britons were routine movie-goers, but one third never went to the cinema at all. Americanization, if it had been pervasive, should have created an increasingly shared monoculture as standards of living rose. Research on reading has painted a more complicated picture. In Norway and the Netherlands, reading books and magazines remains a leisure activity shared by most. In the United States, on the other hand, reading has become a minority pastime, but those who do read ('participants'), read more and more – eighty-seven minutes a day in 1998 (compared to forty-seven minutes devoted to reading by the Norwegians and British).[46] It is debatable whether the internet and other new media is killing reading as a pastime. Magazine-reading has declined, but books are more popular than ever. In the Netherlands and Britain, heavy internet users tend to be more (not less) active readers.[47]

This snapshot of reading habits prompts an interesting hypothesis. It may be that people's leisure patterns are converging in continental Europe, whereas in the United States (and to a lesser extent in Britain) they are diverging. In other words, affluence has made Americans specializers, Europeans generalizers. In America, you either read a lot or you do not read at all; you either do a lot of sport or none at all. In the Netherlands and Norway, by contrast, most people do a bit of both. Consumption is more shared. If Americanization has a particular dynamic, then, it might be internal diversification, not conformity. Everyone lives on their own lifestyle island. One possible reason for the contrast might be that affluence in continental Europe has been conditioned by social democracy, where inequality is less sharp, education more homogeneous and the state has an established role in cultural provision. Britain, tellingly, lies mid-Atlantic, between these two consumption zones. Whether homogeneity is preferable to differentiation is another question.

8

Asia Consumes

Up to this point, the story of consumption has been about more. In contemporary Asia, more became most. The boom that began in Japan in 1955 was the first of a series of waves that lifted up Taiwan and South Korea in the 1970s, China since 1979 and, most recently, India. Between 1990 and 2002, according to the World Bank, 1.2 billion people have moved of poverty; almost 1 billion of them were Asians. Since 2012, growth has slowed. Still, never before in the history of the world did so many people join the ranks of shoppers in such short time. In Western Europe during the post-war miracle, it took ten to fifteen years until half the households had a TV, twenty to twenty-five years until a fridge crossed their doorstep. South Korea managed this in a single decade in the 1970s; China in the 1980s in even less. Washing machines, stereos and VCRs – goods that in the West had arrived one after another over several decades – entered Chinese homes virtually simultaneously, among poor and rich alike.[1]

Superlatives come easily, especially for China. In 2009, it became the greatest polluter in the world, the biggest purchaser of cars, and had the largest proportion of home-owners.[2] The global consequences of China's rise have attracted widespread commentary. There has been a curious mismatch, however, between the attention paid to production and that to consumption, between a broad concern with sweated labour and ecological meltdown, on the one hand, and a much narrower focus on 'consumerism' that takes its cues from luxury malls and the members of the Shanghai Porsche club.

History is not a crystal ball, but it can place the current transformation in a longer perspective and help us understand how and why Asian societies came to consume the way they did. Placing Japan, China and India alongside the unfolding of consumption we have traced in this book, we can immediately see one major difference: several successive stages have been compressed into one. The rise of the middle class, a culture of domestic comfort, urbanization, a boost in discretionary spending and increasing home ownership – these were processes that took four centuries in Europe and the United States. In the booming societies of Japan in the 1950s–'80s, and in China and India since, these transformations happened more or less in parallel.

A second and no less crucial difference concerns the place of consumption in the sequence of historical change. When tea, china and cotton took off in the precocious Netherlands and Britain, these were already urban societies. The Industrial Revolution came after. In addition, in many parts of the West, consumer power drew on traditions of citizenship that invoked political rights, as we have repeatedly seen. Asia is a reminder that history does not like to proceed in a uniform series of steps. In China and Japan, the sequence was reversed. Both started industrialization as predominantly rural societies. They were modern before they were urban. The recent surge of consumption came as part of a great migration, as hundreds of millions set up homes in cities often built from scratch. This would have profound implications, not least for the role of the home. The stages of citizenship, similarly, were reversed. In the West, political rights came first and then expanded into social rights. The Far East skipped the first step. Citizenship meant duties, not rights. In exchange for protection and some social support, a citizen had a duty to support the state. This made for a political habitat fundamentally different from that in the liberal West, where citizen-consumers linked a demand for individual rights to one for social welfare. India took a democratic road, but here, too, the newly independent state asked citizens to be producers and subordinate their personal desires to the collective interest of an independent nation.

As before, the pages to follow do not try to offer encyclopaedic country files, nor do they wish to paint a monochrome picture of East versus West. Rather, with the help of selective and thematic comparisons, they seek to outline principal developments and to identify differences as well as parallels. As the key changes did not happen simultaneously in the Asian countries, we sometimes need to view different time periods alongside each other, that is, to compare Japan in the 1950s–'80s with China in the 1990s–2000s.

Three main questions arise. First, to what degree was the recent, material leap forward a break with the past? Second, is a fast-growing society like China veering towards an American 'throwaway consumer lifestyle', as one China expert has warned?[3] Finally, there is politics. In Britain, France and the United States, the rise of consumption was tied up with the rise of civil society, citizenship and social democracy. What kind of political animal is consumption outside a liberal and republican habitat, in regimes characterized by strong states and weak individual rights?

CRESCENDO

For any story, the starting point shapes the moral. GDP growth of over 10 per cent a year in Japan (1955–73), in China (1979–2011) and close to it in India (8.7 per cent in 2003–8) has been so extraordinary that it is no surprise that most commentators take their respective starting points as the Japanese miracle, Deng Xiaoping's opening of China and India's liberal reforms in 1991. Clearly, the mass purchase of TVs, cars, AC units and much else was made possible by phenomenal growth, a rise in spending power and greater choice.[4]

The issue is whether the recent drama appears as an equally sharp break once we take a longer view. In fact, it was Maoism in China and Nehru's vision for India that were short, if deep, deviations from a longer path of commercial development. Mao turned merchants and shoppers back into peasants. At the birth of the People's Republic of China in 1949, for example, Beijing was thriving, with a good 10,000 restaurants and fast-food snack stands. By 1979, a mere 656 were left. Shortages affected not only goods but the services necessary to maintain them. Shops, knife sharpeners and bicycle-repair men all but disappeared from the urban landscape.[5] India, meanwhile, at the stroke of the midnight hour on 14 August 1947, made its tryst with destiny and turned its back on the world. To Nehru, independence demanded self-sufficiency, building factories and power stations, not shopping. Consumption carried the stain of empire. Once at the crossroads of global exchange, the Indian Ocean came almost to a standstill; India's share of world trade fell from 2.4 per cent to 0.4 per cent between 1947 and 1990.[6] Liberalization since needs to be seen as a return to an older, historical trajectory.

Getting and spending, then, are not recent, alien imports from the 'modern' West into an austere and 'traditional' East. Visions of abundance had deep, indigenous roots. The *Arthashastra*, the ancient Indian 'Wealth of Nations' (c.300 BCE–150 AD), defined a wise king as one who 'endears himself to his people by enriching them and doing good to them'.[7] *Dharma* (spiritual well-being) and *kama* (pleasure), it said, depended on material well-being. There was nothing wrong with either abundance or pleasure as long as they did not spin out of control. In Chinese, 'boy' and 'fish' have the same sound as an 'abundance of things' and are symbols of good fortune. We have noted earlier how fashion and domestic comfort had already left their mark on late Ming China and colonial India. Around 1900, there was a step change with the arrival of branded goods and new technologies that promised a modern life. Some of these came straight from the West, such as German beer, Sheffield cutlery and Swedish matchsticks. Others were local creations, for example Double Pearl toothpaste in China or Kaiser Beer, a Japanese lager that tried to cash in on the popular preference for fermented German-style beer over flat English ale.

Modern consumer culture had its greatest reception in Japan. Shops, restaurants and accessories such as combs and fans were already widespread in eighteenth-century Edo. Innovation gathered pace after Commodore Perry's opening of Japan in 1854 set in motion a revolution in transport and communication. New styles began to circulate faster and wider. The Japanese state's drive to modernize was accompanied by a push to reform lifestyle. Japan picked the best of the West: American baseball and German beer. The fascination with the German model of industrial power and military might in the 1890s and 1900s left its mark on Japanese tastebuds. Army officers, students and businessmen returned from Berlin with a thirst for lager. To be modern one had to drink as well as think like a German: a potent mix. In Kyoto, university professors campaigned for beer on tap. When the members of the 'Berlin Beer Association' gathered in Tokyo, they each reportedly downed three litres: impressive even by German standards.[8]

Western goods and tastes, however, were rarely imported wholesale. They were adapted to fit indigenous fashions and habits. Modernity was made on the ground. The kimono, for example, had undergone its first modern customization in the eighteenth century with the addition of wide sashes (obi). By 1900, silk-cotton mixes added new fabrics, and light shawls and overcoats started to be worn on top. In the inter-war years, some women added fox-fur collars to their kimonos. Others converted their unused ones into Western-style clothing. Male clerks put on Western-style suits but naturalized them with pins and other accessories; once home, many swapped back into Japanese clothes. Western products such as soap and aspirin became household articles, as did curry-rice and other imported hybrid foods. By the 1920s, department stores, Western-style restaurants, beer halls and baseball parks were well established.

We must not exaggerate the transformation. It was piecemeal and patchy, by class as well as region. 'Modern lifestyle' was more often talked about than acted out. In 1925, Kon Wajiro, an architecture professor, surveyed hundreds of women in the Ginza entertainment district and found that a mere handful wore Western dress. The 'flapper' was largely a figment of the imagination. In the rural north, most people had barely any possessions, let alone foreign ones; they even lacked a futon to sleep on. Nonetheless, between 1904 and 1939, personal consumption expenditure grew by 2–3 per cent a year, well short of the 8 per cent in the 1950s–'60s but perfectly respectable for its time. These percentage points translated into more meat on the table and a more varied, higher quality diet all-round. White rice, once an urban luxury, started to be a common necessity, served three times a day. There was more discretionary spending on alcohol, sweets, furniture and entertainment, in dance halls and in cinemas. The pocket watch ceased to be a collector's item, imported from Switzerland, and became a popular accessory, mass-produced in Japan by Seikosha and the Osaka Watch Company. By the end of the 1930s, a radio played in a third of Japanese homes and the share of food in the household budget had fallen below the 50 per cent benchmark. These changes reached beyond the professional elite. In 1927, statisticians found that clerks and workers alike spent 7 per cent of their earnings on alcohol, tobacco and sweets, another 11 per cent on recreation and parties. Workers, as well as Kyoto professors, could afford to drink beer rather than sake.[9]

Across Asia, change was most visible in big cities like Tokyo and Hong Kong, and on Shanghai's Nanking Road. Neon lights and dance hostesses made Shanghai the Paris of the East. The icon of style and confidence was the 'modern woman', celebrated in novels, movies and on poster calendars (see Plate 48).[10] Eileen Chang, the author of *Love in a Fallen City* (1944), spent the money from her first commission on lipstick.

By the inter-war years, drops of this urban consumer culture were trickling through to provincial towns and the surrounding countryside. In the Punjab, in India, steel-plated cutlery from Solingen (Germany) carried greater prestige than local knives, a bar of Pears more than home-boiled *desi* soap.[11] In Sichuan, China, itinerant traders peddled Japanese mirrors and Austrian enamelware. Farmers started to wear Western-style suits, leather shoes and hats.[12] Olga Lang, who observed China on the eve of Mao's revolution, felt that the countryside was undergoing momentous change. Rich peasants had 'clocks and watches,

wash with Western-style soaps, [and] dry themselves with Turkish towels'. Photographs and calendars of branded goods looked down from
the walls. In the homes of landlords, 'one can find foreign mirrors,
razors and hair clippers and sometimes even battery radios.'[13] Everyone
wore galoshes. Often Western goods were turned to local use, such as
the ubiquitous cans of Standard Oil that were converted into buckets,
stoves and roofing material. In the vanguard were cosmetics, drugs and
hygienic products. The face cream White Snow (Baixue) and Peacock
toothpowder promised health and beauty to rural as well as urban consumers. In China, this cosmetic revolution was facilitated by the
1911 revolution, which did away with sumptuary laws forbidding
make-up. The phenomenon, however, was a general one, reflecting the
pull of a modern ideal of consumption that combined personal hygiene
and self-fashioning with a promise of rational efficiency. Peasants, too,
were entitled to a bar of soap and a touch of rouge. By the 1930s, the
dream of capturing *400 Million Customers* for Western merchandise
in China was born.[14]

Part of the confusion about what happened in the transition from
traditional to modern consumer societies stems from a simple misunderstanding. Traditional consumers are presumed to be frugal, meeting
their fixed, basic needs and saving a penny for a rainy day. Their modern successors, by contrast, are imagined to have unlimited wants and
to compulsively spend their additional income and future earnings (via
credit) on more and more stuff. In the words of one eminent sociologist, 'only the modern consumer typically' uses 'surplus income to
satisfy new wants ... the traditional consumer being more inclined
either to save or to translate his extra wealth into leisure', that is, to
work less.[15] This is a neat contrast that can be traced back to the
Enlightenment belief that material desires rouse people out of lazy
self-sufficiency. It has led scholars to focus their attention on how
people have been coaxed out of their modest world of frugality on to a
hamster wheel of getting and spending (and debt). But we have already
seen that it is not necessary to have surplus income to have expanding
wants. In the late eighteenth century, ordinary Britons were pinched by
declining wages yet bought more goods; they simply worked longer.
The Asian experience in the twentieth century affords further insights
into just how misleading this model is for understanding how people
came to consume more.

How 'traditional' were Asian consumers before the miracle years?
A 1934 survey gives a fascinating snapshot of the everyday lives of

Shanghai labourers.[16] Their pay and material conditions were as different as day and night from those of more affluent workers in the United States. Labourers in Shanghai spent 53 per cent of their wages on food, compared to Americans' 38 per cent. Many lived on the edge of hunger. And yet they devoted a quarter of their earnings to 'miscellaneous' items, the same as their American comrades, and far more than workers in London, Paris and Berlin. 'Miscellaneous' was a catch-all category to cover everything that was not food, housing and clothes. Amongst Shanghai labourers, the average family spent $112 a year on it. The biggest items were wine and cigarettes ($19) and gifts and presents ($10). Religious offerings ate up another $5, sanitary and beauty items $8, including hair-dressing and tooth-powder. A further $2.40 went on the theatre and gambling. It was the distribution of these expenses that struck social reformers in their fight against 'superstitious practices' as so irrational. Shanghai labourers starved themselves rather than cut back on weddings and funerals. Yet they were no longer 'traditional' either. Instead of working less or saving for a rainy day, additional earnings were spent on wine, cigarettes and entertainment. Together, the demands of the old and the temptations of the new pulled these labourers deeper and deeper into debt. None of them lived within their means. The average family paid $8 interest to pawnbrokers and credit sharks. In short, they lived a mixed life as customary and modern consumers.

And customary and new spending habits could spiral upwards together. This seems to have been especially true in rural areas, where life was improving, as in the 1920s in the Punjab, India's granary. In the course of his work as registrar of co-operative societies, Malcolm Darling, the Eton-educated son of an Anglican clergyman, met 10,000 Punjabi peasants. He recorded how village life was 'stirring with a new spirit'. Everywhere life was getting better. Comforts were on the rise, and so were aspirations. In the canal colonies in Western Punjab, golden ornaments were taking the place of silver. 'In the old days . . . even among the well-to-do, many women were glad enough to get their husbands' cast-off shoes. Now some are not content till they can trip about in the *zenana* [the inner apartment of a Muslim home] in a pair of fancy slippers.' Only a generation ago, people did not own a shirt. Now almost everyone wore 'some machine-made cloth, and all boast shirt, waistcoat, chaddar and coat. In the old days men had to be content with two meals a day; now they have three. The thatched huts of their fathers . . . are replaced by clean, mud-plastered houses.'[17] A wedding used to cost Rs50, Darling noted. Now it was not uncommon to spend Rs3,000 on the celebration and another Rs2,000 on jewels.

Rather than seeing a sharp break between 'traditional' and 'modern' consumers, one cannot but be struck by the links between the two. Personal possessions and comforts surged alongside spending on communal festivities and rituals. The group driving the process was the Rajput, proud members of an old warrior tribe, who had suffered a decline in status. Conspicuous consumption was a way to reassert their *izzat* (social standing). They made the most of the new cheap credit from America and the Far East; in central Punjab, the interest rate was 6–12 per cent, low by local standards. Whereas in Shanghai debt was a sign of poverty, in the Punjab it was a mark of rising aspirations. The Punjabi peasant did not start to consume more because he earned surplus income. Rather, the multiplication of wants was fuelled by easy credit and status competition. In the pursuit of better homes and bigger weddings, many peasants ended up pledging their land to creditors. The Punjabi peasant of the 1920s was closer to the over-indebted American of the 2000s than to any 'traditional' consumer.

Japan pioneered a new model: save and spend. Looking back at the twentieth century, learning to save was probably as important for the global rise in consumption as learning to want more. It was vital for the Japanese miracle after 1955 and that of Korea and Singapore from the 1970s. Saving generated the investment necessary for industrial development.

The foundations were laid in the decades before the Second World War. Japan had already established postal savings banks in 1875, copied from the British. In the inter-war years, savings promotion grew into an ambitious programme to reform people's lifestyle, both in Japan and in its Korean colony. Stop wasting money on luxurious festivities, housewives were told, and instead keep an account book, plan ahead, prioritize expenses on domestic comforts and conveniences, and save for the future. At the same time, retailers and manufacturers introduced instalment plans to ease purchases. In the 1930s, these accounted for almost 10 per cent of all sales. Japan was developing into an 'instalment plan nation', in the words of one historian.[18] But it was also turning into a super-saver. Consumption was fine, as long as it was 'rational', the result of personal discipline and financial foresight.

Saving was not genetic – the savings rate had been low in the 1920s – but the product of history and policy.[19] In the space of twenty years (1955–75), the household savings rate rocketed from 11 per cent to

23 per cent. In part, Japanese families were saving more because their incomes were growing faster than they could spend them; in part, because the war had destroyed homes and assets and they had to save up from scratch. But they were also subject to considerable moral pressure by the government in collaboration with business, media and civic groups. A Central Council for Savings Promotion started work in 1952, funded by the Bank of Japan. People had barely emerged from the rubble of war when they were warned against 'excesses of consumption'. Children's banks were set up, and women ran model savings groups in their neighbourhoods, subsidized by the state. Before the war, the 'life improvement' campaign had focused on eradicating old customs. After the war, that energy was directed towards promoting Japanese products.

In Western Europe, the eighteenth century had normalized 'luxury'. By stressing the 'innocent' and 'modest' nature of comforts and conveniences, it took the sting out of moral critiques of excess. In post-war Japan, denunciations of 'luxury' returned with a vengeance but at the same time there were national campaigns to promote the latest comforts and technologies. In the 1960s, while Japan still suffered from trade deficits, foreign products were the subject of anti-luxury campaigns. For late modernizers, nationalism offered a moral script that would have far greater consequences than for earlier consumer-patriots such as the American revolutionaries of the 1760s–'70s. Buying national had the full backing of the state. From 1958, the Japan Consumers Association set out to promote 'virtuous consumption' (*shōhi wa bitoku*), which meant buying a Japanese TV. Tellingly, the association was the child of the Japan Productivity Centre and MITI (Ministry of International Trade and Industry). Its *raison d'être* was to encourage demand. Similar campaigns followed in South Korea, which inherited Japan's institutions, and also managed to double its savings rate in the 1970s–'80s. Here, the crusade for a 'wholesome consumer lifestyle' received an additional boost from Korean Presbyterians troubled by materialist excess and moral corruption.

Savings and national product campaigns were not a uniquely Asian phenomenon, of course. Nor was the exhortation for the consumer to be a patriotic shopper. In Germany and Austria, the consumer was mobilized during the First World War to save vital resources. From Egypt to China, nationalist protesters had burnt the clothes of their imperial masters in the inter-war years. It was the scale that was new in Japan and Korea. They were the first to turn saving and consumption into a sustained strategy of state-led development in peacetime. In Europe, significantly, it was late modernizers such as Finland, which followed a similar path in the 1960s, using 'target' saving to tap wages and direct discretionary spending into TVs and washing machines.[20]

Saving and consumption were nationalist pistons of growth, channelling precious capital from private households to Japanese firms. By 1960, every other Japanese home owned a TV and a washing machine. Most of them were bought on instalment. Domestic consumer demand was far more significant for Japan's growth than is sometimes realized in models of export-driven development; exports contributed only 11 per cent to Japan's GDP, half the figure in Western Europe during its miracle years.

Generating such demand for consumer goods was not easy. In 1955, a television cost ¥140,000, almost as much as a modest house in one of the big cities. War and poverty had scarred the country, and most Japanese suffered from poor nutrition and bad housing. Yet, five years later, almost every second Japanese household had its own TV. The speed of adoption was the result of push and pull factors. Families had more money to spend, as incomes rose and taxes fell. Equally important was the idea of a 'bright life' (akurai seikatsu). The big manufacturers worked hand in glove with electricity companies to show how electric goods were the 'Key to Happiness', as one series of exhibitions was called in 1960. Buying consumer durables, they explained, was rational and saved families money and time. A housewife washing her laundry in a wooden tub consumed one third more calories than did her neighbour with an electric machine. Any saving was illusory, since she needed to spend more on food, adverts explained. Giving wives greater leisure time was, moreover, a mark of civilization. In these years, advertising budgets rose fifteen-fold. Matsushita Electric spent a whopping 9 per cent of its sales on adverts and, like other companies, set up its own instalment loan subsidiary. In 1960, it was routine for a family to devote 10 per cent of its budget to repaying such loans.

These corporate persuaders would have been far less successful without two influential supporters: women's groups and sumo wrestlers. Local demonstrations of white goods – sometimes accompanied by free hand-outs of light bulbs and smaller articles – were often conducted under the auspices of women's organizations. During and after the war they had been leading the fight against inflation and black markets. Now they helped to normalize consumption as the enemy of waste. Electric rice cookers were justified as functional rather than frivolous. For the TV set, it was love of sport that clinched the deal. Wrestling attracted huge crowds to public screens and travelling TV-cinemas. In the 1957 film *Ohayo* (*Good Morning*), two boys from a lower-middle-class family go on a silent strike to force their parents to buy a set so they can watch sumo wrestling. In real families, the entertainment of some was funded by the thrift of others. As with the nation, so with families: purchases were aided by a culture of caring, filial duty and sacrifice. Rather than spending it on herself, Hanada Mitsue put aside some of her modest salary, month after month, so that her ailing father could watch his beloved sumo on a discounted TV set: 'I felt it would be such a pleasure for him to watch it at home.'[21]

Among the new technologies, television was the most revolutionary because it transmitted ideas of a new lifestyle to communities separated by distance and custom. This much is obvious. The rapid penetration of rural life by consumer culture is unthinkable without the box. What has been far less appreciated is the role of the state in making rural communities more receptive to consumer culture in the first place. In short, we need to acknowledge the state (as well as the market) as an architect of the contemporary world of goods. This is true for India as well as China under and immediately after Mao, albeit in different ways and sometimes with unintended consequences.

In the Indian countryside, goods were carried by three waves: family planning, the green revolution and electrification. Kerala in the south of India is well known today as a model of high literacy and social equality. Basic needs, however, were secured by creating new wants. The small family unit was integral to development and reformers appealed to parents' material aspirations to create it, putting into practice what the Reverend Malthus had first dared to think a century and a half earlier. At local camps in the 1960s and '70s, the Family Planning Programme dangled consumer goods in front of the rural poor to show what responsible parenting held in store for them. They handed out free wristwatches, radios and stainless-steel pots. In a prize-winning essay, a woman described 'The Family I Dream of' through its possessions: a radio, an electric fan and iron, a pressure cooker and a dressing table. What had been luxuries of the few would be within the reach of the many, with the help of self-restraint and sterilization.[22] Ironically, it was often the extended family that delivered fridges and cars to the lucky few, brought back by 'Gulf workers' on their visits home.[23] A small family was good; a big family with a cousin in Kuwait even better.

Consumer goods had been sold in the Indian countryside since the late nineteenth century. By the 1950s, rich farmers earned enough to spend almost 40 per cent of their income on clothes, furniture, festivities, entertainment and other items not related to food and housing. But these were concentrated in the north, and even here most peasants ate cereals and little else. In poorer Orissa and West Bengal, the current of goods dwindled to a trickle. Most Indians lived on the edge of starvation, their lives untouched by consumer culture. In 1959, half of rural India survived on the cereals they had grown themselves, although in the big cities only 2 per cent of food was home-grown.[24] The droughts of 1965 and 1966 took a terrible toll.

It was the 'green revolution', from the late 1960s, which freed India from dependence on food aid and opened the floodgates to new tastes, habits and lifestyles. State assistance – in the form of price supports, tariffs and high-yielding seed varieties from Mexico – swelled the ranks of peasant consumers; in the course of the 1970s and '80s, the poverty share dropped from over 60 per cent to below 40 per cent.[25] In a predominantly rural society, this state-led development was arguably as crucial to the breakthrough of consumption as the liberal reforms after 1991. Self-sufficient peasants turned into aspiring consumers. They began to buy cooking oil, tea and sugar, drink more milk and eat more meat, put on ready-made clothes and wash their hair with shampoo, sold in little sachets for Rs1. Already in 1989, on the eve of the liberal reform era, people in the countryside bought over 70 per cent of the radios, bicycles, shoes and wristwatches sold in India. Every second tape recorder, ceiling fan, package of biscuits and bar of soap was sold to a rural family.[26]

The Indian village was changing. The overall number of possessions, however, remained modest. Most families had only two or three basic products, such as a radio, a fan and a watch, not more – but the upward trend was unmistakable. More open markets after 1991 accelerated it. Greater urban demand translated in the countryside into more sales, more investment and more spending power. By 2001, for example, in Datia, a district in Madhya Pradesh in central India, 35 per cent of households owned a TV, 20 per cent a radio, 10 per cent a car, another 10 per cent a scooter. At the same time as consumer goods were narrowing the gap between city and country, they sharpened the visible divide between the haves and the have-nots in rural society. Half the households in rural Datia owned neither a radio nor a TV, let alone a motor vehicle.[27] In the Indian village, two nations now lived side by side.

The rural consumer revolution had two allies: banks and electricity. Indeed, it was the uneven expansion of these two which in no small part explains the uneven advance of goods. We noted earlier that easy credit stimulated conspicuous consumption in the Punjab a century ago. The recent expansion of the banking network in South Asia has multiplied these effects. In India alone, almost 300,000 branches of postal, co-operative and rural commercial banks opened their doors in the 1980s–'90s. Those with land and assets were able to take out credit more cheaply. For the many without, the 'tyranny of the collateral' meant they continued to live from hand to mouth, in a daily struggle for cash, at the mercy of loan sharks, without access to either savings or loans to buy big ticket items.[28]

The electric charge has been no less powerful. In less than a decade (1998–2006), the number of Indian homes with electricity went up by a half, to 120 million. In 2005, households overtook industry as the biggest consumer of electricity. Much of this is urban air-conditioners and fridges. A family in West Bengal uses only a quarter of the electricity of a family in Delhi. Many villages in the south are still waiting for the current to arrive. That Indian states count villages as electrified once 10 per cent of homes are connected speaks volumes.[29] These qualifications notwithstanding, the effects of electrification on rural life have been enormous. They are illuminated by developments in Bangladesh.[30] Between 1978 and 2001, the number of rural homes with electricity has increased by more than a thousand times, the combined effort of local co-operatives and international development aid. The initial rationale was to help farmers run irrigation pumps. The repercussions for domestic life turned out to be as profound. Once connected, rural households took on urban habits. They saved more than their neighbours, invested more in the education of their children and bought more consumer goods. Electric lights and fans meant that families spent more time together in the home, able to study and work after sunset, and to relax. TVs and cassette players entertained and at the same time whetted a curiosity for the world outside. They spread ideas of modern life and personal hygiene which showed in the growing use of soap and sanitary latrines. Rural shops with electricity started to install fridges and carry a greater assortment of goods, in turn raising expectations of variety and choice. None of this was new in principle. Manufacturers and energy companies had long advertised electricity's civilizing force in the United States, Japan and Europe. Electricity was integral to 'life improvement', as the Japanese called it. But these were societies that prided themselves on leading the race to modernity. It was news in a poor country that modern history had seemingly forgotten. Development aid and televisions arrived together, as international agencies picked up the baton in the race to modernize the home.

If anything, progress in the countryside was even more spectacular in China after Mao. Between 1979 – when peasants were once again allowed to sell in the market – and 1984 the rural poor shrank by half. Consumption doubled.[31] Rural demand and private entrepreneurship drove the first phase of China's consumer revolution. It was only in the 1990s that the state seized control of growth, prioritized urbanization and cut welfare – breaking the 'iron rice bowl' and a life of guaranteed security. Under Mao, aspirations had centred on the 'four musts': a bicycle, a radio, a watch and a sewing machine. Under Deng Xiaoping, after 1979, they were superseded by the 'eight BIGS': a colour TV, a fridge, a hi-fi, a camera, a motorbike, an electric fan, a washing machine and furniture. Most rural households managed at least five or six, notwithstanding the shift to urban growth and the rise in inequality since the 1990s. By 2007, 94 per cent of rural households had a colour TV, half had a motorbike and a washing machine and a fifth owned a fridge.[32]

Rising disposable income made these purchases possible, but where did the desire come from? Behind these purchases lies a longer history of rising aspirations and private materialism. In 1936, Hsiao-Tung Fei observed country life in the Yangzi Valley and was struck by the pervasive 'cultural control on consumption':

> To be content with simple living is a part of early education. Extravagance is prevented by sanctions. A child making preferences in food or clothes will be scorned and beaten . . . If a mother lets her child develop special tastes in food, she will be criticized as indulging her child. Even rich parents will not put good and costly clothes on their children, for doing so would induce the evil spirits to make trouble.[33]

Except for weddings and other ceremonies, thrift ruled. 'Throwing away anything which has not been properly used will offend heaven, whose representative is the kitchen god . . . Clothes are used by generations, until they are worn out.' Consumption was a matter for the extended family (*jia*), not the individual. It was a world apart from today's 'little emperors', spoilt with toys, cash and Western fast food. Yet change was already on the horizon. Olga Lang sensed the first stirrings in the 1940s. The admonition not to spoil a child was still strong, as was severe punishment until the age of fifteen. But there were also signs that children were becoming less obedient and developing a sense of rights as well as duties. 'Many working boys and girls,' she noted, 'are beginning to regard their earnings as their own and not as the property of their families.' The change was especially noticeable among students. Yes, they all wanted to advance peace and happiness and make 'great contributions to society and the nation', but many now combined these altruistic goals with a desire for 'comfort in my own clothing, food and housing'.[34] The crucial words were 'my own'.

Ironically, Mao was the handmaiden of consumerism. In hard numbers, of course, Mao's policies were the exact opposite. In the 1960s and '70s, the earnings from growth were poured into investment, not consumption. The Mao suit and plain living were de rigueur. At the same time, Mao struck at the family as an outdated feudal institution. Women and youth were mobilized against their elders and given a whole new sense of self. The aim was to transfer their allegiance from their husbands and fathers to the collective. When the collectives started to break up in the 1970s, however, it left behind a generation with a radical sense of individual autonomy. Mao thus accomplished a cultural revolution, though not the one he had intended. If saving was state directed in Japan, so was individualization in China.

Yunxiang Yan, a farmer turned anthropologist who now teaches at the University of California in Los Angeles, lived in Xiajia village in Heilongjiang province in China's north-east in the 1970s and has returned many times since. Under Mao, sociability and entertainment were collective. During the collective era (1956–80), villages and towns had brigades with their own performance troupes, dance parades, basketball tournaments and radio broadcasts; performers were paid by the collectives. At the same time, the revolution fostered a culture of private intimacy. Marriage ceased to be about what parents dictated and became instead about two people in love. Romance and courtship were on the rise in the 1950s–'60s, premarital sex normal by the 1970s. While formally arranged marriages continued, now the couple had often picked each other before getting their families involved. As, over the course of life, a major portion of consumption is concentrated in the wedding through bridewealth, gifts and ceremonies, the romantic revolution had major repercussions for consumer culture. Young women suddenly acquired a voice and choice. Paternalism gave way to individualism. Instead of having presents arranged by and for their parents, by the early 1970s couples were writing their own gift lists.

For brides and grooms, the shopping trip to the provincial capital Harbin became a ritual where they bought their wedding clothes and personal items, sat for professional engagement photos and enjoyed a couple of nights alone in a hotel.

Notwithstanding public policy, bridewealth has been on the rise in the last two generations. Traditionally, it fulfilled the obligations of a groom's family to the bride's kin. Now it increasingly serves private wants – a TV, furniture or, more lately, a washing machine and a car, things that a couple wanted to start out life together. Young people were pressing their parents for more pocket money and, if they did not get enough, resorted to petty theft to obtain what they felt ought to be theirs. The sense of individualism was reflected in the home. By the 1970s, new homes were built to offer some private space on the top floor. Bedrooms became separated from the living room. A decade later, children gained their own room. Families started to watch their preferred programmes in separate rooms on separate TV sets. Life was about 'being able to do what you want' (*xiang gansha jiu gansha*), as villagers put it.[35]

The search for contrasts between 'East' and 'West' naturally leads to the discovery of unique characteristics. But there are intriguing parallels between them as well as differences. One shared pattern has been the asymmetrical take-up of consumer technologies. In 1960s Japan, families bought a TV but made do without their own flush toilet. This was not miles away from the story in many poor homes in British cities in the 1950s, nor so different from Americans' preference for soft furniture and crystal glasses over sanitation and insulation in the late eighteenth century that we encountered earlier.[36] Indian homes today enjoy many domestic comforts while their cities lack constant water and a sewage system.[37] But so did many French cities a century ago. For rural Europeans in the 1950s and '60s, viewing television in a crowd in a country bar was equally the first step on the road to a private set, although Italians preferred game shows with big prizes to big men in loincloths. Again, that many cosmetic items sold once they were marketed in little sachets does not reflect some peculiarly Indian trait.[38] Chocolates and other small luxuries were sold in similarly small packets in the first vending machines in early-twentieth-century Europe. These are characteristics of many emerging mass markets where the poor are enjoying rising but limited discretionary spending.

It would be equally misleading, however, to conclude that parallels demonstrate convergence. Retailing remains hugely diverse. European chains have had mixed success in Asia and had to adapt to high local expectations of customer service. In 2010, the French supermarket chain Carrefour opened a store in Haikou with a sales area of 6,000 square metres and thirty cashiers. Fourteen years later, it had 236 hypermarkets in the 'middle kingdom', but this is in a country with 1.3 billion customers. Imagine a dozen of these stores in the whole of France – hardly a sign of dominance.[39] Shopping habits continue to diverge. A Chinese person will spend nine hours a week shopping here and there, talking to neighbours and family members along the way; an American picks up all the groceries in a single pit stop. A tiny 10 per cent of China's beer market is in foreign hands. Local retailers have stepped up their game. In India, the number of small traditional family stalls has increased since the reform period. In Delhi, thousands flock to Globus, Lifestyle and other glitzy malls in Gurgaon on the weekend, while millions still get what they need from small shops such as the Fancy Boot House, Self Choice – the Flavour of Fashion, Kadrix & Sons Jewellers, the sexologist (Gold medallist), and the countless other food stalls, pan sellers and electronic and household goods stores in Sangam Vihar and other local markets that continue for miles off major thoroughfares like M. B. Road (see Plate 49). In 2012, the government lowered investment barriers to attract foreign chains. So far, not many have set up shop.

Consumption has evolved into distinct national types in Asia. One major difference between the early phase of mass consumption in Japan (1955–73) and that in China since 1979 was that Japan managed growth with equality while China has become one of the most unequal societies on the planet. In Singapore, the state engineered equality by making everyone a home owner, channelling rising incomes into property through a system of compulsory saving funds that could be withdrawn only to buy a house. Here again consumption was shaped by the state.

Japan's economic crisis in 1989–90 set off a new split between savers and spenders. In the 'lost decade' of the 1990s, equality gave way to *kakusa shakai*, a society of disparities. To boost demand, Japan and Korea switched from promoting saving to flaunting credit. Credit-card spending ballooned; savings plummeted. By 2000, a quarter of all purchases were paid for with plastic in Japan. Korea even offered a tax rebate on purchases made by credit card. In Korea, household debt as a share of GDP came to rival that in the USA. Thousands of Japanese committed suicide because of indebtedness. By 2003, the household saving rate in Japan had dropped to 6 per cent, in Korea to 3 per cent, well below the respectable 11 per cent of France, Germany and Italy.[40] So much for the caricature that Asians save and Westerners spend. Meanwhile, fast-growing India and China just kept saving.

The Asian crisis of 1989 left behind a curious paradox. It was the countries hardest hit that were forced to be more consumer friendly. In addition to easier credit, Japan pursued 'price destruction' (*kakaku hakkai*) by slashing the cost of food and breaking the hold of small retailers. Discounters opened their doors; shopping hours became more convenient. Just as they were tightening their belts, Japanese consumers came to enjoy unprecedented choice and cheapness.[41] In booming China, by contrast, consumption became less important. While the cake has been getting bigger, the slice reaching the people has been getting smaller. Yes, consumption doubled in the 1990s, but saving tripled, to an official 23 per cent. The engine pulling the Chinese economy is investment, not consumption – in contrast to India, where household savings are equally high but investment is low. Naturally, 1.3 billion people buy a lot, but in 2005 the average Chinese still spent less than the average Albanian or Sudanese.[42] Personal loans remain a tiny fraction of bank lending when compared to other emerging nations. A Brazilian, for example, carries four times as much consumer debt. We could continue with facts and figures, but the point has been made. There are probably few people further removed today from the popular image of the spendthrift consumer than the Chinese.

The reason is simple, and leads us back to the centrality of the state. When the Communist party began to cut the state workforce and slash welfare services after 1997, it shifted the burden to private households. Health, education and housing – once free – now cost money and worry. A growing chunk of 'private consumption' is absorbed by these three. It is not uncommon for a businessman to spend a quarter of his earnings on the education of his children.[43] On top, young couples face the so-called 4–2–1 phenomenon, with four parents to look after and only one child of their own to help them in the future. It encourages saving. Relatively speaking, buying stuff here and now is less important than planning for the future.

In 2004, China's Premier Wen Jiabo announced that domestic demand had to become the basis of China's development. This has been easier said than done, and until wages, public health and education receive a major boost it is difficult to see how it will happen; health insurance (since

2007) has so far been rudimentary. As we shall see in Part Two, private affluence in the West since the 1950s was helped by 'public consumption', with increased state spending on housing, welfare and leisure. How China will accomplish the former without the latter is unclear. Today, the Middle Kingdom remains as far removed from the kind of consumer society exemplified by the United States as from Europe and Japan. In the course of the last decade, the contribution of consumption (what households spend on goods and services) to GDP has fallen from 42 per cent to below 35 per cent, although official statistics downplay the extra spending on the home.[44] In the USA, it is double that. The rest of Asia stands around 50 per cent, pretty normal by the standards of other developed countries. The Chinese are simply not consumerist, if 'consumerism' is defined as a culture of instant gratification where private spending drives the economy and dominates everyday life.

TRADITIONAL MODERN

These aggregate developments give an impression of the changing terrain of consumption. They do not tell us how Asians experienced it. In the final analysis, consumption is about practices and identities, about doing and belonging. Having a few more yen, yuan or rupees to spend is one thing. How greater spending affects lifestyle and belonging is something else. What does it feel like being a Japanese, Chinese or Indian consumer? Have older customs, hierarchies and mentalities been swapped for a more anonymous, global consumer culture where status and identity are set by one's taste and possessions?

Across contemporary Asia, the single most talked about group has been the middle class. For national governments and foreign investors alike, the middle class has been the litmus test of success: the bigger that group, the more modern one's society. In reality, the middle class has proved difficult to pin down. Measurements have varied hugely, depending on whether 'the middle' has been defined as the statistical average, in terms of their possessions, as anyone between the starving poor and the super rich, or as a combined effect of education, income and lifestyle. In India in the 1990s, estimates ranged from 100 to 500 million people. In a 2000 survey by the Chinese Academy of Social Sciences, almost half the respondents placed themselves in the middle, even though only 3 per cent had the goods and income required to meet the official definition.[45]

Such confusion is not peculiarly Asian or new. The middle class in Brazil is equally elusive. Into the nineteenth century, Europeans used a range of competing categories such as rank, sort, degree and order. The British 'middling sort' found its voice as the 'middle class' only in the course of the struggle over the vote, when it presented itself as the embodiment of constitutional balance and social stability. What is new in Asia since the 1980s is how talk of a new middle class has mainly emanated from governments and corporations, not from a political movement. In China, the very term remains tainted by association with Maoist attacks on the bourgeoisie. Officials prefer to speak more narrowly of a 'middle income group' or 'newly propertied middle strata' (xinzhongchan jieceng). These are economic categories that lack the sense of a shared identity and lifestyle discernible in nineteenth-century Europe. In 1900 Paris, members of the bourgeoisie enjoyed the same culture of consumption, with similar tastes in possessions and in leisure pursuits such as collecting, painting and theatre-going. In 2000 Shanghai, by contrast, researchers found that professionals with almost identical income, education and occupation led vastly different lifestyles.[46]

In a country where power resides in the Communist Party, status is achieved through proximity to that Party, which secures access to land and assets; not through conspicuous consumption. Sociologically as much as economically, then, China is not a consumer society in the classic sense. Everyone has more or less the same stuff. Dramatic inequalities are obscured by the fact that rich and poor alike have TVs.[47] For centuries, over-consumption has been blamed on social emulation and 'keeping up with the Joneses'. Contemporary China ticks according to a different mechanism. It is a highly unequal society, where, ironically, there is little to gain from showing off. Excessive lifestyles have been punished by the Party. Arguably, authoritarianism has done more to check conspicuous consumption in China than appeals to simple living in the democratic West.

Looked at more closely, the middle classes are an amorphous bunch. In China in 2003, the 3-million-yuan ($120,000) millionaires were a world apart from the top 20 per cent urban households, with a disposable income of $2,000 a year. For most people in China, as in India and Asia more generally, being middle class does not mean going to the mall but living on the edge in a daily struggle to pay the bills for schools and hospitals. Most are anxious consumers on a budget.

The constraints on consumption are similarly discernible in South

Asia. Researchers followed clerks and professionals in Kolkata and in Siliguri, a regional town in Northern Bengal, between 1999 and 2006. Most enjoyed rising wages, owned a TV and a fridge. They greeted cable channels and shopping as progressive, even emancipating – 'just because I'm a woman, why do I have to be stuck at home all day cooking and cleaning? I can go out and do a bit of shopping. To go shopping is what they show on television . . . This is the symbol of the new modern woman.' At the same time, rising prices forced them to be frugal. They cut back on cinemas and restaurants, brushed their teeth with Babool instead of Colgate, and went to the library rather than the bookshop. Local sweets replaced branded snacks.[48]

Many continued to rely on gifts, loans and a bit of luck to maintain the façade of middle-class comforts, in a manner that would have been all too familiar to the great theorist of capitalism, Karl Marx. Let us take a look inside the apartment of an office worker for an advertising firm in Sri Lanka in the early 1990s. The living room had a couch, two chairs and a dining table, with a lithograph of a Burmese village scene on the wall. There was a telephone, a radio, a thirteen-year-old black-and-white 'National' TV set and an even older tape player, broken. None of these he had bought himself. The TV was a gift from a European when he still worked as a driver. The tape deck he inherited from another employer. Furniture came from friends and family. The washing machine was on temporary loan from a neighbour who was in China on study leave. The only thing he had bought himself was the set of cheap curtains. The bulk of his salary went on food, medicine for his wife and school fees for his children.[49] Market analysts have been puzzled by the tiny size of the market for second-hand goods in a poor country like India – a mere 8 per cent of radios sold in rural India were second hand.[50] It may reflect an economy of mutual support and hand-me-downs as much as a belief that new is best.

In the course of modern history, the home has been the energy cell of consumer culture. It is where comfort and convenience is generated, families store their memories and individuals shape their identities through things. What was a piecemeal transformation in the West was a revolution in China. In less than a decade, China created a nation of property-owners. By comparison, Herbert Hoover and Margaret Thatcher, the champions of home-owning democracy in the United States and Great Britain, were amateurs. In sixteen months in 1997–98, China sold off Y8 trillion of state housing – an unprecedented transfer of wealth. Most work units sold off flats to their members at

artificially low prices. The housing sale amounted to a stimulus almost
as large as that of the American New Deal in 1933.[51] If home owners
had been made to pay market value, consumer spending would have
taken a nose dive.

Privatization shifted the orientation of life from the work unit (*dan-wei*) to the home. Until the 1990s, the *danwei* was a twenty-four-hour
mini-society. Eating and playing, labour and sociability – life was
organized by and around it. Taking a trip or booking a hotel had to be
approved by the *danwei*. It distributed watches, clothes and other
rationed goods. And it assigned housing. In this system, the home was
little more than a place of shelter, and a miserable one at that. The push
to industrialize in the Great Leap Forward (1958–61) proved a big step
backwards for housing standards. Shortages in steel and cement put a
virtual halt to modern construction. Having to rely on local materials,
builders and towns in the 1960s erected simple houses made of
pressed earth-walls. The overall picture was one of acute shortage,
overcrowding and a lack of privacy. In 1985, the first general survey of
housing found that each person, on average, had less than 4 square
metres to himself. Many families cooked in corridors and shared toilets
and a tap. Two years later, the Party officially buried the ideal of collective living. 'Each unit,' the design policy laid down, 'must be a single
house not sharing an entrance with others. It should have a bedroom,
a kitchen, a bathroom and a storeroom.'[52] By 2002, nine in ten homes
in Shanghai were like this. The private family unit had won. Until then,
space had been measured by 'sleep-type'. Now, the state accepted that
a home was a place to live, not just to sleep. A home needed to have
separate spaces for recreation, sociability and study. And it needed to
grow so that the TV, kitchen range, shower and washing machine
could move in. Within a decade, urban homes had doubled in size.

The building boom gave millions a chance to escape into a private
world. Gated communities mushroomed. One thirty-three-year-old
engineer who had moved into Vanke Garden City in Shanghai explained
that 'where I grew up, my neighbours know how well I scored in my
school exams; whether my family has bought new furniture and even
what we cook for dinner. In my own apartment now, I do not have to
face nosy neighbours who query endlessly about your private life.'[53]
Millions of new apartments were sold as empty shells – without fitted
kitchen and bathroom, wiring or paint – which the proud owners then
turned into homes of their own. In 2000, residents in Shanghai spent
several years' worth of their earnings on decorating their apartment.

IKEA opened its doors in 1998. By 2006, Chinese home fabrics had reached sales of $20 billion.[54] A host of home magazines and interior-design firms started to cater to dreams of 'noble and elegant living enjoyment', be it sleek modern Italian designer sofas or 'England nostalgia' with heavy oak tables and club armchairs;[55] *Better Homes and Gardens* launched its Chinese edition in 2006.

For the last two decades, the sociologist Deborah Davis has followed dwellers and their dwellings in Chinese cities. For many, home decorating became a second job. They visited showrooms and DIY stores during their lunch break, shopped for furniture and materials after work and checked on handymen at the weekend. Many slept for months in a single room while their flat was being done up, and afterwards wondered whether they had, perhaps, not been too extravagant. Others expressed frustration at not being able to afford what glossy magazines promised. Still, overall, what Davis's interviews bring out is the genuine satisfaction of having been able to choose their private home and make it a reality. The majority of her subjects were born between 1948 and 1956. The Cultural Revolution had robbed them of their adolescence and young adulthood. They had to work in the countryside, sleep on pavements or squeeze in with another family. They had grown up without private space. Compared to these horrible memories, the frustrations of being a consumer with limited means were negligible. What mattered to them was that it was they who were in charge of designing their own privacy. Sleeping on the floor and waking up to a bad paint job were worth the sacrifice. As one bride put it, 'I had the home I wanted; the renovation made us very happy (*kaixin*).'[56] The suffering of an entire generation during the Cultural Revolution is one reason why the escalating inequalities that have come with the advance of consumer culture in China have not shaken the regime. Privacy and stability make up for relative deprivation. The question is what will happen when a new generation becomes used to private comfort and the dark memories of the 1960s recede into history.

That foreign things will corrode local identity is a fear as old as trade itself. The cross-cultural flow of things and images has exponentially increased in the modern period. This much is obvious. What is less clear is how local cultures have responded. Has the influx swept away collective identities such as caste and nation, leaving behind a 'flat world'?[57]

'Where could you find a Japan not Americanized?' the writer

Murobuse Takanobu asked as early as 1929. 'I dare to declare that America has become the world; Japan is nothing but America today.'[58] A new world order seemed to be taking shape, based not on military power but on a material civilization of goods and dreams. Such fascination with American culture was home-grown, less a Hollywood import than a tool of modernization. It intersected with an interest in the material foundations of everyday life: clothes and cinema made people. Such ideas were in part inspired by Marx and Heidegger, but in Japan they took a different direction. Rather than lamenting how modern things killed authenticity, many Japanese writers celebrated American movies, bars and the modern home as vehicles of emancipation from feudal customs. For Kon Wajirō, an early ethnographer, consumption was a source of subjectivity.[59] Instead of being told how to dress and behave, people could fashion themselves.

American things multiplied with the American occupation after the Second World War. In 1949, the *Asahi* newspaper started the comic strip 'Blondie' which gave Japanese housewives a snapshot of the American way of life. Chewing gum, jazz and, soon, rockabilly found new fans. Roppongi, the Tokyo base of the US army in the 1950s, attracted trendy Japanese youth, the *Roppongi-zoku*. Urban housing adopted a standardized Western layout, or LDK (living-dining-kitchen). On the inside, however, these foreign spaces were domesticated. Most families set up a Japanese-style room with tatami mats or built alcoves (*tokonoma*) to display antiques, flowers or a scroll. The Japanese room doubled as space for individual relaxation and for religious celebrations. It was here, in the middle of a Western-style apartment, that one still showed one's Japanese taste.

Technology, too, was redefined as Japanese. Japanese firms marketed TVs and other appliances as a fusion of tradition and modernity. A Matsushita advert in the late 1960s quoted a Japanese painter: 'the dehumanized mechanism of the West came to Japan and evolved into something suited to the warmth of human skin. This thing is the National colour television set.' Only a Japanese colour TV was able to reproduce true 'Japanese colour', adverts promised. Stereo commodes and television sets integrated Japanese design features. It was now possible to watch baseball and at the same time feel connected to the imperial past. Matsushita even dressed one of its refrigerators in teak finish and named it Kiso, after a valley in the Japanese Alps which had been Emperor Go-Daigo's stronghold in the early fourteenth century.[60]

Americanization has attracted disproportionate attention in Asian countries less because of the volume of imports than because of fears of cultural contagion.[61] After all, Singapore and its neighbours also buy plenty of Japanese goods without worrying about Nipponization. Japanese products are viewed as a useful gadget rather than an alien virus. In 1992, the Japanese television station Fuji launched *Asia Bagus!*, a Sunday-night talent show, co-produced with Singapore, Malaysia and Indonesia; Taiwan joined two years later. Every season, half a million aspiring performers threw their name in the hat in the hope of becoming the next Asian Idol. The show was hosted jointly by a Japanese and two Singaporean presenters who switched between Japanese, Malay and Mandarin.[62] Such forms of Asianization are probably more important now than Americanization. Japanese popular music has been a major export, in spite of being officially banned in South Korea until 1998. By the 1990s, the future was Japan, not America. Many pan-Asian films would include shots of Tokyo Tower to give them an air of modernity. The Korean wave since and the success of Cantopop from Hong Kong and Mandarin pop from Taiwan in the People's Republic of China reflects the growing importance of this pan-Asian circuit; K-pop (Korean pop) is nurtured by the government with a $1 billion investment fund, another example of the significant role played by states.[63] Similarly, on the Indian subcontinent, Muscat and Dubai have been at least as influential for ideas of modern life as Paris or New York. It was in the Gulf states that economic migrants from South Asia picked up air-conditioning and other new appliances and leisure habits such as dining out.

In India, the legacy of empire made for a more complicated, touchy relationship between consumption and nationalism. Empire gave consumption a bad name. Fashion, foreign goods and the desire for distinction were denounced as an imperialist scheme to keep Indians in subjugation. National identity was defined in opposition to the British empire. Since the empire flaunted its modern goods, to be a free Indian necessarily meant asceticism. The historical irony was that this anti-colonial approach continued to do the work of empire after it was officially dead, by reinforcing the idea of a two-tier world where only some were privileged to be comfortable and the rest were meant to work.

The liberal opening since 1991 has put an end to this dichotomy. Suddenly, to be modern meant to be a consumer. 'We have a great feeling for Gandhi,' one young Kerala woman of the second-rank Hindu Nair caste confessed, 'but I don't think we practise his ideas. In our family we like things from other places.'[64] There are not many left who subscribe to Gandhi's belief that the rich need to live more simply so that the poor may simply live. An IT worker put the new orthodoxy bluntly: 'I think materialism is good . . . it's pathetic the way we think. You know, "I don't need a fridge, I have a black-and-white TV." I mean, come on! That's all crap . . . Somewhere along the line, we've gone and made a virtue out of our poverty and I think it's time to stop doing that.'[65] When Hindu nationalists (BJP) rediscovered swadeshi in the late 1990s, it was pro-global as well as pro-nationalist.

If frugality has been thrown overboard it would be difficult to say the same for India-ness. Being modern in India means buying global products, not adopting a global identity. Individualism remains checked by commitments to family and community. The middle classes in Baroda, in Gujarat's 'golden corridor', for example, perform a delicate balancing act. At the same time as they buy cars, appliances and decorate their homes, they try to preserve traditional values. When they talked in 2004 about their new lifestyle, they compared it unfavourably to an idealized village community. Spending on oneself, fashion and conspicuous display were seen as a moral threat to tradition, family and status. Thus, paradoxically, while consumption has gone up in real terms, it has remained marginal to the group identity of those who do most of it. At least in Baroda, the middle classes take their cue from local ideas of moral worth and community, not from global consumer culture.[66] Elsewhere, expatriate IT workers and businessmen return to live in the motherland so that their children grow up Indian, with respect for family and customs.

Far from killing Indian identities, consumer culture has provided fresh opportunities for articulating them. Female IT workers go to their offices with traditional hairstyles and wearing a *salwar kameez*. When foreign firms entered the Indian market, after 1991, it also created a space for Indian companies to stand out by trumpeting their own distinct value. And what better marker than Indian food. 'Indian Terrain' advertised its casual cruise shirts under the headline 'I made Pizza go Tandoori', with a stylish modern Indian, coiffured with hair gel, giving his philosophy as a consumer:

> Ever heard of the Vegetable Hamburger? Or Masala Tea? Or a Tandoori Pizza? All creations inspired by my refusal to eat exactly like the rest of the world does. So the food chains read the message on the wall (or on their cash registers) and tailored a whole new menu to my taste.[67]

Class and caste were based on one's place in the system of production. Has the rise of consumption eroded them? For the Indian elite, the end of Nehru's bureaucratic 'licence raj' opened up new sources of status. Working for a foreign corporation started to carry more weight than a post in the civil service. Inevitably, liberalization prompted fears that India's elite was 'westoxicated',[68] sacrificing their national soul and concern for the poor on the altar of global materialism. In reality, IT managers and professionals are fairly conservative consumers. Their main priorities remain those of their parents: to buy a house, help the family and invest in their children's education.[69] For social status, a fancy car or flat-screen TV is no substitute for an MBA from an elite institute of technology or a foreign university. In some respects, the economic miracle has hardened inequalities between and within classes. In rural India, big landlords and rentiers have increased their share of consumption, while lowly peasants have lost out, no longer receiving subsidies and at the mercy of moneylenders. In cities, owners and managers in the retail and service sector have gained, while unskilled workers are spending proportionally less.[70]

The top positions in the professions and business continue to go to upper-caste Hindus, but there are signs that caste has softened. An anthropologist 'hanging out' with young men in Bangalore between 2001 and 2006 found that friends shared clothes, cigarettes and motorbikes, irrespective of caste or income.[71] In Uttar Pradesh, outside Delhi, it became common for Dalits, too, to brush their teeth with branded toothpaste rather than chewing on twigs from the local neem tree. Consumer goods have long been vehicles for lower castes to assert themselves, going back at least to the early twentieth century when Dalits, fortunate to acquire a bit of land, put on artificial silk saris. At the top, Brahmins began to sit down to dinner in a shirt rather than a dhoti, eat meat and drink alcohol.[72] This does not mean caste has disappeared, however. In Kerala in the 1990s, the low-caste Pulayas dressed to kill, in red satin shirts and trainers, their hair coiffed like film stars. None of it shook the caste system. The group of labourers above, the Izhavas, looked down on such displays as flashy and foolish. To them, being respectable meant spending on a house, furniture and gold jewellery.[73] Consumption continues to be about securing recognition in one's own group rather than emulating that above.

Low castes are poor, but this does not mean they all live alike. Some consume more than others. In 1993, the Labour Bureau investigated the living conditions of 'scheduled castes workers' in Indore. Families making shoes, it found, ate more meat and drank more milk than sweepers and scavengers, probably because working with leather had lowered a ritual resistance to animal products. Yet sweepers and scavengers had more possessions. Many owned a TV, an electric fan, a bicycle and a wristwatch; several had a sewing machine, a record player and a fridge; one even a camera. By contrast, the homes of shoemakers were barren.[74]

Upper-caste members who find themselves at the bottom of the income scale today are almost ten times as likely to own a TV, a fridge and a car as equally poor, lower-caste Indians. Caste, then, matters, but not on its own. It is connected to a material divide between town and country: upper castes are more likely to live in cities and thus are relatively better off to begin with.[75] Among lower-caste members who have done well and moved to the city, the ownership of TVs and other appliances is closer to that of higher castes. Significantly, it is in the poorest regions where the gulf between castes is highest.

So much of Western commentary equates consumerism with individualism that spending on the family deserves special emphasis. In India, the nuclear family was already the norm before the recent boom, and yet rupees continue to be showered on the extended family. A century of social reformers' denunciations of lavish weddings and funerals have fallen on deaf ears. Arguably, spending on family and customs has increased with the rise of consumer culture, not diminished. In 1994, the film *Hum Aapke Hain Koun ...!* (*Who am I to You ...!*), took India by storm with a drama that rolled family, love and home comfort into one. In this lifestyle romance, the new kitchen and opulent interior are as important as the fashionably dressed stars. Prem, the heart-throb played by Salman Khan, even has a dog, Tuffy, the ultimate sign of a middle-class lifestyle. What sealed its success at the box office was that the love story was framed by a harmonious extended family, including nephews, distant relatives and happy arranged marriages. For audiences, the film proved that it was possible to have more stuff and stay true to the large family ideal.[76] In real life, love and weddings continue to be demonstrations of family loyalty and reciprocity. Dowries, wedding festivities and gifts have soared in value. An Indian wedding outfit can cost as much as a car. Most Indian brides and grooms today marry for love. Yet they would rather wait and not marry than lose their parents' approval; among software engineers, two thirds of marriages are still formally arranged, although the couple is already romantically attached.

Across Asia, the family continues to shape consumption patterns. The washing machines for cousins, the school fees and other remittances sent home by migrant workers all indicate where the priorities lie: with family obligations, not personal luxury. It is the orientation of family life – more than family ties as such – that changed once consumer durables crossed the threshold. The sociologist Ronald Dore lived in a Tokyo ward in 1951 and captured a society in transition. 'Is there any article for use in the home,' he asked housewives, 'which you often think to yourself you would like to have if only you could afford it?' His respondents were divided. Almost half answered more clothing or better furniture. A slightly larger group wanted a washing machine, a vacuum cleaner, a stereo or toaster. The responses reflected the partial breakdown of an older status system. In the past, the most treasured objects had been a way to assert status. Peasants would put on their finest clothes and lay out their best china for special festivities to impress their peer group. Then, when the party was over, it was back to rags and cracked cups. The first group of Dore's Tokyo housewives still reflected that mentality. They desired more of the same and had their eyes on higher-quality clothes. It was normal to sacrifice family comfort to impress others. Parents stinted on food so that their sons had pocket money to keep up with the Joneses. It was among the second group that a new orientation was shining through. Here aspirations centred on novelties that first and foremost promised satisfaction to the family, through entertainment, greater comfort and saving time and effort. In the growing cities, community ties were looser, and this, Dore explained, made 'status and hence the prestige attach[ed] to material possessions of lesser importance'.[77] Conspicuous consumption did not die, but it was now harnessed to the welfare of the family through the purchase of an electric fan, a TV and other new appliances that could be shown with pride to guests and friends.

In Japan from the 1950s onwards, greater consumption was legitimized by two rather different ideals: national strength and social equality. Consuming was fine as long as shoppers did not forget the local peasants, small retailers and manufacturers who belonged to the same nation. Paying a bit more for Japanese rice was the price of national solidarity. At the same time, affluence generated new worries. In the 1970s, Japan looked itself in the mirror and wondered about its 'lifestyle'. In annual surveys, the Prime Minister's office asked people 'Do you feel your lifestyle has improved?' In 1974, the answer turned negative, and has stayed negative since.[78]

The 1980s are now remembered as a golden decade of rising incomes, fashionable teenage tribes and *Gucci on the Ginza*, a 1989 English-language bestseller on Japan's new generation of consumers. Attitudinal surveys in the mid-1980s found that most people put their own satisfaction first. Consumer culture seemed to be breeding a nation of individualists. In reality, this was a blip. Already before the bubble burst in 1989–90, the trend of 'breaking away from things' and enjoying 'things other than things' (*mono igai no mono*) was under way.[79] The post-material search for authentic experiences and happy relationships entered the retail landscape. Tired of technological novelties, customers discovered nostalgia. Seibu department stores opened 'Reborn Pavilions' and herbal-medicine shops. The deep recession and 'lost decade' of the 1990s that followed reinforced this trend, as shoppers tightened their belts and big corporations cut back on ski-trips and expense accounts. The family regained importance. Salarymen no longer spent their evenings in bars with colleagues but at home with their wives, though they still rarely sat down for a shared meal. In 1992, Prime Minister Miyazawa promised to make Japan a 'lifestyle superpower', less stressed and more relaxed.[80] By then, *Gucci on the Ginza* looked like a relic of a bygone age. Instead of individualization, retail analysts worried that the Japanese were all becoming alike.[81] Since 1989, attitudes have been back where they were before the 1980s boom: society and nation come first.[82]

In South Korea, as in Japan, conspicuous consumption was once again treated as a social disease in the late 1980s and '90s. In 1993, 93 per cent of South Koreans felt that 'excessive consumption' (*kwasobi*) was a 'serious social problem', although few were inclined to point the finger at themselves.[83] Spending on schools, leisure, customary gifts of congratulations and condolences attracted the greatest blame. Most of it was directed at women. The Korean media ran scare stories of 'too rich too soon' that painted young, educated women as slaves to shopping; students at Ewha, Seoul's elite private women's university, were rumoured to spend half a million won on a pair of underpants, roughly US $700 at the time. Two groups were in the vanguard of the anti-luxury campaign: Presbyterians and the state. Greater affluence had been demonized by the Seoul YMCA throughout the 1980s. A 'wholesome' lifestyle, they warned, was giving way to a pleasure economy of discos, alcohol and sex. Private extravagance was taking the place of shared sacrifice.

A century earlier, similar alarm bells would have been rung by

European and American reformers worried about commercial leisure corrupting communal life, body and mind. There was one big difference: in Korea, they had the full support of the state. From one day to the next, foreign boutiques disappeared from department stores. Rumours circulated that people who had purchased foreign cars would be investigated on suspicion of smuggling and foreign-currency fraud. For the government, 'excess' was code for foreign products. Grape-fruits from the United States were boycotted. Foreign goods were required to carry a price tag that listed their low import value next to the hefty price in shops. Korean consumers would thus realize that they were paying through the nose for an American video camera or an Italian handbag that, in its original state, was worth a fraction of its retail price.[84] It says something about the strength of nationalist feeling that the government never seems to have worried that the price-tag system might direct consumer anger at the Korean state itself, which, after all, put the heavy duties on foreign goods in the first place.

These campaigns notwithstanding, it is difficult not to conclude that Asian societies have found consumption less of a moral challenge than European ones. Most sermons and bestsellers decrying 'consumerism' hail from the United States and Europe, not Japan, India or China. Asian debates about luxury lack the emotional heat and shrill paranoia of those in the West. Wealth and possessions do not carry the same stigma of sin for Buddhists or Hindus as they do for many Christians. Nationalism and social solidarity provide a shared moral script. As long as consumers act responsibly, affluence is not a problem.

Caring for family and community, therefore, has been an essential precondition for the Asian embrace of consumption. And this attitude extends beyond the human community to the community of things. Earlier, we criticized the view that the modern West has been an object-alien, subject-centred civilization. Western thinkers and writers, in fact, did appreciate that the self was material. Victorian literature taught children that if they cared for their toys, toys would love them back. Asian societies have a particularly strong view of things possess-ing a soul. In Buddhism, objects, as well as experiences, are always in flux and can advance towards liberation. In Shinto, objects have magi-cal powers. Karl Marx argued that the West led capitalism because it cleverly took the spirits out of objects so that it could trade them for profit as abstract commodities. The thesis clearly sits awkwardly with the Asian miracle of the last few decades. Animism – the belief that animals and things have spirits – clearly did not stop consumer capitalism in its tracks in the East. That things have spirits does not mean they cannot also be bought, gifted, desired and exchanged.

Japan is a case in point. The inter-war architect Bruno Taut, who idealized an austere East, would be shocked by the many ornaments, gifts and souvenirs that crowd Japanese homes today. In the past, the *kura*, a storehouse, served the changing demands of the seasons. Goods rotated. Today, small apartments are bursting with permanent storage units to accommodate the multiple sets of clothes for any given season. In a gift society like Japan, the sharp rise of disposable income, together with travel and the commercialization of old and new festivities such as Valentine's Day, have swamped homes with objects. Yet to throw them away might cause bad luck. To this day, gifts and souvenirs cannot easily be transferred unless a new recipient promises to take good care of them. One housewife, for example, hated the three wise men statuettes her husband had brought back from China but worried she might be cursed (*tatari*) if she got rid of them. Appliances, similarly, should not be thrown out if they are still functioning and full of life. To cope with the material deluge, Japanese households have come up with three strategies. One is to have cabinets and alcoves so that the many figurines, flowers and gifts can be appropriately housed and displayed. The second is to favour gifts that can be used up, especially sweets and pickles, but also washing powder. Finally, there are fund-raising bazaars where people can leave their unused things with a farewell card, asking the new owner to look after them well, almost as if dropping off a child at an orphanage.[85]

Consuming, in other words, can be spiritual. It is possible to have more goods and be good. Sects and ghost worship in South-east Asia since the 1980s have risen alongside the world of goods.[86] In China, the Communist Party has rediscovered Confucius and makes offerings on his birthday. The larger religious revival suggests that neo-Confucianism is more than just the product of a state in search of a national ideology after Mao. Temples are being renovated and religious tourism is thriving.[87] Confucianism holds out an ideal of harmony and respect for others, convenient to authoritarian rulers, but it is also a guide (*li*) to virtuous conduct in everyday life. It appeals to individuals worried about avarice and greed yet at the same time keen to use gifts, and getting and spending, to create *guanxi* (social networks) to get on in life.

In societies which mix gift and commodity culture and where consumption is tied to ritual and reciprocity, individuals have to walk a fine line between generosity and self-interest, reciprocity and corruption. Religion offers them a moral balancing rod. The Confucian revival might be one reason for the decline in a work-hard-get-rich mentality reported by Gallup polls between 1994 and 2004. *Ren*, or self-cultivation in the quest of reaching full humanity, is a central concern in Confucianism. Contrary to popular wisdom, the Chinese are not obsessed with work. Their values have shifted to self-expression, personal taste, entertainment and communication. One indication is the phenomenal speed with which DVDs and mobile phones have been adopted – 7 per cent of households in 1997 to 52 per cent and 48 per cent respectively by 2004, much faster than the washing machine and the fridge in earlier decades; by 2013, the average Chinese household had two mobile phones.[88] If this shift from functional to emotional goods is observable in all advanced economies, it is especially pronounced in Asia.

DEMI-GOD, HALF-CITIZEN

It was not exactly what it said on the label. In 1998, Chinese villagers in Shanxi province in northern China treated themselves to bottles of 'Long Life and Double Happiness' during the spring festival. For twenty-seven of them, it was their last celebration. The liquor had been mixed with poisonous methyl alcohol. Such tragedies would have been familiar to the Victorians and have repeated themselves time and again in developing societies. Rising demand and new products create risk as well as pleasure. This was the historical backdrop to debates about consumer rights and protection, from early laws against adulteration in late-nineteenth-century Europe to J. F. Kennedy's Consumer Bill of Rights in 1962, which laid down the rights to be safe, to choose freely, and to be heard, informed and treated with respect. In the United States and much of Western Europe, such policies developed in tandem with democratic politics. Consumers demanded recognition as citizens. In Asia, the discovery of the consumer has been as dramatic as the growth of the economy. Japan, India and China have all rolled out their own consumer bills. By 1997, according to one survey, consumer law had come to matter more to Chinese people than employment and criminal law.[89] Everywhere now, the consumer is recognized as an important being. The question is, what kind of creature is it, and who are its parents? Is it a political citizen, a self-reliant market actor or, as the Chinese have it, a 'god'?

In India, consumer protection had ancient roots. The *Arthashastra* concerned itself a good deal with the many risks facing the public, from fraudulent gamblers to washerwomen wearing their customers' clothes. Merchants were 'all thieves', out to cheat their customers, it said. An over-reaching state was another danger. Two thousand years of history have barely changed the litany of complaints – profiteering, price-fixing, adulteration, the fraudulent use of weights and measures, misrepresentation and deceit – although few consumer advocates today would go as far as the *Arthashastra* in punishing the culprits. A merchant who misrepresented the quality of an item, it recommended, ought to pay eight times the actual value, while a goldsmith working illegally faced a fine of 200 panas or the loss of his fingers; the lowest government official earned 60 panas a year.[90]

Independent India was slow to develop its own consumer regime, but when it did, it did so with a splash. In the 1950s, the government passed a string of laws to control drugs and 'magic remedies', food adulteration and trade and merchandise marks. These, however, were purely preventive and offered consumers no redress. That arrived in 1986, with the Consumer Protection Act, a remarkable measure that catapulted India into pole position in global consumer politics. In addition to protection and information, Indians gained the right to complain and seek redress. Over 3 million complaints have been handled since by the thirty-five state and six hundred-odd District Consumer Fora.[91]

Rights do not automatically translate into consumer power, of course. Twenty years after the law was passed, most Indians continue to be unaware of their rights. Bringing a complaint costs time and money and often involves hiring a lawyer. Most people do not bother. India remains a shadowland of monopolies. Consumers secured the right to participate in proceedings before the Monopolies Commission but, for every monopoly struck down, a new one cropped up. In Jaipur, cable TV companies dictate their terms and schools force pupils to buy their books and uniforms at specified shops. Barber shops and paan dealers fix their prices like in days of old.[92] In many ways, India remains a society where the producer and trader, not the consumer, is king. The Department of Consumer Affairs tries to make the best of a shoe-string budget to raise awareness with video-clips (*Jago Grahak Jago!*; *Awake, Consumer, Awake!*) and radio programmes in Hindi and regional languages, broadcast in homes, postal offices and railway stations. There are parallels here to the state-sponsored media and awareness campaign during the New Deal in 1930s America – with a crucial difference. In the United States, this had been a moment of greater state intervention. In India, by contrast, it was one of economic liberalization and rolling back the state.

If market reform opened up a space for consumer politics in India, this does not mean it has remained a matter for the market. There was also a political thrust behind it. In 1994, a court in Lucknow found in favour of Mr Gupta against the Lucknow Developing Authority in a dispute over housing construction. It was a landmark ruling. The interests of a consumer, it said, concerned 'not only day-to-day buying and selling activity undertaken by a common man, but even such activities which are otherwise not commercial in nature' yet confer some benefit, for example construction and land development. Statutory services, such as public housing, were a 'service to the citizens' that needed to be protected as much as goods bought over the counter.[93] Consumers since have confronted the state when electricity and telecommunications fail. Interestingly, the majority of complaints have concerned shoddy services rather than faulty products.[94] Consumer protection built a bridge between people's private grievances in the marketplace and their public interest as citizens. In 2005, the Right of Information Act handed consumers an additional weapon. Activists and courts have used consumer law to press for greater accountability. In the case of medical damages, for example, the Supreme Court has stressed that the consumer forums did not exist simply to quantify damages but also to 'bring about a qualitative change in the attitude of the service provider'.[95] Greater accountability and good governance mattered as well as product safety.

Some of this language echoed the 'Citizen Charters' agenda of John Major's Tory government in Britain in 1991, which set out to make hospitals, schools and other public services more accountable to users; in fact, some Indian administrators had picked up the idea at the UK's civil service college at Sunningdale. These ideas, however, acquired a more radical flavour in a country like India, where most consumers were (and are) poor and excluded from politics and where corruption has remained widespread. Consumer rights, citizenship and human rights walked together. Neo-liberalism has been tempered by shades of Gandhi. On the one hand, choice and competition came to rule. In that sense, Gandhi's ideas of self-sufficiency and asceticism are dead. On the other, consumer advocates have continued to take inspiration from the mahatma when turning to questions of social inclusion. Official posters in 2007 urged consumers to 'Join a Revolution' and announced

'The Time Has Come for Us to Stand up for Our Rights Again', with an image of Gandhi leading the poor in protest against the British Salt Tax in 1930.

The Indian government supports over 7,000 consumer clubs in schools, where concerned pupils act out the dilemmas of being a consumer in street-plays (nukkad natak) and reflect on the ethics of shopping. 'While buying a product,' the students' column of one club's magazine read, you should ask yourself: "Do you really need this product? . . . Will it last as long as you would like it to?"' What was the 'health fall-out' and impact on the environment? A 'consumer must exercise restraint in consumption to consume responsibly'. At the same time, it was no longer possible to hold up a universal norm of austerity. 'Every segment has its own special consumer profile' and needed to define its own sense of responsibility.[96] In a poor country with a rich moral history, personal excess remains a sore point for middle-class students. Consumer choice is good but should include standing up for the poor. Or, as one advocate of consumer protection put it, 'maybe we can start realizing a "good" in between "God" and "goods",' similar to the Middle Path of Buddha or Aristotle's golden mean.[97] Sometimes, nationalist history is bent to fit that purpose. Gandhi has been reincarnated by government agencies as the friend of the consumer who had the prophetic wisdom to recognize 'the customer' as the 'most important visitor on our premises', the 'purpose' of our work and the element on whom everything depends.[98] Adam Smith had said something like that in the Wealth of Nations. Whether Gandhi would have liked to appear as an Indian mouthpiece of Smith is doubtful.

As early as 1915, passengers irritated with transport services set up an association to voice their complaints. Half a century later, a more general Consumer Guidance Society of India was founded. In the 1980s and '90s, the number of consumer groups jumped from 80 to 1,500. It is this thriving civil society that has been one of the most striking features of India's embrace of consumption, and comes closest in Asia to the parallel growth of goods and associational life in the United States and Western Europe in earlier centuries. One of the most active bodies is CUTS, the Consumer Unity and Trust Society. Founded in a garage in Rajasthan in 1983, CUTS has grown into a global NGO which works on trade, women's rights and rural poverty. There are not many consumer groups in the West that can match its expertise or its staff of three hundred. India no longer just imports but exports policy frameworks. CUTS, for example, has drawn up blueprints for consumer protection for Ghana, South Africa and Vietnam. In the 1990s, when there were plenty of social movements opposed to globalization, CUTS linked free trade to basic needs for all and ran an outreach programme in rural areas. Here was an echo of the British crusade for cheap food and free trade a century earlier. But the balance between private and public services has been almost fully reversed. Nationalization has come and gone. In nineteenth-century London, consumer groups were formed by propertied householders against private monopolies in gas and water. In 1980s–'90s India, the frontier of consumer politics was bad public services. One reason choice appeared so attractive as an instrument of social welfare was that most of the poor had been let down by state schools and power stations; Pradeep Mehta, CUTS' crusading director, has proposed school vouchers, so the poor can pick their school, instead of sitting in a classroom with no teacher at all.

In the 1990s, critics across the globe attacked neo-liberalism for shrinking public life. Privatization, it was said, reduced public-minded citizens to self-centred customers. That argument was the privilege of affluent nations that went to bed without having to worry whether there would be water and electricity in the morning. In developing societies like India, most homes did not enjoy twenty-four-hour basic services. Farmers, it is true, got their electricity free or at subsidized rates, but that was also one reason the network was so overstretched and constantly breaking down. If privatization raised fears, it also created opportunities. It is not possible here to do justice to the complex picture across all regions and services, merely to single out two interesting developments – one affecting the rural poor, the other the urban middle classes.

For many rural poor, being called a customer was a sign of recognition, a step up from being treated as a passive dependent or from never having had access to basic services in the first place. Poor people and poor services were connected in a vicious circle. Because they could not pay, they were in debt to the utility companies. Cut off, they started stealing their water and electric current. The companies, in turn, lacked the revenue to provide a decent service. At home, the lights went out; in the fields, the water pumps fell silent. A project in Rajasthan in 2002 set out to break the circle by turning villagers into paying customers. In Piplod, in the District of Jhalawad, where the electricity transformer burnt out sixteen times a month, the village elders got together and agreed to put an end to the pilferage of electricity and to install tamper-proof cables. In exchange, the electricity company invested in a better transformer that guaranteed the villagers electricity for more hours, without a drop in voltage. A household committee (*vidyut sudhar samiti*) was set up to monitor improvements. Soon, all villages in the district had such a body. In the Indian context, 'customerization', to use an ugly phrase, was not only about making peasants pay but about giving them a stake in their local infrastructure. Neo-liberalism had social-democratic features. Indeed, the reforms in Jhalawad were steered by Indian consumer groups with the help of the Friedrich-Ebert-Stiftung, the German social democratic foundation.[99]

In Indian cities, the middle classes started to put gates around their neighbourhoods in the 1980s. In the United States, such gated communities have been synonymous with privatism. In India, by contrast, the precarious state of basic services has drawn the middle classes into public life and into working with the municipal authorities, which, in a city like Delhi, continue to run water and other services. Such Resident Welfare Associations have evolved into their own hybrid of civic participation and controlled sociability.[100] On the one hand, RWAs promise a refuge from the dangers of the street and unwanted outsiders. Private life and social leisure are safe. Residents organize their own national and religious festivals, dance competitions and consumer fairs. On the other hand, the very premium placed on a lifestyle of comfort and security has drawn residents out of their private shell into working more directly with the municipal authorities. Many RWAs offer a secure water supply and twenty-four-hour power back-up, a not insignificant attraction in a city where disruption is the norm. While friends elsewhere face black-outs, families in an RWA can watch TV, run the washing machine and use their computers. For the city government desperate to improve services, these neighbourhood bodies conveniently organize consumers with a keen interest in things running smoothly. Since 2001, the Delhi government and the RWAs have entered into a kind of private–public partnership. In workshops and meetings, residents sit down with deputies, police and water officials to identify solutions to local problems. In the Bhagidari Scheme, more than a hundred associations work with the Delhi authorities on everything from curbing waste to harvesting rain water. Residents even help collect payment on water and electricity bills. If there has been criticism, it has been about residents not having more power to punish culprits or switch to private services.[101]

In Japan, the springtime of consumer movements were the years immediately following the Second World War. Nihon Shufurengōkai (All-Japan Housewives' Association), better known as Shufuren, was born in 1948. The regional Kansai Shufuren (Kansai federation of house-wives) followed the year after; Chifuren, a more diverse, pro-business group, in 1952. American occupation and support for liberal democracy fostered associational life. In its first year, Shufuren attracted half a million members in Tokyo alone. In Japan, as in Germany, it was war and scarcity that shaped the worldview of the first generation of consumer activists. Their main concern was not variety but survival. Shufuren picked the rice paddle (*oshamoji*) as its symbol. The fight was for fairer rationing, an end to the black market and, most of all, food safety. In 1951, Shufuren's early testing facilities revealed that pickled radish contained carcinogenic dye. The case was heavily publicized and prompted a government ban of the substance, and made adulteration public enemy number one.

In India, consumer politics was the product of a weak state and a relatively strong civil society. In Japan, it was shaped by a strong state and economic nationalism. If housewives' associations were gaining in strength, the state and producers were even stronger. The political system favoured producer groups. Internal divisions between consumer groups did not help. It was not until 1970 that they formed a united front, in a boycott against overpriced colour TVs; MITI caved in on that occasion. Ultimately, the relative weakness of Japanese associations had ideological roots. To be effective, consumers, like other groups, have to define themselves against someone. In Britain and the United States, that enemy was the producer, sometimes the state; in these commercial societies, guilds, corporate mentalities and dependence on local producers had weakened early. In Japan, by contrast, as in imperial Germany before, identities were less differentiated. The ideal was that of *seikatsusha*, a person who tried to harmonize the interests of consumer, farmer and producer.

A weak tradition of civic rights limited consumer influence further. Consumers had obligations, not rights. In 1968, the government passed the Consumer Protection Basic Law. For the first time, consumers were recognized as a unique and often vulnerable group, but they were to be helped by a paternalist state, not empowered. The state was authorized to set safety standards, ensure fair competition and provide citizens with relevant information. The role of consumers was to act 'self-reliantly and rationally' in the marketplace. In the following decade, the state branched out into consumer education – previously the preserve of the housewives' associations – and set up its own network of well-funded local consumer centres, testing facilities and lifestyle consultants. Rights were little more than an afterthought and formally recognized only in the revised Consumer Basic Law of 2004.[102] Policies since then have put the spotlight on 'consumer citizens', whose everyday behaviour holds the key to 'a fair market, social value and higher level of spiritual richness', in the words of the Japanese Cabinet Office.[103] In the West, it has been tempting to see such discourse as a novel product of neo-liberal markets and governmentality, which asks people to rule themselves.[104] The Japanese case suggests it can be consistent with state paternalism, too.

Communist China offers an extreme version of the symbiosis between consumerism and authoritarianism. Instead of greater choice in the shopping mall generating a demand for choice at the ballot box – the Anglo-Saxon democratic trajectory – China has proven the state's ability to co-opt consumers. Consumer politics in China takes the form of a stable non-aggression pact. The regime guarantees its subjects greater comfort and consumer protection. In exchange, consumers direct their anger at fraudulent shopkeepers and property speculators, and agree not to invade the political domain controlled by the Party. For both, fear of upheaval cements the alliance.

The consumer movement in China has been the creature of the state. In itself, this is not as odd as it might seem to liberal readers. Even in the West, there were cases like Imperial Germany, where it was the state that had breathed life into the consumer movement in an effort to harness national resources during the First World War. What sets China apart, in addition to the lack of parliamentary institutions, is that state-driven consumer activism is not an emergency war measure but a normal part of peace-time politics. A responsible, vocal consumer has become the partner of an authoritarian state committed to rapid growth. In Western countries, it took social movements many generations of pressure and campaigning until consumer rights found their way into law. In China, Party rulers simply pressed fast forward and enacted it from the top. On 31 October 1993, the Eighth National People's Congress passed the 'Law of the People's Republic of China on Protecting Consumers' Rights and Interests'. In it, the state took it upon itself to 'protect the legitimate right and interests of consumers' (art. 5). All sections of society shared the responsibility to protect their interests (art. 6). Consumers were entitled to the safety of their person and property, to correct information, quality assurance and accurate measures and to choose their own goods and services (arts. 7–10). In addition, consumers had the right to compensation and to form groups to safeguard their 'legitimate interests.'[105]

After having virtually disappeared from the Chinese lexicon during the Cultural Revolution, 'the consumer' (*xiaofeizhe*) enjoyed a big comeback in the 1990s. The Party newspaper *People's Daily* began to invoke it even more often than 'the worker'. Consumers gained their own TV slots (*Focus*) and radio programmes (*Consumer's Friend*). It is tempting to see this as a belated catching-up with the touted triumph of the consumer in the West, but differences remain. Communist China has so far avoided the narrowing of the consumer into the end-user, so characteristic of the contemporary liberal West. Consumer rights are aimed at rural farmers as much as at urban shoppers. In an effort to boost production, government agencies have distributed hundreds of thousands of legal handbooks to farmers informing them of their rights as consumers to decent seeds and tools. Farmers have brought class-action suits over sub-standard fertilizers. In that sense, China has kept alive part of an older tradition where consumption stood more broadly for the using up of resources, from the raw material to the finished article.

Activism has taken one of two forms: class-action suits and government-sponsored campaigns. A new culture of litigation has sprung up. In 1994 Beijing, three hundred consumers sued six department stores and wholesalers when they realized that the anniversary Mao watch they had bought was not, contrary to adverts, made with real gold and diamonds. A district court in the capital then took out its own newspaper advert and urged anyone else who felt cheated to register their name with the court. In the end, the court ordered the shops to refund the purchase price and to pay legal costs and damages of 3000 yuan per watch. Article 49 of the Consumer Rights Law set the amount of compensation at double the purchase price. Spotting a fake became a lucrative enterprise. From being a small trader in Beijing, Wang Hai rose to media celebrity by exposing a string of fake Sony earphones and counterfeit designer bags. By 1998, he had a dozen fake-busters working for him. But China's answer to Ralph Nader did not take on corrupt institutions, nor did he become a political maverick. Instead, he became the darling of the state. Communist leaders invited him along to meet US President Clinton, celebrating him as a new kind of communist hero who showed it was possible to work for the good of society and make money at the same time.[106]

The regime's watchdog is the China Consumer Association (Zhong-guo Xiaofeizhe Xiehui). Founded in 1984, the CCA oversees consumer education and protection and acts as a local whistle-blower and people's lawyer. It runs food-safety contests on local TV, teaches consumer songs to schoolchildren, organizes 'green shopping day' and holds annual competitions for the 'top ten annoying' complaints; household electronics, including after-sale service, and clothing topped the list in 2012. And it gives advice to consumers who have been cheated. In its first twenty years it handled over 8 million complaints. The range of cases they have dealt with is mindboggling, from the four hundred proud homeowners in Beijing who, on taking possession of their apartment, found that its square footage had shrunk and the promised garden had disappeared from the contracted design, to the forty families who felt cheated by a private coaching school which had advertised that a bit of tutoring and Y20,000 would secure their children a place at a top university. By 1997, the CCA had over 100,000 'volunteers' working for it. Many of these were local officials, but they also included employees in companies and department stores co-opted to address problems at the point of production.[107]

There are two main reasons the regime has been so keen to mobilize consumers. The first is productivity. In a country with poor product standards, vocal consumers perform the job of quality-assurance monitors. No one wants to buy shoes that come apart or cars with stalling engines. For a regime eager to move up the value chain, it makes good sense to celebrate consumer day with a bonfire of fakes. Countries do not get rich on counterfeit DVDs and Rolexes. In addition to cheering on vigilant shoppers, the CCA works with companies and other branches of the state, such as the Administration of Quality Inspection, to raise standards and pre-empt complaints. Faulty products from abroad give additional joy to consumer nationalists; in 2002–4, publicity centred on the safety flaws of the Korean-made MB 100 van and the poor service of a Japanese airline. China's entry into the World Trade Organization (WTO) in 2001 gave consumer protection added significance. As formal barriers to foreign products had to go, other ways to help domestic products gained in significance. Creating demanding shoppers who will pick Chinese products is part of that strategy. Communist rulers today operate in a spirit of consumer nationalism that reaches back to the mass boycotts of foreign goods in the national-products campaign of the early twentieth century.[108] The methods may have changed – the regime today has its own branding policy, complete with a government commission that runs over a hundred corporations. But the goal is the same: make the people buy Chinese.

The second reason is stability. A state-led movement defuses potential conflict. It positions the state as the friend of the helpless shopper in the battle against crooks and fraudsters; tellingly, a new consumer law in 2014 introduced class-action suits but required these to be brought by the official CCA. By providing some organizational structure and setting aside a limited space for protest, consumer protection and home-owner associations also prevent tensions from spinning too far out of control, especially in the ground war with speculators and land developers. In the liberal West, consumer politics put the flashlight on the asymmetry of power. In Communist China, its effect has been to obscure it. Frustration and anger are traced back to an imperfect market, not an imperfect political system. Consumer politics has thus added a dose of soft power to the harder thump of the baton.

Democracy was not accomplished overnight in the West, and it is prudent to recall Western bursts of authoritarian reaction and repression before faulting China for not making faster progress. Historically, what sets China apart from other non-democratic societies is the confident way in which an authoritarian regime has gripped consumption as a tool of political power. The ruling elite in eighteenth-century Britain treated consumers as lesser beings to be squeezed with taxes and regulations. Socialist regimes in the twentieth century saw them either as a selfish enemy who had to be rooted out or, at best, as reformable creatures in need of the state's guiding hand. Communist China rules with consumers, not against them. This is what is unprecedented. People are allowed their private pleasures and comforts, but, in exchange, they are expected to become 'scientific' and 'civilized' consumers. This means that they must break with gambling, porn and other unhealthy habits, and instead learn to balance body and mind, respect the environment and 'actively participate in social supervision', be it protesting about bad fertilizers or burning counterfeit videos. Only in this way will China be able to enjoy 'market order' and 'social harmony'.[109]

The constant appeals to the consumer and, since 2005, to a 'harmonious society' are more than rhetoric. They are about behaviour change, an early-twenty-first-century version of the 'new life' movement that sprang up in Japan a century earlier. As in Japan then, so in China now, the aim is to wean people off old customs and make them more discerning, efficient and self-reliant. The goal, however, is not simply to create the rational market actors so beloved by economists. China is more ambitious than that. It is about cultivating the social and moral qualities needed to live together peacefully in a new material world made up of new towns and neighbours, comforts and frustrations, dangers and temptations. In early modern Europe, books of manners taught the middling sort how to be polite. In China, the civilizing process is a joint project of state and business. The Party, developers and home owners have taken over Mao's project of building a new man. Official guidebooks explain 'How to be a Lovely Shanghainese' with advice on everything from appropriate dress and hospitality to how to behave in a public toilet. Volunteers demonstrate how to queue. In new cities and suburbs, housing developers engineer microcosms of social harmony. Developers in Chengdu, in Sichuan province – home of the giant panda – for example, have their own 'lifestyle office' (*shenghuo fangshi ban*). In addition to putting residents in touch with travel agents and the latest show, it organizes collective leisure activities. Elsewhere in the city, on parkland freshly reclaimed from a garbage dump, a developer put on social events for a year to enlist home-buyers from the start in creating the right ambience. Consumers are expected to do their bit in building a community with a high *suzhi*, or high-quality lifestyle.[110] Indeed, their contribution is vital if new urban spaces and the cultural vacuum left behind by work units are to be filled with the safety, sociability and decorum needed to enjoy the pleasures of privacy. Chinese consumers might not be citizens in the democratic sense, but nor are they just customers in the commercial sense. Their official elevation to 'god' is closer to the truth. After all, they are expected to create their own consumer paradise.

China, India, Japan and South Korea today are consuming societies marked by notable differences, from their propensity to spend to the exercise of rights. In that sense it is misleading to speak of the 'Asian consumer' or to expect, as marketing gurus like to do, that history will repeat itself, as purchasing power spreads across the continent. Nonetheless, looked at in the round, there are also similar patterns that set the experience of these countries apart from the West, especially Britain and the United States. In the Far East, the state and nationalism were the driving forces of expansion. Business was a junior partner. It was the state that acted as the schoolmaster for a new generation of consumers, teaching them how to save and spend. Getting and spending were legitimized in relation to national strength and social solidarity. In no Western country did consumption, state formation and development form such a tight bond.

Possessions, too, have functioned differently. Liberal commercial societies in the West championed a dominion of things that privileged private pleasure and comfort. People invested in being a master over things, rather than over other people. This fostered a more inward-looking material culture, with attention increasingly lavished on private possessions rather than on social networks. That this process was never pure and complete should not blind us to the general rise of this material privatism. What is extraordinary about East Asia as well as India, is how these societies have welcomed things without ditching people. Customary festivities have retained their significance alongside possessions. Where in the West do weddings and funerals consume multiple annual salaries? Luxury is a mass market in these new rich societies, because branded handbags and designer labels are about belonging, rather than distinction. Privatism, to be sure, has been on the rise in Japan, China and India, but it continues to be moderated by spending on social networks, the extended family and gifts for friends and superiors. The big question now, to which only a future historian will have the answer, is whether, with the parallel rise of wealth and inequality, consumption will continue to work as a social glue or, rather, start to dissolve the social fabric of these nations.

PART TWO

Preface

By the late twentieth century, consumption had reached a height unparalleled in the history of the world, in both its material scale and global reach. In the preceding chapters we have followed the dynamics of this great transformation across time, from the Renaissance to twenty-first-century China. As we moved forward in time, we have seen the decisive contribution made by states and empires, war and ideology, as well as markets and money. And we have observed how possessions, comfort and entertainment left their mark on the modern city, the home and politics. Why not stop here? We would have a perfectly presentable work of history. But the story is not over. Consumption has become central to the economy, society, politics, public and private life. Not all life today may be about consuming, but consuming is certainly intrinsic to most aspects of our lives, and that is reflected in the range of heated debates in which it plays a leading role.

Consuming has been criticized as a fundamental threat to wealth and well-being. People had become addicted to consumer credit, it was said when the Great Recession hit in 2008–9. Shopping, materialism and luxury fever have been blamed for longer work hours, stress and time poverty, the rise in inequality and selfishness, and a decline in civic feeling and politics; for good measure, some add that goods killed God. The consequences for the planet are, if anything, even more dramatic. Affluent societies, it is said, no longer make and care about things: they just throw them away. For many observers, the world has been reordered according to a neo-liberal diktat of individual choice and markets. But what about all the consuming that is not about individual choice but collective, and that takes place outside the market, such as welfare services? There are, on the other hand, also those who stress the emancipatory effects of consumption, its breaking down of old barriers of class and sex and setting the young free from established old hierarchies. Most optimistically, some look to consumers to lead us out of the moral, economic and environmental crisis by shopping for fair and sustainable products.

How much truth is there either in these accusations or these hopes? The chapters to come seek to provide some answers. Unlike Part One, where we were travelling forward on the path of history, Part Two reverses the direction. In each of the following chapters, we will start with contemporary debates but then fall back, placing current developments and anxieties in a longer historical perspective, in order to come to a better understanding of our present situation and what it might hold for the future. The main topics we need to examine are credit and saving; the speed and quality of life and leisure; the impact on generations; consuming outside the marketplace; the movement of goods and people and their impact on ethics and identities; the impact on religious life; and, finally, waste and what happens to goods at the end of their life.

9

Buy Now, Pay Later

Diagnoses of 'affluenza' identify consumer credit as a decisive transmitter in the viral spread of excess. Few subjects trigger such strong reactions. A widespread view about what happened in the 1990s and 2000s goes like this: people became addicted to credit they could not afford in order to buy stuff they did not need.[1] Easy credit fed a cult of novelty and luxury, with disastrous consequences. 'Buy now, pay later' made people short-sighted and self-centred, easy prey for advertisers peddling the illusion that more stuff means more self-esteem. Inherited self-restraint was thrown to the wind in pursuit of instant gratification. Depression was pre-programmed, in the psychological as well as economic sense. Individuals were losing their balance, and so were entire economies. When the world recession hit in 2008–9, it was natural to point the finger at silly mortgages and credit-card debt, especially in the Anglo-Saxon world. In the words of one commentator, 'the prevailing evil of our day is extravagance.'

Actually, the last quotation comes from an American writer in 1832, the home economist Lydia Child.[2] It alerts us straightaway to a problem. Warnings against credit and a loss of self-restraint are as old as commercial life itself. Plato, in his *Republic*, dreamt of doing away with credit altogether. Avarice, the early Christian apostle Paul warned, was 'the root of all evil'. Purgatory was invented in the Middle Ages to calculate the afterlife of moneylenders. Dante, in his fourteenth-century *Divine Comedy*, condemned usurers to the seventh circle of hell, alongside sodomites and blasphemers, pulled down by their moneybags on to the burning sand, their fine dress – a sign of their lust for material goods in the world – offering no protection against the rain of fire.[3]

Such moral indignation left its mark on European languages; the German *Schuld* conveniently rolls debt and guilt into one. From the sixteenth century, the Christian critique received additional support

from a republican ideal of free and independent citizens. Debt made
one person slave to another. He 'that goes a-borrowing goes
a-sorrowing', as Benjamin Franklin summed it up in 1732 in his *Poor
Richard's Almanac*, a global bestseller that became the bible for champions of thrift from colonial America to imperial Japan. Vanity and a
lust for things were bad enough, Franklin wrote. But even worse was to
run into debt for 'these superfluities! . . . think what you do when you
run into debt; you give to another power over your liberty'. To avoid
the lender, a debtor would start hiding 'and sink into base, downright
lying . . . Lying rides upon Debt's back.'[4] The Victorians swore by the
three Cs – civilization, commerce and Christianity – and dreaded the
three Ds: debt, dirt and the devil. 'Under the best of circumstances a
man who is in debt is only half a man; his future is not his own,' an
English social reformer wrote in 1896. For a working-class man it was
infinitely worse. Facing weekly visits from debt-collectors and taking
his family's clothes back and forth to the pawnshop, he 'has sold himself into a slavery from which there is no escape but flight'. Such a
person inevitably drifted into 'despair' and 'indifference', dragging his
family down with him. Buying goods on instalments was especially
alarming. Hire-purchase schemes seduced the poor into impulse buying of furniture and sewing machines which they then had to return
before they were able to enjoy them because they could not keep up
with the payments. These 'temporary owners are like spoiled children
with too many toys, always wanting something else'.[5]

Such admonitions about a 'live now, pay later' lifestyle could be quoted
at length, but these examples should be enough to make us sceptical
about the presumed sudden collapse of self-restraint in recent decades.
If people already lacked self-restraint in earlier periods, it is not possible for later generations to have lost it in the 1930s, '60s or '90s. A
second problem concerns the link between debt and excess. From
ancient Romans to today's critics of 'affluenza', debt has been associated
with extravagance, superfluities and false needs. Credit, it was feared,
gave our animal sensations the upper hand over the critical faculties of
reason and foresight on which our moral character and well-being
depended. This is one reason women as the 'weaker sex' have figured so
prominently in moral panics about credit bingeing, past and present.
This moral tradition has inspired commentators to the present day and
is interesting in its own right.[6] Yet it is not especially helpful if we want
to understand the changing realities of consumer credit. It tells us more
about how observers felt people ought to behave rather than why or

how much they in fact borrowed. It always tends to be others who are extravagant. As we have seen earlier, what is excessive or superfluous is relative. There is no fixed line between 'needs' and 'wants'. What appears a 'false need' to one person may appear genuine and authentic to another. The same is true for societies. When fear of 'excessive consumption' reached South Korea in the early 1990s, high tutoring fees were seen to be the main culprit, well ahead of fashion or electronic products.[7]

Credit and debt were a normal part of life long before the credit card. In commercial societies where cash was short and financial institutions embryonic, borrowing was a vital part of day-to-day household management. In England in 1700, every second head of a household left behind unpaid debts at death, and a quarter had debts that exceeded their credit and movable goods.[8] Living beyond one's means was customary in the best quarters. Revd John Crakanthorp of Cambridgeshire, whose detailed account books from the early eighteenth century survive, routinely overspent yet continued to live in the biggest house in the village. His standing meant he commanded good credit in the community. Credit was face to face and built around personal trust. Demonstration of character was critical. Into the nineteenth century, respectable debtors in England benefited from their own charities and enjoyed drink and dance in designated prisons, and a respite from demanding creditors. Debt was treated as a temporary misfortune that could happen to the best, not a sign of recklessness that required stiff punishment to set an example. It was when debt became more firmly associated with the poor that it spelled moral shame.

In shops across Europe in 1900, cash purchases were the exception, not the norm. Rich and poor alike bought on credit. In tailor shops in Jena, Germany, for example, only a quarter of customers paid in cash or settled their bills within three months. Students were notorious for extending their credit, 'sometimes for years', although their parents and university corps saw to it that debts were eventually paid off.[9] For the working poor, borrowing was an unavoidable strategy of survival. Like their superiors, workers used credit to bridge the temporary gap between earnings and expenses. Unlike their superiors, they had neither the assets nor the 'character' to be especially credit-worthy. For them, the gap could be a matter of life and death. Labour was casual and poorly paid. Income was unpredictable. Sudden unemployment, ill health, birth and death – any of these could push them over the edge. For working-class housewives, making ends meet was a weekly,

sometimes daily high-wire act. Being poor and needing a quick loan to
get through the week translated into exorbitant rates of interest.

An investigation of 305 labouring families in Shanghai in 1934 gives
a sense of just how precarious life could be. The average family took in
$417 in wages a year, but it needed to borrow a further $148 to get by.
Much of this came from *hui* funds – a kind of mutual-aid loan society –
and from notorious 'stamp money' (*yin-tse-chien*), advanced by small
moneylenders, 'usually gangsters or Indian constables'. Three in four
families regularly pawned goods. Pawnshops came in three classes.
The large first-class 'Kungtien' charged 2 per cent a month but reserved
its trade for better-quality articles. The poor had to make do with the
smaller third-class 'Ya-pu', which accepted their goods but charged up
to 9 per cent a month for the privilege – a good 181 per cent interest per
year. For most, it was a vicious cycle. Their earnings were barely
enough to redeem half the pledges. 'It is easily conceivable what a miserable life the average working families must have experienced as they
have to live on borrowings which they can not refund and receipts from
pawned articles which they can not redeem.'[10] The daily papers were
full of stories of debtors driven to suicide or to selling their children.

Working families in American and European cities did not sell their
children to meet their obligations but, with local variations, these were
familiar stories. Few managed without the routine visit to 'Uncle'.
Pawnshops were the banks of the people, turning their winter coats
into food and rent in the summer (see Plate 24). In late-Victorian London, pawnshops managed 30 million transactions a year. Moneylending
was ubiquitous. Liverpool, England's unofficial capital of lending, had
1,380 *registered* moneylenders alone in 1925. Many were women who
'carry on business in small streets and from their own houses'. On average they charged a penny in the shilling per week – which may not seem
much but adds up to 433 per cent interest a year. A Liverpudlian
reformer waved a promissory note at a parliamentary committee to
show how it 'simply consists of a series of blank spaces which I think is
typical'.[11] The Shanghai 'stamp money' lender, even if he was neither
Indian nor gangster, would have known exactly what was going on, for
he too liked to leave a blank space for the amount of the loan. That
way, the rate of interest looked quite reasonable.

THE DEMOCRACY OF DEBT

This old regime of credit never entirely disappeared, yet, slowly but surely, it came to be overshadowed by a new regime in the course of the twentieth century. At the same time as recognizing that debt and credit have a very long history, we also need to appreciate that after 1900 they evolved into something qualitatively and quantitatively new. Consumer credit underwent a revolution as dramatic as the revolution on the industrial side that made cheap, mass-produced articles available. Indeed, it was in no small part the growing number of 'buy now, pay later' instruments that turned the dream of possessions into a reality for the many. New credit arrived in a series of overlapping waves, beginning with instalment plans and mortgages, then extending to store cards and personal loans, and, most recently, adding credit cards and equity withdrawal.

Credit injected consumer capitalism with fresh energy. By the inter-war years, paying in instalments already financed 2–6 per cent of consumer expenditure in the United States and Western Europe. By 2006, 'unsecured consumer credit' made up 25 per cent of disposable income in the United States, 24 per cent in Britain, 16 per cent in Germany and Austria, and 9 per cent in Italy.[12] This includes loans, credit cards, instalments and mail order – what, for brevity's sake, we shall simply refer to as consumer credit. But people buy homes as well as things and, once we add mortgages, the credit revolution looks even more dramatic. By 2007, total household debt as share of gross disposable income stood at 180 per cent in the United Kingdom, 140 per cent in the United States, 130 per cent in Japan, and 96 per cent in France and Germany.[13]

As important as the volume of additional purchasing power it released was credit's new social purpose and moral standing. In the old regime, credit had been face to face. For most, it was a revolving door: in and out of the pawnbroker, but rarely getting a foot off the ground. The new regime was more akin to an escalator: credit gave people a chance to accumulate goods and assets and move up in the world. Instead of debt marking a character defect – a lack of prudence and a habit of sacrificing the future for the present – it came to be defended as a sign of virtue: a wise investment in future wealth and happiness. Gradually, credit was liberated from the face-to-face surveillance which had kept a check on what people did with the money loaned to them.

Credit-rating mechanisms took the place of character tests, anonymous financial institutions that of local moneylenders who knew a family's biography inside out and built up their clientele from one generation to the next.

To be sure, this was not a smooth, linear story. Countries evolved their own distinctive credit cultures, some more liberal, some more paternalistic. Today, Anglo-American countries have a penchant for credit cards, Germany for instalment credit and France for personal loans. Similarly, within countries, some households remain thriftier than others. The size and speed of the credit escalator varies, too: some countries still will not let everyone step on to it, while others did away with handrails altogether. Pawnbrokers and pay-day lenders never became extinct but by the late twentieth century they had been pushed to the margins of society. The democratization of credit was neither complete nor painless, but its limits should not distract from its revolutionary force.

It was in the early nineteenth century that Cowperthwaite and Sons in New York first began to sell furniture on instalment. In Paris, Dufayel followed in the 1860s. By 1900, Dufayel had grown into a national system, where customers bought vouchers on instalments which then enabled them to purchase goods at participating stores. Almost every second Parisian used it. Other countries developed their own credit networks – the British had their 'cheque trading', the Germans the 'Königsberg' system, where customers bought their vouchers from a separate credit firm. Whatever the particulars, the general idea was everywhere the same. Stores wanted customers without having to go through the trouble of checking whether they were creditworthy, let alone collecting debts. Instalment banks took care of that, and charged interest in return. By 1930, half the furniture and electrical goods sold in Germany were bought on instalment.[14]

The instalment boom was most dramatic in the United States. By 1881, the United States was still in the rearguard of consumer credit. Most states had laws against usury. In Europe, these had been abolished by the 1850s. With instalment credit, America moved into pole position. A 1936 study found that Americans owed $408 million of instalment debt that year. For every dollar spent, credit added ten cents. National income gained 2 per cent. Most of it was spent on cars (60 per cent), followed by electrical appliances (25 per cent), radios (10 per cent) and furniture (5 per cent).[15] If the average American had chosen to pay cash for his car, he would have had to save up for five years.

Thanks to the instalment plan, he paid 20 per cent down and could drive off into the sunset straightaway, spreading the remaining debt over years to come.

Not all drivers or manufacturers were immediately convinced by such schemes. In the 1920s, one in three car owners still paid in cash. But these were the wealthy few. Henry Ford wanted customers to channel their savings into a weekly purchase plan before getting behind the wheel. In 1926, after three years, his plan had to be dropped. The future belonged to competitors such as General Motors, which offered credit through its own Acceptance Company.[16] European producers started their own credit schemes, too. Philips set up Radiofiduciaire in 1933. In 1953, Cetelem (Compagnie pour le financement des équipements électro-ménagers) brought France's electrical manufacturers together with banks. Soon, every second TV set in France was sold on credit.[17] Instalment credit converted mass production into mass consumption. Economists emphasize how credit allows the 'smoothing' of consumption over the lifecycle, enabling people to draw on future earnings. Equally important, instalment purchases helped smooth production, freeing manufacturers from the headaches caused by idle plants.

Credit's rapid take-off in the United States in part reflected a simple economic truth. Between the 1870s and 1920s, American incomes were rising by around 1 per cent a year. Americans thus not only enjoyed high wages but were beginning to expect even higher wages in the future. This created a mental disposition favourable to 'buy now, pay later'. Growth, rising income, credit and consumption pushed each other forward. Such favourable conditions would reach Western Europe only in the booming 1950s and '60s. Liberal credit, however, also benefited from liberal politics. The wheels of America's credit engine were oiled by democratic culture and government support. It was political culture and institutional regulation as much as incomes that set the United States apart from Europe.

To trust people with money, you need to trust people in the first place. The United States made this transition more quickly than European class societies. In the early twentieth century, the stigma of shame that had stuck to debt was sidelined by a new chorus of voices that championed credit as the road to self-improvement and citizenship. Credit became all-American. 'We Trust the People – Everywhere,' the Spiegel House Furnishing Company advertised in 1905.[18] Social reformers lent a helping hand, training ordinary Americans in the new art of credit. The Provident Loan Society was founded in New York in 1894, the biggest of its kind. Their immediate goal was to liberate workers from loan sharks, but in their campaign for legal lending they ended up laying the foundation for a new system of mass credit. Not only did they offer loans at a low rate of 12 per cent interest, they transformed the look of credit. As their name emphasized, taking out a loan was 'provident', not reckless. It was not even credit, they argued, more like rent. Regular repayments would teach the poor essential skills of saving, discipline and planning. Instead of spending their extra pennies on drink (men) or frills (women), families would put them aside to repay the loan for a larger, 'more sensible' purchase. Similar remedial societies sprang up in Britain, where the Provident Clothing and Supply Company offered customers a 'cheque' worth £1 of goods that had to be repaid in twenty weekly instalments of one shilling, plus one extra for interest; by the 1930s, the company had 1 million customers who converted their cheques at 14,000 shops.[19] The difference was that in inter-war America, these philanthropic societies prepared the way for much larger personal-finance companies. Official lenders multiplied. Shops issued metal 'charge plates', an embryonic credit card (see Plate 52). By the 1940s, many offered revolving credit (at 12 per cent interest), enabling shoppers to keep shopping without having to pay off the balance.

Everywhere, the traditional emphasis on thrift and enterprise had been a way for middle classes to justify their position vis-à-vis the 'feckless' poor on the one hand, and the 'extravagant' elite on the other. The middle class was productive; the rest were not. Now, the American middle class championed credit as the handmaiden of both their personal comfort and the national interest. Driving around in a car and filling the home with goods – all bought on credit – was productive, not wasteful. It was a lifestyle everyone ought to emulate. 'Consumption' shed another layer of its negative image. Buying a washing machine on an instalment plan, its defenders pointed out, did not destroy wealth. It was an investment that provided utility for years before it wore out and 'saved' on servants and laundry services in the meantime. Consumer durables were capital goods, in the language of economists.

In his defence of instalment selling in 1927, the Columbia economist E. R. Seligman explained how such purchases not only increased an individual's standard of living but made him a better, more productive citizen. Credit whetted his appetite for a better life. 'The more varied, the higher, and the finer his tastes . . . the greater will be his intelligence, his efficiency and his capacity for real co-operation.'[20] The entire nation gained. These arguments picked up on David Hume and fellow Enlightenment writers who, two centuries earlier, had defended 'modest luxury' as a way of making people more industrious and sociable.[21] It needed the American high-wage economy and a democratic culture to convert such ideas into reality. 'Going into debt for luxuries is wrong,' one American told pollsters in 1926, '[b]ut instalment buying helps the family on a small income to raise its standard of living.'[22] The democratization of credit completed the democratization of luxury.

For champions like Seligman, freedom of credit and freedom of choice were two sides of the same coin. In an 'age of liberty', it was only natural that credit, too, was freed from paternalist controls.[23] In reality, however, the American government was anything but aloof. The New Deal played a crucial role in boosting the market for personal credit. The world depression (1929–31) had choked mortgages and the entire housing industry. Roosevelt's response was twofold. One was to offer direct help to those facing default via the Home Owners' Loan Corporation. By the time it was shut down in 1936, it had provided assistance to one in ten mortgagors. More decisive in the long run was the Federal Housing Administration, created in 1934. The FHA did not itself lend money. Rather, it acted as an insurer for lenders, underwriting mortgages. It was a lifesaver. The mortgage crunch had been aggravated by the small size of the private banking sector, and banks had largely turned up their noses at private customers. The FHA suddenly made personal loans and mortgages less risky. Before the first year was out, over 8,000 banks had signed up to the scheme. A decade later, almost half of all mortgage funds were federally insured.[24]

It was a golden handshake between the banks and the state, and of historic importance for the expansion of private credit. For one, a home tends to be far more expensive than a radio or a fridge. Mortgages thus make up a much larger part of personal credit than 'unsecured' consumer credit. There is, secondly, a close correlation in modern credit societies between mortgage debt and other consumer credit. The greater the former, the greater tends to be the latter.[25] What is decisive is mortgages rather than home ownership as such. Greece and Italy today have a higher home-ownership rate than the United States, but people there inherit homes and take out less credit.[26] Mortgages, by contrast, simultaneously accustom households to taking on big debt and serve as a collateral that enables them to borrow more for other purposes. Mortgages thus raised the high-water mark of consumer credit generally. Finally, the banks' entry into private credit opened up an untapped pool of capital. Before the New Deal, most loans had come from finance companies. By 1940, commercial banks had out-paced them.[27]

We must not, however, fall into caricatures of free-spending Ameri-cans and frugal Europeans. We are dealing with degrees and tendencies, not absolutes. Not all Americans greeted consumer credit with approval. As late as 1930, eminent Federal Reserve bankers blamed instalment credit for feeding Americans' 'passion for indulgence' and causing the Depression.[28] After the Second World War, J. K. Galbraith and others continued to worry about America being swallowed up by debt. If credit was becoming more democratic, access was never fair or equal. In the 1920s, blacks were twice as likely to buy their furniture on instalments as whites, who were more likely to 'charge it'. With few black merchants around and little collateral, black families were largely excluded from charge cards and in-store credit.[29] The Federal Trade Commission reported similar racial divides in 1969. The European reaction, too, was complex. In Britain, 7 million new hire-purchase agreements were signed in 1936 alone.[30] The Nazis railed against con-sumer credit as anti-German but were unable to stop its expansion. After the war, consumer credit shot up rapidly and paid for 15 per cent of retail sales in West Germany. Enterprising travel agents offered the first holidays on credit. During the 1970s, consumer credit in Germany more than quadrupled.[31]

Ordinary Europeans, then, did not have a natural aversion to bor-rowing. Rather, it was their governors who rationed credit. In Italy, Mussolini's 1936 banking law strictly limited the number of bank branches and credit providers.[32] It is difficult to take out a loan if there are no lenders to go to. In France, after the war, the Conseil National du Crédit, similarly, fixed the number of credit institutes. In 1966, a French customer wishing to buy a TV on instalment had to first make a cash deposit of 25 per cent of the purchase price – a German needed to put down only 10 per cent, a Briton a mere 5 per cent and, on top, they had half a year longer to make the last payment. It should not come as a surprise, therefore, that sales of TVs and other consumer durables were lagging behind in France.[33] Older Christian fears of usury retained their resonance in France longer than in America or Britain, all the way to the 1989 Neiertz law, which capped credit rates at 20 per cent. The West German state, meanwhile, showered savers with favours. Savers were exempt from paying income tax on the first

DM600 interest they earned; in 1993, when automatic withholding was introduced, the exemption was raised to DM6,000.[34] Japan offered similar tax exemptions. By comparison, attempts to control credit in the United States were short-lived. In 1942, a regulation was passed to limit revolving credit to a maximum of eighteen months and a ceiling put on down payments. A decade later, it was gone, after lobbying from shops.

How much more would Europeans have borrowed in a more credit-friendly environment? A fair bit, the evidence suggests. When controls on hire purchase were briefly relaxed in Britain in 1958–60, credit jumped up dramatically.[35] In most of Europe, easy credit had to wait for the liberalization of financial services and for lower interest rates in the 1980s and '90s. In Italy, as late as 1995, every second person who applied for credit was turned down. By 2002, nine out of ten got the credit they wanted.[36] More bank branches and lenders meant cheaper, easier credit.

European caution and control stemmed from a mixture of three factors: fear of inflation, social welfare and class snobbery. In the 1950s, the top priority of governments in France and West Germany was to prevent inflation from killing the economic miracle. Too much credit threatened to divert capital away from investment. It was also feared to sharpen social conflict. Consumers needed to be protected against themselves, especially the most vulnerable classes. The West German social market model aimed at harmony within growth and prioritized saving over borrowing accordingly. Easy credit would only tempt households to fritter away their hard-earned bacon. By contrast, with a little help from the taxman, *Bausparen* and *Vermögensbildung* (putting money into a building society and for wealth formation) would encourage them to save for a home and bolster social equality.

The rise in instalment credit in the early 1950s sparked a moral panic. Newspapers reported cases of workers who were up to their ears in debt and laid down their tools on the eleventh day of a month, calling in sick to avoid having their wages seized by their creditors – legally, sickness pay could not be 'attached'. A lot of this was sensationalism. One investigation found that a mere 1 per cent of all users of instalment credit had ended up in difficulty and had their wages attached.[37] Rather, alarmism reflected paternalism and class bias, and a touch of nationalist pride. After all, was it not savings that had made Prussia great? Strong Germans risked degenerating into a nation of debtors and weaklings, the last thing that was needed after a humiliating defeat.

Unlike for the American middle class, credit continued to leave behind a bitter aftertaste for many German *Bürger* and, the more educated they were, the harder they found it to swallow that ordinary folk might borrow, too. The *Bildungsbürgertum* – the educated bourgeoisie – took a dim view of the lower orders' capacity to derive genuine, civilized pleasures from additional spending. In what remains one of the most original accounts of luxury, first published in 1912, Werner Sombart, a *Bildungsbürger* and patriot par excellence, stressed that the uncultured nouveau riche were naturally extravagant. Their showing-off was a universal of history. Luxury, he wrote, reflected the 'inability of the simple and crude human being to derive any but material pleasure from life'.[38] Such class prejudice cast a long shadow, well into the miracle years of the 1950s and '60s. In public, the middle classes were vocal champions of thrift. In private, interestingly, they topped the league of borrowers. Available data from credit institutes shows that civil servants (*Beamte*) made up a disproportionately large group of customers.[39] It is difficult to avoid the conclusion that the bourgeoisie's paternalist impulse to protect 'ordinary' consumers from themselves drew at least part of its strength from a class interest in keeping credit to itself and hoi polloi at bay.

Where credit was rationed, it gave a boost to older, more informal credit networks. The resilience of the itinerant credit trader and the strength of mail order mirrored the relatively slow advance of private banking in post-war Europe. True, Crédit Lyonnais in France, the Midland Bank in Britain and German banks all introduced personal loans in 1958–9, but these reached a tiny clientele only. A decade later, one in five Frenchmen had a current account, and most British workers were still paid in cash. Banks handled only a small portion of consumer credit – roughly a third in Britain in 1966. Someone who wanted to borrow to buy a car was more likely to go to a finance house. Credit for furniture and clothing came from shops and mail order.

The credit market, then, was segmented, not transparent or competitive.[40] This was one reason Europeans borrowed less. Rationing especially affected big amounts. There was little shopping around for the best credit deal. When turned away by one lender, most families abandoned the search for credit and put the next large purchase on ice. Smaller amounts were a different story. What the suburban department store was in the United States, mail order was in Britain: the primary school of consumer credit. For working-class families, it provided easy access to the world of goods within the comfort of the home. Banks were for toffs, mail order for the people. On post-war housing estates, class, community and personal relations underwrote credit in ways not so different from street lenders a century earlier. In 1970, at their peak, mail-order firms employed 3 million agents, mostly local women with slightly higher status to communicate respectability and a lifestyle to emulate. 'Every Friday evening,' a local catalogue lady recalled, 'my neighbours and friends would come and sit in my kitchen, drink tea, look at the catalogue again – [and] pay their cash.'[41]

SAVING AND SPENDING

It is tempting to treat credit and saving as opposites, but for most households in modern societies they have been complementary strategies. What has changed is their relative function and the balance between them. Like institutional credit, saving was a modern invention. And as with personal loans, saving was initially promoted by social reformers before finding an ally in the state. On both sides of the Atlantic, the first savings banks opened in the early nineteenth century, set up by philanthropists to teach workers and small traders the virtues of thrift, sobriety and independence. Saving, they hoped, would break the vicious cycle of extravagance and poverty and set the poor on a path of industriousness and self-improvement. In the late nineteenth century, postal savings grafted national networks on these local initiatives. It was the two world wars that put the state into the driver's seat. War bonds and savings stamps became a matter of national survival. As with new forms of credit, saving advanced through a transnational network of exchange and emulation. Japanese reformers first took a leaf out of the Belgian and British postal saving books in the 1870s. A century later, they would export savings promotions to South Korea, Singapore and Malaysia. Across the world, schoolchildren deposited their pennies with their teachers in weekly thrift parades. No country rivalled Japan's savings crusades. After the Second World War, 8 million schoolchildren participated in children's banks (kodomo no ginkō). In the 1970s, postal savings halls gave Japanese savers privileged access to swimming pools, hotel rooms and wedding halls. By then, Japan's household savings rate stood at 23 per cent.[42]

There can be no doubt that these savings promotions were among the most extensive campaigns of behaviour change orchestrated by states in the modern period. Their contribution to war and peace is equally clear. Savings kept the war machine running, among victors and the defeated alike. Most Americans entered the Second World War not saving at all but emerged from it holding US savings bonds. In the 1950s–'70s, savings played a vital role not only in Japan and Korea but in other fast-industrializing countries like Finland, channelling capital from households to industry. The question is about the extent to which these campaigns actually moulded new 'habits' and 'enduring cultures of thrift', as one recent historian has argued, and can explain why today 'America spends while the world saves.'[43]

Putting it like this both exaggerates the habitual nature of saving and the gulf between short-sighted, spendthrift Anglo-Saxons and the supposedly forward-looking thrifty rest. Habits are routines that are repeated regularly and acquire a subconscious force of their own. There is little evidence that savings campaigns made thrift habitual. Quite the opposite: the historical record suggests saving is fickle. Households switched behaviour, often dramatically, in response to changing pressures and stimuli. That is precisely why patriotic appeals or coercion was required to get people to save in the first place. Singapore was honest when it called its plan 'forced-saving', by which 50 per cent of a worker's gross wage had to be paid into the Central Provident Fund set up in 1955; the rate was lowered to 36 per cent in 1986, where it has stayed to this day – the employee contributes 20 per cent, the employer 16 per cent.[44] In fascist Italy, the voluntary saving scheme was so unpopular that it had to be shelved in 1931. Several decades of aggressive campaigning did nothing to prevent the rapid collapse of saving in Japan and Korea at the end of the twentieth century, when rates plummeted from 12 per cent and 24 per cent respectively in 1990 to below 1 per cent by 2007. The same schoolchildren who had routinely dropped off their yen in savings drives, week after week, year after year, turned to credit and spending in middle age once stagnation hit and consumer credit became more readily available.[45] It is doubtful whether savings campaigns planted a culture of wise housekeeping and foresight. Financial literacy looks no brighter in Japan or Korea than in Britain, according to the OECD. When South Korea adopted the US bankruptcy code in 2004, a stunning 8 per cent of the population defaulted, twenty times that in the United States.[46]

The large number of savings accounts in Europe tells us nothing about how often or how much money is deposited. In Britain, the post office savings bank had 14 million accounts in the 1930s, but many of these saw no activity once they had been opened. Regular saving fitted neither working people's wallet nor their mentality. Wartime savings campaigns had little lasting effect. Mass Observation noted after the Second World War how ordinary Britons continued to take a cyclical, short-term attitude to saving, tied to 'the cycle of the year and its seasons, spring-clean, summer suit, autumn holiday, Christmas party'. Saving was about scraping together a few shillings for a dedicated, short-term purpose, not a gradual build-up of wealth. As the investigator noted, 'this tradition becomes a difficulty when large amounts are required to be saved. Saving is a matter of shillings, spending a matter of pounds.'[47]

'Temptation resisted and hope rewarded,' was how Samuel Smiles, the Victorian champion of self-help, summed up the 'practical wisdom' of thrift.[48] By the 1950s, and with the full support of governments, savings promotions increasingly lured citizens with cars, TVs and holidays. Self-control was now about resisting small temptations to afford big-ticket items. In Western Europe, barely emerging from the rubble of war, savings banks worked hand in glove with manufacturers in special promotions that gave families the chance to buy a sofa on credit as long as they had saved a third of the price.[49] Savings campaigners built on the new culture of credit, which had rebranded consumption as investment. Buying consumer durables was investment, not spending. This rhetoric was particularly important in fast-growing countries like Finland, where peasants turned into industrial workers in little over a generation. Saving grafted a new, urban consumer culture on to a rural ethos of thrift. In a 1952 book, Prime Minister Urho Kekkonen asked whether the Finnish nation had the patience to prosper. High inflation and low rates of interest meant old-fashioned saving made little sense. Instead, Finns were urged to invest in their home and appliances. The new national hero was the 'target saver', who had a monthly portion of his wages deducted for a radio, furniture or a trip to Paris.[50] In societies undergoing rapid modernization, saving campaigns were a Trojan horse for the world of goods (see Plate 54).

The decisive change between the first two thirds of the twentieth century and the last had to do more with the radical turn-about of state action than the habits of their citizens. Put simply, saving required states to have a project, such as war or modernization. In the 1970s–'80s, states lost that sense of purpose, and with it the will to compel their populations to save. The new mantra was to treat citizens as adults and let them to spend and borrow as they saw fit. A UK parliamentary committee in 1971 put the new orthodoxy plainly: 'our general view is that the state should interfere as little as possible with the consumer's freedom to use his knowledge of the consumer credit market to the best of his ability and according to his judgement of what constitutes his best interest.' The state might use 'persuasion to influence the scale of values implied by their expenditure patterns', but it 'remains a basic tenet of a free society that people themselves must be the judge of what contributes to their material welfare'. To restrict their freedom in order to protect a 'small minority who get into difficulties' was misguided.[51] Here, in a nutshell, was the rationale for credit liberalization, fifteen years before Margaret Thatcher's 'big bang' threw open financial markets more generally.

The decline in saving, which began in the 1970s and then progressed in earnest from the 1990s, has not been a peculiarly American or Anglo-Saxon disease. Finns and Danes, for example, have consistently saved less than Anglo-Saxons since the 1970s. In Germany and Belgium, the household saving rate stubbornly stuck at 9–13 per cent in the 2000s. In Japan, Italy and the Netherlands, meanwhile, the decline in saving has been at least as pronounced as in the USA, Canada and Britain.

Are Danes and Italians saving too little, or are Germans saving too much? The answer can be found only by viewing saving alongside credit, income and assets. For a family without any security, not to put aside some money might be foolish. For another, with a low-interest mortgage and a pension fund, it might be far less so. A rising credit-card bill is a drop in the ocean for households enjoying rising incomes and property values. In Britain, for example, the gross household saving ratio fell sharply from 11 per cent in 1992 to 2 per cent in 2007, and the 'mean' unsecured consumer credit had risen to £10,000 when the 2009 Great Recession hit – that is, as many households owed less than £10,000 as owed more than that. Mean mortgage debt stood at £100,000. These are large figures, but they were dwarfed by mean housing and pension wealth, which was over £200,000.[52]

Economists, by and large, turn to two models to explain what has happened to saving: the lifecycle and the permanent-income hypotheses. Both saw the light of day in the 1950s; Franco Modigliani articulated the former, Milton Friedman the latter.[53] For Keynes, the primary motive for saving had been almost irrational pride: to leave a bequest for posterity. Emerging data showed this did not square with reality. People were saving for their own future, not just for their descendants, Modigliani pointed out. They adjusted their consumption

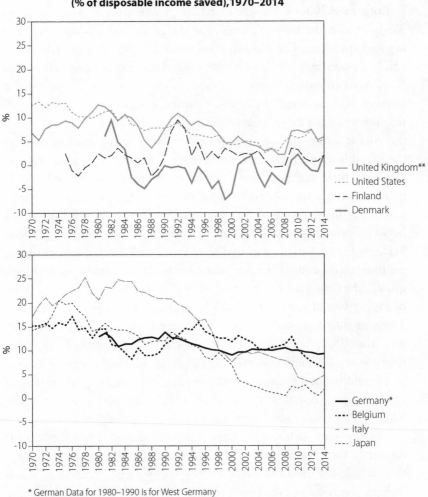

**Household saving ratio
(% of disposable income saved), 1970–2014**

* German Data for 1980–1990 is for West Germany
** UK data is for households' gross saving ratio

Sources: OECD Dataset, *Economic Outlook* no.96 - November 2014 - OECD Annual Projections;
For 1980-1990 West Germany: Statistisches Bundesamt: Fachserie 18, Volkswirtschaftliche
Gesamtrechnungen, Reihe 1.2, Konten und Standardtabellen 1996, Vorbericht.

over time to get the most out of life (to maximize a stable utility function, in the language of economists): saving more when they were young
and had few assets, building up wealth in their peak-income middle
years, and then 'dissaving' and selling off assets during old age. Friedman, similarly, stressed that people took a long view. How much they

consumed depended not on their disposable income at that moment but on what they expected to earn in the future.

Both models took for granted that people were able to build up wealth and make rational, long-term decisions about saving, borrowing and spending. The lifecycle model would have been of little use to earlier generations stuck in a revolving door and condemned to live from hand to mouth. Since the 1970s, these hypotheses have faced a number of challenges. The bequest motive, it was recognized, did matter and could not be written off altogether.[54] So did the precautionary motive for saving. In Germany, the elderly kept saving much more than the lifecycle model predicted, while in the US workers were saving surprisingly little for retirement.[55] The permanent-income hypothesis, meanwhile, was broadly right about the very long run but had little to say about fluctuations in consumption in the short run. Variations between countries posed a further dilemma. The lifecycle hypothesis explained why growth and saving were related; since consumption is assumed to depend on lifetime, not current, income, in periods of high growth the young were getting richer than their parents and so the share of saving would rise over time. The decline in saving since the early 1970s broadly followed what the model predicted, but it was a mystery why the USA, with 2 per cent growth during 1960–85 – where thirty-year-olds could look forward to having double the lifetime income of a grandparent – ended up with the same age consumption profile as Japan, where growth was more than double that and a similar young adult could expect to be four times as rich as a grandparent.[56]

The problem with the permanent-income theory is not that people do not factor in their future earnings, but that they do not always see their whole life ahead of them.[57] They make decisions looking ahead only to the next phase. The future is intermediate and seen in little chunks. And whether it looks rosy or bleak depends on the formative years that came just before. A large-scale survey following German savers between 2003 and 2007 found that those born between 1966 and 1975 saved much more than those born a decade earlier.[58] This generation entered the labour market in the mid-1990s at the very time when the pension system was reformed. Uncertainty about future security, reinforced by the spread of low-paid, part-time jobs, prompted them to tighten their belts and keep them tight, even once conditions, objectively, improved. Such cohort effects are an important piece of the German saving puzzle.

In the world at large, however, savings took a nosedive in the 1980s and '90s, as cheaper credit instruments were rolled out and people began to look beyond saving for their future security. Why stop and save, if it was possible to step on the credit escalator and move up, borrowing against future earnings? Pension plans, shares and bonds and, especially, rising property prices all made saving less relevant.[59] Once of interest to a small elite, the movement of stocks and real-estate value became the breakfast reading matter of the middle classes. Financial products multiplied in leaps and bounds. In the early 1980s, there were thirty-six types of mortgages on offer in Australia: by 2004, an aspiring home-owner could pick from among 3,000.[60] For many, the mortgage took the place of the savings account.

It was in this period, too, that personal banking and credit cards started to reach the poor as well as the rich. The escalator of consumer credit switched gears and got more crowded. To move, it needed the prior *bancarisation* of the people, in the apt French term. In 1966, fewer than two in ten French adults had a current account: ten years later, it was nine out of ten. In earlier generations, lenders had exercised a moral check on the borrower's character and the purpose of a loan. By the 1980s, such paternalism was dead. 'NatWest can give you a personal loan to take to the sales – after that you're on your own,' as one British bank advertised the new spirit of choice.[61] Rising incomes and deregulation encouraged a search for customers. In Britain, the number of people with credit facilities tripled between the mid-1970s and the mid-1990s.

All this does not automatically mean Americans and Britons forgot about saving. It depends on how we measure it. By one estimate, the US saving rate would shoot up from 5 per cent to 10 per cent in the 1990s if capital gains from dividends, interest and rental income were taken into account. Nor does it automatically mean that people save less because they are addicted to consuming more and more. In Britain, the saving ratio was falling between 2000 and 2008 but so was consumption's share of GDP – because people's disposable income as share of GDP was shrinking.[62]

The popular icon of this evolutionary burst was the credit card. Gold, silver, platinum or red (to support the fight against AIDS and malaria), it came in all colours. Revolving credit – the ability to borrow without the need to repay the loan in full at the end of the month – advanced most rapidly in the Anglo-world. In the United States, Citibank launched its credit card in 1961, shortly followed by American Express, but these were for an elite. Credit rationing by class and race remained the norm. It was in the 1990s that risk-based pricing systems delivered unsolicited credit-card offers not only to low-income families but to 'children, dogs, cats, and moose', as Alan Greenspan told the US Senate Committee on Banking during the hearings on his nomination as chairman of the Federal Reserve in 2000. In 1970, only 17 per cent of Americans had a credit card. Thirty years later, it was 70 per cent. In Britain, the number of credit cards in the 1990s jumped from 12 to 30 million.[63]

Revolving credit mattered because shopping with 'plastic' changed shopping behaviour. Already in the 1950s, American department-store managers noted how store cards encouraged customers to shop more frequently, although it did not lead them to spend more per sale than those using a thirty-day charge account.[64] Credit cards did this on a bigger scale. In Britain, outstanding consumer credit as a share of consumer expenditure jumped from 8 per cent to 15 per cent in the 1990s. Arguably, there is a connection between having a credit card and buying more stuff. The uptake of credit cards has, however, remained uneven. Almost nine out of ten Brits, Swedes and Dutch had one in 2004, but only every second Italian. It is also worth pointing out that a high number of credit cards is not only related to a higher propensity to shop but also to higher overall access to banking and assets. Britons, often charged with credit bingeing, also had more life-insurance policies, private pension plans, bonds and interest-bearing deposit accounts than the average European.[65]

Credit cards are sometimes held up as symptomatic of spendthrift Anglo-Saxons vis-à-vis more frugal cultures elsewhere. This is a distorted reading of the evidence. The democratization of consumer credit and rising personal debt in the 1990s and 2000s have been global phenomena. In virtually all developed societies, personal debt jumped to record highs. Some simply started out from a lower base than others; one exception is Japan, where households carried a high burden of debt to begin with and kept it constant. Borrowing on 'plastic' is a small affair compared to overall consumer credit; even in the United States at the height of the credit boom in 2008, credit cards amounted to merely 8 per cent of lending for home purchases. That the French, Germans and Japanese use plastic less frequently than Americans, Britons or, for that matter, the Dutch and the Swedes – and tend to pay back their monthly balance in full when they do – does not mean they do not borrow. They simply use other channels of credit such as personal loans (France), instalment plans (Germany) or cash advance and borrowing from *shinpan kaisha*, consumer finance companies (Japan).[66]

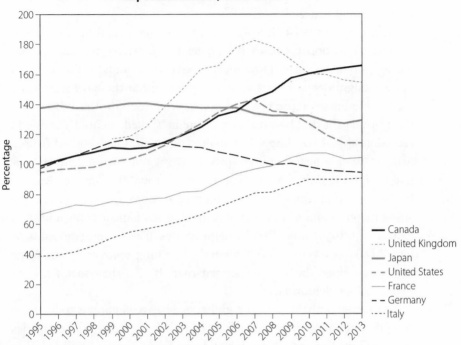

Household debt as a percentage of net disposable income, 1995–2013

Source: OECD *National Accounts at a Glance, 2014*, http://data.oecd.org/hha/household-debt.htm.

The interesting contrast between countries lies less in the growth of personal debt than in its composition. As a share of disposable income, total credit in the Netherlands and Denmark doubled between 1995 and 2007, reaching levels that make American households look positively restrained; Danes are roughly twice as deep in debt as Americans. Virtually all of it was for mortgages, however. Credit for goods and services made up a higher share in Britain and Germany (15–20 per cent); in Poland and Austria, it reached 40 per cent of total personal credit. Mortgages, then, make up the bulk of consumer credit, but they do so to a larger or smaller degree. It is a common misunderstanding to presume that because renting is widespread in the Netherlands and Germany, mortgage debt must be smaller, too. Land and property costs much more in Maastricht and Munich than in Missouri, which means that those Dutch and Germans who buy a home carry a disproportionately large burden of debt. The big difference between the Anglo-world and the rest in the 1990s and early 2000s was that, for the latter, unsecured credit (plastic, instalments, loans) shrunk as a share of private debt. It took the 2008–11 contraction of credit for this to happen in the US and Britain.[67]

Debt does not exist in isolation but must be related to wealth and income. A $1,000 credit-card statement will terrify the pauper but hardly bother a prince. How much assets households sit on, sadly, is not a straightforward matter, as many found out the hard way when the bubble burst in 2008–9 and homes were found to have been seriously overvalued. The escalator of credit stalled. Behind the world recession lurked two larger imbalances of credit. One resulted from a historic realignment between private debt and income, most pronounced in the United States. For a century, roughly from the 1870s to the 1970s, Americans borrowed more and more, but they did so on rising incomes and assets. The big spurt in instalment plans and cash loans in the 1930s was offset by net increases in assets and, indeed, savings.[68] Default was not a problem in the booming 1950s and '60s. Wage stagnation since the 1970s changed that. It was then that America turned into a 'debtor nation'.[69]

The second imbalance was a global one between nations such as the United States and Britain, which loved to buy on credit, and countries such as Germany and China, which loved to sell them cars and clothes but did not like to buy much in exchange and, instead, locked their earnings away in savings. It is an interesting question whether it is more foolish to consume too much or too little. That the Japanese needed to spend more and save less had been a staple of American diplomacy in the 1980s. What made the global imbalance trigger a crisis in 2009 was that debt in the meantime had become a global market. Banks channelled excess savings from one side of the world back into sub-prime mortgages on the other. It was like pouring oil on fire.

Notwithstanding the severity of the world recession, it is important to view the story of debt in the longer context of wealth accumulation. The 1980s to the early 2000s – that is prior to the sub-prime real-estate bonanza – saw real gains in net worth. By 2001, households in the United Kingdom and Japan owned six times as much net wealth as they owed in liabilities; in Germany, it was five times; in the United States, four.[70] The 2009–11 crisis may have wiped off a few years of inflated gains, but it did not cancel the longer rise of wealth built up over decades. Personal debt continues to be dwarfed by private wealth and the more so, the richer the country. Tellingly, the 2004/5 European Social Survey found that British, German and Scandinavian households suffered less from financial stress than their poorer neighbours in Portugal, Greece and Eastern Europe.[71]

The revolution of personal credit advanced furthest in the Anglo-world with the introduction of second mortgages and home-equity withdrawal in the 1990s and 2000s. The home was turned into a cash-point. Historically, this was a radical conclusion to twentieth-century developments which put the private consumer on a par with the business creditor. And it wasn't only that private credit assumed a greater share of credit overall. Consumers started to be treated as miniature businessmen with the right and ability to cash out all their assets to finance other plans; the extension of economic theory to marriage, divorce and childrearing – most famously by the Chicago Nobel Prize-winner Gary Becker in the 1960s – and the treatment of households as units of production and consumption was one part of this broader shift.[72] Age-old distinctions between fixed and mobile wealth were swept aside. Why should brick and mortar be treated differently from, say, a car or jewellery? Why prevent consumers from tapping into the housing wealth they had built up to spend it on something else? For centuries, republican writers had idealized the home as the anchor of citizenship and community in a restless world of commerce. Now, in the Anglo-Saxon world, the anchor was cut loose. The home was swept away by an international market in credit and debt. Beginning in the 1970s, home-equity refinancing was given a boost by Ronald Reagan's 1986 Tax Reform Bill which with one hand gave tax privileges to 'second mortgages' and with the other took them away from all other types of loan. The cheapest point of credit was now the home. In most of continental Europe, by contrast, the home stayed put in its own legal and material zone. Instead of promoting the easy flow from one sphere of credit to another, France, Germany and Italy retained firewalls between them. Mortgages continued to require considerable down payments of 20–40 per cent – one reason why people saved so much in these countries. Flexible mortgages and easy refinancing remained foreign words.

'Cashing out' on the home was the final fillip of the credit revolution. Equity withdrawal was literally that: a bit of value was taken out of the home to pay for something else. In 2003, American households withdrew $139 billion this way, the equivalent of 6 per cent of their disposable income. In Australia, such withdrawal released an estimated 2–3 per cent of additional consumption into the economy.[73] In the original Keynesian model, such extra injections came from the state.

Borrowing on rising property prices replaced this model with a 'privatized Keynesianism'.[74] Perhaps as important as any direct transfers were the indirect links between the price of the home and the ability and willingness to spend. Economists have compared the effect of financial wealth and housing wealth on the propensity to consume and have found remarkable national differences. A rise in share prices had virtually the same effect on consumption in the USA, Japan and the Eurozone; people spent 6 cents for each additional dollar of wealth gained. When it came to the 'wealth effects' of housing, they were worlds apart. When a home shot up in value by, say, $100,000 in America, its owner would spend an additional $5,000. The Japanese or European owner responded to a similar property boom with a meagre $1,500. In all countries, rising house prices triggered rising consumption, but in some much more than in others. In addition to the Anglo-world, Finland, Sweden and the Netherlands have also seen bigger effects. Again, these had not only to do with the rate of home ownership but with the ease with which households could extract liquidity from their home and cash in on the rising value of their property, thanks to equity withdrawal, flexible mortgages and easy refinancing.[75]

GOING FOR BROKE

Where did all the money go? When the 2009 recession hit, many commentators had little doubt about the answer. The rising volume of private debt was an indicator of reckless 'consumerism', an addiction to shopping and living beyond our means. At one stage, the British prime minister Gordon Brown even urged citizens to pay back their credit-card bills; this probably would have brought spending to a halt and only deepened the crisis. The idea was that once people spent less on frivolous stuff, society would return to a healthier balance both at the personal and economic level.

If only it was that easy. Reality was more complex than moral conviction. Neither equity withdrawal nor credit-card spending was mainly for frivolous 'wants'. Admittedly, car dealers in California estimated that on the eve of the recession every third car was bought on a home-equity loan.[76] But, arguably, a car is a 'need' in most of the United States. In any case, car purchases made up a small fraction in the overall use of such loans. One third of home equity was withdrawn to fund home improvements – effectively, an investment – and one half to repay debts or buy other assets. Only 16 per cent went to finance consumer expenditure. Australia and the United Kingdom show similar patterns, though in New Zealand spending on consumption was higher. Far from financing mindless excess, surveys show that equity withdrawal has been disproportionately used by households to tide them over challenging transitions in their lives. Families with young children are especially high equity borrowers – making up for a temporary shortfall in earnings – as are divorcees and those suffering redundancy.[77]

The association of credit with shopping malls and 'unnecessary' stuff stems from a simple misunderstanding. National data captures the volume of unsecured consumer credit regardless of what households decide to use it for. 'Private consumption', similarly, refers to all household spending – medicine and education as well as clothes and holidays. It is a fallacy to suppose that anyone who takes out credit must be on an impulse shopping spree buying a flat-screen TV or yet another pair of designer shoes. One reason for the high volume of personal credit in Britain and America is that it pays for education and basic living expenses – and healthcare in America – and the costs of these services have been rising. In Britain, the average student loan in 2007 was twice the size of a car-finance loan. In the United States that year, a third of all instalment debt was for education.[78] It is not surprising that American college students graduate carrying a millstone of debt around their neck – $20,000 on average – compared to their Danish peers, who pay no fees and receive a monthly allowance from the state on top. For many Americans in the 1990s and 2000s – a period of stagnant wages and rising inequality – the credit card acted as a private substitute for a missing welfare state, paying for medical bills and for food and housing in times of unemployment. The high volume of unsecured consumer credit in the Anglo-world therefore involves a bit of an optical illusion. Loans paid for goods and services provided for free by the state elsewhere.

This raises the intriguing question of how lopsided the American economy really has been. Between the 1960s and the '90s, the household consumption rate (the ratio of household consumption to GDP) climbed from 69 per cent to 77 per cent. But this included spending on health, which multiplied in leaps and bounds in this period. Once medical expenses were taken out of the picture, economists found virtually no change in the consumption profile for these decades. In other words, Americans were not becoming spendthrift shopaholics, or at least not all of them. They spent more on pills, teeth and doctors. Not surprisingly, the increase in the propensity to consume was concentrated

among the elderly. Rising spending was most pronounced among sixty-
to eighty-year-olds. In 1990, they consumed half as much more than
their predecessors had in 1960.[79] Looked at this way, the decline of
saving and the rise in consumer credit appears in a rather different light
from the customary morality tale of affluenza. Should the elderly have
consumed less for the sake of a more balanced economy?

Aggregate trends highlight the expansion of credit-based consumption and variations *between* societies. As the previous observation
suggests, however, it is equally important to recognize differences
within societies. It is a mercantilist mistake to think of the nation as a
household, just bigger. That Germany maintained high saving rates
does not mean that every German was a heroic saver. National averages hide a variety of micro-cultures. A greater appreciation of these
requires us to moderate some of the shriller condemnations of reckless
consumers. A detailed study of Britons' financial lives between 2006 and
2009 revealed that only 4 per cent were behind with their credit commitments by two or more months. The vast majority had no problem
with their repayments; the ratio of repayment to income on unsecured
debts was below 10 per cent for two thirds of people. Savings were low,
but this still meant that 41 per cent had savings worth more than
£5,000.[80] A few years earlier, just one in twenty households used their
credit cards to transfer balance from one card to another. Only 7 per cent
decided 'on the spur of the moment' to buy something on instalment –
the majority had planned it 'all along'.[81] Even in the United States, 40 per
cent of credit-card holders routinely paid their balance in full. The Federal Reserve Board's 'Survey of Consumer Finances for 2007' gives a
fascinating snapshot of the diversity of family budgets in America. Of the
respondents, 6 per cent reported that they usually spent more than they
earned; 16 per cent broke even; 42 per cent saved regularly. The remaining 36 per cent saved primarily for retirement.[82]

Comparing national surveys can be treacherous, but it is difficult to
resist the temptation to place the data from spendthrift America alongside that from *über*-frugal Germany. In the same year, 49 per cent of
German households saved – down from 59 per cent in 2003; interestingly, almost every second young household saved regularly. Most of
these, however, saved only a small portion of their income. What made
the difference was not that Germans in general saved more but that a
tiny, rich minority (8 per cent) saved a stunning 30 per cent of their
income.[83]

For all the millions of credit cards and TVs bought on the instalment plan, attitudes to credit have proved remarkably stubborn. In 1979, 31 per cent of Britons felt that credit was 'never a good thing'. In 2002, after a twenty-year-long credit boom, that number had not changed a bit. In both years, only one in seven was happy to see credit as 'a sensible way of buying'. Others felt it was a convenience. In inter-war Britain, furniture bought on the instalment plan ('hire purchase') was routinely delivered by 'plain vans' to preserve a family's standing.[84] Such ruses, still present in the 1960s, may no longer be common today, but this does not mean that contemporaries openly flaunt credit either. For many, a moral cloud continues to hang over it.

So far we have seen how more consumer credit enabled more consumption. What about the reverse? Did a greater lust for things push people deeper into debt? The charge that excessive consumerism is to blame for excessive debt is an old one. Workers had developed a taste for champagne on lager budgets, social reformers complained around 1900. A century later, the rise in personal bankruptcies at a time of booming credit produced similar soul-searching across the developed world. In the United States, just under 1 million people filed for bankruptcy in 1992. Six years later, it was 1.4 million. In neighbouring Canada, personal bankruptcies rose by 9 per cent a year in the 1990s. In Japan, 217,000 individuals went bankrupt in 2005.[85] Over-indebtedness was a global problem. International comparison is difficult – bankruptcy laws and definitions of over-indebtedness vary between countries and, in addition, have changed over time. One reason for the dramatic spike in bankruptcies was that virtually everywhere legal reforms made it easier for debtors to declare insolvency. Britain passed its Insolvency Act in 1986. Many European countries followed with debt adjustment and bankruptcy laws in the 1990s; Japan in 2005.[86] Experts estimate that, from 1999 to 2004, roughly 2 per cent of Finnish households were over-indebted, 3 per cent in France, 4 per cent in the Netherlands and 7 per cent in Britain and Germany. In the United States, the number of households that declared bankruptcy reached 1.7 per cent in 2004, but the rate of over-indebtedness was probably closer to 12 per cent.[87]

How did they get into such a precarious position? From Germany to the United States, study after study has reached the same conclusion. The road to bankruptcy is paved by unemployment, low income, ill health and divorce. Single parents – and especially low-income mothers – are particularly vulnerable. Poor housekeeping or an excessive lifestyle are the case in only a minority. The descent into bankruptcy among middle-class families in America had more to do with keeping up payments on education and housing on falling incomes than with spending too much at the mall.[88]

The democratization of credit was neither complete nor egalitarian. In the 1980s and '90s it did provide the poor and minorities with easier access to credit and mortgages. But it was no unmitigated blessing. While some joined the escalator, those who already had difficulty repaying their debts were pushed ever deeper into the abyss. As in the past, the very poor today are hit by a double whammy of low income and high credit rates. Financial and social exclusion have remained symbiotic. The location of bank branches gives an almost perfect map of inequality. Between 1975 and 1995, banks opened 30 per cent more branches across the United States. In poor areas, 21 per cent closed their shutters. The vacuum was filled by pay-day lenders and cheque-cashers. In Britain, 7 per cent of the population today lives completely outside the established world of finance, without a bank account, savings, a pension, insurance or a credit card. Over the course of a lifetime, American families without bank accounts pay an estimated $15,000 to pay-day lenders – in fees alone. The going rate of interest at British moneylenders ranges from 100–500+ per cent.[89] This is what 'the poor pay more' means. It is not surprising that British researchers found 'widespread resistance to the use of consumer credit among those on the margins of financial services, coupled with an acceptance that "lumpy" expenditure could not be met without it'.[90] Credit was a last resort, taken out to buy shoes for the kids or a few Christmas presents, rarely to fund a shopping spree.

These numbers are interesting in several, related ways. Poverty, they suggest, not the inability to resist material craving, remains the single biggest cause of credit failure. They are, secondly, a reminder of how, in spite of a creeping upward trend since the 1980s, over-indebtedness in mature credit-based consumer societies is the fate of a small minority, and bankruptcy even more so. In England and Wales, one in a thousand filed for bankruptcy in 2004. The vast majority has handled rising volumes of credit without default. The idea of a more sober, restrained past is the stuff of myth, not history. In 1900, law courts from Prussia to England were clogged with suits for non-payment of outstanding credit on a scale unimaginable to today's readers (and judges). The global proliferation of bankruptcy laws, finally, is a recognition that over-indebtedness is a problem in all affluent societies, including social market and welfare states. The roads taken, however, continue to reflect rival views of the place of consumption in society overall.

22. *top* Central Market Hall, Berlin Alexanderplatz – one of the many covered market halls appearing in cities in the late nineteenth century.

23. *middle* Strong man advertising the miraculous power of his patent medicine at Tianqiao market, Beijing, *c.* 1933–46.

24. *bottom* Uncle Paul's Pawn Shop, Augusta, Georgia, *c.* 1899.

HUSBANDS FETCHING WATER IN THE MORNING.

25. *above* 1882: the first electric arc light in Ginza-dōri, Tokyo, in an 1883 engraving of the scene by Utagawa Shigekiyo.

26. *left* 1898: husbands fetching water with buckets in London's East End during the 'water famine', when constant supply collapsed.

27. *left* Luna Park at night,
with the 'shoot-the-chutes'
amusement ride on the left,
Coney Island, New York
City, 1904.

28. *below* Blackpool,
England, and its 'flying
machines', *c.* 1910.

29. *top* 1912: basic comforts amidst sweated labour – a family making artificial flowers in an overcrowded one-room tenement on Thompson Street, New York City.

30. *left* 1913: the kind of stuffed bourgeois interior loathed by the architect Bruno Taut and fellow modernists, in a photograph from Radautz in the Austro-Hungarian empire (today: Radivtsi, Ukraine). The owner's note proudly points to the electrically operated petroleum lamp.

31. *above right* 1921: the clean lines of modern living championed by Taut, exemplified by the Atelier Berssenbrugge in The Hague.

32. *above* Henkel men advertising washing powder, Germany 1914.   33. *below* Telefunkensuper radio, Germany 1933.

34. *top left* Horse-drawn van advertising gas-heated baths, Norwich, Easter Monday, 1908.

35. *top right* German electricity fair, 1953.

36. *middle left* Mr and Mrs Pickens' first electric cooker, Norwalk, California, 1938.

37. *below* Japanese board game extolling the benefits of gas, c. 1925–43.

38. *top* 'White Label' for goods approved
by the National Consumers League, 1910s,
USA; this one came from a swimsuit.

39. *left* Caricature of an Indian 'Baboo' aping
the West, by Gaganendranath Tagore, 1917.

40. *below* By the 1930s, Gandhi's austere vision
of self-reliance was supplanted by more
colourful *swadeshi* fashions, like this one.

41. Holiday programme of the Nazi leisure organization Strength Through Joy (*Kraft Durch Freude*), 1938.

42. Soviet advertisement: 'In America, a bottle of ketchup stands on every table in a restaurant and in every housewife's cupboard', 1937.

43. The Soviet stand of appliances at the 1959 Moscow exhibition, where Nixon and Khrushchev had their 'kitchen debate'.

Societies with the most liberal approach to credit have also treated bankrupts most liberally. The ease with which an American can file for the liquidation of debts under Chapter 7 mirrors the centrality of credit-based consumption in American society. It demands swift rehabilitation instead of eternal shame. An excommunicated debtor is a lost customer. Much better to give him a 'fresh start' and let him rejoin the pack. Bankruptcy legislation here has been first and foremost about making markets work smoothly, not protecting or educating vulnerable citizens. Debts could be written off easily; too easily, according to some estimates, which reckon that as many as 15 per cent of Americans filing for Chapter 7 could have managed a repayment plan instead. In 2010, 1.5 million Americans filed for $450 billion in debt relief. Americans receive more money through debt relief than from unemployment benefits.[91] Here was yet another instance where consumers gained the privileges previously reserved for businessmen. Market-oriented societies such as Britain have moved closest to the American model, where bankruptcy is about regulating markets.

Social market societies which retained some credit regulation – Germany, for example, capped rates for consumer credit at 23 per cent – have found it more difficult to drop a paternalist attitude completely. In 1999, a new law gave consumers the chance to get rid of their debt, but first they had to undergo debt counselling and show six years of good behaviour. If the Social Democrats (SPD) had had their way, they also would have had to hand over three years' non-exempt income before being discharged; the former Communists found even this too soft and pitched for five years – in vain.[92] The insolvent German, then, was no longer condemned to life-long indebtedness and a shadow existence, but, unlike his American counterpart, he was not set completely free either. A fresh start had to be earned by good behaviour. Tellingly, whereas in America bankrupt citizens enjoyed exemptions in most states that allowed them to hold on to private property worth thousands of dollars (and, in Texas, to their home), German law laid down a tougher standard and protected 'modest' needs only; a colour TV could be repossessed as long as it was replaced with a black-and-white model. Scandinavian welfare regimes have gone furthest in treating over-indebtedness as a social problem calling for social protection; Finland in 2003 introduced 'social loans' to help the most vulnerable escape the vicious cycle of high debt and high interest. Those in debt are visited by a welfare officer, not the repo-man.[93]

INEQUALITY

Over-indebtedness at the bottom of society has been one sign of the rise in inequality that has afflicted most developed societies since the 1980s, from Anglo-Saxon countries to Germany and Sweden. The spectacular rise in millionaires and billionaires at the top has been the other. In the United States, the number of millionaires doubled between 1995 and 2005. By the early twenty-first century, the richest 10 per cent in Anglo-Saxon countries controlled 30–43 per cent of income, a concentration not seen since the 1930s.[94] Inequality is most pronounced at the very top. The super-rich turned into the mega-rich. Between 1995 and 2007, the four richest people in America more than doubled their wealth to over $1 trillion.

The precise causes behind this new era of inequality are a matter of debate – technological change, the rise in single-person households, poorly paid and insecure part-time jobs and less effective tax redistribution are the prime candidates. A large literature shows that inequality is bad for well-being, mental health, civic life and tolerance.[95] What interests us here is whether it is also responsible for over-consumption. Some commentators think so. To them, credit bingeing and an unhealthy lust for things ('materialism') feature as symptoms of the same underlying disease of rising inequality. Greater wealth and bigger bonuses, they argue, have unleashed a 'luxury fever'.[96] The new rich live in a 'self-contained world' of material excess – 'Richistan', in the words of the *Wall Street Journal* special reporter Robert Frank. 'There are so many Richistanis today, with so much money to spend, that they're creating an entirely new level of consumption. Being a truly conspicuous consumer has never been harder, since there are millions of millionaires competing for the same status symbols, and an even greater number of affluent consumers purchasing luxury goods to try to mimic the elite.'[97] A once proudly owned 100-foot yacht suddenly looked embarrassing when a 450-foot yacht pulled up alongside. In a race to keep up with the newest rich on the block, cars, houses and jewellery were all super-sized. Such excess, it is argued, sets off an avalanche of spending, from the super-rich to the mere rich and, from there, to the middle classes and below, each feverishly trying to keep up with their immediate social superiors. Recent psychologists concerned about the mental disorders wrought by inequality add Erich Fromm's distinction between 'having' and 'being'. People, they say, identify themselves too much by what they own, not who they are.[98]

This kind of diagnosis appeals to our sense of injustice but has serious flaws. There is, first of all, little in these accounts that is unique to recent decades of inequality and luxury. Fromm, after all, was already bemoaning a surge of possessiveness in the 1950s–'60s, which, importantly, was an era of growing equality. For Jean-Jacques Rousseau, writing two centuries earlier, luxury fever was a constant of commercial society across time. In his great work *On the Origin of Inequality* (1754), he put it forcefully: the 'savage lives within himself, while social man lives constantly outside himself'.[99] Appearance and the opinion of others meant everything for the latter. Luxury, inequality – and, Rousseau would have added, slavery – drove each other forward. Today's luxury critics write under the long shadow of these ideas, making it difficult to see today's luxury except through the eyes of this older morality. More specifically, it is unclear how the super-rich can inform the lifestyle of the rest while living on a separate planet. Most people would be hard pressed to name a handful of the super-rich and we know very little about how they live. By comparison, 250 million viewers followed the Spanish/Portuguese hit video '*Danza Kuduro*' in 2011, in which Don Omar picks up Lucenzo in a BMW Z4 and enjoys a cruise on a Viking Sport Cruiser V52 (a 'mere' fifty-six-foot motor yacht).[100] In a media society, celebrity culture has a larger pull on material aspirations than a banker or CEO.

The shift in cultural gravity from the wealthy to the movie star and tabloid beauty was already under way in the United States in the middle of the twentieth century. In 1956, the sociologist C. Wright Mills pointedly noted that the cover of *Life* magazine featured not a single debutante 'but no less than 178 movie queens, professional models, and the like . . .'[101] Significantly, it was the post-war decades of rising equality (1950s–'70s) that were also the years of the big consumer boom, in the USA and Western Europe alike. Tail-fins were getting longer in the 1950s. American homes, too, were getting bigger well before McMansions started to mushroom in suburbia in the 1990s. The super-rich were, in fact, downsizing in the 1950s–'60s, abandoning one luxurious mansion in Newport after another for a more 'normal' existence. Interestingly, American houses stopped growing in the 2000s, in spite of dizzying bonuses and escalating inequality.

Many observers continue to take their inspiration from Thorstein Veblen, the great critic of 'conspicuous consumption' in America a century ago, whom we met earlier. Veblen's moral outrage about the wastefulness of elite leisure, however, blinded him to the simple fact

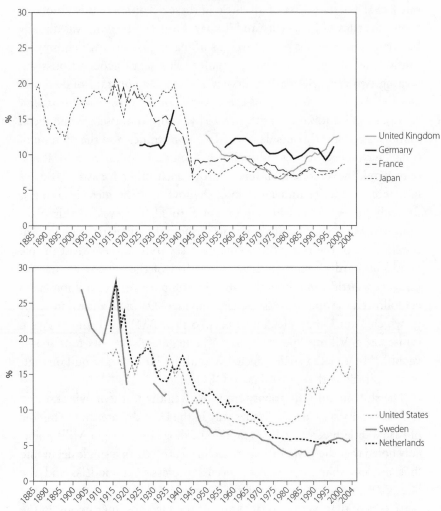

Source: Andrew Leigh, 'How Closely Do Top Income Shares Track Other Measures of Inequality?',
Economic Journal 117 (2007): 589–603.

that consumer culture can reach up as well as down. Once a car, a
home, a TV and a fridge came to be universal points of reference, elite
taste lost a good deal of its autonomy. The 'standard package', as the
sociologist David Riesman called it in 1955, started to operate as 'a
kind of sumptuary guide' on the upper classes. Rather than dictating
taste to others, the elite was being pulled along by the middle-class
mainstream. They started driving the Lincoln required by business etiquette (rather than an eccentric red Jaguar) and wearing the blue jeans

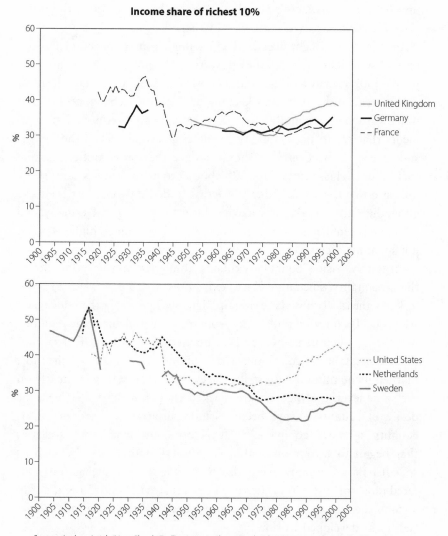

Income share of richest 10%

Source: Andrew Leigh, 'How Closely Do Top Income Shares Track Other Measures of Inequality?', *Economic Journal* 117 (2007): 589–603.

demanded by college life (rather than highly personal bohemian dress).[102]

As we have seen in previous chapters, it would be foolish to think that class has completely ceased to be a marker of taste. The rich may listen to pop, but they also still go to the opera. Nonetheless, the number of acceptable styles from which people pick their identity has proliferated considerably in the last half-century. Distinction looks increasingly in all directions – sideways and downwards as well as upwards. The advancing pluralism in taste has diminished the influence of the rich as style icons even further.[103]

Inequality in recent decades has resulted from a concentration not only of wealth at the top but of poverty at the bottom. Status-anxious people look downwards as well as upwards, seeking to stay ahead of the poorer Smiths as well as keeping up with the richer Joneses. That downward view is equally important and is easily overlooked in arguments that try to tie inequality to material excess. When the Smiths sink deeper into poverty, it should reduce the status anxiety among their middle-class neighbours. Why bother to upgrade one's car if those falling down the social ladder have just traded down or lost their car altogether? In fact, this is what has been happening in Germany and China in recent decades: higher inequality has prompted higher saving, not spending escapades.

Arguably, rising equality explains emulative consumption better than inequality, since it produces extra pressure to buy goods in order to keep ahead of those catching up. This was precisely the conclusion Alexis de Tocqueville took away from his tour of democratic America in 1831–2, when he compared it to his native, more stratified France. 'When inequality of conditions is the common law of society, the most marked inequalities do not strike the eye; when everything is nearly on the same level, the slightest are marked enough to hurt it. Hence the desire of equality always becomes more insatiable in proportion as equality is more complete.'[104] It is no coincidence that societies that began to favour an egalitarian lifestyle more recently, such as socialist East Germany, were also those where consumer goods mattered most for distinction. Luxury goods thrive in South Korea, not in spite of the fact, but perhaps because it is one of the most equal societies in the developed world.

The inegalitarian luxury thesis tends to take the United States today as the norm, but consumer cultures have come in a variety of shapes. In capitalist societies today, extreme personal debt is not only found in countries suffering from high inequality and few welfare services but also in those blessed with high equality and a welfare state, notably Denmark. The difference is that Danes are happy while in debt – they score highest in international happiness surveys. They can go to sleep in the sure knowledge that the state will come to their rescue if they run out of money in the morning. Anglo-Saxon observers often report that conspicuous consumption is unknown in Scandinavia, but this has probably more to do with their inability to read local codes than with its absence. Spending goes on summer houses, interior design and high-end ski wax rather than on wristwatches and SUVs. 'Luxury fever' is not a peculiar disease born out of Anglo-Saxon inequality. Take France, one of the few countries that so far has managed to escape widening income inequality. A high-net-worth French millionaire spends $30,000 on luxury goods a year, $8,000 more than the equivalent American.[105] The inegalitarian thesis would predict the opposite.

When we speak of luxury, we are, in fact, dealing with several markets. The high-end one includes classic Porsches and Tiffany and follows the ups and downs of the stock market.[106] Luxury handbags and watches make up a second, more diffused market with a logic of its own. The demand for luxury accessories is no longer primarily about emulating the very rich. It is about a sense of belonging to a global 'modern' middle class, about vertical inclusion rather than hierarchical distinction. This is one reason for the popularity of luxury brands in Asian markets, including China, with its stellar savings rate. For millions of urban secretaries, going off to work with the same handbag and sunglasses conveys the feeling of being part of the modern world. In the European Union, an estimated three quarters of luxury bags were counterfeit in 2006; Italy alone seized 89 million *falsi* articles that year.[107] Luxury, like consumption and taste more generally, has benefited from the relative loosening of the straitjacket of class-based taste since the 1950s. Formerly, luxury goods were about prestige: they signalled their owner's status. What marketing analysts call 'new luxury' is about experience rather than ownership as such.[108] It promises self-expression and belonging. Luxury is almost a democratic right: everyone is entitled to their own personal version of it. This is the backdrop to the phenomenal growth of luxury groups like LVMH in recent years – it had a revenue of €20 billion in 2010, one third of which came from Asia. Sales to the millions no longer means suicide for an exclusive brand. It is doubtful whether greater equality would change that.

Looking back at consumer credit over the last century, it is striking how successfully most people have mastered the rising volume of credit that came their way. Commentators in 1900 were united in predicting that debt meant moral corruption, social decay and bankruptcy. Some recent writers continue to argue that affluence has softened inherited restraint, leaving individuals unable to cope with the permanent flow of novelty.[109] This is hardly true for credit. By and large, people have proved their moral critics wrong. For every item repossessed there have been thousands of cars, TVs and homes that were loyally paid off. Credit has oriented consumers towards the prospect of ownership. Paying the monthly mortgage or an instalment on a product focused the mind. The number at the mercy of loan sharks and high-interest pay-day lenders is much smaller today than it was a century ago. Yet for the few who have been kept off or pushed off the escalator of credit, being excluded from regular credit is much harder now, because so many features of life today depend on a decent credit rating. Here is one of the first signs of polarization characteristic of contemporary consumer culture.

Not So Fast

The Society for the Deceleration of Time was founded in Klagenfurt, Austria, in 1990 and, in addition to its inspired name, deserves recognition for one of the more imaginative attempts at behaviour change. In town centres, activists planted 'speed traps' to slow down pedestrian traffic. People caught rushing were pulled aside and given a symbolic fine on the spot: a toy tortoise which they had to steer along 50 slow yards, before they were allowed to carry on. The decelerators have not been slow in coming up with other creative disruptions of the hurried pace of life, including setting up hundreds of deck chairs for a collective siesta.[1] Ironically, Austrian towns might strike most readers as in need of acceleration, not deceleration – a researcher who compared walking speeds across the world found Austrians walked more slowly than almost everyone else in Europe.[2]

The tortoise has long been the symbol of a wise, measured lifestyle. In the 1830s, *flâneurs* began promenading the galleries of Paris with live ones on a lead, showing off the pleasures of aimless strolling.[3] The return of the tortoise in the 1990s was part of a larger, global disquiet about the speed of life that reached a crescendo at the close of the twentieth century. A century that had started with promises of time-saving devices and leisure in abundance ended with anxieties about a 'time famine'. In 1900, speed meant modernity and vitalism.[4] Filippo Tommaso Marinetti and other futurist artists glorified it. To be sluggish was for peasants. Today, it is speed that is treated as uncivilized. 'Fast' life is under attack in all its forms: food, fashion, design, travel, tourism, music and sex. In 2005, the artist Ohad Fishof set out on a 'slow walk' across London Bridge to celebrate Longplayer, a loop of music that will be playing until the end of the millennium – it took him 9 hours, 43 minutes and 25 seconds.

The slow movement stretches from the many thousands of 'downshifters' who celebrate 'Take Back Your Time Day' in the USA and

Canada to the few hundreds in the Sloth Club of Japan. Slow Food, the largest group, was born in 1989 in reaction to a McDonald's erecting its golden arches next to the Spanish Steps in Rome. Since then, its initial emphasis on the pleasure of food has widened into an 'eco-gastronomic' politics of sustainability and responsible consumption. It currently counts 100,000 members in 153 countries. Cittaslow (slow city), its partner, followed in 1999, and at the time of writing has signed up 190 towns from Goolwa in Australia to Mungia in Spain; its symbol is the slug.[5] The philosophy (and, we might add, view of history) of these groups is pretty straightforward: in the words of the Slow Food manifesto, the twentieth century 'first invented the machine and then modelled its lifestyle after it. Speed became our shackles ... *Homo sapiens* must regain wisdom and liberate itself from the "velocity" that is propelling it on the road to extinction.'[6]

There is little dispute that the modern period has seen an unprecedented acceleration of life, although it is doubtful this started with the twentieth century. Friedrich Nietzsche worried in 1874 about the 'increasing rush and hurry of life' and the accompanying 'decay of all reflection and simplicity'.[7] He stood in a long line of commentators. Two generations earlier, touring the United States, it struck Alexis de Tocqueville that 'the American' was always in a hurry: 'he is so hasty in grasping at all within his reach that one would suppose he was constantly afraid of not living long enough to enjoy them.'[8]

Acceleration has been driven by three main forces. One is technological innovation: steam engines and the internet, trains, planes and automobiles. A conservative estimate is that the speed of communication increased by a factor of 10^7 in the course of the twentieth century.[9] The second is cultural: we feel the world is moving faster. It is tempting to think our sense of acceleration must have been the child of technological change, but perhaps it also worked the other way around. With the discovery of progress in the eighteenth century, modern societies transformed their sense of time from a wheel, where past, present and future spun in a circle, into an arrow with an open, unpredictable future. Finally, society itself has been speeding up, especially in the last half-century, as jobs and partners are changed more frequently and, with them, our sense of who we are.[10]

The precise interplay between these factors lies beyond the scope of this book. What interests us is what difference our consuming behaviour has made to our use and sense of time. Put crudely, is being time poor the price we pay for being rich in stuff? There have been two slightly different affirmative answers to this question. In the first, quality time appears as the victim of frenetic consumption. Affluent societies squeeze ever greater returns out of every hour worked, but by doing so they also make each leisure hour relatively more expensive in terms of foregone income. To make it worthwhile, people try to get more out of free time by consuming more things more quickly and superficially. Activities that take time and skill are replaced by an ever-growing mountain of stuff that offers novelty and instant gratification. Let's call this thesis the 'kid in the candy store' syndrome. The second proposition goes one step further. In a consumer society, where goods buy status and advertisements are everywhere, it suggests, people become so habituated to wanting more that they trade in leisure for longer work hours in order to finance their rising material aspirations. It is a form of self-enslavement. The quantity as well quality of leisure time suffers. People have to run faster and longer to keep their consuming self fed. This is the hamster-wheel syndrome. How close to reality is either of these answers?[11]

THE LEISURE REVOLUTION: WORK IN PROGRESS

A British man born in the 1840s would have clocked up 124,000 hours in the typical forty years of his life at work. His great-great-great grandson, on retiring in 1981, would similarly have spent forty years in his job but his total work hours would add up to a mere 69,000. And he could also look forward to living twenty years longer. Whereas his ancestor had spent half his waking hours working, he spent a mere 20 per cent.[12] This decline in work hours is so impressive that it raises the obvious question of how anyone could doubt that the twentieth century delivered a leisure revolution. Nonetheless, the nature of this revolution and its very existence have been a subject of intense debate. Not surprisingly, what has happened to work and leisure has been most hotly contested in the first affluent society: the United States.

Optimists can point to the data for work hours gathered by Angus Maddison, a pioneer of quantitative history. In 1900, an American worker worked 2,700 hours a year. By the 1980s, it was 1,600. In 1991, the sociologist Juliet Schor presented the case for the pessimists. Far from enjoying more and more leisure, she found that Americans since the 1960s were working longer hours and feeling increasingly stressed. Schor's thesis was a version of the hamster-wheel scenario, with a twist. The long-hours culture, she argued, had its roots in the power of American capitalists: for them, it was easier to exploit and control a full-time workforce than to deal with flexible or part-time employees. Workers, who might have preferred more leisure, were bought off with higher pay. Over time, this trade-off trapped workers in a consumerist 'work–spend cycle'.

Most time-use scholars who have scrutinized the pessimistic case have found it wanting. John Robinson and Geoffrey Godbey have shown how work hours did continue to fall between 1965 and 1985 – by seven hours for men and six for women. By the latter date, the average American adult had a total of forty hours of free time per week. They similarly threw out the pessimists' discovery of a 'leisure gap'. Instead of women carrying a double or triple burden – juggling kitchen, children and a job – to support their husbands' leisure, they identified an incipient 'androgynous society', with men and women increasingly spending their time in similar fashion.[13]

Whom should a jury of historical readers believe? The competing interpretations reflect in no small measure different methods and lines of inquiry. Schor rested her case on subjective estimates. These captured that Americans increasingly *felt* overworked – there is little dispute that, in the United States and in developed societies more generally, the number of people who feel rushed has been going up since the 1970s.[14] Our subjective sense, however, is a notoriously bad judge of time. 'The happier the time, the quicker it passes,' Pliny the Younger observed 2,000 years ago.[15] It is not surprising that the more stressed people were, the longer work seemed; people's estimates of how they spent their time each day routinely added up to more than twenty-four hours. A more conventional method asks people to keep track of their daily activities in time-use diaries. This was the method employed by Robinson and Godbey. These diaries provide a useful reality check: people worked less, it showed, than they felt they did.

In addition to how much time, we should also ask whose leisure we are tracking. Data such as Maddison's shows us the rise of leisure from the perspective of the individual worker. That is great if you happen to be a typical adult male in paid work. It is not so revealing if you happen to be a woman, unemployed, under fourteen or over sixty-five. Work and leisure, moreover, are not individual experiences. Most people (still) live in households which share paid work, unpaid work and leisure unevenly among their members. If Mr John Smith came home one hour earlier from the office on Friday, it would make little difference to the sum of leisure if Mrs Smith spent an extra hour cooking his meal. One person's leisure can mean another's work. But it does not have to. Mr Smith might decide to lend his wife a hand with the dishes (thirty minutes), in which case each would gain thirty minutes of leisure, and immeasurable marital harmony. It is the distribution between members that matters as well as leisure overall. There are good reasons, then, why, before we can reach a verdict on the leisure revolution, we need to widen our perspective from that of the worker to that of society as a whole.

Thanks to Valerie Ramey and Neville Francis, two economists, we have a comprehensive analysis of time use that allows us to follow the shifting balance between work and leisure in the United States across the twentieth century.[16] Their data captures unpaid work ('home production', i.e. cooking, cleaning, etc.) and schooling, alongside paid work. It also includes adolescents, the elderly and those working for the state, for example soldiers and teachers. The figures reveal several fascinating long-term trends. Working men have indeed been doing less paid work since the 1930s, but women have been doing more. Put together, both sexes aged twenty-five to fifty-four on average worked exactly as many hours in 2005 as they did in 1910: thirty-one hours a week. When it comes to leisure, the picture is mixed. Americans as a whole (aged fourteen+) enjoyed four more hours of leisure a week in 2005 than their ancestors a century earlier. But some generations gained much more than others. The young (aged fourteen to seventeen and eighteen to twenty-four) had five extra hours of free time, the elderly (sixty-five+) as many as fourteen. Everyone was a winner, except the twenty-five- to fifty-four-year-olds. In 2005, they had almost the same amount of free time as in 1900. But look a bit closer and an interesting backsliding becomes visible. The middle-aged, too, had their leisure revolution. It simply went into reverse in the 1980s. For them, 1980 was the apex of leisure – five hours extra compared to 1910. This was quite in line with their younger cohorts. What set them apart was that these additional hours were all lost again between 1980 and 2005.

John Maynard Keynes in 1930 gazed into a crystal ball and saw a future where, thanks to greater productivity, people would enjoy an extra twenty hours of leisure a week by 2030. Clearly, we are a long way from this utopia. At the same time, it is plainly wrong to think there was no leisure revolution at all or to suggest that workers in the 1930s gave up free time in exchange for goods and higher wages.[17] Into the 1970s, Americans across all age groups enjoyed more leisure and did less paid work. It is a fallacy to presume that consuming more must

Average weekly hours of work and leisure for all people aged 14+ in the United States, 1900–2005

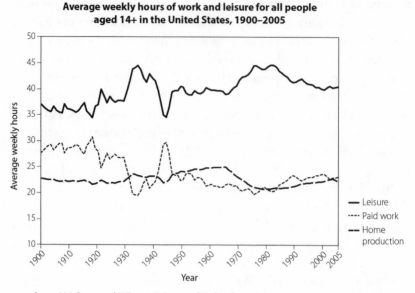

Source: V. A. Ramey and N. Francis, 'A Century of Work and Leisure', *American Economic Journal: Macroeconomics* 1, no. 2 (2009): 189-224.

Average weekly hours of leisure for men by age group in the United States, 1900–2005

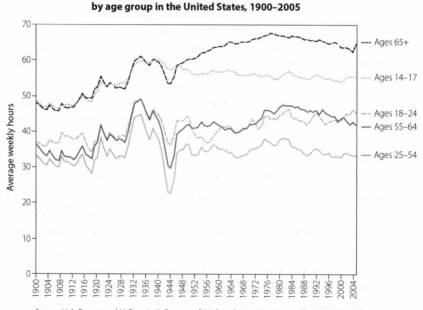

Source: V. A. Ramey and N. Francis, 'A Century of Work and Leisure', *American Economic Journal: Macroeconomics* 1, no. 2 (2009): 189-224.

**Average weekly hours of leisure for women
by age group in the United States, 1900–2005**

Source: V. A. Ramey and N. Francis, 'A Century of Work and Leisure,' *American Economic Journal: Macroeconomics* 1, no. 2 (2009): 189-224.

mean having less leisure. The bulk of the twentieth century shows the opposite is the case.

Does the reversal since the 1970s then prove the pessimists right? Not entirely. American women (aged twenty-five to fifty-four) did eleven hours more paid work in 2000 than they did in 1970. We would expect leisure to suffer. What is remarkable is that their free time declined by only half that amount. In other words, leisure proved quite resilient. Women did not trade in their free time for greater earnings on a 1:1 basis. Since a day has only twenty-four hours, where did the missing hours come from once women started going to the office? They came mostly from taking off their rubber gloves and putting down mops and dusters. Women's weekly unpaid 'home production' has fallen by over eleven hours since 1960. Their husbands and partners picked up some of the slack. Since 1970, the typical middle-aged American man has been chipping in five extra hours a week doing chores at home. This, in part, explains why the leisure revolution came to a full stop for men of working age; incidentally, these were the very years when complaints about feeling rushed started to rise. Many men converted shorter working hours not into leisure but into housework.

Going to work accomplished what Hoovers, washing machines and other domestic technologies had promised for decades but failed to deliver: to save women time.[18] Time devoted to childcare, it should be noted, has expanded, even as the time devoted to cooking and cleaning has fallen.

It is too simple to imagine a straightforward substitution of household labour by goods and services bought in the marketplace, as some economists do.[19] While double-earner families did 'buy in' food rather than cook from scratch, they have been unwilling to let go of all sorts of other housework, including care of their children. The remarkable fact is that an American household spends the same twenty-two hours on home production in 2000 as it did in 1900 – *in spite of* having fewer children, although also *because* of more smaller households that create more work. Instead of substituting one for the other, households buy more goods and services *and* hang on to housework. If those doing it were paid for it, household work alone would amount to a formidable 22 per cent of GDP in the USA today; if the services provided by dishwashers and other consumer durables were added, this figure would rise to 30 per cent.[20] It is no coincidence that the decline in unpaid work since the 1970s has been accompanied by a shift towards casual clothing and eating out. If people were willing to hand over even more unpaid work to the market or accept lower standards of comfort and cleanliness, leisure would benefit considerably; in sum, home production has proved as much a brake on the leisure revolution as work and wages.

To see here the coming of an 'androgynous society' may be a little premature – women at present are still left with two thirds of the housework, and men tend to look after the dog rather than the kids. Still, the large gulf in time use between American men and women has narrowed, a partial convergence echoed across Europe and Canada.[21]

This democratizing trend has been criss-crossed by new class divides. In the 1950s, observers started to notice that ordinary Americans were working less and expressed a greater desire for free time than their bosses. Executives, meanwhile, demonstrated their importance with long days at the office and multiple phones on their desk. Busyness signalled status. Time-use diaries since have documented the widening gulf between these two cultures of work and leisure. Education is a good predictor of leisure. The more Americans have of the former, the less they tend to have of the latter. A high-school graduate gained almost seven hours of extra free time between 1965 and 1985, whereas a university graduate stood still. Long hours were disproportionately clocked up by highly educated men and women. The educational gap was reflected in inequalities of time by income. High earners had four hours less free time than workers on a low income. The poor were the new leisure class, the rich the new working class.[22]

Theories of consumer society often see leisure and work in a zero-sum relationship: the more important one becomes, the less significant the other. Yet the gain in leisure – while modest – has been paralleled by the growing significance of work as a source of wealth. In 1900, being rich meant having a country house or an inheritance. Today, it depends much more on one's salary and qualifications – hence the fascination with bonus pay and the proliferation of university degrees. In the course of the twentieth century, success came to rely increasingly on human capital.[23] Longer hours are one way to accumulate it. Idleness fell victim to career development.

'Extreme *busyness*,' Robert Louis Stevenson wrote in 1877, seven years before shooting to fame with *Treasure Island*, 'whether at school, or college, kirk or market, is a symptom of deficient vitality; and a faculty for idleness implies a catholic [wide-ranging] appetite and a strong sense of personal identity.'[24] The idea that idleness built personality will appear perverse to most readers today. Admittedly, Stevenson managed to combine idle moments with writing thirteen novels, six travel books, collections of essays and poetry, composing – he played the flageolet, a type of flute – and travelling to North America and Samoa, where he cleared land and built a home, all in a life cut short at forty-four. Keynes, too, had a dismal view of work. In his eyes, the rich, if they worked at all, were motivated by avarice, the poor by the need to survive. That work might be a source of pleasure and pride largely eluded him.[25] In post-industrial society, managers and professionals are spending longer hours at the office than their counterparts two generations earlier. In part, they do so because their job is more satisfying today – '*le bonheur du travail*', as the French say.[26]

The contrast between hard-working Americans and idle Europeans is almost a cliché today. In 2006, the financial giant UBS pointed to longer work hours to explain why the American economy was growing faster[27] – an idea that the recession since has surely put to rest. On the face of it, the numbers speak for themselves. According to the OECD, Americans worked on average 1,800 hours in 2005, compared to 1,680 in Britain, 1,550 in France, and around 1,400 in the Netherlands, Germany and Scandinavia.[28] The introduction of the thirty-five-hour

week in France in 2000 was the icing on the cake. In Germany, the
number of paid holidays rose from twenty-three days in the 1970s to
thirty-one days in 2010; after twenty years of service, an American
employee would be lucky to get nineteen days. What lies behind this
divergence? One thesis invokes the deep-rooted Puritan work ethic in
America. This is rather dubious. In the 1950s, a keen observer of social
change like David Riesman worried that America was undergoing an
'anti-Puritan revolution', where leisure, once a 'fringe benefit', 'threatens to push work itself closer to the fringes of consciousness and
significance'.[29] Americans were more idle than Europeans into the early
1980s. A good deal of the recent reversal had to do with stronger
unions, public services and social-democratic politics in the old world.

Such contrasts between national types obscure more than they reveal.
Americans, the argument goes, prefer income and consumption to leisure, whereas Europeans choose to be a bit poorer and take time off. It
depends on one's point of view. To Australian Aborigines, whose simpler
lifestyle requires only three or four hours of work a day, the two alleged
opposites would appear barely different versions of the same modern
time regime.[30] Once we dig beneath the national stereotypes, the parallels become more visible. In 1941, a mere 3 per cent of sixty-five-year-old
Americans cited a preference for leisure as the main reason for leaving
the labour force. By the 1980s, every second did.[31] Ageing Americans,
in other words, are not so different from Europeans. Conversely, many
Europeans share in the trends outlined for the United States. Shorter
official work hours notwithstanding, busyness and overtime have been
on the rise in Europe, too, chipping away at a neat distinction between
working week and leisurely weekend. In Germany, the number working in the evenings has increased from 23 per cent to 30 per cent since
1995; 40 per cent regularly worked on Saturdays, 20 per cent on Sundays in 2007.[32] In the Netherlands, paid work has increased and free
time decreased by almost four hours a week in the last generation.[33]
The gender gap with regard to leisure and unpaid work has narrowed –
although it remains pronounced in Italy and Spain.[34] One reason for
the higher number of hours worked in the United States is that fewer
people in France and Germany do paid work in the first place. This
does not automatically mean the latter wallow in an ocean of leisure.
Rather, they cook more frequently. Once unpaid work is added, the gap
in work hours with the United States shrinks to 10 per cent.[35] Spaniards virtually match American hours in paid work.

Above all, European time has undergone a similar polarization by class. In Germany today, more than half of those in a 'superior position' work more than forty hours a week; a fifth put in more than forty-eight hours. In lower positions, thirty-five hours or less are normal. In the United Kingdom, similarly, men with low human capital had less leisure time in 1961 than their better-educated fellow citizens. Forty years later, they had more. The average British manager gives up four days of his holiday entitlement every year.[36]

All this means that education, gender and household composition shape leisure more than whether one lives in the United States, or Sweden, or France. A chief executive in Stockholm or Paris is closer to his New York counterpart than to the local postman when it comes to free time. Across the board, children are very bad for leisure; living alone with them doubly so. It is these social roles that largely determine who is time rich and who time poor. National policy regimes matter less.

A group of social scientists has tried to capture how much free time people could have if they just worked enough to stay above the poverty line and attended to the bare necessities at home.[37] Like 'discretionary income', people have 'discretionary time', a hidden reserve they could tap in to. Some have more than others. A single adult with no kids gains around eleven hours of discretionary time when tying the knot as the couple starts to share household chores. When the first-born arrives, a double-earning couple loses between seven hours (Sweden) and thirteen hours (United States). A subsequent divorce leaves a Finnish mother twenty-three hours worse off, an American thirty-three hours. As we might expect, time poverty, like other poverty, is less harsh in Scandinavian welfare regimes than in liberal America; although the figures also suggest that the French have even less potential free time.

In real life, of course, time does not have the same kind of 'discretionary' quality as money. It does not come in clear units of dollars and pounds but is tied up in habits, sequences of activities and all sorts of acts of coordination. Counting it in bulk is fraught with problems. Still, the concept of discretionary time makes it possible to distinguish between those who give up leisure by choice and those who do so by necessity. Double earners complain about harriedness, but they could make Keynes's dream a reality tomorrow if they wanted to. While not completely masters of their own destiny, it is hard to treat them as victims of time poverty. The real temporal proletariat are lone parents. What is interesting for our purpose is that Europeans – whether they live in welfarist Sweden or corporatist France – have been just as bad at turning discretionary time into leisure as Americans. A Swede could have eighty-five hours of extra free time a week and still live above the poverty line. In real life, he makes do with just thirty hours of spare time. Similarly, the average American, German and Frenchman each sacrifice forty-six hours a week of potential leisure. The contrast between leisure-loving Europeans and go-getting Americans must not be overdone.

Most people in affluent societies, though, do not want to live just above the bare minimum. Downshifting remains a minority trend.[38] Lots of extra free time is not seen to be worth it if it involves a shabbier apartment, older clothes and furniture and giving up the car, the newest electronic device and exotic holidays. The question is: is it the right choice? Or, is this allocation of time making people less happy than they would be otherwise? The question goes to the heart of what we mean by well-being and how to measure it. In the last generation, a vast literature has challenged the conventional economic yardstick of gross domestic product (GDP) and outlined a number of alternative measures of well-being. We cannot do justice to this extensive scholarship,[39] only hint at implications for the uses of time. The initial focus of research was on the tenuous link between income and happiness in affluent societies. In a seminal paper in 1974, Richard Easterlin noted that, while rich Americans were happier than their poor neighbours, Americans as a whole were no happier in 1970 than in 1946, in spite of being 60 per cent richer (in real income). Once basic human needs were met – around $15,000 a year in 1974 money – additional income ceased to buy more happiness.[40]

Other scholars since have been more optimistic and point out that richer countries do tend to be happier than poorer ones. Danes today are richer *and* happier than they were forty years ago. Whether there is a basic threshold beyond which money does not buy more happiness has also been questioned. A Gallup poll in 2007, for example, found that Americans' reported well-being continued to rise with their money.[41] That happiness has not blossomed in the developed world at large even though money has rained down on us should not be so surprising. A new car or kitchen raises our objective well-being but at the same time it also raises our expectations. Our subjective well-being – which is what most surveys measure – remains unchanged. This is the so-called satisfaction treadmill. It is worth stressing, however, since it is sometimes forgotten, that the data does not show that affluence has made us *less* happy.

It is useful asking people how happy they feel overall, but everyday life is a mix of more or less pleasant activities. We can learn a lot from asking in addition how satisfying or annoying they find particular activities on a given day and then checking how much time they devoted to each. This, put crudely, is the day-reconstruction method developed by the Nobel Prize-winning psychologist Daniel Kahneman. It has been the basis of an innovative inquiry into time use and well-being in France and the United States led by Kahneman, his Princeton colleague Alan Krueger and four other experts. The team interviewed eight hundred women in middle America (Columbus, Ohio) and a similar sample in the middle of France (Rennes) in 2005.[42] The result is a 'U-index', a misery index which measures the percentage of time spent in an unpleasant state. There are many similarities. American, like French women, found sex, exercise and eating far more pleasant than going to work or looking after the children. Watching TV, it is worth noting, was as enjoyable as prayer and conversation, and considerably more so than sleeping and shopping. But there were also significant differences. French women tended to do more of the pleasant stuff, like eating and, yes, sex, and less unpleasant housework and paid work. And they found childcare less irritating than American mothers, which, perhaps, is the result of doing less of it, thanks to greater childcare support and having grandparents nearby.

Overall, however, the differences are not vast. Women in Columbus spent at most 5 per cent more time in unpleasant activities than their counterparts in Rennes.[43] This may, however, be an underestimate, since the data did not include holidays – people who were away, after all, could not be interviewed, and French vacations are three weeks longer. The researchers discounted their importance since across a whole year they add up to a tiny fraction of time. This is surely too simple. Holidays are an integral part of people's identities. They are planned before and relished after. On vacation, families follow a different rhythm. More time is devoted to play, eating, sociability and, presumably, sex, all of which leaves a legacy when people re-enter ordinary life. The number of photos taken and souvenirs on display tell a story of a holiday's lasting effect on well-being, which is insufficiently captured by a method that asks individuals to reconstruct only a normal day.

Research that compares how societies use and experience time is still in its infancy. Plenty of problems remain. What if some societies are simply grumpier than others or take pleasure from different activities?

Time and pleasure

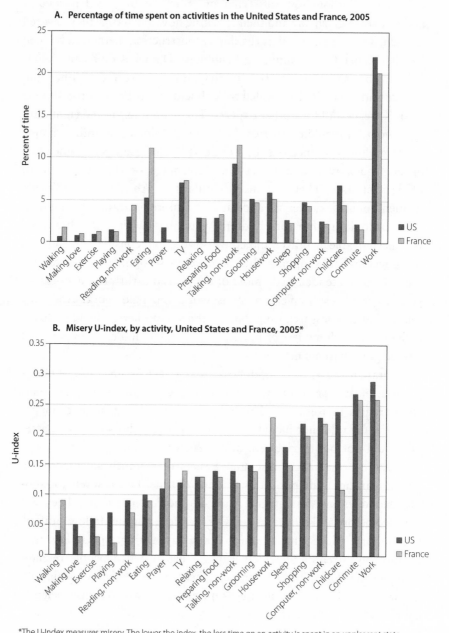

A. Percentage of time spent on activities in the United States and France, 2005

B. Misery U-index, by activity, United States and France, 2005*

*The U-Index measures misery. The lower the index, the less time on an activity is spent in an unpleasant state.

Source: Krueger et al, 2009, 'Time Use and Subjective Well-being in France and the US', *Social Indicators Research* (2009), table 3.

Long lunches may make the French happy, but does that necessarily mean other cultures would (or, indeed, should) follow their example? What is pertinent for us is that the French–American comparison hints at a paradoxical relation between leisure and well-being. It brings us back to the critique that the affluent society is essentially 'joyless'.[44] According to this thesis, affluence favours cheap entertainment technologies and other 'comfort goods' that give instant but short-lived pleasure at the expense of genuinely stimulating 'relational goods'. People sit and watch TV alone instead of meeting friends. Ranking daily activities by their pleasantness suggests this is too simple. Some consumer products give greater joy than others – in France, as in the United States, watching TV is well ahead of computing. More importantly, the French have a greater *joie de vivre* all-round: they watch more TV *and* have more sex. Whether consumer goods have really killed time-intensive leisure and relational goods should be treated as an open question, not a foregone conclusion. It is to the uses of leisure that we must now turn in search of an answer.

WORK HARD, PLAY HARD

Leisure was a discovery of the ancient Greeks. Work and play were fused in an organic whole in hunter-gatherer societies. It was the Greeks who split them apart. Aristotle ranked leisure alongside wisdom and happiness as one of the ends of life. Leisure made the complete person. It allowed for passive contemplation and civic action, and involved the freedom to take a disinterested view of the world. Not by chance do the European words 'school', *Schule* and *scuola* echo the Greek for 'leisure' (*schole*), although the reality of education today may be a far cry from this ideal. Unlike for the moderns, leisure for the ancients was pure and indivisible. The idea that it could be measured in hours and minutes or that someone might have more or less of it would have stunned Aristotle. Leisure and work were mutually exclusive states of existence. The privilege of having the former required a complete freedom from the latter. The leisure of the few was therefore supported by the slavery of the many. It was this that gave 'leisure' a bad name in Victorian times and made 'the leisured classes' a frequent term of abuse. A man with an income of £200,000 a year, the Victorian historian and moralist Thomas Carlyle sharply noted, lived off the labour of 6,666 men and did nothing but shoot partridges.[45]

Industrialization delivered enormous gains in productivity that made it possible to give workers time off. Before it could be enjoyed, however, leisure had to be reclaimed as something good. Into the early twentieth century, leisure appeared a 'threat'. Would workers know what to do with free time, or just drink it away while gambling on a bloody dog fight? The answer, according to middle-class reformers, lay with 'rational recreation' such as reading, sober entertainment and physical exercise. By the early twentieth century, the war over leisure was being won. All societies – democratic, fascist and socialist – embraced leisure as a means to create stronger citizens, although they differed in the purpose to which they put this strength.

In addition to the quantity of free time, therefore, the contest over leisure concerned its quality. Champions of leisure rarely advocated doing nothing. For 'the first time in human history,' an American observer wrote in 1942, 'leisure for recreation and the arts is available to almost all classes. Instead of regarding leisure as dangerous, we should use it as a means of rounding out our personalities . . . Play and creative activities should occupy more of our attention.' [46]

Defining leisure has been far from easy. Leisure implies choice and the ability to do something for its own sake. In 1976, official British statistics included activities in the work environment, such as company sports and clubs. Paid holidays, meanwhile, appeared in the category of employment before they were moved back to leisure in 1988.[47] The international convention since has been to distinguish free time from paid and domestic work on the one hand, and from personal care on the other. The harmonized European time-use survey (HETUS) treats socializing, entertainment, reading, resting and hobbies as free time. Gardening, handicrafts and shopping, on the other hand, are coded as domestic work, together with childcare and cleaning, while eating features as personal care. Of course, such hard-and-fast distinctions blur reality. We must all eat to survive, but some eat for pleasure and like to dine in style; if eating was partly treated as free time, the leisure gap between Americans and Europeans would widen.[48] Gardening, knitting and do-it-yourself projects, similarly, have taken on qualities of leisure. In the following pages therefore, we need to be flexible. Anything else would give a distorted picture about the implication of affluence for leisure.

A final word of caution about a simple yet fundamental difference. Private consumption, for the economist, refers to how much money an individual spends. Leisure, for the sociologist, measures the amount of free time devoted to a certain purpose. The two do not translate into each other. Mr Jones might buy a fancy new car, but if most of his driving was to commute to work, it would show up as travel to work in a time-use diary. Conversely, leisure can involve more or less consumption. An active skier consumes more money and resources than her neighbour who prefers to stay at home and read. Whether more leisure is the inverse of more consumption – as in the idle European, consumerist American stereotype – is a question that calls for empirical verification.

In 1927, Lydia Lueb interviewed 2,000 female textile workers in Westphalia about how they spent their free time. On average, these young women worked fifty-four hours a week, including Saturday mornings. In addition, they did around two hours of housekeeping a day. What was their 'favourite' activity in their own time? she asked them. The biggest single answer was rest (41 per cent). A quarter listed sewing, knitting and domestic work, followed at some distance by reading (8 per cent), cycling/sport (3 per cent) and entertainment (2 per cent). The women had a week's holiday – half spent theirs at home with needlework or in the garden. Only one in five went on a short trip. A tiny minority went hiking. During the working week, some of the women went swimming, but 'sport on the weekend was virtually unknown' among them. Some lived in hostels and factory homes which on evenings and Sundays put on dances and social games as well as courses in cooking and sewing. In the winter months, trade unions organized plays and song recitals for their members. For the majority, Sundays were unchanging: in the morning to church, then housework and lunch. The afternoon was filled with walks and visits with friends and family. A few practised an instrument or rehearsed for a play. Some went on excursions with their singing club. What they appreciated most, however, was the chance to sleep in and rest.[49]

Fast forward to Europe in 2000 and we enter a different time zone. A German woman now enjoyed over five hours of free time a day, a Norwegian almost six. Men, on average, had half an hour more. Around two hours a day was devoted to watching television – one third of all free time in Germany, and over half in Hungary. This is the single biggest shift in the use of leisure time. What rest was for Westphalian workers, TV is for contemporary Europeans. Other activities, however, complicate the picture. A good half of all Europeans spent an hour or so socializing. Reading, too, remained popular, especially in Northern Europe. A quarter of Europeans spent half an hour a day playing a sport and walking. Cultural participation (five to fourteen

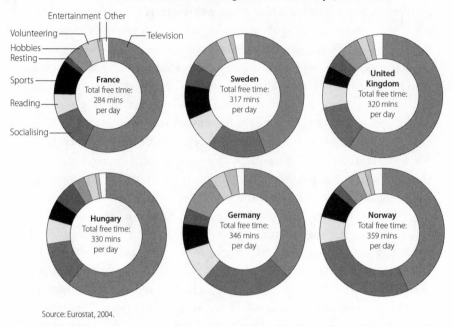

Free-time activities of men aged 20 to 74 in Europe, 1998–2002

France
Total free time:
284 mins
per day

Sweden
Total free time:
317 mins
per day

United
Kingdom
Total free time:
320 mins
per day

Hungary
Total free time:
330 mins
per day

Germany
Total free time:
346 mins
per day

Norway
Total free time:
359 mins
per day

Entertainment Other
Volunteering
Hobbies
Resting
Sports
Reading
Socialising
Television

Source: Eurostat, 2004.

minutes a day) came last, but it looks so small because time-use diaries measure daily averages and people do not go to the theatre or the museum every day. Gardening added ten to thirty minutes a day, shopping another half an hour.[50]

Of course, the two surveys do not allow for a rigorous comparison; the historical study was limited to female workers, not a cross-section of the population. National time-use surveys exist only from the 1960s. Still, placing the two alongside each other points to major changes in the quality of free time, its rhythm, pace and density. First, in the 1920s it was still natural to include housework and needlework as 'free time'; indeed, a quarter of the young women listed these as their favourite activity. By 2000, such tasks had been demoted to 'unpaid work'. Second, the number of leisure activities has grown exponentially. The Westphalian working women either went swimming or did no sport at all. Their great-grand-daughters could choose football, volleyball, tennis, judo and indoor skiing. The greater level of activity, thirdly, is related to greater mobility. Other than the occasional walk, leisure in the 1920s had a fixed residence, at home or in the hostel. Today, Europeans still spend two thirds of their leisure at home, but they have been increasingly restless since the 1960s; in 1961, a British adult spent

Free-time activities of women aged 20 to 74 in Europe, 1998–2002

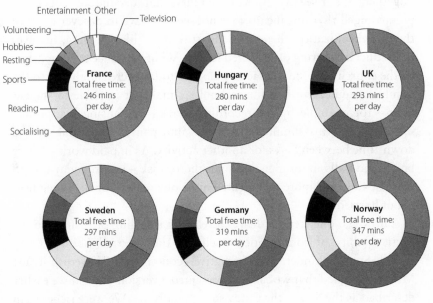

Source: Eurostat, 2004.

eighty-seven minutes a day on shopping and out-of-home leisure; forty years later it was 136. In France, more than a third did not go out at all in the evenings in 1973; a generation later, that number had fallen to a fifth.[51] Going out for a meal was unknown to the Westphalian women, who either ate at home or at work – their ninety-minute lunch break would strike most workers today as equally inconceivable, at least outside France.

Finally, there is the density of activities themselves. Europeans in 2000 do not only watch long hours of television, they also crowd their day with a larger number of other activities than their ancestors. Reading has slightly declined in the last three decades,[52] but the numbers flocking to museums and the outdoors are up. And while no longer as dominant as even half a century ago, socializing remains a significant part of everyday life. In the past, there was less leisure, but what there was came in predictable, sequential chunks: the visit to church, followed by housework, lunch, then the afternoon walk. Today, there is more time off, but leisure is less structured and comes in a greater range of offerings, each with their own demands on time and space. The visit to the gym needs to be coordinated with dropping off the kids for their music lesson and the trip to the supermarket. Europeans today spend more time in their car for the purpose of free time than to get to work.[53] Together, the rise in physical mobility and decline in collective, pre-arranged rhythms means that households have to do ever more of that synchronization themselves. Leisure time, like all time, involves the artificial ordering of scattered reality. What was once accomplished by the church bell and the factory clock is today increasingly left to the family schedule. Information technology makes it possible to stagger time – for example by pre-recording movies or pausing live perfor- mances – but this simultaneously eats into pauses by freeing up the down-time between tasks for another activity. As in paid work – where breaks have all but disappeared since the 1960s[54] – leisure today is both more flexible and more turbulent. This is one reason for the rising feel- ing of harriedness.

Can we go one step further and relate that feeling of rushing to the hectic quality of consumption itself? In the *Harried Leisure Class* (1970), Staffan Linder, a conservative economist and Swedish Trade Minister, argued that we can. He presented a version of what we earlier described as the 'kid in the candy store' syndrome. We were richer than ever before, Linder wrote, but, instead of enjoying a harmonious arca- dia, 'our lives . . . are becoming steadily more hectic.' At the root of this paradox of affluence lay an 'increasing scarcity of time'. Consumption, he noted, takes time as well as money. As productivity increased the relative price of work, it simultaneously made free time more expen- sive. Sitting on a bench and watching the birds looked less attractive if it was possible to earn good money in the same amount of time. In addition, products were becoming progressively cheaper. The natural response to these changes, Linder argued, was to switch from time- hungry, slower cultural activities to cheap goods that offered instant gratification. Consumption, he predicted, would become more and more 'commodity intensive'.[55]

Forty years on, it is possible to take stock. True, cupboards and garages have never been so full of goods and gadgets. But the thesis was not simply about the rate of acquisition. It was about con- sumer goods killing off time-intensive leisure activities. Reading, it is true, has declined in almost all affluent societies since the 1980s, although there are notable differences between countries and age groups. Scandinavians remain twice as avid readers as Southern Euro- peans. Among the French, however, fifty-five- to sixty-four-year-olds today are more likely to read a book than they were ten years ago. In

Britain as a whole, book reading has been on the rise in the last generation.[56]

Plenty of other evidence, however, suggests that free time in affluent societies has not entirely succumbed to turbo materialism. After all, the biggest chunk is spent in front of the television. Adverts may be faster and more frequent than they were half a century ago, and there are shopping channels and channel surfing but, as such, television is not especially 'commodity intensive'. The set is changed every few years, TV dinners arrived and programmes whetted an appetite for the outside world, but otherwise the two hours a day in front of the box are two hours of wasted opportunities for other 'commodity intensive' leisure. A good deal of television viewing, moreover, involves time-intensive sociability. Herr W., a fifty-six- year-old retired digger operator, told German researchers in the 1980s that he watched up to six hours a day when football was on – he was a Borussia Dortmund fan – but did not think it had hurt his social life at all: he often watched with neighbours and they sometimes played games on the side.[57]

Television habits remain uneven across Europe. The more affluent Scandinavians and Germans devote less of their free time to television (c.33 per cent) than Hungarians and Eastern Europeans (50+ per cent). Interestingly, the former also socialize more than the latter, the very opposite of what the harried model would predict. Socializing has declined in some countries, such as the Netherlands. Overall, however, visiting and chatting have been remarkably resilient, and this in spite of materialist temptations and more women joining the workforce. Americans today socialize less with neighbours than two generations ago but in exchange spend more time with friends and family. In Britain, socializing has been stable since the 1970s. In Germany, it may even have increased. And families spend more time with their children. Ironically, and notwithstanding the advance of fast food and eating out, the family meal at home is stronger than ever in some affluent societies today. Germans spent more time eating in 2000 than in 1990 and did most of it within their own four walls.[58]

Social life might have been accelerating, but it is a mistake to presume that it was an oasis of calm a century ago. *The Week-end Book* first appeared in 1924 to provide the British middle classes with suitable material for 'hours of sociable relaxation'. A run-away success, many new editions followed. In the 1931 edition, poems took up 218 pages, games and songs another 116, including the 'Eton Boys', best sung 'with feeling and a nasal Cockney intonation'. Relaxation in the lounge, however, was accomplished through speed in the kitchen. 'As time is usually the chief consideration,' the authors explained, 'menus have been drawn up on a speed-basis.' A good hostess was advised to 'serve unusual dishes that will be remembered' but assured that it was fine to use 'tinned foods' and 'disguise them'. A 'quickish' menu consisted of escalopes of veal – simmered for ten minutes – accompanied by a nut and olive salad, and 'deep-fat-fried potato fingers'. If time was really short, there was always the 'very quick' option of cold mutton slices, followed by 'stewed prunes in claret – boil 10 minutes'. What was not be rushed were the drinks. There were recipes for seven cocktails: 'If possible, ALL COCKTAILS should stand on ice for at least half an hour before shaking and taking.'[59] Fast food and slow drinks summed up the inter-war weekend. A new edition in 1955 added scrambled eggs and hot sandwiches to the list of 'quick dishes' and introduced 'quick sweets' such as tinned pineapple with honey 'fried over low heat'. And, thank God, it discovered espresso for the English. Coffee, it explained, need not be 'Puddle water'.[60] The serious host was urged to acquire an expensive Gaggia machine or at least to 'practise your palate at the Espresso bars' in the meantime. By 2006, coffee had improved, but *The Week-end Book* had dropped both its poetry section (an indication of the decline of shared reading aloud) and its sheet music (a sign of the decline of the house concert and the diffusion of stereos and CD players). The number of cocktails, on the other hand, had jumped from seven to forty – reflecting the rise of exotic travel and the greater range of cultural influences. Foodstuffs and cuisines, too, were more varied than ever before, ranging from Scallops en Coquilles to old-fashioned Tripe and Onions. Speed, interestingly, no longer merited special attention at all.[61]

The Week-end Book first appeared in a period associated with the advent of 'mass consumption'. Since then, a striking number of time-intensive activities have survived the onslaught of cheap, ready-made goods: hobbies and handicraft, sports, gardening, dog walking, music making and participation in cultural life. To be fair, some of these have undergone a relative decline. The number of Americans doing needlework, for example, fell from a third to a quarter in the course of the 1980s.[62] Still, this leaves a proud 5 million who, unfazed by economic models, regularly display their handiwork in public today. And for every story of decline, it is easy to cite one of rise, resilience or renewal. Amateur cultural practices especially have blossomed. In France, women today are three times as likely to play an instrument or sing in a choir than they were in 1973. Every third person is engaged in painting, dancing, writing a novel or pursuing some other amateur art for pleasure, double the number a generation ago.[63] In New Zealand, 71 per cent regularly read for pleasure, 50 per cent potter about in the garden, and 12 per cent sing or tell stories; to put this in perspective, computer games are played by 28 per cent. In the United States, the boom in spectator sport since the 1960s has been paralleled by a no less impressive rise in visits to theatres, opera and non-profit cultural venues. In affluent societies today, many more people play sport and go to a museum than at the time Linder was writing, not fewer.[64]

There are plenty of reasons why the 'kid in the candy store' model does not capture the full reality of consumption in the rich world. One mistake was to imagine a simple trade-off between leisure and work, as if no time was devoted to domestic work, social life or education. Time might be scarce, but contemporaries have scraped it off cooking and cleaning to have more time for gardening and assembling scrapbooks. Sport, museum-going and other time-intensive activities have also benefited from the helping hand of the state; there is a reason cultural participation is strong in Belgium and Germany but has decreased in Eastern Europe, where governments slashed subsidies after the collapse of communism; in Poland, theatres and music halls lost almost half their audiences in the 1990s.[65] Perhaps the fundamental mistake, however, was to treat consumption as a short-lived encounter where a fairly passive consumer took quick satisfaction from one standardized good before moving on to the next. Anthropologists have shown how people take sustained pleasures even from mass-produced goods by making them their own, selecting them with care and integrating them with other possessions, creating their identity in the process.[66] For many, their possessions are the project of a lifetime. Quick 'commodity intensive' distraction offers no short cut. If economists read more Henry James, they would have appreciated this.[67] The consumer's active role as a creator of novelty extends to innovation and skill. These have stimulated new leisure activities as well as perpetuating older ones. Gardening, sewing, home improvement and similar hobbies have an in-built tendency to lead people on to fresh tasks, by creating new skills and expectations in the process.[68] Paradoxically, time-saving products such as hand-held power-drills and quick-fix plumbing have been catalysts of more time-intensive leisure.

Innovation also helps explain why cheaper goods have not wiped out

cultural activities. The ability to reproduce music has vastly extended
its appeal and access. We have seen this for the radio in the early twentieth century.[69] The tape recorder and the MP3 player take this story to
the present. One important difference between the radio age and the
present is that technology now is more modular, giving consumers the
chance to be producers and create their own video or pop song, or
touch up their digital pictures.[70] The mobile phone and social networking sites have spread this process to socializing. The mobile phone is a
good example of how users turned a device that was originally designed
for business into a tool to stay in touch with friends and family. Instead
of accelerating the pace of leisure, it may well have eased time pressure
by giving people unprecedented flexibility to coordinate their schedules, use 'down time' and to stagger commitments. An Australian
study, which compared phone logs, diaries and survey questionnaires
in 2007, found that frequent mobile-phone users did not report a
greater feeling of being rushed. Nor, contrary to popular wisdom, was
there any significant spill-over of work into leisure time. A mobile call
about work interrupted leisure or domestic activities for only 1 per cent
of people. Most calls on mobiles (74 per cent) and texting (88 per cent)
were to friends and family.[71]

Since then, smartphones have multiplied the channels and types of
communication between work and leisure. By 2011, roughly every
third American and European had a smartphone. Measuring what precisely people use their smartphones for is enormously difficult. Still, the
best available data gives some idea about the core functions. In the
United States in 2010, smart phones were most commonly used for
sending text messages (68 per cent), taking pictures (52 per cent),
accessing news (40 per cent), accessing social networks (25 per cent)
and playing games (23 per cent). Only 31 per cent used them to send
emails. In Europe, a large 2009 survey found that usage varied considerable between countries. In Italy, only 8 per cent used their mobile
phone for emails, while it was 20 per cent and 26 per cent in France
and the United Kingdom respectively. In France, 41 per cent used theirs
to play music; in Spain and Britain, it was barely 20 per cent.[72] These
figures suggest smartphones are primarily used for leisure and personal
communication. True, the boundary between work and leisure has
become more porous with smart technologies, but, arguably, it is leisure and private life which are increasingly invading work. Employees
with children or other care responsibilities at home use their personal
mobile phones at the workplace to be readily available. Information

and communication technologies have created a growing expectation that people should be accessible to their friends at all times, including work hours – multiple email accounts and texting are ways to manage this invasion.[73] Thanks to online browser-based software, games can be played on the office computer at any time.[74] How many employees refrain from checking their Facebook page at work?

In addition to using up time, then, consumption has created new uses of time with the aid of more sophisticated products and technologies. It needs a computer and software to manipulate digital photos as well as a digital camera or phone. Thanks to the mobile phone, making a personal film has never been easier. In France, the number of people shooting a film or video doubled between 1997 and 2008.[75] By 2012, iPhones were more widely used than digital cameras. The taking and sharing of photos has skyrocketed with the spread of social networking sites and microblogging platforms which enable users to post and share multimedia. In 2012, according to one estimate, Facebook had 10,000 times more photos than the US Library of Congress. One billion videos are watched every single day on YouTube, the bulk shot with mobile phones. In Germany alone, 14.5 million smartphones were sold in 2011; in the same year, another 7.5 million compact cameras and 1 million digital SLR cameras were purchased. Across the world, digital camera sales that year reached 140 million.[76] And with the new digital technologies have come new types of uses and products. Photos are no longer just printed – but they are processed and manipulated and turned into personalized canvases, calendars, neckties, even bed linen. In sum: instead of swamping leisure with a deluge of cheap stuff, innovative commodities and new time-intensive activities have grown in tandem. The remarkable story of leisure in the late twentieth century is one of symbiosis, not extinction.

We saw earlier how the young and old have snatched the biggest share of free time. Types of leisure, too, are unevenly distributed, especially by education and class. The better educated, the more active people are. That this should be so contains a final clue as to why time-intensive cultural activities have not vanished. Learning to play the piano takes time. A pianola solves that problem: it plays by itself. And yet, the homes of the cultured and upwardly mobile tend to have a piano, not a pianola. In Germany, ten- to eighteen-year-olds spend an impressive hour a day on music-making or creative arts.[77] Why torture innocent ears if it is possible to satisfy the children with cheap, easy downloads of the newest tune? The short answer is: 'It's sociology, stupid.' In addition to any intrinsic pleasure from the sound of music, the time set aside to learn an instrument teaches discipline, how to gain competence and overcome challenges and, above all, cultivates the taste of a 'superior' person. An appreciation of Bach and Berg is a form of cultural capital. Listening to the 'Well-tempered Clavier', going to the opera and visiting metropolitan art galleries are all leisure activities that require time, education and investment and are consequently a mark of high status. Economic capital does not directly translate into cultural capital. Education is decisive. Being cultivated matters to professionals working in media and the arts, whereas for managers and engineers with the same salary it is a minor badge of distinction at best. In France in 2008, a member of the liberal professions was twice as likely to attend a classical concert as a businessman. Such status distinctions are mirrored in who plays an instrument, notwithstanding the growing popularity of music-making overall. A French professor is twice as likely to play an instrument as a skilled worker or an entrepreneur.[78]

Private tastes have public consequences. One explosive issue is whether the best educated also reap the greatest benefits from support for the arts. Are ordinary tax-payers funding the cultural capital of their superiors and their own subordination to boot? The evidence is not clear cut. An investigation in 1973 found that during the weekend, upper-class Germans were seven times as likely to go to the theatre, a concert or a lecture as their fellow lower-class citizens.[79] By contrast, a study in New Zealand three decades later found broadly similar levels of participation across society. Class mattered for the cultural genre preferred, not whether people enjoyed it actively or passively. The poor were not all couch potatoes. They simply preferred singing and folk music to ballet and opera.[80]

New Zealanders, though, are an unusually active bunch. Where education does leave a mark is on the range and frequency of activities, and here New Zealand shares in an international pattern. University graduates go to rock concerts and restaurants *and* to the museum, the theatre, the movies and the gym.[81] And they do so more often than workers. They are also more active in clubs and associations. They personify leisure in action. Contrary to a conventional preoccupation with 'stress' and 'burn-out', some evidence suggests that these typically better-educated, high-status groups enjoy their fast-paced, complex types of leisure, and more so than those with simpler lifestyles.[82] These hyper-active individuals are also the same people, French data shows, who possess the most audio-visual equipment and portable devices and own the greatest

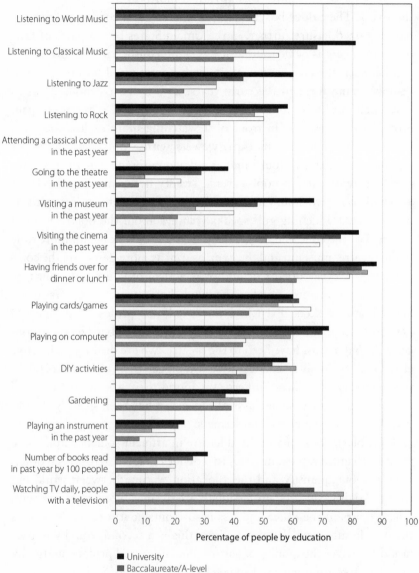

Leisure cultures by educational background, France, 1997

Listening to World Music
Listening to Classical Music
Listening to Jazz
Listening to Rock
Attending a classical concert in the past year
Going to the theatre in the past year
Visiting a museum in the past year
Visiting the cinema in the past year
Having friends over for dinner or lunch
Playing cards/games
Playing on computer
DIY activities
Gardening
Playing an instrument in the past year
Number of books read in past year by 100 people
Watching TV daily, people with a television

Percentage of people by education

■ University
■ Baccalaureate/A-level
▨ Professional training (CAP)
☐ 3 years high school (BEPC)
▨ No diploma or elementary school only

Source: Olivier Donnat, *Les pratiques culturelles des Français: Enquête 1997.*

number of CDs, tapes and long-play records, underscoring the symbiotic relationship between time-intensive and goods-intensive leisure patterns; tellingly, the educational gulf was narrowest for 45rpm pop singles.[83]

'Work hard, play hard' was already a motto in the United States in the 1950s. The cult of busyness in professional and corporate life since has energized leisure further, in the United States but in parts of Europe, too. There is evidence that it has significantly widened the leisure gap between the classes. For all its bad reputation, TV was a radical democratizing force in the early years. By 1970, most households in developed capitalist and socialist societies owned a set and spent around the same time in front of it watching more or less the same programmes. In France in 1974, viewers with a university degree or diploma watched fifty-four minutes a day on average, just twenty minutes less than early school-leavers. Twenty-five years on, the latter watched over two hours a day while graduates watched just half as much.[84] That widening gulf speaks volumes about the polarization of leisure. For the educated, less time in front of the box meant more time in the theatre, museum and the gym, as well as more games on the computer.[85] Not every doctor or author is active, of course. We must be careful not to imagine an absolute divide between active professionals and passive workers. Even in France, half the professional elite has never set foot in an opera house, a symphony hall or been to a pop concert, although most have been to the theatre. We are dealing with active elements, but in some classes these are bigger than in others. Only a tiny minority of skilled workers ever found their way to any of these venues, and in the case of classical concerts it has been steadily shrinking; they could just as well be farmers.[86]

The polarization of work and leisure in affluent societies in the late twentieth century, then, involves two divides that cut across each other. One is about quantity and the allocation of time between work and leisure. Highly educated professionals are the new working class – with longer hours in the office and less leisure outside it; ordinary workers the new leisure class. Running across this is a second, equally important divide over the quality of leisure time. Educated professionals may have less free time but they squeeze the most out of it, juggling a far larger number of frequently changing activities than those without qualifications.[87] Their leisure pattern mimics their work life. As the masses gained leisure and holidays in the sun, idle conspicuous consumption lost some of its charm for the elite. The privileged few now raised their game, seeking refuge and distinction in more demanding activity holidays, cultural tours and personal-fitness regimes. Climbing up Mount Kilimanjaro replaced lazy days on the Riviera. Since their hyper-activism consists of especially time-intensive activities that involve going out, extra mobility and coordination, it is, perhaps, only fair that these are also the very groups that feel most rushed. Fitting it all into twenty-four hours is not easy.

In the final analysis, 'time poverty' is about the quality of leisure, not its quantity. Active practices can be fulfilling but require being in the right place at the right time. The greater their frequency, the greater the challenge of synchronizing them all. Leisure is not much fun if it is constantly interrupted. Women suffer from this problem every day. Men, it has been estimated, enjoy three more hours of pure, undiluted leisure than women, who have to combine theirs with childcare and housework.[88] 'Turbulence of everyday life is evidently female,' the German statistical office put it bluntly in 2004.[89]

The sense of stress also reflects changing expectations about the purpose of free time. A sociologist who interviewed French mothers found that university-educated women experienced leisure in a radically different way to their working-class sisters. For the latter, a 'totally free day' ideally meant spending it with their children. Leisure was family leisure, a reprieve from work and having to earn a living. Looking after the children was not so bad. To the graduates, by contrast, childcare was a task, not leisure. It appeared like a burden. Individual leisure to them did not appear as liberation from paid work but as its equivalent. Tellingly, graduate mothers treated family leisure as part of their 'housework'.[90]

In many ways, these two groups stand for the alternative ideals of leisure that have traded places in the twentieth century, one dominant at its beginning, the other at its end. In 1900, leisure was primarily about restoration after work – time to rest, recover and refuel. The key word was 'recreation'. Cultural activities were an add-on, to pull workers away from drink, gambling and other temptations. By 2000, leisure had undergone an active makeover. Free time was no longer primarily about freedom from work but about the freedom to accomplish things, to acquire and demonstrate one's competence in a range of activities. The latter were simply unpaid. The surge of extreme sports, creative-writing courses, amateur cooking and drama groups is merely the tip of the iceberg of intensified leisure. For many, leisure is serious business. It is no coincidence that professional busyness, active leisure and 'quality time' have arisen together in the late twentieth century, a period when affluent Western societies began the transition from industrial to knowledge-based societies. After centuries of trying to break free from the world of work, leisure today is close to mimicking its rhythm. It is too early to tell whether in post-industrial society leisure and work will once again fuse into an organic whole; the use of social media points in that direction. If they do, it is unlikely to involve the contemplative, disinterested qualities cherished by the ancients.

Slow Food, Cittaslow and similar movements hope to stop the acceleration of life. In the light of the above, their chances of success are slim. The intensification of leisure is the crest of a wave of social, technological and cultural changes. Frequenting slow-food restaurants may help local farmers but it is far too specific an intervention to slow down the overall tempo of life. The 150,000 who visit the annual 'Salon of Taste' do not arrive in Turin by foot or donkey. If the pace of life resulted primarily from consuming products faster, there might be room for hope. It stems, however, primarily from doing more and the pressure to coordinate a greater number of activities. Cultivating a taste for local food can be interpreted as another attempt to build cultural capital and demonstrate aesthetic expertise. It is not clear that it has any impact on the number of other activities, their frequency or the increasingly complex sequencing between them. It may just add to these. A manifesto for a slow lifestyle announces 'we believe multitasking is a moral weakness.'[91] Mobile phones, email and other communication devices give their users greater flexibility to arrange the sequence of tasks. It is unlikely most people will switch off their Facebook sites or stop following Twitter while socializing or working, if movements like Slow Food cannot do without them either. Voluntary simplicity, similarly, faces the challenge that, however much we might want to, it is extremely difficult as an individual to simplify one's lifestyle if the world around us continues to tick to a different rhythm. Voluntary simplifiers find themselves in a position akin to shift-workers whose schedule is out of synch with everyone else's.[92]

Collective changes to everyday rhythms have greater promise. Car-free Sundays appeared during the oil crisis in 1973 and were selectively rediscovered in 2010 by Hamburg, Bern and in Paris along a stretch of the Seine. The French thirty-five-hour week, introduced in 2000, freed up Saturdays for family time and sport. Yet it also increased the number taking weekend breaks.[93] Even collective interventions face their limits in an age of personalized scheduling and the simultaneity of 'timeless time' offered by email and wireless technologies.[94] Faster physical and virtual communication have created the 'long weekend'. The French train network shows greater numbers leaving on Thursday and returning on Tuesdays. No law can stop such a change in rhythm. It would require the collapse of the TGV, budget flights and mobile networks to reverse the move towards 'bi-residence' and holiday homes.

Should we despair? The acceleration of life has its costs, such as 'burn-out'. But that does not mean society is flying off the rails, as some commentators fear. Humans are extraordinarily flexible and adaptive, much more so than they are sometimes given credit for. William James in the 1890s noted how people acquired habits and routines to free up the mind for other, more conscious and directed activities. The 'great thing', James wrote, 'in all education, is to *make our nervous system our ally instead of our enemy* ... [and to] make automatic and habitual, as early as possible, as many useful actions as we can'.[95] The twentieth century has been a long lesson in such habituation. Early listeners gave the radio their full attention. Swedish ads in the late 1920s praised the banana as the ideal quiet snack during radio hours.[96] Gradually, people learnt to listen to the radio and eat their breakfast, talk and read the paper. Similar feats of coordination and multi-tasking happened with the car, the TV, the computer, the mobile phone, and will, presumably, continue to do so with unknown technologies in the future. One act of consumption has served as a platform for another. What is fast and slow, then, is an evolving affair without a given threshold. There is no reason to believe this evolution is finished.

Leisure, we have noted, has been a Western concept, and it was industrial European and American societies which first wrestled with its quantity and quality. The data for non-Western societies is thinner. Still, it is worth pondering at least briefly to what degree the Western story of leisure in the twentieth century is indicative of general trends. Outside the affluent core, the answer probably would be 'not much'. In Africa, colonial rulers constantly complained of 'lazy' natives. Such charges were steeped in racism but they also recorded that time was ticking to a different rhythm. Many Africans who arrived in inter-war Brazzaville (Congo), for example, were used to a four-day week. They were not easily disciplined into a continuous imperial working week with a few dedicated hours for structured leisure on the side. Absenteeism was rife. Before the arrival of football and dance halls, men filled their time playing cards or strolling about. For a woman to be seen with time on her hands, by contrast, marked her out as a bad wife or prostitute. As late as the 1980s, social workers struggled to persuade women in rural Congo that recreation was not dishonourable.[97] Communist China underwent its own revolution in time. Mao ordered workers to sleep in the middle of the work day. A three-hour nap was quite normal, the very opposite of intense leisure and an intervention that makes Western decelerators look positively feeble.[98] Today, the Chinese watch as much television as the heaviest viewers in Europe – two hours and six minutes – but their day in many ways retains its own distinct rhythm. The Chinese spend less time cooking, cleaning and shopping. And 40 per cent take a nap between 1 p.m. and 2 p.m., although few may nod off dreaming of Mao; far fewer Europeans take a siesta.[99] Mao's China, though, was hardly an exemplar of commercial leisure. A look across the Sea of Japan is instructive.

The creative use of free time had long been cherished in Japan as a path to self-discovery. The arts had absorbed the Buddhist idea of self-cultivation in the late Heian period (794–1185 CE). Competence in flute and *kin* – a string instrument – was a measure of one's worth and a central feature of elite culture and identity, as captured in the *Tale of Genji*, the eleventh-century novel about the life and love of an emperor's son. 'Genji was at leisure, and he spent his time at music making of all kinds.' He organized nocturnal dances and had princes and nobles pick up their own favourite instruments and join the professionals. Their 'playing of "Ah, Wondrous Day!" brought the most ignorant manservants in to listen among the horses and carriages crowded by the gate, smiling broadly as though life was at last worth living'.[100]

The opening of Japan to the West in the late nineteenth century ushered in a dramatic revolution of leisure. In Edo, leisure had been communal, taking place in temple festivals and floating worlds (*ukiyo*) with puppet theatres, games and songs. Westernization spread commercial entertainment instead. And it broke the elite's control over leisure. Once the preserve of samurai, *budō* (martial arts) became sport for the masses. The years around 1900 saw the invention of a host of new traditions like judo with their own grades and competitions; women were admitted, too. Bars and cinemas offered dreams of modernity.

Looking back from the vantage point of the early twenty-first century, it would be foolish to deny the impact of Western ideas and practices on Japanese leisure. At the same time, it was not a simple story of one replacing the other but rather of advance through permeation, with new practices drawing strength from inherited customs and ideals. New products and habits were incorporated into an existing leisure culture. The Japanese used to talk of spare time at home as 'killing time' (*hima tsubushi*). A main activity was 'lying around' (*gorone*). With the arrival of TV, surveys recorded a switch to *terene*: lying down to watch TV.[101] In the 1960s, Pachinko, a kind of pinball game, advanced into the national pastime – at its height, in the 1980s, it is said to have contributed 5 per cent to Japan's GDP and, even after a recent decline, one in seven Japanese today regularly put their yen in the slot, spending Y19 trillion ($175 billion) in 2013.[102] Especially popular with young adults on low income, Pachinko offered an escape from the drudgery of everyday life (see Plate 50). As in Edo times, it created public spaces for entertainment.

In Japan, as in the West, recent decades have seen a shift from passive to active leisure, from recovery and recreation to self-improvement. The emphasis on active recreation has been able to draw on an older tradition of creative play and self-cultivation. Hiking, fishing and other active outdoor activities (*asobi*) reached new popularity in the 1970s. Leisure parks started to combine education and fun. The Japanese can visit a reconstruction of the Dresdner Zwinger (Dresden's magnificent Rococo palace) in Arita and learn about porcelain, or visit Huis Ten Bosch – a theme park replica of a Dutch town twice the size of Tokyo Disneyland which opened in Nagasaki prefecture in 1992 – to admire the windmills and experience the force of Dutch floods in a high-tech video diorama.[103] By international comparison, vacations and free time in Japan continue to be the victim of a long-hours culture, notwithstanding government efforts since the 1990s to reduce work hours. Still, the Japanese feel less rushed than Americans, in spite of sleeping less; one reason frequently given is that they are better at demarcating blocks of time for eating, hobbies and conversation.[104] The Japanese tea hour provides a separate time zone to unwind, similar to the long lunch in France. 'Grazing' Americans have lost this sense of time.[105]

THE DAY OF REST?

1949: Sunday in a working-class household in south London. Stella, a twenty-four-year-old housewife; her two-year-old son Steven; her younger sister, Joan (a clerk) and a dog. Stella's husband is away in the army:

8.45 a.m.	Stella gets up . . . makes pot of tea, takes tray to bedroom with *Sunday Pictorial* . . .
9.30 a.m.	Stella comes into kitchen again in pyjamas . . . Starts to cook fritters and fried bread, goes to fetch Steven [and feeds him].
10 a.m.	Makes another pot of tea . . . reading the paper.
10.30 a.m.	Joan gets up . . . They eat at table . . .
11 a.m.	Steven is washed . . . Stella puts on her clothes . . . the wireless provides background music.
12.30 p.m.	Stella preparing pudding for dinner . . .
1 p.m.	Stella cooking. Steven playing. Joan plucking eyebrows in front of kitchen mirror. The two women talking about artists heard at the moment on 'Family Favourites'.
2 p.m.	All have dinner . . . Menu: joint, boiled potatoes, sprouts, suet pudding with golden syrup – pot of tea. Wireless background.
3 p.m.	Stella washes . . . up dinner things – then joins Joan, playing with Steven. They talk. Joan makes a pot of tea.
3.30 to 6 p.m.	Both women . . . reading. Stella, *Red Star Weekly, Women's Own* and *Sunday Pictorial* – Joan, *American Comics*. Steven plays with cards. Dog asleep. Wireless background – light programme. Bursts of conversation – bursts of knitting.
6 p.m.	Stella laying tea . . . in kitchen . . .
8 to 10 p.m.	Like the afternoon again.
10.30 p.m.	Sitting over supper – talking about underwear. Stella writes a letter to her husband. Joan writes a letter too.
11.30 p.m.	Library books open (novels) but both talking . . . The dog is sent down the garden for a few minutes.
12.30 a.m.	They go to bed.[106]

We have this sequence of a normal Sunday thanks to Mass Observation, which, beginning in 1937, sent out volunteer observers to record ordinary life in Britain. It is a good way to start the final leg of our exploration of the changing nature of leisure time. So far we have encountered time in several dimensions: clock time that counts the hours; pace; and density. But time also has a rhythm. The seven-day cycle, with a day of rest following a working week, has been a powerful one, although neither natural, nor universal. The seven-day rhythm was a human invention, a mathematical contrivance with roots in Judaism and astrology. Not all civilizations have shared it. In 1929, in the last serious experiment with an alternative pattern, the Soviets tried to rationalize activity into an 'uninterrupted' work week (*nepreryvka*) and abolished a shared day of rest – it caused so much disruption that it had to be suspended two years later.[107]

For most readers, the slightly abbreviated pattern of Stella's Sunday will look so alien that it might just as well have come from a documentary about a distant tribe. Yet it happened just over sixty years ago in one of the most developed corners of the world. Although recovering from war and austerity, Britain had been in the vanguard of consumer culture. This would be hard to tell from the record of Stella's Sunday. Admittedly, the family drank an impressive volume of tea, and Sunday was the day to get 'stuffed' with a rich meal. Plenty of time went on reading the papers and magazines – many Britons took three or more newspapers on Sundays. Most strikingly, however, by midnight, when Stella sank into bed, the family had not set a foot outdoors, not even to walk the family dog. What consumption there was took place within the four walls of their home. Public spaces, shops and entertainment might just as well not have existed.

The reason, of course, was that most of these were closed on Sundays. Across the border, puritanical Scotland went so far as to put the swings in parks out of use, although shops here could choose to open on Sundays. To be sure, not every Briton was solidly stuck at home. One in seven went to church, slightly more preferred the pub when it opened at 11 a.m. Some fathers took their children to parks and fountains. Nor was entertainment completely absent. Across the River Thames, in working-class Hammersmith, there was a swimming pool, a few tennis courts, two cinemas and theatres, a musical concert and a Lyons tea house. Still, as the mass observers stressed, that was 'not a lot' for 100,000 people. For adolescents, in particular, Sunday was an uphill struggle to find some fun. Here and there, an amusement arcade and skating rink were open, but these were rare oases. A good deal of entertainment was self-made. In Hammersmith, the fourteen- to eighteen-year-old members of the 'White City Racers' turned a waste site into a speedway track for their bicycles, delighting local onlookers with their stunts and 'pseudo-leather' uniforms. In the rest of the country, however, Sundays were largely immobile. A tiny minority (5 per cent) went 'motoring'. In the industrial north, mass observers found the town centres empty. In the countryside, residents rarely strayed beyond the village green. It was as close to 'slow living' as modern Britons got. In pubs, customers sipped their pint of beer more slowly, to pass the empty hours. 'Sunday is a dreary day,' a metalworker's wife told researchers:

'Everywhere is dead.' A fifteen-year-old schoolgirl was slightly more charitable: 'nothing particular ever happens, and yet I would not call it dull.'[108]

One day a week was fenced off as the very opposite of the over-stimulated eventfulness with which consumption is associated. This deserves more attention than it has received. For there was nothing natural about putting Sunday off limits, not even in Christian societies. In colonial North America, settlers trading on a Sabbath were fined. However, when the Spanish brought the seven-day week to Latin America in the sixteenth century they made sure to set up Sunday markets. Sunday was a day for church and commerce, prayer and play. As late as 1857, the municipal Council of Ambato (Ecuador) was worried that the bulk of the population would abstain from Mass if Sunday commerce was prohibited. 'It is a fallacy to believe,' it said, that Sunday 'being given over to vice and complete idleness . . . would favour religious practice and public morality.'[109] To the contrary, allowing people to sell on the way to church made it easier to save souls. The Council was right. Once Sunday was exclusively devoted to the service of God, in the 1860s, attendance at mass began to plummet.

Ecuador was caught up in a larger movement that gathered pace in commercial Christian societies in the middle of the nineteenth century. Some forces were local and specific – prohibition in Ecuador was driven by a devout Catholic magnate, whereas sabbatarianism in Britain was led by evangelicals who tried to ban all recreation and labour on a Sunday as sinful. Other facilitating factors were of a more general sort – advances in transport made it easier for goods and people to reach markets on other days of the week. In England, the 1830 Beer Act limited pub opening hours to 1–3 p.m. and 5–10 p.m. on Sundays. Fairs were prohibited twenty years later. The Lord, however, never gained complete control of Sunday. When sabbatarians joined with temperance reformers in 1855 and tried to prohibit Sunday trading after having reduced drinking hours a year earlier, Londoners started a riot in Hyde Park. Karl Marx believed the English revolution had finally begun. In reality, Britons' revolutionary struggle ended with winning back two and a half additional hours to drink up on Sundays.[110]

Shop hours remained flexible in England until the Shops Act of 1911 entitled all employees to a half-day holiday and required all shops to have an early-closing day; in Canada, Sunday had been designated a weekly day of rest four years earlier with the federal Lord's Day Act. In the nation of shopkeepers, Sunday trading had largely ceased by the 1930s. Britons seeking entertainment elsewhere could go cycling and boating or visit the British Museum, which opened its doors on Sundays in 1896. A 1932 law permitted concerts, zoos and some cinemas to open, but most other forms of recreation struggled for decades before they managed to shake off the sabbatarian straitjacket. Amateur football matches on Sundays went ahead only in 1960; professional games not until 1974. Horse racing and betting had to wait another generation. On the continent, too, shops did not pull down their shutters on Sundays until well into the twentieth century. Bismarck's Berlin was a shopper's paradise. On Sundays, many shops opened at six in the morning and closed only at eleven o'clock at night. Shops had no interest in losing valuable customers who came to town for church or other distractions. In 1892, opening times were limited to five hours in the German empire, but it was not until 1919 that most shopkeepers and salespeople earned a full day of rest. Even then, shops were allowed to stay open on 'Special Sundays' and Christmas Eve.[111]

The partial closing down of Sunday in the century after 1850 points to a number of ironies. At the very moment societies began to enjoy greater purchasing power and greater access to mass consumer goods, they lost precious time to shop and spend. It is a reminder that advanced societies do not only tick to the rhythm of the till. Real wages picked up in the 1870s and consumer culture boomed in the roaring 1920s but they did so in what were predominantly industrial societies. And until the 1960s, they remained such. Sunday closure reflected the influence of churches but, even more so, of trade unions. Legislation was tightened as church attendance was plummeting. The voice of dispersed consumers was no match for that of organized workers. In an era of trade-union power, attention was on shorter working hours, not longer shopping hours.

Another irony concerns the role reversal between otherwise more open and more regimented societies. Commercial societies, it is often said, are naturally more open, flexible and consumer friendly than those where states, producers and traders rely on privileges and restrictions. Hence, it is possible today to shop in an American mall or British supermarket on a Sunday but stand in front of closed doors in Germany. These contemporary positions are far from natural, however. A Berlin housewife in the 1880s had at least as much access to shops on Sundays as one in London. She would have found the limited opening hours in Anglo-Saxon cities a century later distinctly illiberal.

Sunday closing was not some natural default in consumer society but the historic outcome of forces and circumstances specific to each country. The current situation is distinguished by remarkable variety. On one extreme are Austria and Germany, where only shops at railway stations and airports have the right to open on a Sunday. On the other is Finland, where smaller stores can trade around the clock on weekends and larger ones can open from 12 to 6 p.m., and as late as 9 p.m. in December. In between, there is an impressive range of compromises. Spain initially allowed shops to open on Sunday in the 1980s, before restoring some restrictions in the 1990s. Today, most Spanish shops open on the first Sunday of each month. Norway limited Sunday opening to December; France and Belgium to a maximum of five days a year. Mediterranean countries tend to exempt tourist areas, a considerable concession. In England and Wales, the 1994 Sunday Trading Act gave small shops permission to open; shops larger than 280 square metres (3,000 square feet) were limited to six continuous hours between 10 a.m. and 6 p.m. Across the border, in Scotland, such regulations have been unknown.[112]

Deregulation started early in the United States. In 1961, thirty-four states banned Sunday trading. By 1985, the number was down to twenty-two. Discount stores asserted that 'blue laws' supporting the Christian Sabbath were a violation of the First Amendment, which prohibits any law respecting an establishment of religion. A string of court cases subjected Sunday-closing laws to a 'rational basis test': what was the sense of allowing the sale of camera film but not of cameras? California, Florida and many states in the West and Midwest were in the vanguard and lifted their 'blue laws' altogether, aside from the sale of alcohol. Other states kept specific restrictions on the books. New Jersey, which did away with Sunday closing in 1978, continued to outlaw bingo, barbers and beauty parlours.[113] Canada began its deregulation in 1985. It would be a mistake, however, to interpret Sunday opening as an Anglo-Saxon neo-liberal crusade. In Europe, the first to move was social-democratic Sweden in 1971, followed by Belgium and Spain. Margaret Thatcher, the priestess of neo-liberalism, suffered a memorable defeat when she tried to liberate British shops in 1986.

In England and Wales, the situation was messy. The prohibition of Sunday trading after the Second World War was shot through with eccentric loopholes. Corner stores were allowed to sell gin and takeaway food but not dried milk or fish and chips. At their local newsagent, customers could buy porn but not a bible. The 1986 plan was to create a clean slate. Instead it split public opinion and, interestingly, retailers.[114] In one corner were the challengers – the Shopping Hours Reform

Council – a group of retailers, producers and consumer advocates. In the opposite corner stood the Keep Sunday Special Campaign, an alliance of trade unionists and bishops, but with notable support from C&A, a fashion chain, Iceland, a supermarket, and the co-operative societies. Each side claimed their position fostered family and wealth. For the latter, open Sundays threatened to kill 'quality time' for family lunches, worship and recreation. For the liberators, Sunday jobs would give women independence. A Conservative MP quoted one of his constituents, who was a 'Sunday only worker' in Bristol:

> I work on Sundays, because I want the best for my children . . . They have a lot more extras and holidays, clothes and outings . . . When I leave the house on Sunday mornings I leave happy in the knowledge that my husband will be caring for them and that they will all enjoy some 'quality time' together. I also get a well needed break from the children and household . . . I look forward to my own independent time.[115]

Liberators claimed that deregulation would both set families free and generate wealth and employment. The opposing side cited Marks and Spencer, the quintessential British shop, which opposed Sunday trading because it would merely spread six days' business over seven days. The liberators lost. With a twist of historical irony, the same Iron Lady who crushed the mighty unions and deregulated the City failed to crack open shop doors on Sunday. Victory had to wait until 1994.

Is it possible to discern any pattern in the uneven landscape of Sunday trading? Affluence alone is clearly not enough. After all, Germany is wealthier than Britain, France richer than Finland. Religion is a contributing factor, but not in a direct sense of religious attendance. In the United States, Sunday shopping advanced in spite of a religious revival, whereas church-going has declined across Europe; in Thatcher's Britain, merely 10 per cent went to church regularly. Rather, religion has acted as a bulwark in societies where it occupies a central place in the political landscape thanks to strong Christian Democratic parties. In Germany, Sunday opening was a political anathema until 1999, when department stores in Berlin openly called on shoppers to join in demonstrations of civil disobedience and purchase goods speciously labelled 'tourist items'. Such pressure from retailers faced a far tougher political environment than elsewhere. Wolfgang Schäuble, the former leader of the German Christian Democratic Union (CDU), denounced shopping on a Sunday as a 'threat to Judeo-Christian civilization'.[116] Reform stopped at longer Saturday opening hours.

The decisive factor can be found in the changing structure of the economy in combination with the role of women in the workforce. Sunday opening in Britain came on the heels of a shift from industry to services, which gave the retail sector and unions with shop assistants among their members greater weight than in Germany or France. In Britain, the shop workers' union (USDAW) switched from opposing to supporting partial deregulation in order to defend jobs. Retail was at the vanguard of part-time work and its workforce was disproportionately female. Since it is women who do most of the shopping, the more women entered the workforce, the stronger became the case for flexible shopping. It is difficult to work and shop at the same time. Significantly, the societies which have been at the forefront of Sunday opening (Sweden, Finland and the United Kingdom) are also those with the highest female labour participation in Europe.[117]

What difference did Sunday opening make to the rhythm of the day and to consumption more generally? Both camps liked to exaggerate their case. Sunday was never a pure, non-commercial idyll, not even during the prohibitive post-war era. In England and Wales, restrictions applied to department stores and bigger shops, not to smaller corner stores. The law stopped people from buying big-ticket items, not from shopping on Sunday as such. In addition, flouting of legislation was as widespread as opportunities to shop were limited. In Cardiff, people did 3 per cent of their weekly shopping trips on a Sunday in the early 1980s. Almost half their food and grocery purchases were illegal, covering the entire range of prohibited articles from canned fruit to frozen meals.[118] Sundays are a good example of how changes in leisure spill over into shopping. In Britain, the craze for gardening and home improvement in the 1980s added extra pressure on shop opening hours: garden centres and DIY stores decided to open on Sundays. On the eve of the 1994 law, an estimated 40 per cent of English shops already traded on Sundays. A ringing cash till more than compensated for a fine.

Longer hours have made the weekend once more the major shopping event that it had been in the age of the Sunday market two centuries and more ago. In Britain, Saturday and Sunday are the busiest days of trading. Ten per cent of shoppers do their main shopping on a Sunday. Longer shop hours mean lower unit costs and less congestion on the roads. According to one estimate, these translated into savings of £1.4 billion, or £64 per household, in 2001. The story elsewhere has been more muted. In Sweden, longer shop hours reduced prices by a tiny 0.3 per cent. The Australian Productivity Commission doubted whether flexible hours had brought consumers any net benefit. Nor has recreational shopping spilled over effortlessly from Saturday to Sunday. For most Swedes, Sunday is for buying groceries.[119]

More significant has been the impact on work patterns. We have noted how increased female labour participation added pressure to make shopping more flexible, but, in turn, Sunday shopping also reinforced the trend towards greater part-time work, especially for lone mothers. In the Netherlands, shops since 1996 have been allowed to stay open until 10 p.m. during the week and during Sunday afternoons. Since then, time-use data shows that the Dutch shop more but also work more on Sundays and in the evenings, especially women and single men; significantly, Dutch men with a partner shopped more, but worked less.[120] These patterns are a far cry from the London Sunday with which this section started. For most working-class housewives then, Sundays meant one round of cooking, tidying up and washing up after another. 'It's the hardest day of the week,' a forty-year old taxi driver's wife observed in 1949.[121] For many of their husbands, Sundays was the time for a long nap. Sunday opening did not bring to an end centuries of gender inequality. But it did throw open the family home, dispersed its members and by doing so lifted some of the collective burden off women's shoulders.

For a good century, roughly from the 1860s to the 1960s, authorities and societies in the developed world entered into an ingenious compact with regard to time. More and more of people's lives was given over to material goods and desires. Cities became billboards for consumer goods, and governments started to compete about how best to raise the standard of living. Yet, in exchange, Sunday was fenced off as a no-go zone for consumption. Since the 1960s, this compact has been broken. Several affluent societies have already torn it up; in others, its future is precarious. Today, it may look laughable for authorities to try to legislate the quality of a day, but this was a widely shared rationale just a few generations ago. A century's work has been undone in little over two decades.

The spread of the internet since the 1990s has given shopping an altogether new virtual dimension, where the opening hours of a physical shop lose their relevance. In continental Europe, historic towns with small shops in pedestrianized centres are currently reviewing their past opposition to Sunday openings: if the real shops are closed, why bother to visit these cobbled arcades, if one can enter a virtual shop on a tablet? The advance of internet shopping, though, should not be exaggerated. Prophecies of the death of old retail have so far not come true. In Europe and the United States, where internet and mobile devices are now ubiquitous, the majority of people still do most of their shopping in physical stores rather than on the internet. In Europe, the biggest online shoppers are Britons, who in 2014 spent £1,071 or almost 15 per cent of all retail sales online; in Italy and Poland, it was not even 3 per cent. Internet shopping has made the greatest strides with clothes and travel; 21 per cent of European internet users had made a purchase online in 2008; in 2012, it had risen to 32 per cent. A quarter purchased books. But for many other products and services, the internet remains marginal. Not even one in ten Europeans bought food on the internet in 2012, although in Britain one in five had done so. Furniture and other heavy items are rarely purchased with a click. In Switzerland, the world leader in mobile use (85 per cent), smartphones added 1 million mobile shopping sites in 2013–14. Across the Alps in Italy, by contrast, more than two thirds did not shop on line at all.[122]

One of the main reasons for the resilience of the conventional shop is that most people do not simply want to buy goods: they want to touch and try them. Another, ironically, is that most feel the internet is too slow: they want to get a product immediately; ease of return, trust and lower price are additional, yet smaller factors. E-commerce and smart phones have wrought a revolution in retail as we knew it, but, as ongoing Swiss research shows, the outcome has been unexpected hybrids rather than the extinction of the physical by the virtual shop. There are some exclusively online shops, especially for holidays and music, but in many other branches the movement has been towards symbiosis between the old and the new, with physical retailers starting their own webshops and online shops opening showrooms and real sale points.[123]

The abolition of the day of rest was the culmination of the leisure revolution. This revolution, as so many others, failed to deliver what it had promised. The material gains in leisure time in the twentieth century proved more limited and uneven than reformers and visionaries had imagined. A major reason for this was that the early utopia of leisure reflected a narrow view of work, that of the wage-earning male worker. Idyllic pictures of idle Sundays and family roasts which gave coalminers and bank clerks their well-deserved day of rest and recreation tended to forget the enormous amount of female work that made these possible. Free time remains fractured by generation, class and gender. The young and the old have gained the most. Leisure in middle age, by contrast, has been constrained by the growth in women's paid work and men's rising commitment to housework. Since the 1960s, the real revolution has happened elsewhere: the quality of leisure time has been transformed and polarized. In hours and minutes, the leisure gap between the sexes might have narrowed, but women are less likely to enjoy theirs in one, sustained piece. Women's leisure remains a patchwork. The democratization of leisure, finally, has had the unintended consequence of triggering new inequalities of time. Once the doors to idle leisure opened for the common man, leisurely consumption lost its distinction for the privileged few. Since then, the educated classes have thrown their energies into a new activity-packed leisure regime. This hyper-activism has had a paradoxical consequence for consumption, although not the one that critics of affluence predicted. Success means buying more and doing more. The old divide between those who had leisure and those who did not has been replaced by a new one based on how much people do in their leisure time. 'Time poverty' is the price paid for the privilege of being able to combine flexibility and action.

11

From the Cradle to the Grave

Consumption shapes identities. How we dress and eat, where we shop, whether we drive an SUV or an electric car, go to the opera or a football match, all these practices announce who we are and who we'd like others to think we are. Consuming marks our place in the social order and it helps us understand how that order comes about and how it is reproduced. Class and gender identities have loomed especially large, and we have encountered them at various points in these pages, from middle-class ideals of material comfort and anxieties about the female shopaholic in the past to the role of leisure and taste for social status in the present. There is one additional set of identities that now deserves our sustained attention: age. Arguably, it was here that the last hundred years witnessed a historically unprecedented change. This story has been told as the rise of the teenager – a term that first began to circulate in the 1940s. If we cannot ignore them, we should, however, not allow them to crowd out everyone else. Youth is not the only generation. The teenager was merely one species in a larger evolution that gathered pace in the twentieth century, producing ever more finely graded age-specific groups defined by their appearance, possessions and lifestyle. The first to take shape was the child consumer. By the century's end, this group had been joined by elderly 'golden agers'. The image and reality of old age was transformed by the aspiration and ability to consume. Arguably, it was for this generation, more than for any other, that consumption was truly revolutionary.

THE CHILD CONSUMER

Few topics ring as many alarm bells in the rich world today as that of children under siege by a commercial juggernaut of adverts, brands and corporations. Here is a short list of dangers plucked from the large number of books and reports by concerned writers and advocates. Three-year-olds today can recognize McDonald's golden arches before they can recall their own surname. By the age of ten, British children command a knowledge of 350 brands but can name only twenty birds. Mattel created an interactive doll, Diva Starz, which introduced six- to eleven-year-olds to retail therapy, telling them, 'I'm in a bad mood. Let's go shopping.' In Nottingham, England, an eight-year-old girl was bombarded with pre-approved credit-card offers. In the United States, pupils are subject to in-school advertising and branded give-aways. Girl Scouts no longer just learn to build a campfire but can also earn a 'fashion adventure' badge for a trip to the mall and a visit to a pre-teen clothing store. On both sides of the Pond, seven- to eleven-year-olds are working for market researchers, telling them which toys are cool. In 1994, Jean-Paul Guerlain launched a citrus- and mint-scented children's perfume. Other fashion labels followed with baby sprays and eau de toilette. Girls who have not even entered elementary school wear shirts decorated with Playboy bunnies. As with Victorian anxieties about female shoppers, sex and shopping are feared to go hand in hand. Children are being 'stalked' and 'groomed for profit'. Alongside obesity, bulimia and suicide, activists have diagnosed a plague of social marketing diseases. For some writers, childhood today is 'toxic'. Others have pronounced its 'death'.[1]

The fever pitch of these anxieties is matched by the money at stake. Never before in history have children controlled so much spending power. In Britain, those under nineteen years of age spent £12 billion in 2008 – almost £1 billion went towards snacks, sweets and soft drinks. Once the money their parents spend on them is added, this figure rises to an estimated £99 billion a year. In the United States, the market influenced by kids is said to be worth $670 billion, and more than $15 billion is spent on advertising and marketing to children.[2] In short, little angels are big spenders, and it is this clash between ideal and reality that lies behind the moral panic and unease.

To be sure, there are many aspects which deserve concern and demand action. This is a matter for campaigners, politicians and regulators. What history can do is something else, but no less useful. It can guard against a lazy nostalgia for a golden age where children were once pure and innocent, untouched by the market. And it can explain how we got to where we are. Just like the dollars and pounds spent on direct marketing, so contemporary ideas of childhood are the product of change over time. What we need to understand, then, is how childhood became so mixed up with choice and spending in the first place. This is a longer history, in which educators, parents, doctors and politicians played as decisive a role as corporations; children were not entirely passive in this process either.

As late as the 1970s, historians treated childhood as the invention of bourgeois modernity. It was only in the seventeenth and eighteenth centuries, they argued, that brutality and emotional distance gave way to a more affectionate, child-oriented and permissive culture. More recent historians have thrown cold water on the thesis of a sentimental bourgeois revolution.[3] There is plenty of evidence of love and grief, play and toys in earlier centuries, in West and East. Nonetheless, what is new and marks 1900 as a turning point is that childhood gained its own special place in the marketplace. Children had always consumed, but now they started being treated as customers in their own right, with their own age-specific needs, fashions and, soon, spending money.

The spread of age-specific clothing in the United States shows the speed of change. Before the First World War, clothing was stocked by article and size, not by age group. Stockings for children were displayed next to those for their parents. By the Second World War, children's clothing had moved to a separate floor, and often to a separate shop altogether. Saks Fifth Avenue and other department stores opened floors for young people with colour coding for different age groups. By 1929, there were over a thousand stores for infants and children. Two decades later, the number of such shops had shot up to six thousand. Their stock came from a growing number of factories dedicated to making children's clothing. Stores began to organize baby contests and baby weeks which marketed pre-assembled clothes for the newborn – the 'layette' – to expecting parents. In the 1930s and '40s, age gradation became more finely grained. Fashion for six- to fourteen-year-old girls was separated from that for their three- to six-year-old sisters. The 'toddler' acquired a separate persona and its own space on the sales floor, away from the infant. Saleswomen were instructed to play up to their emerging personality and cater to their individual style. Universal 'bulgy bloomers of yesteryear' were replaced by stylish dress for each sex – 'dainty pastels' for girls, 'tailored' garments for boys. No one did more to embody and popularize the new style than Shirley Temple, the Hollywood child actress, with her pinafore look – no belt and no trimming other than a bow of baby ribbon. Her fame on and off the screen made Temple the ambassador of the new look, with trademark dresses in her name for the toddler range.[4]

Shops, cinemas and advertisers were pushing these age-specific fashions, but they would hardly have managed to get their hands so easily into parents' purses had it not been for the fortuitous convergence of several larger currents. These involved, on the one hand, a shift in the relation between work and consumption, and new attitudes towards child-rearing on the other. The first change meant clothes were less often made at home and increasingly purchased ready-made. Unless they were a trained dressmaker with plenty of time on their hands, few mothers would have relished making age-specific clothes for their little ones. Influence over clothing design thus moved from the mother's needle to the market. This was only a favourable precondition, however. What made parents captive customers was that shop assistants were echoing what experts and authorities were preaching about the personality of the child. In the early twentieth century, child-rearing literature began to stress that children had rights. Parents were advised to pay more attention to the perspective of the child and their changing impulses and desires.

In 1929, President Hoover called a conference on child health at the White House. It led to the passage of a Children's Charter which defended the 'understanding and the guarding' of a child's personality as 'his most precious right'.[5] Women's magazines went one step further and announced 'Your Child's Right to Beauty'. And that personality was evolving, requiring adults to keep step with its growth. Advertisers applied the discovery of developmental stages to age-specific product categories: four- to six-year-olds were said to be developing their imagination, which made them ideal customers for fantasy toys; seven- to nine-year-olds mixed enthusiasm with purpose, which made them collectors.[6] Freudian psychology encouraged parents to be more accepting of their children's material desires. Educational experts at the White House conference warned that too often the child was an 'alien in his home'.[7] Chairs, tables and plates were too big and there was not enough consideration for his toys and needs. Squeezing the child into an adult environment led to moral and physical retardation. Excessive thrift bottled up unmet needs, with potentially dangerous consequences later. Possessions were vital for personal development and mental health.

What linked these twin transformations in work and mentality was the child's role reversal in the market place. Children ceased to be workers who contributed to the family income and instead were embraced as consumers. In the words of the sociologist Viviana Zelizer, the more children were becoming economically useless, the more they appeared to be emotionally 'priceless'.[8]

As children put down their tools and picked up their schoolbooks, earnings were replaced by allowances. Already in the nineteenth century, bourgeois families had used pocket money to teach their children thrift and financial discipline. By the 1930s, half of American professional families were giving their children an allowance; in the semi-skilled working class, it was a quarter. Rather than only teaching the art of saving, moreover, the focus now widened to the art of spending. As one textbook for child study groups explained in 1932, 'emphasis is always placed on the saving of money, but with the increased opportunity and necessity for handling money in the purchase of commodities it is increasingly necessary that children have training in spending money.' 'Modern American life . . . glorifies the idea of spending.' It now also needed to train young people how to do it.[9]

Pocket money announced a new truce: kids were given the opportunity to fulfil their own desires while parents kept a check on their wallets. That children had rights as consumers had particular importance for communities battling discrimination: it demonstrated they had some independence and choice. The African-American paper the *Chicago Defender* sponsored parties with toy prizes and candy for its young readers. The growing acceptance of the child consumer's position in the family mirrored the appreciation of consumption as a positive force in society at large, so precocious in inter-war America. By the time the White House Conference on Child Health and Protection met in 1936, allowances were accepted as the natural entitlement of future citizen consumers. As autonomous beings, experts said, children naturally deserved a democratic voice in the family budget. Children themselves were absorbing the new wisdom fast, a survey taken at the time suggests. When asked to imagine themselves as parents in the future, many said they planned to hold weekly family councils for a spending review.[10]

Work never completely disappeared from children's lives, not even in the affluent world. Still, it was the emphasis on play and fun that progressively shaped the idea of childhood, and with it notions of what children should do with their time and money. Toys illustrate the shifting balance. In Europe, children already played with wooden toy sets in the early modern period. Customized paper dolls appeared in Britain and Germany at the end of the eighteenth century when the first toy shops opened their doors. Most toys, however, had an educational purpose – to learn by playing, as urged by John Locke – or to prepare the young directly for the craft and business skills of the world of work. From the late nineteenth century, such older customs started being overshadowed by a new commerce in fantasy and desire. Christmas – once a communal holiday, celebrated with neighbours and servants – shrunk into a family affair. The middle-class ideal of intimate domesticity carved out a special place for children's longing and wonder. Wish lists got longer and longer.[11] The success of Walt Disney's *Snow White* (1937) reflected the new acceptance of play for play's sake. In the United States, the sales value of toys and games skyrocketed from $8 million in 1899 to $103 million thirty years later. In the two decades after the Second World War, American spending on toys doubled again.

These developments were not unique to the United States. Japan was as precocious. The comic *The Adventures of Sei-chan* produced spin-off cards and toy hats as early as 1924. The market for fantastic characters and heroes with superhuman powers has been getting bigger ever since. Parents were crucial collaborators in this process. By the middle of the twentieth century, parents had not only made their peace with the new culture of play but began to participate in it, getting in touch with their own 'inner child'.[12]

The commercialization of childhood, then, has been deeply paradoxical. Age differences were simultaneously sharpened and diluted. What began as a movement to champion the distinctive needs and rights of the young evolved into a commercial phenomenon which made childhood a place of the imagination, open to all, where biological age ceased to matter.

Children's exposure to advertising took a big jump with television. By the 1980s, the average American child under twelve watched over four hours of television a day. In the course of a year, they would have been exposed to 20,000 adverts. By 2004, the American Academy of Pediatrics had raised this figure to 40,0000.[13] There is no denying that children are more than ever bombarded by commercial images and that advertising is employing increasingly sophisticated techniques, such as advergames. What is harder is interpreting these figures. For some experts, advertising is directly responsible for rising rates of obesity and violence. For others, its effects are indirect and modest, doing little more than influencing the choice between brands.[14] For yet others, adverts are an indispensable educational tool for growing up in a media-saturated world of goods, a kind of commercial grammar. Only Sweden has banned advertising during and immediately after programmes that are intended for children; the use of characters from children's programmes in commercials is also prohibited.

A good deal hinges on how vulnerable or savvy kids are presumed to be. What research on advertising has made clear is that it is unhelpful to generalize about 'children'. The ability to distinguish between commercials and programmes varies greatly with age. Some children as young as three are aware of the difference. Still, a 1985 study found that, before the age of five, only 10 per cent could tell the difference. For five- to six-year-olds it rose to 62 per cent. Even once children reached the age of eight or nine, there were still 15 per cent who were unable to spot the intent to push goods. The older children became, the more easily they lost interest and adopted a sceptical attitude.[15] From exposure and reception, however, it is still some way to the point of purchase. When Quebec introduced a law that banned commercials directed at children in 1980, researchers found that English-speaking children in Montreal with access to neighbouring US stations were buying more cereal than their French-speaking neighbours.[16] As critics pointed out, however, this might have had to do with different breakfast cultures in the two groups. Advertising has some effect on what children buy, but it is only one of several factors. Age, education, peer culture, income and family life are at least as significant. What TV adverts do accomplish is to reinforce children's existing demands for products.

Anxieties about the loss of childhood often rest on an ideal of inner purity and innocence at risk of pollution by external forces of corporate greed. This narrative is unhelpful. After all, it was partly in the marketplace that children were first recognized as separate persons. Children are vulnerable, but they are not passive. In reality, children never completely left the world of work and exchange. Today, growing up continues to happen within the economy, not outside it.[17] Chores, paid work, gifts and exchange remain normal features of children's lives. Friendships are cemented through trade in cards and food. In the late 1980s, 21 per cent of American children's income came from household chores, 10 per cent from paid work outside the home; 45 per cent was from allowances, the remaining 24 per cent from gifts. In 1997, American nine- to twelve-year-olds spent over six hours per week on household work.[18] In England, a large survey of thirteen- to fourteen-year-olds in England found that one quarter held a paid job for four hours a week; eight out of ten helped with chores around the house.[19]

Poor children in the United States carried particularly large responsibilities for the purchase of food and clothing. In return, they enjoyed disproportionately high allowances. For all the surround-sound of corporate branding and pressures for emulative spending, most of these kids showed remarkable discipline in balancing material desires with financial reality. Poorer children saved as much as their more affluent peers; they simply did not put their money in a bank. A German study found that children overwhelmingly displayed 'rational consumer behaviour'. In a representative sample of one thousand ten- to seventeen-year-olds, the vast majority lived within their means. A mere 6 per cent were in debt to their peers – mainly to pay for fast food, going out and clothing. Interestingly, such 'excess' was scattered across the rich as well as the poor.[20] Most of these debts were small – €72 on average, less than what these children received each month. More than three quarters of those questioned in the sample were confident that they could meet all their debts within a month's time. There is a certain irony, then, in adults' moral alarm about children being seduced by the shiny world of goods. When it comes to debt and credit, the vast majority of children have been more responsible and restrained than their parents.

In the early 1990s, the anthropologist Elizabeth Chin observed how black children in New Haven, Connecticut, handled money and goods. She gave the participants in her study $20 to spend as they wished. What did they do with it? One ten-year-old girl spent her unexpected windfall on a pair of cheap denim sandals for herself and a pair of golden slip-ons as a birthday gift for her mother, some pink hair rollers for her grandmother and a bag of bubblegum to share with her sister. It was hardly a display of selfish materialism or conspicuous consumption. In many ways, children have taken the place in popular discourse once assigned to the poor and women: their excess and inability to restrain desires are seen to threaten the moral and social order. As in the past, this may say more about middle-class angst than about children or the poor. In reality, there are few lessons that teach financial discipline so well as having to make ends meet. Most of the children Chin interviewed knew the worth of their Christmas gifts down to the penny and understood that some hoped-for presents simply lay beyond their family's means. The arrival of a Barbie doll did not mark a complete surrender to mainstream consumer culture. Girls were aware that Barbie was a 'dope' or stereotype. Some, in playing with them, mocked white middle-class norms. Others made the doll their own by braiding its blond waves into black hairstyles.[21]

From the vantage point of the early twenty-first century, we can see the rise of the child consumer as part of a historic bargain between children and the adult world. Children gained commercial power and choice but in exchange forfeited a certain degree of autonomy to adult control and regulation. Instead of roaming city streets and dance halls in the early twentieth century and mingling with adults, they were confined to 'safe' spaces of education, the home and fenced-in playgrounds. In the last generation, digital media and internet gaming have progressively undercut this arrangement. Growing parental fears over the loss of childhood reflects this loosening of control.

Yu-Gi-Oh! is a Japanese mixed-media series about a high-school boy with the supernatural powers of an Egyptian pharaoh. Its magical world reveals some of the emerging forms of childhood consumption.[22] One is the symbiotic relationship between old and new media. *Yu-Gi-Oh!* began life as a manga series in the *Shonen Jump* magazine in 1996 before taking off as an animated TV series and Playstation game. Its digital success rested on the popularity of card trading. In 2000, according to one survey, every single student in a Kyoto elementary school owned *Yu-Gi-Oh!* cards. In this fantasy world, the balance of power between children and adults is overturned, as child players take on supernatural powers with the help of monsters and magic.

A second implication concerns the creativity and intellectual skills that come with consuming in the digital age. *Yu-Gi-Oh!*, in many ways, exemplifies the stereotype of consumerism as a treadmill: the more children play it, the more they hunger to buy new cards to strengthen their hand, the greater the options and number of cards for sale. Yet, notwithstanding the commercial interests involved, *Yu-Gi-Oh!* also shows how this kind of game has outpaced the old critique of 'mass consumption'.[23] As they create their own characters, children become sophisticated traders and diplomats, negotiating their way through a thicket of passionately debated rules. Internet sites and digital gaming provide serious players with additional points of entry into the fantasy world. Finally, this is a world for virtual as well as real children. There were adults who fantasized about being cowboys or Indians a century ago, but digital media and social networks have given the escape back into childhood a whole new scale and respectability. In Japan, a third of all fantasy-character goods are bought by adults. This adult invasion of youth has come with its own dangers, not least the sexualization of childhood. Yet it has also had a liberating effect, freeing adults from the ideal of disciplined, purposeful 'rational leisure' that became dominant with industrial society and restoring a little bit of the pleasure of play familiar to our ancestors in earlier times.

The generic 'child consumer' has attracted so much contemporary concern that it is important to remember that children, like any other age group, are hugely diverse. True, certain trends have minimized differences across the globe. Pocket money, the birthday party, fast-food snacks and toy tie-ins are no longer the preserve of Los Angeles but are found in Beijing and Taiwan. Still, even after discounting the hundreds of millions of children in the world too poor to go to school and just concentrating on rich and middle-income countries, children's lives continue to be shaped by culturally specific attitudes to childhood and money. In Taiwan in 1990, for example, most children were spending independently at the age of five; not so different from Americans. However, this included buying their own school supplies. Spending was balanced by moral dictates of saving and education. Tellingly, Taiwanese children saved more of their pocket money.[24] Nor were they paid for doing chores. They just did them.

Even children's power over their own and their family's spending is easily exaggerated. The previously mentioned 2005 German survey of ten- to seventeen-year-olds found that in only 11 per cent of families were children entirely free to decide what to buy. A third of parents advised their children, and almost half decided for them when it came to larger purchases; spending on mobile phones was the main source of conflict. Similarly, in only 14 per cent of cases did the young influence larger family purchases. Children may have gained all sorts of freedoms since the 1960s, but in financial affairs they continue to be kept 'on a short leash', at least in prosperous Germany.[25]

The shift in relations between children and the adult world has nowhere been more dramatic than in China after Mao. In the past, adults might have reminisced about the favourite foods they enjoyed as children but, as late as 1979, dictionaries did not have a single word for 'children's food'. With the exception of 'old rice powder', children ate adult food. Since then, Chinese cities are full of American and home-grown fast-food outlets, shelves stacked high with baby food and children's medicinal food (*ertong yaoshan*), and billboards targeting fun-loving kids. Peng, an eleven-year-old boy of the Hui Muslim minority, in 1997 recorded what he ate during a typical day:

8 a.m.:	One bottle of soda, no price given. One package of crisps (*guoba*), 1 yuan (*c*.15 US cents).
12.30 p.m.:	a cooked beef sandwich, prepared by his father. Three pieces of chocolate, from the family cupboard. One ice cream bar, purchased from a street store.

5 p.m.:   another ice cream bar, purchased from a street store.
                       One banana, no price.
7 p.m.:   fried eggplant and fried egg, purchased from a
                       restaurant down the street. 11 yuan
8.30 p.m.:   another package of crisps, 1.3 yuan.[26]

The child consumer in China has been catapulted forward by several
forces: a rise in discretionary income; the one-child policy; the transfer
of leisure from a state-controlled workplace to family and home; and a
backlash against the privations of the Cultural Revolution. By the late
1990s, there were some 65 million single-child families. As families
shrank, so aspirations were more intensely focused on the single child –
in the so-called '4-2-1' family, all eyes are on the single child, much
more so than in a family where the child has to compete with four or
five siblings for attention. Arguably, it was in school, not at home,
where the absence of siblings really intensified the pressure to consume.
At home, many children did not act spoiled at all and ate conserva-
tively. In their own peer groups, however, toys, new snacks and products
became all-powerful communicators of identity, belonging and standing. Researchers who visited two primary schools in the Haidian
district in Beijing in 1995 were struck by the importance of goods and
brand knowledge for *panbi*, 'climbing and comparing'. Children without trendy snacks were ostracized or beaten up. For parents, snack and
spending money was, in part, a way to compensate for their own lost
childhood during the Cultural Revolution. But it was also an instrument to exercise control and to incentivize and reward their children's
performance in an intensely competitive environment. After decades of
conformity, parents more than anything wanted their children to be
'special' and stand out. It made it difficult to resist the latest fashion
and novelty snack.[27]

THE TEENAGER

In 1914, the Collegiate Special Advertising Agency started targeting
American youth with images of cigarettes and cars. In Europe,
age-specific marketing had already been employed by the book trade.
Now, young Americans received direct mailings advertising the 'var-
sity' look. By the 1920s, there were special promotions for free tobacco
and billiard lessons. The Knox Hat Company led clothing firms in

setting up a university-style advisory board. These boards recruited students from Ivy League colleges on the East Coast as well as from big state universities such as Michigan. Twice a year, student members met in New York to give new fashions their stamp of approval. 'These men know style,' promotional material assured customers: 'Dunlap spring hats are fashioned to the ideal of the young man and the man who stays young.'[28]

No one yet talked of the 'teenager' but, already by the 1920s, American companies and market researchers had their eyes on the youth market. Budget studies in 1929 revealed that daughters over the age of fifteen were the biggest consumers of clothing in rich and poor families alike. Eighteen- to thirty-year-old Americans ruled the market in dress goods, records, hosiery and, indeed, furniture. The focus on college students was no coincidence. Their wardrobes were bursting. A typical male Harvard student in the 1920s bought every year 7 shirts, 8 neckties, 6 pieces of underwear, 12 handkerchiefs, 12 pair of socks and 3 pair of shoes. At Penn, the average young woman added to her collection annually 7 dresses, 5 sweaters, 3 skirts, 3 hats, 4 pair of shoes, 3 purses, 25 items of hosiery and 12 pieces of lingerie.[29] That was a lot of clothes at a time when two dress shirts and three ties were considered a 'fair' standard for an adult man, with one skirt and nine plain cotton stockings for his wife.[30]

American students were merely a few steps ahead in the international rise of the youth consumer. By the 1950s, Britons, Germans and the French were discovering their own teenage markets.[31] More than ever before, to be an adolescent meant to have fun and spend money. Initially a metropolitan and college story, by the 1940s it was reaching small towns and the countryside. A study of Danish birth generations shows how far-reaching the change in the experience of coming of age was in this period. Young Danish seamstresses, shop assistants and agricultural workers born before 1900 did not mention leisure once in their autobiographies. For those born in the 1930s, movies, excursions and Saturday-night dances until dawn were an essential part of their youth. This does not mean this age group stopped working, simply that identity was increasingly defined by leisure. Only a small minority now handed over their pay packet to their parents, in stark contrast to earlier generations.[32]

The teenager emerged from several forces. For one, young men and women had more money to spend; their wages shot up during and after the First World War. Secondly, thanks to longer and more widespread schooling, they lived increasingly separate lives, magnifying the influence of cliques and peer groups. Finally, they responded to a cult of youth promoted by their elders. Some of this was commercial, as firms and advertisers started vying for the youth market. Yet the new generational identity was nurtured by politics, too. The contribution of Romanticism and nationalism to ideals of youth is well known. Just as critical were political efforts to cultivate new citizens after the horrors of the Second World War. For every commercial milk bar and dance hall in post-war Europe, there was a state-sponsored youth club. The French government targeted students with domestic-science competitions; Denise Chicault from Dijon was crowned the 'fairy of the household' in 1949. By the 1960s, over 300,000 youths frequented the *maisons des jeunes* (youth centres), which offered everything from ping-pong and creative arts to lectures. For its organizers, these were nurseries of citizenship, in the best Tocquevillian sense.[33] The 1950s, too, were the golden age of the youth hostel, although its origins reach back to the early twentieth century.

None of this fits the popular image of the teenage rebel, made famous by James Dean, which created a moral panic in the wake of the 1958 rock 'n' roll riots in European cities. Yet the official courting of youth was just as important in endorsing the special status of the teenager, making it about more than sex and shopping. This may help explain why so few were willing to join the much feared war of generations. As we saw in Chapter 6, most teenagers looked up to their parents, valued work and saved for a moped or to start a family; it is worth recalling that in Western Europe in the 1960s every second marriage was to a man who had not reached his twenty-fifth birthday.[34] Commentators such as Richard Hoggart, one of the founding fathers of cultural studies in Britain, scorned the 'candy-floss world'[35] and failed to see that hedonism was often matched by civic engagement. After all, it was the young who would march for peace, civil rights and the environment in these years.

The cult of the teenager has tended to conjure up an image of a single, homogeneous generation. In reality, this age group was just as divided by class as the rest of society. Young people longed for novelty, variety and mobility, for sure. But many poor teenagers were unable to afford any of these. A 1975 study of a housing estate in the south-east of England recorded the following conversation among a group of thirteen- to fifteen-year-old girls about their leisure pursuits. 'When it's raining, we listen to the wireless in our room ... or we stand in the passage [between terraces]. When it is not raining, we go to the park, or go for a walk.'[36] The local youth club was only for those aged fifteen-plus. Some of the girls did not even have the 5 pence to go to the movies. The bus fare ruled out a trip to town.

The teenager struck so many alarm bells because it was feared that an entire generation was drifting further and further apart from their elders. But was this true? Were teenagers in the 1970s a more thorough, hardened generational type than their original trailblazers a few decades earlier? The American sociologist August B. Hollingshead had first observed the youth of Elmtown, a small Midwestern town, in 1941–2. He returned thirty years later to find the overall generational pattern of leisure had barely changed. The gap between what adults deemed 'good' and what kids desired had not narrowed, but it had not widened either. 'The activities and behaviour of the present generation of adolescents,' he wrote in 1973, 'are only minimally different from that of their parents when they were adolescents.'[37] A few smoked marijuana, but, by and large, teenagers were less transgressive or, at least, the community was better organized to prevent them from stepping over the line of decency. In the 1940s, clothes had been a constant battle between young and old. Now, the new high school operated a strict dress code. Boys and girls had to wear socks or hose at all times. Clothing with obscene writing on it was prohibited. Boys were banned from sporting a moustache or a beard. Girls had to wear 'appropriate' underwear and their dresses had to reach at least three inches below the buttocks; Hollingshead does not say who applied the measuring tape. Leisure patterns varied by social status as much as age. Most kids followed their parents' habits.

Of course, Elmtown was not frozen in time. By 1973, cinema had lost its central position in popular entertainment; only one screen survived. On the other hand, plenty of leisure continued to be organized by churches, unions and local women's and farmers' organizations. Commercialization had its limits. In many ways, the post-war decades were the golden age of local, self-organized shows and festivals. Elmtown held its first 'corn festival' in 1949. By 1972, it was the highlight of the autumn calendar. These were family events, and teenagers played their part. A thousand families had one or more members who devoted several weeks to setting up decorations and exhibits – not bad for a town with a total population of 14,211. High-school students decorated store windows. The 135 home-made floats were followed by a festival queen and twenty-seven bands. There was a football game and a roller-skating rink for several hundred teenagers. But the climax was the greased-pig contest at the local airport, in which contestants wrestled with slippery, half-grown pigs. The evening ended with rock music and dancing.

It was not just in Elmtown that teenagers proved to be more than the passive prey of mainstream celebrity culture. There have been rebellious youth subcultures from the Scuttler gangs in 1890s Manchester to the *blousons noirs* in 1950s Paris, and Mods and Rockers in the 1960s (see Plate 56). It would be a mistake, however, to divide teenagers into two opposite camps, conformists on one side and deviants on the other. Young people have played an active role in developing their own fashions in a wide variety of ways. Subcultures have not been the preserve of rebelliousness, masculinity and adrenalin. In Japan, the 'lost decade' of the 1990s saw teenage girls take flight in a whole series of new styles and identities. Pushed-down, loose white knee socks were one of the first fashion trends among high-school girls in this period. By 1996, shops stocked thirty-five kinds of such loose socks. In the mid-1990s, the Kogal look added the plaid skirt. Then came the Ganguro, or black-face, fashion with dark-tanned skin, bleached hair, short pants and platform boots. Teenage consumers became fashion producers, creating new markets as much as responding to them. Some looks split into their own distinct subsets, such as the Mamba, subdivided into the Lomamba style, which borrowed from *Lolita*, in contrast to the Coccomba, which championed the Cocolulu brand. The Gothic Lolitas, who blended Victorian and Gothic elements, would hardly have impressed the tough Manchester Scuttlers, but they were no less playful and original in creating their own style out of elements of consumer culture. Crucially, stars and celebrities had little influence on the evolution of these Japanese fashions. A *Popteen* survey in 1999 did not find a single celebrity among the top five role models. Instead, teenagers looked up to amateur high-school models and salesgirls, who played a key role in shaping new trends.[38]

OUT OF THE ROCKING CHAIR

In 1936, the Bradenton Kiwanis Club founded a trailer park in their town of Manatee County, Florida. Within fifteen years, it had over a thousand units. Most residents stayed for six or seven months a year, added patios and, sometimes, like on camping grounds, permanent structures, too. Unlike on a camping ground, everyone in the Bradenton trailer park was elderly. The mean age of the community was sixty-nine years, but some regulars reached ninety. The park was one of the first retirement communities, although a few of the early residents still did a bit of part-time or seasonal work. It was a self-conscious experiment in a new lifestyle of active ageing. Many initially came for the warm climate but stayed for the sociability and fun. The weekly schedule of events left no room for loneliness or boredom. On Mondays there was bingo, on Tuesdays square-dancing lessons and the star club. Wednesday offered bible classes for the devout and movies for the rest. Thursday belonged to the hobby club. There was choir and ballroom dancing on Friday. On Saturday, there was more bingo and a chance for people to give group performances. Each week ended with a Sunday Church service and a family hour. The park was generously equipped, with nineteen shuffle-board courts and eight horseshoe courts, framed by small grandstands for the two weekly tournaments. The card room was open every day from eight in the morning to ten o'clock at night.[39]

The Bradenton trailer park was an early sign of what was arguably the most dramatic transformation experienced by any age group in the twentieth century. Consumption redefined old age. Mostly poor and dependent at the beginning of the twentieth century, elderly people were celebrated as active, well-off and fun-loving consumers by its end.

The old have always been with us. It is a common mistake to presume that old age is an invention of the twentieth century. In the Italian town of Arezzo in 1427, for example, every sixth citizen was sixty or older. Elsewhere, numbers were lower, but elderly people were a common sight in early modern societies. What radically changed in the twentieth century was the proportion of older people, their longevity and their status in society. In the 1880s, those over sixty made up between 5 and 10 per cent of the population across Europe and the United States. A century later, their share had doubled. And more and more of them enjoyed longer lives. In 1953, there were 825,000 people who were eighty or older in the Federal Republic of Germany. Fifty years later, they reached almost 6 million.[40] Longer life and better health were preconditions for active ageing. Although illness, disability and loneliness persist, it is easier to enjoy old age with a hearing aid, dentures and a good pair of glasses than 'sans teeth, sans eyes, sans taste, sans everything', to quote Shakespeare's As You Like It (1600). This physiological transformation went hand in hand with a revolution in the material resources and cultural ideals of old age.

As with children, the forces behind this change gathered early momentum in the United States. Pension plans made it not only easier to retire but possible to do so and retain independence. As late as 1880, three quarters of American men aged over sixty-four were in work. By 1930, the figure had dropped to 55 per cent, by 1990 to around 20 per cent. While modest by today's standards, the Union Army pension – which reached 21 per cent of sixty-five to sixty-nine-year-old men in 1900 – indicated early on the close correlation between pensions and the decision to stop working. Union Army veterans were twice as likely to retire as their fellow Americans. These were federal monies. The first private pension fund was started by American Express in 1875. By 1930, around one in ten American workers was covered by a retirement plan. In other words, when elderly people continued to work, it was out of necessity, not choice. The retirement plan opened the door to leisure and independence.[41]

It needed additional cultural and political factors to push the elderly across the threshold. Pensions loosened up the authority of family and work. In the nineteenth century, to be the head of a household meant that you were a worker. For the old and frail, to stop work meant having to move in with their children. By the middle of the twentieth century, it was possible to be a pensioner and yet continue to live on one's own; by 1970, fewer than 30 per cent of retired Americans were living with their extended families. For some, of course, it has ended in loneliness – 'solo living' can be seen as one of the diseases of affluence. To many, however, it has meant greater independence. In the process, work lost a good deal of its authority as the essence of life.

The embrace of leisure over work was not automatic. Companies, doctors, the government and civic groups all played their part. In the 1940s, only 3 per cent of elderly Americans collecting social security benefits gave a preference for leisure as the main reason for retirement. Leisure remained the privilege of the rich elderly. It was during the 1950s–'70s that it reached the rest; by 1982, 48 per cent of retirees cited leisure as the main reason for stopping to work.[42] Companies and insurers introduced schemes to prepare workers for retirement and organized hobby clubs. The Prudential launched its pre-retirement programme in 1949. In Bridgeport, Connecticut, the General Electric Company started to counsel its workers five years prior to retirement and offered additional check-ups after it.[43] In the hands of the pension business, retirement lost the bitter taste of 'maladjustment' and was reborn under the slogan 'the best of life is yet to come'.[44] Suddenly, old age was something to look forward to. The American Association of Retired Persons, founded in 1955, began to promote an image of vigorous, independent seniors. Ten years later, as part of Lyndon B. Johnson's 'great society', the Older American Act made it a duty for government to help the elderly not only in cases of need or poor health but to assist them in the 'pursuit of meaningful activity'.[45]

The general transformation of old age lies beyond the scope of this book. Two facilitating forces, however, deserve special attention in order to understand the ascendance of active ageing. The first involved a shift in cultural and medical attitudes and can be illustrated by comparing two canonical texts written thirty years apart: Hall's *Senescence*, written in 1922, and Havighurst and Albrecht's *Older People*, published in 1953.

After devoting his professional career to the study of childhood, the American psychologist G. Stanley Hall retired and added a book on *Senescence*. It is a depressing read from start to finish. The book opens with a personal confession of how press notices of his own retirement left him with a sense of 'anticipatory death', and ends with a chapter devoted to death proper. In between, life in old age is portrayed as a series of unflattering defects. The old smell, they have problems with the toilet, they are fussy, pedantic, always moody and uniquely sensitive to changes in the weather; the association between old age and disease had tightened in the late nineteenth century with the invention of 'senility' and age-related pathologies such as senile pneumonia. Being old in these pages was no fun, and where it might be, it ought not to be. Sex did not stop with the 'closed season', Hall acknowledged. Yet it was not to be indulged in either. To do so would just lead to 'follies' and sap the little 'vitality' old people had left. Hall's advice was to 'rigorously ignore and suppress all such manifestations in this field': 'complete chastity, psychic and somatic, should be the ideal of the old'. 'Just living' and 'contemplating nature' was pleasure enough. All this did not mean that the elderly should withdraw from society completely, simply that their true mission was to be a conservative, quiet force that spread wisdom and restrained youth. Old and young were opposite poles, and the task of the former was to balance the latter, or as Hall put it, the morning and evening of life were not alike. It was only childhood that was active and buoyant.[46]

By the 1930s, more cheerful voices could be heard. *Who Says Old!*, Elmer Ferris, a retired New York professor, challenged his contemporaries in 1933. Age was an opportunity, no less than youth. Ferris's advice was to stay fit by walking five miles a day to build up an appetite, indulging in nice meals and a daily cigar, watching baseball and becoming more 'extrovert'. Above all, he recommended investing in the latest fashions, for 'to be dressed in style means that one is in the swim'. One gained 'a daily sense of refreshment by dressing for every occasion'.[47] Notwithstanding such advice books, however, scholarly opinion largely remained of the view that old age involved a progressive withdrawal from the world of action.

It was in the 1950s that social gerontology took off and psychologists began to replace this model of disengagement with an active conception of 'successful ageing'. In *Older People*, R. J. Havighurst and Ruth Albrecht offered a strikingly new, upbeat portrait. 'To some readers', they confessed, their book 'will seem too optimistic, with its reports of the happiness and economic security of the majority of older people'. But this was the truth. 'The old-age group is as much to be envied as to be pitied.'[48] The elderly they had studied in Prairie City were neither intrinsically passive, nor bored and miserable. It was a mistake to presume that there was a biological break between an active and a passive lifestyle. True, a third of their elderly sample were passive and the overall level of leisure activity declined in age, but, importantly, their sample also revealed large variation. People's sense of play and fun was a personality trait they largely took with them from middle age into retirement. In part, it was a function of social status; people of lower status tended to be less active, travel less, read less and rarely went to the movies. Older people included the 'well-adjusted' retired professional who travelled with his wife to Florida in the winter and enjoyed a range of hobbies and entertainment as well as the farmer whose whole identity had been defined by work and who, on retirement, found himself worthless and cut off. The elderly, in other words, were just as inclined to leisure as their juniors, at least those able to enjoy their golden years in reasonably good health.

One reason for the continuing interest in leisure in old age, the authors argued, was that society as a whole was increasingly happy to see itself as a leisure society. Play was no longer defined negatively – as a relief from work – but raised to a positive level alongside work; indeed, sometimes above it. 'The person who makes a hobby of woodworking or pottery making, or plays golf or bridge "just for the fun of it", or travels during vacations,' Havighurst and Albrecht wrote, 'is getting the same values from his play as if he was doing work for the sheer enjoyment of the work itself.'[49] Leisure brought entertainment, curiosity, self-esteem and social prestige. Havighurst and Albrecht dubbed it 'the principle of equivalence of work and play'. Many of the elderly people interviewed by the authors were energetic and fun-loving. For some, leisure more than compensated for the loss of work. What was the point of making a living, one retired man wondered, if one did not have a chance to enjoy its riches?

Havighurst and Albrecht were not naïve. They were all too aware that for many elderly people leisure was no paradise. 'What passes for recreation is too often just sitting' and many seniors 'run the danger of being mentally passive'.[50] Still, their attention to stories of successful ageing and their link between levels of active leisure and states of happiness was a revelation. Retirement no longer had to mean social death. Recreation gave it purpose and meaning. The task now was to prepare people to make more and better use of it. Although the theory of disengagement continued to have its advocates, the future of social gerontology belonged to active ageing.[51]

The second force which encouraged recognition of the active old was politics, and emerged out of the mid-twentieth-century crisis, with its concerns over the future of democracy. The first Golden Age Club in Chicago was founded in 1940 by Oskar Schulze, an émigré from Germany who had witnessed the appeal of extreme doctrines to the elderly after the hyper-inflation of 1923 wiped out their pensions. Poor, lonely and disaffected seniors were easy prey for the enemies of democracy. A rich cultural programme, Schulze said, helped to keep 'their interest alive in community and national affairs so that they do not feel out of it'.[52] The club offered Chinese checkers and cards, picnics and boating trips, and special celebrations on birthdays and golden-wedding anniversaries. By 1946, there was a whole network, with sixteen clubs in Cleveland alone. Similar clubs sprang up across the country. Recreation for the elderly was essential in a democratic society, binding together generations in a reciprocal spirit of trust and community. 'In his life-time, the older person has made his contribution,' Harry Levine, the founder of the Hodson centres, explained in 1952. 'We owe him the opportunity to prolong his usefulness ... to the life around him.' In New York City, twelve day centres opened their doors to local seniors, with a pool, dancing, costume making and even wedding parties. In this democratic vision, choice and a 'motivation to do' took the place of charity and dependence. For Levine, it was 'fundamental' that the centres offered choice. It was choice that nourished 'experience and growth'. Instead of drifting into numb isolation, seniors were stimulated to be creative and play their part in the community.[53] The golden-age club movement was yet another manifestation of the influence of John Dewey's blend of pragmatism, democracy and choice.[54]

In Washington, too, the Second World War and the Korean War five years later made senior citizens more valuable than ever before. The first National Conference on the Aging [*sic*] met between May 1950 and August 1951, at President Truman's request. Oscar Ewing, the Administrator of the Federal Security Agency, explained that America was 'no longer a nation of young people'. Almost 12 million Americans were aged sixty-five or older; this happened to include Truman, who had just turned sixty-six. Those who reached sixty-five, on average lived to seventy-eight. Rather than looking at this age group as a burden, Ewing said, they should be recognized as 'great national assets'. Their well-being was everyone's business and essential to the strength of 'the local community and the Nation as a whole'. The idea that older people ought to avoid exertion had been discredited. Senior citizens played softball and went camping, Ewing pointed out. They had plenty of vitality left. There was a 'spark of genius' in each and every one of them. Recreation had the ability to foster new talents and rekindle the 'will to do'. And it was the 'impulse to do' which led the individual into new activities and relationships. Active leisure, in this view, made for democratic as well as personal growth. With the young serving in the Korean War, the United States could not possibly afford to waste the potential of its older citizens at home.[55]

These were words. What was the relation between rhetoric and reality? Which came first: the language of active ageing or the lifestyle itself? On the one hand, the stereotype of the elderly as smelly, bored and senile did obscure the many healthy and vigorous members in their midst. 'Old' tends to be used to describe others, rarely oneself. In that sense, Havighurst and like-minded researchers made visible the many retired people who already led an active life, who travelled for pleasure, played sport and socialized. On the other, the new discourse of active ageing clearly widened the opportunities for leisure and strengthened the desire and compulsion to remain active in old age.

In 1929, the US Bureau of Labor Statistics found idleness to be a serious problem in old people's homes. Many 'inmates' resisted doing even light duties. Some homes took a lesson from occupational therapy, which had been shown to improve the health of wounded soldiers after the First World War. Still, men, in particular, were reluctant participants. They had come to rest, not to work, they said.

In the course of the twentieth century, the room for rest and idleness progressively shrank. Leisure was energized. Golden-age and sunshine clubs, 'old-timers' and 'Live Long and Like It' groups mushroomed in the 1940s and '50s and outdid each other with parties and excursions. These were the years that gave birth to the Golden Age Hobby Show. The first, in Cleveland in 1945, attracted 200 exhibitors and 4,000 visitors. In addition to demonstrations of weaving and toy-making, there was live entertainment by the old for the old. In Chicago and New York, seniors put on variety shows and comedy acts.[56] Nurses started to take note. In 1955, the *American Journal of Nursing* praised the ABC Groups (Always Be Cheerful), which organized parties, trips and resident rhythm bands. Entertainment, 'a pretty dress', and 'nurses' knowledge of a resident's personal wishes' were recognized as a central part of therapy, as important as comfort and security. Age might have reduced their physical capacity but not their ability and right to enjoy their favourite pastimes.[57]

Of course, not all the activities were about fun. There were talks for the elderly, too, on the concentration camps, and other serious topics. Still, the overall number and sheer variety of leisure programmes shot up exponentially. A survey of thirty-four homes in Cook County, Illinois, found that most offered musicals, holiday celebrations and organized shopping trips and visits to the movies; a third had their own auditoriums for showing films. With one exception, these homes were privately run. Half had hobby and sewing rooms. The calendar at the Home for Aged Jews was especially full, with festivities on birthdays and holidays, bingo parties and pinochle (a trick-taking card game) tournaments. Each room had its own radio. 'They have parties in their own rooms whenever they desire them.'[58] Not all groups were so fortunate. Four homes in Cook County had nothing to offer but a chapel. and people barely ever left their rooms. African-Americans had only three small homes to turn to. Nonetheless, few groups were entirely bypassed by the general drive for recreation. After the Second World War, cities opened summer camps for elderly African-Americans. Baltimore started one in 1953, 25 miles outside the city. A welfare officer who had worked with golden-age clubs recruited the first party of forty-six campers: their average age was seventy-three; one was a hundred and five years old. In addition to hymn singing, there was fishing and hiking, checker contests, parties and, for the men, a shooting match. 'The senior citizens,' a staff member noted, 'actually proved to be much less frail than we had expected.' The only illness that occurred was from 'overeating'.[59]

Before pursuing the advance of leisure in old age further, let us briefly pause and make two general observations. Chronologically, the interest in recreation for the elderly coincided with the rise of the teenager. It has been difficult to see this, for the simple reason that the teenager has been given great prominence in cultural studies whereas the elderly ended up in the pages of gerontology journals. Putting them alongside each other suggests that, rather than being a solitary pioneer, the teenage consumer was part of a bigger historical moment in which recreation redefined generations. Secondly, the turn to active leisure further illuminates one of the forces behind the cult of busyness we have discussed earlier. It is too simple to lay the blame for hurriedness exclusively at the feet of advertisers, corporations and materialist shoppers. Active leisure had support, too, from doctors, civic leaders, welfare officers and pension advisers. It played no small part in raising the status and well-being of retired people. Whatever the strain of hurriedness, it is naïve to treat 'slow' life as a panacea for all. Idleness, the elderly remind us, has costs, too.

For older Europeans wanting a bit of fun and action, there were few places to turn to after the Second World War. A social survey of Merseyside painted a grim picture of old age in England's north-west. There were few concessions for the elderly – in Bootle, bowls were free but, 4 miles south in Liverpool, had to pay 2½d, almost the full rate. Holidays were effectively unknown – a mere fifty applicants had been treated to a trip to the Hoylake hostel before the war. There were only two regular clubs; one, the Rendezvous, had a few easy chairs but no canteen, although the atmosphere was reported to be 'cheerful and friendly'. The Old Age Pensions Association offered talks, lantern shows, weekly entertainment and tea, though the tea only materialized 'sometimes'.[60] Only 2 per cent of the elderly were in a retirement home. In London, most lived in small, overcrowded flats or unfurnished rooms. Pastimes were almost exclusively home-bound and solitary. A study of one hundred people over seventy years of age in Hammersmith in 1954 discovered that almost half had no activities outside the home at all; only one in eight regularly visited the pub, a cinema or church. Only a handful belonged to a club. Couples, in general, tended to read more and have more pets but, for many, life was pinched, monotonous and cold. It is not easy to engage with the world, without the money to pay for a radio, buy a ticket for the cinema, or go out, decently dressed, to meet others in a pub.

By the 1950s, the seeds for a richer, more consumer-oriented and diverting lifestyle for the elderly had been planted. Yet, across the world, the soil varied greatly, with different levels of wealth, welfare systems and attitudes to the elderly. The progress of the elderly consumer was consequently piecemeal and uneven. A comparison of Europe and North America in 1960 concluded that in 'all the countries an active, creative use of leisure time by older people is respected,' but in reality 'it is expected that older people will be happy if they can "take things easy".'[61] The situation differed considerably from country to country. In the United States, Great Britain and Scandinavia, active leisure pursuits were most pronounced. In Sweden, welfare boards had hobby rooms; here, an impressive 40 per cent of men and women aged between sixty-eight and seventy-three spent more time on hobbies than they had in middle age. In France and the Netherlands, by contrast, elderly people lived a more passive life. In The Hague, the Catholic Union of Diocesan Associations of Old People ran over twenty clubs and tried to introduce seniors to cultural activities, 'but mostly the members are not much interested. They like to say, "We are here for our pleasure, not to learn anything or to be really active."' They might dress up for Carnival but classical music and cultural films were 'not much liked'.[62] Members preferred to chat or play cards. A few liked knitting. In Germany, a survey concluded that 'it is not expected . . . that older people will discover or develop new leisure activities or that they will be strenuously active in such things.' In the Ruhr, retired miners kept a goat or two and did some gardening, but that was about it. Culture and entertainment were all but absent. Even reading and listening to the radio were minority pursuits.[63]

By the end of the 1980s, later life had been transformed beyond recognition. Admittedly, some still did not pursue any leisure activities and were depressed, but they were now in a minority. Most Britons in their sixties, seventies and eighties, researchers found, were intensely active and happy; only one in five of those over eighty-five needed care. Dancing and gardening were especially popular. Many, including widows, went to clubs and enjoyed socializing. The majority were happy with how they looked – what was important was to keep 'smart' and 'proper'. Most felt in good health. Disability and disease were not central to how they saw themselves. In their own self-image, they were active, energetic, even youthful, just like other members of society. If they disliked one thing, it was being patronized.[64] A study of five hundred elderly Berliners in the 1990s similarly captured the remarkably high levels of activity. More than half the seventy- to eighty-four-year-olds enjoyed travel, excursions and eating out. Among those over eighty-five, it was still a third. Not surprisingly, those living on their own were the most active but, strikingly, even a quarter of those living in old-age homes now went on excursions or visited restaurants.[65] Ageing involved a gradual change in the kinds of activity and engagement under-taken, not a sudden disengagement all-round. As French women moved into their mid-seventies, some stopped getting on their bicycles and ceased to do gymnastics, but more played Scrabble and did crosswords. Interestingly, most seventy-five-year-olds listened to music and visited museums and cinemas as often as they had when they were sixty.[66]

The enrichment of retirement went hand in hand with a dramatic improvement in elderly people's finances. In 1900, the aged had been just as poor as anyone else. By mid-century, however, rising wages for the employed, on the one hand, and limited welfare provision for the retired on the other, made old age synonymous with poverty. In 1970 Britain, pensioners made up every second household below the poverty line. Thirty years later, this had dwindled to a mere quarter. In the United States, in the 1980s, the elderly ceased to be poorer than the rest of the nation. By now, the Dutch, the Italians, the French and the Germans were leapfrogging Americans into early retirement, although Scandinavians remained industrious – fewer than a third of fifty-five to sixty-four-year-old Italians and Belgians were in paid work in 2005; in Germany, it was 41 per cent, while in Denmark and Sweden it was 62 per cent.[67] In Germany in 2003, the average pensioner household was worth a quarter of a million euros. In Japan at the same time, eld-erly households (sixty-plus) held four times the financial wealth of their younger neighbours.[68] Across the developed world, the 1960s–'90s were the golden years for seniors, although widows and singles contin-ued to find themselves more easily trapped in poverty. Pensions came to stand for a salary rather than charity, and redistributed wealth from young to old. European welfare regimes accepted that the elderly in care homes, too, had a right to at least some discretionary spending.

Under affluence, the definition of basic needs widened. In Germany, the 'basic pocket money' (*Grundtaschengeld*) had been calculated in 1964 to cover the simplest needs: every person on welfare benefits should be able to afford half a bar of soap, 80 grams of noodles and three bottles of beer per month. By 1980, most pensioners received DM66 on top of the 'basic' DM90. When, in 1982, the government proposed cutting into the extra pocket money, there was an outcry. The minister in charge, Antje Huber, was bombarded with complaints from old-age homes. The Grey Panthers demonstrated in Bonn, the capital. 'PENSION CUT: GRANNY COMMITS SUICIDE', announced the headline of one tabloid newspaper. What united the protesters was simple. To age decently and stay connected in an affluent society, half a bar of soap and three bottles of beer were no longer enough. Old people had a right to pursue their small pleasures and enjoy a bit of entertainment and distraction – the monthly trip to the hairdresser, a visit to the cinema, a nice blouse, musical records and presents for the grandchildren. One outraged labour charity itemized for the minister what the elderly in care homes actually spent to meet their 'basic needs' and participate in social life – the list included a monthly pedicure and ten cigarettes a day, flowers and magazines, visits to restaurants and the theatre. The pocket money needed to be doubled, not cut, it said. In the end, the luckless coalition government gave in and agreed to a compromise. The extra money was cut, but the basic pocket money was raised from DM90 to DM120 and renamed 'cash for personal use'. Those who lived in homes and contributed to their cost from their pension received another 5 per cent of income on top. Across the land, hairdressers and confectioners breathed a sigh of relief.[69]

The living conditions of the elderly edged closer and closer to those of the rest of society. By the mid-1990s, consumer spending by older couples in Finland and the United Kingdom reached 81 per cent and 85 per cent of that of younger cohorts; and this figure excluded housing. In Germany, Japan and New Zealand, they even outdid the young. Active ageing translated into yen and euros. An elderly Japanese couple, for example, spent 132 per cent as much on recreation and culture as a younger one; in Germany it was 115 per cent.[70] These figures manifested a historic shift: working income ceased to be the all-important ticket into the world of consumption.

Possessions, travel and beauty – all signalled the apotheosis of the elderly consumer. In London in the 1950s, most septuagenarians made do with a few old clothes and chairs and a small number of photographs and personal possessions. Single elderly men and widows especially lived barren material lives. The Hammersmith survey of 1954 listed the budget of a single man who 'cooked only once a week and made things last over, eating one potato only for dinner . . . He was still wearing clothes he had had since 1914 and they and his furniture were in a very poor condition.'[71] Many elderly people possessed only bedroom slippers for shoes. From 1947, local authorities in Britain were required to register all belongings on admitting someone to an old-age home. Such inventories make for grim reading. In his ground-breaking investigation of homes for the aged, Peter Townsend in 1962 catalogued page after page of 'one broken wall-clock; two wooden chairs, one with a loose leg; one role of yellowing wall-paper'; a single cardboard box filled with 'broken ornaments, hairpins, rusty screws, a broken pair of scissors'.[72]

At first, televisions, telephones and consumer durables were slow to reach the households of the old. By 1990, elderly Britons had caught up. A decade later, the sixty-five- to seventy-four-year-olds could lay a greater claim than the twenty-five- to thirty-four-year-olds to that most precious possession: a home.[73] Cramped rooms and council flats had largely given way to home ownership. A similar trend is evident elsewhere. A Swedish study of over 100,000 households in 2004 found that thirty- to fifty-nine-year-olds on average had 'access' to 5.5 of the following: a second home, a car, a boat, a caravan, a video recorder, a dish washer, a daily newspaper and a holiday. Those aged seventy still enjoyed five items from this group and were slightly ahead of those in their twenties. Even in their early eighties Swedes managed to enjoy at least four of these.[74]

Behind these rising rates of ownership lay two developments. One was simply that a new cohort arrived, those born during the post-1945 baby boom, who had reached adolescence in the age of affluence and carried their material lifestyle with them into old age. This so-called 'cohort effect' is visible, for example, in their disproportionately high rate of VCR ownership, in which the baby-boomers had acted as trendsetters. Yet when it came to televisions, and telephones and household goods more generally, all cohorts showed rising levels of ownership, those born in the 1920s and '30s as much as those born in the '40s and '50s – sign of a 'generational effect'.

The main lesson to take away from these trends is that seniors have come to be equal participants in consumer society. With the partial exception of car ownership, crossing the threshold into old age no longer triggers dispossession.[75] And with equality came greater independence and personal choice. It was not that elderly people had been completely bypassed by goods in the past, but, once they stopped working and were unable to support themselves, they became dependent consumers, at the mercy of their children or the community for food, fire and a bed. In eighteenth-century England, the country with the most generous welfare system, a good deal of aid had been in kind, although some parishes gave the aged poor cash in addition. In Puddletown, Dorset, in the 1770s, for instance, the septuagenarian widow Judith Biles received fuel and one new under-gown a year, plus a 'purging mixture' and medical 'drops'.[76]

The recent surge of possessions has not reached all elderly equally. Residential homes and geriatric hospitals are not the same as private homes, and the minority living in the former – 3 per cent in Spain and Italy, 12 per cent in France, the Netherlands and Ireland – continue to make do with few personal belongings.

In the post-war period, possessions gained new advocates among gerontologists across the West. There was a growing recognition that things were an anchor of personality and mental health. Research in the 1950s highlighted the psychological damage concentration-camp inmates suffered from being stripped of their possessions. In the following decade, studies diagnosed similar effects of 'depersonalization' in long-term care. Canadian advocates for the elderly started to speak up for seniors' rights to property and individuality. To take their possessions away was to take away a piece of their identity. In 1961, psychiatrists compared three mental hospitals in Britain and noted a correlation between high levels of disturbance and low levels of personal possessions and leisure. In one, almost all female schizophrenic patients had their own dress and make-up, comb, mirror and jewellery – in the more 'disturbed' one, only the minority did.[77] A decade later, the Department of Health issued guidelines for geriatric hospitals on the minimum required clothing. The health authority in Yorkshire in 1988 required all residential units to give individuals a chance to experience a degree of the independence, choice and individuality they would have enjoyed in their own homes. Such directives notwithstanding, progress was painfully slow. In the late 1980s, two British psychiatrists were 'appalled' that a generation after the well-publicized exposures of institutional misery, many of the Alzheimer's patients they visited were still 'denied personal property to the extent that some aspects of the concentration camp are being replicated and basic human rights (such as the wearing of one's own underwear) are not being met'.[78]

The last half-century has been an age of unprecedented mobility, for old and young. Travel, too, has become a natural part of active ageing. The Long Beach recreation department started its 'Golden Tours' in 1957 for anyone aged fifty or over. There were excursions to

Disneyland and Yellowstone, Las Vegas and Santa Monica. Most cost $2.25. Travel ceased to be a luxury. In six years, the Golden Tours covered 240,000 miles, a trip further than to the moon, as one volunteer cheerfully pointed out. 'See Earth First!' was their motto.[79] A study of three US corporations in 1980 noted that frequent travel shot up when employees retired.[80] In Britain, SAGA began offering holidays for the over-fifties in 1951; by 2003, it had a turnover of £383 million.

The taste for holidays developed into a desire for a more permanent place in the sun. In the United States, elderly snowbirds started their migration to the sunny south in the 1930s. By the 1970s, one in four Americans above the age of sixty-five lived in three states: Florida, California and New York. In St Petersburg ('Sunshine City'), one in three residents was over sixty-five, in Miami every other, although St Petersburg took the honour of having the biggest shuffleboard club in the world.[81] For others, being on the move came to define retirement. Trailers had been a part of the American landscape since the 1930s, but then they were primarily about offering a cheap, mobile home to the poor and to migrant workers. In the 1960s, nomadic seniors took to the road and founded trailer clubs; by 1991, more than 8 million recreational vehicles (RVs) were registered in the United States. 'My wife and I have completely changed our lifestyle since retirement,' one former accountant who had retired early, at sixty, recalled in 1972. For the first couple of years they travelled around the country. Then they joined the Wally Byam Caravan Club International and found new friends. In the summer, they travelled with their thirty-one-foot trailer to visit family and sightsee along the way. Come November, they would drive to Melbourne, Florida, where 'we . . . square dance and party all winter'.[82]

Without a Florida of their own, elderly Britons did the next best thing – they moved to the English south coast, to Spain, or to Australia. In 1981, pensioners made up a third of the population in ten towns on England's 'Costa Geriatrica'. In the course of the decade, the number of British and German residents in Spain doubled. Many were elderly. The Royal British Legion has over a thousand members on the Costa del Sol. The Germans had tried hard to claim their own 'place in the sun' in the scramble for colonies in the 1890s. They were not to be beaten this time. The first wave of winter tourists arrived in November 1962, when Luis Riú struck a deal with a charter company and kept his hotel in Mallorca open in winter. By 2005, the holiday Club Schwalbe (swallow) hosted 4,000 seniors on Mallorca. The consul general in Malaga estimates that up to half a million Germans aged sixty or over spend a good part, or most, of the year in Spain; another 100,000 are believed to have picked South Africa.[83]

Cheaper travel, better health and, in the case of Western Europe, transferrable pensions and health services all facilitated the move to the sun. It would be misleading, though, to treat it entirely as a new commercial phenomenon born out of the charter and holiday boom of the 1960s. Earlier experiences of migration and war had already whetted the taste for a peripatetic life and retirement in foreign lands. In the case of Britain, the empire left a distinct legacy. Raymond Flower, the first Briton to buy a farm in Italy's Chianti, for example, had been raised in Egypt and served in Italy during the Second World War. On the Algarve, a property developer recalled the '60s, when many of the early British residents came straight from East Africa, after independence: 'it was a bit like the days of the Raj down here then . . . Servants were a-plenty, booze was cheap and the climate was good.'[84]

A host of age-specific initiatives has courted the expanding 'silver market'. The American Association of Retired Persons (AARP) introduced a Grand Circle for elderly travellers as early as 1955, but the real take-off came in the 1980s and '90s. In the meantime, old age has started earlier and earlier. In Tokyo, in 1984, the Yutaka Club introduced a tourism club and cruises for those over sixty-five. Neckermann, the German travel group, offers special city tours for seniors over fifty-nine; the AARP introduced its own waiting rooms at JFK Airport in 1986. Austria and Switzerland pioneered a network of '50plus Hotels' that combined discounts with the 'pronounced hospitality' supposedly prized by that age group. Scotland has a Club 55 card for rail travellers. Only in rich Norway does one have to reach sixty-seven to qualify for discounts on the Hurtigruten cruise.

These commercial campaigns do not exist in a vacuum. Ever younger ageing consumers have also become the darling of public authorities. Like so many elements of contemporary consumption, they are partly the creature of public policy. In 1999, Nordrhein-Westphalia, the biggest state in Germany, established a special resort for Seniorenwirtschaft to stimulate markets and services for the elderly. The Teutoburg Forest, where German warriors once ambushed Romans, now lures those over fifty with 'wellness' packages. Swords and battleaxes were replaced by Nordic walking sticks. Some towns have built 'smart homes' designed for the elderly and provided seniors with their own internet cafés. European regions started a silver economy network (SEN@ER). In ageing societies, the old became the market of the future.

If we step back and look at these various forms of active ageing together, they reveal a central tension at the heart of ageing in affluent societies. On the one hand, active ageing stressed that people were only as old as what they did and how they felt. The barrier with younger cohorts was blurred. Seniors had just as much right to have fun, go on a city break and pick up new hobbies as anyone else. In a 1990 British study, there was nothing that united the sixty- to eighty-year-olds as much as a dislike of old people's clubs run by younger members of the middle classes who treated them as passive. People, they said, liked to get together because of shared interests, not a pre-determined bio-logical birth age.[85] On the other hand, there was an exodus to trailer parks and retirement communities that gave rise to new forms of age segregation, particularly pronounced in the United States but also vis-ible in 'geriatric' seaside communities in Europe.

'Wake up and live in Sun City', a radio advert urged listeners in 1960, 'for an active new way of life ... Don't let retirement get you down! Be happy in Sun City; it's paradise town.'[86] The retirement com-munity in Arizona offered each resident a 'Lip' (Leisure Interest Profile) – at one point, there were plans to build a Legoland for the eld-erly (see Plate 59). 'Leisure World', a gated retirement community in California, was built in the late 1960s. By 1971, it had 14,000 inhabit-ants who lived in 8,300 units spread across 918 acres, with its own tennis courts, theatre productions, picnics and hobby sales. Such exclu-sive, resort-style retirement communities have attracted their share of criticism. A sociologist who planted himself for one year in one such community in California in the early 1970s left with a dismal verdict. The settlement had a town-hall-activity centre, but neither mayor nor politics. It had 92 clubs and offered 150 daily activities, but only one in ten of the 5,600 residents – all white – regularly heeded the town motto to enjoy an 'active way of life'. Even shopping was no fun, because there was little choice and no public transport. Many, in fact, went out of town to shop and play golf, because it was better and cheaper there. The streets were clean, the ranch-style houses orderly, but all looked alike and unlived in. Those who arrived hoping for paradise were in for a shock. Other studies have been more optimistic. A survey of the 5,000 senior clubs and centres in the United States by the National Council on Aging put the figure for those participating in active and creative activities higher, at three to four out of ten. A leisure expert who had advised the Walters-Gould Corporation behind Sun City found that most residents felt their needs were met.[87]

The ageing body was simultaneously liberated and shackled by the ideal of staying young and active. Old age is no longer treated as a bar to exercise and adventure. Seniors cruise through powder and enjoy après-ski in the Alps.[88] No challenge is high enough. In 2012, seventy-three-year-old Watanabe Tamae from Japan became the oldest woman to climb Mount Everest; a seventy-six- year-old Nepalese holds the record for men. More and more, the cage of biological age has opened up. The 1950s introduced the 'third age' as a new life-stage of creative fulfilment, before the descent into a 'fourth age' of ill health, dependence and death; in addition to the initial third-age universities, there are now online gaming clubs and other services.[89] In recent years, even that distinction has been loosened. The fourth age is not necessarily all bad, just as the third age is not all good, critics point out. There are octogenarian athletes. A study of male and female athletes in Australia has noted how sport continued to be about fun, sociability and competition for those aged into their eighties. Few were in denial of their age. Sport was about keeping their body moving so they did not 'rust up'.[90]

At the same time, the culture of active ageing shifted the responsibility to stay young and fit on to the elderly. Old age was no longer destiny. It was an individual lifestyle choice, even an obligation. The new-found freedom simultaneously made ageing more fun and more painful; brilliantly mocked by Federico Fellini in his 1986 film *Ginger and Fred*, when an elderly TV-gym instructor announces 'old age has ceased to exist' and instructs viewers to eliminate their wrinkles with bizarre face-stretching exercises, grimacing and frowning.[91] Immortality has been a dream of humans ever since the Babylonian legend of Gilgamesh. In the late twentieth century, the quest for eternal youth reached new heights. Consumer culture was not the only stimulus – there was also the medicalization of age – but it certainly helped give unprecedented credence to the belief that age could and ought to be arrested altogether. According to one estimate, the anti-ageing market was worth $43 billion in the United States in 2002. A year earlier, the AARP reported that every second American baby-boomer was depressed about getting old. Every third woman admitted using anti-ageing cosmetics, and one in ten was contemplating surgery. In Brazil, plastic surgery is considered natural, with 360,000 interventions in 2000. Nor is it just women who try to halt the inevitable sagging of the chin. The number of Brazilian men turning to the scalpel shot up exponentially in the 1990s.[92]

While on the rise globally, active ageing has taken a variety of forms, depending on long-standing traditions and understandings of old age.

In Japan, individuals are seen to have some power to stem the tide of *boke* – the disintegration of the self – or at least to slow it down. To be idle is to encourage *boke* and let the community down as well as one-self. The elderly (*rojin*) are expected to demonstrate their value to themselves and to society. They are pushed to develop an *ikigai*, or personal hobby. Health and active leisure are treated not as a matter of personal choice but as part of a social contract between the elderly and the community, This contract was formally recognized by the Law for the Welfare of the Aged in 1963 and followed by the birth of Old People Clubs, elder colleges and government support for sports and recreation for the over-sixty-fives. In rural Japan, old persons' clubs are crucial. In the hamlet of Jonai, for example, every fifth resident belongs to the local *rojin kurabu*. Being active, of course, does not automatically entail being an active consumer. Some leisure activities come cheap, such as the boardgame Go and singing in a choir. Others, however, carry a larger price tag. One of the most popular pastimes among Japanese seniors is Gateball (*geeto booru*), a fast-paced type of croquet. A decent stick easily costs Y40,000, or $500.[93]

Since the 1960s, Japanese elderly have been subject to two competing pressures. On the one hand, the flight of the young from the countryside to the city and the rise of single elderly households have widened the generation gap, leaving a feeling of isolation and worthlessness. In rural areas, suicides have shot up dramatically. Neglect and abuse were widespread, and community care was minimal prior to the introduction of long-term care insurance in 2000. On the other hand, the value of the elderly as consumers has received unprecedented attention in attempts to capture the 'silver market'; in 2002, only 4 per cent of households headed by a pensioner were low-income. In the shops arrived electrical goods that talked, internet software designed for seniors, specialized mattresses and insurance packages. Shiseido, the cosmetics firm, has run beauty sessions in homes for the elderly since 1975; they are popular with men as well as women. In the 1990s, Itôchû, a large trading company, began sending photographers to visit seniors in their homes for market research. Other companies introduced phones with large buttons and stylish light-weight walking sticks. The Elderly Service Providers Association launched a 'silver mark' for products that met its welfare and comfort standard. By 1999, 1,000 firms carried the label. Age-appropriate hotels carried silver stars. Ageing Europe turned to Japan for inspiration.[94]

None of these commercial overtures should be surprising. What is remarkable, given how much spending the elderly control, is how limited they have been. In contrast to their fascination with teenagers, advertisers and companies all but ignored their grandparents' new affluence. The elderly were virtually absent from billboards and TV screens; in the United States and Japan, elderly actors appeared in a mere 2 per cent of prime-time television and commercials in the 1970s.[95] In the 1960s, some marketers urged companies to wake up to the unique $40 billion market made up of 'old folks'. Their call fell on deaf ears.[96] The first proper study of the 'mature market' did not appear until 1980, in the *Harvard Business Review*. It was only in the following decade, with the help of US census data, that marketing experts began to break down the ageing consumer into smaller cohorts and distinguish the lifestyles and spending power of the GI generation born before 1930 from that of the war babies and post-war baby boomers. Early attempts to capture that market often backfired; Kellogg's had to recall their 'forty-plus' cereal after six months in 1989 in the face of complaints about ageism and charges by the Iowa attorney-general that it was deceptive advertising to suggest that people over forty had special dietary needs. Marketing to the over-sixties continues to be the Cinderella of the business world. According to the Center for Mature Consumer Studies, many companies still do not grasp why they should reach out to older consumers. When they do, they often treat them as homogeneous, whereas, in reality, they are more diverse than their juniors.[97] With the exception of Viagra and stairlifts, older consumers continue to be largely invisible.

In sum: the more positive image of the elderly, of active leisure and the third age have made seniors an integral part of affluent consumer societies. But this shift was driven by gerontology, civic culture and better pensions and welfare provision, not by corporations. It has yet to conquer Madison Avenue. At least in the commercial world, the elderly are prisoners of youth.

So far, we have dealt with affluent seniors in affluent countries but, of course, from a global perspective, these are the minority. Only a third of the world's elderly live in Europe and North America. In 1999, over half were in Asia, where the ageing of societies has been at least as dramatic. Japan made the transition to affluence in the 1960s and has already been discussed. In the rest of Asia, it was in the late twentieth century that development and urbanization brought about a sharp decline in fertility. In Singapore, for example, seven births per woman

were typical in the 1950s. Twenty years later, the two-child family was
the norm. Korea makes the European story of ageing look like it happened in slow motion – in 1990, for every Korean over the age of
sixty-five, there were five children under fifteen; by 2020, the ratio will
be 4:5, close to equal.

To what degree has old age in Asian societies also become a more
intensive consumer experience mirroring the Western trend towards
more independent, leisurely elders? The answer is complicated by historically different living arrangements between the generations that
impinge on the resources and opportunities to spend time and money –
living alone is a world apart from living under one's children's roof. In
Thailand in the late 1980s, only one in ten elderly people lived apart
from their children. In the United States, it was three out of four.[98] This
divergence is not the result of some unchanging cultural DNA, however. In Taiwan, the number of elderly living with their kids dropped
from two thirds to one half in the 1980s. Rather, a main difference
between East and West is that in Europe the extended family had long
ceased to exist by the time department stores opened their doors,
whereas in Asia consumer culture encountered multi-generational families intact when it took off in the late twentieth century.[99]

This encounter has taken various shapes. In more affluent Singapore, the state has put its resources and authority behind the three-
generation family, with tax breaks and laws on filial piety. Almost
85 per cent of seniors continue to live together with their children. The
family remains the first line of support. At the same time, the government has discovered its seniors as a 'valuable resource' and supports
'active lifestyles', with Gateball courts and spaces for *taiji quan*
martial-art exercises.[100]

In India, by contrast, a national survey in 1995–6 revealed that over
two thirds of the aged depended on others for their day-to-day existence. Almost every second old person was still working. Most lived
with their spouse, a third with their children, mostly by necessity rather
than choice. Only 5 per cent lived alone, though many more would
have liked to. A mere 1 per cent received institutional care, and while
some homes had TVs and radios, there was little interest in activities.[101]
Most elderly were poor and spent their twilight years as dependent
consumers, preoccupied with shelter, food, medicine and clothing.
Compared to their German and Japanese cousins, their spending on
entertainment and leisure was tiny.

The economic life of the household remains complex. It tends to be assumed that in South Asia the old move in with their married son, but often it is the other way around. Money, similarly, flows in both directions. Many elderly support their unmarried children, while others are at the mercy of their married sons. What is clear is that the rising demands of the conjugal family have made filial support less forthcoming. 'They don't need it, and I can't give it' is a common refrain by sons today. That pleasure is the preserve of the young is an old Indian notion, but the advance of consumer culture and rising aspirations since the 1980s have reinforced it. More than ever, the young are the natural consumers. Here is a major difference with the affluent West. While the elderly in the West have seen their needs expand, the elderly poor in India have seen theirs contract. Old age marks the end of the right to consume and enjoy goods. In the South Indian state Tamil Nadu, there is a saying that the elderly have had their life (*vaalkai mudinchi pochu*). Why waste money and goods on those who are finished? Old people are expected to have little appetite and no need for comfort and convenience. Consequently, they receive little food and medicine – far too little. Instead of a colourful sari, dull cast-off cloth will do. Since being old is not defined by biological age but by a decline of activity and sensual appetite, the very idea of fun-packed active golden years is an oxymoron.[102]

Old age looks different for the Indian middle class, however. Here, as among their Western peers, consumer goods have been on the rise. In the 1990s in the middle-class district of Deccan Gymkhana in Pune, over a third of women over sixty had a mixer, grinder and oven; one in nine boasted a washing machine. Along with their remittances, successful migrants have also brought back with them from America new ideas of ageing. The first retirement communities have sprung up. On the whole, however, old age for affluent Indians, too, remains a far cry from the Western pursuit of independent living and active leisure. In 2000, over half lived with their children. In Rana Pratap Bagh, an upper-middle-class neighbourhood in north-west Delhi, one in five elderly people kept contributing to the family income, working as accountants or shop owners. The lives of the retired were not untouched by commercial leisure – many went to the movies or watched TV – but they were not defined by it either. Most free time was devoted to visiting shrines and relatives. Only one in eight had an active hobby.[103]

SOLIDARITY

Today's world is sometimes said to be 'liquid', to use the image of the sociologist Zygmunt Bauman. People no longer form 'real' solid bonds but pass from one 'virtual' momentary engagement to another like restless eels.[104] In this view, consumer culture, with its dream worlds, its material temptations and its licence for the pursuit of personal desire, is the chief – if the not only – solvent of solid human relationships.

We have looked at each generation in turn. Now, in conclusion, it is vital to look briefly at the relations between them. Has the growing number and significance of possessions for lifestyle and age-specific identities blown generations asunder? What difference have goods, tastes and material comfort had for the family as the principal institution through which generations care for each other?

It would be easy to point to physical manifestations of individualism. Most Americans had stopped living with their kids by the 1950s. Even in Japan, the number of three-generational households dropped by half in the 1980s and '90s while the number of single elderly doubled. Yet, the decline in co-residence does not automatically tell us about the emotional life of families. In the West, it is worth recalling, the multi-generational family was dead long before consumer goods and leisure forged the teenager and the active senior. There is little evidence that living apart has weakened generational bonds. In France in 1992, nine out of ten of the war babies (born 1939–42) provided domestic help for their elderly parents.[105] In any case, transport and telecommunication have shrunk space and, with it, softened the effects of physical distance. Most German seniors live less than an hour away from their children; south of the Alps, many stay in the same community, sometimes the same apartment building. Family members got on much better once they started to live around the corner instead of with each other.

Consumption has acted as a glue between generations in three main ways. First, there are the things themselves, the many gifts and possessions that parents collect and take with them into old age as reminders of their children. Second, as markers of personal taste and identity, the diffusion and range of goods and leisure have prompted greater tolerance and respect between children and their parents for their individual lifestyles, teaching them to live with difference. Of course, families today continue to live with tension and violence, though it would be naïve to think they had not also done so before consumer goods crossed the doorstep. Leisure and entertainment have created spaces and experiences shared by old and young. Authority may have been different, but so, in the process, has conflict. A study in London's East End in the mid-1960s found that most adolescent boys felt their parents to be understanding; in Germany, too, researchers at the time noted that 'the family today was no longer a typical place for hard and sustained generational conflict'.[106] The relationship between sons and fathers is undoubtedly warmer and more understanding at the end of the twentieth century than it was at its beginning. The shift in social values from work to leisure has further eased relations with the elderly. Retirement today no longer carries the same stigma of uselessness. Active leisure reintegrated the elderly into society. Everyone was a consumer now.

Finally, there is the transfer of resources that funds consumption, both within families and within nations. Rather than pulling families apart, consuming and caring work in symbiosis today. In affluent societies, middle-aged women are carers as well as consumers. They look after their elderly parents when the elderly are not picking up the grandchildren from school. Seniors give their children and grandchildren gifts, time and money as well as love. The available data suggests that affluence has strengthened, not weakened, this circulatory system. Significantly, in the United States, gifts and assistance from the elderly to their children and grandchildren rose in the 1960s, the golden decade of consumer society.[107] In Germany in 1996, every third senior transferred an average €3,700 to their children or grandchildren, the equivalent of 10 per cent of the public pension.[108] How many homes, holidays and appliances would young households have been able to afford without such parental transfers or the free childcare that so many offer? Grandchildren's wardrobes and bedrooms would be half empty. At national level, states oversee large generational transfers that enable most senior citizens to participate in consumer society. Without pensions, the elderly would drift back into poverty and dependence. At the time of writing, governments may try to raise the pension age and change contributions. Still, even during the worst recession since the Second World War, no one dreams of scrapping the compact between generations altogether. Class war has not been superseded by a war between generations. For this, consumption deserves some credit.

12

Outside the Marketplace

People enter a shop, compare the cost and appeal of the items on offer, check their wallet, then make a choice and pay at the counter. This, in a few words, is a widespread view of how consumption works. For critics and champions alike, consumption has been synonymous with individual choice in the marketplace. They may disagree about the virtues of choice, but not its centrality.[1] There are, of course, good reasons we are so preoccupied with choice. Never before have people had so much of it, at least in the rich world. Americans can pick among three hundred brands of cereal, Europeans from a hundred deodorants, Australians from a thousand mortgages. It sometimes seems as if society has turned into one enormous mall. Students are encouraged to shop around for courses, patients for doctors, and so forth.

The fixation with choice, however, comes at a price. For one, it encourages us to see in the past only what we can recognize as precursors of the present. The supermarket, advertising and the credit card emerge as milestones on the way to the neo-liberal trinity of choice, individualism and markets in the late twentieth century. From this perspective, the historic surge in consumption results from the unabashed triumph of private choice. We have already seen that such a view misses the longer influence of empire, ideology and power and the role of social habits and conventions. By treating consumption as choice's twin, secondly, it appears as the natural enemy of civic life and collective interests. Contemporary history comes to resemble a seesaw: as consumption went up, social democracy went down. The more private choice, the less shared purpose.

Yet, even now, plenty of goods and services reach people through collective channels where choice and markets are absent or limited, from public housing to the company car. In England and Wales, public hospitals in the National Health Service served over 200 million meals in 2000, more than KFC and Domino's Pizza combined; only

McDonald's served more.[2] In the twentieth century, the advance of consumption was as profound outside the marketplace as within it. If we want to understand the latter, we must therefore also appreciate the former, and especially the contribution of two institutions: the firm and the state.

THE FIRM

In 1792, Samuel Slater opened a free Sunday school to recruit boys for his cotton mill at Pawtucket in Rhode Island. A century later, company services had expanded to such a degree that many firms ran their own mini welfare state. In Europe as in America, industrialization and rapid growth confronted employers with the same dual challenge: how to attract skilled workers but keep out unions. Company housing, health clinics, sport and education were the price of a loyal, disciplined workforce. It is difficult to strike if it means eviction from the company flat. Many pension funds were introduced in the wake of strikes and limited entitlements to those with ten years of service or more. Krupp, the German steel maker, started out with seven employees in 1827. On the eve of the First World War, it had 42,000 workers in Essen alone. At that time, the firm owned or leased 7,000 flats for its workers. Their rent, on average, was 20 per cent less than on the open market. A first social insurance fund was set up in the 1860s. Krupp paid in half, the employee the other half. A dental clinic opened in 1903, a convalescent home followed four years later. Housewives bought their sausages and cheese at the firm's own *Konsumanstalt*, at discounted prices. The 50,000 volumes in the company library provided educational uplift.[3] The electrical giant Siemens started sending female employees and needy children to the Baltic coast before the First World War. In 1920, the firm's five holiday homes accommodated 2,000 employees and 1,000 children across the year. At that time, the company pension was double that offered by the state.[4]

For Alfred Krupp and Werner von Siemens, as for the Levers and Cadburys in England and countless paternalist entrepreneurs elsewhere,[5] the head of the firm was like a father to its workers and their dependents. Founder's days with fancy-dress competitions, a Christmas bonus for loyal staff, and – in the case of Lever – a co-partnership scheme with a share of profits, were ways of keeping the family together. Many bosses were driven by a genuine humanitarian impulse, but

humanitarianism was also good business. The gains from fewer stop-
pages, higher retention and higher productivity easily outweighed the
cost of pensions and other services.[6]

The company town was the most complete version of this kind of
collective consumption. It was genuinely global, stretching from Le
Creuset's iron works in northern France to the steel town of the Com-
panhia Siderúrgica Nacional in Volta, Brazil.[7] There was never a single
model, however. Most towns were erected in the middle of nowhere
but, ultimately, the quality and scope of their social provisions depended
on the type of business and skills needed. Where margins were low and
company owners relied mainly on unskilled labour, exploitation
trumped benevolence. The Panama Canal was built with blood, sweat
and tears.[8] Mining towns were notorious for poor conditions and lack
of services. Decent company services could make all the difference
between a loyal and a rebellious workforce. One lightning rod was the
company store. It was notorious for cheating workers out of their
hard-earned dollars. In the United States, an investigation during the
New Deal found that food cost 2–10 per cent more in company stores.[9]
As late as 1968, workers at the American Can Company had their
shopping bill from its grocery store in Bellamy, Georgia, deducted from
their wages. Elsewhere, owners opted for peace rather than a quick
buck and refused to run their own shops. In 1938, Frank Gilchrist
designed a grocer, liquor store and dry cleaner for his mill town in
Oregon, but did not own or manage any of them. Other bosses encouraged their workers to make use of mail order and itinerant traders. The
most contentious issue by far was the quality and quantity of company
food. A bad canteen was a recipe for unrest. In the Pacific Northwest
during the First World War, army officers found that loggers received
double a soldier's ration and enjoyed six different pastries for breakfast. In Mason City, a reporter noted that a 'man is not a man unless he
can eat his own weight three times a day', only mildly exaggerating. A
daily T-bone steak with one third of a pound of bacon on the side was
the norm.[10]

In railway towns and shipyards, where skilled labour was needed,
collective provision was in a different league. When the Pullman Palace
Car Company built its town in Illinois in 1881 it featured a hotel, a
theatre, an arcade of shops and a church, in addition to company housing. Pullman, Illinois, was a model of a closed-loop economy, creating
a virtuous circle between farm and fork. In company shops, workers
bought vegetables which had been fertilized on the company farm with

their own human waste collected by the local sewage network. Recreational facilities were the pride of benevolent company towns. In Indian Hill, home of the engineering firm Norton, just outside Worcester, Massachusetts, workers could play ball on the company baseball diamond or go rowing and trap-shooting. There were company clubs for amateur gardeners, photographers and stamp collectors. On summer evenings, the Norton bathhouse offered a retreat on the local lake.[11]

Company towns offered an important countervailing trend to the commercialization of leisure and its separation from communal life that is so often seen to be characteristic of consumer society. Production and consumption were one. Nowhere did this vision find a clearer expression than in Zlín, the Moravian base of the Bat'a shoe empire in what is today the Czech Republic. Tomáš Bat'a opened his first small workshop in 1894. By 1931, his factory produced 35 million shoes and, directly or indirectly, employed the bulk of the town's 30,000 inhabitants. The firm also produced plastics, tyres and, from 1927, had its own film department. Tomáš Bat'a was the town's employer, landlord and mayor. An admirer of Henry Ford, he turned the company town into a grand experiment in modern living. Standardized mass production was matched by standardized living. Housing colonies were a chessboard of functionalist two-storey, two-family cubes, each 8.5 by 9 metres. The company won over Le Corbusier, the pioneer of modernism, who judged the designs for workers' flats – Bat'a's town, the architect said, felt like 'a whole new world with, it seems, enough happiness to go around'.[12] What workers did in their leisure time was in one way or another organized by the shoe company. The local orchestra was the factory orchestra. Health and sport were company-based. Over the town towered the ten-storey 'community house' which contained the hotel and a bowling alley. Bat'a's 2,500-seater grand cinema, the largest in Europe at the time, offered free shows to inhabitants. Appropriately, in a town built on shoes, films were also shown during pedicure sessions. By the time the Nazis marched into Moravia on 15 March 1939, the Bat'a empire extended to satellite towns across the globe, from Bataville near Strasbourg and East Tilbury in Essex all the way to Batatuba in Brazil, founded by Tomáš's half-brother Jan. In Europe, Bat'a football teams played each other for the company cup (see Plate 66).[13]

Company towns have largely been understood in terms of industrial discipline, their welfare services as a tool to keep workers quiet. American unionists a century ago denounced their 'hellfare' services. The historical verdict has been mixed. In some companies, better services bought loyalty and peace, while, in others, they failed to contain strikes.[14] Our concern here, however, is not primarily with productivity and work discipline. Companies were equally important for consumption. They were schools of a new lifestyle that inculcated new habits and tastes and taught workers how to spend their time and money.

Their contribution took several forms. The first is perhaps an obvious one about space, but is nonetheless worth emphasizing. Many company towns were literally in the middle of nowhere and the only place far and wide to offer workers any kind of entertainment. In the Pacific Northwest and many other distant regions, mining, logging and the railways put shops, bars and theatres on the map. More widely, companies played a crucial role in diffusing a new culture of competitive sports (see Plates 64 and 65). Manchester United, the English soccer team, started life as a railway team; the Green Bay Packers, the American football team, in the canned-meat industry.[15] Dynamo Dresden, Lokomotive Moscow and similarly named clubs continue to wear their industrial origins on their sleeves. Already by the inter-war years, management and sport were entering a symbiotic relationship as businesses were discovering the value of sport for corporate image and company morale. Peugeot, in France, promoted sport as 'the moral and physical educator of youth' and stressed its psychological benefits in teaching employees to work together for a shared goal. When mayor of Cologne in the 1920s, Konrad Adenauer, West Germany's future post-war chancellor, similarly saw 'sport as the practical doctor at the sickbed of the German people'. In the 1920s, in a city like Hamburg, 166 company sports clubs were competing with 14 run by the municipal authorities, none bigger than the police club.[16]

Secondly, the scale of social services deserves recognition, for freeing up purchasing power and enhancing well-being. Siemens, in the mid-nineteenth century, gave workers an annual Christmas bonus worth a month's salary. Not every company flat was a bargain but, overall, they probably enabled families to save on rent. At a time when government welfare was virtually non-existent, these company services were doubly important. In the United States in 1916, 1,000 firms provided housing for 600,000 workers plus their families; for comparison, there were 1.3 million units of public housing in 1989.[17] Of course, not all services were free. A survey of Chicago in 1939 found that only one in eight firms paid for all their employees' recreation.[18] Other programmes were either self-supporting, or the cost was split with staff. However limited, such non-wage benefits made a significant contribution to the actual level of consumption which is missing from statistics relying on wages. Equally important were dynamic, long-term effects. Health and recreational services were not just savings now but raised the future quality of life and with it the potential to consume more later. Economists have emphasized such effects for developing nations,[19] but they played a similarly important role in Western societies in the heat of industrialization. That companies had their own profit motives for introducing such services should not obscure their contribution to well-being.

Many company towns were openly dedicated to what today would be called lifestyle change. Their mission was to socialize peasants and immigrants into a 'wholesome' pattern of consumption, not so different from what Stalinists tried in Russia in the 1930s. A good deal of this was about discipline and restraint. Dollars spent on flashy jewels and showing off might trigger jealousy among neighbours and demands for higher wages. In Granite City, Illinois, Commonwealth Steel had home visitors who checked on indebted workers and gave them lessons on how to live within their means. Idleness was disparaged. With their endless range of clubs and civic organizations, companies bear some responsibility for the spread of hyper-active leisure. In Indiana in 1940, an American researcher visited one large company where six hundred horseshoe teams were competing during the lunch break.[20] Workers busy throwing horseshoes or competing for the best garden had neither time nor energy to be revolutionaries, managers said.

At the same time, companies steered rural and foreign workers into a new world of comfort, convenience and material desire. In Moravia, Bat'a supervisors dropped in on housewives to ensure that their modern homes were matched by modern standards of cleanliness. In American company towns, 'neighbourhood houses' gave lessons in cooking with gas and electricity. It was here that many families listened to their first Victrola phonograph.[21] Few had greater faith in the power of material civilization than Henry Ford, who, in an effort to create a rubber plantation (Fordlandia) in Brazil in the late 1920s and '30s, brought electricity to the heart of the jungle.[22] Radio, records and company films, he believed, would Americanize the mixed races working on the plantation. The scheme failed to deliver the rubber for a single car tyre. What it did do was to leave behind a taste for mass-manufactured goods.

By the 1950s, American companies no longer just offered sport to their male workers but leisure activities for the entire family. A

contemporary survey found that the fashion show was the most popular part of the recreation programme for women. Many companies put
one on every season, with the help of local department stores, which
gladly provided the latest styles and in many cases sent 'live models to
display them'.[23] Company stores started selling apparel and electronic
goods. In club rooms, vending machines sold soft drinks and candy
bars to help pay for recreation programmes. The workplace often provided the basic units of the private world of consumption. When
Giuliana married Antonio M. in Milan on 25 April 1966, her co-workers
from the pharmaceutical laboratory presented them with a washing
machine on their wedding day; his office mates contributed a fridge.[24]
Such gifts were customary in many European countries during the miracle years.

Company services involved a contentious trade-off between free
provision and free choice. When workers at Fordlandia were informed
three days before Christmas 1930 that table service had been abolished, they smashed up the cafeteria. The anger was about more than
being served. Their demands included the freedom to choose their own
leisure activities and an end to the ban on liquor. In Europe and America, many company towns were a golden cage. In his *English Journey*
(1934), J. B. Priestley stopped at Cadbury's Bournville, outside Birmingham. 'What progressive people all over the world are demanding
for humanity,' he wrote, 'these workers have here.' They enjoyed comfortable housing and pension plans, sports pavilions and club
rooms. The factory had its own concert hall and 'is almost as busy in
the evenings as it is in the daytime. Games, music, drama, lectures,
classes, hobbies, conferences, all keep the place in full swing.' And yet,
there was something unnerving about the place. The firm was a total
society. Workers, he worried, were paying for their benefits with their
independence. 'I would infinitely prefer,' he wrote on leaving the village, 'to see workers combining to provide these benefits . . . [and] to
see them using their leisure, and demanding its increase, not as favoured
employees but as citizens, free men and women.'[25]

By the 1950s and '60s, the golden cage was losing some of its shine.
The main reason firms had been able to control leisure was location.
The main reason they lost their grip was the motor car. Mobility shrank
physical space and reduced their monopoly on entertainment. The Australian experience is indicative. At the end of the Second World War,
recreation and travel was still largely a collective endeavour. Going on
an excursion meant going with co-workers on the company bus. By

1959, such joint, work-based activities were in decline. The 'excitement and gaiety associated with a group travel to picnic sites by special train, ferries or buses', a government official noted, was 'losing appeal in the face of growing preference by families for travel in their own cars and in their own time'.[26] Greater private access to planes and automobiles repeated this story across the rich world.

Was this the end of corporate-led consumption? It has been customary to treat the 1930s as the high-water mark of welfare capitalism. Most writers have taken their cue from the American story. The New Deal, it is argued, took away the core attractions of company-based welfare by, on the one hand, providing alternative state services and, on the other, prohibiting firms from using recreation committees to side-step unions.[27] Why bother building a gym if the company had to give up control over its use? In the depressed 1930s, it is true, many facilities were shut down. One third of summer camps and a quarter of sports programmes were dissolved; half the women social directors were sacked.[28] Company housing, too, was being sold off. Yet this does not mean workers were left with nothing. To focus only on the paternalist side of welfare capitalism distracts from how firms continued to contribute to collective consumption after the Second World War. The war did not see the end of company services but their mutation. This matters even for the American story. It matters still more for the rest of the world.

In the United States, the demands of war production gave a new stimulus to plant-based recreation. Leisure was a way to integrate women and other new workers in the war effort, just as it had been for immigrants earlier. Patriotic spirit and support from the Federal Security Agency soothed fears that industrial recreation aimed to crush unions. 'Play ball and win the war' was the motto. Companies taught Americans to bowl together. More than ever, raising productivity and eliminating absenteeism were crucial. Some firms even did the Christmas shopping for employees, and took out their laundry. After the war, companies no longer had to worry about powerful unions, thanks to the Taft–Hartley Act of 1947. However, they still needed workers to show up at work, be alert and do their best. Recreation was rediscovered as a management tool. By 1953, 30,000 companies spent some $800 million to organize recreational programmes for 34 million workers, more than was devoted to all the schools in the United States.[29] The proliferation of clubs at Boeing gives a snapshot. A golf association was founded at Puget Sound on the Pacific coast in 1946 and has held company tournaments ever since. An alpine society followed in 1963, with mountaineering and snowshoeing courses. Three years later, the Ski Club, with support from the company's recreation department, bought a seventy-two-bed lodge at Crystal Mountain, complete with game room, fireplace, a TV room and a 'fully equipped commercial kitchen [with] pancake mix, syrup, coffee, tea, cocoa, sugar, creamer & some condiments provided'.[30] At lower altitude, there was tango and foxtrot, basketball, canoeing, chess, shooting and, naturally, flying – and all these were just in the Puget Sound area.

By the 1970s, the paternalist boss, so dominant even half a century earlier, was largely a thing of the past, in Europe as in America. So, increasingly, was the culture of the personal gift, which bosses used to cement loyalty and discipline. The days of the golden watch for decades of service were numbered. Ironically, the decline of paternalism – and, in the United States, the decline of union power – was paralleled by a rise in company spending. Nurseries, recreation, pensions and – especially in America – medical insurance all expanded and began to be treated as a basic entitlement rather than a special favour. In 1954, 20 per cent of payroll in American firms went to non-wage incentives. Twenty-five years later, it was 37 per cent.[31]

The rise of 'wellness' since the 1970s and attempts to promote a healthier lifestyle are best understood as variations on a historic theme, not a new departure. As in the early days of Ford, perks and services continued to have two main functions: to attract skilled staff and to reduce the number of hours lost to stoppage and absenteeism. What changed was their form, in response to changes in lifestyle. Hi-tech firms in Silicon Valley today offer Botox as well as baseball. In addition to building team spirit, fitness programmes started to target individual lifestyle. The National Cash Register Company introduced morning and afternoon exercise for its employees as early as 1944. By the 1970s, the soaring health-care costs from smoking and coronary heart disease caused headaches for firms, large and small. Lincoln Plating, a metal finishing company in Nebraska, started with free blood-pressure checks in the 1970s. A decade later, they added 'lunch and learn' educational lessons. By 2000, a 'wellness programme' was in place, with sticks and carrots. Smoking on site was prohibited. Quarterly check-ups and personal wellness goals were mandatory and workers received free pedometers to monitor their daily activity. The company sponsored 'wellness Wednesdays' and an annual 14,000-feet mountain challenge. Those who managed to lower their cholesterol and blood pressure gained credit on the 'consumer-directed' health plan. Gym membership was reimbursed for staff and their families. Since its inception, the programme has saved the firm half its health-insurance costs. The aircraft maker Lockheed reduced absenteeism by an estimated 60 per cent with the help of its wellness services.[32]

How typical are such success stories? 'Wellness' is now part of a global management culture, but a 2009 survey found significant regional differences about what this means in practice. Workers might sweat on Wednesdays at Lincoln Plating, but in the rest of the United States wellness is first and foremost about immunization and flu shots. The gym is secondary. In Europe, with more comprehensive public-health systems, the priorities are the reverse. Asian companies devote most energy to biometric health screening and on-site health classes.[33]

It is tempting to imagine that the enormous growth of commercial consumer culture in the last half-century must have spelled the death of company recreation. This would be too simple. That there is more commercial leisure today than two or three generations ago is undeniable. Company teams have withered while private fitness studios have mushroomed. Bars and restaurants have replaced working men's social clubs. Even this trend must not be blown out of proportion, however. In France, 2.5 million employees belong to one of 8,000 company clubs. There are inter-company competitions and, in 2000, the ministry of youth and sport launched a national day (17 June) in support of company sports.[34] As many Finns today exercise at their workplace as at a commercial gym. In Scandinavian countries especially, companies continued to invest in their recreational facilities. In Kristinedal, Gothenburg, the Swedish ball-bearing manufacturer SKF in the 1970s erected a dedicated leisure hall the size of a football pitch. The basement housed a pool and gym and a central kitchen; the first floor a dining room and the main sports hall. On the top floor, workers had access to hobby rooms and their own TV studio. For a tiny fee, they could play ping-pong or relax in the sauna, any time between 6 a.m. and 10 p.m. Today, the complex remains in the hands of the SKF staff fund, while members of the public now also enjoy access to the facilities.[35]

Commercial fast food has made its way into firms and schools in the United States and Britain, but in many affluent countries the company canteen remains as important in people's lives as it was a century ago, if not more so. In Scandinavia, the share of food prepared away from home doubled in the 1970s–'80s as women entered the workforce. This benefited the collective as well as the commercial food sector, and was facilitated by union agreements and public support until subsidies were cut in the 1990s. In 1997, most Finnish employees ate in a canteen or brought a packed lunch; only 4 per cent went to a restaurant. In continental Europe, according to a 2003 estimate, one third of all eating away from home took place in canteens, worth 6 billion euros of sales a year. In half the cases, firms subsidize canteen meals. In Paris, two out of three employees have their lunch in a company cafeteria; to give a sense of perspective, in an early industrial canteen like that of Sandoz in Basel, numbers had barely reached one in five in the 1920s. In Denmark, some firms have introduced canteen take-away services for the whole family to enjoy.[36]

Companies, moreover, also subsidize commercial recreation and entertainment. Many firms may no longer run their own gym or cinema club, but they continue to support such activities outside their walls. The Swiss pharmaceutical giant Roche, for example, offers a free culture pass which entitles employees and their families to reduced tickets to cinemas and theatres, the circus and the 'bird's-eye jazz club'; tickets to the Basel Symphony are half price. The employee association, founded in 1950, has long ceased to be a simple 'salmon and salami club' handing out food baskets at the Christmas ball. There is hardly anything in the vicinity of Basel which members cannot buy at a discount, from massages, dry cleaning and domestic heating oil to up to 40 per cent off on appliances. Workers receive CHF100 when they sign up with a fitness club. In addition, the firm offers a special mortgage package. Similarly, Boeing operates a discount programme that stretches from cars and computers to flowers and fitness centres.[37] Many private gyms would fold without such company schemes. Rather than viewing them as mutually exclusive, with the rise of one leading to the extinction of the other, it is better to think of 'private' consumer culture and 'collective' services as completing each other. The latter helps prop up the former.

The most extensive braiding of these two strands has occurred in France and was set in motion by the Liberation. Too many bosses had been discredited by collaboration with the Nazis to allow a simple return to pre-war paternalism. Unions wanted a voice, the government industrial peace to rebuild the country. The compromise was a system of work councils, established by the decree of 22 February 1945. In practice, these *comités d'entreprise* (CEs) fell short of delivering genuine participation. They have been largely consultative. What they lacked in managerial muscle, however, they made up for with a sizable budget for culture and tourism. Any firm with more than fifty employees was required to have a CE, and support it. On average, firms today devote 1 per cent of their payroll to their social and cultural activities – at the Banque de France it is a whopping 7 per cent. With 11 million employees belonging to a CE in France, that is a lot of collectively funded consumption – €11 billion in 2009, to be precise, with €2.6 billion coming directly from the employer and an additional €7.8 billion from salaries. Most of it goes to fund holidays, sport and nurseries. The Chèques Vacances, a network introduced in 1982 for employees in small firms, distributes coupons for hotels and restaurants worth another €1.3 billion. It also supports a social tourism programme for single parents and the disabled.[38]

Thanks to their CE, workers can play tennis on the company court and borrow the newest books, DVDs and video games from the multimedia library; smaller firms can use a 'bibliobus' with 3,000 books on board that stops by once a month. Above all, they can travel cheaply. Most CEs have their own *offres touristiques* that put together everything from a day-trip to a cruise. Others run their own ski chalets and youth hostels. In 1994, all CEs together owned one quarter of a million beds of accommodation, from holiday villages in the Savoie to camping sites on the Côte d'Azur. When it comes to 'perks' in France, the subsidized camping van is vastly more important than the company car. The average French worker effectively goes on holiday at half the cost. A third of the staff at Canon's French branch in Courbevoie spend their annual holidays at the firm's holiday village. Messier, the aircraft-landing-gear manufacturer, subsidizes one flight per family per year, as well as ferries to Corsica and Morocco. Other firms give staff 50 per cent discounts on package tours to Disneyland and Parc Astérix. Admittedly, though collectively funded, very few of these trips are any longer collectively enjoyed. Families do not travel as work teams but drive away into the sunset in their private car. Equally, we must not get too nostalgic. Most workers did not travel together in the years after Liberation either. In the 1960s, barely a quarter of French firms had a CE, and those that existed spent a minuscule amount on holidays.[39] The big expansion only came in the next few decades, alongside the boom in commercial charter flights and package holidays, not in spite of it.

Holidays for the masses had been an integral element in the clash of ideologies in the inter-war years. Fascists had their leisure organizations, social democrats and trade unions theirs; the Workers Travel Association in Britain started in 1921, initially arranging trips to the battlefields of the Great War before discovering holiday camps; the Swedish RESO (Folkrörelsernas Reseorganisation) in 1937. Danish trade unions copied Butlin's holiday resorts. Little of that energy survived the Second World War. A Bureau International du Tourisme Social (BITS) was founded in Brussels in 1963, but 'social tourism' has proved no match for the private car and package tour. The Belgian trade union organization Vacances et Santé, born in 1938, still exists, and has holiday homes catering for 1.5 million nights of accommodation a year,[40] but this is barely more than what two cruise ships manage together. The French *comités d'entreprise* steered social tourism in a new direction, as a partner rather than the enemy of commercial holidays. The work council did for millions of ordinary French workers what fascist leisure organizations like the Nazi Kraft durch Freude had done for a largely middle-class clientele: they paved the road to mass tourism.[41] This was, perhaps, the CE's main historical contribution.

Perks had a special significance in post-war Japan. Japanese firms competed for skilled employees on benefits rather than wages. In the 1950s, 'non-wage benefits' ranged from 8 per cent up to 25 per cent of a salary. In 2002, according to a survey, a third of employees were living in a company flat or receiving a housing allowance. Another third received congratulatory or condolence payments. One in six workers went to a subsidized canteen. The 'lost decade' of the 1990s simultaneously pressed companies to cut costs and to meet their workers' demand for more flexible benefits. The answer was the 'cafeteria plan', which allowed staff to order from a menu of benefits. Seiyu, the department store, introduced its plan in 1996, with choices ranging from help with a babysitter and the mortgage to a 'subsidy for using Western food'. A decade later, around 10 per cent of Japanese firms had switched to a 'cafeteria plan'. Company housing was cut back and leisure subcontracted. By 2008, perks had shrunk to an estimated 5 per cent of cash wages, the lowest since the 1950s. Still, at the time of writing, what is impressive is how much has stayed, not just not how much has gone. Toyota has not only kept its baseball teams and philharmonic orchestra but also its own hospitals. In Japanese firms, half the perks continue to go to housing. Support for cultural activities and sport has increased since the 1990s.[42]

While the company town proper, then, became more marginal in the second half of the twentieth century, consumption continues to benefit from sponsorship by firms in a variety of ways. Its persistence is visible not only in the old industrialized West but also among recent newcomers such as South Korea. Into the 1980s, Korean companies resembled boot camps. Canteen food and leisure facilities were the preserve of privileged managers. Cramped dormitories and dirty baths were a constant complaint and helped spark strikes in the 1970s and '80s. The decisive change came after military rule collapsed in 1987. As growth slowed down, the government was forced to intervene in wage negotiations. Greater benefits were a way to restrain wages, contain strikes and to incorporate workers on shorter hours into a company culture. Korean companies reinvented themselves, shedding their authoritarianism for family values. Hyundai built athletic fields for sports teams and corporate flats for single workers. At LG, employees could play golf or learn a foreign language together to create team spirit. At its headquarters, all staff, from top to bottom, would meet once a month in the basement company pub, with free beer on tap.[43]

Globally, the greatest assault on firm services came with the wave of privatization in Eastern Europe after the fall of communism in 1989, and China's so far successful attempt to escape a similar fate by liberalizing its economy. Privatization meant a change in ownership, but, more than that, it pushed firms to focus on their 'core business' and divest themselves of their stake in the community. State enterprises had been practically their own commonwealths, overseeing everything from housing and health to sport and music. In Russia in the early 1990s, social spending by state enterprises amounted to 4 per cent of GDP. A typical Russian state enterprise spent around 20 per cent of its profits on housing and feeding its workers and looking after their children. In Poland, it was 10 per cent. In China, benefits made up as much as 40 per cent of pay.[44]

As in the West, privatization has reduced this figure. Yet many services managed to survive. The Russian story, in particular, has been one of adaptation rather than extinction. Paternalism lived on, and with it the suspicion of free unions. A manager of an equipment plant in Krasnoyarsk in Siberia explained in 1996 why his firm knew best: 'We provide our employees with various services. We sell them food and consumer goods at discount. We finance the hospital, housing and schools. We have property in the Crimea for their vacations. We do everything – we have pigs and we grow mushrooms for them.'[45] All the new trade union did was criticize. So, he said, it was only right to abolish it. Across Russia, the second half of the 1990s saw a vast transfer of flats, kindergartens and sports fields from enterprises to municipalities. Still, in 2000, one in six firms ran their own summer camps and cultural facilities. The number of cafeterias had barely changed and, while most firms no longer owned their own sports grounds, they now subsidized their workers' recreation. Interestingly, almost half the foreign-owned firms provided housing; more than Russian-owned ones did.[46]

Size matters. Recreation and welfare services were never the sole preserve of the giants of industry – the Krupps, Toyotas and Bat'as. In the inter-war years, light industries, banks and services, too, started to sponsor company teams.[47] Still, the scale of services fell sharply with the size of a firm. A family firm with a dozen employees does not tend to build a pool. This was why the French state introduced the *chèques vacances* to give workers in small firms at least some indirect benefits. Big companies with a few hundred employees or more are the norm in Sweden, Germany and Britain, but the exception in Greece and Italy. As a space of consumption, the world of work was therefore sharply divided. On one side were corporations that organized life and leisure. On the other were small enterprises and family shops which did little more than throw a Christmas party. Inevitably, our search for company activities has biased us towards the former. Before we finish, therefore, it would be useful to step back briefly and regain a sense of proportion by remembering that most workers in modern capitalist societies never dipped their toe in a company pool. The majority of Japanese workers make their living in small or medium-sized enterprises, not as 'salarymen' at Hitachi. What is their leisure like? The anthropologist James Roberson observed the lives of the fifty-five employees of a metals company in Tokyo in 1989–90. The company did belong to a 'resort trust', had a baseball club and handed out gifts and alcohol at four festivals a year, but that was the limit of its contribution. Contrary to the popular idea that, in Japan, life after work continued to revolve around the work group, he found that most employees spent their free time with friends from their *nakama* groups – non-kin networks – not their co-workers. Occasionally, colleagues went out drinking together, but most of their leisure time was spent alone or with friends playing Pachinko, going dancing or fishing.[48]

THE STATE

If the firm's contribution to consumption in the twentieth century was considerable, that of the state was even greater. Of course, kings and governments have always left their mark on their subjects' way of life.

In eighteenth-century France, the fine wool worn by officials accounted for a significant share of the luxury trade. In 1871, the short-lived Paris Commune gave schoolteachers free furniture. In early modern England, the destitute could turn to the Poor Law for help. Still, prior to the 1930s, state spending on health, housing, education and welfare was tiny. The economic historian Peter Lindert, who has put together the most comprehensive statistics, found that in the nineteenth century not a single country spent even 3 per cent of its gross domestic product (GDP) on social programmes. By 1930, a small group of Scandinavian countries, Germany, Britain and New Zealand led the developed world with between 2 per cent and 5 per cent of GDP.[49] By 2007, that figure had climbed to 20 per cent in the developed world; in France it was 29 per cent.[50]

These figures capture 'social spending' – especially pensions, health and income support – but they are only one portion of overall 'public consumption', which extends from warheads to museums. The state is a voracious consumer. In the European Union today, 16 per cent of the gross national product goes towards the public purchase of goods and services; public authorities buy almost 3 million desktop computers a

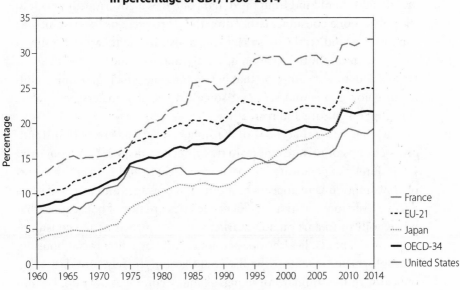

Public social spending in selected OECD countries, in percentage of GDP, 1960–2014

Source: OECD Social Expenditure database (2012, 2014), www.oecd.org/els/social/expenditure.

year. As a consumer, the state packs a big punch, for the environment
as well as the economy. A report by the National Health Service found
that in 2004 English hospitals emitted as much carbon as all of Estonia; some of this was from buildings and transport, but three fifths
came from the procurement of drugs, food and equipment.[51]

The state also facilitates consumption indirectly. One of its jobs is to
provide 'public goods' which are shared by all but which markets would
not spontaneously create by themselves.[52] Everyone benefits from peace
and safety, whether they pay taxes or not. In the long run, a peaceful
commonwealth makes for a more prosperous nation. Other types of
state action enable particular kinds of private consumption. A car
would be little fun without roads. National statistics treat such spending on infrastructures as investment; in the European Union,
government expenditure on transport, energy and communication
amounted to 4 per cent of GDP in 2009.[53] 'Public consumption', on the
other hand, is defined as all purchases of goods and services undertaken by government, ranging from schools and healthcare to pensions
and submarines. This definition generates a very big shopping list and
is fraught with problems. It could be said, for example, that education
is an investment and does not belong under 'public consumption', but
to remove it would add a new distortion since 'private consumption'
includes what households spend on schooling. For our purposes, spending on national defence is of less interest. Its benefits are more diffused
and of a different kind from the dollars or euros a government puts into
the pockets of a consumer either directly – through a pension or income
support – or indirectly, by subsidizing a visit to the theatre or a dip in
the public pool. In the following, we are mainly concerned with those
types of public consumption that have a tangible effect on people's ability to enjoy goods and services: so-called social transfers and public
spending on culture and recreation.

The conventional account of consumer society has rested on standard measures of private market activity, such as disposable income and
GDP. Public expenditure has been ignored. Mr and Mrs Smith's level
of consumption here appears as a function of wages and prices. This is
a naïve oversimplification. Affluent societies are full of households that
rely wholly or in part on non-market sources for their actual consumption: state schools, healthcare, pensions, child benefits, social housing,
unemployment benefits – the list could go on. To rely on GDP as an
indicator of the standard of living, as many commentators do, is similarly problematic. As the name indicates, gross domestic product

measures what is produced for the market. It does not tell us about everything that is consumed. Just how crucial public services and spending are is suggested by the Nobel Prize-winning team of Joseph E. Stiglitz, Amartya Sen and Jean-Paul Fitoussi, who have developed fresh ways of measuring economic performance. In France and Finland, they show, household final consumption expenditure jumps by 20 per cent once social transfers are taken into account. In 2007, the French government channelled €290 billion to households, mainly in the form of health services and education. In the United States, by contrast, such transfers add only 10 per cent.[54] Real consumption in France and Finland, then, is much closer to that in the United States than standard national accounts would have us believe. A previously hidden world of consumption comes into view.

Since the 1950s, it has been natural to criticize affluent societies for promoting private consumption at the expense of public goods. This powerful idea was most brilliantly expressed by J. K. Galbraith in his 1958 bestseller *The Affluent Society*.[55] It is very bad history. The record of the last half-century tells a quite different story. The richer a nation got, the more public money it devoted to health, pensions and education. Some countries, it is true, continue to spend much more on social benefits than others – social spending is 30 per cent of GDP in France but only around 20 per cent in the United States and 10 per cent in Korea. Still, the overall trend has been almost universally upwards. In 1960, average social spending in the OECD was 10 per cent of GDP. By 2007, its share had almost doubled, to 19 per cent. Even Korea spends three times more of its GDP on welfare today than it did a generation ago. The relative decline in the Netherlands and Ireland since 1985 has been an exception to the rule. Since 2009, a few countries have slightly reduced their social spending relative to GDP (Britain and Germany by 2 per cent), but for rich countries as a whole – the OECD group – it stands in 2014 exactly where it stood before the 2009 Great Recession, at just over 21 per cent (social spending ratio to GDP); indeed, Japan, Finland and Spain increased theirs by 4 per cent. Austerity measures have especially hurt the poor and disadvantaged, but it remains to be seen whether most governments will be able to reverse the historic surge in public spending in the long run, especially those with ageing populations.[56]

The age of affluence (1949–73) is now remembered for the boom in private consumption. This is only half the picture. In the United States, federal consumption expenditure (excluding defence) grew by an

average 2.7 per cent a year in the 1950s and '60s, rising to 4 per cent a
year in the 1970s; state and local consumption expenditure rose by
4 per cent and 6 per cent a year respectively in the 1950s and '60s. In
1958, the year Galbraith published his *Affluent Society*, US government spending grew by over 5 per cent, twice as fast as private consumer
expenditure. In most years, it is true, private consumer spending grew
faster than public. But the important point is that throughout these
golden years, public consumption did not contract but expanded, both
in total dollars and as share of GDP. By 1978, public spending on social
security and medicare exceeded military expenditure.[57]

What difference government spending makes for wealth and welfare
has divided economists ever since Keynes, and it would be presumptu-
ous for a historian to try to settle the debate in a few quick words.
Public spending is not automatically a boon: in certain contexts it can
displace private spending. In the high-growth decades of the post-war
miracle, with high employment, public monies probably did not 'crowd
out' that much private spending. Measuring the direct effects is difficult. In Canada, for example, federal transfers played an important
part in boosting consumption immediately after the war but then lost
their force as inflation eroded the family allowance; from 1949, a rise
in consumer credit and a fall in saving came to matter more.[58] But a lot
of the dynamics from public spending for consumption were indirect,
such as the support for home ownership in Canada and the GI Bill and
mortgage relief south of the border in the United States. Over a million
new homes were built in Canada in the 1950s, mostly detached. How
many fridges and cars would have been sold without such government
support for houses and roads?

A few general observations on historical patterns might be helpful.
The dramatic rise in public spending does not appear to have hurt
affluence. Otherwise, France, Sweden and Germany would be in the
poor house. The United States was much better off in 1964 than in
1954, a period during which its welfare bill doubled. For all their alternative models of capitalism, and all the heated debates between
self-proclaimed liberals and defenders of the welfare state, the club of
rich nations has pretty much travelled on the same road towards greater
social spending, some a bit further along than others, but all moving in
the same direction. As countries get richer, private consumption makes
up less of GDP.[59] Modern history does not reveal a second road, where
diminishing welfare spending leads to greater affluence – at least, not
yet. If anything, the pace on the welfarist road of development has

quickened with time. In 2000, spending by Sri Lanka and Panama on social transfers was more than twice that of the most advanced European countries in 1930.[60] Nor must the differences between welfarist Scandinavians and liberal Anglo-Saxons be exaggerated. Swedish and Danish benefits look generous on paper but, in reality, a good deal of what these states give out with one hand, they take back with the other, through fine-tuned taxes. Conversely, public spending in the United States and Britain remained high in the neo-liberal 1980s; Margaret Thatcher managed to cut it in only a single year (1985), Ronald Reagan not even that.[61]

How sustainable is this state of affairs? In the 1950s and '60s, high growth and investment generated money for hospitals and pensions. Since the 1970s, however, growth has slowed and the rise in public consumption has been accompanied by a drop in public investment; in the United States and the core European Union (EU12), public investment fell from 4 per cent of GDP in 1975 to around 3 per cent in 2005. For some commentators, this shift from public investment to consumption sets off a dangerous downward spiral, leading to lower productivity and private investment, and ultimately to lower wages, recession and bankruptcy.[62] Yet it is historically risky to castigate public consumption as if it is all about a hand-out of cash benefits which trickle away without a trace. It also means better health and education, which is good for development. Interestingly, the eurozone country which experienced the biggest fall in public investment also happened to be the one which has emerged strongest from the 2009 crisis: Germany.[63]

A last observation concerns social spending. Statisticians speak of 'social transfers'. This is technically correct, since the state uses income support, state pensions and housing benefits to move money from one section of society to another; these transfers are not always from the richest to the poorest – unlike in Britain, Northern Europe and Australia, in Mediterranean countries most cash benefits go to fairly well-off households with a strong employment and pension record.[64] What happens in the course of such transfers has been the subject of long-standing debate. Harold Wilensky, an American expert, in the 1960s argued that such welfare schemes had a 'negligible' effect on equality. The poor stayed poor. The real winners, he argued, were the poor's better-off relatives, who would otherwise have picked up the bill to look after them. Now, instead, they had money to spend on themselves.[65] This is doubtful. Private charity in the past was never on the same scale as public benefits would be from the 1930s. Most needy individuals would have faced destitution. Public welfare has probably made people more, not less, charitable in the course of the twentieth century.[66]

Most importantly, social spending does not stop with the transfer of money. It has changed the nature of private consumption. The rich and the poor carry with them quite different shopping baskets – so-called 'consumption bundles'. To a millionaire, a few thousand pounds lost in taxes is peanuts. It might mean one luxury watch less but it makes no difference to his diet, comfort or convenience. To a pauper, a few thousand pounds gained makes all the difference in the world. It means regular meals instead of going hungry, being able to run the radiator rather than sitting in the cold, having a TV instead of not having one. Social transfers did not eliminate inequality. They did, however, play a crucial role in lifting the disadvantaged and the poor into a society of mass consumption from which they had been excluded. By the late 1960s, TV screens were flickering in housing projects as much as in suburban villas across the developed world.[67] Without the rise in social spending, the bottom would have fallen out of the boom in consumer durables. Public consumption deserves at least some of the credit (and blame) for the rapid advance of private consumer goods.

The expansion of public consumption is even more impressive once we remember that Western nations scaled back their defence spending at the same time. The Cold War saw a great shift in spending from military to social purposes. In the United States, defence was 14 per cent of GDP at the end of the Korean War in 1953, 9 per cent at the height of the Vietnam War in 1968, but had dropped to 5 per cent at the time of bin Laden's death in the 'War on Terror' in 2011.[68] The United Kingdom devoted half its public consumption to defence at the height of the Korean War. By 1980, it was down to a quarter. The big winners were health and education; the latter doubled its share in Britain during these years.[69] Since then, ageing populations have meant a further rise in spending on health and pensions. Within this broadly shared international trend, many national peculiarities remain. Depending on national priorities and benefit systems, some groups have benefited more from public consumption than others. Among rich nations, the United States spends disproportionately on healthcare but leaves only crumbs for those on income support. In Denmark and Sweden, the elderly, disabled and families with young children receive five times as much support as in the United States or Spain. Public pensions are a major transfer in Italy, France and Austria (12–14 per cent of GDP), but tiny in Australia, Ireland and Iceland (less than 4 per cent). Those in need of public housing are more likely to find it in Canada than south of the border.[70]

Let us now turn away from social transfers to focus on a few other zones where the state has left its mark on how people consume: food, recreation and culture. Armies teach fighting, and schools teach maths, but they also shape tastes and leisure. In 2005, the American forces were 1.4 million strong. Their recreation centres now offer everything from horse riding and boating to car washes and travel services. More than half of army spouses use its fitness centres. The largest child-care programme in America is run by the military.[71] In some cases, armies have revolutionized national food and identity. In inter-war Japan, nutritionists were convinced that beriberi, a disease affecting the central nervous system, was caused by a lack of protein. This was wrong – vitamin B1 deficiency was to blame – but had far-reaching consequences. Army canteens started to serve up hamburger dishes and doughnuts, and use curry and Chinese stir fries to flavour and disguise cheap meats; curry dishes had made their appearance at the Nakamuraya restaurant in Tokyo in the 1920s, introduced by the exiled Indian revolutionary Rash Behari Bose. After the war, army chefs and nutritionists took their multicultural recipes to restaurants and company cafeterias. The Japanese curry, doughnuts with mustard and other miracles of fusion food were the result. Food in Japan has never been the same.[72]

In the home of the doughnut, schoolchildren were subject to rather different influences. In the 1930s, social reformers on both sides of Atlantic seized on the school meal as a way to build stronger citizens.[73] In the United States, it was also a way to absorb vast surplus food. The New Deal was already serving lunches in thousands of schools at the outbreak of war. By 1942, the Surplus Marketing Administration was dumping 5 million pounds of food on schoolchildren. In 1946, the National School Lunch Program passed into law. School meals had a broad alliance of support. They turned rickety kids into strong citizens. They gave nutritionists a chance to put their expertise to use. And they promised to forge a shared American way of life – unions supported the scheme under the motto 'Kids Eat Democracy'. Above all, they pleased farmers eager to get rid of their surplus. Tellingly, the 1946 bill emerged from the Department of Agriculture. A subsidy to agriculture was dressed up as a service to the nation's young. In practice, combining the two goals was problematic. Fruit and vegetables, after all, had their distinct growing season. Some schools were deluged with apples for weeks, and there were only so many that kids were willing to eat. Many ended up in toilets. The farming lobby also looked at schoolchildren as captive customers for new foods. This may have worked in the long run, but in the short run it often backfired. In Maryland, children refused to eat surplus grapefruit and, instead, played catch with them.[74]

By 1970, the school-meals programme cost $2 billion. Parents paid half, but this still left the federal government and states to pay the other half. It was then, under Richard Nixon, that the priorities shifted. Instead of aiming at healthy food for all, school meals turned into a welfare scheme to feed the poor. By 1972, 8 million kids ate a free lunch. Once meals were earmarked as an anti-poverty scheme, however, paying kids started to drop out and local government lost the will to contribute. Schools fired their nutritionists and called in private caterers. By the time the Reagan administration slashed federal support and redefined ketchup as a vegetable in 1981, the main damage had already been done. French fries, soda and candy were the new American school meal. Apples and carrots were pushed off the tray by milkshakes and cheeseburgers, fortified with vitamins to meet dietary guidelines. It would be too easy to blame the school meal for obesity – Italian children have also become fatter in spite of a Mediterranean lunch. It would be equally foolish to deny that it disposed a generation towards a high-fat and high-sugar fast-food lifestyle. Here is an example where a shift in a tiny portion of public consumption – 0.1 per cent – has had a disproportionate long-term legacy for private consumption and all the private and public costs that come with it.

We noted earlier how consumers have become ever more active, especially in the second half of the twentieth century. Leisure benefited from state support of recreation as well as from commercial development. In the United States, the cult of motoring for fun and outdoor recreation was oiled by the extensive state park system. In 1955, state parks covered 5 million acres and attracted over 200 million visits. The number of public pools almost doubled between 1948 and 1955. American children threw balls on 15,000 baseball and softball diamonds. Recreation was not always free. The government built pools but then charged families to use them. It put a tax on sporting goods. Such inconsistencies notwithstanding, the rise in public spending on recreation was impressive, even if it slightly lagged behind the phenomenal rise in income in the 1940s–'60s.[75]

The fitness wave reached Europe and Japan in the 1960s and '70s. The cult of physical exercise had been central to nineteenth-century nationalism. In the inter-war years, fascists, socialists, and conservatives, too, had lined up thousands in gymnastic rows. In France, pools and sports grounds were one of the legacies of the short-lived left-wing Popular Front (1936–8). But, in general, sports facilities were few and far between before the 1960s. In Finland, for example, there were only 1,600 facilities in 1930. By 1970, there were ten times as many. Most were owned by local authorities.[76] Across the developed world, governments discovered 'sport for all': the young, the old and the bulging middle-aged. Germany opened fitness trails, Sweden built communal leisure halls – the Hallonbergen housing estate near Stockholm included a sauna, a fitness centre and a shooting range.[77] France, in 1978, established a separate department dedicated to 'sport for all'. The response was impressive. In 1967, one in seven French citizens practised a sport. Twenty years later, it was every second.[78] By 1995, the Japanese state spent almost 1 per cent of its budget on sport; half the facilities were public, not counting schools. In Korea, public grounds mushroomed in the 1990s and far outnumbered commercial sites. Without this kind of public support for recreation, the take-off in fashionable sports shoes and leisure wear since the 1960s would be inconceivable.[79]

In 1991, Prime Minister Kiichi Miyazawa promised to make Japan a 'lifestyle superpower' (seikatsu taikoku). The state's direct interest in leisure had a long history. As early as 1912, the Japanese government turned itself into the travel agency for foreign visitors, drawing in precious foreign currencies. The railways department was a main promoter of domestic tourism in the inter-war years. The embrace of leisure in the 1970s was far tighter. If Japan was to catch up with the West, officials reasoned, the Japanese people needed to be taught more active, Western leisure. An introspective tea ceremony was no longer good enough. Unlike in the West, the Japanese state turned the right to recreation into a function of government. Leisure was not a private affair. In 1972, the Ministry of International Trade and Industry (MITI) set up a Leisure Development Industrial Office. Governing leisure reached its climax with the 1986 resort law, which released subsidies and low-interest loans for marine resorts and golf courses.[80]

Nowhere did governments try harder to direct the leisure of their subjects than in socialist countries. Nowhere did they fail so badly. The gulf between utopia and reality was most pronounced in the Soviet Union. 'Free time', Brezhnev reminded Russians as late as 1972, did not mean time free from responsibility towards society. Socialism effectively gave earlier bourgeois ideals of 'rational recreation' a second lease of life. 'Houses of culture' sought to mould appropriate Soviet tastes and activities. By the 1930s, there were over 100,000 of these in the USSR. Forty years later, many stood empty. A survey of eight Russian towns in the early 1980s found that no more than 5 per cent of hobbies were collectively organized. In Smolensk, barely one in fifteen adults regularly went to a house of culture. Some tried to survive by mixing socialist education with disco music; the Leningrad house of culture even offered breakdancing courses. Few youths were taken in. In Voronezh in 1982, they simply danced in front of the slide projector, blocking the educational part of the evening. The flight from organized socialist culture was well under way years before perestroika. In Hungary, a spot-check in 1967 found that barely any house of culture bothered to celebrate the official Women's Day. In most, people were watching a movie and drinking beer. Others were closed altogether. Poles boycotted theirs in the 1970s.[81]

Instead of blossoming into schools of socialist living, houses of cultures withered into refuges for stamp collectors and small children with nowhere else to go. In the ideologically charged years of the Cold War, it was tempting to see this as the triumph of commercial over collective leisure. But the flight was not all down to the disco or other products of the capitalist 'culture industry'. In 1977, youths in Eisenach, East Germany, spent more of their free time in the garden or on housework than sitting in front of the television. What it was really about was a retreat into privacy. An official inquiry by the Institute of Youth Research found that even the most loyal pupils and young workers barely devoted two hours per month to the socialist youth movement (Freie Deutsche Jugend). The vast majority just wanted to relax, listen to music or hang out with friends.[82] Ironically, the socialist drive for collective culture accomplished the very opposite of what it had set out to do: it made people value leisure as something private.

Today, the state plays a crucial role in cultural consumption and private taste on both sides of the former Iron Curtain. Theatre, opera, museums and libraries – few of these manage without support from the state. In Germany, each spectator in a public theatre is subsidized by €87.[83] How much time would audiences spend with Schiller or Brecht if they had to cough up the full price? In the United States, admittedly, direct funding for the arts is smaller, but this does not mean the state can be ignored altogether. A good deal of private and corporate sponsorship relies on tax relief, which is an indirect form of state support. In Portugal, the private Calouste Gulbenkian Foundation contributes an impressive 40 per cent to spending on culture, but this is an extreme case. Virtually everywhere in Europe, the state is the main benefactor of cultural life. That states continue to subsidize their citizens' taste for art, music, literature and drama deserves emphasis, because it runs counter to what we might expect in an age of cultural relativism, where all tastes are said to be equal, and neo-liberalism, where markets and private choice supposedly rule. Those who like to listen to Shakespeare or Verdi have their own welfare state. So do artists, most notably in Sweden, where 16 per cent of the total cultural budget goes directly to them. In the 1980s and '90s, states everywhere started knocking at the door of corporations to get them to invest more in culture. What has ultimately happened in these neo-liberal decades, however, is not the withdrawal of the state but a handover of funds from government to more or less autonomous arts councils and foundations.

These are general observations. Pinning down the specific role of individual states is more difficult. In Europe – supposedly moulded by a shared culture – no two countries agree on what they mean when they support 'culture'. Behind such problems of definition lurk fundamental differences about national tastes and policy priorities. Denmark, for example, includes sport and libraries in its support for culture; Hungary also includes religious activities. Germany focuses on the performing arts; Italy on heritage. In some countries, TV viewers pay a licence fee. In others, the state picks up the bill. In the Netherlands, public cultural expenditure grew by one third in the early 2000s, but that was in part because the licence fee was abolished. Support for culture in many countries is spread between different ministries and local and central authorities. In Italy, the European Parliament found in 2006, data was 'still not regularly collected'.[84]

All this makes comparison difficult. What is clear is the considerable and ongoing diversity. Public support for cultural consumption amounts to 0.2 per cent of GDP in Ireland but 1.9 per cent in Estonia; in Belgium, Austria and the Scandinavian countries it is just under 1 per cent; in Germany and Portugal only 0.4 per cent. Just because culture is cheap, or there is more of it, does not mean that people automatically consume more of it. Still, it is noteworthy that more people attend theatre, music and dance performances where government spending is most generous: the Scandinavian countries and Estonia. Attendances are also above average in Germany, where government spends fairly little, but what it does spend it gives mainly to the performing arts.[85]

Sociologists have stressed the influence of class and education on taste. Equally important may be how states favour certain tastes and practices over others. It is, probably, no coincidence that people today rarely go to a theatre or concert hall in Italy – the home of *bel canto* – where the performing arts have to live off the few crumbs left over by 'heritage'. It could be argued that societies simply opt for a different mix of private and public consumption. Households in Britain and Germany spend above average on culture, while their governments are rather stingy by European standards. More widespread, however, is a symbiosis: individuals spend more on culture where governments do so, too. Danes, Finns and Austrians commit almost twice the share of their household budget to culture as do the Italians, the Spanish and the Portuguese.[86] Here may be as good an illustration of the influence of public for private consumption as any: where states value cultural activities, so do their citizens, at least in democratic societies.

TOO MANY CHOICES

Since the middle of the twentieth century, then, the rise in private consumption has been accompanied by a dramatic rise in public consumption. Ever greater choice in the marketplace arrived alongside more schools, hospitals and social benefits funded by the state. By the end of the century a big question emerged: how should public services respond to the profusion of private choice? Why should a patient in a public hospital be treated differently from someone paying for any other service? Were they not all consumers?

Welfare reform preoccupied many affluent countries, but the zeal was greatest in the United Kingdom in the years around 2000. Tony Blair made the 'consumerization' of public services the mantra of his New Labour government. 'Open and competitive markets', a government white paper stressed, were 'the best guarantee of a good deal for consumers'.[87] And not only at the cash register. 'I believe,' Blair said, 'people do want choice, in public services as in other services.'[88] New Labour, in this view, was merely responding to a social transformation. Britain had changed beyond recognition since the early days of the welfare state. Affluence had created a society of consumers who expected to be treated as individuals. The state needed to change accordingly. The middle classes already worked the system, jumping queues or opting out altogether. Giving the poor the power to choose between providers would give them the same power. And it would put pressure on public hospitals and schools to raise their game. Some on the Left were appalled. Choice in public services, they said, would favour the winner over the rest. It would reinforce a selfish individualism at the expense of fairness and solidarity. The more consumer, according to this view, the less citizen.[89]

These opposing positions made good political sense at the time. For the Blair government, 'consumerizing' public services, to use official language, was a way to fix an image problem. New Labour had opened the taps of public spending. Queues for hospital treatment were getting shorter, and there were more nurses and doctors. Statistics showed heart disease was killing fewer. Yet poll after poll showed Britons to be deeply pessimistic, even cynical, about the government's record. Public services had a bad reputation – they attracted over a million complaints a year – and few trusted the government to fix them.[90] The government took a leaf out of the basic handbook of customer service: choice would improve the customer experience and finally give New Labour the credit they deserved. Being 'consumer-focused' also addressed a legitimacy deficit. Party membership was falling, and so was turnout at elections. What was the authority of a government if 40 per cent of voters stayed at home? One answer was that parties, too, needed to respond to affluence by reaching out to citizens as consumers; as so often, this was a rather insular British view, which ignored the fact that Germany, Spain and other affluent countries enjoyed high turnouts at elections. There were, similarly, good reasons the Left was so alarmed about choice. Blair's reforms built on the Citizens' Charters introduced by the Conservatives in 1991: the 'third way' seemed a slippery slope to neo-liberalism.

From a historical perspective, however, these two portrayals of the consumer are equally unhelpful. They involve two basic misunderstandings. One is about sequence. The consumer was not the child of post-war affluence but had already reached maturity by then. The second is about consumers' DNA. Choice was only one strand. Social justice and democratic rights were just as important. It was these together that had catapulted consumers to the centre of public life around 1900. In Britain, the consumer who had defended the freedom to buy cheap goods in 1906 had been equally concerned with bread for the poor and democratic accountability. In early-twentieth-century America, progressives fought monopolies and fraud, not only because they harmed individuals ('consumer detriment') but because they corroded public life. In Paris, Vienna and Berlin, meanwhile, shoppers' leagues felt their choices ought to be used to improve the welfare of workers and sales-people. The idea that citizen and consumer were opposites, let alone mutually exclusive, would have baffled these earlier generations just as much as the idea that choice was all about individual satisfaction.[91]

It is, similarly, unwise to see governments' embrace of the consumer as a sudden response to the inescapable demands of affluence. States' responsiveness to consumers has a longer history. The apotheosis came on a cold Thursday in March 1962 in Washington DC, when President Kennedy gave an address to Congress on protecting the consumer interest. Kennedy laid down four basic rights: the right to safety, to be informed, to choose and to be heard. These four points have become the global cornerstone of consumer protection, remembered every 15 March (World Consumer Rights Day). They are now so often recited that they barely attract attention. It is therefore worth listening to the speech as a whole to recapture its larger spirit. 'Consumers,' Kennedy began, 'include us all.' They were the largest group in the economy. Yet they were the one group 'whose views are often not heard'. Americans were better off than ever before. At the same time, they were exposed to an avalanche of new, complex products and subject to 'increasingly impersonal' marketing – 90 per cent of prescription drugs, he noted, had been unknown twenty years earlier. Advertisers were using 'highly developed arts of persuasion'. To assess the value, safety and quality of a product, the 'housewife is called upon to be an amateur electrician, mechanic, chemist, toxicologist, dietitian and mathematician'. Even then, vital information was hidden from her. Kennedy's call for consumer rights, however, was about more than fixing market imperfections. Government, he stressed, also had to 'meet its responsibility to consumers'. 'Nearly all' its programmes were of 'direct or inherent importance to consumers', from medical care and mass transit to parks and power.

Kennedy gave his speech at the height of affluence, but it was indebted to a progressive tradition that reached back to the bleak 1930s and the unequal 1890s. The fight against monopoly, hazardous drugs and dangerous foods, the call for 'truth in lending' and 'truth in packaging' – these battles had been waged by earlier activists and muckrakers. In addition to strengthening existing regulations, however, Kennedy assigned government new responsibilities. These included low-cost housing for 'moderate income families', safer transport and a cheap and adequate supply of natural gas. Choice was about more than letting individuals shop freely in the marketplace. Consumer rights would raise the standard of living for all. They were part of a democratic philosophy which recognized, in Kennedy's concluding words, that 'we share an obligation to protect the common interest.'[92]

Europeans with memories of war and hunger would have marvelled at Kennedy's reference to the 6,000 separate food items on display in an American supermarket. Still, in consumer policy, the wind was almost everywhere blowing in a similar social liberal direction. Rich and poor were promised choice, but also a guarantee they were not being ripped off. The emerging consensus was for a mix of competitive markets and consumer protection. Where countries differed was how they struck the balance between the two and who did the protecting. Britain leant towards the market and trusted information to do the job. Government looked on from the sidelines as the Consumers' Association kept an eye on three of Kennedy's principles (choice, safety and information). *Which?*, the watchdog's house magazine, started comparative testing in 1957. Ten years later, it had over half a million subscribers. A government-sponsored National Consumer Council was not set up until 1975. In countries with a statist tradition, by contrast, product testing was more likely to be housed within the state. In Denmark, the government's Home Economic Council tested products and handled consumer complaints. Sweden in 1957 set up a National Consumer Council (Statens konsumentråd), and a National Institute for Consumer Issues (Statens institut för konsument-frågor), alongside a cartel board. In Scandinavian countries, the state recognized consumers not simply out of charity but because it made it possible to co-opt them for rational planning. The state wanted to guide consumers as much as protect them. They had to be taught to make the most of the limited resources available so as to increase the nation's productivity.

France tried to have the best of both worlds, an active state and a vibrant associational culture. In addition to two general bodies (the testing organization UFC-Que Choisir and CLCV/Consommation, logement et cadre de vie), there were by the 1980s seven women's and family consumer groups, six associations inspired by syndicalist ideas of common ownership and a number of tenant and other specialist groups. It was a crowded marketplace with plenty of voices speaking on behalf of the consumer. It was in the 1970s and '80s that the state entered the fray in earnest. Consumers, Giscard d'Estaing, the republican economic minister, said in 1972 were treated as 'silent extras' rather than as the main characters they were. Four years later, now President, he created a Secretary of State for Consumption and appointed Christiane Scrivener, a Harvard Business School graduate, inevitably christened 'Madame Consommation' by the press. Not to be outdone, the socialists, under François Mitterrand, set up an entire ministry of consumption in 1981. The following year, a law gave consumer representatives seats on councils in nationalized enterprises.[93]

Progress at the global level proved more difficult. In theory, consumers were the quintessential citizens of the world, the recipients of goods from near and far. The renaissance of globalization since the 1960s might have been expected to catapult them to the centre stage of global politics. The first few steps were encouraging. In 1960 at The Hague, seventeen national associations came together to form the International Organization of Consumer Unions, the forerunner of Consumers International. In the 1970s and '80s, consumer movements took off in India, Singapore and Malaysia. The IOCU now had a global constituency and turned to the United Nations to protect consumers everywhere. Yet as the movement spread, ideological divides began to open up between North and South. In part, this reflected a gulf in material conditions. Protecting consumers in affluent America meant one thing, doing so in developing Malaysia something quite different. Here it was first and foremost about access to food and shelter, clean water, education and other basic goods. Choice was for the rich. Anwar Fazal, the IOCU's Asian regional president, went so far as to drop choice off the list of consumer rights altogether.[94]

The South left its mark on the IOCU's increasingly ambitious programme. Its 1978 Charter put poverty relief and the environment at the heart of consumer protection. The right to consume was balanced by the social and ecological responsibilities that came with it. Such appeals were not without their crusaders in the rich North. Ralph Nader, who shot to fame in the United States in the late 1960s with his exposures of exploding cars and corporate abuse, campaigned for a shift from conspicuous to conscientious consumption. The UN's Guidelines on Consumer Protection (1985) were proof consumers had arrived in the corridors of international politics. Kennedy's principles had grown into an international bill of consumer rights, including an emphasis on just, equitable and sustainable development. From Finland to Brazil, the guidelines became the point of reference for new consumer laws.[95]

Yet the guidelines' birth was far from simple and foreshadowed troubles to come. Having led the battle for consumer protection at home, the United States dragged its feet internationally. American companies protested against interference in their foreign markets. When the UN General Assembly voted for an international list of unsafe, banned products, the United States provided the one vote of dissent. The American delegation fought the 1985 guidelines tooth and nail and, while it was unable to stop them, made sure that its provisions fell short of those at home.

Back in Washington, consumer protection and 'Nader's Raiders' had set off a corporate backlash against regulation. The post-war settlement, symbolized by Kennedy's bill, had balanced individual choice with a better life for all. The Reagan administration tore it up. What was left was choice. Deregulation looked to business to keep its house in order. The Federal Trade Commission was told by Congress to suspend its investigation of children's television adverts and similar subjects. The Consumer Product Safety Commission survived efforts to abolish it by the skin of its teeth but now focused more on voluntary standards.

Internationally, all eyes turned to opening up trade. The very moment the consumer movement reached the corridors of global politics, the action moved behind closed doors as the Uruguay Round of trade talks got under way in 1986. It took a decade for the talks to be completed and for the World Trade Organization to be set up, in 1995. In low- and middle-income countries tariffs fell from around 39 per cent in the early 1980s to 13 per cent by 2000.[96] Consumers might be the beneficiaries of the freer movement of goods, but they were certainly not invited to the negotiating table. Worse, free trade put those who saw it as the consumers' best friend at loggerheads with many activists in the South who felt it ran roughshod over social justice and local development.

The momentum for choice was top-down, sponsored by the architects of the neo-liberal 'Washington Consensus'. Equally interesting was a second, bottom-up dynamic. This was not spearheaded by lawyers, economists and businessmen, nor was it about waving the magic wand of the market in foreign lands. It came from ordinary people who demanded to be heard as users of public services. Today, the welfare state is often mocked as the 'nanny state', from which Thatcher and Reagan liberated downtrodden citizens. Yet it was not all bossy and stubborn. Public services contributed their own laboratory for choice. At first, some choice was granted at the discretion of officials and providers. Eventually, recipients began to assert their rights for themselves.

A major arena was public housing. In Britain, the first support for choice came from above as slum clearance got seriously under way in

the 1930s. Who was to decide what colour curtain graced a new block
of flats: government or tenant? The housing director in Leeds
was R. A. H. Levitt, a trained architect who, inspired by the Karl Marx
Hof in Vienna, brought high-rise living to England with the eight-storey
Quarry Hill flats. He brushed aside those who clamoured for uniformity. The 'taste of the tenant is not always good', he agreed, and they
might need advice, but it 'would be a retrograde step to rob the tenants
of that little expression of individuality'. Control in public housing was
necessary, 'but it should be limited . . . after all, we in this country still
pride ourselves in being democratic'.[97] After the war, and notwithstanding austerity and fuel shortages, authorities in Manchester let
tenants choose whether they wanted a gas or an electric cooker when
they moved into a new council home. Yet choice had its limits: future
tenants were stuck with that first decision for good.[98]

By the end of the 1950s, such gestures were no longer good enough.
Tenants began to complain that their local authorities were high-handed,
unresponsive and negligent. An earlier generation had been grateful to
be rescued from private slum landlords. As slum conditions ceased to
be the norm, tenants became more demanding. The mood swing
resulted from two forces coming together, one material, the other cultural. Tight budgets and poor planning forced cities such as Manchester
to build flats on the quick. Labour had promised the New Jerusalem.
When tenants opened the door to their new home they often found
damp and mould instead. On the Beswick estate in Manchester, windows came crashing down to earth because the fastenings were not
strong enough.

Equally significant were the rising expectations that came with rising incomes. The home – its comfort, possessions and the social life
they made possible – was their manifestation. In the 1950s, spending
on household goods doubled. By the early 1960s, many tenants gained
the right to move partition walls as they liked. An official report for the
Ministry of Housing recognized the need for greater accountability as
well as choice. Tenants expected fair treatment and to have the right to
complain.[99] It left the thorny issue of redress unanswered. After all,
council tenants, unlike private ones, did not have the option to move
house if they were dissatisfied. For Conservatives, this distinction
remained axiomatic. 'In a free country,' the 1963 Conservative housing
policy stressed, 'the householder must be prepared to meet the cost of
his house where he is able to do so. Otherwise he will have little freedom of choice.'[100] This was unlikely to appease council tenants asked to

pay rising rents while waiting for repairs. As the decade progressed, some took councils to court. Others joined protest marches and tenant associations. Poor people might be dependent on the state. Nonetheless, one association said, they should have the 'indisputable right' to take decisions that concerned their everyday lives, their homes and their community.[101] In her dual plan in 1979 for a 'right to buy' and a Tenants' Charter for those who chose not to, Thatcher capitalized on that earlier wave of anger. She did not create it.[102]

The movement for patient rights was the second major arena in which users were asserting greater voice vis-à-vis professional experts and authorities. Although healthcare was provided by a mix of public, private and charitable bodies, the issues of choice and voice were similar to those in the public sector. By the early 1970s, the 'health consumer' had entered the political lexicon. As with tenants, patients' metamorphosis into consumers did not begin with neo-classical economics but with a critique of authority and a revival of voluntarism. Patient groups signalled a new confidence in self-help. The origins of this reach back to the 1930s with Alcoholics Anonymous in the United States and increasing interest in homeopathic medicine. The real burst came in the decades after the Second World War – in Britain, these years saw the birth of MIND, the National Spastics Society, the Muscular Dystrophy Group, the Patients' Association and a host of other mutual support groups.[103]

There was one major difference between patients' groups and tenants' associations. Unlike in housing, where there was never enough funding to fix all the holes, healthcare saw more doctors and pills than ever before. Voluntarism was a reaction to what critics called the 'medical-industrial complex' and its monopoly on expensive, by-prescription-only medication. Doctors were challenged for being over-specialized, distant and too reliant on pharmaceutical handouts. They needed to stop playing God and listen to their patients. In addition to older calls for safe medication, American and British activists demanded greater privacy, legal protections for those suffering from mental illness and a stop to hospital trials without consent; that such experiments continued notwithstanding laws following Nazi atrocities was especially galling. Cure, they insisted, ought to be more patient-led. These demands came to the fore the very moment the consumer movement was targeting unaccountable business and government more generally. Nader's first branch of his consumer advocacy group Public Citizen was the Health Research Group. The American Civil Liberties Union started to defend the rights of the 'medical consumer'. The voice of the patient chimed with that of the citizen-consumer.

Like the proverbial genie, once the health consumer was out of the bottle, it was difficult to control. At first, it looked as if patients' activists had struck a victory. England and Wales established Community Health Councils in 1973. These were intended as a consumer watchdog to help patients with everything from complaints and more flexible visiting hours to better hospital food. In reality, most councils did not dare to bark. As the 1970s progressed, the health consumer was hijacked by the state and business.

In Britain, where the state ran a National Health Service, the government's interest in self care was fiscal as much as medical: healthier citizens and active volunteers were a cure for unhealthy public finances. 'Everyone knows that there is going to be less money,' Dr David Owen, the then Labour health minister and a trained neurologist, pointed out in 1976. People had to learn that 'health is not just something that is provided for by the NHS, but that each individual has a responsibility for his own well-being.' Volunteers needed to get involved in looking after the sick, the elderly and, he added, 'psychiatric patients who have been discharged'.[104] A year earlier, Owen had given a government grant to the Patients' Association. The principles of self-help and voluntarism were first co-opted, and then managed by the state. The return to power of the Conservatives in 1979 accelerated this process. The more the Thatcher and Major governments celebrated choice, however, the more choices were made on behalf of rather than by patients. Ironically, reforms ended up delivering new powers for doctors and managers. For campaigners, choice had originally been a capacious ideal, accommodating collective concerns about equality of access alongside demands for individualized treatment. Some even proposed that consumers as taxpayers be brought into overseeing health providers – after all, it was they who paid for the NHS. By the time the Tories launched their Patient's Charter in 1991, the health consumer had shrunk to an individual customer in a 'quasi-market'.[105]

A similar deflation of choice happened in the United States, only more swiftly, in the absence of a comprehensive public health service. Consumer and patient groups – never the most coherent coalitions at the best of times – were outflanked by the medical and pharmaceutical lobby. By the 1990s, half of Americans' health insurance was financed through government taxes.[106] Struggling to check the spiralling cost of Medicare, government pushed doctors to be more competitive and encouraged private HMOs (Health Maintenance Organizations) to drive down costs. Patient empowerment became a commercial venture. Consumers had wanted more information and choice. Now they were swamped with them, as long as they were able to pay. For those without medical coverage, choice was irrelevant. Even in Scandinavia, choice pressed its way into welfare services. In 2003, Denmark gave the elderly a choice between private and public care. The freedom to choose, the Finance Ministry waxed philosophically, articulated a democratic view of human nature: citizens, not the system, knew what was best for them.[107]

Tenants and patients fought for warm homes and better treatment, but they also signalled a general shift in political atmosphere in Western democracies in the post-war years. Public services were under pressure to put their users first instead of treating them as deserving objects of charity. The reorientation towards users put to the test the most fundamental relationship between state and citizen, that between governors and governed. What was government for if not the people? Who protected citizens against wrongdoing at the hands of the state? The answer came from Sweden: the Ombudsman.

The office of Ombudsman had been created in 1809 to keep an eye on state officials and ensure laws were executed as the king intended. A strong state was checked by the rule of law. It was in the twentieth century that the Ombudsman switched from a guardian of royal interests into a tribune of the people. His main business was to protect their civil rights against an overarching state. Appointed by parliament, he had the power to inquire about judges. In the 1950s, thousands of Swedes filed grievances about court actions, administrative malpractices and heavy-handed police. Internationally, it was the one Swedish word on everyone's lips. Denmark introduced its first Ombudsman in 1955. New Zealand got one seven years later. From there, the office reached the United Kingdom in 1967. Ombudsmen arrived in Spain and Portugal in the 1980s, after the fall of dictatorship, and in Poland and Hungary, after the collapse of communism. At the time of writing, Britain has twenty-four Ombudsmen, whose remits range from police complaints and helping consumers who were missold insurance policies to adjudicating football complaints.[108]

Why did the Ombudsman's global career take off when it did? One reason was the particular social democratic constellation of the period. Ombudsmen helped societies to reconcile a fast-growing state with a commitment to markets and democracy. This is the standard explanation.

A second, perhaps equally important reason has to do with the changing habits of citizens. If everyone took malpractice on their chin, there would be nothing for the Ombudsman to do.

There are indications that greater affluence has encouraged complaining, in part because of rising expectations, in part because the channels encouraging us to complain and the ease of doing so have increased exponentially. Some of this reflects the expansion of customer service in businesses, although standards continue to diverge hugely. Yet states deserve credit, too. In a bustling marketplace, it is easy for a dissatisfied shopper to move their custom elsewhere. If there is only one water company in town, this is impossible. State-sponsored consumer complaints boards and the promotion of 'alternative dispute resolution' have given 'voice' a new outlet. Where collective redress mechanisms exist, consumers make use of them – Spain and Portugal are good examples. In countries where action requires a mandate by each individual victim (as in France) or out-of-court settlements are difficult (as in the Netherlands), consumers don't. The Portuguese Association for Consumer Protection is part of an especially successful model of class action; when it brought a case against Portugal Telecom on behalf of the country's consumers, it won a settlement of damages worth €120 million. Similarly, in Spain, where collective redress mechanisms are in place, consumers tend to use them, as when the Association of Bank Users (ADICAE) filed a lawsuit against 101 banks on behalf of 20,000 claimants about illegal mortgage clauses.[109]

Technology has facilitated 'voice', too. Consumers who feel defeated by their electricity bill are now just one click away from venting their frustration. Whether they do depends in part on whether they trust that their complaint will be handled fairly. And this varies enormously between societies. Institutions and cultures of complaint reinforce each other. It is probably no coincidence that the greatest complainers live in those countries that have the strongest tradition of Ombudsmen, complaint procedures and trust in the rule of law. One in three Swedes made a formal complaint in 2008, and every fourth Dane, Briton and German. In Italy, it was not even one in ten.[110] Some have turned complaining to creative use. In Helsinki in 2005, a group of Finns pioneered a complaints choir (Valituskuoro), grumbling that 'we always lose to Sweden in hockey and Eurovision . . .' Since, similar choirs have formed in St Petersburg, Melbourne, Singapore and two dozen other cities; in Hamburg, the singers' complaint is directed at the overly complicated German tax form. The Budapest choir claims that Hungarians are the world champions of complaining.[111] Even in England, home of the stiff upper lip, a first choir has started in Birmingham.[112]

The Ombudsman was an example of the lively flow of ideas and institutions between countries. Such transnational exchanges had long been a part of consumer movements, reaching back to the buyers' leagues in 1900 and to the anti-slavery boycotts a century earlier. The European Union added a new, supranational dimension. It took a surprisingly long time for European bureaucrats to fall in love with the consumer. The 'consumer' was barely on anyone's lips in Brussels in the 1960s. It was only from the mid-1970s that the European Court of Justice began to harmonize national measures on safety and quality, and only in 1987 that the Single European Act included a 'high level' of consumer protection.[113] There were good reasons for the late awakening. Ever since the French Revolution of 1789, the spirit of law was about upholding universal civic rights. There would be no special protection. Granting special rights to consumers would have violated the autonomy of contracts between equals. Lawyers and economists alike fell back on the convenient fiction that the consumer was naturally 'sovereign' in the marketplace. The 1970s broke the silence. As the engine of political integration hit the buffers, European officials and judges switched tracks to economic integration. The consumer would be the locomotive; choice and competition the fuel. A new European citizen was born: the 'market citizen'. After centuries, German beer makers were told in 1987 that their beer was no healthier than Belgian lager and to remove their restrictive purity laws. It was for consumers to choose which beer they wanted, and any national hurdles that stood in their path had to be cleared away. Choice would empower consumers – this was the official justification. It also empowered the European Commission.

From directives on package holidays to doorstop selling, a good deal of European policy reinforced the growing emphasis within member states on individual choice and competitive markets as the best defence of the consumer interest. One could stop here and only see neo-liberal forces at work. Yet that would be too simple. The European story is ongoing and has also breathed new life into concerns about basic needs and social obligations that had inspired consumer movements in the past. The European consumer is more than the shopper who hops across the border to fill the car with cheap booze. One of them was Yvonne Watts, a seventy-five-year-old British citizen who suffered from severe arthritis in the hip. In March 2003, in constant pain, Mrs Watts abandoned her attempts to move off the waiting list of her local hospital in Bedford and went to France, where she paid the equivalent of £3,900 for a new French hip. When her request for reimbursement from the NHS was rejected, she went to the European Court and won. Waiting times had to be 'acceptable' on the basis of a medical assessment of a patient's clinical needs. Britain was forced to change how it managed hospital waiting lists.[114]

'Vulnerable consumers', too, received renewed attention. The European Economic and Social Committee, a consultative body of the European Union (EU) observed in 1999 that 'not everybody has the necessary self-assurance and assertiveness to make his or her own choices and to come to sensible decisions.'[115] At the bottom of society, it noted, many were shut out from housing and other basic goods. For choice to be meaningful to low-income groups and single mothers, they had to be empowered first. Perhaps more than any other problem, climate change pushed the EU to a more rounded view of the consumer as citizen. Consumers were also producers of environmental harm – a topic to which we shall return in the chapter on waste (see Chapter 15). For the European Union, individual choice in the present had to be moderated by social responsibility for the future. This is a noble aspiration, but it also contains a real dilemma. For European integration has been all about the free movement of goods and people. A low-carbon environment requires less driving and fewer flights and lorries. Unless the laws of physics give way, it is difficult to see how the European project can possibly have it both ways.

The apotheosis of the consumer, then, is full of paradoxes. The more tenants, patients, students and many others came to assert their rights as consumers, the more fragmented and diffuse the identity became. This left consumer advocates with a serious problem. In Britain, for example, the National Consumer Council in 2007 concluded that, in a pluralistic society, it no longer made sense to appeal to a uniform citizen: services needed to respond to the diversity of consumers instead; the following year, the NCC was abolished.[116] Whatever we personally may think about this diagnosis, the lesson from history seems clear. Today, in the age of the consumer, it is far harder to organize consumers than it was a century ago. Choice deserves some of the blame, but we must not exaggerate. Tellingly, the same NCC also stood up for the elderly in care homes, and for water users and others who had no choice whatsoever.

Nowhere has the crusade for choice been louder than in Britain, and this has attracted most attention. Yet the British experience is equally instructive for the remarkable gulf that remains between political ambition and social reality, between what politicians say and want and what people on the ground hear and do. When it came to public services, researchers found that appeals to choice and the customer grated with most users and providers. As a police officer put it bluntly: 'We are not Tesco's, Marks and Sparks [Marks and Spencer], or BT [British Telecom]. We are not in consumables or domestic appliances . . . we are the police service . . . we serve the public [as] a public service.' Calling the police or going to the hospital was simply not like going shopping. 'If I am in a shop,' one health-service user said, 'I am just there to buy something, I don't have any relationship with them . . . [at the doctor's] I don't want to be a customer. I want to be a patient.' People wanted the local leisure centre to respond to their needs, but not at the expense of others. Decades of policy initiatives and cheering for choice had done little to dislodge a deep-seated commitment to fairness in public services.

In spite of what many politicians believe, it is not at all clear that affluence has led to political apathy. Media research shows that Britons have a strong sense of public connection and interest in politics – they simply distrust politicians. It is doubtful whether boycotts and other kinds of consumer politics necessarily sap the energy of older forms of civic engagement. To the contrary, history suggests the former often reinforced the latter, as in the radical movements for the vote in the early nineteenth and, again, in the early twentieth century. Today, those most likely to boycott a product are also the ones who are most active in local politics.[117]

13

Home and Away

Consumption, we have seen, has transformed time. Equally important, it has transformed space. Products and people travel greater distances than ever before in human history. What effect did this have on people's relationship to goods and those who produce them? This is, obviously, a very big question which would require a full book to answer. The next chapter has to be more modest and tries to provide some suggestive answers by travelling along three spatial axes: the purchase of goods to express a concern for others; the rediscovery of local food and its role for identity; and, finally, the effect of people's migration on the diffusion of new tastes and products.

ETHICS FOR SALE

We live in the age of 'fair trade'. There are some 27,000 'Fairtrade' products today,[1] assuring consumers that distant producers in the developing world receive a fair deal for their sweat and toil. In 2007, 20 million fair-trade roses blossomed. Two years later, global sales of fair-trade products reached €3.4 billion, benefiting over a million farmers and workers. Fair-trade towns have mushroomed – Garstang, in Lancashire, England, the first in 2000, has since been joined by over 1,000 in twenty-four countries. In 2006, 'Fairtrade Fortnight' put on some 8,000 activities across Britain, from meetings with banana producers to fashion shows and 'ladies pamper nights'. There was 'Mango Mania' in Lothian, and toddler and senior meetings in Dorset.

A fringe movement when the label was first introduced in the Netherlands in 1988, fair trade has entered the citadels of capitalism. Even the discounter Asda began promoting fair-trade oranges in 2006. In the United States, you can dunk a doughnut into fair-trade coffee in the popular chain of that name. Global brands such as Starbucks and

Cadbury's Dairy Milk made 100 per cent commitments. There are few aspects of life and leisure that are untouched by fair trade these days. In 2007, the Dutch National Bank started using fair-trade cotton for its €10 banknotes. Those so inclined can be buried in a fair-trade bamboo coffin made in Bangladesh. Film stars give their time as ambassadors on well-publicized visits to cotton growers in Burkina Faso. Ethical trade has even entered the football pitch: on 4 March 2011, the German soccer giant BVB Dortmund used its home game to promote the campaign 'Fair Play Meets Fair Trade'. In the family wing, fans had a chance to acquaint themselves with the 'high quality of fair-trade products'. At half-time, stars joined in a penalty shoot-out and the stadium screen was given over to the principles of fair trade. The Dortmund coach, Jürgen Klopp, posed with a fair-trade banana in his living room. Not to be left behind, the local rival in Gelsenkirchen offered its very own 'play fair/drink fair' *Schalke-Kaffee*.[2]

What does this fanfare for fairness mean? Advocates and critics alike have emphasized the importance of individual choice and markets. For the former, fair trade has taken off because millions of shoppers have come to realize the ethical power of their purse. Some commentators have announced the coming of a 'new moral economy'.[3] Critics, by contrast, see little more than an ethical fig leaf that allows consumers in the affluent North to feel good about themselves but leaves global trade and inequality effectively as they are. But fair trade is about more than individual choices, whether self-serving or not. It has been shaped as much by politics, religion and social movements as by shoppers.

Fair trade is a hugely diverse phenomenon, by product and by country. Its success has come from a handful of articles, especially coffee, chocolate, bananas, flowers and sugar. Expansion in other commodities and higher-value products has been disappointing. Sales in fair-trade cotton, for example, declined in the late 2000s. Even the advance of fair-trade coffee on Western high streets looks less impressive when put in a global context. In 2009, it made up only 1 per cent of the world coffee trade. In part, fair-trade growth looks so remarkable because it started from a very low level, but the reality is that fair-trade products still rarely find their way into shopping baskets. Swiss consumers lead the world but even they spend a total of only €21 a year per person on them. The average Briton spent €11 in 2008, a German only €1.70, the equivalent of a dozen bananas in a whole year. It is instructive to place these figures alongside the general price of

Annual fair-trade consumption per capita in 2007, in euros

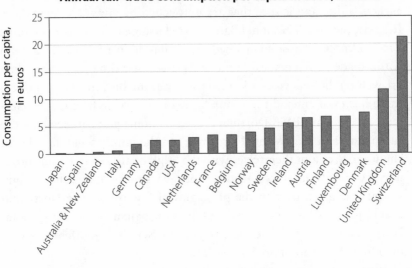

Number of world shops/fair-trade shops, 2007

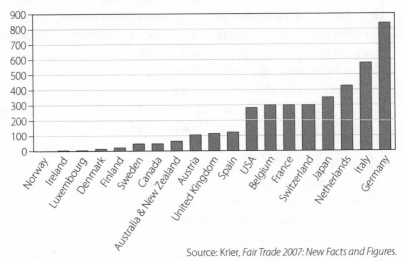

Source: Krier, *Fair Trade 2007: New Facts and Figures.*

food. The period between 1975 and 2007 was the golden era of cheap food; overall cost fell by a third. Western households made huge savings at the check-out: the ethical premium got the small change. Since 2007, food prices have escalated. Initially, fair-trade products continued their forward march regardless. In 2014, it came to a halt. For the first time in twenty years, fair-trade sales dropped, by 4 per cent. Whether it has reached a plateau or in future will be able to regain momentum and withstand the pressure from discounters remains to be seen.

Fair trade today comes in two dominant forms. One is commercial, with rising sales in supermarkets but with weak grass-roots activism – Great Britain is a pronounced case. The second is as a social movement, where sales are small but made in local 'world shops', *Weltläden* and *botteghe del commercio*, with their devoted volunteers who try to raise awareness for trade justice as well as selling handicrafts and foodstuffs from the developing world; these are more widespread in the Netherlands, Germany and Italy.

These two sides reflect an ideological divide within the movement about the best way to make trade fairer: work with the market or fight for an alternative? When the multinational Nestlé adopted the fair-trade label for its Nescafé Partner's Blend in 2005 it caused a lot of soul searching among ethical consumers. For some, the spread of fair-trade products in supermarkets was an act of betrayal. For the twenty-seven-year-old Matteo in Italy, Nestlé was the 'very antithesis' of what fair trade stood for: 'Big supermarkets were one of the things we should be fighting against.' Their fair-trade products were 'mere consumerism' and distracted from the fundamental question of global inequality and the causes of poverty. Andrea (thirty-five), by contrast, was more pragmatic. Supermarkets were a 'double-edged sword'.[4] True, they did not give shoppers the full picture of trade justice they got in the smaller *botteghe*. At the same time, they might help spread fair-trade products. For him, goods bought in a *bottegha* were of a higher quality, but, he acknowledged, the hypermarket was more convenient, and that is where he bought fair-trade products when he was short of time. Elena, a working woman in her fifties, agreed.

The ambivalence about brands and supermarkets articulated a more fundamental disagreement about what 'fair' meant. Was it about giving farmers a fair deal, or should fairness extend from farm to fork, along the entire food chain, including processing, shipping and distribution? In 2006, the French government's standards agency (AFNOR) made an effort to define fair trade, and failed. Big companies were unlikely to agree with the small Minga Fair Trade Imports, for whom fairness had to include small-scale local exchange between producers and consumers. In practice, it has been 'Max Havelaar' and 'Fairtrade' – the main Dutch and British labelling organizations – which since the 1990s have increasingly defined the issue as one of fair wages for producers plus certified health and safety standards. The label was a crucial step in the commercial advance of fair trade. It made it ready for the supermarket shelf. Corporate brands were able to strike selective deals for certain product lines without having to renounce capitalism all round. People no longer had to change their entire lifestyle. Fairness was for sale piecemeal.

The label shifted the balance within the movement. This is not because world shops have disappeared or churches have stopped selling fair-trade products. Far from it – most churches in Bavarian towns have regular fair-trade stands. Rather, since the late 1990s, the labelling organizations have outpaced everyone else. By 2007, less than 10 per cent of sales were still done via 'alternative trading organizations'. Even in Germany and the Netherlands, where a thousand-odd worldshops did respectable business at that time, they were now outflanked by over 30,000 supermarkets that carried 'fair-trade' products.

Diversity extends to the uneven uptake of what is the most popular article: coffee. No one drinks more coffee than Scandinavians – Finns have a statutory coffee break – but so far they have largely shunned the fair-trade variety. It is mainly Brazilians, Americans and Britons who sip it. In Finland, a mere 0.4 per cent of the 12kg of beans consumed per person per year is fair trade. Are Finns less ethical than Anglo-Saxons? This is doubtful. National tastes have been moulded by retail environments and drinking habits. Spontaneous acts of choice have less to do with it. Finns, for example, have long been accustomed to a light-roasted blend of Colombian and Santos beans from Brazil, a mix that is claimed to be uniquely suited to Finland's soft water. In the twentieth century, it was marketed as 'Finnish' coffee by the 'Paula girls', who toured the country for the Paulig company in national Sääksmäki dress offering advice on how to prepare a decent cup (see Plate 18). Here is a legacy of the Western rebranding of distant 'exotic' commodities as part of their own national identity that we observed earlier.[5] The more aromatic, hand-picked Arabica beans preferred by fair trade simply taste 'unFinnish' to many. In Britain and America, the diffusion of fair-trade coffee has been driven by coffee chains and supermarkets. They make the choice for the consumer. In these countries, the new taste for espressos and speciality coffees, drunk in cafés or on the go, offered an outlet for small roasters and fair-trade beans. In Finland, by contrast, most coffee is brewed and drunk at home. Heavy discounts favour the big 'Finnish' blends which are regularly on promotional sale. In general, where big discounters dominate the retail landscape, as in Norway, there is less breathing space for fair-trade products and the smaller shops that give them an initial foothold.[6]

All this does not mean we can ignore choice. Choice as the instrument to promote trade justice has dominated fair-trade campaigns since the 1990s, when labels took off. There were political as well as cultural reasons for the apotheosis of the ethical consumer. The collapse of an international architecture of coffee agreements (1962–89) and marketing boards left behind a vacuum.[7] Shoppers were asked to fill it. With their wallets, they would help small farmers let down by global politics.

But fair trade also tapped into a more general decline of trust in companies and the state. Corporate health, labour and environmental standards were scrutinized and found wanting. Jonah Peretti's 2000 battle with Nike to get the company to personalize his sneakers with the word 'sweatshop' was just one of several *causes célèbres* that registered the new mood. In demonstrations, fair-trade activists resurrected the old, radical image of the big, fat boss to personify the raw, selfish force of neo-liberalism. Unlike in earlier muckraking exposés, consumers now felt less confident in looking to the state for help. They took consumer protection into their own hands, rewarding 'good' companies and boycotting others. Ethics became a regular part of shopping; according to a 2011 survey, two thirds of Germans routinely applied ethical criteria in their purchasing decisions.[8] Significantly, this trend has not been shared by all rich societies alike. The sense of consumer power is high in liberal countries like Britain. In Norway, by contrast, fewer than one in ten consumers feel their voice matters: most rely on the government to deal with any problem.[9] Paternalism does not nurture ethical consumers.

Choice promised empowerment. 'People who feel disempowered by the political system,' the editor of *New Consumer*, a monthly magazine championing ethical living, wrote during the 'Make Poverty History' campaign in 2005, 'know that they can make a difference by purchasing fair-trade goods . . . We've shopped our way into this mess and we can shop our way out.'[10] Shopping was the new democratic politics. And, on top of it, it was fun! The call to conscience increasingly mobilized the joy of shopping. Fair trade presented itself as a 'lifestyle' movement. It made peace with consumption. Adverts came to mirror those of mainstream consumer culture, tickling a desire for exotic luxuries and cheap deals. Brilliant Earth, for example, gives its customers the chance to enjoy 'luxury with a conscience' by ordering their own conflict-free diamond ring. Attuned to the German love of *Schnäppchen* (bargains), GEPA (the biggest fair-trade company, founded in

1975, which supplies world shops) offers 'treasures of the world' at 'fair discounts'.[11]

The fair-trade consumer, then, was a perfect fit for neo-liberal times. This does not, however, mean that choice was the direct cause of success. The link was more indirect. In campaigns to promote fair-trade towns, the figure of the ethical consumer was a way to win over public providers, retailers and food producers. Given the focus on individual choice, it was, ironically, corporations and public bodies that gave fair trade the decisive boost. In 2008, Tate & Lyle, the big refiner that had invented the sugar cube, switched all its retail sugar to fair trade. Morrisons, the supermarket, started stocking fair-trade sugar only. A year later, Cadbury's Dairy Milk also switched. Lovers of Britain's most popular chocolate now automatically ate fair-trade cocoa. More often than not, shoppers had ethical products chosen for them. Of course, in return, companies used these commitments to signal their ethical credentials to consumers and shareholders, but, at the point of purchase, individual choice had little to do with it. Similarly, in fair-trade towns, local authorities switched their collective procurement. Some residents were not even aware of the change.[12] In the Netherlands, most ministries, municipalities and schools serve fair-trade beverages. In Sweden, the Fair Trade association receives government subsidies; in France, preferential rates to advertise in public media. In 2003, the city of Munich supported a 'One World' initiative with fair-trade tea and coffee in municipal buildings, the Olympic park and the zoo. It was now that shops and restaurants started to take notice and to offer more fair-trade beverages. Across the Alps, in Switzerland, government support has been crucial for the high level of awareness.[13]

Some see in fair trade a sign that we increasingly care for distant others, a kind of ethical response to globalization. Philosophers have long been divided over whether such concern is even possible. For David Hume, in the mid-eighteenth century, sympathy was limited to those near us. It was impossible to love mankind. By contrast, Friedrich Nietzsche, a century later, denounced *Nächstenliebe* as selfish and rotten and called for a higher love of distant others and unknown futures (*Fernstenliebe*) that in its highest form would stretch to things, and even spirits.[14]

Clearly, it matters what we mean by 'caring'. Buying a certified banana because it might help a small farmer on the other side of the world is not the same as looking after a child or elderly person, day in, day out. 'Caring for' is more demanding than 'caring about'.[15] The former requires physical contact and an understanding of the needs and abilities of the person cared for. Fair trade, by contrast, creates a more distant, fleeting relationship and one that often gives a distorted sense of the subjects of concern. Exhortations to Northern consumers have invoked images of powerless, dependent Southern producers. 'You choose – because he has no choice,' fair-trade adverts read in 2007, accompanied by an image of a starving African child.[16] Small farmers' skills all but disappeared from view, as well as the fact that they, too, were consumers. While bridging distance in one sense, such campaigns have also had the side-effect of creating a new sense of distance between powerful consumers in the North and powerless producers in the South.

In reality, fair trade relies on Southern consumers as much as on Northern ones. In Brazil, it was grafted on to the movement for rural solidarity in 2002; the government helped farmers with advance payment systems. Brazilian farmers have been encouraged to produce for Brazilian consumers, not for Americans or Europeans. Africans, similarly, are consumers as well as producers: half the fair-trade goods produced in Africa stay on that continent.[17]

Fair trade today manifests the contradictions of globalization. As the food chain got longer and longer, consumers came to know less and less about the people who grew their food. At the same time, the world has shrunk and people are more aware than ever of the plight of their cousins on the other side of the globe. The tension between these two forces can be traced back to the eighteenth century and before. What is new is that in our digital-media age it is all but impossible to shut out images of poverty, hunger and violence, however far away.[18] Fair trade is a relatively easy way of turning such sympathy into practical action, certainly less demanding than, say, sacrificing a fifth of one's income to famine relief or volunteering time. In reality, though, it has been all but easy. Ethical consumption in general has been troubled by a paradoxical gap between sentiment and action. In survey after survey, European and North American consumers stress their ethical credentials. In a MORI poll in 2000, every second European said they would be prepared to pay extra for ethical products. French consumers said they would pay up to 25 per cent more for clothes not made by children. And yet, in the real world of shopping, ethical products, led by fair trade, amount to a minuscule sliver of the cake. What explains this contradiction?

That people like to think well of themselves but find it difficult to translate good intentions into practice is hardly surprising, but the gap has to do with more than hypocrisy. In part, fair trade is wrestling with a problem of scale, the gulf between a small type of local action (purchase) and a vast global problem arising from the world-trade system and inequality. People do not have to be hard-hearted to be sceptical about whether spending a few extra pennies will cure global poverty. Some simply feel overwhelmed. 'It shouldn't be down to the consumer,' a British woman told a recent researcher. 'It should be up to the governments to fair-trade with other countries, not us buying one kind of chocolate over another.'[19] Others prefer to give to charity. Germans, for example, on average give over thirty times as much to humanitarian aid as they spend on fair-trade products.[20] However significant shopping might be to people's identity, it is wide of the mark to think that most ethics today are expressed at the check-out. Moreover, a variety of causes and labels are competing for attention in the ethical marketplace. For some, caring for children, animals or the planet takes precedence over caring for distant others.

Above all, shopping involves stubborn habits. A study in Ghent, Belgium, placed consumers in a close-to-reality setting to see how much more they were prepared to pay for the fair-trade label. When it came down to it, a mere 10 per cent of the sample were willing to put their money where their mouth was and pay the Belgian 27 per cent premium. This group tended to be better educated, in their thirties and forties, and more idealistic; other studies have found women, teachers, Christians and high-income groups over-represented. For the majority, flavour, price and, especially, brand trumped the ethical label.[21] In real life, people are not accustomed to making new choices daily. There is a certain irony in all this. Fair-trade campaigns have looked to choice as the high road to ethical purchases. But ethical calculations, like price calculations, are only part of what goes on when people consume. To create ethical lifestyles, ingrained habits would need to change, too.

Fair trade exists as a social movement, and it is its political promise as much as the actual products purchased that has guaranteed it attention. Like boycotts and buycotts more generally, it has been the poster-boy of a new type of 'life politics', said to be typical of 'late modernity', where the personal is political.[22] Daily life here appeared as a new arena of citizenship, where individuals deliberate and take their stand, creating a new link between the local and the global. Opinion about its impact on political life has been divided. On the one hand, political consumption has been seen to give a voice to people who did not have one before. Consumers become citizens, and in the process open up new spaces of politics, above and below the nation-state. On the other, it might suck the energy out of established institutions, as boycotts took the place of elections, and consumer networks that of parties and parliaments.

There is no question that more people are active as political consumers now than a generation ago. In 1990, for example, 22 per cent of Danes had boycotted at least once. In 2004, the proportion had doubled. Still, neither of the two prognoses has been borne out by reality. In Britain, fair trade mainly recruits people who are already politically aware and engaged. Nor did it have a 'crowding out' effect. A study of 1,000 young adults in Brussels and Montreal found that political consumers were twice as likely to join political groups and parties as regular shoppers. While they were critical of political institutions, they at the same time had a high degree of trust in their fellow citizens. In short, new and old politics reinforced each other.[23]

THE TWISTED ROAD TO FAIR TRADE

Fair trade has attracted attention not only because of its rising turnover but because it is often greeted as a new era in global ethics. The late twentieth century, in this view, gave rise to a new moral economy. This is a deeply flawed view of past and present. Fair trade did not appear out of nowhere. To understand its appeal, its prospects and its contradictions we need to reconstruct its longer history. The labelling initiatives grew out of a longer transformation in human sympathy that urged consumers to take responsibility for the consequences of their actions for distant others. While fair trade today speaks a distinctive language of individual choice, it taps into a moral geography of care that has taken shape over the last two centuries.

When political consumers stepped forth in the modern period, they did not march in a straight line towards global compassion. Their sense of responsibility towards producers was conditioned and constrained by empires and nations as well as liberalism. It was in the eighteenth century that the international flow of goods made people more aware of their interdependence. No other product symbolized the moral chain between consumer and producer as much as sugar. In 1791, when the British parliament threw out a bill to abolish the British slave trade, it triggered a wave of boycotts of slave-grown sugar. These boycotts revealed a new moral geography at work – but also its limits. Boycotters hoped to put an end to the British slave trade, not slavery in general.

From a political perspective, this strategy made good sense. After all, they were trying to change British policy and save British souls. At the same time, approaching the slave trade as a question of national sin meant personal ethics stopped at imperial borders. Taste for activism diminished once Britain had abolished the slave trade (1807) and freed its slaves (1833), even though slavery continued elsewhere. The same people who had boycotted sugar from the British West Indies continued to wear slave-grown cotton and smoke tobacco from the American South. Very few abolitionists felt their responsibility as consumers extended to distant producers in general.[24]

The tension between personal and national responsibility would be resolved in two opposite ways. Liberals looked to free trade. By allowing goods to enter freely, it gave all producers an equal chance to sell their wares at the best possible price, irrespective of their country of orgin. In a way, in Victorian and Edwardian Britain, free trade was the original fair-trade movement, linking consumption to an ethic of reciprocity; free traders invoked the Golden Rule: Do unto others as you would have them do unto you. While free trade made moral sentiment more global in reach, in practice, it made it far less personal. Consumers were relieved of any direct responsibility for how distant producers were treated. If other countries were foolish enough to erect trade barriers and tolerate horrible working conditions, that was their problem. The best thing Britain could do was to throw its own door wide open and lead by example. A few radicals believed that free trade would teach consumers an 'increased regard for quality of life' and gradually make them favour goods made under decent conditions,[25] but how it would do so was left vague. For most, buying cheap was fair enough.

The liberal moment peaked before the First World War. Afterwards, a rival, conservative strategy was in the ascendance, as popular imperialists discovered consumer power. Empire shopping weeks urged British housewives to care for their cousins in the colonies and shop with a sense of imperial duty. Paying a bit extra was the price of imperial solidarity. Of course, the philosophy of these campaigns was essentially different from that of fair trade today. It was racially motivated, seeking for the most part to help white farmers in Canada and Australia, not distant producers in general or exploited coolies in the colonies. In that sense, it was a narrower vision. In another, though, it was less lop-sided than today's moral geography, for it recognized that distant producers were consumers, too. Buying apples from Canada was important because it would enable Canadians in turn to buy more manufactured products from Manchester and Birmingham. In its methods, the inter-war 'Buy Empire Goods' campaign showed remarkable similarity with fair trade today. Processions and food stalls put a human face to the food chain. There were baking and costume competitions to promote colonial products, while Kenyan coffee had its own tasting demonstration.[26]

In the end, it was war, not peace and commerce, that forged a more global moral geography. Already in the 1930s, the League of Nations had concluded that it was impossible to improve nutrition among consumers in one continent without also improving the conditions of producers in another.[27] Co-operatives finally established an International Trading Agency of their own in 1937. The Second World War brought home the lessons of mutual dependence with a vengeance. It also gave rise to the idea that a global body should coordinate global needs and supplies. The Cold War intervened to limit these ambitions, and the United Nations' Food and Agriculture Organization (FAO) worked to raise living standards, not to eliminate world hunger through a world food plan. Yet the shift towards a more global ethic of care outlasted this institutional defeat. 'Fifty years ago would anyone have thought about a WORLD food problem?' British co-operators asked their members in the 1950s. 'When famine struck India [in 1876], or the potato blight struck Ireland [in 1845], other people heard of *India*'s or *Ireland*'s food problem.' They did not see it as a 'world food problem that the WORLD should do something about solving'.[28]

Such structural understandings of the uneven distribution of food were reinforced by diagnoses of the unfair terms of trade between primary producers and industrial nations. Hans Singer and Raúl Prebisch, two economists at the UN, wrote in 1949 about how the developed North was feeding off the underdeveloped South.[29] Proposals to help primary producers ranged from tariffs at the national level to international commodity agreements which sought to iron out the disastrous boom-and-bust cycles of the inter-war years with the help of buffer stocks and quotas; these ranged from wheat (1949–70) to coffee (1958–89). This structural view of global trade was troubling for consumers as well as economists: what if their cheap breakfast table was built on the poverty of Southern farmers? To tackle global poverty, individual acts of charity were no longer enough. A new repertoire of consumer activism was taking shape among Christian missions, youth groups and Third World movements. It resonated with a wider soul-searching about affluence.

One beginning was the charity gift shop. In 1947, five years after its birth, the Quaker-led Famine Relief Committee Oxford (Oxfam) opened their first gift shop on 17 Broad Street – it helped first Greek, then German refugees. Clothes drives and the sale of cards and gifts for famine victims had already been under way in the late-Victorian period, but these had been episodic affairs. What was new about Oxfam was that it turned buying for charity into a self-sustaining business model. Income was ploughed back into additional shops and aggressive marketing introduced. By 1966, there were fifty stores, seven years on, over five hundred. Initially, the roles were the reverse of fair trade today. In its first decade, Oxfam sent British goods to needy foreigners and refugees, not exotic goods to British consumers. In the United States, Mennonites had begun selling embroidered textiles from Puerto Rico in 1946. In Britain, a first sign of change came in 1959, when Pastor Ludwig Stumpf of the Lutheran World Service arrived in Oxford with a suitcase full of pin cushions and embroidered boxes made by Chinese refugees in Hong Kong. They were sold in the Huddersfield Oxfam shop. Two years later, the Christmas sale featured African and Chinese handicrafts. The African beads and ornaments had been sourced by Tristram Betts from Bechuanaland, a retired colonial officer with progressive leanings. By the 1970s, handicrafts from India and Bangladesh were everywhere.

Ethical consumerism drew on a Christian–colonial nexus. In Oxfam shops in Britain, embroidered wall-hangings from Gujarat were made by widows and the disabled in workshops sponsored by missionaries. In the Netherlands, the founding fathers of the first fair-trade label were a missionary from Oaxaca and an economist from Solidaridad, an ecumenical development body. Third-world products were responsible for half the sales of Oxfam trading, set up in 1975. Oxfam illustrates how the means and ends of helping by buying shifted in this period. At first, selling exotic handicrafts was all about raising money for Oxfam and its relief work – to give the artisans a fair deal had not crossed anyone's mind. Fair trade was an afterthought. By the late 1960s, some members were accusing Oxfam of hypocrisy, buying cheap and selling dear. It was only in the 1970s that a new model won out ('the Bridge') which marketed purchases as a way to help artisans in what was then called the Third World.

The two groups that were more than any other behind the transition from charity to trade justice were Christian youth and students. Their role was especially pronounced in the Netherlands and Germany, where world shops took off in the 1970s. The first one opened its doors in Breukelen, outside Utrecht, in April 1969. Two years earlier, a group of youths in the Catholic aid charity SOS (Steun voor Onderontwikkelde Streken/ Support for Under-developed Regions) had started importing wood-carvings from the slums of Port-au-Prince and bamboo ashtrays and other handicrafts from the Philippines. World shops responded to the call for 'trade not aid' at the time. In the Netherlands, some activists had taken to the streets to sell Caribbean cane sugar in plastic bags.[30] In the early 1970s, world shops were opening in Germany, initially as *Dritte Welt* or Third World shops before abandoning the hierarchical label for the more inclusive *Weltladen*. The church-hall and missionary exhibitions were vital conduits. Churches held services on the Third World. Afterwards, the congregation had an opportunity to buy woven baskets brought back by missionaries from Papua New Guinea. Coffee from co-operative farmers arrived via missionaries in Tanzania; in Italy, world shops received crafts from Italian missionaries in Brazil. For the ethical career of fair trade, the churches were crucial: in their hands, the products appeared morally clean, untainted by the blood and suffering of the global commodity trade.

University towns such as Göttingen and Freiburg were often the first to open a fair-trade shop in a region, but the movement reached more widely into small towns and secondary schools. In sleepy Schorndorf, outside Stuttgart, young Christians of the YMCA had held special promotions to support Nigeria during the town festival in 1972. On the second Sunday of Advent that year, pupils from the local secondary school exhibited texts and handicrafts to illustrate the link between the rich world and the poor. Was it not high time that Schorndorf adopted a partner town from the developing world? a poster asked. In Hildesheim, Catholic and Protestant youth were selling peanuts in 1969. Three years later, the first world depot opened in a cowshed, shortly followed by a proper Latin American market in a former fishmonger's; this would be among the first to join the El Puente foundation, which imported fair-trade handicrafts. By the early 1980s, there were over three hundred such world shops across Germany, with more than 2,000 support groups (*Aktionsgruppen*).[31]

Trade justice received a lift from several forces. One was a religious turn towards global solidarity. In the 1950s, Catholic and Protestant youths organized fasts and action groups for the starving people of the world. From here it was a short step to the sale of Third World goods to raise awareness in the battle against hunger, as Protestant youth did in their hunger march in 1970. Trade justice received significant support from Church leaders. Fair trade would eliminate the need for aid, the Bishop of Recife said. Pope Paul VI, in his encyclical letter *'Populorum progressio'* ('The Development of Peoples') in 1967 questioned the basic principle of liberalism. 'Prices which are freely set in the market' produced mutual gains if the parties were in relatively equal positions, but in an unequal world they had 'unfair results'. 'Freedom of trade,' he wrote, 'is fair only if it is subject to the demands of social justice';[32] as a cardinal, he had seen poverty in Brazil and Africa with his own eyes. Fair trade was a global extension of the right to a just wage. Crucially, such critiques linked material poverty in the South to moral poverty in the North. Love of possessions was displacing love for one's fellow man. In Britain, Christian Aid held harvest festivals similarly critical of 'consumer society' at this time.

Secondly, alternative trade could be linked to a struggle for an alternative society at home. This took a number of forms. For some, it was a rallying cry for simple living. In Germany, the group Kritischer Konsum organized special campaigns in the run-up to Christmas in 1969 and 1970 in which they attacked the seasonal churchgoer who gave a few marks for 'bread for the world', yet at the same time enjoyed chunks of chocolate 'which he can only buy so cheaply because the farmer in Cameroon or Ghana is paid a famine wage'.[33] Christmas revealed poverty in the South and 'the organized orgy of wasteful consumption' in the North to be two sides of the same coin. Trade justice, consequently, was not something external but required Westerners to break free from the dream worlds and manipulations spun by advertisers and producers.

Both of these developments gained a good deal of their momentum from a third factor: the growth in student activism and anti-colonial politics. Like the peace and social movements of the 1960s and '70s, fair trade benefited from the unprecedented expansion of higher education in these years. Colonial struggles gave the Third World greater public visibility, beginning with the solidarity campaign for Algeria in 1954 and reaching its high point with support for the Sandinista liberation movement in Nicaragua in the 1980s. World shops were extensions of this milieu, boycotts their recruiting ground. The Dutch network led the boycott against Angolan coffee in 1972 and the solidarity movement for Vietnam and Suriname the following year. World shops mushroomed as a consequence, their number reaching almost two hundred by 1974.[34] The German campaigns for 'Nica coffee' and 'Jute instead of Plastic' (*Jute statt Plastic*) had a similar effect in the early 1980s. Across the West, apartheid was fought with boycotts of South African fruit. Dutch fair traders took the name 'Max Havelaar' for their label from the hero of the eponymous 1860 novel about the struggle against colonial abuses in Java, a curiously local choice for a movement with global ambition. It was not all about opposition from below, however. Interest in the Third World was actively supported by West European governments and churches, initially to counter the Red Peril and keep the young on side. By the 1970s, 'development' had its own state department in Germany.[35]

Simple living had its followers in the United States, but here attention to the problems of the Third World also gave rise to movements that looked for change in political structures. In the wake of the oil and food crises of the early 1970s, the ecumenical network 'Bread for the World' connected famine relief and trade justice abroad with support for workers and the poor at home. A 'more modest style of life can be a powerful witness in the struggle against hunger', its director, Arthur Simon, wrote in 1975, but only if it was accompanied by better government policies of production and distribution. Lifestyle 'can . . . lull us with a false sense of fulfilment'. Eating no meat or throwing out the television set might be 'morally satisfying' to the individual. By itself, however, it did not put more food on the table of the world's poor. Worse, it 'may do nothing more than put people out of work'. What was needed were international and domestic interventions that complemented each other. The West had to lower its tariff barriers and, in addition, give the poorest countries preferential treatment and minimum-price agreements. At home, the United States government should guarantee its citizens work and a basic 'economic floor'. 'The appeal that is primarily needed is not for less personal consumption, but for a greater share of per capita US growth,' Simon said.[36] In Western European welfare states, radical students founder it easier to dream of simple living: they had a secure 'floor' under their feet. In America, with fewer benefits, redistribution could not be ignored.

Today, Britain is among the world leaders in the fair trade market (£26 or Euro 35 per person in 2014), but in that earlier phase it was lagging behind the Netherlands and Germany. Why? After all, like the Netherlands, it was a commercial society with an imperial past and had, if anything, an even stronger line of critics of colonialism to draw on. It had affluence, radical students and a counter-culture, like the rest of Western Europe. True, Britain had Traidcraft and Christian Aid, but it was not until the 1990s that fair trade came into its own. The reason was that the return of the ethical consumer coincided with the crisis of the social movement that had been its natural champion in the past: the co-operatives. In the 1960s and '70s, the Co-ops were losing members and closing shops, squeezed by the supermarkets. When, in 1973, a television programme revealed how a cup of tea was so cheap because of the appalling conditions on tea plantations, including Co-op ones, some members were outraged. Yet, the Co-ops went on cutting prices further. It was only in the 1990s that they rediscovered that ethics did sell, stocking fair-trade products in all their stores by the end of the decade.[37]

What do we learn from placing fair trade today in a longer historical context? Fair trade has only been the latest wave in a longer ebb and flow of efforts to moralize the economy. It is quite misleading to think moral economy was killed by industrial capitalism, as the Marxist historian E. P. Thompson famously argued,[38] or to treat the present as a sign of its sudden resurrection, in reaction to neo-liberalism and individual choice. The modern world has always had moral economies. Caring for distant others by way of buying (or boycotting) their goods has never been entirely selfless, though. It has always been linked to caring for one's own community – be it to save one's own soul, create jobs, build a strong empire or promote justice at home. It is worth recalling that 'fair trade' was not originally the slogan of shoppers but of manufacturers and farmers who in 1880s Britain campaigned against 'unfair' competition from foreign producers who benefited from tariffs and subsidies. In the United States, fair-trade laws in the 1930s were about helping small businesses against the big chain stores by allowing producers to fix a minimum retail price.

There are intriguing parallels between our own times and that earlier era of globalization in the years around 1900. In both, consumer activism flourished alongside the greater flow of goods, in Europe as well as in America. There is a major difference, however. In the earlier period, boycotts and white lists sought to bring fair wages and decent working conditions to local shopgirls and sweated labour. Today, by contrast, fair trade is resolutely international in its focus. There is little sense that shoppers should do for poorly paid seasonal farmhands picking their local strawberries what they do for coffee farmers in Tanzania. Fair trade operates in the wake of welfare states and labour regulations which their historical predecessors could only dream of.

For farmers in the South, tensions persist between the ideal of fair trade and reality on the ground. Liberal economists warn that the premium paid by Northern consumers (however well intentioned) props up Southern farmers in unviable sectors already suffering from overproduction. Nor is 'fair trade' the monopoly of small farmers. Picking coffee is labour intensive. In Costa Rica, the fair-trade harvest still depends on landless labourers and seasonal migrants from Nicaragua; whether well-run plantations qualify as fair trade has divided the movement in the United States. Moreover, the elaborate certification process has created a layer of middlemen and can act as a barrier for small farmers.

Other inequalities persist. On the page, fair trade stands for gender equality. In reality, a study in Guatemala found that benefits are disproportionately reaped by men who control cash-crop farming and household income. Women on co-operative boards, like at the Asociación Maya de Pequeños Agricultores, continue to be rare exceptions.[39] Northern consumers might see their premium as the font of fairness, but for farmers in the South it is often the coffee roaster who decides their fate. In Ghana, it has been the government which fixed the price of cacao, and there is some evidence that farmers who operated outside fair trade benefited as well.[40] None of this is to minimize the benefits fair trade has brought to many communities, from greater security to education, health and co-operative institutions and access to high-value markets; without the fair-trade premium, coffee farmers in Tanzania and Uganda would have been swept away by the collapse in prices in 2001.[41]

Fair trade has left behind a curious split in moral geography and how consumers see themselves in relation to the people who feed and clothe them, and the consequences this entails for an ethical lifestyle. Never before, perhaps, have people learnt so much about global commodity chains and how their choices affect the lives of distant others, thanks to the work of fair-trade groups in schools, shops and churches – an interest manifest in the popular biographies of sugar and other exotic foods. At the same time, we are more prone to forget that our choices have local as well as global consequences. London, New York and other world cities struggle to give workers a living wage, but there is little sense among their residents that this might also be their personal responsibility. Compared to the original world shops of the 1960s and '70s, fair trade today is both bigger and thinner. Entering supermarkets and coffee chains on the high street has boosted sales and helped many more farmers than ever before. At the same time, it has lost the earlier ambition to build an alternative world of getting and spending. The labelling organizations continue to fight against unfair trade barriers but no longer strive to build a parallel trading system, let alone a new society at home.

A TASTE FOR THE LOCAL

'We people in the city have lost touch with the soil and the people, from whom comes what we need to live.' So commenced a Thanksgiving service in Munich's Heilig Geist church in 2003: 'Bananas from a banana freighter, tomatoes from a container-lorry . . . pork chops from the slaughter-house – but where does it all really come from?' It was time for a change of 'lifestyle': 'to maintain the natural basis of humans, animals and plants and to improve them with the help of a regional cycle [Kreislauf] of producing and consuming.' God had placed man in the Garden of Eden to cultivate it. Regional food would fulfil this divine mission. 'It is important that consumers and farmers know and appreciate each other as humans . . . The greenhouse in Holland has no face and no name.' For this purpose, the church had invited members of UNSER Land (OUR Land) to stand at the altar next to the harvest crops. They were 'no saints'. They did not give away their bread for free but sold it. Still, they symbolized God's grace. Locals bought their bread from local bakers who received their flour from local mills. UNSER Land was solidarity in action, uniting local producers, retailers and consumers – not forgetting the animal kingdom, with dog food made from local beef and chicken, untouched by genetic technology.[42]

The Bavarian UNSER Land network, which originated in Fürstenfeldbruck in 1994, is just one of a large number of regional and local food initiatives that have sprouted across the West since the late twentieth century. 'Slow food' has radiated outwards from its original home in Northern Italy to over a hundred countries. From New Mexico to New England, America is now peppered with community-supported agriculture (CSA) groups. Unknown in England before 1997, today, over five hundred farmers' markets set up their stalls, week after week. Urban gardens in Paris and New York, food-box deliveries in Bristol, award-winning restaurants in Copenhagen that serve locally foraged mushrooms – the quest for authenticity in local food appears unstoppable. Those who really want to know where their salami comes from can adopt their own suino nero (black pig) in Puglia's Monti Dauni for a modest €100.[43]

We know a fair bit about these concerned foodies. The typical shopper at a British farmer's market, for example, is female, over forty, retired or in full employment, and comfortably off.[44] Local, for them, means fresh, healthy, quality food. Although, strictly speaking, local and organic (or 'bio') food are separate categories, in practice the two are often joined or confused, and it would be impossible to treat the career of the former in isolation from the latter. In the 1990s, more and more people turned to organic food, free of chemicals, for a healthy diet, notwithstanding scientific doubts about the connection between the two; in the United States the market for organic foods jumped from $78 million in 1980 to $6 billion in 2000. For some it was part of a wider lifestyle change, to vegetarianism or alternative medicine. For most, however, it was the arrival of a child that put food in a new light. Unsurprisingly, it is mothers who have been the organic consumers par excellence.[45] On their own, though, these facts do not offer much of an explanation. Mothers have always wanted to raise healthy children. Why all the interest in local food now?

For activists and supporters, it is a battle between David and Goliath. Local food is a revolt against an industrial food system that is big, fast, anonymous and tasteless. Slow food seeks to rediscover regional tastes and traditions that have been all but erased by an 'alimentary monoculture', to quote its founder, Carlo Petrini.[46] Such views tend to cast local and modern food as cultural and historical opposites, one traditional, authentic and full of pleasure, the other industrial, artificial and cheap but essentially dull, with the latter making mincemeat of the former in the course of the nineteenth and twentieth centuries.

There is no question that farms, supermarkets and fast-food chains are bigger than ever before. Yet, ultimately, this way of looking at it is too simple. It draws on a foundational myth of modernity which sees community (tradition) being progressively eroded by commercial capitalism (modernity) – it is the moral cousin of the idea we encountered earlier that 'moral economy' died with modern capitalism. It is worth stressing here that Ferdinand Tönnies, the late-nineteenth-century thinker with whom these concepts are most associated, never saw *Gemeinschaft* (community) and *Gesellschaft* (commercial society) as sequential stages but as social systems that interacted with each other in any given period. Sometimes the former predominated; sometimes the latter.[47] Local food cultures, similarly, have been shaped by modernity rather than existing outside it.

What counts as 'local' is a complicated matter. In Belize today, treasured local dishes have their roots in imperial trade, which prized imported fish and tinned fruit over the local catch. The new local is the old global. Notwithstanding the rise of processed food, most food in the world is still cooked at home, mostly by women, and is subject to local habits, technologies and cultures of eating. As anthropologists have shown, cola in Trinidad is a distinctly local drink; bottled on the island, Coca-Cola is treated by locals as Trinidadian not foreign, naturalized with rum. It competes with a range of other 'red' and 'black' sweet drinks that carry particular local associations, such as the soft drink produced by the Muslim Jaleel company which thrives on its ethnic connection in the south.[48] Across the world, plenty of foods carry local or regional labels, but what this means varies enormously. Unser Norden (Our North), a brand of the German coop, specifies that food must have been processed in northern Germany, but its ingredients can come from almost anywhere; alongside Hamburger *Labskaus* and apple juice, its products include banana chips and salted pistachios. Unsere Heimat (Our Homeland), an in-house brand of the EDEKA chain, by contrast, puts origin first and requires all ingredients to come from south-west Germany.[49] Which local products are fit to carry a certified label and which aren't has never been so complicated. A chicken or cut of beef reaching Italian tables must have its origin declared, but pork and lamb needn't. Puréed tomatoes announce 'Made in Italy' even if the fruit was grown in China, as long as they were processed in the *bel paese*.[50] Agro-businesses are happy with territorial certification as long as the criteria are not too stringent. This is one reason for the simultaneous proliferation of regional products and their ambivalent nature.

Farmers' markets are similarly riddled with ambiguity. In English provincial towns, for example, local farmers might come from 25 miles away. In London, the radius is a generous 100 miles. And these are the remits for the farmers, not necessarily for the produce they sell. There is no rule on how long a cow has to have stayed on a local farm before it qualifies as 'local'. Stall-holders can sell pork even if they do not have pigs on their farm. Industry and restaurants have stretched the geographic imagination, offering 'Devon ham' and 'Welsh lamb' that hailed from Denmark and New Zealand. British inspectors in 2011 found one in five restaurants was offering fake 'local' foods. When it comes to what 'local' means in an integrated global food system, there are plenty of bones to pick. Is a fish caught off the coast of Devon still 'local' if it is then filleted in China before ending up again in a Devon shop? The regulators thought not. There is a code of practice, but, significantly, the law is silent. When traders were asked to define 'local', answers ranged from 'less than 5 miles' to 'within the country'.[51]

Local markets may come in a great variety, but they play to a shared script: to give consumers the feeling of being connected to farmers and the land. Locality and a face-to-face encounter at stalls create trust and simultaneously promise quality food and a sense of community. Local chicken from a local farmer has added emotional value missing from the anonymous bird on the supermarket shelf. A good deal of what happens in these markets, therefore, is about personalizing food. Customers do not only buy some eggs but want to know from farmers how many eggs their chicken laid; if they buy pork, they want to know when the pig was reared and killed and what might be a tasty way to roast it. Stall-holders learn to act their part, selling an image of tradition, local stewardship and rustic farming. Locality, in other words, is not a geographical fact but a stage: origin has to be performed. Local markets are democratic successors to Marie Antoinette's model farm in the gardens of Versailles. People feel they are keeping tradition alive. For parents, it is a way to show their children what 'real' food used to be before industrial farming. The demands on heritage require appropriate display and packaging: tweeds and sheepdogs; cheese wrapped in paper, not plastic; a little soil on vegetables to indicate their natural freshness.

In reality, of course, heritage is an industry like any other and local markets exist in the modern world, not outside it. Local farmers, too, use abattoirs. Nor are vegetables automatically organic because they are local, as many customers presume. In her classic study of the regional market in Carpentras, near Avignon, Michèle de la Pradelle reconstructed this theatre of illusion and self-deception. Potatoes here were deliberately kept muddy and presented in bulk to suggest they came straight from the farm. In reality, very few small farmers survived in the region. The salespeople were retailers who bought from wholesalers; some hailed from Paris. Olives were imported from Tunisia, just as in the supermarket. The demand for authenticity reversed the conventional price signal. If something was too cheap, it created suspicion and customers moved on. Friday after Friday, the market was bustling because it gave customers a sense of community and of a shared past, of being part of *la Provence éternelle*.[52]

These markets reflect the dialectic of globalization. At the same time as it flattened distinctions, it triggered a search for new ones. The result has been a bi-polar moral geography, with local food looking in the opposite direction from fair trade. Whereas global commerce stretched the ethics of care to far and distant strangers, local markets concentrate on the nearest and dearest. Local farmers guarantee good, safe food and look after nature. Consumers, in turn, are asked to reward them with their custom. 'You do like to think that in buying their products you are benefiting your neighbours,' as one London woman told researchers.[53]

The appetite for local food is an indicator of how trust and caring can diminish with distance. This is a major point, but we must add an equally important addendum: distance here is not a geographic unit, measured in kilometres, but a political one. For many local foodies, trust in the food chain stops at the border. 'When you go to the supermarket and pick up some tomatoes, they could be from anywhere,' one English woman explained: 'I suppose the good thing about the FM [farmer's market] is that it is British produce.' It matters little that Dutch farms are closer to London than those in Wales or Scotland.

Local food articulates popular disquiet about global agro-business and fast food. It gives consumers a chance to respond to a growing sense of risk manifest in food scandals and anxieties about increasingly complex and invisible food chains. But to see it only in these terms would be unhelpful. We must also understand it in relation to the state and national systems of provision. Trust in the food system varies considerably across the rich world. Britons, interestingly, have the highest trust in food in Europe, notwithstanding the catastrophic outbreaks of mad cow disease in 1992–3 and foot and mouth in 2001. Their strong sense of consumer power is matched by their confidence in the state and in supermarkets. Germans and Italians have less of either. Norwegians live in the shadow of corporate paternalism: the state, they believe, will ensure that their food is safe. In Norway, the state has traditionally bolstered agricultural producers, making national food a byword for health. In such a setting, organic food has found it hard to get a foot in the door. According to a manager of a producer co-operative, 'nothing can be closer to ecological than traditional Norwegian meat production.'[54]

Many Finns, similarly, treat national origin as a mark of 'natural' quality. 'What's relevant in organic foods, is the origin,' one Finn told researchers in 2004. 'I feel it's more trustworthy if it's domestic,' another added. Someone who bought organic foods regularly explained

that 'if you have to choose between Italian organic tomatoes and Finnish normal tomatoes, then I will buy the Finnish ones.' In general, there
was a consensus that organic food from Finland was purer, safer and
tastier than organic food from abroad. 'I think that the "organicness"
is totally lost' on the way from central Europe, a young woman said,
even though food from northern Finland travelled a greater distance to
a Helsinki dinner plate than from farms across the Baltic. Natural food
here is not imagined as slow or small-scale but in the first place as
national. As one Finnish consumer put it, with 'domestic organic products, you can imagine there's a real farmer or producer somewhere in
Finland. But if it's Belgian, it can be anything.'[55] The legacy of nationalism for perceptions of nature could not be clearer. Natural food
comes from one's own people, foreign food from some unknown, artificial process.

Local food networks that look like a radical 'alternative' to global
neo-liberalism from Bristol, Berkeley or Barcelona appear more like a
continuation of conventional orthodoxy if we view them from Oslo or
Tokyo, where national food has long expressed the solidarity between
consumers and producers. In Japan, the Seikatsu Club, founded in the
1980s, now delivers local produce from several thousand farmers to
30,000-odd households a week. On a smaller scale, though more
demanding, is the *tekei* system, where consumers enter into a partnership with organic farmers, pledge to take whatever the harvest delivers
and even help with weeding. Shinto traditions and cleaning rituals to
eliminate contamination from the outside probably reinforced a preference for local over foreign foods. More immediately, such initiatives
grew out of the Japanese consumer movement and politics after the
Second World War, which made food safety a top priority and called
on urban housewives to remember their dependence on their cousins in
the fields. The experience of war and hunger meant reliable Japanese
rice was favoured over the cheap, imported variety. Consumers were
conditioned to see their interests as being tied up with those of producers. It is no coincidence that the foods which attracted the greatest flak
from Japanese critics of GM (genetically modified) produce were the very
ones where Japan had come to depend on imports: soybean and corn.[56]

In Europe, buying groups started to crop up in the 1990s. In Fidenza,
near Parma, Italy, fifty families got together in 1994 as a '*gruppo
d'acquisto solidale*' to purchase organic products for mutual benefit.
What started as a buying club developed into an education in food
miles and solidarity. Today, there are around nine hundred of these

GAS in Italy.[57] Over 2,000 communities have declared themselves GM free. Local food has had a helping hand from the state as well as from concerned consumers. By 2009, many Italian provinces had their own laws to provide schools and hospitals with organic food. Organic here had to be local. Local authorities help organize farmers' markets. Calabria, in its 2011 law, spelled out the vision of local solidarity: 'bringing the end-consumer and farmer closer together was an effective way to raise the added value for the producer and make it cheaper for the consumer to obtain certified local produce that was distinctly fresh.'[58] In France, Parisians and tourists can sample pâtés, liqueurs and other delicacies from the Lozère in the Maison de la Lozère sponsored by that department's tourist board.

'Terroir' is no longer a French speciality. In neighbouring countries, too, local foods invoke the emotional and cultural qualities of the soil as well as its distinctive mineral composition. In Germany, local food is inseparably tied to Heimat, a sense of the homeland. All regional states have their own food schemes and labels, although their criteria and philosophy vary considerably; Hesse requires 100 per cent of the main ingredient to come from within its boundaries; Thuringia takes a more relaxed view, with 50.1 per cent. Across Germany, there are some five hundred regional food initiatives. Together with state television, the Federal Ministry of Nutrition, Agriculture and Consumer Protection has organized culinary competitions for the best regional dishes. The winner in 2012 was a Bavarian pork roast with dumplings made from pretzels and topped with beer gravy.[59]

Today's search for the local repeats the pattern of the late nineteenth century that we observed in Chapter 3.[60] Both were periods of intense globalization that made farmers and traders turn to local tradition and regional customs to fight off foreign competitors. The years around 1900 saw the birth of local certification regimes and regional product brands such as champagne. Dresden's Striezelmarkt, today one of the world's biggest Christmas markets, took off in the 1890s in response to toy competition not only from Japan but also from Nuremberg. Such well-marketed regional customs were part of a broader momentum towards 'invented traditions'.[61]

What has changed? Several important things. Probably the major one concerns the expanding role of the state. In 1900, food-safety policies were in their infancy and there were no agencies to regulate or check on origin. By and large, producers had the field to themselves. Today, 'Protected Designation of Origin', 'Protected Geographical

Indication' and 'Traditional Specialities Guaranteed' are the subjects of national and European governance – in 2011, the European Union registered the thousandth food name under these schemes, the Piacentinu Ennes, an Italian cheese made from raw sheep's milk, saffron crocus and salt. (Almost a quarter of protected foods come from Italy.)[62]

When consumers say they find it easier to trust a local market or a farmer from their country, or slow fooders' first response to a food scandal is to ask their local butcher for a special cut of meat and have it minced under their eyes, they take for granted that national mechanisms are in place to protect them against being poisoned. Before governments took on greater responsibility for food safety, consumers were just as likely to be struck down by old meat from the shed next door as from abroad; indeed, a consumer in Edwardian London might have been safer with French food, thanks to more advanced regulation across the Channel.

Alimentary localism is unthinkable without the state. This is true for fascist and socialist as well as capitalist countries; Mussolini's Italy gave a boost to regional dishes and Dresden's Stollen (Christmas bread) and local crafts had the support of the East German state. The current worry and confusion about local food results from the tug of war between states and supranational organizations as well as from fears about anonymous agro-business. Origin is a zone of conflict between rival liberal and national conceptions of food, between the European Union's mission to promote the competitive, free flow of goods on the one hand, and states' efforts to protect national farmers on the other. Today's consumers have to negotiate a jungle of local product claims and a thicket of labels unimaginable to their great-grandparents. In 1999, the 'week of Saxony', for example, offered over 3,000 *heimische* (native) products from the region. Dresden no longer just prides itself on its Stollen but on Dresdner Brie, Gouda, even shampoo.

Local food, then, is part of modern life. We have already noted the stake of producers in the promotion of regional and national brands. Tesco, Britain's biggest chain, introduced a 'Cheese Challenge' for regional varieties and asked customers to 'Enjoy the Taste of Scotland'. Walmart, the American giant that would be difficult to mistake for a farmer's market, declares 'when produce has been grown and picked closer to home, it tastes wonderful.'[63] Supporters of local food, likewise, live inside consumer culture, not outside it. One manifestation is a drive for distinction. The huge drop in the price of food from the 1960s to mid-2000s meant that class-based diets were eroding in the affluent

West. The poor began filling their shopping baskets with many of the same items as the rich. The phenomenal jump in the consumption of meat and soft drinks in this period speaks volumes. A special trip to a farm, rather than to the supermarket down the road, is partly a way to regain distinction. Cooking and serving local food to dinner guests involves time, knowledge and taste. Appreciating seasonal patterns of cultivation and, perhaps, knowing the name of the cow or chicken and their surroundings, sets a host aside from hoi polloi who toss convenience food into a microwave. It is telling, too, that farmers' markets echo the key words of mainstream consumption: freshness, choice and diversity. Regular customers contrast the 'crisp and fresh' vegetables at local markets with the pre-packaged ones on the supermarket shelf. The current concern with freshness, however, is not something natural but itself a product of modern history, engineered in the last century and a half by advances in refrigeration (in the home and in shipping), transport and packaging, food science and, yes, supermarkets.[64]

There are clear limits to how far today's consumers are prepared to go back in time and eat subject to the seasons. For most, local food is not a radical alternative to supermarkets but an add-on that increases further the range of food already available. 'I'm quite keen on supporting smaller local producers,' one English woman explained, 'because I think that way you get diversity, more competition and different qualities . . . it is a way of making sure we maintain choice.'[65] This is a far cry from the dull and repetitive diet that ruled when food was really local. Tellingly, the regional market of Carpentras today offers greater variety in winter than in summer.[66] Commentators like to stress the potential of local food networks. It is equally important to recognize the limits of people's commitment. In the United States, Community Supported Agriculture initiatives have found it difficult to survive once the enthusiasm of the first harvest is over. For many members, a CSA is little more than a food-buying club. In New Mexico, they lose half their members every year.[67]

ON THE MOVE

Fernando Sánchez left his native Mexico for Los Angeles in the 1920s. Across the border, he found a new material civilization where homes had hot baths and electrical lights and people listened to the radio and drove to the local movie palace in a private car. Sánchez, a typesetter

from the city of Saltillo in north-eastern Mexico, enjoyed his share of
the new comfort and conveniences. He owned a record player and,
occasionally, would go to the cinema, too. But new technology did not
mean an entirely new way of life. Instead of a smoky wood stove, he
now cooked with gas – it made for 'better taste' – but the food he ate
was the same as in Mexico. 'I follow my Mexican customs and I won't
change them for anything in the world,' Sánchez said. He did not let his
sisters cut their hair, nor 'go around like the girls here with all kinds of
boys'. On Sundays he met with friends in the park, where they played
Mexican songs on their guitars. 'I have a great many records of Mexican song and also many American ones, but I have the latter because
they are the ones my children like.'[68]

Sánchez was one of many thousands of Mexicans who in the 1920s
crossed to 'the other side'. Many stayed; others returned. An official list
of 2,000 returning immigrants registered what they took back with
them to Mexico. On average, a repatriate had two trunks full of
American-made clothes. Three in four had bought beds and mattresses.
One in five had a phonograph, some even a piano. One in four drove
home in a Ford.[69]

Migration is a major channel for goods, taste and desire. When
people move, so do things. The material flow, however, is in more than
one direction. Migrants take from the lifestyle in the host country but
at the same time add their own customs to it. Sánchez's compromise
with the American way of life shows how assimilation was often piecemeal. Moreover, a large effect of the flow does not concern the migrants
and host country directly. The families who are left behind receive not
only a share of the migrants' earnings but also a taste of their experiences in the form of gifts and stories. In addition to moving labour,
then, migration moves things, lifestyles and aspirations back and forth
between the richer and poorer regions of the world. How this circulatory system works in all its global complexity we still do not fully
understand. What the following pages are meant to do is to illuminate
some of the material currents and cross-currents that happen in the
wake of labour migration. To be clear, our focus is on 'free' migrants,
not slaves, indentured labourers or internal migrants, although they,
too, have played a role in these exchanges.

In 2012, global remittances exceeded $500 billion, according to the
World Bank. People in poor countries received an impressive two thirds
of such cross-border person-to-person payments. How much does this
matter? It depends on the home country. In Lesotho, Nepal and

Moldova, remittances make up a quarter of the entire economy. Private transfers from the US to Haiti are roughly the same. Every year, Mexicans in the USA send back around $12 billion to their families south of the border. Thanks to the break-up of Yugoslavia and migration within the European Union, rich regions such as Europe, too, have witnessed an increase in such flows. In Serbia, the money sent from neighbouring Austria accounted for 10 per cent of GDP in 2010.[70]

Remittances, like migration, of course, are nothing new. The wave of people who left the old world for the new a century ago – a time when one in ten Norwegians and Italians emigrated – was as large, if not larger, than recent movements. Scattered evidence suggests how migrants were already then leaving their mark on the old country. In the British empire, money earned in the colonies was sometimes left in bequests for churches and charities back home. In the Belhelvie parish in Aberdeenshire, for example, it was Jamaican and Indian money that paid for local schools and poor relief.[71] The introduction of the Imperial Postal Order Service in 1904 made transfers simpler than ever. Between 1873 and 1913, around £170 million worth of private transfers reached Britain, just under 1 per cent of GDP at the time. The bulk came from generous cousins in the United States. Within the empire, it was Britons in South Africa who gave most. Cornwall then was to South Africa what Haiti is to the United States today. Without the weekly 'home pay' from Cornish miners working in the goldmines of the Transvaal, wives and mothers back home would have had to tighten their belts.[72]

Such antecedents notwithstanding, the rise in remittances in the last half-century has been unprecedented. The European miracle sucked in guest workers from Greece, Turkey, Morocco and Algeria, who, by 1975, sent $5 billion back home, roughly a quarter what these countries earned from their exports. For many developing countries, remittances were bringing in as much as tourism. The oil boom in the Middle East pulled in workers from India, Egypt and Yemen, who collectively sent back $1.5 billion. By 2000, Saudi Arabia had almost caught up with the United States as the source of the most generous transfers. In the last decade, remittances to Africa have quadrupled (to $40 billion in 2010), today exceed official aid and are close to the level of foreign direct investment.[73]

What did the lucky recipients do with the money? Remittances do not equal consumption. After all, the money might be used to set up a business or buy a tractor. There is good evidence that remittances help such investment and, with it, long-term development, but this is another subject.[74] We are interested in the more immediate difference migration and transfers make to the way people live, that is, their food, dress, comfort and lifestyle. At first glance, the answer looks straightforward. In 1982, the sociologist Douglas Massey and his colleagues compared the possessions and spending patterns of Mexican non-migrant households with those of their neighbours who had someone earning money in the United States. In Altamira, a rural town in southern Jalisco, migration made all the difference. In non-migrant households, only a small minority owned a fridge and a washing machine. The rate climbed up steadily the longer a family's migrant experience. After ten years, three in four households with a family member who had migrated had a fridge and a washing machine. In the industrial town of Santiago, Jalisco, by contrast, it did not matter whether one stepped into a home with or without a family member working in the States. In both, most had such appliances.[75]

The effect of migration depends on the level of development, or, more precisely, on the gap in material civilization between home and away. The American way of life has had a more profound impact on rural than on industrial communities south of the border. Just as important as conditions in the receiving country is where remittances come from, for migrants bring back ideas of the good life as well as money. In 2009, the World Bank conducted household surveys for the Africa Migration Project and compared who had a mobile phone, radio, TV and access to a computer. In Kenya, Nigeria, Senegal and Burkina Faso, there was a difference between households receiving remittances from within Africa and those without remittances, but it was minor; in the case of Ghana, the former group even scored lower, although that may have been the result of the small Ghanaian sample. Throughout, it was families who received money from outside Africa that were the best equipped.

Tracing the effects of remittances is enormously complicated. Transfers reach home communities in a great variety of ways – cheques, money orders, cash and gifts – which makes it hard to know for sure their value. In his pioneering study, Massey sidestepped this problem by looking only at how migrants spent their savings from their last journey of work. Money first went towards food, clothing and consumer goods. A second chunk – between 20 per cent and 40 per cent – went into bricks and mortar, into buying or building a house, or repairs. Only the little that was left was invested in land or business.[76]

Use of remittances by recipient households in selected African countries, by source of remittances (% of total remittances), 2009

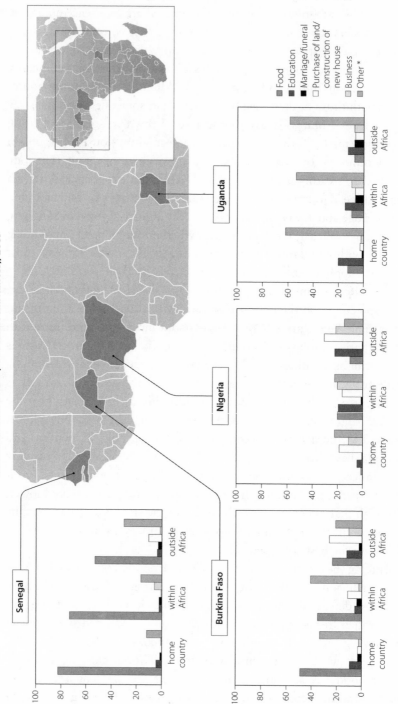

Food
Education
Marriage/funeral
Purchase of land/ construction of new house
Business
Other*

*'Other' includes health, rent (house/land), cars/trucks, rebuilding of house, improvement of farm and investment.

Source: World Bank, 2011, *Leveraging Migration for Africa (2011)*, table 2.3, p. 64.

When remittances took off in the 1970s and '80s, there were frequent complaints that recipients frittered them away on flashy clothes and lavish ceremonies, indulging in short-lived pleasures rather than committing themselves to long-term development.[77] This view mirrored anxieties in the affluent North over 'wasteful' conspicuous consumption, but, just as for the North, it is misleading. For one, from the migrant's point of view, building a home is an investment in the future, not consumption. It keeps the family together, ties money down and prevents it from being spent on baubles and fripperies. In Nigeria, many houses stand empty, ready for the owner's return. Migrant communities today continue to live according to the Italian motto of an earlier era of migration: 'Whoever crosses the ocean, he will buy a house.' Secondly, remittance cultures have varied considerably across the world. While not unique, the high spending on consumption in Mexico is not representative. In rural Egypt, Pakistan and Guatemala in the 1990s, most money sent home found its way into business, land, education and health. Spending on weddings and funerals was only a tiny fraction.[78]

Finally, it is unclear whether remittances really are so special. Some economists have argued that they are just like any other source of income.[79] Our perspective may have been warped because we are not comparing like with like. A Nigerian family, say, receiving a monthly transfer from London, will behave differently from poorer neighbours. Yet do they consume any differently from a neighbour who banks an equivalent pay rise? The jury is out. While migrant households do consume more in total, remittances in fact reduce the relative amount spent on food and dress. After all, these families are better off and can afford to put extra money aside for land and business. In that sense, they are no different from generations of upwardly mobile people before them. On the other hand, remittances are in some ways distinctive. Most strikingly, they flow in a counter-cyclical fashion, that is, they go up when depression and disaster strike, at the very moment when other investments and wages go down. For families in developing countries, they are, therefore, hugely important – a cushion in hard times. Unlike a pay rise, moreover, migrant families tend to view remittances as a temporary gain. It is uncertain when the foreign well will dry up. Interestingly, this does not encourage a mad binge, where the windfall is consumed on the spot. Quite the opposite: it prompts prudent, forward-looking behaviour and investment. For many families in Africa and elsewhere, migration is a carefully planned path. Step by step, one or

Household access to information and communication technology in selected African countries, by source of remittances (% of households with devices), 2009

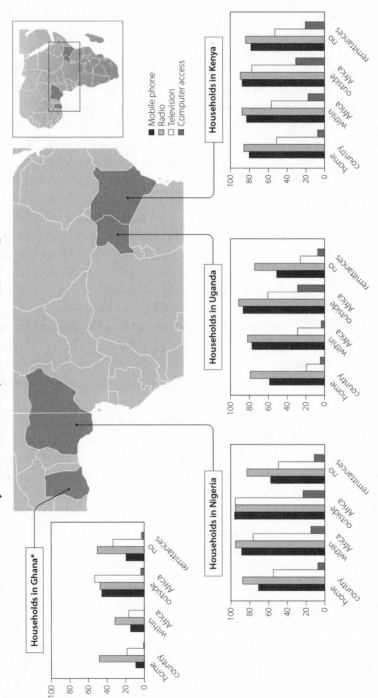

*Ghana data from 2005.

Source: World Bank, 2011, *Leveraging Migration for Africa* (2011), table 2.5, p. 71.

two family members move to a more distant, better-paid job. And with every step, the family moves up in the world. The Africa Migration Project suggests that the further migrants move afield, the more remittances are invested in health, education and a new house.[80]

Contrary to negative stereotypes, then, migration has progressively favoured investment over consumption. This is not to say that we should ignore the often dramatic effects remittances have had on local lifestyles. A pronounced example is Chen village, a farming community in southern China, which a group of anthropologists has been following since the 1960s. In 1979, several hundred men moved to Hong Kong, where they were able to earn ten to twenty times as much on construction sites as when ploughing their ancestral land back home. Their remittances and gifts on visits during the Chinese New Year transformed life for their families beyond recognition. Three years after they had left, every second home had a Hitachi colour television equipped to show Hong Kong programmes. Instead of going to political meetings, peasants stayed at home to watch variety shows. They wore fashionable Hong Kong clothes. The transfers set off a spiral of competitive gift-giving. While the construction workers themselves lived in overcrowded rooms in exile, their hard-earned savings funded Hong Kong-style villas with tiled bathrooms for their kin back home. That some parents actually chose to stay put in their old house was a separate matter. A modern house demonstrated a family's worth and a son's filial piety. Rising expectations shattered inherited values and created a culture of dependence. Idleness, instead of being a stigma, advanced into a mark of success. Hard work in the fields was now looked down upon as a 'backward' activity, practised only by those lesser families without a dutiful son earning big in Hong Kong. In the village, young men started lounging about, either subsidized by their cousins' generosity or propping themselves up with smuggling and theft, rather than taking up a local job that paid a pittance in comparison.[81]

Chen village may be an extreme case, but it does point to some more general patterns. Economic migration probably exacerbates social inequality. It tends to be the better off and better educated who manage to leave. With the remittances they send back their families edge still further ahead. Migrant families may invest *relatively* more than they consume, but what less fortunate neighbours see is their *absolute* accumulation of possessions. Remittances can thus sharpen a sense of relative deprivation by making inequality more visible. So far, we have presumed that remittances are necessarily a private family affair. Of course, there have been many times in history when they were not and migrants have given their fortune to their church or town; initially, in Chen village, emigrants would bring gifts to the local Communist Party secretary. It is specifically gifts in the form of consumer goods that have had a privatizing effect. Electric fans, TV sets and modern bathrooms – and the domestic habits that come with them – tighten family ties while loosening those with the community. Status progressively resides in a family's material comfort. The lavish private wedding takes the place of the communal Saint's Day, a shift noticeable in Mexico.[82]

So far, we have looked at the return flow of money and things to home societies. But what about the migrants themselves and the role of lifestyle, taste and possessions for their own identity and their impact on their host society? There is probably no social group for whom things matter quite so much as for people on the move. Personal possessions provide an anchor for people adrift, a reminder of home, their family and self.

Migration is not necessarily, as often presumed, from a place without things to one overflowing with stuff. Some migrations are triangular, as in the case of Indian professionals who worked in Aden in the 1960s, accustomed to a life of modern comfort and conveniences, until Britain pulled out of Yemen in 1967, when they first moved back to India, into homes without running water, before moving on again to Britain. Decolonization resulted in the mass exodus of Indians and Pakistanis from East Africa to Britain. An anthropologist who studied South Asian families in north London who had been expelled from Kenya and Uganda in 1972 has noted the symbolic significance of Asian objects and food in their homes. Without the customary public space for expressing their identity, their private homes grew into substitute shrines. Many families had never lived in South Asia but surrounded themselves with Peshawari silk paintings and mass-produced carvings. In East Africa, one woman said, they did not have any displays on their walls, but now her husband collected animal pictures. Families acknowledged that the many copper plates would be considered kitsch in East Africa, but in England they had real value, a reminder of their Sangat identity. An elephant-foot stool, complete with hair and skin, brought a piece of Africa to Harlesden.[83]

What is true for objects in general is especially so for food, which, physiologically and sensually, is a uniquely intimate form of consumption. For the South Asian families in Harlesden, cooking and eating kept their identity alive. They prepared *saag*, a Punjabi spinach dish, in a terracotta *mati ka handi*, not a metal pot. Purified water was served in a terracotta jug. Across the world, there are countless examples of local foods serving migrants as reminders of the homeland and maternal love, from Polish sausages to the local care packets that Greek mothers would send their sons abroad. 'Home food' in a migrant community, however, rarely resembles everyday diet back home. It tends to be super-charged, a menu of special offerings, such as Polish *flaczki* (a thick tripe soup), that evokes feast days and family gatherings. Home food is about more than an authentic sausage. When South Asian corner shops in Britain started stocking Polish foods in the 2000s, Polish migrants continued to flock to their Polish shops, which were laid out and lit to evoke the motherland and where they were greeted by a Krakowianka doll. Ethnic shops provide a shared sense of place as much as native food and drink.[84]

For host societies, the arrival of migrant food cultures has been no less transformative. The take-off of Indian, Italian and Greek take-aways and restaurants since the 1960s is sometimes viewed as a milestone, a culinary revolution that, at last, opened Anglo-Saxon, German and Scandinavian tastebuds to previously unknown foreign delights. There is no dispute about the size of this market. A German today is as likely to bite into a Döner Kebap as into a grilled sausage. In Britain in 1997, 10 per cent of all eating-out purchases happened in ethnic restaurants and take-aways – a figure that does not include the many curries sold in pubs after a few pints of beer.

What is debatable is chronology and causation. Food cultures were not closed or frozen in national cuisines before the 1960s. Inter-war Britain, for example, had Jewish fried fish, Italian ice cream and Chinese restaurants. Indian restaurants, such as Veeraswamy's, which opened in London's exclusive West End in 1926, may have been rare sights, catering mainly to retired colonial officials from the Raj, yet dishes inspired by the subcontinent, such as kedgeree (a rice and smoked haddock version of the lentil dish *khichari*) already featured in the more plebeian recipe book *Dainty Dishes for Slender Incomes* in 1895.[85] 'National' cuisines with dedicated menus and cookbooks were themselves an invention of the mid-twentieth century, a culinary reaction to the foreign and colonial people and influences arriving in Europe. In his *Traditional Dishes of Britain* (1953), Philip Harben disingenuously presented fish and chips as a model British food, ignoring its mixed Jewish and French provenance. A study of restaurants and recipes in Germany points to a similar dialectic. Foreign-sounding dishes were a common sight on menus until the Nazis launched their culinary Aryanization programme. The delicate *entrecôte* became the more chewy *Doppelrumpfstück*.[86] The classic nineteenth-century cookbook *Mrs Beeton's Household Management* (1861) was organized by type of food and preparation, not by national cuisine. English roast beef was followed by instructions on 'the Dutch way to salt beef', Folkestone Pudding-pies (a puff-pastry custard tart with currants and lemon peel), by *Dampfnudeln* (sweet, steamed German buns). Mrs Beeton also included Indian chutneys and a 'Fowl Pillau' with generous amounts of cardamom.[87]

Part of the problem is pinning down what exactly is meant by 'foreign' and 'national' foods, since plenty of what people ate and drank in 1800 and 1900 was not originally grown in their own backyard but came from across the oceans – foodstuffs that would have been exotic novelties only a few centuries earlier: potatoes, tea and coffee for Europeans; pork for Latin Americans; maize for the Chinese. The changes that have taken place since the 1960s should be seen in the context of earlier waves of migration and globalization.

Between 1860 and 1920, some 30 million people migrated to the United States.[88] Most came from Europe – Chinese and Asians were barred from the 1880s. It was an unprecedented exodus. Between the 1880s and 1920s, 4 million Italians alone arrived in the United States; in the decade after 1900, more than 10 per cent of the Italian population made the journey. They were joined by the Irish, Scandinavians, and Jews escaping pogroms in Eastern Europe. In the United States, we therefore have a real-life experiment about what happens to different eating cultures on the move.

Italians have been singled out as 'culinary conservatives'.[89] In one sense, this is correct. Italian immigrants did not switch to the foods and menus of earlier Anglo-Saxon and German settlers but favoured Italian macaroni, tomato sauce and salami. However, they did change their diets radically. Most Italian migrants came from the poor, rural south, where they had been used to a diet of beans, potatoes and dry bread soaked in boiling water, with a bit of salt or olive oil for flavouring. Pasta was found in cities and was mainly a luxury of the well-off. In Calabria, there were peasants who had never seen meat. Italian-American food, then, turned a previously imagined land of cockayne – a fantastic land of milk and honey – into reality. Wheat replaced rye and chestnut flour. Above all, meat became a must, now eaten daily. In

New York City, any self-respecting Italian family had at least one pep-
peroni hanging from the ceiling. A budget survey in 1904 revealed how
an Italian family who spent $9 a month on rent devoted almost the
same amount to beef, veal and chicken, in spite of the breadwinner, a
stone-cutter, being frequently out of work. Back in Sicily and Puglia,
families had drunk beverages made of roasted grains. In the New
World, they had real coffee. Candy and cake transformed breakfast. Social workers frequently complained about the damaging effects
on health and household budgets. 'A three-year-old boy's lunch fur-
nishes an extreme example,' one researcher in New Haven reported in
1938: 'he sat in a high-chair holding a cup of strong, black sweet Italian
coffee with a trace of whiskey in it and dipping doughnuts in powdered
sugar before eating them. "My girl," asserted the mother of a six-year-
old to the school nurse, "she likes candy." '[90]

Perhaps, most decisively, the Italian-American meal became prized as
a shared family affair. In the old country, people had eaten together on
feast days and special occasions, but rarely in everyday life. Peasants who
had to walk several miles to work did not have a chance to sit down for
a family meal. They ate alone. While prized ingredients, then, did come
from the old world, what and how Italian migrants ate was very new.

Italian life in America was an example of how high-status food from
the homeland became the cornerstone of ethnic identity in the New
World. Social workers despaired over poor migrant families' insistence
on cooking with expensive, imported olive oil and eating tinned Italian
tomatoes. Yet, whatever the drain on the weekly budget, the Italian
meal gave these families a sense of pride and authority in the host society: Italians knew how to cook and eat well. They commanded taste,
which, over time, gained them acceptance and status. It did not matter
that meatballs in tomato sauce was a recent invention.

For the homeland, the migrant food culture had ripple effects, too.
Demand for tomatoes and pasta in New York City boosted the tinning
and food industry in Italy. As the price of voyages on steamships fell,
half the migrants returned home, bringing their newly acquired eating
cultures with them. All this helped elevate pasta and sauce into a
national dish, notwithstanding Mussolini's attempt to make everyone
eat local rice. Without the earlier mass migration from the *mezzo-
giorno*, pizza and pasta would be neither the national staple nor the
global success story they are today.

The Irish experience was the polar opposite of the Italian. The Irish
diaspora made do without Irish food. There were no Irish delicatessens

or Irish meals on St Patrick's Day. Identity was defined by dance and drink. When it came to eating, Irish-Americans preferred a fusion cuisine that mixed Anglo-Saxon and European influences. In 1912, the Ancient Order of Hibernians held their annual Irish picnic in Milwaukee. On the menu were roast beef (the food of the English enemy since the eighteenth century); sliced tomatoes (a Mediterranean fruit that had been transplanted from Mexico); and hot coffee and pie. Even the potatoes – the closest to an Irish staple – were dressed up as a Wiener potato salad from Austria. Like their Italian neighbours, a lot of Irish immigrants were poor and from the countryside. Italian peasants, too, had been visited by hunger. Unlike them, however, the Irish arrived with the national trauma of the potato famine (1845–50) imprinted on their minds. Irish identity was defined by the lack of food, not its pleasures.[91]

Jewish migrants reached their own compromise between culinary traditionalism and selective innovation, defending regional dishes and elements of kosher while at the same time developing a taste for foreign foods. Gefilte fish and borscht kept their symbolic centrality for Eastern European Jews but were increasingly reserved for the Sabbath and other special days. Regular meals incorporated meatloaf and meat soups. From German Jews, they discovered Frankfurters and pastrami. In reverse, German Jews picked up gefilte fish. Such gastronomic exchanges were not self-contained Jewish affairs but open to cuisines from further afield. By the 1920s, Yiddish cookbooks featured French soup and dishes with Parmesan. Gradually, kosher lost its rigour and accepted selected American products, including Wrigley's gum. In New York, a Chinese meal became a ritual that marked the end of Sabbath for many Jewish families. Chinese restaurants started putting kosher chow mein on their menu, a tradition that lives on on Manhattan's Upper West Side.[92]

Migration might appear as a wonderful harbinger of multiculturalism, a constant injection of new tastes, but the arrival of some ethnic food cultures is always accompanied by the decline and disappearance of others. In London, little remains of the culinary footprint of Jewish and German communities from Victorian and Edwardian times. Gone are the many kosher outlets and German beer halls. Chinese and Indian restaurants have taken their place; the latter increased ten-fold in the 1980s. Such transitions are rarely smooth and easy, and we must resist the temptation to see in every ethnic restaurant a shining example of multicultural tolerance. At times, ethnic food was a lightning rod for racial prejudice. In the 1960s and '70s, just as Indian restaurants made their first appearance in provincial towns, British landlords complained of South Asians 'stinking' of curry. Some British tenants asked their council either to give them a rent rebate because of the 'smell' or to be moved away from their Asian neighbours; in Germany, citizens complained about 'noisy' Italians who left restaurants singing and shouting, without respect for German privacy and night rest (*Nachtruhe*).[93] Before the craze for al fresco dining on cold, wet Northern streets, ethnic restaurants could appear a threat to indigenous cultures of public space.

Exotic influences had to be massaged to make them safe, as in the famous case of 'chicken tikka masala', a meal that had to be invented before it could be devoured as a quintessential national dish by British politicians and customers. Other influences had to be disguised. Indian restaurants in Britain rarely shout about their Islamic roots, even though the vast majority are run by Muslims from the Punjab and Kashmir. For understandable reasons, most enterprising restaurateurs played it safe and opted for a generic standardized menu where India is everywhere and nowhere. Regional and religious authenticity were sacrificed. British authorities played their role in marketing an airbrushed 'India' that fitted their local interests. De-industrializing old industrial towns began to reinvent themselves as regional curry capitals. In the 1980s, Bradford promoted a 'curry trail' for visitors. Birmingham pushed wok-style balti cooking as its civic trademark.[94] The effects of these invented hybrids must not be exaggerated. Eating in an ethnic restaurant may give locals a sense of difference, however inauthentic the dish or decor might be, but it is little more than multiculturalism at a distance. There is a big difference between living with strangers and occasionally ordering food from them. The millions of curries served in Britain every year have not extinguished racial discrimination and conflict.

Continuity and change are mirrored within migrant families. On the one hand, people are extraordinarily stubborn when it comes to food. Taste, after all, is one of the most intimate aspects of our lives, a powerful sense that reaches back all the way to early childhood, perhaps the womb. On the other, people are also extraordinarily flexible, suddenly falling in love with foods that carried age-old stigmas, such as raw fish and sushi. These tensions are particularly acute for migrants, who have to navigate their way in a host society with a strange food culture. How are they resolved?

It is worth recalling that eating is about more than the food on the plate. It concerns the format of the meal and the habits and spaces of eating as well. Migrants have managed to preserve their identity by adapting some elements and conserving others. An ethnography of Bengali-American households in the Chicago area, conducted a decade ago, gives the following meal plan for a family: on Sunday, omelette and toast for breakfast, with lamb curry for dinner; fish and rice on three days during the working week; Thursday dinner: roast chicken leg with an American-style salad and French dressing. On Friday, the family went to Red Lobster, the steak and seafood chain. These families continued to eat a lot of fish and rice, like their cousins back in Bengal and unlike their American neighbours. The meal that had changed most dramatically was the one with the lowest symbolic value: breakfast. What had shifted, too, was the space and format of the family meal. In Calcutta, the weekend meal had been a private affair, eaten at home. In Chicago, families went out and ate in public.[95] Such selective rearrangements can continue for generations without leading necessarily to a loss of ethnic identity. Italian-Americans in the 1990s ate less macaroni than their great-grandparents. During the week, they alternated between stews and American platters. Come Sunday, however, Italian-style dishes would multiply in a great family feast that celebrated eating together.

Status is as important as tastebuds for the survival of an ethnic food culture in exile. It determines whether migrant communities have the power and interest to hold on to inherited customs. The Bengali households in Chicago were distinguished by high status – there was little insecurity or perceived need among them to stop eating fish and copy all things American. A study of Japanese workers on a sugar plantation in Hawaii, conducted in the 1930s, affords a case in contrast. In Japan itself, working families with rising incomes moved to higher-quality, polished rice. Among similar Japanese families on Hawaii, the reverse happened. Only the elderly were clinging to a diet of rice. The rest progressively switched to American crackers, white bread, butter, jam and coffee. In American Hawaii, unlike in Japan, polished rice signalled poverty. Plantation workers were eager to leave it behind as they tried to climb up the social ladder. For the new generation, traditional food was losing its taste fast. 'I don't like Japanese foods,' a female graduate from an American high school said. 'Fish smells bad and the rice takes too long to cook.'[96]

Migrants are not the only carriers of foreign tastes. In the sixteenth and seventeenth centuries, travellers played a critical role in spreading the craze for coffee, cocoa and other exotic novelties. Since the 1950s, mass tourism has raised the exposure to foreign culinary influences to unprecedented levels, although the two world wars were already stepping stones along the way. Tourism has certainly played its part in the popularization of foreign cuisines. The German holiday exodus to Italy in the 1950s and '60s epitomized a new hedonism. Food and wine, beach and sun took the place of ancient ruins and Goethe's *Italienische Reise*. Back home, the neighbourhood Italian restaurant, with fishing nets on the wall and straw-bottles of Chianti on the table, offered everyone, for a couple of hours, a holiday feeling and a carefully packaged taste of Mediterranean romance, complete with the seductive 'Mario'; *padroni* and waiters were invariably men and addressed by their first name, even if the 'authentic' food that emerged from the kitchen was often prepared by their German wives or by Turkish cooks. In the Canale Grande in Munich, customers enjoyed a life-size replica of Venice's Bridge of Sighs, although the city authorities put a stop to their plan of mooring a real gondola outside on the Nymphenburg canal.[97]

Some historians have detected in the global advance of Mediterranean cuisine the birth of a new 'style generation'.[98] What is more debatable is the general influence of tourism on taste, at least when it comes to food. With the partial exception of 'Italian' and 'Greek' food, the orders taken in ethnic restaurants have not followed the popular tourist trail; even in the Italian case, many establishments had their roots in the *gelaterie* of the inter-war years, well before the German masses reached Rimini. Chinese and Indian restaurants abound in Western Europe but, until recently, very few Europeans travelled there. Millions of Britons, meanwhile, have returned from Spain without an appetite for *bacalao* (salted cod). Instead, charter holidays brought mushy peas to Torremolinos. The limited and highly selective effect of travel for taste deserves greater attention than it has received. England is a popular tourist destination for Italians and Arabs, but we do not find Yorkshire puddings served on the Arno or the Nile.

The reason for this uneven appropriation is two-fold. Tourism may make people more receptive to strange foods overall, but it also needs migrants to open and run the places to serve them. Where ethnic restaurants have been successful, they have been able to draw on prior labour migrations, be they of Turks and Greeks to Germany or Indians and Hong Kong Chinese to Britain. Secondly, the ethnic shape of the culinary landscape has been dependent on state regulation as well as consumer choice. On the European continent, unlike in the United

Kingdom or the United States, non-European migrants who wished to set up a restaurant faced often insuperable obstacles. Prior to reforms in 1978, German law discriminated against Turkish guest workers in favour of Italians and other immigrants from the European economic community, who needed no special permission to stay in order to open a restaurant; it gave Italian pizzerias a formidable head start. In Switzerland, Turks and migrants from Yugoslavia were allowed to work in Swiss kitchens but prevented from starting their own. The strength and variety of ethnic cuisines, then, is not only about the diversification of consumer taste in a post-industrial leisure society. It is also a comment about a host society's self-understanding vis-à-vis immigrants and the power of the state to enforce it. Where migrants were treated as temporary 'guest workers', it was natural to keep a cap on ethnic restaurants. After all, they were expected to return after a few years. Neither the people nor their food were seen as valuable, permanent additions to the host culture.

The ethnic restaurant may tell a story of advancing diversity in the affluent world since the 1960s. Yet there are equally important countervailing trends. We need to look at diversity from a global and social perspective as well as that of the individual. From the perspective of the prairies and oceans, the twentieth century saw a sharp decline in biodiversity, reversing 10,000 years of history in which humans had added to the gene pool of plants and animals. At the beginning of the twenty-first century, over three quarters of all crop varieties in Europe and the Middle East had vanished. In the United States, according to one survey, the figure is as high as 97 per cent. A quarter of the world's fish stock is facing extinction today.[99] Everyone wants a piece of tuna. Convergence has been accelerated by a near-universal, growing appetite for meat, the global integration of food systems and retailing, and the mono-cultures of agro-business. Put differently, while most individuals are enjoying a richer and more varied diet, the varied spices and sauces of their meals increasingly flavour the same kind of wheat, rice and chicken.

A similar contradiction exists when it comes to eating as a social practice. On the one hand, the rise in the standard of living and the decline in the price of food – first in the late nineteenth century, then with a second, major drop in the late twentieth – have narrowed the previously vast dietary gulf between rich and poor. The stark contrast between the feasts of the elite and monotony for the rest is gone.[100] All social classes eat meat and snack on processed foods, although some princes may prefer the organic variety from their own certified farm. Supermarkets have weakened (though not eliminated) regional food cultures. Together, TV, leisure and relative affluence have popularized cooking and baking as serious hobbies and a sign of distinction, where hosts play chef and perform in the kitchen. In the process, elite haute cuisine lost its dominant status.

At the same time, there is evidence that food cultures may be as diverse today as they were half a century ago, before TV and eating out took off; the inter-war years, probably, marked a bigger change, as the middle classes lost their cooks and suddenly had to cook for themselves. Eating in affluent societies may simply have articulated fresh differences. The most nuanced study we have – on British society – has found ongoing differentiation. Regional differences declined, but what food people bought and cooked continued to diverge by class, gender and age in the late 1980s as much as a generation earlier. Professionals were more receptive to state recommendations on healthy eating than manual workers. Yes, everyone was eating out more. But for educated elites, a restaurant meal with a good bottle of French wine was a way to express their taste and knowledge, affirming their status in their peer group, and that, culturally, they were miles apart from young working-class men going for a curry. Much has been made of individualization and the reign of private choice. But as the sociologist Alan Warde has noted, if this were true we would expect far greater interpersonal variation in diet than the evidence supports.[101] Personal taste remains socially structured. The imagined worlds that people enter when they eat, as well as the company they eat with, continue to be shaped by class, community and the state.

14

Matters of the Spirit

Affluence challenged old hierarchies of class and taste and forged new ones. So far, we have looked at secular dimensions, but we should also ask about matters of the spirit. Did goods kill God?

The idea that greater consumption must be the enemy of religious life has come in a variety of guises. When affluence arrived in Western Europe in the 1960s, people stopped going to Church and went shopping instead, some commentators said. In the 1980s and '90s, Pope John Paul II attacked 'consumerism' for making people 'slaves of "possession" and immediate gratification', promoting 'having' over 'being', and damaging people's 'physical and spiritual health'. Some writers go so far as to say that materialism is the new religion: people want goods, not gods.[1]

Lurking behind these verdicts is an instinctive way of looking at religion in opposition to the material world. The life of the spirit and that of things here appear locked in rivalry – more of the latter must mean less of the former. This idea has been pronounced in strands of Christian thought but reaches back to Plato. It received fresh impetus from Enlightenment philosophers and, in the early twentieth century, from thinkers such as Max Weber who were pondering the transformative effects of modern capitalism. The advance of reason, money and modernity, in this view, naturally led to secularization, be it by exposing the irrationality of religious beliefs or by undermining the institutional power of churches. The shift from tradition to modernity shattered people's solid sense of themselves and their world and unleashed so many different life projects that the space for a unified belief system vanished. The death of religion was just a matter of time.

To what degree are these views borne out by history? What exactly have products and possessions done to religious life? To answer these questions, we need to look at what has happened in affluent societies in the Christian West but we should also cast our inquiry wider and consider the advance of goods in earlier periods as well as in developing societies and other religions since.

The case of Western Europe is the most straightforward. Nowhere has secularization made greater strides than in what was once the centre of Christendom. In 1910, from Scandinavia to the Mediterranean, 98 per cent of people belonged to a Christian Church or chapel. A century later, less than two thirds identified themselves as Christian and only a small fraction of those regularly attended a religious service.[2] Still, the loss of faith did not suddenly happen in the affluent 1960s. As we have seen earlier, in England, church-going had already begun to collapse in the inter-war years, and concerned contemporaries were pointing their finger at a selfish culture of instant gratification in the late 1940s, in the midst of austerity and rationing. In Britain, the best-documented case, every generation born after the First World War has been less religious than the one before.[3]

Outside this rich little corner of the world, however, the trend since the 1970s has all been in the opposite direction. Eastern and central Europe today is not only richer in things than under communism; it also has more Christian believers; the revival of the Orthodox Church has been especially pronounced. In the Arab world, new oil wealth aided the Islamic revival, not secularism. In China, similarly, rapid growth and urbanization coincided with a growth in Buddhism – up from 13 per cent in 1970 to 19 per cent of the population in 2010 – as well as mass conversions to Protestantism, many from the educated and enterprising middle classes. No movement, however, has multiplied as fast as Pentecostalism, which stresses a believer's personal experience of God through baptism with the Holy Spirit and the power of spiritual gifts, including speaking in tongues. In 1970, 5 per cent of all Christians in the world were Pentecostalists. By 2010, every fourth Christian was a Pentecostalist, or 500 million in total. Revivalism has taken off not only in poor countries such as Jamaica and North Korea but also in Brazil and other developing countries. In sum, the last three decades have thrown up plenty of counter-examples to the supposedly unstoppable forward march of secularization – and all at a time when an unprecedented number of people on the planet were lifted out of poverty. Even in rich Western Europe, it is worth remembering that, after half a century of self-service supermarkets, charter holidays and TV game shows, Christians still outnumber agnostics and atheists by two to one.[4]

The United States holds one set of clues to how religion has been able to turn commercial culture to its advantage. A large part of our confused thinking stems from the simple yet deep-seated error of assuming that 'traditional' communities must have lived in a golden age of religion from which there could only have been a fall as people became 'modern'. In reality, the very opposite happened in America. Americans were less (not more) religious at the time of George Washington than that of Ronald Reagan. In 1776, when the United States declared its independence, Church membership in New England was a lowly 20 per cent. Religious life started to quicken only in the second half of the nineteenth century. By 1890, 45 per cent belonged to a Church, chapel or synagogue. Thirty years later, the number had climbed to 59 per cent; in the early twenty-first century, it hovers around 62 per cent. Far from retreating, religion advanced with modern commerce and consumer goods. It was an affluent society which, in 1954, put 'In God We Trust' on all its coins and banknotes.[5]

Nor did religiosity automatically arrive with the millions of poor Irish and Italian immigrants in the late nineteenth century. As Archbishop Corrigan of New York pointed out to Cardinal Manning in 1888, there 'are 80,000 Italians in this city, of whom only two per cent ... have been in the habit of hearing Mass'.[6] Rather, it was the result of an increasingly urban, rich and competitive marketplace in which preachers and missionaries made the most of an expanding commercial consumer culture by skilfully harnessing media, entertainment and the seductive power of fine things.

The American Tract Society was founded in 1825. By the end of the decade, it had printed 5 million items, with snippets of the bible to make it 'entertaining' as well as 'useful'. The evangelical revival on the eve of the Civil War (1861–5) pioneered a new kind of religious advertising, putting millions of mass-produced images of Christ, heaven and angels into circulation. New churches relied on fun as well as the gospel to attract disciples. Brigham Young, the 'American Moses', led a group of Mormons to Salt Lake Valley in 1847. Three years later, this isolated place would boast an amusement resort, soon followed by a social hall and musical concerts. On Fridays, Mormons would dance the night away. The theatre sat 7,000 people.[7]

In the 1870s, the Evangelical revivalists Dwight Moody and Ira Sankey became religious pop stars on both sides of the Atlantic, with millions flocking to see them in the major cities. Their hymn books were bestsellers, and their fame encouraged a brisk trade in unauthorized porcelain statues and other memorabilia for their hungry fans. In

1875, the two rented Barnum's Hippodrome in New York City – today's Madison Square Garden – for $1,500 a week and made religion the greatest show on earth.[8] Their services were carefully staged performances. The doors opened at 7.15, with 5,000 people rushing to find a seat in the space of ten minutes. The congregation would join the choir in the simple but memorable hymns of Moody and Sankey's hymn book. Then Sankey, the 'sweet singer of Methodism', would give a solo performance on the melodeon, a reed organ. But the highlight came when Moody rose for one of his biblical lectures. 'His voice is rough, pitched on one key, and he speaks straight before him, rarely turning to the sides,' one listener remembered. 'But how real he makes the men! How visibly the deceiving, scheming Jacob stands before us! And how pointedly he applies the lessons of the patriarch's life to the men and women before him!'[9] Then there was more singing and weeping. In Philadelphia, outside the tabernacle, statuettes of Moody sold for $2 a piece.

The rapprochement between Christianity and consumption was facilitated by the tools of commerce, but, just as importantly, it involved a shift in belief and doctrine. Like the other world religions, Christianity had a strain that was deeply suspicious of material possessions, with plenty of warnings about their power to lead the faithful astray from the true path of God, as in the story of the Golden Calf, when Aaron moulded golden earrings into the idol of a calf, after Moses had gone up on Mount Sinai to receive the Ten Commandments. The mid- and late nineteenth century saw the coming of a more gentle, beautiful God who, rather than standing aloof and in judgement, was immersed in the world and in the people and things within it. This doctrinal shift was not caused by possessions or hedonism: immanentism, as one version was called, was a reaction to the crisis of faith caused by science and evolution and attracted many Victorian romantics and socialists who loathed consumer culture.[10] But the idea that God was everywhere did help to make the pursuit of precious things a virtuous, even pious, path. If God's beauty was unfolding in the world, how could it not be Christians' duty to surround themselves with things that radiated that divine beauty?

The coming of the railway aided the circulation of things. Diaries of the 1860s–'80s show that Mormons devoted increasing attention to stylish objects and fashion as a way of becoming tasteful people, with entries on a 'beautiful silk china handkerchief' or 'a beautiful Morocco bound case lined inside with rose colored satin, while the cover contains a plate glass mirror ... Altogether ... most elegant'. 'The foundation of our society has been laid,' the *Desert News* announced in 1860: now 'the work of ornamentation, adornment and more perfect development becomes a matter of judicious attention'.[11] Excess continued to be frowned upon, but austerity was just as bad. A good Christian needed to cultivate the style and fashion best suited to their person.

Of course, earlier Christians had indulged in fine living, as we have seen, notably in the Netherlands and England in the seventeenth and eighteenth centuries. What was new in the late nineteenth century was that many churches lost their old qualms about material corruption and openly preached that God promised material abundance for everyone. Henry Ward Beecher, a Congregationalist social reformer and abolitionist, told American audiences that luxury was the sign of pious men. Beecher himself liked jewellery and shopping. It helped that he commanded a speaking fee of $1,000 for each of the sixty lectures he gave in eighteen states in 1876.[12] For Beecher, 'the instinct for producing wealth was God's educating power in the world'. 'Wealth gives culture.'[13] People had a right to enjoy it for themselves, especially by creating a beautiful home, but they should also spend it on their church and community.

None of this was peculiarly American. The idea that stylish objects radiated a spark of divine beauty also had its champions in Europe, as we have seen in earlier chapters.[14] What made American churches distinctive was that they turned the moral defence of prosperity into a business model, tapping into their members' success to finance their own expansion. The preachers of the 'prosperity gospel' in the 1960s and televangelism and mega-churches since need to be seen in this longer historical context, although they lost the progressive mission of the earlier 'social gospel' ministers. God offered believers a material–spiritual new deal: give yourself over to Him and, in exchange, He will increase your wealth. A powerful proponent of this view was Kenneth Hagin, the father of the Faith movement in the 1960s, who trained thousands of evangelists at his Rhema Bible Center in Tulsa, Oklahoma, spawning 1,440 congregations; he also sold an estimated 53 million books. Hagin preached that God's blessing of Abraham with financial prosperity in the Old Testament applied to the here and now as well: God wants his children 'to wear the best clothing. He wants them to drive the best cars, and He wants them to have the best of everything.'[15]

The televangelist Jim Bakker, a former Assemblies of God minister, raised conspicuous consumption to new heights. TV testimonials resembled shopping lists, and he flaunted his own luxurious lifestyle as a sign of God's grace; in 1984, he bought a 1939 Rolls-Royce and a 1953 Silver Dawn Rolls-Royce, on the same day;[16] his dogs enjoyed air-conditioning in their kennel. In the 1939 Rolls, Bakker would drive generous givers around Heritage USA, his theme park in Fort Mill, South Carolina, which blended bible schools with a luxury mall and the 501-room Heritage Grand Hotel; at its height, it was the third most visited entertainment park in the United States, bringing in $126 million a year, until, in the late 1980s, a combination of sex and tax scandals brought Bakker down to earth. For the evangelical faithful, Heritage USA was proof that Christian love and luxury belonged together. As one female visitor put it, 'Christians don't have to accept second class. I worship luxury and make no secret of it.'[17]

What accounts for the contrast between religious vitality in America and religious sclerosis in Western Europe? From Adam Smith in the eighteenth century to Alexis de Tocqueville in the nineteenth and the *Economist* in the early twenty-first, many writers have found the answer in America's uniquely open marketplace, where churches and sects have to compete with each other to survive, without being bolstered by state subsidies or other privileges.[18] This makes them more entrepreneurial and more entertaining. Pat Robertson's 700 Club, a popular TV programme that began in 1966, for example, is staffed by over 4,000 volunteers who make 4 million prayer calls a year and generated the bulk of the Christian Broadcasting Network's annual income of $233 million.[19]

Religious life in Europe has never been entirely divorced from commerce. The Crusaders traded relics in the Middle Ages and millions of candles and medals have been purchased every year at Lourdes since Mary's apparition there in 1858. Michele Ferrero ('Mr Nutella'), a fervent Catholic, attributed his success to the Madonna of Lourdes and, in 1982, designed and named his Ferrero Rocher chocolates after the rocky grotto; he also placed statues of the 'Madonnina' outside all the factories of his global sweets empire.[20] Still, this is nothing compared to the profusion of Christian rock albums, bible-based video games, children's 'pray clothes' and scripture cookies in the United States.[21] The American marketplace is a fertile ground for mega-churches, especially among revivalist and non-denominational groups without an established home. The Second Baptist of Houston, a mega-church with

17,000 members, fields sixty-five softball teams and has craft and fitness rooms. Even some Catholic churches such as St Timothy's in Mesa, Arizona, have grown into mega-churches, complete with music, entertainment and radio shows.[22]

In Western Europe, it is said, the strength of established churches, benefiting from tax, revenue and other privileges, all but eliminates the need to innovate and entertain. There is some truth in this, but it is only a partial argument. After all, in the eighteenth century, the Church of England was more powerful than it is now, but this did not stop the popular Methodist revival. Moody and Sankey, it is worth pointing out, took America by storm in 1875 after having completed an equally successful tour of Britain. The established Churches today have lost many of their former privileges, but mega-churches and revivalist groups have not filled the void.

Arguably, just as important as the religious marketplace is the nature of the social state. In America, religious bodies offer not only spiritual guidance but community, self-help, social services and leisure. Willow Creek, a mega-church in Illinois, runs a food pantry and an employment bureau, offers childcare and support groups for parents, divorcees and recovering addicts, and even has volunteer mechanics who fix the cars of single mothers free of charge.[23] In other words, American churches continue to do a lot of the work that has been taken over by welfare states in Europe since the Second World War, although austerity measures are starting to test this division of labour.

So far, the discussion has followed religious bodies, but religion is not the preserve of institutions. It is possible to believe without belonging to a church or a temple. William James, in 1902, defined religion as the 'feelings, acts and experiences of individual men in their solitude' in relation to a divine force. This force could be a single God but just as well might do without a God (as in the case of Buddha, who stands in his place), or be trandescendentalist, whereby men and women have a divine spark within them and the power to connect with the mystical truth in nature. What difference has consumer culture made to religious experience?

That agnostics even in Western Europe today remain a minority (c.20 per cent), tells us something about the remarkable flexibility of religious feelings in the face of secular change. In Denmark and Finland as well as Ireland and Italy, over 80 per cent of people still define themselves as Christians, even if they never set foot in a church.[24] Three in four Americans believe in God or some higher power. But belief can mean a lot of things. According to the US General Social Surveys of 1991 and 2006, for example, 70 per cent of Americans see God as a 'healer'. Two thirds viewed God as a 'friend'; the same percentage also believed in the devil. One in two Americans said they 'definitely' believed in miracles.

Baby boomers have been diagnosed as 'spiritual seekers', who, since the 1970s, have mixed their own cocktail of beliefs, blending elements of Eastern religion with Christian traditions and adding a touch of New Age spirituality. A physical therapist living near Boston, when asked by a researcher in 1996 whether she had checked out other religions after experimenting with drugs and Scientology, responded, 'Oh yes . . . I read all the books I could on Buddhism . . . I liked the fact that it encouraged me to . . . look within myself and to find out what was right and true for me. I also like *Star Trek* – is that a religion? I don't know.'[25]

Still, it is debatable how representative this kind of do-it-yourself religion is. A large-scale study of American teenagers carried out between 2001 and 2005 found that most of them were remarkably conventional in their religious lifestyle, following loyally in the mainstream denominational footsteps of their parents; only 4 per cent tried to integrate Zen, Buddhism or Hinduism into their Christian faith, and only 0.3 per cent had joined pagan or Wiccan cults. Hardly anyone went church shopping. At the same time, and notwithstanding spending many a Sunday in a church, most of them had little or no understanding of the Gospel. Some Catholic teenagers believed in reincarnation, while many of their Protestant peers felt they would go to heaven if they did 'the right thing . . . and nothing really bad', in ignorance of the doctrine of justification by faith alone on which Protestantism was founded. American teenagers looked to God as a 'cosmic therapist' on demand, in the words of the researchers.[26] As we have already noted, the idea that people and the world carried a divine spark was already on the rise in the nineteenth century. It is, therefore, a mistake to treat it simply as the result of materialist individualism after the Second World War. Still, advertising and consumer culture arguably did make Christian belief more self-centred and self-serving than before. For most Americans, God is no longer a judge but a healer and a buddy.[27]

From a global perspective, however, Christianity's main momentum is no longer in the North but in the South, driven by the Pentecostalist revival in Africa and Latin America. In 1970, one in seven Christians in Nigeria was a Pentecostalist. By 2010, it was every second. In Brazil, the percentage jumped from 7 per cent to 25 per cent of the Christian population in these years. Some leaders, such as the Nigerian Enoch Adeboye, who heads the Redeemed Christian Church of God (RCCG), were inspired by their charismatic brethren in the United States, such as Kenneth Hagin and his word-faith movement. In general, however, these are locally financed, indigenous success stories, not American imports. What made Pentecostalism so attractive in the 1980s and '90s was that it offered a material as well as a spiritual response to globalization and the challenges and opportunities that came with it. At a time of inflation, unemployment and uncertainty, Pentecostalist churches offered a message of self-help, education and work, promising to liberate believers from dependence on old elites and giving them a chance to forge their own life.

Since the 1970s, Pentecostalists have invoked the 'spirit of poverty' doctrine. Africans, in this view, were poor because they remained under the spell of witchcraft, ancestor worship and indolence. A better life required rebirth and discipline. Pentecostalism held out both. For those under the spell of the 'spirit of poverty', foreign goods were temptations by the devil that dragged them into debt, alcohol and ruin. By contrast, those who had been baptised in the Holy Spirit would learn to accumulate a fortune and enjoy the good life. The power of the word purified consumer goods, keeping the devil at bay.

Anthropologists in Ghana and Zimbabwe have documented the interplay between spiritual and material rebirth. Instead of spending their hard-earned money on expensive customs and on gifts for the extended family, believers were taught how to invest in themselves, their nuclear family and their church. Pentecostalist churches offered literacy classes and advice on managing money. They tapped into a pre-existing culture that looked to individual willpower to overcome poverty. As the state retreated from social support in the neo-liberal 1980s, Pentecostalism filled the gap. The message of self-help and security appealed to the poor in the countryside as well as to the upwardly mobile in urban mega-churches; in Brazil, Pentecostalism initially attracted the poorest of the poor, although it has moved up the social ladder since the 1990s, cashing in on the new opportunities for wealth in a growing economy.[28]

In the seventeenth century, Calvinists would sometimes interpret their financial success as a sign of belonging to 'the elect', even as their sermons continued to warn of excess and its temptations. In the years around 1900, Christian missions in Africa showed a similar ambivalence, as we have seen, on the one hand promoting material comfort alongside the Gospel, on the other bemoaning their new flock's hunger for fashion and little luxuries.[29] In the 1980s, Pentecostalists went a big step further and started to preach openly in favour of material riches. In 1981, when Adeboye took over the RCCG in Nigeria, the Church was poor and did not take offerings at all. Adeboye abandoned the asceticism of earlier Pentecostalists and introduced a new culture of giving for believers and for local churches, which now had to pay tithes to the centre – God, congregations were assured, would repay such investment many times over. In 2005, Adeboye announced that he had been mandated by God to set up a 'Redeemers' Club' for members pledging the equivalent of £50,000. The sum of £5,000 bought a place on a cruise from Miami to the Bahamas on the SS *Wonderland* and an opportunity to hear Adeboye preach. Christ, he said, had died for our prosperity. His suffering provided us with infinite credit. 'God is the God of the rich': He wanted people to prosper and have 'cars, a house, clothes, land, anything money can buy'.[30]

The RCCG's success illustrates the combination of factors at work in the Pentecostalist surge: charismatic preachers, a message of hope and prosperity at a time of economic uncertainty and weak states, and new media and skills. The RCCG maintains nine separate tape ministries, with audiocassette sermons in Yoruba, Igbo and Hausa as well as in English and French; a single sermon sells half a million audiocassettes in Nigeria each month. It also exploits the internet, video and digital technology. Instead of disco, there is 'praise-co' music. The Church has special arrangements for retail outlets with Nestlé Foods and 7UP as well as with local traders. And it has its own university and local business schools.[31]

How does this symbiosis between religion and riches in the Christian revival compare with the relationships forged in other world religions? In the United States, commercialization also left its mark on Jewish life. For Jewish immigrants in the years around 1900, possessions were an important ticket into the new nation and showed that one was no longer a 'greenhorn' (*oysgrinen zich*). Chanukah, like Christmas, did not originally involve gifts, but by the 1890s both were becoming part of a new shopping season; new furniture and bedding was bought during Passover.[32]

The life of the spirit was even more saturated with things in Asian religions, such as Shinto and Buddhism, which do not have a single creator deity and where the divine takes material shape in rocks, trees and also possessions. In Japan, religious rituals are tightly interwoven with the purchase of objects and gifts. Ceramic rabbits and bird statues, as well as practical objects such as cups and rice scoops, are bringers of good fortune (*engimono*). Standing on television sets or in alcoves, these good-luck charms help their owners to connect with deities, ward off evil and ease their return to normal life after an illness. In shamanic rituals in Korea, imported whiskey, toys and foodstuffs serve as 'travel money' to enable the living to make peace with their ancestors' ghosts.[33]

It has been Islam where the encounter between religion and consumer culture has given rise to the most heated debate, both within the Islamic world and in the West. The Iranian Revolution in 1979 at first seemed to herald a new clash of cultures between an Islamic republic and Western materialism. In the West, commentators began to diagnose a battle of 'Jihad *vs* McWorld', with traditional religious groups striking back at global consumer capitalism.[34] In Iran itself, the Ayatollah Khomeini, who had led the revolution, gave his verdict in his final testament in 1989. Western advertising, radio, television and cinemas, he said, had been 'successfully used to intellectually anaesthetize nations, and especially the youth'. For the last half-century, they had worked as 'a propaganda tool against Islam', not only marketing 'luxury items', cosmetics, drinks and clothing but promoting 'a form of life as a prestigious model, so much so that to look like westerners in every aspect of one's daily life became a status symbol'. This consumer-oriented lifestyle corrupted hearts and minds, leading to envy and social conflict, estranging men, women and the young, in particular, from their country, their culture and their religion. And fashion and the taste for expensive products translated into political dependence, because 'cosmetics, entertainment, alcoholic beverages . . . toys and dolls' and other 'modish extravaganzas' were paid for with the export of oil and other resources, leaving Iran a colony of the West.[35]

We tend to think of the 'luxury wars' as a European debate that was over by the nineteenth century, settled in favour of consumption, growth and development. This is too parochial. The Iranian Revolution opened a new front. Like Rousseau two centuries earlier, Khomeini pointed to a causal chain between luxury, status-seeking and envy, social conflict, corruption and dependence. Unlike Rousseau – a profligate spender and lover of women – Khomeini also lived the idea and banished luxury from the new society. Film, books and media were censored. Almost half the cinemas in Iran were shut down or burnt in the immediate aftermath of the revolution. Alcohol was outlawed, and women's hair and bodies disappeared behind headscarves and plain overcoats. In the 1979 revolution, the figure of the 'warrior brother' was matched by that of the 'veiled sister' and her weapon of the *hijab* and black *chador*.[36]

After the head-on assault, however, there was rapprochement. The government accepted that it was impossible to stop Iranians from watching banned films in their own homes; a law against the private use of satellite dishes proved impossible to police. The late 1980s saw a revival of Iranian cinema, and the regime embraced it as a showpiece of Islamic culture. Women returned to take part in sports and appeared again in the stands as spectators. The 1998 World Cup gave proof that football mania had returned to the Republic. Iran beat the United States 2–1 before being itself knocked out of the competition; the winning goal in the eighty-fourth minute was scored by Mehdi Mahdavikia ('the Rocket'), who went on to be Asian Footballer of the Year and to play for Hamburg SV. What has changed since 1979 is that, in general, more leisure happens within the family and friendship groups than in commercial spaces. Still, a lot of consumption continues, even if only as an escape from the morality policy. Iranian women might not be allowed to wear short dresses or colourful clothing, but they can buy branded sunglasses, lipstick and rouge. As a primary-school teacher explained in 2013, 'women don't have enough facilities here and wearing make-up for me and people like me is a kind of fun.' Iran is the second-biggest cosmetics market in the Middle East, after Saudi Arabia, with a thriving trade in counterfeit products from China and Turkey.[37]

The fundamentalist attack on the Western consumer lifestyle has received fresh publicity with the expansion of the Islamic State in Iraq and Syria since 2011. 'It is well known that the material societies today are built up on the ideology of an atheist,' the all-female Al-Khanssaa Brigade stated in its manifesto on women in February 2015. Fashion and cosmetics were the work of Iblis, the devil, who was seeking to take away a woman's clothes, 'wishing to bring her from her Paradise of covering and decency, and encourage her to spend huge amounts of money to change God's creation, demand that surgeons change the nose, ear, chin and nails'. It was only the establishment of the caliphate, an Islamic government, that restored decency and respect for women's bodies, thanks to coverings and the full *hijab* which shielded their face from the eyes of corrupt onlookers.[38]

Yet fundamentalism must not be equated with the Islamic revival, nor with Islam more generally. Most Islamic communities in the Middle East, Arabia and parts of Asia have developed working relationships with consumer culture. In the early 1980s, the Gulf region attracted Liberty, Marks & Spencer and other major Western shops. The following decade saw a boom in shopping malls. The two largest shopping malls in the world are in Dubai – the Dubai Mall, built in 2008, has 1,200 outlets, including Bloomingdale's, cinemas, an ice-rink and an aquarium. But the phenomenon reaches further. Oman got its Muscat City Centre mall, with a Carrefour. Ankara, in Turkey, can boast two dozen malls, even as Islamist politics has grown in strength. Hypermarkets have encroached on traditional souqs. From Saudi Arabia to Turkey, Ramadan in the 1990s and 2000s acquired the aura of a shopping holiday, like Christmas and Chanukah before it. Instead of celebrating at home or helping the poor and needy, the ritual of daily prayers and fasting is increasingly followed by sunset feasts, a trip to the mall or a visit to some night-time entertainment.[39]

The Islamic revival itself has in no small part drawn strength from a strategic alliance with consumer goods. New Islamic products, even fashion, and new media and technologies have played a vital role in the diffusion of Muslim identity and lifestyle. The American Barbie doll, for example, was outlawed as indecent, first in Saudi Arabia in 1994, only to see its place filled by the Fulla doll a few years later, which arrived from Syria in a *hijab*, but also with lipstick and high heels. Fulla also sold prayer sets. The attacks on Pepsi and Coca-Cola did not do away with the sweet soft drink but saw its substitution with Zam Zam Cola in Iran and similar regional brands elsewhere. Muslim children play with videogames that light up with the 'Name of God' when enemy planes are shot down on the screen. For those who prefer old-fashioned games, there is the Quran Challenge Board Game, a 'fun way to learn about the Quran'. There are prayer clocks, prayer dolls and even interactive prayer machines with sensors, digital camera and vibrating motors that track and improve proper body movement.[40] The Islamic revival has been not so much anti-consumerist as about creating a distinctive style of consuming with its own range of products. The halal market – which certifies permissible use under Islamic law – has seen a rapid expansion not only in meat but also in everything from music and film to cosmetics and hotels; in the Middle East and Malaysia, halal cosmetics accounted for 20–25 per cent of sales in 2014.[41]

In the last decade, there have been consumer jihads that boycotted foreign firms such as Nestlé and other brands for sponsoring American imperialism and helping Israel. But, even here, the target was the perceived anti-Islamic conduct of particular companies, not goods and appliances as such. In Turkey in 2008, Muslim shoppers turned against products by Beko, the large Turkish manufacturer of white goods, to protest at the parent company's announcement that it would not hire workers with a moustache or beard, which are customary among Islamists. Fridges, televisions and appliances from other companies were fine.

The single most important consumer item for popularizing Islam has been the audiotape. Cassette sermons are sometimes associated with fanaticism – they were originally used by the Muslim Brotherhood in the 1970s. Since then, however, they have become a much wider fixture of public life, responding to the Quran's particular sensibility for listening: 'God seals the hearts of those who refuse to hear' (Quran 7:100). In turn, they have created new religious spaces and communities. Sermons no longer emanate only from mosques but from loudspeakers in cafés, taxis and at home. The tapes drew a new generation to prayer. The most popular preachers (khutaba), such as Muhammad Hassan, have become media stars, although so far the genre has escaped the fate of a standardized culture industry and continues to circulate in tapes produced by small firms and under the oversight of the Council on Islamic Research. As a type of media, these tapes illustrate the capacity of religion to exploit entertainment technologies rather than surrendering to them. This has not been a one-way street, though. With new technologies came new genres of speech, and preachers started to sound a little bit like stars of television and the silver screen.[42]

The veil, too, has undergone a fashionable makeover in the last couple of decades. The metamorphosis has been especially pronounced in Turkey, where unveiling had been an integral part of building a modern, secular state after Mustafa Kemal Atatürk, in 1923, proclaimed the republic and abolished the Ottoman caliphate. While veils were not formally outlawed, their use was heavily stigmatized. Beginning in the late 1970s, the veil started to make a sudden comeback – and in cities and among young professional, educated women; not only in rural villages. For many, putting on a veil was a way of regaining security and respect at a time of deep political and economic turmoil; Turkey went through a major debt crisis, followed by a military takeover in 1980, hyper-inflation and, finally, under the auspices of the International Monetary Fund, threw open its market. Islamic faith, dress and all-female clubs offered stability and community. Like Pentecostalism in

Africa and Latin America, then, the revival of Islam was at least in part a reaction against liberalization and the uncertainties that came with it.

In the early 1980s, the *tesettür* style of covering, an outfit character-ized by a large scarf that covered head and shoulders and a long, dark, shapeless overcoat that covered everything else but the hands, spread rapidly; the large scarf also set it apart from the smaller ones worn in the countryside. It was now that the Turkish government banned veils from schools and public buildings. Instead of retreating, however, the veil found fresh commercial support. The career of the *tesettür* since is testimony to the ability of fashion and Islamic lifestyle to work together. Once modest and plain, the scarf and accompanying overcoat have gained a splash of colour and a stylish cut. In 1992, Tekbir, a large Islamic clothing company, sponsored the first *tesettür* fashion show in Turkey. Tekbir's mission was to attract women to the veil by making 'covering beautiful'. Headscarves became smaller. Overcoats were trimmed or altogether replaced by tighter, body-hugging jackets and pants. Inevitably, there has been tension between piety and fashion. Luxury scarves with French and Italian designer labels are not liked everywhere. To some housewives and Quran instructors in poorer neighbourhoods in Istanbul, they display a self-indulgence not befitting a 'true' Muslim woman, who is meant to be moderate and altruistic. A growing number of wealthy and professional women are donning a veil in Turkey and elsewhere. Veiled middle-class women who have several dozen stylish outfits in their wardrobe relax in beach-side resorts, play tennis during the day and go dancing in the all-female disco at night.[43]

In Indonesia, the country with the largest Muslim majority, univer-sity students today go to Quran study sessions and talk about their fashionable headscarves. Veils are decorated with carefully chosen accessories. *NOOR*, an Islamic women's magazine, advertises 'girly accent' floral sunglasses, and fashionable models in the 'Shadow of Preppy' alongside exhortations of 'worship to Allah'; it also gives the latest tips on interior design. A thirty-five-year-old Indonesian woman who bought up to seven headscarves a week explained to an anthro-pologist in 2008 why she was so irritated by teenagers who wore oversized headscarves (*jilbabs*): they made Islam look 'rigid, unfash-ionable, whereas in fact our God likes beauty'.[44]

Piety and style, then, were not automatically enemies. They could be friends. Here was an argument for spiritual beauty that was not so dif-ferent from the Christian defence of material possessions that we encountered earlier: if God's beauty manifested itself in the material world, it was only natural for his followers to want to express their piety by surrounding themselves with beautiful things.

Contrary to the idea – still popular in the West – that modernity must lead to secularization, religion has proved remarkably vibrant and innovative. Consumer culture has been one source of that innovation, clearly discernible in recent revivals but already visible in earlier centuries. Mainstream religious institutions have suffered, especially in Christendom, but religious experience is alive and well today. Products, entertainment, taste and fashion have played a vital role in communicating and, indeed, asserting religious faith and identity. The religious revivals since the 1970s have, similarly, demonstrated the remarkable ability of consumer culture to adapt itself to new realities and work with a range of communities of faith. As with secular ideologies, so with world religions: consumption has proved an extremely flexible partner. The belief that the world of the spirit is 'higher' than the 'base' world of things and that the true believer should aspire to the former and resist the temptations of the latter is long-standing. Yet, in the real world, religious life does not exist in a purely spiritual form. It is saturated with things. Affluence, and development more generally, are not only a challenge for religion but also an opportunity.

15

Throwaway Society?

In the world's oceans today, some 18,000 pieces of plastic are swimming on the surface of every square kilometre of water.[1] On International Coastal Clean-up day in 2011, 600,000 volunteers scoured 20,000 miles of coastline for rubbish. By the end of the day, they had collected almost 10 million pounds in weight. Their haul included 250,000 items of clothing, a million pieces of food packaging and several hundred TV sets, mobile phones and bicycles. That year, the United States alone produced 210 million tons of municipal waste – enough to fill a convoy of garbage trucks and circle the equator nine times. Just the food thrown out by British households each year could fill almost 5,000 Olympic pools.[2]

We appear to be drowning in waste. The thesis of the 'throwaway society' was the natural twin of the 'affluent society'. Americans had barely had time to sit down in front of their new television sets and grab a cold drink from the fridge when Vance Packard, in 1960, launched his attack on *The Waste Makers*. The United States, Packard warned, in what became a bestseller, had developed into a 'hyper-thyroid economy', where ever greater artificial stimuli created ever greater wastefulness. A disposable lifestyle was taking over, defined by plastic, one-way bottles, tins and convenience meals. Cars were no longer prized for their working engine but for their fashionable looks, dumped for a new one the minute styles changed. Packard did not have a problem with change as such, as long as it was related to functional improvements. His target was planned obsolescence dictated by fashion and the pursuit of change for change's sake.

Packard touched a nerve. Things no longer seemed to last as long as they used to. They were made to break. Today, concern about waste is mainly about environmental pollution. Then, it was about national decline and moral decay. The United States, Packard worried, was turning from a 'have' into a 'have-not' nation, wasting its precious oil and copper and risking dependence on foreigners. There were neo-Malthusian undertones: together with a growing population, the reckless love of novelty was pushing the United States beyond its natural limits. The shift from frugality, quality and durability to a 'wasteful, imprudent and care-free' lifestyle was corroding the 'American character'. The young were becoming 'soft' and decadent, lacking the discipline of their fathers. And the cult of consumer goods tended to 'disenfranchise' the housewife, tak-ing away her skill and identity. Instead of mending shirts and darning socks, she took a job to buy more goods, leaving the family in a 'morass'.[3]

As these remarks indicate, waste, like consumption, is a deeply mor-alistic subject. The narrative of waste has tended to follow that of consumer culture, with the twentieth century progressing inexorably towards ever greater wastefulness. Waste mountains appear as a phys-ical reminder both of our addiction to more and our careless disregard for objects and the resources that go into creating them. Writing in 1999, the American historian Susan Strasser noted how, for her fellow citizens, 'discarding things is taken to be a kind of freedom'. They had lost the 'stewardship of objects' of their nineteenth-century forebears. A culture of re-use – where broken earthenware was mended by boiling it in milk and materials were recycled – was displaced by a culture of disposal. For Strasser, the loss of caring for things reflected a switch in the United States from being a nation of producers to one of consum-ers. Repairing and recycling, she writes, came 'more easily to people who make things'.[4]

The rise of the 'throwaway society' has defined the way we think about waste. How much of it is true, though? In attempting to answer this question, our focus will largely have to be on affluent societies, not on waste and scavenging in poorer ones, because we are interested in whether societies when they get richer become more careless and waste-ful. There are three dimensions to this question which call for particular attention and shape the main lines of inquiry of the pages to come. The first is a classic problem of history and concerns the nature and direc-tion of change over time. The throwaway thesis presumes not only a parallel rise between consuming and wasting. It sees history as a suc-cession of stages, where, in the course of the twentieth century, one social order ('traditional', re-using) gave way to another ('modern', throwing away). The second issue is about comparison. As the original protagonist, the United States naturally features in the historical van-guard of the throwaway society. Just as other societies have charted their own paths to consumer culture, however, it is worth pondering whether all affluent societies necessarily end up with the same waste heap.

Finally, there is the problem of how we track wastefulness across time and space. This is, perhaps, the most intriguing issue. In part, it is about what we count. Developed societies at the beginning of the twenty-first century are much richer than a century ago. Many more objects enter households today, so we would expect households to throw out more than their poorer ancestors; low-income societies today produce less waste than high-income ones. What is more interesting is whether they are also *relatively* more wasteful. To know this, we cannot treat throwing away in isolation but must see it as just one way of getting rid of stuff among others, including gifting and giving things to charity shops or storing them in the garage. It also matters where we look for waste. The throwaway thesis takes the private consumer as the unit of analysis. But materials and objects have a long journey behind them before they cross the threshold of the home. These stages can be more or less wasteful and may have little or nothing to do with the relative thrift or prodigality of Mr and Mrs Consumer. To know how wasteful modern societies are, we should also ask about the materials and energy that go into the buildings, cities and infrastructures that enable our high levels of consumption in the first place. After looking at household waste, therefore, we need to look at discarding and material flows more generally.

THE MAKING OF WASTE

Let us start by lifting the lid on the garbage can. With its dense population and shortage of vacant land, New York City kept a close eye on the changing composition of refuse from the early twentieth century onwards. Residents had to segregate it into three categories for separate collection: ash, 'garbage' (mainly food waste) and all other 'rubbish'. Thanks to the engineer Daniel Walsh, who has mined the samples recorded by the city, we have a snapshot of change between 1905 and 1989.[5] The most dramatic change affected ash, which declined as coal gave way to oil and natural gas for heating and cooking. At the start of the century, waste was mainly ash. From the mid-century, a new kind of 'affluent waste' emerges: ash free but heavy in paper and, from the

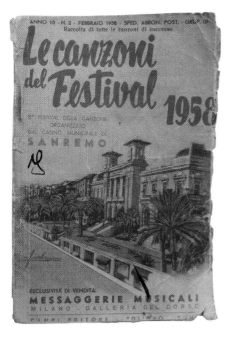

44. *top left* 1958 brochure of the eighth Italian song festival at Sanremo.

45. *top right* Domenico Modugno taking off with the winning song 'Nel blu dipinto di blu' (Volare), inspired by two Chagall paintings, at Sanremo, 1958.

46. *middle* Rural nostalgia: a 1997 stamp celebrating Finnish Tango.

47. *below* Commercial reality: the annual festival of Finnish Tango, 2013.

48. *top left* Shanghai modern: a calendar with a Scandinavian beer advertisement, 1938.

49. *top right* South Delhi market, India, 2010.

50. *middle* Pachinko gambling parlour, Tokyo, 2014.

51. *below* China Consumer Association playing cards, 2006, alerting consumers to watch for misleading claims about products, with the famous Monkey King, from the classic *Journey to the West*, smashing fake and poor quality goods.

52. *top* Before the credit card: an embossed metal 'charga-plate' for the department store Thalhimers in Richmond, Virginia, c. 1938.

53. *middle right* Benjamin Franklin thrift bank, United States, 1931.

54. *middle left* Save – and appliances and a trip to Paris will follow, according to this Finnish savings poster from the early 1950s.

55. *bottom right* A Japanese housewife proudly shows her savings book, in a poster celebrating eighty years of postal saving and financial planning, 1955.

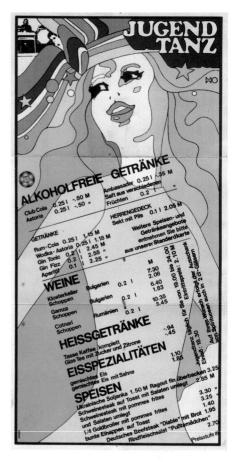

56. *top left* Mugshot of the violent Scuttlers in Manchester, 1894, with their trade-mark neckerchiefs and 'donkey-fringe' hairstyle, cut short in the back and with angled fringe in the front.

57. *top right* Poster for a youth dance in socialist East Germany, 1973, with rum-cola, grilled chicken and chips and Ukrainian solyanka.

58. *below* Latino Zoot Suiters on their way to LA County Jail, 1943.

59. *top* Fit and active in old age: morning fitness in Sun City, the retirement community in Arizona.

60. *left* Shanghai, People's Park, 2006.

61. *right* Sun City aerial view, *c.* 1970.

62. *top* The 110-foot 'municipal plunge', the South Pasadena City Pool, built in 1939 with a grant from the Public Works Administration.

63. *bottom* Fast food: 19 cent Hamburger outlet, 1952, Culver City, LA. Open 11 a.m.– 1 a.m. every day, and Friday to Saturday until 2.30 a.m.

64. *top left* Electric Edison baseball team, California, 1904.

65. *top right* Edison Girls' basketball team, California, 1932.

66. *middle* The shoe-manufacturer Bata's 1947 football competition between French and English company teams, with the winning team from Vernon, France.

67. *below* Housing, leisure, library and social services at Henkel, the German laundry detergent producer, 1937.

Werksbücherei

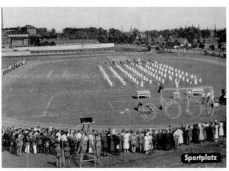

Sportplatz

Werkshäuser

Kinderfürsorge

68. *top left* Chiffonier (rag picker) and his donkey, Lozére, France, *c.*1900.

69. *top right* Boys picking garbage on 'the Dumps', Boston, 1909.

70. *middle left* Manhattan self-storage advertisement, 2012.

71. *middle right* E-scrapping of old computers, Guiyu, Guangdong province, China, 2005.

72. *bottom left* Robert Rauschenberg, *Monogram*, 1955–9.

Kilograms of residential waste discarded per capita/annually in New York City in the 20th century: total and by fraction

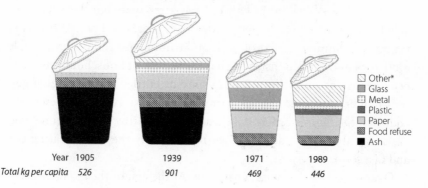

	Other*
	Glass
	Metal
	Plastic
	Paper
	Food refuse
	Ash

Year	1905	1939	1971	1989
Total kg per capita	526	901	469	446

*'Other' includes: textiles, hazardous, rubber, leather, wood, garden refuse, miscellaneous.
Source: Adapted from D. C. Walsh 'Urban Residential Refuse Composition and Generation Rates for the Twentieth Century', in *Environmental Science & Technology* 36, no. 22 (2002): 4936-42.

1960s, with rising amounts of plastic. New Yorkers were now throwing away less glass and metal – a combined result of the plastic bottle, the aluminium can and 'lightweighting', which made it possible to produce thinner glass bottles and metal tins. The results become more startling once ash is taken out of the equation. Food refuse made up the same share in 1905 as it did in 1989. In 1939, bins contained more paper than fifty years later. Stunningly, New Yorkers threw out more ash-free waste in 1939 than at any time since – 500kg per person, compared to roughly 440kg a year since the 1980s. Equally remarkable, it was the era of affluence (the 1950s–'60s) which saw residential waste plummet to its lowest point in the twentieth century: around 360kg per person.

The example of New York City is a reminder of the long trail of waste, especially paper. At the same time, it illustrates how difficult it is to translate such historic data into conclusions about how wasteful we are. Most old samples measured weight, but this gives only part of the picture. One reason less waste ended up in New York bins in the 1960s was that it was now being diverted and burnt in residential incinerators; Walsh estimates that around 25 per cent went up in flames. This still leaves waste in the 1960s lighter than in the 1930s. If we asked about volume and material substance instead, we would arrive at a different picture. The decline of ash and the rise in packaging shifted the challenge of waste from weight to volume, and this makes comparison across time treacherous. Plastics and other new materials also have longer life spans and have introduced previously unknown forms of environmental pollution. Nor do we know precisely what was thrown away. Food waste fell in the half-century after 1939, but this was probably because the rise of frozen foods, ready meals and peeled fruit and vegetables eliminated a lot of peels and trimmings. Today, more edible food goes into the bin instead. That the weight of household waste has been persistent since the 1980s, in spite of bottles and packaging getting lighter, suggests people throw more items away, not fewer. In addition, the figures report only what people throw away at home and are silent about the additional waste caused by the rise in eating out and fast food.

Overall, we are left with a paradox. At the end of the twentieth century, New Yorkers were eight times richer than at the beginning, but their rubbish weighed slightly less. At the same time, they were throwing out many more bottles, containers and meals. From the point of view of material mass, they were less wasteful; from that of human behaviour, more so.

We have so far used the term 'waste' freely, as if it is self-explanatory, but it was only in the late nineteenth century that it acquired its modern meaning, referring to the disposal of unwanted stuff. In Old English, 'waste', from the Latin *vastus*, referred to wild or empty land. It could imply squandering, as in the biblical parable of the young man who left his home to 'waste his substance on riotous living' (Luke 15). Around 1800, Europeans used 'waste', *Abfall* and *déchet* to capture the loss of a substance in the course of production, such as the woodchips on an artisan's floor or the chaff in threshing. There was a synergy between such physical and metaphysical associations, but they were not about garbage. Under *Abfall*, in their German dictionary (1852), the Brothers Grimm follow the example of the leaf 'falling off' the tree with that of the angel falling away from God.[6] Humans had long thrown away bones, food and objects that were no longer wanted; the first landfills in Knossos date back to 3000 BCE, and we know from archaeologists that Mayans in Belize in 900 CE threw away perfectly good items.[7] But it was only in the late nineteenth century, once these material remnants were put in dedicated bins and separated from human faeces and urine, and cities took over collection from rag pickers, that they acquired a distinct identity as 'waste'. 'Municipal solid waste' (MSW) was born, separated from human liquid waste.

MSW is a tricky category, since it records what cities pick up rather than what households dispose of. To this day, it includes rubbish from schools, parks, some shops and firms, and farms to various degrees. In Copenhagen, for example, household waste makes up only 30 per cent of MSW; in the United States it is 60 per cent, in Britain 89 per cent. How waste is defined matters hugely. Japan, which follows a different nomenclature, treats paper, glass and other refuse as valuable resources. It does not include them in its official waste figures, which, consequently, look minuscule. In an ideal world, we would want to capture everything that a consumer throws out, from the paper at home to the Styrofoam cup at work and the left-over food on the plate in a restaurant. Sadly, in the real world, data is organized by who does the collecting, not by who generates waste. Where possible I have tried to give separate figures for household waste, but in the following pages it is important to bear this caveat in mind.

There are probably few concepts in modern times that have attracted a greater variety of interpretations than waste. For many writers and artists, it has encapsulated the human condition. Sigmund Freud imagined the psyche as a constant system that created waste as it generated excitement – a notion he borrowed from thermodynamics and its recognition that all work involved the waste of energy through heat loss.[8] More recent writers have defined waste as a way of 'holding things in a state of absence'.[9] Many invoke the anthropologist Mary Douglas, who famously defined dirt as 'matter out of place', a byproduct of categorizing something as clean in the first place.[10] There is a vast gulf between these approaches and the pages of waste-management journals, where engineers analyse material density, incinerators and recycling mechanisms. Readers of the former rarely bother with the latter, and vice versa. This is a shame because, to understand the evolution of waste, we need both. Waste is relative, a matter of culture and shifting meanings. But it is also physical matter, shaped by products and practices, infrastructures and technologies of collection and disposal. In fact, it was engineers who already in the years around 1900 argued that garbage was not 'worthless waste but matter in the wrong place', in the words of Hans Thiesing, a scientific member of the Royal Testing Station for water supply and waste-water removal in Berlin, the oldest institute for environmental health in Europe.[11] Domestic refuse, Thiesing stressed, included food waste that, once separated, made excellent fertilizer. Waste is not something that humans have always repressed or tried to hide, as some writers like to imagine, nor is it naturally the opposite of value.

Since the mid-nineteenth century waste has undergone a series of remarkable metamorphoses that changed its value and the places, people and practices connected with its disposal and recovery. We can loosely distinguish three transitions: from dustyards (where 'dust' or coal ash was collected) and rag pickers to municipal control in the pursuit of cleanliness and public health in the late nineteenth century; the rise of 'burn or bury' engineering solutions in the early and mid-twentieth century which treated rubbish as cost; and its resurrection as a valuable material since the 1970s, with citizen-consumers doing the recycling. None of these transitions was smooth or perfect. Let us have a closer look at how they played out in different settings.

Dustyards and rag-and-bone men were central actors in the systems of re-use and recycling that pervaded Western cities in the nineteenth century. Rags, bones and other secondary materials were important industrial inputs at a time when raw materials were scarce and technological substitution limited – rags were turned into paper and wallpaper, bones into glue. As late as 1884, there were around 40,000 rag pickers (*chiffoniers*) in Paris; across France, recycling is estimated to have employed half a million people, most of them women and children. By the mid-century, a dual system was emerging in many European cities, with licensed collectors picking up rubbish in the morning and informal gatherers operating at night. In early-nineteenth-century London, dustyards took recycling to a new level, recovering 'soil' (coal ash), 'breeze' (bits of coal) and cinders. Dust made good fertilizer but, as London grew, it was even more valuable for making bricks. By the 1840s, the dustyards' days were numbered, as cheap 'Oxford clay' and new forms of brickmaking took over.[12]

Recycling created a virtuous link between consumers, industry and agriculture. It would be wrong, though, to imagine it as a closed loop or a self-sufficient local metabolism in which material energy keeps circulating through the same veins. Materials were re-used, but not necessarily by the same community that threw them out. Local economies got injections from far-away places. A good deal of Londoners' dust ended up in the bricks used to rebuild Moscow after the 1812 fire. Shirts and jackets discarded by their Parisian owners were worn across Europe, North Africa and Latin America; in 1867, over 800 tons of old clothes were exported from France.[13] The rag trade was a global business. Britain, the United States and Germany each sucked in tens of thousands tons of rags.[14] With the Lancashire cotton industry in full swing, British rags, not surprisingly, were especially rich in cotton (50 per cent), not a plant that grew on British soil fertilized by British sewage. The growing portions of Danish butter and American beef consumed by Londoners equally contained a lot of embedded energy and water that never found its way back into their original eco-systems. In brief, local recycling fed off the international extraction and permanent transfer of materials.

In the light of today's concerns about landfill sites and pollution, it is tempting to extol a Victorian mentality of thrift and recycling. However, all this recycling probably says more about infrastructures than minds or habits. Rag pickers and second-hand dealers existed because people were buying new, increasingly cheap and mass-manufactured clothes and getting rid of old items rather than recycling them into napkins or curtains, as the Pepys family still did in the 1660s. In 1830s America, families had no problem with throwing out an eight-place porcelain table setting that was barely damaged.[15] Things were recovered only where systems of recovery were in place. Without them, consumers picked their own methods of disposal. In 1893 Boston, the sanitary committee observed how many residents burnt their refuse 'while others wrap it up in paper and carry it on their way to work and drop it when unobserved, or throw it into vacant lots or into the river'.[16] Whether burnt or set adrift, it would have contained paper and food waste that could have been re-used or composted. The Mississippi and Hudson were, similarly, treated as dumping grounds. Households in British cities were notorious for profligately throwing away partly burnt coal.

The waste bin announced the coming of a new era. On 24 November 1883, the prefect of the Seine, Eugène Poubelle, ordered all Parisians to put their refuse in a bin and place it outside for collection, between 6.30 and 8.30 in the morning during summertime, and between 8 and 9 a.m. in the winter; neither shards of glass or pottery nor oyster shells were allowed. Poubelle won the honour of giving his name to the French dustbin (*la poubelle*), but not without a fight. What right did the city have to take over waste collection? Was rubbish not the property of the householder? And what about the *chiffoniers*, how were they to earn a living? A year later, a compromise was reached. Residents were allowed to put out their rubbish from nine o'clock in the evening and no longer had to separate oyster shells. The *chiffoniers* were granted permission to sort through the rubbish before the next morning, as long as they did so on top of a large blanket to contain the mess.[17]

Across the West, the dustbin symbolized the ideal of the sanitary city and of clean, democratic living. Its early years were plagued with problems – bins were of different materials and sizes, sometimes without lids. In Hamburg, they originally belonged to households, which caused endless headaches, since they were often thrown away together with the trash; the city introduced municipal bins only in 1926. Still, within a generation, the bin revolutionized waste. It simultaneously made it more convenient for residents to throw away more and marginalized rag pickers and existing channels of recycling; as bins got bigger, so did the amount of waste.[18]

The municipal takeover was paved with good intentions. Refuse and manure in streets were major health hazards, killing thousands of children through diarrhoea and infecting others, not least the rag pickers themselves. Clean streets would improve public health and raise civic spirit. The approach was not necessarily based on new scientific knowledge of germs. George Waring, the sanitation commissioner whose broom swept garbage off the streets of New York City, believed to his death in 1898 that disease was caused by miasma. The attack was three-pronged, combining sanitary reform and civic action with modern technologies to extract value from waste. For the progressive 'colonel' – Waring had served in the bright red Garibaldi Guards during the Civil War – waste producers were also citizens. They had to do their bit to create a clean, civilized community. Children, women's groups and civic associations were mobilized to help the official 'White Wings'. For Waring, civic awareness extended to disposal at home. Residents had to separate garbage (food waste) and rubbish (rags, paper, metal, glass) from ash; fifty officers went from door to door to instruct them. Individual sorting was crowned with a municipal sorting and 'reduction' plant on Barren Island, the first of its kind; its conveyor belt was fired by burning garbage. Rags were sold on to paper mills; grease and ammonia to soap makers and chemical industries. Ash was used to increase the size of Rikers Island.[19]

Waring's war on waste soon hit an insuperable enemy: cost. The reduction plant was shut down for lack of funds. Complaints from residents about the smell did not help. The First World War was not over before the city was again dumping its refuse into the ocean.

The case of New York City was emblematic of the dialectic of urban waste at the time. Cities simultaneously caused growing volumes of waste and pioneered new solutions, such as the reduction plant and incinerators; by 1914, Budapest, Amsterdam and London all had their own sorting plants. The new standards of cleanliness made society less tolerant of waste and, at the same time, made it produce more, with wrappers and packaging to keep products clean and new disposable products such as Kleenex, which arrived in 1924. Above all, collecting bins from every household was hugely expensive, adding a major item to city budgets and taxes. Rising wages added to the bill. The earnings from Waring's recycling plant had been barely enough to pay the women sifting through the rubbish there. Waste started losing some of its value, partly because its composition was changing as urban residents bought more prepared foods with fewer scraps, partly because industries found new substitutes for previously precious waste byproducts. In the fields, Fritz Haber's process converted atmospheric nitrogen into ammonia. Fertilizer was plucked from the air instead of the toilet. In paper making, wood pulp (processed with sulphites) eliminated the dependence on rags; the first chemical pulping mill opened in 1890, in Sweden. The earlier regime of recycling, in which waste from households flowed back to farms and industry, unravelled at both ends.

Waring's philosophy relied on the collaboration of citizens, but residents proved less conscientious than rag pickers about separating materials. Physical analyses of rubbish revealed how much valuable material now ended up in the bin. In Washington DC in 1914, 10 per cent of household rubbish was tinware; another 10 per cent bottles. In New York, at the slip station on 13th Street, almost half consisted of marketable objects; a third was paper.[20] All of this made recycling increasingly challenging and unattractive to cities. Food waste was notoriously heavy. It was much easier to instruct residents to burn it on their coal fire, as many American and European cities did in the early twentieth century. That way, municipal collectors had a lighter load. Homes became little incinerators; tellingly, in winter, the amount of food waste in bins dropped to a fraction of that in summertime.[21] In 1903, Charlottenburg, then still its own city west of Berlin, was one of the first emulators of New York City's sorting model. Households had a special garbage cabinet with three parts – kitchen waste went into the top-right half, ash and dust in the drawer below, and other bulky rubbish into the left side. The food waste was then cleaned, boiled and strained before being served to pigs. It was an expensive operation, because the kitchen waste rarely arrived pure, and dangerous items had to be picked out manually. Swine fever was the final nail in the coffin. In 1917, after less than a decade, the swill enterprise was dead.[22]

Municipal waste management, then, had many unintended consequences. What had started as a crusade for public health and civic renewal ended up in the hands of engineers who focused on finding the best and cheapest technologies for getting rid of waste by either burying or burning it. In Britain, the first 'destructor' opened in Leeds in 1874. On the eve of the First World War, there were five hundred incinerators across Britain. The first 'sanitary landfills' appeared in the 1920s; America's first opened in Fresno in 1934.[23] By the 1960s, 'controlled tipping' took care of around 90 per cent of household waste in Britain and the United States. In France and Germany, it was around 70 per cent with another 20 per cent going up in flames in incinerators. The changing composition of waste – with its higher calorific value – and the sheer difficulty of handling the growing volume led to a new appreciation of waste as primary energy, with waste-to-energy plants mushrooming in European cities in the 1960s. None of these technological solutions guaranteed perfect elimination. Fly-tipping was a common sight. Cleanliness provided no immunity against the growing wave of packaging, plastic and other consumer waste. In 1972, German chambers of commerce guessed that one in thirteen unwanted cars was dumped in the woods or abandoned on a quiet road; in Saarbrücken, it was one in four.[24]

It is important to stress how haphazard and uneven the adoption of these new strategies of waste disposal has been. Different cities confronted quite different challenges. Partly, this reflected standards of living and degrees of commercialization. New Yorkers in 1900 threw away three to four times as much as Londoners, Parisians and Berliners. But even among cities with fairly similar conditions, there were astonishing differences. In Vienna, glass made up 22 per cent of household waste in one district; in nearby Prague it was only 3 per cent.[25] Composting did not suddenly disappear – or at least not everywhere. In the 1930s, the Netherlands installed a plant that by the early 1950s turned 163,000 tons of domestic refuse from The Hague and Groningen into agricultural compost a year; locomotives carried the waste to Wyster, where it was dumped six foot deep into composting cells, regularly sprinkled with water and then left to decompose for six months, before a grab crane pulled it out, leaving tins and bottles behind.[26] Even in New York City, over 600 tons of swill a day were still collected for pigs in the early 1950s – not as much kitchen waste as what was burnt in incinerators but still a fairly impressive 16 per cent. It was only after the outbreak of a national swine virus and the discovery that uncooked meats were the source of parasites that could be transmitted to humans that this kind of recycling went rapidly out of fashion.[27] In 1955 Hamburg, with the post-war boom in full swing, there were

185 *Altwarenläden*, shops buying and selling old goods. 'Old iron' traders and rag-and-bone men could still be seen in European cities in the 1960s and 1970s. In much of rural Europe, the municipal waste revolution had yet to arrive; communal waste collection did not reach one in three Bavarians at this time.[28]

Outside the West, the notion of a simple progression from a traditional to a modern waste regime is even less helpful. Colonialism did export the municipal approach. In Tel Aviv, in the 1920s, for example, British authorities rolled out the foot-pedal dustbin, fined locals for throwing garbage into their yards and ran education campaigns. Here, as in London and Liverpool, the municipal conquest of waste was inspired by ideals of public health and cleanliness, but it was reshaped by colonial ideology. It was a top-down effort, not a shared project for active citizens, as it had been for progressives like Waring. The dominant language was one of command and punishment, since, after all, the natives were not ready to clean their own villages, let alone run them. Colonial authorities rarely had the inclination or money for a comprehensive separation of human from solid waste. Thus Tel Aviv got compulsory European toilets in the 1930s but no sewage system to carry the excrement away. Municipal services tended to favour the districts of the colonial rulers, reinforcing their identity as clean and civilized masters reigning over dirty and barbarian subjects.[29]

In Shanghai, the epitome of modernity in the East, recycling, bins, landfill and incineration all complemented each other. In 1905, the Municipal Council ruled that from then on all refuse had to be placed in designated receptacles for collection; the galvanized iron bins could be obtained from the Convict Labour Department at the city jail. The containers were to be taken directly by Chinese barrows to garbage chutes on the creeks. From there, the waste would be shipped to nearby farms or the depot. All this was easier said than done. At the end of the year, the Council reported 'much difficulty . . . in changing the old habits of native residents of indiscriminately throwing all refuse out of the door'. Over 1,000 offenders were prosecuted. For every single one fined, several new migrants arrived with their own ways of dealing with refuse. Boat coolies continued to dump refuse into the Soochow Creek. Plague prevention – Shanghai was hit by cholera in 1907 – saw the introduction of a standard concrete house-refuse container with an 'efficient and satisfactory lock', devised by the 'ingenuity of Inspectors', to prevent rag pickers from going through the rubbish and strewing it about the alleyways. But these concrete receptacles were more suitable for large foreign buildings than for Chinese houses, which lacked the watchmen to supervise their appropriate use. By 1924, there were still an estimated 2,000 rag pickers in the streets every morning. For the council, public health and recycling continued to go hand in hand: 'the return of all refuse to the soil is the ideal to be strived for.' Some 40 per cent of house refuse was sold to farmers in the 1920s. At the same time, residents were urged to burn 'all combustible refuse, such as vegetable matter, paper, straw, etc'. Landfill and incineration were supplementary technologies. After two years in landfill, the refuse was considered pure enough to raise low-lying land. Waste regimes were seasonal. Farmers were interested in waste in spring and summer. Come September, they took very little. It was in autumn that the 'destructor' sprung into action. Millions of tons of human excrement were barged to the countryside as fertilizer as late as the 1980s.[30]

The municipal revolution is a well-known chapter in urban history, but it was only part of the story. A second, equally important revolution was under way at the same time. In the early twentieth century, waste became a veritable keyword of social, moral and economic reform. There were campaigns for social, industrial and national efficiency.[31] All were animated by a similar diagnosis: unnecessary waste was causing unemployment, inequality and national decline. In November 1920, Herbert Hoover was appointed president of the newly founded Federation of American Engineering Societies. One of his first acts was to launch an ambitious inquiry into waste in industry. Waste, the commission reported, was not an individual failing but systemic – the result of boom and bust, speculation, high labour turnover and inefficiency. Half of it was the fault of business owners and managers; a mere 20 per cent the fault of labour. But the consumer was also to blame. 'In certain industries,' the commission concluded, 'the consuming public is to a degree responsible for seasonal fluctuations because of the eagerness with which it accepts or adopts changes in style.' The clothing industry attracted particular ire with its ever faster changes of fashion – a customer was able to choose between 1,100 varieties of cloth. Style should be constrained by the 'standpoint of usefulness and economy'.[32] For Hoover and like-minded champions of productivity, the future lay with standardization. Car makers such as Henry Ford and home builders were leading the way.

Critics of the throwaway society tend to view industry as the culprit, but it is important to recognize that industry, in addition to creating more products and more waste, also provided some of the answers by re-using materials in new ways. The gradual (if never complete) retreat of rag-and-bone men and recycling consumers was accompanied by industry taking over the role of scavenging. From the point of view of the materials, what changed was who did the collecting. Data does not allow us to say whether industrial recycling was more or less prodigal than private efforts. What available figures do suggest is that a lot of secondary materials found their way back into the cycle of production in the era normally associated with heedless waste. In 1951 America, electric light bulbs were 60 per cent broken glass. Up to 50 per cent of cullet (broken glass) was recovered overall. Disposable nappies used cotton waste. Four thousand firms sourced fats, grease and blood from meat waste to make cosmetics, gloves and guitar strings. A decade later, 2,000 firms were busy reconditioning carburetors and clutches, and Chrysler offered a warranty on rebuilt parts. Department stores had their own salvage paper bales. The Bell System, the telephone giant, scooped up old telephones and cables and ran its own smelting and refining works to get at the copper needed for wires; it recovered 20 per cent of the 2 million tons of copper consumed in the USA.[33] Waste-material dealers filled the space vacated by the rag-and-bone man and sourced non-ferrous scrap metals for industry. Forty-five per cent of US steel was made from secondary materials. By 1970, the paper industry still took 20 per cent of its raw material from recovered waste, down from 35 per cent at the end of the Second World War – not, perhaps, enough to save the planet but still significant enough to save a forest of 200 million trees; in Britain at the time, it was 42 per cent. Even plastic – the synthetic material that more than any other symbolized the throwaway culture – did not all end up in landfill in the 1960s. Some 10 per cent was recovered, finding its way back into toys and the heels of shoes. In the United States, corporations made $8 billion from recycling, according to a contemporary expert.[34]

The dilemma of the post-war boom was that such efforts were out-paced by an avalanche of consumer waste and a simultaneous drop in the price of virgin materials. Put bluntly, it had never been so cheap to buy new, nor so convenient to dispose of materials. As packaging and self-service spread, the concomitant rise in rubbish was stunning. In 1950 West Germany, peas, lentils and rice were mostly still sold loose. By the end of the decade, they all came pre-packaged. In the 1960s, household waste shot up from 200kg to 300kg a person a year, but, most worryingly, its volume doubled. In Berlin and Paris, half the rubbish was now packaging, mostly paper and cardboard; plastic still made up only 3 per cent of waste in 1971.[35] In Canada, beer continued to be served in returnable bottles but, elsewhere, a new culture of convenience took over. Across the border, only eight out of every hundred containers were still returnable in 1966. People stopped returning bottles, and the drinks industry abandoned deposits. In New York City, the typical bottle now made only two trips to and from the store before it ended up as solid waste. In West Germany, the number of one-way bottles doubled in the course of the 1970s to reach 3 billion.[36]

Disposable products polarized opinion. There were those who, in the 1960s, started to put the throwaway society on trial. In his sculpture *Poubelle de Jim Dine* (1961), Arman Feer exhibited a Plexiglass cylinder filled with the empty cigarette packs, cosmetic bottles and other packaging discarded by his Pop-artist friend. Conceptual artists set out to dematerialize art by placing concept over object. 'The world is full of objects, more or less interesting,' the American Douglas Huebner famously said in 1969. 'I do not wish to add any more.' Artists who piled up disbanded TV screens and car wrecks or who shredded their private possessions in front of museum audiences have been part of the art world ever since.

Yet for every counter-cultural critic there were others who took a more cheerful attitude to waste or who openly celebrated rapid product turnover. Disposability and transience were an influential strand in modern art, aesthetics and architecture. For readers who have grown up in an age concerned with climate change, this might seem surprising. In their 1914 'Manifesto of Futurist Architecture', Antonio Sant'Elia and F. T. Marinetti promised that 'things will endure less than us.'[37] For them, impermanence and material change were the mark of a dynamic society. Every generation ought to have its own new city, buildings and interiors. Conservation meant stagnation. For Archigram, a British group of avant-garde architects, material and stylistic obsolescence was the sign of a vibrant, sophisticated culture. Fashion literally became disposable when, in 1967, Bernard Holdaway created paper furniture and paper dresses; the dress sold for a pound, a fraction of its cotton rival.[38] 'Pop' went the object.

In visual arts, the twentieth century saw the rise of waste art. In 1913, the French Dadaist Marcel Duchamp installed a bicycle wheel in his studio, the first of a string of mass-manufactured objects he turned into so-called 'readymade' pieces of art. In Germany after the First World War, and then from 1941 in exile in England, Kurt Schwitters similarly turned his attention to discarded objects, combining string, bits of newspapers and a pram wheel in installations and collages. In the 1950s, the American Robert Rauschenberg picked up where Duchamp and Schwitters had left off, playfully assembling metal scraps, Coca-Cola bottles and other debris in his 'combine paintings'; Rauschenberg had seen some of Duchamp's work and would meet him in 1959. Recycling ran in the family. Rauschenberg's mother went as far as turning the suit in which her younger brother had been laid out into a skirt; later, in *Yoicks*, her son made a painting from strips of fabric. In college, Rauschenberg drove a garbage truck. As a young, poor artist in Manhattan, he collected umbrellas and objects off the street. 'I really feel sorry,' he said, 'for people who think things like soap dishes or mirrors or Coke bottles are ugly.' In *Monogram* (1955–9), he wrapped a car tyre around the midriff of a stuffed angora goat; Rauschenberg had picked up the goat for $35 at a struggling office-supply store on Eighth Avenue in Manhattan (see Plate 72).

Rauschenberg found beauty in waste and set in train a cultural revaluation of rubbish. This did not make him a critic of the affluent society, though. In fact, he was an optimistic waster. At home, he had a TV set in almost every room, running day and night. He was quite at ease with the affluent society that furnished him with the secondary materials for his art. In 1963, when a gallery in Florence put on a show of his *scatole contemplative* – wooden 'thought boxes' of junk he had collected on his European travels – an irritated Italian critic suggested they should be thrown into the Arno. Rauschenberg thanked him and took him at his word – it took care of the packing problem, he said.[39]

Outside the art world, people were equally ambivalent about the rubbish rising around them. The salvage campaigns of the two world wars are sometimes portrayed as short-lived blips in the unstoppable advance of a culture of disposability and carelessness, as if only military zeal or a brute struggle for survival were momentarily able to entice people to conserve resources. This may be too cynical a view. What is striking is how many civic groups and individuals conscientiously collected glass and paper in the decades before and after the Second World War at the same time that their neighbours were throwing more of them in their bins. In Britain, commentators in the mid-1930s noted a rise in salvage – the recovery of paper alone ran to 1.5 million tons in 1937. In the 1960s, most local councils still collected paper, and *The Times*, in its 'Home Forum', advised people to compost kitchen waste, as if it was the most normal thing in the world. Many youth groups and charities routinely ran paper collections; almost a third of Britain's paper consumption was reclaimed in 1971. The 1973 oil crisis showed how easily people responded to calls for salvage. Boy scouts, schoolchildren and voluntary organizations picked up a record 200,000 tons of paper off the streets the following year. The problem was finding a buyer. The price of waste paper at mills had dropped from £30 to £21 a ton. It was this that made most local authorities pull out of recycling. When Bristol stopped its paper collection because of expense, the Revd F. B. Welbourn took the matter into his own hands and painstakingly separated newsprint and glossy paper from magazines with glued bindings that made them unacceptable to industry. By 1977, such stalwart efforts were no longer good enough. Bales of unwanted paper were piling up in sheds and church halls.[40]

Bad prices, not bad people, were what caused the decline in recycling in the age of affluence. The unprecedented drop in the price of materials squeezed the margins for recycling in industry. The fortunes of collecting and re-use also reflected technological developments. The history of the tin can is a good illustration. Few objects were as complicit in the triumph of disposability. Patented in 1810 by a British merchant, the tin can, by sealing and preserving food, revolutionized food culture; curiously, the dedicated tin-opener emerged only half a century later. Ham, beans and condensed milk could now travel long distances and be available when needed. The Crimean War and the American Civil War might have taken different courses without the tin can. It was military campaigns like these that popularized tins and processed food such as corned beef. Tin was a crucial element, because it stopped the can from rusting and spoiling the contents. The problem was how to re-extract it from the millions of cans once the corned beef had been devoured. In 1905, a German factory, Goldschmidt, developed a process to do just that. Washed and dried, old tins were thrown into sealed iron containers where the air was sucked out and chlorine pumped in; the latter reacted with the tin, leaving behind iron scrap. The de-tinned scrap went straight to Goldschmidt's neighbour, Siemens, which made new steel from it. The secondary tin found its way back to the tin industry. Collecting old tins became big business. By the 1920s, around half of all the tin used in Germany and the United States was reclaimed. All this changed as the canning industry, in the inter-war years, found ways to produce lighter cans with a thinner coat of tin (lightweighting). The US abandoned de-tinning in 1929. Goldschmidt clung on, briefly rewarded by the boom in cans in the 1960s and '70s.

But the odds were stacked against it. The tin cover was getting thinner and thinner, and soda cans now had an aluminium top. The global drop in the price for tin was the final nail in the coffin.[41]

The 1970s and '80s set in motion a recycling renaissance. Campaigns against litter were older. A 'Keep Britain Tidy Group' was launched in 1958, although it was more concerned with abandoned cars and how they scarred views of the green and pleasant land than with environmental pollution as such; the chairman of the group, T. R. Grieve, was the managing director of the oil marketing giant Shell-Mex and BP.[42] By the early 1970s, a new environmentalism was gaining followers. They had read Rachel Carson's warnings about chemicals' lethal effects on birds, wildlife and humans in *Silent Spring* (1962) and were shaken by the Club of Rome's *Limits to Growth* (1972), with its scenarios of rampant growth and consumption eating up the finite resources of the planet.[43] Waste confronted a new species of eco-citizen. In 1971, in one of their first campaigns, Friends of the Earth dumped thousands of non-returnable bottles outside Schweppes's London headquarters. Recycling became a moral duty to the planet.

The sense of environmental risk was matched by a concern about future resources. Significantly, some of the earliest recycling initiatives were joint affairs between industry and social movements. In York, in 1975, Oxfam struck a deal with the Redfearn Glass manufacturer over recycled glass. The first bottle bank, in Oxford, was opened two years later by the Glass Manufacturers' Federation. Some of this was an effort to contain an environmental backlash. In Berlin, for example, it was the private recycling firm RGR (Recyclinggesellschaft für Rohstoffgewinnung) that worked together with a citizen initiative to start separate collections of paper and glass in 1975.[44]

On their own, it is doubtful how much these efforts would have accomplished. The oil crisis turned out to be a temporary spike in the long decline of material prices. In the past, salvage had risen and fallen on such tides. What has been different since the 1970s is that governments have started to interfere. Laws and regulation kept recycling afloat at low tide, when the price of secondary materials was falling. Rising demand from Asia since the 1980s further propped it up. After decades of being burnt or shovelled underground, waste resurfaced as valuable stuff – *Wertstoff*, to use the apt German term. A range of measures was used, from making it more expensive to dump waste to requiring companies to take back products at the end of their life. Regulations governing material recovery by manufacturers were introduced in Germany (1972), France (1975) and Sweden (1975), followed by polluter-pay principles. Japan passed its waste law in 1970; the European Community followed five years later with its waste directive, which laid out the hierarchy of the three 'R's: reduce, re-use and recycle. The new ideal (formalized in law in the 1990s) was of the economy as a circular metabolism instead of a one-way road to the dump.[45]

One country was lagging behind: Britain. In 1974, the Labour government had called for a 'war on waste' and agreed that the world 'cannot afford the luxury of a throwaway society'.[46] It considered incentives for consumers to return waste as well as charges for industries using non-recycled materials. In the end, cost and the Conservatives trumped conservation. With privatization and competition the new gospel, the Thatcher government was not going to run to the rescue of the paper industry and local councils when the market for secondary materials hit a new low. By 1985, there was only one outer borough in London left which offered a kerb-side recycling collection. Not surprisingly, 'bring systems' made for disappointing recycling rates. Even the 'dirty man of Europe', however, ultimately cleaned up its act – with a little help from Brussels. The 1999 European Landfill Directive, which English law was forced to implement, set a maximum landfill level of 50 per cent by 2013 for municipal waste, accompanied by stiff fines.

The picture since the 1970s has been uplifting and depressing in equal measure. In the United States, a mere 7 per cent of materials was recovered in 1970 – not counting composting. Two decades later, it was 14 per cent; by 2010, it had crossed the 25 per cent threshold. Today, Americans recycle a third of all their glass containers and PET (Polyethylene terephthalate) bottles. In the European Union, too, paper recycling has steadily gone up, reaching over 70 per cent today. At the same time, advanced consumer societies continue to generate large volumes of waste. In 2010, the average French person threw out four times as much as in 1970. In the United States, waste fell slightly in 2008–09 – waste tends to decline in a recession – but it was a temporary dip, and in 2010–12 levels stabilized.

Europe has performed a bit better and managed to lower waste generation by 8 per cent between 2000 and 2013 – especially in Germany, Britain and Spain – as well as stepping up recycling efforts. But that still means people on the old continent on average generated 481kg of waste in 2013, a phenomenal amount in the annals of human history and bringing it down only to the already high levels of the 1990s; only 131kg of this was recycled in 2013. If we get our hands dirty and pick through the bins, however, it is far from clear whether these figures translate into an actual decline of municipal waste. Large-scale tests in German cities, for example, have revealed that up to 50 per cent of what people threw into the yellow bin designated for packaging was 'incorrect' and consisted of other waste. The household bin may be a little bit lighter but only because some non-recyclable waste ends up in a recycling bin. And not everything that ends up in a recycling bin is actually recyled. In the case of plastics, for example, German sorting plants manage to fish out only 15 per cent of materials that will then be re-used in production.[47] The bulk is either burnt (for heat) or exported to China, both processes that turn waste into value but hardly genuine recycling. Whether waste can be reduced much further only time will tell. It will certainly be a formidable challenge. Between 1997 and 2004, for example, packaging waste in the EU-15 increased by 10 million tonnes; it was only because 12 million tonnes made it to recycling that bins did not burst.

Putting these figures alongside each other prompts a number of

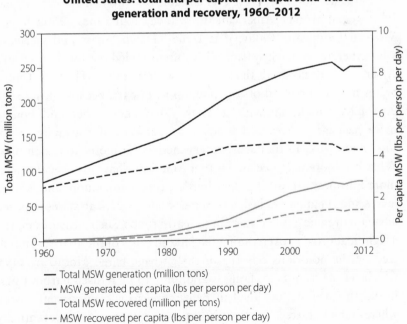

United States: total and per capita municipal solid-waste generation and recovery, 1960–2012

— Total MSW generation (million tons)
--- MSW generated per capita (lbs per person per day)
— Total MSW recovered (million per tons)
--- MSW recovered per capita (lbs per person per day)

Source: US Environmental Protection Agency, *Municipal Solid Waste in the United States: 2011 Facts and Figures* (2013).

thought-provoking observations. It is quite misleading to see today's
passion for recycling as a return to the lifestyle of a century or so ago.
Recycling co-exists with an intensive, high-volume disposable lifestyle
that has kept waste levels at a plateau reached in the 1970s–'80s and
far exceeds anything seen in earlier periods; recycling bins even encouraged the triumph of the disposable bottle over the returnable version.
Today's Americans discard as much packaging waste as their grandparents – and that is after recycling bottles and newspapers. Bins
continued to get bigger and fuller during the early stages of the green
revolution, in spite of bottle banks and landfill directives. Only
since 2000 has household waste levelled off. Yet, while waste has been
reined in, it has scarcely been reduced, at least among households. It is
worth noting here that municipal waste is only a small share of total
waste – around 10–15 per cent in developed societies – and that commercial and industrial waste has fallen more sharply.[48] All that
Americans, for example, have managed to do is to roll back their personal garbage to the levels of the 1970s. Even after all the recycling and
composting, the bin today is 10 per cent fuller than it was in 1960 during the peak of affluence when the throwaway mentality came under
attack.[49]

There has, secondly, been a remarkable role reversal among nations.
In 1965, an average American threw away four times as much as a
Western European. Today, it is Danes, Dutch, Swiss and Germans
who generate the most waste. While often singled out for their excess,
Americans are no more than average wasters today. That the United
States has been pushed off the podium is, in part, because other societies have caught up with it as they have got richer and bought
more packaged, processed foods – 87 per cent of packaging is for
food and drink. In that sense, everyone is a bit more American now.
What is less often appreciated is that Americans have also become a bit
more European, returning their bottles, composting more and leaving
leaves and cut grass on the lawn. Some twenty American states imposed
a ban on organic garden waste in the early 1990s. Such measures played
a significant role in overcoming the landfill crisis of the 1980s, symbolized by the notorious odyssey of the garbage barge *Mobro* in 1987,
which set off from Islip, Long Island, only to be refused harbour first
in North Carolina and then in Belize, and to end up virtually back
where it had started, in New York, where its waste was eventually
incinerated.

Household waste generation in selected countries, 1980–2005

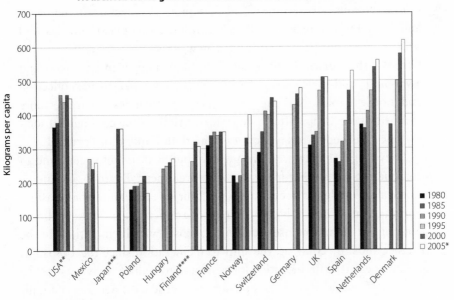

* Or latest available year.

** US figures for 1980 and 1985 have been adapted from US official data source, on the basis that, on average, household waste makes up 60% of municipal solid waste in the United States.

*** I have revised these figures upwards, since official Japanese figures count only waste after recycling and do not include the portion of household waste that is collected by private commercial recycling firms, which is considerable. See: Allen Hershkowitz and Eugene Salerni, Garbage Management in Japan (1987).

**** I have revised the figures for Finland slightly upwards, since household waste makes up 64% of municipal solid waste according to recent Finnish estimates, which is slightly higher than the figure underlying the OECD data. Source: *OECD Environmental Data Compendium 2006–2008*, Table 2A, with above-mentioned recalculations.

Waste, these divergent national trends show, cannot be treated as shorthand for national consumerism. Consumer cultures vary. People can be thrifty with money (the Germans and the Swiss) yet throw away more than people who live on credit (Americans). Germans go through a lot of plastic (5.5 million tons a year) but also recycle a lot of it (42 per cent). It is, similarly, wrong to imagine a natural affinity between making things and caring for them at the end of their lives, on the one side, and between a service–leisure society and wastefulness on the other. Britons and Americans started to recycle more at the very time they stopped making cars and clothes.

The speed with which recycling has been taken up by countries previously stigmatized as throwaway societies means we should be cautious about interpretations that see waste behaviour as rooted in national traditions and culture. Salvage drives and the pursuit of self-sufficiency

during the Nazi years did not automatically predispose later generations of Germans to become world champions in recycling: in the 1960s
and '70s, they were notorious for throwing out plastic bottles and
packaging. It was the state and a new grassroots movement – the
Greens – that turned habits around through changes in law, taxes and
awareness, and through smaller bins in the home, kerb-side collection
and bottle banks. Nor are recent peasant societies naturally more
inclined to recycling. After a slow start, Britain – the commercial society par excellence – today recycles more than Finland or Portugal.

Recycling has increased everywhere, but at different speeds and in
conjunction with other forms of waste treatment. By 2010, Germany,
Austria and Belgium recycled 60 per cent of their municipal waste –
Portugal and Greece barely managed 20 per cent; Turkey almost
nothing. In Japan, intense recycling co-exists with incineration. In the
Netherlands, by contrast, the shift to incineration since the 1980s has
meant there is little incentive for residents to reduce their waste. The
content of bins also continues to vary. In Sweden, 68 per cent of municipal waste is paper – in France and Spain, it is merely 20 per cent.[50]
Swiss and Danes dispose of lots of textiles; Germans don't.

Roughly, Europe today is made up of three waste regions: a Northern one, stretching from Belgium and Germany to Scandinavia, with
few landfills and a lot of recycling but also a lot of household waste; a
Mediterranean one, where landfills continue to be more plentiful and
recycling is modest; and Eastern Europe, where hardly anything is
recycled and the bulk of municipal waste ends up in a landfill. The typical fee and taxes to send non-hazardous municipal waste to landfill in
Northern Europe is three to four times higher than in Eastern Europe.
For all the progress made towards greater harmony by the European
Union, plenty of dissonances remain. Bio-waste (food and garden), for
example, lacks a common standard. Plenty of Dutch and Spaniards
recycle theirs, whereas it goes to landfill in Croatia and Portugal.[51]

Nowhere was the road to recycling more twisted and dramatic than
in Eastern Europe, where socialism charted its own path. In the communist lexicon, waste was a capitalist phenomenon and typified the
reckless squandering of human energy and material resources for
short-sighted profit and imperial expansion. In the hands of socialists,
it was valuable 'old raw' or 'secondary material', a source that never
dried up, as propaganda had it. In a way, socialists picked up the earlier
capitalist crusade for efficiency led by Hoover and others. Shortage
of raw materials – the result of geographic destiny and inefficient

Municipal waste generated and recycled: the three waste regions of Europe, 1995–2013

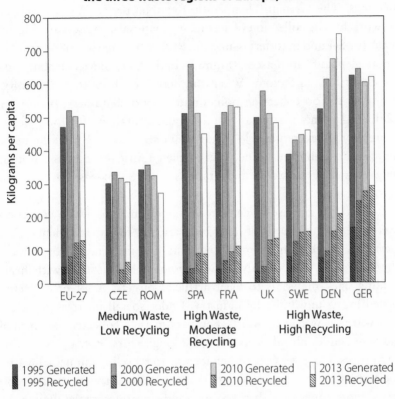

Source: Eurostat, *Municipal Waste Generation and Treatment 1995–2013.*

planning – made recycling an everyday concern in the Eastern bloc during the Cold War. Collecting waste saved hard currency. Hungary had lost territories and faced an embargo, which made salvaging everything from metal scraps to door handles a matter of life and death for its metal industries. In 1951, when collections got under way, 2,000 tons of iron were gathered in a single week. For the Communist Party, 'the material squanderers must be subject to disciplinary action'.[52] But people also had to be enticed. Socialist ideals were not enough. Rags paid for shoes; bits of hog leather could be traded in for pepper and rice. In 1950s East Germany, half a kilo of used paper secured a precious roll of wallpaper; a kilo of bones one bar of hand soap (*Feinseife*).

Salvage drives were the socialist equivalent of the fair-trade campaigns in the West. Instead of consuming ethical coffee, young pioneers showed their 'solidarity with Vietnam' by gathering old newspapers and rags. The German Democratic Republic perfected a nationwide network for the collection of secondary materials, the so-called Kombinat für Sekundärstofferfassung (SERO), which in the 1980s brought a pink elephant – its mascot, 'Emmy' – to the lakes of Mecklenburg and the chalk hills of Saxony. When the Berlin Wall fell in 1989, SERO operated 17,200 collecting points and 55,000 containers; there were additional points for metal recycling and containers for food waste. More, not fewer, returnable bottles made the rounds.[53] East Germans recycled an estimated 40 per cent of their refuse – something Britons only managed in 2010 and Italians and Spaniards have yet to accomplish.

It would be unwise to get too nostalgic, though. Waste collection was driven by the needs of dirty industry, not the environment – East Germany raised some 10 per cent of its raw materials through recycling. A good deal of salvage was immensely wasteful, with firms holding back materials to meet artificial targets. A lot of old scrap rusted away, unwanted by industry. Under socialism, recycling went backwards as well as forwards. Hungary in 1960 collected one third of old tyres, miles ahead of its capitalist neighbours. But, by 1973, this had dropped to 3 per cent. When it came to recycling municipal waste, socialist states fell behind in the 1980s; West Germans already collected more paper than their brothers and sisters across the Wall in the 1970s. Nonetheless, the collapse of socialism amounted to a major disruption in existing channels and habits of recycling. Within a couple of years of the fall of the Berlin Wall, only a hundred collection points were left in East Germany. Elsewhere back-purchase systems lost their subsidies and gave way to cheaper, privatized forms of disposal. In the Czech Republic, paper and glass collection all but collapsed. If the 1990s were golden years for recycling in the West, they were a lost decade east of the Elbe.[54] Recycling had to start again from scratch.

The first consumer society to get a grip on waste was Japan. With limited geological options for landfill and few raw materials of its own, Japan might be thought naturally prone to recycle. In the booming 1960s, however, waste was spinning out of control – between 1967 and 1970, it jumped up by half, from 650 to 920 grams per person per day. What Japan managed in the early 1970s was first to reduce its garbage and then keep a lid on it. It is a lesson in how waste regimes from different historical eras could be effectively combined. Incineration and recycling have complemented each other. By the 1980s, Japan was recycling 50 per cent of its paper – twice as much as in the mid-1950s – and more than 90 per cent of its beer bottles. The average sake bottle was re-used twenty times. In cities, a third of waste was gathered by private collectors – and thus does not appear in national statistics. In their lorries, traders would roam the streets and shout 'Chirigami kōkan', handing out tissues and toilet paper in exchange for old newspapers. Alongside, and subsidized by their city, civic and neighbourhood groups were collecting cans, bottles, metals and old textiles.

In Machida City, near Tokyo, public officials in the 1980s went from door to door once a year to explain source separation – the city separated seven materials: paper, glass, cans, bulk waste, non-combustible hard plastic and scrap metal, and combustible waste (including kitchen waste). In third and fourth grade, children had dedicated lessons on the system. Over a hundred civic groups were active, collecting 70 per cent of the city's aluminium cans – a major achievement in the land of the vending machine. Bulky furniture and bicycle parts went to a recycling centre, where disabled citizens made them fit for new life.[55]

Getting people to sort their rubbish, cities found, was much more effective than charging them for their waste. Nagoya in 1998 set itself the target to reduce its waste by a quarter. 'Challenge 100' urged each citizen in this city of 2 million to reduce their daily garbage by 100g. A recycling crusade got under way. Schools opened centres for recycling. Over 2,000 meetings were held to explain sorting. There was 'naming and shaming' for those who refused to do it, with stickers identifying those who had not properly sorted their garbage; Tokyo introduced transparent bin bags that put residents' civic and environmental standards on public display. Glass and cans had to be taken to collection stations. The retailer had to come to pick up fridges and other appliances. Paper went to the kerb, but with newspaper separated from magazines and cardboard. Milk and juice cartons had to be unfolded and dried out before they could be taken to the supermarket or the local government office. All these various efforts helped reduce CO_2 emissions by a third, thanks to the diminished inflow of material.[56] In 2000, a new national recycling law came into effect and shifted the balance from incineration to the recovery of packaging materials. In the countryside, most livestock waste made it back on to the field; in some areas, there was too much waste for farmland to take.[57]

Just how much Japanese households actually reduced their waste is a subject of debate – one waste survey found that bins ended up 10 per cent lighter because people, in addition to composting, burnt some of their waste in their backyard. Few lived by the pledge of civic campaigns to stop buying what was likely to be wasted.[58] Still, compared to Europe and the United States, these campaigns look pretty impressive. Not that there were no success stories elsewhere. In Los Angeles, for example, the School District eliminated trays in their food service to discourage pupils from piling up extra food which would later end up in the bin – it cut waste by half a million tons. American communities introduced Pay-As-You-Throw (PAYT) or Save Money and Reduce Trash (SMART) schemes. In Sweden, municipalities which operated pay-by-weight schemes saw a 20 per cent drop in the household waste collected, although, interestingly, it had no effect on recycling behaviour.[59] In Italy, several cities in 2002 started to ban the distribution of unsolicited advertisements; placing a flyer under a windshield in Turin lands a fine of up to €500.[60]

But these have been specific initiatives that lacked the integrated Japanese approach to reduction, re-use and recycling, which combined municipal subsidies, commercial dealers, civil society and moral pressure. European attempts to tackle waste have been far less able to rely on civic groups and neighbourhood activism, with the exception, perhaps, of Switzerland. Elsewhere, some localities have managed to co-opt residents in addition to charging them for garden waste and separate food-waste collections; the Somerset Waste Partnership in England is an example. Stirling, in Scotland, hands out yellow and red cards to residents who ignore its 'Bin Lids Down' rules: the first time, an over-full wheelie bin would not be collected; a repeated offence was punished with a £50 penalty. Such measures lowered waste by 5 per cent on some estates. For every Somerset and Stirling, though, there is a Cumbria or Barking, with loads of waste and little recycling.[61] Efforts to stem the tide of unsolicited mail and print publicity have been largely disappointing. In 1999, the Brussels region launched an 'anti-pub' campaign, to much fanfare. A few years on, barely one in ten people was taking part. Across the European Union, instead of receding, the avalanche of paper and plastic has continued to swell. In the United States, the drop in newspaper sales has been all but made up for by the rise in office-type paper, making a mockery of the much lauded 'paperless office'.[62] Europe has so far turned the famed waste pyramid on its head: almost all the money flows into recycling. Waste reduction has received minuscule support.

Food waste illustrates the many factors that conspire against change.

Europeans throw out 90 million tonnes of food a year. The average American household today puts around 600 grams of food in the bin every day, worth $600 a year. Around 25 per cent of food bought ends up in the bin, not the stomach, experts estimate. The poor do it as well as the rich, although slightly less so. Whichever way we look at it, this is a perverse state of affairs at a time when millions go hungry and the planet is heating up; if Britons were to buy only the food they would actually eat, they would cut CO_2 emissions by 17 million tonnes – equivalent to taking every fifth car off the roads.

Wasting food is nothing new. In fact, it is quite normal under capitalism. In the 1930s, millions of gallons of milk were poured into rivers and grain was burnt when demand and trade collapsed. What is new in recent decades is that food is wasted while demand is high, a result of buying too much, not too little. Instead of the 'under-consumption' that so troubled progressives a century ago, we are today dealing with a new kind of over-consumerist waste. Food is also lost at different points on the way from farm to fork. With affluence and development, waste has shifted from producer to consumer. In rich societies today, one quarter of edible food is wasted. Before the Second World War, it had been 3 per cent; kitchen waste was mainly peel and bones, rarely a whole head of lettuce or a half-eaten steak. Farmers and retailers are still not entirely innocent, of course. Two-for-one specials encourage over-shopping. An obsession with cosmetically perfect fruit and vegetables and poor demand management are responsible for 10 per cent wastage in the food chain in the United Kingdom. Still, there is no doubt that so-called 'post-harvest loss' has declined with development. In developing countries, about half the avocados grown are lost before they reach market; for citrus, the percentage is even higher. By contrast, only 10 per cent of horticultural and perishable crops suffer that fate in Britain and the United States. More than ever, the real culprit is the consumer.[63]

Why does so much edible food end up in the bin? In the media, it has been tempting to point the finger at thoughtless consumers who simply do not care about the world. But this misses the social and technical forces at play. A recent close-up look at households in Manchester found that most people felt guilty when they emptied parts of their fridge into the bin.[64] Nonetheless, on the next shopping trip, they would once again buy too much. An explanation for this behaviour can be found in the kind of food that ends up in the bin. Most of it consists of lettuce, fresh fruit and vegetables.[65] A wilted leaf or a brown spot is often enough to consign food to the bin. The arrival of the fridge has been a mixed blessing. On the one hand, refrigeration vastly improved food preservation and helped families to save money while enjoying nutritious food year around; in Scandinavia, women household economists were keen advocates of the freezer, which gave families a chance to store salmon, venison and fruit for the long winter.[66] On the other hand, it was an invitation to buy and store more, making meal planning a more complicated affair than in the past. And it raised expectations about the fresh appearance of food and sticking to sell-by dates. There is always a forgotten piece of cheese hiding in the back of the fridge or an exotic vegetable which looked appetizing in the shop but just did not fit the dinner plan. More than half the food wasted in the United Kingdom is because it is not used in time. Another third is the result of people cooking and serving too much. Pets these days get only a few scraps from such over-provisioning. In that sense, there has been a major disruption in the ecology of modern cities, where animals once had been one stage in the elimination of waste, with swill being served to pigs. Today's pets create waste.[67]

Some may blame a decline in cooking skills and household management for the rise in food waste, but this would be too easy. Culinary skills are far more widely diffused today than a century ago. What has changed is the variety of food, the rhythm of meal times and the pressures of social life. When the pioneering archaeologist of waste, William Rathje, was digging with his students through people's bins in Arizona in the 1970s, they spotted a close correlation between the diversity of diets and the amount wasted. Mexican-Americans who routinely used the same ingredients threw away 20 per cent less food than their neighbours. The more people ate the same thing day after day, the less they wasted. Rathje called it the first principle of food waste. The pull of variety has been reinforced by the diffusion of cosmopolitan taste and ethnic cuisines. Who now dares to serve guests ordinary bread, cold cuts and an apple? Children, too, have acquired greater voice over their culinary preferences, which can clash with the carefully planned menu of healthy food brought home from the supermarket. On top of it all, food in the fridge has to compete with unforeseen opportunities to eat out. A sudden call from friends, going out for pizza or a curry, and the fresh fish and vegetables planned for that evening are forgotten and later binned. This is one reason single households, with less structured meal and leisure times, tend to produce more food waste.

Hard times might be expected to be a cure for all this, but this is probably naïve. Rathje, in the 1970s, found that the amount of meat thrown away went up during a recession, as people bought discounted larger packets and cheaper cuts of meat but then did not know how to prepare them.[68] In recent years, campaigners have tackled misconceptions about 'best before' dates and tried to educate people to check their cupboards and plan their meals for the week before filling up the shopping trolley. Supermarkets started to advise customers on how to store fruit in the fridge, and some companies introduced re-sealable packs for fish fingers. Small loaves of bread appeared on the shelves. After a 'Love Food Hate Waste' initiative in one British community, avoidable waste in bins went down by 15 per cent.[69] This is a step in the right direction but hardly a giant leap. Some of the recent decline, furthermore, may be a result of the recent recession and people buying less fresh fruit and vegetables. Food waste needs to be recognized as a by-product of the busy lifestyle, with its competing, multiple demands on time, as we have discussed in Chapter 10. Individual morals and lack of information are not the primary problem. The sad truth is not that people do not understand or care about the food they waste. They care about world hunger and global warming, yet their fragmented social schedules override personal ethics and lead them to waste regardless.

Rather than being the natural end point of affluence, the 'throwaway era' of the 1950s and '60s was merely one stage in a longer transformation of people's relationship to their waste. At the beginning of the twenty-first century, we are both wasting more and recycling more. Indeed, we are more directly implicated in handling and sorting our rubbish than our Victorian forebears. It is not certain that all developing societies will necessarily follow the trajectory of American and European cities in the past and replace 'backward' rag-and-bone men with 'modern' technological solutions. In Colombia and Brazil, authorities have recognized scavengers as valuable partners in waste management and organized co-operatives since the 1980s; in India today, over 3 million waste pickers recycle almost 7 million tons of scrap a year, saving municipalities Rs452 million.[70] In the rich West, however, a wondrous new constellation has appeared. The sifting and separating once done by lowly rag-and-bone men is now done by all citizens. Rich and poor alike are getting their hands dirty, separating old bottles from cardboard and smelly food. Recycling has turned an old hierarchy of value upside down. Since ancient times, handling and sorting rubbish has been the fate of the lowest of the low, hence the

stigma of the 'untouchables'. Today, it is a sign of environmental awareness that marks one out as a responsible citizen. Instead of sending their
collective rubbish to highly sophisticated sorting machines, the richest
people on the planet insist on doing it themselves and for free, as if
wanting to defy the economic law of the division of labour. Recycling is
no longer treated as backward or traditional. It has become the ally of
high-octane consumption, a kind of ersatz sacrament that cleanses us of
our stuff. A new steady state of waste has emerged. Instead of 'waste
not, want not' the new maxim is to use more, recycle more.

Where does all the waste and recycling go? The PET bottles, paper
and the TV sets and computers that are no longer wanted have to end
up somewhere if the local landfill is shut. Between 2000 and 2010, the
fifteen member states of the European Union raised the packaging
waste they recycled from 33 to 46 million tonnes and doubled the
amount of plastic packaging recycled, from 2.2 to 4.3 million tonnes.[71]
Rich societies today recycle more than ever, but they also send more of
their waste across their borders than ever before. In essence, this is
nothing new. In the nineteenth century, there was a lively international
trade in second-hand clothes and rags. But this fades into insignificance
when compared to today's transboundary movement of waste, and the
money as well as the environmental consequences involved; in the EU,
the export of plastic waste jumped from 1 million tonnes in 1999 to
almost 6 million tonnes in 2011, while the export of copper, aluminium and nickel wastes doubled.

The revival of recycling since the 1980s, then, has come with a curious paradox. At the same time as affluent consumers have been giving
their household waste greater personal attention – sorting their bottles
and separating plastic and paper – the overall waste stream has increasingly moved out of sight and out of mind. Contrary to popular wisdom,
however, the flow has not been down a one-way street, from the rich
North to the poor South. The European Union exports most of its plastic waste to China, but the bulk of its more precious metal waste
(copper, aluminium, iron and steel and precious metals) travels from
one European country to another. Hazardous waste is almost entirely
(97 per cent) traded within the EU, most of it ending up in wealthy
Germany. Similarly, in the United States, the majority of recycled or
refurbished electronic products are sold there. Some American and
European televisions and circuit boards end up in Ghana and Nigeria,
but Africa also sends its own electronic waste to Korea and Spain; the
Middle East sends its to Korea.[72]

Shifting one's waste to distant places is not necessarily a bad thing. Recovered plastic and scraps of precious metal can save virgin resources and reduce the pollution that would otherwise be caused by their extraction. The PET bottle collected in a European town returns as a warm fleece jacket made in China. The problem is that such a virtuous "open loop" is only one aspect of the global waste trade which also involves a more destructive stream of hazardous materials and used goods from the rich world ending up in countries that lack the technologies and regulations to recycle them appropriately. Precious materials are lost, leading to further depletion of virgin resources. European cars, for example, have catalytic converters that are rich in platinum group metals. Since 2000, all vehicles scrapped in the EU had to have the platinum recycled from their converters. Yet 100,000 used cars are shipped every year from the port of Hamburg to Africa and the Near East, where, ultimately, the platinum ends up in scrapyards or in the ground.

Even more worrying is the considerable illegal trade in hazardous electronic waste, which causes serious environmental pollution if improperly recycled. In Guiyu, the Chinese centre for e-scrap recycling in Guangdong province, workers melt printed circuit boards over charcoal to remove the microchips from the molten lead, before trying to recover copper and gold with the help of acid (see Plate 71). The majority of children in the region suffer from respiratory diseases. In 2000 and 2001, China and Vietnam banned the import of used electrical equipment, but both made an exception for products that would be rebuilt for re-export. This has opened the door to a large and profitable smuggling trade across their border.[73] Europe has even stricter regulations on the treatment of electronic waste, but a lot of it continues to travel under the radar of European inspectors, disguised as used goods. Spot checks in Denmark and the German port of Hamburg in 2006 suggest that, each year, 250,000 tonnes of used TVs, computers, screens and fridges are shipped from Europe to non-OECD countries. Although hard numbers are impossible to come by – several European countries do not report illegal shipments at all – many containers probably include appliances that are either dead or beyond repair and thus are true waste. According to the Secretariat of the Basel Convention (which introduced an international check on the movement of hazardous waste in 1992), one third of all the electronic equipment Europe sent to Ghana in 2010 did not work, and was thus illegal.[74]

It is hard not to conclude that rich consumers today may recycle more but, with a habit of swapping old models for new, they also dump more of their lifestyle on distant places.

GOOD RIDDANCE

So far, we have followed stuff from the kitchen and the cupboard to the bin. But this is not the only route possessions take. To know how wasteful we are, we need to view throwing things away alongside other channels and strategies for coping with more stuff, such as gifting, passing on, repairing and storing.

Giving stuff away, either for free or at a price, is one way to keep goods in circulation. Charity shops, eBay and Freecycle have brought this strategy a lot of recent attention. In Britain alone, there are some 7,000 charity shops. Car-boot sales attract a million people every week.[75] At the time of writing, Freecycle has close to 10 million members across the world who pass on everything from unwanted cutlery to mobile homes. Websites and social networks enable owners to upload their unwanted items to a virtual skip. Fashion lovers can swap or 'swish' their unwanted designer bags online; gardeners have their seed-swapping sites.

We should not get over-excited about these trends. A new culture of sharing has not replaced individual wastefulness. For one, the things shared are quite limited. They make barely a dent in the big picture of material resource use. Car-sharing and giving away olds sofas and TVs may be beneficial, but such gains have been more than cancelled out by a declining willingness to share housing and the rise of solo living, where each individual has a fridge, washing machine and TV all to themselves. The number of solo dwellers in the world has risen sharply in the last couple of decades, from 153 million in 1996 to 277 million in 2011. In the United States today, every fourth household has only one resident; in the United Kingdom, it is almost every third. It would be unwise to put the blame for this trend solely at market-driven materialism. In welfare states such as Sweden and Norway, more than 40 per cent of households are solo. Since optimists point to the young as the harbingers of a new culture of sharing, it is worth noting that, unlike in the past, it is young people in their twenties and thirties who make up the fastest-growing group of solo dwellers.[76]

Yes, the internet has made it easier for people to sub-let and share their holiday homes, but that does not automatically mean that resource use has fallen or the number of holiday homes has declined. Data on secondary homes is not consistently collected in Europe, and by some countries not at all. Still, what is available suggests a rapid and ongoing increase in their number. In France in 2005, there were 2.9 million vacation homes, and the share of non-resident owners had increased from 6 per cent to 9 per cent since 1997. In Spain, the Ministry of Housing combined census data with surveys of inbound visitors, and reached the conclusion that 1.5 million homes in the country in 2008 were secondary dwellings. They made up 37 per cent of the increase in total housing stock between 2001 and 2008. That is a lot of bricks and mortar, and a lot of appliances and furniture to go inside. About 58 per cent of these dwellings were in the prime tourist areas by the sea. The number of English people owning a second home abroad doubled in the decade after 1997, reaching a quarter of a million in 2007; that of Norwegians quadrupled between 2002 and 2008.[77]

Of course, champions of the sharing economy might respond that, nonetheless, online services such as airbnb provide shared, alternative lodging that makes more efficient use of existing resources, meaning that fewer hotels are required. On New Year's Eve in 2014, more than half a million people on this planet stayed on sofas and in flats rented via airbnb. Studies have certainly shown a correlation between the spread of airbnb lodgings on offer and a fall in hotel bookings, especially among cheaper hotels. In January 2015, hotel revenue in New York City was 19 per cent lower than in the previous year, the result, partly, of lots of snow and a weak euro, but partly also of more private rooms readily available on the site. Lower demand for cheap hotel rooms, however, does not necessarily translate into lower demand for goods and resources. Private holiday rentals hurt hotel owners, not their customers. In fact, hotels responded by lowering their rates, leaving tourists with more money to spend on other things. More and cheaper private accommodation may have encouraged airbnb customers to take more city holidays and mini-breaks, a kind of touristic rebound effect. And, finally, their temporary hosts gained additional income. Sharing only reduces resources if hosts throw open their homes to strangers and stay put, or temporarily move in with friends around the corner. But many hosts rent out their entire apartment and combine letting with going on holiday themselves. Reduction and displacement of resources and demand in some cases is matched, perhaps even outdone, by growth in others. Indeed, airbnb itself has responded to its critics by emphasizing that they are bringing more business and cash to city centres and their shops and restaurants.[78]

We must, moreover, not forget that people have always passed on goods. What is new is not the sharing of stuff but that it is less and less with family and friends and more and more with strangers, with the help of the internet. The technology of sharing responds to a society of more fleeting relationships and more people living alone. But this does not mean that sharing is new. Car sharing was widespread in the inter-war years.[79] Even in the affluent 1950s and '60s it was normal for families to pass on clothes, toys and furniture from one child or cousin to another. So was the trade in second-hand goods; mothers' groups sell 'nearly new' children's clothes and toys in church halls across London to this day.[80]

In the seventeenth and eighteenth centuries, second-hand was a way of life for most Europeans – in rural Flanders as much as in bustling Antwerp, for rich and poor. Auctions circulated beds, sheets and pillows through society but, above all, kitchen utensils and clothing. Initially, many second-hand dealers sold new and old. In Antwerp, mercers pressed the city to restrict their operations from the 1670s.[81] It was the start of their social and commercial marginalization. True, second-hand dealers never entirely disappeared. But their relative position vis-à-vis shopkeepers who sold 'new' steadily deteriorated. As clothes became cheaper and less sturdy and as the fashion cycle accelerated, their second-hand value dropped, and with it the profits and standing of their dealers. By 1900, second-hand was largely for the poor, although the invention of vintage did give it a new lease of life at the top of society, too.

Relative decline within Europe, however, has been accompanied by expansion outside it. In the 1980s–'90s, the global export of second-hand clothing increased more than six-fold.[82] In Sub-Saharan Africa, a third of all textile imports were second-hand in these years. The twin channels which fed this system were already taking shape in the late nineteenth century: Christian charities and commercial operators. The anthropologist Karen Hansen followed the twists and turns taken by clothes on their way from European to Zambian wardrobes in the 1990s. Few Western donors and Zambian consumers were aware that most clothes did not come via the charity shop. Most donations, in fact, never made it inside the shop. Instead they were collected, pressed and sold in large 2,000lb bales to textile salvagers and exporters. The will to do good and give away rather than throw away overwhelmed charities' ability to process the textiles. Once the clothes arrived in Lusaka, they were altered and refashioned by local *salaula* (rummaging) traders. Trims, gold buttons and a new cut turned old clothes into new. Buying used clothes had less to do with imitating the West, Hansen found in her fieldwork, or with the subcultural irony that has preoccupied cultural theorists. They dressed up, according to Hansen, 'to escape their own economic powerlessness, momentarily and vicariously'.[83] Zambians, in fact, did not talk about 'Western' clothes but about shirts and dresses from the 'outside', which could mean Hong Kong as well as Hollywood.

In Zambia, used clothes went up as the economy went downhill in the 1970s. But second-hand clothing also boomed in rich countries. In Britain, such shops doubled their turnover in the 1990s. How beneficial has this renaissance of re-use been for the environment? Do people who give away clothes, books and other possessions help save the planet by reducing material use, as some environmentalists have pleaded,[84] or do they harm it by putting still more stuff into circulation?

The answer depends on context and the item in question. A detailed study of fifty-nine households in Nottingham, England, found that they disposed of a total of 4,500 objects in a single year. Just under a third was binned, 10 per cent each was either sold or moved to the loft, half was given away to family, friends or charity shops. The flow of things illustrates the interconnection between the desire for novelty and an impulse to do good by giving stuff away. 'Sarah' went through her wardrobe twice a year to separate those items that were 'no longer me'. A once 'groovy' coat was ready for charity – 'I'd seen too many really boring people wearing it.'[85] The charity shop stands at the end of a chain of self-fashioning in which new things are needed to redefine who we are. Passing on old but fully functioning toasters and electronic goods to family members simultaneously demonstrates one's care for people and for things. At the same time, it creates space for a shiny replacement. In addition, selling used cars and similar goods where money can be made gives owners the cash to buy a new model. Their purchase presumes that such goods can be resold later.

The changing life span of things matters here. Packard, in *The Waste Makers*, singled out planned obsolescence and warned of ever faster product cycles. The introduction, in the 1950s, of 'printed circuits', for example, made transistor radios all but unrepairable. Since then, the 'death-dating' of components has added sophistication to the art of 'made to break'.[86] Consumers have been strangely divided in their attitudes to durability. A 2005 British study found them evenly split between those who wished products lasted longer and those who were happy with their lifespan. Five years for a computer was felt to be all right.[87] Mobile phones and computers turn into dinosaurs long before they fall apart. According to one estimate, 49 per cent of all mobile devices were replaced in the United States in 2014. This is an extraordinary number for any product, but the figure hides two trends that may be pulling in opposite directions. The percentage of devices that go through an annual replacement cycle has gone up (from 45 per cent in 2013 to 49 per cent in 2014). But what about the remainder? Interestingly, the percentage of mobiles that were replaced only when they reached obsolescence also went up (from 15 to 30 per cent). In 2010–12, every second mobile phone was changed after two years – 'New Every Two', in the words of one provider's slogan. In 2014, this figure was down to 16 per cent. One reason for phones being changed more slowly was the introduction of Equipment Installment Plans (EIP) which offered annual upgrades on existing phones and discounted service pricing. Another was the death of smaller handset providers and a decline in profits, which discouraged the rapid development of new products. Whether the relative ageing of mobile phones is a good thing or whether it might slow down innovation, speed and efficiency in the long run is a separate matter.[88]

The point here is that contemporary life is not all about ever faster obsolescence. There are also counter-trends of senescence. Personal computers in the 1990s and 2000s were often replaced every two years. But these were years of rapid innovation in chips and technology. Since then, the potential for innovation has diminished, with the result that PCs stick around for five to seven years. The rise in life expectancy has been particularly pronounced for automobiles. Since the 1973 oil crisis, cars in the United States extended theirs by 50 per cent. This has made for a more lucrative second-hand car market, where sales have doubled. In these ways, passing on and second-hand are partners of rising demand rather than thrift.

Causation, though, also runs in the opposite direction.[89] Not every used good is a valuable asset like a car. Try and sell a second-hand copy of Harry Potter. EBay carries entire libraries of unsold, used books. The effect of second-hand trade on demand and resources depends on the articles in question. Most clothes are cheap and have little resale value. Their value, in turn, is conditioned by politics. Second-hand markets, like markets in general, are political creatures. The big wave of second-hand clothes flowing into developing countries seriously repressed the sale of new clothes. That is why so many countries in the

1980s and '90s banned such imports, to protect their own textile industries, although the market stalls in Zambia suggested there were plenty of loopholes for clothes from outside to slip through. It has been pressure from the World Trade Organization (WTO), since the late 1990s, which has lifted many bans on used goods. Rather than being a radical alternative to it, second-hand has flourished in a liberal market order.

Repairing is the second major process in the repertoire of keeping things alive and out of the bin. It is a topic about which we know surprisingly little. As with second-hand markets, the focus has been on textiles. Anecdotal evidence paints a picture of terminal decline. Who today under the age of sixty darns their socks, let alone knows how to turn a suit into a dress, as Rauschenberg's mother did? The age of the sewing machine – that most coveted consumer durable of the inter-war years – is over, at least for the vast majority of people in the affluent West. It is less clear why we should mourn its passing. The long hours of sewing and darning did not just reflect a love of things but also a low regard for the people who did it. Women's labour was cheap, and in the home it was free. Once wages were rising, repair inevitably became less attractive; greater productivity and the drop in the price of clothing made it even less so. Repair has become an optional, sometimes expensive hobby, less an exercise in thrift. The large German time-use survey in 2001–2 revealed that one in five men was regularly busy doing repairs around the home, fixing a bicycle, maintaining an appliance or engaged in some form of craftsmanship, for one and a half hours a day. In neighbouring Austria, a quarter of women routinely sewed and knitted, as many as went to church, and almost as many as went shopping for pleasure.[90]

In the long history of consumer society, the disappearance of the repairman has been a recent and partial phenomenon. They have come and gone as new products and technologies arrived and then, over time, became cheaper to replace. The car brought with it not only glitzy showrooms but grimy auto-repair shops – in 1967, there were 139,243 of these across the United States. The 1950s and '60s – the age of affluence – saw a four-fold increase in the value of all the various repair services in America, a bigger rise than that enjoyed by the retail trade. People spent more money on new TVs and radios, but the amount spent on having them fixed rose even faster. By the late 1960s, there were 45,000 proprietors of electrical repair shops and 20,000 furniture upholsterers.[91] Forty years later, their number had plummeted. For every four TV repairmen and appliance service technicians then, only one is still around today. Older trades tell a similar story. The disappearance of the shoe repairman from American and European street corners is characteristic. In America in 1967, over 9,000 were still fixing heels. By 2004, fewer than 3,000 were left. Thanks to the Asian miracle, many shoes, shirts, umbrellas and other articles are so cheap that taking them for repair to a cobbler or seamstress who earns even a minimum wage no longer makes sense. Anyone who has marvelled at umbrella repairmen in Delhi and Beijing and wondered why they are never around in London or Amsterdam when one needs them will appreciate the economic logic of this change.

Fortunately, there are trends in reverse as well, especially in high-end electronic products where governments have had the courage to counter the commercial tide of low-cost replacement and disposal. Japan's treatment of old personal computers (PCs) is a shining example. In 2001, a voluntary take-back and recycling scheme was introduced for used business computers. Two years later, it was extended to home computers. Instead of ending up on the trash heap, by 2004, two thirds were saved and refitted for domestic use or export. Of the 7 million used PCs thrown out every year, over 1 million PCs and laptops now find their way into a second-hand market, according to the Refurbished Information Technology Equipment Association (RITEA), the trade body of PC re-use companies. RITEA established labels and qualification schemes, including guidelines on erasing data.[92] Cheap Chinese production may have eliminated cobblers and TV repairmen in New York and Berlin, but at the same time it has given rise to a new generation of consumers hungry for refitted, second-hand products. This effect of development is easily overlooked. India, Brazil and Africa hold out a similar potential. How soon it will be tapped is unclear. At present, however, the number of refitted Japanese PCs that reach new users abroad is dwarfed by the mountains of non-functional machines and toxic electronic waste (containing lead, mercury and cadmium) that are dumped in places such as Lagos and the Ivory Coast.[93]

A final strategy of diversion is storage. In the biography of goods, lofts, garages and storage units are holding stations before 'end-of-life management' either breaks objects into recyclable pieces or buries them in a landfill. Humans have stored their valuables since they first had them. In ancient China, people kept objects in clay pots in public underground storage. In European port cities in the eighteenth century, commercial warehouses started to cater for sailors and their possessions. In the United States, professional storage traces its roots to the Civil War. The real take-off, however, came in the 1960s–'80s, with the spread of self-storage. The United States today counts 50,000 self-storage facilities which together offer a space three times the size of Manhattan.[94] One in ten households uses them. Developed countries elsewhere are following in American footsteps. In Seoul, as in Manhattan, balconies are no longer for sitting out on but for stuff; in the former, the elimination of storage inside new-built apartments added to the pressure.[95]

Never before, perhaps, in human history have hoarding and clutter given rise to so much soul-searching. As a large billboard for 'mini-storage' in Manhattan puts it: 'Material Possessions Won't Make You Happy Or Maybe They Will.' (see Plate 70) There are Clutterers Anonymous and professional organizers who coach people suffering from 'Disposophobia TM', that is, the fear of getting rid of stuff: 'Call 1 800 ThePlan'.[96] The promotion of novelty has simultaneously reinforced the urge to collect and preserve old stuff, be it for a sense of physical security, status or immortality. Collectoronline.com lists over 2,000 clubs devoted to one form of collectible or another, from glass and vintage cars to corkscrews and beer bottles. Capron, Illinois, is home to a vacuum cleaner collectors club, with dedicated members in North America and Europe. Edgar in Belgium is the proud owner of 'Holland electro toppys (his masters voice edition rare!!)'. On Vacuumland, their web-based library, aficionados can admire the 1908 Hoover Model O in action.[97] A genetic study has identified linkages to compulsive hoarding on chromosome 14 in families with Obsessive Compulsive Disorder.[98] Genetics, however, cannot explain how storage has developed into a normal part of everyday life in such a short period of time. It mainly came about because a rising number of possessions intersected with a steep rise in personal mobility, as people moved house and work more frequently.

To observe life with clutter, two American anthropologists visited the garages of middle-class families in Los Angeles between 2002 and 2004. Most had two- or three-car garages. Yet only six of the twenty-four families they studied still parked their cars in them. One had converted the garage into a bedroom; others had carved out an office or a leisure space. But most gave it over to storing old appliances and possessions. 'From construction materials to excess furniture and toys, we find items blocking driveways . . . or spilling out of garages [into back yards].' Most garages were 'usually quite jumbled and chaotic'. Only five families actively used their garage – all for recreational purposes. Half the sample did not visit theirs once.[99]

The loft and the garage were probably as crucial as recycling in rescuing the United States from its landfill crisis in the late twentieth century. The impulse to hoard was far greater than to throw away. Anthropologists in Tucson in the 1980s found that when old objects were replaced, only 6 per cent were actually thrown away. Half were given away or sold to family and friends, just under a third to strangers or shops. One third was hoarded at home.[100]

In its major surveys, the US Environmental Protection Agency (EPA) gives an indication of the mountain of stuff that is stored. American homes have turned into veritable mines of untapped materials. In 2009, some 70 million computers and 104 million TV sets lay idle in storage, most of them at home. For every three or four computers and TVs in use, there is one old one packed up in a box in a loft. An old electronic product is almost as likely to be hoarded as to be recycled.

The impulse to hoard complicates the conventional picture of wasteful consumers, but not in an entirely cheerful way. It certainly qualifies simple moralistic verdicts of a heedless disregard for things. On the contrary, people do care, perhaps too much. From a material and environmental point of view, this creates its own problems. They want replacement items but without letting go of old ones. This simultaneously sucks in more materials and blocks the release of existing ones. Lofts and garages have thus turned into a contemporary version of the pre-modern *vastus*, an uncultivated electronic wasteland strewn with computers, TVs and cameras. Hoarding works like a dam, stopping the flow of these materials back into circulation and use elsewhere. This places a serious limit on the potential of recycling. The World Re-use, Repair and Recycling Association estimates that two thirds of TV sets that are recycled are either refurbished or remanufactured into new TVs or monitors abroad. But in the United States, for example, only 17 per cent of TVs that are ready for end-of-life management are collected for recycling – a larger number sit in storage. In 2011, the EPA reckoned that it took thirteen years before even half of the old black-and-white TV sets and cathode-ray tube monitors (CRT) were thrown out – for desktop computers it was ten years.[101] By the time they are all released, people in developing countries will themselves have switched to flat screens. Who will free the machines?

Recycling of used electronics has made progress in the last two decades; in the USA, according to the latest figures (2009), a quarter of

Products in use, in storage and at end of life in US, 2009
(out of all products sold, 1980–2009)

Mobile devices
Total sold: 1,660,000,000

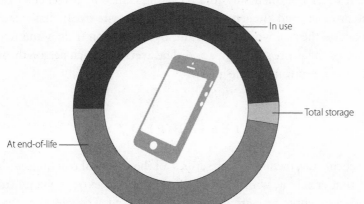

———— In use

———— Total storage

At end-of-life ————

Computers
Total sold: 857,000,000

TV's
Total sold: 772,000,000

Computer monitors
Total sold: 653,000,000

Printers, scanners, copiers
& fax machines
Total sold: 471,000,000

Source: US Environmental Protection Agency, *Electronics Waste Management in the United States through 2009* (2011).

electronics were collected for recycling. The slice has been getting bigger, but so has the cake. Between 1987 and 2007, the sale of electronic products shot up seven-fold, to 426 million units in America. A third of old computers are recycled, but other technologies, such as mobile phones, never find their way to a recycling firm. The presence of electronic products and kitchen appliances in the waste stream has steadily risen across the rich world. In Britain, over 2 million fridges and freezers entered the waste stream in 2006. The average French person throws out 25kg of electronic waste a year.[102]

MATERIAL FLOWS

In biochemistry, metabolism describes all the chemical reactions within a cell that enable it, with the help of enzymes, to extract energy from the environment to live, grow and reproduce itself. The idea of applying the concept to human society had occurred to Marx, who referred in *Das Kapital* to the metabolism (*Stoffwechsel*) between man and nature. Since the 1980s, 'social metabolism' has emerged as a key concept to capture the flow of materials and resources that societies take from the earth in order to transform them into the products, buildings and infrastructures that make up the material fabric of everyday life, and the waste and emissions generated in the process.[103]

Previously, we have followed goods from the moment they are desired and acquired to the point where they end up in the bin, the garage or a landfill. These are important stages in the journey of stuff. What might appear like a linear biography of things – from birth to death – is in fact circular from the perspective of ecology. Matter is transformed and moved: it does not die or disappear. Whether recycled, buried or burnt, material particles flow back into eco-systems, be it as sludge or CO_2 emissions. Cars, shoes and games consoles do not grow on trees. Iron and copper had to be mined and smelted, grasslands had to be created for cows to graze so as to produce the hide, and chemical factories had to be fired to create the components for toys and appliances. What we take home in our shopping bag carries with it a material past and future. And these are considerable. In a groundbreaking analysis in 1997, the World Resources Institute reckoned that, in rich industrial societies, the typical consumer would have had to carry an additional three hundred shopping bags every week, filled to the brim with all the materials that had been needed to give them the products and lifestyle they were accustomed to. Imagine carrying a large car on your back. The problem of household waste shrinks into a tiny matter when placed next to the 45,000–85,000kg of all the material used by an individual in such advanced societies every year.[104]

The analysis of material flows, made possible by new efforts of national accounting in the last fifteen years, enables us to follow this gargantuan transformation of matter over time and ask not only how much but also how well societies have made use of material resources. Direct Material Input (DMI) captures all the materials that go into processing and manufacture – the logs used to make the kitchen table, the petroleum that goes to the refinery, the iron that had to be mined to make cars, and so forth. A lot of material, however, is dug up or pulverized in the process and never makes it into the final article – to get at the iron ore, a lot of other matter has to be removed in the first place. It all adds up to the Total Material Requirement. To visualize this, Friedrich Schmidt-Bleek of the Wuppertal Institute came up with the image of the 'ecological rucksack'.[105] This is not about the weight of a product itself, nor about the materials used directly, but about the hidden material burden it carries on its shoulder, from the petrol used to ship it to the resources needed to get rid of it. We also want to know how wasteful or efficient societies have been when squeezing value out of matter, that is, the 'material intensity', or productivity, of stuff.

Material-flow analysis is not perfect. The flow has mainly been measured using national accounts. These include how much material a society imports and exports, but, since they are national, they do not count the hidden resources that are embedded in foreign products before they cross the border. A car made in Britain in a factory fired by British gas adds many more tons to the British account than a car imported from Korea which appears as if by immaculate conception, with the weight of its body only. The ecological burden of our lifestyle on distant others through the soil degradation and pollution involved in production tends to disappear from sight. National borders and statistics are rather meaningless when it comes to environmental cost. Unlike a cell, a society does not strictly speaking have one metabolism. It has lots of them. Through some households and regions, material rushes like a wild torrent; in others, it is a trickle. A lot depends on how (and how intensely) things are used, not just the total material and its value as such. Moreover, the analysis tells us about overall flow, without telling us about the effects of different materials on the environment, which vary greatly. A 24-carat diamond will have done vastly more damage than a renewable wood pellet. Water, too, is generally excluded from material-flow analyses. This is understandable – water weighs a lot and would distort the picture – but means that all the water needed to produce food and other products (so-called 'virtual' water) evaporates from sight.[106]

A final problem is that material flows are measured in relation to the value of all products made in a country (GDP). Of course, it is useful to know whether a society needs two lumps of coal to produce a product worth $9.99 or finds ways to do so with just one. But using money as a shorthand for material productivity has the unfortunate downside of obscuring the different environmental consequences between high-end and low-end versions of the same product. A person who spends $100 on a T-shirt in a designer boutique walks out of the shop with a lighter ecological rucksack than someone who buys twenty T-shirts for that price at a bargain outlet. A study of Swiss households suggests that richer families tend to consume better as well as more, preferring higher-quality goods with relatively lower environmental impact, although, in total, of course, they have more stuff than their poorer neighbours.[107] Still, however rough and limited, material-flow analysis does give us at least a sense of the general picture of how much material is needed to prop up our way of life.

Humans have interfered with the environment, clearing land and extracting resources for 12,000 years, ever since settlers first started farming in southern China and the Near East; the Chinese mined coal and used it for cooking 3,000 years ago. Methane levels started to increase 5,000 years ago and continued to do so through the industrial era. The killer gas was released by the switch to irrigation and the cultivation of rice fields, in particular. Forest clearances set free carbon. The anthropogenic impact on climate thus goes back a long way. What changed in modern times, from around 1800, was the speed and intensity of human interference. Between 1000 and 1700, the proportion of the earth's surface that was turned into cropland rose from 1 per cent to 2 per cent. By 2000, it had reached 11 per cent; the area used for pasture grew from 2 per cent to 24 per cent. Coal and industry peppered the landscape with smoke stacks. Humans started to be a bigger influence on climate than nature itself. The acceleration of global warming in the last 150 years is the result.[108]

Thanks to a team of Austrian social ecologists, we can follow material flows at a global level for the last hundred years.[109] Between 1900 and 2009, the total amount of materials extracted from the earth rose

Global development of material use, material intensity, population and GDP, 1900–2009; indexed (1900 = 1)

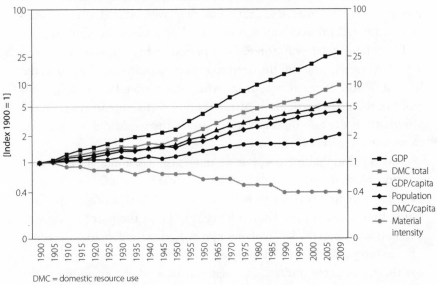

DMC = domestic resource use

Source: Krausmann et al., 'Growth in Global Materials Use, GDP and Population', *Ecological Economics* (2009).

ten-fold. Population growth was one factor – and in China was the main one until the 1980s – but what was decisive was the quickening metabolism of industrial societies. In the early 2000s, a person went through twice as much matter as in 1900. Worse – from the perspective of nature – development and the rising standard of living brought a shift in the kind of matter extracted. Renewable biomass (crops, wood) and energy, which are literally used up and, in part, find their way back into the soil (throughput materials) have increasingly given way to materials that stick around, such as cement and metals (accumulation materials). Making cement is a major source of CO_2, responsible for 8 per cent of CO_2 emissions in 1980 but a stunning 16 per cent in 2005.[110] Here, at last, is evidence of the material burden created by the global pursuit of a better life, as manifest in apartment blocks, migration to the city and the proliferation of single households that rarely feature in more optimistic pictures of consumer waste for these years.

From the point of view of a merchant or engineer, the twentieth century is an impressive success story of unprecedented efficiency gains. In 2005, it needed only a third of the materials and half the energy to produce stuff of the same value as in 1900. For nature, it nonetheless meant a bigger material burden. GDP grew faster than matter, but the world was still loosening its belt to accommodate its bulging mass. Human societies were wasting less stuff, but they were still devouring ever more. Material productivity was outpaced by a faster metabolism.

There have been only three short periods when the world enjoyed actual dematerialization: the deep recession of 1929–32, the end of the Second World War, and 1991–2, when the Soviet Union collapsed. None of these are particularly attractive models to emulate. Even in the aftermath of the two oil crises in the 1970s the world did not manage to reverse its metabolic hunger.

This is the global picture, but we must also ask about the changing position of countries relative to each other. Here, charting the total passage of materials through national statistics gets murkier, as illustrated by the case of the United Kingdom. From the point of view of national accounts, the UK emerges as a posterboy of dematerialization. The country successfully 'decoupled' growth from material input, to use the fashionable phrase. The material base of the economy is the Total Material Requirement (TMR), which includes everything that is extracted in the UK and everything that is imported, from finished products to raw materials and semi-manufactured items. Since 1970, Britain has managed to more than double its GDP with only an additional 18 per cent of TMR; for comparison, Austria, similarly, needed only half the material to produce goods of the same value as in 1960.[111] Since 2001, Britain's TMR has even fallen, by 4 per cent. In addition to the recession since 2008 – recessions slow down the metabolism – the major factor has been the decline of mining and home construction.[112] Fewer new homes meant less sand, gravel and cement, notwithstanding kitchen and basement extensions. Some accounts also suggest that Britons eat less today than a decade ago, though not necessarily more healthily.

We should be cautious, however, before jumping to the conclusion that a country such as Britain has managed to reduce its pressure on the planet.[113] While the recent decline might be heartening, from a historical perspective it is so far little more than a blip. Material intensity has failed to reverse the major increase in Britain's material bulk in the 1970s–'90s. Most worryingly, the picture of dematerialization might be a statistical illusion. At home, the balance has shifted from industry to services. Here is a major cause for the rise in material productivity. Less stuff is needed to create a £ or a $ from consulting than from extracting a lump of coal or making steel for the frame of a car. But, of course, Britons have not stopped buying stuff. They simply import more goods and resources. Material-flow figures include the weight of imported steel, cars and tinned tomatoes, but they tend to be silent about all the material and fossil fuels that have to be extracted to create and deliver these imports. Petrol imported is counted, but aviation fuel used by foreign airlines is not. For the environment, it is of little comfort that fewer Britons drive to Blackpool if more fly off to Marbella. The picture would be far less rosy if these embedded material flows were included. Britain has pushed the damage caused by its material appetite offshore; by one count, some 13 per cent of carbon emissions are embodied in manufactured imports.[114] In the British Isles, greenhouse-gas emissions have fallen by 1 per cent a year in the last twenty years. At the same time, British consumers have more than made up for this with their rising appetite for imported stuff.[115] Perhaps not surprisingly, rich countries have been loath to switch from territorial accounts to consumption-based emission accounts. The only region in the world that can claim to have accomplished all-round dematerialization is Central Asia, which went into freefall when the Soviet Union broke up.

In the 1970s, campaigners for environmental justice in the United States added 'Nimby' to the political vocabulary, drawing attention to how white middle-class neighbourhoods had mobilized around a 'Not in My Back Yard' sentiment and then dumped their waste and pollution on to poor and black communities. Material-flow analysis reveals an even more dramatic global version of Nimby-ism. In the 1950s, Europe and the United States, by and large, still lived mainly off their own resources. In the last fifty years, and especially since the 1970s, they have increasingly offloaded the burden of resource extraction to other regions. A study of the physical trade balances in the world found that developed countries shifted some 185 billion tonnes of material to developing and transition countries between 1962 and 2006.[116] The ecological rucksack of traded goods grew faster than the volume of traded goods themselves. Unlike with domestic Nimby-ism, the global imbalance runs from north to south as well as from rich to poor. The biggest environmental burden has ended up on Australian and Latin American shoulders. From here come copper, iron, meat, wool, and much more. Australia's physical trade deficit rose almost eight-fold between 1970 and 2005. Since 1980, even the United States – hugely rich in resources – has outsourced its environmental burden. Significantly, it is not only Japan, Germany and Britain that have shifted their ecological rucksack offshore but also Pakistan, Vietnam and China; naturally, small islands and tourist havens like the Bahamas and the Seychelles are also shifting theirs. In the last half-century, the world has thus come to resemble an organized mountaineering party, with some well-fed tourists striving to the top, followed by a large group of sherpas who carry their food and kit.

Ultimately, of course, we want to know what materials do as well as where they come from. The universe of consumer goods does not exist in a vacuum. It needs a supporting infrastructure. A car is no use without a road. A fridge, a hot bath and TV need electricity, gas pipes, four walls and a roof. In addition to the energy embodied in goods, therefore, we need also to consider the energy needed to make use of them. In other words, we want to know about flow as well as stock. Thanks to Patrick Troy and colleagues, we have some idea what this looked like for six districts in Adelaide in Australia in the 1990s. Troy's team reconstructed what historic data they could find on the built environment, from the thickness of the walls in houses and whether floors were made of wood or concrete to the size and age of vehicles and water pipes. This was their embodied energy. They then compared it to the operational energy needed to run the show, that is, the gas that fired the boiler, the electricity that ran the appliances and the fuel to drive from A to B. As they acknowledged, their method was not perfect – they were able to estimate how much energy was buried in the transport network but found it impossible to do the same for the gas and electric networks, other than that which went through the pipes themselves. Non-residential developments, too, escaped them. Still, it does give us a helpful rule of thumb about the energy stuck in things in relation to that needed to run them. In all six districts, people used three to four times as much operational energy as embodied energy on an annual basis. In other words, in an average year in the 1990s, it took three times as much energy to heat space and water and to drive about than the annual share it had taken to make the pipes, radiators and cars. Almost half of all operational energy was used in transport.

Things cast a huge shadow even in their afterlife. In this book, we have followed the ups and downs of recycling. Today, many cities pride themselves on being committed to zero waste and point to ambitious goals of increasing recycling and diverting waste from landfill. But genuine zero waste would have to mean zero depletion. Two sustainable designers have proposed a zero-waste index to measure how well cities perform. Their comparison of three self-proclaimed zero-waste cities – Adelaide, San Francisco and Stockholm – is sobering. Adelaide has banned shopping bags and recycles half its municipal solid waste. Still, its zero-waste index was a mere 0.23 – recovering only 23 per cent of resources from everything thrown away. In Stockholm, it was a dire 0.17 – of a Stockholmer's 480kg of annual waste, only 79kg succeeded in replacing virgin materials. Only San Francisco managed to recover half of its waste. Since many products carry a lot of embedded energy with them, recovery can make a huge difference – San Francisco substituted almost twice as much energy from the materials it recovered as Adelaide and Stockholm. By avoiding more landfill, San Francisco also saved twice as many greenhouse-gas emissions as the other two cities.[117]

All this does not mean we should belittle the advances in energy efficiency and waste management that have taken place in the last half-century. These have been nothing short of spectacular. Notwithstanding earlier campaigns for greater efficiency, the rich world was a hugely wasteful place in 1973 when the first oil crisis hit. Art Rosenfeld, who as a young man cut his teeth in particle physics with the Nobel-Prize-winner Enrico Fermi, before maturing into the father of energy efficiency in California, recalled how in November 1973 he decided to switch off the lights in the twenty offices of the Berkeley Radiation Laboratory, only to find that the switches were hidden behind filing cabinets, bookcases and posters. The lights were on twenty-four hours a day. In public as in private life, waste was endemic. One investigation the following year found that Americans encountered ten times as much artificial light outside as inside the home, even though they worked during daylight and spent their evenings at home.[118] There were two ways to meet California's hunger for energy: build new power stations or squeeze more out of existing energy. New building codes, heat-mirror windows that reflected nearby infrared radiation and prevented invisible heat from leaking out, the use of high-frequency ballasts that made it possible for 16-watt compact fluorescent lamps (CFLs) to radiate as much light as the old 70-watt incandescent light bulb and lasted longer, more efficient appliances and car engines – together, these measures saved huge amounts of energy. Better homes and building standards alone saved California the annual output of two and a half 1-gigawatt power plants. In a single decade (1975–85), the energy used in a new home per square foot for heating and cooling fell by a staggering 50 per cent.[119]

The real problem is not efficiency but why these measures have not been enough. In California, it is true, demand for power was no longer rising at the rate of 6 per cent a year per person as it had since the end of the Second World War, but it was not falling either. All efficiency measures did was to keep things steady, at the high plateau that had been reached by the early 1970s. In the rest of the country, Americans used twice as much electricity in 2008 as in 1968. In other advanced societies, many experts in these years predicted that private energy use would fall or at least stay put.[120] Reality proved otherwise. In Britain, for example, domestic energy consumption rose fairly steadily, by 30 per cent between 1970 and 2005, though it has fallen again since. In the old European Union (EU15), residential electricity use jumped by 40 per cent in the 1990s and 2000s; only Germany and Bulgaria managed to keep it static.[121] More generally, prognoses of saturation have been belied by the proliferation of stuff in our lives. As in the case of waste reduction, in their use of energy and materials, private households have proved far more stubborn and far less responsive than shops and industries. Why?

In a way, the answer has already been given in this book. It has followed how consumption has changed across time and space and stressed that rising demand is not a simple economic function, nor just a play for status, but is shaped by the interplay between political, social and cultural forces. This is as true for the period since the 1970s as it is for the five previous centuries. Those predicting in the 1970s that households in advanced, rich societies would become saturated once everyone had a TV, a fridge, and most had a car were wrong because they ignored a fundamental dynamic of consumer societies: standards, norms, technologies and habits change.

For one, efficiency carried with it the in-built dilemma that it saved people money, which could be spent on bigger things or greater comfort. Efficiency and consumption shadowed each other. Indeed, the latter often outfoxed and undercut the former – the so-called rebound effect.[122] Fridges became more efficient, but they also doubled in size. Appeals to consumers to curb their waste have often been naïvely complicit here. As an official campaign urging French people to switch off lights and keep their thermostats at 19 degrees explained in 2011: save on heat and you have more money to go on holiday.[123] Engines were made more fuel-efficient, allowing car makers and owners to expect more horsepower under the hood. The energy used per square foot in new American homes may have fallen, but the houses themselves ballooned. Total energy use in American homes has remained constant since 1978. What was saved thanks to 'low-E' windows and more efficient heating was blown away through air conditioners and a greater number of appliances.[124] A generation ago, offices in cities like Vienna were cooled by opening the window. Today, half of them are air-conditioned, as new office designs have eliminated through-flow to make the most out of rentable space. In Sweden – a pioneer of energy saving – efficiency gains have been eaten up by a 40 per cent increase in the number of homes.[125]

The shrinkage of families and the rise of single households has been a contributing factor. This does not mean that all singles are more wasteful. Solo living includes thrifty grannies as well as profligate youngsters. Intriguingly, a 1972 survey of roadside collection in New Haven, Connecticut, found that the bigger the family, the larger the waste bin, relatively and absolutely; a mother who had to look after four or five children rather than one, it was reasoned, bought more goods and fewer services.[126] From a general perspective of material use, however, such snippets are exceptions to the rule. Individuals who live on their own depend proportionally on a larger amount of embedded material and operational energy, just as the small carton of a pint of milk proportionally uses more paper than a two-gallon one. The problem is compounded by the individual ownership of appliances. In 2009 in the United States, every one-person household had a television – a third of them had two, and 13 per cent even three sets. Two thirds had their own washing machine and dryer. Every second single household had their own dishwasher.[127] Many had a large 19–22 cubic feet fridge: why go for a small fridge just because you are a small household? Freecycle and virtual sharing is nice but it means little as long as singles in their own homes live by the motto of 'to everyone their own machine'.

Inside the home, standards of comfort and more intensive habits and practices have risen in tandem. Central heating – still a rarity in 1950s Europe – has not only diffused warmth to previously chilly rooms but has helped to raise the temperature considered normal by several degrees; from 16°C to 19°C in Britain in little over a decade since 1990. Smarter boilers, a cult of fitness and busyness and ideas of athletic beauty mean that most people in the rich world no longer wash over the sink or have a weekly bath but have a hot shower at least once a day, if not more. People and their clothes have never been cleaner. The volume of laundry has risen five-fold in Britain in the course of the twentieth century. In the USA, most singles run two to five loads a week, which hints at the great frequency with which clothes are changed these days.[128] With the homes, bathrooms, urban infrastructures and leisure spaces they design, urban planners, architects and policy-makers are busy encrypting such 'normal' conventions and practices into the material fabric of our future lives. It is difficult to revert to communal bathing once the bathhouse has been sold off and turned into condominiums.[129]

More than ever before, the home has morphed into one gigantic socket. In the United Kingdom, the electricity used by household appliances has doubled in the three decades since the 1973 oil crisis. Bigger freezers and bigger TVs are part of the story, but so is the influx of a new generation of gadgets, from Game Boys to digital phones and cameras which need their batteries recharged. In 2009, the average British home had more than ten times as many consumer electronic goods as in 1990. Notwithstanding energy efficiency and an attack on the silent waste of stand-by, energy consumption rose six-fold. In the United States, 5 million desktop computers were sold in 1983. Twenty years later, it was 35 million. New technological features, such as plasma screens, ensured that older products, too, never reached a point of saturation. In 2003, almost twice as many TVs were sold in the USA as in 1983.[130]

The home mirrors the faster circulation of material flows at a global level. Our material metabolism has quickened – not for every person but for most. New stuff and gadgets have grabbed the attention, but what is, perhaps, more troubling is that the proliferation has affected older kinds of articles and more conventional goods just as much. In 2006, British women bought twice as many clothes as they had ten years earlier. It is not only more electronic goods but more furniture that ends up on the waste heap; in the USA, the amount of furniture in municipal solid waste almost doubled between 1960 and 2009, reaching 9.9 million tons.[131] Greater access to storage outside the home has failed to stop the pressure for space within it – quite the opposite. Professional storage and loft and kitchen extensions are symptoms of the same problem, just in different places. In the United States, the typical large kitchen in 2004 contained 330 different and a total of 1,019 items. Even a small one had a total of 655 items – three times as many as in 1948. Waffle irons, blenders, grapefruit spoons and espresso cups are all competing for space. Countertops have consequently been getting bigger, as have drawers. The ideal of the eat-in-kitchen, where hosts can demonstrate their culinary skills, has added recipe books and specialized equipment, even if these are rarely used. In Britain, this ideal of the kitchen as a social rather than a work space has had particularly sharp consequences, because new British homes, uniquely, have shrunk rather than grown. The arrival of a dishwasher or a fancy cappuccino maker quickly overwhelmed the available space, especially once the kitchen was meant to be the heart of the home and accommodate a table and chairs. The only solution was to renovate the kitchen, move walls or dig out the basement.[132]

We can imagine two ideal worlds of material efficiency. One is ruled by a culture of austerity, where people live by the mantra of 'use it up, wear it out, make it do'. The other is a more dynamic and intense regime where lots of things race at high speed without causing waste and damage because the flow is circular and so efficient that old is constantly turned into new. At present, we are a long way from the first but not much nearer to the second. In popular mentality and everyday life, the debate about wastefulness has been dominated by the waste bin and the recycling container – so much so that it often seems as if we hold the answer to the problem of waste in our own hands as long as we remember to return bottles and espresso pods and sort our garbage responsibly. A study of five European cities in 2002 found that, everywhere, waste was the one environmental issue that mattered most to consumers. Using second-hand goods and eating less meat, by contrast, 'were not important at all'.[133] This is a dangerously lop-sided state of affairs. For the planet, re-using glass bottles and separating food waste is a nice gesture, but it is the busy, energy-hungry lives we lead at home and on the roads and in the air that are the real threat. Domestic waste needs to be put in perspective. In a rich society such as Britain, almost a third of all CO_2 emissions come from our homes. Personal travel raises it to 47 per cent. Recycling has been little more than a comforting distraction from the stuff that really matters.

Epilogue

What is to be done?

Our lifestyle is characterized by high and rising levels of consumption, in rich societies and increasingly in developing societies, too. Yet resources are finite and consuming them carries significant environmental costs. Most readers will be aware of this problem. There is now an industry of forecasts and models, utopias and dystopias, and global conferences setting goals for a more sustainable world by 2020 or 2050. Most of these begin in the present and then project forward to a better future. This book, on the other hand, offers a historical perspective. It looks to the past to bring to light the long-term forces and deeper currents that have made consumption ever more central in modern societies. It is this longer history that continues to shape the way we use, live with and think about things.

A good deal of current analysis and policy is restless, always in search of the next best technological solution or regulatory goalpost. History is often little more than a point of departure from which to escape. Or it can serve as a backdrop to contrast the present with an unspecified industrial or pre-industrial era, as if the past was cast out of solid blocks. Some of the sentiment is understandable. A lot of environmental damage has already been done, so it is tempting to draw a line now and focus on more sustainable forms of consumption in the future. Historical knowledge can appear an indulgence when compared to the hard sciences and engineering which are cracking on with the immediate task of developing more efficient products and delivering cleaner energy. It therefore rarely makes it into the tool kit.

But the past is not just a costly page in the ledger of humanity that we can turn over as simply as that. Our material history is not prior: we carry it with us today and it is bound to affect our future. By revealing the diversity and dynamics of change, historical knowledge also enables us to look with fresh eyes at what today can appear to be normal, natural and immutable – for what is normal today was not so in the past and, inversely, a lot of what appeared normal to previous cultures would strike us as abnormal today. A historical perspective is therefore essential if we want to understand the surge of consumption and its underlying causes, and the first step before we can evaluate what are more or less promising remedies.

In recent discourse, the critique of 'consumerism' has, notably, come in two guises. For the first, the root of the problem is a social and moral failure: people want constantly more than they *really* need, egged on by brands, advertisers and corporations and by their own desire to show off and emulate their superiors. The second sees 'consumerism' as part of a larger obsession with economic growth that triumphed after the Second World War.[1] Liberate rich societies from the gospel of growth and switch to 'zero growth', and the unsustainable surge of material goods will come to a stop. Sometimes, the two views work together. Neither offers a compelling historical account.

Complaints about conspicuous consumption by the rich and by others who spend beyond their means in an attempt to imitate them are as old as human civilization. There is nothing particularly new or modern about it. In the first century CE, the Roman philosopher Seneca worried constantly about the way riches turned lesser mortals into slaves to pleasure.[2] In the mid-eighteenth century, Rousseau and other thinkers attacked the corrupting lust for luxury. But the world's material metabolism has accelerated enormously since. Clearly, status-seeking cannot be the principal explanation for our unprecedented levels of consumption. To focus on shopping sprees, branded accessories or luxury yachts misses the wood for the trees. True, some goods and leisure practices involve showing off. In the larger picture, though, these represent just a small fraction of our voracious material desire. Most goods and services are acquired and used for other purposes, such as creating a comfortable home and fashioning one's identity, in the pursuit of activities and entertainment, or being with friends and family. In brief, the focus on showing off comes from an ancient moral script that is out of synch with the present scale of consumption and the threat it poses to the planet. Even if it were possible to outlaw all luxury bags, designer watches and other items of conspicuous consumption tomorrow, it is hard to see how this would make a big difference to what is currently an unsustainable use of material resources. Nor is it clear that such measures would necessarily be fair and democratic. Who would decide what is conspicuous or excessive for whom? The lesson of the sumptuary laws in early modern Europe is that it was patrician men who used such measures mainly to repress the material lives of women. It tends to be well-off commentators, like Seneca, who berate others for being in the grip of material temptations. It is rarely common people. Such voices, in other words, should not be taken at face value. Rather, they are one side of the pendulum of consumption that has swung back and forth between more goods and the disquiet they set off.

The idea that rising consumption was born out of the growth model adopted after the Second World War, by contrast, takes too short a view. Zero-growth advocates continue to orbit in the mental universe of J. K. Galbraith's *The Affluent Society*. The 'affluent society', as we have seen, was a brilliant thesis and constituted a major political intervention. But even at the time it was dubious history. Now, half a century later, its weaknesses are clear. The high-growth years of the postwar boom amplified and intensified consumption: they did not prompt a sudden take-off. Almost all the forces driving up consumption were in place by the time Western states embraced sustained growth in the 1950s: the rise in domestic comfort, fashion and novelty; shopping for pleasure; a taste for articles from faraway lands; rising levels of water and energy use; the cult of domestic possessions and hobbies; urban entertainment and pleasure; credit and debt; and the notion of the 'material self', which recognized that things are an inextricable part of what makes us human.

In this book, we have followed the history of these strands and how they came to be woven together. To attribute the rise in consumption to postwar growth or to neo-liberalism is both historically wrong and politically wrong-headed. The yearning for more goods and services was not the child of standardized mass production. Demand for fashionable cotton, comfortable bedding or an exotic cup of tea or cocoa, for example, were rising before the Industrial Revolution gathered steam in the late eighteenth century. Compared to the booming West in the 1950s and 1960s, early modern Europe and late Ming China were low-growth societies, but this does not mean their material appetites were stagnant. Commerce and culture fed their expansion, thanks to new tastes and habits as well as lower prices. How zero-growth today would automatically curb such expansion is difficult to see in the light of this longer history.

Slow or no growth also tends to lead to unpleasant distributional conflicts. It is unlikely that any resulting reductions in the use of material resources would be distributed fairly, either within nations or across the globe. Why would powerful elites in the rich West give up their fair share of goods and services? And why would groups on low incomes embrace zero growth as likely to increase their share of a diminishing cake? For poor and developing countries, similarly, such a paradigm shift in the West would hardly be attractive: how would the standard of living of the global South rise without demand for their goods from the affluent North? The Nobel Prize-winner Joseph Stiglitz and other economists have repeatedly warned how rising inequality since the 1970s has come at a high price: it represses growth.[3] Conversely, low growth threatens to cement inequality, both within the West and between the affluent West and the less fortunate rest. It also makes it more difficult to turn dirty growth into green growth. Countries that are stagnant or growing slowly resemble vehicles that are standing still: they are much harder to move and steer in a new direction than those on the move.

This book, then, offers a dose of historical realism. Whether we like it or not, we need to face up to the considerable power and resilience that consumer culture has demonstrated over the last half-millennium. In addition to stressing the long duration of this process, the preceding chapters have revealed several characteristics that have tended to be ignored or misunderstood.

Many commentators speak of 'consumer society' in the singular, a tendency that harks back to the early twentieth century, when the concept was associated with the United States and the American way of life, with its then unrivalled level of material comfort and consumer spending. In reality, consumer societies have taken on a variety of guises and arrived via different pathways. What sets them apart is how high levels of consumption have been created, funded and distributed, not their material metabolism as such. Germany, Japan and Finland, for example, took the road of saving (instead of credit) to develop into high-consumption societies. The United States continues to rely disproportionately on private consumer spending. Scandinavia and France, by contrast, afford a different model, where the state makes up for lower private consumer spending with pensions, benefits and other kinds of public support.

The label 'consumer society' also disguises considerable variation within countries. If a country has a huge credit-card bill, it does not automatically follow that its inhabitants are excessive and wasteful all round. Rising consumption is not some sort of virus that transforms the entire social body equally. Germans save and use credit cards with extreme caution, for example, but it does not mean they do not also produce a lot of waste; they throw away as much as Americans. Similarly, variations apply to social groups. Highly educated professional elites pursue multiple, highly active and resource-intensive leisure activities that set them apart from their less privileged neighbours, with their more settled pastimes.

As a way of life and as an ideal, consumption has shown remarkable adaptability over time. It has been difficult to see this because of the fixation with the United States, and the associated belief that consumption was a testimony to the superiority of Anglo-Saxon markets and liberal democracy. The decline of the American empire and the resurgence of China since the 1980s have shaken up this seemingly self-evident truth. Chinese state capitalism is only the latest in a global series of political systems that have embraced consumption. Markets certainly expanded the scope for new tastes and products in the past but, as we have repeatedly seen, they were rarely acting in a political vacuum. Empires, totalitarian states and social movements spread material norms and expectations of the good life, in addition to interfering with supply and demand. By one route or another, all modern regimes ended up promising their subjects more goods. This included socialist as well as fascist societies. Of course, the track record of delivering the goods differed. What is remarkable, though, from a world-historical perspective, is how the vision of high and rising levels of consumption managed to install itself as the undisputed cultural ideal. Ideals of frugal self-reliance have been no match, or have been limited to short-lived and self-destructive experiments like that of the Khmer Rouge in Cambodia, between 1975 and 1979.

What accounts for this extraordinary fitness to adapt and spread? Older radicals and Marxists pointed the finger at corporations and advertisers for manipulating people's desires. Liberals defended markets for giving people what they wanted. Neither of these views offers a particularly satisfactory account of change over time in a variety of settings. In addition to markets (and advertisers), two institutions deserve greater attention: states and consumer movements. Both were especially crucial for mass consumption in the twentieth century. Consumer movements gave consumption political legitimacy. They established consumers as citizens with rights and duties, widening the scope of politics and public life, especially for women, who did not have a formal vote in most countries in the early twentieth century. We can debate how successful consumer movements have been, but the point here is to stress how consumption successfully entrenched itself in political life, continuing to this day with fair trade, boycotts and other ethical initiatives.

Private consumption, however, would be in a much weaker position had it not received help from the public hand. This has ranged from subsidized mortgages in the United States to public housing in Europe, Canada and Singapore. Some of the assistance has been indirect and came in the shape of transport infrastructures and water and energy networks, which laid the basis for greater private material use, in the home and on the road. Other sources were more direct, such as public pensions, social transfers and benefits and cash allowances. Where these are 'progressive' and distribute money from the richest to the poorest – as they continue to do in Scandinavia, Britain and Australia – they boost mass consumption. But even where they are not – as in the case of public pensions in Greece and Italy – they still increase the propensity to consume by reducing the need to save for a rainy day. Today, the comparatively high saving and low consumption rate in China, where the communist state has drastically scaled back earlier welfare services, indicates how crucial the welfare state was for mass consumption in the West after the Second World War. To recognize this is also to question the old tale of inequality as a stimulus to competitive spending. Greater equality, not inequality, propelled mass consumption after the war. Today, inequality is a brake on growth in the West and East, and so, too, on consumption. The historical record suggests that there is no reason why we should assume that greater equality would suddenly temper people's material appetite for more things.

We have stressed the contribution of states, ideologies and social movements. This does not mean that consumers have been passive bystanders, merely that these institutions shaped the context in which they lived their lives. In the last analysis, consumption is so strong because it affects so much of our lives, from eating and drinking to fashioning who we are, from our hobbies and most precious possessions to social norms of comfort and pleasure. It is, ultimately, how people use goods (such as the radio in the interwar years, or mobile phones since the 1990s) that makes consumer culture what it is. Critics tend to single out shopping binges and frivolous luxury as a distraction from the good life, but a focus on such extremes misses those situations where things have given people a new identity, a better quality of life and, indeed, a sense of liberation. The rise of teenage culture is well known. This book has also highlighted the elderly generation as a major beneficiary of greater consumption in the last half-century. Just because some objects or leisure pursuits may strike some people as shallow does not mean that a lot of consumption is not deeply meaningful to those doing it, and often for good reasons. To have any chance of success, proposals that hope to create more sustainable lifestyles need to appreciate the personal and social meaning people take from their things.

The greater historical realism advocated by this book has implications for how we assess our current situation and evaluate the prospect of moving in a materially lighter and healthier direction. Some of it calls for scepticism, even pessimism, but, as we shall see, a better sense of the past also leaves us with a glimmer of hope for the future.

According to a number of recent commentators, we are already living in the twilight years of the empire of things. They announce the coming of 'dematerialization' and 'post-consumerism', marked by a growing interest in experiences, emotions and services, a revival of repairing, and the spread of leasing initiatives and sharing networks enabled by the internet.[4] By 2015, almost a thousand repair cafés had sprung up in the richest corners of consumer societies in Western Europe and North America. In the ten years since its birth in 2003, the non-profit Freecycle network, which recycles stuff for free to keep it out of the rubbish bin, has grown into a global movement with over 7 million members. People lend their sofa to travellers (couchsurfing), turn food waste into meals for strangers and hire evening dresses for a party rather than buying new. We should certainly support this growing trend: as consumers, we can (and should) make much better use of our existing possessions and extend their lives. Governments, too, could do more, for example by exempting repair services from VAT: in some countries this measure is already in place to help cobblers and bicycle-repair shops.[5] The question is whether such initiatives are part of a larger trend and will become widespread enough to tackle the scale of the empire of things and its material legacy.

The main evidence marshalled in support of dematerialization is the growing significance of services in the world economy. In value-added terms, services contributed 30 per cent to world trade in 1980. By 2008, this had risen to 40 per cent, while the share of goods was falling.[6] What we are seeing here, however, is a relative shift in value, not an absolute fall in the volume of goods. All that has happened is that services have grown slightly faster than goods. Goods have expanded, nonetheless – indeed, in gross terms, they still make up 80 per cent of world exports in 2008 (83 per cent in 2000). The latest available figures for merchandise trade offer little evidence of dematerialization. In the fifteen years between 1998 and 2013, world merchandise trade (which does not include services) doubled, in spite of the significant dip of the 2009 recession. A good chunk of that growth was made up of oil, gas and iron, coal and grain. But even just looking at other dry cargoes, the increased material flow on the oceans is astounding: it grew from 717 million tons in international seaborne trade in 1970 to 3,784 million tons in 2013. By that year, four times as many containers travelled back and forth between Europe and Asia as in 1995.[7]

These are traded materials, but the picture does not get much rosier if we turn to material consumption. In the OECD – the club of the thirty-four richest societies – domestic material consumption grew by a third between 1980 and 2007. The world's material appetite was, predictably, depressed by the 2009 recession, but already by 2012 it was once again bigger than in 2008. True, in Europe, *domestic* material consumption has fallen since the 1980s, but this is partly because a lot of production is now outsourced and the heavy materials (such as coal and pig iron) used in the manufacture of cars and gadgets for Europeans have disappeared from their national statistics. We may have seen a relative decoupling of material use from growth – that is, fewer materials are now needed to create the same amount of value as thirty years ago. Still, in the OECD as a whole, there has been no absolute fall in material appetite. The outlook gets more worrying when we quantify all the resources that are being used in the process of creating our material world – from oil, coal and aluminium all the way to the cement needed to build not only apartments but the shops and service centres of our allegedly 'dematerialized' lifestyles. In 2010, the latest available data, *total* material consumption in the OECD was 45 gigatonnes, the equivalent of 100kg per person per day.[8] That is a lot of stuff.

The immediate challenge is not a scarcity of materials as such, but the pollution, conflict and environmental damage that currently goes hand in hand with their mining, production, transportation and disposal. Aluminium, for example, is the third most abundant element in the crust of the earth (after oxygen and silicon). It is, perhaps, the element par excellence of our current consumer lifestyle, finding its way into everything from packaging, refrigerators and soft-drinks cans to car wheels, mobile phones and snowboard bindings. But its mining is often dirty, spilling out 'red mud' with polluting alkaline. Smelting and casting produces greenhouse gases. Aluminium production is responsible for 1 per cent of all man-made greenhouse-gas emissions – the growing demand for so-called rare-earth elements (used in computer hard drives, loudspeakers and hybrid cars) carries the additional risk of radioactive waste. Since 1960, global aluminium production has increased eightfold. This is not a simple story of mindless waste. The truth is more inconvenient. As industrial countries have developed and got richer, they have built up stocks of aluminium and other metals. It is estimated that three quarters of all aluminium mined in the course of the twentieth century is still in use today – a quarter of this sits in our electrical appliances. Even in high-income countries, though, aluminium production has not fallen but merely levelled off. Consequently, the OECD predicts that, without major efficiency measures in production and a switch to renewable energy, 'absolute global emissions from aluminium production are expected to continue to rise.'[9]

Not every consumer society has the same material metabolism – some are more efficient than others, some are endowed with more natural resources and churn through them more hungrily than others. Averages, therefore, need to be used with caution. What do these very large figures mean for the number of products and appliances people in rich societies consume in their daily lives? Let us look briefly at one country which has a track record both as an environmental pioneer and as a model of welfare and equality, until the social democrats lost power in 2006: Sweden. For many Anglo-Saxon commentators, the country was the healthy Nordic alternative to Anglo-American 'consumerism'. Thanks to the government's Waste Minimization Programmes for 2014 and 2020, we know in detail how many goods and products Swedes have been consuming. On the bright side, Stockholm did manage to lower its consumption of fossil fuels by 25 per cent between 1996 and 2012 – although there was no reduction in Sweden as a whole. In all other respects, however, the appetite for more has been unabated. In the 1990s, the average Stockholm resident bought 6kg of clothing each year. By 2007, it was 12kg, in 2011 over 19kg. The number of skin products and perfumes purchased has multiplied fourfold in the last twenty years. Meat consumption has risen by a quarter. In 1995, the 750,000 burghers of Stockholm bought around 1,000 large and a 1,000 small household appliances. Twelve years later, it was 2,200 and 5,000 respectively. The best that can be said is that the demand for appliances reached a plateau in 2007 and has levelled off since. The number of electronic devices, by contrast, has continued its steep ascent and tripled between 1995 and 2014.[10] If there is a trend from stuff to fluff, it has not reached Sweden.

It is a mistake to assume that services and the internet are ethereal. Leisure and communication require equipment, infrastructure and energy. In France, for example, information and communications technology (ICT) accounts for 15 per cent of the service sector's electricity consumption. In 2007, the French travelled 52 billion kilometres to do their shopping, 42 billion to pursue their hobbies and another 12 billion to eat and drink in cafés and restaurants – those staffing the service sector added another 90 billion travelling to work.[11] That is a lot of tarmac, vehicles and fuel for supposedly 'light' services.

The account in this book has raised serious questions about the idea that we are in the midst of moving from a hard, product-based economy to an experience economy. Yes, the last two decades have seen a phenomenal rise in the number of people flocking to music and film festivals, going on wellness holidays or being pampered in a day-spa. In 2000, the sale of CD albums in the United States was worth $13 billion; by 2008 it had dropped to $2 billion, as listeners were increasingly downloading their music or, more recently, streaming it. The vinyl record has had a comeback in the last decade, but this still leaves it with no more than 3 per cent of the US market in recorded music. Two thirds of music sales are now digital.[12] Is this not a clear illustration of the general switch from a culture based on the ownership of physical products to one focused on servicing experiences?

Not really, because it wrongly assumes that consuming in the past was rock solid. Many of the features of an expanding consumer economy we have encountered in this history were all about tickling the senses: the pleasure gardens of eighteenth-century London, the department stores in Paris, Moscow and Tokyo a century later, the excitement at Tianqiao market in 1920s Beijing with its diverse retailers and entertainers, shooting the chutes at Coney Island, the millions flocking to cinemas several times a week, and the craze for dance halls, to name just a few milestones. People in the past were not lacking in experiences or fun. Communication, pleasure and entertainment have been a growing feature of the emotional economy for several centuries.[13] The internet has added a new layer, not created a revolutionary break.

As visual reminders of our bulging lifestyle, things have had a bad press in recent years.[14] By shedding possessions, in this view, we will save not only the planet but also ourselves. Freeing ourselves from the shackles of material property, we will enjoy authentic experiences once again. Facing up to the environmental consequences of our things, however, should not automatically erase an awareness of the emotional work they do, as recognized by novelists and philosophers as well as anthropologists, psychologists and those working in marketing. It is a fundamental mistake to draw a sharp line between things and emotions. The empire of things expanded in part because possessions became increasingly important carriers of identity, memory and emotions. To the collector, things are friends and family, not dead matter. Clothes, cars and many other objects are prized for the feelings they generate within their owners as well as their practical use.

It is uncertain whether ICT, the internet and sharing networks will automatically lead to greater sustainability. It will depend on how consumers put these technologies to use and what they do with the savings of money and time made possible by them. The internet, computing and telecommunications are currently contributing 2 to 2.5 per cent of greenhouse-gas emissions in the world, and their share has been rising fast with the global diffusion of mobile phones, the greater power needed for higher processing speed and the growing ownership of multiple devices which are constantly 'on'.[15] In 2008, the Global e-Sustainability Initiative, sponsored by ICT companies, predicted that 'smart' technologies would by 2020 be able to save over five times their own ecological footprint by facilitating more efficient transport and buildings and by dematerializing the way we live, as things will give way to electronic and virtual alternatives.[16] What such prognoses tend to ignore is what people do with the resources freed up by 'smart' technologies. ICT, for example, has encouraged home-working and home delivery, cutting down commuting time and multiple trips to shops. These direct reductions would be significant if people stayed at home and enjoyed the time and money saved without changing anything else in their lives. The environmental gains quickly disappear, however, if they are spent on additional electronic items, a new set of clothes or an extra holiday. Innovative 'smart' technologies have been a mixed blessing so far, as the spread of new software and innovative apps to phones, computers and, increasingly, washing machines and other appliances is accelerating the product-cycle, making machines that had worked perfectly fine in a less smart environment suddenly obsolescent.

The twentieth century saw huge efficiency gains in the use of materials and energy. Refrigerators today are much more economical than they were a generation ago. Radiators are more efficient, bottles are lighter, and so forth. But it has not meant that a household's consumption has consequently declined. Instead, fridges have got bigger, central heating has raised indoor temperature throughout the home, and one-way bottles have replaced reusable ones. On top of this, additional purchasing power and leisure time are being devoted to an expanding set of new goods and services, previously undreamt of. Material use has indeed been decoupled from growth since the 1980s in rich OECD countries, but it has not declined in absolute terms, nor diminished in environmental impact.

It is not clear why the latest technology (ICT and the internet) would break with this historical pattern. Business flights and conference trips are more frequent than ever, notwithstanding the availability of Skype and videoconferencing. The crux of the matter is that new technologies don't automatically replace existing patterns of use. They often complement or add to them. In addition to virtual consumption, telecommunication and the internet have, arguably, reinforced physical consumption by expanding the awareness of the objects and places that exist in the world and making it easier to buy and visit them.

For the internet of things to displace the empire of things, it would need to replace the existing culture of use with a radically new one. This is the hope many attach to a sharing and leasing economy. The internet, in this view, will not only bring greater efficiency but wean people off ownership and socialize them into a sharing lifestyle characterized by collaboration, long product-cycles, maintenance and reuse and a low carbon footprint. So far, the sharing economy has been limited to very specific sectors, especially car travel and accommodation, while leasing mainly takes place between businesses.[17] We need to have a sense of proportion. In 2014, 92,000 vehicles belonged to car-sharing programmes – in the entire world. By comparison, 2.5 million new cars were registered in the United Kingdom alone that year, the fourth largest figure on record. In the United States, 1 million drivers belong to car-sharing schemes, and this is estimated to have reduced the sales of new private cars by half a million. That is a considerable achievement, as far as the number of cars is concerned. But it does not necessarily follow that the same members have become universal sharers, fed up with personal ownership, or that they have taken their foot off the material accelerator. People may increasingly share a car or an electric drill, but, in West and East alike, they almost all aspire to have their own apartment with private comfort and conveniences – and 'their own' more and more means exactly that – living solo, not with family or friends.[18] How many communes have grown up around car-sharing schemes?

The savings from sharing networks overwhelmingly flow back into a society centred on private ownership and pleasure. As one car-sharer told the *Wall Street Journal* in 2014, she used the money saved to go skiing in Utah, holidaying in Bermuda and touring Europe.[19]

Reuse, recycling, cradle-to-cradle product design and greater fuel and technological efficiency – we will still need to encourage all these measures. But on their own they do nothing to curb our material appetite for more. They just make resources go round more efficiently. We should also think about the consumption side and how changes to lifestyle could lower the demand for products and resources in the first place. History cannot provide a detailed list of policy measures. What it can do is give us a perspective on change across time and, in doing so, a fresh way of thinking about current problems. So far, we have stressed the long and deep roots of an increasingly resource-intensive consumer lifestyle that defies quick fixes. But, by showing us how this upward momentum came about, the same history also provides us with lessons about the types of interventions that might help change lifestyles in a more sustainable direction.

Today, the discussion of change is mainly framed in terms of choice, markets and the sovereign consumer. Behavioural economists have added the concept of 'choice architecture' to show that consumers do not make decisions in a vacuum but are influenced by available information as well as their own inertia, procrastination or unfounded optimism.[20] Their analysis has encouraged a libertarian paternalism, a mix of measures that gently nudges people towards more sustainable behaviour by improving the 'architecture' with the help of more salient information, default rules and opinion from valued groups, while preserving freedom of choice overall. This is a step in the right direction but, from a historical perspective, does not go far enough. The rise of consumption entailed greater choice but it also involved new habits and conventions, and these were social and political outcomes, not the result of individual preferences. Domestic comfort, exotic holidays, eating and drinking routines, shopping hours, what it means to be clean, fit and fashionable: these and many other aspects of our lifestyles are the historical product of social norms, expectations and arrangements.

To be sure, consumers need to play their part in change, as indeed do companies, but a sole focus on choice and markets distracts from the active role played by states, cities and social movements in laying down material infrastructures and promoting ideals of a higher material standard of living for all. This is not to argue that the era of slums, poverty and disease was a better time or that we should go back to it. But we should recognize that, however desirable from a social point of view, higher standards of housing and hygiene, the expansion of roads, water and energy infrastructures and welfare services have all been implicated in the rise and diffusion of materially more intensive lifestyles. Because these interventions have been progressive does not mean they have been benign in terms of material-resource use or for the environment. It is disingenuous for states today to say that their hands are tied and that they cannot interfere too much because they need to respect the sovereign consumer. It amounts to an abdication of collective historical responsibility.

For consumers and producers, it is critical that the carbon and water embedded in goods and services are properly priced. Without that, it is difficult for people to gain a sense of the consequences of their lifestyles for the planet and for those mining, producing and dismantling the materials for these products. On their own, however, correct pricing and labels are unlikely to be enough to change what are often deep-seated habits. For this to happen, we need a more honest public debate about how standards and habits have come to be what they are, a keener appreciation of changes in the past and alternatives for the future, and a recognition that, even today, in rich societies the most materially intensive practices are not distributed evenly. One lesson from history is that we are wrong to take our current standards as given or to assume that our lifestyles will and ought to continue into the future, just more efficiently serviced. Air-conditioning, hot showers, fast fashion and budget city-breaks are not an inherent part of human civilization. The high-flying, multitasking consumer lifestyle, in particular, which requires so much coordination and with it mobility and resources, has been a quite recent phenomenon, driven by the highly educated professional middle classes, who have taken standards of productivity from the world of work and injected them into the world of leisure, radically intensifying it in its course. It is easy to forget that, even sixty or so years ago, the same kind of people lived more sedentary, relaxed lives and that other groups continue to enjoy fewer, less hectic and less mobile pastimes. 'Slow living' advocates have tried to counter this trend, but for the most part they have been marginal and ineffective. Society as a whole continues to tick to a faster rhythm. There has to be a more general appreciation of the pleasures from a deeper and longer-lasting connection to fewer things.

Our lifestyles, and their social and environmental consequences, should be the subject of serious public debate and policy, not left as a matter simply of individual taste and purchasing power. There are plenty of opportunities for intervention, from shared housing and different standards of heating and cooling to more sustainable forms of mobility, all the way to public-information campaigns about the damage done by ever more frequent showers and changes of clothes.

Such a debate has to be bold and envisage different lifestyles and the concomitant changes to housing, transport and culture. It will need more people to remember that, as consumers, they are citizens and not just customers. And it will need historical imagination.

Acknowledgements

This book has consumed a lot of my time and thought over the last seven years. It would have been impossible without help from many people. The original idea for it came to me at the end of the Cultures of Consumption programme, a research network of over sixty experts from fashion and geography to law and business which I had the good fortune to direct. Thanks to everyone involved, including Stefanie Pearce, my superb administrator, the advisory group and to the Arts and Humanities Research Council and the Economic and Social Research Council for funding this unique and rewarding multidisciplinary endeavour. The sociologist Elizabeth Shove and the anthropologist Rick Wilk have continued to be sources of inspiration since.

Several institutions provided me with time to research and to think. I am grateful to the European University Institute for a Fernand Braudel Senior Fellowship, to Caltech for awarding me a Moore Distinguished Fellowship, to the Sustainable Consumption Institute, Manchester, and for visiting professorships at the University of St Gallen and the École des hautes études en sciences sociales, Paris. Thanks to colleagues in all these places for many stimulating conversations. Ironically, the more I followed the surge of consumption in the past, the more the present was adding new chapters to the story, as British governments decided that students, too, should be treated as consumers in an educational marketplace: that the consumer could be a citizen as well as a customer was forgotten. Financial reform and bureaucratic red tape were the results. More than ever, therefore, my deepest thanks go to my home institution, Birkbeck College, and to the Master and Dean for steering us safely through the resulting turbulence, as well as to all colleagues, students and staff for keeping Birkbeck a special place of critical inquiry, teaching and learning which makes books like this one possible.

Over the years, I have benefitted from countless opportunities to try out ideas and early drafts in lectures and seminars across the globe. I am grateful to organizers and audiences for discussion and comments in New York, Pasadena, Rio de Janeiro, Helsinki, Oslo, Gothenburg, Amsterdam, London, Oxford, Cambridge, Berlin, Cologne, Munich, Paris, Florence, Delhi, Tokyo and Beijing. Additional thanks to local experts who helped me in foreign places – in Beijing: Bingzhong Gao, Yunxiang Yan, the officers of the China Consumers' Association, and also to Karl Gerth and Julia Lovell for their advice; in Rio: Livia Barbosa; in Helsinki: Jukka Gronow; in Tokyo: Sheldon Garon and Hiroki Shin; and in Delhi: Gurcharan Das, Anjali Garg, Sanjay Srivastava, Suresh Mishra and the National Council of Applied Economic Research.

Three scholars generously read the entire manuscript and gave me the benefit of their unrivalled knowledge of culture, economy and society: John Brewer, Martin Daunton and Gerhard Haupt. My debt to them is immense. Thanks also to Sheila Fitzpatrick and Jonathan Wiesen for reading an early draft of the chapter 'Age of Ideologies', and to Chris Coggins and Heike Weber for leading me to dig deeper into waste. Ed Mayo, at the then National Consumer Council (UK), generously shared with me his knowledge of consumer advocacy, as did Robin Simpson of Consumers International. Throughout, Heather Chappells has been an ingenious research assistant.

At Harper, in New York, I have had the great pleasure and privilege to work with Jonathan Jao and his team. My thanks to them for believing in this book and bringing it to American readers. In London, Stuart Proffitt and Laura Stickney have been exceptional editors, and I am grateful to them and everyone at Allen Lane/Penguin for all their support. From start to finish, David Godwin, my agent, provided just the right mix of enthusiasm and advice, and I am greatly indebted to him and everyone at DGA.

My final thanks go to my family and are immeasurable. I have been blessed with a partner who is not only caring and supportive but, on top, is the best in-house editor any writer could wish for: thorough, demanding and critical. There is not a page in this book that has not benefitted from Lizza Ruddick's eye for style, clarity and reasoning. This book, however, is dedicated to our children, Julia and Oscar, who have enriched this journey of the material world with their humour, curiosity and tolerance, and who can finally breathe a sigh of relief and say: *consummatum est.*

Frank Trentmann
London, August 2015

Notes

The following notes list the sources directly related to the text, but these are only the tip of the research iceberg on which this book rests. Readers who wish to delve deeper into the specialized literature on a particular theme can browse my 260-page working bibliography at: http://www.bbk.ac.uk/frank-trentmann/empire-of-things/.

INTRODUCTION

1. Britons today, for example, replace their dresses and jackets every two to three years. See WRAP (Waste & Resources Action Programme), *Valuing Our Clothes* (Banbury, 2012); the figure is for Britons aged 16+. *Süddeutsche Zeitung*, 26 April 2011. For American garages: Jeanne E. Arnold, *Life at Home in the Twenty-first Century: Thirty-two Families Open Their Doors* (Los Angeles, 2012). For contrast, see the role of possessions in rural Hungary: Tamás Hofer, 'Gegenstände im dörflichen und städtischen Milieu', in: *Gemeinde im Wandel*, ed. Günter Wiegelmann (Münster, 1979), 113–35. **2.** The English title of Georges Duby's seminal 1977 book of essays. An alternative to this sequential scheme was to see history as a clash between rival identities, as in Werner Sombart's famous portrayal of the First World War as a fight between calculating English merchants and primordial German heroes: W. Sombart, *Händler und Helden* (Munich, 1915); see also: David Priestland, *Merchant, Soldier, Sage: A New History of Power* (London, 2012). **3.** For emissions, see the Intergovernmental Panel on Climate Change, *Fifth Assessment Report, Working Group III – Mitigation of Climate Change* (2014), esp. chs. 8 and 9. Emissions from transport have more than doubled since 1970, faster than any other energy end-use sector. The bulk of this increase (80%) has come from road vehicles. See also: International Energy Agency, *Energy Efficiency Indicators: Essentials for Policy-makers* (Paris, 2014); International Energy Agency, *Worldwide Trends in Energy Use and Efficiency* (Paris, 2008); for meat and nitrogen, see the Royal Society, *People and the Planet* (London, 2012). For the electronic-waste trade, see ch. 15 below. **4.** See Dominik Schrage, *Die Verfügbarkeit der Dinge: Eine historische Soziologie des Konsums* (Frankfurt am Main 2009), 43–50. **5.** Adam Smith, *An Inquiry into the Nature and Causes of the Wealth of Nations* (Chicago, 1776/1976), bk IV, ch. 8, 179. **6.** The quotation is from Neal Lawson,

'Do We Want to Shop or to Be Free?', *Guardian*, 3 Aug. 2009, 24. See also: George Monbiot in the *Guardian*, 26 Nov., 4 Feb. 2015, and 5 Jan. 2010; Lynsey Hanley, 'Shopping: How It Became Our National Disease', *New Statesman*, 18 Sept. 2006. See also: Naomi Klein, *No Logo: Taking Aim at the Brand Bullies* (New York, 1999); Oliver James, *Affluenza* (London, 2007); and Neal Lawson, *All Consuming: How Shopping Got Us into This Mess and How We Can Find Our Way Out* (London, 2009). In a more academic vein, see esp. Juliet B. Schor, *The Overspent American: Why We Want What We Don't Need* (New York, 1999); Barry Schwartz, *The Paradox of Choice: Why More is Less* (New York, 2005); Avner Offer, *The Challenge of Affluence: Self-control and Well-being in the United States and Britain since 1950* (Oxford, 2006); and Zygmunt Bauman, *Consuming Life* (Cambridge, 2007).   **7.** Milton and Rose Friedman, *Free to Choose* (New York, 1979), 3. See also the US Center for Consumer Freedom, https://www.consumerfreedom.com.   **8.** Lizabeth Cohen, *A Consumers' Republic: The Politics of Mass Consumption in Postwar America* (New York, 2003). Compare: David Steigerwald, 'All Hail the Republic of Choice: Consumer History as Contemporary Thought ', *Journal of American History* 93, no. 2, 2006: 385–403.   **9.** Tony Blair, *Guardian*, 24 June 2004, 1. See further: Tony Blair, *The Courage of Our Convictions: Why Reform of the Public Services is the Route to Social Justice* (London, 2002). The earlier point on social democrats paraphrases C. A. R. Crosland, *The Future of Socialism* (London, 1956).   **10.** Two milestones are Mary Douglas & Baron Isherwood, *The World of Goods: Towards an Anthropology of Consumption* (London, 1996, 2nd edn); and Daniel Miller, *The Comfort of Things* (Cambridge, 2008). See also: Michel de Certeau, *The Practice of Everyday Life* (Berkeley, CA, 1974/1984). For different academic approaches, see: Daniel Miller, ed., *Acknowledging Consumption: A Review of New Studies* (London, 1995); Martyn J. Lee, *The Consumer Society Reader* (Malden, MA, 1999); and Juliet B. Schor & Douglas B. Holt, eds., *The Consumer Society Reader* (New York, 2000).   **11.** Daniel Kahneman & Amos Tversky, eds., *Choices, Values, and Frames* (Cambridge, 2000). **12.** John Kenneth Galbraith, *The Affluent Society* (New York, 1958), 203.   **13.** *The Works of Aurelius Augustine, Vol. II : The City of God* (Edinburgh, 1871), 518.   **14.** 'History and Literature', repr. in T. Roosevelt, *History as Literature and Other Essays* (New York, 1913), 27. For other approaches, see F. Trentmann, 'The Politics of Everyday Life': in *The Oxford Handbook of the History of Consumption*, Frank Trentmann, ed. (Oxford, 2012), 521–47.   **15.** Fernand Braudel, *The Structures of Everyday Life* (New York, 1979/1981), 23, 28.   **16.** Neil McKendrick, John Brewer & J. H. Plumb, *The Birth of a Consumer Society: The Commercialization of Eighteenth-century England* (Bloomington, IN, 1982).   **17.** Victoria de Grazia, *Irresistible Empire: America's Advance Through Twentieth-century Europe* (Cambridge, MA, 2005).   **18.** OECD, Social Expenditure Update, November 2014, http://www.oecd.org/els/soc/OECD 2014-Social-Expenditure-Update-Nov2014-8pages.pdf.   **19.** See esp. Robert H. Frank, *Luxury Fever: Money and Happiness in an Era of Excess* (Princeton, NJ, 1999), and the discussion below at 434–9.   **20.** Readers interested in this debate might wish to turn to: Angus Deaton, *Understanding Consumption* (Oxford, 1992); Herbert A. Simon, *Models of Bounded Rationality* (Cambridge, MA, 1982); and D. Southerton A. Ulph, eds., *Sustainable Consumption* (Oxford, 2014). **21.** Thorstein Veblen, *The Theory of the Leisure Class: An Economic Study of Institutions* (New York, 1899/1953). **22.** For this emerging field, see, e.g., Jukka Gronow Alan Warde, eds., *Ordinary Consumption* (London, 2001); A. Warde D. Southerton, eds., *The Habits of Consumption* (Helsinki, 2012); and Elizabeth Shove, Mika Pantzar & Matthew Watson, *The Dynamics of Social Practice: Everyday Life and How It Changes* (London, 2012). **23.** W. G. Runciman, *Relative Deprivation and Social Justice: A Study of Attitudes to Social Inequality in Twentieth-century England* (London, 1966). **24.** In the United Kingdom in 2013, homes were directly responsible for 77 Mt or 17% of all carbon emissions, more than the entire business sector (16%); most of it was from heating space and water. 'Directly', because government statistics treat CO_2 emissions from the energy-supply sector separately (38%); see Department of Energy and Climage Change, 2013 UK Greenhouse Gas Emissions, etc., at: https://www.gov.uk/government/uploads/system/uploads/attachment_data/file/295968/20140327_2013_UK_Greenhouse_Gas_Emissions_Provisional_Figures.pdf. **25.** Thirty-five experts give critical overviews of their regions, periods and topics in: *Oxford Handbook of the History of Consumption*, ed. Trentmann. **26.** Two short exceptions with a comparative European focus are: Heinz-Gerhard Haupt, *Konsum und Handel: Europa im 19. und 20. Jahrhundert* (Göttingen, 2002); and Marie-Emmanuelle Chessel, *Histoire de la consommation* (Paris, 2012).

CHAPTER I

1. Antonia Finnane, 'Yangzhou's "Mondernity": Fashion and Consumption in the Early Nineteenth Century', *Positions: East Asia Cultures Critique* 11, no. 2, 2003: 395–425. I am grateful to Antonia Finnane for discussion. Alternatively, we could have started with the proliferation of shops, fashion and desire in late-seventeenth-century Japan, captured in the contemporary source: Ihara Saikaku, *The Japanese Family Storehouse, or the Millionaires' Gospel Modernized*, trans. G. W. Sargent (Cambridge, 1688/1959). **2.** Neil McKendrick et al, *The Birth of a Consumer Society*; Braudel entitled his discussion of the lack of fashion in China 'When Society Stood Still', in: *Civilization and Capitalism, 15th–18th Century*, I, 312. **3.** Joan Thirsk, *Economic Policy and Projects: The Development of a Consumer Society in Early Modern England* (Oxford, 1978); Chandra Mukerji, *From Graven Images: Patterns of Modern Materialism* (New York, 1983); John Goldthwaite, 'The Empire of Things: Consumer Demand in Renaissance Italy', in: *Patronage, Art and Society in Renaissance Italy*, eds. Francis Kent & Patricia Simons (Oxford, 1987); Lisa Jardine, *Worldly Goods: A New History of the Renaissance* (London, 1997); Craig Clunas, *Superfluous Things: Material Culture and Social Status in Early Modern China* (Chicago, 1991); Christopher Dyer, *An Age of Transition? Economy and*

Society in England in the Later Middle Ages (Oxford, 2005); and Maryanne Kowaleski, 'The Consumer Economy', in: Rosemary Horrox & W. M. Ormrod, *A Social History of England, 1200–1500* (Cambridge, 2006), 238–59. **4.** Ruth Barnes, *Indian Block-printed Textiles in Egypt: The Newberry Collection in the Ashmolean Museum* (Oxford, 1997). **5.** In the first half of the seventeenth century, Chinese sugar (powdered and candied) was a growing part of consignments to Europe, as conflict between the Dutch and Portuguese disrupted supply from Brazil; in 1637, over 4 million pounds of Chinese sugar were sent to Europe. Shipments to Amsterdam stopped in the 1660s once Brazil recovered, but they continued to Persia and Japan. See Sucheta Mazumdar, *Sugar and Society in China: Peasants, Technology, and the World Market* (Cambridge, MA, 1998), 83–7. **6.** 1.3% per annum in the sixteenth century, 0.7% in the seventeenth, and 1.3% in the eighteenth, according to K. H. O'Rourke & J. G. Williamson, 'After Columbus: Explaining the Global Trade Boom: 1500–1800', *Journal of Economic History* 62, 2002: 417–56. See now in greater depth, Ronald Findlay & Kevin H. O'Rourke, *Power and Plenty: Trade, War and the World Economy in the Second Millenium* (Princeton, NJ, 2007), chs. 4–5. **7.** Angus Maddison, *The World Economy: Historical Statistics* (Paris, 2003), 260–3. **8.** John E. Wills, 'Maritime China from Wang Chih to Shih Lang: Themes in Peripheral History', in: *From Ming to Ch'ing: Conquest, Reign and Continuity in Seventeenth-century China*, eds. Jonathan Spence & John Wills (New Haven, CT, 1979), 201–28. **9.** Antonio de Morga, *Sucesos de las Islas Filipinas* (1609) [*History of the Philippine Islands*], quoted at 405–8, available at: http://www.gutenberg.org/dirs/etext04/8phip10.txt. **10.** William Atwell, 'Ming China and the Emerging World Economy' in: Denis Twitchett & Frederick W. Mote, eds., *Cambridge History of China, Vol 8: The Ming Dynasty, 1368–44, Part 2* (Cambridge, 1998), 388–92. **11.** W. L. Idema, 'Cannon, Clocks and Clever Monkeys', in: *Development and Decline of Fukien Province in the 17th and 18th Centuries*, ed. Eduard B. Vermeer (Leiden, 1990). **12.** Jan De Vries & A. M. van der Woude, *The First Modern Economy: Success, Failure and Perseverance of the Dutch Economy, 1500–1815* (Cambridge, 1997), 437, table 10.4; F. S. Gaastra & J. R. Bruijn, 'The Dutch East India Company', in: J. R. Bruijn & F. S. Gaastra, *Ships, Sailors and Spices: East India Companies and Their Shipping in the 16th, 17th and 18th Centuries* (Amsterdam, 1993), table 7.2, 182. **13.** De Vries & Woude, *First Modern Economy*, 457–8. **14.** Ralph Davis, *English Overseas Trade, 1500–1700* (London, 1973). **15.** Richard Ligon, *A True & Exact History of the Island of Barbados* (London, 1657), 40. I use the original spelling but have dropped the many italics. **16.** Phyllis Deane & William Alan Cole, *British Economic Growth, 1688–1959* (Cambridge, 1962), 87; and Ralph Davis, 'English Foreign Trade, 1700–74', *Economic History Review* (2nd series) XV, 1962: 285–303. **17.** For the importance of this 'miracle food', see: Sucheta Mazumdar, 'China and the Global Atlantic: Sugar from the Age of Columbus to Pepsi–Coke and Ethanol', *Food and Foodways* 16, no. 2, 2008: 135–47. **18.** See Richard Goldthwaite, *The Economy of Renaissance Florence* (Baltimore, MD, 2009); Robert S. DuPlessis, *Transitions* to *Capitalism in Early Modern Europe* (Cambridge, 1997); and Harry A. Mis-kimin, *The Economy of Later Renaissance Europe, 1460–1600* (Cambridge, 1977). **19.** Patricia Fortini Brown, *Private Lives in Renaissance Venice: Art, Architecture and the Family* (New Haven, CT, 2004), 149 f. **20.** See Marta Ajmar-Wollheim & Flora Dennis, eds., *At Home in Renaissance Italy* (London, 2006), esp. the chapters by Reino Liefkes on 'Tableware' and Marta Ajmar-Wollheim on 'Sociability', 254–66, 206–21. **21.** Pietro Belmonte, *Institutione della sposa* (1587), quoted in Ajmar-Wollheim, 'Sociability', in Ajmar-Wollheim & Dennis, eds., *At Home in Renaissance Italy*, 209. **22.** Jacob Burckhardt, *The Civilization of the Renaissance in Italy* (New York, 1860/1958), 364 & 369–70. **23.** Ajmar-Wollheim & Dennis, eds., *At Home in Renaissance Italy*; and Jardine, *Worldly Goods*. **24.** Norbert Elias, *The Civilizing Process* (Oxford, 1939/1994). **25.** Ajmar-Wollheim & Dennis, eds., *At Home in Renaissance Italy*. **26.** Paula Hohti, 'The Innkeeper's Goods: The Use and Acquisition of Household Property in Sixteenth-century Siena', in: Michelle O'Malley & Evelyn Welch, eds., *The Material Renaissance* (Manchester, 2007), 242–59. **27.** The inventory is given in Isabella Palumbo-Fossati, 'L'interno della casa dell'artigiano, e dell'artista nella Venezia del cinquecento', *Studi Veneziani* (new series) 8, 1984: 126–8 **28.** Goldthwaite, *The Economy of Renaissance Florence*, 381. **29.** Brown, *Private Lives in Renaissance Venice*, 173–82. **30.** Gasparo Segizzi, who died in 1576; see Palumbo-Fossati, 109–53, esp. 138–45. **31.** Goldthwaite, *The Economy of Renaissance Florence*, 384. **32.** Bruno Blondé, 'Tableware and Changing Consumer Patterns: Dynamics of Material Culture in Antwerp, 17th–18th Centuries', in: *Majolica and Glass from Italy to Antwerp and Beyond*, ed. Johan Veeckman (Antwerp, 2002). **33.** Jardine, *Worldly Goods*, 33–4. **34.** Goldthwaite, 'The Empire of Things'. **35.** The conservatism was noted by contemporary observers such as the humanist Benedetto Varchi, cited in Paolo Malanima, *Il lusso dei contadini: consumi e industrie nelle campagne toscane del sei e settecento* (Bologna, 1990), 24. **36.** Robert C. Davis, *Shipbuilders of the Venetian Arsenal* (Baltimore, MD, 1991), 100. **37.** Elizabeth Currie, 'Textiles and Clothing', in: Ajmar-Wollheim & Dennis, eds., *At Home in Renaissance Italy*, 349. **38.** Evelyn Welch, *Shopping in the Renaissance: Consumer Cultures in Italy, 1400–1600* (New Haven, CT, 2005), quoted at 234. **39.** Welch, *Shopping in the Renaissance*, 68–72; Garzoni quoted at 68. **40.** Plato, *The Republic*, Book II, 'The Luxurious State' (372–37CE), trans. R. E. Allen (New Haven, CT, 2006), 55–6. See further: Christopher Berry, *The Idea of Luxury* (Cambridge, 1994); and William Howard Adams, *On Luxury: A Cautionary Tale* (Washington, DC, 2012, 1st edn). **41.** Matthew 6:19–21 (King James Bible). See also: *The Works of Aurelius Augustine, The City of God* (Edinburgh, 1871). **42.** Patricia Allerston, 'Consuming Problems: Worldly Goods in Renaissance Venice' in: O'Malley & Welch, eds., *The Material Renaissance*, 22. **43.** 1564, cited in O'Malley & Welch, eds., *The Material Renaissance*, 19. **44.** Vincent Cronin, *The Florentine Renaissance* (London, 1972), 288f. **45.** This paragraph draws on Patricia Fortini Brown, 'Behind the Walls: The Material Culture of Venetian Elites' in: John Martin &

Dennis Romano, *Venice Reconsidered: The History and Civilization of an Italian City-state, 1297–1797* (Baltimore, MD, 2000), quoted at 324 & 326. **46.** Paola Pavanini, 'Abitazioni popolari e borghesi nella Venezia cinquecentesca', *Studi Veneziani* (new series) 5, 1981: 63–126, esp. 111–12, 125–6. **47.** Ulinka Rublack, 'Matter in the Material Renaissance', *Past & Present* 219, 2013: 41–84. **48.** Kent Roberts Greenfield, *Sumptuary Law in Nürnberg: A Study in Paternal Government* (Baltimore, MD, 1918), 109. **49.** Greenfield, *Sumptuary Law in Nürnberg.* **50.** Sheilagh Ogilvie, 'Consumption, Social Capital and the "Industrious Revolution" in Early Modern Germany', *Journal of Economic History* 70, no. 2, 2010: 287–325, 305. **51.** 24 Hen. VIII. C. 13 (1532–3), in: *Statutes of the Realm*, Vol. III: 1509–45 (London, 1817), eds. T. E. Tomlins & W. E. Taunton, quoted at 430. **52.** Frances Elizabeth Baldwin, *Sumptuary Legislation and Personal Regulation in England* (Baltimore, MD, 1926), 231f. **53.** Greenfield, *Sumptuary Law*, 109, 128–30. **54.** Madeline Zilfi, 'Goods in the Mahalle', in: *Consumption Studies and the History of the Ottoman Empire, 1550–1922*, ed. D. Quataert (New York, 2000). **55.** Roy Porter, 'Consumption: Disease of the Consumer Society?', in John Brewer & Roy Porter, eds., *Consumption and the World of Goods* (London & New York, 1993), 58–81; Dominik Schrage, *Die Verfügbarkeit der Dinge: Eine historische Soziologie des Konsums* (Frankfurt am Main, 2009), 43–51; Frank Trentmann, 'The Modern Genealogy of the Consumer: Meanings, Identities and Political Synapses', in: *Consuming Cultures, Global Perspectives: Historical Trajectories, Transnational Exchanges*, eds. John Brewer & Frank Trentmann, (Oxford & New York, 2006), 19–69. **56.** Alan Hunt, *Governance of the Consuming Passions: A History of Sumptuary Law* (Basingstoke, 1996), quoted at 73. **57.** Andreas Maisch, *Notdürftiger Unterhalt und gehörige Schranken: Lebensbedingungen und Lebensstile in württembergischen Dörfern der frühen Neuzeit* (Stuttgart, 1992), 366–70. **58.** Hans Medick, *Weben und Ueberleben in Laichingen, 1650–1900: Lokalgeschichte als allgemeine Geschichte* (Göttingen, 1996), esp. 387–437. **59.** Daniel Roche, *The Culture of Clothing: Dress and Fashion in the 'Ancien Régime'* (Cambridge, 1989/1994), 56. **60.** Sheilagh C. Ogilvie, *A Bitter Living: Women, Markets and Social Capital in Early Modern Germany* (Oxford, 2003); and Ogilvie, 'Consumption, Social Capital and the "Industrious Revolution" in Early Modern Germany'. **61.** Matteo Ricci, *China in the Sixteenth Century: The Journals of Matthew Ricci: 1583–1610, trans. from the Latin by Louis J. Gallagher* (New York, 1583–1610/1953), 25, 550. **62.** Semedo, *The History of That Great and Renowned Monarchy of China* (1655; 1st Portugese edn, 1641), at https://archive.org/download/historyofthatgreooseme/historyofthatgreooseme.pdf. **63.** Timothy Brook, *The Confusions of Pleasure: Commerce and Culture in Ming China* (Berkeley, CA, 1998), 123, and for the following, more generally. **64.** Semedo, *History of That Great and Renowned Monarchy of China,* 23. **65.** Brook, *Confusions of Pleasure*, 198. See also: Bozhong Li, *Agricultural Development in Jiangnan, 1620–1850* (Basingstoke, 1998). **66.** Sarah Dauncey, 'Sartorial Modesty and Genteel Ideals in the Late Ming' in: Daria Berg & Chloe Starr, *The Quest for*

Gentility in China: Negotiations beyond Gender and Class (London, 2007), 137. **67.** Daria Berg, *Women and the Literary World in Early Modern China, 1580–1700* (London, 2013). **68.** Wu Jen-shu, *Elegant Taste: Consumer Society and the Literati in the Late Ming* (Taipei, 2007). Wu Jen-shu, 'Ming–Qing Advertising Forms and Consumer Culture' (forthcoming), with thanks to Wu Jen-shu for sharing this paper. **69.** Brook, *Confusions of Pleasure*, 6, 220. **70.** See Clunas, *Superfluous Things*, 37 f. **71.** *The Plum in the Golden Vase, or Chin P'ing Mei*, trans. David Tod Roy (Princeton, NJ, 1618/1993), Vol. I, 126, 133–4. **72.** Brook, *Confusions of Pleasure*, 153–4. **73.** The cost of funerals, Shen Bang said, could run into thousands of taels (a low-ranking official earned 35 silver taels a year); see Dauncey 'Sartorial Modesty', in: Berg & Starr, *The Quest for Gentility in China*, 134–54. **74.** Ping-Ti Ho, 'The Salt Merchants of Yang-chou', *Harvard Journal of Asiatic Studies* 17, 1954: 130–68, quoted at 156. **75.** Werner Sombart, *Luxus und Kapitalismus* (Munich, 1912), 96–7. **76.** Yue Meng, *Shanghai and the Edges of Empires* (Minneapolis, MN, 2006), 143–6. See also: Antonia Finnane, 'Chinese Domestic Interiors and "Consumer Constraint" in Qing China', *Journal of the Economic and Social History of the Orient* 27, 2014: 112–44. **77.** Cited in Brook, *Confusions of Pleasure*, 144. See also: Kenneth Pomeranz, *The Great Divergence: China, Europe and the Making of the Modern World Economy* (Princeton, NJ, 2000); Roy Bin Wong, *China Transformed: Historical Change and the Limits of European Experience* (Ithaca, NY, 1997); and Hanchao Lu, 'Arrested Development: Cotton and Cotton Markets in Shanghai, 1350–1843', in: *Modern China* 18, no. 4, 1992: 468–99. **78.** Clunas, *Superfluous Things*, 35, 38, 44. **79.** Quoted in Clunas, *Superfluous Things*, 74. **80.** Clunas, *Superfluous Things*, 111. **81.** See Kathlyn Maurean Liscomb, 'Social Status and Art Collecting: The Collections of Shen Zhou and Wang Zhen', *Art Bulletin* 78, no. 1 (1996): 111–35. **82.** *The Plum in the Golden Vase, or Chin P'ing Mei*, 223, and 383–4 for the previous quotation, which is given with the original Wade–Giles system of transliteration, and Pinyin in brackets. **83.** Dauncey, 'Sartorial Modesty', in: Berg & Starr, *The Quest for Gentility in China* , 140f. **84.** Many of Bourdieu's analytical insights about the Parisian bourgeoisie in the 1960s have a remarkable resonance for the late Ming and Qing. See, e.g., his reflections on the 'aesthetic disposition' and the continuing attraction of the 'scholastic world of regulated games and exercise for exercise' for bourgeois adolescents and housewives who lack the economic capital of the male earner. 'Economic power,' he notes by contrast, 'is first and foremost a power to keep economic necessity at arm's length. This is why it universally asserts itself by the destruction of riches, conspicuous consumption, squandering, and every form of *gratuitous* luxury'; Pierre Bourdieu, *Distinction: A Social Critique of the Judgment of Taste* (Cambridge, MA, 1984/1979), 54f. **85.** Craig Clunas, *Empire of Great Brightness: Visual and Material Cultures of Ming China, 1368–1644* (London, 2007), 137–51. **86.** Ho, 'The Salt Merchants of Yang-chou', esp. 156–60; to make the spelling consistent with the standard Pinyin system of transliteration used elsewhere in this book, I have converted the names from the older Wade–Giles system used by Ho: Ma Yüeh-kuan and Ma Yüeh-lu). **87.** Timothy Brook, *Vermeer's Hat: The Seventeenth Century and the Dawn of the Global World* (London, 2008), 74–83, quoted at 82. **88.** Smith, *Wealth of Nations*, bk. IV, ch. 8, 179. **89.** Charles Wilson, 'Cloth Production and International Competition in the Seventeenth Century', *Economic History Review* 13, no. 2, 1960: 209–21. **90.** C. Lis et al., eds., *Guilds in the Early Modern Low Countries: Work, Power and Representation* (London, 2006). **91.** This paragraph draws especially on De Vries and Woude, *First Modern Economy*; see also: DuPlessis, *Transitions to Capitalism in Early Modern Europe*; Bas van Bavel, 'The Organization of Markets as a Key Factor in the Rise of Holland', *Continuity and Change*, 27, no. 3, 2012, 347–78. **92.** Jan De Vries, *The Dutch Rural Economy in the Golden Age, 1500–1700* (New Haven, CT, 1974), 218–22. **93.** Atwell, 'Ming China and the Emerging World Economy', in: Twitchett & Mote, eds., *Cambridge History of China, Vol VIII: The Ming Dynasty, 1368–44, Part 2*, 396. **94.** For this and the following, see Simon Schama, *The Embarrassment of Riches* (Berkeley, CA, 1988), chs. 3 & 5. **95.** Clunas, *Empire of Great Brightness*, 141: **96.** Brant van Slichtenhorst; see Schama, *The Embarrassment of Riches*, 193–201. **97.** Dyer, *An Age of Transition?*; and Kowaleski, 'A Consumer Economy'. **98.** William Harrison, *A Description of England* (London, 1577/1587), ch. 8, 151–6, available at: https://archive.org/stream/elizabethanengla32593gut/pg32593.txt. For fashion in this period, see Carlo Belfanti, 'The Civilization of Fashion: At the Origins of a Western Social Institution', *Journal of Social History* 43, no. 2, 2009: 261–83. **99.** Linda Levy Peck, *Consuming Splendour: Society and Culture in Seventeenth-century England* (Cambridge, 2005). **100.** Thirsk, *Economic Policy and Projects*. See also now: Sara Pennel, 'Material Culture in Seventeenth-century "Britain"' in: Trentmann, ed., *Oxford Handbook of the History of Consumption*, ch. 4. **101.** Daniel Defoe, *A Tour through England and Wales*, II (London 1727/1928), 126. **102.** Jane Whittle & Elizabeth Griffiths, *Consumption and Gender in the Early Seventeenth-century Household: The World of Alice Le Strange* (Oxford, 2013), 120–4, 144–53. On the growing variety of products, their qualities and prices, see further: Thirsk, *Economic Policy and Projects*. **103.** Lorna Weatherill, *Consumer Behaviour and Material Culture in Britain, 1660–1760* (London, 1996, 2nd edn), table 3.3, 49. **104.** Edward Roberts & Karen Parker, eds., *Southampton Probate Inventories 1447–1575* (Southampton, 1992), Vol. I, 54–5. **105.** Ann Smart-Martin, 'Makers, Buyers and Users: Consumerism as a Material Culture Framework', in: *Winterthur Portfolio* 28, no. 2/3, 1993: 141–57, p. 154. See also: Cary Carson, 'The Consumer Revolution in Colonial British America: Why Demand?' in: *Of Consuming Interests: The Style of Life in the Eighteenth Century*, eds. Cary Carson, Ronald Hoffman & Peter J. Albert (Charlottesville, VA, 1994), 483–697; and Carole Shammas, *The Pre-industrial Consumer in England and America* (Oxford, 1990). **106.** Peter King, 'Pauper Inventories and the Material Lives of the Poor in the Eighteenth and Early Nineteenth Centuries', in: *Chronicling Poverty: The Voices and Strategies of the English Poor, 1640–1840*, eds. Tim Hitchcock, Peter King & Pamela

Sharpe (New York, 1997), 155–91.   **107.** John Styles, 'Lodging at the Old Bailey: Lodgings and Their Furnishing in Eighteenth-century London', in: *Gender, Taste and Material Culture in Britain and North America, 1700–1830*, eds. John Styles & Amanda Vickery (New Haven, CT, 2006).   **108.** Charles P. Moritz, *Travels, Chiefly on Foot, through Several Parts of England in 1782* (London, 1797, 2nd edn), 24.   **109.** Shane White & Graham White, 'Slave Clothing and African-American Culture in the Eighteenth and Nineteenth Centuries', *Past & Present* 148, 1995: 149–186, quoted at 156.   **110.** See Frank Salomon, 'Indian Women of Early Quito as Seen through Their Testatements', *The Americas* 44, no. 3, 1988: 325–41, esp. 334–7; and now Elena Philips, 'The Iberian Globe', in: Amelia Peck, ed., *Interwoven Globe: The Worldwide Textile Trade, 1500–1800* (New York, 2013), 28–45.   **111.** John Irwin & P. R. Schwartz, *Studies in Indo-European Textile History* (Ahmedabad, 1966). For the global expansion of cotton cultivation, see now: Sven Beckert, *Empire of Cotton: A New History of Global Capitalism* (London, 2014).   **112.** 'First Report' (24 Dec. 1783), *in Reports from the Committee on Illicit Practices Used in Defrauding the Revenue* (1783–4), Vol. XI, quoted at 228, figures from appendix 4, 204-1. See also: William J. Ashworth, *Customs and Excise: Trade, Production and Consumption in England, 1640–1845* (Oxford, 2003), 149–50. For French smugglers, see now: Michael Kwass, *Contraband: Louis Mandrin and the Making of a Global Underground* (Cambridge, MA, 2014), esp. 106–8, 218–20; and Giorgio Riello, *Cotton: The Fabric That Made the Modern World* (Cambridge, 2013), 121. For smuggling of silk, see: William Farrell, 'Silk and Globalization in Eighteenth-century London', PhD thesis, Birkbeck College/ University of London, 2013, 148–95.   **113.** Maxine Berg, 'In Pursuit of Luxury: Global History and British Consumer Goods in the Eighteenth Century', *Past & Present* 182, no. 1, 2004: 85–142.   **114.** J. F., *The Merchant's Ware-House Laid Open: Or, the Plain Dealing Linnen-Draper. Shewing How to Buy All Sorts of Linnen and Indian Goods* (London, 1696), A3, 7, 27, 29–30. For the sheer variety of patterns available, even to poorer consumers, see John Styles: *Threads of Feeling: The London Foundling Hospital's Textile Tokens, 1740–70* (London, 2010).   **115.** On France: Roche, *Culture of Clothing*, 126–39. For silk, see Natalie Rothstein: 'Silk in the Early Modern Period, *c*.1500–1780', in: D. T. Jenkins, *The Cambridge History of Western Textiles* (Cambridge, 2003), 528–61; and Farrell, 'Silk and Globalization in Eighteenth-century London'. See now also: S. Horrell, J. Humphries & K. Sneath, 'Consumption Conundrums Unravelled', in: *Economic History Review* (online version 17 Dec. 2014).   **116.** Roger-Pol Droit, *How are Things? A Philosophical Experiment*, trans. Theo Cuffe (London, 2005), 52.   **117.** Fourteen ducats in 1546, see Patricia Allerston: 'Clothing and Early Modern Venetian Society', in: *Continuity and Change* 15, no. 3, 2000: 367–90, at 372.   **118.** 1765, quoted in Beverly Lemire, *Fashion's Favourite: The Cotton Trade and the Consumer in Britain, 1660–1800* (Oxford, 1991), 94. See now also: Prasannan Parthasarathi & Giorgio Riello, eds., *The Spinning World: A Global History of Cotton Textiles, 1200–1850* (Oxford, 2009).   **119.** Roche, *Culture of Clothing*, 108–11; and

John Styles, *The Dress of the People: Everyday Fashion in Eighteenth-century England* (New Haven, CT, 2007). **120.** Andrew Bevan & D. Wengrow, eds., *Cultures of Commodity Branding* (Walnut Creek, CA, 2010). **121.** McKendrick, in McKendrick, Brewer & Plumb, *Birth of a Consumer Society*, 141. **122.** Phyllis G. Tortora & Keith Eubank, *Survey of Historic Costume: A History of Western Dress* (New York, 1998, 3rd edn), 147–9, 158–60. **123.** Quoted in Om Prakash, 'The Dutch and the Indian Ocean Textile Trade', in: Parthasarathi & Riello, eds., *The Spinning World*, 149. **124.** Quoted in Woodruff D. Smith, *Consumption and the Making of Respectability, 1600–1800* (London, 2002), 50. **125.** *Magazine à la Mode, or Fashionable Miscellany* (January 1777), 49–51. **126.** McKendrick in: McKendrick, Brewer & Plumb, *Birth of a Consumer Society*, 43–7. **127.** Pomeranz, *Great Divergence*; compare Prasannan Parthasarathi, 'The Great Divergence', *Past & Present* 176, 2002: 275–93; Robert Brenner & Christopher Isett, 'England's Divergence from China's Yangzi Delta: Property Relations, Microeconomics and Patterns of Development', in: *Journal of Asian Studies* 61, no. 2, 2002: 609–22; and Kenneth Pomeranz, 'Standards of Living in Eighteenth-Century China: Regional Differences, Temporal Trends, and Incomplete Evidence', in: *Standards of Living and Mortality in Pre-industrial Times*, eds. Robert Allen, Tommy Bengtsson & Martin Dribe (Oxford, 2005), 23–54. **128.** Robert C. Allen, *The British Industrial Revolution in Global Perspective* (Cambridge, 2009); Robert C. Allen et al., 'Wages, Prices and Living Standards in China, Japan and Europe, 1738–1925', GPIH Working Paper no. 1, (2005); and Stephen Broadberry & Bishnupriya Gupta, 'The Early Modern Great Divergence: Wages, Prices and Economic Development in Europe and Asia, 1500–1800', *Economic History Review* 59, no. 1, 2006: 2–31. Compare now: Jane Humphries, 'The Lure of Aggregates and the Pitfalls of the Patriarchal Perspective: A Critique of the High Wage Economy Interpretation of the British Industrial Revolution', *Economic History Review* 66, 2013: 693–714; and Robert C. Allen, 'The High Wage Economy and the Industrial Revolution: A Restatement', *Economic History Review* 68, no. 1, 2015: 1–22 **129.** Kenneth Pomeranz, 'Chinese Development in Long-run Perspective', in: *Proceedings of the American Philosophical Society* 152, 2008: 83–100; and Prasannan Parthasarathi, *Why Europe Grew Rich and Asia Did Not: Global Economic Divergence, 1600–1850* (Cambridge, 2011), 37–46. **130.** Bozhong Li, 'Xianminmen chi de bucuo', *Deng Guangming xiansheng bainian shouchen jinian wenji* (2008). I am grateful to Bozhong Li for an English version of this article. For opium, see Zheng Yangwen, *The Social Life of Opium in China* (Cambridge, 2005). **131.** Tokugawa Japan was more equal still, but it was also closed to international commerce. Japanese living standards in this period may have been underestimated, because many peasant households received land shares of their outputs as well as enjoying additional income from wives, children and non-agricultural jobs; see now: Osamu Saito, 'Growth and Inequality in the Great and Little Divergence Debate: A Japanese Perspective', *Economic History Review* 68, 2015: 399–419; and Osamu Saito, 'Income Growth and Inequality over the Very Long Run: England, India and Japan

Compared', (2010), at: http://src-h.slav.hokudai.ac.jp/rp/publications/noo2/ P1-C1_Saito.pdf. **132.** Neil McKendrick, 'Home Demand and Economic Growth', in: N. McKendrick, ed., *Historical Perspectives* (London, 1974), 209 **133.** Daniel Defoe, *Everybody's Business is Nobody's Business* (1725), De Foe's Works, Vol. II (London, 1854 edn), 499f., 504. **134.** See Styles, *Dress of the People.* **135.** Jan De Vries, 'The Industrial Revolution and the Industrious Revolution', *Journal of Economic History* 54, no. 2, 1994: 249–70. **136.** The following draws on Craig Muldrew, *Food, Energy and the Creation of Industriousness: Work and Material Culture in Agrarian England, 1550–1780* (Cambridge, 2011). **137.** Hans-Joachim Voth, *Time and Work in England, 1750–1830* (Oxford, 2001). Whether late-medieval workers enjoyed so much more leisure is debatable; see: Gregory Clark & Ysbrand van der Werf, 'Work in Progress? The Industrious Revolution', *Journal of Economic History* 58, no. 3, 1998: 830–43. **138.** Frederic Morton Eden, *The State of the Poor: Or, an History of the Labouring Classes in England* (London, 1797), Vol. II, 87–8. **139.** Julie Marfany, 'Consumer Revolution or Industrious Revolution? Consumption and Material Culture in Eighteenth-century Catalonia'; for the limited number of new objects, see J. Torras & B. Yun, eds., *Consumo, condiciones de vida y comercialización: Cataluña y Castilla, siglos XVII–XIX* (Castile and León, 1999); Jan De Vries, 'Peasant Demand Patterns and Economic Development: Friesland 1550–1750', in: *European Peasants and Their Markets*, eds. W. N. Parker & E. L. Jones (Princeton, NJ, 1975); and Mark Overton, Jane Whittle, Darron Dean & Andrew Hann, *Production and Consumption in English Households, 1600–1750* (London, 2004). **140.** Ogilvie, 'Consumption, Social Capital, and the "Industrious Revolution" in Early Modern Germany'. **141.** Quoted in DuPlessis, *Transitions to Capitalism in Early Modern Europe*, 36. **142.** Regina Grafe, *Distant Tyranny: Markets, Power and Backwardness in Spain, 1650–1800* (Princeton, NJ, 2012). **143.** Fernando Carlos Ramos Palencia, 'La demanda de textiles de las familias castellanas a finales del Antiguo Régimen, 1750–1850: ¿Aumento del consumo sin industrialización?', in: *Revista de historia económica* 21, no. S1, 2003: 141–78; and Torras & Yun, eds., *Consumo, condiciones de vida y comercialización.*

CHAPTER 2

1. Girolamo Benzoni, *La historia del Mondo Nuouo* (1572 edn; 1st edn, Venice, 1565), 103, my translation. **2.** George Sandys, *Travels* (1615), quoted in Anon., *The Vertues of Coffee* (London, 1663), 8, reprinted in Markman Ellis, ed., *Eighteenth-century Coffee-house Culture, Vol. IV* (London, 2006). **3.** J. H. Bernadin de Saint-Pierre, *Voyage à l'Îsle de France* (1773). **4.** Sidney Mintz, *Sweetness and Power: The Place of Sugar in Modern History* (New York, 1985). **5.** Arjun Appadurai, ed., *The Social Life of Things: Commodities in Cultural Perspective* (Cambridge, 1986). See also: Robert J. Foster, 'Tracking Globalization: Commodities and Value in Motion', in: *Handbook of Material*

Culture, eds. Christopher Tilley, et al. (London, 2006); Felipe Fernández-Armesto, *Food: A History* (London, 2002). **6.** Elias, *The Civilizing Process*. Gabriel Tarde had formulated a similar top-down model in the 1890s. **7.** Jürgen Habermas, *The Transformation of the Public Sphere* (Cambridge, 1989; 1st German edn, Germany, 1976). **8.** Wolfgang Schivelbusch, *Tastes of Paradise: A Social History of Spices, Stimulants and Intoxicants* (New York, 1992). **9.** Mintz, *Sweetness and Power*. **10.** Compare the more Eurocentric treatment by Fernand Braudel, *The Structures of Everyday Life* (New York, 1979/1981), 249–60. **11.** Heinrich Barth, *Reisen und Entdeckungen in Nord- und Zentralafrika in den Jahren 1849–55* (Wiesbaden, 1858/1980), 238, my translation. **12.** Antonio de Alcedo, 1786, quoted in Ross W. Jamieson, 'The Essence of Commodification: Caffeine Dependencies in the Early Modern World', *Journal of Social History*, 2001: 269–94, 278. For the above and the following, see also: William Gervase Clarence-Smith, *Cocoa and Chocolate, 1765–1914* (London, 2000); and William Gervase Clarence-Smith & Steven Topik, eds., *The Global Coffee Economy in Africa, Asia and Latin America, 1500–1989* (Cambridge, 2003). **13.** Johann Kaspar Riesbeck, 1780, quoted in Christian Hochmuth, *Globale Güter – lokale Aneignung: Kaffee, Tee, Schokolade und Tabak im frühneuzeitlichen Dresden* (Konstanz, 2008), 64, my translation. **14.** Roman Sandgruber, *Bittersüße Genüße: Kulturgeschichte der Genußmittel* (Vienna, 1986), 80f. **15.** Retained imports of tea were 540 tons in 1724, but tea leaves produce around four times as much beverage as coffee, by unit. My estimate takes into account loss of weight during roasting. Calculated from retained import data in Elizabeth Boody Schumpeter, *English Overseas Trade Statistics 1697–1808* (Oxford, 1960), table XVIII. **16.** For this and the following, see Jamieson, 'Essence of Commodification', Marcy Norton, 'Tasting Empire: Chocolate and the European Internalization of Mesoamerican Aesthetics ', *American Historical Review* 111, no. 3, 2006: 660–91; Michael D. Coe & Sophie D. Coe, *The True History of Chocolate* (London, 1996); and Kenneth F. Kiple & Kriemhild Ornelas, eds., *The Cambridge World History of Food*, 2 vols. (Cambridge, 2000). **17.** Jacob Spon, *De l'usage, du caphé, du thé, et du chocolate* (Lyon, 1671); I quote from the contemporary English translation by John Chamberlayne, *The Manner of Making Coffee, Tea and Chocolate* (London, 1685), reprinted in Ellis, ed., *Eighteenth-century Coffee-house Culture*, Vol. IV , 105–11. **18.** Quoted from John Chamberlayne, *The Natural History of Coffee, Tea, Chocolate, Tobacco* (London, 1682), 4–5. **19.** Chamberlayne, *The Manner of Making Coffee*. For Red Sea piracy, see K. N. Chaudhuri, *The Trading World of Asia and the English East India Company, 1660–1760* (Cambridge, 1978), 361. **20.** James Howell, 1650s, cited in *The Vertues of Coffee*. Pepys's diary, 24 April 1661. **21.** James Howell, 1650s, cited in *The Vertues of Coffee*. **22.** Habermas, *Transformation*; Brian Cowan, *The Social Life of Coffee: The Emergence of the British Coffeehouse* (New Haven, 2005); Hochmuth, *Globale Güter*; James Livesey, *Civil Society and Empire* (New Haven, CT, 2009); Jean-Claude Bologne, *Histoire des cafés et des cafetiers* (Paris, 1993). **23.** P. 'Considerazioni sul Lusso', in: *Il Caffè* (Milan, 1764), 110, my translation. **24.** Amanda Vickery, *The Gentleman's Daughter: Women's Lives in Georgian England* (New Haven, CT, 1998), 206–8. **25.** Michael North, *Genuß und Glück des Lebens: Kulturkonsum im Zeitalter der Aufklärung* (Cologne, 2003), 209. **26.** Jean de La Roque, *An Historical Treatise Concerning the Original [sic] and Progress of Coffee, as well as in Asia as Europe* (1715; London edition, 1732), repr. in: Ellis, ed., *Eighteenth-century Coffee-house Culture, Vol. IV* , 277–312. For de La Roque, see Ina Baghdiantz McCabe, *Orientalism in Early Modern France: Eurasian Trade, Exoticism and the Ancien Regime* (Oxford, 2008), 172f. **27.** Anne McCants, 'Poor Consumers as Global Consumers: The Diffusion of Tea and Coffee Drinking in the Eighteenth Century', *Economic History Review* 61, 2008: 172–200; Wouter Ryckbosch, 'A Consumer Revolution under Strain: Consumption, Wealth and Status in Eighteenth-century Aalst', PhD thesis, Antwerp (2012); John Styles, 'Lodging at the Old Bailey: Lodgings and Their Furnishing in Eighteenth-century London', in: *Gender, Taste and Material Culture in Britain and North America, 1700–1830*, eds. John Styles & Amanda Vickery (New Haven, CT, 2006); and Lorna Weatherill, *Consumer Behaviour and Material Culture in Britain, 1660–1760* (London, 1996, 2nd edn). **28.** Edward Eagleton, 1785, quoted in Hoh-cheung Mui & Lorni Mui, *Shops and Shopkeeping in Eighteenth-century England* (London, 1987), 257. For variety, see Jon Stobart, *Sugar and Spice: Grocers and Groceries in Provincial England, 1650–1830* (Oxford, 2013), 50–6. **29.** Hochmuth, *Globale Güter*, 134, 142. **30.** Robert Batchelor, 'On the Movement of Porcelains: Rethinking the Birth of the Consumer Society as Interactions of Exchange Networks, China and Britain, 1600–1750', in: *Consuming Cultures, Global Perspectives*, 95–122. **31.** The above draws on Maxine Berg, *Luxury and Pleasure in Eighteenth-century Britain* (Oxford, 2005), 52–75, 128–49; Chaudhuri, *Trading World of Asia*; Chuimei Ho, 'The Ceramics Trade in Asia, 1602–82', in: *Japanese Industrialization and the Asian Economy*, ed. A. J. H. Latham & Heita Kawakatsu (London, 1994), 35–70; Fang Lili, *Chinese Ceramics* (Beijing, 2005). **32.** Jonas Hanway, *Letters on the Importance of the Rising Generation of the Labouring Part of Our Fellow-subjects* (London, 1757), II, letter XXX, 174–85. **33.** Legrand d'Aussy, *Histoire de la vie privée des François* (Paris, 1815; 1st edn 1783), 145, my translation. **34.** La Roque, *Progress of Coffee*, 366. **35.** Dr Fothergill to J. Ellis, 2 September 1773: in John Ellis, *An Historical Account of Coffee* (London, 1774), 38, repr. in Ellis, ed., *Eighteenth-century Coffee-house Culture, Vol. IV*. **36.** Postlethwayt, *The African Trade* (1745), quoted in Eric Williams, *Capitalism and Slavery* (Chapel Hill, NC, 1944/1994), 52. **37.** Joseph E. Inikori, *Africans and the Industrial Revolution in England* (Cambridge, 2002); 'Roundtable, Reviews of Joseph Inikori, Africans and the Industrial Revolution in England', *International Journal of Maritime History* XV, no. 2, Dec. 2003: 279–361. Patrick O'Brien, 'Fiscal and Financial Preconditions for the Rise of British Naval Hegemony 1485–1815', working paper 91 (2005), http://www.lse.ac.uk/collections/economicHistory/pdf/WP9105.pdf. **38.** S. D. Smith, 'Accounting for Taste: British Coffee Consumption in Historical Perspective', *Journal of*

Interdisciplinary History 27, 1996: 183–214.   **39.** La Roque, *Progress of Coffee*; Zedler's *Universal-lexikon*, quoted in Annerose Menninger, *Genuß im kulturellen Wandel: Tabak, Kaffee, Tee und Schokolade in Europa (16.–19. Jahrhundert)* (Stuttgart, 2004), 317.   **40.** Fothergill to Ellis, 2 September 1773, in Ellis, *An Historical Account of Coffee* (London, 1774), 30.   **41.** Edward Gibbon Wakefield, *England and America* (New York, 1834), 84.   **42.** As in the case of the wool industry in the West Riding of Yorkshire.   **43.** Berg, 'Pursuit of Luxury'. I write 'favoured' because consumer demand in the empire was not by itself a sufficient cause for the Industrial Revolution. At the same time, the many feedbacks between overseas and domestic developments make it unhelpful to draw an overly sharp distinction between exogenous and endogenous factors. For Europe's advance in science and technology, see Joel Mokyr, *The Gifts of Athena: Historical Origins of the Knowledge Economy* (Princeton, NJ, 2002).   **44.** Jan De Vries, *European Urbanization, 1500–1800* (Cambridge, MA, 1984); Paul Bairoch, *De Jéricho à Mexico: Villes et économie dans l'histoire* (Paris, 1985); Peter Clark, ed., *The Oxford Handbook of Cities in World History* (Oxford, 2013). Li Bozhong's recent research suggests that as many as 20% of the population in the Jiangnan region might have been urban during the Qing era. My point here is about degrees, not absolutes. China did not lack towns and cities, it just had fewer of them.   **45.** Weatherill, *Consumer Behaviour and Material Culture in Britain, 1660–1760*, table 4.2. As she notes, the exceptions were less conspicuous items such as books.   **46.** Andrew Hann & Jon Stobart, 'Sites of Consumption: The Display of Goods in Provincial Shops in Eighteenth-century England', *Cultural and Social History* 2, 2005: 165–87, esp. 177.   **47.** Bernard Mandeville, *The Fable of the Bees* (1714; London, 1989), Remark (M), 152. A widespread observation, e.g. John Rae: 'In town Molly Seagrim would have been admired as a fantastical fine lady; in the country she got herself mobbed': *Statement of Some New Principles on the Subject of Political Economy* (Boston, 1834), 280.   **48.** Stephen D. Greenblatt, *Renaissance Self-fashioning* (Chicago, IL, 1960); see also P. D. Glennie & N. J. Thrift, 'Modernity, Urbanism and Modern Consumption', *Environment and Planning D: Society and Space* 10, 1992: 423–43.   **49.** According to Wim van Binsbergen, in Wim M. J. van Binsbergen & Peter L. Geschiere, eds., *Commodification: Things, Agency and Identities (The Social Life of Things Revisited)* (Münster, 2005) quoted at 33. See also: Igor Kopytoff, 'The Cultural Biography of Things', in Appadurai, ed., *Social Life of Things*, esp. 84. Whether this is a satisfactory view of Descartes or Kant is a different matter. That the Cartesian self was more than the mind is explored in Karen Detlefsen, ed., *Descartes' Meditations: A Critical Guide* (Cambridge, 2013).   **50.** Bruno Latour, 'From Realpolitik to Dingpolitik', in: *Making Things Public: Atmospheres of Democracy*, ed. Bruno Latour & Peter Weibel (Cambridge, MA, 2005); Bruno Latour, *We Have Never Been Modern* (Cambridge, MA, 1993); see further, Frank Trentmann, 'Materiality in the Future of History: Things, Practices and Politics', *Journal of British Studies* 48, no. 2, 2009: 283–307.   **51.** The term is Cook's, on whose book, Harold J. Cook, *Matters of Exchange: Commerce, Medicine and Science in the*

Dutch Golden Age (New Haven, CT, 2007), I have drawn here. **52.** Brook, *Vermeer's Hat,* quoted at 82. See also: Schama, *The Embarrassment of Riches.* **53.** Thomas Mun, *England's Treasure by Forraign Trade* (London, 1664), 108. **54.** *Some Considerations Touching the Usefulness of Experimental Natural Philosophy* (Oxford, 1663) in: *Works of the Honorable Robert Boyle* (1744), 56. **55.** Bishop of Rochester, Thomas Sprat, *The History of the Royal Society of London* (London, 1667), 381, 384. **56.** Nicholas Barbon, *A Discourse of Trade* (London, 1690), 14–15. **57.** Bernard Mandeville, *The Fable of the Bees* (1714; London, 1989), 68, 69. **58.** As does Clunas, *Superfluous Things,* 146. **59.** Daniel Defoe, *A Plan of the English Commerce* (Oxford, 1728/1927), 77, 144–6. John Cary, *An Essay on the State of England* (Bristol, 1695), esp. 147. See further, Richard C. Wiles, 'The Theory of Wages in Later English Mercantilism', *Economic History Review,* new series, XXI/1 (April 1968), 113–26; Paul Slack, 'The Politics of Consumption and England's Happiness in the Later Seventeenth Century', *English Historical Review* CXXII, 2007: 609–31; Cosimo Perrotta, *Consumption as an Investment I: The Fear of Goods from Hesiod to Adam Smith* (London and New York, 2004). **60.** Berry, *The Idea of Luxury*; Perrotta, *Consumption as Investment*; Maxine Berg and Elizabeth Eger, eds., *Luxury in the Eighteenth Century: Debates, Desires and Delectable Goods* (Basingstoke, 2003). **61.** Michael Kwass, 'Consumption and the World of Ideas: Consumer Revolution and the Moral Economy of the Marquis de Mirabeau', *Eighteenth-century Studies* 37, no. 2, 2004: 187–213. See also: James Livesey, 'Agrarian Ideology and Commercial Republicanism in the French Revolution', *Past and Present,* no. 157, 1997: 94–121. **62.** Montesquieu, *L'Esprit des lois* (1748), bk VII. **63.** David Hume, 'Of Refinement in the Arts' (1741), repr. in: *Political Essays* (Cambridge, 1994), 108, 112. See also: 'Of Commerce', 93–104. **64.** Hume, 'Of Refinement in the Arts', 107. **65.** David Hume, *A Treatise of Human Nature* (1739), 116. For Spinozism, see Jonathan Israel, *Radical Enlightenment* (Oxford, 2001). See also: Annette C. Baier, 'David Hume, Spinozist', *Hume Studies* XIX/2 (Nov. 1993), 237–52. **66.** 'Novelty, and the Unexpected Appearance of Objects', Henry Home/Lord Kames, *Elements of Criticism* (London, 1762/1805, I, 211–21, quoted at 221. Compare Addison's essay on the pleasures of the imagination in the *Spectator,* no. 412. **67.** Adam Smith, *The Theory of Moral Sentiments* (London, 1759), Part IV, ch.1. I quote from the 1976 edited reprint of the 6th edn (1790), 179–87. **68.** Smith, *Wealth of Nations* bk II, ch. 3, 362–7. **69.** Adam Smith, *Wealth of Nations,* 412 (bk III, ch. 2) and 437–40 (bk III, ch. 4). See further, Albert O. Hirschman, *The Passions and the Interests: Political Arguments for Capitalism before Its Triumph* (Princeton, NJ, 1977). **70.** William Blackstone, *Commentaries on the Laws of England* (1765–9; 18th edn, 1829, London), II, ch. 1/11. **71.** Anne Granville Dewes, quoted in Keith Thomas, *The Ends of Life: Roads to Fulfilment in Early Modern England* (Oxford, 2009), 127. In addition, see Vickery, *Gentleman's Daughter,* 183–94; Laurel Thatcher Ulrich, 'Hannah Barnard's Cupboard: Female Property and Identity in Eighteenth-Century New England', in: *Through a Glass Darkly: Reflections on Personal*

Identity in Early America, eds. Ronald Hoffman, Mechal Sobel & Fredrika J. Teute (Chapel Hill, NC, 1997), 238–73; Sandra Cavallo, 'What Did Women Transmit? Ownership and Control of Household Goods and Personal Effects in Early Modern Italy', in: Moira Donald & Linda Hurcombe, eds., *Gender and Material Culture in Historical Perspective* (Basingstoke, 2000), 38–53. **72.** Fredrik Albritton Jonsson, *Enlightenment's Frontier: The Scottish Highlands and the Origins of Environmentalism* (New Haven, CT, 2013), 18–26, 237–9. **73.** Jonathan Lamb, 'The Crying of Lost Things', *English Literary History* 71, no. 4: 949–67; Mark Blackwell, ed., *The Secret Life of Things: Animals, Objects and It-Narratives in Eighteenth-century England* (Lewisburg, 2007); Julie Park, *The Self and It: Novel Objects in Eighteenth-century England* (Stanford, 2010). **74.** Bernard Mandeville, *A Treatise of the Hypochondriack and Hysterick Diseases* (New York, 1976 repr. of 1730 edn; 1st edn 1711), 233. **75.** Fredrik Albritton Jonsson, 'The Physiology of Hypochondria in Eighteenth-century Britain', in: *Cultures of the Abdomen: Dietetics, Obesity and Digestion in the Modern World*, eds. Christopher Forth & Ana Cardin-Coyne (New York, 2010). Roy Porter, 'Consumption: Disease of the Consumer Society?' in: *Consumption and the World of Goods*, eds. John Brewer & Roy Porter (London and New York, 1993), 58–81. **76.** William Winstanley, *The New Help to Discourse* (London, 1684, 3rd edn), 272, 282, 293–4. **77.** Lawrence E. Klein, 'Politeness for Plebes', in: John Brewer & Ann Bermingham, eds., *The Consumption of Culture, 1600–1800* (London, 1995), 362–82. **78.** See Susan Hanley, *Everyday Things in Premodern Japan* (Berkeley, CA, 1997). **79.** Roy Porter, *English Society in the Eighteenth Century* (London, 1990), 222. **80.** *The Connoisseur*, 1756, quoted in Robert W. Jones, *Gender and the Formation of Taste in Eighteenth-century Britain* (Cambridge, 1998), 13–14. For the culture of sensibility and refinement, see John Brewer, *The Pleasures of the Imagination* (New York, 1997). **81.** Thomas Sheraton, *Cabinet Dictionary*, 1803, quoted in Amanda Vickery, ' "Neat and Not Too Showey": Words and Wallpaper in Regency England', in: *Gender, Taste and Material Culture in Britain and North America, 1700–1830*, eds. John Styles & Amanda Vickery (New Haven. CT, 2006), 201–24, 216. See also in the same volume: Hannah Greig, 'Leading the Fashion: The Material Culture of London's Beau Monde', 293–313. **82.** Zheng Yangwen, *The Social Life of Opium in China*. **83.** John Millar, *The Origin of the Distinction of Ranks* (Edinburgh, 1771/1806), 89, 100–102. See further Mary Catharine Moran, 'The Commerce of the Sexes', in: *Paradoxes of Civil Society*, ed. F. Trentmann (New York, 2000), 61–84, and Karen O'Brien, *Women and Enlightenment in 18th-century Britain* (Cambridge, 2009). **84.** The best discussion now is T. H. Breen, *The Marketplace of Revolution: How Consumer Politics Shaped American Independence* (New York, 2004), although the repetitive use of the label 'consumers' is out of historical context. **85.** John Dickinson, *The Late Regulations Respecting the British Colonies* (London, 1766), 27. **86.** Gordon S. Wood, *The Creation of the American Republic, 1776–87* (Chapel Hill, NC, 1998), 573–7. **87.** Richard Wrigley, *The Politics of Appearances: Representations of Dress* *in Revolutionary France* (Oxford, 2002), ch. 5; and Leora Auslander, *Cultural Revolutions: The Politics of Everyday Life in Britain, North America and France* (Oxford, 2009), ch. 5. **88.** John Thelwall, *Poems Written in Close Confinement in The Tower and Newgate* (1795), sonnet V. **89.** Karl Marx, 'On the Jewish Question', repr. in Marx, *Early Political Writings*, ed. J. O'Malley (Cambridge, 1994), 28–56. **90.** Karl Marx, *Das Kapital*, I (Frankfurt am Main, 1987; repr. of 1872 edn; 1st edn 1867), 35, 17. **91.** Marx, *Das Kapital*, I, 50, my translation. **92.** Karl Marx, *Gesamtausgabe* (MEGA), *Karl Marx, Friedrich Engels, Briefwechsel*, 21 January 1858, my translation. **93.** MEGA, *Briefwechsel*, vols. V, VI, VII, VIII, IX, letters from Marx to Engels, 27 February 1852; 15 July 1858; 28 April 1862; 27 May 1862; 8 January 1863; 4 July 1864 15 July 1858, my translations. See also: Peter Stalybrass, 'Marx's Coat', in: *Border Fetishisms: Material Objects in Unstable Spaces*, ed. Patricia Spyer (London, 1998), 183–207; Francis Wheen, *Karl Marx* (London, 1999), ch. 8. **94.** Nicholas Crafts T. C. Mills, 'Trends in Real Wages in Britain, 1750–1913', in: *Explorations in Economic History* 31, 1994: 176–94. **95.** Galbraith, *The Affluent Society* (New York, 1958), 37. **96.** T. R. Malthus, *An Essay on the Principle of Population* (London, 1817, 5th edn), III, book IV, ch. 8, 302–4. See further, E. A. Wrigley, 'Malthus on the Prospects for the Labouring Poor', *Historical Journal* 31, no. 4, 1988: 813–29. **97.** M. von Prittwitz, *Die Kunst reich zu werden* (Mannheim, 1840), 485, see also 488–91, my translation. **98.** Wilhelm Roscher, *Principles of Political Economy* (1878), 191, 230, 552; the first German edition was published in 1854. **99.** [Anon.], *Hints on the Practical Effects of Commercial Restrictions on Production, Consumption, and National Wealth, with Remarks on the Claims of the Silk Trade. By a Consumer* (London, 1833), 14, 24–5, italics in the original. **100.** Albert Tanner, *Arbeitsame Patrioten, wohlanständige Damen: Bürgertum und Bürgerlichkeit in der Schweiz, 1830–1914* (Zurich, 1995), 284–92, 323–6; Moser quoted at 328. **101.** Tanner, *Arbeitsame Patrioten*, von Fischer quoted at 303, my translation.

CHAPTER 3

1. See now: Steve Pincus, 'Addison's Empire: Whig Conceptions of Empire in the Early 18th Century', *Parliamentary History* 31, no. 1, 2012: 99–117. See also: Carl Wennerlind & Philip J. Stern, eds., *Mercantilism Reimagined: Political Economy in Early Modern Britain and Its Empire* (Oxford, 2013). **2.** Peter M. Solar, 'Opening to the East: Shipping between Europe and Asia, 1770–1830', *Journal of Economic History* 73, no. 3, 2013: 625–61. For a visual illustration of the European empires' changing trade routes between the 1750s and 1820s, drawing on a thousand ship logs, see the maps created by the EU CLIWOC project at: http://pendientedemigracion.ucm.es/info/cliwoc/Cliwoc_final_report.pdf. **3.** Pomeranz, *Great Divergence*; Parthasarathi, 'The Great Divergence'; P. H. H. Vries, 'Are Coal and Colonies Really Crucial?' *Journal of World*

History 12, 2001: 407–46; and Findlay & O'Rourke, *Power and Plenty: Trade, War and the World Economy in the Second Millenium*, 330–64.   **4.** William T. Rowe, *China's Last Empire: The Great Qing* (Cambridge, MA, 2009), ch. 6.   **5.** Allen, *The British Industrial Revolution in Global Perspective*, ch. 11.   **6.** There were tensions between the two in the 1830s–'40s. Even then, however, for many liberals, justice to Africa and free trade in Britain were symbiotic: poor Britons would have little sympathy for freed slaves if it meant their sugar was going to be more expensive to protect the West Indies. The sugar duty had to go. See Richard Huzzey, 'Free Trade, Free Labour and Slave Sugar in Victorian Britain', *Historical Journal* 53, no. 2, 2010: 359–79.   **7.** Nick Draper, *The Price of Emancipation* (Cambridge, 2009).   **8.** The differential impact of slavery and domestic service on consumption deserves more attention than it has received, or we can give it here. 'Objectification' should be understood as a general direction, a process rather than an accomplished fact. Speed and degree varied; *captifs* were widespread in Guinea into the twentieth century, and it was still common for children to be sold in China before 1949. Sombart rightly noted the process of objectification (*Versachlichung*) for early-modern Europe but exaggerated when he diagnosed it as the triumph of women (*Sieg des Weibchen*); Sombart, *Luxus und Kapitalismus* (Munich, 1912), 112. Their husbands simply invested themselves in other articles (wine, cigars, smoking jackets, horses, libraries, etc). Servants, of course, continued to be part of European middle-class households into the 1950s, but their role is different from that of client slaves. Servants in the twentieth century were mainly substitutes for washing machines and other labour-saving technologies. They were rarely liveried manifestations of status. Ultimately, they complemented and maintained a culture of things rather than distracting from it. For a detailed study of how control of people and wealth was translated into social rank and spiritual worth among the Igbo in Eastern Nigeria, see Jane I. Guyer, *Marginal Gains: Monetary Transactions in Atlantic Africa* (Chicago, 2004).   **9.** Philip D. Curtin, *Economic Change in Precolonial Africa: Senegambia in the Era of the Slave Trade* (Madison, WI, 1975); Stanley B. Alpern, 'What Africans Got for their Slaves: A Master List of European Trade Goods ', *History in Africa* 22, 1995: 5–43; David Eltis, 'Trade between Western Africa and the Atlantic World before 1870', *Research in Economic History* 12, 1989: 197–239; A. G. Hopkins, *An Economic History of West Africa* (London, 1973); and Herbert S. Klein, 'Economic Aspects of the Eighteenth-century Atlantic Slave Trade', in: *The Rise of Merchant Empires*, ed. James D. Tracy (Cambridge 1990), 287–310. Eltis's figures for West Africa show a smaller share for iron than Curtin's but a similar declining trend.   **10.** Johann Krapf, quoted in Jeremy Prestholdt, 'East African Consumerism and the Genealogies of Globalization', PhD thesis, Northwestern University (Evanston, IL) 2003, 93. See now: Jeremy Prestholdt, *Domesticating the World: African Consumerism and the Genealogies of Globalization* (Berkeley, CA, 2008).   **11.** Quoted in Elizabeth Elbourne, *Blood Ground: Colonialism, Missions and the Contest for Christianity in the Cape Colony and Britain, 1799–1853* (Montreal, 2002), 213.   **12.** Robert Moffat, *Missionary*

Labours and Scenes in Southern Africa (London, 1842), 503–7. See also: Jean Comaroff & John Comaroff, 'Colonizing Currencies: Beasts, Banknotes and the Colour of Money in South Africa', in: *Commodification: Things, Agency and Identities (The Social Life of Things revisited)*, eds. Wim van Binsbergen & Peter L. Geschiere (New Brunswick, 2005). **13.** *Church Missionary Traces: The Village Missionary Meeting, A Dialogue* ... (London, 1852). **14.** John Philip, *Researches in South Africa* (London, 1828), 72–3. **15.** T. Fowell Buxton, *The African Slave Trade and Its Remedy* (London, 1840), 367–73. See similar judgements by CSM missionaries about the desire for furniture and comforts among native Americans such as the Choctaws, *Missionary Register 1829*, 472. **16.** Samuel Crowther, *Journal of an Expedition up the Niger and Tshadda Rivers*. With a new introduction by J. F. Ade Ajayi (London, 1854/1970), 11. **17.** Quoted in Charlotte Sussman, *Consuming Anxieties: Consumer Protest, Gender and British Slavery, 1713–1833* (Stanford, CA, 2000), 40. **18.** William Fox in 1791, quoted in Sussman, *Consuming Anxieties*, 115. **19.** Henry Nevinson, *A Modern Slavery* (London, 1906). Further, see Kevin Grant: *A Civilised Savagery: Britain and the New Slaveries in Africa, 1884–1926* (New York, 2005); and Lowell J. Satre, *Chocolate on Trial: Slavery, Politics and the Ethics of Business* (Athens, OH, 2005). In September 1907, the *Review of Reviews* pointed out that one fifth of cocoa was mixed with the blood of slaves. Ultimately, it was Cadbury and other European cocoa makers who settled the issue among themselves by agreeing not to source their cocoa from the islands. **20.** Adam Jones & Peter Sebald, *An African Family Archive: The Lawsons of Little Popo/Aneho (Togo) 1841–1938* (Oxford, 2005). **21.** Quoted in K. Onwuka Dike, *Trade and Politics in the Niger Delta, 1830–85* (Oxford, 1956), 113–14. **22.** Joseph Thomson, quoted in Prestholdt, 'East African Consumerism', 125. **23.** Christopher Fyfe, *A History of Sierra Leone* (Oxford, 1962), 411–68. **24.** Dike, *Trade and Politics in the Niger Delta, 1830–85*, 207. **25.** Thomas. J. Lewin, *Asante before the British: The Prempean Years, 1875–1900* (Lawrence, KS, 1978); and William Tordoff, *Ashanti under the Prempehs, 1888–1935* (London, 1965). See now also: G. Austin, 'Vent for Surplus or Productivity Breakthrough? The Ghanaian Cocoa Take-off, c.1890–1936', in: *Economic History Review*, Vol. 67, issue 4, 2014: 1035–64; and E Frankema & M. van Waijenburg, 'Structural Impediments to African Growth? New Evidence from Real Wages in British Africa, 1880–1965', Centre for Global Economic History working paper no. 24 (2011). **26.** Jonathon Glassman, *Feasts and Riot: Revelry, Rebellion and Popular Consciousness on the Swahili Coast, 1856–88* (Portsmouth, NH, 1995). **27.** Quoted in Laura Fair, *Pastimes and Politics: Culture, Community and Identity in Post-Abolition Urban Zanzibar, 1890–1945* (Athens, OH, 2001), 64, and see 64–109 for the above. **28.** Lynn Schler, 'Bridewealth, Guns and Other Status Symbols: Immigration and Consumption in Colonial Douala', *Journal of African Cultural Studies* 16, no. 2, 2003: 213–34. **29.** Marion Johnson, 'Cotton Imperialism in West Africa', *African Affairs* 73, no. 291, 1974: 178–87. **30.** D. Bavendamm, 1894, cited in Birgit Meyer, 'Christian Mind and Worldly Matters: Religion and Materiality in the Nineteenth-century Gold Coast', in: Richard Fardon, Wim van Binsbergen & Rijk van Dijk, eds., *Modernity on a Shoestring: Dimensions of Globalization, Consumption and Development in Africa and Beyond* (Leiden, 1999), 167–9. **31.** Quoted in H. Maynard Smith, *Frank: Bishop of Zanzibar: Life of Frank, Weston, D.D. 1871–1924* (London, 1926), 187. **32.** Klaus J. Bade, *Friedrich Fabri und der Imperialismus in der Bismarckzeit* (Freiburg, 1975); and Horst Gründer, *Christliche Mission und deutscher Imperialismus, 1884–1914* (Paderborn, 1982). **33.** Friedrich Michael Zahn in: *Allgemeine Missions-Zeitschrift: Monatshefte für geschichtliche und theoretische Missionskunde*, Vol. XIV (1887), 46, my translation. **34.** For the changing spectrum, see A. N. Porter, *Religion Versus Empire? British Protestant Missionaries and Overseas Expansion, 1700–1914* (Manchester, 2004); and Roland Oliver, *The Missionary Factor in East Africa* (London, 1952). **35.** Bruno Gutmann, 'The African Standpoint', *Africa* 8, no. 1, 1935: 1–19, quoted at 7. **36.** Chika Onyeani, *Capitalist Nigger: The Road to Success* (Timbuktu, 2000). **37.** For example, the otherwise excellent James Walvin, *Fruits of Empire: Exotic Produce and British Taste, 1660–1800* (London, 1997) concludes with metaphors of contagion, infection and affliction, 174–83. **38.** W. H. Ingrams quoted in Fair, *Pastimes and Politics*, 76. See also: Richard Austin Freeman, *Travels and Life in Ashanti and Jaman* (London, 1898/1967), 380. **39.** Godfrey Wilson, *An Essay on the Economics of Detribalization in Northern Rhodesia*, Rhodes–Livingstone papers, nos. 5, 6 (Livingstone, Northern Rhodesia 1941), 20. **40.** 'Flexible racism' in the words of Mona Domosh, *American Commodities in an Age of Empire* (New York, 2006). Compare de Grazia, *Irresistible Empire*. **41.** Abdul Halim Sharar, *Lucknow: The Last Phase of an Oriental Culture* (Oxford, 1975 edn), 73, 121–5. **42.** Maya Jasanoff, *Edge of Empire: Lives, Culture and Conquest in the East 1750–1850* (New York, 2005), esp. ch. 2. **43.** Quoted in Robin D. Jones, *Interiors of Empire: Objects, Space and Identity within the Indian Subcontinent, c.1800–1947* (Manchester, 2007), 95. **44.** C. A. Bayly, ' "Archaic" and "Modern" Globalization in the Eurasian and African Arena, c.1750–1850', in: *Globalization in World History*, ed. A. G. Hopkins (London, 2002), 45–72, quoted at 52. **45.** Russell W. Belk, *Collecting in a Consumer Society* (London and New York, 2001). **46.** Hosagrahar Jyoti, 'City as Durbar', in: *Forms of Dominance: On the Architecture and Urbanism of the Colonial Enterprise*, ed. Nezar Al Sayyad (Aldershot, 1992), 85–103. **47.** Christopher Alan Bayly, *Rulers, Townsmen and Bazaars: North Indian Society in the Age of British Expansion, 1770–1870* (Cambridge, 1983). **48.** Douglas Haynes, *Rhetoric and Ritual in Colonial India: The Shaping of a Public Culture in Surat City, 1852–1928* (Berkeley, CA, 1991). **49.** John Crawfurd, *A Sketch of the Commercial Resources and Monetary and Mercantile System of British India*, 1837, repr. in *The Economic Development of India under the East India Company, 1814–58: A Selection of Contemporary Writings*, ed. K. N Chaudhuri (Cambridge, 1971), quoted at 233, 241. **50.** See Tirthankar Roy, *The Economic History of India, 1857–1947* (Oxford, 2006). Compare B. R. Tomlinson, *The New Cambridge History of India, 3: The Economy of Modern*

India, 1860–1970 (Cambridge, 1993). **51.** David Cannadine, *Ornamentalism* (London, 2001); and *The Great Delhi Durbar of 1911* (London, 1911). **52.** This does not mean, of course, that gifts stopped to play other social functions; see Margot C. Finn, 'Colonial Gifts: Family Politics and the Exchange of Goods in British India', in: *Modern Asian Studies* 40, no. 1, 2006: 203–31. **53.** Joseph A. Schumpeter, *Imperialism and Social Classes* (Oxford, 1919/1951), 14. **54.** Veena Talwar Oldenburg, *The Making of Colonial Lucknow, 1856– 1877* (Princeton, NJ, 1984). **55.** Haynes, *Rhetoric and Ritual in Colonial India.* **56.** C. A. Bayly, *The New Cambridge History of India: Indian Society and the Making of the British Empire* (Cambridge, 1988). **57.** Rita Smith Kipp, 'Emancipating Each Other: Dutch Colonial Missionaries' Encounter with Karo Women in Sumatra, 1900–1942', in: *Domesticating the Empire: Race, Gender and Family Life in French and Dutch Colonialism*, eds. Julia Clancy-Smith & Frances Gouda (Charlottesville, VA, 1998), ch. 11. **58.** Bernard S. Cohn, *Colonialism and Its Forms of Knowledge* (Princeton, NJ, 1996), 106–62; and Emma Tarlo, *Clothing Matters: Dress and Identity in India* (London, 1996). **59.** Abigail McGowan, 'Consuming Families', in: Douglas Haynes et al., eds., *Towards a History of Consumption in South Asia* (Oxford, 2010), 155–84. **60.** Shib Chunder Bose, *The Hindoos as They Are* (London, 1881), 191–208. **61.** G. F. Shirras, *Report on an Enquiry into Working-class Budgets in Bombay* (Bombay, 1923). **62.** Bose, *The Hindoos as They Are*, 195. **63.** Haruka Yanagisawa 'Growth of Small-scale Industries and Changes in Consumption Patterns in South India, 1910s–50s', in: Haynes et al., eds., *Towards a History of Consumption in South Asia*, 51–75. **64.** Kate Platt, *The Home and Health in India and the Tropical Colonies* (London, 1923), 16. See further: Elizabeth Buettner, *Empire Families: Britons and Late Imperial India* (Oxford, 2004). **65.** This and the following draws on Jones, *Interiors of Empire*, quoted at 1. **66.** *Selections from the Calcutta Gazettes, 1784–88* (Calcutta, 1864), 47, 50–4, 60. **67.** Jones, *Interiors of Empire*, 105. **68.** Platt, *Home and Health in India and the Tropical Colonies*, 64. **69.** Edward Braddon, *Life in India*, 1872, cited in Jones, *Interiors of Empire*, 85. **70.** Jones, *Interiors of Empire*, 137. **71.** Arnold Wright, *Twentieth-century Impressions of Ceylon* (London, 1907), 709–11, and 487, 692, 697, 720 for additional examples. **72.** Charles Feinstein, 'Changes in Nominal Wages, the Cost of Living and Real Wages in the United Kingdom over the Two Centuries, 1780–1990,' in: *Labor's Reward: Real Wages and Economic Change in 19th- and 20th-century Europe*, eds. P. Scholliers & V. Zamagni (Aldershot, 1995). **73.** Ernst Engel, 'Die Productions- und Consumtionsverhältnisse des Königreichs Sachsen', in: *Zeitschrift des statistischen Büreaus des K. Sächsischen Ministeriums des Innern*, 22 Nov. 1857. For contemporary misinterpretations, see Carle C. Zimmerman, 'Ernst Engel's Law of Expenditures for Food', *Quarterly Journal of Economics*, 47/1 (Nov. 1932), 78–101. For Engel's impact, see Erik Grimmer-Solem, *The Rise of Historical Economics and Social Reform in Germany, 1864– 1894* (Oxford, 2003). **74.** Lawrence B. Glickman, *A Living Wage: American Workers and the Making of Consumer Society* (Ithaca, NY, 1997).

75. William C. Beyer, Rebekah P. Davis & Myra Thwing, *Workingmen's Standard of Living in Philadelphia: A Report by the Bureau of Municipal Research of Philadelphia* (New York City, 1919). For wages at the time, see Lindley Daniel Clark, *Minimum-wage Laws of the United States: Construction and Operation* (Washington, DC, 1921).   **76.** Shirras, *Report on an Enquiry into Working-class Budgets in Bombay*, 14. For a critique of the Western yardstick, see Radhakamal Mukerjee, *The Foundations of Indian Economics* (London, 1916).   **77.** J. S. Mill, *Essays on Some Unsettled Questions of Political Economy* (London, 1844), 132.   **78.** William Stanley Jevons, *The Theory of Political Economy* (London, 1871/1888), ch. 3, 43.   **79.** 1863, quoted in Donald Winch, *Wealth and Life* (Cambridge, 2009), 155.   **80.** R. M. Robertson, 'Jevons and His Precursors', *Econometrica*, Vol. XIX, 1951: 229-49; R. C. D. Black, *Economic Theory and Policy in Context* (Aldershot, 1995).   **81.** W. Stanley Jevons, *The State in Relation to Labour* (London, 1882/1887), 41.   **82.** Lionel Robbins, 'The Place of Jevons in the History of Economic Thought', *Manchester School of Economics and Social Studies*, VII (1936), 1.   **83.** Alfred Marshall, *Principles of Economics* (London, 1890/1920), 72, 74-5.   **84.** Marshall, *Principles of Economics*, 113.   **85.** Karl Oldenberg, 'Die Konsumtion', in *Grundriss der Sozialökonomie*, II, eds. Fr. Von Gottl-Ottlilienfeld et al. (Tübingen, 1914), 103-64. The Irish Cliffe Leslie had similarly argued that 'without habits of considerable superfluous expenditure a nation would be reduced to destitution' in his *Essays in Political and Moral Philosophy* (1879), 223.   **86.** Simon N. Patten, *The Consumption of Wealth* (Philadelphia, 1889), vi.   **87.** Simon N. Patten, *The New Basis of Civilization* (New York, 1907), 143. Further: Daniel M. Fox, *The Discovery of Abundance: Simon N. Patten and the Transformation of Social Theory* (Ithaca, NY, 1967).   **88.** *Current Opinion*, 54 (1913), 51-2.   **89.** T. H. Marshall, *Citizenship and Social Class and Other Essays* (Cambridge, 1950).   **90.** Charles Gide, *La Cooperation: Conférences de propaganda* (Paris, 1900), 227, my translation.   **91.** Ellen Furlough, *Consumer Cooperation in France: The Politics of Consumption, 1834-1930* (Ithaca, NY, 1991), 80-97.   **92.** Kathryn Kish Sklar, *Florence Kelley and the Nation's Work* (New Haven, CT, 1995).   **93.** Elisabeth von Knebel-Doeberitz, 'Die Aufgabe und Pflicht der Frau als Konsument', in: *Hefte der Freien Kirchlich-Sozialen Konferenz*, 40 (Berlin, 1907), 39, my translation.   **94.** Alain Chatriot, Marie-Emmanuelle Chessel & Matthew Hilton, eds., *Au nom du consommateur: Consommation et politique en Europe et aux États-Unis au XX siècle* (Paris, 2004); Louis L. Athey, 'From Social Conscience to Social Action: The Consumers' Leagues in Europe, 1900-1914', *Social Service Review* 52, no. 3, 1978: 362-82; and Matthew Hilton, *Consumerism in Twentieth-century Britain* (Cambridge, 2003).   **95.** *La Liberté: Journal politique, religieux, social*, 26 Sept. 1908, 1, my translation.   **96.** Women's Co-operative Guild, *28th Annual Report, 1910-11*. Gillian Scott, *Feminism and the Politics of Working Women: The Women's Co-operative Guild, 1880s to the Second World War* (London, 1998).   **97.** Teresa Billington Greig, *The Consumer in Revolt* (London, 1912), quoted at 4, 52.   **98.** J. A. Hobson, *Imperialism: A Study* (London, 1902),

86. 99. J. A. Hobson, *Evolution of Modern Capitalism* (London, 1897), 368–77; *Work and Wealth* (London, 1914). 100. See references in the following notes, and Benjamin S. Orlove, 'Meat and Strength: The Moral Economy of a Chilean Food Riot,' *Cultural Anthropology* 12, no. 2, 1997: 234–68. 101. Christoph Nonn, *Verbraucherprotest und Parteiensystem im wilhelminischen Deutschland* (Düsseldorf, 1996), 78. 102. Marie-Emmanuelle Chessel, *Consommateurs engagés à la Belle Époque: La Ligue sociale d'acheteurs* (Paris, 2012); and Marie-Emmanuelle Chessel, 'Women and the Ethics of Consumption in France at the Turn of the Twentieth Century', in: *The Making of the Consumer: Knowledge, Power and Identity in the Modern World*, ed. Frank Trentmann, (Oxford, 2006), 81–98. 103. Walter E. Weyl, *The New Democracy* (New York, 1912), 254. 104. The quote is from Alfred Mond, the chemical industrialist. See Frank Trentmann, *Free Trade Nation: Commerce, Consumption and Civil Society in Modern Britain* (Oxford, 2008). 105. Michael Edelstein, *Overseas Investment in the Age of High Imperialism* (New York, 1982); Lance E. Davis & Robert A. Huttenback, *Mammon and the Pursuit of Empire* (Cambridge, 1986); Avner Offer, 'Costs and Benefits, Prosperity and Security, 1870–1914', in: *The Oxford History of the British Empire*, ed. Andrew Porter (Oxford, 1999), 690–711. 106. Stephen Constantine, ' "Bringing the Empire Alive": The Empire Marketing Board and Imperial Propaganda, 1926–33', in: *Imperialism and Popular Culture*, ed. John M. MacKenzie (Manchester, 1986), 192–231; and Trentmann, *Free Trade Nation.* 107. Trevor Burnard, *Mastery, Tyranny and Desire: Thomas Thistlewood and His Slaves in the Anglo-Jamaican World* (Jamaica, 2004). 108. Joanna de Groot, 'Metropolitan Desires and Colonial Connections', in: Catherine Hall & Sonya Rose, eds., *At Home with the Empire* (Cambridge, 2006), 186. 109. Mintz, *Sweetness and Power*, 157. 110. From 731,000lbs in 1745 to 2,359,000lbs the following year; Ashworth, *Customs and Excise: Trade, Production and Consumption in England. 1640–1845*, 178. 111. Kwass, *Contraband.* 112. Clarence-Smith, *Cocoa and Chocolate, 1765–1914*; W. G. Clarence-Smith & Steven Topik, *The Global Coffee Economy in Africa, Asia and Latin America, 1500-1989* (Cambridge, 2003). 113. Ernst Neumann, *Der Kaffee: Seine geographische Verbreitung, Gesamtproduktion und Konsumtion* (Berlin, 1930), 141–3; the French figure is for 1927. 114. Neumann, *Kaffee, 69*, 151. Denmark had small colonies in the Virgin Islands, from where it took its rum, but mainly imported its coffee from Brazil and Guatemala. 115. Michelle Craig McDonald & Steven Topik, 'Americanizing Coffee', in: Alexander Nützenadel & Frank Trentmann, eds., *Food and Globalization: Consumption, Markets and Politics in the Modern World* (Oxford, 2008), 109–28. 116. Martin Bruegel, 'A Bourgeois Good? Sugar, Norms of Consumption and the Labouring Classes in Nineteenth-century France,' in: Peter Scholliers, *Food, Drink and Identity: Cooking, Eating and Drinking in Europe since the Middle Ages* (Oxford, 2001), 99–118. 117. Hamburger Staatsarchiv, 314-1/B VIII 8, 'Berichte von Angestellten der Deputation über Konsumverhältnisse in ihnen bekannten Orten', 20 May 1878, my translation. 118. Julia Laura Rischbieter, 'Kaffee im

Kaiserreich', PhD thesis, Frankfurt (Oder), 2009, 283; see now her book: *Mikro-Ökonomie der Globalisierung* (Cologne, 2011). Hamburger Staatsarchiv, 314-1/B VIII 8, 12 May 1878 (on Magdeburg). For brandy and coffee in France, see W. Scott Haine, *The World of the Paris Café: Sociability among the French Working Class, 1789–1914* (Baltimore, 1998). **119.** In Essen, it stopped serving beer during work hours only in 1910. **120.** For example, the St Georg hospital in Hamburg 1875, Hamburger Staatsarchiv, HH 314-1, B VIII, no. 19. **121.** *Illustrated London News*, August 1885; *Graphic*, 19 Sept. 1896; and *Penny Illustrated Paper*, 1 Aug. 1896, 66, and 26 Oct. 1901, 272. **122.** Roman Rossfeld, *Schweizer Schokolade: Industrielle Produktion und kulturelle Konstruktion eines nationalen Symbols, 1860–1920* (Baden, 2007). **123.** Jan De Vries, *The Economy of Europe in an Age of Crisis, 1600–1750* (Cambridge, 1976), 71–3. **124.** J. R. Peet, 'The Spatial Expansion of Commercial Agriculture in the Nineteenth Century', *Economic Geography* 45, 1969: 283–301. **125.** David T. Courtwright, *Forces of Habit: Drugs and the Making of the Modern World* (Cambridge, MA, 2001), 53–66. **126.** See further: David Anderson et al., *The Khat Controversy: Stimulating the Debate on Drugs* (Oxford, 2007). **127.** Erika Rappaport, 'Packaging China: Foreign Articles and Dangerous Tastes in the Mid-Victorian Tea Party', in: Frank Trentmann, ed., *The Making of the Consumer: Knowledge, Power and Identity in the Modern World* (Oxford, 2006), 125–46, quoted at 131 (1851). **128.** See Peter H. Hoffenberg, *An Empire on Display: English, Indian and Australian Exhibitions from the Crystal Palace to the Great War* (Berkeley, CA, 2001), quoted at 115. **129.** Colonial provenance, this suggests, continued to matter in cases where it signalled white Anglo-Saxon control of the value chain. This extends to the white settler colonies, as in the marketing of 'Canadian salmon'. **130.** Kolleen M. Guy, *When Champagne became French: Wine and the Making of a National Identity* (Baltimore, MD, 2003). **131.** Kai-Uwe Hellmann, *Soziologie der Marke* (Frankfurt am Main, 2003), Part I. See now also: T. da Silva Lopes & Paulo Guimaraes, 'Trademarks and British Dominance in Consumer Goods, 1876–1914', in: *Economic History Review*, Vol. 67, issue 3, 2014: 793–817. **132.** Quoted from Manuel Llorca-Jana, *The British Textile Trade in South America in the Nineteenth Century* (Cambridge, 2012), 92. **133.** John Potter Hamilton, *Travels through the Interior Provinces of Colombia* (London, 1827), Vol I, 139 and Vol. II, 76, quoted at 120. I am grateful to Ana Maria Otero-Cleves for this reference, whose 2011 Oxford PhD thesis ('From Fashionable Pianos to Cheap White Cotton: Consuming Foreign Commodities in Nineteenth-century Colombia') discusses these flows in greater detail. **134.** Benjamin Orlove, ed., *The Allure of the Foreign: Imported Goods in Post-colonial Latin America* (Michigan, 1997). **135.** See Gary Magee & Andrew Thompson, *Empire and Globalization: Networks of People, Goods and Capital in the British World, c.1850–1914* (Cambridge, 2010), and the roundtable in *British Scholar Journal*, III, Sept. 2010. **136.** Richard Wilk, *Home Cooking in the Global Village: Caribbean Food from Buccaneers to Eco-tourists* (Oxford, 2006). For approaches to commodity chains, see Foster:

'Tracking Globalization: Commodities and Value in Motion'. **137.** Thomas Richards, *The Commodity Culture of Victorian England: Advertising and Spectacle, 1851–1914* (Stanford, CA, 1990), 144. **138.** Anne McClintock, *Imperial Leather: Race, Gender and Sexuality in the Colonial Contest* (London, 1995), 36. **139.** *Whitehall Review Annual*, 1881–2, repr. in Anandi Ramamurthy, *Imperial Persuaders: Images of Africa and Asia in British Advertising* (Manchester, 2003), 67. **140.** *Penny Illustrated Paper*, 23 Feb. 1901, 144, and 26 Oct. 1901, 272. **141.** *The Times*, 24 Oct. 1910, 14. **142.** Arthur Girault, *The Colonial Tariff Policy of France* (Oxford, 1916); and Rae Beth Gordon, 'Natural Rhythm: La Parisienne Dances with Darwin: 1875–1910', *Modernism/modernity* 10, no. 4, 2003: 617–56. **143.** Deutsches Historisches Museum, Berlin, P 57/1452 (Hofer, Kaffee-Messmer); Rischbieter, 'Kaffee im Kaiserreich', 227–31; Volker Ilgen & Dirk Schindelbeck, *Am Anfang war die Litfasssäule* (Darmstadt, 2006), plate 13 (Stollwerck). Of the 400 coffee and cocoa posters in the collection of Les Arts Decoratifs in Paris, there are, similarly, only a handful with exotic images. Some coffee makers retained a Moorish association, but even here ethnic image and regional origin could be confused, as in the case of 'Mohren-Kaffee', by A. L. Mohr, Hamburg-Bahrenfeld, which was a mix of genuine exotic beans and local substitutes, advertised for making a stronger (*kräftiger*) brew than real beans of average quality. **144.** Claudia Baldioni & Jonathan Morris, 'La globalizzazione dell'espresso italiano', *Memoria e Ricerca*, XIV, 23, 2006, 27–47.

CHAPTER 4

1. Sombart, *Luxus und Kapitalismus*, 28–41. **2.** Max Weber, *Economy and Society*, 1922/1978, eds. G. Roth & C. Wittich (Berkeley, CA), 125–6. **3.** Bairoch, *De Jéricho à Mexico: Villes et économie dans l'histoire*, 373–6, 516–42. For different types of cities, see now: Jürgen Osterhammel, *Die Verwandlung der Welt* (Munich, 2009), section VI. **4.** Julius Rodenberg, 'Die vierundzwanzig Stunden von Paris', in: *Paris bei Sonnenschein und Lampenlicht*, ed. Julius Rodenberg (Berlin, 1867), 1–54, quoted on 40, my translation. He refers to 40,000 public lamps. The actual number was half that; see references in the next note. **5.** Commission Internationale de l'Éclairage, *Recueil des travaux et compte rendu des séances, sixième session, Genève – Juillet, 1924* (Cambridge, 1926), 288; Léon Clerbois, 'Histoire de l'éclairage public à Bruxelles', *Annales de la société d'archéologie de Bruxelles* 24, 1910, 175. **6.** *The Gas World Year Book 1913* (London, 1913); J. C. Toer & Asociados, eds., *Gas Stories in Argentina, 1823–1998* (Buenos Aires, 1998). Electricity spread later and is discussed in the chapter on the home; for these networks, see Thomas P. Hughes, *Networks of Power: Electrification in Western Society, 1880–1930* (Baltimore, MD, 1983). **7.** *Journal of Gas Lighting, Water Supply, etc.*, CX (1910), 10 May 1910, 371–5; John F. Wilson, *Lighting the Town: A Study of Management in the North-west Gas Industry, 1805–1880* (Liverpool, 1991), 167; Charles

W. Hastings, *Gas Works Statistics* (1880; 1884); *The Gas World Year Book 1913*; and *Gas in Home, Office and Factory: Hints on Health, Comfort and Economy – Popular Lectures at the National Gas Congress and Exhibition, London, October 1913* (London, 1913). **8.** J. T. Fanning, *A Practical Treatise on Hydraulic and Water-supply Engineering* (New York, 1902, 15th edn), 41. Throughout the text I have converted figures into US gallons (3.8 litres) for consistency. One imperial (UK) gallon, which ceased to be a legal unit in 2000, is 4.5 litres. **9.** Richard L. Bushman & Claudia L. Bushman, 'The Early History of Cleanliness in America', in: *Journal of American History* 74, no. 4, 1988: 1213–38; see also: E. Shove, *Comfort, Cleanliness and Convenience: The Social Organization of Normality* (Oxford, 2003). **10.** John Simon, *English Sanitary Institutions* (London, 1897, 2nd edn), 466. **11.** Jean-Pierre Goubert, *The Conquest of Water: The Advent of Health in the Industrial Age* (Princeton, NJ, 1989), 150–1. **12.** A. R. Binnie, *Royal Commission on Metropolitan Water Supply 1893–94*, XL, Part I, 18 June 1892, para. 3235. **13.** Elizabeth Otis Williams, *Sojourning, Shopping and Studying in Paris: A Handbook Particularly for Women* (London, 1907), 34; Shanghai Municipal Council, *Annual Report*, 1935, 188; Hanchao Lu, 'The Significance of the Insignificant: Reconstructing the Daily Lives of the Common People of China', in: *China: An International Journal* 1, no. 1, 2003: 144–58; and Goubert, *Conquest of Water*, 62. **14.** Shanghai Municipal Archive, *Annual Report of the Shanghai Municipal Council*, 1905, 152; Shahrooz Mohajeri, *100 Jahre Berliner Wasserversorgung und Abwasserentsorgung 1840–1940* (Stuttgart, 2005), 71 f.; Maureen Ogle, 'Water Supply, Waste Disposal and the Culture of Privatism in the Mid-nineteenth-century American City', in: *Journal of Urban History* 25, no. 3, 1999: 321–47; R. Wilkinson & E. M. Sigsworth, 'A Survey of Slum Clearance Areas in Leeds', in: *Yorkshire Bulletin of Social and Economic Research*, Vol. 15/1, 1963, 25–47; Clemens Zimmermann, *Von der Wohnungsfrage zur Wohnungspolitik* (Göttingen, 1991); Petri S. Juuti & Tapio S. Katko, eds., *From a Few to All: Long-term Development of Water and Environmental Services in Finland* (Finland, 2004), 19f.; and Petri S. Juuti & Tapio S. Katko, eds., *Water, Time and European Cities* (Tampere, 2005). **15.** Ruth Rogaski, *Hygienic Modernity: Meanings of Health and Disease in Treaty-port China* (Berkeley, CA, 2004), 212–24; and Sidney D. Gamble, *Peking: A Social Survey* (London, 1921), 31. **16.** F. Bramwell in a memorandum to the Royal Commission on Water Supply (1900), Vol. 39, Appendix Z, 6, 406. **17.** Vanessa Taylor & Frank Trentmann, 'Liquid Politics: Water and the Politics of Everyday Life in the Modern City', in: *Past & Present* 211, 2011: 199–241. **18.** Ruth Schwartz Cowan, 'The Consumption Junction: A Proposal for Research Strategies in the Sociology of Technology', in: *The Social Construction of Technological Systems: New Directions in the Sociology and History of Technology*, eds. Wiebe E. Bijker, Thomas P. Hughes & Trevor J. Pinch (Cambridge, MA, 1987), 261–80. **19.** Clémentine Deroudille, *Brassens: Le Libertaire de la chanson* (Paris, 2011), 26–7. **20.** Constance Williams & Arthur Martin in *Gas in Home –Popular Lectures*, 49–72. See further: Martin Daunton, *House and Home in the Victorian City* (London, 1983); and

Judith Flanders, *The Victorian House* (London, 2004), 168–73. **21.** Henry Letheby, 'Report on the Coal Gas Supplied to the City of London' (London, 1854); John Simon, 'Report by the Medical Officer of Health on Complaints of Nuisance from the City of London Gas Company's Works' (London, 1855); and Toer & Asociados, eds., *Gas Stories in Argentina*. **22.** Manuel Charpy, 'Le Théâtre des objets: espaces privés, culture matérielle et identité bourgeoise, Paris 1830–1914', PhD thesis, Université François-Rabelais de Tours, 2010, Vol. I, 249–71. **23.** Jun'ichirō Tanizaki, *In Praise of Shadows* (1933/1977). **24.** Jens Hanssen, *Fin de siècle Beirut: The Making of an Ottoman Provincial Capital* (Oxford, 2005), 200; and Edward Seidensticker, *Low City, High City: Tokyo from Edo to the Earthquake* (London, 1983), 80–1. **25.** Haydn T. Harrison, 'Street Lighting', in: *Commission Internationale de l'Éclairage*, 1924, 277, and for the 1911 tests. **26.** *Journal of Gas Lighting, Water supply, etc.* CXII (1910), quoted at 473 and 471. **27.** Lynda Nead, *Victorian Babylon: People, Streets and Images in Nineteenth-century London* (New Haven, CT, 2000); Joachim Schlör, *Nights in the Big City* (London, 1998); Wolfgang Schivelbusch, *Lichtblicke: Zur künstlichen Helligkeit im 19. Jahrhundert* (Munich, 1983); and Chris Otter, *The Victorian Eye: A Political History of Light and Vision in Britain, 1800–1910* (Chicago, 2008). **28.** Robert Millward, 'European Governments and the Infrastructure Industries, c.1840–1914', in: *European Review of Economic History* 8, 2004: 3–28, also for below. Martin V. Melosi, *The Sanitary City* (Baltimore, MD, 2000). **29.** P. J. Waller, *Town, City and Nation: England 1850–1914* (Oxford, 1983), 300. See further Robert Millward & Robert Ward, 'From Private to Public Ownership of Gas Undertakings in England and Wales, 1851–1947', *Business History* 35, no. 3, 1993: 1–21; and Wilson, *Lighting the Town*. **30.** John Henry Gray, *Die Stellung der privaten Beleuchtungsgesellschaften zu Stadt und Staat* (Jena, 1893); Martin Daunton, 'The Material Politics of Natural Monopoly: Consuming Gas in Victorian Britain', in: *The Politics of Consumption: Material Culture and Citizenship in Europe and America*, eds. Martin Daunton & Matthew Hilton (Oxford, 2001), 69–88. **31.** W. H. Y. Webber, 'Gas Meter', and John Young, 'Hints to Gas Consumers', in: *Gas in the Home –Popular Lectures*, 1913, 85–99; and Graeme J. N. Gooday, *The Morals of Measurement: Accuracy, Irony and Trust in Late-Victorian Electrical Practice* (Cambridge, 2004). **32.** Christopher Hamlin, 'Muddling in Bumbledom: On the Enormity of Large Sanitary Improvements in Four British Towns, 1855–1885', *Victorian Studies* 32, 1988: 55–83; and M. J. Daunton, 'Public Place and Private Space: The Victorian City and the Working-class Household', in: *The Pursuit of Urban History*, eds. Derek Fraser & Anthony Sutcliffe (London, 1983). **33.** Taylor & Trentmann, 'Liquid Politics'. **34.** A. Dobbs, *By Meter or Annual Value?* (London, 1890), 30, my emphasis. **35.** James H. Fuertes, *Waste of Water in New York and Its Reduction by Meters and Inspection: Report to the Committee on Water-supply of the Merchants' Association of New York* (New York, 1906), 84. **36.** *Royal Commission on Metropolitan Water Supply 1893–94*, XL, Part I, Minutes of Evidence, 5 Oct. 1892, 7353–4. **37.** *Royal Commission on Water Supply*

(1900), Cd. 25, Final Report, para. 178, 74. **38.** Fuertes, *Waste of Water*, 100. **39.** Fuertes, *Waste of Water*, 56. **40.** Fuertes, *Waste of Water*, 42. **41.** *Royal Commission on Water Supply* (1900), Cd. 25, Final Report, paras 176–80. See also: W. R. Baldwin-Wiseman, 'The Increase in the National Consumption of Water', in: *Journal of the Royal Statistical Society* 72, no. 2, 1909: 248–303, esp. 259. **42.** *Royal Commission on Metropolitan Water Supply, 1893–94*, XL, Part I, 5 Oct. 1892, 7358. **43.** Patrick Joyce, *The Rule of Freedom: Liberalism and the Modern City* (London, 2003); and Tom Crook, 'Power, Privacy and Pleasure: Liberalism and the Modern Cubicle', in: *Cultural Studies* 21, no. 4–5, 2007: 549–69. **44.** Richard Wollheim, *Germs: A Memoir of Childhood* (London, 2004), 132; Fuertes, *Waste of Water*, 30; and Goubert, *Conquest of Water*, 131. **45.** Roger-Henri Guerrand, *Les Lieux: Histoire des commodités* (Paris, 1997), 157. **46.** M. Thiele & W. Schickenberg, *Die Verhältnisse von 534 Stadthannoverschen kinderreichen Kriegerfamilien* (Hanover, 1919), 8; and Clemens Wischermann, *Wohnen in Hamburg* (Münster, 1983). **47.** Interview no. 28, P. Thompson & T. Lummis, *Family Life and Work Experience before 1918, 1870–1973*, Colchester, Essex: UK Data Archive. **48.** Madeleine Yue Dong, *Republican Beijing: The City and Its Histories* (Berkeley, CA, 2003), ch. 6. For South City, see Gamble, *Peking: A Social Survey*, 235–9. **49.** Claire Holleran, *Shopping in Ancient Rome: The Retail Trade in the Late Republic and the Principate* (Oxford, 2012). **50.** Sombart, *Luxus und Kapitalismus*. **51.** Rosalind H. Williams, *Dream Worlds: Mass Consumption in Late-nineteenth-century France* (Berkeley, CA, 1982), 67. **52.** S. Faroqhi, *Towns and Townsmen of Ottoman Anatolia* (Cambridge, 1984). **53.** Claire Walsh, 'The Newness of the Department Store: A View from the Eighteenth Century', in: Geoffrey Crossick & Serge Jaumain, eds., *Cathedrals of Consumption: The European Department Store, 1850–1939* (Aldershot, 1999), 46–71; Claire Walsh, 'Shops, Shoppping and the Art of Decision Making in Eighteenth-century England', in: *Gender, Taste and Material Culture in Britain and North America, 1700–1830*, eds. John Styles & Amanda Vickery (New Haven, CT, 2006); Welch, *Shopping in the Renaissance*; Jon Stobart, *Sugar and Spice: Grocers and Groceries in Provincial England, 1650–1830* (Oxford, 2012); Tammy Whitlock, *Crime, Gender and Consumer Culture in Nineteenth-century England* (Aldershot, 2005); Karen Newman, *Cultural Capitals: Early Modern London and Paris* (Princeton, NJ, 2007); John Benson & Laura Ugolini, eds., *A Nation of Shopkeepers: Five Centuries of British Retailing* (London, 2003); and Isobel Armstrong, *Victorian Glassworlds: Glass Culture and the Imagination, 1830–1880* (Oxford, 2008), 134–41. **54.** The literature is too vast to list in full. In addition to later references, I have drawn especially on Michael B. Miller, *The Bon Marché: Bourgeois Culture and the Department Store, 1869–1920* (London, 1981); Crossick & Jaumain, eds., *Cathedrals of Consumption*; Bill Lancaster, *The Department Store* (Leicester, 1995); H. Pasdermadjian, *The Department Store: Its Origins, Evolution and Economics* (London, 1954); and Erika D. Rappaport, *Shopping for Pleasure: Women and the Making of London's West End* (Princeton, NJ, 2000).

55. Richard Dennis, *Cities in Modernity* (Cambridge, 2008), 311; see also: Richards, *The Commodity Culture of Victorian England: Advertising and Spectacle, 1851–1914*. **56.** Roger Gravil, *The Anglo-Argentine Connection, 1900–1939* (Boulder, CO, 1985), 92–4, 107; and Wellington K. K. Chan, 'Selling Goods and Promoting a New Commercial Culture', in: Sherman Cochran, *Inventing Nanking Road: Commercial Culture in Shanghai, 1900–1945* (Ithaca, NY, 1999), 19–36. **57.** Harrod's Stores Ltd, *Harrod's Catalogue 1895* (Newton Abbot, 1972 facsimile), 816, 879, 1128, 1156. **58.** Harrod's Stores Ltd, *A Story of British Achievement, 1849–1949* (London, 1949). **59.** *Olivia's Shopping and How She Does It: A Prejudiced Guide to the London Shops* (London, 1906), 62–3. For sales and credit in eighteenth-century shops, see now: Natacha Coquery, *Tenir boutique à Paris au XVIIIe siècle: Luxe et demi-luxe* (Paris, 2011), ch. 7. **60.** Émile Zola, *The Ladies' Paradise*, trans. Brian Nelson (Oxford, 1883/1995), 397–8, 418–19. **61.** Zola, *The Ladies' Paradise*, 77, 104, 117, 240. **62.** See Perez Galdos's novel, *La da Bringas* (1884). Lara Anderson, *Allegories of Decadence in Fin-de-siècle Spain: The Female Consumer in the Novels of Emilia Pardo Bazán and Benito Pérez Galdós* (Dyfed, 2006). **63.** Miles Ogborn, *Spaces of Modernity: London Geographies, 1680–1780* (New York, 1998), 116–57. **64.** Nead, *Victorian Babylon*, 62–79; and Krista Lysack, *Come Buy, Come Buy: Shopping and the Culture of Consumption in Victorian Women's Writing* (Athens, Ohio, 2008). **65.** Zola, *The Ladies' Paradise*, 422; Elaine Abelson, *When Ladies Go A-Thieving* (Oxford, 1989); Detlef Briesen, *Warenhaus, Massenkonsum und Sozialmoral: Zur Geschichte der Konsumkritik im 20. Jahrhundert* (Frankfurt am Main, 2001); and Uwe Spiekermann, 'Theft and Thieves in German Department Stores, 1895–1930', in: Crossick & Jaumain, eds., *Cathedrals of Consumption*, 135–59. See also: Mona Domosh, 'The "Women of New York": A Fashionable Moral Geography', *Environment and Planning D: Society and Space* 19, 2001: 573–92. **66.** Paul Göhre, *Das Warenhaus* (Frankfurt am Main, 1907). **67.** Georg Simmel, *The Philosophy of Money* (London, 1900/1990), 449–61. **68.** Walter Benjamin, *The Arcades Project*, trans. Eiland Howard & Kevin McLaughlin (Cambridge, MA, 1999), 389, K1, 4. **69.** Benjamin, *The Arcades Project*, 408, L2, 4. **70.** Benjamin, *The Arcades Project*, 540, R2, 3. **71.** Benjamin, *The Arcades Project*, 43, A4, 1; see also 60, A12, 5. For different readings, see Beatrice Hanssen, ed., *Walter Benjamin and the Arcades Project* (London, 2006); Susan Buck-Morss, *The Dialectics of Seeing: Walter Benjamin and the Arcades Project* (Cambridge, MA, 1989); Esther Leslie, *Walter Benjamin* (London, 2007); and Esther Leslie, 'Flâneurs in Paris and Berlin', in: *Histories of Leisure*, ed. Rudy Koshar (Oxford and New York, 2002). **72.** Benjamin, *The Arcades Project*, pp. 370f AP, J 81, 1. **73.** Rappaport, *Shopping for Pleasure*, 132–41. **74.** Göhre, *Das Warenhaus*, 141–2, my translation. Warren G. Breckman, 'Disciplining Consumption: The Debate about Luxury in Wilhelmine Germany, 1890–1914', in: *Journal of Social History* 24, no. 3, 1991: 485–505. **75.** Rachel Morley, 'Crime without Punishment: Reworkings of Nineteenth-century Russian Literary Sources in Evgenii Bauer's *Child of the Big City*', in: *Russian and*

Soviet Film Adaptations of Literature, 1900–2001, ed. Stephen Hutchings & Anat Vernitski (London, 2004), 27–43.   **76.** Julius Hirsch, *Das Warenhaus in Westdeutschland* (PhD thesis, Friedrich-Wilhelms-Universität zu Bonn, 1909), 28. At the Les Grands Magasins du Louvre in Paris, the average sale price was 20 francs.   **77.** Quoted in Susan Matt, *Keeping up with the Joneses: Envy in American Consumer Society, 1890–1930* (Philadelphia, 2003), 78.   **78.** Brent Shannon, 'ReFashioning Men: Fashion, Masculinity and the Cultivation of the Male Consumer in Britain, 1860–1914', in: *Victorian Studies* 46, no. 4, 2004: 597–630; and Christopher Breward, *The Hidden Consumer: Masculinities, Fashion and City Life, 1860–1914* (Manchester, 1999).   **79.** E. E. Perkins, *The Lady's Shopping Manual and Mercery Album* (London, 1834), vi, emphases in original.   **80.** Margot C. Finn, *The Character of Credit: Personal Debt in English Culture, 1740–1914* (Cambridge, 2003), esp. 264–73; and Whitlock, *Crime, Gender and Consumer Culture*.   **81.** Fred W. Leigh, 'Let's Go Shopping' (London, 1913).   **82.** Uwe Spiekermann, *Basis der Konsumgesellschaft: Entstehung und Entwicklung des modernen Kleinhandels in Deutschland, 1850–1914* (Munich, 1999), 380f.   **83.** William Leach, *Land of Desire: Merchants, Power, and the Rise of a New American Culture* (New York, 1994), 62.   **84.** Sarah Elvins, *Sales and Celebrations: Retailing and Regional Identity in Western New York State, 1920–40* (Athens, OH, 2004).   **85.** Huda Sha'arawi, *Harem Years: The Memoirs of an Egyptian Feminist, 1879–1924*, quoted in the sourcebook: Reina Lewis & Nancy Micklewright (eds.), *Gender, Modernity, Liberty: Middle Eastern and Western Women's Writings* (London, 2006), 192. For sales assistants, see Nancy Young Reynolds, *Commodity Cultures: Interweavings of Market Cultures, Consumption Practices and Social Power in Egypt, 1907–61* (PhD, Stanford University, 2003), ch. 3.   **86.** Werner Sombart, *Der Moderne Kapitalismus* (Munich, 1916, 2nd edn), Vol. II, Part I, ch. 28.   **87.** T. K. Dennison, *The Institutional Framework of Russian Serfdom* (Cambridge, 2011), 199–212.   **88.** David Blanke, *Sowing the American Dream: How Consumer Culture Took Root in the Rural Midwest* (Athens, OH, 2000). See also: Roman Sandgruber, *Die Anfänge der Konsumgesellschaft: Konsumgütergesellschaft, Lebensstandard und Alltagskultur in Österreich im 18. und 19. Jahrhundert* (Vienna, 1982); and Michael Prinz, ed., *Der lange Weg in den Überfluss: Anfänge und Entwicklung der Konsumgesellschaft seit der Vormoderne* (Paderborn, 2003).   **89.** John Benson, 'Large-scale Retailing in Canada', in: John Benson & Gareth Shaw, eds., *The Evolution of Retail Systems, c.1800 –1914* (Leicester, 1992), 190ff.   **90.** Karl Marx, *Das Kapital*, I (Frankfurt am Main, 1867/1969), 314. See also: Braudel, *Structures of Everyday Life*, I, ch. 8.   **91.** Sombart, *Der Moderne Kapitalismus*, II, 379; and Miller, *Bon Marché*, 61f.   **92.** Harvey Pitcher, *Muir and Mirrielees: The Scottisch Partnership that became a Household Name in Russia* (Cromer, 1994), 145–7.   **93.** Rita Andrade, 'Mappin Stores: Adding an English Touch to the Sao Paulo Fashion Scene', in: Regina A. Root, ed., *The Latin American Fashion Reader* (Oxford, 2005), ch. 10; Orlove, ed., *The Allure of the Foreign: Imported Goods in Post-colonial Latin America*; and Christine Ruane, 'Clothes

Shopping in Imperial Russia: The Development of a Consumer Culture', in: *Journal of Social History* 28, no. 4, 1995: 765–82. **94.** Reynolds, *Commodity Cultures in Egypt*, 75–88. For Isma'il Pasha's modernization, see Janet L. Abu-Lughod, *Cairo: 1001 Years of the City Victorious* (Princeton, NJ, 1971), 98–117. **95.** James Jefferys, *Retail Trading in Britain, 1850–1950* (Cambridge, 1954), 21–30. **96.** Spiekermann, *Basis*; H.-G. Haupt, 'Der Laden', in: *Orte des Alltags*, ed. H.-G. Haupt (Munich, 1994), 61–7; and H.-G. Haupt & Geoffrey Crossick, eds., *The Petite Bourgeoisie in Europe, 1780–1914* (London, 1998). **97.** Martin Philips, 'The Evolution of Markets and Shops in Britain', in: Benson & Shaw, eds., *The Evolution of Retail Systems, c.1800 –1914*, 54. See also: Margot Finn, 'Scotch Drapers and the Politics of Modernity', in: *The Politics of Consumption: Material Culture and Citizenship in Europe and America*, eds. Martin J. Daunton & Matthew Hilton (Oxford, 2001), 89–107. Charlotte Niermann, ' "Gewerbe im Umherziehen" – Hausierer und Wanderlager in Bremen vor 1914', in: *Der Bremer Kleinhandel um 1900*, ed. H.-G. Haupt (Bremen, 1982), 207–55. **98.** Spiekermann, *Basis*, 277–95, 382–415, 736–41. **99.** G. J. Holyoake, inaugural address, 19th Co-operative Congress (Manchester, 1887), 11. **100.** G. D. H. Cole, *A Century of Co-operation* (London, 1944); Ellen Furlough & Carl Strikwerda, eds., *Consumers against Capitalism? Consumer Cooperation in Europe, North America and Japan, 1840–1990* (Lanham, 1999); Michael Prinz, *Brot und Dividende: Konsumvereine in Deutschland und England vor 1914* (Göttingen, 1996); and Martin Purvis, 'Societies of Consumers and Consumer Societies: Co-operation, Consumption and Politics in Britain and Continental Europe *c.*1850–1920', in: *Journal of Historical Geography* 24, no. 2, 1998: 147–69. **101.** James Schmiechen & Kenneth Carls, *The British Market Hall* (New Haven, CT, 1999). Andrew Lohmeier, '*Bürgerliche Gesellschaft* and Consumer Interests: The Berlin Public Market Hall Reform, 1867–1891', in: *Business History Review* 73, no. 1, 1999: 91–113. **102.** Lange, 1911, quoted in Spiekermann, *Basis*, 183. **103.** Henri Lefebvre, *The Production of Space*, trans. Donald Nicholson-Smith (Oxford, 1991) 57. **104.** Shanghai Municipal Archive, Municipal Council, Annual Report 1929, 169, 170–2. **105.** Rosemary Bromley, 'Market-place Trading and the Transformation of Retail Space in the Expanding Latin American City', in: *Urban Studies* 35, no. 8, 1998: 1311–33; G. M. Zinkhan, S. M. Fontenelle & A. L. Balazs, 'The Structure of Sao Paolo Street Markets', in: *Journal of Consumer Affairs* 33, no. 1, 1999: 3–26. **106.** Schmiechen & Carls, *The British Market Hall*, 192. **107.** Christina M. Jiménez, 'From the Lettered City to the Sellers' City: Vendor Politics and Public Space in Urban Mexico, 1880–1926', in: Gyan Prakash & Kevin M. Kruse, eds., *The Spaces of the Modern City* (Princeton, NJ, 2008), 214–46. **108.** Henri Lefebvre, *Rhythmanalysis: Space, Time and Everyday Life* (London, 2004/1992), 40–1. **109.** Elizabeth Shove, Frank Trentmann & Richard Wilk, eds., *Time, Consumption and Everyday Life* (Oxford, 2009). See also below, 233–4. **110.** George R. Sims, ed., *Living London: Its Work and Its Play, Its Humour and Its Pathos, Its Sights and Its Scenes*, 3 vols. (London, 1904), Vol. II, 13, 380; Vol. III, 143. **111.** See Schmiechen & Carls, *The*

British Market Hall, 142–75. **112.** Lefebvre, *The Production of Space*, 86. **113.** Stephen Kern, *The Culture of Time and Space, 1880–1918* (Cambridge, MA, 1983); compare James Chandler & Kevin Gilmartin, eds., *Romantic Metropolis: The Urban Scene of British Culture, 1780-1840* (Cambridge, 2005). **114.** What Max Weber called *Lebensführung*. **115.** Georg Simmel, 'Die Grossstädte und das Geistesleben', in: *Die Grossstadt. Vorträge und Aufsätze zur Städteausstellung, Jahrbuch der Gehe-Stiftung* 9, 1903: 185–206, repr. in *Gesamtausgabe*, Vol. VII (1995), and transl. as 'The Metropolis and Mental Life', in: *The Sociology of Georg Simmel*, ed. Kurt Wolff (New York, 1950). **116.** 'Die kleinen Ladenmädchen gehen ins Kino', March 1927, repr. in Siegfried Kracauer, *Das Ornament der Masse* (Frankfurt am Main, 1977), quoted at 279–80, emphasis in original; 'Kult der Zerstreung', 4 March 1926, repr. in Kracauer, *Ornament*, quoted at 311, 313, my translations. **117.** Deutsche Kinemathek, Berlin, permanent exhibition. **118.** Michael M. Davis, *The Exploitation of Pleasure: A Study of Commercial Recreations in New York City* (New York, 1912), 21; Douglas Gomery, *Shared Pleasures: A History of Movie Presentation in the United States* (London, 1992); Joseph Garncarz, 'Film im Wanderkino', in: *Geschichte des dokumentarischen Films in Deutschland: Vol. I: Kaiserreich, 1895–1918*, eds. Uli Jung & Martin Loiperdinger (Stuttgart, 2005); Jon Burrows, 'Penny Pleasures: Film Exhibition in London during the Nicklodeon Era, 1906–14', *Film History* 16, no. 1, 2004: 60–91; and Luke McKernan, ' "A Fury for Seeing": London Cinemas and Their Audiences, 1906–1914 (Working Paper no. 1),' (AHRC Centre for British Film and Television Studies, 2005). See also the searchable database at www.london-film.bbk.ac.uk. **119.** Jean-Jacques Meusy, *Paris-Palaces, ou le temps de cinemas (1894–1918)*, (Paris, 1995), 173f. For Ireland, see Kevin Rockett & Emer Rockett, *Magic Lantern, Panorama and Moving Picture Shows in Ireland, 1786–1909* (Dublin, 2011). **120.** C. H. Rolph, *London Particulars* (Oxford, 1980), 105. **121.** Georges Dureau, quoted in Meusy, *Paris-Palaces*, 255, my translation. **122.** Simmel, 'Grossstädte'. **123.** Quoted in Meusy, *Paris-Palaces*, 229. V. Toulmin, S. Popple & P. Russell, eds., *The Lost World of Mitchell and Kenyon: Edwardian Britain on Film* (London, 2004); and Lynda Nead, 'Animating the Everyday: London on Camera *circa* 1900', in: *Journal of British Studies* 43, 2004: 65–90. **124.** Melvyn Stokes & Richard Maltby, eds., *American Movie Audiences* (London, 1999); Richard Butsch, *The Making of American Audiences: From Stage to Television, 1750–1990* (Cambridge, 2000), 142–7; and Kathy Peiss, *Cheap Amusements: Working Women and Leisure in Turn-of-the-Century New York* (Philadelphia, 1986). **125.** Emilie Altenloh, *Zur Soziologie des Kino: Die Kino-Unternehmung und die sozialen Schichten ihrer Besucher* (Jena, 1914), 67–8. **126.** Peter Bailey, *Leisure and Class in Victorian England* (London, 1978). **127.** George Barton Cutten, *The Threat of Leisure* (New Haven, CT, 1926), 17, 72, 90. **128.** Granville Stanley Hall, *Adolescence: Its Psychology and Its Relations to physiology*, Vol. I (New York, 1904); and John R. Gillis, *Youth and History: Tradition and Change in European Age Relations, 1770–Present* (New York, 1981 edn). **129.** Staatsarchiv

Hamburg, 424-24/88, 14 Jan. 1922, Herr Lorenzen, department of youth wel-
fare, Altona, my translation. For the United States, see David Nasaw, *Children
of the City* (New York, 1985).   **130.** Davis, *Exploitation of Pleasure* (1912), 3,
and 9 for the previous quotation.   **131.** Henry W. Thurston, *Delinquency and
Spare Time: A Study of a Few Stories Written into the Court Records of the
City of Cleveland* (Cleveland, 1918), 22-3, 79, 85.   **132.** Michael M. Davis Jr,
*The Exploitation of Pleasure: A Study of Commercial Recreations in New York
City* (New York, 1912), 14.   **133.** Raymond Moley, *Commercial Recreation*
(Cleveland, 1920), 87, and 91 for the above.   **134.** Staatsarchiv Hamburg,
614-1/18/57, 'Kampf gegen Schmutz und Schund in Wort und Bild', Dec.
1921 and 24 Oct. 1922.   **135.** Davis Jr, *Exploitation of Pleasure*, 44.   **136.**
Roy Rosenzweig, *Eight Hours for What We Will: Workers and Leisure in an
Industrial City, 1870–1920* (Cambridge, 1983), 147. For Manchester, see H. E.
Meller, *Leisure and the Changing City, 1870–1914* (London 1976). For
Cologne: *Hans Langenfeld in Zusammenarbeit mit Stefan Nielsen/Klaus Rein-
arz und Josef Santel*, 'Sportangebot und -nachfrage in grossstädtischen Zentren
Nordwestdeutschlands (1848–1933)', in: Juergen Reulecke, ed., *Die Stadt als
Dienstleistungszentrum* (St Katharinen, 1995), 461.   **137.** Roland S. Vaile,
Research Memorandum on Social Aspects of Consumption in the Depression
(New York, 1937), 25.   **138.** For Coney Island and Blackpool, see Gary S.
Cross & John K. Walton, *The Playful Crowd: Pleasure Places in the Twentieth
Century* (New York, 2005), quoted at 109.   **139.** Wong Yunn Chii & Tan Kar
Lin, 'Emergence of a Cosmopolitan Space for Culture and Consumption: The
New World Amusement Park – Singapore (1923–70) in the Inter-War Years', in:
Inter-Asia Cultural Studies 5, no. 2, 2004: 279–304; Philip Holden, 'At Home
in the Worlds: Community and Consumption in Urban Singapore', in: *Beyond
Description: Singapore Space Historicity*, eds. Ryan Bishop, John Phillips &
Yeo Wei-Wei (New York, 2004), 79–94; and Yung Sai Shing & Chan Kwok
Bun, 'Leisure, Pleasure and Consumption: Ways of Entertaining Oneself', in:
Past Times: A Social History of Singapore, eds. Kwok Bun Chan & Tong Chee
Kiong, (Singapore, 2003), 153–81.   **140.** In the 1970s, Manuel Castells argued
that industrial capitalism led to the disappearance of the city as an autonomous
social system, in *The Urban Question* (London, 1978).

CHAPTER 5

1. Bruno Taut, *Die neue Wohnung* (Leipzig, 1924/1928: 5th rev. edn), quoted at
10–12, 59–60, my translation.   **2.** Barbara Miller Lane, *Architecture and Politics in Germany, 1918–45* (Cambridge, MA, 1968); for Taut as architect, see
Erich Weitz, *Weimar Germany* (Princeton, NJ, 2007), 169–83.   **3.** Clarence
Cook, *The House Beautiful* (New York, 1881), 49.   **4.** Deborah Cohen, *Household Gods: The British and Their Possessions* (New Haven, CT, 2006), 36.   **5.**
Edward Young, *Labor in Europe and in America* (Washington, DC, 1875),
tables, 822–5.   **6.** Sergej Prokopowitsch, 'Haushaltungs-budgets Petersburger

Arbeiter', in: *Archiv für Sozialwissenschaft und Sozialpolitik* 30, 1910, 66–99, so-called summer tenants (*Sommermieter*). **7.** Daunton, 'Public Place and Private Space: The Victorian City and the Working-Class Household', 227. **8.** Report by Mr Andrews, the Hon. Minister for the USA in Stockholm, 1873, in Young, *Labor in Europe and in America*, 698. See also: the Amuri district in Tampere, Finland, now a museum of workers' housing. **9.** Taut, *Die neue Wohnung*, 98, my translation. **10.** For this, and much more, see the excellent thesis by Charpy, 'Le Théâtre des objets', Vol. I. See also: Walter Benjamin, *Berlin Childhood around 1900* (Cambridge, MA, 2006). **11.** Louise, d'Alq, *Le Maître et la mâitresse de maison* (1885), quoted in Charpy, 'Le Théâtre des objets', I, 179. See also: Jean-Pierre Goubert, ed., *Du luxe au confort* (Paris, 1988). **12.** Judy Neiswander, *The Cosmopolitan Interior: Liberalism and the British Home, 1870–1914* (New Haven, CT, 2008). **13.** Sonia Ashmore, 'Liberty and Lifestyle', in: David Hussey & Margaret Ponsonby, eds., *Buying for the Home: Domestic Consumption from the Seventeenth to the Twentieth Century* (Aldershot, 2008). **14.** Natacha Coquery 'Luxe et demi-luxe: Bijoutiers et tapissiers parisiens à la fin du XVIIe siècle', in Stephane Castelluccio (ed.), *Le Commerce de luxe à Paris au XVIIe et XVIIIe siècle* (Bern, 2009). **15.** Between 1820 and 1890, London trade directories show a rise in the number of furniture brokers from 2 to 390, furniture dealers from 2 to 47, upholsterers from 165 to 468; Clive Edwards & Margaret Ponsonby, 'Desirable Commodity or Practical Necessity?', in: Hussey & Ponsonby, *Buying for the Home*, 123–4. For Paris, see Charpy, 'Le Théâtre des objets', I, esp. 507–614. **16.** Steven M. Gelber, *Hobbies: Leisure and the Culture of Work in America* (New York, 1999), 139. See also: Belk, *Collecting in a Consumer Society*; and Raphael Samuel, *Theatres of Memory* (London, 1994). **17.** See the discussion in ch. 3. **18.** Veblen, *The Theory of the Leisure Class: An Economic Study of Institutions*, 69. David Riesman distinguished between the inner-directed conspicuous consumer and a more conformist outer-directed type in *The Lonely Crowd* (1950/1953), 143f. **19.** Veblen, *Leisure Class*, 69. **20.** Veblen, *Leisure Class*, 69. **21.** Charlotte Perkins Gilman, *The Home: Its Work and Influence* (1903/2002), 120. **22.** Taut, *Die Neue Wohnung*, 87. For a critique of Veblen and other universal theories, see Jean-Pascal Daloz, *The Sociology of Elite Distinction* (Basingstoke, 2010). **23.** George & Weedon Grossmith, *The Diary of a Nobody* (London, 1892/1999), 31–5. **24.** Max Weber, 'Zwischenbetrachtung', in: *Gesammelte Aufsätze zur Religionssoziologie* I (1920/1988), esp. 568–71, my translation. In English, *From Max Weber: Essays in Sociology*, eds. Hans Heinrich Gerth & Charles Wright Mills (Oxford, 1946). **25.** Leora Auslander, *Taste and Power: Furnishing Modern France* (Berkeley, CA, 1996). **26.** Jackson Lears, *Fables of Abundance: A Cultural History of Advertising in America* (New York, 1994), 49. By 1900, according to Lears, alternative ways of thinking 'had lost nearly all intellectual legitimacy' and were limited to a few 'idiosyncratic writers and artists', 19. **27.** Bill Brown, *A Sense of Things: The Object Matter of American Literature* (Chicago, 2003). **28.** Graham Wallas, *Human Nature in Politics* (London, 1908). **29.** Henry James, *The Spoils of Poynton*

(London, 1897/1987), 30. **30.** James, *Spoils of Poynton*, 43. **31.** William James, *Principles of Psychology* (New York, 1890/1950), Vol. I, 291, emphases in original, and 292–3 for the following. They were not exactly the same, he conceded, but they operated 'in much the same way for all'. At the end of his life, James speculated whether plants, animals and Earth had their own consciousness: see Bruce Wilshire, 'The Breathtaking Intimacy of the Material World: Williams James's Last Thoughts', in: *The Cambridge Companion to William James*, ed. Ruth Anna Putnam (Cambridge, 1997), ch. 6. George Herbert Mead would develop some of these ideas further, stressing the ways in which humans and objects sustained each other in co-operative relationships: G. H. Mead, *The Philosophy of the Act* (Chicago, 1938), ed. Charles Morris; see also the discussion by E. Doyle McCarthy, 'Toward a Sociology of the Physical World: George Herbert Mead on Physical Objects', in: *Studies in Symbolic Interaction* 5, 1984: 105–21. **32.** James, *Principles of Psychology*, I, 125. **33.** James, *Principles of Psychology*, I, 122. **34.** Russell's *History of Western Philosophy* devotes eight pages to James, zero to Heidegger. In his *Wisdom of the West* (New York, 1959), Russell allows one note: 'One cannot help suspecting that language is here running riot. An interesting point in his speculations is the insistence that nothingness is something positive. As with much else in existentialism, this is a psychological observation made to pass for logic', 303. **35.** Martin Heidegger, 'Das Ding' (1949), in: *Gesamtausgabe*, Vol. III, 79: *Bremer and Freiburger Vorträge* (1994), 5–23; in English in: *Poetry, Language, Thought* (New York, 2001), 161–84. **36.** Documentary images can be viewed at /www.youtube.com/watch?v=Mqsu72ZlJ2c. **37.** Martin Heidegger, *Sein und Zeit*, 1927, 69–84. **38.** A sentiment that would be given new force by the architect Sigfried Giedion in his *Mechanization Takes Command* in 1948. **39.** Heidegger, *Sein und Zeit*, 126–7, my translation. The original is *man*. This is often translated as 'they'. 'People' captures better the singular, conformist qualities Heidegger is writing about. **40.** Fiona C. Ross, 'Urban Development and Social Contingency: A Case Study of Urban Relocation in the Western Cape', in: *Africa Today* 51, no. 4, 2005: 19–31. **41.** Godfrey Wilson, *An Essay on the Economics of Detribalization in Northern Rhodesia* (Rhodes–Livingstone Papers, 1941), 18. **42.** Eurostat, *Housing Statistics in the European Union 2004*, table 3.5, 50. **43.** Herbert Hoover, *American Individualism* (Garden City, NY, 1923), 27, 32, 38. See also: David Burner, *Herbert Hoover: A Public Life* (New York, 1979). For a contemporary paen, see Walter Friar Dexter, *Herbert Hoover and American Individualism* (New York, 1932). **44.** De Grazia, *Irresistible Empire*. **45.** Michael Sandel, *Democracy's Discontent: America in Search of a Public Philosophy* (Cambridge, MA, 1996). **46.** W. E. Du Bois, *The Philadelphia Negro* (Philadelphia, 1899), 195f. **47.** Hazel Kyrk, *Economic Problems of the Family* (New York, 1929), 417. **48.** Elaine Lewinnek, *The Working Man's Reward: Chicago's Early Suburbs and the Roots of American Sprawl* (Oxford, 2014), 64–84, 94–105. **49.** 48%. For numbers, see Heinz Umrath, 'The Problem of Ownership', in: *International Labor Review*, 1955, issue 2, p. 110; Bruno Shiro, 'Housing Surveys in 75 cities, 1950 and 1952', in: *Monthly Labor Review*,

1954, 744–50; and the 1930 census figures cited in Kyrk, *Economic Problems of the Family*, 416. **50.** Quoted in Marina Moskowitz, *Standard of Living: The Measure of the Middle Class in Modern America* (Baltimore, 2004), 140; and 163–73 for below. **51.** Regina Lee Blaszczyk, *Imagining Consumers: Design and Innovation from Wedgwood to Corning* (Baltimore, 2000), 176–81. **52.** James Hutchisson, *The Rise of Sinclair Lewis, 1920-30* (University Park, PA, 1996), 88. **53.** Sinclair Lewis, *Babbitt* (London, 1922), 95–6. **54.** Lewis, *Babbitt*, 23–4. **55.** Lewis, *Babbitt*, 103–4, italics in original. **56.** M. Mead Smith, 'Monthly Cost of Owning and Renting New Housing, 1949–50', in: *Monthly Labour Review*, Aug. 1954, 852. **57.** Jordan Sand, *House and Home in Modern Japan: Architecture, Domestic Space and Bourgeois Culture, 1880-1930* (Cambridge, MA, 2003), 298. **58.** Peter Clarke, *Hope and Glory: Britain 1900-1990* (London, 1996), 144–50; Peter Scott, 'Marketing Mass Home Ownership and the Creation of the Modern Working-class Consumer in Interwar Britain', in: *Business History* 50, no. 1, 2008: 4–25; and Peter Scott, 'Did Owner-occupation Lead to Smaller Families for Inter-war Working-class Households', in: *Economic History Review* 61, no. 1, 2008: 99–124. For France, see Alexia Yates, 'Selling *la petite propriété*: Marketing Home Ownership in Early-twentieth-century Paris', in *Entreprises et histoire* 64, no. 3, 2011: 11–40. **59.** W. E. Dwight, 'Housing Conditions and Tenement Laws in Leading European Cities', in: Robert W. Deforest & Lawrence Veiller, eds., *The Tenement House Problem* (New York City, 1903), 174–84. For the 1920s, see Daniel T. Rodgers, *Atlantic Crossings: Social Politics in a Progressive Age* (Cambridge, MA, 1998), 381–91. **60.** See now Peter Scott, *The Making of the Modern British Home: The Suburban Semi and Family Life between the Wars* (Oxford, 2013), ch. 2. **61.** In Finland, it jumped up from 19% in 1980 to 26% in 2003; in Britain from 16% to over 18%; see National Board of Housing, Sweden et al., *Housing Statistics in the European Union* (2004), 61. I discuss the effects of housing wealth on consumption on 243–5 below. **62.** Quoted from Madeline McKenna, 'The Development of Suburban Council Housing Estates in Liverpool between the Wars', PhD thesis, Liverpool University, 1986, Vol II, Mrs F., Settington Road, Norris Green, interview no. 12, 428–9. **63.** Bruno Shiro, 'Housing Surveys in 75 cities, 1950 and 1952', *Monthly Labor Review*, 1954, 744–50. Strict rent control and tax rules have had a similar effect in the Federal Republic of Germany since the 1960s: with secure tenancies, people invest in modernizing their rented flats. **64.** European Mortgage Federation, Hypo Stat, 2009. **65.** Quoted in Vera Dunham, *In Stalin's Time: Middle-class Values in Soviet Fiction* (Cambridge, 1976), 48. **66.** Michael McKeon, *The Secret History of Domesticity: Public, Private and the Division of Knowledge* (Baltimore, 2005), 259–64. **67.** One child was to sleep in the living room. Royal Meeker, 'Relation of the Cost of Living to Public Health', in: *Monthly Labor Review*, Jan. 1919, Vol. VIII, no. 1, 5. Meeker was the Commissioner of the Bureau. **68.** For example, Beyer, Davis & Thwing, *Workingmen's Standard of Living in Philadelphia*, 1. **69.** V. Volkov, 'The Concept of *Kul'turnost*', in: Sheila Fitzpatrick, ed., *Stalinism: New Directions*

(London, 2000), 210–30. **70.** John E. Crowley, *The Invention of Comfort: Sensibilities and Design in Early Modern Britain and Early America* (Baltimore, MD, 2001). See also: Shove, *Comfort, Cleanliness and Convenience.* **71.** Kyrk, *Economic Problems of the Family*, 368. **72.** White House Conference on Child Health and Protection, *The Young Child in the Home: A Survey of Three Thousand American Families* (New York, 1936), 274. **73.** 'The Demand for Domestic Appliances', in: *National Institute Economic Review* 12, Nov. 1960, tables 2, 5 and 6, 24–44. **74.** Robert L. Frost, 'Machine Liberation': in *French Historical Studies*, Vol. XVIII, no. 1, spring 1983, 124. See further, Sue Bowden & Avner Offer, 'Household Appliances and the Use of Time: The United States and Britain since the 1920s', in: *Economic History Review* 47, no. 4, 1994: 725–48. **75.** 'The Demand for Domestic Appliances', 27f. **76.** David E. Nye, *Consuming Power: A Social History of American Energies* (Cambridge, MA, 1998), 170f.; and Ruth Schwartz Cowan, *More Work for Mother* (New York, 1983), 91. **77.** Robert S. Lynd & Helen Merrell Lynd, *Middletown: A Study in Modern American Culture* (New York, 1929), quoted at 97–8; see also 175. See also the survey data in: Federal Emergency Administration of Public Works, Housing Division, Bulletin no. 1: *Slums and Blighted Areas in the United States* (Washington, DC, 1935). **78.** R. Wilkinson & E. Sigsworth, 'A Survey of Slum Clearance Areas in Leeds', in: *Yorkshire Bulletin of Economic and Social Research*, Vol. XV/1, 1963, 25–47; François Caron, *Economic History of Modern France* (New York, 1979); and Karl Ditt, *Zweite Industrialisierung und Konsum: Energieversorgung, Haushaltstechnik und Massenkultur am Beispiel nordenglischer und westfälischer Städte, 1880–1939* (Paderborn, 2011), 452–63. **79.** Hughes, *Networks of Power: Electrification in Western Society, 1880–1930.* **80.** H. Schütze, *Elektrizität im Haushalt* (Stuttgart, 1928), 22, 59. **81.** *Energiewirtschaftliche Tagesfragen*, Vol. XIV, issue 123 (1964), 155f. **82.** Shanghai Municipal Archive (SMA), Shanghai Municipal Council Report for 1923, 5 A, and Report for 1924, 2 A, 6 A. **83.** SMA, Municipal Gazette, 30 March 1937, 98–100; and Bureau of Social Affairs, the City Government of Greater Shanghai, *Standard of Living of Shanghai Laborers* (Shanghai, 1934), 135–48. **84.** Vereinigung der Elektrizitätswerke, *Fortschritte in der Elektrifizierung des Haushalts* (Berlin, 1932), 106. **85.** The kitchen was exhibited at the V&A's Modernism exhibit in 2006; see *Modernism: Designing a New World*, ed. Christopher Wilk (London, 2006), 180; a picture of the original is at: www.vam.ac.uk/vastatic/microsites/1331_ modernism/files/94/1926_frankfurt_lihotzky.jpg. See also: Michelle Corrodi, 'On the Kitchen and Vulgar Odors', in: Klaus Spechtenhauser, ed., *The Kitchen: Life World, Usage, Perspectives* (Basel, 2006), 21–42. **86.** Nederlandse Vereniging van Huisvrouwen (NVvH), see Onno de Wit, Adri de la Bruheze & Marja Berendsen, 'Ausgehandelter Konsum: Die Verbreitung der modernen Küche, des Kofferradios und des Snack Food in den Niederlanden', *Technikgeschichte*, 68 (2001), 133–55. **87.** Shanghai Municipal Council, *Annual Report for 1924*, illustration facing 7 A; Deborah S. Ryan, *Daily Mail – Ideal Home Exhibition: The Ideal Home through the Twentieth Century* (London, 1997),

49–55, 93; Robert L. Frost, 'Machine Liberation: Inventing Housewives and Home Appliances in Interwar France', in: *French Historical Studies*, Vol. 18, no. 1 (Spring, 1993), 127.   **88.** *Energiewirtschaftliche Tagesfragen* 13, issue 114/115 (1963), quoted at 247, my translation; Nicholas Bullock, 'First the Kitchen: Then the Façade', in: *Journal of Design History*, Vol. I, no. 3/4 (1988), 188–90. Margaret Tränkle, 'Neue Wohnhorizonte', in: Ingeborg Flagge, ed., *Geschichte des Wohnens: Von 1945 bis Heute*, Vol. V (Stuttgart, 1999), 754–5.   **89.** Hilla Mann lived in Meyer's Hof from 1932. The interview is in J. F. Geist K. Kürvers, *Das Berliner Mietshaus, 1862–1945*, Vol. II (Munich, 1984), 535–6, my translation.   **90.** Jacques Berque, *Egypt: Imperialism and Revolution* (London, 1967/1972), 332.   **91.** Schler, 'Bridewealth', in: *Journal of African Cultural Studies*, 2003.   **92.** Ellen Hellmann, *Rooiyard: A Sociological Survey of an Urban Native Slum Yard* (Cape Town, 1948), esp. 10, 28, 31 (budget no. 2), 115. The book was based on her 1935 MA thesis.   **93.** *American Home*, 1934, quoted in Arwen P. Mohun, *Steam Laundries: Gender, Technology and Work in the United States and Great Britain, 1880–1940* (Baltimore, 1999), 259.   **94.** Turin, 1956, quoted in Enrica Asquer, *La rivoluzione candida: Storia sociale della lavatrice in Italia, 1945–70*, (Rome, 2007), 71, my translation; and Wolfgang König, *Geschichte der Konsumgesellschaft* (Stuttgart, 2000), 231–2.   **95.** Mohun, *Steam Laundries*, 256; Susan Strasser, *Never Done: A History of American Housework* (New York, 1982), 104–24.   **96.** Joy Parr, *Domestic Goods: The Material, the Moral and the Economic in the Post-war Years* (Toronto, 1999), ch. 10.   **97.** Simon Partner, *Assembled in Japan: Electrical Goods and the Making of the Japanese Consumer* (Berkeley, CA, 1999), 141, 181–3.   **98.** Helen Meintjes, 'Washing Machines Make Women Lazy: Domestic Appliances and the Negotiation of Women's Propriety in Soweto', *Journal of Material Culture* 6, no. 3, 2001: 345–63.   **99.** John Kenneth Galbraith, *Economics and the Public Purpose* (Boston, 1973).   **100.** Henkel Archiv, Düsseldorf, *Gesolei Tagesberichte*, 1926, unnumbered, *Gesundheitspflege, soziale Fürsorge und Leibesübungen* (GeSoLei), my translation.   **101.** Wilfried Feldenkirchen & Susanne Hilger, *Menschen und Marken: 125 Jahre Henkel* (Düsseldorf, 2001), 75–6.   **102.** Henkel Archiv, Düsseldorf, *Blätter vom Hause*, 17. Jhg, 1937, 49, and report in H 482, quoted at 349 (1936). For the above, see also the files H 310: *Waschvorführung*; H 480, Gesolei; *Gesolei Tagesberichte*, 1926; *Henkel-Bote*, 18 Sept. 1937 on infant mortality charts; *Blätter vom Hause*, 17. Jhg, 1937, 46, 49, 137; 1928, 266; and film: *Das Ei des Kolumbus*.   **103.** *President's [Hoover] Conference on Home Building and Home Ownership, Household Management and Kitchens* (Washington, 1932), Foreword. See also: Margaret Horsfield, *Biting the Dust: The Joys of Housework* (London, 1998).   **104.** Barbara Sato, *The New Japanese Woman: Modernity, Media and Women in Inter-war Japan* (Durham, NC, 2003), 102. Compare Joanna Bourke, 'Housewifery in Britain, 1850–1914', *Past and Present*, 143/1 (1994), 167–97.   **105.** In the words of the top official, Ministerialrat Dr Gertrud Bäumer, president of the 1928 exhibition *Heim und Technik: Amtlicher Katalog, Ausstellung München 1928* (1928), 45.   **106.** Sand, *House and*

Home, 21–94. **107.** Quoted in Sand, *House and Home*, 183; 187 for health and safety, and see Ch. 5 for the above. See also: Sheldon Garon, 'Luxury is the Enemy: Mobilizing Savings and Popularizing Thrift in Wartime Japan', in: *Journal of Japanese Studies* 26, no. 1, 2000: 41–78. **108.** Amy Hewes, 'Electrical Appliances in the Home', in: *Social Forces* 2, Dec. 1930: 235–42, quoted at 241. **109.** For calculations, see Joel Mokyr, 'Why "More Work for Mother?" Knowledge and Household Behavior, 1870–1945', in: *Journal of Economic History* 60, no. 1, 2000: 1–41. **110.** G. Silberzahn-Jandt, *Waschmaschine* (Marburg, 1991) 74. **111.** Cowan, *More Work*, quoted at 100, and see 159–99. **112.** Lee Rainwater, Richard P. Coleman & Gerald Handel, *Workingman's Wife: Her Personality, World and Life Style* (New York, 1959), 179. **113.** Lynd & Lynd, *Middletown*, 174; for later data, see Jonathan Gershuny, *Changing Times: Work and Leisure in Post-industrial Society* (Oxford, 2000), 46–75. Given the different types of datasets, any generalization is fraught with danger. In contrast to Gershuny, the adjusted estimates in Ramey's article show a rise in 'home production' for employed women in the United States across the twentieth century: Valerie A. Ramey, 'Time Spent in Home Production in the Twentieth-century United States: New Estimates from Old Data', in: *Journal of Economic History* 69, no. 1, 2009: 1–47. See also 443–51 below. **114.** Ramey, 'Time Spent', 26–7. **115.** Unni Wikan, *Life among the Poor in Cairo* (London, 1976/1980), 133–65; Homa Hoodfar, 'Survival Strategies and the Political Economy of Low-income Households in Cairo', in: Diane Singerman & Homa Hoodfar, eds., *Development, Change and Gender in Cairo: A View from the Household* (Bloomington, IN, 1996), 1–26. **116.** For a more contemporaneous example, see Wim van Binsbergen, 'Mary's Room: A Case Study on becoming a Consumer in Francistown, Botswana', in: Richard Fardon, Wim Van Bimsbergen & Rijk van Dijk (eds.), *Modernity on a Shoestring: Dimensions of Globalization, Consumption and Development in Africa and Beyond* (Leiden, 1999), 179–206. **117.** Quoted in Steven M. Gelber, 'Do-it-yourself: Constructing, Repairing and Maintaining Domestic Masculinity', in: *American Quarterly* 49, no. 1, 1997: 66–112, 86. See also: Gelber, *Hobbies*. **118.** *Jardin ouvrier de France*, Sept. 1941, quoted in Florence Weber, *L'Honneur des jardiniers: Les Potagers dans la France du XXe siècle* (Paris, 1998), 197, my translation, and 138–45 for inter-war growth. In Britain, there were 609,352 allotments in 1935, and still half a million in 1990; David Crouch & Colin Ward, *The Allotment: Its Landscape and Culture* (Nottingham, 1997), 64–81. In Germany in 2009, there were 1 million *Kleingärten*, according to the Bundesverband Deutscher Gartenfreunde e.V. **119.** Michael Prinz, *Der Sozialstaat hinter dem Haus: Wirtschaftliche Zukunftserwartungen, Selbstversorgung und regionale Vorbilder; Westfalen und Südwestdeutschland, 1920–1960* (Paderborn, 2012), 95–8, 322–4. **120.** W. V. Hole & J. J. Attenburrow, *Houses and People: A Review of User Studies at the Building Research Stations* (London, 1966), 54–6; a 1960 survey showed that 60% of British households had done some DIY in the previous ten months, 55. **121.** 'Prime-age' American men spent a mere 3.9 hours on home production in 1900 and 1920, which rose to 9 hours by 1950.

This aggregate includes non-employed men. Significantly, employed men shared in the upward trend, up from 3 hours to 8.1 hours; Ramey, 'Time Spent', table 7, 29. **122.** Reports of the Committees on Household Management, and on Kitchens and other Work Centers; part of the President's Conference on Home Building and Home Ownership (1932), section on Management of Household Operations. **123.** Ramey, 'Time Spent'. **124.** Tan Sooi Beng, 'The 78 RPM Record Industry in Malaya Prior to World War Two', in: *Asian Music* 28, no. 1, 1996/97: 1–41; Roland Gelatt, *The Fabulous Phonograph* (London, 1956); Friedrich A. Kittler, *Gramophone, Film, Typewriter* (Stanford, 1986/1999); Mark Hustwitt, ' "Caught in a Whirlpool of Aching Sound": The Production of Dance Music in Britain in the 1920s', in: *Popular Music* (1983) 3, 7–31; and James J. Nott, *Music for the People: Popular Music and Dance in Inter-war Britain* (Oxford, 2002). **125.** Frederik Nebeker, *Dawn of the Electronic Age: Electrical Technologies in the Shaping of the Modern World, 1914–1945* (Piscataway, NJ, 2009), 133f. **126.** 15,000 of 35,000 schools; Archives Nationales Luxembourg, FI-547, *Radio-Revue Luxembourgeoise*, Ire année, no. 8 (April 1932), citing *Der Schulfunk* (June 1931), at 115–16. **127.** John Tigert, *Radio in Education* (New York, 1929). Of course, the rise of entertainment did not mean that the radio ceased to be a tool for education or propaganda, including at the colonial village level; Joselyn Zivin, 'The Imagined Reign of the Iron Lecturer: Village Broadcasting in Colonial India', in: *Modern Asian Studies*, 32/3 (1998), 717–38. **128.** Archives Nationales Luxembourg, FI-547, *Radio-Revue Luxembourgeoise*, Ire année, no. 9 (May 1932), 140; no. 7 (March 1932), 104 for the Telefunkensuper 653; 2e année, no. 6 (July 1933), 68; and Shaun Moores, 'The Box on the Dresser', in: *Media, Culture and Society* 10/1 (1988), 23–40. **129.** One radio for every six persons; Archives Nationales Luxembourg, FI-547, Commission d'Études Radioelectriques, 'Rapport sur l'exploitation de la radiodiffusion, 1936', 3–4. The figure for Argentina is for 1938, cited in Paul F. Lazarsfeld & Frank N. Stanton, (eds.), *Radio Research 1941* (NY, 1941), 227. **130.** In 1943, 3.5 hours for a single-person household, 6 hours and 8 minutes for a family of five in America: Matthew Chappell & C. E. Hooper, *Radio Audience Measurement* (New York, 1944), 203. **131.** Michael Brian Schiffer, *The Portable Radio in American Life* (Tucson and London, 1991), 76. **132.** Susan J. Douglas, *Listening In: Radio and the American Imagination* (Minneapolis, MN, 2004), 77; and Andrew Stuart Bergerson, 'Listening to the Radio in Hildesheim, 1923–53', in: *German Studies Review* 24, no. 1, 2001: 83–113. **133.** Beng, 'Record Industry in Malaya', 15. **134.** Archives Nationales Luxembourg, FI-547, *Radio-Revue Luxembourgeoise*, 2e année, no. 4/5 (May–June 1933), 41–2. **135.** For example, the Methodist Revd G. Reid Smith in Georgia, 1936; Kathy M. Newman, *Radio Active: Advertising and Consumer Activism, 1935–1947* (Berkeley, CA, 2004), 81–2. **136.** Marian Parker, quoted in Roland R. Kline, *Consumers in the Country: Technology and Social Change in Rural America* (Baltimore, MD, 2000), 123. **137.** A woman from Chicago's South Side, interviewed in 1946, quoted in Ruth Palter, 'Radio's Attraction for Housewives', in: *Hollywood Quarterly* 3, no. 1, 1948: 248–57, 253.

138. Quoted in Palter, 'Radio's Attraction for Housewives', 251; Azriel Eisenberg, *Children and Radio Programs* (New York, 1936); Paul F. Lazarsfeld, *Radio and the Printed Page* (New York, 1940); and Matthew Chappell & C. E. Hooper, *Radio Audience Measurement* (New York, 1944). **139.** T. W. Adorno 'The Radio Symphony', in: Paul F. Lazarsfeld & Frank N. Stanton (eds.), *Radio Research 1941* (New York, 1941), 131. **140.** Stefan Müller-Doohm, *Adorno: A Biography* (Cambridge, 2005), 46. **141.** Adorno, 'Radio Symphony', 112, 131, 137; and T. W. Adorno, 'Zur gesellschaftlichen Lage der Musik', in *Zeitschrift für Sozialforschung*, I (1932), esp. 373. **142.** Quoted in Edward Suchman, 'Invitation to Music', in: Lazarsfeld & Stanton, *Radio Research 1941*, 149 and 186. In the United States, sales of pianos declined in the 1920s but, looking at the whole twentieth century, what is remarkable is the relative resilience of music making. See p. 463 below. **143.** Karin Nordberg, 'Ljud över landet: Centrum och periferi i tidig svensk radiohistoria', *Lychnos*, 1995, 145–78, quoted at 160, my translation. **144.** Douglas, *Listening In*, 93–6; Drew O. McDaniel, *Broadcasting in the Malay World: Radio, Television and Video in Brunei, Indonesia, Malaysia and Singapore* (Norwood, NJ, 1994), 21–48; Cantril & Allport, *Psychology of Radio*, 28; Sato, *New Japanese Woman*, 86; Nott, *Music for the People*. **145.** John Gray Peatman, 'Radio and Popular Music', in Paul. F. Lazarsfeld & Frank N. Stanton, *Radio Research 1942–1943* (New York, 1944), 354; all programmes together amounted to 60,000 hours in 1938. **146.** Marshall D. Beuick, 'The Limited Social Effect of Radio Broadcasting', in: *American Journal of Sociology*, 32/4 (Jan. 1927), 622. **147.** Cantril Allport, *Psychology of Radio* (London, 1935) 10. **148.** A Chicago woman in 1946 about why she liked *Pepper Young's Family*; Palter, 'Radio's Attraction for Housewives', at 255. **149.** Herta Herzog, 'What Do We Really Know about Day-time-serial Listeners', in: Lazarsfeld & Stanton, *Radio Research 1942–1943*, 8, 24. For the mix of solidarity and self-gratification, see also the study of *Professor Quiz*, in: Paul F. Lazarsfeld, *Radio and the Printed Page* (New York, 1940), 64–93. **150.** Edward Bellamy, *Looking Backward: If Socialism Comes, 2000–1887* (London, 1887/1925), 71. **151.** John R. Seeley, R. Alexander Sim & Elizabeth W. Loosley, *Crestwood Heights* (London, 1956), 221. Crestwood Heights was Forest Hill. **152.** For a moving ethnographic study of the importance of things in people's lives today, see Daniel Miller, *The Comfort of Things* (Cambridge, 2008). A fictional treatment is Orhan Pamuk, *Masumiyet Müzesi/Das Museum der Unschuld* (Munich, 2008). **153.** Seeley, Sim and Loosley, *Crestwood Heights*, 58. **154.** J. M. Mogey, *Family and Neighbourhood* (Oxford, 1956), 73; Kirsi Saarikangas, 'What's New? Women Pioneers and the Finnish State Meet the American Kitchen', in: Ruth Oldenziel & Karin Zachmann, *Cold War Kitchen: Americanization, Technology and European Users* (Cambridge, MA, 2009), ch. 12. **155.** Hole & Attenburrow, *Houses and People*, 36, from a 1956 survey. **156.** Leslie Kent from Luton, quoted in Fiona Devine, *Affluent Workers Revisited: Privatism and the Working Class* (Edinburgh, 1992), 161. See further: Dennis Chapman, *The Home and Social Status* (London, 1955); Margaret Tränkle, 'Neue

Wohnhorizonte', in: Flagge, ed., *Geschichte des Wohnens: Von 1945 bis Heute*, esp. 722–37.

CHAPTER 6

1. Bundesarchiv Koblenz, Germany, B 146/394, f.532 (5 Dec. 1952), name changed. **2.** Smith, *Wealth of Nations*, IV, ch. 8, 179. **3.** Robert Schloesser, 'Die Kriegsorganisation der Konsumenten', in *Genossenschaftliche Kultur* 19/20, 1917, 1–31; and Carl von Tyszka, *Der Konsument in der Kriegswirtschaft* (Tübingen, 1916). **4.** Schloesser, 'Kriegsorganisation', 25f. **5.** Avner Offer, *The First World War: An Agrarian Interpretation* (Oxford, 1989); Belinda J. Davis, *Home Fires Burning: Food, Politics and Everyday Life in World War I Berlin* (Chapel Hill, NC, 2000). **6.** Hamburger Staatsarchiv: Konsumenten-kammer Hamburg (371-12), X A II 1b; Arthur Feiler, 'The Consumer in Economic Policy', in: *Social Research* 1, no. 4, 1934, 287–300; Trentmann, *Free Trade Nation*, ch. 4; and Hilton, *Consumerism in Twentieth-century Britain*, 53–78. **7.** Julie Hessler, *A Social History of Soviet Trade: Trade Policy, Retail Practices and Consumption, 1917–53* (Princeton, NJ, 2004). In the 1930s, the gap between manual and brain workers narrowed, according to Hessler's data (227–30). **8.** In 1933, see Elena Osokina, *Our Daily Bread: Socialist Distribution and the Art of Survival in Stalin's Russia, 1927–1941* (Armonk, NY, 2001), 84. **9.** Leon Trotsky, *The Revolution Betrayed* (Dover, 1937/2004), 85. **10.** E. P. Thompson, 'The Moral Economy of the English Crowd in the Eighteenth Century', in: *Past and Present* 50, 1971: 76–136; Bernard Waites, 'The Government of the Home Front and the "Moral Economy" of the Working Class', in: *Home Fires and Foreign Fields: British Social and Military Experience in the First World War*, ed. Peter H. Liddle (London, 1985), 175–93. For critiques, see Frank Trentmann, 'Before "Fair Trade": Empire, Free Trade and the Moral Economies of Food in the Modern World', in: *Environment and Planning D* 25, no. 6, 2007: 1079–102. **11.** Staatsarchiv Hamburg: Konsu-mentenkammer (371-12), I A IV 2 (1926); *Bericht der Konsumentenkammer*, 1924, 23; VI A II 14: *Automatenverkauf*, my translation. **12.** Claudius Torp, 'Das Janusgesicht der Weimarer Konsumpolitik', in: Heinz-Gerhard Haupt & Claudius Torp, eds., *Die Konsumgesellschaft in Deutschland, 1890–1990* (Frankfurt am Main, 2009), 264; Claudius Torp, *Konsum und Politik in der Weimarer Republik* (Göttingen, 2011); and Mary Nolan, *Visions of Modernity: American Business and the Modernization of Germany* (Oxford, 1994). **13.** Robert Millward & Jörg Baten, 'Population and Living Standards 1914–45', in: S. N. Broadberry & Kevin H. O'Rourke, eds., *The Cambridge Economic History of Modern Europe* (Cambridge, 2010). **14.** *Historical Statistics of the United States*, Vol. III, Part C (Cambridge, MA, 2006), 271. **15.** Marie Jahoda, Paul F. Lazarsfeld & Hans Zeisel, *Die Arbeitslosen von Marienthal: Ein Soziographischer Versuch über die Wirkungen langdauernder Arbeitslosigkeit.* (Suhrkamp, 1933/1975), 55, my translation, and 83–92 for changing rhythms. Lazarsfeld was responsible for method; Jahoda wrote the narrative. Interviews on the ground were mainly conducted by Lotte Danzinger. **16.** Jahoda, Lazarsfeld and Zeisel, *Marienthal*, 72, my translation, and 73. **17.** Jahoda, Lazarsfeld and Zeisel, *Marienthal*, 76, my translation. **18.** Maurice Halbwachs, *L'Évolution des besoins dans les classes ouvrières* (Paris, 1933). See now : Hendrik K. Fischer, *Konsum im Kaiserreich: Eine statistisch-analytische Untersuchung privater Haushalte im wilhelminischen Deutschland* (Berlin, 2011). **19.** Vaile, *Research Memorandum on Social Aspects of Consumption in the Depression*, 19, 32, 35. The number of cars visiting national parks went up by 20%. **20.** Robert S. Lynd & Helen Merrell Lynd, *Middletown in Transition: A Study in Cultural Conflicts* (New York, 1937), 265–7. **21.** David Fowler, *The First Teenagers: The Lifestyle of Young Wage-earners in Inter-war Britain* (London, 1995); and Selina Todd, 'Young Women, Work and Leisure in Inter-war England', in: *Historical Journal* 48, no. 3, 2005: 789–809. **22.** Andrew Davies, *Leisure, Gender and Poverty: Working-class Culture in Salford and Manchester, 1900–1939* (Buckingham, 1992). **23.** Herbert Blumer, *Movies and Conduct* (New York, 1933), 31–40. **24.** Blumer, *Movies and Conduct*, 156, and 159 and 64 for the above. **25.** J. P. Mayer, *British Cinemas and Their Audiences: Sociological Studies* (London, 1948), 25 (shoes); 74 (neat appearance). **26.** Mayer, *British Cinema Audiences*, 116, undated c.1944; she was looking back on the previous ten years. **27.** Nolan, *Visions of Modernity*; Jackie Clarke, 'Engineering a New Order in the 1930s', in: *French Historical Studies* 24, no. 1, 2001: 63–86; and de Grazia, *Irresistible Empire*. **28.** Staatsarchiv Hamburg, Z3 14/14, *Bericht der Konsumentenkammer*, 1926, 40. **29.** Published in English as Georges Duhamel, *America: The Menace – Scenes from the Life of the Future* (Boston, 1931). **30.** José Ortega y Gasset, *The Revolt of the Masses* (London, 1930/1932), 19, 46–7, 108–10. **31.** J. Huizinga, *In the Shadow of Tomorrow: A Diagnosis of the Spiritual Distemper of Our Time* (London, 1935/1936), 119, and 25, 115, 157, 187, 193 for the above. He developed the theme of play in his *Homo ludens* in 1938. **32.** 'Saving and Spending' (1931), in: John Maynard Keynes, *Essays in Persuasion* (London, 1931/1972), 137–8. The line of thought has most recently been refreshed by Robert Skidelsky & Edward Skidelsky, *How Much is Enough?: The Love of Money and the Case for the Good Life* (London, 2012). **33.** Keynes, *Essays in Persuasion*, 330–1. Keynes's argument here was about 'absolute needs'; he allowed that 'relative needs' might continue, such as the satisfaction of feeling superior to others. **34.** W. H. Hutt, *Economists and the Public* (London, 1936); Furlough, *Consumer Cooperation in France*, 275ff.; and further: Trentmann, 'Genealogy of the Consumer', 43–8. **35.** *The American Way: Selections from the Public Addresses and Papers of Franklin D. Roosevelt* (1944), 32. **36.** Lizabeth Cohen, 'The New Deal State and the Making of Citizen Consumers', in: Susan Strasser, Charles McGovern & Matthias Judt, eds., *Getting and Spending: European and American Consumer Societies in the Twentieth Century* (Cambridge, 1998), 111–26; and Alan Brinkley, *The End of Reform: New Deal Liberalism in Recession and War*

(New York, 1995). **37.** Meg Jacobs, *Pocketbook Politics: Economic Citizenship in Twentieth-century America* (Princeton, NJ, 2005), 104–35; Newman, *Radio Active: Advertising and Consumer Activism, 1935–1947*, 145–65; and Lawrence Glickman, *Buying Power: A History of Consumer Activism in America* (Chicago, 2009). **38.** Charles F. McGovern, *Sold American: Consumption and Citizenship, 1890–1945* (Chapel Hill, NC, 2006), ch. 6. **39.** E.g., Speech to the Daughters of the American Revolution, 19 April 1926; http://www.presidency.ucsb.edu/ws/index.php?pid=393; and Coolidge, *The Price of Freedom* (1924). **40.** Stuart Chase, *The Economy of Abundance* (New York, 1934), 274, 308. **41.** 1937, in Roland Marchand, *Creating the Corporate Soul: The Rise of Public Relations and Corporate Imagery in American Big Business* (Berkeley, CA, 1998), 213; and 48–87 for AT&T. **42.** Marchand, *Corporate Soul*, 278–82. **43.** 'The Need for a New Party', in: *New Republic* 66 (18 March, 25 March, 1 April & 8 April 1931), repr. in *John Dewey, The Later Works, 1925–1953*, Vol. VI: *1931–1932*, ed. Jo Ann Boydston (Carbondale, 1985), 159–81. Public letter to Roosevelt, May 1933, in: Dewey, *Later Works*, Vol. IX, 265f. **44.** See esp. John Dewey, *Human Nature and Conduct: An Introduction to Social Psychology* (New York, 1922); Alan Ryan, *John Dewey and the High Tide of American Liberalism* (New York, 1995); and Martin Jay, *Songs of Experience: Modern American and European Variations of a Universal Theme* (Berkeley, CA, 2005), ch. 7. **45.** Kyrk, *Economic Problems of the Family*, 396; Hazel Kyrk, *A Theory of Consumption* (London, 1923); F. W. Innenfeldt, 'Teaching Consumer Buying in the Secondary School,' in: *Journal of Home Economics*, 26/5 (1934); and H. Harap, 'Survey of Twenty-eight Courses in Consumption', in: *School Review* (September 1937), 497–507. **46.** Horace M. Kallen, *The Decline and Rise of the Consumer* (New York, 1936), ix. Kallen wanted consumers to be self-organized, not by New Deal agencies. **47.** See, e.g., Steigerwald, 'All Hail the Republic of Choice: Consumer History as Contemporary Thought'. **48.** Adam Tooze, *The Wages of Destruction: The Making and Breaking of the Nazi Economy* (New York, 2006); and Hartmut Berghoff, 'Träume und Alpträume: Konsumpolitik im Nationalsozialistischen Deutschland', in: Haupt & Torp, eds., *Konsumgesellschaft*, 268–88. **49.** See Adam Tooze, 'Economics, Ideology and Cohesion in the Third Reich: A Critique of Götz Aly's *Hitler's Volksstaat*', http://www.hist.cam.ac.uk/academic_staff/further_details/tooze-aly.pdf. Cf. Götz Aly, *Hitler's Beneficiaries: Plunder, Racial War and the Nazi Welfare State* (New York, 2007). **50.** Colin Campbell, *The Romantic Ethic and the Spirit of Modern Consumerism* (London, 1987/2005). **51.** Tooze, *Wages of Destruction*, 154–6. **52.** S. Jonathan Wiesen, 'Creating the Nazi Marketplace: Public Relations and Consumer Citizenship in the Third Reich', in: *Citizenship and National Identity in Twentieth-century Germany*, eds. Geoff Eley & Jan Palmowski (Stanford, 2008), 146–63. **53.** Moscow Sonderarchiv, 1521-53-1, Richard Richter-Pössneck, 'Eine K.d.F Seereise nach Norwegen', 1936, 17. **54.** Shelley Baranowski, *Strength through Joy: Consumerism and Mass Tourism in the Third Reich* (Cambridge, 2004). **55.** Henkel Archiv, Düsseldorf, Henkel-Bote 14/6,

10 July 1937, 262–65. W. E. Maiwald, *Reichsausstellung Schaffendes Volk* (Düsseldorf, 1937); and Stefanie Schäfers, *Vom Werkbund zum Vierjahresplan* (Düsseldorf, 2001). **56.** Joseph Stalin, *Anarchism or Socialism?* (1907) in *Works*, I: 1901–07 (Moscow, 1953). **57.** The complete score was reconstructed by Mark Fitz-Gerald and performed in 2003 in Den Bosch, Holland, and in 2006 in London. For Odna, see Denise Youngblood, *Soviet Cinema in the Silent Era, 1918–35* (Ann Arbor, MI, 1985), 226 f. **58.** Sheila Fitzpatrick, *Everyday Stalinism: Ordinary Life in Extraordinary Times: Soviet Russia in the 1930s* (Oxford, 1999); Jukka Gronow, *Caviar with Champagne: Common Luxury and the Ideals of the Good Life in Stalin's Russia* (Oxford, 2003); and Victor Buchli, *An Archaeology of Socialism* (Oxford, 1999). **59.** At the All-Union conference of Stakhanovites, quoted in Lewis H. Siegelbaum, *Stakhanovism and the Politics of Productivity in the USSR, 1935–41* (Cambridge, 1988), at 228. For Western Europe, see Charles Maier (ed.), *In Search of Stability*, (Cambridge, 1987). **60.** Siegelbaum, *Stakhanovism and the Politics of Productivity in the USSR, 1935–41*, 228. **61.** Elias, *The Civilizing Process*; Oleg Kharkhordin, *The Collective and the Individual in Russia: A Study of Practices* (Berkeley, CA, 1999), 164–230; and Stephen Kotkin, *Magnetic Mountain: Stalinism as a Civilization* (Berkeley, CA, 1995). **62.** Hessler, *Soviet Trade*; Gronow, *Caviar with Champagne*, 25; for distinctions, see Fitzpatrick, *Everyday Stalinism*, 107–9. **63.** Sarah Davies, 'Us against Them', in: Fitzpatrick, ed., *Stalinism: New Directions*, 64f. **64.** Julie Hessler, 'Cultured Trade', in: Fitzpatrick, ed., *Stalinism: New Directions*, 182–209; and Amy E. Randall, *The Soviet Dream World of Retail Trade and Consumption in the 1930s* (Basingstoke, 2008), esp. 134–57. **65.** Hessler, *Soviet Trade*, 207–9, 241. **66.** Tarlo, *Clothing Matters*, esp. 60–71. **67.** M. K. Gandhi, *Hind Swaraj or Indian Home Rule* (Ahmedabad, 1908/1996), 33. **68.** Gandhi, *Hind Swaraj*, 55. **69.** C. A. Bayly, 'The Origins of Swadeshi (Home Industry): Cloth and Indian Society, 1700–1930', in: *The Social Life of Things: Commodities in Cultural Perspective*, ed. Arjun Appadurai (Cambridge, 1986), 285–321. **70.** *Young India*, 15 January 1928, repr. in M. K. Gandhi, *Khadi: Why and How*, ed. B. Kumarappa (Ahmedabad, 1955), 66. **71.** *Young India*, 22 September 1927, repr, in Gandhi, *Khadi*, 104f. **72.** *Young India*, 8 December 1921, repr. in Gandhi, *Khadi*, 14. **73.** Lisa Trivedi, *Clothing Gandhi's Nation: Homespun and Modern India* (Bloomington, ID, 2007), 30–6. For distinct elite styles, see also: Tarlo, *Clothing Matters*, 105–17. **74.** Shanghai Municipal Archive, *Municipal Gazette*, 12 December 1920, 48; 11 March 1920, 71; 17 June 1920, 237; see also: *Annual Report of the Shanghai Municipal Council*, 1905, 30–3; Karl Gerth, *China Made: Consumer Culture and the Creation of the Nation* (Cambridge, MA, 2003); and Jane Leung Larson, 'The 1905 Anti-American Boycott as a Transnational Chinese Movement', in: *Chinese Historical Society: History & Perspectives* 21, 2007: 191–8. **75.** Quoted in Reynolds, *Commodity Cultures in Egypt*, 300. **76.** Gerth, *China Made*, 279f., 285–332. **77.** Quoted in Reynolds, *Commodity Cultures in Egypt*, 364. **78.** The above draws on the excellent PhD thesis by Reynolds, *Commodity Cultures in Egypt*, 175–7, 281–400. **79.** *Home and*

Politics, June 1924, 23. Trentmann, *Free Trade Nation*, 228–40; Constantine, '"Bringing the Empire Alive": The Empire Marketing Board and Imperial Propaganda, 1926–33'. **80.** For Soviet data, see also: Igor Birman, *Personal Consumption in the USSR and the USA* (Basingstoke, 1983), who offers comparable figures by population. **81.** Giovanni di Somogyi, 'Il boom dei consumi', in: *Storia dell'economia mondiale, V: La modernizzazione e i problemi del sottosviluppo*, ed. Valerio Castronovo (Rome, 2001), 149–70. **82.** Reaching 7% in 1966–70; see Seweryn Bialer, *Stalin's Successors* (Cambridge, 1980), table 6, 153. **83.** Detlef Siegfried, *Time is on My Side: Konsum und Politik in der westdeutschen Jugendkultur der 60er Jahre* (Göttingen, 2006), 37–42. **84.** Raising it to 4.2 hours. **85.** Ivan T. Berend, *An Economic History of Twentieth-century Europe* (Cambridge, 2006), 253–5. **86.** Written by Marcello Marchesi and produced by Carlo Ponti. **87.** David Forgacs, 'Cultural Consumption, 1940s to 1990s', in: *Italian Cultural Studies*, eds. David Forgacs & Robert Lumley (Oxford, 1996), 273–90, 278. **88.** Michael Wildt, 'Continuities and Discontinuities of Consumer Mentality in West Germany in the 1950s', in: *Life after Death: Approaches to a Cultural and Social History of Europe During the 1940s and 1950s*, eds. Richard Bessel & Dirk Schumann (Cambridge, 2003), 211–30, 222. **89.** Vera Dunham, *In Stalin's Time: Middle-class Values in Soviet Fiction* (Cambridge, 1976), 43–8. For film and fashionability, see Juliane Fürst, 'The Importance of Being Stylish', in: Juliane Fürst, ed., *Late Stalinist Russia: Society between Reconstruction and Reinvention* (London, 2006), 209–30. **90.** Jean Fourastie, *Les Trente Glorieuses, ou la revolution invisible de 1946 à 1975* (Paris, 1979), 17: in 1975 there were 212 homes, of which 210 had a fridge; 197 gas or electric cooking; 100 central heating. They owned 280 cars; 250 radios; 200 TVs; 180 washing machines; 150 interior WCs. **91.** Galbraith, *The Affluent Society*, 199f., and 128–9, 203 and 218 for the above. On the production of wants, Galbraith was developing the argument made by his young Harvard colleague James Duesenberry in: *Income, Saving and the Theory of Consumer Behavior* (Cambridge, MA, 1949). **92.** Crosland, *Future of Socialism*, 355, 357, 175 and 214, 216 for the above. **93.** Galbraith, *The Affluent Society*, 203. **94.** Steven Fielding, 'Activists against "Affluence": Labour Party Culture During the "Golden Age", *circa* 1950–1970', in: *Journal of British Studies* 40, 2001: 241–67; and Lawrence Black, *The Political Culture of the Left in Affluent Britain, 1951–64: Old Labour, New Britain?* (Basingstoke, 2003), ch. 6. **95.** Daniel Horowitz, *The Anxieties of Affluence: Critiques of American Consumer Culture, 1939–1979* (Amherst, MA, 2004), 102–8. **96.** Galbraith, *The Affluent Society*, 218f. **97.** *Historical Statistics of the United States*, Vol. III, 291. **98.** Spending by federal government grew from 3% of GDP in 1925 to 16% in 1950. Federal spending on social security and medicare was 0.2% of GDP in 1948, rising to 1.7% in 1958, when *The Affluent Society* was published; by 1968 it had reached 3.3%. State and local government spending rose from 5.5% of GDP in 1948 to 8.2% in 1958. Defence spending declined from the 15% peak at the end of the Korean War in 1953 to around 10% for the rest of the 1950s and '60s. See the official data in: Congressional

Budget Office, 3 July 2002: *Long-range Fiscal Policy Brief*, and table 15.5: 'Total Government Expenditures as Percentages of GDP: 1948–2006', at: www. gpoaccess.gov/USbudget/fy08/sheets/hist15z5.xls. See further: 537–44 below. **99.** Cohen, *Consumers' Republic.* **100.** *Life* magazine, 12 July 1948, 94–113, quoted at 97, 104. **101.** Richard F. Kuisel, *Seducing the French: The Dilemma of Americanization* (Berkeley, CA, 1993), ch. 4. **102.** Priestley, *Thoughts in the Wilderness* (London, 1957), 23. **103.** Kuisel, *Seducing the French*, 38. **104.** Maria Mitchell, 'Materialism and Secularism: CDU Politicians and National Socialism, 1945–1949', in: *Journal of Modern History* 67, no. 2, 1995: 278–308; and Axel Schildt, *Moderne Zeiten: Freizeit, Massenmedien und 'Zeitgeist' in der Bundesrepublik der 50er Jahre* (Hamburg, 1995), 354–61. **105.** Quoted in Peter Clarke, *Liberals and Social Democrats* (Cambridge, 1978), 288. **106.** B. Seebohm Rowntree & G. R. Lavers, *English Life and Leisure: A Social Study* (London, 1951), p. 277; and pp. 225–27; 249–50 and 363ff. **107.** de Grazia, *Irresistible Empire*; Roberta Sassatelli, 'Impero o mercato? Americanizzazione e regimi di consumo in Europa', in: *Stato e Mercato*, no. 80, 2007: 309–23. See also: Charles S. Maier, *Among Empires: American Ascendancy and Its Predecessors* (Cambridge, MA, 2006). **108.** Sheryl Kroen, 'Negotiations with the American Way', in: *Consuming Cultures, Global Perspectives*, eds. John Brewer & Frank Trentmann (Oxford, 2006), 251–77. **109.** Bundesarchiv Koblenz, B 146/1138, 3 December 1952, my translation. The official English translation was 'A Higher Standard of Living', which fails to capture the prescriptive meaning of the original. **110.** Bundesarchiv Koblenz B 146/389 and B 146/1138. **111.** Ralph Harris, Margot Naylor & Arthur Seldon, *Hire Purchase in a Free Society* (1961), 28. **112.** Kelly Longitudinal Study, interview with Lucille Windam, quoted in E. T. May, *Homeward Bound: American Families in the Cold War Era* (New York, 1999), 180. See also: Erica Carter, *How German is She? Post-war West German Reconstruction and the Consuming Woman* (Ann Arbor, MI, 1997). **113.** Glen H. Elder, *Children of the Great Depression: Social Change in Life Experience* (Colorado, 1974/1999). **114.** Richard Easterlin, 'The American Baby Boom in Historical Perspective', in: *American Economic Review* LI, no. 5, 1961: 869–911. **115.** Bundesarchiv Koblenz B 146/389 (1950). **116.** 'Der Verbraucher sichert Lohn und Brot', in: *Freude im Alltag* (July 1951), 13, in Bundesarchiv Koblenz B 146/384. **117.** Ludivine Bantigny, *Le Plus Bel Âge? Jeunes et jeunesse en France de l'aube des "Trente Glorieuses" à la guerre d'Algérie* (Paris, 2007); Georges Lapassade, *L'Entrée dans la vie* (Paris 1963); Fürst, ed., *Late Stalinist Russia*; Juliane Fürst, *Stalin's Last Generation: Soviet Post-war Youth and the Emergence of Mature Socialism* (Oxford, 2010); Uta Poiger, *Jazz, Rock and Rebels: Cold War Politics and American Culture in a Divided Germany* (Berkeley, CA, 2000); and Paola Ghione & Marco Grispigni, eds., *Giovani prima della rivolta* (Rome, 1998). **118.** Kunsten en Wetenschappen Netherlands Ministerie van Onderwijs, *Maatschappelijke Verwildering der Jeugd* (The Hague, 1952), 17–18, 35, my translation. **119.** Kunsten en Wetenschappen Netherlands Ministerie van Onderwijs, *Bronnenboek bevattende gegevens ten* *grondslag liggend aan rapport Maatschappelijke verwildering der jeugd, etc.* (1953). **120.** 1956, quoted in Siegfried, *Time is on My Side*, 327, my translation. For the cult of speed, see Kristin Ross, *Fast Cars, Clean Bodies: Decolonization and the Reordering of French Culture* (Cambridge, MA, 1996). **121.** Bantigny, *Le Plus Bel Âge?*, 140f. **122.** Bantigny, *Le Plus Bel Âge?*, 71f. **123.** Peter Wilmott, *Adolescent Boys of East London* (1966/1969), 20. **124.** Bantigny, *Le Plus Bel Âge?*, 53 **125.** August B. Hollingshead, *Elmtown's Youth: The Impact of Social Classes on Adolescents* (New York, 1949), 397. **126.** Susan E. Reid & David Crowley, *Style and Socialism: Modernity and Material Culture in Post-war Eastern Europe* (London, 2000). **127.** Juliane Fürst, 'The Importance of being Stylish', in: Fürst, ed., *Late Stalinist Russia*, 224. **128.** Rowntree & Lavers, *English Life and Leisure*, 214. **129.** Thurston, *Delinquency and Spare Time: A Study of a Few Stories Written into the Court Records of the City of Cleveland*, 165. **130.** Françoise Giroud, *La Nouvelle Vague: Portraits de la jeunesse* (Paris, 1958), 331–2. **131.** 16–22-year-olds in Nuremberg, interviewed by Reinhold Bergler, 'Dimensionen der Wunsch – und Erlebniswelt Jugendlicher', in: Ludwig v. Friedeburg, ed., *Jugend in der modernen Gesellschaft* (Cologne, 1965), 513–30. **132.** Kaspar Maase, 'Establishing Cultural Democracy: Youth, "Americanization" and the Irresistible Rise of Popular Culture', in: Richard Bessel & Dirk Schumann, eds., *Life after Death* (Cambridge, 2003), 428–50. **133.** Rowntree & Lavers, *English Life and Leisure*, 383f. **134.** Thomas Frank, *The Conquest of Cool: Business Culture, Counterculture and the Rise of Hip Consumerism* (Chicago, 1997), 189–97. **135.** Guia Croce, ed., *Tutto il meglio di Carosello, 1957–77* (Turin, 2011). **136.** Umberto Eco, *Apocalittici e integrati* (Milan, 1964/1988), 29–64. **137.** Ernest Dichter, *The Strategy of Desire* (New York, 1960), 18, 90, 169, 263. Compare Horowitz, *Anxieties of Affluence*, ch. 2; David Bennett, 'Getting the Id to go Shopping', in: *Public Culture* 17, no. 1, 2005: 1–26; and Stefan Schwarzkopf & Rainer Gries, eds., *Ernest Dichter and Motivation Research* (Basingstoke, 2010). **138.** Betty Friedan, *The Feminine Mystique* (New York, 1963). **139.** Ernest Dichter, *Handbook of Consumer Motivations: The Psychology of the World of Objects* (New York, 1964), 5; 458–69 on saving and life insurance. **140.** Herbert Marcuse, *One-dimensional Man: Studies in the Ideology of Advanced Industrial Society* (London, 1964/2002), 150. **141.** See Richard S. Tedlow, *New and Improved: The Story of Mass Marketing in America* (New York, 1990); and Stuart Ewen, *Captions of Consciousness: Advertising and the Social Roots of the Consumer Culture* (New York, 1976). **142.** The above draws on Josh Lauer, 'Making the Ledgers Talk: Customer Control and the Origins of Retail Data Mining, 1920–1940', in: Hartmut Berghoff, Philip Scranton & Uwe Spiekermann, *The Rise of Marketing and Market Research*, (New York, 2012), 153–69; and Susan Strasser, *Satisfaction Guaranteed: The Making of the American Mass Market* (New York, 1989), esp. 211–20. See also: Hartmut Berghoff, ed., *Marketinggeschichte: Die Genese einer modernen Sozialtechnik* (Frankfurt am Main, 2007). **143.** Christiane Lamberty, *Reklame in Deutschland, 1890–1914: Wahrnehmung, Professional-*

isierung und Kritik der Wirtschaftswerbung (Berlin, 2001). **144.** Sean Nixon, 'Mrs Housewife and the Ad Men: Advertising, Market Research and Mass Consumption in Post-war Britain', in: Hartmut Berghoff, Philip Scranton & Uwe Spiekermann, eds., *The Rise of Marketing* (New York, 2012), 193–213. See also: Sean Nixon, *Hard Sell: Advertising, Affluence and Transatlantic Relations*, c.*1951–69* (Manchester, 2013). **145.** Stefan Schwarzkopf, 'Respectable Persuaders: The Advertising Industry and British Society, 1900–1939', PhD, Birkbeck College, University of London, 2008 ; Stefan Schwarzkopf, 'Markets, Consumers and the State: The Uses of Market Research in Government and the Public Sector in Britain, 1925–55', in: Berghoff, Scranton & Spiekermann, eds., *Rise of Marketing*, 171–92; and Kerstin Brueckweh, ed., *The Voice of the Citizen Consumer: A History of Market Research, Consumer Movements, and the Political Public Sphere* (Oxford, 2011). **146.** Starch Inra Hooper Group and International Advertising Association, *Sixteenth Survey of Advertising Expenditures Around the World: A Survey of World Advertising Expenditure in 1980* (1981). **147.** R. Van der Wurff & P. Bakker, 'Economic Growth and Advertising Expenditures in Different Media in Different Countries', in: *Journal of Media Economics* 21, 2008: 28–52, table 1. **148.** Gerhard Schulze, *Die Erlebnisgesellschaft* (Frankfurt am Main, 1992). **149.** Hermann Gossen, *Entwicklung der Gesetze des menschlichen Verkehrs und der daraus fliessenden Regeln für menschliches Handeln* (1854); and Sergio Nistico, 'Consumption and Time in Economics: Prices and Quantities in a Temporary Equilibrium Perspective', in: *Cambridge Journal of Economics*, 2005, 29: 943–57. **150.** *The Times*, 17 May 1968, 12. Guy Debord, *La Société du spectacle* (Paris, 1967); and Thomas Hecken & Agata Grzenia, 'Situationism', in: Martin Klimke & Joachim Scharloth, eds., *1968 in Europe* (Basingstoke, 2008), ch. 2. **151.** See the opinion survey in Kuisel, *Seducing the French*, 189. **152.** Detlef Siegfried, 'Aesthetik des Andersseins', in: K. Weinhauer, J. Requate & H.-G. Haupt, *Terrorismus in der Bundesrepublik* (Frankfurt am Main, 2006), 76–98. **153.** Württembergische Landesbibliothek Stuttgart, Collection 'Neue Soziale Bewegungen', D0895, flyers nos. 7 & 8, both 24 May 1967. **154.** Quoted in Gerd Koenen, *Vesper, Ensslin, Baader: Urszenen des deutschen Terrorismus* (Frankfurt am Main, 2005), 142, 176. See also: Stephan Malinowski and Alexander Sedlmaier, ' "1968" als Katalysator der Konsumgesellschaft', in: *Geschichte und Gesellschaft* no. 2, April–June, 2006: 238–67 **155.** Kunzelmann of Kommune 1. **156.** Marcuse, *One-dimensional Man*. **157.** Rainer Langhans & Fritz Teufel, *Klau mich* (Frankfurt am Main, 1968). **158.** Personal information. **159.** Gudrun Cyprian, *Sozialisation in Wohngemeinschaften: Eine empirische Untersuchung ihrer strukturellen Bedingungen* (Stuttgart, 1978), 81–5; the research was conducted in 1974. **160.** Pier Paolo Pasolini, *Scritti corsari* (Milan, 1975/2008), see esp. 9 Dec. 1973, 22–5; and 10 June 1974, 39–44, my translation. **161.** Jean Baudrillard, *Société de consommation* (1970) (English: *The Consumer Society: Myths and Structures* (London, 1970/98), 27, emphasis in original, my translation. **162.** Alexander Solzhenitsyn, *Letter to Soviet Leaders* (London, 1974), 21–4. **163.** Kuisel, *Seducing the French*, 153. **164.** Jean-François Revel, *Without Marx or*

Jesus, trans. J. F. Bernard (New York, 1970/1971). **165.** Michel de Certeau, *The Practice of Everyday Life* (Berkeley, CA, 1974/1984); Mary Douglas & Baron Isherwood, *The World of Goods: Towards an Anthropology of Consumption* (London, 1979); and Schama, *The Embarrassment of Riches*. For disciplinary routines, see Henri Lefebvre, *Critique of Everyday Life: Foundations for a Sociology of the Everyday, Volume 2* (London, 2002 (1961)); and Lefebvre, *Rhythmanalysis: Space, Time and Everyday Life*; see the chapter 'Not so Fast!', below. **166.** The quotes are from King's 'Drum Major Instinct' sermon in Atlanta, 4 February 1968; full text at: http://mlk-kppo1.stanford. edu/index.php/encyclopedia/documentsentry/doc_the_drum_major_instinct/.See further: Horowitz, *Anxieties of Affluence*, ch. 6. **167.** Felicia Kornbluh, 'To Fulfil Their "Rightly Needs": Consumerism and the National Welfare Rights Movement', in: *Radical History Review* 69, 1997: 76–113. **168.** 15 July 1979, available at: www.pbs.org/wgbh/amex/carter/filmmore/ps_crisis.html. **169.** Energy Information Administration, *Monthly Energy Review*, Sept. 2013. The share of all renewable energy sources together has not changed much since 1973; it currently stands at 9%. **170.** Jean Saint-Geours, *Vive la société de consommation* (Paris, 1971), 28, 33, 128–9, my translation. **171.** Imogene Erro, 'And What of the Consumer?', in: *Problems of Communism* (1963), 34–7. **172.** Reid & Crowley, *Style and Socialism*, 42; Philip Hanson, *Advertising and Socialism: The Nature and Extent of Consumer Advertising in the Soviet Union, Poland, Hungary and Yugoslavia* (London, 1974); and Patrick Hyder Patterson, 'Truth Half Told: Finding the Perfect Pitch for Advertising and Marketing in Socialist Yugoslavia, 1950–1991', in: *Enterprise & Society* 4, no. 2, 2003: 179–225. **173.** Robert H. Haddow, *Pavilions of Plenty: Exhibiting American Culture Abroad in the 1950s* (Washington, DC, 1997). Riesman had anticipated this diplomacy of goods in his 1951 satire 'The Nylon War', repr. in David Riesman, *Abundance for What? And Other Essays* (London, 1964), 65–77. **174.** Mark Landsman, *Dictatorship and Demand: The Politics of Consumerism in East Germany* (Cambridge, MA, 2005). **175.** Pence, ' "A World in Miniature": The Leipzig Trade Fairs in the 1950s', in: David F. Crew, ed., *Consuming Germany in the Cold War* (Oxford, 2003), 21–50; and Judd Stitziel, 'On the Seam between Socialism and Capitalism: East German Fashion Shows', in: Crew, ed., *Consuming Germany*, 51–86. **176.** '*Überholen und Einholen*'; this is sometimes rendered as '*Überholen ohne einzuholen*'. I follow Ina Merkel's version, in 'Konsumpolitik in der DDR ', in: Haupt & Torp, eds., *Konsumgesellschaft*, 291. **177.** Katherine Verdery, *National Ideology under Socialism: Identity and Cultural Politics in Ceausescu's Romania* (Berkeley, CA, 1991); and Thomas W. Simons, Jr. *Eastern Europe in the Post-war World* (Basingstoke, 1993, 2nd edn), 106–13. **178.** See Landsman, *Dictatorship and Demand*, esp. 195–7. **179.** Walter Hixson, *Parting the Curtain: Propaganda, Culture and the Cold War, 1945–1961* (New York, 1997); Haddow, *Pavilions of Plenty*, 201–29; and David Caute, *The Dancer Defects: The Struggle for Cultural Supremacy during the Cold War* (Oxford, 2003), 42–9. **180.** Jürgen Barsch, *Freizeiteinstellung und Freizeitverhalten weltanschaulich unter-*

schiedlich eingestellter Jugendlicher (Leipzig, 1974). **181.** Natalya Chernyshova, *Soviet Consumer Culture in the Brezhnev Era* (London, 2013), quoted at 50. **182.** *Ty I Ja*, cited in David Crowley, 'Warsaw's Shops, Stalinism and the Thaw', in: Reid & Crowley, *Style and Socialism*, 42. **183.** Bundesarchiv Berlin, DL 102/543 (Institut für Marktforschung), 'Zur Entwicklung Sozialistischer Verbrauchs- und Lebensgewohnheiten der Bevölkerung der DDR' (1971), 17. **184.** Zentralinstitut für Jugendforschung, 'Jugend und Mode', Leipzig 1979, mimeogram in Bundesarchiv Lichterfelde, Library, B 6123, table 2. **185.** Janine R. Wedel, *The Private Poland* (Oxford, 1986). **186.** Bundesarchiv Berlin, DL 102/591, 'Tendenzen der Entwicklung der Wohnbedürfnisse', 1971. **187.** Bundesarchiv Berlin, DY 30/2589, *Eingaben an Honecker*, 'Informationen über eingegangene Eingaben im 1. Halbjahr 1980', 15 August 1980. **188.** Bundesarchiv Berlin, DL 102/99, 'Internationaler Vergleich ... langlebiger Konsumgüter', August 1967; DL 102/1425, 'Zur Differenzierung des Verbrauchs ... nach Klassen und Schichten ... 1970–80'; in 1980, 55% of 'intelligentsia' households had a washing machine, versus 27% workers. DL 102/1472, 'Urlaubsreisetätigkeit ... 1971–80'. See further: Ina Merkel, *Utopie und Bedürfnis: Die Geschichte der Konsumkultur in der DDR* (Cologne, 1999); and Mary Fulbrook, *The People's State: East German Society from Hitler to Honecker* (New Haven, CT, 2005). **189.** Bundesarchiv Berlin, DL 102/543, 'Zur Entwicklung Sozialistischer Verbrauchs- und Lebensgewohnheiten der Bevölkerung der DDR', appendix 7, table 2: husbands' share was 12%; other household members' 8%. **190.** Bundesarchiv Berlin, DL 102/1471 and DL 102/1471; it was a third amongst 12–15-year-old boys. **191.** Bundesarchiv Berlin, DL 102/366, 'Einkaufsgewohnheiten bei Industriewaren nach der Einführung der durchgängigen 5-Tage-Arbeitswoche', table 134. Most shops selling clothes opened only one Saturday a month. **192.** Bundesarchiv Berlin Lichterfelde, Library, FDJ/6147: Zentralinstitut für Jugendforschung, 'Freizeit 69, Abschlussbericht', *Vertrauliche Dienstsache*, Oct.–Nov. 1969. **193.** Marc-Dietrich Ohse, *Jugend nach dem Mauerbau* (Berlin, 2003). **194.** Bundesarchiv Berlin, Lichterfelde (Library): FDJ 6243, Zentralinstitut für Jugendforschung, 'Freizeit und Freizeitnutzung junger Arbeiter und Schüler in der Wartburgstadt Eisenach' (Leipzig, 1977), and 'Jugend und Mode', Leipzig, 1979, 18. **195.** Chernyshova, *Soviet Consumer Culture in the Brezhnev era*, 111. **196.** George Gomori, 'Consumerism in Hungary', in: *Problems of Communism* XII, no. 1, 1963: 64–6. **197.** Wolf Oschlies, *Jugend in Osteuropa, Vol. II: Polens Jugend* (Cologne, 1982), 166–90. **198.** Václav Havel, 'Power of the Powerless' (1978), repr. in *Living in Truth* (London, 1989), esp. 63–5, referring to the trial of the 'Plastic People of the Universe'. **199.** See 589–96 below. **200.** Annette Kaminsky, *Wohlstand, Schönheit, Glück: Kleine Konsumgeschichte der DDR* (Munich, 2001), 145. **201.** Bundesarchiv Berlin, DY 30/3261, 14 Sept. 1976. See further: Jonathan Zatlin, *The Currency of Socialism* (Cambridge, 2007). **202.** Bundesarchiv Berlin, DG/7/1768, 17 March 1986, name changed, my translation. **203.** Bundesarchiv Berlin, DY 30/3261, anonymous, 26 February 1987. An inquiry established that he did have a private Citroën as well as a Lada for business trips. **204.** Bundesarchiv Berlin, DG 7/1769, 26 September 1986; my translation. **205.** Bundesarchiv Berlin, DY 30/3261, 12 Feb. 1981, my translation. **206.** Merkel, *Utopie und Bedürfnis*, 357–409. **207.** Bundesarchiv Berlin, DY 30/3261, 6 Dec. 1985, name changed, my translation. **208.** For their later nostalgic revaluation and the identity politics of 'Ostalgie', see Ina Merkel 'From Stigma to Cult: Changing Meanings in East German Consumer Culture', in: Trentmann (ed.), *Making of the Consumer*, 249–70.

CHAPTER 7

1. Statistisk sentralbyrå, NOS Forbruksundersøkelse, http://www.ssb.no/vis/histstat/histo5.html. OECD, *National Accounts of OECD Countries, 1953–69* (Paris, 1970), 158–9, 242–3. United Nations, *National Accounts Statistics* (New York, 2004), table 3.2, 976. **2.** OECD, *Towards Sustainable Household Consumption?* (Paris, 2002), fig. 1 a–d (household food consumption), 23; and Carol Helstosky, *Garlic and Oil: Food and Politics in Italy* (Oxford, 2004). **3.** See references in notes 1 and 2 for this chapter and, for other EU countries, Eurostat, *Household Final Consumption Expenditure in the European Union, 1995–99* (2002), chs. 2 & 4. **4.** Gronow & Warde, eds., *Ordinary Consumption*. **5.** Workers up from 5.7% to 6.4%, *cadres supérieurs* down from 12% to 7%, 1959 to 1979; Nicolas Herpin & Daniel Verger, *La Consommation des Français* (Paris, 1988), 114. **6.** Shinobu Majima, 'Affluence and the Dynamics of Spending in Britain, 1961–2004', *Contemporary British History* 22, no. 4, 2008: 573–97. **7.** George A. Lundberg, Mirra Komarovsky & Mary Alice McInerny, *Leisure: A Suburban Study* (New York, 1934), 83. See also: William H. Whyte, *Organization Man* (New York, 1956). **8.** Lundberg et al., *Leisure*, 189. **9.** Lundberg et al., *Leisure*, 149f., 155, 189; Bennett M. Berger, *Working-class Suburb: A Study of Auto Workers in Suburbia* (Berkeley, CA, 1960), esp. 58–65. **10.** Alison J. Clarke, 'Tupperware', in: Roger Silverstone, ed., *Visions of Suburbia* (London, 1997), ch. 5. **11.** Gail Cooper, *Air-conditioning America: Engineers and the Controlled Environment, 1900–1960* (Baltimore, MD, 1998), 157–73; and M. Ackerman, *Cool Comfort: America's Romance with Air-conditioning* (Washington, DC, 2002). **12.** Siegfried Stratemann, *Das grosse Buch vom eigenen Haus: Eine Entwurfslehre f.d. Eigenheim*, 2 (Munich, 1954; 2nd rev, edn), 15, my translation. **13.** Berger, *Working-class Suburb*. **14.** Rainwater, Coleman & Handel, *Workingman's Wife: Her Personality, World and Life Style*, 146–51 for the quotations below. See further: Lizabeth Cohen, 'The Class Experience of Mass Consumption', in: *The Power of Culture*, eds. Richard W. Fox & T. J. Jackson Lears (Chicago, 1993). **15.** Katona, Strumpel & Zahn, *Zwei Wege zur Prosperität* (Düsseldorf, 1971). **16.** 1960: US 16%, EU area 20%; 1978: US 19%, EU 21%; Barry Bosworth, 'United States Saving in a Global Context', fig. 5; www.brookings.edu/testimony/2006/0406macroeconomics_bosworth.

aspx. **17.** Ferdynand Zweig, *The British Worker* (Harmondsworth, 1952); Ferdynand Zweig, *The Worker in an Affluent Society* (London, 1962); and Ferdynand Zweig, *The New Acquisitive Society* (Chichester, 1976). **18.** Alan Bennett, *Enjoy* (London, 1980). **19.** See, esp. Vol. III, John H. Goldthorpe, et al., *The Affluent Worker in the Class Structure* (Cambridge, 1971), 85–156. **20.** Zweig, *The New Acquisitive Society*, 15. For class cultures before the 1950s, see Ross McKibbin, *Classes and Cultures: England 1918–1951* (Oxford, 1998). **21.** Mike Savage, 'Working-class Identities in the 1960s', in: *Sociology* 39, no. 5, 2005: 929–46. See also: John Foot, *Milan since the Miracle: City, Culture and Identity* (Oxford, 2001). **22.** Devine, *Affluent Workers Revisited: Privatism and the Working Class*, 57–74, 134–52. **23.** Tony Bennett et al., *Culture, Class, Distinction* (London, 2009), 9. **24.** Bourdieu, *Distinction*, 56, 241. **25.** Bourdieu, *Distinction*, 274–8, and chs. 6 & 7. **26.** Julien Vincent, 'The Sociologist and the Republic: Pierre Bourdieu and the Virtues of Social History', in: *History Workshop Journal* 58, no. 1, 2004: 128–48. **27.** Altenloh, *Zur Soziologie des Kino: Die Kino-Unternehmung und die sozialen Schichten ihrer Besucher*, 67f. **28.** Bernard Lahire, *La Culture des individus: Dissonances culturelles et distinction de soi* (Paris, 2004) ; and Elizabeth B. Silva, 'Homologies of Social Space and Elective Affinities', in: *Sociology* 40, no. 6, 2006: 1171–89. **29.** Bennett et al., *Culture, Class, Distinction*. Unfortunately, we do not have international research to compare the British situation with societies that have stronger traditions of public theatres. For a different approach, see T. W. Chan & J. H. Goldthorpe, 'Social Stratification and Cultural Consumption', in: *European Sociological Review* 23/1 (2007), 1–19. **30.** For changing leisure practices, see the chapter 'Not so Fast!' below. **31.** Ioné Acquah, *Accra Survey: A Social Survey of the Capital of Ghana, Formerly Called the Gold Coast, Undertaken for the West African Institute of Social and Economic Research, 1953–56* (London, 1958), 154–63; and Phyllis M. Martin, *Leisure and Society in Colonial Brazzaville* (Cambridge, 1995). **32.** Philip Mayer & Iona Mayer, *Townsmen and Tribesmen: Conservatism and the Process of Urbanization in a South African City* (Cape Town, 1961); see also their postscript to the 1971 edition. Some of this communal drinking culture re-emerged around hostels: see Leslie Bank, 'Men with Cookers: Transformations in Migrant Culture, Domesticity and Identity in Duncan Village, East London', in: *Journal of Southern African Studies* 25, no. 3, 1999: 393–416. See also: B. A. Pauw, *The Second Generation: A Study of the Family among Urbanized Bantu in East London* (Cape Town, 1963/1973). **33.** Adam Mack, 'Good Things to Eat in Surburbia: Supermarkets and American Consumer Culture, 1930–1970', PhD thesis, University of South Carolina, 2006. **34.** De Grazia, *Irresistible Empire*, 395, and ch. eight in general. **35.** Stewart Howe, ed., *Retailing in the European Union* (London, 2002). **36.** Mack, 'Supermarkets', 165–73. **37.** Emanuela Scarpellini, *Comprare all'americana: Le origini della rivoluzione commerciale in Italia 1945–71* (Bologna, 2001); Emanuela Scarpellini, 'Shopping American-style: the Arrival of the Supermarket in Post-war Italy', in: *Enterprise & Society* 5, no. 4,

2004: 625–68. **38.** Luciano Bianciardi, *La vita agra* (Milan, 1962), 171, my translation. **39.** Andrew Alexander, et al. 'The Co-creation of a Retail Innovation: Shoppers and the Early Supermarket in Britain', in: *Enterprise & Society* 10, no. 3, 2009: 529–58, quoted at 547. See further: A. Alexander, S. Phillips & G. Shaw, 'Retail Innovation and Shopping Practices: Consumers' Reactions to Self-service Retailing', in: *Environment and Planning A* 40, 2008: 2204–21; Paul du Gay, 'Self-Service: Retail, Shopping and Personhood', in: *Consumption, Markets and Culture* 7, no. 2, 2004: 149–63; Emanuela Scarpellini, *L'Italia dei consumi* (Rome, 2008), 229–31; *Independent*, 26 Oct. 1998 (Sainsbury obituary); Charles Debbasch & Jean-Marie Pontier, *La Société française* (Paris, 1989), 228. **40.** James L. Watson, ed., *Golden Arches East: McDonald's in East Asia* (Stanford, CA, 1997). **41.** My translation. **42.** Janne Poikolainen, 'Anglo-American Pop Music, Finnish Tango and the Controversial Images of Modernity in Finland in the 1960s', in: Visa Heinonen & Matti Peltonen, eds., *Finnish Consumption: An Emerging Consumer Society between East and West* (Helsinki, 2013), quoted at 142 (the musician was M. A. Numminen). **43.** The song is by Jukka Poika. Ermanno Labianca, *Canzone per te: Appunti di musica leggera, 1957–2007* (Rome, 2007); Dario Salvatori, *Sanremo 50: La vicenda e i protagonisti di mezzo secolo di Festival della canzone* (Rome, 2000); Bantigny, *Le Plus Bel Âge?*, 66; and Pirjo Kukkonen, *Tango Nostalgia: The Language of Love and Longing* (Helsinki, 1996). For later hybrids, see Marco Santoro & Marco Solaroli, 'Authors and Rappers: Italian Hip Hop and the Shifting Boundaries of *Canzone d'Autore*', in: *Popular Music* 26, no. 3, 2007: 463–88. **44.** *Loi no. 86-1067 du 30 septembre 1986 relative à la liberté de communication* (Loi Léotard) is available at: http://www.legifrance.gouv.fr/affichTexte.do?cidTexte=LEGITEXT000006068930. **45.** Alan Warde et al., 'Changes in the Practice of Eating: A Comparative Analysis of Time-use', in: *Acta Sociologica* 50, no. 4, 2007: 363–85; Shu-Li Cheng et al., 'The Changing Practice of Eating: Evidence from UK Time Diaries, 1975–2000', in: *British Journal of Sociology* 58, no. 1, 2007: 39–61. Claude Fischler & Estelle Masson, *Manger: Français, Européens et Américains face à l'alimentation* (Paris, 2008). **46.** Dale Southerton et al. 'Trajectories of Time Spent Reading as a Primary Activity: A Comparison of the Netherlands, Norway, France, UK and USA since the 1970s', CRESC Working Paper 39, 2007; http://www.cresc.ac.uk/publications/documents/wp39.pdf. **47.** W. Griswold, T. McDonnell & N. Wright, 'Reading and the Reading Class in the Twenty-first Century', in: *Annual Review of Sociology* 31, 2005: 127–41; and J. Gershuny, 'Web-use and Net-nerds: A Neo-functionalist Analysis of the Impact of Information Technology in the Home', in: *Social Forces* 82, no. 1, 2003: 139–66.

CHAPTER 8

1. China, *Statistical Yearbook* (1988 and 1993); for 2009: see http://www.stats.gov.cn/tjsj/ndsj/2009/indexeh.htm. For Korea, see Laura C. Nelson, *Measured*

Excess: Status, Gender and Consumer Nationalism in South Korea (New York, 2000), 87; for Japan, Partner, *Assembled in Japan*, tables 6, 1. Diffusion in the United States had been faster than in Britain, see Offer, *Challenge of Affluence*, esp. 173–80. **2.** If we measure purchasing power parity – that is, what money really buys on the ground – China's $10 trillion were only second in spending power to the United States in 2009. **3.** The most forceful, recent version of this thesis is Karl Gerth, *As China Goes, So Goes the World: How Chinese Consumers are Transforming Everything* (New York, 2010), quoted at 192. **4.** A separate issue is whether miraculous growth has been an optical illusion, produced by conventional measurements. The costs from environmental pollution and degradation would eat up around 10% GDP a year, according to Elizabeth C. Economy, 'The Great Leap Backward', in: *Foreign Affairs*, 86/5, 2007, 38–59. **5.** Across the country, the number of shops fell almost five times, while the population was growing; see Martin King Whyte & William L. Parish, *Urban Life in Contemporary China* (Chicago, 1984), 98–9. **6.** It has since risen to 2.9%, according to the WTO. **7.** Kautilya, *The Arthashastra*, trans. L. N. Rangarajan (London, 1992), 1.7.1, 145. **8.** See Harald Fuess, *Transnational History of Beer in Japan* (forthcoming), ch. 3. **9.** T. Matsuda, 'The Japanese Family Budget Enquiry of 1926–1927', in: *International Labour Review* 23, 1931: 388–98. For watches: Pierre-Yves Donzé, 'Des importateurs suisses de Yokohama aux fabricants d'horlogerie japonais', in: *Revue d'histoire moderne et contemporaine* 57, no. 1, 2010: 168–89. The above further draws on Hiroshi Hazama, 'Historical Changes in the Life Style of Industrial Workers', in: *Japanese Industrialization and Its Social Consequences*, ed. Hugh Patrick (Berkeley, CA, 1976), 21–51; Sato, *New Japanese Woman*; and Penelope Francks, *The Japanese Consumer: An Alternative Economic History of Modern Japan* (Cambridge, 2009). For Hitoshi's survey of the North and attitudes to modernity more generally, see Harry Harootunian, *Overcome by Modernity: History, Culture and Community in Interwar Japan* (Princeton, NJ, 2000). **10.** Leo Ou-Fan Lee, *Shanghai Modern: The Flowering of a New Urban Culture in China, 1930–1945* (Cambridge, MA, 1999). **11.** Prakash Tandon, *Punjabi Century, 1857–1947* (London, 1961), 110–11. **12.** Frank Dikötter, *Things Modern: Material Culture and Everyday Life in China* (London, 2006), 55–6, 196–200, and 205–13 for cosmetics, below. See also: Cochran, *Inventing Nanking Road: Commercial Culture in Shanghai, 1900–1945*. **13.** Olga Lang, *Chinese Family and Society* (New Haven, CT, 1946), 74. **14.** The title of Carl Crow's book, published in 1937. **15.** Campbell, *The Romantic Ethic and the Spirit of Modern Consumerism*, 18. **16.** Shanghai Library, Bureau of Social Affairs, The City Government of Greater Shanghai, 'Standard of Living of Shanghai Laborers' (1934), 102–4, 157, table XLI. **17.** Malcolm Lyall Darling, *The Punjab Peasant in Prosperity and Debt* (London, 1925), quoted at xiv, 144, 164–6. **18.** Andrew Gordon, 'From Singer to Shinpan: Consumer Credit in Modern Japan', in: Sheldon Garon & Patricia L. Maclachlan, eds., *The Ambivalent Consumer: Questioning Consumption in East Asia and the West* (Ithaca, NY, 2006), 137–62, at 141. **19.** The following draws on: Garon, 'Luxury is the Enemy'; Sheldon Garon, 'Japan's Post-war "Consumer Revolution", or Striking a "Balance" between Consumption and Saving', in: *Consuming Cultures, Global Perspectives*, eds. John Brewer & Frank Trentmann (Oxford, 2006); and Charles Yuji Horioka, 'Are the Japanese Unique?', in: Garon & Maclachlan, eds., *Ambivalent Consumer*, ch. 5. **20.** Turo-Kimmo Lehtonen and Mika Pantzar, 'The Ethos of Thrift: The Promotion of Bank Saving in Finland during the 1950s', in: *Journal of Material Culture* 7, no. 2, 2002: 211–31. See also: Minna Lammi, '"Ett" varttuisi Suomenmaa. Suomalaisten kasvattaminen kulutusyhteiskuntaan kotimaisissa lylhytelokuvissa 1920–69' (Helsinki, 2006). **21.** This and the above draw on Partner, *Assembled in Japan,* quoted at 163. **22.** J. Devika, 'Domesticating Malayalees: Family Planning, the Nation and Home-centred Anxieties in Mid-20th-century Keralam' (Kerala: Centre for Development Studies: WP340, 2002), 46–9. **23.** Harold Wilhite, *Consumption and the Transformation of Everyday Life: A View from South India* (Basingstoke, 2008), 89–103. **24.** Indian Statistical Institute, *The National Sample Survey, 11th and 12th Rounds, Aug. 1956–Aug. 1957, no. 46, Tables with notes on Consumer Expenditure of Agricultural Labour Households in Rural Areas* (Delhi, 1961). **25.** Ashok Gulati & Shenggen Fan (eds.), *The Dragon and the Elephant: Agricultural Rural Reforms in China and India* (Oxford, 2007). **26.** S. L. Rao & I. Natarajan, *Indian Market Demographics: The Consumer Classes* (Delhi, 1996); NCAER, *India Market Demographics Report 2002* (Delhi, 2002). **27.** Madhya Pradesh, *Human Development Report 2007* (Oxford, 2007), 180. **28.** World Bank, New Delhi: 'Scaling-up Access to Finance for India's Rural Poor' (Dec. 2004), report no. 30740-IN: 87% of the rural poor had no access to credit, 71% no savings. The story is similar in Nepal: see Aurora Ferrari, *Access to Financial Services in Nepal* (Washington, DC, 2007). **29.** The Energy and Resources Institute (TERI), *Energy Data Directory* (Delhi, 2009), 139–41; and Madhya Pradesh, *Human Development Report 2007*, 13. **30.** Human Development Research Centre and National Rural Electricity Co-operative Association (NRECA), 'Economic and Social Impact Evaluation Study of the Rural Electrification Program in Bangladesh' (Dhaka, 2002), with thanks to Anjali Garg for pointing me to this document. In 2007, Bangladesh's GDP per capita was the 155th lowest in the world ($1,241 PPP), barely ahead of Gambia and Tanzania. It ranked 146th in the overall human development index. See also: Md. Motaher Hossain, 'Role of Technology in Consumption and Everyday Life in Rural Bangladesh,' in: *Technology in Society*, XXXII/2 (2010), 130–6. **31.** Linda Chao & Ramon H. Myers, 'China's Consumer Revolution: The 1990s and Beyond', in: *Journal of Contemporary China* 7, no. 18, 1998: 351–68, 354, table one. For the shift to state-led growth, see Yasheng Huang, *Capitalism with Chinese Characteristics: Entrepreneurship and the State* (Cambridge, 2008). **32.** China Statistical Yearbook 2009, http://www.stats.gov.cn/tjsj/ndsj/2009/indexeh.htm. **33.** Hsiao-Tung Fei, *Peasant Life in China: A Field Study of Country Life in the Yangtze Valley* (London, 1939), 119. **34.** Lang, *Chinese Family and Society*, 239–44, 279–80, quoted at 338. **35.** Yunxiang Yan, *Private Life under Socialism: Love,*

Intimacy and Family Change in a Chinese Village, 1949–99 (Stanford, CA, 2003); and Yunxiang Yan, *The Individualization of Chinese Society* (Oxford, 2009). See also: Anita Chan, Richard Madsen & Jonathan Unger, eds., *Chen Village: The Recent History of a Peasant Community in Mao's China* (Berkeley, CA, 1983), 219, 252–4; and Edward Friedman, Paul G. Pickowicz & Mark Selden, *Revolution, Resistance and Reform in Village China* (New Haven, CT, 2005), 227–32. **36.** See 61, 179 above. **37.** In 2006, Rajkot and Indore, for example, had only 45 minutes of water a day; National Institute of Urban Affairs, *Report on Water Services* (2006). **38.** See the case studies in Rama Bijapurkar, *We are Like That Only: Understanding the Logic of Consumer India* (New Delhi, 2007). **39.** Jos Gamble, 'The Rhetoric of the Consumer and Customer Control in China', in: *Work, Employment and Society* 2, no. 1, 2007: 7–25. For Carrefour's stores in 2013, see http://www.carrefour.com/sites/default/files/PARCGB 31122013.pdf. **40.** Souichirou Kozuka & Luke R. Nottage, 'The Myth of the Cautious Consumer: Law, Culture, Economics and Politics in the Rise and Partial Fall of Unsecured Lending in Japan', in: *Consumer Credit, Debt and Bankruptcy: National and International Dimensions*, eds. J. Niemi-Kiesilainen, I. Ramsay & W. Whitford, (Oxford, 2009); and Horioka, 'Are the Japanese Unique?', in: Garon & Maclachlan, eds., *Ambivalent Consumer.* **41.** Jeff Kingston, *Japan's Quiet Transformation* (New York, 2004). **42.** In converted US dollars; World Bank, *2005 ICP Global Results* (Washington, 2005), table 5. **43.** Marcos D. Chamon & Eswar S. Prasad, 'Why are Saving Rates of Urban Households in China Rising?' in: *American Economic Journal: Macroeconomics*, (2010) 2(1): 93–130; and Elizabeth Croll, *China's New Consumers* (London, 2006), 85. For the tiny share of public spending on education and health by international comparison, see OECD, *Challenges for China's Public Spending: Toward Greater Effectiveness and Equity* (Paris, 2006), ch. 2. **44.** Unofficial estimates raise it to 41%; see *The Economist*, 26 May 2012, 15–17. **45.** Xiaohong Zhou, 'Chinese Middle Class: Reality or Illusion?', in: Christophe Jaffrelot & Peter Van der Veer, eds., *Patterns of Middle-class Consumption in India and China* (Los Angeles, 2008), ch. 5; P. K. Varma, *The Great Indian Middle Class* (Delhi, 1998); McKinsey Global Institute, 'The "Bird of Gold": The Rise of India's Consumer Market' (San Francisco, 2007); NCAER, *The Great Indian Market* (New Delhi, 2005); Ernest Young, 'Great Indian Middle Class'; David S. G. Goodman, ed., *The New Rich in China: Future Rulers, Present Lives* (New York, 2008); and Cheng Li, *China's Emerging Middle Class: Beyond Economic Transformation* (Washington, DC, 2010). See also 434–9 below on luxury. **46.** Jun Wang & Stephen Siu Yu Lau, 'Gentrification and Shanghai's New Middle Class: Another Reflection on the Cultural Consumption Thesis', *Cities* 26, no. 2, 2009: 57–66; and Xin Wang, 'Divergent Identities, Convergent Interests', in: *Journal of Contemporary China* 17, no. 54, 2008. **47.** Deborah Davis & Wang Feng, *Creating Wealth and Poverty in Post-socialist China* (Stanford, 2008). For the proximity of the new middle class to the Party, see Li Jian & Niu Xiaohan, 'The New Middle Class in Peking: A Case Study', in: *China Perspectives*, Jan.–Feb.

2003. **48.** Hindu woman quoted in R. Ganguly-Scrase & T. J. Scrase, *Globalization and the Middle Classes in India: The Social and Cultural Impact of Neo-liberal Reforms* (London, 2009), 98, no age given. **49.** Steven Kemper, *Buying and Believing: Sri Lankan Advertising and Consumers in a Transnational World* (Chicago, 2001), 200–5. **50.** S. L. Rao & I. Natarajan, *Indian Market Demographics: The Consumer Classes* (Delhi, 1996), 162. **51.** Bill Adams, 'Macroeconomic Implications of China Urban Housing Privatization, 1998–1999', *Journal of Contemporary China* 18, no. 62, 2009: 881–8. **52.** Quoted in Junhua Lü, Peter G. Rowe & Jie Zhang, eds., *Modern Urban Housing in China, 1840–2000* (Munich, 2001), 241. **53.** In 2004, quoted in Choon-Piew Pow, 'Constructing a New Private Order: Gated Communities and the Privatization of Urban Life in Post-reform Shanghai', in: *Social & Cultural Geography* (2007) 8/6, 813–33, at 826. **54.** *China Business Weekly*, 7–13 Aug. 2006, 9. **55.** http://residence.net.cn/main.htm. **56.** 2004, quoted in Deborah Davis, 'Urban Consumer Culture', in: *China Quarterly*, 2005: 692–709, 706. See also: Deborah S. Davis, ed., *The Consumer Revolution in Urban China* (Berkeley, CA, 2000). **57.** Thomas L. Friedman, *The World is Flat: A Brief History of the Globalized World in the Twenty-first Century* (London, 2005). **58.** Shunya Yoshimi, 'Consuming America, Producing Japan,' in: Garon & Maclachlan, eds., *Ambivalent Consumer*, 64. **59.** Harootunian, *Overcome by Modernity*, esp. chs. 2–3. **60.** Shunya Yoshimi, 'Consuming America, Producing Japan', in: Garon and Maclachlan, eds., *Ambivalent Consumer*, ch. 3. See also: Shunya Yoshimi, 'Made in Japan: The Cultural Politics of "Home Electrification" in Post-war Japan ,' in: *Media, Culture & Society* 21, no. 2, 1999: 149–71. **61.** For this, see Chua Beng Huat, *Life is Not Complete Without Shopping: Consumption Culture in Singapore* (Singapore, 2003). **62.** Koichi Iwabuchi, 'Return to Asia? Japan in Asian Audiovisual Markets', in: Kosaku Yoshino, ed., *Consuming Ethnicity and Nationalism* (Richmond, Surrey, 1999), ch. 8. **63.** Chua Beng Huat, 'Transnational and Transcultural Circulation and Consumption of East Asian Television Drama,' in Jaffrelot & Veer, eds., *Middle-class Consumption in India and China*, ch. 10. Euny Hong, *The Birth of Korean Cool* (New York, 2014). **64.** Quoted from Wilhite, *Consumption and Everyday Life*, 134. **65.** S. Radhakrishnan, 'Professional Women, Good Families: Respectable Femininity and the Cultural Politics of a "New" India', in: *Qualitative Sociology* (2009) 32: 195–212, 205. **66.** Margit van Wessel, 'Talking about Consumption: How an Indian Middle Class Dissociates from Middle-class Life', *Cultural Dynamics* 16, 2004: 93–116. **67.** W. Mazzarella, *Shoveling Smoke: Advertising and Globalization in Contemporary India*, (Durham, NC 2003), 277. **68.** Dipankar Gupta, *Mistaken Modernity: India between Worlds* (New Delhi, 2000). **69.** E.g., Carol Upadhya, 'Rewriting the Code: Software Professionals and the Reconstitution of Indian Middle-class Identity', in: Jaffrelot & Veer, eds., *Middle-class Consumption in India and China*, ch. 3. **70.** Vamsi Vakulabharanam, 'Does Class Matter? Class Structure and Worsening Inequality in India', in: *Economic & Political Weekly*, XLV/29 (17 July 2010), 67–76. **71.** Nicholas Nisbett, 'Friendship,

Consumption, Morality: Practising Identity, Negotiating Hierarchy in Middle-class Bangalore,' in: *Journal of the Royal Anthropological Institute* 13, 2007: 935–50. See further: Chandra Bhan Prasad, 'Markets and Manu: Economic Reforms and Its Impact on Caste in India', in: *CASI Working Paper Series*, no. 08-01, Jan. 2008. For the loosening of caste in Nepal and efforts by the middle classes to balance local and global identities, see Mark Liechty, *Suitably Modern: Making Middle-class Culture in a New Consumer Society* (Princeton, NJ, 2003). See also 143 above. **72.** Haruka Yanagisawa, 'Growth of Small-scale Industries and Changes in Consumption Patterns in South India, 1910s–'50s', in: Douglas Haynes et al. (eds), *Towards a History of Consumption in South Asia* (Oxford, 2010), 51–75; and Yogendra Singh, *Culture Change in India: Identity and Globalization* (Jaipur, 2000). **73.** Filippo & Caroline Osella, *Social Mobility in Kerala: Modernity and Identity in Conflict* (London, 2000), esp. 119–22. **74.** *Report on the Working and Living Conditions of the Scheduled Castes Workers in the Selected Occupations at Indore, 1993* (Labour Bureau, Government of India, Chandigarh/Shimla, 1997), tables 3.11 A–C. **75.** Rajesh Shukla, Sunil Jain & Preeti Kakkar, *Caste in a Different Mould* (New Delhi, 2010). **76.** Patricia Uberoi, 'Imagining the Family: An Ethnography of Viewing *Hum Aapke Hain Koun . . . !*' in: Rachel Dwyer & Christopher Pinney (eds.), *Pleasure and the Nation: The History, Politics and Consumption of Public Culture in India* (Oxford, 2001). **77.** Ronald Philip Dore, *City Life in Japan: A Study of a Tokyo Ward* (London, 1958), 62–80. **78.** White Paper on the National Lifestyle, Fiscal Year 1995, 'Looking Back on 50 years . . . and Forward, in Search of an Affluent and Diversified National Lifestyle for Japan,' Economic Planning Agency, Government of Japan, http://www5.cao.go.jp/seikatsu/whitepaper/h7/life95so-e-e.html. **79.** Lonny Carlile, 'The Yoahan Group', in: Kerrie L. MacPherson (ed.), *Asian Department Stores* (Richmond, Surrey, 1998), 233–52. **80.** Jeff Kingston, *Japan's Quiet Transformation* (New York, 2004). **81.** John L. McCreery, *Japanese Consumer Behavior: From Worker Bees to Wary Shoppers* (Richmond, Surrey, 2000). **82.** White Paper on the National Lifestyle, Fiscal Year 1995, Government of Japan. **83.** Seung-Kuk Kim, 'Changing Lifestyles and Consumption Patterns of the South Korean Middle Class and New Generations,' in: Chua Beng Huat, ed., *Consumption in Asia: Lifestyles and Identities* (London, 2000), ch. 3. **84.** Nelson, *Measured Excess.* **85.** The above draws on Inge Daniel's ethnography of thirty homes in the Kansai region in central Japan conducted in 2002–3: *The Japanese House: Material Culture in the Modern Home* (Oxford, 2010). Her findings question the picture of a throwaway society, e.g., John Clammer, *Contemporary Urban Japan: A Sociology of Consumption* (Oxford, 1997), 79–80. **86.** Robert W. Hefner (ed.), *Market Cultures: Society and Morality in the New Asian Capitalisms* (Boulder, CO, 1998). **87.** Elizabeth Croll, 'Conjuring Goods, Identities and Cultures', in: Kevin Latham, Stuart Thompson & Jakob Klein, eds., *Consuming China: Approaches to Cultural Change in Contemporary China* (London, 2006), 22–41; and Robert Well, 'Divided Market Cultures in China', in: Hefner, *Market Cultures*, ch. 2. **88.** *China Statistical Yearbook*, 2014.

W. McEwen et al., 'Inside the Mind of the Chinese Consumer', in: *Harvard Business Review*, March 2006; 84(3): 68–76. **89.** For this and general discussion, see Beverley Hooper, 'The Consumer Citizen in Contemporary China', in: Centre for East and South-east Asian Studies Working Paper 12, 2005. **90.** *Arthashastra*, 86, 245–8. **91.** 'Cases filed, disposed and pending', data compiled by Centre for Consumer Studies, IIPA, New Delhi, 2008. **92.** Pradeep S. Mehta, ed., *Competition and Regulation in India* (CUTS/Jaipur, 2007), #0715. **93.** (1994) 1SCC243, quoted in IIPA, *Housing and Consumer* (Delhi, 2006). **94.** In 2008, 17% of complaints filed were about defective goods, compared to 27% about electricity, mainly billing and disruption. Data compiled by CCS, IIPA, Delhi, 2008. **95.** 7 SCC 688, Charan Singh *vs.* Healing Touch Hospital, quoted in S. S. Singh & Sapna Chadah, *Consumer Protection in India* (New Delhi, 2005), 26. **96.** *Awaken*, Consumer Club Bulletin of Kamala Nehru College, 3 (Aug. 2008), 9. **97.** V. Prabhu, in E. Rajaram, K. Durai, M. Jeyakumaran & E. Yavanarani (eds.), *Consumer Protection and Welfare* (Chennai, 2008), ch. 22. **98.** Quoted, e.g., on the homepage of the Centre for Consumer Studies, Indian Institute of Public Administration, which oversees the government programme of consumer awareness and training. The quote, too, hangs on the walls of many business offices. I am grateful to Suresh Mishra and everyone at the IIPA for discussion and information. Gandhi's 98 volumes of works are now on line, at http://www.gandhiserve.org/cwmg/cwmg.html. **99.** Water and Sanitation Program, *Engaging with Citizens to Improve Services* (2007), ch. 6. For Piplod, see also the account at http://www.cuts-international.org/psr-04.htm. **100.** Sanjay Srivastava, 'Urban Spaces, Post-nationalism and the Making of the Consumer-Citizen in India', in: *New Cultural Histories of India*, eds. Partha Chatterjee, Tapati Guha Thakurta & Bodhisattva Kar (New Delhi, 2014), ch. 13. **101.** E.g., 'Bhagidari: Good Intention, Bad Implementation?' by the liberal Centre of Civil Society, http://www.ccsindia.org/ccsindia/interns2003/chap7.pdf. **102.** Patricia L. Maclachlan, *Consumer Politics in Post-war Japan: The Institutional Boundaries of Citizen Activism* (New York, 2002); and Takao Nishimura, 'Household Debt and Consumer Education in Post-war Japan', in: Garon & Maclachlan, eds., *Ambivalent Consumer*, ch. 11. **103.** Cabinet Office of Japan, White Paper on the National Lifestyle: Prospects for Consumer Citizenship (2008), intro.; http://www5.cao.go.jp/seikatsu/whitepaper/h20/06_eng/index.html. **104.** Nikolas Rose, *Powers of Freedom: Reframing Political Thought* (Cambridge, 1999). **105.** The full text is at http://www.cca.org.cn/english/EnNewsShow.jsp?id=38&cid=983. **106.** 'Class Action Litigation in China', in: *Harvard Law Review* 111, no. 6, 1998: 1523–41; Hooper, 'The Consumer Citizen in Contemporary China'. **107.** China Consumers' Association, *Annual Report* 2004, 2005; Haidian CCA, 'The Dynamics of Consumption', monthly magazine, 47 (2003), 35. **108.** In 2002, the regime set up the State-owned Assets Supervision and Administration Commission (SASAC). In 2008, the promotion of national brands was incorporated into the government's National Strategy. See Gerth, *As China Goes*, ch. 5. **109.** Chinese Consumers' Association, 'A Guide to Scientific Consumption

2008', at http://www.cca.org.cn/english/EnNewsShow.jsp?id=184&cid=982.
110. Luigi Tomba, 'Of Quality, Harmony and Community: Civilization and the Middle Class in Urban China', in: *Positions: East Asia Cultures Critique* 17, no. 3, 2009: 592–616.

CHAPTER 9

1. John De Graaf, David Wann & Thomas H. Naylor, *Affluenza: The All-consuming Epidemic* (San Francisco, 2001); Clive Hamilton & Richard Denniss, *Affluenza: When Too Much is Never Enough* (Crows Nest, NSW, 2006); and James, *Affluenza*. Avner Offer diagnoses a rise in instant gratification and the decline of 'commitment devices' from the 1950s onwards, Offer, *Challenge of Affluence*.   **2.** Lydia Maria Francis Child, *The American Frugal Housewife* (Boston, 1835, 16th edn), p. 89 – it was dedicated to 'those who are not ashamed of economy'.   **3.** King James Bible, 1 Timothy 6:10; Jacques Le Goff, *Your Money or Your Life: Economy and Religion in the Middle Ages* (New York, 1988); Dante Alighieri, *Divine Comedy* (1308–21), *Inferno*, Canto XVII, third round of the seventh circle; and Rosa-Maria Gelpi & François Julien-Labruyère, *The History of Consumer Credit: Doctrines and Practice* (Basingstoke, 2000).   **4.** Benjamin Franklin, *Poor Richard's Almanac* (Philadelphia, 1732), 25; Franklin, *The Way to Wealth* (London, 1758), 13.   **5.** Helen Bosanquet, 'The Burden of Debts', in: *Economic Journal*, 6/22 (June 1896), 212–25, quoted at 220, 223.   **6.** Daniel Horowitz, *The Morality of Spending: Attitudes towards the Consumer Society in America, 1875–1940* (Chicago, 1992); Horowitz, *Anxieties of Affluence*.   **7.** Seung-Kuk Kim, 'Changing Lifestyles and Consumption Patterns of the South Korean Middle Class and New Generations', in: Beng Huat, ed., *Consumption in Asia: Lifestyles and Identities*, 71–3.   **8.** Craig Muldrew, *The Economy of Obligation: The Culture of Credit and Social Relations in Early Modern England* (Basingstoke, 1998), 68, 117–18. For a continental European example, see S. Ogilvie, M. Kuepker & J. Maegraith, 'Household Debt in Early Modern Germany: Evidence from Personal Inventories', in: *Journal of Economic History* 72, no. 1, 2012: 134–67.
9. Julius Pierstorff, 'Drei Jenaer Handwerke', in: *Schriften des Vereins für Socialpolitik* LXX, no. 9, 1897, quoted at 50.   **10.** Bureau of Social Affairs, The City Government of Greater Shanghai, 'Standard of Living of Shanghai Laborers' (1934), 108 and tables 15, 16.   **11.** *1924–25 (153) Report by the Joint Select Committee of the House of Lords and the House of Commons on the Moneylenders Bill [H. L.] and the Moneylenders (Amendment) Bill*, 78: Dorothy Keeling of the Liverpool Women Citizen's Association. See further: Paul Johnson, *Saving and Spending: The Working-class Economy in Britain, 1870–1939* (Oxford, 1985).   **12.** Camille Selosse & Lorna Schrefler, 'Consumer Credit and Lending to Households in Europe', (European Credit Research Institute, 2005), fig. 6.   **13.** http://www.oecd-ilibrary.org/economics/oecd-factbook_18147364.   **14.** J. Logemann & U. Spiekermann, 'The Myth of a Bygone Cash

Economy: Consumer Lending in Germany from the Nineteenth Century to the Mid-twentieth Century', in: *Entreprises et histoire*, no. 59, 2010: 12–27; Sean O'Connell, *Working-class Debt in the UK since 1880* (Oxford, 2009), ch. 2; and Lendol Calder, *Financing the American Dream: A Cultural History of Consumer Credit* (Princeton, NJ, 1999), ch. 4.   **15.** National Bureau of Economic Research, *The Pattern of Consumer Debt, 1935–36: A Statistical Analysis*, ed. Blanche Bernstein (1940).   **16.** Calder, *Financing the American Dream*, 184–99.   **17.** Isabelle Gaillard, 'Télévisions et crédit à la consommation: Une approche comparative France–Rfa 1950–1970', in: *Entreprises et histoire*, no. 2, 2010: 102–11.   **18.** Calder, *Financing the American Dream*, 175, and ch. 3 for the following.   **19.** O'Connell, *Working-class Debt in the UK since 1880*, 58–66.   **20.** Edwin R. A. Seligman, *Economics of Instalment Selling: A Study in Consumers' Credit* (1927), 222.   **21.** See 101–2 above.   **22.** Quoted in Calder, *Financing the American Dream*, 235.   **23.** Seligman, *Economics of Instalment Selling*, 224.   **24.** Louis Hyman, *Debtor Nation: The History of America in Red Ink* (Princeton, NJ, 2011), ch. 2.   **25.** It is, of course, also true that high-income households tend to have higher debt. The interplay between these factors is complex. See further: Sarah Bridges, Richard Disney & Andrew Henley, 'Housing Wealth and the Accumulation of Financial Debt', in: Giuseppe Bertola, Richard Disney & Charles Grant, eds., *The Economics of Consumer Credit* (Cambridge, MA, 2006), 135–79; and Richard Disney, 'The UK's Household Debt Problem: Is There One? And, If So, Who's at Risk?' (London: Institute for Fiscal Studies, 2007).   **26.** According to the European Mortgage Federation, per capita mortgage debt in Greece in 2010 was €7,120 and €5,830 in Italy – in the United States, it was four times that (€27,040); http://www.hypo.org/Content/Default.asp?pageId=414.   **27.** Martha L. Olney, *Buy Now, Pay Later: Advertising, Credit and Consumer Durables in the 1920s* (Chapel Hill, NC, 1991), table 4.6, 108.   **28.** George Norris, governor of the Philadelphia Federal Reserve Bank, cited in P. J. Kubik, 'Federal Reserve Policy during the Great Depression: The impact of Inter-war Attitudes Regarding Consumption and Consumer Credit', in: *Journal of Economic Issues* 30, no. 3, 1996: 829–42, at 833. For intellectuals' ongoing ambivalence, see Horowitz, *Anxieties of Affluence*.   **29.** M. L. Olney, 'When Your Word is Not Enough: Race, Collateral and Household Credit', in: *Journal of Economic History* 58, no. 2, 1998: 408–31.   **30.** P. Scott, 'The Twilight World of Inter-war British Hire Purchase', in: *Past & Present* 177, no. 1, 2002: 195–225.   **31.** From DM27 billion at the beginning of 1970 to DM115 billion at the end of 1979. See the Bundesbank Zeitreihe PQ 3150 'Sonstige Kredite an ... Privatpersonen'. While not perfect, this data series gets us closer to the volume of consumer credit than the MFI-Zinsstatistik, used by some writers, which includes credit to individual traders and non-profit-making organizations; http://www.bundesbank.de/statistik/statistik_zeitreihen.php?lang=de&open=banken&func=row &tr=PQ3150.   **32.** Luca Casolaro, Leonardo Gambacorta & Luigi Guiso, 'Regulation, Formal and Informal Enforcement, and the Development of the Household Loan Market: Lessons from Italy', in: Bertola, Disney & Grant, eds.,

The Economics of Consumer Credit, 92–134.   **33.** See Gaillard, 'Télévisions et crédit', 108f; in 1960, 70% of consumer goods were bought on credit in the USA and Canada, 60% in Britain, 55% in West Germany, but only 35% in France.   **34.** A. Börsch-Supan, 'Savings in Germany – Part II: Behavior', in: James M Poterba, ed., *International Comparisons of Household Saving* (Chicago, 1994).   **35.** Great Britain. Dept of Trade and Industry, Committee on Consumer Credit, 'Consumer Credit. Report of the Committee. Chairman: Lord Crowther, etc.' (1971), Cmnd. 4596, 123.   **36.** Casolaro et al., 'Lessons from Italy', in: Bertola, Disney & Grant, eds., *The Economics of Consumer Credit*, 120f.   **37.** P. Horvath, 'Die Teilzahlungskredite als Begleiterscheinung des westdeutschen Wirtschaftswunders, 1948–1960', in: *Zeitschrift für Unternehmensgeschichte* (1992) 19–55, esp. 35–7.   **38.** Sombart, *Luxus und Kapitalismus*, 96, my translation.   **39.** Horvath, 'Teilzahlungskredite', 22.   **40.** Crowther Committee on Consumer Credit (1971), tables 2.1 & 2.4, 52–55.   **41.** 'Beryl' in Hemel Hempstead, in a 1997 interview, quoted in O'Connell, *Working-class Debt in the UK since 1880*, 120.   **42.** The above draws on Sheldon Garon, *Beyond our Means: Why America Spends while the World Saves* (Princeton, NJ, 2011).   **43.** Garon, *Beyond our Means*, 10.   **44.** A. Chandavarkar, 'Saving Behaviour in the Asian-Pacific Region', in: *Asian-Pacific Economic Literature* 7, no. 1, 1993: 9–27; www.cpf.gov.sg.   **45.** C. Y. Horioka, 'Are the Japanese Unique? An Analysis of Consumption and Saving Behavior in Japan', in: *Osaka University Institute of Social and Economic Research, Discussion Paper 606*, (Osaka, 2004); Victoria de Grazia, *The Culture of Consent: Mass Organization of Leisure in Fascist Italy* (Cambridge, 1981), 154–9. See also 371–2 above.   **46.** Soogeun Oh, 'Personal Bankruptcy in Korea', in: Johanna Niemi, Iain Ramsay & William C. Whitford, *Consumer Credit, Debt and Bankruptcy: Comparative and International Perspectives* (Oxford, 2009), 375–93.   **47.** Quoted in Johnson, *Saving and Spending*, 213f.   **48.** Samuel Smiles, *Self-help; with Illustrations of Character, Conduct and Perseverance* (London, 1859/1866), 295.   **49.** E.g., the 1949 *Möbelsparaktion* by savings banks in Lower Saxony; Horvath, 'Teilzahlungskredite', 21.   **50.** Lehtonen & Pantzar, 'The Ethos of Thrift: The Promotion of Bank Saving in Finland during the 1950s' . See also: Visa Heinonen, 'Talonpoikainen etiikka ja kulutuksen henki. Kotitalousneuvonnasta kuluttajapolitiikkaan 1900-luvun Suomessa' ('Peasant Ethic and the Spirit of Consumption'), in: *Bibliotheca Historica* (1998) 33; Visa Heinonen, Minna Lammi & Esko Varho, ' "Ei nimittäin haluttu valmistaa tavallista reklaamifilmiä ..." Mainonta ja valistus suomalaisissa lyhytelokuvissa', *Lähikuva* 4/1995, 34–47. With thanks to Visa Heinonen and Minna Lammi for showing me film adverts of the target saver.   **51.** (Crowther) Committee on Consumer Credit, Report, Cmnd 4596, IX.1 (1971) , 151, 153; Lord Crowther, the head of the 1971 committee, had studied with Keynes and taken over *The Economist* the day before Munich 1938, but, perhaps equally significantly, he was a keen observer of the American economy, married an American and had a (not entirely happy) experience with the property market and hotel groups.   **52.** Unlike in most OECD countries,

British official data is for the gross saving ratio. The net ratio is slightly lower because it deducts the consumption of fixed capital in respect of owner-occupied dwellings, that is, it takes into account the fall in value in homes owned through wear and tear. For credit, see (UK) Department for Business, Innovation & Skills, 'Credit, Debt and Financial Difficulty in Britain, 2009/10' (June 2011), http://www.bis.gov.uk/assets/biscore/consumer-issues/docs/c/11-963-credit-debt-in-britain-2009-10.pdf. Mean housing wealth was £204,500 in 2008, see 'Wealth in Great Britain: Main results, 2006/08'; http://www.bris.ac.uk/geography/research/pfrc/themes/psa/pfrc0914.pdf.   **53.** Franco Modigliani & Richard H. Brumberg, 'Utility Analysis and the Consumption Function: An Interpretation of Cross-section Data', in: *Post-Keynesian Economics*, ed. Kenneth K. Kurihara (New Brunswick, NJ, 1954), 388–436; Andrew B. Abel, ed., *The Collected Papers of Franco Modigliani* (Cambridge, MA, 1980), Vol. II; and Milton Friedman, *A Theory of the Consumption Function* (Princeton, NJ, 1957).   **54.** As Modigliani himself acknowledged in Franco Modigliani, 'Life Cycle, Individual Thrift and the Wealth of Nations', in: *American Economic Review* 76, no. 3, 1986: 297–313.   **55.** A. Börsch-Supan, *Life-cycle Savings and Public Policy: A Cross-national Study of Six Countries* (Amsterdam, 2003); A. Lusardi, 'Information, Expectations, and Savings for Retirement', in: *Behavioral Dimensions of Retirement Economics*, 1999: 81–115; B. D. Bernheim, J. Skinner & S. Weinberg, 'What Accounts for the Variation in Retirement Wealth among US Households?' in: *American Economic Review*, 2001: 832–57. The precautionary motive of saving is ruled out by the certainty equivalence assumption underlying the permanent-income hypothesis rules; see Deaton, *Understanding Consumption*, 177–9.   **56.** Christopher D. Carroll & Lawrence H. Summers, 'Consumption Growth Parallels Income Growth: Some New Evidence', in: *National Saving and Economic Performance*, ed. B. Douglas Bernheim & John B. Shoven (Chicago, 1991), 305–48, esp. 315–18.   **57.** Deaton, *Understanding Consumption*, 163.   **58.** Axel Börsch-Supan et al., 'The German "SAVE" Study' (2009) http://www.mea.uni-mannheim.de/fileadmin/files/polstudies/3aferngyoiaowiys_MEA_Study_6.pdf.   **59.** Everywhere, the rich save more than the poor, but British research for 1970–2007 also found that those who rented a council flat saved significantly more than comparative households who had a mortgage; Thomas Crossley & Cormac O'Dea, *The Wealth and Saving of UK Families on the Eve of the Crisis* (Institute for Fiscal Studies, 2010).   **60.** See Elizabeth Lanyon, chair of the law council of the Australia Financial Services Committee, in Consumers International, 'Living on Credit', in: *Asia Pacific Consumer* 35/36, no. 1/2, 2004: 1–51, 11. The above draws further on Luigi Guiso, Michael Haliassos & Tullio Japelli, eds., *Household Portfolios* (Cambridge, MA, 2002); Elaine Kempson & Claire Whyley, *Kept out or Opted out?: Understanding and Combating Financial Exclusion* (Bristol, 1999). In the United States, the number of households holding mutuals and pension funds as well as direct stocks shot up from 32% to 49% in the 1990s.   **61.** Quoted in Jackie Botterill, *Consumer Culture and Personal Finance: Money Goes to Market* (Basingstoke, 2010), 149.   **62.** For the United

States: R. Peach & C. Steindel, 'A Nation of Spendthrifts? An Analysis of Trends in Personal and Gross Saving', in: *Current Issues in Economics and Finance/ Federal Reserve Bank of New York* 6, no. 10, 2000: 1–6. For Britain: S. Berry, M. Waldron & R. Williams, 'Household Saving', *Bank of England Quarterly Bulletin* Q3, 2009: 191–209. **63.** http://www.bostonfed.org/education/ ledger/ledger04/sprsum/credhistory.pdf. Greenspan's hearing was on 26 January 2000 (S. HRG.106-526), available at: www.fraser.stlouisfed.org.; the computer had reversed names. See further: Robert D. Manning, *Credit Card Nation: The Consequences of America's Addiction to Credit* (New York, 2000); and Richard Berthoud & Elaine Kempson, *Credit and Debt: The PSI Report* (London, 1992). **64.** Hyman, *Debtor Nation*, 150f. **65.** Eurobarometer, *Consumers' Opinions on Services of General Interest, no. 230* (Luxembourg, 2005). **66.** Ronald J. Mann, 'Credit Cards and Debit Cards in the United States and Japan', in: *Vanderbilt Law Review* 55, no. 4, 2002: 1055– 108. Schufa, *Schuldenkompass 2004: Empirische Indikatoren der privaten Ver- und Überschuldung in Deutschland* (Wiesbaden, 2004). **67.** In 2006, Americans owed $801 billion on credit cards and $13 trillion on loans (including mortgages). By 2010, it was $754 billion and $13.4 trillion respectively; OECD.StatExtracts, meta data 'Household assets', http://stats.oecd.org/Index. aspx, data extracted 1 Sept. 2011. **68.** National Bureau of Economic Research, *Pattern of Consumer Debt, 1935–36*, 110. Only the poorest families experienced dissaving. **69.** Hyman, *Debtor Nation*, ch. 7. **70.** I have drawn on the OECD data series for 2000–2010. 'Households' Financial and Non-financial Assets and Liabilities', extracted from http://stats.oecd.org/Index.aspx on 14 Nov. 2011. **71.** Catarina Frade & Cláudia Lopes, 'Overindebtedness and Financial Stress: A Comparative Study in Europe', in: Niemi, Ramsay & Whitford, *Consumer Credit, Debt and Bankruptcy*, 249–71. **72.** The starting point is: Gary S. Becker, 'A Theory of the Allocation of Time', in: *Economic Journal* 75, no. 299, 1965: 493–517. **73.** Helen Jarvis 'Housing to Manage Debt and Family Care in the USA' and Carl Schwartz et al., 'A Survey of Housing Equity Withdrawal and Injection in Australia', both in: *The Blackwell Companion to the Economics of Housing*, Susan J. Smith & Beverley A. Searle (eds.) (Oxford, 2010) chs. 7 & 16. **74.** The term was coined by Colin Crouch, 'What Will Follow the Demise of Privatized Keynesianism?' in: *Political Quarterly* 79, no. 4, 2008: 476–87, though it should be stressed that this was not exclusively an Anglo-Saxon phenomenon. **75.** C. Kerdrain, 'How Important is Wealth for Explaining Household Consumption over the Recent Crisis?', OECD Economics Department Working Papers, no. 869, 2011. **76.** *The Economist*, 18 Sept. 2010, 86. **77.** Sharon Parkinson et al., 'Mortgage Equity Withdrawal in Australia and Britain: Towards a Wealth-fare State?' in: *European Journal of Housing Policy* 9, no. 4, 2009: 365–89; Jarvis, 'Housing to Manage Debt in the USA'; and Schwartz et al., 'Equity Withdrawal in Australia', in: *Blackwell Companion to the Economics of Housing*, chs. 7 & 16. **78.** 'Changes in US Family Finances from 2004 to 2007: Evidence from the Survey of Consumer Finances', *Federal Reserve Bulletin*, Feb. 2009, A 46, table 15. **79.** In the early

1960s, those aged 65 and over made up 11% of household consumption and 14% of the population. By 1988, they accounted for 18% of consumption and 16% of the population. Jagadeesh Gokhale et al., 'Understanding the Post-war Decline in US Saving: A Cohort Analysis', *Brookings Papers on Economic Activity*, 1996, no. 1, 1996: 315–407.   **80.** (UK) Department for Business, Innovation & Skills, 'Credit, Debt and Financial Difficulty in Britain, 2009/10'.   **81.** Elaine Kempson, *Over-indebtedness in Britain: A Report to the Department of Trade and Industry* (London, 2002), 43, 48.   **82.** 'Changes in US Family Finances from 2004 to 2007', A9–10.   **83.** Börsch-Supan et al., 'The German "SAVE" study'.   **84.** Kempson, *Over-indebtedness in Britain*, 19; for white vans, see Scott, 'The Twilight World of Inter-war British Hire Purchase'; and O'Connell, *Working-class Debt*.   **85.** Birgitta Klingander, Jean Lown & Sue McGregor, 'Comparative Analysis of Canadian, American and Swedish Bankruptcy Policy: Why do Governments Legislate Consumer Debt?' *International Journal of Consumer Studies* 25, no. 3, 2001: 208–27.   **86.** Udo Reifner et al., *Consumer Over-indebtedness and Consumer Law in the European Union: Final Report Presented to the Commission of the European Communities, Health and Consumer Protection Directorate-General* (2003); and I. Ramsay, 'Comparative Consumer Bankruptcy', in: *University of Illinois Law Review* 241, 2007: 241–73.   **87.** Udo Reifner & Helga Springeneer, 'Die private Überschuldung im internationalen Vergleich – Trends, Probleme, Lösungsansätze,' in: *Schuldenkompass 2004*, 174.   **88.** Reifner et al., *Consumer Over-indebtedness in the European Union*; Oliver J. Haas, 'Over-indebtedness in Germany', International Labour Office, Working Paper no. 44 (2006); Elaine Kempson & Claire Whyley, *Kept Out or Opted Out?: Understanding and Combating Financial Exclusion* (Bristol, 1999); Nicola Jentzsch & Amparo San José Riestra, 'Consumer Credit Markets in the United States and Europe', in: Bertola, Disney & Grant, eds., *The Economics of Consumer Credit*, 34–9; and A. Raijas, A. R. Lehtinen & J. Leskinen, 'Over-indebtedness in the Finnish Consumer Society', in: *Journal of Consumer Policy* 33, no. 3: 209–23.   **89.** Gregory D. Squires, 'Inequality and Access to Financial Services', in: Niemi, Ramsay & Whitford, *Consumer Credit, Debt and Bankruptcy*, 11–30; and Angela C. Lyons, 'How Credit Access Has Changed over Time for US Households', in: *Journal of Consumer Affairs* 37, no. 2, 2003: 231–55.   **90.** Kempson & Whyley, *Kept Out or Opted Out?*, quoted at p. 42.   **91.** See Will Dobbie and Jae Song, 'Debt Relief and Debtor Outcomes: Measuring the Effects of Consumer Bankruptcy Protection', in: *American Economic Review*, Vol. 105(3) (2015), 1272–311.   **92.** Jason J. Kilborn, 'The Innovative German Approach to Consumer Debt Relief', in: *North-western Journal of International Law & Business*; 24, no. 2, 2004: 257–97.   **93.** Reifner & Springeneer, 'Private Überschuldung im internationalen Vergleich'; and Ramsay, 'Comparative Consumer Bankruptcy'.   **94.** James D. Davies, 'Wealth and Economic Inequality', in: Wiemer Salverda, Brian Nolan & Timothy M. Smeeding, eds., *The Oxford Handbook of Economic Inequality* (Oxford, 2009), ch. 6. And see now at length: Thomas Piketty, *Capital in the*

Twenty-first Century (Cambridge, MA, 2014). In this section, I am focusing on income inequality (not wealth), because earned income, rather than inherited country houses, became the main marker in the twentieth century. Piketty focuses on capital's share of income (such as dividends and capital gains) and argues that we are seeing a return to a widening gulf between capital and labour that scarred the nineteenth century. But the inequality that has come since the 1970s is not primarily between capital's and labour's share of income, it is within labour between CEOs on high salaries and low-earning manual and clerical labour. **95.** Richard G. Wilkinson & Kate Pickett, *The Spirit Level: Why Equality is Better for Everyone* (London, rev. edn, 2009). OECD, 'Divided We Stand: Why Inequality Keeps Rising' (OECD: 2011). It is a matter of debate whether 'stress' and 'depression' have actually increased since the 1950s or whether rising numbers reflect a rise in diagnostic tests and categories. **96.** Frank, *Luxury Fever: Money and Happiness in an Era of Excess.* See also the books on affluenza in note 1. **97.** Robert Frank, *Richistan: A Journey through the 21st-century Wealth Boom and the Lives of the New Rich* (London, 2008), 3, 122. **98.** Erich Fromm, *To Have or to Be?* (New York, 1976) is a source of inspiration for Oliver James, *The Selfish Capitalist: Origins of Affluenza* (London, 2008), esp. 46–54; James, *Affluenza*, esp. 65–7. **99.** Jean-Jacques Rousseau, A *Discourse on the Origin of Inequality*, ed. G. D. H. Cole (Chicago, 1952), 362. **100.** On Vevo, according to Universal Music, http://universalmusica.com/donomar/. In cases where the lifestyle of millionaires reaches broader audiences, it has had to ape celebrity culture, as in reality shows such as *Made in Chelsea* (UK) or *Mulheres Ricas* (Brazil). **101.** C. Wright Mills, *The Power Elite* (New York City, 1956), 75. See further: F. Trentmann, 'Past and Present: Historical Perspectives on Inequality and Collective Provision in Modern Consumption', in: Southerton & Ulph, eds., *Sustainable Consumption*, 243–76. **102.** David Riesman with Howard Roseborough, 'Careers and Consumer Behaviour' (1955), repr. in Riesman, *Abundance for What? And Other Essays*, quoted at 122. According to US census data, the average floor area of a new American home was 2,324 square feet in 2001 and 2,392 sq ft in 2010: http://www.census.gov/const/C25Ann/sftotalmedavgsqft.pdf. It is debatable whether the size of homes illustrates inequality and status seeking; in the United Kingdom, new-built homes have shrunk in the late twentieth century. **103.** For a measured critique of top–down views of social distinction, see Daloz, *The Sociology of Elite Distinction.* **104.** Alexis de Tocqueville, *Democracy in America* (New York, 1840/1994), Vol. II, ch. 13, 138. **105.** Euromonitor International, 'Global Luxury Goods Overview', June 2011; http://www.wisekey.com/en/Press/2011/Documents/Euromonitor_Report_for_FT_Business_of_Luxury_Summit_2011.pdf. **106.** Y. Ait-Sahalia, J. A. Parker & M. Yogo, 'Luxury Goods and the Equity Premium', *Journal of Finance* 59, no. 6, 2004: 2959–3004. **107.** 'Falso di moda', symposium at Palazzo Medici Riccardi, Florence, 30 Nov. 2007. **108.** Pamela N. Danziger, *Let Them Eat Cake: Marketing Luxury to the Masses – As Well as the Classes* (Chicago, 2005). **109.** Offer, *Challenge of Affluence.* The decline of self-control is case specific and should not be overstated. It is best documented for obesity. Other types of excessive consumption have their own trajectories. Americans, for example, drank more in the 1860s than in the 1980s, at least outside university fraternities. In Western Europe, serious drug use has declined in the last decade.

CHAPTER 10

1. The deck chairs were in Rorschach on the Swiss side of Lake Constance; http://www.zeitverein.com/framesets/fs_zeitverein.html. See further: Carl Honoré, *In Praise of Slowness: Challenging the Cult of Speed* (New York, 2004), esp. 37–9; Fritz Reheis, *Die Kreativität der Langsamkeit* (Darmstadt, 1998); James Gleick, *Faster: The Acceleration of Just about Everything* (London, 1999); Stefan Klein, *The Secret Pulse of Time: Making Sense of Life's Scarcest Commodity* (Cambridge, MA, 2007). 2. R. N. Levine, *A Geography of Time: On Tempo, Culture and the Pace of Life* (New York, 2008), 131f. 3. Benjamin, *The Arcades Project*, 106. 4. Kern, *The Culture of Time and Space, 1880–1918*. 5. http://www.cittaslow.org/section/association; Wendy Parkins & Geoffrey Craig, *Slow Living* (Oxford, 2006). 6. Slow Food Manifesto: http://www.slowfood.com/international/2/our-philosophy. Carlo Petrini, *Slow Food: Le ragioni del gusto* (Rome, 2001); compare: R. Sassatelli & F. Davolio, 'Consumption, Pleasure and Politics', in: *Journal of Consumer Culture* 10, no. 2: 202–32; and Richard Wilk, ed., *Fast Food/Slow Food: The Cultural Economy of the Global Food System* (Lanham, 2006); http://longplayer.org/what/whatelse/slowwalk.php. 7. 'Schopenhauer als Erzieher' (1874) in: *Complete Works of Friedrich Nietzsche* (London: 1909), transl. Adrian Collins, Vol. V, Part II, para. 4, 136. 8. Alexis de Tocqueville, *Democracy in America* (New York, 1840/1994), Book 2, ch. 13, 136. 9. See Hartmut Rosa, *Beschleunigung: Die Veränderung der Zeitstrukturen in der Moderne* (Frankfurt am Main, 2005), 126. 10. Rosa, *Beschleunigung*; Reinhart Koselleck, *Zeitschichten* (Frankfurt, 2000) and *Futures Past: On the Semantics of Historical Time* (New York, 2004). 11. The first answer was most forcefully put by Staffan Burenstam Linder, *The Harried Leisure Class* (New York, 1970), the second by Juliet B. Schor, *The Overworked American: The Unexpected Decline of Leisure* (New York, 1991). I discuss both below. 12. J. H. Ausubel & A. Grübler, 'Working Less and Living Longer: Long-term Trends in Working Time and Time Budgets', in: *Technological Forecasting and Social Change* 50, no. 3, 1995: 195–213. 13. Angus Maddison, *Monitoring the World Economy, 1820–1992* (Paris, 1995), Appendix J; Angus Maddison, *Phases of Capitalist Development* (Oxford, 1982); Schor, *Overworked American*; P. Robinson & G. Godbey, *Time for Life: The Surprising Ways Americans Use Their Time* (University Park, PA, 1997), quoted at 196. 14. E.g., see the Dutch data in Koen Breedveld et al., *De Tijd Als Spiegel: Hoe Nederlanders Hun Tijd Besteden (Time as a Mirror: How the Dutch Spend Their Time)* (The Hague, 2006); Klein, *Secret Pulse of Time*, ch. 8. There is some evidence that in the United

States the sense of rush may have slowed in the early 1990s; see Robinson & Godbey, *Time for Life*, 231–9. **15.** '*Tanto brevius omne quanto felicius tempus*', Pliny the Younger, *Epistles*, Book VIII, letter 14. **16.** V. Ramey & N. Francis, 'A Century of Work and Leisure', in: *American Economic Journal: Macroeconomics* 1, no. 2, 2009: 189–224. **17.** The thesis of Gary Cross, *Time and Money: The Making of Consumer Culture* (London, 1993). **18.** See 250–9 above. **19.** Jan De Vries, *The Industrious Revolution: Consumer Behaviour and the Household Economy, 1650 to the Present* (Cambridge, 2008), ch. 6. The lack of attention to childcare and emotions more generally is striking. Many scholars erroneously presume that modern consumer culture must have meant the end of home production and provisioning. A useful corrective is V. A. Ramey, 'Time Spent in Home Production in the Twentieth-century United States: New Estimates from Old Data', in: *Journal of Economic History* 69, no. 01, 2009: 1–47. **20.** To give a sense of comparison, the figures for France are 30% and 32% respectively. Joseph E. Stiglitz, Amartya Sen & Jean-Paul Fitoussi, 'Report by the Commission on the Measurement of Economic Performance and Social Progress, www.stiglitz-sen-fitoussi.fr' (2009), 130. **21.** Gershuny, *Changing Times*, ch. 5. **22.** A. Heckscher & S. de Grazia, 'Executive Leisure', in *Harvard Business Review* 37, no. 4, 1959: 6–12; Robinson & Godbey, *Time for Life*, 128f. See also: Mark Aguiar & Erik Hurst, 'Measuring Trends in Leisure: The Allocation of Time over Five Decades', Working Paper no. 06-2: Federal Reserve Bank of Boston, 2006; although their numbers for leisure are inflated by treating childcare as leisure (rather than as unpaid work). **23.** For this and other reasons why Keynes was wrong, see Lorenzo Pecchi & Gustavo Piga, eds., *Revisiting Keynes: Economic Possibilities for Our Grandchildren* (Cambridge, MA, 2008). **24.** 'An Apology for Idlers', in: *Cornhill Magazine*, 36 (July 1877), repr. in *The Novels and Tales of Robert Louis Stevenson* (1895 edn), 73; emphasis in original. **25.** This applies to Thorstein Veblen as well, whose theory of the idle rich ignored the hard-working Rockefellers and more thrifty members of the elite. For a more balanced picture, see Frederic Cople Jaher, 'The Gilded Elite, American Multimillionaires, 1865 to the Present', in: *Wealth and the Wealthy in the Modern World*, ed. W. D. Rubinstein (London, 1980), 189–276. **26.** Alain Chenu & Nicolas Herpin, 'Une pause dans la marche vers la civilisation des loisirs?' *Economie et statistique* (2002), 352–3. **27.** USB, 'Income and Leisure: Two Differently Valued Elements of Prosperity' in the 2006 edition of *Prices and Earnings*, 36–8. Echoes in Niall Ferguson, *Civilisation: The Rest and the West* (London, 2011), 265f., who treats paid work in isolation. **28.** http://www.oecdobserver.org/news/fullstory.php/aid/2480/Counting_the_hours.html. **29.** David Riesman with Warner Bloomberg, 'Work and Leisure: Fusion or Polarity?' (1957), repr. in Riesman, *Abundance for What?*, 147. **30.** Marshall David Sahlins, *Stone Age Economics* (Chicago, 1972). **31.** D. L. Costa, 'The Evolution of Retirement: Summary of a Research Project', in: *The American Economic Review* 88, no. 2, 1998: 232–6, 234. **32.** Dominik Hanglberger, 'Arbeitszufriedenheit und flexible Arbeitszeiten: Empirische Analyse mit Daten des sozio-oekonomischen Panels', SOEP paper no. 304,

2010. **33.** Breedveld et al., *Tijd Als Spiegel*. **34.** For comparative data on the Netherlands, Norway, Finland, Hungary, Finland and the United Kingdom, see Gershuny, *Changing Times*, ch. 5. **35.** See M. Burda, D. Hamermesh & P. Weil, 'The Distribution of Total Work in the EU and US', in *Institute for the Study of Labor (IZA)*, no. 2270, 2006. **36.** Siebter Familienbericht: *Familie zwischen Flexibilität und Verlässlichkeit – Perspektiven für eine lebenslaufbezogene Familienpolitik*, Deutscher Bundestag. 16. Wahlperiode. Drucksache 16/1360 (26.04. 2006), 223; Jonathan Gershuny, 'Busyness as the Badge of Honor for the New Superordinate Working Class', in: *Social Research* 72, no. 2, 2005: 287–314; and Chartered Management Institute, reported in the *Guardian*, 15 June 2006. **37.** Robert E. Goodin et al., *Discretionary Time: A New Measure of Freedom* (Cambridge, 2008). **38.** According to the US Panel Study of Income Dynamics, 9% of all employees were downshifters who opted for lower earnings at some stage during the period 1983 to 1992; R. E. Dwyer, 'Downward Earnings Mobility after Voluntary Employer Exits', in: *Work and Occupations* 31, no. 1, 2004: 111–39. **39.** Daniel Kahneman, Ed Diener & Norbert Schwarz, eds., *Well-Being: The Foundations of Hedonic Psychology* (New York, 1999); Richard Layard, *Happiness: Lessons from a New Science* (New York, 2005); and Luigino Bruni & Pier Luigi Porta, eds., *Economics and Happiness: Framing the Analysis* (New York, 2006). Of course, happiness extends beyond behavioural economics: for other approaches see: Dieter Thomä, Christoph Henning & Olivia Mitscherlich-Schönherr, eds., *Glück: Ein interdisziplinäres Handbuch* (Stuttgart, 2011). **40.** Richard Easterlin, 'Does Economic Growth Improve the Human Lot? Some Empirical Evidence', in: *Nations and Households in Economic Growth: Essays in Honor of Moses Abramovitz*, eds. Paul A. David & Melvin W. Reder (New York, 1974), 89–125. **41.** Compare M. R. Hagerty & R. Veenhoven, 'Wealth and Happiness Revisited: Growing National Income Does Go with Greater Happiness', in: *Social Indicators Research* 64, no. 1, 2003: 1–27; R. A. Easterlin, 'Feeding the Illusion of Growth and Happiness: A Reply to Hagerty and Veenhoven', in: *Social Indicators Research* 74, no. 3, 2005: 429–43; R. Veenhoven & M. Hagerty, 'Rising Happiness in Nations, 1946–2004: A reply to Easterlin', in: *Social Indicators Research* 79, no. 3, 2006: 421–36; and Betsey Stevenson & Justin Wolfers, 'Subjective Well-being and Income: Is There Any Evidence of Satiation?' in: *American Economic Review* 103, no. 3, 2013: 598–604. **42.** A. B. Krueger et al., 'Time Use and Subjective Well-being in France and the US', in: *Social Indicators Research* 93, no. 1, 2009: 7–18. They discuss their method at greater length in 'National Time Accounting: The Currency of Life', Working Paper no. 523 (April 2008), Industrial Relations Section, Princeton University, http://www.krueger.princeton.edu/data/ATUS/523alan.pdf. **43.** And this is in the upper quintile of the U-index distribution. The difference shrinks in the fourth quintile and virtually disappear in the third; see Krueger et al, 'Time Use', fig. 1, 12. **44.** Tibor Scitovsky, *The Joyless Economy: The Psychology of Human Satisfaction* (New York, 1976). **45.** Ida Craven, 'Leisure', in: *Encyclopaedia of the Social Sciences* (New York, 1933; repr. 1949), IX–X, 402–6;

Sebastian de Grazia, *Of Time, Work and Leisure* (New York, 1962); and Bailey, *Leisure and Class in Victorian England*. For collective and company leisure, see chapter 12 below. **46.** Harry Elmer Barnes, *The American Way of Life: Our Institutional Patterns and Social Problems* (New York, 1942), 525. **47.** J. I. Gershuny & K. Fisher, 'Leisure in the UK across the 20th Century', Institute for Social and Economic Research Working Paper, no. 99-03, 1999. **48.** Stiglitz, Sen & Fitoussi, 'Measurement of Economic Performance and Social Progress', 126f. **49.** Lydia Lueb, *Die Freizeit der Textilarbeiterinnen* (Münster, 1927), tables 8, 10, 19, 22, 30, quoted at Part II, para. 11. **50.** Eurostat, *How Europeans Spend Their Time: Everyday Life of Women and Men: Data 1998–2002* (Luxembourg, 2004). **51.** Olivier Donnat, *Les Pratiques Culturelles des Français: Enquête 1997* (Paris, 1998), 45. Jonathan Gershuny, 'What Do We Do in Post-industrial Society? The Nature of Work and Leisure Time in the 21st Century', Working Paper no. 2005-7: Institute for Social and Economic Research, 2005), table 1; Jukka Gronow & Dale Southerton, 'Leisure and Consumption in Europe', in: *Handbook of European Societies*, eds. Göran Therborn & Stefan Immerfall (New York, 2010), 355–84. **52.** With a slight delay in Nordic countries, http://tilastokeskus.fi/til/akay/2009/05/akay_2009_05_2011-12-15_tie_001_en.html. See also: Statistisches Bundesamt, *Alltag in Deutschland* (2004). **53.** 35 minutes a day in the United Kingdom (compared to 24 minutes to get to work or study), 34 minutes each in Germany and Norway (*vs* 21 and 24 minutes for work). Only Hungarians spend four more minutes for travelling to work than for free-time purposes. Of course, not all travel is by car or motorbike, but two thirds is in Western Europe, and for men it is slightly higher. Eurostat, *How Europeans Spend Their Time*, tables 8.6–8.8, 116–21. For coordination, see further: Dale Southerton, ' "Squeezing Time": Allocating Practices, Coordinating Networks and Scheduling Society', *Time and Society* 12, no. 1, 2003: 5–25; and Dale Southerton, 'Re-ordering Temporal Rhythms', in: Shove, Trentmann & Wilk, eds., *Time, Consumption, and Everyday Life*, ch. 3. **54.** J. P. Robinson & S. Martin, 'Changes in American Daily Life: 1965–2005', *Social Indicators Research* 93, no. 1, 2009: 47–56, fig. 2. **55.** Linder, *The Harried Leisure Class*, 1–3, 78. **56.** Olivier Donnat, 'Les Pratiques Culturelles des Français à l'ère numérique: Éléments de synthèse 1997–2008', in: *Culture études*, 2009-5, 7. The number-one readers in Europe in 2000 were Finnish women, who read 47 minutes a day; French women read for only 23 minutes: Eurostat, *How Europeans Spend Their Time*, 92. **57.** Quoted in Gerald Straka, Thomas Fabian & Joerg Will, *Medien im Alltag älterer Menschen* (Düsseldorf, 1989), 164. **58.** Dutch researchers have found a shift from time-intensive to commodity-intensive leisure, but their actual data is more ambiguous and interesting than this. The time for social contacts declined by over three hours between 1975 and 2005. Sport, on the other hand, increased by over an hour, in spite of Dutch adults spending four hours more on paid and unpaid work: Breedveld et al., *Tijd Als Spiegel*, 52f. For the United States, see Robinson & Godbey, *Time for Life*, 268f. For Britain: J. Gershuny & K. Fisher, 'Leisure', in: *Twentieth-century British Social Trends*, eds. A. H. Halsey & J. Webb (Basingstoke, 2000), ch. 18. For Germany, compare the data for 1972 in Kaspar Maase, *Lebensweise der Lohnarbeiter in der Freizeit* (Frankfurt am Main, 1984), 76, with Eurostat, *How Europeans Spend Their Time*, 84-7. For mealtimes: Siebter Familienbericht, *Familie zwischen Flexibilität und Verlässlichkeit*, 212; and Cheng, Olsen, Southerton & Warde, 'The Changing Practice of Eating'. **59.** Vera Mendel & Francis Meynell, *The Week-end Book* (London, 1931), xiv, xv, 267, 441, 452, emphasis in original. **60.** Francis Meynell, *The Week-end Book* (London, 1955), 468-70. **61.** Francis Meynell, *The Week-end Book* (London, 2006). **62.** John P. Robinson & Geoffrey C. Godbey, 'United States of America: Time-use and Cultural Activities', in: G. Cushman, A. J. Veal & J. Zuzanek, *Free Time and Leisure Participation: International Perspectives* (Wallingford, 2005), 277. **63.** Donnat, 'Les Pratiques Culturelles des Français à l'ère numérique', 10: http://www.pratiques-culturelles.culture.gouv.fr/doc/evolution73-08/T7-PRATIQUES-MUSICALES-EN-AMATEUR.pdfhttp://www.pratiquesculturelles.culture.gouv.fr/doc/evolution73-08/T8-PRATIQUES-ARTISTIQUES.pdf. **64.** At the time of the 1959 Rome Olympics, one in thirty Italians practised some sport. In 2005, it was one in three. ISTAT, 'Lo sport che cambia', *Argomenti* 29, 2005, 17-19. In France, 33% visited museums and exhibitions at least once a year in 1973. In 2008 it was 37%: http://www.pratiquesculturelles.culture.gouv.fr/doc/evolution73-08/T17-FREQUENTATION-MUSEE-EXPOSITION.pdf. For New Zealand, see the chapter by Sue Walker, Mary Donn & Allan Laidler, in: Cushman, Veal & Zuzanek, *Free Time and Leisure Participation*, ch. 12; for American trends, see W. B. Beyers, 'Cultural and Recreational Industries in the United States', in: *Service Industries Journal* 28, no. 3, 2008: 375-91. **65.** Bohdan Jung, 'Poland', in: Cushman, Veal & Zuzanek, *Free Time and Leisure Participation*, ch. 13. **66.** Mihaly Csikszentmihalyi & Eugene Rochberg-Halton, *The Meaning of Things: Domestic Symbols and the Self* (Cambridge, 1981); and Miller, *The Comfort of Things*. **67.** See above, 231-3. **68.** Elizabeth Shove et al., *The Design of Everyday Life* (Oxford, 2007). See also: Alan Warde, 'Consumption and Theories of Practice', in: *Journal of Consumer Culture* 5, no. 2, 2005: 131-53. **69.** See above, 264-6. **70.** M. Bianchi, ed., *The Active Consumer: Novelty and Surprise in Consumer Choice* (London, 1998); and M. Bianchi, 'Time and Preferences in Cultural Consumption', in: *Value and Valuation in Art and Culture*, eds. M. Hutter & D. Throsby (Cambridge, 2007). **71.** M. Bittman, J. E. Brown & J. Wajcman, 'The mobile phone, perpetual contact and time pressure', *Work, Employment & Society* 23, no. 4, 2009: 673-691; the authors acknowledge that mobile communication may have intensified pressures at work. See also: J. Wajcman et al., 'Enacting Virtual Connections between Work and Home', in: *Journal of Sociology* 46, no. 3, 2010: 257-75; and Nelly Oudshoorn & Trevor Pinch, eds., *How Users Matter: The Co-construction of Users and Technology* (Cambridge, MA, 2003). **72.** Leopoldina Fortunati & Sakari Taipale, 'The Advanced Use of Mobile Phones in Five European Countries', in: *British Journal of Sociology* 65, no. 2, 2014: 317-37. **73.** Emily Rose, 'Access Denied: Employee Control of Personal

Communications at Work', in: *Work, Employment and Society* 27, no. 4, 2013: 694–710. **74.** 10% of online gaming in the United States takes place at work, according to research undertaken in 2006; D. Deal, 'Time for play – An Exploratory Analysis of the Changing Consumption Contexts of Digital Games', in: *Electronic International Journal of Time-use Research* 5, no. 1, 2008. **75.** Olivier Donnat, *Les Pratiques Culturelles des Français à l'ère numérique: Enquête 2008* (Paris, 2009), 193–7. **76.** See Photokina 2012, *Trends in the Photo and Imaging Market*, http://www.prophoto-online.de/img/ftp/broschueren/Trends-in-the-photo-and-imaging-market-photokina-2012.pdf; see also: http://mashable.com/2012/11/17/photography/. **77.** C. Wingerter, 'Time Spent by the Population in Germany on Cultural Activities', *Wirtschaft und Statistik*, no. 4, 2005: 318–26. **78.** 16% and 7% respectively, see http://www.pratiquescul-turelles.culture.gouv.fr/doc/evolution73-08/T7-PRATIQUES-MUSICALES-EN-AMATEUR.pdf. We can only note here that, in contrast to their growing attendance of theatre and popular music, French workers have fled symphony halls in the last quarter-century; see http://www.pratiquesculturelles.culture.gouv.fr/doc/evolution73-08/T15-FREQUENTATION-CONCERT-R%20J.pdf. For the United States, see Steven Brint & Kristopher Proctor, 'Middle-class Respectability in 21st-century America: Work and Lifestyle in the Professional–Managerial Stratum', in: *Thrift and Thriving in America: Capitalism and Moral Order from the Puritans to the Present*, eds. Joshua Yates & James Davison Hunter (Oxford, 2011), ch. 19. **79.** R. Nave-Herz & B. Nauck, *Familie und Freizeit* (Munich, 1978), tables 24 and 28. **80.** Sue Walker, Mary Donn & Allan Laidler, 'New Zealand', in: Cushman, Veal & Zuzanek, *Free Time and Leisure Participation*, 183f. **81.** Statistics New Zealand, '2002 Cultural Experiences Survey', in: *Key Statistics*, Oct. 2003, 9–11. **82.** Georgios Papastefanou & Ewa Jarosz, 'Complexity of Leisure Activities over the Weekend: Socio-economic Status Differentiation and Effects on Satisfaction with Personal Leisure', GESIS Working Paper 2012-26. Cologne, Germany: GESIS – Leibniz-Institut für Sozialwissenschaften, (2012). **83.** Donnat, *Pratiques Culturelles des Français: Enquête 1997*, 101–3. **84.** Chenu & Herpin, 'Une pause dans la marche vers la civilisation des loisirs?', 35; the official 1997 inquiry gives even higher viewing times for those without diploma or Bac: Donnat, *Pratiques Culturelles des Français: Enquête 1997*, 77. **85.** This is a bold generalization, but not without some empirical support. In France, those spending less than 14 hours a week watching television go twice as often to the theatre, cinema and museum as those who watch 30 hours or more. Some of that might be explained by old age but not all of it – the elderly watch most television and experience a decline in cultural participation. Donnat, *Pratiques Culturelles des Français: Enquête 1997*, 73–5. For higher activity levels among British managers, see A. Warde & T. Bennett, 'A Culture in Common: The Cultural Consumption of the UK Managerial Elite', in: *Sociological Review* 56, 2008: 240–59. **86.** Only 5–25% of skilled workers had ever frequented any of these venues; Donnat, *Pratiques Culturelles des Français: Enquête 1997*, 251. Similarly, in sport, there are sharp divides in the level of participation and its intensity: two in three German children play no sport at all, whereas one third play over two hours a day; Statistisches Bundesamt, *Alltag in Deutschland*, 171   **87.** A study of twenty households in Bristol found that those with higher education also pursued more irregular activities: Dale Southerton, 'Analysing the Temporal Organization of Daily Life: Social Constraints, Practices and their Allocation', in: *Sociology* 40, no. 3, 2006: 435–54.   **88.** Michael Bittman & Judy Wajcman, 'The Rush Hour: The Character of Leisure Time and Gender Equity', in: *Social Forces* 79, no. 1, 2000: 165–95.   **89.** Statistisches Bundesamt, *Alltag in Deutschland*, 110.   **90.** Nicky Le Feuvre, 'Leisure, Work and Gender: A Sociological Study of Women's Time in France', in: *Time & Society* 3, no. 2, 1994: 151–78, quoted at 171, 173.   **91.** International Institute of Not Doing Much, http://slowdownnow.org/.   **92.** Reinhard Rudat, *Freizeitmögli-chkeiten von Nacht-, Schicht-, Sonn- und Feiertagsarbeitern* (Stuttgart, 1978); and *Voluntary Simplicity: Toward a Way of Life that is Outwardly Simple, Inwardly Rich*, Duane Elgin (ed.) (Fort Mill, SC, 1993).   **93.** Jean Viard, *Le Sacre du temps libre: La Société des 35 heures* (La Tour d'Aigues, 2004), esp. 148–55.   **94.** Manuel Castells, *The Rise of the Network Society* (Oxford, 2000, 2nd edn) Vol. I, ch. 7.   **95.** 'Habit' (1892), repr. in Robert Richardson, ed., *The Heart of William James* (Cambridge, MA, 2010), 110.   **96.** Orvar Löfgren, 'Excessive Living', *Culture and Organization* 2007, no. 13, 2007: 131–43, 136.   **97.** Martin, *Leisure and Society in Colonial Brazzaville*.   **98.** Brigitte Steger & Lodewijk Brunt, 'Introduction: Into the Night and the World of Sleep', in: *Night-time and Sleep in Asia and the West*, Brigitte Steger & Lodewijk Brunt (eds.) (London, 2003), 1–23.   **99.** China National Bureau of Statistics, 'Summary on 2008 Time-use Survey, transl. Henry Lee for the Australian Time-use Research Group', 2008. On average, Chinese sleep over an hour longer than Japanese, and a day and forty minutes longer than Britons. The data also suggests they spend less time on social interaction. Only around 10% of Greeks, Italians and French take a midday nap; in Northern Europe, the number is even smaller; see HETUS: https://www.h2.scb.se/tus/tus/AreaGraphCID.html; Wilse B. Webb & David F. Dinges, 'Cultural Perspectives on Napping and the Siesta', in: *Sleep and Alertness: Chronobiological, Behavioral and Medical Aspects of Napping*, eds. David F. Dinges & Roger J. Broughton, (New York, 1989), 247–265.   **100.** Murasaki Shikibu, *The Tale of Genji* (Penguin, 2003 edn), 443, 446.   **101.** S. Linhart, 'From Industrial to Post-industrial Society: Changes in Japanese Leisure-related Values and Behavior', *Journal of Japanese Studies* 14, no. 2, 1988: 271–307.   **102.** *The Economist*, 27 Sept. 2014, 68.   **103.** Sepp Linhart & Sabine Frühstück, eds., *The Culture of Japan as Seen through Its Leisure* (Albany, 1998); and Joy Hendry & Massimo Raveri, *Japan at Play: The Ludic and the Logic of Power* (London, 2002).   **104.** Levine, *A Geography of Time*, 145; Robinson & Godbey, *Time for Life*, 268.   **105.** Americans are not alone. In Scandinavian countries, eating is similarly spread across the day; see the HETUS graphs 'how time is used during the day': https://www.h2.scb.se/tus/tus/AreaGraphCID.html. To the best of my knowledge, there is, unfortunately, no comparative research to test the relationship between snacking cultures and harriedness. **106.** Mass Observation, *Meet Yourself on Sunday* (London, 1949), 9f. **107.** See the fascinating study by Eviatar Zerubavel, *The Seven-day Circle: The History and Meaning of the Week* (Chicago, 1985). **108.** Mass Observation, *Meet Yourself on Sunday*, quoted at 22, 57. **109.** 1857, quoted in Rosemary Bromley & Robert J. Bromley, 'The Debate on Sunday Markets in Nineteenth-century Ecuador', in: *Journal of Latin American Studies* 7, no. 1, 1975: 85–108, at 98. **110.** John Wigley, *The Rise and Fall of the Victorian Sunday* (Manchester, 1980); and Brian Harrison, 'The Sunday Trading Riots of 1855', in: *Historical Journal* 8, 1965: 219–45. **111.** J. A. Kay et al., *The Regulation of Retail Trading Hours* (London, 1984); Douglas A. Reid, ' "Mass Leisure" in Britain', in: *Twentieth-century Mass Society in Britain and the Netherlands*, eds. Bob Moore & Hen van Nierop (Oxford, 2006), 132–59. Uwe Spiekermann, 'Freier Konsum und soziale Verantwortung zur Geschichte des Ladenschlusses in Deutschland im 19. und 20. Jahrhundert', in: *Zeitschrift für Unternehmensgeschichte* 49, no. 1, 2004: 26–44. **112.** The above takes into account the Finnish law of 2009 which extended the 1994 liberalization; *Helsingin Sanomat*, 19 Nov. 2009. The Scottish situation has been under review. http://www.scotlandoffice.gov.uk/scotlandoffice/10245.html. For an extensive overview of the situation in 2006, see John Hargreaves et al., 'The Economic Costs and Benefits of Easing Sunday Shopping Restrictions on Large Stores in England and Wales: A Report for the Department of Trade and Industry' (May 2006). **113.** David N. Laband & Deborah Hendry Heinbuch, *Blue Laws: The History, Economics and Politics of Sunday-closing Laws* (Lexington, MA, 1987); and M. Skuterud, 'The Impact of Sunday Shopping on Employment and Hours of Work in the Retail Industry: Evidence from Canada', in: *European Economic Review* 49, no. 8, 2005: 1953–78. **114.** P. Richter, 'Seven Days' Trading Make One Weak? The Sunday Trading Issue as an Index of Secularization', in: *British Journal of Sociology*, 1994: 333–48. **115.** 22 Jan. 1993, Michael Stern, House of Commons, col. 638, http://www.publications.parliament.uk/pa/cm199293/cmhansrd/1993-01-22/Debate-3.html. **116.** R. Halsall, '*Ladenschluss* revisited: Will Germany Learn to Love Shopping on a Sunday?' in: *Debatte* 9, no. 2, 2001: 188–209, quoted at 202. **117.** In 1994, the female employment rate was 68% in Sweden, 61% in the United Kingdom and 59% in Finland, compared to 35% in Italy, 51% in France and 55% in Germany. See table 5.2 in http://epp.eurostat.ec.europa.eu/portal/page/portal/employment_unemployment_lfs/data/main_tables. See further: Imelda Maher, 'The New Sunday: Reregulating Sunday Trading', in: *Modern Law Review* 58, no. 1, 1995: 72–86; and J. Price & B. Yandle, 'Labor markets and Sunday Closing Laws', in: *Journal of Labor Research* 8, no. 4, 1987: 407–14. The Spanish story is distinctive: here, early relaxation came on the heels of major tourist and commercial development after Franco. **118.** N. Wrigley, C. Guy & R. Dunn, 'Sunday and Late-night Shopping in a British City: Evidence from the Cardiff Consumer Panel', *Area* 16, no. 3, 1984: 236–40. **119.** Hargreaves et al., 'Costs and Benefits of Easing Sunday Shopping Restrictions'. **120.** J. P. Jacobsen & P. Kooreman, 'Timing Constraints and the

Allocation of Time: The Effects of Changing Shopping Hours Regulations in the Netherlands', in: *European Economic Review* 49, no. 1, 2005: 9–27. In Britain, the rate of lone parents in employment shot up from 42% to 56% in the decade after Sunday opening. 10% of Sunday workers work in retailing. **121.** Mass Observation, *Meet Yourself on Sunday* (London, 1949), 57. **122.** Eurostat news release, 147/2013, 15 Oct. 2013; Price Waterhouse Cooper, 'Annual Global Total Retail Consumer Survey, Feb. 2015', at: http://www.pwc.com/gx/en/retail-consumer/retail-consumer-publications/global-multi-channel-consumer-survey/assets/pdf/total-retail-2015.pdf; Centre for Retail Research, 'Online Retailing: Britain, Europe, US and Canada 2015': http://www.retail-research.org/onlineretailing.php. **123.** Thomas Rudolph et al., *Der Schweizer Online-Handel: Internetnutzung Schweiz 2015* (St Gallen, 2015).

CHAPTER 11

1. Compass, 'The Commercialization of Childhood' (London, 2006); Juliet Schor, *Born to Buy: The Commercialized Child and the New Consumer Culture* (New York, 2004); Ed Mayo & Agnes Nairn, *Consumer Kids: How Big Business is Grooming Our Children for Profit* (London, 2009), which includes a list of advocacy organizations; Victoria Carrington, ' "I'm in a Bad Mood. Let's Go Shopping": Interactive Dolls, Consumer Culture and a "glocalized" Model of Literacy', in: *Journal of Early Childhood Literacy* 3, no. 1, 2003, 83–98; Sue Palmer, *Toxic Childhood: How the Modern World is Damaging Our Children and What We Can Do about It* (London, 2006); and David Buckingham, *After the Death of Childhood: Growing Up in the Age of Electronic Media* (Oxford, 2000). Compare: Stephen Kline, *Out of the Garden: Toys, TV, and Children's Culture in the Age of Marketing* (London, 1993). **2.** James McNeal, *The Kids Market: Myths and Realites* (Ithaca, NY, 1999); Mayo & Nairn, *Consumer Kids*, 5–18. **3.** Linda A. Pollock, *Forgotten Children: Parent–Child Relations from 1500 to 1900* (Cambridge, 1983). For the older view, see Philippe Ariès, *Centuries of Childhood* (London, 1962); and Lawrence Stone, *The Family, Sex and Marriage in England, 1500–1800* (London, 1977). **4.** Daniel Thomas Cook, *The Commodification of Childhood: The Children's Clothing Industry and the Rise of the Child Consumer* (Durham, NC, 2004); see here appendix, fig. 4, for the number of infants' and children's stores. **5.** Children's Charter (1931), full text at http://www.presidency.ucsb.edu/ws/?pid=22593. **6.** Quoted in Cook, *Commodification of Childhood*, 80, and 75–80 for age divisions. **7.** *White House Conference on Child Health and Protection* (1929), Section Three: Education and Training, 39. Full text at http://www23.us.archive.org/stream/homechildsectionoofjke/homechildsectionoofjke_djvu.txt. **8.** Viviana A. Zelizer, *Pricing the Priceless Child: The Changing Social Value of Children* (New York, 1985). **9.** Alice Cora Brill & Mary Pardee Youtz, *Your Child and His Parents* (New York, 1932), quoted at 301, with thanks to Sandra Maß for pointing me to this soure.

10. Lisa Jacobson, *Raising Consumers: Children and the American Mass Market in the Early Twentieth Century* (New York, 2004); and Lisa Jacobson, *Children and Consumer Culture in American Society: A Historical Handbook and Guide* (Westport, CT, 2008). **11.** D. Hamlin, 'The Structures of Toy Consumption: Bourgeois Domesticity and Demand for Toys in Nineteenth-century Germany', in: *Journal of Social History* 36, no. 4, 2003: 857–69. For the earlier period, see J. H. Plumb, 'The New World of Children in Eighteenth-century England', in: *Past and Present*, no. 67, 1975: 64–95. **12.** G. Cross & G. Smits, 'Japan, the US and the Globalization of Children's Consumer Culture', in: *Journal of Social History*, 2005: 873–90; Gary Cross, *Kids' Stuff: Toys and the Changing World of American Childhood* (Cambridge, MA, 1997). **13.** Report of the APA Task Force on Advertising and Children, Section: 'Psychological Issues in the Increasing Commercialization of Childhood', 20 February 2004. **14.** Sonia Livingstone, 'Assessing the Research Base for the Policy Debate over the Effects of Food Advertising to Children', in: *International Journal of Advertising* 24, no. 3, 2005: 273–96. **15.** Barrie Gunter & Adrian Furnham, *Children as Consumers: A Psychological Analysis of the Young People's Market* (London, 1998), esp. chs. 5–6. D. R. John, 'Consumer Socialization of Children: A Retrospective Look at Twenty-five Years of Research', in: *Journal of Consumer Research* 26, no. 3, 1999: 183–213. **16.** Marvin E. Goldberg, 'A Quasi-experiment Assessing the Effectiveness of TV Advertising Directed to Children', in: *Journal of Marketing Research* 27, no. 4, 1990: 445–54. Compare: Gunter & Furnham, *Children as Consumers*, 151–4. **17.** See especially Viviana Zelizer, 'Kids and Commerce', *Childhood* 9, no. 4, 2002: 375–96; Lydia Martens, Dale Southerton & Sue Scott, 'Bringing Children (and Parents) into the Sociology of Consumption: Towards a Theoretical and Empirical Agenda', in: *Journal of Consumer Culture* 4, no. 2, 2004: 155–82. **18.** S. L. Hofferth & J. F. Sandberg, 'How American Children Spend Their Time', in: *Journal of Marriage and Family* 63, no. 2, 2001: 295–308. **19.** McNeal, *Kids Market*, 69–71. 'The Longitudinal Study of Young People in England (Next Steps) Summary Report of Wave 1' (2004). **20.** Elmar Lange & Karin R. Fries, *Jugend und Geld 2005* (Münster, 2006). **21.** Elizabeth M. Chin, *Purchasing Power: Black Kids and American Consumer Culture* (Minneapolis, MN, 2001), esp. 82–5, 126, 161–2. **22.** The following draws on Mizuko Ito, 'Play in an Age of Digital Media: Children's Engagements with the Japanimation Media Mix', in: *Abe Seminar Paper*, 2002; and M. Ito, 'Mobilizing the Imagination in Everyday Play: The Case of Japanese Media Mixes', in: *International Handbook of Children, Media and Culture*, eds. Kirsten Drotner & Sonia Livingstone (Thousand Oaks, CA, 2008), 397–412. **23.** See the discussion on 266–7 above. **24.** J. U. McNeal & C. H. Yeh, 'Taiwanese Children as Consumers', in: *European Journal of Marketing* 24, no. 10, 1990: 32–43. **25.** Lange & Fries, *Jugend und Geld 2005*. **26.** From the food diaries collected by Bernadine Chee in Jun Jing, ed., *Feeding China's Little Emperors: Food, Children and Social Change* (Stanford, CA, 2000), appendix, 215. **27.** Jing, ed., *Feeding China's Little Emperors*, esp. the chapter by Bernadine

Chee, 'Eating Snacks and Biting Pressure', 48–70. Deborah Davis & Julia Sensenbrenner, 'Commercializing Childhood', in: Davis, ed., *The Consumer Revolution in Urban China*, 54–79. **28.** Stanley C. Hollander & Richard Germain, *Was There a Pepsi Generation before Pepsi Discovered It? Youth-based Segmentation in Marketing* (Lincolnwood, IL, 1993), esp. 13–48, quoted at 64. **29.** Hollander & Germain, *Pepsi Generation*, 15. **30.** William C. Beyer, Rebekah P. David & Myra Thwing, 'Workingmen's Standard of Living in Philadelphia: A Report by the Bureau of Municipal Research of Philadelphia, NY, 1919: 67. **31.** See 310–14 above. **32.** B. Søland, 'Employment and Enjoyment: Female Coming-of-age Experiences in Denmark, 1880s–1930s': in Mary Jo Maynes, Birgitte Søland & Christina Benninghaus, eds., *Secret Gardens, Satanic Mills: Placing Girls in European History, 1750–1960* (Bloomington, IN, 2005), 254–68. **33.** Richard Ivan Jobs, *Riding the New Wave: Youth and the Rejuvenation of France after the Second World* (Stanford, CA, 2007), 80 and 106–12. **34.** See 313 above, and Dorothea-Luise Scharmann, *Konsumverhalten von Jugendlichen* (Munich, 1965); Friedhelm Neidhart, *Die Junge Generation*, issue 6 (Opladen, 1970, 3rd rev. edn). **35.** Richard Hoggart, *The Uses of Literacy*, (1957), ch. 7. **36.** Rhona Rapoport & Robert N. Rapoport, *Leisure and the Family Life Cycle* (London, 1975), quoted at 108. **37.** August B. Hollingshead, *Elmtown's Youth and Elmtown Revisited* (New York, 1975), quoted at 375. Hollingshead, *Elmtown's Youth: The Impact of Social Classes on Adolescents*. **38.** Yuniya Kawamura, 'Japanese Teens as Producers of Street Fashion', *Current Sociology* 54, no. 5, 2006: 784–801. **39.** G. C. Hoyt, 'The Life of the Retired in a Trailer Park', in: *American Journal of Sociology*, 1954: 361–70. **40.** David I. Kertzer & Peter Laslett, *Aging in the Past: Demography, Society and Old Age* (Berkeley, CA, 1995); Paul Johnson & Pat Thane, eds., *Old Age from Antiquity to Post-modernity* (London, 1998); *Fünfter Bericht zur Lage der älteren Generation in der Bundesrepublik Deutschland: Potenziale des Alters in Wirtschaft und Gesellschaft*, Berlin, Aug. 2005: 35. **41.** Dora L. Costa, *The Evolution of Retirement: An American Economic History 1880–1990* (Chicago, 1998). **42.** Costa, 'The Evolution of Retirement: Summary of a Research Project', at 234. **43.** *Recreation*, May 1952: 99. **44.** William Graebner, *History of Retirement: The Meaning and Function of an American Institution 1885–1978* (New Haven, CT, 1980). **45.** W. Andrew Achenbaum, *Shades of Grey* (Boston, 1983); and W. Andrew Achenbaum, *Old Age in the New Land: The American Experience since 1790* (Baltimore, MD, 1978). **46.** Granville Stanley Hall, *Senescence: The Last Half of Life* (New York, 1922), quoted at xi, 376–8. **47.** Elmer E. Ferris, *Who Says Old!* (New York, 1933). **48.** Robert James Havighurst & Ruth Albrecht, *Older People* (New York, 1953), v. **49.** Havighurst & Albrecht, *Older People*, 130; the book shows the palpable influence of David Riesman's reassessment of leisure. **50.** Havighurst & Albrecht, *Older People*, 141. **51.** Elaine Cumming & William E. Henry, *Growing Old: The Process of Disengagement* (New York, 1961). Compare: Wilma Donahue, Harold L. Orbach & Otto Pollak, 'Retirement: The Emerging Social Pattern', in: Clark Tibbitts, ed., *Handbook of Social*

Gerontology: Social Aspects of Aging (Chicago, 1960), 330–406. Paul B. Baltes & Margret M. Baltes, *Successful Aging: Perspectives from the Behavioral Sciences* (Cambridge, MA, 1990). **52.** Oskar Schulze, 'Recreation for the Aged', in: *Journal of Gerontology*, IV (1949), 312. **53.** Harry A. Levine, 'Community Programs for the Elderly', in: *Annals of the American Academy of Political and Social Science* 279, 1952: 164–70, quoted at 164 & 169; and Arthur Williams, *Recreation for the Aging* (New York, 1953). An earlier Three-quarter-century Club had been founded in New York City in 1932. I am grateful to Vanessa Taylor for bibliographical references. **54.** For Dewey, see 288–9 above. **55.** US Federal Security Agency, *1st National Conference on the Aging, Man and His Years* (Washington, DC, 1951), quoted at 1, 43, 181, 199. **56.** *Geriatrics*, 6 (1951), 314–18. For this and other material for this period, I have found invaluable Nathan Wetheril Shock, *A Classified Bibliography of Gerontology and Geriatrics. Supplement 1, 1949–1955* (Stanford, CA, 1957), nos. 15037–17250. **57.** 'Recreation for the Aged', in: *American Journal of Nursing*, 55/8 (Aug. 1955), 976–8. **58.** M. Zahrobsky, 'Recreation Programs in Homes for the Aged in Cook County, Illinois', in: *Social Service Review* 24, no. 1, 1950: 41–50, quoted at 47. **59.** Felisa Bracken, 'Senior Citizens Go Camping', in: *Nursing Outlook*, 2/7 (July 1954), quoted at 362. **60.** Ellinor I. Black & Doris B. Bead, *Old People's Welfare on Merseyside* (Liverpool, 1947), 40–6. **61.** Havighurst, in Ernest Watson Burgess, ed., *Aging in Western Societies* (Chicago, 1960), 351. **62.** Dr Robert van Zonneveld, of the National Health Research Council, in: Burgess, ed., *Aging in Western Societies*, 447 **63.** Havighurst, in Burgess, ed., *Aging in Western Societies*, quoted at 321. **64.** Paul Richard Thompson, Catherine Itzin & Michele Abendstern, *I Don't Feel Old: The Experience of Later Life* (Oxford, 1990). **65.** J. Smith et al., 'Wohlbefinden im hohen Alter', in: Karl U. Mayer & Paul B. Baltes, eds., *Die Berliner Altenstudie* (Berlin, 1996), 497–524, table 4 (p. 532). 43% of those aged 70–84 practised sport, a level that dropped to 12% after the age of 85. **66.** Joëlle Gaymu & Christiane Delbès, *La Retraite quinze ans après (Cahier no. 154 de INED)* (Paris, 2003), 95. **67.** *Fünfter Bericht zur Lage der älteren Generation in der Bundesrepublik Deutschland*, 35ff. See also: Jay Ginn & Janet Fast, 'Employment and Social Integration in Midlife: Preferred and Actual Time Use across Welfare Regime Types', *Research on Aging* 28, no. 6, 2006: 669–90. **68.** M. Cirkel, V. Gerling & J. Hilbert, 'Silbermarkt Japan' in: Institut Arbeit und Technik, *Jahrbuch 2001/2*, 73–91. **69.** Bundesarchiv Koblenz, B 189/21915, 'Taschengeld, 1965–82': 'Resolution' of the Councils of Old-age Homes, Aachen, to Antje Huber, 11 Feb. 1982; Herr Radtke (Arbeiterwohlfahrt, Essen) to Huber, 10 Feb. 1982; the headline appeared in the *Express*, 22 Feb. 1982. **70.** Bernard Casey & Atsuhiro Yamada, 'Getting Older, Getting Poorer? A Study of the Earnings, Pensions, Assets and Living Arrangements of Older People in Nine Countries' Organization for Economic Co-operation and Development, 2002, table 2.4. **71.** National Council of Social Service, *Over Seventy: Report of an Investigation into the Social and Economic Circumstances of One Hundred People of over Seventy Years of Age* (London 1954),

54. **72.** Peter Townsend, *The Last Refuge: A Survey of Residential Institutions and Homes for the Aged in England and Wales* (London, 1962), 244. **73.** See Ian Rees Jones, Paul Higgs & David J. Ekerdt, eds., *Consumption and Generational Change* (New Brunswick, NJ, 2009), esp. ch. 6 by Martin Hyde & colleagues and ch. 7 by Fanny Bugeja. **74.** J. Vogel, 'Ageing and Living Conditions of the Elderly: Sweden 1980–1998', *Social Indicators Research* 59, no. 1, 2004: 1–34. **75.** Jones, Higgs & Ekerdt, eds., *Consumption and Generational Change*, ch. 6. **76.** S. Ottaway, 'Providing for the Elderly in Eighteenth-century England', *Continuity and Change* 13, 1998: 391–418. **77.** J. K. Wing & G. W. Brown, 'Social Treatment of Chronic Schizophrenia: A Comparative Survey of Three Mental Hospitals', in: *British Journal of Psychiatry* 107, no. 450, 1961: 847–61. **78.** The above draws on Gail Mountain & Peter Bowie, 'Possessions Owned by Long-stay Psychogeriatric Patients', in: *International Journal of Geriatric Psychiatry* 7, no. 4, 1992: 285–90, quoted at 290. **79.** 'How Active are They?', in: *Recreation*, May 1964, 228. **80.** From 13% to 37% after retirement, Dean W. Morse & Susan H. Gray, *Early Retirement – Boon or Bane: A Study of Three Large Corporations* (Montclair, NJ, 1980). **81.** Max Kaplan, *Leisure, Lifestyle and Lifespan: Perspectives for Gerontology* (Philadelphia, PA, 1979), 84. **82.** Morse & Gray, *Early Retirement*, quoted at 59. See further: Dorothy Ayers Counts & David R. Counts, *Over the Next Hill: An Ethnography of RVing Seniors in North America* (Peterborough, NH, 1997). **83.** *Fünfter Bericht zur Lage der älteren Generation in der Bundesrepublik Deutschland*, 441. For Mallorca, see Armin Ganser, 'Zur Geschichte touristischer Produkte in der Bundesrepublik', in: *Goldstrand und Teutonengrill: Kultur- und Sozialgeschichte des Tourismus in Deutschland, 1945–1989*, ed. Hasso Spode (Berlin, 1996), 185–200. **84.** Quoted in Russell King, Tony Warnes & Allan Williams, *Sunset Lives: British Retirement Migration to the Mediterranean* (Oxford and New York, 2000), 85. See also: Andrew Blaikie, *Ageing and Popular Culture* (New York, 1999), ch. 7. **85.** Thompson, Itzin & Abendstern, *I Don't Feel Old*, 247. **86.** Quoted in Marc Freedman, *Prime Time: How Baby Boomers Will Revolutionize Retirement and Transform America* (New York, 1999), 32. **87.** Kaplan, *Leisure, Lifestyle and Lifespan: Perspectives for Gerontology*, 101–4. **88.** E.g., see the senior weeks organized by the Austrian alpine club (OeAV), http://www.oeav-events.at/service/jahresprogramme/austria/2012/Inhalt/Aktiv-2012-web-18-21.pdf. **89.** The British historian Peter Laslett was one of the trail-blazers: Peter Laslett, *A Fresh Map of Life: The Emergence of the Third Age* (London, 1989). **90.** Rylee Dionigi, 'Competitive Sport as Leisure in Later Life: Negotiations, Discourse and Aging', in: *Leisure Sciences* 28, no. 2, 2006: 181–96. **91.** My translation. **92.** A Leibing, 'The Old Lady from Ipanema: Changing Notions of Old Age in Brazil', in: *Journal of Aging Studies* 19, no. 1, 2005: 15–31. Robert H. Binstock, Jennifer R. Fishman & Thomas E. Johnson, 'Anti-aging Medicine and Science', in: Robert H. Binstock & Linda K. George, eds., *Handbook of Aging and the Social Sciences* (Boston, MA, 2006, 6th edn), 436–55; James Harkin & Julia Huber, *Eternal Youths: How the Baby Boomers are*

Having Their Time Again (London, 2004). **93.** John W. Traphagan, *The Practice of Concern: Ritual, Well-Being and Aging in Rural Japan* (Durham, NC, 2004). See also: John W. Traphagan, *Taming Oblivion: Aging Bodies and the Fear of Senility in Japan* (New York, 2000). **94.** For the above, see Vera Gerling & Harald Conrad, 'Wirtschaftskraft Alter in Japan: Handlungsfelder und Strategien Expertise', a study for the German Ministry of Family, Seniors, Women and Youth (BMFSFJ), 2002, http://www.ffg.uni-dortmund.de/medien/publikationen/Expertise%20Japanischer%20Silbermarkt.pdf. **95.** A. W. Achenbaum, *Older Americans, Vital Communities: A Bold Vision for Societal Aging* (Baltimore, MD, 2005), 40–1. **96.** E. Gidlow, 'The Senior Market', in: *Sales Management*, October 1961: 35–9, 108–11; L. Morse, 'Old Folks: An Overlooked Market?', in: *Duns Review and Modern Industry*, 1964: 83–8. **97.** See George P. Moschis, *The Maturing Marketplace: Buying Habits of Baby Boomers and Their Parents* (Westport, CN, 2000). For marketing studies in the 1970s, see H. L. Meadow, S. C. Cosmas & A. Plotkin, 'The Elderly Consumer: Past, Present and Future', in: *Advances in Consumer Research* 8, no. 1, 1981: 742–7. **98.** Carole Haber 'Old Age through the Lens of Family History', in: Binstock & George, eds., *Handbook of Aging and the Social Sciences*, 41–75. **99.** As always, there are, of course, exceptions, such as Hungary and Northern Italy, where widows were expected to move in with their son's families: Kertzer & Laslett, *Aging in the Past*. **100.** Committee on Ageing Issues, *Report on the Ageing Population 52* (Singapore, 2006); and A. Chan, 'Singapore's Changing Age Structures', in: Shripad Tuljapurkar, Ian Pool & Vipan Prachuabmoh, eds., *Population, Resources and Development*, Vol. I (Dordrecht, 2005), ch. 12. **101.** Ministry of Planning, Government of India, National Sample Survey Organization, 'The Aged in India: A Socio-economic Profile: NSS 52nd Round (July 1995–June 1996); Report no. 446 (52/25.0/3)' (1998); and Kumudini Dandekar, *The Elderly in India* (London, 1996). **102.** Penny Vera-Sanso, 'They Don't Need It and I Can't Give It: Filial Support in South India', in: *The Elderly without Children: European and Asian Perspectives*, eds. P. Kreager & E. Schroeder-Butterfill (Oxford, 2004), 76–105. **103.** John Van Willigen & N. K. Chadha, *Social Aging in a Delhi Neighborhood* (Westport, CN, 1999); Usha Bambawale, Ageing and the Economic Factor in Later Life', in: Indrani Chakravarty, *Life in Twilight Years* (Calcutta, 1997); and Ashish Bose & Mala Kapur Shankardass, *Growing Old in India: Voices Reveal, Statistics Speak* (Delhi, 2004). **104.** Zygmunt Bauman, *Liquid Love: On the Frailty of Human Bonds* (Cambridge, 2003), xii; and Bauman, *Consuming Life*. **105.** Claudine Attias-Donfut, ed., *Les Solidarités entre générations: Vieillesse, familles, État* (Paris, 1995). **106.** Neidhart, *Die Junge Generation*, 64; any translation. For London, see Wilmott, *Adolescent Boys of East London*, 66–8. **107.** Assistance to children went up from 60% to 70%, to grandchildren from 50% to 71%, see Robert H. Binstock & Ethel Shanas, eds., *Handbook of Aging and the Social Sciences* (New York, 1985), 322. **108.** M. Kohli, 'Private and Public Transfers between Generations: Linking the Family and the State', in: *European Societies* 1, no. 1, 1999: 81–104. This paragraph further draws on

Martin Kohli, 'Ageing and Justice', in: Binstock & George, eds., *Handbook of Aging and the Social Sciences*, 456–78; and Attias-Donfut, ed., *Solidarités*.

CHAPTER 12

1. Schwartz, *The Paradox of Choice: Why More is Less*. **2.** UK Audit Commission, 'Acute Hospital Portfolio: Review of National Findings' (2001): 220 million meals. McDonald's sold around 700 million meals at the time in the whole of the United Kingdom. **3.** Eugene C. McCreary, 'Social Welfare and Business: The Krupp Welfare Program, 1860–1914', in: *Business History Review* 42, no. 1, 1968: 24–49. **4.** Wilfried Feldenkirchen, *Siemens, 1918–1945* (Munich, 1995), 348–52. **5.** John Griffiths, ' "Give my Regards to Uncle Billy": The Rites and Rituals of Company Life at Lever Brothers, c.1900–c.1990', in: *Business History* 37, no. 4, 1995: 25–45; and Charles Delheim, 'The Creation of a Company Culture: Cadburys,1861–1931', in: *American Historical Review* 92, 1987: 13–46. **6.** See the calculations by Jakub Kastl & Lyndon Moore, 'Wily Welfare Capitalist: Werner von Siemens and the Pension Plan', in: *Cliometrica, Journal of Historical Economics and Econometric History* 4, no. 3, 2010: 321–48. **7.** Oliver J. Dinius & Angela Vergara, eds., *Company Towns in the Americas: Landscape, Power, and Working-class Communities* (Athens, GA, 2011); and Hardy Green, *The Company Town* (New York, 2010). **8.** Julie Greene, *The Canal Builders: Making America's Empire at the Panama Canal* (New York, 2009). **9.** Stuart Dean Brandes, *American Welfare Capitalism, 1880–1940* (Chicago, 1976), 45. **10.** Linda Carlson, *Company Towns of the Pacific Northwest* (Seattle, 2003), quoted at 51, and ch. 8 for the above. **11.** Margaret Crawford, *Building the Workingman's Paradise: The Design of American Company Towns* (London, 1995), ch. 6. For Pullman, see Brandes, *American Welfare Capitalism, 1880–1940*, 16f. **12.** Quoted in Jean-Louis Cohen, ' "Unser Kunde ist unser Herr": Le Corbusier trifft Bat'a', in: *Zlín: Modellstadt der Moderne*, ed. Winfried Nerdinger (Berlin, 2009), 123, my translation. **13.** Katrin Klingan, ed., *A Utopia of Modernity: Zlín – Revisiting Bat'a's Functional City* (Berlin, 2009). See also: http://batawa.ca/batawahistorys33.php; http://www.batamemories.org.uk/. **14.** For a nuanced discussion: Crawford, *Building the Workingman's Paradise*. **15.** Robert F. Wheeler, 'Organized Sport and Organized Labour: The Workers' Sports Movement', in: *Journal of Contemporary History* 13, no. 2, 1978: 191–210; and Gerald R. Gems, 'Welfare Capitalism and Blue-collar Sport: The Legacy of Labour Unrest', in: *Rethinking History* 5, no. 1, 2001: 43–58. **16.** For Peugeot: P. Fridenson, 'Les Ouvriers de l'automobile et le sport', *Actes de la recherche en sciences sociales* 79, no. 1, 1989: 50–62, quoted at 53, my translation. For Germany: Hans Langenfeld in collaboration with Stefan Nielsen, Klaus Reinarz and Josef Santel, 'Sportangebot und – Nachfrage in grossstaedtischen Zentren Nordwestdeutschlands, 1848–1933', in: Reulecke, ed., *Die Stadt als Dienstleistungszentrum*, Adenauer quoted at 473, my translation. **17.** For the above, see

Brandes, *American Welfare Capitalism, 1880–1940*; and 38 for the 1916 survey. For data from the 1989 American Housing Survey, see US Department of Housing and Urban Development, 'Public Housing: Image Versus Facts', at http://www.huduser.org/periodicals/ushmc/spring95/spring95.html. **18.** Leonard James Diehl, Floyd R. Eastwood & Purdue University, *Industrial Recreation: Its Development and Present Status* (Lafayette, IN, 1942), 20. **19.** Amartya Sen, *Development as Freedom* (Oxford, 1999); and Partha Dasgupta, *An Inquiry into Well-being and Destitution* (Oxford, 1993). **20.** Diehl, Eastwood & Purdue, *Industrial Recreation*, 52. Inhabitants in Canadian railtowns in the 1960s were much busier with sports and volunteering than those in neighbouring small towns: see Rex Archibald Lucas, *Minetown, Milltown, Railtown: Life in Canadian Communities of Single Industry* (Toronto, 1971), esp. 196. **21.** Arnold R. Alanen, *Morgan Park: Duluth, US Steel and the Forging of a Company Town* (Minneapolis, MN, 2007), ch. 7. **22.** Elizabeth Esch, 'Whitened and Enlightened: The Ford Motor Company and Racial Engineering in the Brazialin Amazon', in: Dinius & Vergara, eds., *Company Towns*, ch. 4, for this and the following. **23.** Jackson Moore Anderson, *Industrial Recreation: A Guide to Its Organization and Administration* (New York, 1955), 125. **24.** Enrica Asquer, *Storia intima dei ceti medi: Una capitale e una periferia nell'Italia del miracolo economico* (Rome, 2011), 19. **25.** J. B. Priestley, *English Journey* (London, 1934), 95, 100. **26.** S. E. G. Imer of the Industrial Welfare Division, in 1959, quoted in: Nikola Balnave, 'Company-sponsored Recreation in Australia: 1890–1965', in: *Labour History*, no. 85, 2003: 129–51, at 137. **27.** Brandes, *American Welfare Capitalism, 1880–1940*. **28.** Anderson, *Industrial Recreation*, 63. **29.** Anderson, *Industrial Recreation*, 64–8, and p. 8 for Christmas shopping during the war. **30.** http://www.skibacs. org/; http://www.boeing.com/companyoffices/aboutus/recreation/puget.html. **31.** Elizabeth Fones-Wolf, 'Industrial Recreation, the Second World War and the Revival of Welfare Capitalism, 1934–1960', in: *Business History Review* 60, no. 2, 1986: 232–57, 256. **32.** For Lincoln Plating, see the article at the Society for Human Resource Management: http://www.shrm.org/hrdisciplines/benefits/Articles/Pages/CMS_013248.aspx; B. W. Simonson, 'Corporate Fitness Programs Pay Off', in: *Vital Speeches of the Day* 52, no. 18, 1986: 567–9; and Richard L. Pyle, 'Performance Measures for a Corporate Fitness Program', in: *Human Resource Management* 18, no. 3, 1979: 26–30. **33.** Buck Consultants, 'Working Well: A Global Survey of Health Promotion and Workplace Wellness Strategies' (2009). **34.** Assemblée Nationale, no. 2624, annexe no. 33, 'Jeunesse et sports', esp. section 4 c), at http://www.assemblee-nationale.fr/budget/plf2001/b2624-33.asp. See also: B. Barbusse, 'Sport et entreprise: des logiques convergentes?' in: *L'Année sociologique* 52, no. 2, 2002: 391–415. **35.** Walter Schmolz, 'Freizeit und Betrieb' in: W. Nahrstedt, *Freizeit in Schweden* (Düsseldorf, 1975). **36.** E. Roos, S. Sarlio-Lähteenkorva & T. Lallukka, 'Having Lunch at a Staff Canteen is Associated with Recommended Food Habits', in: *Public Health Nutrition* 7, no. 01, 2004: 53–61; NPD Insight, 'Report on Away-from-home Eating', Aug. 2003. The figure for company subsidies is for

1993, see John S. A. Edwards, 'Employee Feeding – an Overview', in: *International Journal of Contemporary Hospitality Management* 5, no. 4, 1993: 10–14. For France, see the series of articles in *Libération*, Oct. 2003. B. E. Mikkelsen, 'Are Traditional Foodservice Organizations Ready for Organizational Change? (A Case Study of Implementation of Environmental Management in a Work-place Canteen Facility)', in: *Foodservice Research International* 15, no. 2, 2004: 89–106; Marianne Ekström, Lotte Holm, Jukka Gronow, Unni Kjærnes, Thomas Lund, Johanna Mäkelä and Mari Niva, 'The Modernization of Nordic Eating', in: *Anthropology of Food* S7, 2012. In Denmark, 'food on wheels' and public catering for the elderly alone makes up 10% of the entire food sector; see Instituttet for Fødevarestudier & Agroindustriel Udvikling-IFAU, *Food service i Danmark 2007: Udvikling og tendenser i QSF markedet* (Hörsholm, 2007), with thanks to Karen Hamann at the IFAU. For Sandoz, see Jakob Tanner, *Fabrikmahlzeit: Ernährungswissenschaft, Industriearbeit und Volksernährung in der Schweiz, 1890–1950* (Zürich, 1999), 193–5. **37.** http://www.entrez-basel. roche.ch/; http://www.avroche.ch/; http://www.avroche.ch/_verguenstigungen/ discountlist.php?print=1; see the AVR newsletters nos. 55 (June 1997), no. 65 (Dec. 2002) and 66 (May 2003): http://www.avroche.ch/_info-archiv/infos-archiv.php. For Boeing, see http://www.boeing.com/empinfo/discounts.html. **38.** Georges Mouradian, ed., *L'Enfance des comités d'entreprise, de leur genèse dans les conditions de la défaite de 1940 à leur enracinement dans les années 1950* (Roubaix, 1997). Direction de l'Animation de la Recherche des Études et des Statistiques (DARES) and Institut de Recherches Économiques et Sociales (IRES), *Les Comités d'entreprise: Enquête sur les élus, les activités et les moyens* (Paris, 1998); and Conseil National du Tourisme, 'Évolution des pratiques sociales des comités d'entreprise en matière de vacances' (Paris, 2010), http://www. tourisme.gouv.fr/cnt/publications/evolution-pratiques-sociales.pdf. **39.** For this and the above: Conseil National du Tourisme, 'Évolution des pratiques sociales des comités d'entreprise'. See also: 'Les Activités sociales et culturelles des CE – Crise de sens' in; *Le Nouvel Économiste*, 26 Jan. 2012. **40.** http://www. bits-int.org/fr/; http://www.reka.ch/. **41.** Hasso Spode, 'Fordism, Mass Tourism and the Third Reich: The "Strength through Joy" Seaside Resort as an Index Fossil', in: *Journal of Social History*, 2004: 127–55; and Victoria De Grazia, *The Culture of Consent: Mass Organization of Leisure in Fascist Italy* (Cambridge, 2002). **42.** K. Nishikubo, 'Current Situation and Future Direction of Employee Benefits', in: *Japan Labor Review* 7, no. 1, 2010: 4–27; Toyota, sustainability report 2011, 'Approaches to Stakeholders: Relations with Employees'; and Tamie Matsuura, 'An Overview of Japanese Cafeteria Plans' (NLI Research Institute, 1998), http://www.nli-research.co.jp/english/socioeconom-ics/1998/li9803.html. **43.** Seung-Ho Kwon & Michael O'Donnell, *The Chaebol and Labour in Korea: The Development of Management Strategy in Hyundai* (London, 2001); and Jim Barry, *Organization and Management: A Critical Text* (London, 2000), 113–16. **44.** S. Kikeri, 'Privatization and Labour: What Happens to Workers When Governments Divest?' World Bank Technical paper 396 (1998), World Bank, Washington, DC. **45.** Quoted in

Joseph Raphael Blasi, Maya Kroumova & Douglas Kruse, *Kremlin Capitalism: The Privatization of the Russian Economy* (Ithaca, NY, 1997), 112f. **46.** According to a survey of 404 mid-sized and large manufacturing firms: see Pertti Haaparanta et al., 'Firms and Public Service Provision in Russia', Bank of Finland, Institute for Economies in Transition, BOFIT Discussion paper no. 16 (2003), Helsinki. **47.** Michael Heller, 'Sport, Bureaucracies and London Clerks 1880–1939', in: *International Journal of the History of Sport* 25, no. 5, 2008: 579–614. **48.** James E. Roberson, *Japanese Working-class Lives: An Ethnographic Study of Factory Workers* (London, 1998). The classic study of the salaryman is Ezra Feivel Vogel, *Japan's New Middle Class: The Salary Man and His Family in a Tokyo Suburb* (Berkeley, CA, 1963). **49.** Peter H. Lindert, *Growing Public: Social Spending and Economic Growth since the Eighteenth Century* (Cambridge, 2004). **50.** http://www.oecd.org/document/9/0,3746 ,en_2649_33933_38141385_1_1_1_1,00.html. **51.** PricewaterhouseCoopers, Significant and Ecofys, 'Collection of Statistical Information on Green Public Procurement in the EU' (2009), at http://ec.europa.eu/environment/gpp/pdf/statistical_information.pdf. NHS Sustainable Development Unit, 'England Carbon Emissions' (Jan. 2009), 4, at: http://www.sdu.nhs.uk/documents/publications/1232983829_VbmQ_nhs_england_carbon_emissions_carbon_footprint_mode.pdf. **52.** P. A. Samuelson, 'The Pure Theory of Public Expenditure', in: *Review of Economics and Statistics* 36, no. 4, 1954: 387–9. **53.** Eurostat, 'General Government Expenditure Trends 2005–10: EU Countries Compared', in: *Statistics in Focus* 42/2011. **54.** Stiglitz, Sen & Fitoussi, 'Measurement of Economic Performance and Social Progress', esp. 30–2, 89–90. **55.** See Galbraith's new Introduction to the Penguin fifth edition (1999) of this book and also Mike Berry, *The Affluent Society* (Oxford, 2013). **56.** See 'Social Expenditure – Aggregated Data' at OECD.StatExtracts: http://stats.oecd.org/Index. aspx?datasetcode=SOCX_AGG; W. Adema, P. Fron & M. Ladaique, 'Is the European Welfare State Really More Expensive?: Indicators on Social Spending, 1980–2012', *OECD Social, Employment and Migration Working Papers*, no. 124,2011;http://www.oecd.org/els/soc/OECD2014-Social-Expenditure-Update-Nov2014-8pages.pdf. **57.** (United States of America) Bureau of Economic Analysis/ Department of Commerce, 'Tables on Government Consumption Expenditure and Personal Consumption Expenditure', at http://www.bea.gov/. **58.** See Robert Malcolm Campbell, *Grand Illusions: The Politics of the Keynesian Experience in Canada, 1945–1975* (Peterborough, Canada, 1987), 78–9; I am grateful to Bettina Liverant for this reference. See now also: Bettina Liverant, 'Strategic Austerity on the Canadian Home Front', in: Hartmut Berghoff, Jan Logemann & Felix Römer, eds., *The Consumer on the Home Front: Second World War Civilian Consumption in Transnational Perspective* (Oxford, in press), ch. 11. For the GI Bill and federal support in the United States, see Cohen, *Consumers' Republic*, chs. 3–5. **59.** In 1960, private consumption made up 63% of GDP in industrialized countries. In 1976, it had fallen to 58%. In low-income countries the figures were 79% and 81%. World Bank, *World Development Report* (Washington, DC, 1978), tables 4 and 5, 82–5. **60.** See

Lindert, *Growing Public*, 218. **61.** See OECD data. In addition to levying high indirect taxes, which hit ordinary consumers hardest, Scandinavian countries also impose substantial direct taxes and social security contributions on benefit recipients. In 2007, Denmark and Sweden clawed back more than a quarter of social transfers through such direct taxes; the OECD average is 9%. As Adema and colleagues show, the net total social spending in most OECD countries, including the USA and the United Kingdom, hovers somewhere between 22 and 28% of GDP: Adema, Fron & Ladaique, 'Is the European Welfare State Really More Expensive?'. **62.** R. Straub & I. Tchakarov, 'Assessing the Impact of a Change in the Composition of Public Spending: A DSGE Approach. IMF Working Paper WP/07/168', (International Monetary Fund, 2007). **63.** Interestingly, too, embattled Spain had seen a rise in public investment. **64.** See: http://www.oecd.org/els/soc/OECD2014-Social-Expenditure-Update-Nov2014-8pages.pdf. **65.** Harold L. Wilensky, *Industrial Society and Social Welfare: The Impact of Industrialization on the Supply and Organization of Social Welfare Services in the United States* (New York, 1958/ 1965), xiiif. **66.** In the United States, the rich gave 7% of estates worth over £10 million to charity in 1922. Fifty years later it was 31%; Jaher, 'The Gilded Elite, American Multimillionaires, 1865 to the Present', 209f. **67.** In housing projects in New York City, all but 5% had a TV as early as the early 1960s, see Wilensky, *Industrial Society and Social Welfare*, xxx. **68.** 'Historical Tables', Budget of the United States Government, table 3.1, http://www.whitehouse.gov/sites/default/files/omb/budget/fy2012/assets/hist.pdf. **69.** J. P. Dunne, P. Pashardes & R. P. Smith, 'Needs, Costs and Bureaucracy: The Allocation of Public Consumption in the UK', in: *Economic Journal* 94, no. 373, 1984: 1–15. **70.** Adema, Fron & Ladaique, 'Is the European Welfare State Really More Expensive?'; 'other social services' (childcare, home care for the elderly and similar services) make up a formidable 5% of GDP in Denmark and Sweden, but only 1% in the USA and Southern European countries. **71.** B. Booth, M. W. Segal & D. B. Bell, 'What We Know about Army Families: 2007 Update. Prepared for the Family and Morale, Welfare and Recreation Command' (2007). **72.** K. J. Cwiertka, 'Popularizing a Military Diet in Wartime and Post-war Japan', in: *Asian Anthropology* 1, 2002: 1–30; and Katarzyna Cwiertka, *Modern Japanese Cuisine: Food, Power and National Identity* (London, 2006). **73.** Peter J. Atkins, 'Fattening Children or Fattening Farmers? School Milk in Britain, 1921–1941', in: *Economic History Review* 58, no. 1, 2005: 57–78; and James Vernon, *Hunger: A Modern History* (Cambridge, MA, 2007). **74.** This, and the following paragraph, are indebted to Susan Levine, *School Lunch Politics: The Surprising History of America's Favorite Welfare Program* (Princeton, NJ, 2008). **75.** M. Clawson, 'Statistical Data Available for Economic Research on Certain Types of Recreation', in: *Journal of the American Statistical Association*, 1959: 281–309; and C. L. Harriss, 'Government Spending and Long-run Economic Growth', in: *American Economic Review* 46, no. 2, 1956: 155–70. **76.** T. Ståhl et al., 'The Importance of Policy Orientation and Environment on Physical Activity Participation: A Comparative Analysis between Eastern Germany, Western Germany and Finland', *Health Promotion International* 17, no. 3, 2002: 235–46   **77.** Sigurd Agricola, 'Freizeit, Planung, Paedagogik und Forschung', in: Nahrstedt, *Freizeit in Schweden*, 78–102. **78.** Institut National de la Santé et de la Recherche Médicale (Inserm), *Physical Activity: Context and Effects on Health* (Paris, 2008).   **79.** Lamartine Pereira da Costa & Ana Miragaya, *Worldwide Experiences and Trends in Sport for All* (Oxford, 2002). See now also: Thomas Turner, 'The Sports Shoe: A Social and Cultural History, *c.*1870–*c.*1990', PhD thesis, Birkbeck College/University of London, 2013.   **80.** David Richard Leheny, *The Rules of Play: National Identity and the Shaping of Japanese Leisure* (Ithaca, 2003).   **81.** Anne White, *De-Stalinization and the House of Culture: Declining State Control over Leisure in the USSR, Poland and Hungary, 1953–1989* (London, 1990). **82.** Bundesarchiv Berlin Lichterfelde, Zentralinstitut für Jugendforschung, 'Freizeit und Freizeitnutzung junger Arbeiter und Schüler in der Wartburgstadt Eisenach' (Sept. 1977), pp. 15–20, 60–5.   **83.** Statistisches Bundesamt Deutschland, *Datenreport 2002*, 152.   **84.** Directorate General Internal Policies of the Union, 'Financing the Arts and Culture in the European Union', IP/B/CULT/ST/2005_104 (30 Nov 2006), quoted at 17, and for below. **85.** Eurostat, *Cultural Statistics*, 2011 edition (Luxembourg, 2011), figure 8.7, 171. In 2006, 50% of Danes went between one and six times to such live performances and 5% went seven to twelve times. In Italy, the respective figures were half these. The suggested correlation between spending and attendance is reinforced by Orian Brook, 'International Comparisons of Public Engagement in Culture and Sport' (UK Department for Culture, Media and Sport, Aug. 2011), 21–2.   **86.** Eurostat, *Cultural Statistics*, fig. 9.1, 201.   **87.** UK Department of Trade and Industry, *Modern Markets: Confident Consumers* (London, 1999).   **88.** Tony Blair, quoted in *Guardian*, 24 June 2004, 1. See further: Blair, *The Courage of Our Convictions: Why Reform of the Public Services is the Route to Social Justice* and his 'Progress and Justice in the Twenty-first Century', Inaugural Fabian Society Annual Lecture, 17 June 2003.   **89.** Lawson, *All Consuming: How Shopping Got Us into This Mess and How We Can Find Our Way Out.*   **90.** Wendy Thomson (Head of the Prime Minister's Office of Public Services Reform), 'Consumerism as a Resource for Citizenship', seminar on consumers as citizens, HM Treasury, 22 April 2004.   **91.** See 154–60, 286–9 above.   **92.** John F. Kennedy Presidential Library (Boston, MA), Speech Files, JFKPOF-037-028, special message to Congress on protecting consumer interest, 15 March 1962; WH-0800-03; to listen to the audio file: http://www. jfklibrary.org/Asset-Viewer/Archives/JFKWHA-080-003.aspx.   **93.** Alain Chatriot, Marie-Emmanuelle Chessel & Matthew Hilton, eds., *The Expert Consumer: Associations and Professionals in Consumer Society* (Aldershot, 2006); see further the special issue 'Verbraucherschutz in internationaler Perspektive', *Jahrbuch für Wirtschaftsgeschichte* 1, 2006; Iselin Theien, 'Planung und Partizipation in den regulierten Konsumgesellschaften Schwedens und Norwegens zwischen 1930 und 1960', *Comparativ* 21, no. 3, 2011: 67–78. **94.** For this and the following, see Matthew Hilton, *Prosperity for All:*

Consumer Activism in an Era of Globalization (Ithaca, NY, 2009); and Stephen Brobeck, ed., *Encyclopedia of the Consumer Movement* (Santa Barbara, CA, 1997). **95.** Anon., 'Consumer Protection Report of the Secretary-General of the United Nations', in: *Journal of Consumer Policy* 16, no. 1, 1993: 97–121. **96.** Smith Institute *Is Free Trade Fair Trade?* (London, 2009). For a view from the North at the time, see the British National Consumer Council, *The Uruguay Round and Beyond: The Consumer View* (London, 1994). **97.** R. A. H. Livett, 'Modern Flat Building', in: *Journal of the Royal Society for the Promotion of Health* 61, no. 2, 1940: 48–57, 57. **98.** Greater Manchester County Record Office, Housing Committee, Minutes, 5 Nov. 1953. **99.** Central Housing Advisory Committee Housing Management Sub-committee, *Councils and Their Houses* (London, 1959). **100.** Ministry of Housing and Local Government, 1963, quoted in I. A. N. Greener and M. Powell, 'The Evolution of Choice Policies in UK Housing, Education and Health Policy', in: *Journal of Social Policy* 38, no. 01, 2009: 63–81, at 66. **101.** Manchester and Salford Housing Association, 1973, quoted in Peter Shapely, *The Politics of Housing: Power, Consumers and Urban Culture* (Manchester, 2007), 171 and ch. 6 for the above. **102.** Shapely, *Politics of Housing*. **103.** Malcolm L. Johnson, 'Patients: Receivers or Participants', in: Keith Barnard & Kenneth Lee, *Conflicts in the National Health Service* (London, 1977), 72–98. **104.** Dr Owen, interview with *The Times*, 9 Feb. 1976, 1. **105.** Chris Ham, 'Power, Patients and Pluralism', in: Barnard & Lee, *Conflicts in the National Health Service*, 99–120; Martin Blackmore, 'Complaints within Constraints: A Critical Review and Analysis of the Citizen's Charter Complaints Task Force', in: *Public Policy and Administration* 12, no. 3, 1997: 28–41; A. Mold, 'Patient Groups and the Construction of the Patient-Consumer in Britain: An Historical Overview', in: *Journal of Social Policy* 39, no. 04, 2010: 505–21. **106.** The official figure is 45%, but some experts calculate it as high as 60%: S. Woolhandler & D. U. Himmelstein, 'Paying for National Health Insurance – and Not Getting It', in: *Health Affairs* 21, no. 4, 2002: 88–98. **107.** Danish Finance Ministry, *Frihed til at vælge* (Copenhagen, 2004); and Nancy Tomes, 'Patients or Healthcare Consumers? Why the History of Contested Terms Matters', in: *History and Health Policy in the US : Putting the Past Back In*, eds. R. A. Stevens, C. Rosenberg & L. R. Burns, (New Brunswick, NJ, 2006), 83–110. In 1994, the World Health Organization published its 'Principles of the Rights of Patients in Europe'. Five years later, an International Alliance of Patient Organizations was formed: A. van der Zeijden, 'The Patient Rights Movement in Europe', in: *Pharmacoeconomics* 18, no. Supplement 1, 2000: 7–13. **108.** S Jägerskiöld, 'The Swedish Ombudsman', *University of Pennsylvania Law Review* 109, no. 8, 1961: 1077–99; P. Magnette, 'Between Parliamentary Control and the Rule of Law: The Political Role of the Ombudsman in the European Union', in: *Journal of European Public Policy* 10, no. 5, 2003: 677–94; Frank Stacey, *The British Ombudsman* (Oxford, 1971); and Glen O'Hara, 'Parties, People and Parliament: Britain's "Ombudsman" and the Politics of the 1960s', in: *Journal of British Studies* 50, no. 3, 2011: 690–714. **109.** Ed Mayo, investigation report for Consumer Focus (UK), Aug. 2012; Citizens' Advice Bureau (UK), *Access for All* (2011). **110.** Eurostat, *Consumers in Europe* (Luxembourg, 2009), fig. 1.65, 104. In Britain, Energywatch alone received 109,578 complaints in 2002–3 – almost half were about billing. Elsewhere in the European Union, mobile phones and postal service top the list. National Audit Office, 'Benchmarking Review of Energywatch and Postwatch' (March 2004), 11f. **111.** See www. complaintschoir.org. Finland finally won Eurovision in 2006. **112.** Although complaining remains uneven and, indeed, has been falling in recent years in some services notorious for poor standards (like trains); http://dataportal. orr.gov.uk/displayreport/report/html/6870b367-965b-4306-819b-8eafdbacdd7a. **113.** For this and the following, see: Michelle Everson, 'Legal Constructions of the Consumer', in: Trentmann, ed., *Making of the Consumer*, 99–121; Jim Davies, *The European Consumer Citizen in Law and Policy* (Basingstoke, 2011); and Stephen Weatherill, *EU Consumer Law and Policy* (Cheltenham, 2005). **114.** Summary of Judgement, Case C-372/04, Watts *v* Bedford Primary Care Trust and Sec. of State of Health: http://eur-lex.europa.eu/LexUriServ/LexUriServ.do?uri=CELEX:62004J0372:EN:HTML. **115.** EESC, 'On the Consumer Policy Action Plan, 1999–2001', cited in Davies, *The European Consumer Citizen in Law and Policy*, 41. **116.** NCC, 'Consumer Futures' and 'Consumer: What's in a Name?' (2007). **117.** The above barely skims the surface of a very large literature and research. See esp. John Clarke et al., *Creating Citizen-Consumers: Changing Publics and Changing Public Services* (London, 2007), quoted at 132; R. Simmons, J. Birchall & A. Prout, 'User Involvement in Public Services: "Choice about Voice"', in: *Public Policy and Administration* 27, no. 1, 2012: 3–29; Yiannis Gabriel & Tim Lang, *The Unmanageable Consumer: Contemporary Consumption and Its Fragmentations* (London, 1995); Mark Bevir & Frank Trentmann, eds., *Governance, Citizens and Consumers: Agency and Resistance in Contemporary Politics* (Basingstoke, 2007); Nick Couldry, Sonia Livingstone & Tim Markham, *Media Consumption and Public Engagement: Beyond the Presumption of Attention* (Basingstoke, 2007); M. Micheletti, D. Stolle & M. Hoogh, 'Zwischen Markt und Zivilgesellschaft: Politischer Konsum als bürgerliches Engagement', in: *Zivilgesellschaft – national und transational*, eds. D. Gosewinkel et al. (Berlin, 2003), 151–71.

CHAPTER 13

1. Since the 1990s, the official name and label has been 'Fairtrade'. For literary convenience, and to accommodate earlier spellings, I have used separate words unless when specifically referring to the organization. **2.** For Dortmund: http://www.fairtrade-deutschland.de/mitmachen/kampagnen-von-transfair/gelungene-kampagnen/fairtrade-kampagne/joachim-krol-in-dortmund/?tx_jppageteaser_pi1%5BbackId%5D=534; for Schalke: http://schalkespieltfair.de/. 'Fairtrade Labelling Organizations International, Growing Stronger Together: Annual Report 2009-10'; www.transfair.org/top/news 4 March

2011; and Jean-Marie Krier, *Fair Trade 2007: New Facts and Figures from an Ongoing Success Story* (Culemborg, 2008). 3. Gavin Fridell, *Fair-trade Coffee: The Prospects and Pitfalls of Market-driven Social Justice* (Toronto, 2007); and Gavin Fridell, 'Fair Trade and Neoliberalism: Assessing Emerging Perspectives', in: *Latin American Perspectives* 33, no. 6, 2006: 8–28. 4. Quoted in Luigi Ceccarini, 'I luoghi dell'impegno: tra botteghe del mondo e supermarket', in: Paola Rebughini & Roberta Sassatelli, eds., *Le nuove frontiere dei consumi* (Verona, 2008), 150, 153, my translation. 5. See 171–3 above. 6. The Norges chain carries some fair-trade products: http://www.fairtrade.at/fileadmin/user_upload/PDFs/Fuer_Studierende/FromBeanToCup_2005.pdf?PHPSESSID=8b44ffe3cef7deocf13d8cca979c90f8. 7. Latin American producers had already agreed on export quotas in 1958. The 1962 agreement, which included the United States, used export quotas to stabilize the price of coffee. It was amended in 1968 with a special fund to prevent coffee from being overplanted. The agreement collapsed in 1989 as consuming countries turned to cheap coffee outside the cartel. For a short overview, see Michael Barratt Brown, *Fair Trade: Reform and Realities in the International Trading System* (London, 1993), ch. 7. 8. Otto, 'Otto Group Trend Studie 2011 (3. Studie zum ethischen Konsum: Verbraucher–Vertrauen)' (2011). 9. Magnus Boström et al., *Political Consumerism: Its Motivations, Power and Conditions in the Nordic Countries and Elsewhere* (Copenhagen, 2005); and Unni Kjærnes, Mark Harvey & Alan Warde, *Trust in Food: A Comparative and Institutional Analysis* (Hampshire, 2007). 10. Mel Young editorial, *New Consumer*, May/June 2005, 7. 11. See www.brilliantearth.com; http://www.gepa.de/produkte/kaffee-tee/kaffee.html. 12. Kathryn Wheeler, *Fair Trade and the Citizen-consumer* (Basingstoke, 2012), 79–81. 13. Council of Europe: http://www.coe.int/t/dg3/socialpolicies/socialcohesiondev/forum/2004monatzederschulze_en.asp. 14. Friedrich Nietzsche, *Thus Spake Zarathustra*. 15. Joan C. Tronto, *Moral Boundaries: A Political Argument for an Ethic of Care* (New York, 1994); and Andrew Sayer, 'Moral Economy and Political Economy', in: *Studies in Political Economy* 61, 2000: 79–104. 16. Amanda Berlan, 'Making or Marketing a Difference? An Anthropological Examination of the Marketing of Fair-trade Cocoa from Ghana' in: Geert De Neve et al., 'Hidden Hands in the Market', in: *Research in Economic Anthropology* 28, 2008: 171–94 171–94; see also: Michael K. Goodman, 'Reading Fair Trade: Political Ecological Imaginary and the Moral Economy of Fair-trade Goods', *Political Geography* 23, 2004: 891–915. 17. John Wilkinson & Gilberto Mascarenhas 'The Making of the Fair-trade Movement in the South: The Brazilian Case' in: Laura T. Raynolds, L. Murray Douglas & John Wilkinson, eds., *Fair Trade: The Challenges of Transforming Globalization* (London, 2007); for the size of local markets, see *Fair-trade Facts and Figures 2010*, figures 3.8–3.10: http://www.fairtrade.de/cms/media//pdf/Facts_&_Figures_2010.pdf. 18. Luc Boltanski, *Distant Suffering: Morality, Media and Politics* (Cambridge, 1999). 19. Wheeler, *Fair Trade*, 173. 20. Around €140 in 2011 for humanitarian aid compared to €3 per person on fair-trade retail sales (2009); compare Deutscher Spendenrat, *Bilanz des Helfens*,

2011, with *Fair-trade Facts and Figures 2010*, fig 2.8.   **21.** Patrick De Pels-macker, Liesbeth Driesen & Glenn Rayp, 'Do Consumers Care about Ethics? Willingness to Pay for Fair-trade Coffee', in: *Journal of Consumer Affairs* 39, no. 2, 2005: 363–85.   **22.** Anthony Giddens, *Modernity and Self-identity* (Cambridge, 1991); Sarah Lyon, 'Evaluating Fair-trade Consumption: Politics, Defetishization and Producer Participation', in: *International Journal of Consumer Studies* 30, no. 5, 2006: 452–64.   **23.** Micheletti, Stolle & Hoogh, 'Zwischen Markt und Zivilgesellschaft: Politischer Konsum als bürgerliches Engagement'; Boström et al., *Political Consumerism*; and Wheeler, *Fair Trade*, chs. 5 and 7.   **24.** Compare Thomas L. Haskell, 'Capitalism and the Origins of the Humanitarian Sensibility, Part 1', in: *American Historical Review* 90, no. 2, 1985: 339–61, and 'Capitalism and the Origins of the Humanitarian Sensibility, Part 2', in: *American Historical Review* 90, no. 3, 1985: 547–66; with Richard Huzzey, 'The Moral Geography of British Anti-slavery Responsibilities', in: *Transactions of the Royal Historical Society* (6th series) 22, 2012: 111–39, who stresses the limits of the 'free produce' and notes that even among British abolitionists themselves, very few followed Joseph Sturge's example and ordered ethically unpolluted underwear.   **25.** J. A. Hobson, *The Evolution of Modern Capitalism* (London, rev. edn 1897), 368–80.   **26.** Constantine, ' "Bringing the Empire Alive": The Empire Marketing Board and Imperial Propaganda, 1926–33'; and Trentmann, *Free Trade Nation*, 228–40.   **27.** *Final Report of Mixed Committee of the League of Nations on the Relation of Nutrition to Health, Agriculture and Economic Policy* (Geneva, 1937); and Frank Trentmann, 'Coping with Shortage: The Problem of Food Security and Global Visions of Coordination, c.1890s–1950', in: *Food and Conflict in Europe in the Age of the Two World Wars*, eds. Frank Trentmann & Flemming Just (Basingstoke, 2006), 13–48.   **28.** 1955, 'Co-operative Notes for Speakers on the Food and Agriculture Organization', quoted in Trentmann, 'Coping with Shortage', 39–40.   **29.** John Toye and Richard Toye, 'The Origins and Interpretation of the Prebisch–Singer Thesis', in: *History of Political Economy* 35, no. 3, 2003: 437–67.   **30.** The journalist Dick Scherpenzeel had called for dedicated shops to sell sugar at fair prices at the 1968 United Nations Conference on Trade and Development (UNCTAD) in New Delhi.   **31.** For Schorndorf, see: http://www.elmundo.de/neu/index.php?option=com_content&task=view&id=62&Itemid=64; for Hildesheim, see the newsletter *El Puente Informiert* 2010, 44.   **32.** *Populorum progressio*, full text at: http://www.newadvent.org/library/docs_pao6pp.htm.   **33.** 1970, quoted in Werner Balsen & Karl Rössel, *Hoch die internationale Solidarität: Zur Geschichte der Dritte-Welt-Bewegung in der Bundesrepublik* (Cologne, 1986), 284.   **34.** Hans Beerends, *De Derde Wereldbeweging: Geschiedenis en toekomst* (Utrecht, 1993), 126–30.   **35.** Claudia Olejniczak, *Die Dritte-Welt-Bewegung in Deutschland: Konzeptionelle und organisatorische Strukturmerkmale einer neuen sozialen Bewegung* (Wiesbaden, 1999), pp. 140–41, notes that by the end of the 1980s non-governmental organizations received 14 per cent of their funding from the state.   **36.** Arthur Simon, *Bread for the World* (New York, 1975), quoted at 56–7, 98–101.   **37.** Matt Anderson,

'Cost of a Cup of Tea: Fair Trade and the British Co-operative Movement, *c.* 1960–2000', in: *Consumerism and the Co-operative Movement in Modern British History*, eds. Lawrence Black & Nicole Robertson, (Manchester, 2009). **38.** Thompson, 'The Moral Economy of the English Crowd in the Eighteenth Century'. Compare: Trentmann, 'Before "Fair Trade": Empire, Free Trade, and the Moral Economies of Food in the Modern World'. **39.** Sarah Lyon, 'Fairtrade Coffee and Human Rights in Guatemala', in: *Journal of Consumer Policy* 30, no. 3, 2007: 241–61. **40.** Amanda Berlan, 'Making or Marketing a Difference?' in: De Neve et al., 'Hidden Hands in the Market'. **41.** A. Tallontire et al., Diagnostic Study of FLO, DFID (2001). **42.** See www.unserland.info and 'Network Unser Land' brochures. **43.** *La Repubblica*, 24 Oct. 2009. **44.** James Richard Kirwan, 'The Reconfiguration of Producer–Consumer Relations within Alternative Strategies in the UK Agro-food System: The Case of Farmers' markets', unpubl. PhD thesis, University of Gloucestershire, 2003, 37–8. **45.** Renée Shaw Hughner et al., 'Who are Organic Food Consumers? A Compilation and Review of Why People Purchase Organic Food', in: *Journal of Consumer Behaviour* 6, no. 2–3, 2007: 94–110. **46.** Petrini, *Slow Food: Le ragioni del gusto*. In fact, most people's diet was far more monotonous in the centuries before the supermarket and modern food science than after: see now Rachel Laudan, *Cuisine and Empire: Cooking in World History* (Berkeley, CA, 2013). **47.** Jose Harris, ed., *Tönnies: Community and Civil Society* (Cambridge, 2001); the German original appeared in 1887. **48.** Daniel Miller, 'Coca-Cola: A Black Sweet Drink from Trinidad', in: Daniel Miller, ed., *Material Cultures: Why Some Things Matter* (London, 1998), ch. 8.; and Wilk, *Home Cooking in the Global Village*. **49.** http://www.bmelv.de/SharedDocs/Downloads/Ernaehrung/ Kennzeichnung/Regionalsiegel-Gutachten.pdf?__blob=publicationFile, 13; www. unser-norden.de. **50.** *Guardian*, 27 Feb. 2013. **51.** Local Government Regulation, A Local Authority Survey: 'Buying Food with Geographical Descriptions – How 'Local' is 'Local'? Jan. 2011; http://www.devon.gov.uk/lgr_-_how_local_is_ local_report_-_february_2011.pdf. **52.** Michèle de la Pradelle, *Market Day in Provence*, trans. Amy Jacobs (Chicago, 2006); Keith Spiller, 'Farmers' Markets as Assemblage Social Relations: Social Practice and the Producer/Consumer Nexus in the North-east of England', unpubl. PhD thesis, University of Durham, 2008. **53.** Kirwan, 'Reconfiguration of Producer–Consumer Relations', 155. **54.** 2003, quoted in Boström et al., *Political Consumerism*, 477; I have slightly rephrased the quote for the sake of grammar. **55.** Mari Niva, Johanna Mäkelä & Jouni Kujala, ' "Trust Weakens as Distance Grows": Finnish Results of the Omiard Consumer Focus Group Study on Organic Foods', in *Working Papers 83*: National Consumer Research Centre, 2004. **56.** Patricia L. Maclachlan, 'Global Trends *vs.* Local Traditions: Genetically Modified Foods and Contemporary Consumerism in the United States, Japan, and Britain', in: Garon & Maclachlan, eds., *Ambivalent Consumer*, esp. 248–50 ; see also: Maclachlan, *Consumer Politics in Post-war Japan: The Institutional Boundaries of Citizen Activism*. **57.** See http://www.retegas.org. **58.** See: http://www.consiglio.regione.fvg.it/consreg/documenti/approfondimenti/%5B20091203_103833

%5D_849178.pdf, my translation. **59.** See FiBL (Forschungsinstitut für biologischen Landbau), 'Entwicklung von Kriterien für ein bundesweites Regionalsiegel: Gutachten im Auftrag des Bundesministeriums für Ernährung, Landwirtschaft und Verbraucherschutz' (Frankfurt, 2012), at: http://www.bmelv. de/SharedDocs/Downloads/Ernaehrung/Kennzeichnung/Regionalsiegel-Gutachten. pdf?__blob=publicationFile. **60.** See 169 above. **61.** E. J. Hobsbawm & T. O. Ranger, eds., *The Invention of Tradition* (Cambridge, 1983). **62.** European Commission, 'Geographical Indications and Traditional Specialities', see documents at http://ec.europa.eu/agriculture/quality/schemes and http://euroalert. net/en/news.aspx?idn=11727. M. Schramm, *Konsum und regionale Identität in Sachsen, 1880–2000: Die Regionalisierung von Konsumgütern im Spannungsfeld von Nationalisierung und Globalisierung* (Stuttgart, 2002); and *La Repubblica*, 13 Feb. 2013, 29–31. **63.** http://instoresnow.walmart.com/ Food-Center-locally-grown.aspx. **64.** Susanne Freidberg, *Fresh: A Perishable History* (Cambridge, MA, 2009). **65.** Quoted in Kirwan, 'Reconfiguration of Producer–Consumer Relations', at 155. **66.** De la Pradelle, *Market Day in Provence*, 111–13. **67.** Lois Stanford, 'The Role of Ideology in New Mexico's CSA (Community-supported Agriculture)', in: Wilk, ed., *Fast Food/Slow Food: The Cultural Economy of the Global Food System*, ch. 12. **68.** Quoted from Manuel Gamio, *The Mexican Immigrant: His Life-story* (Chicago, 1931), 68. **69.** Manuel Gamio, *Mexican Immigration to the United States* (Chicago, 1930), 67–9 and appendix V. **70.** World Bank, *Migration and Development Brief*, no. 19 (20 Nov. 2012). **71.** Alexia Grosjean, 'Returning to Belhelvie, 1593–1875', in: *Emigrant Homecomings: The Return Movement of Emigrants, 1600–2000*, ed. Marjory Harper (Manchester, 2006), 216–32. **72.** The figure here is the net gain from remittances, from which smaller outward flows have been deducted. See Magee & Thompson, *Empire and Globalisation: Networks of People, Goods and Capital in the British World, c. 1850–1914*, 97–105; and James Belich, *Replenishing the Earth: The Settler Revolution and the Rise of the Anglo-world, 1783–1939* (Oxford, 2009), esp. 128, 189. **73.** World Bank, *World Development Report* (Washington, DC, 1978), 11. *The Economist*, 28 April 2012: 65; World Bank, Global Remittances Working Group (GRWG), http://www.worldbank.org/en/topic/paymentsystems remittances/brief/global-remittances-working-group; and J. A. Garçia, 'Payment Systems Worldwide: A Snapshot' (Washington, DC, World Bank, 2008). **74.** Ian Goldin, Geoffrey Cameron & Meera Balarajan, *Exceptional People: How Migration Shaped Our World and Will Define Our Future* (Princeton, NJ, 2011); Dilip Ratha et al., 'Leveraging Migration for Africa: Remittances, Skills and investments' (Washington, DC, World Bank, 2011). **75.** Douglas S. Massey, *Return to Aztlan: The Social Process of International Migration from Western Mexico* (Berkeley, CA, 1987), 220–31. **76.** Massey, *Return to Aztlan*, table 8.1, 218. **77.** Shahid Perwaiz, *Pakistan, Home Remittances* (Islamabad, 1979); see also his 'Home Remittances', *Pakistan Economist*, 19 Sept. 1979. Cf. A. G. Chandavarkar, 'Use of Migrants' Remittances in Labor-exporting Countries', *Finance and Development* 17, no. 2, 1980: 36–9. **78.** Ratha et al.,

'Leveraging Migration for Africa', ch. 2. Richard H. Adams, 'The Economic Uses and Impact of International Remittances in Rural Egypt', in: *Economic Development and Cultural Change* 39, no. 4, 1991: 695–722; Richard H. Adams, Jr., 'Remittances, Investment, and Rural Asset Accumulation in Pakistan', in: *Economic Development and Cultural Change* 47, no. 1, 1998: 155–73; and Richard H. Adams & Alfredo Cuecuecha, 'Remittances, Household Expenditure and Investment in Guatemala', in: *World Development* 38, no. 11, 2010: 1626–41. **79.** Richard H. Adams, Alfredo Cuecuecha & John M. Page, 'Remittances, Consumption and Investment in Ghana' (Washington, DC, World Bank, 2008). For methodological problems with earlier surveys, see also: J. Edward Taylor & Jorge Mora, 'Does Migration Reshape Expenditures in Rural Households? Evidence from Mexico', in: *Policy Research Working Paper Series no. 3842* (Washington, DC, World Bank, 2006). **80.** Ratha et al., 'Leveraging Migration for Africa'. **81.** Anita Chan, Richard Madsen & Jonathan Unger, eds., *Chen Village: The Recent History of a Peasant Community in Mao's China* (Berkeley, CA, 1984/1992), 267–99. **82.** Jeffery H. Cohen, 'Remittance Outcomes and Migration: Theoretical Contests, Real Opportunities', in: *Studies in Comparative International Development* 40, no. 1, 2005: 88–112. **83.** Divya Praful Tolia-Kelly, 'Iconographies of Diaspora: Refracted Landscapes and Textures of Memory of South Asian Women in London' (PhD thesis, UCL, 2002). **84.** Kathy Burrell, 'Materializing the Border: Spaces of Mobility and Material Culture in Migration from Post-socialist Poland', in: *Mobilities* 3, no. 3, 2008: 353–73. **85.** Panikos Panayi, *Spicing up Britain: The Multicultural History of British Food* (London, 2008), 120. **86.** Panayi, *Spicing up Britain*; Maren Möhring, *Fremdes Essen: Die Geschichte der ausländischen Gastronomie in der Bundesrepublik Deutschland* (Munich, 2012), pp. 63–6. **87.** Isabella Beeton, *Mrs Beeton's Household Management* (Ware, 1861/2006), 290–2, 451, 618–20. **88.** Timothy J. Hatton & Jeffrey G. Williamson, *The Age of Mass Migration: Causes and Economic Impact* (New York, 1998). **89.** Donna R. Gabaccia, *We Are What We Eat: Ethnic Food and the Making of Americans* (Cambridge, MA, 1998). **90.** Phyllis H. Williams, *South Italian Folkways in Europe and America: A Handbook for Social Workers, Visiting Nurses, School Teachers, and Physicians* (New Haven, CT, 1938). **91.** I follow here Hasia R. Diner, *Hungering for America: Italian, Irish and Jewish Foodways in the Age of Migration* (Cambridge, MA, 2001). **92.** Diner, *Hungering for America*, 194–216; Gabaccia, *We Are What We Eat*, 104, 176ff. **93.** For this, and the following, see Elizabeth Buettner, 'Going for an Indian: South Asian Restaurants and the Limits of Multiculturalism in Britain', in: *Journal of Modern History* 80, no. 4, 2008: 865–901; Möhring, *Fremdes Essen*, 254f. **94.** Buettner, 'Going for an Indian'; Steve Shaw, 'Marketing Ethnoscapes as Spaces of Consumption: Banglatown – London's Curry Capital', in: *Journal of Town and City Management* 1, no. 4, 2011: 381–95. **95.** Krishnendu Ray, *The Migrant's Table: Meals and Memories in Bengali-American Households* (Philadelphia, 2004), appendix 3 for the menu, and 97 for the following. **96.** Jitsuichi Masuoka, 'Changing Food

Habits of the Japanese in Hawaii', in: *American Sociological Review* 10, no. 6, 1945: 759–65. **97.** Möhring, *Fremdes Essen*, 253–70. **98.** Till Manning, *Die Italiengeneration: Stilbildung durch Massentourismus in den 1950er und 1960er Jahren* (Göttingen, 2011). **99.** Erik Millstone & Tim Lang, *The Atlas of Food: Who Eats What, Where and Why?* (Berkeley, CA, 2008), 54–5; K. Hammer, T. Gladis & A. Diederichsen, 'In Situ and On-farm Management of Plant Genetic Resources', in: *European Journal of Agronomy* 19, no. 4, 2003: 509–17; and Food and Agriculture Organization, 'Biodiversity for Food and Agriculture: Contributing to Food Security and Sustainability in a Changing World' (Rome, 2010). **100.** Stephen Mennell, *All Manners of Food: Eating and Tasting in England and France from the Middle Ages to the Present* (Oxford, 1985), ch. 12. **101.** Alan Warde, *Consumption, Food and Taste: Culinary Antinomies and Commodity Culture* (London, 1997).

CHAPTER 14

1. Encyclical Letter of John Paul II, *On the Hundredth Anniversary of Rerum Novarum*, 5 Jan. 1991, see ch. 36, at https://capp-usa.org/social_encyclicals/45#chapter_36. For affluence as the cause of religious decline, see Mark Lynas, *New Statesman*, 15 Jan. 2007; Callum G. Brown, *The Death of Christian Britain: Understanding Secularisation, 1800–2000* (London, 2000); and Mark Mazower, *Dark Continent: Europe's Twentieth Century* (New York, 1998), 302. **2.** In the 2011 Census, 59 per cent of English and Welsh people identified themselves as Christian; http://www.ons.gov.uk/ons/rel/census/2011-census/detailed-characteristics-for-local-authorities-in-england-and-wales/sty-religion.html. **3.** Alasdair Crockett & David Voas, 'Generations of Decline: Religious Change in Twentieth-century Britain', in: *Journal for the Scientific Study of Religion* 45, no. 4, 2006: 567–84. See also 306 above. **4.** Centre for the Study of Global Christianity, 'World Christian Database', http://www.worldchristian-database.org/wcd/. For an accessible overview, esp. on the United States, see John Micklethwait & Adrian Wooldridge, *God is Back: How the Rise of Faith is Changing the World* (London, 2010). **5.** Roger Finke & Rodney Stark, *The Churching of America, 1776–2005: Winners and Losers in Our Religious Economy* (New Brunswick, NJ, 2005); Dianne Kirby, 'The Cold War' in: Hugh McLeod, ed., *The Cambridge History of Christianity: Vol. IX, World Christianities, c.1914–c.2000* (Cambridge, 2006). **6.** Shane Leslie, *Henry Edward Manning: His Life and Labour* (London, 1921), quoted at 358. **7.** R. Laurence Moore, *Selling God: American Religion in the Marketplace of Culture* (New York, 1994), 95–8; David Morgan, *Protestants and Pictures: Religion, Visual Culture and the Age of American Mass Production* (New York, 1999). **8.** Bruce Evensen, *God's Man for the Gilded Age: D. L. Moody and the Rise of Modern Mass Evangelism* (New York, 2003), 88–96. **9.** William Hoyt Colement, quoted in William Revell Moody, *The Life of Dwight L. Moody* (New York, 1900), 278. **10.** See Mark Bevir, 'Welfarism, Socialism and Religion:

On T. H. Green and Others', in: *Review of Politics* 55, no. 4, 1993: 639–61.
11. Greg ('Fritz') Umbach, 'Learning to Shop in Zion: The Consumer Revolution in Great Basin Mormon Culture, 1847–1910', in: *Journal of Social History* 38, 2004: 29–61, quoted at 44, 48. **12.** Moore, *Selling God*, 206–9. **13.** Lecture on 'The Ministry of Wealth', at the Dowse Institute, Cambridge, MA, *Cambridge Chronicle*, XXXI/47, 18 Nov. 1876: 1. **14.** See 97, 118 above. **15.** Quoted from http://hopefaithprayer.com/faith/kenneth-hagin-faith-lesson-no-15-faith-for-prosperity/. See also: www.rhema.org; and Kenneth E. Hagin, *Biblical Keys to Financial Prosperity* (Broken Arrow, OK, 1973). **16.** *Los Angeles Times*, 22 May 1987. **17.** 1988, quoted by Thomas C. O'Guinn & Russell W. Belk, 'Heaven on Earth: Consumption at Heritage Village, USA', in: *Journal of Consumer Research* 16, no. 2, 1989: 227–38, at 234. **18.** Finke & Stark, *Churching of America*; Micklethwait & Wooldridge, *God is Back*; and *The Economist*, 24 Dec. 2005, 59–61. **19.** Richard N. Ostling, 'Power, Glory – and Politics', *Time*, 24 June 2001. **20.** Obituaries: *Corriere della Sera*, 15 Feb. 2015; *La Stampa*, 15 Feb. 2015; *The Economist*, 21 Feb. 2015. **21.** Colleen McDannell, *Material Christianity: Religion and Popular Culture in America* (New Haven, CT, 1995). **22.** Richard Cimino & Don Lattin, *Shopping for Faith: American Religion in the New Millennium* (San Francisco, 1998), 56–63. **23.** http://www.willowcreek.org/. See further: Nancy Tator Ammerman, *Pillars of Faith: American Congregations and Their Partners* (Berkeley, CA, 2005); and Richard Kyle, *Evangelicalism: An Americanized Christianity* (New Brunswick, NJ, 2006). **24.** Hugh McLeod 'The Crisis of Christianity in the West: Entering a Post-Christian Era?', in: McLeod, ed., *Cambridge History of Christianity* IX, ch. 18. **25.** Wade Clark Roof, *Spiritual Marketplace: Baby Boomers and the Remaking of American Religion* (Princeton, NJ, 2001), quoted at 31. See also: Adam Possamai, 'Cultural Consumption of History and Popular Culture in Alternative Spiritualities', in: *Journal of Consumer Culture* 2, no. 2, 2002: 197–218. **26.** Christian Smith & Melinda Lundquist, *Soul Searching: The Religious and Spiritual Lives of American Teenagers* (New York, 2005), quoted at 136, 165. **27.** When asked which image of God was 'extremely likely' to come to their mind by the US General Social Survey (1972–2006), 70% picked 'healer', 63% 'friend' and only 48% 'judge'. See database 'Images of God', under Religion, at http://www3.norc.org/GSS+Website/. **28.** David Maxwell, ' "Delivered from the Spirit of Poverty?": Pentecostalism, Prosperity and Modernity in Zimbabwe', in: *Journal of Religion in Africa* 28, no. 3, 1998: 350–73; and Birgit Meyer, 'Make a Complete Break with the Past: Memory and Post-colonial Modernity in Ghanaian Pentecostalist Discourse', in: *Journal of Religion in Africa* 28, no. 3, 1998: 316–349. For Brazil, see Andrew Reine Johnson, 'If I Give My Soul: Pentecostalism inside of Prison in Rio de Janeiro', PhD thesis, University of Minnesota, 2012. **29.** See 133–5 above. **30.** Enoch Adeboye, *How to Turn Your Austerity to Prosperity* (Lagos, 1989), quoted in Asonzeh Ukah, *A New Paradigm of Pentecostal Power: A Study of the Redeemed Christian Church of God in Nigeria* (Trenton, 2008), 185f. **31.** Ukah, *Pentecostal Power*; see also: Ogbu Kalu, *African*

Pentecostalism: An Introduction (New York, 2008).   **32.** Andrew R. Heinze, *Adapting to Abundance: Jewish Immigrants, Mass Consumption and the Search for American Identity* (New York, 1990).   **33.** Inge Maria Daniels, 'Scooping, Raking, Beckoning Luck: Luck, Agency and the Interdependence of People and Things in Japan', in: *Journal of the Royal Anthropological Institute* 9, 2003: 619–38; Laurel Kendall, *Shamans, Nostalgias and the IMF: South Korean Popular Religion in Motion* (Honolulu, 2009).   **34.** Benjamin Barber, *Jihad vs. McWorld: How Globalization and Tribalism are Reshaping the World* (New York, 1996), following on from his 1992 article in *Atlantic Monthly*. **35.** 'The Political and Religious Testament of the Leader of the Islamic Revolution and the Founder of the Islamic Republic of Iran, Imam Khomeini' (1989), reproduced in the appendix of H. Fürtig, *Liberalisierung als Herausforderung: Wie stabil ist die Islamische Republik Iran?* (Berlin, 1996), *Arbeitshefte* 12, appendix, quoted at 128f.   **36.** Minoo Moallem, *Between Warrior Brother and Veiled Sister: Islamic Fundamentalism and the Politics of Patriarchy in Iran* (Berkeley, CA, 2005).   **37.** William H. Martin & Sandra Mason, 'The Development of Leisure in Iran', in: *Middle Eastern Studies* 42, no. 2, 2006: 239–54; Aliakbar Jafari & Pauline Maclaran, 'Escaping into the World of Make-up Routines in Iran', in: *Sociological Review* 62, no. 2, 2014: 359–82; http://www.cosmeticsdesign-asia.com/Market-Trends/Iran-cosmetics-market-begins-to-boom-again.   **38.** 'A Manifesto on Women by the Al-Khanssaa Brigade', transl. and edited by Charlie Winter, Feb. 2015, for Quilliam, a counter-extremist thinktank, http://www.quilliamfoundation.org/wp/wp-content/uploads/publications/free/women-of-the-islamic-state3.pdf, quoted at 14, 21.   **39.** Özlem Sandikci & Sahver Omeraki, 'Globalization and Rituals: Does Ramadam Turn into Christmas?' *Advances in Consumer Research* 34, 2007: 610–15; Rakesh Belwal & Shweta Belwal, 'Hypermarkets in Oman: A Study of Consumers' Shopping Preferences', in: *International Journal of Retail and Distribution Management* 42, no. 8, 2014: 717–32.   **40.** Johanna Pink, ed., *Muslim Societies in the Age of Mass Consumption* (Newcastle upon Tyne, 2009); Leor Halevi, 'The Muslim Xbox' (31 May 2013), in: *Reverberations: New Directions in the Study of Prayer*, http://forums.ssrc.org/ndsp/2013/05/31/the-muslim-xbox/; and http://www.islamicbookstore.com/publisher-goodword-books. html.   **41.**   http://www.worldhalalsummit.com/the-global-halal-market-stats-trends/; Jonathan Wilson et al., 'Crescent Marketing: Muslim Geographies and Brand Islam', in: *Journal of Islamic Marketing* 4, no. 1, 2013: 22–50.   **42.** This paragraph draws on the fascinating research by Charles Hirschkind, *The Ethical Soundscape: Cassette Sermons and Islamic Counterpublics* (New York, 2006); see also: Charles Hirschkind, 'Experiments in Devotion Online: The YouTube Khutba', in: *International Journal of Middle East Studies* 44, no. 1, 2012: 5–21.   **43.** Özlem Sandikci & Guliz Ger, 'Veiling in Style: How Does a Stigmatized Practice become Fashionable?' in: *Journal of Consumer Research* 37, no. 1, 2010: 15–36. For critical voices in Istanbul, see Elif Izberk-Bilgin, 'Infidel Brands: Unveiling Alternative Meanings of Global Brands at the Nexus of Globalization, Consumer Culture and Islam', in: *Journal of Consumer*

Research 39, no. 4, 2012: 663–87. **44.** Quoted in Carla Jones, 'Materializing Piety: Gendered Anxieties about Faithful Consumption in Contemporary Urban Indonesia', in: *American Ethnologist* 37, no. 4, 2010: 617–37, at 619. Compare: http://www.noor-magazine.com/2014/10/shadow-of-preppy/.

CHAPTER 15

1. See www.oceanconservancy.org.: 'The Ocean Trash Index' (2012). **2.** For American data, see the reports by the US Environmental Protection Agency, for British figures, those by WRAP: http://www.epa.gov/epawaste/nonhaz/munici-pal/pubs/msw_2010_rev_factsheet.pdf; www.wrap.org.uk/media_centre/key_facts/index.html. **3.** Vance Packard, *The Waste Makers* (London, 1961), quoted at 6–9, 236f. **4.** Susan Strasser, *Waste and Want: A Social History of Trash* (New York, 1999), 10, 16, 21. **5.** D. C. Walsh, 'Urban Residential Refuse Composition and Generation Rates for the Twentieth Century', in: *Environmental Science & Technology* 36, no. 22, 2002: 4936–42. **6.** Jacob & Wilhelm Grimm, *Deutsches Wörterbuch*, at: http://dwb.uni-trier.de/de/; Sabine Barles, *L'Invention des déchets urbains: France, 1790–1970* (Seyssel, 2005), 229–31; Ludolf Kuchenbuch, 'Abfall: Eine stichwortgeschichtliche Erkundung', in: *Mensch und Umwelt in der Geschichte*, eds. J. Calließ, J. Rüsen & M. Striegnitz (Pfaffenweiler, 1989); John Hollander, 'The Waste Remains and Kills', *Social Research* 65, no. 1, 1998: 3–8; and John Scanlan, *On Garbage* (London, 2005). **7.** William Rathje & Cullen Murphy, *Rubbish: The Archaeology of Garbage* (New York, 1992). **8.** Suzanne Raitt, 'Psychic Waste: Freud, Fechner and the Principle of Constancy', in: Gay Hawkins & Stephen Muecke, eds., *Culture and Waste: The Creation and Destruction of Value* (Lanham, MD, 2003), 73–83. **9.** Kevin Hetherington, 'Second-handedness: Consumption, Disposal and Absent Presence', *Environment and Planning D: Society and Space* 22, 2004: 157–73, at 159. **10.** Mary Douglas, *Purity and Danger: An Analysis of the Concepts of Pollution and Taboo* (London, 1966), 44. Her approach framed the exhibition on dirt and waste at the Wellcome Trust, London, in 2012. The definition of 'dirt' as 'a thing in a wrong place' was already common among Victorians and was used by Lord Palmerston in 1852. See also: Zsuzsa Gille, *From the Cult of Waste to the Trash Heap of History: The Politics of Waste in Socialist and Post-socialist Hungary* (Bloomington, IN, 2007); and Gavin Lucas, 'Disposability and Dispossession in the Twentieth Century', in: *Journal of Material Culture* 7, no. 1, 2002: 5–22. **11.** Cited in M. A. Jinhee Park, 'Von der Müllkippe zur Abfallwirtschaft: Die Entwicklung der Hausmüllentsorgung in Berlin (West) von 1945 bis 1990', PhD thesis: Technische Universität Berlin, 2004), p. 22, my translation. **12.** C. A. Velis, D. C. Wilson & C. R. Cheeseman, 'Nineteenth-century London Dust-yards: A Case Study in Closed-loop Resource Efficiency', in: *Waste Management* 29, no. 4, 2009: 1282–90. **13.** Manuel Charpy, 'Formes et échelles du commerce d'occasion au XIXe siècle: L'Exemple du vêtement à Paris', *Revue d'histoire du XIXe siècle* 24, 2002:

125–50. **14.** Barles, *L'Invention des déchets urbains*, 32–4. **15.** William L. Rathje, 'The Garbage Decade', in: *American Behavioral Scientist* 28, no. 1, 1984: 9–29. **16.** Quoted from Martin Melosi, *Garbage in Cities: Refuse, Reform and the Environment, 1880–1980* (College Station, TX, 1981), 23. **17.** Barles, *L'Invention des déchets urbains*, 167–9. **18.** See Hildegard Frilling and Olaf Mischer, *Pütt un Pann'n: Geschichte der Hamburger Hausmüllbeseitigung* (Hamburg, 1994). See further: Heather Chappells & Elizabeth Shove, 'The Dustbin: A Study of Domestic Waste, Household Practices and Utility Services', in: *International Planning Studies* 4, no. 2, 1999: 267–80. **19.** Martin Melosi, *Garbage in Cities: Refuse, Reform and the Environment, 1880–1980*, (Pittsburgh, rev. edn., 2005), ch. 2; and Daniel Eli Burnstein, *Next to Godliness: Confronting Dirt and Despair in Progressive Era New York City* (Urbana, IL, 2006). **20.** Rudolph Hering & Samuel A. Greeley, *Collection and Disposal of Municipal Refuse* (New York, 1921), 50. **21.** Hering & Greeley, *Collection and Disposal of Municipal Refuse*, 19, 34; and J. C. Wylie, *Fertility from Town Wastes* (London, 1955), esp. 200; see also: J. C. Wylie, *The Wastes of Civilization* (London, 1959). **22.** See Park, 'Von der Müllkippe zur Abfallwirtschaft', 24–6. **23.** G. E. Louis, 'A Historical Context of Municipal Solid-waste Management in the United States', in: *Waste Management and Research* 22, no. 4, 2004: 306–22. **24.** *Müll und Abfall*, Feb. 1973, 35–6. **25.** Johann Eugen Mayer, *Müllbeseitigung und Müllverwertung* (Leipzig, 1915). **26.** Wylie, *Fertility from Town Wastes*. **27.** Matthew Gandy, *Recycling and the Politics of Urban Waste* (New York, 1994), 74. **28.** Bayerisches Statistisches Landesamt, *Die Müllbeseitigung in Bayern am 30. Juni 1963* (Munich, 1965), 7. **29.** Anat Helman, 'Cleanliness and Squalor in Inter-war Tel Aviv', in: *Urban History* 31, no. 1, 2001: 72–99. See also: Joshua Goldstein, 'Waste', in Trentmann, ed., *Oxford Handbook of the History of Consumption*, esp. 337–41 and for further references. **30.** Shanghai Municipal Archive, Annual Report of the Shanghai Municipal Council, 1905: 149–51; 1906: 172–3; 1920: 128A–130A; 1923: 135; 1935: 213. **31.** Geoffrey Russell Searle, *The Quest for National Efficiency: A Study in British Politics and Political Thought, 1899–1914* (Oxford, 1971). **32.** Commitee on the Elimination of Waste in Industry of the Federated American Engineering Societies, *Waste in Industry* (Washington, DC, 1921), 30, 97. **33.** See the fascinating film *Scrap* by the Nassau Recycle Corporation in 1974 from the AT&T Archives at http://techchannel.att.com/play-video. cfm/2011/10/12/AT&T-Archives-Scrap. **34.** Charles H. Lipsett, *Industrial Wastes: Their Conservation and Utilization* (New York, 1951); and C. L. Mantell, *Solid Wastes: Origin, Collection, Processing and Disposal* (New York, 1975), 753–5. **35.** Waste-industry experts began to speak of 'the age of packaging' e.g. C. Basalo of Paris at the International Solid Waste and Public Cleaning Association conference, cited in *Müll und Abfall*, 4/1970: 131; see also: *Müll und Abfall*, 1/1972: 9. **36.** Roland Salchow, *Zeitbombe Müll* (Hamburg, 1992), 30. **37.** Quoted in Kern, *The Culture of Time and Space, 1880–1918*, 100. **38.** Nigel Whiteley, 'Toward a Throwaway Culture: Consumerism, "Style Obsolescence" and Cultural Theory in the 1950s and 1960s', in *Oxford Art Journal* 10, no. 2, 1987: 3–27; and Andrea El-Danasouri, *Kunststoff und Müll: Das Material bei Naum Gabo und Kurt Schwitters* (Munich, 1992). **39.** *New York Times*, 23 Dec. 2005; *New York Times*, 14 May 2008; Barbican Art Gallery, London: 'The Bride and the Bachelors: Duchamp with Cage, Cunningham, Rauschenberg and Johns', 14 February 2013–9 June 2013. Gallery Gagosian, *Robert Rauschenberg: Catalogue, with texts by James Lawrence and John Richardson* (New York, 2010); Calvin Tomkins, *The Bride and the Bachelors: Five Masters of the Avant-garde* (Harmondsworth, expanded edn, 1976), 207f. **40.** *The Times*, 11 May 1977: 24. Between 1964 and 1977 the number of local authorities involved in waste-paper recycling fell from 744 to 196. See further: Timothy Cooper, 'War on Waste? The Politics of Waste and Recycling in Post-war Britain,1950–1975', *Capitalism Nature Socialism* 20, no. 4, 2009: 53–72. **41.** Susanne Köstering, 'Hundert Jahre Entzinnung von Konservendosen: Ein Wettlauf zwischen Altstoffrückgewinnung und Rohstoffeinsparung', in: *Müll von Gestern? Eine umweltgeschichtliche Erkundung in Berlin und Brandenburg*, eds. Susanne Köstering & Renate Rüb, (Münster, 2003), 151–64. **42.** Civic Trust, 'Civic Amenities Act, 1967, Part 3: Disposal of Unwanted Vehicles and Bulky Refuse' (London: 1967), 32. **43.** For the reception of Carson's book, see Priscilla Coit Murphy, *What a Book Can Do: The Publication and Reception of 'Silent Spring'* (Amherst, 2005). **44.** Park, 'Von der Müllkippe zur Abfallwirtschaft', 109–11; *The Times*, 4 Sept. 1974: 19; 20 Aug. 1975: 16; 25 Aug. 1977: 17. See now also the special issue edited by Ruth Oldenziel & Heike Weber, 'Reconsidering Recycling', in: *Contemporary European History* 22, no. 3, 2013. **45.** Council Directive of 15 July 1975 on waste (75/442/EEC). **46.** Quoted in *The Times*, 12 Sept. 1974: 25. **47.** Rat für Nachhaltige Entwicklung, *Ressourcenmanagement und Siedlungsabfallwirtschaft (Challenger Report)* (Berlin, 2014). **48.** In Britain, commercial waste has fallen by a quarter since 2002/03; http://www.bis.gov.uk/assets/biscore/business-sectors/docs/f/11-1088-from-waste-management-to-resource-recovery. In Berlin, the drop in municipal solid waste from 2.1 million to 1.68 million in the decade after 1996 was almost entirely due to the fall in commercial waste: see Zhang Dongqing, Tan Soon Keat & Richard M. Gersberg, 'A Comparison of Municipal Solid Waste Management in Berlin and Singapore', in: *Waste Management* 30, no. 5, 2010: 921–33. **49.** US Environmental Protection Agency, 'Municipal Solid Waste in the United States: 2009 Facts and Figures' (Washington, DC, 2010), tables 18–22, 89–93, and 94 for packaging waste. In the above, I refer to per capita figures. Of course, population growth has meant that total waste has skyrocketed in these years, from 88 million tons in 1960 to 250 million tons in 2010. **50.** Eurostat, 'Waste Generated and Treated in Europe Data, 1995–2003' (Luxembourg, 2005). **51.** European Environment Agency, *Managing Municipal Solid Waste – A Review of Achievements in 32 European Countries* (Copenhagen, 2013). **52.** Quoted in Gille, *From the Cult of Waste to the Trash Heap of History*, 71, on which I have also drawn below. **53.** Susanne Hartard & Michael Huhn, 'Das SERO System', in: *Umweltschutz in der DDR: Analysen und Zeitzeugenberichte*, eds. Hermann

Behrens & Jens Hoffmann (Munich, 2007); and Jakob Calice, ' "Sekundär-rohstoffe – eine Quelle, die nie versiegt": Konzeption und Argumentation des Abfallverwertungssystems in der DDR aus umwelthistorischer Perspektive' (MA thesis, Vienna, 2005). **54.** DHV CR Ltd, 'Waste Management Policies in Central and Eastern European Countries: Current Policies and Trends', in: *Final Report* (Prague, 2001). See also the country reports by the European Environment Agency at http://www.eea.europa.eu/publications/managing-municipal-solid-waste. **55.** Allen Hershkowitz & Eugene Salerni, *Garbage Management in Japan: Leading the Way* (New York, 1987). **56.** http://www.city.nagoya.jp/en/cmsfiles/contents/0000022/22536/guide_e.pdf; http://www.japanfs.org/en/public/gov_01.html. **57.** H. Itoh, *Waste Management in Japan* (Southampton, 2004); and Fumikazu Yoshida, *The Economics of Waste and Pollution Management in Japan* (Tokyo, 2002). **58.** Yoshida, *The Economics of Waste and Pollution Management in Japan*. **59.** Dahlén Lisa & Anders Lagerkvist, 'Pay as You Throw: Strengths and Weaknesses of Weight-based Billing in Household Waste-collection systems in Sweden', in: *Waste Management* 30, no. 1, 2010: 23–31. On Sweden, see now also: K. Wheeler & M. Glucksmann, *Household Recycling and Consumption Work* (London, in press). **60.** WasteWise, *Annual Report 2007.* **61.** Resource Futures WR0121 – *Understanding Waste Growth at Local Authority Level, Final Report to Defra* (2009), http://randd.defra.gov.uk/Document.aspx?Document=WR0121_8316_FRP.pdf. **62.** Eurostat figures for 2004–8: paper waste rose by 7%; plastic by 20%. In the USA, newspapers' contribution to MSW rose from 7 million tons in 1960 to 15 million in 2000. By 2009 it had fallen to 8 million. Office-type paper meanwhile jumped from 1.5 million in 1960 to 5.4 million in 2009: see US Environmental Protection Agency, http://www.epa.gov/waste/nonhaz/municipal/pubs/msw2009rpt.pdf, table 15. **63.** Julian Parfitt, Mark Barthel & Sarah Macnaughton, 'Food Waste within Food Supply Chains: Quantification and Potential for Change to 2050', in: *Philosophical Transactions of the Royal Society B: Biological Sciences* 365, no. 1554, 2010: 3065–81. See also: Tristram Stuart, *Waste: Uncovering the Global Food Scandal* (London, 2009). **64.** David Evans, 'Beyond the Throwaway Society: Ordinary Domestic Practice and a Sociological Approach to Household Food Waste', in: *Sociology* 46, no. 1, 2012: 41–56; and David Evans, 'Binning, Gifting and Recovery: The Conduits of Disposal in Household Food Consumption', in: *Environment and Planning D: Society and Space* 30, no. 6, 2012: 1123–37. **65.** In Britain in 2006/7, fresh vegetables and salads amounted to 811,358 tons of 'possibly avoidable' food waste, more than twice that of all other food combined; WRAP, *Household Food and Drink Waste in the UK* (2009). WRAP, *New Estimates* (2012), table 4. **66.** Terje Finstad, 'Familiarizing Food: Frozen Food Chains, Technology and Consumer Trust, Norway 1940–1970', *Food and Foodways* 21, no. 1, 2013: 22–45. **67.** WRAP, *Household Food and Drink Waste in the UK*, 5. **68.** Rathje, 'The Garbage Decade'. **69.** WRAP, 'New Estimates for Household Food and Drink Waste in the UK' (2011), 15–16. **70.** http://globalrec.org/2013/11/11/report-national-green-assembly-on-waste-legislation-and-waste-pickers/. See also: Martin Medina,

'Scavenger Co-operatives in Asia and Latin America', in: *Resources, Conservation and Recycling* 31, no. 1, 2000: 51–69; and Kaveri Gill, *Of Poverty and Plastic: Scavenging and Scrap-trading Entrepreneurs in India's Urban Informal Economy* (Oxford, 2009). **71.** European Environment Agency, *Movements of Waste across the EU's Internal and External Borders* (Copenhagen: 2012), section 4.2. **72.** European Environmental Agency, 'Movements of Waste'; and Josh Lepawsky & Chris McNabb, 'Mapping International Flows of Electronic Waste', in: *Canadian Geographer* 54, no. 2, 2010: 177–95. **73.** Takayoshi Shinkuma & Nguyen Thi Minh Huong, 'The Flow of E-waste material in the Asia Region', in: *Environmental Impact Assessment Review* 29, 2009: 25–31. International Labour Office, 'The Global Impact of E-waste' (Geneva: 2012). **74.** European Environmental Agency, 'Movement of Waste', sections 5 and 6. **75.** Sally Hibbert, Suzanne Horne & Stephen Tagg, 'Charity Retailers in Competition for Merchandise: Examining How Consumers Dispose of Used Goods', in: *Journal of Business Research* 58, no. 6, 2005: 819–28. **76.** Eric Klinenberg, *Going Solo: The Extraordinary Rise and Surprising Appeal of Living Alone* (London, 2012). In Britain in 2013, 7.7 million households, or 29%, had single dwellers (up from 6.6 million in 1996): see Office of National Statistics, *Families and Households, 2013*, table 5. **77.** See United Nations, Economic Commission for Europe, Economic and Social Council, ECE/CES/GE.20/2015: 'Vacation Home Ownership in a Globalized World', and see the UNECE's http://www.unece.org/fileadmin/DAM/stats/groups/wggna/GuideByChapters/Chapter_12.pdf. **78.** A study of Austin, with data from 2008 to 2014, estimated that each 10% increase in airbnb supply resulted in a 0.35% decrease in monthly hotel-room revenue; for this and further references: see Georgios Zervas, Davide Proserpio & John W. Byers. 'The Rise of the Sharing Economy: Estimating the Impact of Airbnb on the Hotel Industry' (Boston, 2014). **79.** Sean O'Connell, *The Car and British Society: Class, Gender and Motoring, 1896–1939* (Manchester, 1998), 34–6. **80.** Alison Clarke, 'Mother Swapping: The Trafficking of Nearly-new Children's Wear', in: *Commercial Cultures: Economics, Practices, Spaces*, eds. Peter Jackson et al. (Oxford, 2000), ch. 4. **81.** Ilja van Damme, 'Changing Consumer Preferences and Evolutions in Retailing. Buying and Selling Consumer Durables in Antwerp, c.1648–c.1748', in: *Buyers and Sellers: Retail Circuits and Practices in Medieval and Early Modern Europe*, ed. P. Stabel et al. (Turnhout, 2006), 199–224; and Ilja Van Damme & Reinoud Vermoesen, 'Second-hand Consumption as a Way of Life: Public Auctions in the Surroundings of Alost in the Late-eighteenth Century', in: *Continuity and Change* 24, 2009: 275–305; see also 190, 227 above. **82.** In the United Kingdom, some 300,000 tons of garments are collected each year. Only half is of sufficiently high grade to be sold on. 10% ends up recycled in industrial products such as as rags or filler for car seats. **83.** Karen Tranberg Hansen, *Salaula: The World of Second-hand Clothing and Zambia* (Chicago, 2000), 226. **84.** E. D. Larson, M. Ross & R. H. Williams, 'Beyond the Era of Materials', in: *Scientific American* 254, no. 6, 1986: 34–41; Robert H. Williams, Eric D. Larson & Marc H. Ross, 'Materials, Affluence and Industrial

Energy Use', in: *Annual Review of Energy* 12, no. 1, 1987: 99–144. **85.** Nicky Gregson, Alan Metcalfe & Louise Crewe, 'Identity, Mobility and the Throwaway Society', in: *Environment and Planning D: Society and Space*, 2006, 682–700, quoted at 688. See further: Nicky Gregson & Louise Crewe, *Second-hand Cultures* (Oxford, 2003); and Nicky Gregson, *Living with Things: Ridding, Accommodation, Dwelling* (Oxford, 2006). **86.** Giles Slade, *Made to Break: Technology and Obsolescence in America* (Cambridge, MA, 2006). **87.** Tim Cooper, 'Inadequate Life? Evidence of Consumer Attitudes to Product Obsolescence', in: *Journal of Consumer Policy* 27, 2004: 421–49. **88.** Rober Entner, '2014 Mobile Phone sales fall by 15%', Recon Analytics: http://reconanalytics.com/2015/02/2014-us-mobile-phone-sales-fall-by-15-and-handset-replacement-cycle-lengthens-to-historic-high/; and David Pogue, 'Should You Upgrade Your Phone Every Year?', in: *Scientific American*, 20 Aug. 2013. **89.** For these opposite dynamics, see Valerie M. Thomas, 'Demand and Dematerialization Impacts of Second-hand Markets', *Journal of Industrial Ecology* 7, no. 2, 2003: 65–76. **90.** The data from the German 2001–2 time budget study can be viewed at https://www.destatis.de/DE/Publikationen/Thematisch/EinkommenKonsumLebensbedingungen/Zeitbudgeterhebung/ZeitbudgetsTabellenband1_5639102029005.xls?__blob=publicationFile. For Austria, see the research by the Ludwig Boltzmann Institut für Freizeit in 2002: http://www.freizeitforschung.at/data/forschungsarchiv/2002/ft_07_2002.pdf. **91.** US Department of Commerce, *Statistical Abstract of the United States 1971* (Washington, DC, 1971) 200, 722, 741–3. **92.** Aya Yoshida & Tomohiro Tasaki, 'Material-flow Analysis of Used Personal Computers in Japan', in: *Waste Management* 29, no. 5, 2009: 1602–14. **93.** Of the 400,000 used computers that reach Lagos every month, only a quarter are functional, according to Oladele Osibanjo, 'The Waste Challenge in Urban Development' (University of Ibadan, Nigeria, 2006). For electronic waste, see the briefing papers available from the Basel Action Network at: http://www.ban.org/library-page/#briefing. **94.** According to the Self Storage Association, 2.3 billion square feet: http://www.selfstorage.org/ssa/content/navigationmenu/aboutssa/factsheet/. **95.** D. S and I. W. Yoon Oh, 'A Study on the State of Balcony Usage and the User's Attitude with Relation to Balcony Layout', in: *Housing Studies, Journal of Korean Association for Housing Policy Studies* 7, no. 2, 1999: 125–32. **96.** http://ronalford.theplan.com/; the National Association of Professional Organizers currently has 4,000 members: http://www.napo.net/who/. **97.** See http://www.collectoronline.com; http://www.vacuumland.org; and Russell Belk, Magnus Morck & Karin M. Ekstrom, 'Collecting of Glass: A Multi-sited Ethnography', in: *European Advances in Consumer Research* 7, 2005: 404–8. **98.** Don Jefferys, 'Pathological Hoarding', in: *Australian Family Physician* 37, no. 4, 2008. **99.** J. E. Arnold and U. A. Lang, 'Changing American Home Life: Trends in Domestic Leisure and Storage among Middle-class Families', in: *Journal of Family and Economic Issues* 28, no. 1, 2007: 23–48, quoted at 36, 43. **100.** Richard A. Gould & Michael B. Schiffer, *Modern Material Culture: The Archaeology of Us* (New York, 1981). **101.** EPA, *Electronics Waste Management in the United States through*

2009 (May 2011), table 4, 16. **102.** Barely one in ten old mobile phones is recycled in the USA today; EPA, *Electronics Waste Management in the United States through 2009* (May 2011), table 13, 27. For British figures, see Market Transformation Programme, 2005/6, 10. For France: Agence de l'Environnement et de la Maîtrise de l'Energie, Déchets d'Équipements Électriques et Électroniques (DEEE) (2010). **103.** See esp. Alfred Schmidt, *The Concept of Nature in Marx* (London, 1971); John Bellamy Foster, *Marx's Ecology: Materialism and Nature* (New York, 1999); Albert Adriaanse et al., *Resource Flows: The Material Basis of Industrial Economics* (Washington, DC, 1997); Marina Fischer-Kowalski et al., *Gesellschaftlicher Stoffwechsel und Kolonisierung von Natur* (Amsterdam, 1997); and R. P. Sieferle et al., *Das Ende der Fläche: Zum gesellschaftlichen Stoffwechsel der Industrialisierung* (Cologne, 2006). **104.** Adriaanse et al., *Resource Flows*. **105.** Friedrich Schmidt-Bleek, *Wie viel Umwelt braucht der Mensch?* (Berlin, 1994). **106.** M. Dittrich et al., 'Green Economies around the World: Implications of Resource Use for Development and the Environment' (Vienna: SERI, 2012), 12, 57–8. The Food and Agriculture Organization and the European Union include the water content (up to 15%) of grasses: Eurostat, 'Material Use in the European Union, 1980–2000: Indicators and analysis' (Luxemburg, 2002). **107.** B. Girod & P. De Haan, 'More or Better? A Model for Changes in Household Greenhouse-gas Emissions due to Higher Income', in: *Journal of Industrial Ecology* 14, no. 1: 31–49. **108.** William F. Ruddiman, *Plows, Plagues & Petroleum: How Humans Took Control of Climate* (Princeton, NJ, 2005); for land use, I draw on the new historical database of the environment (HYDE) developed by Kees Klein Goldewijk, see http://www.mnp.nl/en/themasites/hyde/index. html. **109.** F. Krausmann et al., 'Growth in Global Materials Use, GDP and Population during the Twentieth Century', in: *Ecological Economics* 68, no. 10, 2009: 2696–705, with thanks to Fridolin Krausmann for allowing me to reproduce these figures. DMC equals the total amount of resources extracted (DE), plus imports minus exports. Since one country's exports are another's imports, DMC is the same as DE for the world. **110.** Dittrich et al., 'Green Economies', 60. **111.** Eurostat, 'Economy-wide Material-flow Accounts and Derived Indicators' (Luxembourg, 2001), 40. **112.** Ian Gazley & Dilan Bhuvanendran, 'Trends in UK Material Flows between 1970 and 2003', in *Economic Trends* 619 (London: Office for National Statistics, 2005). **113.** Goodall notes that Britons ate 4% less in 2007 than in 2000; Chris Goodall, ' "Peak Stuff": Did the UK Reach a Maximum Use of Material Resources in the Early Part of the Last Decade?',   http://www.carboncommentary.com/wp-content/uploads/2011/10/ Peak_Stuff_17.10.11.pdf, 2011. Compare the critique by George Monbiot in his blog: http://www.guardian.co.uk/environment/georgemonbiot/2011/nov/03/ peak-consumption-hypothesis-correct. **114.** Andrew W. Wyckoff & Joseph M. Roop, 'The Embodiment of Carbon in Imports of Manufactured Products: Implications for International Agreements on Greenhouse-gas emissions', in: *Energy Policy* 22, no. 3, 1994: 187–94; Roldan Muradian, Martin O'Connor & Joan Martinez-Alier, 'Embodied Pollution in Trade: Estimating the

"Environmental Load Displacement" of Industrialized Countries', in: *Ecological Economics* 41, no. 1, 2001: 51–67. **115.** According to the UK Energy Research Centre, territorial-based emissions declined by 19% between 1990 and 2008, while consumption-based emissions increased by 20%; government figures give higher figures for the former: HC 1646, 18 April 2012, House of Commons, Energy and Climate Change Committee: *Consumption-based Emissions Reporting, Twelfth Report of Session 2010–12, Vol. I.* **116.** M. Dittrich, S. Bringezu & H. Schutz, 'The Physical Dimension of International Trade: Part 2: Indirect Global Resource Flows between 1962 and 2005', in: *Ecological Economics* 79, 2012: 32–43. **117.** Atiq Uz Zaman & Steffen Lehmann, 'The Zero Waste Index: A Performance Measurement Tool for Waste Management Systems in a "Zero Waste City" ', in: *Journal of Cleaner Production* 50, 2013: 123–32. **118.** American Physical Society, *Efficient Use of Energy: The APS Studies on the Technical Aspects of the More Efficient Use of Energy* (New York, 1976), no. 25, 77. **119.** Arthur H. Rosenfeld, 'The Art of Energy Efficiency: Protecting the Environment with Better Technology', in: *Annual Review of Energy and the Environment* 24, no. 1, 1999: 33–82. **120.** E.g., 12th Congress of the World Energy Conference, New Delhi, 18–23 Sept. 1983, division 2, section 2.3.12: Naoto Sagawa, 'Prospects for Japan's Energy Supply–Demand System', 22. **121.** Department of Energy and Climate Change, 'Energy Consumption in the United Kingdom', 2012; Eurostat: http://epp.eurostat.ec.europa.eu/tgm/table.do?tab=table&plugin=1&language=en&pcode=tsdpc310. **122.** The size of the rebound effect and how to measure it remains a subject of considerable controversy. The International Energy Agency, in its *World Energy Outlook* in 2012, reckoned it to be a modest 9%. Other experts reach 50%: e.g. Ted Nordhaus, Michael Shellenberger & Jesse Jenkins, *Energy Emergence: Rebound and Backfire as Emergent Phenomena* (Oakland, MD, 2011). **123.** 2011 'Consommation durable' fair, Paris: ADEME (French environment and energy management agency), *Petites réponses*, 9. **124.** 1993: 10.01 quadrillion Btu vs 10.17 quadrillion Btu in 2009: US Energy Information Administration, *Residential Energy Consumption Survey, 2009.* **125.** Swedish Parliament, 'Think Twice! An Action Plan for Sustainable Household Consumption', in: *Government Communication 2005/06:107* (Stockholm, 2005). **126.** Peter Kemper & John M. Quigley, *The Economics of Refuse Collection* (Cambridge, MA, 1976), 83. **127.** See the 2009 residential data by the US Energy Information Administration, esp. table HC 3.4, at: http://www.eia.doe.gov/consumption/residential/data/2009/excel/HC3.4%20Appliances%20by%20Number%20of%20Household%20Members.xls. **128.** DTI, *Energy Consumption in the United Kingdom* (2004). For American singles, see the EIA data cited in the previous note 127. **129.** Shove, *Comfort, Cleanliness and Convenience: The Social Organization of Normality*; and Shove, Pantzar & Watson, *The Dynamics of Social Practice: Everyday Life and How It Changes.* **130.** For the UK, see Energy Saving Trust, *The Rise of the Machines: A Review of Energy Using Products in the Home from the 1970s to Today* (London, 2006), and the follow-up report, *The Elephant in the*

Living Room: How Our Appliances and Gadgets are Trampling the Green Dream (London, 2011). In the USA, 426 million electric units were sold in 2007, seven times as many as in 1987: see New York State Department of Environmental Conservation, *Beyond Waste* (New York, 2010), 63f. **131.** EPA, *Municipal Solid Waste in the United States 2009*, ch. 2. For clothes in Britain, see *Guardian*, 28 Feb. 2006. **132.** K. Parrott, J. Emmel & J. Beamish, 'A Nation of Packrats: Rethinking the Design Guidelines for Kitchen Storage', in: *Housing on the Urban Landscape Conference* (Chicago, 2004). See further: Oriel Sullivan & Jonathan Gershuny, 'Inconspicuous Consumption: Work-rich, Time-poor in the Liberal Market Economy', in: *Journal of Consumer Culture* 4, no. 1, 2004: 79–100, esp. 95–6; Martin Hand, Elizabeth Shove & Dale Southerton, 'Home Extensions in the United Kingdom: Space, Time and Practice', in: *Environment and Planning D* 25, no. 4, 2007: 668–81. **133.** The cities were Fredrikstad, Groningen, Padova, Guildford and Sodermalm/Stockholm: see Eivind Stø et al., 'Consumption and Environment in Five European Cities: European Report' (2002).

EPILOGUE

1. Serge Latouche, *Le pari de la décroissance* (Paris, 2006); Tim Jackson, *Prosperity without Growth: Economics for a Finite Planet* (London, 2009); Paul Ariès, *La simplicité volontaire contre le mythe de l'abondance* (Paris, 2010); Niko Paech, *Befreiung vom Überfluss: Auf dem Weg in die Postwachstumsökonomie* (Munich, 2012). Compare: Irmi Seidl and Angelika Zahrnt (eds), *Postwachstumsgesellschaft: Konzepte für die Zukunft* (Marburg, 2010). **2.** See now, Emily Watson, *Seneca: A Life* (London, 2015). **3.** Joseph E. Stiglitz, *The Great Divide* (London, 2015). **4.** Rachel Botsman and Roo Rogers, *What's mine is yours: the rise of collaborative consumption* (New York, 2010); B. Joseph Pine and James H. Gilmore, *The experience economy* (Boston, Mass., 1999); Jon Sundbo and Flemming Sørensen (eds), *Handbook on the experience economy* (Cheltenham, 2013); Juliet Schor, *Plenitude: the new economics of true wealth* (New York, 2010). See also now the overviews by Juliet Schor and Connor Fitzmaurice, 'Collaborating and connecting' and by Maurie J. Cohen, 'Toward a post-consumerist future?' in Lucia Reisch and John Thøgersen (eds), *Handbook of Research on Sustainable Consumption* (Cheltenham, 2015), pp. 410–25, 426–39. **5.** See http://repaircafe.org/locations/; 200 of these are in Germany, where craftsmanship has remained strong. **6.** Arvind Subramanian and Martin Kessler, 'The Hyperglobalization of Trade and its Future', in Franklin Allen et al. (eds), *Towards a Better Global Economy* (Oxford, 2014), pp. 216–76; see also the commentary by Bernard Hoekman in the same volume, pp. 278–88. **7.** United Nations Conference on Trade and Development (UNCTAD), *Review of Maritime Transport* (New York, 2014), ch. 1. **8.** OECD, *Material Resources, Productivity and the Environment* (Paris, 2015), p. 82 and pp. 69–82 for the above. **9.** OECD, *Material Resources, Productivity and the*

Environment, p. 116. **10.** See Yuliya Kalmykova, Leonardo Rosado and João Patrício, 'Resource consumption drivers and pathways to reduction: economy, policy and lifestyle impact on material flows at the national and urban scale', *Journal of Cleaner Production* 30, 2015: 1–11. **11.** See Charlotte Fourcroy, Faiz Gallouj, and Fabrice Decellas, 'Energy consumption in service industries: Challenging the myth of non-materiality', *Ecological Economics* 81, 2012: 155–64. **12.** See: https://musicbusinessresearch.wordpress.com/2014/03/21/the-recorded-music-market-in-the-us-2000-2013/ . **13.** Ann Bermingham and John Brewer (eds), *The Consumption of Culture 1600–1800: Image, Object, Text* (London, 1995). See now also Michael Hutter, *The Rise of the Joyful Economy: Artistic invention and economic growth from Brunelleschi to Murakami* (Abingdon, 2015). **14.** In addition to references in the Introduction and notes 1 and 4 above, see most recently: James Wallman, *Stuffocation: how we've had enough of stuff and why you need experience more than ever* (London, 2015). **15.** See the International Telecommunication Union: http://www.itu.int/themes/climate/docs/report/02_ICTandClimateChange.html . **16.** Global e-Sustainability Initiative, 'SMART 2020: Enabling the low-carbon economy in the information age' (2008); http://gesi.org/About_ICT_sustainability. **17.** See Susanne Fischer et al. (Wuppertal Institute), *Leasing Society: report for the European Parliament's Committee on Environment, Public Health and Food Safety* (Brussels, 2012). **18.** See page 654 above. **19.** Wall Street Journal, 3 February 2014. For UK figures, see the Society of Motor Manufacturers and Traders: http://www.smmt.co.uk/2015/01/uk-new-car-registrations-december-2014/ . Similar reservations apply to the hope some attach to 3-D printing: why assume that the opportunity for the personalized, bespoke making of stuff will only be used to prolong the life of objects and that people will stop wanting novelty and variety? **20.** Richard H. Thaler and Cass R. Sunstein, *Nudge: Improving decisions about health, wealth and happiness* (London, 2009). For a short overview, see Cass Sunstein, 'Behavioural economics, consumption and environmental protection' in Reisch and Thøgersen (eds), *Handbook of Research on Sustainable Consumption*, pp. 313–27.

Index

About the Author

Frank Trentmann is a professor of history at Birkbeck College, University of London, and directed the £5 million Cultures of Consumption research program. His last book, *Free Trade Nation*, won the Royal Historical Society's Whitfield Prize. He was educated at Hamburg University, the LSE and Harvard. He has been Fernand Braudel Senior Fellow at the European University Institute, Florence, as well as a visiting professor at Bielefeld University, the University of St. Gallen, the British Academy and at the École des hautes études en sciences sociales, Paris. In 2014 he was awarded the Moore Distinguished Fellowship at the California Institute of Technology.